LIFESPAN
DEVELOPMENT

LIFESPAN DEVELOPMENT

Helen Bee

HarperCollins*College*Publishers

Acquisitions Editor: Meg Holden
Developmental Editor: Rebecca Kohn
Project Editor: Melonie Parnes
Design Supervisor/Cover Design: Wendy Ann Fredericks
Text Design: Edward Smith Design, Inc.
Cover Photo: © Marie Lynn Spoto
Photo Researcher: Rosemary Hunter
Production Manager: Willie Lane
Compositor: CRWaldman Graphic Communications
Printer and Binder: R. R. Donnelley & Sons Company
Cover Printer: The Lehigh Press, Inc.

Lifespan Development

Library of Congress Cataloging-in-Publication Data
Bee, Helen L.,
  Lifespan development / Helen Bee.
      p.   cm.
  Includes bibliographical references and indexes.
  ISBN 0-06-500981-9 (student ed.).—ISBN 0-06-500982-7 (instructor's ed.)
    1. Developmental psychology.   I. Title.
  BF713.B435 1994
  155—dc20   93-20091
                                                                                    CIP

95 96 9 8 7 6 5 4 3

To all the wonderful women friends
who have been part of my convoy:

Diane

Ellen

Jane

Kathy

Linda Jo

Maisie

Miriam

Molly

Neila

Nora

Sandy

Sarah

Tilli

BRIEF CONTENTS

DETAILED CONTENTS

10 Social and Personality Development From 6 to 12   228

11 Physical and Cognitive Development in Adolescence   253

TO THE STUDENT

To my admittedly prejudiced view, the study of human development is one of the most fascinating of all subjects. Because humans are astonishingly complex, understanding comes slowly and with great effort. But the process of trying to achieve understanding is full of wonderful puzzles and questions, blind alleys, theoretical leaps forward. And because it is *ourselves* we are studying, there is an added element of intrigue. One of my great hopes in writing this book is that I can draw you into the excitement and fascination.

I have used every strategy I know to lure you. I have written the book in the first person so you will know it is a live person talking to you. In the process, I have told you my opinions, shared some of my concerns, and said clearly when we do not know or cannot answer some question. I have also talked about how to apply the research and theory to your own life, both in extended discussions in "real world" boxes and in the text itself.

But I hope that the greatest attraction is the science itself—the enormous amount of research by skillful people who are attempting to understand human development more and more fully. My wish is that your journey through this book will be intriguing and full of learning, just as your everyday life over the years is fascinating and full of opportunities for growth.

Helen Bee

TO THE INSTRUCTOR

This book has been a first for me. Not a first text, obviously, because I have been writing texts on human development for many years. But this is the first time I have organized the material chronologically rather than topically. I have always taught this subject topically, so naturally I have thought and written about it in that format. When Harper-Collins asked me to do a chronological version of a lifespan text, I initially demurred because it was not clear that I could write it in that format. But then I started thinking about the challenge it presented and the potential fruitfulness of organizing the subject in a new fashion, and I agreed. It has been a fascinating enterprise, and I have indeed learned a great deal. I come away in the end with the conclusion that both organizational rubrics are useful and necessary, and that all of us would benefit from using both at different times. In particular, the chronological format, far more than the topical system, forces the author and the instructor to think about how the various simultaneous developments at any given age may be linked to one another.

❭ Goals

My goal in this book, as in every text I have written, is to entice the student into the fascination of scientific inquiry. The enticements are of several kinds: a personal writing style in which I talk directly to students as if I were having a conversation with them; personal examples and practical applications, to show that the theory and research is linked to everyday experience; descriptions of the most current research and theories, to illustrate that ideas are constantly revised, new questions are being asked and answered, and many uncertainties still remain. Throughout, I have aimed for a careful balance of theory, research, and application. Although the book reads easily, I have never shied away from difficult concepts and complex theories. I have consistently challenged the students to think about the material—and themselves—in new ways.

❭ Special Features

The book has several special features, designed to further these basic goals. First, to encourage the students to ponder, analyze, and think more creatively, I have included **critical thinking questions** in every chapter. These questions appear in the margins and ask the student to pause and consider a particular point before going on. Often they ask the reader to consider how the material may apply to his or her own life. In other cases, they ask the student to think about how one could design a piece of research to answer a particular question. Sometimes they ask theoretical questions or ask the student to analyze her or his own point of view on the subject at issue. These questions may be useful for provoking class discussion; it is also my hope that they will make the reading process more active and thus provide for deeper learning.

The **interludes** that cap each section are a second special feature. Many chronological texts are mere catalogues of behavior changes at each age, without a focus on the key underlying processes. The interludes are designed to fill that gap by providing a brief review and analysis of the age period covered in that section. They may also provide a good study tool for the students as they review the material in the book and in the course.

Each chapter also contains a number of *boxes*, a common feature of current texts, which allow excursions into interesting side channels or practical applications. In this book there are five types of boxes:

Across Cultures boxes focus on two aspects of cross-cultural or cross-ethnic group research: evidence showing that basic developmental processes are the *same* in children or adults of every culture, and research cataloging the variations in life experience or developmental patterns as a function of culture or subcultural differences. An example of the first type is a box on common patterns of early language development around the world in Chapter 7; an example of the second type is a box on adult kin relationships in African-American and Hispanic-American families in Chapter 14.

Research Reports are more detailed descriptions of individual research projects or highly specific research areas, such as Anne Streissguth's studies of fetal alcohol exposure (Chapter 3), studies of ethnic differences in styles of parenting (Chapter 8), or alternative explanations of the greater longevity of women compared to men (Chapter 15).

The Real World boxes all explore some practical application of research or theory, such as a discussion of how much weight a woman should gain in pregnancy (Chapter 3), how to choose a toy for a child (Chapter 7), the effects of cohabitation on subsequent marital success (Chapter 14), or the pros and cons of hormone replacement therapy after menopause (Chapter 15).

Across Development boxes touch on links between child and adult development. For example, in the chapter on early attachment (Chapter 6), there is a box discussing the connections between the adult's internal model of attachment and the security of the infant's attachment. And in the chapter on peer relationships among school-age children (Chapter 10), there is a box on the links between early unpopularity or aggressiveness with peers and later juvenile delinquency or adult deviance. Boxes of this type are not as common as the others, since we lack good long-term longitudinal information in many cases. But I thought it important to remind the students, whenever possible, that there is continuity as well as change operating across the life span.

Soap Boxes are the last and least common type. In these features I have commented on pressing social policy issues: the importance of prenatal care and the need for a national family policy. I have put these strong personal opinions in boxes, rather than in the main text, to make it clear that these are my views. I have included them because I think it is important for students to be confronted with such issues.

One final special feature of the book is the photo program. HarperCollins departed from standard procedures and involved me in this aspect of the project. I worked directly with a photo researcher from the beginning of the project. In many cases, of course, I asked for a photo of a very specific kind and the long-suffering photo researcher had to find one that fit. But more often we worked in the other direction, with the researcher sending me hundreds of striking photos of children and adults, from which I was able to select those that were good illustrations of important points. This has been a wonderful way to work, and it allowed us to pick the most interesting and engaging photos. I think you will see the difference in the quality of the pictures in the book.

❯ Projects and Other Pedagogy

Those of you who have used any of my other texts on child development or lifespan development will know that I have always included student projects in the text itself. Each project lays out a plan for the student to observe a child or adult, to collect some data, or to investigate programs available for children or adults in their community. For this text I have changed that strategy and put the projects in the *Instructor's Manual*, in order to give instructors more control over the process of obtaining informed consent for such endeavors. The *Instuctor's Manual* includes three types of projects:

Twenty *Research Projects*, each of which involves students' observing or testing one or more individual subjects of some age, such as listening to the language of a 2-year-old or asking adults of various ages about their personal social networks.

Six *At Home Projects*, each of which involves some analysis that can be done at home, without having to locate individual subjects or obtain any informed consent. Examples: analyzing aggression or sex roles on TV programs; analyzing one's own diet and comparing it to lists of risk factors for cancer and heart disease; estimating one's own likely longevity.

Four *Investigative Projects*, each of which is designed for a single student or a small group of students to determine the availability of certain kinds of services within your own community, such as day-care options, birth options, or the like.

In order to make it possible for each instructor to select appropriate projects and to tailor the projects or the project instructions to his or her own needs, HarperCollins will also provide a computer disk containing all the projects.

In addition to the projects and the critical thinking questions, this text includes a number of useful pedagogical aids:

Chapter Summaries, which highlight the key points and provide the students with a focus for their reviews

Key Terms, boldfaced in the text, and defined in a glossary

Suggested Readings for each chapter, annotated, to direct students to the next level of scientific discussions, or practical applications

❯ Supplements

Naturally there are a variety of supplements available to the Instructor and the Student.

For the Instructor

Instructor's Manual.   Written by Michelle Breault of Northeast Missouri State College, this manual contains a wealth of teaching aids for the Lifespan instructor. Each chapter contains lecture notes, in-class exercises, discussion questions, and transparency masters, which are all keyed to the chapter outlines. I have contributed student projects with detailed instructions for each chapter, as well as lecture ideas that I either have used in class or were recommended by reviewers. In addition, the manual includes many references to related print, film, and video resources. This manual is available on disk in both IBM and Macintosh formats from the software support line (1-800-677-6337).

Test Bank.   Written by Darryl Dietrich of the College of St. Scholastica, this test bank contains 2000 questions. Reviewed on content and question type by professors and testing experts, each chapter includes approximately 90 multiple-choice and 10 essay questions. Each question is referenced by learning objective, level of difficulty, and text page. As an added feature, 15 percent of the multiple choice questions also appear in the student study guide and are indicated as such in the test bank.

Software

TestMaster Computerized Testing System.   This flexible, easy-to-master computerized test bank includes all of the test items in the printed test bank. The TestMaster software allows instructors to edit existing questions and add their own items. Available in IBM or Macintosh formats.

QuizMaster.   This new software program, available to instructors, allows students to take TestMaster generated tests on computer. QuizMaster gives the students their scores right away as well as a diagnostic report at the end of the test. This report lets the students know what topics or objectives they may need to study to improve their scores. Test scores can be saved on disk, allowing instructors to keep track of scores for individual students, class sections, or whole courses.

For the Student

Written by Peggy Skinner of South Plains College, the **Study Guide** includes study aides such as chapter outlines, review questions, summaries, glossary terms, essay questions, matching, and true/false questions, including 300 multiple choice questions provided by the Testbank author.

▌ Some Bouquets

No book is an independent project, even one written by a single author. In this case I have had remarkable assistance from a number of editors at HarperCollins, who have collectively made this one of the smoothest and simplest writing projects I have ever undertaken. Anne Harvey, whose idea it was to do this text, was capable, flexible, supportive, and enthusiastic. The developmental editor, Becky Kohn, has been equally splendid. She has adapted to my writing schedule and my somewhat quirky travel plans, given me excellent feedback on style and format, and run interference for me with all the production experts. My deepest thanks to them both, and to all the others at Harper-Collins, including Joanne Tinsley and Susan Driscoll, who were involved in the planning and execution of this book, and to the photo researcher, Rosemary Hunter, who adapted wonderfully to a novel way of working and found dozens of remarkable pictures for us to use.

Equally critical for any text are the comments, criticisms, and suggestions from the many colleagues who served as reviewers at various stages of manuscript preparation. I have greatly appreciated the thought and care given to the text by each of these individuals: Frank Barnett, Kansas State University; Michele Breault, Northeast Missouri State University; Darryl Dietrich, College of St. Scholastica; Susan Doyle, University of Oklahoma; James A. Frost, Cuyahoga Community College; Patricia Guth-Kent, Westmoreland County Community College; David Klein, Stark Technical College; Deborah R. McDonald, New Mexico State University; Phillip Mohan, University of Idaho; Linda Palm, Edison Community College; Judy Raibranum, South Dakota State University; Bonnie Seegmiller, Hunter College; Peggy Skinner, South Plains College; Thomas Spencer, San Francisco State University; Granville Sydnor, San Jacinto College; Thomas Tighe, Moraine Valley Community College; Joe M. Tinnin, Richland College; and Nancy Wallis; Pierce College.

Finally, I need to express my thanks to my husband, Carl de Boor, and to my friends and family, who form my own personal "convoy," without whom an intensive effort like this could not be undertaken, let alone completed on schedule.

Helen Bee

LIFESPAN DEVELOPMENT

Helen L. Bee

ISBN: 0-06-500981-9

Helen Bee's inimitable voice is ever present in her latest text, *Lifespan Development.* Organized chronologically, with parallel chapters on physical/cognitive development and social/personality development for each stage, this text gives students a thorough understanding of human development; it includes an abundance of special, high-interest features and learning aids. It is important to note that though this text is extremely accessible, it is also consistently challenging. Its careful balance of theory, research, and applications inspires readers to think about the material and their own lives in new ways.

PRENATAL DEVELOPMENT AND BIRTH

3

Like any good story, human development has a beginning, a middle, and an end. So let us start the story at the beginning—with conception and with the months of prenatal development. What does normal prenatal development look like? What forces shape it, and what forces can deflect it from its normal path? For example, how much can the mother's health or her health practices help or hinder the process? These questions have great practical importance for those of you who expect to bear (or father) children in the future. But they are also important basic issues as we begin the study of lifespan development. The heredity passed on to the new individual at the moment of conception, and the neurological and other physical developments in these first months, set the stage for all that is to follow.

▶ Conception

The first step in the development of a single human being is that moment of conception when a single sperm cell from the male pierces the wall of the ovum of the female—a moment captured in the photo shown here (Figure 3.1). Ordinarily, a woman produces one **ovum** (egg cell) per month from one of her two ovaries. This occurs roughly midway between two menstrual periods. If the ovum is not fertilized, it travels from the ovary down the **fallopian tube** toward the **uterus,** where it gradually disintegrates and is expelled as part of the next menstruation.

But if a couple has intercourse during the crucial few days when the ovum is in the fallopian tube, one of the millions of sperm ejaculated as part of each male orgasm may travel the full distance through the woman's vagina, cervix, uterus, and fallopian tube and penetrate the wall of the ovum. A child is conceived. Interestingly (and perhaps surprisingly to you), only about half of such conceptuses are likely to survive to birth (and

Figure 3.1 The moment of conception when a single sperm has pierced the shell of the ovum.

CHAPTER OPENING OUTLINES

Prepare the students for what's to come by outlining the organization of the chapter.

What kind of study would you have to do to figure out whether it is OK for pregnant women to maintain high levels of exercise, such as running 30 miles a week?

that are significantly heavier, more alert, and less likely to die in the first year of life (Brown, 1987).

The Mother's Age. One of the particularly intriguing trends in modern family life is that more women are postponing their first pregnancy into their late twenties or early thirties. In 1989, roughly 20 percent of all first births in the United States were to women over 30, double the rate in 1970 (Berkowitz et al., 1990; U.S. Bureau of the Census, 1991). Of course there are many reasons for such delayed childbearing, chief among them the increased need for second incomes in families and the desire of young women to complete job training and early career steps before bearing children. The more education a young women has completed, the more likely she is to delay childbearing into her thirties—a pattern I'll be talking about in the chapters on early adulthood. The key issue for us here is the impact of maternal age on the mother's experience of pregnancy and on the developing child.

The evidence tells us that for the woman, the optimum time for childbearing is in her early twenties. Mothers over 30 (particularly those over 35), are at increased risk for several kinds of problems, including miscarriage (McFalls, 1990), complications of pregnancy such as high blood pressure or bleeding (Berkowitz et al., 1990), and death during pregnancy or delivery (Buehler et al., 1986). For example, in one large recent study of nearly 4000 women in New York, all of whom had received adequate prenatal care, Gertrud Berkowitz and her colleagues (1990) found that women 35 and older during their first pregnancies were almost twice as likely as women in their twenties to suffer some pregnancy complication. These effects of age seem to be exacerbated if the mother has not had adequate prenatal care or has poor health habits. For example, the negative effects of maternal smoking on birth weight is considerably *greater* among women over 35 than among young women (Wen et al., 1990).

On the infant's side of the equation, the news is more positive. Other than the increased risk of Down Syndrome, there is little indication that babies of older mothers are at increased risk for disabilities or problems. Berkowitz found that older mothers were only slightly more likely to have low-birth-weight infants and no more likely to have premature deliveries than were mothers in their twenties. Other epidemiologists (Baird, Sadovnick & Yee, 1991) have found no increased risk of birth defects for older mothers.

Although Berkowitz's study points to increased risks even among older mothers with good prenatal care, other evidence suggests that the effect of age on pregnancy is even

in poverty or among those with poor prenatal care (e.g., ... suggest that age may interact with other factors, such as the

... reased risks for mother and child among teenage mothers. ... at this effect was due to some inherent inadequacy of the ... rmal pregnancy. But recent findings suggest that the height- ... or other nonoptimal outcomes among very young mothers is more a consequence of inadequate prenatal care for teenagers than of age per se. Among those teenagers who have decent diets and adequate prenatal care, problems of pregnancy, preterm delivery or low birth weight are no more frequent than among women in their twenties (Strobino, 1987).

Taking these two sets of data together, it looks as if knowing the mother's age may help us predict the average rate of problems in pregnancies, but it is probably not the age itself that is most critical for most difficulties. More important is the kind of prenatal care a woman receives, the adequacy of her diet, and her general physical health.

The Mother's Emotional State. Finally, the mother's state of mind during the pregnancy may be significant, although the research findings are decidedly mixed (Istvan, 1986). Results from infrahuman studies are clear: exposure of the pregnant female to stressors such as heat, light, noise, shock, or crowding significantly increases the risk of

---

BOXES

Each chapter contains a number of boxes which allow excursions into interesting side channels or practical applications. *Lifespan Development* features **five types of boxes:**

1. "THE REAL WORLD" BOXES

All of these boxes explore some practical application of research or theory.

2. "SOAP BOXES"

In both of these boxes, the author expresses her personal views on pressing social policy issues: the importance of prenatal care and the need for a national family policy.

Other Drugs. There is no room to list or discuss the many other drugs that appear to have some teratogenic effect, but let me give two more brief examples:

Diethylstilbestrol (DES) is a synthetic estrogen that at one time was commonly given to pregnant women to prevent miscarriages. The daughters of such women have been found to have higher rates of some kinds of cancers, and as many as 30 percent of the sons have been found to be infertile (Rosenblith & Sims-Knight, 1989).

One of the most widely used drugs, *aspirin*, is teratogenic in animals when given in high doses. Humans rarely take high enough doses to produce such effects directly, but it turns out that aspirin in moderate amounts can have negative effects on the fetus if it is ingested along with benzoic acid, a chemical widely used as a food preservative, such as in catsup. This combination, especially in the first trimester, seems to increase the risk of physical malformations in the embryo/fetus.

▶ Other Influences on Prenatal Development

Diet. Another risk for the fetus is poor maternal nutrition. In periods of famine, for example, preterm births and low birth weight are greatly increased, as is the death rate for infants in the first year of life (e.g., Stein et al., 1975). Studies of famine show that the consequences are most detrimental if the malnutrition occurred during the last three months of the pregnancy, when neurons are beginning a rapid expansion of dendritic density. Malnutrition or subnutrition associated with poverty appears to have similar negative effects, a conclusion reinforced by the repeated observation that poor (presumably malnourished) women given nutritional supplements during pregnancy have babies

5. "ACROSS CULTURES" BOXES

These boxes focus on two aspects of cross-cultural or cross-ethnic group research: evidence showing that basic developmental processes are the same in children or adults in every culture, and research cataloging the variations of developmental patterns as a function of cultural or subcultural differences.

ACROSS CULTURES
Universals and Variations in Early Language

In the early years of research on children's language development, linguists and psychologists were strongly impressed by the apparent similarities in the vocabularies and early sentences children constructed. You'll remember some of the cross-cultural comparisons of early vocabulary from Chapter 5, which show strong similarities. Studies in a wide variety of language communities, including Turkish, Serbo-Croatian, Hungarian, Hebrew, Japanese, a New Guinean language called Kaluli, German, and Italian, have revealed other important similarities:

- The prelinguistic phase seems to be identical in all language communities. All babies coo, then babble; all babies understand language before they can speak it; babies in all cultures begin to use their first words at about 12 months.
- In all language communities studied so far, a one-word phase precedes the two-word phase, with the latter beginning at about 18 months.
- Language learning is affected by the child's own actions. So, for example, in every language studied so far, when children first add verb inflections such as the past tense, they are more likely to add them to verbs that describe actions that bring visible results, such as *drop*, *fall*, *break*, or *spill*.
- In all languages studied so far, prepositions describing locations are added in essentially the same order. Words for *in*, *on*, *under*, and *beside* are learned first. Then the child learns the words *front* and *back* (Slobin, 1985a).
- Children seem to pay more attention to the ends of words than the beginnings, so they learn suffixes before they learn prefixes.

At the same time there are marked differences among languages and in children's early attempts to construct sentences in the language they are hearing. For example:

- The specific word order that a child uses in early sentences is not the same for all children in all languages. In some languages a noun/verb sequence is fairly common, in others a verb/noun sequence may be heard.
- Particular inflections are learned in highly varying orders from one language to another. Japanese children, for example, begin very early to use a special kind of marker, called a *pragmatic* marker, that tells something about the feeling or the context. For instance, in Japanese, the word *yo* is used at the end of a sentence when the speaker is experiencing some resistance from the listener; the word *ne* is used when the speaker expects approval or agreement. Japanese children begin to use these markers very early, much earlier than other inflections appear in most languages.
- Most strikingly, there are languages in which there seems to be no uninflected Stage 1 grammar at all. Children learning Turkish, for example, use essentially the full set of noun and verb inflections by age 2 and never go through a stage of using uninflected words. Their language is simple, but it is rarely ungrammatical from the adult's point of view (Aksu-Koc & Slobin, 1985).

Obviously any theory of language acquisition must account for both the common ground and the wide variations from one language to the next.

and on syllables in the stream of sounds they hear, that they pay attention to sound rhythm, and that they prefer speech of a particular pattern, namely motherese. Slobin also proposes that babies are preprogrammed to pay attention to the beginnings and endings of strings of sounds and to stressed sounds. Together, these operating principles would help to explain some of the features of children's early grammars.

The fact that this model is consistent with the growing information about apparently built-in perceptual skills and processing biases is certainly a strong argument in its favor. But it is still early days in the exploration of this approach, and there are other compelling alternatives. In particular, there are theorists who argue persuasively that what is important is not the built-in biases, but the child's *construction* of language as part of the broader process of cognitive development. In this view, the child is a "little linguist," applying her emerging cognitive understanding to the problem of language, searching for regularities and patterns.

Constructivist Theories of Language. Melissa Bowerman (1985) is the clearest proponent of this view. She puts the proposition this way: "When language starts to come in, it does not introduce new meanings to the child. Rather, it is used to express only those meanings the child has already formulated independently of language" (1985, p. 372).

The amount and kind of contact an adult has with kin are strongly influenced by proximity. Adults who live within two hours of their parents and siblings see them far more often than is true of those who live at longer distance. But long distance does not prevent a parent or sibling from being part of an individual adult's convoy. These relationships can provide support in times of need, even if physical contact is infrequent.

Friendships in Early Adulthood

Friends, too, can be important members of a convoy. We choose our friends as we choose our partner, from among those we see as like ourselves in education, social class, interests, family background, or family life-cycle stage. Cross-sex friendships are more common among adults than they are among 10-year-olds, but they are still outnumbered by same-sex friendships. Young adults' friends are also overwhelmingly drawn from their own age group. Beyond this basic filter of similarity, close friendship seems to rest on mutual openness and personal disclosure.

There are some hints that the number of friends in the convoy may be at a peak in

ACROSS CULTURES
Kin Relationships in Black and Hispanic Families

You may well wonder whether the description of young adult kin relationships I've given you is equally valid for all subgroups or subcultures. In fact it is not. In the United States, both black and hispanic family relationships differ from those in the Anglo culture.

Hispanic Kin Relationships. Among Hispanics, particularly Mexican-Americans, the convoy is strongly dominated by family ties, a pattern strengthened by the fact that Hispanic families typically choose to live nearer to one another than is true of Anglos. Given a choice, many non-Hispanics move *away* from kin networks in early adulthood while Hispanics move *toward* them (Vega, 1990). In the Hispanic culture, extensive kin networks are the rule rather than the exception, with frequent visiting and exchange not only with parents, children, and siblings, but with grandparents, cousins, aunts, and uncles (Keefe, 1984). These frequent contacts are not only perceived as enjoyable, they are seen as vital signs of the closeness of kin relationships. It is not enough to write or talk on the phone; to maintain close ties you need to see and touch your relatives and friends. Among Hispanics, an individual's self-esteem may also be more strongly related to the valuation given by the kin group. William Madsen describes the difference this way:

When an Anglo fails, he thinks first of how this failure will affect him and his status in society. When a Chicano fails, his first evaluation of the failure is in terms of what it will do to his family and how it will affect his relationship to other family members. (1969, p. 224)

There is some indication that this pattern is stronger in first-generation immigrants, who rely almost exclusively on family members for emotional support and problem solving. Second-generation immigrants seem to have more extensive non kin networks. But in both generations, the extended family clearly plays a more central role in the daily life of Hispanics than it does in the Anglo culture.

Black Kin Relationships. The same is true of African-Americans, although the reasons are somewhat different. There is a whole set of demographic differences between black and white families in the United States that create markedly different kin contacts. Young adult blacks are much less likely to marry than are whites. Many live in cohabiting relationships, but many others live in multigeneration households with their parents, grandparents, or other relatives. The National Survey of Black Americans, a nationally representative sample studied in 1980, showed that 21.8 percent of all black families were of this extended type. Among black families headed by a young adult, the rate was 50 percent, most of these consisting of a two generations of adult women and one or more children (Hatchett, Cochran & Jackson, 1991). Over the period of young adulthood, six out of ten black women live in such a household at least for a period of time, compared to only about 30 percent of white women (Beck and Beck, 1989). As a result, parent-adult child relationships seem to be particularly central to young adult convoys in African-American culture, especially the relationship between mothers and their adult daughters.

Frequent and supportive contact with kin and other network members is also a significant part of the daily life of most black adults who do not live in extended family households. In one large national survey of black Americans (Taylor, 1986), 37 percent reported that they had contact with family members nearly every day. African-Americans also are more likely to form what have been called pseudokin networks or "fictive" kin relationships—close familylike relationships with neighbors or peers, in which a wide variety of aid is exchanged (Taylor et al., 1990).

such differences in rate are consistent over time. Questions of this kind about infant development have an important practical implication: If we could accurately measure differences in infants' rate (or pattern) of development in the early months of life, then it might be possible to identify infants who are later going to have problems learning to read or to perform in school in other ways. It might then be possible to intervene very early, perhaps thereby averting or at least ameliorating the problem.

One of the motivations behind the development of the various infant IQ tests was just such a hope that test scores could be used to help identify infants with current or prospective problems. Typically, these tests are constructed rather like IQ tests for older children: They include a series of items identified as suitable for children of particular ages, or a series of items of increasing difficulty. The child's performance is then compared to the average performance of other children the same age to yield an IQ-like score. In the case of infant tests, the items measure primarily sensory and motor skills, such as:

Reaching for a dangling ring (a 3-month-old item)

Uncovering a toy hidden by a cloth (8 months)

Putting cubes in a cup on request (9 months)

Building a tower of three cubes (17 months)

In the most widely used modern version of such a test, the **Bayley Scales of Infant Development** (Bayley, 1969), the score is subdivided into two parts, one reflecting mental development and the other motor development.

Many (but not all) of those who devised such infancy tests assumed that they were measuring the same basic intellectual processes as are measured by the tests for older children. But empirical results do not support that assumption. Scores on infant tests do not predict later IQ test scores at all well. The typical correlation between a 12-month Bayley mental test score and a 4-year-old IQ score is only about .20 to .30 (e.g., Bee et al., 1982)—significant, but not robust. Bayley's test and others like the Denver Developmental Screening Test are effective in identifying children with serious developmental delays (Frankenberg et al., 1975; M. Lewis & Sullivan, 1985). But as a more general predictive tool to forecast later IQ or school performance, such tests have not been nearly as useful as many had hoped. Ten years ago, Robert McCall summarized the empirical findings flatly:

Nearly 50 years of research shows that [correlations] from infant behavior to later I.Q. are sufficiently low to be conceptually uninteresting and clinically useless. (McCall, 1981, p. 141)

Building a tower of three cubes is an item at the 17-month-level on the Bayley Scales of Infant Development.

It seems reasonable to guess that referential and expressive style babies would differ from each other in other ways as well. Can you make any guesses about just what those differences might be?

CRITICAL THINKING QUESTIONS

Critical Thinking Questions,

appearing frequently in the margins of each chapter, encourage students to think more critically and read more actively. Some questions ask readers to relate the chapter material to their own lives. Others ask students to think about ways to design a piece of research in response to specific questions. Still others ask theoretical questions or require students to analyze his or her own point of view on a given subject or issue.

ART PROGRAM

Helen Bee worked hand-in-hand with the photo researcher from the beginning of this project. Hence, striking and engaging photographs of children and adults, all of which clearly illustrate important points, are woven throughout. The quality of the photos as well as the line art in this book is unsurpassed.

▶ **Birth**

Once the 38 weeks of gestation are over, the fetus must be born into the world—an event that holds some pain as well as a good deal of joy for most parents. In the normal process, labor progresses through three stages of unequal length.

The First Stage of Labor. Stage 1 covers the period during which two important processes occur: dilation and effacement. The cervix (the opening at the bottom of the uterus) must open up like the lens of a camera (**dilation**) and also flatten out (**effacement**). At the time of actual delivery of the infant, the cervix must normally be dilated to about 10 centimeters (about 4 inches), as you can see in Figure 3.10 (page 70). This part of labor has been likened to putting on a sweater with a neck that is too tight. You have to pull and stretch the neck of the sweater with your head in order to get it on. Eventually the neck is stretched wide enough so that the widest part of your head can pass through.

Customarily, stage 1 is itself divided into phases. In the *early* (or *latent*) phase, contractions are relatively far apart and are typically not too uncomfortable. In the *late* phase, which begins when the cervix is about halfway dilated and continues until dilation has

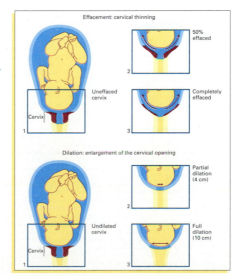

Figure 3.10 The process of effacement and dilation during labor. (*Source:* Stenchever, 1978, Figure 5-4, p. 84.)

INTERLUDES

Interludes synthesize the developmental patterns and processes of each age period. They answer critical questions like, "What are the Key or basic processes at work?," "What external influences affect those processes?," and " What are the relationships among the various threads of development in that age period?".

SUMMING UP MIDDLE CHILDHOOD DEVELOPMENT

Basic Characteristics of Middle Childhood

The table below summarizes the changes and continuities of middle childhood. You can see from the table that there are many gradual changes: greater and greater physical skill, less and less reliance on appearance and more and more attention to underlying qualities and attributes, and greater and greater role of peers. The one period in which there seems to be a more rapid change is right at the beginning of middle childhood, at the point of transition from the preschooler to the school child. And of course at the other end of this age range, puberty causes another set of rapid changes.

The Transition Between 5 and 7. Some kind of transition into middle childhood has been noted in a great many cultures. There seems to be widespread recognition that a 6-year-old is somehow qualitatively different from a 5-year-old: more responsible, more able to understand complex ideas. Among the Kipsigis of Kenya, for example, the age of 6 is said to be the first point at which the child has ng'omnotet, translated as *intelligence* (Harkness & Super, 1985). The fact that schooling begins at this age seems to reflect an implicit or explicit recognition of this fundamental shift.

Psychologists who have studied development across this transition have pointed to a whole series of changes.

• Cognitively, there is a shift to what Piaget calls concrete operational thinking. The child now understands conservation problems, seriation, and class inclusion. More generally, the child seems to pay less attention to surface properties of objects and more to underlying continuities and patterns. We see this not only in children's understanding of physical objects but in their understanding of others, of relationships, and of themselves. In studies of information processing, we see a parallel rapid increase in the child's use of executive strategies.

• In self-concept, we first see a global judgment of self-worth at about age 7 or 8.

• In peer relationships, gender segregation becomes virtually complete by age 6 or 7, especially in individual friendships.

The apparent confluence of these changes is impressive and seems to

A Summary of the Threads of Development During Middle Childhood

Aspect of development	Age in years					
	6	7	8	9	10	11	12
Physical development	Jumps rope; skips; may ride bike	Rides two-wheeled bike	Rides bike well	Puberty begins for some girls		Puberty begins for some boys
Cognitive development	Gender constancy; various concrete operations skills, including some conservation, class inclusion, various memory strategies, executive processes (metacognition)		Inductive logic; better and better use of concrete operations skills; conservation of weight			Conservation of volume
Self/personality development	Concept of self increasingly more abstract, less tied to appearance; descriptions of others increasingly focused on internal, enduring, qualitites					
			Global sense of self-worth			
			Friendship based on reciprocal trust			
		Gender segregation in play and friendships almost total				
		Enduring friendships appear, continue throughout these years				

---

provide some support for the existence of a Piaget-like stage. On the surface, at least, there seems to be some kind of change in the basic structure of the child's thinking that is reflected in all aspects of the child's functioning. But impressive as these changes are, it is not so clear that what is going on here is a rapid, pervasive, structural change to a whole new way of thinking and relating. Children don't make this shift all at once in every area of their thinking or relationships. For example, while the shift from a concrete to a more abstract self-concept may become noticeable at 6 or 7, it occurs quite gradually and is still going on at ages 11 and 12. Similarly, a child may grasp conservation of quantity at age 5 or 6, but typically does not understand conservation of weight until several years later.

Furthermore, expertise, or the lack of it, strongly affects the pattern of the child's cognitive progress. Thus, while I think most psychologists would agree that there is a set of important changes that normally emerge together at about this age, most would also agree that there is no rapid or abrupt reorganization of the child's whole mode of operating.

Central Processes

In trying to account for the developmental shifts we see during middle childhood, my bias has been to see the cognitive changes as most central, the necessary but not sufficient condition for the alterations in relationships and in the self-scheme during this period. A good illustration is the emergence of a global sense of self-worth, which seems to require not only a tendency to look beyond or behind surface characteristics, but also the use of inductive logic. The child appears to arrive at a global sense of self-worth by some summative, inductive process.

Similarly, the quality of the child's relationships with peers and parents seems to rest, in part, on basic cognitive understanding of reciprocity and perspective taking. The child now understands that others read him as much as he reads them. Children of 7 or 8 will now say of their friends that they "trust each other," something you would be very unlikely to hear from a 5-year-old.

Such a cognitive bias dominated theories and research on middle childhood for many decades, largely as a result of the powerful influence of Piaget's theory. This imbalance has begun to be redressed in recent years, as the central importance of the peer group and the child's social experience have been better understood. There are two aspects of this revision of thinking. First, we have reawakened to the (obvious) fact that a great deal of the experience on which the child's cognitive progress is based occurs in social interactions, particularly in play with other children. Second, we have realized that social relationships make a unique set of demands, both cognitive and interactive.

People simply ne of water, other thi ally, and informat ther, unlike relationships with objects, relationships with people are mutual and reciprocal. Other people talk back, respond to your distress, offer things, get angry.

Children also have to learn social scripts, those special rules that apply to social interactions, such as politeness rules, or rules about when you can and cannot speak, or rules about power or dominance hierarchies. Such scripts change with age, so at each new age the child must learn a new set of roles, a new set of rules about what she may and may not do. To be sure, these changes in the scripts are partly in *response* to the child's growing cognitive sophistication. But they also reflect changes in the child's role in the social system. One obvious example is the set of changes when children start school. The script associated with the role of "student" is simply quite different from the one connected with the role of "little kid." School classrooms are more tightly organized than are preschools or day care centers, expectations for obedience are higher, and there are more drills and routines to be learned. These changes are bound to affect the child's pattern of thinking.

Just what role physical change plays in this collection of developments I do not know. Clearly there *are* physical changes going on. Girls, in particular, begin the early steps of puberty during elementary school. But we simply don't know whether the rate of physical development in these years is connected in any way to the rate of the child's progress through the sequence of cognitive or social understandings. There has been virtually stances in which they rarely have much control over their lives may be more likely to develop a low sense of self-efficacy or little optimism. The point is that these psychological processes and enduring personality characteristics affect not only our roles and relationships, they affect our physical health as well, beginning in early adulthood.

Summary

1. Although it is an arbitrary division, we can segment the adult years into three periods, with young adulthood comprising the years from 20 to about 40.
2. Sorting out the effects of basic maturational change (which we call *aging*) from other causes of change in adult life has proven difficult. Both disease and reduced activity may also contribute to observed patterns.
3. Nonetheless, it is clear that between 20 and 40, adults are at their peak both physically and cognitively. In these years a person has more muscle tissue, more calcium in the bones, more brain mass, better sensory acuity, greater aerobic capacity, and a more efficient immune system.
4. These differences are smaller when we study only healthy individuals longitudinally, but there is still some decline.
5. Studies of heart and lung function show no age change under resting conditions, but performance declines with age when tests are given during or after exercise.
6. A number of these changes contribute to a loss of speed with age—both speed in moving and response time to some stimulus. This decline is observed even (or especially) in top athletes.
7. Changes in the immune system may be especially critical in accounting for what we think of as the aging process, because they mean the older adult is more susceptible to disease.
8. Increases in disease and disability with age are earlier and larger for lower class than upper-class adults, even when health habits and stress levels are taken into account.
9. In contrast, mental health is *worse* in early adulthood; young adults *are* more likely to be depressed, anxious, or lonely than are the middle aged.
10. Measures of cognitive skill, like physical skill, show declines with age, but the decline is quite late for well exercised abilities like vocabulary, everyday memory problems, and normal problem solving.
11. There *may* also be a change in cognitive structure in adult life, with several varieties of post-formal-operational stages suggested by theorists.
12. Exercise of either physical or cognitive abilities can improve performance at any age, although the upper limit may decline over time.
13. There are wide individual variations in the rate of physical and cognitive loss. Some of this difference seems to be explained by varying health habits. Adults with good health habits have lower risk of death and disease at any age.
14. Social support and a sense of personal control also affect the rate of disease and death, especially in the face of stress.

CHAPTER SUMMARIES

These learning aids highlight key points and provide students with focuses for review.

KEY TERMS

Important new words are boldfaced in the text and then defined in a text-ending glossary.

Key Terms

crystallized intelligence	locus of control	self-efficacy
fluid intelligence	maximum oxygen uptake	

Suggested Readings

Seligman, M. E. P. (1991). *Learned optimism.* New York: Alfred A. Knopf. (A very readable description of Seligman's influential theory of optimism and learned helplessness, written for the lay reader. A wide-ranging and thought-provoking book.)

Salthouse, T. A. (1991). *Theoretical perspectives on cognitive aging.* Hillsdale, NJ: Lawrence Erlbaum Associates. (An extremely thorough, detailed analysis of all the evidence on cognitive changes from early to late adulthood. This book is not for the casual reader, but it is an excellent source of further references on virtually any aspect of this complex subject.)

Schneider, E. L., & Rowe, J. W. (Eds.) (1990). *Handbook of the biology of aging,* 3rd ed. San Diego, CA: Academic Press. (A compendium of technical papers describing current knowledge about various facets of biological aging, including changes in the brain, the circulatory system, and the immune systems.)

SETTING THE STAGE: BASIC CONCEPTS AND METHODS

1

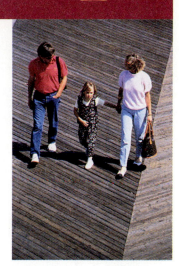

Each summer I spend several months at a unique family camp in the state of Washington. Because many of the same people come back year after year, bringing their children (and often later their grandchildren), I see many people in once-a-year snapshots. When a family arrives, I am immediately struck by how much the children have changed. We all seem to find ourselves saying to the kids, "Good grief, you've grown a foot," or "Last time I saw you, you were only this big." (I say these things, even remembering full well how much I hated it when people said these things to me at the same age. Of *course* I had grown. And because I was always taller than anyone my age, I didn't like to be reminded of this peculiarity.)

But when we see the adults, we are much less struck by the changes. We are more likely to say something like, "You look great," or "You haven't changed a bit." If we notice change, it is more likely to be something peripheral like a new hairdo or a weight loss. Some of this may be flattery: we assume that adults don't like to be reminded that they're getting older, so we may lie a little when we say someone hasn't changed. But there is a basic difference in our reactions to a child and to an adult. We *expect* a child to change; we expect an adult to remain the same. Yet children also show continuity, and adults also change—albeit over longer periods. The shy 2-year-old is still likely to be more shy than average at 8 or 12. And the 40-year-old not only looks different from the 20-year-old, he also is likely to have different attitudes, different values, a different life pattern. In fact, as adults most of us feel as if we are changing, growing, and learning. Many of us resent assumptions by family or friends that we are just the same as we always were.

All of this means that to understand development, we must look at both change and continuity across the entire age range from conception to death. What kinds of changes do we see, and at what ages? We also need to understand which of those changes (or continuities) are shared by individuals in all cultures, and which are unique to a given culture, to a group within a culture, or to a particular individual. For example, most of us assume that mental abilities decline as we move into old age. Certainly that is true on

If you think of yourself as you are now, and as you were when you were 10 or 12, in what ways are you the same, and in what ways have you changed? Have your siblings and friends changed in similar ways?

average, but is it true for everyone? Is it an inevitable change that is part of the shared, normal process of aging, or is it true only of some people and not others?

At the same time, we need to try to understand the origins of these patterns of development, both the shared and the unique. This issue is typically framed in terms of biology versus environment, nature versus nurture. But of course nature and nurture are both involved in almost every developmental pattern we see. Older adults could become slower in their thinking processes because of basic biological change in the nervous system, for example. Or perhaps they are slower because they are simply out of practice. More probably, it is both, in varying amounts for different individuals. Even if everyone is experiencing a basic physiological decline in old age, it could still be the case that those adults who remain the most mentally active decline the least.

Throughout these chapters, I will try to sort out the relative impact of nature and nurture in each domain of development and at each age. What you need at this point is a grounding in some of the basic concepts and theories that form the framework for such an analysis. Let me begin by looking at change with age and what might cause it.

▶ Explaining Changes over the Life Span

Psychologists and sociologists who study development talk about three basic categories of change with age: (1) shared, age-graded changes common to every individual in a species, (2) changes that are common to a particular subgroup growing up together—either a particular culture or a particular generation within a given culture, and (3) individual changes resulting from unique, nonshared events (Baltes, Reese & Lipsitt, 1980).

Shared, Age-Graded Changes

When most of us think about "developmental change," we're thinking about the shared, age-graded changes. Changes in this category are basic to human behavior, inevitable for all of us, and linked to age. At least three forces could produce such age-graded changes.

Biologically Influenced Changes.   The most obvious candidate to account for shared, age-graded changes is some kind of basic biological process common to all humans. The infant who shifts from crawling to walking, the teenage girl who develops breasts and begins to menstruate, the older adult whose skin becomes progressively more wrinkled, all seem to be following a ground plan laid down in the physical body, most likely in the genetic code itself. The term most often used to describe this kind of change is **maturation**. Arnold Gesell, who introduced this concept many years ago (1925), defined maturation as *genetically programmed sequential patterns of change*. Changes in body size and shape, changes in hormones at puberty, changes in muscles and bones, changes in the circulatory system in middle and old age, all may be programmed in this way, a kind of **biological clock** ticking away in the background.

Like all of us, this boy has passed through a clear sequence of maturational changes, from babyhood through early childhood and into adolescence.

Gesell thought that maturationally determined development occurred regardless of practice or training. You don't have to practice growing pubic hair or be taught how to walk; you do not try to slow down your reaction time as you get older. Despite these obvious examples, researchers since Gesell's day have found clear evidence that no such "pure" maturational effects exist. The environment always has some effect. Even powerful, apparently automatic maturational patterns such as brain growth in the first year of life require at least some minimal environmental support. The baby whose environment is severely impoverished is not going to develop the same density of neural connections in the brain as will an infant who grows in a complex environment. And at the other end of the age spectrum, experience may retard or hasten the basic maturational processes. Exercise may help to slow down the compression of the spine, good diet may affect the loss of elasticity in the skin.

I should point out that the term *maturation* does not mean the same thing as *growth*, although the two terms are sometimes used as if they were synonyms. *Growth* refers to a step-by-step change in quantity, for example in size. We speak of the growth of the child's vocabulary or the growth of her body. Such changes in quantity *may* be the result of maturation, but not necessarily. A child's body might grow because of a change in diet, which is an external effect, or because muscles and bones have grown, which is probably a maturational effect. To put it another way, the term *growth* is a *description* of change, while the concept of maturation is one *explanation* of change.

Shared Experiences. The biological clock is not the only one ticking. There is also a **social clock** that can shape all (or most) lives into shared patterns of change (Helson, Mitchell & Moane, 1984). The social clock defines a sequence of shared cultural experiences, typically occurring at common ages, which collectively help to create shared patterns of development. For example, all over the world children start school somewhere between the ages of 5 and 7. This shared timing may reflect a recognition by adults in many cultures that this is about the age at which children are ready to deal with school tasks. But the fact that children go to school at this age also shapes their development, since schooling itself helps to spur children on to more complex forms of thinking (e.g., Stevenson et al., 1991). So many of the cognitive changes we see in children between 7 and 12 may be the product of the common experience of schooling, rather than (or in addition to) biological changes.

In adulthood the social clock is particularly noisy. Sociologist Matilda White Riley (1976, 1986) points out that virtually every society is organized in **age strata**—periods in the life span when there are common tasks, common expectations, common societal norms. In every culture, young adults are expected to form families, to reproduce. Those in middle and later years have greater power and authority, and "elders" have still different roles, sometimes ceremonial or religious. These age strata tend to shape all lives into similar trajectories.

Obviously, developmental patterns based on shared experiences are less likely to be universal than are maturationally based, biological-clock patterns. The large majority of children go to school, but not all; every culture has age norms, but not all those norms are precisely the same. Despite these variations, though, we need to look for shared experiences within a culture, or even across cultures, that may help to account for the common threads of development we see.

Shared Internal Changes. At a still deeper level, there may be shared inner changes that are the result of the way we respond to the developmental pressures of the biological and social clocks. For example, learning to walk not only makes the baby physically more independent, it may also stimulate a shift toward greater psychological independence at about the same age in all children. Thus the physical change triggers a much broader shift in perspective. In the same fashion, perhaps the greater cognitive skill that comes at about age 7 (in part from schooling) contributes to the child's growing ability to make global assessments of others and of himself. It is at this age, for example, that children first develop a sense of global self-esteem, an overall assessment of their own worth, which in turn affects both motivation and relationships.

Similarly, the common biological and social changes of adolescence and adulthood may form the framework for a set of predictable changes in personality, in style of thinking, in values. One example is a set of personality changes that seem to occur between early and middle adulthood.

In every culture that I know of, young adults are required to learn and perform a complex set of roles—marrying and forming a family, bearing and rearing children, working. By middle adulthood, though, the roles are less confining, partly because at this point they are well learned, and partly because children are mostly grown and demand less

Keeping physically active and fit, like this 97-year-old gardener, will not allow you to evade the inevitable maturational decline of old age, but it may significantly retard the process.

Write a sentence or two about the characteristics of each major adult age stratum in our culture. How do you think our expectations of 20-year-olds differ from our expectations of 70-year-olds?

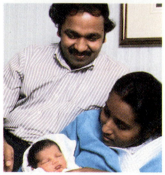

In every culture, early adulthood is the time for forming families.

attention. This shift in the social clock seems to be accompanied by—and may indeed trigger—a deeper psychological change, marked by a movement toward a greater sense of autonomy, greater assertiveness and self-confidence. Figure 1.1 shows the results from one study illustrating this change. In this study, the same individuals were interviewed repeatedly from early childhood through late mid-life. You can see that in their late thirties these subjects experienced a sharp rise in self-confidence. These results alone do not tell us that such a shift is universal or even common, nor do they reveal the cause. But the results do illustrate a shared psychological change that *may* be triggered by common social tasks or biological maturation.

Cultural and Cohort Effects

Development is also shaped by less universally shared experiences. Each culture has its own expectations, its own standards and age patterns. In some cultures, for example, girls typically marry at age 12 or 13; in others marriage occurs at least a decade later. *Within* each culture, there are many shared age-linked patterns, but those patterns are not the same from one society to the next. This is a simple truth we must keep in mind as we look at research on development over the life span. The vast bulk of our research base is made up of studies on children and adults in the United States or in other western or industrialized countries. We must be careful not to assume that patterns of development that occur in our culture will necessarily appear in every culture, or even for every subgroup within our own society.

An equally important source of variation in life experience comes from historical forces that affect each generation somewhat differently. Social scientists use the word **cohort** to describe groups of individuals born within some fairly narrow band of years, who share the same historical experiences at the same times in their lives. Within any given culture, successive cohorts may have quite different life experiences. For example, my father, born in 1914, was a teenager when the Great Depression hit in the United States. He and all his cohort were profoundly affected by that experience.

Figure 1.1 These results are from a famous study in Berkeley and Oakland, California, of a group of subjects, some born in 1920 and some in 1928. They were tested frequently in childhood and adolescence, as well as three times in adulthood. Here you can see the sharp rise in self-confidence that occurred for both men and women in this group in their thirties—a pattern that *may* reflect a shared personality change triggered by the common experiences of the social clock. (*Source:* Haan, Millsap & Hartka, 1986, Figure 1, p. 228.)

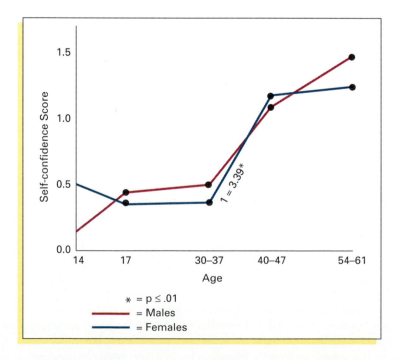

RESEARCH REPORT
Children and Adolescents in the Great Depression of the 1930s: An Example of a Cohort Effect

Research by Glen Elder on children and adolescents who grew up during the Great Depression illustrates exceptionally clearly that the same historical event can have very different effects on adjacent cohorts (Elder, 1974, 1978; Elder, Liker & Cross, 1984). Elder used information from one of the most famous long-term studies in the psychological literature, the Berkeley/Oakland Growth Study. The several hundred subjects who were involved in this study had been born either in 1920 or in 1928. All have been studied in detail over the succeeding years, with the most recent assessments completed when they were in their fifties. Those in the 1920 group were in their teens during the depression; those born in 1928 were still young children during the worst economic times.

Elder was able to compare the experiences of children whose families had lost more than 35 percent of their pre-depression income with those whose economic condition was better. In the most general terms, he found that the economic hardship was largely beneficial to the cohort born in 1920, who were teenagers when the depression struck full force, while the experience was generally detrimental to the cohort born in 1928.

Most of the teenagers whose families experienced the worst economic hardship were pushed into prematurely adult responsibilities. Many worked at odd jobs, earning money that was vitally important to the family's welfare. They felt, and were, needed by their families. As adults, they had a strong work ethic and a strong commitment to family.

Those who were born in the late 1920s had a very different experience. These children were quite young during the hardest years and so spent a larger proportion of their early years under conditions of hardship. Because of the economic stress, their families frequently experienced a loss of cohesion and warmth. They had little time to meet the emotional needs of their younger children. The consequences were generally negative for the children, especially the boys. These youngsters were less hopeful and less confident than their less economically stressed peers; in adolescence they did less well in school, completed fewer years of education, and were less ambitious and less successful as adults.

These two cohorts were only eight years apart, yet their experiences were strikingly different because of the timing of a key event in their lives.

An example that may be a bit closer to home is that of the Baby Boom—the major increase in birth rate that occurred in the United States as well as in many other industrialized countries right after World War II, peaking between 1955 and 1965. This significant change created a cohort far larger than those on either side. The very largeness of the cohort has shaped the experiences and opportunities of those born within it. If you are part of that cohort, you went to crowded schools, had a harder time getting into college because the competition for each space was greater, and you competed with more people for jobs. Those of us in the much smaller cohort born right before the Baby Boom (as I am, born in 1939) have had much less competition at many stages of our lives. Thus the timing of one's birth may have long-term consequences for the experiences we will have, the way in which we will develop, and the attitudes we will have.

These examples show that the concept of a cohort can help us in two ways. It can help to explain why people in a given age group are similar to one another, and it can help to explain why groups close in age may have very different developmental trajectories.

The concept of a cohort becomes particularly important as we try to interpret studies of adults. A great deal of research on adulthood involves comparisons of sets of subjects from different age groups—a strategy called a *cross-sectional study*. Each age group is assessed on a particular variable, such as work satisfaction, loneliness, depression, or cognitive skill. The average scores for each age group can then be compared. But when we compare those averages, we are comparing cohorts as well as age groups, which makes the results very difficult to interpret.

For instance, in a recent article on self-esteem, *Newsweek* magazine (Feb. 17, 1992, p. 50) reported on results from a Gallup poll. Several hundred adults from across the

In the 1950s and 1960s, the average woman in the United States had between three and four children, a pattern that created the famous Baby Boom. By the late 1970s, the number had dropped to less than two. This simple statistical difference has had a profound effect on the life experiences of two adjacent cohorts.

Those adults now in their fifties, who will soon be moving into retirement and old age, represent the leading edge of a cohort that experienced a massive increase in women's labor force participation and in divorce rates. What effects might these demographic characteristics have on the aging experiences of this cohort that are likely to be different than the old-age experiences of cohorts that preceded them?

country were asked which of a variety of situations would make them feel very bad about themselves. The following results were typical:

	Age Groups		
	18–29	39–49	50+
Would feel very bad about being unable to pay their bills	51%	57%	80%
Would feel very bad about doing something embarrassing in public	26%	25%	50%

How would you interpret age differences like these? Do they mean that there is a basic developmental shift toward more self-criticism as we get older, or do they show only a cohort difference? Perhaps the cohorts now over 50 grew up at a time when there were different cultural values, including a greater emphasis on personal responsibility. There is nothing in the statistics themselves that permits us to choose between these possibilities.

It is important to keep these culture- and cohort-specific variations in mind as we go along. They make the job of sorting out shared, basic developmental patterns much more difficult, but at the same time they can be immensely informative and interesting. To understand human development we need to do more than merely identify those patterns of change with age that occur regardless of environmental variation. We also need to understand how specific experiences can shift whole groups of people into different pathways. Cohort comparisons can shine an enormous amount of light on just such questions.

Unique, Nonshared Events

In the same vein, we have to try to understand the ways in which highly individual experiences shape the lives of children and adults. What is the impact of a divorce on a child? Does the child's age at the time of the divorce make a difference? What about a man being laid off from work in his early thirties, or a girl giving birth to a child at age 14, or a couple delaying childbirth until their forties? And what of those chance encounters with a single individual—a remarkable teacher, a rapist, a mentoring boss—that may alter an individual's life path (Bandura, 1982a, 1989)? Each individual's development is shaped by a unique combination of specific events. While we cannot study every individual, we can look for basic processes or rules that seem to govern how individual experiences will affect an individual's pathway of development.

Timing of Experience. Many psychologists have concluded that a key factor is the *timing* of specific experiences. Timing effects have been central in studies of both children and adults, but the issue is phrased differently in the two cases.

In theories of child development, the significant concept is that of a **critical period**. The basic idea is that there may be specific periods in development when an organism is especially sensitive to the presence (or absence) of some particular kind of experience. In baby ducks, the period about 15 hours after hatching is a critical period for the development of attachment and following. They will follow any duck or any other quacking, moving object that happens to be around them at that critical time. If nothing is moving or quacking at that critical point, they don't develop any attachment or following response at all (Hess, 1972).

We can see similar critical periods in the action of various **teratogens** in prenatal development. A teratogen is an outside agent, such as a disease organism or chemical, that can adversely affect the developmental process. Most teratogens have negative effects only during some critical period. For example, if a mother contracts the disease rubella (commonly called *German measles*) during the first three months of pregnancy, some damage or deformity is very likely to occur in the fetus. Infection with the same virus after the third month of pregnancy is much less risky.

In the months after birth, too, there seem to be critical periods in brain development—specific weeks or months during which the child needs to encounter certain types of stimulation or experience for the nervous system to develop normally and fully (Hirsch & Tieman, 1987).

A broader and somewhat looser concept of a **sensitive period** is also widely used. A sensitive period is a span of months or years during which a child may be particularly responsive to specific forms of experience or particularly influenced by their absence. For example, the period from 6 to 12 months of age may be a sensitive period for the formation of a core attachment to the parents.

In studies of adults, the central timing concept has been the contrast of *on time* versus *off time* events (Neugarten, 1979). The basic idea is that any experience occurring at the normal, expectable time for that culture (or that cohort) will pose far fewer difficulties for the adult's adaptation than is true for an off time experience. Thus, being widowed at 30 or laid off from work at 40 is far more likely to produce serious life disruption or pathology such as depression than is being widowed at 70 or ending your work life at 65.

It may seem at first glance that the concept of critical or sensitive periods and the concept of on-timeness are quite different notions. But there is an underlying similarity. In both cases the basic idea is that the normal trajectory of development rests on a foundation of common experiences occurring in a particular sequence at particular times. Any individual—child or adult—whose life experiences deviate from that normal sequence or timing may be thrown off track in some way.

This baby's brain is developing at a furious rate. In fact, the first year of life may be a critical period for certain aspects of brain development. Certain types of experience may be required in these months in order for the baby's brain to develop optimally. Later stimulation apparently cannot make up the lack.

We now see many adults in our society choosing to delay childbearing until their thirties or forties, thus significantly postponing the "normal" timing. What do you think are the likely effects of such a different timing? List as many effects as you can think of.

▶ Explaining Continuity over the Life Span

Because this is a book about *development* over the life span, you will not be surprised that we will spend most of our time looking at changes that occur with age. But we can't ignore the continuities either. We have a number of alternative approaches to choose from in describing and explaining such continuities.

Biological Explanations of Consistency

The concept of maturation assumes that all members of a given species share basic genetic codes that shape the patterns of normal development. But our genetic heritage is individual as well as collective. Each of us inherits a wide range of unique characteristics or tendencies as well. And because those characteristics or tendencies are laid down in the genes, they tend to persist throughout our lives.

The range of behaviors now known to be at least partially influenced by hereditary differences is remarkably broad (Plomin, Rende & Rutter, 1991). Included in the list are not only obvious physical differences such as height, body shape, or a tendency to skinniness or obesity, but also cognitive abilities such as general intelligence, or more specific cognitive skills like spatial visualization ability. Many aspects of temperament or personality are also clearly heritable, including extraversion versus introversion, emotionality, activity, and openness to experience (Plomin et al., 1988; Plomin & Rende, 1991; Loehlin, 1989). Newer research is also showing that many aspects of pathological behavior are also genetically influenced, including alcoholism, schizophrenia, excessive aggressiveness, even anorexia (Plomin, Rende & Rutter, 1991).

You may wonder, by the way, just how behavior geneticists figure out whether some particular characteristic is influenced by heredity. They use two basic techniques, the study

RESEARCH REPORT
How Do Behavior Geneticists Identify Genetic Effects?

There are two basic ways of searching for a genetic influence on a trait. You can study identical and fraternal twins, or you can study adopted children.

Identical twins share exactly the same genetic patterning, because they develop from the same fertilized ovum. Fraternal twins each develop from a separate ovum, separately fertilized. They are therefore no more alike than are any other pair of siblings, except that they have shared the same prenatal environment and grow up in the same sequential niche within the family. If identical twins turn out to be more like one another in any given trait than fraternal twins, that would be evidence for the influence of heredity on that trait.

An even more powerful variant of the twin strategy is to study twins who have been reared apart from one another. If identical twins are still more like one another on some dimension, despite having grown up in different environments, we have even clearer evidence of a genetic contribution for that trait.

In the case of adopted children, the strategy is to compare the degree of similarity between the adopted child and his birth parents (with whom he shares genes but not environment) and adopted child to his adoptive parents (with whom he shares environment but not genes.) If the child should turn out to be more similar to, or his behavior or skill better predicted by the characteristics of his *birth* parents than by characteristics of his adoptive parents, that would again demonstrate the influence of heredity.

Let me give you some examples of results from studies of each type. The twin method has been widely used in studies of the heritability of IQ. Bouchard and McGue (1981) have combined the results of dozens of such studies, with the following results (from Figure 1, p. 1056):

Identical twins reared together	.85
Identical twins reared apart	.67
Fraternal twins reared together	.58
Siblings (including fraternal twins) reared apart	.24

The numbers here are correlations—a statistic I'll explain more fully later in this chapter. For now, you need to know only that a correlation can range from 0 to +1.00 or −1.00. The closer it is to 1.00, the stronger the relationship it describes. Thus you can

see that identical twins reared together have IQs that are highly similar, much more similar than what occurs for fraternal twins reared together. You can also see, though, that environment plays a role since identical twins reared apart are less similar than are those reared together.

A somewhat weaker but still significant genetic effect is evident in twin studies of personality. One set of data comes from Sweden, which has kept a registry of twins since 1886, nearly 25,000 pairs in all. From this set Robert Plomin and his colleagues (Plomin et al., 1988) were able to locate 99 pairs of adult identical twins reared apart, 229 pairs of fraternal twins reared apart, and matched pairs of twins reared together. All these individuals were given a standardized test of personality, which measured a variety of dimensions. The results for one scale that measured fearful emotionality (including such items as "I am easily frightened") look like this (Table 3, p. 47):

Identical twins reared together	.49
Identical twins reared apart	.37
Fraternal twins reared together	.08
Fraternal twins reared apart	.04

Once again it is clear that the identical twins are more alike than are the fraternal twins, even when they are reared apart, a finding matched in a number of other large studies of personality in twins (Loehlin, 1989).

I know of no adoption studies of the heritability of personality, but there are a number of adoption studies in which IQ has been the focus. Here are some results from a study of roughly 100 adopted children by Scarr and Weinberg (1983, Table 1, p. 262), again expressed in terms of correlations between the child's IQ and:

The natural mother's IQ	.33
The natural father's IQ	.43
The adoptive mother's IQ	.21
The adoptive father's IQ	.27

These results, like the results of twin studies of IQ, tell us that there is indeed a substantial genetic component in what we measure with an IQ test, just as there is a substantial genetic component in many dimensions of personality.

of identical and fraternal twins and the study of adopted children, both of which I've explained in the "research report" above.

None of these characteristics is completely fixed by a person's genetic heritage. Nor will they be entirely consistent over a person's lifetime. The particular behavior an individual shows will *always* be a joint product of the genetic pattern and the environment the individual has grown up in or exists in as an adult. Still, it is clear that we are born with certain response patterns that shape our reaction to the world. Because we carry those same response patterns with us through our lives, some aspects of our behavior tend to be at least moderately consistent over time as well.

Environmental Sources of Continuity

Continuity is also fostered by the environment and by our own behavior (Caspi, Bem & Elder, 1989). For example, we tend to choose environments that fit our characteristics, creating a unique "niche" for ourselves within our family, among our peers, in our workplace (Scarr, 1992). As children we choose activities we think we might be good at and avoid those we think we can't do. (Being somewhat gawky and uncoordinated, I always avoided any competitive sports, because I was afraid I would be embarrassed by my klutziness or let down the team). As adults we choose jobs that match our skills and personality. This protects us from experiences that might force change and thus helps to create continuity in behavior. Continuity is also fostered by the fact that as we are growing up, we learn particular types of interaction or strategies for solving problems that are successful for us. Faced with some new situation, we try what we know.

At the same time, our habitual patterns trigger reactions from others that are likely to perpetuate those patterns. For instance, a neurotic, complaining adult is likely to generate criticism or countercomplaints more often than will a sunny-dispositioned person. The criticism then further strengthens the complaining behavior and creates continuity over time.

Avshalom Caspi and his colleagues have some fascinating data illustrating the combined effect of all these forces for continuity from childhood into adulthood, based on the same set of subjects Elder studied in his research on the impact of the Great Depression (Caspi, Elder & Bem, 1987, 1988; Caspi & Elder, 1988). In this case, Caspi has looked at the histories of 214 children born some time in the 1920s, and since followed into middle adulthood. (The same subjects, by the way, are represented in Figure 1.1.) Among these subjects, Caspi has traced the development of two separate groups: shy children and ill-tempered children. Let me just give you a taste of their findings.

Men who had been ill-tempered boys had very different life pathways than did more even-tempered men. They completed fewer years of school, had lower-status jobs, and were twice as likely to be divorced by age 40. They also changed jobs more often, but as you can see in Figure 1.2 (page 10), that was only true for those in low-status jobs. Ill-tempered boys who were able to move into jobs with higher status had stable job careers. Why the difference? Caspi suggests that the difficulty for these men is that they react to any kind of authority with ill-temper. Higher-status jobs are likely to give the individual more independence, less supervision. Initially ill-tempered men who reach such jobs are thus less likely to have their ill-tempered pattern elicited. But those who are in low-status jobs with hovering authority figures continue to react in their usual way, which in turn calls forth displeasure from the supervisor and may lead to job loss.

Caspi and Elder are not arguing against heredity here. It may well be that the original tendency toward shyness or ill-temper has a genetic origin. But such patterns persist in large part because of environmental forces for continuity, and can be broken if the environment no longer sustains them.

▶ Nature and Nurture

Let me turn now to the equally broad and basic issue of the role of nature and nurture in shaping development. The so-called nature/nurture controversy has its roots in very old philosophical arguments. Plato, for example, believed that certain ideas were innate. British empiricists, such as John Locke, and the American behaviorists who followed them, such as J. B. Watson, and B. F. Skinner, scoffed at the notion of innate ideas. But there has been a considerable revival of this notion among developmental psychologists in the past decade or so, in the form of the concept of *inborn biases*. Today there are many theorists who argue that babies are born with built-in biases in the way they experience

Figure 1.2   In this study, based on the same sample shown in Figure 1.1, men who had been ill-tempered as boys changed jobs more often in adult life than did those who had been more even-tempered—but only if the men were in low-status, low-autonomy jobs. (*Source:* Caspi & Elder, 1988, Figure 6.3, p. 128.)

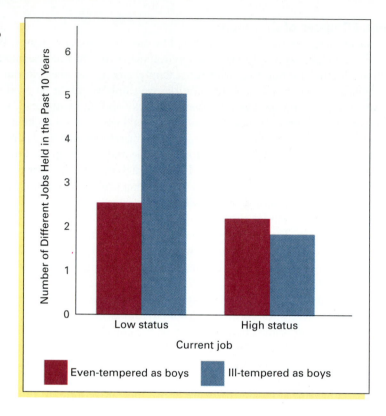

and respond to the world. For instance, from the earliest days of life babies seem to listen more to the beginnings and ends of sentences than to the middle (Slobin, 1985a), and they respond visually to motion and to shifts from dark to light (Haith, 1980). These built-in biases are the starting point. Subsequent development is a result of experience interacting with these initial biases.

Internal Models of Experience

Another concept prevalent in current theories about child development, and increasingly evident in thinking about adult development, is that of an **internal model** of experience. The key idea is that the effect of some experience, some environmental event, lies in an individual's *interpretation* of it, the *meaning* the individual puts on that experience rather than on any objective properties of the experience. If you think about it, you can come up with lots of everyday examples of this principle. For instance, if your friend says something to you that he thinks is innocuous but that you take as a criticism, what matters for you is how you interpreted the concept, not how he meant it. If you regularly hear criticism in other people's comments, we would say that you have an internal model of yourself and others that includes a basic expectation that might be like this: "I usually do things wrong so other people criticize me."

Theorists who emphasize the importance of such meaning systems argue that each child creates a set of internal models—a set of assumptions or conclusions about the world, about himself, and about relationships with others—through which all subsequent experience is filtered (Epstein, 1991). John Bowlby (1969, 1980) expressed this idea when he talked about the child's "internal working model" of attachment. A child with a secure model of attachment may assume that someone will come when he cries and that affection and attention are reliably available. A child with a less secure model may assume that if a grown-up frowns it probably means she will be yelled at. These expectations are based on actual experiences, to be sure, but once formed into an internal model, they generalize beyond the original experience and affect the way the child interprets future experiences. A child who expects adults to be reliable and affectionate will be more likely to interpret the behavior of new adults in this way and will re-create friendly and affectionate relationships with others outside the family; a child who expects hostility will read hostility into otherwise fairly neutral encounters.

A child's self-concept seems to operate in much the same way, as an internal working model of "who I am" (Bretherton, 1991). This self-model is based on experience, but it also shapes future experience.

The concept of internal models, which originated in studies of infants and young children, has now begun to appear in studies of adults as well. For example, Deborah Cohn and her colleagues (Cohn et al., 1991) have found that adult couples in which both partners have insecure working models of attachment report more conflict and less positive interaction than do other couples.

Research on stress and social support sends us a similar message. Again and again researchers have found that the objective amount of stress an adult experiences, or the number of friends or family members she may have in her support network, is not what matters; the crucial factor is how the adult *perceives* the stress and the support. If she perceives the support as adequate, then her chance of illness, depression, or other dysfunction as a result of stress goes down. If she perceives it as inadequate, no matter how much objective support there may appear to be, her risks go up (Cohen & Wills, 1985).

The concept of internal models obviously also helps us account for continuity of behavior over time. The models we create in childhood are not unchangeable, but they do tend to be carried forward and continue to shape and define our experiences as adults. This concept also helps us understand why the same experience seems to have such varying effects on different individuals.

Eight-year-old Brian's internal model of himself may include the sense that "I am good at sports," or even more generally, "I am physically capable." Such internal models are partly based on experience. Brian may have found that he is coordinated enough to learn many physical skills easily. But once the internal model is established, it will affect Brian's choices and his interpretation of future experiences.

Can you think of other examples of internal models that might affect a child's or adult's behavior?

The Ecological Perspective

Another facet of current thinking about environmental influences is a growing emphasis on the importance of casting a very wide explanatory net. To understand a child's development, it is not enough to look just at the child and his immediate family. We must also understand the entire ecological setting in which the child is growing: his neighborhood and school, the occupations of his parents and their level of satisfaction in these occupations, the relationships his parents have with each other and their own families, and so on and on (e.g., Bronfenbrenner, 1979, 1986, 1989; Pence, 1988). A child growing up in a poverty-stricken inner-city neighborhood, with cocaine sold on every street corner and violence a part of everyday life, is coping with a radically different set of problems than is a suburban child in a safe neighborhood. Similarly, when parents are overwhelmed with the problems in their own lives and are isolated from family or friends who might provide help, they are bound to create a very different family environment than will parents whose lives are more stable and supported.

A particularly nice example of research that examines many aspects of this larger system of influences is Gerald Patterson's work on the origins of antisocial behavior in children (Patterson, DeBarsyshe & Ramsey, 1989; Patterson, Capaldi & Bank, 1991). His studies show that the initial cause of excessive aggressiveness in children lies in parental response to a child's behavior. Parents who use poor discipline techniques and monitor the child poorly are more likely to have noncompliant or antisocial children. But once established, the child's antisocial behavior pattern has repercussions in other areas of his life, leading to rejection from peers and academic difficulty. These problems, in turn, are likely to push a young person toward a deviant peer group and still further delinquency (Dishion et al., 1991). So a pattern that began in the family is maintained and exacerbated by interactions with peers and the school system.

Patterson expands the net still further, as you can see in Figure 1.3, by asking about

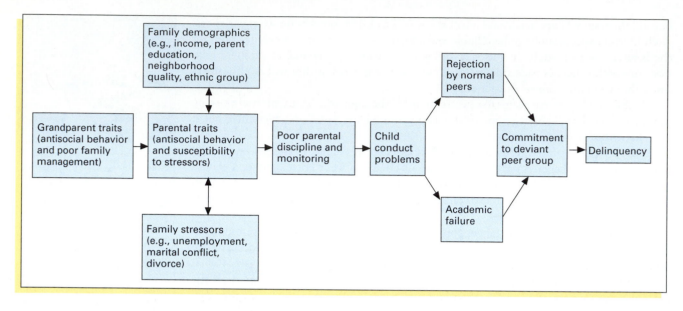

Figure 1.3 Patterson takes quite a broad ecological approach in this model of the many factors that influence the development of delinquency. In his view, the core of the process is the interaction between the child and the parent. But the parents' ability to handle the child effectively is, in turn, affected by their own history and by their current support and life satisfaction. (*Source:* Patterson, DeBarsyshe & Ramsey, 1989, Figures 1 and 2, pp. 331, 333.)

Think back to your own childhood experiences. How much do you think your life was affected by the way your mother or father felt about their jobs, or by the relationships they had with friends or other family members?

the factors in the parent's lives that make it more or less likely that they will use poor discipline techniques in the first place. He finds that those parents who were themselves raised using poor disciplinary practices are more likely to use those same strategies with their children, so the "sins of the fathers" are visited on the children. But even parents who possess good basic child-management skills may fall into ineffective patterns when the stresses in their own lives are increased. A recent divorce or unemployment raises the likelihood that poor disciplinary practices will be used, increasing the chances that the child will develop a pattern of antisocial behavior.

In studying adult development, too, we need to look well beyond the adult's immediate family, or even his job. We also have to understand the impact of larger social forces that may be affecting his cohort. For example, the immensely rapid change in women's roles occurring in our culture in the past several decades has surely affected every adult in our society—but it has affected them differently, depending on their age and the pattern of their upbringing.

Interactionist Approaches

Patterson's model, and the many others like it, takes us a long way toward a more complete look at development. But he has not included any "nature" in the model. What happens if we add that to the system?

It's not such a big step. In the case of Patterson's model, we need only assume that children begin life with different temperaments. Some are cranky and hard to handle; others are sunny-dispositioned and easy to care for. For a parent with a cranky or difficult baby, it will take more skill to avoid spiraling into a pattern that ends up reinforcing the child's defiance. Thus the qualities the child brings to the interaction creates an initial bias in the system to which the parents, and others in the environment, must respond.

A more general version of such an interactionist model is implicit in the ideas of **vulnerability** and **resilience** (Masten, Best & Garmezy, 1990; Garmezy & Masten, 1991; Garmezy & Rutter, 1983; Rutter, 1987). According to this view, each child is born with certain vulnerabilities, such as a difficult temperament, a physical abnormality, allergies, a genetic tendency toward alcoholism, and so on. Each child is also born with some *protective factors*, such as high intelligence, good coordination, an easy temperament, or a lovely smile, that tend to make her more resilient in the face of stress.

These vulnerabilities and protective factors then interact with the child's environment. Frances Horowitz has proposed a particularly clear model of such an interaction (1987, 1990). As you can see in Figure 1.4, the environmental variable she describes is something called "facilitativeness." A highly facilitative environment is one in which the child has loving and responsive parents and is provided with a rich array of stimulation. Horowitz proposes that when different levels of facilitativeness are combined with initial vulnerabilities, the result is not merely addition of the two factors. Rather, they interact. A resilient child (one with many protective factors and few vulnerabilities) may do quite well in a poor environment, because such a child can take advantage of all the stimulation and opportunities available; similarly, a vulnerable child may do quite well in a highly facilitative environment. According to this model it is only the double whammy—the vulnerable child in a poor environment—that leads to really poor outcomes for the child.

A growing body of research provides support for Horowitz's model. For example, very low IQ scores are most common among children who had a low birth weight *and* were reared in poverty-level families, while low-birth-weight children reared in middle-class families develop essentially normal IQs, as do normal-weight infants reared in poverty-level families (Werner, 1986). What this means is that the same environment can have very different effects, depending on the qualities or capacities the child brings to the equation.

Vulnerabilities (and resilience) are probably also cumulative. A child whose initial environment is insufficient to support optimum development will become more vulnerable and place a still greater demand on the environment to meet further needs.

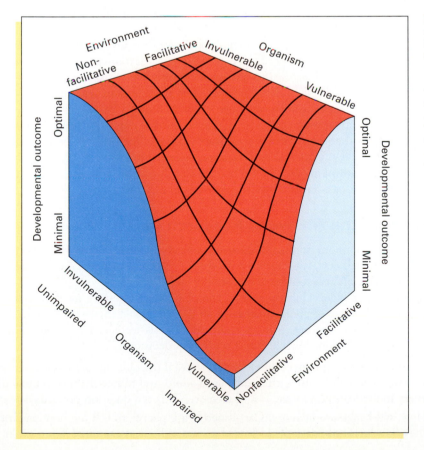

Figure 1.4 Horowitz's model describes one possible type of interaction between nature and nurture. In this case she is arguing that the child's vulnerability interacts with the facilitativeness of the environment. The surface of the curve describes the level of some developmental outcome, such as IQ or skill in social relationships. You can see that she is suggesting that only the combination of high vulnerability and poor environment will consistently produce poor outcomes. (*Source:* Horowitz, 1987, Figure 1.1, p. 23.)

You might explain this little boy's behavior by saying he is in the "terrible twos." The phrase assumes that there is something distinctly different about 2-year-olds that makes them more cranky and more difficult. Stage concepts like this are common in everyday language and in developmental theory. But many current developmental psychologists think that such concepts are misleading.

The same concepts can also help to understand responses to stress in adulthood. Faced with some upheaval in our lives, which of us will fall apart and which of us will cope well? If we look at each person's vulnerabilities and protective factors, we can make some reasonable guesses. Good emotional support from others is one protective factor, as is the cognitive skill to evaluate alternative courses of action. Poor relationships with others, insecure working models, low self-esteem, a sense of being unable to control events, are all vulnerabilities that increase the likelihood that a person will respond poorly to some crisis or stress. Some of these vulnerabilities and resources can be acquired in adult life, but many of them are carried forward from childhood and adolescence.

What Is the Nature of Developmental Change?

A third basic question we must address as we go along—and which all theorists have had to address—concerns the nature of developmental change itself. Are changes qualitative or quantitative? A 2-year-old is not likely to have individual friends among her playmates, but an 8-year-old will probably have several. We could think of this as a change in amount from zero friends to some friends (a *quantitative* change). Or we could think of it as a change from one sort of peer relationship to another (a *qualitative* change). We could think of the cognitive changes in middle adulthood and old age in terms of gradual loss of speed or memory capacity (a quantitative change), or we might look for a qualitative change, such as an increase in wisdom.

Stages and Sequences.   A very important related question concerns the presence or absence of *stages* in the course of development. If development consists only of additions (quantitative change), then the concept of stages is not needed. But if development involves reorganization of old skills or the emergence of wholly new strategies or skills (qualitative change), the concept of stages may become attractive. The very fact that courses on development tend to be organized chronologically, in stage-like chapters, reflects the appeal of the concept of stages. And in everyday language we hear a great deal of "stagelike" terms such as the "terrible twos" or "midlife crisis."

But to what extent does development across the life span really progress in stages? Certainly we can mark the years off in age strata, as Matilda Riley suggests. The chapters of this book are organized in precisely that way. But the existence of age strata does not necessarily mean that there are major qualitative changes between one period, one "stage," and the next. I believe I can make a persuasive argument that 12-year-olds are qualitatively different in their thinking and their social relationships from 2-year-olds. But it is not so clear that 20-year-olds are qualitatively different from 40-year-olds.

Finding the Answers: Research on Development

I've asked an enormous number of questions already in this chapter. But before you can understand the answers, you need to have some familiarity with the methods researchers use when they explore questions about development.

For example, older adults frequently complain that they have more trouble remembering people's names or phone numbers than they did when they were younger. Suppose I want to find out whether memory really declines as we age. How would I go about answering this question? I would face a number of decisions:

- Should I compare groups of different ages to see if the older groups have lower memory scores? Or should I start with middle-aged adults and follow them over time to see if every individual shows some loss of memory? This is a question of *research design*.

- How will I measure memory? Can I merely ask people to tell me how much trouble they have remembering, or do I need a standardized assessment? What other things might I want to know about each of my subjects? These are questions of *research methodology*.

- How will I interpret the results? Is it enough to know that older adults do or do not show a decline in memory skill? What other analyses might I do that would make the results clearer? These are questions of *research analysis*.

▌ Research Design

Choosing a research design is crucial for any research, but especially so when the subject matter you are trying to study is change (or continuity) with age. You have basically three choices: (1) You can study different groups of people of different ages, called a **cross-sectional** design. (2) You can study the *same* people over a period of time, called a **longitudinal** design. (3) Or you can combine the two in some fashion, using what is called a **sequential** design (Schaie, 1983a).

Cross-Sectional Designs

The key feature of a cross-sectional design is that separate age groups are assessed, with each subject tested only once. To study memory cross-sectionally I might select groups of subjects at each of a series of ages, such as groups of 25-, 35-, 45-, 55-, 65-, 75-, and 85-year-olds. I'd assess each person with my measure of memory skill and then see whether the scores go down steadily with age. Figure 1.5 shows the results of just such a study in which adults of different ages listened to lists of letters being read to them one letter per second and then had to repeat the letters back in the order given—a task not unlike what you have to do when you try to remember a phone number someone has read off to you. You can see that there was a sharply lower performance among the 60- and 70-year olds.

Because these findings fit our hypothesis, it is tempting to conclude that memory ability *declines* with age. But this is precisely what we cannot say with cross-sectional data, since these adults differ not only in age but in cohort. Among other things, we know that

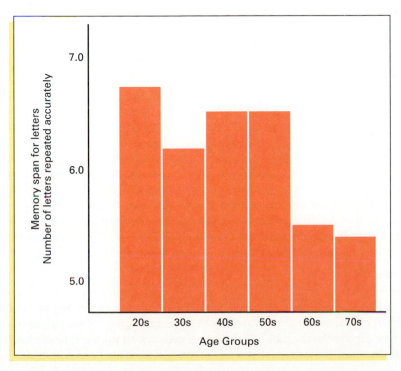

Figure 1.5 In this study, adults of various ages listened to an experimenter reading a series of letters, one letter per second. The subject's task was to try to repeat back the list in the order it had been read. The scores shown here are the average number of letters each age group could repeat back. Can we legitimately interpret these results as meaning that memory ability *declines* with age? (*Source:* Botwinick & Storandt, 1974.)

in our society today, older cohorts have had fewer years of education than younger cohorts. The differences in memory might reflect education differences (or some other cohort difference) and not changes actually linked to age or development.

Suppose a cross-sectional study of sex-role attitudes reveals that the most egalitarian attitudes occur among adults between ages 20 and 50, with both teenagers and those over 50 having more traditional attitudes. How could you interpret these results?

Cross-sectional research is often enormously useful. It is relatively quick to do, and by revealing age differences it can suggest new hypotheses about developmental processes. But in any cross-sectional study, age and cohort are entirely *confounded*—that is, they vary simultaneously, so we cannot sort out their differential effect. In addition, cross-sectional research cannot tell us much about *sequences* of development, such as the sequence of concepts children have about their own gender. A cross-sectional study might show that 2-year-olds have a different idea of gender than 4-year-olds, but that won't tell us whether there are steps in between or whether every child acquires this concept in the same sequence. Similarly, cross-sectional studies will not tell us anything about the consistency of individual behavior over time. Are those adults with good memories at 40 still likely to have good memories at 60 or 80?

Longitudinal Designs

Longitudinal designs seem to solve all these problems because they follow the *same* individuals over a period of time. They allow us to look at sequences of change and individual consistency or inconsistency over time. And because they compare performances by the same people at different ages, they get around the obvious cohort problem.

Short-term longitudinal studies, in which groups of children or adults are studied for a period of several years, have become common in recent years. There are also some famous long-term longitudinal studies that have followed groups of children into adulthood, or groups of adults from early to late adult life.

The Berkeley/Oakland Growth Study, which I've already talked about several times, is one of the most famous of this type of longitudinal study (Eichorn et al., 1981). The Grant study of Harvard men is perhaps equally famous (Vaillant, 1977). In this study, several hundred men were studied from age 18 until they were in their sixties.

Sounds perfect, doesn't it? Unfortunately, longitudinal designs are not as perfect as they seem at first. There are two major difficulties.

Selective Attrition and Drop Out.   One significant problem is that not everyone sticks with the program. You can imagine that it might become quite intrusive to have researchers coming back year after year to ask you endless questions. Some subjects just say no after a while. Others move and can't be located. Some die. As a general rule, it is the healthiest and best educated who stick it out, and that fact biases the results, particularly if the study covers the final decades of life. Each succeeding testing includes proportionately more and more healthy adults, which may make it look as if there is less change, or less decline, than actually exists.

Time of Measurement Effects.   More important, longitudinal studies don't really get around the cohort problem. The Grant study and the Berkeley/Oakland Growth Study both observed and tested subjects born in the same decade (1918–1928). Even if both studies showed the same pattern of change with age, we wouldn't know if that pattern was unique to that cohort or reflected more basic developmental changes that would be found in other cultures, other cohorts. This is referred to as a *time of measurement effect*. One way to avoid this problem is to use a *sequential* design.

Sequential Designs

All sequential designs involve studying more than one cohort over time, but there are a number of alternatives, shown in Figure 1.6. At the top of the figure are years of birth of each cohort; on the left are the years in which we might take some measurement on a given cohort. Entered in the table are the *ages* of each cohort at that time of measurement. Within this matrix, you can see that a cross-sectional study involves a comparison across

	Year of birth of each cohort							
Year in which measurement was obtained	1905	1915	1925	1935	1945	1955	1965	1975
1920	15							
1930	25	15						
1940	35	25	15					
1950	45	35	25	15				
1960	55	45	35	25	15			
1970	65	55	45	35	25	15		
1980	75	65	55	45	35	25	15	
1990	85	75	65	55	45	35	25	15
2000	95	85	75	65	55	45	35	25
2010		95	85	75	65	55	45	35
2020			95	85	75	65	55	45

Figure 1.6 I know this figure is complicated, but a bit of time spent trying to understand it will repay you in the end. Each entry in the table is the age of some group of individuals, born in a particular cohort, at some particular time of measurement. Cross-sectional studies involve studies of parts of any one row, longitudinal studies any one column. Sequential studies involve combinations of these, of which the most complex is a cohort-sequential design, which would involve both multiple cross-sectional and multiple longitudinal studies, such as the set of cells in the blue rectangle. The yellow circles illustrate a time-lag design, described more fully in the text.

any one row in the table, while a longitudinal study involves part of any single column.

The remaining logical possibilities are the following:

1. Time-lag design: The simplest of the sequential designs involves studying several cohorts at the *same ages*, and thus involves comparisons along one of the diagonals, such as the yellow circled entries in the figure. You may have seen reports in a newspaper of periodic assessments of drug use in adolescents. Every few years, a new sample of teenagers is asked about their drug use to see if there has been any rise or decline since the last observation. This kind of design looks directly at cohort differences without the confounding of age.

2. Time-sequential design: A more complex possibility is to do several cross-sectional studies, several years apart. In Figure 1.6, this would involve studying parts of any two or more rows. For example, if I had done a cross-sectional study of memory in 1960, I might repeat the same cross-sectional study in 1980. If I found the same pattern of age differences, I could be more confident that the pattern was related to age and not just to cohort effects.

3. Cohort-sequential design: The next logical possibility is to do two or more longitudinal studies, each with a different cohort. In the figure, this would mean studying more than one column. If the Grant study investigators, who originally studied men who were Harvard freshmen in 1937, had later studied another group, perhaps those who were freshmen in 1960, they would have a cohort-sequential design.

4. Cross-sequential design: The remaining possibility would be to study multiple rows *and* multiple columns, such as the blue box outlined in the figure. The researcher would begin with several age groups and study each group longitudinally. A good example of this is one of the Duke Longitudinal Studies of Aging (Palmore, 1981, I. Siegler, 1983). The investigators started by testing a sample from each of five age groups: 45, 50, 55, 60, and 65. They then retested all the subjects in each age group every two years for six years.

Sociologists frequently use a variant of the cross-sequential design that they call a *panel* study. They select a large (often nationally representative) sample that covers a wide age range, then follow every subject over a period of years, sometimes decades. One particularly rich example is the Michigan Panel Study of Income Dynamics (Duncan & Morgan, 1985), which started in 1968 with a nationally representative sample of 5000 families. Each year since the beginning, one member of each family has been interviewed at length about the entire family.

All these sequential designs are becoming much more prevalent as researchers struggle to find ways to uncover basic developmental patterns.

Experimental Designs

All the research designs I have described so far are alternative ways to look at changes with age. But if we are interested in examining a basic process—such as learning or memory—or in *explaining* any observed phenomena, we may do **experiments**.

An experiment is normally designed to test a specific hypothesis, a particular causal explanation. Suppose, for example, I think that the observed age differences in memory span are a function of how often adults of various ages actually use their memories. I could test this hypothesis by providing special memory practice to some older adults, and no such training to another group the same age. If the trained adults can remember more letters or numbers than they did before training, and the no-training group shows no change, this would be consistent with my hypothesis.

A key feature of an experiment, then, is that subjects are assigned *randomly* to participate in one of several groups. Subjects in the **experimental group** receive the treatment the experimenter thinks will produce an identified effect (such as memory practice), while those in the **control group** receive either no special treatment or a neutral treatment. The presumed causal element in the experiment is called the **independent variable** (in this case the training), and any behavior on which the independent variable is expected to show its impact is called a **dependent variable** (in this case a score on the memory test).

This particular design could be made more complex, and far more interesting, by repeating the whole experiment several times with subjects of different ages. In this way I could discover whether training had an equal effect on subjects of all ages, or whether it had a larger beneficial effect for older subjects than for younger ones—a result that would provide much stronger support for my hypothesis.

Problems with Experiments in Studying Development.   Experiments like this are essential for our understanding of many aspects of development. But two special problems in studying child or adult development limit the use of experimental designs.

First, many of the questions we want to answer have to do with the effects of particular unpleasant or stressful experiences on individuals—abuse, prenatal influences such as alcohol or tobacco, low birth weight, poverty, unemployment, widowhood. For obvious ethical reasons, we cannot manipulate these variables. We cannot ask one set of pregnant women to have two alcoholic drinks a day and others to have none; we cannot randomly assign adults to become unemployed. So, to study the effects of such experiences we must rely on nonexperimental designs, including longitudinal and sequential studies.

Second, the independent variable in which we are often most interested is age itself, and *we cannot assign subjects randomly to age groups*. We can compare 4-year-olds and 6-year-olds in their approach to some particular task, such as searching for a lost object, but the children differ in a host of ways in addition to their ages. Older children have had more and different experiences. Thus, unlike psychologists studying other aspects of behavior, developmental psychologists *cannot* systematically manipulate many of the variables we are most interested in.

To get around this problem, we can use any one of a series of strategies that are sometimes called *quasi experiments*, in which we compare groups without assigning the subjects randomly. Cross-sectional comparisons are a form of quasi experiment. So are studies in which we select naturally occurring groups that differ in some dimension of

RESEARCH REPORT
Ethical Issues in Research on Development

Any time we try to understand human behavior by observing, testing, asking questions, we are probing into personal lives. If we go into someone's home to observe the way they interact with their children, we are invading their privacy. We may even inadvertently give the impression that there must be something wrong with the way they are raising their family. If we give adults or children laboratory tests, such as those illustrated in Figure 1.5 that measure memory span, some subjects will do very well, others will not. How will the less-successful subject interpret this experience? What is the risk that some subject will become depressed over what he perceives as a poor performance?

Any research on human behavior involves some risks and raises some ethical questions. Because of this, psychologists and other social and biological scientists have established clear procedures and guidelines that must be followed before any observation can be undertaken, any test given. In every school or college—the settings in which most such research is done—there is a committee of peers who must approve any research plan involving human subjects. The most basic guideline is that subjects must always be protected from any potential mental or physical harm. More specific principles include:

Informed Consent. Each adult subject must give written consent to participate. In the case of research on children, informed consent must be obtained from the parent or guardian. In every case, the procedure and its possible consequences must be explained in detail. If there are potential risks, these must be de-

scribed. For example, if you were studying patterns of problem solving in married couples, you might want to observe each couple while they talked about some unresolved issue between them. As part of your informed consent request, you would have to explain to each couple that while such discussions often lead to greater clarity, they also occasionally increase tension between the pair. And you would need to provide support and debriefing at the end of the procedure, to assist any couple who found the task stressful or destabilizing.

Right of Privacy. Subjects must be assured that highly personal information they may provide will be kept entirely private—including information about income, attitudes, or illegal behavior like drug taking. Researchers can use the information *collectively*, but they cannot report it individually in any way that will associate a subject's name with some piece of data—unless the subject has specifically given permission for such use.

In virtually all cases, it is also considered unethical to observe through a one-way mirror without the subject's knowledge, or to secretly record behavior.

Testing Children. These principles are important for any research, but particularly so for research on children. Any child who balks at being tested or observed must *not* be tested or observed; any child who becomes distressed must be comforted; any risk to the child's self-esteem must be avoided.

interest, such as children whose parents choose to place them in day-care programs compared to children whose parents rear them at home, or adults who have been laid off from work compared to those who are still employed in the same industry.

Such comparisons have built-in problems, because groups that differ in one way are likely to be different in other ways as well. Families who place their children in day care, compared to those who rear them at home, are also likely to be poorer, may more often be single-parent families, and may have different values or religious backgrounds. If we find that the two groups of children differ in some fashion, is it because they have spent their daytime hours in different places or because of these other differences in their families? We can make such comparisons a bit cleaner if we select our comparison groups initially so that they are matched on those variables we think might matter, such as income or marital status or religion. But quasi experiments, by their very nature, will always yield more ambiguous results than will a fully controlled experiment.

▶ Research Methods

Choosing a research design is only the first crucial decision an investigator must make. Equally important is to decide what subjects to study and how to study them.

Choosing the Subjects: Because we would like to uncover basic developmental patterns that are true for all children, all adolescents, or all adults, the ideal strategy would

One way of collecting information is by direct observation, such as in this nursery school. This observer may be keeping a running record of the child's behavior or counting certain specific behaviors.

be to select a random sample of all people in the world to study. Clearly impractical. Sociologists and epidemiologists frequently try to get around the problem by selecting large samples that are representative of some subgroup or population. The National Survey of Black Americans, for example, involves a nationally representative sample of over 2000 black adults in the United States, interviewed in 1979 and 1980 (e.g., Taylor & Chatters, 1991).

Psychologists typically choose to study much smaller groups in greater depth and detail, in an attempt to uncover very basic processes. For instance, Alan Sroufe and his colleagues (Sroufe, 1989; Sroufe, Egeland & Kreutzer, 1990) have studied a group of 267 children and their families, beginning before the birth of the child. Families were deliberately chosen from among those thought to be at high risk for later care-giving problems, such as low-education single mothers with unplanned pregnancies. The children have now been repeatedly studied, each time in considerable detail. A subset of the children attended a special preschool run by Sroufe and his coworkers; some later attended special summer camps at which observers were able to evaluate a broad array of child behavior. The sample is not representative of the population as a whole, but it is enormously informative nonetheless, and may tell us more about the process of emotional and social development than we could possibly glean from larger samples studied more broadly. Neither strategy is better than the other; both are useful. In either case, we need to remember that the conclusions we can draw will be limited by the sample we studied.

Collecting the Information from Your Subjects.   Having chosen your basic design and the subjects you wish to study, you then need to decide how to assess them. The options are usually grouped into two subsets, *naturalistic* and *laboratory* research, but in fact there are many shadings in between. On the far end of the naturalistic category are completely unstructured observations in natural settings, such as observations of children on playgrounds or elderly adults in a nursing home. At the opposite end of the continuum would be highly structured tasks given to subjects in controlled laboratory settings. In between lie many semistructured test situations, often used in studies of children, as well as a vast array of interviews, questionnaires, and pencil-and-paper tests widely used in studies of adults.

Each of these alternatives has costs and benefits. Structured laboratory tests give the experimenter excellent control over the situation so that each subject is confronted with the same task, the same stimuli. But because they are artificial, such tests may not give us an accurate portrayal of how individuals behave in the more complex natural environment. Interviews, especially very open-ended ones in which the subject is only guided toward general topics, may give a rich picture of an individual's thoughts and feelings, but how do you reduce the answers to comparable scores? Questionnaires solve part of this problem, but the trade-off may be the richness and individuality of replies. Often the best strategy—although one not always possible because of cost in time or money—is to collect many different kinds of information from each subject.

▶ Research Analysis

Finally, you need to analyze the results of your research. In studies of development, there are two broad forms of analysis.

First, we can compare different age groups by simply calculating the average score of each group on some measure, precisely as Botwinick and Storandt did in the data I showed in Figure 1.5. You might make this particular comparison more informative if you subdivided each age group, say according to level of education, and then calculated averages for each subgroup. But the strategy is the same. You will see *many* examples of exactly this kind of analysis as you go through the book.

A second strategy allows us to look at relationships between two separate variables, using a statistic called a **correlation**. A correlation is simply a number ranging from -1.00 to $+1.00$, that describes the strength of a relationship between two variables. A zero correlation indicates that there is no linear relationship between those variables. For instance, you might expect to find a zero or near-zero correlation between the length of big toes and IQ. People with toes of all sizes have high IQs, and those with toes of all sizes have low IQs. The closer a correlation comes to -1.00 or $+1.00$, the stronger the relationship being described. If the correlation is positive, it indicates that high scores on the two dimensions tend to go together, and low scores tend to go together, such as length of big toes and shoe size, for example. Height and weight are also strongly positively correlated, as (probably) are age and memory span.

If the correlation is negative, it describes a relationship in which high scores on one variable are associated with low scores on the other. There is a negative correlation between the amount of disorder and chaos in a family and the child's later IQ (high chaos is associated with lower IQ, and low chaos with higher IQ).

Perfect correlations (-1.00 or $+1.00$) do not happen in the real world, but correlations of .80 or .70 do occur and correlations of .50 are common in psychological research, indicating a relationship of moderate strength.

Correlations are an enormously useful descriptive tool. If I want to know if shy 4-year-olds are still shy at 20, and I have a suitable set of longitudinal data, I would use a correlation to look at the degree of consistency. If I want to know whether better-educated mothers are more likely to have children with larger vocabularies, I would use a correlation. But correlations do not tell us about *causal* relationships.

For example, several researchers have found a moderate positive correlation between the "difficultness" of a child's temperament and the amount of punishment the child receives from his parents: the more difficult the temperament the more punishment the child experiences. But which way does the causality run? Do difficult children *elicit* more punishment? Or does a greater rate of punishment lead to a more difficult temperament? Or is there some third factor that may cause both, such as perhaps some genetic contribution both to the child's difficultness and to the parent's personality? The correlation alone does not allow us to choose among these alternatives. Stating the point more generally: no correlation, standing alone, can prove causality. A correlation may point in a particular direction, or suggest possible causal links, but to discover the causes, we must then explore such possibilities with other techniques, including experiments.

Researchers have found a positive correlation between a mother's age at the birth of her child and the child's later IQ: very young mothers have children with lower IQs. How many different explanations of this correlation can you think of?

▶ A Final Word

It may seem to you that these details about research design are of interest and value only to professional researchers. But that is not true. There are many practical daily applications for knowledge of this kind, even if you never take another course in psychology. An example: An issue of *Time* magazine I read recently included an article about a new system for providing stimulation for the unborn baby. The mother-to-be apparently wears a belt full of audio equipment on which are played tapes of various complex patterns of heartbeat sounds. The article reported that the maker of this gadget had done some research to demonstrate that this procedure produces smarter, faster-developing babies. To quote *Time*: "Last year 50 of the youngsters [whose mothers had worn the belt], ranging in age from six months to 34 months, were given standardized language, social and motor-skills tests. Their overall score was 25% above the national norm." (Sept. 30, 1991, p. 76)

I hope you would not go out and buy this apparatus on the basis of that finding! After reading what I've said about research design, you should to be able to see immediately why one can't conclude anything helpful from this reported result. There are equivalent reports of research on children, on adolescents, on adults in the newspapers and popular magazines every day. Obviously I want you to be critical analysts of the research I'll talk about in this book. But if nothing else, I want you to become very critical consumers of popularly presented research information. Some of it is very good. A lot of it is bunk, or at the very least inconclusive. I hope you are now in a better position to tell the difference.

Summary

1. In studying development over the life span, we need to understand both change and continuity, shared and individual patterns of development, and the relative influences of nature and nurture.

2. One major type of change is a shared, age-graded change, which might be the product of maturation (biological clock), common social prescriptions (social clock), or inner changes triggered by either biological or social clock.

3. Cultures, and individual cohorts within cultures, may define the social clock differently. Different cohorts also live through different historical periods at different points in their development, all of which can alter the underlying pattern of development.

4. Awareness of potential cohort differences is especially crucial in studies of adults, in which comparisons of different age groups are inevitably confounded with cohort effects.

5. Individual life pathways are also affected by unique, nonshared experiences. The timing of such individual experiences may be especially important in shaping an individual's developmental pattern.

6. Consistency over time can also be explained in biological terms. Using studies of twins and adopted children, behavior geneticists have found significant genetic influence on a wide range of behavior.

7. Consistency in behavior over time may also be fostered because of the cumulative effects of early behaviors, and because children and adults tend to select niches in which their basic behaviors fit well.

8. Historically psychologists and philosophers have argued about nature *versus* nurture, but we now know that every behavior, every developmental change, is a product of both. In studying nurture, it is important to look well beyond the immediate family and consider the larger cultural influences, and the impact of the entire environmental system.

9. Babies appear to begin life with a wide variety of inborn biases in their ways of responding to the stimulation around them.

10. Each child, and each adult, also creates internal models of meaning to interpret past experience and to understand new experience.

11. Inborn or acquired vulnerabilities and resilience resources interact with the richness of the environment in nonadditive ways. The only seriously detrimental combination appears to be a high level of vulnerability combined with a poor environment.

12. Researchers and theorists differ about whether development should be conceived as purely quantitative, or whether there are also qualitative dimensions to change. Similarly, there is disagreement about whether there are distinct, qualitatively different stages of development over the life span.

13. In studying any aspect of development, three main types of research design are possible: cross-sectional designs, in which separate age groups are each tested once, longitudinal designs, in which the same individuals are tested repeatedly over time, and sequential designs, which offer combinations of the first two.

14. Longitudinal or sequential research is required to study sequences of development, or consistency over time.

15. To test specific hypotheses, experimental designs are also possible in which subjects are assigned randomly to treatment or control groups. However, there are limitations in the use of experimental designs in studies of development.

16. The choice of subjects may have a major effect on the generalizability of results from any one study.

17. Correlational research, common in studies of development, can be informative, but correlations do not describe causal relationships, so care is needed in interpretation.

Key Terms

age strata

biological clock

cohort

control group

correlation

critical period

cross-sectional design

dependent variable

experiment

experimental group

independent variable

internal model

longitudinal design

maturation

resilience

sensitive period

sequential design

social clock

teratogen

vulnerability

Suggested Readings

Bornstein, M. H. (Ed.) (1987). *Sensitive periods in development. Interdisciplinary perspectives.* Hillsdale, NJ: Erlbaum. (Bornstein's own paper in this collection is an excellent introduction to the concept of sensitive periods. There are also several other excellent papers analyzing the evidence for critical or sensitive periods in a number of areas of development, including language and social relations.)

Neugarten, B. L. (1979). Time, age, and the life cycle. *American Journal of Psychiatry, 136,* 887–894. (This is the best brief discussion of the effects of timing of experience on adult life that I have found.)

Rowe, J. W., Wang, S. Y., & Elahi, D. (1990). Design, conduct, and analysis of human aging research. In E. R. Schneider & J. W. Rowe (Eds.), *Handbook of the biology of aging* (3rd ed.) (pp. 63–71). San Diego, CA: Academic Press. (Included in this paper is a particularly good—albeit high-level—discussion of the pros and cons of longitudinal research designs in studies of adulthood and aging.)

Seitz, V. (1988). Methodology. In M. H. Bornstein & M. E. Lamb (Eds.), *Developmental psychology: An advanced textbook* (2nd ed.) (pp. 51–84). Hillsdale, NJ: Erlbaum. (A well-organized, clearly written review of many of the methodological issues I have talked about in the chapter.)

2

THEORIES OF DEVELOPMENT

S tudents often tell me that they hate reading about theories. What they want are the facts. But it is a fallacy to assume that facts can simply stand alone, without any explanation or framework. Even in your everyday interactions with friends, family, and acquaintances, you *always* interpret, try to make sense out of what others do or say. If a friend frowns when you expected a smile, you try to *explain* his behavior to yourself. You have developed a kind of mini-theory about this friend, based on his past behavior, so you interpret his current frown in light of that theory. Social psychologists call this process *attribution*; you attribute the other person's behavior to a specific cause, either some internal property of the individual, or some outside force. The internal models of relationships or of the self that I talked about in Chapter 1 are also a kind of theory: a set of propositions or assumptions about the way the world is organized that help you to organize and interpret experiences.

The same is true of research facts. For example, here is a fact: In a series of recent studies in the United States, researchers have found that a slightly higher percentage of infants in day care have an "insecure" attachment to their mothers than is true of infants reared at home (Clarke-Stewart, 1990). The difference is small (36 percent versus 29 percent) but has been found quite consistently in a number of studies. What does this fact mean?

There are many possible meanings. Because we know that parents who place their children in day care differ in a variety of ways from those who do not, there could be some self-selection factor involved. So it may not be day care at all that is producing this effect. But let's assume for the moment that we have ruled out all explanations of this type and that there is still a difference to be explained. Why might such a difference occur? Does it mean that day care is damaging to children? If so, what (if anything) might we do to alter the pattern? Only theory can help us here—theories about how attachments are formed in the early months of life and about the importance of such attachments.

Here's another fact: Studies in the United States and in other developed countries show that in the months immediately after the death of a spouse, men are more likely than women to fall ill, to commit suicide, or to die of other causes (Stroebe & Stroebe, 1986). Again there may be some methodological explanations. We know that adult men die at earlier ages than women anyway, so we'd have to be sure that the apparent effect of widowhood was not simply a result of different basic death rates between men and women. But let us again assume that the fact remains after we have eliminated such possible explanations. Now what? As soon as you try to go beyond methodological explanations you are in the realm of theory, such as theories about the possible role of social networks in providing support in times of crisis, and theories about the origins of differences in social networks between men and women.

Have I persuaded you? The creation of models or theories is a natural and necessary process to make sense out of our experience. Theories also guide our collection of facts by suggesting what patterns we ought to observe. For example, I might explain the different response of men and women to widowhood by proposing that, in general, men have smaller social networks and less intimate social relationships, which leaves them especially vulnerable after the loss of their spouse. If that is a valid explanation (a good theory), then I ought to be able to subdivide widowers into those with, and those without, extensive and intimate social networks. I should find notably higher rates of death and disease only among those lacking such networks. Thus the theory suggests a specific hypothesis that guides the next empirical investigation.

A theory need not offer a grand scheme to be classed as a theory. Mini-theories that account for a narrow range of empirical observations are much more common than are grand schemes. I'll be describing many such mini-theories as we go along. What I want to do here is to introduce you to some of the grand schemes—those major theories of human development that have shaped our thinking and our research over the past decades.

▶ Theories About Human Development

To help you organize all the various theories in your mind, let me offer you a kind of theory of theories—a framework or matrix that lets you place each theory in relation to the others. You can see in Figure 2.1 (page 26) that I have organized the options along two dimensions, both of which will be familiar from Chapter 1. The first dimension is simply whether the theory proposes any kind of stages of development or not. The second is more complex, similar to the distinction between qualitative and quantitative change. On one end of this dimension are theories proposing that the change we see with age is not just qualitative but has some identifiable goal or direction and involves real structural change. On the other end of the continuum are theories that see change with age as being primarily quantitative, or as having no direction or goal and no structural change. I could put it another way by saying that one group of theories emphasizes mere *change*, while the other group emphasizes some kind of *development*, some kind of systematic restructuring of the individual's skills or characteristics that takes place with increasing age. This two-dimensional classification scheme gives us four types of theories—although you can be sure that all shades and variations along these dimensions actually exist in present-day theories. And of course there are many other dimensions I could have chosen as well, such as the relative degree of emphasis on nature versus nurture. But this will still give you a structure on which to hang the theoretical hats. Let me describe several theories of each type.

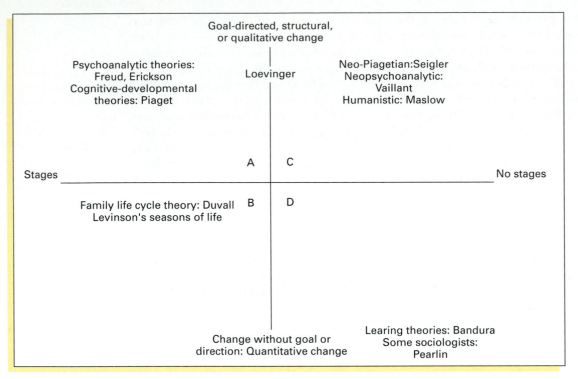

Goal-directed, structural,
or qualitative change

Psychoanalytic theories: Freud, Erickson Cognitive-developmental theories: Piaget	Loevinger	Neo-Piagetian:Seigler Neopsychoanalytic: Vaillant Humanistic: Maslow

Stages   A   C   No stages

Family life cycle theory: Duvall Levinson's seasons of life	B	D

Change without goal or
direction: Quantitative change

Learing theories: Bandura
Some sociologists:
Pearlin

Figure 2.1 The dozens of theories of human development can be organized along many possible dimensions. Here they are arrayed on two dimensions: stages versus no stages and goal-directed/structural change versus quantitative or non-goal-directed change.

▌ Type A Theories: Qualitative/Structural Change in Stages

The theories in this group share the assumption that development has some end point, some direction, some goal, whether that is conceptualized in terms of increasing maturity, greater integrity, a more integrated sense of identity, or more complex forms of thinking. Further, these theorists assume that each of us moves toward this end point in fixed, shared stages.

Psychoanalytic Theories

There is a whole family of theorists called *psychoanalytic,* including Sigmund Freud (1905, 1920/1965), Carl Jung (1916, 1939), Alfred Adler (1948), and Erik Erikson (1959, 1964, 1974). All have been interested in explaining human behavior by understanding the underlying processes of the *psyche,* a Greek term meaning "soul," "spirit," or "mind." Sigmund Freud is usually credited with originating the psychoanalytic approach, and his terminology and many of his concepts have become part of our intellectual culture, even while his explicit influence on developmental psychology has waned.

Freud's Theory.   One of Freud's most distinctive theoretical contributions is the idea that behavior is governed not only by conscious but by *unconscious* processes. The most basic of these unconscious processes, according to Freud, is an instinctual sexual drive he called the **libido**, present at birth and forming the motive force behind virtually all our behavior. Further unconscious material is also created over time through the functioning of the various **defense mechanisms**—those automatic, normal, unconscious strategies for reducing anxiety that we all use on a daily basis, such as repression, denial, or projection.

Freud also argued that personality has a structure, and that such a structure develops over time. Freud proposed three parts: the **id**, in which the libido is centered, the **ego**, a

THE REAL WORLD
We All Use Defense Mechanisms Every Day

I suspect many of you, hearing the phrase *defense mechanisms,* think of some kind of abnormal or deviant behavior. It is important for you to understand, though, that Freud conceived of them not only as unconscious but as entirely normal. Their primary purpose is to help us protect ourselves against anxiety. Since we all feel anxious some of the time, we all use some form of defense.

Suppose I send a paper to a professional journal and it comes back with a rejection letter. I feel anxious. I might be able to handle this anxiety realistically by looking objectively at my paper to see how it could be improved, doing another study to prove the point I was trying to make, or something equivalent. More likely, I wouldn't be able to handle all the anxiety this way. So I would resort (unconsciously) to some kind of defense mechanism.

All defense mechanisms distort reality to some extent, but they vary in the amount of distortion involved. At one extreme end is *denial*. I might deny that I had ever submitted the paper or that it had ever been rejected. Or I could use *distortion,* such as by persuading myself that the journal really loved the paper but that there hadn't been enough space.

A notch less distorting are mechanisms such as *projection*, in which I push my feelings onto someone else. ''Those people who rejected this paper are really stupid! They don't know what they're doing.'' In this way, I ascribe to others the qualities I fear may be true for me, in this instance stupidity. I might also *repress* my feelings, insisting that I really don't mind at all that my paper is rejected. Or I could use *intellectualization*, in which I consider, in emotionally very bland terms, all the reasons why the paper was rejected. Intellectualization sounds quite rational and open, as if there were no defense involved. But what has been pushed away is the emotion.

Another defense that is about equivalently distorting is *displacement*. If I am upset about the rejection but cannot direct my distress at the appropriate target—such as the editor of the journal, whom I cannot afford to alienate—I might displace my emotion onto someone else. I might find myself being overly critical of a student or unexpectedly angry at my husband, or pushing the cat off my lap when it bids for some attention.

The least distorting defenses include such things as *suppression*, in which I allow myself to be aware of my distress but still shove it away for a while by saying, à la Scarlett O'Hara, ''I'll think about it tomorrow.'' So I push it away, but not so firmly into the unconscious as is true for repression. Or I could have prepared myself for the possibility of rejection by *anticipation*, rehearsing how I will feel or figuring out ahead of time where I will send the paper if it is rejected by the first journal.

Not long ago I was reminded very forcibly just how powerful these defensive processes can be. I received a phone call at noon one day from a friend, who told me of the death of a mutual friend—a man who was very dear to me. I said all the right things at the time, finished my lunch, and went back to work, pressing to meet a deadline. At dinner that evening, I had this vague feeling that there was some important news I meant to tell my husband, but I *couldn't remember what it was.* I went to a choir rehearsal that evening and was unbearably grumpy and irritable, but couldn't figure out why. As I got into my car to drive home, the memory of my friend's death suddenly returned, and I burst into tears in the parking lot. This is a perfect example of repression. I couldn't deal with the news when it first arrived, so I pushed it out of my conscious memory long enough to get me through the day.

Can you think of equivalent examples in your own life? When was the last time something uncomfortable happened to you. How did you handle it? Bear in mind that these defenses are entirely normal.

much more conscious element that serves as the executive of the personality, and the **superego**, the center of conscience and morality, incorporating the norms and moral strictures of the family and society. In Freud's theory, these three parts are not all present at birth. The infant and toddler are all id, all instinct, all desire, without the restraining influence of the ego or the superego. The ego begins to develop in the years from 2 to about 4 or 5 as the child learns to adapt his instant-gratification strategies. Finally the superego begins to develop just before school age, as the child incorporates the parents' values and cultural mores.

Freud also proposed a series of five **psychosexual stages,** (summarized in Table 2.1) through which the child moves in a fixed sequence strongly influenced by maturation. In each, the libido is invested in that part of the body that is most sensitive at that age. In a newborn, the mouth is the most sensitive part of the body, so libidinal energy is focused there. The stage is therefore called the *oral* stage. As neurological development progresses, the infant has more sensation in the anus (hence the *anal* stage), and later the genitalia (the *phallic* and eventually the *genital* stages).

TABLE 2.1 Freud's Stages of Psychosexual Development

Stage	Age	Erogenous Zones	Major Developmental Task (potential source of conflict)	Some Adult Characteristics of Children Who Have Been Fixated at this Stage
Oral	0–1	Mouth, lips, tongue	Weaning	Oral behavior, such as smoking, overeating; passivity and gullibility.
Anal	2–3	Anus	Toilet training	Orderliness, parsimoniousness, obstinacy, or the opposite.
Phallic	4–5	Genitals	Oedipus complex	Vanity, recklessness, and the opposite.
Latency	6–12	No specific area	Development of defense mechanisms	None: fixation does not normally occur at this stage.
Genital	13–18	Genitals	Mature sexual intimacy	Adults who have successfully integrated earlier stages should emerge with a sincere interest in others, and mature sexuality.

The most famous of these stages is probably the phallic, since it is here that the *Oedipus conflict* is said to occur. Freud proposed that at about age 4 or 5, the boy begins to have a sort of sexual attachment to his mother and to regard his father as a sexual rival. His father sleeps with his mother, holds her and kisses her, and generally has access to her body in a way that the boy does not. The boy also sees his father as a powerful and threatening figure who has the ultimate power—the power to castrate. The boy is caught between desire for his mother and fear of his father's power.

Most of these feelings and the resultant conflict are unconscious. The boy does not have overt sexual feelings or behavior toward his mother. But unconscious or not, the result of this conflict is anxiety. How can the little boy handle this anxiety? In Freud's view, the boy responds with a defensive process called **identification:** the boy "incorporates" his image of his father, and attempts to match his own behavior to that image. By trying to make himself as like his father as possible, the boy not only reduces the chance of an attack from the father, he also takes on some of the father's power as well. Furthermore, it is the "inner father," with his values and moral judgments, that serves as the core of the child's superego.

A parallel process is supposed to occur in girls. The girl sees her mother as a rival for her father's sexual attentions, and also has some fear of her mother. Like the boy, she resolves the problem by identifying with the same-sexed parent.

Optimum development requires an environment that will satisfy the unique needs of each period. The baby needs sufficient oral and anal stimulation; the 4-year-old boy needs a father present with whom to identify and a mother who is not too seductive. An inadequate early environment will leave a residue of unresolved problems and unmet needs, which are then carried forward to subsequent stages.

This emphasis on the formative role of early experience, particularly early family experience, is a hallmark of psychoanalytic theories. In this view, the first five or six years of life are a kind of sensitive period for the creation of the individual personality.

Erikson's Theory.   Other than Freud, the psychoanalytic theorist who has had the greatest influence on the study of development has been Erik Erikson. Erikson shares most of Freud's basic assumptions, but there are some crucial differences between their theories. First, Erikson deemphasizes the centrality of sexual drive and instead focuses on a stepwise emergence of a sense of **identity.** Second, although he agrees with Freud that the early years are highly important, he argues that identity is not fully formed at the end of adolescence, but continues to move through further developmental stages in adult life. You can see in Table 2.2 that he proposes eight stages, three of which are reached only in adulthood.

In Erikson's view, maturation plays relatively little role in the sequence of stages. Far more important are common cultural demands for children of a particular age, such as the demand that the child become toilet trained at about 2, that the child learn school skills at age 6 or 7, or that the young adult form an intimate partnership. Each stage, then, centers on a particular dilemma, a particular social task. Thus he calls his stages **psychosocial stages** rather than psycho*sexual* stages.

Table 2.2 will give you some familiarity with the names and basic descriptions of all eight of these stages. Of the eight, four have been the focus of the greatest amount of theorizing and research: trust in infancy, identity in adolescence, intimacy in early adulthood, and generativity in mid adulthood.

Erikson believes that the behavior of the major caregiver (usually the mother) is critical to the child's establishment of a sense of basic trust. For a successful resolution of this task, the parent must be consistently loving and respond predictably and reliably to the child. Those infants whose early care has been erratic or harsh may develop *mis*trust.

TABLE 2.2   The Eight Stages of Development Proposed by Erik Erikson

Approximate Age	Ego Quality to be Developed	Some Tasks and Activities of the Stage
0–1	Basic trust versus mistrust	Trust in mother or central caregiver and in one's own ability to make things happen. A key element in an early secure attachment.
2–3	Autonomy versus shame, doubt	New physical skills lead to free choice; toilet training occurs; child learns control but may develop shame if not handled properly.
4–5	Initiative versus guilt	Organize activities around some goal; become more assertive and aggressive; Oedipus conflict with parent of same sex may lead to guilt.
6–12	Industry versus inferiority	Absorb all the basic cultural skills and norms, including school skills and tool use.
13–18	Identity versus role confusion	Adapt sense of self to pubertal changes, make occupational choice, achieve adultlike sexual identity, and search for new values.
19–25	Intimacy versus isolation	Form one or more intimate relationships that go beyond adolescent love; form family groups.
26–40	Generativity versus stagnation	Bear and rear children, focus on occupational achievement or creativity, and train the next generation.
41 +	Ego integrity versus despair	Integrate earlier stages and come to terms with basic identity. Accept self.

In either case, the child carries this aspect of basic identity through development, affecting the resolution of later tasks. This conceptualization had a strong influence on theorists such as John Bowlby, who recast the trust versus mistrust dilemma in terms of the process of *attachment*. Bowlby's thinking has in turn prompted a rich and fascinating body of research on early attachments and their consequences for the child's later functioning—all of which I'll talk about in Chapter 6.

Erikson's description of the central adolescent dilemma of *identity versus role confusion* has also been highly influential. He argued that every adolescent, in order to arrive at a mature sexual identity and occupational identity, must reexamine his identity and the roles he must occupy. He must achieve a reintegrated sense of self, of what he wants to do and be, and of his appropriate sexual role. The risk is that of confusion, arising from the profusion of roles opening to the child at this age.

Expanding on this idea, James Marcia (1966, 1980) proposes that the process of adolescent identity formation has two parts, a *crisis* and a *commitment*. A crisis is a period of decision making when old values, old choices are reexamined. This may occur either gradually or abruptly, but the outcome of the reevaluation process is a commitment to some specific role or some particular ideology. If you put these two elements together, as in Figure 2.2, you can see that four different **identity statuses** are possible: (1) **Identity achievement**. The person has been through a crisis and reached a commitment. (2) **Moratorium**. A crisis is in progress, but no commitment has yet been made. (3) **Foreclosure.** A commitment has been made without any reassessment of old positions. Instead, the young person has simply accepted a parentally defined commitment. (4) **Identity diffusion**. The young person is not in the midst of a crisis and no commitment has been made. Diffusion may represent either an early stage in the process (before a crisis), or a failure to reach a commitment after a crisis.

In Chapter 12 you'll see that Marcia's category system, firmly rooted in Erikson's theory, has been a helpful way of looking at the adolescent identity process.

In the next stage, which Erikson labels *intimacy versus isolation*, the young adult builds upon the identity established in adolescence. Erikson defines intimacy as "the ability to fuse your identity with someone else's without fear that you're going to lose something yourself" (Erikson, in Evans, 1969). One implication of this definition is that—if Erikson is correct—intimacy cannot be achieved unless or until the young person has successfully arrived at a clear identity.

The key task of middle adulthood is *generativity versus stagnation*, the sense of passing on the flame in some fashion to the new generation, of contributing one's energy, thoughts, and work products to the society at large. The rearing of children is one obvious way to achieve such a sense of generativity, but it is by no means the only way. Creative

If a clear identity is necessary for real intimacy to be established, then we might guess that happy marriages, such as this pair seem to have, could be predicted by knowing which couples had achieved clear separate identities before they married. Does this hypothesis make sense to you?

Figure 2.2 The four identity statuses proposed by Marcia, based on Erikson's theory. To achieve a full identity, the young person must move through a crisis in which goals and values are examined, and arrive at a commitment to a particular role or set of values. (*Source:* Marcia, 1980.)

	Degree of crisis	
	High	Low
Degree of commitment to a particular role or values — High	Identity achievement status (crisis is past)	Foreclosure status
Low	Moratorium status (in midst of crisis)	Identity diffusion status

work, service to organizations or society, serving as mentor to younger colleagues—all these can help the mid-life adult achieve a sense of generativity. Failing that, the self-absorbed, nongenerative adult may feel a sense of stagnation.

A key idea to take away with you from this very brief presentation of Erikson's theory is that each new task, each dilemma, is thrust upon the developing person because of changes in social demands. We might rephrase this idea in Matilda Riley's terms by saying that each age strata has its own central psychological task. Because age marches along, willy nilly, the developing person is confronted with new tasks whether she has successfully resolved earlier dilemmas or not. The unresolved issues will be carried forward as excess baggage, making successful or complete resolution of later dilemmas more difficult. The very earliest tasks are thus especially important because they set the stage for everything that follows.

Other Psychoanalytic Theorists.   A number of other theorists who have had an important influence on current thinking about development have been strongly influenced by psychoanalytic theory. Jane Loevinger (1976) has focused on ego development, which she sees as progressing from childhood through adulthood in a series of ten stages or steps. Loevinger's model departs in an important way from Freud and Erikson, however, in that she does not think these stages are tied to age. There is a *sequence* of steps that people move through in the same order, but not all individuals will progress to the same level or move at the same speed. In Figure 2.1, Loevinger's theory falls somewhere in the middle on the dimension of stages. But she is on the very upper end of the qualitative/quantitative dimension. In her view, each new step or stage—if it is achieved at all—represents a radical restructuring, a new perspective, a new way of understanding oneself and one's relationship to the world.

For example, the fifth stage in Loevinger's sequence is called the *conformist stage*, and is typically (but not invariably) reached in late adolescence or early adulthood. An individual in this stage identifies his own welfare with that of some group—family, work group, religious group, or whatever. He *defines himself* in terms of his membership in that group or subgroup, and tends to define others as either being one of "us" or one of "them." Within this stage, there is a good deal of stereotyping of others and insensitivity to individual differences. Inwardly, he understands his own emotions in parallel ways, such as either happy or sad, good or bad, but without many gradations in between.

After passing through a transitional phase Loevinger calls the self-aware level, the adult *may* eventually move out of the conformist stance and arrive at the *conscientious stage*. A radical change is involved in this transition. In the conformist stage, authority is external to the self; in the conscientious stage, authority is taken inward. The person now creates her own rules and attempts to live by them. She has a much richer inner life, with many more shadings of feeling, and perceives others in more subtle and individualistic terms as well.

As evidence against strict age-linked stages has accumulated, the sequential-but-not-inevitable aspect of Loevinger's proposed stages has become more attractive to many current researchers.

Critique of Psychoanalytic Theories.   The very endurance of psychoanalytic theories over so many decades is one indication that this perspective has had powerful attractions. The concept of unconscious motivations has been a profoundly important idea whose traces we can certainly see in current theories emphasizing internal models. Freud and Erikson also focused our attention on the importance of the child's relationship with her caregivers in shaping the child's internal models, habit patterns, and personality. At the same time, by emphasizing that the child comes to this encounter with certain tasks to accomplish, an agenda of development if you will, psychoanalytic theorists emphasized the *transactional* nature of the developmental process. It is not that the child is a passive

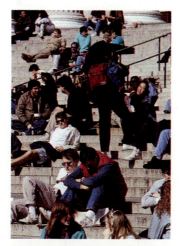

Chances are that if you asked these young people to define themselves, the word *student* would be part of the definition. According to Loevinger, most young adults like these are in the *conformist* stage, in which people understand and define themselves with reference to the group to which they belong or the roles they fill.

recipient of the family's influence; rather the child enters the system with needs and tasks of her own. This is a particularly attractive element of such theories, because so much of our current research is pointing us more and more strongly toward just such a transactional conceptualization.

On the other side of the ledger are several significant weaknesses. Both Freud's and Erikson's theories were based primarily on clinical observations rather than on any systematic research. In Freud's case, the clinical observations all involved individuals who had come to him for psychotherapy. This may have led Freud to his strong emphasis on pathological and negative psychological processes. This criticism is less valid for Erikson's theory, however, since he emphasizes constructive and healthy adaptations as well as negative ones.

An even greater weakness in all the psychoanalytic approaches is their fuzziness. As Jack Block puts it (1987, p. 2):

> For all the richness, insight, and seriousness of psychoanalytic theory regarding the understanding of personality functioning, it has also been imprecise, overly facile with supposed explanations, and seemingly inaccessible scientifically.

Because of such imprecision, researchers have often found it hard to turn Freud's and Erikson's concepts into valid and reliable measures. This has meant, in turn, that the theories themselves are difficult to test and thus difficult to disconfirm. Current psychoanalytically flavored theories, such as Loevinger's or Bowlby's, are markedly more precise, which has led to a resurgence of interest in this approach in recent years.

Cognitive-Developmental Theories

A second theoretical tradition that emphasizes qualitative changes in stages is the cognitive-developmental approach. Like psychoanalytic theorists, cognitive-developmentalists strongly emphasize the role of the child as the most active participant in the process of development. Both also describe clear, qualitatively different stages of development. But the similarity largely stops there, in part because the two theoretical traditions have turned their attention to very different facets of the child's development. Psychoanalytic theorists have focused almost exclusively on personality development. Cognitive-developmentalists, as the name implies, have attempted to explain the development of the child's thinking, and have paid relatively little attention to the specifics of the child's relationship with caregivers.

The central figure in cognitive-developmental theory has been Jean Piaget (1952, 1970, 1977; Piaget & Inhelder, 1969), a Swiss psychologist whose theories have shaped the thinking of several generations of developmental psychologists. Piaget, along with other early cognitive theorists such as Lev Vygotsky (1962) and Heinz Werner (1948), was struck by the great regularities in the development of children's thinking. He noticed that all children seemed to go through the same kinds of sequential discoveries about their world, making the same sorts of mistakes and arriving at the same solutions. For example, 3- and 4-year-olds all seem to think that if you pour water from a short, fat glass into a tall, thin one, there is now more water, because the water level is higher in the thin glass than it was in the fat glass. But most 7-year-olds realize that there is still the same amount of water in either case. If a 2-year-old loses her shoe, she may look for it briefly and haphazardly, but she is unable to undertake a systematic search. A 10-year-old, in contrast, is likely to use such good strategies as retracing her steps or looking in one room after another.

Piaget's detailed observations of children's thinking led him to several assumptions, the most central of which is that it is the nature of the human organism to *adapt* to its environment. This is an active process. Piaget does not think that the environment *shapes* the child but that the child (like the adult) actively seeks to understand his environment. In the process, he explores, manipulates, and examines the objects and people in his world.

The Concept of Scheme.   A pivotal concept in Piaget's theory is that of a **scheme** (sometimes written as *schema*). In Piaget's view, knowledge itself is a repertoire of *actions*, either physical or mental, such as looking at something, or holding it a particular way, or categorizing it mentally as *a ball*, or labeling it with the word *ball*, or comparing it to something else. Piaget used the word scheme to refer to such actions. The baby begins life with a small repertoire of built-in sensory or motor schemes, such as looking, tasting, touching, hearing, or reaching. For the baby, an object *is* a thing that tastes a certain way, or feels a certain way when it is touched, or has a particular color. Later the baby clearly has mental schemes as well, creating categories, comparing one object to another, learning words for specific categories; by adolescence, we see such complex schemes as deductive analysis or systematic reasoning. But how does the child get from those simple, built-in, sensorimotor schemes to the more internalized, increasingly complex mental schemes we see in later childhood? Piaget proposed three basic processes to account for the change: **assimilation, accommodation,** and **equilibration.**

Assimilation.   Assimilation is the process of *taking in*, of absorbing some event or experience to some scheme. When a baby looks at and then reaches for a mobile above his crib, Piaget would say that the baby had assimilated the mobile to his looking and reaching schemes; when an older child sees a dog and labels it *dog*, she is assimilating that animal to her dog category or scheme. When you read this paragraph you are assimilating the information, hooking the concept onto whatever other concept (scheme) you have that may be similar.

The key here is that assimilation is an *active* process. For one thing, there is selectivity in the information we assimilate. If I am trying to learn tennis and watch my instructor demonstrate a good forehand, I do not assimilate the entire set of information because my existing scheme is simply not close enough to the model. So I assimilate part of it, and can only imitate the part that I have absorbed. In addition, the very act of assimilating changes the information that is assimilated. If I see a friend wearing a new dress in an unusual color of orangish red, I may label the color *red* in my mind (assimilate it to my "red" scheme) even though it is not precisely red. Later, when I remember the dress, I will remember it as being redder than it really is. The process of assimilation, then, has changed the perception.

Accommodation.   The complementary process is accommodation, which involves *changing the scheme* as a result of the new information you have taken in by assimilation. After seeing my friend's dress, my "red" scheme may be expanded somewhat to include this unusual new variation. If I now learn a new word for this special shade of red, I will accommodate still further, perhaps by creating a new subcategory (a new scheme) altogether. The baby who sees and grasps a square object for the first time will accommodate her grasping scheme, so that next time she reaches for an object of that shape her hand will be more appropriately bent to grasp it. Thus in Piaget's theory, the process of accommodation is one key to developmental change. Through accommodation, we reorganize our thoughts, improve our skills, change our strategies.

Equilibration.   The third aspect of adaptation is equilibration. Piaget assumed that in the process of adaptation, the child is always striving for coherence, to stay "in balance," to have an understanding of the world that makes overall sense. What Piaget is proposing is not unlike what a scientist does when she develops a theory—just what I am talking about in this chapter. She wants a theory that will make sense out of every observation and that has internal coherence. When new research findings come along, she assimilates them to her existing theory; if they don't fit perfectly, she might simply set aside the deviant data, or she may make minor modifications in her theory. But if enough noncon-

Using Piaget's language, we would say that 9-month-old Jesse is assimilating this spoon to her grasping scheme.

Think of three or four more examples of assimilation and accommodation in your everyday life.

firming evidence accumulates, she may have to throw out her theory altogether and start over, or she may need to change some basic theoretical assumptions, either of which would be a kind of equilibration.

Piaget thought that a child operated in a similar way, creating coherent, more or less internally consistent models or theories. Because the infant starts with a very limited repertoire of schemes, her early "theories" or structures are inevitably primitive and imperfect. Piaget thought that over the following years, the child makes a series of significant changes in the internal structure.

Piaget saw three particularly significant reorganizations or equilibration points, each ushering in a new stage of development. The first is at roughly 18 months, when the toddler shifts from the dominance of simple sensory and motor schemes to the first really internal representations. The second is at roughly age 5 to 7, when the child adds a whole new set of powerful schemes Piaget calls **operations.** These are far more abstract and general mental actions, such as mental addition or subtraction.

The third major equilibration is at adolescence, when the child figures out how to "operate on" ideas as well as events or objects. These three major equilibrations create four stages:

The *sensorimotor stage,* from birth to 18 months

The *preoperational stage,* from 18 months to about age 6

The *concrete operational stage* from 6 to about 12

The *formal operational* stage, from age 12 onward

Table 2.3 expands somewhat more fully on these stages, each of which I will describe in greater detail in the appropriate age-based chapters. The key for now is to understand that in Piaget's view, each stage grows out of the one that precedes it, and—like Loevinger's stages of ego development—each involves a major restructuring of the child's way of thinking. Also like Loevinger, Piaget does not conceive of progress through all these stages as inevitable. He thought the sequence was fixed, so that if the child made cognitive progress it would be in this order, but not all children would necessarily reach the same end point or move at the same speed. Piaget thought that virtually all children would move to at least preoperational thought, and the vast majority would achieve concrete operations. But not all would necessarily achieve formal operations.

Other Cognitive-Developmental Theorists. Piaget did not think there were any further structural changes in cognition after adolescence. In recent years, though, a number of theorists have proposed further equilibrations in the adult years. Gisela Labouvie-Vief (1980, 1990), for example, argues that the highly analytic mode characteristic of formal operations may be adaptive when one is still in school, but for most of us a more pragmatic, specialized form of thinking emerges in adulthood. We also become better able to understand and deal with both metaphor and paradox.

Another cognitive-developmental theorist who has pushed the process of cognitive development into adulthood is Lawrence Kohlberg (1964, 1976, 1981, 1984), whose theory of the development of moral reasoning has been both fascinating and enormously influential. Kohlberg's work, which I'll be describing in Chapter 11, was clearly based solidly on Piagetian concepts. Each of the six stages of moral development Kohlberg described involves a restructuring of the previous way of thinking; each is a movement toward a more complex, more elaborated understanding. But unlike Piaget, he thought that the final few stages were typically achieved only in adulthood, if then. At the same time, Kohlberg shared with Piaget the assumption that the basic stages developed in the same sequence in all children (and adults) in all cultures. The *rate* may vary from one culture or from one individual to the next, but the *sequence* is precisely the same.

TABLE 2.3 Piaget's Stages of Cognitive Development

Age	Stage	Description
0–2	Sensorimotor	The baby understands the world in terms of her senses and her motor actions. A mobile is how it feels to grasp, how it looks, how it tastes in the mouth.
2–6	Preoperational	By 18–24 months, the child can use symbols to represent objects to himself internally and begins to be able to take others' perspectives, to classify objects, and to use simple logic.
7–12	Concrete operations	The child's logic takes a great leap forward with the development of powerful new internal mental operations, such as addition, subtraction, and class inclusion. The child is still tied to specific experience but can do mental manipulations as well as physical ones.
12+	Formal operations	The child becomes able to manipulate ideas as well as events or objects. She can imagine and think about things she has never seen or that have not yet happened; she can organize ideas or objects systematically and think deductively.

Critique of Cognitive-Developmental Theories.   It would be difficult to overstate the impact that Piaget's ideas have had on the study and understanding of children's development. His work has been controversial precisely because it called into question so many earlier, more simplistic views. Piaget also devised a number of remarkably clever techniques for exploring children's thinking—techniques that often showed unexpected and counterintuitive responses from children, as you can see in the "research report" on page 36. So not only did he offer us a theory that forced us to think about children and their development in a new way, he provided a set of empirical facts that were impossible to ignore and difficult to explain.

By being quite explicit about many hypotheses and predictions, Piaget also enabled others to test his theory. When those tests have been done, Piaget has often turned out to be wrong. He has been wrong about the specific ages at which children understand certain concepts; researchers have consistently found evidence of complex concepts at much earlier ages than Piaget proposed. More profoundly, it now looks as if he is wrong about the central concept of stages of development. Most 8-year-olds, for example, show "concrete operational" thinking on some tasks but not on others, and they are much more likely to show complex thinking on a task with which they are very familiar than one with which they have little experience. The whole process is a great deal less stagelike than Piaget proposed, and more influenced by specific experience than Piaget had thought.

These disconfirmations of Piaget have not meant that Piaget's theory has lost its influence. Many of Piaget's basic concepts have been absorbed into our common base of ideas (much as Freud's concept of the unconscious has been accepted), and his theory continues to set the agenda for a great deal of the research on children's thinking.

▶ Type B Theories:
Stages, but Without End Point or Goal

When we move into the lower left quadrant of Figure 2.1, to Type B theories, the concept of stages remains, but the stages are not moving toward some higher state, such as greater

As part of their adult roles, these Japanese women have learned strict rules of etiquette, including rules for bowing.

RESEARCH REPORT
Piaget's Clever Research

Piaget had an enormous impact on developmental psychologists not only because he proposed a novel and provocative theory, but because of the cleverness of many of the strategies he devised for testing children's understanding. These strategies often showed children doing or saying very unexpected things—results that other theorists found hard to assimilate into their models.

The most famous of all Piaget's clever techniques is probably his method for studying *conservation*. Piaget would begin with two equal balls of clay, show them to the child, and let the child hold and manipulate the clay until she agreed that they had the same amount. Then in full view of the child, Piaget would squash one of the balls into a pancake or roll it into a sausage. Then he'd ask the child whether there was still the same amount, or whether the pancake or the ball had more. Children of 4 and 5 consistently said that the ball had more; children of 6 and 7 consistently said that they were still the same.

Or Piaget would start with two identical water glasses, each containing exactly the same amount of liquid. The child would agree that there was the same amount of water or juice in each one. Then in full view of the child he'd pour the water from one glass into a shorter, fatter glass, so that the water level in the new glass was lower than the water level in the original. Then he'd ask again whether there was the same amount of water in both. Four- and 5-year-olds thought the amounts were now different, while 6- and 7-year-olds knew that there was still the same amount no matter what size glass the liquid was poured into. Thus the older child has acquired the concept of conservation; she understands that the quantity of water or clay is *conserved* even though it is changed in some other dimension.

In another study, Piaget explored the concept of *class inclusion*—the understanding that a given object can belong simultaneously to more than one category. Fido is *both* a dog and an animal; a high chair is both a chair and furniture. Piaget usually studied this concept by having children first create their own classes and subclasses and then asking them questions about them. One 5½-year-old child, for example, had been playing with a set of flowers and had made two heaps, one large group of primroses and a smaller group of other mixed flowers. Piaget then had this conversation with the child:

> Piaget: "If I make a bouquet of all the primroses and you make one of all the flowers, which will be bigger?"
> Child: "Yours."
> Piaget: "If I gather all the primroses in a meadow, will any flowers remain?"
> Child: "Yes." (Piaget & Inhelder, 1959, p. 108).

The child understood that there are other flowers than primroses, but did *not* yet understand that all primroses are flowers—that the smaller, subordinate class, is *included in* the larger class.

In these conversations with children, Piaget was always trying to understand how the child thought, rather than whether the child could come up with the right answer or not. So he used a "clinical method" in which he followed the child's lead, asking probing questions or creating special exploratory tests to try to discover the child's logic. In the early days of Piaget's work, many American researchers were critical of this method, since Piaget did not ask precisely the same questions of each child. Still, the results were so striking, and often so surprising, that they couldn't be ignored. And when stricter research techniques were devised, more often than not the investigators discovered that Piaget's observations were accurate.

maturity or greater complexity of thinking. They are simply shared stages, caused by physiological changes such as puberty or menopause, or by the set of roles we normally take up in a particular sequence in our lives. Two notable theories of adult lives fall in this category.

Family Life Cycle: A Sociological Stage Theory

The first of these is a theory that emerges from the field of family sociology. To understand the basic notion, I have to give you a more precise definition of the concept of **role**, a term I have used loosely so far.

Any social system can be thought of as being made up of a series of interlocking *positions* (also called *statuses*), such as "employer" and "worker," "supervisor," or "teacher" and "student." A role is the *content* of a social position: the behaviors and characteristics expected of a person filling that position. Thus a role is a kind of job description. A teacher, for example, is expected to be knowledgeable, able to communicate, a good "role model" for others, prepared, well organized, clear, and so forth. This set of expected behaviors or qualities defines the *role* of teacher.

Several aspects of the concept of roles are important for our understanding of development. First, they are at least partially culture- and cohort-specific. "Teacher" may be a different role (a different set of expected behaviors) in one culture versus another, or in the same culture from one time to another. A hundred years ago in the United States, women teachers were generally expected to be unmarried and to live a morally pure life. Nowadays it is illegal even to ask a prospective teacher if she (or he) is married.

Second, occupying the multiple roles each of us fills at any one moment inevitably involves frictions of various kinds. I am a psychologist, wife, mother, stepmother, grandmother, daughter, sister, sister-in-law, aunt, niece, friend, author. Sociologists use the term **role conflict** to describe any situation in which two or more roles are at least partially incompatible, either because they call for different behaviors or because their separate demands add up to more hours than there are in the day. At the moment, for example, I am in conflict over my inability to find time for several valued friendships because the demands of my work role are especially intense.

Role strain occurs when an individual's own qualities or skills do not measure up to the demands of some role. A parent who feels incompetent because she just can't figure out how to keep her 2-year-old from drawing on the walls is experiencing role strain. A newly minted Ph.D. in her first professional job, who feels anxious about her ability to do high-quality research, is also experiencing role strain. (I remember both of these!)

The final important point about the concept of roles is that they change systematically with age and occur in particular sequences. Most notably, *family* roles change with age. Sociologists such as Evelyn Duvall (1962) have argued that we can understand adult life in terms of the movement through such family roles. Table 2.4 lists the eight stages of the family life cycle Duvall proposed, each of which involves either adding or deleting some role, or changing the content of a central role.

The concept of family life stages does not imply that each succeeding role is any better, more complex, or more mature than those that preceded it. Stages occur in a particular sequence, and each set of roles shapes the experiences of the individuals in it. But there is no goal, no deeper kind of change proposed.

Levinson's Model of Seasons of Adulthood

Daniel Levinson also talks about adult life in terms of rhythms and shared patterns (1978, 1980, 1986, 1990), without growth or goal. His central concept is that of the **life structure**,

List all the roles you now occupy. What role conflict, or role strain, do you experience?

TABLE 2.4 Family Life Cycle Stages

Stage	Description
1	Adult is newly married, no children. Spousal role is added.
2	First child is born; role of parent is added.
3	Oldest child is between 2 and 6; role of parent has changed.
4	Oldest child is between 6 and 12; role of parent has changed again as child enters school.
5	Oldest child is an adolescent; role of parent changes again.
6	Oldest child has left home; sometimes called the *launching center* phase, as parents assist children to become independent.
7	All children have left home; dramatic change in parental role; sometimes called the *empty nest* or *postparental* stage.
8	One or both spouses has retired; sometimes called "aging families."

Source: Duvall, 1962.

which is the "underlying pattern or design of a person's life at a given time" (1986, p. 6). The life structure obviously includes roles, but it also includes the quality and pattern of the relationships one has, all filtered through one's personality or temperament. Life structures are not permanent. Precisely because roles and relationships change, life structures must change too. In fact Levinson proposes that each adult creates a series of life structures at specific ages, with transitional periods in between when the old life structure is either given up or reexamined and changed. You can see his model more precisely in Figure 2.3.

Levinson divides the life span into a series of broad *eras*, each lasting perhaps 25 years, with a major transition between each era. Within each era, he proposes three periods: the creation of an initial or entry life structure, described as a *novice phase*, an intermediate readjustment of that life structure, and a *culminating phase* life structure created at the end of the era.

He also proposes that each phase, transition, or era has a particular content, a particular set of issues or tasks. For example, the mid-life transition, between 40 and 45, is centered around the growing awareness of one's own mortality, and the realization that the dreams of one's youth may never be realized.

Of course Levinson is not saying that all adult lives are exactly alike. That is clearly nonsense. Nor is he saying that each new life structure is in any way better or more integrated or elegant than the one that went before. He *is* saying that there is a basic alternation between stable life structures and transition periods. And he is saying that this orderly pattern, including the basic tasks or issues associated with each era and age, is shared by *all* people in all cultures.

Critique of Type B Theories

The major difficulty with theories in this group, particularly the concept of family life stages, is that the model no longer describes the majority of life patterns. Considerably

Figure 2.3 Levinson's model of adult development. Each stable life structure is followed by a period of transition in which that structure is reexamined. (*Source:* Levinson, 1986, adapted from Levinson, 1978. Copyright 1978 by Daniel J. Levinson. Reprinted by permission of Alfred A. Knopf, Inc.)

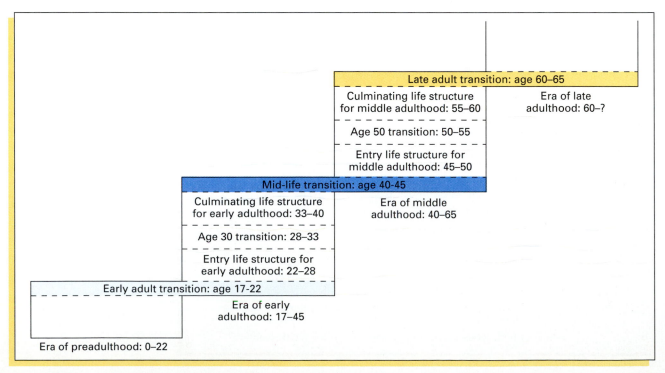

less than half of adults in the United States today follow the life cycle stages as Duvall outlined. Not everyone marries or has children. Those who marry frequently divorce, perhaps marrying again later, or spending years as a single parent. So in a literal way, Duvall's model is simply not accurate.

I also find it difficult to accept Levinson's hypothesis that all adults, in every culture and every cohort, move through eras and transitions at precisely the same ages, such as one at 30 and another between 40 and 45. Among other things, his own original research was done entirely with men and so is hard to generalize to women's lives. More recent research evidence, including studies of both women and men, provides very lukewarm support for this aspect of his theory (e.g., Harris, Ellicott & Holmes, 1986; Reinke, Holmes & Harris, 1985).

At the same time, there is much that is appealing about these views of human development, particularly the notion that there is a basic rhythm to adult life, and perhaps to childhood and adolescence as well. Certainly there is a biological rhythm, marked by such changes as motor development in infancy, puberty at adolescence, and the climacteric in middle adulthood.

The social clock, too, may be characterized by a basic rhythm. If we look at role changes in very general terms, I think a good case can be made that virtually all adults move through a shared series of changes. In early adulthood we *acquire* a whole range of new roles, whether we marry or have children or not. These include new work roles, new definitions of friendship, a new role as an independent person. In middle adulthood we *redefine* our roles. We may have more authority in work; our children may be grown and gone, so the nature of parenthood changes. In late adulthood, we *shed* roles. The specifics may not follow the particular role sequence Duvall proposed, but I think there is still a pattern of role change that is characteristic of nearly all our lives.

Thus what I find most useful from theories like Levinson's or Duvall's is not the

Levinson proposes that everyone, in every culture, goes through some kind of transition between ages 40 and 45. How could you test this hypothesis?

How are Erikson's stages and family life cycle stages the same, and how do they seem to differ?

Many adults, like this struggling single mother, do not find that their lives move through tidy family life stages like the ones Duvall describes.

specific stages proposed—though they can be helpful in understanding some groups—but the idea of a basic shared alternation between stable life structures and transition, and the notion of a basic pattern of acquisition and elimination of roles.

Both the Type B theories I have talked about describe adult development. Can you imagine a theory of *child* development that would fall in the same category?

▶ Type C Theories: Structural, Directional Change Without Stages

When we shift to the right-hand side of Figure 2.1, what disappears is the notion of stages. But there is still divergence on the question of the nature of the change that is occurring. Included in the upper right corner of Figure 2.1 are several neo-Piagetian and neopsychoanalytic theories that have moved away from the notion of strict stages but retain the concept of qualitative change.

For example, George Vaillant (1977), a psychiatrist who has been one of the chief investigators of the Grant study sample of Harvard men, has proposed a psychoanalytically based model of the development of adult maturity. He retains the notion that development occurs in a sequence and with direction, but rejects the concept of fixed stages. Vaillant suggests that one aspect of increasing maturity in adulthood is the gradual abandonment of the most reality-distorting forms of defense mechanisms, such as repression or denial, and the increasing use of more reality-based mechanisms such as suppression or intellectualization. The shift from one type of defense to the other is gradual when it occurs, and does not occur at all in every adult. Thus Vaillant is suggesting something even less stagelike than Loevinger's model. He defines a pathway and argues that movement toward maturity must occur along this pathway, but he does not mark off the pathway into stages, nor does he assume that all adults will move the same distance along the path.

Similarly, there are now a number of neo-Piagetian approaches that emphasize sequence rather than stages, including John Flavell's model of the child's development of strategies for remembering (1985), and Robert Siegler's theory of the development of cognitive "rules" (1981, 1984, 1988; Siegler & Jenkins, 1989), both of which I will talk about in Chapter 9.

Humanistic Theories

A very different type of model that nonetheless falls in this same cluster of theories is the *humanistic* approach, typified by Abraham Maslow's famous hierarchy of needs (1968, 1970a, 1970b, 1971). Humanists, including notably Carl Rogers as well as Maslow, have taken issue with the emphasis on pathology that often pervades psychoanalytic approaches. They assume instead that each individual is born with a basic drive to realize his or her full potential, to achieve *self-actualization* in Maslow's terms. Thus there is a direction to development and qualitative change, as the individual moves toward greater self-realization, but no stages are proposed.

Maslow's greatest interest was in the development of motives or needs, which he divided into two subsets: **deficiency motives** and **being motives.** Deficiency motives involve drives to maintain physical or emotional homeostasis, such as the drive to get enough to eat or drink, the sexual drive, or even obtaining sufficient love or respect from others. Being motives involve the desire to understand, to give to others, and to grow. It is the satisfaction of being motives, Maslow thought, that produces optimum health.

Do you know anyone you would think of as "self-actualized"? What are that person's qualities or characteristics?

Maslow described these various needs or motives in a *needs hierarchy*, shown in Figure 2.4. He argued that the needs must be met from the bottom up. Only when the physiological needs are met do safety needs come to the fore; only when love and esteem needs are met can the need for self-actualization become dominant. For that reason, Maslow thought that being needs were likely to be significant only in adulthood and only in those

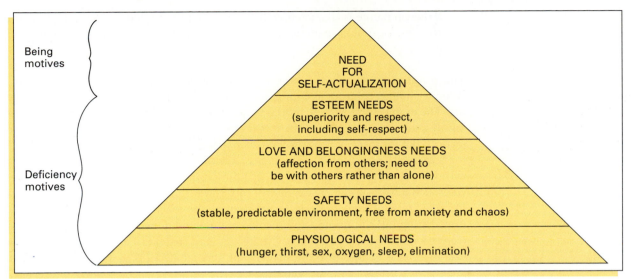

Figure 2.4 Maslow's needs hierarchy. In Maslow's view, needs operate from the bottom up. Until physiological needs are met, no other need will be prominent; until love needs are met, esteem needs will not emerge, etc. Similarly, there is a developmental aspect: A baby is primarily dominated by physiological needs, a toddler by safety needs, and so forth. Only in adulthood may the need for self-actualization become central. (*Source:* Maslow, 1968, 1970b.)

individuals who had found stable ways to satisfy both love and esteem needs—needs which sound very similar to Erikson's stages of intimacy and generativity.

Maslow, like Vaillant and Siegler and many others, thus proposed a *potential* sequence of development, but one that will not be completed by all children or adults.

Critique of Type C Theories

It is my strong impression that theories of this type represent the leading edge of a good deal of current thinking about development in adults as well as in children. Strict stage theories have become less and less attractive for a variety of reasons. In many cases, specific experience seems to be a more powerful influence than age in determining an individual's skill, behavior, or perspective. The concept of shared *sequences* allows us to retain the obviously attractive notion that children and adults develop in common ways, and at the same time leaves room for much more individual variation and a far larger role for specific environment or experience.

Yet most theories of this type are still quite new and none is yet fully formed into a "grand scheme" of development of the same magnitude as Piaget's or Freud's or Erikson's. So it is too early to tell whether they will offer the kind of synthesis that will advance our understanding still further.

▶ Type D Theories: Quantitative Change Without Stages

Finally, we come to the last type of theory, in which change over the course of a lifetime is seen as neither stagelike nor qualitative. Foremost among the theorists in this group are those that emphasize the role of basic learning processes in creating and shaping human behavior from birth to death. But learning theorists are not alone in seeing behavior over the life span in these terms. There are also several sociological theorists who argue strongly against any concept of stages and against any assumption that development has direction or structural change.

Learning Theorists

Although there is a good deal of variation among learning theorists in the particulars, all would agree with Albert Bandura when he says:

[H]uman nature is characterized by a vast potentiality that can be fashioned by direct and vicarious experience into a variety of forms within biological limits. (1989, p. 51)

This is not to say that there is no genetic base or built-in biases. Rather, theorists of this group see human behavior as enormously plastic, shaped by predictable processes of learning. The most central of these processes are classical conditioning and operant conditioning. If you have encountered these concepts in earlier courses, you can skim the next section. But for those of you who lack such a background, a brief description is needed.

Classical Conditioning.   This type of learning, made famous by Pavlov's experiments with his salivating dogs, involves the acquisition of new signals for existing responses. If you touch a baby on the cheek, he will turn toward the touch and begin to suck. In the technical terminology of **classical conditioning**, the touch on the cheek is the **unconditioned stimulus**; the turning and sucking are **unconditioned responses**. The baby is already programmed to do all that; these are automatic reflexes. Learning occurs when some *new* stimulus is hooked into the system. The general model is that other stimuli that are present just before or at the same time as the unconditioned stimulus will eventually trigger the same responses. In the typical home situation, for example, a number of stimuli occur at about the same time as the touch on the baby's cheek before feeding. There is the sound of the mother's footsteps approaching, the kinesthetic cues of being picked up, and the tactile cues of being held in the mother's arms. All of these stimuli may eventually become **conditioned stimuli** and may trigger the infant's response of turning and sucking, even without any touch on the cheek.

Although the study of classical conditioning has not been a hot research topic, it continues to be of interest for several reasons. First, if we knew how early an infant or child can be classically conditioned, we would know more about what kind of neurological connections are possible early in life. Classical conditioning is also of interest because of the role it plays in the development of emotional responses. For example, things or people present when you feel good will become conditioned stimuli for that same sense of goodwill, while those previously associated with some uncomfortable feeling may become conditioned stimuli for a sense of unease or anxiety. This is especially important in infancy, since a child's mother or father is present so often when nice things happen—when the child feels warm, comfortable, and cuddled. In this way mother and father usually come to be a conditioned stimulus for pleasant feelings, a fact that makes it possible for the parent's mere presence to reinforce other behaviors as well. But a tormenting older sibling might come to be a conditioned stimulus for angry feelings, even after the sibling has long since stopped the tormenting. Such conditioned emotional reactions are formed in adulthood as well. I feel a surge of embarrassment every time I drive by a town in which I gave a particularly poor lecture; I feel peaceful each time I visit, or even imagine visiting, a particular beach, or stand by a particular tree.

These classically conditioned emotional responses are remarkably powerful. They begin to be formed very early in life, continue to be formed throughout childhood and adulthood, and profoundly affect each individual's emotional experiences.

Operant Conditioning.   The second major type of learning is most often called **operant conditioning**, although you will also see it referred to as *instrumental conditioning*. Unlike classical conditioning, which involves attaching an old response to a new stimulus, operant conditioning involves attaching a new response to an old stimulus by the application of appropriate principles of reinforcement. Any behavior that is reinforced will be more likely to occur again in the same or in a similar situation. There are two types of reinforcements. A **positive reinforcement** is any event which, following some behavior, increases the chances that the behavior will occur again in that situation. There are certain classes of pleasant consequences, such as praise, a smile, food, a hug, or attention, that serve as reinforcers for most people most of the time. But strictly speaking, a reinforcement is defined by its effect; we don't know something is reinforcing unless we see that its presence increases the probability of some behavior.

The second major type is a **negative reinforcement**, which occurs when something an individual finds *unpleasant* is *stopped*. Suppose your little boy is whining and begging you to pick him up. At first you ignore him, but finally you do pick him up. What happens? He stops whining. So your picking-up behavior has been *negatively reinforced* by the cessation of his whining, and you will be *more* likely to pick him up the next time he whines. At the same time, his whining has probably been *positively reinforced* by your attention, so he will be more likely to whine on similar occasions.

Both positive and negative reinforcements strengthen behavior. **Punishment**, in contrast, is intended to weaken some undesired behavior. Sometimes punishments involve eliminating nice things (like "grounding" a child, or taking away TV privileges, or sending her to her room); often they involve administering unpleasant things such as a scolding or a spanking. This use of the word *punishment* fits with the common understanding of the term and shouldn't be too confusing. What *is* confusing is the fact that such punishments don't always do what they are intended to do: they do not always suppress the undesired behavior. If your child had thrown his milk glass at you to get your attention, spanking him may be a positive reinforcement instead of the punishment you had intended.

Virtually every child finds a hug reinforcing.

Reinforcements do not strengthen a behavior permanently. The reverse process is **extinction**, which is a decrease in the likelihood of some response after repeated nonreinforcements. If you simply stopped reinforcing whining behavior in your child, eventually the child would stop whining, not only on this occasion but on subsequent occasions.

In laboratory situations, experimenters can be sure to reinforce some behavior every time it occurs, or to stop reinforcements completely so as to produce extinction of the response. But in the real world, consistency of reinforcement is the exception rather than the rule. Much more common is a pattern of **partial reinforcement**, in which some behavior is reinforced on some occasions but not others. Studies of partial reinforcement show that children and adults take longer to learn some behavior under partial reinforcement conditions, but once established, such behaviors are much more resistant to extinction. If you smile at your daughter only every fifth or sixth time she brings a picture to show you (and if she finds your smile reinforcing), she'll keep on bringing pictures for a very long stretch, even if you were to quit smiling altogether.

The same principle might help us understand why some marriages endure, even though there seems to be little vitality or affection remaining. The reinforcement rate may be very low—few smiles, few hugs, or other affection—but it may nonetheless be sufficient to sustain "staying behavior," making it remarkably resistant to extinction.

Subvarieties of Learning Theory.   All theorists who emphasize the central role of learning would agree on the importance of these basic processes. But beyond that basic agreement there are significant theoretical variations.

On one end of the theoretical continuum are the *radical behaviorists*. These theorists, strongly influenced by the work of B. F. Skinner, take an extreme environmental position. Donald Baer (1970) refers to this as an "age-irrelevant concept of development." That is, theorists of this persuasion assume that the basic principles of learning are the same no matter how old the learner may be.

Few developmental psychologists today would take such an extreme position. Many trained in this tradition have broadened their theoretical scope and introduced interactive and ecological concepts, as has Gerald Patterson, whose model is shown in Figure 1.3 (page 12). More common today is a second subvariety of learning theory normally called

Think of examples in your everyday life in which your behavior is affected by classical or operant conditioning, or in which you use these principles to affect others' behavior.

THE REAL WORLD
Learning Principles in Real Family Life

All parents, whether they are aware of it or not, reinforce some behaviors in their children by praising them or by giving them attention or treats. And all parents do their best to discourage unpleasant behavior through punishment. But parents often *think* they are reinforcing one thing when in fact they are doing something quite different. I might think I am rewarding behaviors I like and ignoring those I don't like, and yet the results don't seem to be quite what I'd expected. When this happens, it may be because there was more than one learning principle operating at once, or because I—as might any parent—have misapplied the principles.

Suppose you have a favorite armchair in your living room that is being systematically ruined by the dirt and pressure of little feet climbing up the back of the chair. You want the children to *stop* climbing up the chair. So you scold them. After a while you may even stoop to nagging. If you are really conscientious and knowledgeable, you may carefully stop your scolding when they stop climbing in an effort to have your scolding operate as a negative reinforcer. But nothing works. They keep on leaving those muddy footprints on your favorite chair. Why? It could be because the children *enjoy* climbing up the chair. So the climbing is intrinsically reinforcing to the children, and that effect is clearly stronger than your negative reinforcement or punishment. One way to deal with this might be to provide something *else* for them to climb on.

Or you might inadvertently create a partial reinforcement schedule. Suppose your 3-year-old son repeatedly demands your attention while you are fixing dinner—a common state of affairs, as any parent of a 3-year-old can tell you. Because you don't want to reinforce this behavior, you ignore him the first six or eight times he says "Mommy" or tugs at your clothes. But after the ninth or tenth repetition, with his voice getting louder and whinier each time, you can't stand it any longer and finally say something like "All right! What do you want?" Since you have ignored most of his demands, you might well be convinced that you have not been reinforcing his demanding behavior. But what you have actually done is to create a partial reinforcement schedule; you have rewarded only every tenth demand or whine. And we know that this pattern of reinforcement helps to create behavior that is *very* hard to extinguish. So your son may continue to be demanding and whining for a very long time, even if you succeed in ignoring it completely.

Because many parents have difficulty with situations just like this and with seeing exactly what it is they are reinforcing, many family therapists ask families to keep detailed records of their child's behavior and their responses to it. Gerald Patterson, in his book *Families: Applications of social learning to family life* (1975), lays out a plan for parents to follow in doing this. He has used such strategies with good success in treating families with highly aggressive or noncompliant children, and you may find it helpful as well. When you see, through your own records and observations, just what it is you are doing to reinforce whining or noncompliance or destructive behavior or whatever, it is much easier to change your pattern of response.

social-learning theory. The key figure here is Albert Bandura (1977a, 1982b, 1989), a theorist whose views have undergone some interesting changes over the years. Bandura accepts the importance of classical and operant conditioning, but he makes several additional assertions.

First, he argues that learning does not always require direct reinforcement. Learning may also occur merely as a result of watching someone else perform some action. Learning of this type, called **observational learning** or **modeling,** is involved in a wide range of behaviors. Children learn ways of hitting from watching other people in real life and on TV. They learn generous behaviors by watching others donate money or goods. Adults learn job skills by observing or being shown by others.

Bandura also calls attention to another class of reinforcements called **intrinsic reinforcements** or intrinsic rewards. These are reinforcements internal to the individual, such as the pleasure a child feels when she finally figures out how to draw a star, or the sense of satisfaction you may experience after strenuous exercise. Pride, discovery, that "aha" experience are all powerful intrinsic rewards, and all have the same power to strengthen behavior as do extrinsic reinforcements such as praise or attention.

Third, and perhaps most important, Bandura has gone far toward bridging the gap between learning theory and cognitive-developmental theory by emphasizing important *cognitive* elements in learning. Indeed he now even refers to his theory as "social cognitive theory" (Bandura, 1986, 1989). For example, Bandura now stresses the fact that modeling

Children learn a wide variety of skills and behaviors through modeling.

can be the vehicle for the learning of abstract as well as concrete skills or information. In this *abstract modeling*, the observer extracts a rule that may be the basis of the model's behavior, and learns the rule as well as the specific behavior. In this way a child or adult can acquire attitudes, values, ways of solving problems, even standards of self-evaluation through modeling. Furthermore, what we learn from observing someone else is influenced by other cognitive processes, such as selecting what we pay attention to, by our ability to make sense out of and remember what we saw, and by our actual capacity to repeat the observed action. (I will never become an expert tennis player merely by watching Martina Navratilova play!) To my ear, all of this sounds a great deal like Piaget's concept of assimilation.

Bandura introduces other cognitive components as well. In learning situations, children and adults *set goals*, *create expectations* about what kinds of consequences are likely, and *judge* their own performance. The addition of concepts like these makes Bandura's learning theory an *age-relevant* theory, because children of different ages (and probably adults of different ages, too) are highly likely to observe or notice different things and to analyze or process those observations differently. Thus what is learned in any given situation may vary systematically by age.

Critique of Learning Theories

Several implications of this theoretical approach are worth emphasizing. First of all, learning theorists can handle either consistency or change in child or adult behavior. If a child is friendly and smiling both at home and at school, this could be explained by saying that the child was being reinforced for that behavior in both settings rather than by assuming that the child had a "gregarious temperament." But it is equally possible to explain how an adult can be friendly and helpful in a work setting, and unhelpful and frowning at home. We need only assume that the reinforcement contingencies are different in the two settings. To be sure, because individuals tend to choose settings that maintain their accustomed behavior, and because a person's behavior will tend to *elicit* similar responses (reinforcements) from others in many settings, there is a bias toward consistency. But learning theorists have less trouble accounting for normal "situational variability" in behavior than do other theorists.

A related implication is that learning theorists tend to be optimistic about the possibility of change. Children's behavior can change if the reinforcement system or their beliefs about themselves change. So "problem behavior" can be modified.

The great strength of this view of social behavior is that it seems to give an accurate picture of the way in which many behaviors are learned. It is perfectly clear that children do learn through modeling, and it is equally clear that children and adults will continue to perform behaviors that "pay off" for them. The addition of the cognitive elements to Bandura's theory adds further strength, since it offers a beginning integration of learning models and cognitive-developmental approaches.

On the debit side of the ledger, from my view, is the fact that this approach is really not developmental. That is, it doesn't tell us much about change *with age*, either in childhood or adulthood. Thus it can help us understand human *behavior* more fully than it can help us understand human *development*.

Other Nonstage Theories of Change

A number of psychologists and sociologists who study adult lives (e.g., Fiske, 1980; Pearlin, 1980) have become highly disenchanted with any variation of stage theories. Leonard Pearlin, for example, says:

> Because people are at the same age or life cycle phase, it cannot be assumed that they have either traveled the same route to reach their present locations or that they are headed in the same future directions. (1982, p. 64)

Many are equally convinced that it is a mistake to assume that adult life is "going anywhere" except toward death. Pearlin sees adult life, instead, as "a continuing process of adjustment to external circumstances" (1980, p. 180). According to this view, real understanding of the experience of adult life is going to come only when we give up trying to think of it in stagelike or developmental terms, and try instead to uncover basic processes that are valid for adults of any age, such as the ways adults respond to stress or major upheaval. Theorists in this tradition grant that the demands of adult life are likely to change with age. But it is the way we meet those demands, not the demands themselves, that shape adult lives. I certainly would not disagree with the importance of such demands in shaping each life. For me, however, an interesting question remains: Is it possible that the meanings we attribute to an experience, or our ways of meeting those demands, change as we age? This seems clearly to be the case when we look at children. It may also be true in adulthood, as a result of changes in life structures, changes in the type of defense mechanisms or reasoning we typically use, or deeper changes such as a shift in Loevinger's stages. On the whole, then, I think that theories in this last group focus our attention on vital basic processes that are applicable to all ages. But we need not throw out the notion of sequences, perhaps even stages, in order to include some of these basic processes in our theorizing.

▶ An Afterword

I wouldn't be surprised if you are a bit bleary-eyed after all these theories. It's hard to make the theoretical issues real to you before you have delved into the data. And at the same time, it is hard for you to assimilate and integrate the data without having some theoretical models to hook them onto. At the least I hope you can see that there are some real disagreements here, some basic differences in the assumptions theorists make about the very nature of development or about the proper subject matter for our study.

For example, learning theories, even Bandura's remarkably cognitive version, emphasize the vital role of experience in *shaping* the individual. Piaget, on the other hand, believes that the child uses experience to *construct* her own reality, her own understanding. Psychoanalytically inclined theorists fall somewhere between these two poles. This is not a trivial disagreement. It leads to very different questions, very different kinds of research.

Similarly, those who study adulthood ask very different questions and interpret results very differently, depending on their theoretical persuasion or even the academic discipline from which they begin. Sociologist Dale Dannefer (1984a, 1984b, 1988) has rather scathingly pointed out that psychologists, in the face of anything that looks like an age-linked pattern, are likely to jump immediately to the conclusion that they have uncovered a basic developmental process. Presented with the same set of data, a sociologist is likely to look for the social forces that might have shaped the responses of different cohorts or different subgroups within the population. To psychologists, cohort differences are "noise" in the system, distorting their attempt to uncover basic human patterns. To sociologists, cohort differences are the very stuff of interest, since they tell us about how the individual and the society interact.

As we move into the descriptive chapters, I will be coming back again and again to these theoretical perspectives, trying to show not only how the data we've collected have been shaped by the theoretical assumptions researchers have made, but also how the different theoretical perspectives can help us to understand the information that has accumulated. So hang in there. These ideas will turn out to be useful, helping you (and me) to create some order out of the vast array of facts.

Summary

1. Facts alone will not add up to an explanation of any phenomenon, including development. Theory is also required.

2. Theories about human development can be divided along at least two important dimensions: whether or not they posit stages of development, and whether or not they assume that there is some direction to development and/or some structural change.

3. Among those assuming directional change in stages are psychoanalytic theorists such as Freud and Erikson and cognitive-developmental theorists such as Piaget.

4. Freud emphasized that behavior is governed by unconscious as well as conscious motives and that the personality develops in steps: first the id, then the ego, then the superego.

5. Freud also proposed a set of five psychosexual stages: oral, anal, phallic, latency, and genital. The Oedipal crisis occurs in the phallic stage.

6. Erikson emphasized social forces, more than unconscious drives, as motives for development. The key concept is the development of identity, said to occur in eight psychosocial stages over the course of the life span: trust, autonomy,

initiative, industry, identity, intimacy, generativity, and ego integrity.

7. Another psychoanalytically oriented theorist is Loevinger, who proposes a set of ten stages which will be achieved in a given sequence, but not at specific ages and not by everyone.

8. Piaget focused on the development of thinking rather than personality. A key concept is that of adaptation, made up of the subprocesses of assimilation, accommodation, and equilibration.

9. The result of several major equilibrations is a set of four cognitive stages, each of which Piaget thought resulted in a coherent cognitive system: sensorimotor, preoperational, concrete operations, and formal operations.

10. Among theories that propose stages without a defined goal or direction are sociological theories of the family life cycle and Levinson's theory of seasons of adult life.

11. A key concept is that of a role, which is a job description for a specific position or status within a culture, such as the role of teacher or even a sex role. Roles change systematically with age, especially in adulthood.

12. Levinson proposes an ebb and flow between stable life structures and transition periods.

13. Among those proposing qualitative change without stages are both neo-Piagetian and neopsychoanalytic theorists, as well as humanistic theorists such as Maslow.

14. Maslow argued that each individual has not only "deficiency drives," but also a drive toward self-actualization.

15. In the last group of theorists are those who see change with age as being neither stagelike nor directional, including learning theorists and many sociological theorists.

16. Basic learning principles, such as classical and operant conditioning and modeling, clearly govern the acquisition and maintenance of many behaviors.

17. No one of these theories can adequately account for all the available evidence on human development, but each offers useful concepts, and each may provide a framework within which we can examine bodies of research data.

Key Terms

accommodation	identity	operations
assimilation	identity achievement	partial reinforcement
being motives	identity diffusion	positive reinforcement
classical conditioning	identity statuses	psychosocial stages
conditioned stimulus	intrinsic reinforcement	punishment
defense mechanisms	libido	role
deficiency motives	life structure	role conflict
ego	modeling	role strain
equilibration	moratorium	scheme
extinction	negative reinforcement	superego
foreclosure	observational learning	unconditioned response
id	operant conditioning	unconditioned stimulus
identification		

Suggested Readings

Lerner, R. M. (1986). *Concepts and theories of human development* (2nd ed.). New York: Random House. (A very good discussion of most of the major theoretical approaches I have described here.)

Smelser, N. J., & Erikson, E. H. (1980). *Themes of work and love in adulthood.* Cambridge, MA: Harvard University Press. (It would be hard to find a better collection of papers by leading theorists on adult life. Levinson and Pearlin both have papers here, as do other major thinkers. The articles are not overly technical.)

Thomas, R. M. (Ed.) (1990). *The encyclopedia of human development and education. Theory, research, and studies.* Oxford: Pergamon Press. (This is a very useful volume. It includes brief descriptions of virtually all the theories I have described in this chapter as well as a helpful chapter on the concept of stages. Each chapter is quite brief but covers many of the critical issues.)

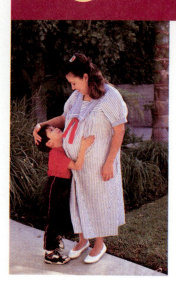

3

PRENATAL DEVELOPMENT AND BIRTH

L ike any good story, human development has a beginning, a middle, and an end. So let us start the story at the beginning—with conception and with the months of prenatal development. What does normal prenatal development look like? What forces shape it, and what forces can deflect it from its normal path? For example, how much can the mother's health or her health practices help or hinder the process? These questions have great practical importance for those of you who expect to bear (or father) children in the future. But they are also important basic issues as we begin the study of lifespan development. The heredity passed on to the new individual at the moment of conception, and the neurological and other physical developments in these first months, set the stage for all that is to follow.

▶ Conception

The first step in the development of a single human being is that moment of conception when a single sperm cell from the male pierces the wall of the ovum of the female—a moment captured in the photo shown here (Figure 3.1). Ordinarily, a woman produces one **ovum** (egg cell) per month from one of her two ovaries. This occurs roughly midway between two menstrual periods. If the ovum is not fertilized, it travels from the ovary down the **fallopian tube** toward the **uterus**, where it gradually disintegrates and is expelled as part of the next menstruation.

But if a couple has intercourse during the crucial few days when the ovum is in the fallopian tube, one of the millions of sperm ejaculated as part of each male orgasm may travel the full distance through the woman's vagina, cervix, uterus, and fallopian tube and penetrate the wall of the ovum. A child is conceived. Interestingly (and perhaps surprisingly to you), only about half of such conceptuses are likely to survive to birth (and

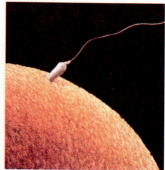

Figure 3.1 The moment of conception when a single sperm has pierced the shell of the ovum.

50

such survival is rarer for male conceptuses than for female). About a quarter are lost in the first few days after conception, often because of a flaw in the genetic material. Another quarter are spontaneously aborted ("miscarried") at a later point in the pregnancy (Wilcox et al., 1988).

▶ The Basic Genetics of Conception

It is hard to overestimate the importance of the genetic events accompanying conception. The combination of genes from the father in the sperm and from the mother in the ovum create a unique genetic blueprint—the **genotype**—that characterizes that specific individual. To understand how that occurs, I need to back up a few steps.

The nucleus of each cell of our bodies contains a set of 46 **chromosomes**, arranged in 23 pairs. These chromosomes include all the genetic information for that individual, including not only genetic information controlling highly individual characteristics like hair color, height, body shape, temperament, and aspects of intelligence, but also all those characteristics shared by all members of our species, such as patterns of physical development.

The only cells that do *not* contain 46 chromosomes are the sperm and the ovum, collectively called **gametes** or *germ cells*. In the early stages of development, gametes divide as all other cells do (a process called *mitosis*), with each set of 23 chromosome pairs "unzipping" and duplicating itself. But in gametes there is a final step, called *meiosis*, in which each new cell receives only one chromosome from each original pair. Thus each gamete has only 23 chromosomes instead of 23 *pairs*. When a child is conceived, the 23 chromosomes in the ova and the 23 in the sperm combine to form the 23 *pairs* that will be part of each cell in the newly developing body.

The chromosomes, in turn, are composed of long strings of molecules of a chemical called **deoxyribonucleic acid** (DNA). In an insight for which they won the Nobel prize, James Watson and Francis Crick (1953) deduced that DNA is in the shape of a *double helix*, a kind of twisted ladder. The remarkable feature of this ladder is that the rungs are made up in such a way that the whole thing can "unzip" and then each half can guide the duplication of the missing part, thus allowing multiplication of cells with each new cell containing the full set of genetic information.

The string of DNA that makes up each chromosome can be further subdivided into segments, called **genes**, each of which controls or influences some specific feature or a portion of some developmental pattern. A gene controlling some specific characteristic, such as blood type or hair color, always appears in the same place (the *locus*) on the same chromosome in every individual of the same species. The locus of the gene that determines whether you have type A, B, or O blood is on chromosome 9; the locus of the gene that determines whether you have the Rh factor in your blood is on chromosome 1, and so forth (Scarr & Kidd, 1983). Geneticists have made remarkable strides in recent years in mapping the loci for a great many features or characteristics—a scientific achievement that has allowed similarly giant strides in our ability to diagnose various genetic defects or inherited diseases before a child is born.

Dominant and Recessive Genes

Because each individual inherits *two* of each chromosome (one from each parent), the genetic instructions at any given locus may be either the same (*homozygous*) or contradictory (*heterozygous*). If you receive a gene for blue eyes from both parents, your inheritance is homozygous and you will have blue eyes. But what if you receive heterozygous information, such as a gene for blue eyes from one parent and one for brown eyes from the other?

Heterozygosity is resolved in several different ways, depending on the particular genes involved. Sometimes the two signals appear to blend, resulting in some intermediate characteristic. For example, the children of one tall parent and one short parent generally have height that falls in between. Another, rarer, outcome is that the child expresses *both* characteristics. For example, type AB blood results from the inheritance of a type A gene from one parent and a type B gene from the other. The most common outcome is that one of the two genes is *dominant* over the other, and only the dominant gene is actually expressed. The "weaker" gene, called a *recessive* gene, continues to be part of the genotype and can be passed on to offspring through meiosis, but it has no effect on visible characteristics or behavior.

A large number of specific diseases appear to be transmitted through the operation of dominant and recessive genes, such as Tay-Sachs disease, sickle-cell anemia, and cystic fibrosis. Figure 3.2 shows how this might work in the case of sickle-cell anemia, which is caused by a *recessive* gene. For an individual to have this disease, she or he must inherit the disease gene from *both* parents. A *carrier* is someone who inherits the disease gene from only one parent. Such a person does not actually have the disease but can pass the disease gene on to his or her children. If two carriers have children together (example 3 in the figure), or if a carrier and someone with the disease have children (example 4 in the figure), their offspring may inherit disease genes from both parents and thus have the disease.

Unlike this simple example, most human characteristics are affected by many more than one gene. Temperament, intelligence, rate of growth, even apparently simple characteristics such as eye color, all involve the interaction of multiple genes. Very exciting new genetic research has also pointed toward totally unexpected additional complexities. For example, researchers studying muscular dystrophy, a recessive gene disease, have observed that this disease often becomes more severe from one generation to the next, apparently through some kind of multiplication of the DNA in the section of the chromosome that signals the disease (e.g., Fu et al., 1992). Other genetic researchers have discovered that, contrary to the long-accepted theory, the outcome may be different if a particular gene comes from the mother or from the father, even though the genes appear to signal precisely the same genotypic characteristic (Rogers, 1991; McBride, 1991). Research like this is beginning to unlock the secrets of genetic transmission, but there is an enormous amount that we still do not know.

The inheritance pattern for eye color is that brown is dominant over blue. Can you figure out what your parents' genotype for eye color has to be, based on the color of your eyes, your siblings' eyes, and that of your grandparents?

Figure 3.2 Some examples of how a recessive-gene disease, like sickle-cell anemia, is transmitted. In section I, a mother who has the disease passes her sickle-cell disease gene to all her children, but since her partner is normal, none of the children actually express the disease. In section II, a normal mother and a carrier father have no children with the disease, but each of their children has a 50/50 chance of carrying the SCA gene. The child can inherit the actual disease in any of three ways: with two affected parents, in which case all the children have the disease; with two carrier parents, as shown in section III; and with one carrier parent and one affected parent (section IV).

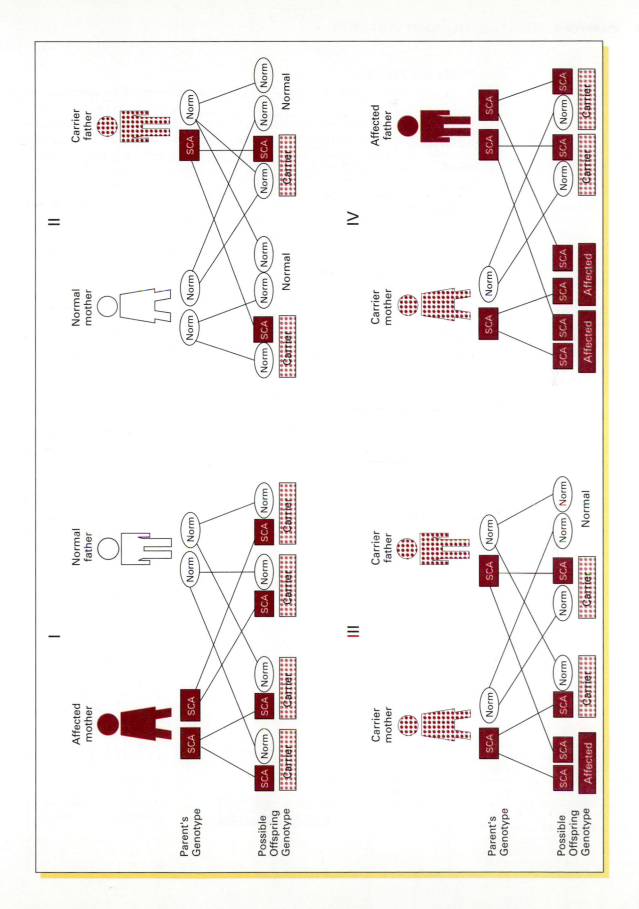

Males and Females

In 22 of the chromosome pairs, called *autosomes*, the members of the pair look alike and contain exactly matching genetic loci. The 23rd pair, however, operates differently. The chromosomes of this pair, which determine the child's gender and are therefore called the *sex chromosomes*, come in two types, referred to by convention as the X and the Y chromosomes. A normal human female has two X chromosomes on this 23rd pair (an XX pattern), while the normal human male has one X and one Y (an XY pattern). The X chromosome is considerably larger than the Y and contains many genetic loci not matched on the Y.

Note that the sex of the child is determined by the sex chromosome it receives from the sperm. Because the mother has *only* X chromosomes, every ovum carries an X. But the father has both X and Y chromosomes. When the father's gametes divide, half the sperm will carry an X, half a Y. If the sperm that fertilizes the ovum carries an X, then the child inherits an XX pattern and will be a girl. If the fertilizing sperm carries a Y, then the combination is XY, and the infant will be a boy.

Geneticists have recently discovered that only one very small section of the Y chromosome actually determines maleness—a segment referred to as *TDF*, or *testis-determining factor* (Page et al., 1987). Fertilized ova that are genetically XY but that lack the TDF develop physically as female.

A second important consequence of the difference between X and Y chromosomes is that a boy inherits many genes from his mother on his X chromosome that are not matched by, or counteracted by, equivalent genetic material on the smaller Y chromosome. Among other things, this means that recessive diseases or other characteristics that have their loci on the nonmatched parts of the X chromosome may be inherited by a boy directly from his mother, a pattern called *sex-linked* transmission, illustrated in Figure 3.3 with the disease hemophilia.

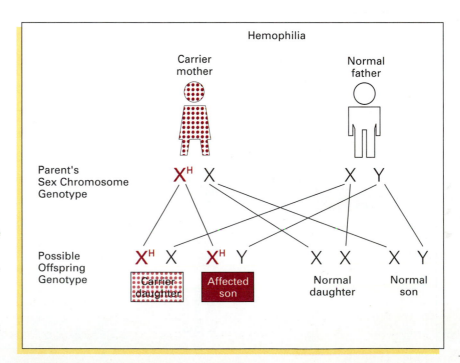

Figure 3.3 Compare the pattern of sex-linked transmission of a recessive disease with the patterns already shown in Figure 3.2. In a sex-linked inheritance, like this example with hemophilia, a carrier mother can pass on the disease to half her sons (on average) because there is no offsetting gene on the Y chromosome. But a daughter of a carrier mother will not inherit the disease itself unless her father has the disease.

You can see that for females, sex-linked recessive genes operate just as they do in other recessive diseases: The girl will have the characteristic only if she inherits the recessive gene from both parents. But a male will inherit the characteristic by receiving the recessive gene only from his mother. Since his Y chromosome from his father contains no parallel loci for these characteristics, there are no counteracting instructions and the mother's recessive gene causes the disorder or other characteristic. For sex-linked characteristics like muscular dystrophy or hemophilia, half the sons of women who carry the recessive disease gene will have the disease, and half the daughters will be carriers of the gene. These daughters, in turn, will pass the disease on to half their sons.

Twins and Siblings

In the great majority of cases, babies are conceived and born one at a time. But multiple births occur roughly once in a hundred cases. The most common type of multiple birth is *fraternal twins*, when more than one ovum has been produced and both have been fertilized, each by a separate sperm. Such twins, also called *dizygotic* twins, are no more alike genetically than any other pair of siblings, and need not even be of the same sex. In rarer cases, a single fertilized ovum may divide and each half may develop into a separate individual. These are *identical*, or *monozygotic*, twins and have identical genetic heritages because they come from precisely the same original fertilized ovum. You'll remember from Chapter 1 that comparisons of the degree of similarity of these two types of twins is one of the two major research strategies in the important field of behavior genetics.

Genotypes and Phenotypes

Using data from twin and adoption studies, behavior geneticists have made great strides in identifying those skills, characteristics, or traits that are influenced by heredity. But no geneticist proposes that an inherited combination of genes fully *determines* any outcome for a given individual. Geneticists (and psychologists) make an important distinction between the genotype, which is the specific set of "instructions" contained in a given individual's genes, and the **phenotype**, which is the actual observed characteristics of the individual. The phenotype is a product of three things: the genotype, environmental influences from the time of conception onward, and the interaction between the environment and the genotype. A child might have a genotype associated with high IQ, but if his mother drinks too much alcohol during the pregnancy there may be damage to the nervous system resulting in mild retardation. Another child might have a genotype for a "difficult" temperament but have parents who are particularly sensitive and thoughtful, making it possible for the child to learn other ways to handle himself.

The distinction between genotype and phenotype is an important one. Genetic codes are not irrevocable signals for this or that pattern of development or this or that disease. The eventual developmental outcome is also affected by the specific experiences the individual may have from conception onward.

Can you think of other examples where the phenotype would be different from the genotype?

▶ Development from Conception to Birth

If we assume that conception takes place two weeks after a menstrual period, when ovulation normally occurs, then the period of gestation of the human infant is 38 weeks (about 265 days). Most physicians calculate gestation as 40 weeks, counting from the last menstrual period. All the specifications of weeks of gestation I've given here are based on the 38-week calculation, counting from the presumed time of conception.

Biologists and embryologists divide the weeks of gestation into three subperiods of unequal length. These are: the *germinal*, which lasts roughly two weeks, the *embryonic*, which continues until about 8 to 12 weeks after conception, and the *fetal* stage, which makes up the remaining 26 to 30 weeks.

The Germinal Stage: From Conception to Implantation

Some time during the first 24 to 36 hours after conception, cell division begins; within two to three days there are several dozen cells and the whole mass is about the size of a pinhead. This mass of cells is undifferentiated until about four days after conception. At that point the organism, now called a *blastocyst*, begins to subdivide. A cavity begins to appear within the ball of cells, and the mass divides into two parts. The outer cells will form the various structures that will support the developing organism, while the inner mass will form the embryo itself. When it touches the wall of the uterus, the outer shell of cells in the blastocyst breaks down at the point of contact. Small tendrils develop and attach the cell mass to the uterine wall, a process called *implantation.* You can see the sequence schematically in Figure 3.4 and a more detailed depiction of implantation in Figure 3.5. When implantation occurs, normally ten days to two weeks after conception, there are perhaps 150 cells in the blastocyst (Tanner, 1978).

The Embryonic Stage

The embryonic stage begins when implantation is complete and continues until the various support structures are fully formed and all the major organ systems have been laid down in at least rudimentary form, a process that normally takes another six to ten weeks.

Support Structures. Two of the key support structures that develop out of the outer layer of cells are the **amnion**, which is the sac or bag filled with liquid in which the baby floats, and that marvelous organ, the **placenta**, a platelike mass of cells that lies against the wall of the uterus. The placenta, which is fully developed by about four weeks of gestation, serves as liver, lungs, and kidneys for the embryo and fetus. Through this large filter, nutrients such as oxygen, proteins, sugars, and vitamins from the maternal blood can pass through to the embryo or fetus, while digestive wastes and carbon dioxide from the infant's blood pass back through to the mother, whose own body can eliminate them (Rosenblith & Sims-Knight, 1989). At the same time, many (but not all) harmful substances, such as viruses, are too large to pass through the various membranes in the placenta and are filtered out, as are most of the mother's hormones. Most drugs and anesthetics, however, do pass through the placental barrier, as do some disease organisms.

Figure 3.4 In this schematic drawing, you can see the sequence of changes during the germinal stage, with the first cell division and the first differentiation of cell function normally occurring in the fallopian tube.

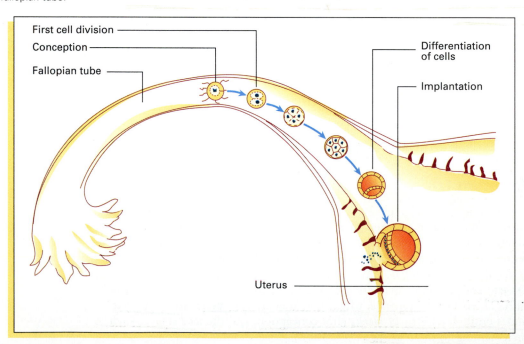

First cell division
Conception
Fallopian tube
Differentiation of cells
Implantation
Uterus

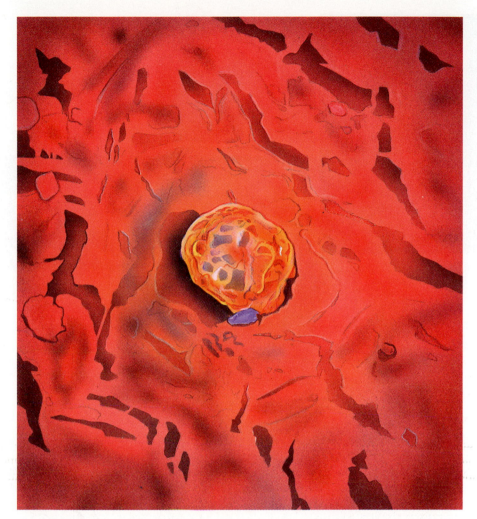

Figure 3.5 The point of implantation. You can see that the cell mass has two types of cells: the outer layer will form the various support structures; the inner mass will form the embryo.

Development of the Embryo. At the same time, the mass of cells that will form the embryo is itself differentiating further into several types of cells that form the rudiments of skin, sense receptors, nerve cells, muscles, circulatory system, and internal organs. Such differentiation is remarkably swift. By eight weeks of gestation, the embryo is roughly 1½ inches long, has a heart that beats, a primitive circulatory system, the beginnings of eyes and ears, a mouth that opens and closes, legs, arms, and a primitive spinal cord.

The Fetal Stage

The seven months of the fetal stage involve primarily a process of refining all the primitive organ systems already in place, much like what happens in constructing a house, when the framework is created quickly but the finishing work is lengthy. The photos in Figure 3.6 show the remarkable changes taking place during these months (see page 58).

Development of the Nervous System. One of the least well developed elements at the end of the embryonic period is the nervous system, which is composed of two basic types of cells, **neurons** and **glial cells**. The glial cells are the glue that holds the whole nervous system together, providing firmness and structure to the brain (Kandel, 1985). It is the neurons that do the job of receiving and sending messages from one part of the brain to another or from one part of the body to another.

Figure 3.6 Some of the changes during the fetal period.

(*a*) 10–12 weeks' gestation: The sex of the child can be determined; muscles, eyelids, lips are present, feet have toes and hands have fingers.

(*b*) 16 weeks: The mother usually feels the first fetal movement about now; bones begin to develop; the ear is better formed.

(*c*) 22 weeks: The eyes are formed (but closed, as you can see), as are hair, fingernails, sweat glands, and taste buds. Some infants born at 22 or 24 weeks survive, but the survival rate is low, and the incidence of problems is very high.

(*d*) 28–30 weeks: The nervous system, blood, and breathing systems are all well enough formed to support life, although the baby is still very tiny and the nervous system has only begun its spurt of dendritic development.

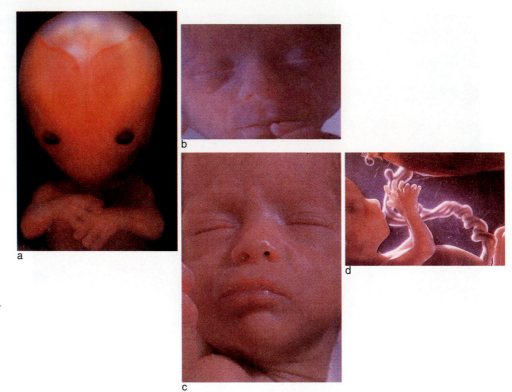

Can you think of any practical consequences of the fact that all the neurons one is ever going to have are present by about 28 weeks of gestation?

Neurons have four main parts, which you can see in the drawing in Figure 3.7: (1) a cell body, (2) branchlike extensions of the cell body called **dendrites**, which are the major *receptors* of nerve impulses, (3) a tubular extension of the cell body called the **axon**, which can extend as far as 1 meter in length in humans (about 3 feet), and (4) branchlike terminal fibers at the end of the axon that form the primary *transmitting* apparatus of the nervous system. Because of the branchlike appearance of dendrites, physiologists often use botanical terms to describe them, speaking of the "dendritic arbor" or of "pruning" of the arbor.

The point at which two neurons connect, where the axon's transmitting fibers come into close contact with another neuron's dendrites, is called a **synapse**. The number of such synapses is vast. A single cell in the part of the brain that controls vision, for instance, may have as many as 10,000 to 30,000 synaptic inputs to its dendrites (Greenough, Black & Wallace, 1987).

Glial cells begin to develop at about 13 weeks after conception and continue to be added until perhaps two years after birth. Neurons begin to appear at about 12 weeks, and are virtually all present by 28 weeks. But at this early stage the neurons consist largely of the cell body. Axons are short, and there is little dendritic development. It is in the last two months before birth and the first few years after birth that the lengthening of the axons and the major growth of the "dendritic arbor" occur, making possible the vast numbers of synapses necessary for all aspects of human functioning (Parmelee & Sigman, 1983). Thus those final months of gestation and the first two years of life can be thought of as a critical period for dendritic growth.

Development of Length and Weight. Similarly, the major growth in fetal size occurs late in the fetal period. The fetus is about half its birth length by about 20 weeks of gestation, but it does not reach half its birth weight until nearly 3 months later, at about 32 weeks.

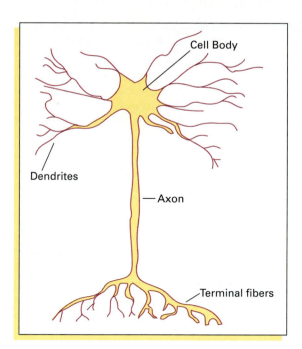

Figure 3.7 The structure of a single developed neuron. The cell bodies are the first to be developed, primarily between weeks 12 and 24. Axons and dendrites develop later, especially during the final 12 weeks, and continue to increase in size and complexity for several years after birth.

An Overview of Prenatal Development

One of the most important points about the child's prenatal development is how remarkably regular and predictable it is. If the embryo has survived the early, risky period (roughly the first 12 weeks), development usually proceeds smoothly, with the various changes occurring in what is apparently a fixed order, at fixed time intervals, following a clear maturational ground plan.

This sequence of development is not immune to modification or outside influence, as you'll soon see in detail. But before I begin talking about the various things that can go wrong, I want to make sure to state clearly that the maturational system is really quite robust. Normal prenatal development requires an adequate environment, but "adequate" seems to be a fairly broad range. *Most* children are quite normal. The list of things that *can* go wrong is long, and getting longer as our knowledge expands. Yet many of these possibilities are quite rare, many are partially or wholly preventable, and many need not have permanent consequences for the child. Keep this in mind as you read through the next few pages.

The potential problems fall into two large classes: genetic errors and those damaging environmental events called *teratogens.* Genetic errors occur at the moment of conception, and there is little that can be done about them. Teratogens may affect development any time from conception onward.

Genetic Errors

In perhaps 3 to 8 percent of all fertilized ova (Kopp, 1983), the genetic material itself contains errors because either the sperm or the ova has failed to divide correctly, so that there are either too many or too few chromosomes. Current estimates are that perhaps 90 percent of these abnormal conceptuses are spontaneously aborted. Only about one percent of live newborns have such abnormalities.

Figure 3.8 This 20-month-old Down syndrome toddler shows the distinctive eyes and flattened face that are characteristic of this disorder.

Over 50 different types of chromosomal anomaly have been identified, many of them very rare. The most common is **Down syndrome** (also called *mongolism* and *trisomy 21*), in which the child, because of a failure of proper meiosis in either sperm or ovum, has three copies of chromosome 21 rather than the normal two. Other forms of trisomy also occur, of course, but Down syndrome is by far the most frequent. Estimates of the incidence of this abnormality differ, but all fall in the range of 1 out of 600 to 1 out of 1000 (Hook, 1982; Nightingale & Goodman, 1990). These children have distinctive facial features (as you can see in Figure 3.8) and are typically retarded.

The risk of bearing a child with this deviant pattern is greatest for mothers over 35 (although there is also a heightened risk for teenage mothers). Among women 35 to 39, the incidence of Down syndrome is about one in 280 births; among those over 45 it is as high as one in 50 births (Kopp, 1983). Recent research by epidemiologists is also revealing a link between exposure to environmental toxins of various kinds and the risk of offspring with Down syndrome. For example, one large study in Canada shows that men who work as mechanics, farm laborers, or sawmill workers, who are regularly exposed to solvents, oils, lead, and pesticides, are at higher risk for fathering Down syndrome children than are men who work in cleaner environments (Olshan, Baird & Teschke, 1989). Findings like this suggest that chromosomal anomalies may not be purely random events, but may themselves be a response to various teratogens.

Sex-Chromosome Anomalies. A second class of anomalies is associated with an incomplete or incorrect division of either sex chromosome, which occurs in roughly 1 out of every 400 births (Berch & Bender, 1987). The most common is an XXY pattern, called Klinefelter's syndrome, which may occur as often as once in 500 births. This pattern results in boys who often have very long legs, poor coordination, poorly developed testes, sterility, and sometimes mild mental retardation. Not quite as common is the XYY pattern. These children also develop as boys, are typically unusually tall, with mild retardation. A single-X pattern (XO), called Turner's syndrome, and a triple-X pattern (XXX) may also occur, and in both cases the child develops as a girl. Girls with Turner's syndrome are exceptions to the rule that embryos with too few chromosomes do not survive. These girls show stunted growth, are usually sterile, and often perform particularly poorly on tests that measure spatial ability. On tests of verbal skill, however, Turner's syndrome girls are at or above normal levels (Scarr & Kidd, 1983). Girls with an XXX pattern are of normal size but are slower than normal in physical development. They also have markedly poor verbal abilities (Rovet & Netley, 1983). As a general rule, children with sex chromosome anomalies are not as severely affected as what we see in Down syndrome, but they do show unusual physical features and some cognitive deficits.

Fragile X-Syndrome. A quite different type of genetic anomaly which has received a good deal of attention lately involves not an improper amount of chromosomal material, but rather a break or gap at a specific location on the X chromosome (McBride, 1991). Both boys and girls may have a fragile X, but boys, lacking the potentially overriding influence of a normal X, are much more susceptible to the negative intellectual or behavioral consequences. The affected child appears to have a considerably heightened risk of mental retardation; current estimates are that among males, 5 to 7 percent of all retardation is caused by this syndrome (Zigler & Hodapp, 1991).

Single-Gene Defects. As I have already indicated, a child may also inherit a gene for a specific disease. In a few cases, such diseases may be caused by a dominant gene. The best known example is Huntington's disease, a severe neurological disorder resulting in rapid loss of both mental and physical functioning, with symptoms usually appearing only at mid-life. Dominant-gene diseases are relatively rare because the affected parent would almost always know that he or she was suffering from the disorder and may be unable or unwilling to reproduce. Far more common are recessive-gene diseases, some of which I've

TABLE 3.1 Some Common Inherited Diseases

Phenylketonuria
A metabolic disorder caused by a recessive gene that prevents metabolism of a common amino acid (phenylalanine). Treatment consists of a special phenylalanine-free diet. The child is not allowed many types of food, including milk. If not placed on the special diet shortly after birth, the child usually becomes very retarded (IQs of 30 and below are not uncommon). Affects only one in 8000 children. Cannot be diagnosed prenatally, but can be detected at birth with a test now routinely given.

Tay-Sachs disease
An invariably fatal recessive-gene degenerative disease of the nervous system; virtually all victims die within the first three to four years. The gene is carried primarily by those of Eastern European Jewish ancestry, among whom the risk is roughly one in 3600 births. Can be diagnosed prenatally.

Sickle-cell anemia
A sometimes fatal blood disease, transmitted with a recessive gene, characterized by joint pain, increased susceptibility to infection, and other symptoms. The gene is carried by an estimated 2 million Americans, primarily blacks, among whom 1 in 400 infants inherits the disorder. Can now be diagnosed prenatally.

Cystic fibrosis
A fatal disease affecting the lungs and intestinal tract. Many children with CF now live into their twenties. This recessive gene is carried by over 10 million Americans, most often whites, among whom one in 1600 infants inherit the disease. Carriers cannot be identified before pregnancy, and affected children cannot yet be diagnosed prenatally, although the locus of one CF gene has now been identified. If a couple has had one CF child, however, they know that each successive child has a one in four chance of being affected.

Muscular dystrophy
A fatal muscle-wasting disease, carried on the X chromosome, found almost exclusively among boys. The gene for the most common type of MD, Duchenne's, has just been located, so prenatal diagnosis may soon be available.

Source: Nightingale & Goodman, 1990.

listed in Table 3.1. The few examples listed in the table do not begin to convey the diversity of such disorders. Among known causes of mental retardation, there are 141 diseases or disorders with known genetic loci and 361 more whose locus has not yet been identified (Wahlström, 1990).

Geneticists estimate that the average adult carries genes for four different recessive diseases or abnormalities (e.g., Scarr & Kidd, 1983), but for any one disease the distribution of genes is not random. For example, sickle-cell genes are more common among blacks; Tay-Sachs is most common among Jews of Eastern European origin.

▶ Teratogens: Diseases and Drugs

Deviant prenatal development can also result from variations in the environment in which the embryo and fetus is nurtured. I pointed out in Chapter 1 that the effect of most teratogens seems to depend heavily on their *timing* (Vorhees & Mollnow, 1987), an example of *critical periods*, or *sensitive periods*. The general rule is that each organ system is most vulnerable to disruption at the time when it is developing most rapidly (Moore, 1988). At that point it is most sensitive to outside interference, whether that be from a disease organism that passes through the placental barrier, inappropriate hormones, drugs, or whatever. Because most organ systems develop most rapidly during the first 12 weeks of gestation, this is the period of greatest risk for most teratogens. Of the many teratogens, the most critical are probably drugs the mother may take and diseases she may have or may contract during the pregnancy.

THE REAL WORLD
Prenatal Diagnosis of Genetic Errors

Not so many years ago, when a child was conceived, that child was born with whatever deformities, diseases, or anomalies happened to come along. The parents had no choices. That is no longer true. Parents today may have access to genetic testing, genetic counseling, and any one of several prenatal diagnostic tests that can detect fetal abnormalities.

Prepregnancy Genetic Testing. Before conceiving, you and your spouse can have blood tests done that will tell you whether you are carriers of genes for those specific diseases for which the loci are known, such as Tay-Sachs or sickle-cell anemia. Because the locations of genes for all genetic diseases have not yet been located, carriers of many diseases (such as cystic fibrosis) cannot yet be identified in this way. But testing may still be an important step if you and your spouse belong to a subgroup known to be likely to carry particular recessive genes.

Prenatal Diagnosis of the Fetus. Four prenatal diagnostic strategies are now available. Two of these, the **alpha-fetoprotein test (AFP)** and **ultrasound**, are primarily used to detect problems in the formation of the *neural tube*, the structure that becomes the brain and spinal cord. If the tube fails to close at the bottom end, a disability called *spina bifida* occurs. Children with this defect are often partially paralyzed, and many (but not all) are retarded.

Alpha-fetoprotein is a substance produced by the fetus that is detectable in the mother's blood. If the level is abnormally high, it suggests that there may be some problem with the spinal cord or brain. The blood test is normally not done until the second trimester. If the AFP value is high, it does not mean there is definitely a problem; it means there is a higher *risk* of problems and further tests are usually indicated.

One such further test is ultrasound, which involves the use of sound waves to provide an actual ''moving picture'' of the fetus. It is frequently possible to detect, or rule out, neural tube defects—or other physical abnormalities—with this method. The procedure is not painful, and it gives parents an often delightful chance to see their unborn child moving, but it cannot provide information about the presence of chromosomal anomalies or inherited diseases.

If you want the latter information, you have two choices: **amniocentesis** or **chorionic villus sampling (CVS)**. In both cases, a needle is inserted and cells are taken from the developing embryo. In CVS, the sample is taken from what will become the placenta; in amniocentesis, the sample is from the amniotic fluid.

Both CVS and amniocentesis will provide information about any of the chromosomal anomalies and about the presence of genes for many of the major genetic diseases. Each technique has its own advantages and disadvantages. Amniocentesis was developed earlier and is the more widely used of the two. Its major drawback is that because the amniotic sac must be large enough to allow a sample of fluid to be taken with very little danger to the fetus, the test cannot be done until the sixteenth week of gestation, and the results are typically not available for several more weeks. If the test reveals an abnormality and the parents decide to abort, it is quite late for an abortion to be performed. CVS, in contrast, is done between the ninth and eleventh weeks of gestation. Early studies suggested that CVS was somewhat riskier than amniocentesis, with higher rates of miscarriage caused by the procedure. More recent research, however, suggests that the risks are about the same for the two procedures (Nightingale & Goodman, 1990).

By the time you are facing this choice, there may be still newer options using maternal blood samples. Experimental evidence already indicates that such a technique may be suitable for diagnosing Down syndrome or even the sex of the fetus (Wald et al., 1988; Lo et al., 1989). But no matter what technique you may select, the moral and ethical choices you may be called upon to make are far from easy.

For example, consider the case of diseases that can occur in mild or moderate as well as severe forms—such as sickle-cell anemia. Prenatal tests can tell you if the child will inherit the disease, but they cannot tell you how severely the child will be affected. Equally difficult is a decision when a chromosomal anomaly is detected, but one so rare that little information about outcome may be available. Genetic counselors may play a very helpful role, but ultimately each couple has to make its own decisions.

Diseases of the Mother

There are at least three mechanisms by which a disease in the mother can affect the embryo or fetus. Some diseases, particularly viruses, can attack the placenta, reducing the nutrients available to the embryo. Some others have molecules small enough to pass through the placental filters and attack the embryo or fetus directly. Examples of this type include rubella and rubeola (both forms of measles), cytomegalovirus (CMV), syphilis, diphtheria, influenza, typhoid, serum hepatitis, and chicken pox. Or, disease organisms present in the mucous membranes of the birth canal may infect the infant during birth itself. Genital herpes, for example, is transmitted this way. As far as researchers now know,

AIDS may be transmitted in any of three ways: prenatally through the placenta, during delivery, or after birth through breast milk (Van de Perre et al., 1991). Of all these diseases, probably the most dangerous for the child are rubella, AIDS, and CMV.

Rubella.   Rubella (also called *German measles*) is riskiest during the first month of gestation. Half of infants exposed during this time show abnormalities of the ears, eyes, or heart, while only a quarter show effects if they are exposed in the second month (Berg, 1974; Kopp, 1983). Deafness is the most common outcome.

Fortunately, rubella is preventable. Vaccination is available and should be given to all children as part of a regular immunization program. Adult women who were not vaccinated as children can be vaccinated later, but it must be done at least three months before a pregnancy to provide complete immunity.

AIDS.   At present, there are approximately 3000 infants with AIDS, a relatively low rate in comparison to many other diseases of childhood. But because the number of infected women of childbearing age continues to grow, the number of infants born infected with the HIV virus will also grow. In areas with a high population of drug users, as many as 3 to 5 percent of all pregnant women are now HIV-infected (Heagarty, 1991). The only good news in all of this is that not all infants born to HIV-infected mothers themselves become infected. Estimates range from 13 percent in a European study (European Collaborative Study, 1991) to 30 percent in U.S. studies (e.g., Hutto et al., 1991). Researchers are still searching for good explanations for this pattern of transmission.

CMV.   A much less well known but remarkably widespread and potentially serious disease is cytomegalovirus (CMV), a virus in the herpes group. It is now thought to be the single most important known infectious cause of both congenital mental retardation and deafness.

As many as 60 percent of *all* women have antibodies to CMV, but most have no recognized symptoms. One to two percent of babies whose mothers have CMV antibodies become infected prenatally. Among mothers whose disease is in an active phase, the transmission rate is more like 40 to 50 percent (Blackman, 1990). As with AIDS, researchers have not yet uncovered all the details of the mechanisms of transmission, nor

Women readers: Have you been vaccinated for rubella? If you don't know, find out; if you have not been, arrange for such a vaccination—but only if you are sure you are not pregnant!

THE REAL WORLD
Rh Factor Incompatibility: Another Type of Genetic Problem

Another possible problem, Rh factor incompatibility, is neither a genetic defect nor an inherited disease, but rather an incompatibility between the mother's genes and the baby's. One of the many factors in the blood is the presence or absence of a red-cell antigen, called the *Rh factor* because rhesus monkeys have it. Humans who have this factor are called *Rh positive* (Rh +), while those who lack it are *Rh negative* (Rh −). Only about 15 percent of whites and 5 percent of blacks in the United States are Rh −; the Rh − factor is quite rare among Asians and Native Americans.

Problems arise if the mother is Rh − and the baby is Rh +. Because Rh + is dominant, a baby with an Rh + father could inherit an Rh + gene from him, even though the mother is Rh −. If the mother's and the fetus's blood mix in the uterus, the mother's body considers the fetus's Rh + factor to be a foreign substance, and her immune system tries to fight it off by producing antibodies. These antibodies cross the placenta and attack the baby's blood, producing a chemical substance in the baby called

bilirubin. Babies with high levels of bilirubin look quite yellow; if untreated, brain damage can occur.

The risk of damage to the fetus increases with each succeeding pregnancy in which an Rh − mother carries an Rh + baby. Normally, the placenta keeps the two blood systems separate, but during birth some mixing usually occurs. So after the first baby, the mother produces some antibodies. With a second incompatible baby, these antibodies attack the infant's blood, producing negative effects.

This problem used to be treated with rather heroic measures, such as complete exchange of the infant's blood shortly after birth to remove all the antibodies. Fortunately, scientists have now discovered a much simpler and safer treatment. Within three days of the birth of her first child, an Rh − mother can be injected with a substance called rhogam, which prevents the buildup of antibodies and thus protects subsequent infants, even if they are also Rh +.

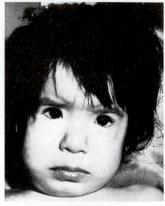

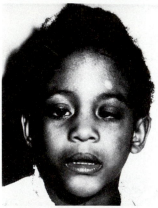

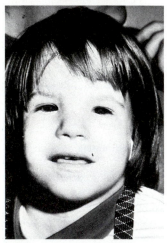

Figure 3.9 Fetal alcohol syndrome children, too, have distinctive features, whatever their familial racial heritage. (*Source:* Streissguth et al., *Science, 209* [July 18, 1980]: Figure 2, p. 355. Copyright 1980 by the American Association for the Advancement of Science.)

have they understood why only about 5 to 10 percent of babies infected prenatally show clear symptoms of the disease at birth. But the 2500 babies born each year in the United States who do display symptoms of the disease have a variety of serious problems, often including deafness and widespread damage to the central nervous system. Most are mentally retarded (Blackman, 1990).

Drugs Taken by the Mother

There is now a huge literature on the effects of prenatal drugs, involving everything from aspirin to antibiotics to alcohol and cocaine. Sorting out their effects has proven to be an immensely challenging task, not only because it is clearly not possible to assign women randomly to various drug groups, but also because in the real world most women take multiple drugs during their pregnancy. Women who drink alcohol are also more likely to smoke; those who use cocaine are also likely to take other illegal drugs or to smoke or drink to excess. What is more, the effects of drugs may be subtle, visible only many years after birth in the form of minor learning disabilities or increased risk of behavior problems. Still, we are creeping toward some fairly clear conclusions in several areas. Let me give you some examples.

Smoking.   One of the most extensive bodies of research is on the effect of smoking. Two consistent results stand out: infants of mothers who smoke are *on average* about half a pound lighter at birth than are infants of nonsmoking mothers (Vorhees & Mollnow, 1987), and are about twice as likely to be born before the full 38 weeks of gestation (Shiono, Klebanoff & Rhoads, 1986). This does not mean that every mother who smokes has a very small or early baby. It does mean that the risk of such an outcome is higher for mothers who smoke.

The causal mechanism seems to work this way: Nicotine constricts the blood vessels, which reduces blood flow to the placenta, in turn reducing nutrition to the fetus. In the long term, such nutritional deprivation seems to increase slightly the risk of learning problems or poor attention span at school age (Naeye & Peters, 1984).

Although research on the effects of smoking is not always easy to interpret, because women who smoke are likely to differ in other ways from those who do not, the moral seems clear: the safest plan is not to smoke during pregnancy. This research also shows a relationship between the "dose" (the amount of nicotine you are taking in) and the severity of the consequences for the child. So if you cannot quit entirely, at least cut back.

Drinking.   Recent work on the effects of maternal alcohol ingestion on prenatal and postnatal development also carries a clear message: To be safe, don't drink during pregnancy.

The effects of alcohol on the developing fetus range from mild to severe. At the extreme end of the continuum are children who exhibit a syndrome called **fetal alcohol syndrome (FAS)** (Jones et al., 1973). Their mothers are heavy drinkers or alcoholics, and the infants themselves are generally smaller than normal, with smaller brains. They frequently have heart defects, and their faces are distinctively different (as you can see in Figure 3.9). As children, adolescents, and adults, they continue to be shorter than normal, have smaller heads, and IQ scores in the range of mild mental retardation. Indeed, FAS is the leading known cause of retardation in the United States, exceeding even Down syndrome (Streissguth et al., 1991b)

But the effects of alcohol during pregnancy are not confined to cases in which the mother is clearly an alcoholic or a very heavy drinker. Recent evidence also points to milder effects of "social" drinking. Children of mothers who drank at this level during pregnancy are more likely to have IQs below 85 and show poorer attention spans. I've given some details about one of the best studies in the "Research Report" on the opposite page, so you can see how investigators have gone about studying this problem.

We do not yet know if there is any safe level of alcohol consumption during pregnancy, although most of those who work in this field are convinced that there is a linear relationship between the amount of alcohol ingested and the risk for the infant. This means that even at low dosage there is *some* increased risk. Probably it also matters when in the pregnancy the drinking occurs, and it clearly matters how many drinks the mother drinks on any one occasion. Binge drinking has been shown to be significantly riskier than regular smaller doses (e.g., Streissguth, Barr & Sampson, 1990). In the face of our remaining ignorance, the *safest* course is not to drink at all.

Cocaine. Significant numbers of pregnant women also take various illegal drugs, most notably cocaine. A recent study in Chicago showed the rate to be about 8 percent of mothers; in New York City it may be as high as 10 to 20 percent (Neerhof et al., 1989; Heagarty, 1991). Cocaine appears to cross the placental barrier quite readily and to have a variety of negative effects, including a heightened risk of premature birth, still birth, low birth weight, crib death in the first year of life, retarded growth prenatally, heart defects, and neurological abnormalities that may show up years later as significant learning disabilities (Kaye et al., 1989; Neerhof et al., 1989; Lipshultz, Frassica & Orav, 1991).

Cocaine-affected newborns display a variety of symptoms, including jerky movements, flushed skin, grating cry, grimaces, averted or closed eyes. These babies have smaller heads (which may be a sign of poorer neural growth), are easily agitated and hard to soothe, and have a difficult time establishing predictable sleep cycles—all of which makes the mother's task even more difficult (Lester et al., 1991). Thus a cycle of poor mother-infant interaction may also develop as a secondary effect of the cocaine.

Other Drugs. There is no room to list or discuss the many other drugs that appear to have some teratogenic effect, but let me give two more brief examples:

Diethylstilbestrol (DES) is a synthetic estrogen that at one time was commonly given

---

RESEARCH REPORT
Streissguth's Study of Prenatal Alcohol Exposure

The best single study of the consequences of alcohol exposure prenatally has been done by Ann Streissguth and her colleagues (1980a, 1980b, 1981, 1984, 1989, 1990, 1991a), who have followed a group of over 500 women and children beginning in early pregnancy. Since the study was begun before there were widespread warnings about the possible impact of alcohol during pregnancy, the sample includes many well-educated, middle-class women with good diets who did not take many other recreational drugs but who did drink alcohol in moderate or even fairly heavy amounts while pregnant—a set of conditions that would be impossible to duplicate today, at least in the United States or other countries in which the risks are well advertised.

Streissguth tested the children repeatedly, beginning immediately after birth, again later in infancy, at age 4, at school age, and again at age 11. She found that the mother's alcohol consumption in pregnancy was associated with sluggishness and weaker sucking in infancy, lower scores on a test of infant intelligence at 8 months, lower IQ at 4 and 7 years, and problems with attention and vigilance at 4, 7, and 11. Teachers also rated the 11-year-olds on overall school performance and on various behavior problems, and on both measures those whose mothers had drunk the most during pregnancy were rated significantly lower.

Streissguth also was careful to obtain information about other drug use in pregnancy, including smoking, and asked mothers about their diet, their education, their life habits. She has found that the links between alcohol consumption and poor outcomes for the child hold up even when all these other variables are controlled statistically.

Setting aside those cases in which the child was diagnosed with the full fetal alcohol syndrome, the effects of moderate levels of alcohol use during pregnancy are not large in absolute terms, but they have significant practical consequences. For example, the difference in IQ scores at age 7 between children of abstainers and children of women who drank 1 ounce or more of alcohol per day during their pregnancy was only about 6 points in Streissguth's sample (Streissguth, Barr & Sampson, 1990). But this relatively small absolute difference means that three times as many alcohol-exposed children have IQs below 85 than is true among children of abstainers. Alcohol-exposed children are thus greatly overrepresented in special classes in schools and probably also appear in over-large numbers among high school dropouts and the underemployed in adulthood—although those links remain for longer-term longitudinal studies to confirm.

to pregnant women to prevent miscarriages. The daughters of such women have been found to have higher rates of some kinds of cancers, and as many as 30 percent of the sons have been found to be infertile (Rosenblith & Sims-Knight, 1989).

One of the most widely used drugs, *aspirin*, is teratogenic in animals when given in high doses. Humans rarely take high enough doses to produce such effects directly, but it turns out that aspirin in moderate amounts can have negative effects on the fetus if it is ingested along with benzoic acid, a chemical widely used as a food preservative, such as in catsup. This combination, especially in the first trimester, seems to increase the risk of physical malformations in the embryo/fetus.

▶ Other Influences on Prenatal Development

Diet.   Another risk for the fetus is poor maternal nutrition. In periods of famine, for example, preterm births and low birth weight are greatly increased, as is the death rate for infants in the first year of life (e.g., Stein et al., 1975). Studies of famine show that the consequences are most detrimental if the malnutrition occurred during the last three months of the pregnancy, when neurons are beginning a rapid expansion of dendritic density. Malnutrition or subnutrition associated with poverty appears to have similar negative effects, a conclusion reinforced by the repeated observation that poor (presumably malnourished) women given nutritional supplements during pregnancy have babies that are significantly heavier, more alert, and less likely to die in the first year of life (Brown, 1987).

The Mother's Age.   One of the particularly intriguing trends in modern family life is that more women are postponing their first pregnancy into their late twenties or early thirties. In 1989, roughly 20 percent of all first births in the United States were to women over 30, double the rate in 1970 (Berkowitz et al., 1990; U.S. Bureau of the Census, 1991). Of course there are many reasons for such delayed childbearing, chief among them the increased need for second incomes in families and the desire of young women to complete job training and early career steps before bearing children. The more education a young women has completed, the more likely she is to delay childbearing into her thirties—a pattern I'll be talking about in the chapters on early adulthood. The key issue for us here is the impact of maternal age on the mother's experience of pregnancy and on the developing child.

The evidence tells us that for the woman, the optimum time for childbearing is in her early twenties. Mothers over 30 (particularly those over 35), are at increased risk for several kinds of problems, including miscarriage (McFalls, 1990), complications of pregnancy such as high blood pressure or bleeding (Berkowitz et al., 1990), and death during pregnancy or delivery (Buehler et al., 1986). For example, in one large recent study of nearly 4000 women in New York, all of whom had received adequate prenatal care, Gertrud Berkowitz and her colleagues (1990) found that women 35 and older during their first pregnancies were almost twice as likely as women in their twenties to suffer some pregnancy complication. These effects of age seem to be exacerbated if the mother has not had adequate prenatal care or has poor health habits. For example, the negative effects of maternal smoking on birth weight is considerably *greater* among women over 35 than among young women (Wen et al., 1990).

On the infant's side of the equation, the news is more positive. Other than the increased risk of Down Syndrome, there is little indication that babies of older mothers are at increased risk for disabilities or problems. Berkowitz found that older mothers were only slightly more likely to have low-birth-weight infants and no more likely to have premature deliveries than were mothers in their twenties. Other epidemiologists (Baird, Sadovnick & Yee, 1991) have found no increased risk of birth defects for older mothers.

What kind of study would you have to do to figure out whether it is OK for pregnant women to maintain high levels of exercise, such as running 30 miles a week?

THE REAL WORLD
How Much Weight Should You Gain in Pregnancy?

Until fairly recently, many physicians advised a weight gain of only about 2 pounds per month during pregnancy. The argument was that smaller babies would be easier to deliver and that the fetus would act as a sort of ''parasite'' on the mother's body, taking whatever nourishment it needed even if the mother gained little weight. But newer research has shown that the amount of weight the mother gains is directly related to the infant's birth weight and to the risk of a preterm birth (Abrams et al., 1989). And both low birth weight and preterm birth are associated with a whole range of risks for the child.

Because of such evidence, physicians now advise a gain of approximately 25 to 30 pounds for a woman who is at her normal weight before pregnancy, and slightly more for a woman who is underweight before pregnancy (Seidman, Ever-Hadani & Gale, 1989). Women who gain less than this may have infants who suffer from some fetal malnutrition and who are thus born underweight for their gestational age.

Furthermore, it matters *when* the weight is gained. During the first three months, the woman needs to gain only 2 to 5 pounds. But during the last six months of the pregnancy, the woman should be gaining at the rate of about 14 ounces (350 to 400 grams) per week in order to support fetal growth (Pitkin, 1977; Winick, 1980). So if you've gained 20 pounds or so during the first four or five months, you should *not* cut back in order to hold your weight gain to some magic total number. Restricting caloric intake during those final months is exactly the wrong thing to do.

Although Berkowitz's study points to increased risks even among older mothers with good prenatal care, other evidence suggests that the effect of age on pregnancy is even greater among women living in poverty or among those with poor prenatal care (e.g., Roosa, 1984). Such findings suggest that age may interact with other factors, such as the overall health of the mother.

There are also some increased risks for mother and child among teenage mothers. Early researchers thought that this effect was due to some inherent inadequacy of the young body for sustaining a normal pregnancy. But recent findings suggest that the heightened risk of low birth weight or other nonoptimal outcomes among very young mothers is more a consequence of inadequate prenatal care for teenagers than of age per se. Among those teenagers who have decent diets and adequate prenatal care, problems of pregnancy, preterm delivery or low birth weight are no more frequent than among women in their twenties (Strobino, 1987).

Taking these two sets of data together, it looks as if knowing the mother's age may help us predict the average rate of problems in pregnancies, but it is probably not the age itself that is most critical for most difficulties. More important is the kind of prenatal care a woman receives, the adequacy of her diet, and her general physical health.

The Mother's Emotional State.   Finally, the mother's state of mind during the pregnancy may be significant, although the research findings are decidedly mixed (Istvan, 1986). Results from infrahuman studies are clear: exposure of the pregnant female to stressors such as heat, light, noise, shock, or crowding significantly increases the risk of low birth weight. Studies of humans, however, have not pointed to such a clear conclusion, in part because it has been very difficult for investigators to agree on a definition of stress. The most reasonable hypothesis at the moment seems to be that long-term, chronic stressors have little direct impact on a specific pregnancy, while abrupt *increases* in anxiety or stress during a pregnancy may have more deleterious effects. For example, Emmy Werner (1986) found that among middle-class women in a major longitudinal study in Hawaii, those who had negative feelings about their pregnancy or who experienced some psychological trauma during the pregnancy had more birth complications and more infants with low birth weight than did those with lower stress or anxiety. But these same patterns did not hold among poor women in this study, many of whom lived in states of chronic stress or disorganization.

Folklore in virtually all cultures certainly assumes a causal link between the mother's emotional experiences during her pregnancy and the outcome for the child. But at

---

SOAP BOX
The Crucial Importance of Prenatal Care

One of the clearest findings in research on prenatal development is that many disabilities, diseases, preterm births, and low birth weights could be prevented if all mothers received adequate prenatal care. Let me give just one research example. Jann Murray and Merton Bernfield (1988), in a study of over 30,000 births, found that the risk of giving birth to a low-birth-weight infant was more than three times as great among women who had received inadequate prenatal care as among those receiving adequate care, and this pattern held among both blacks and whites. That we nonetheless do not provide such care to all women in the United States is, to my eyes, a scandal.

In 1988, 21 percent of white mothers and 39 percent of black mothers had no prenatal care in the first trimester; 4.9 percent of whites and 10.5 percent of blacks had either no care at all or first saw a physician in the seventh month or later (Wegman, 1991). In many inner cities, these figures are far higher (Heagarty, 1991).

Given such statistics, it is perhaps not surprising that the United States continues to have a relatively high rate of infant mortality. These rates have declined steadily in recent years, which is all to the good. But the 1990 United States rate of 9.1 infant deaths per 1000 live births was worse than 20 other countries in the world. Virtually all European countries have lower infant mortality rates, as do Japan (with the lowest rate in the world), Hong Kong, and Singapore. Nearly all the countries with such low infant mortality have either free or very low-cost prenatal care available to all mothers. We also know that when low-cost or free prenatal care has been made easily available to the poor in particular parts of the United States, the infant mortality rate in that area has dropped sharply (Kessner, 1973), suggesting strongly that there is a causal link between availability of care and infant deaths.

I find myself in complete agreement with an impassioned statement recently made by physician Margaret Heagarty (1991), who is director of pediatrics at a large New York hospital. She says:

I am forced daily to confront the facts that about 10% to 20% of infants born in city hospitals of New York have cocaine in their urine at birth, [and] that the neonatal and infant mortality rates in the urban disadvantaged communities, always well above the national average, have risen dramatically in the past few years . . . If we are to stop the destruction of these children . . . we must make a substantial change in our nation's value system, because although we loudly proclaim our belief in the preeminent worth of children, our national actions suggest that we do not believe that children are important. (pp. 8–9)

Even if this moral argument is not persuasive to everyone, there is an equally potent financial argument: it is far cheaper in the long run to provide good, accessible prenatal care to every pregnant woman than it is to pay for extended hospital care for preterm infants or special education classes in schools for retarded or learning disabled children. The place to begin to change this is in one's own community, with one's own representatives. We are throwing away a generation of children.

What three pieces of advice would you want to give a pregnant friend, based on this chapter? Why those three?

the moment the best I can say is that the hypothesis is still plausible but not clearly substantiated.

▶ Sex Differences in Prenatal Development

Because nearly all prenatal development is controlled by maturational codes that are the same for all members of our species—male and female alike—there aren't very many sex differences in prenatal development. But there are a few, and they set the stage for some of the physical differences we'll see at later ages.

- Sometime between four and eight weeks after conception, the male hormone *testosterone* begins to be secreted by the rudimentary testes in the male embryo. If this hormone is not secreted or is secreted in inadequate amounts, the embryo will be "demasculinized," even to the extent of developing female genitalia. This infusion of testosterone also affects the brain so that the proper male hormones are secreted at the right moments later in life. Girls do not secrete any equivalent hormone prenatally.

- Girls are a bit faster in some aspects of prenatal development, particularly skeletal development. They are about one to two weeks ahead in bone development at birth (Tanner, 1978).

- Despite the more rapid development of girls, boys are heavier and longer at birth (Tanner, 1978).

- Boys are considerably more vulnerable to all kinds of prenatal problems. Many more boys than girls are conceived—on the order of about 120 to 150 male embryos to every 100 female—but more of the males are spontaneously aborted. At birth, there are about 105 boys for every 100 girls. Boys are also more likely to experience injuries at birth (perhaps because they are larger), and they have more congenital malformations (Zaslow & Hayes, 1986). And among those infants who experience severe complications during delivery, boys are more likely to die (e.g., Werner, 1986).

The striking sex difference in vulnerability is particularly intriguing, especially since it seems to persist. Older boys are more prone to problems as well, as are adult men. Males have shorter life expectancy, higher rates of behavior problems, more learning disabilities, and usually more negative responses to major stresses, such as divorce. One possible explanation for at least some of this sex difference may lie in the basic genetic difference. The XX combination affords the girl more protection against the fragile-X syndrome and against any "bad" genes that may be carried on the X chromosome. For instance, geneticists have found that a gene affecting susceptibility to infectious disease is carried on the X chromosome (Brooks-Gunn & Matthews, 1979). Because boys have only one X chromosome, such a gene is much more likely to be expressed phenotypically in a boy.

▶ Birth

Once the 38 weeks of gestation are over, the fetus must be born into the world—an event that holds some pain as well as a good deal of joy for most parents. In the normal process, labor progresses through three stages of unequal length.

The First Stage of Labor. Stage 1 covers the period during which two important processes occur: dilation and effacement. The cervix (the opening at the bottom of the uterus) must open up like the lens of a camera (**dilation**) and also flatten out (**effacement**). At the time of actual delivery of the infant, the cervix must normally be dilated to about 10 centimeters (about 4 inches), as you can see in Figure 3.10 (page 70). This part of labor has been likened to putting on a sweater with a neck that is too tight. You have to pull and stretch the neck of the sweater with your head in order to get it on. Eventually the neck is stretched wide enough so that the widest part of your head can pass through.

Customarily, stage 1 is itself divided into phases. In the *early* (or *latent*) phase, contractions are relatively far apart and are typically not too uncomfortable. In the *late* phase, which begins when the cervix is about halfway dilated and continues until dilation has reached 8 centimeters, contractions are closer together and more intense. The last two centimeters of dilation are achieved during a period usually called *transition*. It is this period, when contractions are closely spaced and strong, that women typically find the most painful. Fortunately, transition is also ordinarily the shortest phase. Following this comes the urge to help the infant out by "pushing." When the birth attendant (physician or midwife) is sure the cervix is fully dilated, she or he will encourage this pushing, and the second stage of labor begins.

The length of this first stage of labor varies widely from one woman to the next. The average length of stage 1 is roughly 8 hours for women delivering a first infant without anesthesia, with a range from 3 to 19 hours (Kilpatrick and Laros, 1989). Women delivering second or later children typically have shorter labors, while those with some form of anesthesia typically have slightly longer labors.

Second Stage of Labor. The second stage is the actual delivery, when the baby's head moves past the stretched cervix, into the birth canal, and finally out of the mother's body. Most women find this part of labor markedly less distressing than the transition phase because it is here that they can assist the delivery process by pushing. It typically lasts less than an hour and rarely takes longer than two hours.

Most infants are delivered head first, facing toward the mother's spine. Perhaps three percent, however, are oriented differently, either feet first or bottom first (called *breech* presentations). In the United States today, infants in breech positions are nearly all delivered through an abdominal incision (a **cesarean section**) rather than vaginally (Taffel, Placek & Liss, 1987)

In most delivery situations in the United States, once the baby has emerged he is immediately placed on the mother's abdomen or given to her (and the father) to hold after the cord has been cut and the baby is cleaned up a bit—a matter of a few minutes. For most parents, this first greeting of the baby is a time for remarkable delight, as they stroke the baby's skin, count the fingers, look at the baby's eyes.

The Third Stage of Labor. The anticlimactic but essential stage 3 is the delivery of the placenta (also called the *afterbirth*) and other material from the uterus.

Figure 3.10 The process of effacement and dilation during labor. (*Source:* Stenchever, 1978, Figure 5-4, p. 84.)

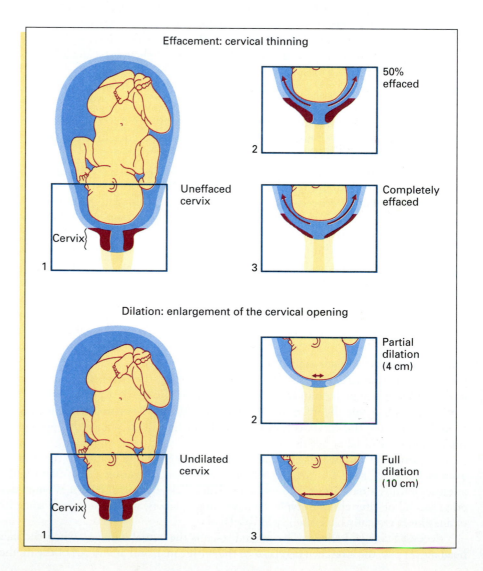

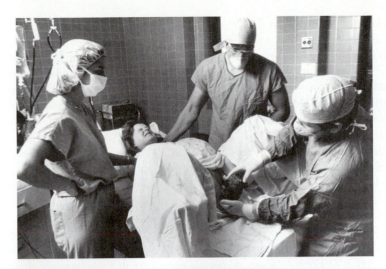

The head just emerging. Notice that the face is downward, as it is in most deliveries. Also notice that the father is present (on the far side of the table), as is now customary in the United States.

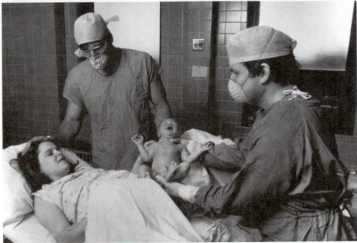

Hello, Baby!

Birth Choices

In the United States and in many industrialized countries, mothers (and fathers) can make a variety of choices about the delivery—choices that may affect the psychological or physical comfort the mother may experience. There are decisions about whether to receive painkilling drugs during delivery, whether to deliver in a hospital or at home, or whether the father should be present during the birth. Because many of you will face these choices at some point in the future, let me say just a word about each of them.

Drugs During Delivery.   One key decision concerns the use of drugs during delivery. Three types of drugs are commonly used: (1) *analgesics* (such as the common drug Demerol) which are given during stage 1 of labor to reduce pain; (2) *sedatives* or *tranquilizers* (such as Nembutol, Valium, or Thorazine) given during stage 1 labor to reduce anxiety; and (3) *anesthesia*, given during transition or the second stage of labor to block pain either totally (general anesthesia) or in portions of the body (local anesthesia). Of the three, anesthesia is least often used (at least in the United States currently), but the great majority of women receive at least one of these types of drugs (Brackbill, McManus & Woodward, 1985).

Studying the causal links between such drug use and the baby's later behavior or development has proven to be monumentally difficult. Controlled experiments are obviously not possible, since women cannot be randomly assigned to specific drug regimens.

And drugs are given in myriad different combinations. But there are a few reasonably clear conclusions.

First, it's clear that nearly all drugs given during labor pass through the placenta and enter the fetal bloodstream and may remain there for several days. Not surprisingly, then, infants whose mothers have received any type of drug are typically slightly more sluggish, gain a little less weight, and spend more time sleeping in the first few weeks than do infants of nondrugged moms (Maurer & Maurer, 1988). These differences are quite small but have been observed repeatedly.

Second, beyond the first few days there are no consistently observed effects from analgesics and tranquilizers, and only a few hints of long term effects of anesthesia (e.g., Rosenblith & Sims-Knight, 1989; Sepkoski, 1987), and then only in a few studies. Given such contradictory findings, only one specific piece of advice seems warranted: If you have received medication, you need to bear in mind that your baby is also drugged, and that this will affect her behavior in the first few days. If you allow for this effect and realize that it will wear off, your long-term relationship with your child is likely to be unaffected.

The Location of Birth.   A second choice parents must make is *where* the baby is to be born. Today there are typically four alternatives: (1) a traditional hospital maternity unit, (2) a hospital-based birth center or birthing room, which is located within a hospital but provides a more homelike setting, with labor and delivery both completed in the same room and family members often present throughout; (3) a freestanding birth center, like a hospital birth center that is located apart from the hospital, with delivery typically attended by a midwife rather than (or in addition to) a physician; and (4) home delivery.

Only about 1 percent of infants in the United States are now born at home, but such an alternative is far more common in many European countries, where it is thought to be both more natural and less expensive for the medical care system. The counter argument, of course, is that if there are complications at the time of delivery, a hospital delivery is far safer.

Because of the importance of safety, home deliveries are encouraged in Europe only in uncomplicated pregnancies in which the women have received good prenatal care. Among this group of women, if there is a trained birth attendant present at delivery, studies in both Europe and the United States show that the rate of delivery complications or infant problems is no higher in home or birth center deliveries than in hospital deliveries (Rooks et al., 1989; Tew, 1985). In contrast, infant mortality rates are significantly higher in home deliveries if they are *unplanned*, if they occur without trained attendants, or if the mother had experienced some complication of pregnancy (Schramm, Barnes, & Bakewell, 1987).

Incidentally, there is no evidence that babies born at home or in birthing centers are in any way better off in the long run than are babies born in more traditional hospital settings. Assuming appropriate safety precautions, then, the choice should be based on what is most comfortable for the individual woman or couple.

After reading this, which birthing location would you choose, and why?

The Presence of Fathers at Delivery.   A third important decision is whether the father should be present at delivery. In the United States today this hardly seems like a "decision." As recently as 1972 only about a quarter of U.S. hospitals permitted the father to be present in the delivery room; by 1980, four-fifths of them did (Parke & Tinsley, 1984), and today the father's presence has become absolutely the norm.

There have been several compelling arguments offered in favor of such a norm: The father's presence may lessen the mother's anxiety and give her psychological support; by coaching her in breathing and other techniques, he may help her control her pain; and he may become more strongly attached to the infant by being present at the birth. There is at least some evidence in support of the first two of these arguments, but—perhaps unexpectedly for some of you—little support for the third.

When fathers are present during labor and delivery, mothers report lower levels of pain and receive less medication (Henneborn & Cogan, 1975). And when the mother has a coach (the father or someone else), the incidence of problems of labor and delivery goes down, as does the duration of labor (Sosa et al., 1980). Furthermore, at least one study shows that women are more likely to report that the birth was a "peak" experience if the father was present (Entwisle & Doering, 1981). But presence at the delivery does not seem to have any magical effect on the father's emotional bond to the baby (Palkovitz, 1985). A father who sees his child for the first time in the newborn nursery, or days later at home, may nonetheless become as strongly attached to the infant as are those fathers who were present at the birth.

This statement is not in any way intended as an argument against fathers' participation in the delivery process. The fact that the father's presence seems to help the mother control pain, reduce medication and labor duration, and may enhance the husband-wife relationship all seem to me to be compelling reasons for encouraging continued high levels of paternal participation. In addition, of course, most fathers report powerful feelings of delight at being present at the birth of their children. Reason enough.

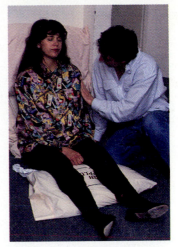

More and more fathers are taking special prenatal classes like this one, so that they can provide support and coaching to their wives during labor.

Problems at Birth

As with prenatal development, there are some things that can alter the normal pattern I have been describing. One of the most common problems is that the delivery itself may not proceed normally, leading to a surgical delivery through an abdominal incision, called a cesarean section (usually abbreviated C-section). A second common problem is that the infant may be born too early.

Cesarean-Section Delivery.   The frequency of C-sections has risen rapidly in many industrialized countries in the past few decades, including Australia, Canada, Britain, Norway, and other European countries (Jonas, Chan & MacHarper, 1989; Borthen et al., 1989); in the United States the increase has been particularly striking, more than quadrupling in the past 25 years. Today roughly one in every four births in the United States is a C-section (U.S. Bureau of the Census, 1990), a pattern that has been the subject of lively (even heated) discussion among physicians for at least the past decade (e.g., Berkowitz et al., 1989; de Regt et al., 1986; Taffel, Placek & Liss, 1987). C-sections are now routinely done for breech births, in cases of active herpes infection (which could otherwise be passed to the baby during vaginal delivery), and when fetal monitors suggest that the fetus may be in some distress. Women who have had previous C-section deliveries may also require C-section for subsequent births, although this is not done as routinely as was the case even a few years ago. These may all be good reasons for C-sections; still, most physicians today agree that the rate has become too high.

Low Birth Weight.   In talking about various teratogens I have often mentioned low birth weight as one of the clearest negative outcomes. Several different labels are used to describe infants with less than optimal weight. All babies below 2500 grams (about 5.5 pounds) are described with the most general term of **low birth weight (LBW).** Those below 1500 grams (about 3.3 pounds) are usually called *very low birth weight*, while those below 1000 grams are called *extremely low birth weight*. The incidence of low birth weight has declined in the United States in the past decade, but it is still high. In 1987, 6.9 percent of all newborns were below 2500 grams—a total of about 45,000 infants each year. Roughly 7800 of those were below 1500 grams (U.S. Bureau of the Census, 1990).

There are a variety of reasons for low birth weight, of which the most common is that the infant is born before the full 38 weeks of gestation. Such infants are usually labeled *premature* or *preterm*. Any birth before 36 weeks of gestation is usually labeled in this way. It is also possible for an infant to have completed the full 38-week gestational period but still weigh less than 2500 grams, or to weigh less than would be expected for

Why might the recent rapid increase in cesarean section deliveries be troubling to psychologists or physicians? How could you decide if this is a negative trend?

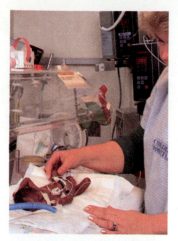

Low-birth-weight infants are kept in special isolettes, like this one, so that the temperature can be controlled. These babies are not only small, they are also more wrinkled and skinny because the layer of fat under the skin has not fully developed.

the number of weeks of gestation completed, however long that may have been. Such an infant is called *small for date*. Infants in this group appear to have suffered from prenatal malnutrition, such as might occur from constriction of blood flow from the mother's smoking, or from other significant problems prenatally. Preterm infants, in contrast, may be early but may have been developing normally in other respects.

All low-birth-weight infants share some characteristics, including markedly lower levels of responsiveness at birth and in the early months of life (DiVitto & Goldberg, 1979; Barnard, Bee & Hammond, 1984). They also have a higher risk of experiencing respiratory distress in the early weeks and may be slower in motor development than their normal-weight peers.

Infant mortality is also correlated with birth weight. About 80 percent of all low-birth-weight infants survive long enough to leave the hospital, but the lower the birth weight, the greater the risk of neonatal death. What is surprising is how many of the really tiny babies survive when they have state-of-the-art neonatal care. In hospitals with especially modern and aggressive neonatal intensive care units, as many as half of infants as small as 500 to 1000 grams at birth (1–2 pounds) may survive (e.g., Astbury et al., 1990).

You might think that all babies this small who do survive will have major developmental problems. But that is not the case. The long-term outcomes depend not only on the quality of care available when (and where) the baby was born, but on just how small the baby was and what kind of family he or she grew up in. Because medical advances in the care of LBW infants have been enormous in the past few decades, the more recently such a baby was born, the better the long-term prognosis seems to be (Kitchen et al., 1991). And, not surprisingly, the smaller the baby, the greater the likelihood of later problems.

The great majority of those above 1500 grams who are not small for date catch up to their normal peers within the first few years of life. But those below 1500 grams, especially those below 1000, have significantly higher rates of long-term problems, including neurological impairment, lower IQs, smaller size, and greater problems in school (Hack et al., 1991; Collin, Halsey & Anderson, 1991; Saigal et al., 1991). You can get a better sense of both the type and incidence of such problems from the data in Table 3.2, which lists the results of two recent studies.

TABLE 3.2 Two Examples of Long-Term Outcomes for Very Low-Birth-Weight Infants

	Australian Study[a]	U.S. Study[b]
Number of babies followed	89	249
Weight at birth	500–999 grams	< 1500 grams
Age at testing	8 years	8 years
Percent with severe problems of some type (IQ below 70, deafness, blindness, cerebral palsy, etc.)	21.3%	15.7%
Additional percent with significant learning problem or IQ between 70 and 85	19.1%	15.4%

[a]Victorian Infant Collaborative Study Group, 1991. The study included all surviving children of 500–999 grams born in a single state (Victoria) in Australia between 1979 and 1980. A total of 351 infants were born in that weight range, so only a quarter survived.
[b]Hack et al., 1991. The study included originally 490 children below 1500 grams born in a single Cleveland, Ohio, hospital between 1977 and 1979. Sixty-four percent (316 children) survived to age 8, of which 249 were examined.

Two points are worth making about the findings from follow-up studies like those shown in the table. First, problems may not show up until school age, when the child is challenged by a new level of cognitive task. Many surviving LBW children who appear to be developing normally at age 2 or 3 later show significant problems in school. Second, even in the extremely low birth weight group, the majority of children seem to be fine. So it is not the case that *all* LBW children are *somewhat* affected, but rather that *some* LBW children are significantly affected while others develop normally. Unfortunately, physicians and researchers have not yet found reliable ways to predict which babies are likely to have later difficulties, which means that parents of LBW infants may be left in suspense for many years.

❱ A Final Word: A More Optimistic View of Risks and Long-Term Consequences of Prenatal and Birth Problems

As I write this chapter I am aware that the list of things that can go wrong seems to get longer and longer and scarier and scarier. Physicians, biologists, and psychologists keep learning more about prenatal and birth risks, so the number of warnings to pregnant women seems to increase yearly, if not monthly. One of the ironies of this is that too much worry about such potential consequences can make a woman more anxious, and anxiety is on the list of warnings for pregnant women! So before you begin worrying too much, let me try to put this information into perspective.

First, remember again that *most* pregnancies are normal and largely uneventful, and most babies are healthy and normal at birth. Second, there are specific preventive steps that any woman can take to reduce the risks for herself and her unborn child. She can be properly immunized; she can stop smoking and drinking; she can watch her diet and make sure her weight gain is sufficient; and she can get early and regular prenatal care.

Third, the consequences of prenatal and birth problems are not always permanent. Of course, some negative outcomes *are* permanent and have long-term consequences for the child. Chromosomal anomalies are clearly permanent and nearly always associated with lasting mental retardation or school difficulties. Some teratogens also have permanent effects, such as fetal alcohol syndrome, deafness resulting from rubella, or AIDS. And a significant fraction of very low-birth-weight infants experience lasting problems.

But many of the negative outcomes I have talked about in this chapter may be detectable only for the first few years of the child's life, and then only in some families. In fact, the relationship between prenatal or birth problems and long-term outcomes illustrates the very pattern of interaction between nature and nurture that Horowitz suggests in her model, shown in Figure 1.4: A biological problem may be amplified by an unstimulating environment but greatly reduced by a supportive one. For example, there are numerous studies showing that low-birth-weight infants, those with poor prenatal nutrition, or those with equivalent difficulties, are likely to show persisting problems if they are reared in unstimulating or unsupportive environments, but develop much more normally if reared in more intellectually and emotionally nurturing families (Breitmayer & Ramey, 1986; Kopp, 1990; Beckwith & Rodning, 1991). So it is not the prenatal or birth problem alone that is the cause of the child's later problem; rather, a nonoptimal prenatal environment may make the infant more vulnerable to later environmental inadequacy. Such children may require a better family environment to develop normally, but in many cases such normal development *is* possible. So don't despair when you read the long list of cautions and potential problems. The story isn't as gloomy as it first seems.

Summary

1. At conception, the 23 chromosomes from the sperm join with 23 from the ovum to make up the set of 46 that will be reproduced in each cell of the new child's body. Each chromosome consists of a long string of deoxyribonucleic acid (DNA), divisible into specific segments called *genes*.

2. The child's sex is determined by the twenty-third pairs of chromosomes, a pattern of XX for a girl and XY for a boy.

3. Geneticists distinguish between the genotype, which is the pattern of inherited characteristics, and the phenotype, which is the result of the interaction of genotype and environment.

4. During the first days after conception, called the germinal stage of development, the initial cell divides, travels down the fallopian tube, and is implanted in the wall of the uterus.

5. The second stage, the period of the embryo, includes the development of the various structures that support fetal development, such as the placenta, as well as primitive forms of all organ systems.

6. The final 30 weeks of gestation, called the fetal period, are devoted primarily to enlargement and refinements in all the organ systems.

7. Normal prenatal development seems heavily determined by maturation—a "road map" contained in the genes. Disruptions in this sequence can occur; the timing of the disruption determines the nature and severity of the effect.

8. Deviations from the normal pattern can be caused at conception by any of a variety of chromosomal anomalies, such as Down syndrome, or by the transmission of genes for specific diseases.

9. Prior to conception, it is possible to test the parents for the presence of genes for many inherited diseases. After conception, several diagnostic techniques exist that identify chromosomal anomalies or recessive-gene diseases in the fetus.

10. Some diseases contracted by the mother may affect the child, including rubella, AIDS, and CMV. Any of these may result in disease or physical abnormalities in the child.

11. Alcohol, nicotine, and cocaine all appear to have significantly harmful effects on the developing fetus; the greater the dose, the larger the potential effect appears to be.

12. The mother's diet is also important. If she is severely malnourished, there are increased risks of stillbirth, low birth weight, and infant death during the first year of life.

13. Older mothers and very young mothers also run increased risks, but many of these risks are greatly reduced or eliminated if the mother is in good health and receives adequate prenatal care.

14. High levels of anxiety or stress in the mother may also increase the risk of complications of pregnancy or difficulties in the infant, although the research findings here are mixed.

15. Sex differences in prenatal development are few. Boys are slower to develop, bigger at birth, and more vulnerable to most forms of prenatal stress.

16. The normal birth process has three parts: dilation, delivery, and placental delivery.

17. Most drugs given to the mother during delivery pass through to the infant's bloodstream and have short-term effects on infant responsiveness and feeding patterns. There may be some longer-term effects, but this is in dispute.

18. In uncomplicated, low-risk pregnancies, delivery at home or in a birthing center is as safe as hospital delivery.

19. The presence of the father during delivery has a variety of positive consequences, including reduced pain experience for the mother, but does not

appear to affect the father's attachment to the infant.

20. Nearly one-fourth of all deliveries in the United States are now by cesarean section—a statistic that has been the cause of considerable debate.

21. Infants born weighing less than 2500 grams are designated as low birth weight; those below 1500 gm are very low birth weight; those below 1000 are extremely low birth weight. The lower the weight, the greater the risk of significant lasting problems, such as low IQ or learning disabilities.

22. Some prenatal or birth difficulties can produce permanent disabilities or deformities, but many disorders associated with prenatal life or with birth can be overcome if the child is reared in a supportive and stimulating environment.

Key Terms

alpha-fetoprotein test	deoxyribonucleic acid	genotype
amniocentesis	dilation	glial cells
amnion	Down syndrome	low birth weight
axon	effacement	neurons
cesarean section	fallopian tube	ovum
chorionic villus sampling	fetal alcohol syndrome	phenotype
chromosomes	gametes	synapse
dendrites	genes	uterus

Suggested Readings

The Boston Women's Health Collective. (1984). *The new our bodies, ourselves: A book by and for women* (2nd ed.). New York: Simon & Schuster. (This revision of a popular book has an excellent discussion of health during pregnancy and good descriptions and diagrams showing stages of prenatal development and birth. You may not be entirely in sympathy with all the political views included, but it is nonetheless a very good compact source of information on all facets of pregnancy and delivery.)

Nightingale, E. O., & Goodman, M. (1990). *Before birth. Prenatal testing for genetic disease.* Cambridge, MA: Harvard University Press. (This is an extremely informative, clearly written, helpful small book.)

Nilsson, L. (1990). *A child is born.* New York: Delacorte Press. (This is a remarkable book, full of the most stunning photographs of all phases of conception, prenatal development, and birth.)

Rosenblith, J. F., & Sims-Knight, J. E. (1989). *In the beginning. Development in the first two years of life.* Newbury Park, CA: Sage. (This is a first-rate text covering prenatal development and infancy. It is an excellent next step in your reading if you are interested in this area.)

Vorhees, C. V., & Mollnow, E. (1987). Behavioral teratogenesis: long-term influences on behavior from early exposure to environmental agents. In J. D. Osofsky (Ed.), *Handbook of infant development* (2nd ed.) (pp. 913–971). New York: Wiley. (A thorough review of the literature on the effects of various commonly discussed teratogens such as alcohol and smoking, this article also covers many other teratogens, such as lead, anticonvulsants, PCBs, hormones, radiation, and aspirin.)

4 PHYSICAL DEVELOPMENT IN INFANCY

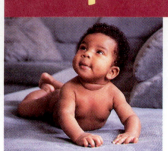

I spoke recently with a friend, the mother of a 6-month-old. When I asked her how things were going, she said three very typical things: "No one told me how much fun it would be," "No one told me how much work it would be," and "I didn't expect it to be this fascinating. She's changing every day. Now she seems like a real person, sitting up, crawling, beginning to make wonderful noises."

I suspect that someone had indeed told her all those things, but she didn't hear them. Only when you are with a child every day, care for the child, and love the child, does the reality of the whole amazing process come home to you. I'll do my best to convey that amazement to you, but some of what I am going to say may not be "real" to you unless and until you help to rear a child yourself. Let me begin by describing the child's physical development during the first 18 to 24 months, starting with a snapshot of the newborn.

▶ The Newborn

Assessing the Newborn

It has become customary in most hospitals to evaluate an infant's status immediately after birth and then again five minutes later, to detect any problems that may require special care. By far the most frequently used assessment system is something called an **Apgar score,** developed by a physician, Virginia Apgar (1953). In this system, the newborn is rated on the five criteria I've listed in Table 4.1, and given a score of 0, 1, or 2 on each criterion, with a maximum score of 10. A score of 10 is fairly unusual immediately after birth because most infants are still somewhat blue in the fingers and toes at that stage. At the five-minute assessment, however, 85 to 90 percent of infants are scored as 9 or 10 (National Center for Health Statistics, 1984). Any score of 7 or better indicates that the baby is in no danger. A score of 4, 5, or 6 usually means that the baby needs help establishing normal breathing patterns. A score of 3 or below indicates a baby in critical condition, although babies with such low Apgar scores can and do often survive.

TABLE 4.1 Evaluation Method for Apgar Scoring

Aspect of Infant Observed	Score Assigned		
	0	1	2
Heart rate	Absent	< 100/min	> 100/min
Respiratory rate	No breathing	Weak cry and shallow breathing	Strong cry and regular breathing
Muscle tone	Flaccid	Some flexion of extremities	Well flexed
Response to stimulation of feet	None	Some motion	Cry
Color	Blue; pale	Body pink, extremities blue	Pink all over

Source: After Robinson, 1978, Table 5–2, p. 102.

Reflexes

Infants are born with a large collection of **reflexes,** which are physical responses triggered involuntarily by a specific stimulus. Many of these reflexes are still present in adults, so you should be familiar with them, such as the knee jerk the doctor tests for, your automatic blink when a puff of air hits your eye, or the involuntary narrowing of the pupil of your eye when you're in a bright light.

The newborn's reflexes can be roughly grouped into two categories. First, there are many *adaptive reflexes* that help the baby survive in the world into which he is born. Sucking and swallowing reflexes are prominent in this category, as is the rooting reflex—the automatic turn of the head toward any touch on the cheek, a reflex that helps the baby get the nipple into his mouth during nursing. These reflexes are no longer present in older children or adults, but are clearly highly adaptive for the newborn.

Other adaptive reflexes do persist over the whole life span, including a withdrawal reaction from a painful stimulus, the opening and closing of the pupil of the eye to

What would be different about development and about adult-baby interactions if babies were born *without* any reflexes, but instead had to learn every behavior?

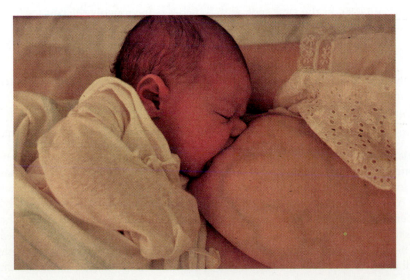

Fortunately, babies are born with a sucking reflex.

variations in brightness, and many others. Finally, there are some reflexes that were adaptive in evolutionary history and that are still present in newborn humans, even though they are no longer helpful. The grasping reflex is one clear example. If you place your finger across a newborn baby's palm, he will reflexively close his fist tightly around your finger. If you do this with both palms, the baby's grasp is strong enough so that you can lift him up by his hands in this way. This reflex is also seen in monkeys and apes, for whom it is highly useful, since the infant must be able to cling to the mother's body while she moves about, or to a tree branch or vine. Most observers assume that this reflex in humans is merely one residual from our evolutionary past.

A second category includes the *primitive reflexes*, so called because they are controlled by the more primitive parts of the brain, the medulla and the midbrain, both of which are close to being fully developed at birth. By about 6 months of age, when the portion of the brain governing such complex activities as perception, body movement, thinking, and language has developed more fully, these primitive reflexes begin to disappear, as if superceded by the more complex brain functions.

For example, if you make a loud noise or startle a baby in some other way, you'll see her throw her arms outward and arch her back, a pattern that is part of the *Moro*, or *startle, reflex*. Stroke the bottom of her foot and she will splay out her toes and then curl them in, called the *Babinsky reflex*. These patterns are of interest primarily because their presence past the age of roughly 6 months may signal the existence of some kind of neurological problem. The Babinsky reflex, in particular, is used as a diagnostic tool by neurologists who may suspect the existence of some dysfunction in a child or adult.

These two categories of reflexes obviously overlap. Many adaptive reflexes—including the sucking and rooting reflexes—begin to fade late in the first year of life, indicating that they are controlled by the more primitive parts of the brain. But I think it is still helpful to distinguish between those reflexes that continue to have daily usefulness for the baby and those that are more purely reflections of the status of the nervous system, without other adaptive functions.

Initial Perceptual Skills: What the Newborn Sees, Hears, and Feels

Babies also come equipped with a surprisingly mature set of perceptual skills. I'll be describing the development of those skills in the next chapter, but I do want you to have some sense of the starting point. The newborn can:

- Focus both eyes on the same spot, with 8 inches being roughly the best focal distance. Within a few weeks the baby can at least roughly follow a moving object with his eyes, and by one or two months he can discriminate Mom's face from other faces.

- Easily hear sounds within the pitch and loudness range of the human voice; roughly locate objects by their sounds, and discriminate some individual voices, particularly the mother's voice.

- Taste the four basic tastes (sweet, sour, bitter, and salty) and identify familiar body odors, including discriminating Mom's smell from the smell of a strange woman.

Brief as this summary is, several points nonetheless stand out. First of all, newborns' perceptual skills are a great deal better than most parents believe—better than most psychologists or physicians believed until a few years ago. The better our research techniques have become, the more we have understood just how skillful the new baby is.

Even more striking is how well adapted the baby's perceptual skills are for the interactions he will have with the people in his world. He hears best in the range of the human voice; he can discriminate mother (or other regular care giver) from others on the basis of smell or sound almost immediately, and by sight within a very few weeks; he can focus

Newborns are pretty nearsighted, but they can focus very well at about 8 to 10 inches—just about the distance in this picture, or between a mother's face and the baby's eyes when the baby is held in Mom's arms for feeding.

his eyes best at a distance of about 8 inches, which is just about the distance between the infant's eyes and the mother's face during nursing.

As you'll see in Chapter 5, there is still a long way to go in the development of sophisticated perceptual abilities. But the newborn begins life able to make key discriminations and to locate objects through various perceptual cues.

Initial Motor Skills: Moving Around

In contrast, the motor skills of the newborn are unimpressive. She can't reach for things she's looking at. She can't hold up her head, roll over, or sit up. Some of these skills emerge rapidly in the early weeks. By 1 month, for example, the baby can hold her chin up off the floor or mattress. By 2 months, she is beginning to use her hands to swipe at objects near her. But babies start their progress in motor development at a much lower level than they start the development of sophisticated perceptual skills.

▶ A Day in the Life of a Baby

What is it like to live with a newborn? How is the infant's day organized? What sort of natural rhythms occur in the daily cycles? What can you expect from the baby as you struggle to adapt to and care for this new person in your life?

Researchers who have studied newborns have described five different states of sleep and wakefulness in infants, referred to as **states of consciousness,** which I've summarized in Table 4.2. You can see that the baby spends more time sleeping than anything else. Of the time awake, only about two to three hours is spent either quietly or actively awake rather than fussing.

The five main states tend to occur in cycles, just as your own states occur in a daily rhythm. In the newborn, the basic period in the cycle is about 1½ or 2 hours. Most infants move through the states from deep sleep to lighter sleep to fussing and hunger and then to alert wakefulness, after which they become drowsy and drop back into deep sleep. This sequence repeats itself about every two hours. By about 6 weeks of age most infants begin to string two or three of these periods together without coming to full wakefulness, at which point we say that the baby can "sleep through the night" (Bamford et al., 1990). One of the implications of this rhythm, by the way, is that the best time for really good

Calves, foals, lambs, and newborns of virtually all mammals besides humans can stand and walk within a few hours after birth. Can you think of any useful evolutionary function for the greater motor helplessness of the human newborn?

TABLE 4.2 The Basic States of Infant Sleep and Wakefulness

State	Characteristics	At Birth	At 1 Month
Deep sleep	Eyes closed, regular breathing, no movement except occasional startles.	16–18 hr	14–16 hr
Active sleep	Eyes closed, irregular breathing, small twitches, no gross body movement.		
Quiet awake	Eyes open, no major body movement, regular breathing.	6–8 hr	8–10 hr
Active wake	Eyes open, with movements of the head, limbs, and trunk; irregular breathing.		
Crying and fussing	Eyes may be partly or entirely closed, vigorous diffuse movement, with crying or fussing sounds.		

Sources: Based on the work of Prechtl & Beintema, 1964; Hutt, Lenard & Prechtl, 1969; Parmelee, Wenner & Schulz, 1964.

social encounters with a young infant is likely to be just after she is fed, when she is most likely to be in a state of quiet awakeness.

Let me take a somewhat more detailed look at the major states.

Sleeping

The child's sleep periods are important to parents because they provide breaks in what may otherwise seem like constant care. Newborns have little day-night rhythms (circadian rhythms) to their sleeping patterns; they sleep about equal amounts at any given time of day. By 6 weeks, however, most have established at least the beginnings of a circadian rhythm, although they still spend an average of about 15 to 16 hours sleeping each day. At 6 months, babies are still sleeping a bit over 14 hours per day, but the regularity and predictability of the baby's sleep increases a good deal over those months. Not only do most 6-month-olds have clear nighttime sleep patterns, they also begin to nap during the day at more predictable times.

I've given you the average figures, but of course babies vary a lot in their sleep patterns. Of the 6-week-old babies in one recent study, there was at least one who slept only 8.8 hours per day, and another who slept nearly 22 hours (Bamford et al., 1990). And some babies do not develop a long nighttime sleep period until late in the first year of life—a characteristic many parents find dismaying.

Aside from the duration and timing of the child's sleep periods, psychologists have been interested in two aspects of babies' sleep. First, irregularity in a child's sleep patterns may be a symptom of some disorder or problem. You may remember from Chapter 3 that one of the characteristics of babies born to drug-addicted mothers is that they seem unable to establish a pattern of sleeping and waking. Brain-damaged infants often have the same kind of difficulties, so any time an infant fails to develop clear sleep-waking regularity, it *may* be a sign of trouble.

The other interesting thing about sleep in newborns is that they show the external signs that signify dreaming in older children or adults, a fluttering of the eyeballs under the closed lids, called **rapid eye movement sleep**, or REM sleep. REMs are not seen in very young preterm infants, so there is clearly some neurological maturity required for this pattern of activity. Among normal-term newborns, though, REM sleep actually makes up a larger portion of sleep time than is true in adults. In adults, REMs typically occur in brief bursts periodically over the sleep period; in newborns they occur more steadily over the entire sleep period (Berg & Berg, 1987). Just what these differences in pattern may mean about the development of the nervous system or about dreaming in very young infants, is not so clear. But some sort of very busy activity seems to be going on during the baby's sleep time.

Crying

For many parents, the infant's crying may be largely disturbing or irritating, especially if it continues for long periods and the infant is not easily consoled. But crying is a crucial signal from the infant, telling the caregiver that the baby needs care. What is more, infants have a whole repertoire of cry sounds, with different cries for pain or anger or hunger. The basic cry, which often signals hunger, usually begins with whimpering or moaning and then works up to a rhythmical pattern: cry, silence, breath, cry, silence, breath, with a kind of whistling sound often accompanying the in-breath. An anger cry is louder and more intense than the basic cry, while the pain cry differs primarily by having a very abrupt onset rather than beginning with whimpering. However, not all infants cry in precisely the same way, so the parents must learn the appropriate discriminations. Alen Wiesenfeld and his colleagues (Wiesenfeld, Malatesta & DeLoach, 1981) found that mothers (but not fathers) of 5-month-olds could discriminate between taped episodes of anger and pain cries in their own babies, while neither parent could reliably make the same discrimination with the taped cries of another baby.

Newborns actually cry less of the time than you might think—something between 2 and 11 percent (Korner et al., 1981). Crying seems to increase over the first six weeks of life, and then decreases. Initially, infants cry most in the evening, later shifting their crying toward times just before feedings.

In all of this, as in the nature of the cries themselves, there are wide individual differences. Fifteen to twenty percent of infants develop a pattern called *colic*, which

The obvious explanation of the mother's greater ability to discriminate among the different cries of her baby is that she spends more time in care-giving than does the father. What kind of study could you design to test this hypothesis?

RESEARCH REPORT
Variations in Children's Cries

Parents have always known that some babies have cries that are particularly penetrating or grating; other babies seem to have much less unpleasant crying sounds. Researchers have confirmed this parental observation in a wide range of studies.

Many groups of babies with known medical abnormalities have different-sounding cries, including those with Down syndrome, encephalitis, meningitis, and those with many types of brain damage. In recent work, Barry Lester has extended this observation to studies of babies who appear physically normal but are at risk for later problems because of some perinatal problem, such as preterm or small-for-date babies (e.g., Lester, 1987; Lester & Dreher, 1989; Zeskind & Lester, 1978). Such babies typically make crying sounds that are acoustically distinguishable from what you hear in a normal, low-risk baby. In particular, the cry of such higher-risk babies has a more grating, piercing quality.

On the assumption that the baby's cry may reflect some basic aspect of neurological integrity, Lester also wondered whether one could use the quality of the cry as a *diagnostic* test. Among a group of high-risk babies, for example, could one predict later intellectual functioning from a measure of the gratingness or pitch of the baby's cry? The answer seems to be yes. Lester found that among preterms, those with higher-pitched cries in the first days of life had lower scores on an IQ test at age 5 (Lester, 1987). The same kind of connection has also been found among both normal babies and those exposed to methadone prenatally. In all these groups, the higher the pitch and more grating the cry, the lower the child's later IQ or motor development (Huntington, Hans & Zeskind, 1990).

Eventually, it may be possible for physicians to use the presence of such a grating or piercing cry as a signal that there may be some underlying physical problem with the infant, or to make better guesses about the long-term outcomes for individual babies at high risk of later problems, such as low-birth-weight babies.

involves intense daily bouts of crying, totaling three or more hours a day. The crying is generally worst in late afternoon or early evening—a particularly inopportune time, of course, because parents are tired and need time with one another then, too. Colic typically appears at about 2 weeks of age and then disappears spontaneously at 3 or 4 months of age. Neither psychologists nor physicians know why colic begins or why it stops without any intervention. It is a difficult pattern to live with, but the good news is that it *does* go away.

Eating

Eating is not a "state," but it is certainly something that newborn babies do frequently! Given that the baby's natural cycle seems to be about 1½ hours long, a newborn may eat as many as ten times a day. By 1 month the average number is down to about 5½ feedings, with a very gradual decline from that number over the first year (Barnard & Eyres, 1979). Both breast-fed and bottle-fed babies eat at about the same frequency, but these two forms of feeding do differ in other important ways.

ACROSS CULTURES
Cultural and Social Class Differences in Patterns of Breast-Feeding and Their Consequences

If you look at the incidence of breast-feeding in countries around the world over the past 40 or 50 years, you'll find some very curious patterns. In the 1950s and 1960s, breast-feeding declined dramatically in most Western countries, including the United States. By 1971, only 25 percent of U.S. women breast-fed even for a few weeks. At the same time, breast-feeding continued to be the normative method of infant feeding in non-Western countries, including virtually all third-world countries (World Health Organization, 1981).

In the decades since, these two trends have reversed. Breast-feeding has risen sharply in most industrialized countries as evidence of its importance came to light; by 1984, 60 percent of U.S. women breast-fed for at least a few weeks (Ryan et al., 1991). In the same years, however, rates of breast-feeding began to drop in many third-world and developing countries. In most such countries the great majority of mothers continued to breast-feed in the early weeks of the infant's life, but the duration of breast-feeding began to decline—an alarming development from the point of view of public health, because it was accompanied by sharp increases in infant mortality.

For example, in Brazil in 1981, over 90 percent of women breast-fed for at least a few weeks, but the average duration of breast-feeding was only 43 days (Rea, 1990)—a considerable decline over previous decades. In the Philippines, the decline was not as large, but between 1963 and 1982, the average duration of breast-feeding dropped from 14.5 months to 12 months (Williamson, 1990).

The Consequences of Formula Feeding in the Third World

A decade ago, the World Health Organization concluded that the marketing of infant formula worldwide was a significant contributor to the declining levels of breast-feeding in many countries (World Health Organization, 1981). Manufacturers of formula have given free samples or free feeding bottles to new mothers and assured women that formula is as good or better for babies, while frequently failing to provide adequate instruction on how formula is to be given. Some women, knowing no better and faced with extreme economic hardship, have diluted their infant's formula with water in order to make it stretch further. And many women have not understood the importance of, or were simply not equipped to handle, the sterilization of bottles and nipples. Worldwide, the concern aroused by this change in normal feeding practices was sufficient to cause the World Health Organization to issue an "International Code of Marketing of Breast-milk Substitutes" in 1981. That code has made some difference; marketing practices have been modified. Yet the decline in breast-feeding has continued, as mothers around the world have increasingly moved into the labor force and into urban living (e.g., Stewart et al., 1991).

Such a decline is cause for real concern. Bottle-fed babies are at far higher risk of serious disease or death. In Bangladesh, for example, the risk of death from diarrhea is three times higher among bottle-fed than among breast-fed babies; in Brazil, the risk of death from various kinds of infections ranges from 2½ to 14 times higher among the bottle-fed. In all these studies, the risk is also related to the sanitary conditions in which the baby is reared. In Malaysia, for example, the risk of death in the first year for those fed formula ranges from 28 to 153 per 1000 infants, depending on whether or not the family lives in a home with piped water and toilet facilities (Cunningham et al., 1991). Breast-feeding is thus better for two reasons: it provides the baby with needed antibodies against infection, and it is likely to expose the baby to less infection in the first place.

Breast- Versus Bottle-Feeding.   After several decades of extensive research in many countries, physicians and epidemiologists have reached clear agreement that breast-feeding is nutritionally substantially superior to bottle-feeding. Breast milk provides important antibodies for the infant against many kinds of diseases, especially gastrointestinal and upper respiratory infections (Cunningham, Jelliffe & Jelliffe, 1991). Human breast milk also appears to promote the growth of nerves and intestinal tract (Carter, 1988), and may stimulate better immune system function over the long term.

Those women who find breast-feeding logistically difficult because of work or other demands may take some comfort from the fact that the research indicates that babies derive some protection from as little as one breast-feeding per day. There is also comfort in the observation that the *social* interactions between mother and child seem to suffer no ill effects from bottle-feeding. Bottle-fed babies are held and cuddled in the same ways as are breast-fed babies, and their mothers appear to be just as sensitive and responsive to their babies as are mothers of breast-fed infants (Field, 1977).

I do not want this set of statements to provoke intense guilt in those of you who find

The benefits of breast-feeding, however, are not restricted to the third world. Even in countries in which the majority of children are reared in good sanitary conditions, breast-fed babies are healthier and less likely to die in the first year (Cunningham et al., 1991).

Who Chooses to Breast-feed?

In view of such findings, it is disturbing to find that in the United States the trend line is again downward. Between 1984 and 1989 the number of women beginning breast-feeding dropped from 60 to 52 percent, while the number still breast-feeding after six months dropped from 23.8 to 18.1 percent (Ryan et al., 1991). At both time points, however, it is the same subgroups that are more likely to breast-feed:

- Caucasian women, more than either blacks or Hispanics. In 1989, the respective rates in the first weeks of the baby's life were 58%, 23%, and 48% (Ryan et al., 1991).
- Older mothers. The older the mother, the more likely she is to breast-feed.
- Higher-education mothers.
- Higher-income mothers.

The very low rates of breast-feeding among poor women in the United States is especially troubling, because rates of infant mortality and illness are already higher among infants born into such families. In one recent study (MacGowan et al., 1991), physicians found that among poverty-level mothers in rural Georgia enrolled in a nationally funded special supplemental food program (the Women, Infants, and Children program, called *WIC*), only 24 percent breast-fed in the first few weeks of their baby's life; only 6 percent continued for at least six months. Within this group, breast-feeding was five times as common among those with high school education as among those with less than ninth grade.

A mother's work status also makes an obvious difference in her decision about breast- or bottle-feeding, but it is *not* the deciding factor in many cases. Most studies show that the decision to begin breast-feeding is only weakly related to whether a mother expects to go back to work or to begin employment shortly after giving birth. At the point at which a mother returns to work, there is indeed a drop in breast-feeding, but it does not drop to zero. In Ryan's 1989 study of a nationally representative sample (Ryan et al., 1991), 8.9 percent of women who worked full-time, 21.1 percent of those who worked part-time, and 21.6 percent of those who were not employed were still breast-feeding at six months. Clearly employment is not the crucial issue here, because four-fifths of the women who were *not* working were also not breast-feeding past the earliest months of the baby's life.

Two things strike me about these results. First of all, it is impressive that many women find creative ways to combine employment and breast-feeding. These findings also provide another bit of evidence in favor of more generous maternal leave policies—policies in place in many European countries but not in most parts of the United States. If remaining at home for the first three or six months enabled more women to continue breast-feeding, it would benefit the children, and thus in the long run would benefit the whole society.

But more importantly, it is clear that there is still a large public health task remaining, not only in the United States but around the world, to educate women still further about the importance of breast-feeding.

that you are physically or otherwise unable to breast-feed. Babies can and do thrive on formula. But it is clear that *if* you have a choice, babies will derive real benefits from breast-feeding.

▶ Physical Change from Birth to 18 Months

As my friend with the 6-month-old has already observed, one of the remarkable things about babies is just how fast change. If I need any further reminder of this fact, I need only look in my briefcase, where I carry pictures of my brand-new grandson. The newborn pictures are (of course!) charming, but the 4-month-old Sam shown in my most recent batch of pictures is remarkably different. He's beginning to sit up with a little help; he's reaching for things; he smiles a lot more. By the time he's 12 or 18 months old, he'll have a whole repertoire of striking new abilities.

Basic Patterns of Physical Changes in Infancy

The sequence of physical changes we see in these early months follows two broad patterns: development proceeds from the head downward, called **cephalocaudal**, and from the trunk outward, called **proximodistal**. We see the operation of these two principles in visible behavior, such as the baby's being able to hold up his head before he can sit, and sit before he can crawl. But we also can document the same patterns in the development of the nervous system.

Changes in the Nervous System

Figure 4.1 shows the main structures of the brain. The most completely developed of these structures at birth are the **midbrain** and the **medulla**, which regulate such basic tasks as attention and habituation, sleeping, waking, elimination, and movement of the head and neck. And as you've just seen, these are all tasks a newborn can perform at least moderately well.

The least-developed part of the brain at birth is the **cortex,** the convoluted gray matter that wraps around the midbrain and is involved in perception, body movement, and all complex thinking and language. The cortex does have all its neurons and some dendritic development at birth. What happens between birth and 18 months is the cre-

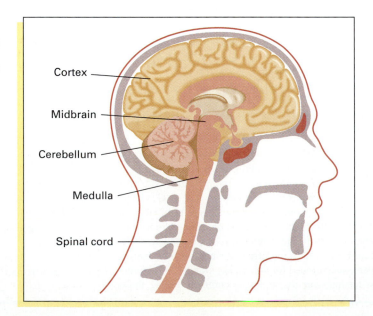

Figure 4.1　The medulla and the midbrain are largely developed at birth. In the first two years after birth it is primarily the cortex that develops, with each neuron going through an enormous growth of dendrites and a vast increase in synapses.

Cortex

Midbrain

Cerebellum

Medulla

Spinal cord

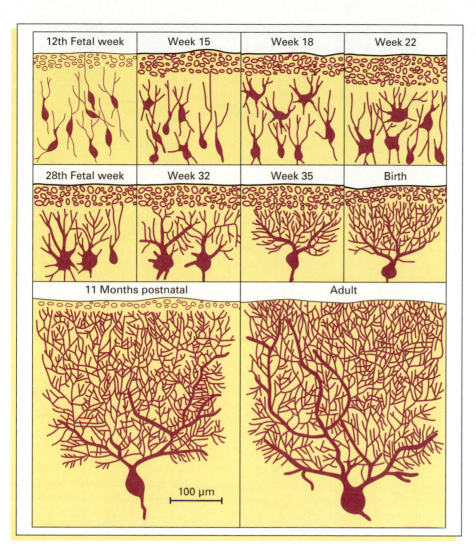

12th Fetal week	Week 15	Week 18	Week 22

28th Fetal week	Week 32	Week 35	Birth

11 Months postnatal	Adult

100 μm

Figure 4.2 You can see here in schematic form both the remarkable growth of dendrites occurring in the year after birth and also the pruning of the ''dendritic arbor'' after age 1, when redundant synapses appear to be eliminated.

ation of a vast number of synapses, which involves enormous growth of the dendritic arbor as well as of axons and their terminal fibers. Because of this rapid multiplication of fibers, the overall weight of the brain triples between birth and 2 years of age (Nowakowski, 1987).

Development of Neurons and Synapses. Dendritic development is not smooth and continuous. Neurophysiologists have found that there is an initial burst of synapse formation, followed by a "pruning" of synapses at about age 2. Redundant connections are eliminated and the "wiring diagram" is cleaned up (Greenough, Black & Wallace, 1987). You can see both the rapid increase and the pruning depicted graphically in Figure 4.2.

For example, early in development each skeletal muscle cell seems to develop synaptic connections with several motor neurons in the spinal cord. But after the pruning process has occurred, each muscle fiber is connected to only one neuron. In an argument reminiscent of the concept of "inborn biases" I mentioned in Chapter 1, some neurophysiologists such as Greenough (Greenough et al., 1987) have suggested that the initial surge of development of dendrites and synapses follows a built-in pattern; the organism is programmed to create certain kinds of neural connections and does so in abundance, creating redundant pathways. According to this argument, the pruning that then takes place at

Developmental psychologists have been very excited about the discovery of dendritic pruning in the second year of life. Why is this such an intriguing finding?

Because motor development is both cephalocaudal and proximodistal, both 7-month-old Helen and 5-month-old Laura are better at reaching and grasping than they are at crawling.

about age 2 is a response to specific experience, so that the most used or the most efficient pathways are selectively retained. Putting it more briefly, "experience does not create tracings on a blank tablet; rather experience erases some of them" (Bertenthal & Campos, 1987). Interestingly, there appears to be another pruning of synapses at adolescence, suggesting that there may be a further reorganization of pathways at that time.

Greenough and his colleagues do not think that all synaptic development is governed by such built-in programming. He suggests that other synapses are formed entirely as a result of specific experience, and go on being created in this way throughout our lives. But the emergence of neuronal control of the basic motor and sensory processes may initially follow built-in patterns, with pruning then based on experience.

Myelinization.   Another crucial process is the development of sheaths around individual axons, which insulate them from one another and improve the conductivity of the nerve. This sheath is made up of a substance called **myelin**; the process of developing the sheath is called **myelinization.**

The sequence with which nerves are myelinized follows the basic cephalocaudal and proximodistal patterns. Thus nerves serving muscle cells in the arms and hands are myelinized earlier than are those serving the lower trunk and the legs. Myelinization is largely complete by age 2, although some continues in the brain well into adolescence.

To understand the importance of myelin, it may help you to know that *multiple sclerosis* is a disease in which the myelin begins to break down. An individual with this disease gradually loses motor control, with the specific symptoms depending on the portion of the nervous system in which the myelin is affected.

Changes in Bones and Muscles

These changes in the nervous system are paralleled by changes in other body structures, including bones and muscles, although here the changes occur fairly gradually from infancy through adolescence, rather than in the remarkable spurt we see in the nervous system.

Bones.   The hand, wrist, ankle and foot all have fewer bones at birth than they will have at full maturity. For example, in an adult's wrist there are nine separate bones. In the 1-year-old, there are only three. The remaining six develop over the period of childhood, with complete growth by adolescence.

In one part of the body, though, the bones fuse rather than differentiating. The skull of a newborn is made up of several bones separated by spaces called **fontanels.** Fontanels allow the head to be compressed without injury during the birth process, and they also give the brain room to grow. In most children, the fontanels are filled in by bone by 12 to 18 months (Kataria et al., 1988) creating a single connected skull bone.

All the infant's bones are also softer, with a higher water content, than adults' bones. The process of bone hardening, called **ossification**, occurs steadily from birth through puberty, with bones in different parts of the body hardening in a sequence that follows the typical proximodistal and cephalocaudal patterns. So, for example, bones of the hand and wrist harden before those in the feet.

You may well be thinking that bone hardening is pretty boring and irrelevant stuff, but it has some fairly direct practical relevance. Soft bones are clearly needed if the fetus is going to have enough flexibility to fit into the cramped space of the uterus. But that very flexibility contributes to a newborn human's relative helplessness. Newborns are remarkably floppy; they cannot even hold their own heads up, let alone sit or walk. As the bones stiffen, the baby is able to manipulate his body more surely, which increases the range of exploration he can enjoy and makes him much more independent.

Muscles. As is true of neurons, the newborn baby has virtually all the muscle fibers she will ever have (Tanner, 1978). But like the infant's bones, muscle fibers are initially small and watery, becoming longer, thicker, and less watery at a fairly steady rate until adolescence. The sequence is again both proximodistal and cephalocaudal. So the baby gains muscle strength in the neck fairly early, but does not have enough muscle strength in the legs to support walking until some months later.

Size and Shape

All these internal changes obviously affect the baby's size and shape. Babies grow very rapidly in the first months, adding 10 to 12 inches in length and tripling their body weight in the first year. By age 2, after adding another 2 or 3 inches, babies are *half as tall as they will be as adults*—a fact I put in italics because it is so surprising to most of us. We are deceived in part by the fact that the baby's body proportions are quite different from those of an adult. Most strikingly, babies have proportionately much larger heads—obviously needed to hold that nearly full-sized brain.

▶ Motor Development

All these physical changes form the substrate on which the child's rapidly improving motor skills are constructed. And of course it is precisely those new physical abilities that are so striking and remarkable to parents (and grandparents!).

Robert Malina (1982) suggests that we can divide the wide range of motor skills into three groups, *locomotor* patterns, such as walking, running, jumping, hopping, and skipping; *nonlocomotor* patterns, such as pushing, pulling, and bending; and *manipulative* skills, such as grasping, throwing, catching, kicking, and other actions involving receiving and moving objects. In Table 4.3 I've summarized the developments in each of these three areas over the first 18 months, based primarily on two large recent studies, one in the United States and one in the Netherlands. The U.S. study (Capute et al., 1984) involved 381 babies tested by their pediatricians at regular visits through the first two years; the Dutch study (Den Ouden et al., 1991) included 550 babies who had been tested repeatedly for their first five years. The sequence of milestones described in these two studies is highly similar, as were the ages at which babies passed each test.

These milestones are striking to watch, but even brief observation of a baby will tell you that there are a lot of other kinds of movement going on besides creeping or crawling. Young infants also show a lot of what Esther Thelen (1981) has called *rhythmical stereotypies*—those patterns of kicking, rocking, waving, bouncing, banging, rubbing, scratch-

The remarkable rapidity of motor development in the early months is easy to illustrate. The 9-month-old at the top can sit alone, the 11-month-old in the middle is obviously a skillful crawler, and the 13-month-old on the bottom is joyously walking.

TABLE 4.3 Milestones of Motor Development in the First Two Years

Age	Locomotor Skills	Nonlocomotor Skills	Manipulative Skills
1 mo	Stepping reflex.	Lifts head slightly; follows slowly moving objects with eyes.	Holds object if placed in hand.
2–3 mo		Lifts head up to 90 degrees when lying on stomach.	Begins to swipe at objects in sight.
4–6 mo	Rolls over; sits with some support; moves on hands and knees ("creeps").	Holds head erect in sitting position.	Reaches for and grasps objects.
7–9 mo	Sits without support; crawls.		Transfers objects from one hand to the other.
10–12 mo	Pulls himself to standing; walks grasping furniture ("cruising"); then walks without help.	Squats and stoops.	Some signs of hand preference; grasps a spoon across palm but has poor aim of food to mouth.
13–18 mo	Walks backward and sideways; runs (14–20 mo).	Rolls ball to adult.	Stacks two blocks; puts objects into small containers and dumps them.

Sources: Primary sources are Capute et al., 1986, and Den Ouden et al., 1991. Other sources: Connolly & Dalgleish, 1989; The Diagram Group, 1977; Fagard & Jacquet, 1989; Mathew & Cook, 1990; Thomas, 1990.

ing, and swaying that the infant repeats over and over and in which he seems to take great delight. These repeated, rhythmical patterns seem to peak at about 6 or 7 months of age, although you can see some such behavior even in the first weeks, particularly in finger movements and leg kicking. While this type of movement does not seem to be totally voluntary or coordinated, it also does not appear to be random. For instance, Thelen has observed that kicking movements peak just before the baby begins to crawl, as if the rhythmic kicking were a part of the preparation for crawling.

This kind of observation reminds us that the baby's new motor skills do not spring forth full-blown. Each emerges from the coordination of a wide range of component abilities, perceptual as well as motor (Thelen, 1989; Thelen & Ulrich, 1991). Using a spoon to feed oneself, for example, requires development of muscles in the hand and wrist, bone development in the wrist, eye-hand coordination skills that allow one to readjust the aim of the spoon as you move it toward your mouth, and coordination of all of these with properly timed mouth opening (Connolly & Dalgleish, 1989).

Most of us are unaware of this complex of developmental processes when we watch an infant. What we are struck with is the daily change in the baby's behavior and skill.

◗ Explaining Early Physical Development

When we search for explanations for the series of physical changes I've been describing, there are some obvious candidates: maturation, heredity, and various environmental factors, including both diet and practice.

Maturation and Heredity

Maturational sequences seem necessarily to be part of the explanation, especially for such central patterns as neuronal changes and changes in muscles and bones. In all these areas, while the *rate* of development varies from one child to the next, the *sequence* is virtually the same for all children, even those with marked physical or mental handicaps. Mentally retarded children, for example, typically move through the various motor milestones more slowly than do normal children, but they follow the same sequence. Whenever we find such robust sequences, maturation of some kind seems an obvious explanation.

At the same time, our genetic heritage is individual as well as species-specific. In addition to being programmed for many basic sequences of physical development, each of us also receives instructions for unique growth tendencies. Both size and body shape seem to be heavily influenced by such specific inheritance. Tall parents tend to have tall children; short parents tend to have short children (Garn, 1980). And there are similarities between parents and children in such things as hip width, arm length (some ancestor certainly passed on a gene for long arms to me!), and long or short trunk.

Rate or tempo of growth, as well as final shape or size, seems to be an inherited pattern as well. Parents who were themselves early developers, as measured by such things as bone ossification, tend to have children who are faster developers too (Garn, 1980).

Environmental Effects: Diet and Practice

I mentioned in the last chapter that mothers who are malnourished during pregnancy are more likely to have stillborn infants or infants who die in the first year. The baby's diet after birth is also an obvious ingredient in the equation, although detecting the unique contribution of postnatal malnutrition has been a difficult research challenge, because most babies who are malnourished are also growing up in environments that are deficient in other respects as well.

You already know that the period of maximum dendritic and synaptic growth is in the final three to five months of pregnancy and the first two to three years after birth. Severe malnutrition during that time appears to produce a slow rate of physical and motor development (Malina, 1982). Children whose diet later improves may partially catch up in height or growth rate, but they are typically shorter and slower than their peers. Research with animals and some parallel studies of the brains and nervous systems of malnourished children who have died, show that the main physical effects of malnutrition are a reduction in the size of the dendritic arbor and in the number of synapses, and a slowing of the rate of myelinization (Dickerson, 1981; Ricciuti, 1981). As a consequence, the cortex does not become as heavy. If the child's diet continues to be poor for the first two or three years, the effects appear to be permanent.

The effects of more mild malnutrition, typically referred to as either "subnutrition" or "undernutrition," are harder to detect. We really don't know how poorly the child must be nourished before we see the effects in growth rate or motor coordination. It does appear, however, that chronic subnutrition affects the child's level of energy, which in turn can affect the nature of the interactions the child has with both the objects and the people around him (Barrett, Radke-Yarrow & Klein, 1982; Lozoff, 1989).

Practice.   We can also think of environmental influences on physical development in terms of the child's own practice of various physical activities. Does a baby who spends a lot of time in a toy called an *infant walker*, which holds up the baby while he moves around, learn independent walking any sooner than a baby who never has that practice? Does a toddler who has a chance to try to climb stairs learn to climb them sooner, or more skillfully, than a toddler who is rarely exposed to stairs?

The answer is both yes and no. We know that when normal opportunities to practice certain motions are greatly *restricted*, children's motor development is retarded. A classic study by Wayne Dennis (1960) of children raised in Iranian orphanages is a good example of such an effect. The babies in the poorest of the institutions Dennis observed were routinely placed on their backs in cribs with very lumpy mattresses. They had little or no experience of lying or moving on their stomachs as a normal baby would, and even had difficulty rolling over because of the hollows in the mattresses. These babies almost never went through the normal sequence of learning to walk—presumably because they didn't have enough opportunity to practice all the on-the-stomach parts of the skill. They did learn to walk eventually, but they were about a year late.

It would appear from this and equivalent research (e.g., Razel, 1985), that for the development of such universal, basic skills as crawling or walking, some minimum amount of practice is needed just to keep the system working as it should. On the other hand, practice above and beyond the minimum amount doesn't speed up these basic sequences. Babies who spend a lot of time in walkers, for example, do not walk any sooner (Ridenour, 1982); babies who have practice climbing stairs do not learn skillful stair climbing much, if any, sooner than those with limited stair experience.

When we move beyond these universal motor skills, however, and look at skills like throwing a ball or climbing a tree, maturation may help to determine when a child *can* learn the skill, but practice is clearly necessary for effective performance. The strength and coordination required to throw a basketball high enough to reach the basket undoubtedly does develop in predictable ways over the early years, providing the environment is sufficiently rich to provide needed maintenance. But to develop the skill needed to get the ball through the hoop with regularity, from different angles and distances, requires endless practice, just as does the development of smooth, coordinated skill in almost any complex motor task.

The comparison of babies who have used walkers and those who have not is a nice way to study the impact of practice on early motor skills. Can you think of another way to study this?

▶ Health

Infant Mortality.   I mentioned in the last chapter that the infant mortality rate—the number of deaths in the first year of life—now stands at 9.1 deaths per 1000 live births in the United States. The risk of death will not be so high again in any year until age 65 (Wegman, 1991).

Most infant deaths occur in the *neonatal* period—the first month of life—and are directly linked either to congenital anomalies or to low birth weight. Only about 3.5 deaths per 1000 occur in the remainder of the first year, and nearly half of those are cases of **sudden infant death syndrome (SIDS),** in which an apparently healthy infant dies suddenly and unexpectedly. In 1988, about 5500 babies in the United States died of SIDS (Wegman, 1991). Some babies are more at risk for this syndrome than others, particularly blacks, males, and those with low birth weight. Young mothers, or those who were ill during their pregnancy, or who smoked, used drugs, or had another baby who died of SIDS, are also at higher risk for bearing a child who will die of this syndrome (Kandall & Gaines, 1991; Mitchell et al., 1991).

Despite extensive study, physicians still know little about SIDS, also called *crib death.* In fact it is called a *syndrome* precisely because there is no known disease involved. The most plausible explanation at the moment seems to be that it may result from some abnormality in the way the brain regulates breathing. Many—but not all—SIDS babies had had irregular breathing patterns with periods of *apnea* (temporary suspension of breathing), or had recently had a cold (Hunt & Brouillette, 1987). There is also growing evidence that SIDS is more common in cold weather and in colder parts of the world. But, of course, the great majority of babies have colds and do not die of SIDS. The search goes on for a clear explanation and appropriate preventive measures.

The higher risk of SIDS for black infants in the United States is part of a persisting

It may seem surprising, but research tells us that a baby who gets to practice a lot of stair climbing is not going to develop skillful ability to climb stairs much sooner than a baby who never sees a stair until just about the "right time" for this skill to appear.

pattern. Black infants have more than twice the rate of infant mortality as whites—17.6 versus 8.5 per 1000 in 1988. Native American babies also die at twice the rate of whites (Honigfeld & Kaplan, 1987). These persisting and disturbing differences appear to reflect variations in the availability of adequate prenatal care as well as lack of support for poor mothers and their infants after delivery. Poor infants, including both blacks and Native Americans, are less likely to receive appropriate immunizations, are more likely to be ill, less likely to be seen by a doctor when they are ill, and more likely to die of such entirely preventable diseases as gastroenteritis (Starfield, 1991).

Illnesses in the First Two Years: Virtually all babies get sick, most of them repeatedly. Data from the United States indicate that within the first year, babies have an average of seven respiratory illnesses. (That's a lot of nose-wipes!) In the second year of life the number actually increases to about eight illnesses. Interestingly, there is now a whole series of studies showing that the incidence of such disorders is higher among babies in day care than among those reared entirely at home, presumably because there is greater exposure to varied germs and viruses in group care settings (Hurwitz et al., 1991). In general, the more different people a baby is exposed to, the more often she is likely to be sick (e.g., Wald, Guerra & Byers, 1991). But this is not the unmitigated negative that it may appear to be. Children reared entirely at home, with low exposure to others, have very high rates of illness at later ages when they first attend school. Attendance at day care simply means that the baby is exposed earlier to the various microorganisms that cause upper respiratory infections.

Individual Differences in Early Physical Development

I've already touched on several kinds of differences among babies that affect their physical development in the first few years: diet, feeding experience, specific practice, and adequacy of prenatal and postnatal medical care. Let me sketch several other differences.

Preterm Babies.   Preterm or low-birth-weight babies move more slowly through all the developmental milestones I listed in Table 4.3. You can get some sense of the degree of difference from Table 4.4, which gives several comparisons. The data here are from the Dutch study of normal development I cited in Table 4.3. Den Ouden and her colleagues (1991) tested 555 normal and 555 preterm babies. The latter group included all the otherwise physically normal preterms born at less than 32 weeks of gestation in the Netherlands in 1983. You can see that the preterms are about 10 to 15 weeks behind their

TABLE 4.4 Comparison of Preterm and Normal-Term Babies in Developmental Milestones in the First Two Years

Developmental Milestone	Age at Which 50% of Babies Passed	
	Preterm (< 32 weeks)	Normal Term
Lifts head slightly	10 weeks	6 weeks
Transfers object hand to hand	36 weeks	23 weeks
Rolls over	37 weeks	24 weeks
Crawls	51 weeks	36 weeks
Pulls to standing position	51 weeks	42 weeks

Source: Den Ouden et al., 1991, from Table V, p. 402.

full-term peers on most physical skills. This is entirely what we would expect, of course, because the preterm baby is, in fact, maturationally younger than the full-term baby. If you correct for the baby's "gestational age," most (but not all) of the difference disappears. Parents of preterms need to keep this in mind when they compare their baby's progress with that of a full-term baby. By age 2 or 3, the physically normal preterm will catch up to his peers, but in the early months he is definitely behind.

Boys and Girls. I'll bet that your first question, when you hear that a friend or family member has had a new baby, is, "Is it a boy or a girl?" You might assume that such a preoccupation exists because boy and girl babies are really very different from one another. But in fact they are not. There are remarkably few sex differences in physical development in young infants. As was true at birth, girls continue to be a bit ahead in some aspects of physical maturity, and boys continue to be more vulnerable, with higher infant mortality rates. Male infants also have more muscle tissue than do girls. More mixed are the findings on activity level. When researchers observe a difference, it is likely to be boys who are found to be more active (e.g., Eaton & Enns, 1986), but many investigators report no difference at all (e.g., Cossette, Malcuit & Pomerleau, 1991). There are actually bigger differences between babies from different ethnic groups—described in the "across cultures" box below—than there are between boys and girls.

The physical development of infants is probably more clearly governed by built-in sequences and timetables and more similar from one baby to another than any other aspect of development we'll be looking at. What is striking to the observer is not "boyness" or "girlness," or blackness or whiteness, but "babyness."

ACROSS CULTURES
Differences in Early Physical Development

The sequence of physical changes I've been describing in this chapter do seem to hold true for babies in all cultures. But there are nonetheless interesting differences.

Black babies—whether born in Africa or elsewhere—develop somewhat faster, both prenatally and after birth. In fact, the gestational period for the black fetus seems actually to be slightly shorter than for the white fetus (Smith & Stenchever, 1978). Black babies also show somewhat faster development of motor skills, such as walking, and are slightly taller than their white counterparts, with longer legs, more muscle, and heavier bones (Tanner, 1978).

In contrast, Asian infants are somewhat slower to achieve many early motor milestones. This could reflect simply differences in rate of maturation. Or it could reflect some ethnic differences in the baby's level of activity or placidity, a possibility suggested by research by Daniel Freedman (1979).

Freedman has observed newborn babies from four different cultures: Caucasian, Chinese, Navaho, and Japanese. Of the four, he found that the Caucasian babies were the most active and irritable and the hardest to console. Both the Chinese and the Navaho infants he observed were relatively placid, while the Japanese infants responded vigorously but were easier to quiet than the Caucasian infants.

One specific illustration: When Freedman tested each baby for the Moro reflex he found that the Caucasian babies showed the typical pattern in which they reflexively extended both arms, cried vigorously and persistently, and moved their bodies in an agitated way. Navaho babies, on the other hand, showed quite a different pattern. Instead of thrusting their limbs outward they retracted their arms and legs, rarely cried and showed little or very brief agitation.

Because such differences are visible in newborns they cannot be the result of systematic shaping by the parents. But the parents, too, bring their cultural training to the interaction. Freedman and other researchers have observed that both Japanese and Chinese mothers talk much less to their infants than do Caucasian mothers. These differences in mothers' behavior were present from their first encounters with their infants after delivery, so the pattern is not a response to the baby's quieter behavior. But such similarity of temperamental pattern between mother and child may strengthen the pattern in the child, which would tend to make the cultural differences larger over time.

One of the key points from this research is that our notions of what is "normal" behavior for an infant may be strongly influenced by our own cultural patterns and assumptions.

Summary

1. Newborns are typically assessed using the Apgar score, which is a rating on five dimensions.
2. Infants have both adaptive and primitive reflexes. The former group includes such essential reflexes as sucking and rooting; primitive reflexes include the Moro and Babinsky, which disappear within a few months.
3. At birth the baby has a far wider array of perceptual skills than psychologists had supposed. In particular, she can see and hear well enough for most social encounters.
4. Babies move through a series of "states of consciousness," from quiet sleep to active sleep to fussing to eating to quiet wakefulness, in a cycle that lasts roughly 1½ to 2 hours.
5. Persisting irregularity of sleep patterns or a particularly high-pitched or grating cry may be indications of some neurological problem.
6. Breast-feeding has been shown repeatedly to be better for the baby nutritionally, providing needed antibodies and reducing the risk of various infections.
7. Changes in the nervous system are extremely rapid in the first two years. Dendritic and synaptic development reaches its peak between 12 and 24 months, after which there is a "pruning" of synapses. Myelinization of nerve fibers is also largely complete by 2 years.
8. Bones increase in number and density; muscle fibers become larger and less watery.
9. Babies triple their body weight in the first year, and add 12 to 15 inches in length before age 2.
10. Rapid improvement in locomotor and manipulative skills occurs in the first two years, as the baby moves from crawling to walking to running, and from poor to good grasping ability.
11. These virtually universal sequences of development are clearly influenced strongly by common maturational patterns. But individual heredity also makes a difference, as does diet.
12. Sufficient practice of even basic skills is required to maintain the physiological system. Practice beyond that minimum, however, does not speed up basic skill development.
13. Most infant deaths in the first weeks are due to congenital anomalies or low birth weight; past the first weeks, sudden infant death syndrome is the most common cause of death in the first year.
14. On average, babies have seven to eight respiratory illnesses in each of the first two years. This rate is higher among infants in day care.
15. Preterm infants are behind their full-term peers in achieving the milestones of development, but they normally catch up within a few years.
16. There are relatively few differences between boys and girls in early physical development. Ethnic differences do exist, however. Black infants develop somewhat more rapidly, Asian infants somewhat slower.

Key Terms

Apgar score
cephalocaudal
cortex
fontanels
medulla
midbrain
myelin
myelinization
ossification
proximodistal
rapid eye movement sleep
reflexes
states of consciousness
sudden infant death syndrome

Suggested Readings

The Diagram Group. (1977). *Child's body*. New York: Paddington Press. (Although not new, this is a nifty book, designed as a parents' manual and full of helpful information about physical development, health, and nutrition.)

Maurer, D., & Maurer, C. (1988). *The world of the newborn*. New York: Basic Books. (An excellent description of the newborn, written for the lay reader but based very clearly and strongly on research.)

Rosenblith, J. F., & Sims-Knight, J. E. (1989). *In the beginning. Development in the first two years of life*. Newbury Park, CA: Sage. (A fine basic text on infant development.)

Slater, A. M., & Bremner, J. G. (Eds.) (1989). *Infant development*. Hillsdale, NJ: Lawrence Erlbaum Associates. (Like the Maurer and Maurer book, this one was written by scientists, based on research, but is aimed at the lay reader. In this case each chapter was written by a separate expert.)

PERCEPTUAL AND COGNITIVE DEVELOPMENT IN INFANCY

5

For the past several years I have been half-heartedly trying to teach myself German. At times this feels like a hopeless task, because languages have never been my long suit. But I have persisted in an on-again-off-again way; having married a man whose native language is German, it seems only reasonable that I learn his language—vocabulary, complex grammar, pronunciation, and all.

In our everyday lives, each of us faces myriad tasks that call for the same kinds of skills as I have had to use to learn a new language. We study for exams, try to remember what to buy at the grocery store, balance the checkbook, remember phone numbers, use a map. Not all of us do these things equally well or equally quickly. But all of us perform such activities every day of our lives.

These activities are all part of what we normally describe as *cognitive functioning* or "intelligence." What I will be exploring here, and in the parallel chapters on cognition in each age period, is how we all acquire the ability to do all these things. One-year-olds cannot use maps or balance a checkbook. How do they come to be able to do so? And how do we explain the fact that not all children learn these things at the same rate or become as skilled?

▶ Theoretical Perspectives

Answering questions like these has been complicated by the fact that there are three distinctly different views of cognition or intelligence, each of which has led to a separate body of research and commentary.

Three Views of Intelligence

Historically, the first approach to studying cognitive development or intelligence was focused on individual differences. It is inescapably true that people differ in their intellectual skill, their ability to remember things, the speed with which they solve problems, the number of words they can define, their ability to analyze complex situations. When we say someone is "bright" or "very intelligent," it is just such skills we mean, and our label is based on the assumption that we can rank-order people in their degree of "bright-

These babies may look as though they are merely playing, but they are also engaged in important cognitive activities—trying to understand the world around them.

ness." The very same assumption led to the development of intelligence tests, which were designed simply to give us a way of measuring individual differences in intellectual *power*.

The intellectual power approach, which Robert Sternberg (1979) refers to as the *differential approach* because of its emphasis on individual differences, held sway for many years. But it has one great weakness. It does not deal with the equally inescapable fact that cognitive skills become increasingly complex and abstractly organized with age. If you give a 5-year-old a mental list of things to remember to buy at the grocery store, she will have trouble remembering more than a few of them, and she will not use many good strategies to aid her memory. An 8-year-old would remember more things and probably would rehearse the list under his breath or in his head as he was walking to the store. Or, he might remember that there were three vegetables on the list, a strategy that makes it more likely that he will remember to buy all three.

The fact that intelligence develops in this way forms the foundation of the second great tradition in the study of cognitive development, the cognitive developmental approach of Jean Piaget and his many followers. Piaget focused on the development of cognitive *structures* rather than intellectual power, on patterns of development that are *common* to all children rather than on individual differences.

These two traditions have lived side by side for some years now, like polite but not very friendly neighbors. In the past few years, though, the two have developed a mutual friend—a third view, called the **information processing** approach, that partially integrates power and structure approaches. Proponents of this third view, such as Robert Sternberg (1985), Earl Butterfield (Butterfield, Siladi & Belmont, 1980), and Robert Siegler (1986; R. Siegler & Richards, 1982), are attempting to identify and understand the *underlying processes* or strategies that make up all cognitive activity. What are the building blocks, the basic elements, such as memory processes or planning strategies? Once we have identified the basic processes, we can then ask both developmental and individual difference questions: Do these basic processes change with age, and do people differ in their speed or skill in using them?

These three themes will appear again and again as we look at cognitive development over the life span. But the research in each tradition is not equally distributed across the several age strata. In particular, Piaget's theory has been the most clearly dominant in research on infant intelligence—perhaps because he was really the first theorist to think of the infant's behavior in terms of intelligence. So most of what I will be talking about in this chapter has been cast in a Piagetian framework rather than a cognitive power or information processing frame.

Piaget's View of the Sensorimotor Period

Recall from Chapter 2 that Piaget assumes that from the beginning, the baby is engaged in an *adaptive* process, trying to make sense out of the world around her. She assimilates incoming information to the limited array of schemes she is born with—looking, listening, sucking, grasping—and accommodates those schemes based on her experiences. This is the starting point for the entire process of cognitive development, according to Piaget. He called this primitive form of thinking *sensorimotor intelligence*, and the entire stage he called the **sensorimotor period**.

Basic Features of Sensorimotor Intelligence. In Piaget's view, the baby comes equipped with only sensory and motor schemes. So that is where she must start. In the beginning, she is entirely tied to the immediate present, responding to whatever stimuli are available. She does not remember events or things from one encounter to the next, and does not appear to plan or intend. This gradually changes during these first 18 months as the baby comes to understand that objects continue to exist even when they are out of sight, and she is able to remember objects, actions, and individuals over periods of time. But Piaget insisted that the sensorimotor infant is as yet unable to *manipulate* these early mental images or memories, nor does she use *symbols* to stand for objects or events. It is the new ability to manipulate internal symbols, such as words or images, that marks the beginning of the next stage, *preoperational thought*, at roughly 18 to 24 months of age. John Flavell (1985) summarizes all this very nicely:

> [The infant] exhibits a wholly practical, perceiving-and-doing, action-bound kind of intellectual functioning; she does not exhibit the more contemplative, reflective, symbol-manipulating kind we usually think of in connection with cognition. The infant "knows" in the sense of recognizing or anticipating familiar, recurring objects and happenings, and "thinks" in the sense of behaving toward them with mouth, hand, eye, and other sensory-motor instruments in predictable, organized, and often adaptive ways. . . . It is the kind of noncontemplative intelligence that your dog relies on to make its way in the world. (p. 13)

This 2-week-old baby is using two basic sensorimotor schemes at the same time: looking and grasping.

The change from the limited repertoire of schemes available to the newborn to the ability to use symbols at roughly 18 months is gradual. Piaget described six substages, which I've summarized in Table 5.1, on page 100.

Each substage represents some specific advance over the one that came before. Substage 2 is marked especially by the beginning of those important coordinations between looking and listening, reaching and looking, and reaching and sucking that are such central features of the 2-month-old's means of exploring the world. The term *primary circular reactions* refers to the many simple repetitive actions we see at this stage, each centered around the infant's own body. The baby accidentally sucks his thumb one day, finds it pleasurable, and repeats the action. *Secondary circular reactions*, in substage 3, differ only in that the baby is now repeating some action in order to trigger a reaction outside his own body. The baby coos and Mom smiles, so the baby coos again, apparently in order to get Mom to smile again. These initial connections between body actions and external consequences are pretty automatic, very like a kind of operant conditioning. Only in substage 4 do we see the beginnings of real understanding of causal connections, and at this point the baby really moves into exploratory high gear.

In substage 5 such explorations become even more marked with the emergence of what Piaget calls *tertiary circular reactions*. In this pattern the baby is not content merely to repeat the original behavior but tries out variations. The baby in substage 5 might try out many other sounds or facial expressions to see if they would trigger Mom's smile, or try dropping a toy from various heights to see if it made different sounds or landed in different places. There is a purposeful, experimental quality to the baby's behavior. Nonetheless, Piaget thought that even in substage 5 the baby does not have internal *symbols* to stand for objects. The development of such symbols is the mark of substage 6.

You can also deduce from Table 5.1 that there is a parallel progression in the baby's ability to imitate other people. Piaget thought that the newborn could not or would not imitate at all. By substage 3, the baby can imitate the actions of others if the action is already in his own repertoire—if he already has that scheme. In substage 4, the baby can now learn something new from imitation. And in substage 6, the toddler is capable of deferred imitation in which he sees some action and then imitates it at a later point—a skill that appears to require some ability to represent the action internally and remember it.

Piaget's descriptions of this sequence of development, largely based on remarkably detailed observations of the early months of his own three children's lives, have provoked a very rich array of research, some of which confirms the general outlines of his proposals, some of which does not. Let me talk about several specific lines of research—on early learning, on early perceptual skills such as the ability to combine data from more than one sense, on imitation, and on the object concept. Not all this research has been done within an explicitly Piagetian framework, but it nonetheless helps us not only to get a sense of what the baby can do but also to evaluate aspects of Piaget's theory.

TABLE 5.1 Substages of the Sensorimotor Period According to Piaget

Substage	Age	Piaget's Label	Characteristics
1	0–1 mo	Reflexes	Practice of built-in schemes or reflexes, such as sucking and looking. Primitive schemes begin to change through very small steps of accommodation. No imitation; no ability to integrate information from several senses.
2	1–4 mo	Primary circular reactions	Further accommodation of basic schemes, as baby practices them endlessly—grasping, looking, sucking. Beginning coordination of schemes from different senses, so that baby now looks toward a sound and sucks on anything he can reach and bring to his mouth. But the baby does not yet link his body actions to some result outside his body.
3	4–8 mo	Secondary circular reactions	Baby becomes much more aware of events outside his own body and makes them happen again in a kind of trial-and-error learning. Not clear that there is understanding of the causal links yet, however. Imitation may occur, but only of schemes already in the baby's repertoire. Beginning understanding of the "object concept" also detected in this period.
4	8–12 mo	Coordination of secondary schemes	Clear intentional means-ends behavior. The baby not only goes after what she wants, she may combine two schemes to do so, such as knocking a pillow away to reach a toy. Imitation of novel behaviors occurs, as does transfer of information from one sense to the other (cross-modal transfer).
5	12–18 mo	Tertiary circular reactions	"Experimentation" begins, in which the infant tries out new ways of playing with or manipulating objects. Very active, very purposeful, trial-and-error exploration.
6	18–24 mo	Beginning of representational thought	Development of use of symbols to represent object or events. Child understands that the symbol is separate from the object. Deferred imitation occurs first here, because it requires ability to represent internally the event to be imitated.

◗ Research Evidence

Learning and Habituation

Most of the work on learning in infancy has been stimulated not by Piaget's theory but by the broader nature/nurture controversy. Those who argue that a child's behaviors and characteristics are a product of experience, rather than being genetically patterned, must be able to demonstrate that an infant can indeed learn from such experience.

From a practical point of view the question is also important, if only because it affects the sort of advice parents may be given about suitable stimulation for their child. For example, if a child's perceptual abilities develop largely through maturation rather than learning, experts would be less likely to advise parents to buy mobiles to hang above the baby's crib. But if learning is possible from the earliest days of life, then various kinds of enrichment would be beneficial.

What does the evidence tell us?

Classical Conditioning. The bulk of the research suggests that it is very difficult to establish a classically conditioned response in a newborn, but by 3 or 4 weeks of age classical conditioning occurs easily. In fact, babies probably learn many important things about their world in this way, such as connections among sounds and smells and touches. The baby learns that the feeling of being picked up, accompanied by Mom's smell, is followed by being touched on the cheek and then food. Soon the baby shows rooting and sucking as soon as she is picked up. Emotional responses are also established through this means, as I pointed out in Chapter 2.

Operant Conditioning. Newborns also clearly learn by operant conditioning. Both the sucking response and head turning have been successfully increased by the use of reinforcements such as sweet-tasting liquids (Sameroff & Cavanaugh, 1979) or the sound of the mother's voice or heartbeat (DeCasper & Sigafoos, 1983; Moon & Fifer, 1990). Among other things, results like this tell us something interesting about the sorts of reinforcements that are effective with very young children; the fact that the mother's voice is an effective reinforcer is surely highly significant for the whole process of mother-infant interaction.

Schematic Learning. In recent years, many theorists have also begun to talk about a third type of learning, sometimes referred to as *schematic learning,* which draws both its name and many of its conceptual roots from Piaget's theory. The basic idea is that from the beginning the baby organizes her experiences into expectancies, into "known" combinations. These expectancies, often called *schemas,* are built up over many exposures to particular experiences, but thereafter help the baby to distinguish between the familiar and the unfamiliar. Carolyn Rovee-Collier (1986) has suggested that we might actually think of classical conditioning in infants as being a variety of schematic learning. When a baby begins to move her head as if to search for the nipple when she hears Mom's footsteps coming into the room, this may not reflect automatic classical conditioning but rather a more explicitly cognitive process of developing expectancies. From the earliest weeks, the baby seems to begin to map links between events in her world—between the sound of her mother's footsteps and the feeling of being picked up, between the touch of the breast and the feeling of a full stomach. These allow her to recognize the familiar and the unfamiliar, and also to anticipate certain patterns or events.

Habituation. A very important related concept is that of **habituation**. Habituation is the automatic reduction in the strength or vigor of a response to a repeated stimulus. Suppose you live on a fairly noisy street. The sound of cars going by is repeated over and over during each day. But after a while, you not only don't react to the sound, you *do not perceive it as being as loud.* The ability to do this—to dampen down the intensity of a physical response to some repeated stimulus—is obviously vital in our everyday lives. If

Can you think of examples of classically conditioned emotional responses that might develop in early infancy?

we reacted constantly to every sight, sound, and smell that came along, we'd spend all our time responding to these repeated events and not have energy or attention left over for things that are new and deserve attention.

The ability to *dishabituate* is equally important. When there is some change in a habituated stimulus, such as a sudden extra-loud screech of tires on the busy street by your house, you again respond fully. Thus the reemergence of the original response strength is a sign that the perceiver—infant or child or adult—notices some significant change.

The ability to habituate obviously rests on the ability to recognize something as "the same" or "different." Thus if it is present in the newborn, it suggests that the baby has far more ability to remember and compare than Piaget thought. In fact, newborns *do* habituate and dishabituate (Lipsitt, 1982). A baby will stop looking at something you keep putting in front of her face; she will stop showing a startle reaction (Moro reflex) to loud sounds after the first few presentations, but will again show a startle response if the sound is changed. Such habituation itself is not a voluntary process; it is entirely automatic. But in order for it to work, the newborn must be equipped with the capacity to "recognize" familiar experiences. That is, she must develop schemas of some kind.

The existence of these processes in the newborn has an added benefit for researchers: It has enabled them to figure out just which things an infant responds to as if they were "the same" and which things she responds to as "different." If a baby is habituated to a stimulus, such as a sound or a particular picture, the experimenter can then present slight variations on the original stimulus to see the point at which dishabituation occurs.

Results of research of this type tells us that Piaget underestimated the very young infant. Newborns have a good deal to work with besides just primitive schemes, applied one at a time. They can learn connections between their own actions and environmental results from the earliest weeks of life, they create expectancies about events that go together, and they have some ability—however automatic—to store information about previously occurring events so that habituation and dishabituation are possible.

Perceptual Development in the First Two Years

Much the same story emerges from the very rich array of research on early perceptual skills: Piaget underestimated the baby. You already know from Chapter 4 that at birth, or in the early weeks of life, the baby can focus his eyes, follow a moving object at least

Try to imagine a baby who was unable to habituate. What might the consequences be of such a lack?

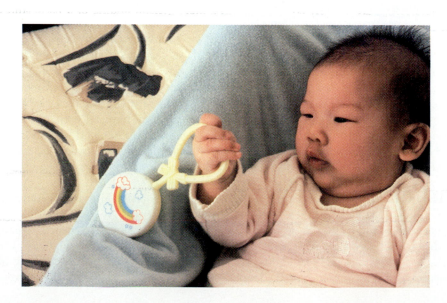

Three-month-old Andrea may be showing a secondary circular reaction here, repeating the sound of the rattle, but she is probably also habituating to the sound it makes.

roughly, taste the major tastes, hear most pitches. These are obviously important skills. They enable the baby to enter into the key interactions with the caregivers, and to react to objects around him. Far more interesting, though, is the recent evidence that very young infants can make remarkably fine discriminations among sounds, sights, and feelings, and that they pay attention to and respond to *patterns*, not just to individual events. We can only sample this fascinating new body of research, but a few examples will give you the flavor—and may amaze you as much as they amaze most researchers.

Discriminating Mom from Other People.   Until quite recently, most psychologists thought that the newborn or very young baby simply couldn't tell the difference between one person and another, even between Mom or Dad and a stranger. But we're beginning to realize that we were wrong.

It looks as if babies first distinguish between one person and another, particularly between Mom and other people, by using their hearing. DeCasper and Fifer (1980) have found that newborns can tell their mother's voice from another female voice (but not their father's voice from another male voice) and prefer the mother's, possibly because the baby has become familiar with the mother's voice while still in utero. By 6 months, babies can even match voices with faces. If you put an infant of this age in a situation where she can see both her father and mother and can hear a tape recorded voice of one of them, she will look toward the parent whose voice she hears (Spelke & Owsley, 1979).

The ability to discriminate by smell also seems to be part of the baby's very early repertoire. Babies as young as a week old can tell the difference between their mother's smell and the smell of a stranger, although this seems to be true only for babies who are being breast-fed and spend quite a lot of time with their noses against the mother's bare skin (Cernoch & Porter, 1985).

Last to develop is the ability to discriminate Mom from others by sight alone, although this too seems to develop within the first two to four weeks (C. Nelson, 1989). Babies as young as 4 to 6 weeks can even discriminate between a picture of their mother and a picture of another female. These early discriminations seem to be based mostly on differences in the shapes of edges, such as the line between hair and forehead. When researchers took pictures of the mother and a stranger when both were wearing a bathing cap, thus disguising any variations in hairline, these young babies could no longer tell the difference (Bushnell, 1982). By 3 months of age, however, infants seem to be able to discriminate mother from stranger in almost any guise (C. Nelson, 1989).

These results are entirely consistent with a more general finding of a basic shift at about 6 to 8 weeks of age in the way babies look at objects around them. From the first days of life babies scan the world around themselves—not very smoothly or skillfully, to be sure, but nonetheless regularly, even in the dark (Haith, 1980). They will keep moving their eyes until they come to a sharp light/dark contrast, which typically signals the edge of some object. Having found such an edge, the baby stops searching and moves his eyes back and forth across and around the edge. For example, when they look at faces, very young babies look mostly at the hairline and the chin, which is why disguising the hairline makes it impossible for the baby to discriminate among different faces.

These rules seem to change at about 2 months, perhaps because the cortex has then developed more fully or perhaps because of experience, or both. Whatever the cause, at about this time the baby's attention seems to shift from *where* an object is to *what* an object is. Put another way, the baby seems to move from a strategy designed primarily to *find* things to a strategy designed primarily to *identify* things. Babies this age begin to scan rapidly across an entire figure, rather than getting stuck on edges. When looking at faces, for example, they now look more at internal features, especially the eyes.

Discriminating Emotional Expressions.   A few months later, babies are paying attention not just to facial features, but to facial expressions. By 5 or 6 months, babies can

How many hypotheses can you think of to explain the fact that newborns can discriminate between Mom's voice and a stranger's, but not between Dad's voice and a stranger's?

RESEARCH REPORT
Langlois's Studies of Babies' Preferences for Attractive Faces

Of all the current research on infant perception that seems to point toward the conclusion that there are many more built-in abilities and preferences than we had supposed, the most surprising and intriguing to me have been Judith Langlois's studies of infant preferences for attractive faces. Langlois has found that babies as young as 2 months old will look longer at a face that adults judge to be attractive than at one adults judge to be less attractive.

In the first work in this series, Langlois and her colleagues (Langlois et al., 1987) tested 2- to 3-month-olds and 6- to 8-month-olds. Each baby, while seated on Mom's lap, was shown pairs of color slides of 16 adult Caucasian women, half rated by adult judges as attractive, half rated as unattractive. On each trial, the baby saw two slides simultaneously shown on a screen in front of him/her, with each face approximately life-size, while the experimenter peeked through a hole in the screen to count the number of seconds the baby looked at each picture. Each baby saw some attractive/attractive pairs, some unattractive/unattractive pairs, and some mixed pairs.

The crucial trials are obviously the ones in which there was one attractive and one unattractive face. The results, which are on the left side of the table below, show that even the 2- to 3-month-olds preferred to look at the attractive faces.

One of the nice features of this study is that they used a variety of attractive and unattractive faces, which makes the conclusion clearer. But because they used only Caucasian females, that leaves open the generality of the result. In a newer study (Langlois et al., 1991), Langlois used the same procedure but showed some 6-month-old infants pictures of (*a*) both unattractive and attractive men and women, or (*b*) attractive and unattractive black women's faces, or (*c*) baby faces varying in attractiveness, all with neutral expressions. You can see the results on the right half of the table below. Once again the results are consistent: In every case babies look significantly longer at the attractive than the unattractive faces.

In another exploration of this same issue, Langlois, Roggman, and Rieser-Danner (1990) have reported that 1-year-old babies interacting with an adult wearing either an attractive or an unattractive mask, showed more positive affective tone, less withdrawal, and more play involvement with the stranger in the attractive mask.

It is hard to imagine what sort of learning experiences could account for such a preference in a 2-month-old. Instead, these findings raise the possibility that there is some inborn template for the "correct" or "most desired" shape and configuration for members of our species, and that we simply prefer those who match this template better. If that's true, what kind of consequences might it have for child and adult development, especially the development of the less attractive baby, child, or adult?

	Average Looking Time				
	Age Groups		**Types of Photos**		
	2–3 mo. olds	**6–8 mo. olds**	**Male & Female**	**Black Women**	**Baby Faces**
Attractive faces	9.22[a]	7.24[a]	7.82[a]	7.05[a]	7.16[a]
Unattractive faces	8.01	6.59	7.57	6.52	6.62

Results from Two Langlois Studies

[a]Contrast between attractive and unattractive faces is statistically significant.
Sources: Langlois et al., 1987, from Table 1, p. 365; Langlois et al., 1991, Table 1, p. 81.

discriminate among faces displaying different emotions. At the same age they respond differently to voices speaking with varying emotional tones. They can tell the difference between happy and sad voices (Walker-Andrews & Lennon, 1991), and between happy, surprised, and fearful faces (C. Nelson, 1987). By roughly 10 months, infants use such emotional cues to help them figure out what to do in novel situations, such as when a stranger comes to visit, or in the doctor's office, or even when a new toy is put in front of them. Babies this age will first look at Mom's or Dad's face to check for the adult's emotional expression. If Mom looks pleased or happy, the baby is likely to explore the new toy with more ease or to accept the stranger with less fuss. If Mom looks concerned or frightened, the baby responds to those cues and reacts to the novel situation with equivalent fear or concern. Researchers have described this as a process of **social refer-encing** (e.g., Hirshberg & Svejda, 1990; Walden, 1991).

Responding to Patterns.   To me, the most surprising discovery to come out of the surge of new research on perception is that babies as young as 3 or 4 months old pay attention to *relationships* among objects or among features of objects. For example, suppose you show babies a series of drawings, one at a time, each of which shows a small object above a larger object of the same shape—something like the ones in the top row of Figure 5.1. After seeing a series of such pictures, babies will habituate. That is, they will look for shorter and shorter periods of time until they are barely glancing at a new version of the figure before looking away. "Ho hum, another one of those." Once habituation is established, you can then throw in a test picture, like the one shown at the bottom of Figure 5.1, that illustrates the opposite pattern, big-over-small. What you are likely to find is that babies of 3 and 4 months will show renewed interest in this different pattern, which tells us that the baby's original habituation had not been to the *specific* stimuli but to a *pattern* (Caron and Caron, 1981).

Using auditory stimuli, you can find the same awareness of pattern in even younger babies. Another study by DeCasper (DeCasper & Spence, 1986) is a particularly striking example. He had pregnant women read a children's story like Dr. Seuss's *The Cat in the Hat* out loud each day for the final six weeks of their pregnancy. After the infants were born, he played recordings of the mother reading this same story, or another previously unheard story, to see which the infant preferred. The newborns clearly preferred the sound of the story they had heard in utero.

Further evidence for the same point comes from the observation that babies as young as 6 months listen to melodies and recognize the patterns. Sandra Trehub and her colleagues (Trehub, Thorpe & Morrongiello, 1985; Trehub, Bull & Thorpe, 1984) trained 6-month-old babies to turn their heads toward a loudspeaker for a particular six-tone melody, and then tested to see if the babies would still turn their heads when they heard melodies that varied in a number of ways. The babies kept turning their heads to new melodies if they had the same contour (notes going up and down in the same sequence)

How might a parent use knowledge of the process of social referencing?

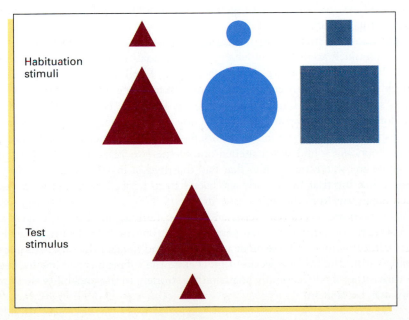

Figure 5.1 Caron and Caron used pictures like this in a study designed to check whether babies were paying attention to the patterns or the relationships among stimuli. Babies were first habituated to a series of pictures, each of which displayed the same pattern, like those in the upper row. Then they were tested either on more of the same or on one with a reverse pattern, like the one on the bottom. Three- and 4-month-old babies show renewed interest in the test stimulus, which indicates that they noticed the pattern and see that it has now changed.

Habituation stimuli

Test stimulus

At older ages, children vary quite a lot in how easily they are able to "carry a tune." You might hypothesize that babies who were especially good at discriminating melodies would also be better at keeping to a tune at later ages. How might you test this hypothesis with research?

and were in approximately the same range. They did not turn their heads if the contour (melody) changed, or if the notes were much higher or much lower. So within the first few months of life, babies appear to pay attention to and respond to pattern and not just the specific sounds. Whether the tendency to respond to patterns in this way is built into the neurological system, or whether it is the result of the child's learning after birth, is still a matter of theoretical and empirical debate (e.g., Morrongiello, 1988), although it seems difficult to argue that it is all learning, given DeCasper's *Cat in the Hat* study. Whatever the source, it is remarkable that babies are paying attention to patterns and relationships among sounds and sights.

Cross-Modal Transfer. If you think about the way you receive and use perceptual information, you'll realize quickly that you rarely have information from only one sense at one time. Ordinarily you have *both* sound and sight, or touch and sight, or still more complex combinations of smell, sight, touch, and sound. You are able to combine this information so that you know the sound that goes with a particular sight or the feel that goes with a particular sight. You can also transfer information from one sense to another. If you have seen an object but not touched it, you could probably still pick it out in the dark; you know what it *ought* to feel like, based on what you saw—an example of **cross-modal transfer**.

If you look again at Table 5.1, you'll see that Piaget believed that the most primitive integration of sensory information, such as looking in the direction of some sound or watching your hand if you touch or grasp something, did not happen until at least substage 2, and that cross-modal transfer did not develop until substage 4, at about 8 months of age or later. Both these assumptions have now been questioned. Babies obviously combine at least vision and hearing immediately after birth, because they will turn their heads to look toward the source of a sound. And it now looks as if cross-modal transfer is possible as early as 1 month of life and is common by 6 months (Rose & Ruff, 1987).

For example, if you attach a nubby sphere to a pacifier and let a baby suck on it, you can test for cross-modal transfer by showing the baby pictures of the nubby sphere and a smooth sphere. If the baby looks longer at the nubby sphere, that would indicate cross-modal transfer. When Meltzoff and Borton (1979) did this, they found that 1-month-old babies preferred to look at the picture of the object they had sucked on earlier. Other investigators have not always found such transfer in infants as young as 1 month, so the phenomenon is not robust at this age.

In older infants, intersensory integration or transfer is more consistently found, not only between touch and sight, but between other modalities such as sound and sight. For instance, in several delightfully clever experiments, Elizabeth Spelke has shown that 4-month-old infants can connect sound rhythms with movement (1979). She showed babies two films simultaneously. One film showed a toy kangaroo bouncing up and down, the other a donkey bouncing up and down, with one of the animals bouncing at a faster rate. Out of a speaker located between the two screens the infant heard a tape recording of a rhythmic bouncing sound that matched one of the two rates. In this situation, babies spent more time watching the film that had the rhythm matching the sound they were hearing, indicating that by an early age babies have hooked up sound with vision and expect the patterns from the two sources to match.

This burgeoning research on cross-modal transfer has raised some interesting theoretical issues. For one thing, it is now perfectly clear that the baby does not need language to transfer information from one mode to another. And the fact that at least some transfer is possible within the first few weeks of life, before the infant has had much direct experience with either mode, certainly points rather strongly to the possibility that *some* connections may be built in.

Eight-month-old Ruth may not be looking at this toy while she is chewing on it, but she is nonetheless learning something about how it *ought* to look, based on how it feels in her mouth and in her hands.

All in all, Piaget seems to have been wrong not only about the specific ages at which things develop, but perhaps even in whether they need to "develop" at all. It begins to look as if there is a great deal of basic understanding about the events in the world that is already built in at birth—a conclusion buttressed by recent studies of the object concept.

Development of the Object Concept

One of Piaget's most striking observations of infants was that they seem not to have a grasp of certain basic properties of objects that adults all take completely for granted. You and I know that objects exist outside our own actions on them. My computer exists independent of my looking at it, and I know that it continues to sit here in my office even if I am somewhere else—an understanding that Piaget called **object permanence.** Piaget thought that babies did not initially know any of these things about objects and acquired this understanding only gradually during the sensorimotor period (Piaget 1952, 1954; Flavell, 1985).

In substages 1 and 2, the baby may follow a person or object with his eyes until it is out of view, but then appears to lose interest. Out of sight, literally out of mind. Piaget believed that a young infant did not understand in any way that other people or objects have independent existence and that they continue to exist even when he cannot see them or act on them.

In substage 3 the baby begins to anticipate the movement of objects. If he drops a toy over the edge of his high chair, he may look over the edge to the place where it is likely to have dropped. If you cover part of a toy with a cloth while the baby is reaching for it, he may continue to reach for it. But if you fully cover the toy he will stop reaching and show no further interest—a pattern you can see in the photos in Figure 5.2.

In substage 4, starting at roughly 8 months of age, the baby will continue reaching for the object or will pull away a cover he has seen you put over some desired object. But babies this age show a curious limitation in this new behavior. Suppose you hide a toy several times in one place, and the baby successfully uncovers it each time. Then—in full view of the baby—you now hide the toy in a second place or cover it with a different cloth. Babies in substage 4 will now search for the toy in the *first* location. Piaget thought that this showed that the baby doesn't yet have a full internal representation of the object

Figure 5.2 A baby in substage 3 of the development of object constancy. She stops reaching as soon as the screen is put in front of the toy and shows no sign that she knows that the toy is still there.

or an understanding that the object can be moved around. Instead, he has developed a sensorimotor scheme that links the toy with reaching in the first location. In learning theory terms, he has developed a simple sensorimotor habit rather than a full understanding of the permanence of objects.

In substage 5 the baby searches wherever the toy was most recently seen. Thus the baby is separating the objects from his own actions to retrieve it, a major new step on the road to object permanence.

This sequence of development has been so compelling, so interesting, and so surprising to many researchers (and parents) that it has been the subject of reams of research. Until recently, most researchers had concluded that Piaget's description of the sequence of development of the object concept was correct. Certainly, if you follow Piaget's procedures, you will see essentially the same results among children in all cultures.

Newer research, though, points to the possibility that very young babies have far more understanding of the properties of objects, including their permanence, than Piaget supposed. For example, Rene Baillargeon (1987; Baillargeon, Spelke & Wasserman, 1985; Baillargeon & DeVos, 1991), in a series of clever studies, has shown that babies as young as 3½ or 4 months show clear signs of object permanence if you use a *visual* response rather than a reaching response to test it. Similarly, in a whole series of experiments, Elizabeth Spelke (1991) has shown that young infants respond to objects in a far less transitory and ephemeral way than Piaget thought. In particular, 2- and 3-month-olds are remarkably aware of what kinds of movements objects are capable of—even when they are out of sight. They expect objects to continue to move on their initial trajectory, and show surprise if the object appears somewhere else. They also seem to have some awareness that solid objects cannot pass through other solid objects.

In one experiment, Spelke (1991) used the procedure shown schematically in the

---

ACROSS CULTURES
Sensorimotor Development in African Babies

If Piaget is correct about the universality of the sequences of development he describes, then we ought to see essentially the same patterns in children in every culture, regardless of the specifics of the child's upbringing. A variety of studies in other cultures show precisely that.

For example, in Zambia babies are typically carried about in a sling on their mother's back. They have few toys to play with and actually spend very little time on the floor or in any position in which they have much chance of independent movement until they are able to sit up at about 6 months. At that point they are usually placed on a mat near the mother, but mothers in this culture do not see it as their role to provide play or stimulation for the baby. Susan Goldberg (1972), who observed 38 babies in Zambia from 2 months of age until the end of their first year, found that at 6 months they were ahead of the American norms on a measure of the object concept. The pattern was reversed when the babies were 9 and 12 months old. At both these ages, the Zambian babies were slightly behind the U.S. norms, a difference Goldberg attributes to the fact that at these ages the Zambian babies were highly fearful of the strange white experimenter, and thus very difficult to test.

Studies in other African cultures generally show African babies to be slightly ahead of French or American comparison groups in most aspects of sensorimotor development (Dasen & Heron, 1981). At the same time, there are striking commonalities. Here's one example:

In one item of [a French test of sensorimotor development], the baby is given a red plastic tube and a chain of paperclips without any instruction on what to do with these objects. All French babies, once they have reached Piaget's substage 5, are observed to make some attempt to have the chain pass through the tube, and they gradually solve the problem in a series of successive adaptations. African babies (Dasen et al., 1978), although they have never seen such strange objects as a plastic tube and paperclips, combine them in exactly the same way, making the same errors and finding the same progressively adapted solutions. (Dasen & Heron, 1981, pp. 305–306)

upper part of Figure 5.3. Two-month-old babies were repeatedly shown a series of events like that in the "familiarization" section of the figure: A ball starting on the left-hand side was rolled to the right and disappeared behind a screen. The screen was then taken away and the baby could see that the ball was stopped against the wall on the right. After the baby got bored looking at this sequence (habituated), he or she was tested with two variations, one "consistent" and one "inconsistent." In the consistent variation, a second wall was placed behind the screen and the sequence run as before, except now when the screen was removed, the ball could be seen resting up against the nearer wall. In the inconsistent variation, the ball was surreptitiously placed on the *far* side of the new wall. When the screen was removed the ball was visible in this new and presumably impossible place. Babies in this experiment were quite uninterested in the consistent condition, but showed sharply renewed interest in the inconsistent condition, as you can see in the lower part of Figure 5.3, which shows the actual results of this experiment.

Findings like this have reopened the debate about Piaget's description of the development of object constancy. More generally, they have sparked a new discussion of that old friend, the nature/nurture issue (e.g., Fischer & Bidell, 1991; Diamond, 1991; Karmiloff-Smith, 1991). Just how much is built in at birth? Piaget, of course, never said that *nothing* was built in. He assumed that the baby came equipped with a repertoire of sensorimotor schemes. But his most fundamental theoretical proposal was that the child *constructed* his understanding of the world based on experience. On the other side of this new argument are those who see the baby as being endowed not only with specific knowledge about the world but with built-in constraints in the ways he processes information.

Spelke's own conclusion is that the development of the understanding of objects is

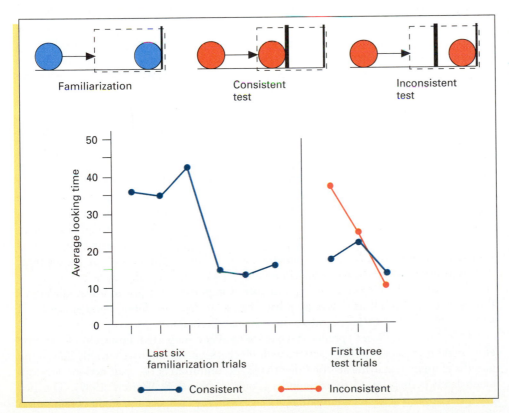

Figure 5.3 The top part of the figure shows a schematic version of the three conditions Spelke used. The bottom half shows the actual results. You can see that the babies stopped looking at the ball and screen after a number of familiarization trials, but showed renewed interest in the inconsistent version—a sign that the babies saw this as somehow different or surprising. The very fact that the babies found the inconsistent trial surprising is itself evidence that infants as young as 2 months have far more knowledge of objects and their behavior than Piaget thought. (*Source:* Spelke, 1991, Figures 5.3 and 5.4.)

Eight- to 12-month-old babies all over the world love to play peek-a-boo. The pleasure seems to come from knowing that the face or person still exists when it is covered up. When the face reappears, this confirms the baby's expectancy, and he is delighted.

Spelke contends that her research shows that babies have a great deal of knowledge about objects built-in from the beginning. How might a confirmed Piagetian reply?

more a process of elaboration than discovery. Newborn or very young babies may have considerable awareness of objects as separate entities, following certain rules. Certainly all the research on the perception of patterns suggests that babies pay far more attention to relationships between events than Piaget's model had led us to suppose. Indeed, the research on babies' preferences for attractive faces, which I talked about in the box on page 104, suggests that there may be built-in preferences for particular patterns. Still, even Spelke would not argue that the baby comes equipped with full-fledged knowledge of objects or a well-developed ability to experiment with the world. It remains to be seen just how much of Piaget's view will need to be changed because of work of this type, but it has raised a whole host of new questions.

Imitation

As a final example of research on infant cognition that has flowed from Piaget's theory, let me say just a word about studies of imitation. Piaget thought that infants could imitate actions they could see themselves make, such as hand gestures, as early as the first few months of life. But it wasn't until substage 4 (8–12 months) that Piaget thought the baby could imitate someone else's facial expressions. To do this seems to require some kind of cross-modal transfer: you must transfer information from the visual cues you get from seeing the other's face to the kinesthetic cues you get from your own facial movement. Otherwise, how could you match the expression? Finally, Piaget thought that deferred imitation, in which the baby sees something at one time but imitates it at a later time, did not occur until substage 6, when internal representation has already begun.

The issue of how soon a baby can imitate is important not just as a test of Piaget's theory. It may also tell us how soon a baby can learn from modeling—a major form of learning proposed by social-cognitive theorists like Bandura.

In broad terms Piaget's proposed sequence has been supported. Imitation of someone else's hand movements or their actions with objects seems to improve steadily during the months of infancy, starting at 1 or 2 months of age; imitation of two-part actions develops much later, perhaps at 15 to 18 months (Poulson, Nunes & Warren, 1989). The two exceptions to this general confirmation of Piaget's theory have been in studies of imitation in newborns and deferred imitation.

The study of imitation in newborns has been somewhat controversial. Several early studies showed that newborn babies would imitate certain facial gestures, particularly tongue protrusion (e.g., Meltzoff & Moore, 1983; Field et al., 1982). But this key finding has not always been replicated (Poulson et al., 1989). The critical factor seems to be how long the model demonstrates the action. If the model holds her tongue out for at least 60 seconds, newborns will imitate it; less time than that and the baby will not imitate (Anisfeld, 1991).

There is also a new dispute about how early deferred imitation can be seen. Meltzoff (1988) has found some ability to defer imitation over a 24-hour period in babies as young as 9 months; the more typical finding is that it occurs at 14 to 18 months, which is closer to what Piaget proposed.

These findings, like so many I have been describing to you in this chapter, suggest that babies may be more skillful than Piaget thought and that there may be more abilities built in from the beginning than he suggested. But they leave open the deeper question of whether the baby is *constructing* his understanding of the world through his experience or whether both his understanding and his experience is *constrained* by powerful built-in biases. You will not be surprised to know that many of these same issues arise yet again when we look at the early stages of the development of language in these same months.

▶ The Precursors of Language

Most of us think of "language" as beginning when the baby uses her first words, which happens (to the delight of most parents) at about 12 months of age. But there are all sorts of important developments that precede the first words.

Perception of Speech Sounds

Let's start with the basic perceptual skills. A baby cannot learn language until he can hear the individual sounds as distinct. Just how early can he do that? If you hadn't just read the rest of this chapter, you might be surprised by the answer. But by now, you know how this song goes. The answer is, remarkably early.

As early as 1 month, babies can discriminate between speech sounds like *pa* and *ba* (Trehub & Rabinovitch, 1972). By perhaps 6 months of age, they can discriminate between two-syllable "words" like *bada* and *baga* and can even respond to a syllable that is hidden inside a string of other syllables (like ti*bati* or ko*bako*) (Morse & Cowan, 1982; Goodsitt et al., 1984). It doesn't even seem to matter what voice quality the sound is said in. By 6 months, babies respond to individual sounds as the same, whether they are spoken by male or female voices or adult versus child voices (Kuhl, 1983).

Even more striking is the finding that babies are actually better at discriminating

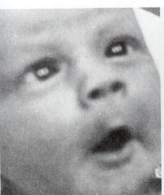

Figure 5.4 This mom was asked to model an exaggerated "surprise" expression to her newborn—an expression the baby imitated, providing further evidence that at least some complex kinds of imitation may be possible far earlier than Piaget thought. (*Source:* T. M. Field, Social perception and responsivity in early infancy. In T. M. Field, A. Huston, H. C. Quay, L. Troll & G. E. Finley [Eds.], *Review of human development.* Copyright 1982 by John Wiley & Sons, New York, p. 26.)

some kinds of speech sounds than adults are. Each language uses only a subset of all possible speech sounds. Japanese, for example, does not use the *l* sound that appears in English; Spanish makes a different distinction between the *d* and *t* sound than we do in English. It turns out that up to about 12 months of age, babies can accurately discriminate all sound contrasts that appear in *any* language, including sounds they do not hear in the language spoken to them. By 1 year of life, this ability has largely disappeared.

An unusually complete study by Janet Werker and Richard Tees (1984) illustrates the point. Combining cross-sectional and longitudinal designs, they first studied 6- to 8-month-old, 8- to 10-month-old, and 10- to 12-month-old babies being raised in English-speaking homes. Each baby was tested on three sound pairs, one heard in English (*ba* versus *da*), one from a North American Indian language, Salish (*ki* versus *qi*), and one from Hindi, a language from the Indian subcontinent (*ṭa* versus *ta*). You can see in Figure 5.5 that the 6- to 8-month-old English-environment babies could easily hear and respond to both the Hindi and Salish contrasts, but very few of the 10- to 12-month-olds could do so. When Werker and Tees later retested some of the 6-month-olds at 9 and 12 months, they found the same pattern. These babies *lost* the ability to make these discriminations. In separate tests, Werker and Tees found that 12-month-old Hindi infants could easily discriminate the Hindi contrast, and Salish toddlers could still hear the Salish contrast.

Results like these seem to be consistent with what we now know about the pattern of synaptic growth in the early months of life. You'll remember from Chapter 4 that many connections are initially created, followed by pruning. Thus young babies are "wired" in a way that allows discriminations along all possible sound continua. But only those pathways that are actually used in the language the child hears are retained; other synapses are pruned. Whether this is the explanation or not, it is certainly clear that the baby is paying attention to very detailed aspects of speech sounds from the earliest days of life.

Early Sounds and Gestures

The early ability to discriminate among sounds is not matched right away by much skill in producing sounds. From birth to about 1 month, the most common sound an infant makes is a cry, although there are other fussing, gurgling, and satisfied sounds. This repertoire expands at about 1 or 2 months, when we begin to hear some laughing and **cooing** vowel sounds, like *uuuuuu*. Sounds like this are usually signals of pleasure in babies, and may show quite a lot of variation in tone, running up and down in volume or pitch.

Figure 5.5 All the results shown here are for babies growing up listening to English. But each baby was tested on non-English language sounds. Specifically, each baby was tested for his or her ability to make discriminations between language sounds that appear in Salish and in Hindi, but not in English. The left side of the figure shows cross-sectional comparisons; the right side shows longitudinal data for a small number of babies tested three times over six months. You can see that at 6 and 8 months they were still able to make such discriminations, but they had lost the ability by 12 months. (*Source:* Werker & Tees, 1984, Figure 4, p. 61.)

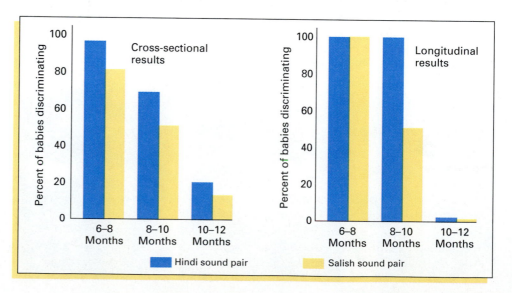

Consonant sounds appear only at about 6 or 7 months, frequently combined with vowel sounds to make a kind of syllable. Babies this age seem to begin to play with these sounds, often repeating the same sound over and over (such as *babababababa* or *dahdahdah*). This new sound pattern is called **babbling,** and it makes up about half of babies' noncrying sounds from about 6 to 12 months of age (Mitchell & Kent, 1990).

Any parent can tell you that babbling is a delight to listen to. It also seems to be an important part of the preparation for spoken language. For one thing, we now know that infants' babbling gradually acquires some of what linguists call the *intonational pattern* of the language they are hearing—a process Elizabeth Bates refers to as "learning the tune before the words" (Bates, O'Connell & Shore, 1987). At the very least, infants do seem to develop at least two such "tunes" in their babbling. A babbling sequence with a rising intonation at the end seems to signal a desire for a response; a falling intonation requires no response.

A second important point about babbling parallels the Werker and Tees findings. When babies first start babbling, they typically babble all kinds of sounds, including some that are not part of the language they are hearing. But at about 9 or 10 months, their sound repertoire gradually begins to drift toward the set of sounds they are listening to, with the unheard sounds dropping out (e.g., Oller, 1981). Findings like these do not tell us that babbling is *necessary* for language development, but they certainly make it look as if babbling is part of a connected developmental process that begins at birth.

Gestures in the First Year.   Another part of that connected developmental process may be a kind of gestural language that develops at around 9 or 10 months. At this age we first see babies "demanding" or "asking" for things using gestures or combinations of gestures and sound. A 10-month-old baby who apparently wants you to hand her a favorite toy may stretch and reach for it, opening and closing her hand, accompanied by whining sounds or other heartrending noises. There is no mistaking the meaning. At about the same age, babies will enter into those gestural games much loved by parents, like "patty-cake," or "soooo-big," or "wave bye-bye" (E. Bates, Camaioni & Volterra, 1975; E. Bates et al., 1987).

Interestingly, the infant's ability to *understand* the meaning of individual words (which linguists call **receptive language)** also seems to begin at about 9 or 10 months. In one recent study, Elizabeth Bates and her colleagues asked mothers about their 10-month-old babies' understanding of various words (Bates, Bretherton & Snyder, 1988). On average, the mothers listed 17.9 words understood. By 13 months, that number was up to nearly 50 words. Because infants of 9 to 13 months typically do not speak any individual words, findings like these make it clear that receptive language comes before **expressive language**. Children understand before they can speak.

Adding up these bits of information, we can see that a whole series of changes seems to come together at 9 or 10 months: the beginning of meaningful gestures, the drift of babbling toward the heard language sounds, imitative gestural games, and the first comprehension of individual words. It is as if the child now understands something about the process of communication and is intending to communicate to the adult.

The First Words

Somewhere in the midst of all the babbling, the first words appear, typically at about 12 or 13 months (Capute et al, 1986). The baby's first word is an event that parents eagerly await, but it's fairly easy to miss. A *word*, as linguists usually define it, is any sound or set of sounds that is used consistently to refer to some thing, action, or quality. But it can be *any* sound. It doesn't have to be a sound that matches words the adults are using. Brenda, a little girl studied by Ronald Scollon (1976), used the sound *nene* as one of her first words. It seemed to mean primarily liquid food, because she used it for *milk*, *juice*, and

At 9 months, Alexandra probably hasn't spoken her first word, but chances are she already understands quite a few. Receptive language is usually ahead of expressive language.

bottle. But she also used it to refer to *mother* and *sleep.* (You can see some of Brenda's other early words in Table 5.2.)

Often, a child's earliest words are used only in one or two specific situations and in the presence of many cues. The child may say "doggie" or "bow-wow" only to such promptings as "How does the doggie go?" or "What's that?" Later the child may use a word spontaneously and in a wider variety of contexts, as if she had grasped the basic *symbolic* characteristic of language—that things have names (Bates, Bretherton & Snyder, 1988).

Adding New Words. Once the milestone of the first word is reached, toddlers typically go through a period of slow growth until they reach a vocabulary of perhaps 30 words. After that, it is common for children to spurt ahead, adding 10, 20, or 30 words in a period of weeks. You can see just such a pattern of slow and then rapid growth in

TABLE 5.2 Brenda's Vocabulary at 14 Months	
Sound	**Apparent Meaning**
aw u	I want, I don't want
nae	no
daedi	daddy, baby, picture in magazine
daeyu	down, doll
nene	liquid food
e	yes
maem	solid food
ada	another, other

Source: R. Scollon, *Conversations with a one year old.* Honolulu: The University Press of Hawaii, 1976, pp. 47.

RESEARCH REPORT
Early Gestural "Language" in the Children of Deaf Parents

Deaf children of deaf parents are a particularly interesting group to study if we want to understand language development. The children do not hear oral language, but they are exposed to *language*—sign language. Do these children show the same sequence of language development as do hearing children, only using gestural language?

The answer seems to be yes. Deaf children show a kind of "sign babbling" between about 7 and 11 months of age, much as hearing children babble sounds in these same months. Then at 8 or 9 months of age, deaf children begin using simple gestures, such as pointing, which is just about the same age that we see such gestures in hearing babies of hearing parents. At about 12 months of age, deaf babies seem to display their first *referential* signs—that is, signs in which a gesture appears to stand for some object or event, such as signalling that they want a drink by making a motion like a cup being brought to the mouth (Petitto, 1988).

Folven and Bonvillian (1991) have studied an equally interesting group—hearing children of deaf parents. These babies are exposed to sign language from their parents and to hearing language from their contacts with others in their world, including

TV, teachers, other relatives, playmates. In this small sample of nine babies, the first sign appeared at an average age of 8 months, the first referential sign at 12.6 months, and the first spoken word at 12.2 months. What is striking here is that the first referential signs and the first spoken words appear at such similar times and that the spoken words appear at such a completely normal time, despite the fact that these children of deaf parents hear comparatively little spoken language.

In a further parallel, Petitto (1988) notes that deaf children make many of the same kinds of linguistic mistakes, at the same ages we see/hear them in hearing children. For example, deaf children using sign language have difficulty with the signs for *you* and *me*, acquiring these pronouns only at about the time we hear them in a speaking child, even though in sign language such pronouns involve straightforward pointing—a gestural skill the child seems to have before age 1.

This marked similarity in the sequence and timing of early language steps in the deaf and the hearing child provides strong support for the argument that the baby is somehow primed to learn "language" in some form, be it spoken or gestural.

Figure 5.6, which shows the vocabulary growth curves of six children studied longitudinally by Goldfield and Reznick (1990).

These early words are most likely to be names for things or people, like *ball, car, milk, doggie, he,* or *that.* Verblike words tend to develop later, perhaps because they label *relationships* between objects rather than just a single object (Gleitman & Gleitman, 1992). For example, over half the first 50 words of the eight children Katherine Nelson studied were nounlike words, while only 13 percent were action words (Nelson, 1973). The same

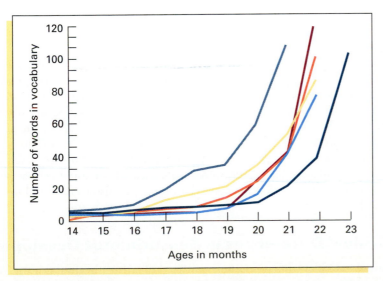

Figure 5.6 Each of the lines in this figure represents the vocabulary growth of one of the 13 children studied by Goldfield and Reznick in their longitudinal study. The six children shown here each acquired new words in the most common pattern: slow initial growth followed by a fairly rapid spurt. Other children in this same study, however, acquired their early words in a more gradual fashion, without the spurt. (*Source:* Goldfield & Reznick, 1990, Figure 3, p. 177.)

ACROSS CULTURES
Early Words by Children in Different Cultures

Children in every culture studied by linguists have shown the same tendency to learn words for people or things before they learn words for actions or other parts of speech. See the table below for (translated) samples from the very early vocabularies of one child from each of four cultures, all studied by Dedre Gentner (1982).

Isn't it impressive how very similar these early vocabularies are? Of course there are some variations, but all these children had names for Mommy and Daddy, for some other relative, for other live creatures, for food. All but the Chinese child had words for toys or clothes. All four had also learned more naming words than any other type, with very similar proportions. They don't know the *same* words, but the pattern is remarkably similar.

	German Boy	English Girl	Turkish Girl	Chinese Girl
Some of the words for people or things	Mommy	Mommy	Mama	Momma
	Papa	Daddy	Daddy	Papa
	Gaga	babar	Aba	grandmother
	baby	baby	baby	horse
	dog	dog	food	chicken
	bird	dolly	apple	uncooked rice
	cat	kitty	banana	noodles
	milk	juice	bread	flower
	ball	book	ball	wall clock
	nose	eye	pencil	lamp
	moon	moon	towel	
Total percentage of naming words	67%	69%	57%	59%
Some of the nonnaming words	cry	run	cry	go
	come	all gone	come	come
	eat	more	put on	pick up
	sleep	bye-bye	went pooh	not want
	want	want	want	afraid
	no	no	hello	thank you

pattern has been found in studies of children learning other languages as well, as you can see in the "across cultures" box above.

However, this noun-before-verb pattern does not hold for all children. Katherine Nelson (1973) first noticed that some toddlers use what she called an **expressive style**. For them, most early words are linked to social relationships rather than to objects. They often learn pronouns (*you, me*) early, and use many more of what Nelson calls "personal-social" words, such as *no, yes, want,* or *please*. Their early vocabulary may also include some multiword strings, like *love you* or *do it* or *go away*. This is in sharp contrast to children who use what Nelson calls a **referential style**, whose early vocabulary is made up predominantly of nounlike words. Observations like this remind us that we need to search not just for common developmental pathways, but also to note and try to understand individual variations.

It seems reasonable to guess that referential and expressive style babies would differ from each other in other ways as well. Can you make any guesses about just what those differences might be?

▶ Individual Differences in Sensorimotor Development

Discussions of individual differences in cognitive skill are nearly always cast in "cognitive power" terms. We ask whether there are differences in *rate* of development, and whether such differences in rate are consistent over time. Questions of this kind about infant development have an important practical implication: If we could accurately measure differences in infants' rate (or pattern) of development in the early months of life, then it might be possible to identify infants who are later going to have problems learning to read or to perform in school in other ways. It might then be possible to intervene very early, perhaps thereby averting or at least ameliorating the problem.

One of the motivations behind the development of the various infant IQ tests was just such a hope that test scores could be used to help identify infants with current or prospective problems. Typically, these tests are constructed rather like IQ tests for older children: They include a series of items identified as suitable for children of particular ages, or a series of items of increasing difficulty. The child's performance is then compared to the average performance of other children the same age to yield an IQ-like score. In the case of infant tests, the items measure primarily sensory and motor skills, such as:

Reaching for a dangling ring (a 3-month-old item)

Uncovering a toy hidden by a cloth (8 months)

Putting cubes in a cup on request (9 months)

Building a tower of three cubes (17 months)

In the most widely used modern version of such a test, the **Bayley Scales of Infant Development** (Bayley, 1969), the score is subdivided into two parts, one reflecting mental development and the other motor development.

Many (but not all) of those who devised such infancy tests assumed that they were measuring the same basic intellectual processes as are measured by the tests for older children. But the empirical results do not support that assumption. Scores on infant tests do not predict later IQ test scores at all well. The typical correlation between a 12-month Bayley mental test score and a 4-year-old IQ score is only about .20 to .30 (e.g., Bee et al., 1982)—significant, but not robust. Bayley's test and others like the Denver Developmental Screening Test are effective in identifying children with serious developmental delays (Frankenberg et al., 1975; M. Lewis & Sullivan, 1985). But as a more general predictive tool to forecast later IQ or school performance, such tests have not been nearly as useful as many had hoped. Ten years ago, Robert McCall summarized the empirical findings flatly:

Nearly 50 years of research shows that [correlations] from infant behavior to later I.Q. are sufficiently low to be conceptually uninteresting and clinically useless. (McCall, 1981, p. 141)

Building a tower of three cubes is an item at the 17-month-level on the Bayley Scales of Infant Development.

McCall concluded that we should give up the search for a link between the speed or sequence of development of sensorimotor intelligence and later cognitive skills. But McCall—and many other psychologists as well—has changed his mind because of newer work emerging from an information processing framework.

Ten or fifteen years ago, a number of researchers began to argue that we were looking in the wrong place for infant predictors of later intellectual functioning (e.g., Fagan & McGrath, 1981; M. Lewis & Brooks-Gunn, 1981; Miranda & Fantz, 1974). We needed instead to measure the infant's ability to process information in some very fundamental way. The strategy they suggested was to measure rate of habituation in 3- and 4-month-old infants. In the typical procedure, researchers count how many repeated exposures it takes before a baby stops responding with interest to a stimulus. The speed with which such habituation takes place may tell us something about the efficiency of the perceptual/conceptual system and its neurological underpinnings. And if such efficiency lies behind some of the characteristic we normally call "intelligence," then it is possible that individual differences in rate of habituation in the early months of life may predict later intelligence test scores.

That is exactly what researchers have now found. The rate of habituation shown by 4- to 6-month-old babies is correlated positively with IQ and language development in preschool and elementary school. That is, slower habituation is associated with lower IQ and poorer language and faster habituation is associated with better IQ (Bornstein, 1989; Colombo & Mitchell, 1990; Fagan, 1984; Sigman et al., 1991). The average correlation is in the range of .45 to .50, which is certainly not perfect but is notably higher than the correlations we see between standard infant IQ scores and later IQ or school performance. Given the difficulties involved in measuring habituation rate in babies, the correlations are actually quite remarkably high.

Certainly these correlations do not prove that intelligence, as we measure it on an IQ test, is only a reflection of some kind of "speed of basic processing." But results like these underline the potential importance of looking at the underlying components of information processing if we want to understand individual differences in skills in early infancy. They also suggest the direction we might go to devise more predictive tests of infant intelligence. In fact, Fagan has developed just such a test, based heavily on measures of habituation rate in early infancy (Fagan & Shepherd, 1986).

▶ Cognitive Development in Infancy: An Overall Look

In a number of important respects, Piaget seems to have underestimated the ability of infants to store, remember, and organize sensory and motor information. Very young babies pay much more attention to patterns, to sequence, to prototypical features than Piaget thought, and can apparently remember them over at least short intervals. Many current theorists have taken this evidence to mean that the baby comes equipped with a wide range of built-in knowledge or inborn constraints on his ways of understanding the world around him.

On the other side of the argument, however, is the obvious fact that newborns, despite their remarkable perceptual and cognitive abilities, are *not* as skilled as 6-month-olds or 12-month-olds. Newborns do not use gestures to communicate, they do not talk, they do not show deferred imitation. Six-month-olds do not combine several strategies to achieve some goal and do not seem to experiment with objects in the same way as do older babies. Even at 12 months toddlers do not seem to use symbols to stand for things in any general way. They use a few words, but they don't yet show pretend play, for example. So despite all the new and fascinating evidence that casts some doubt on some of Piaget's observations and on his basic theorizing, it still appears to be correct to describe the infant as

If you believed that newborn infants could not see, could hear only a little, and could not learn—as many pediatricians did believe until fairly recently—how would you behave differently than you would after reading this chapter?

sensorimotor rather than *symbolic* in her thinking. Over the first 18 to 24 months the baby seems to be building toward such symbol use, a shift that John Flavell correctly sees as remarkable:

> A cognitive system that uses symbols just seems . . . to be radically, drastically, qualitatively different from one that is not. So great is the difference that the transformation of one system into the other during the first 2 years of life still seems nothing short of miraculous to me, no matter how much we learn about it. (1985, p. 82)

Summary

1. When we study the development of intelligence or cognition, we need to distinguish between three traditions, one focusing on intellectual power, a second on intellectual structure, and the third on information processing skills.

2. Studies of infant cognition have been most strongly influenced by Piaget's structural view of intelligence.

3. Piaget described the sensorimotor infant as beginning with a small repertoire of basic schemes, from which she moves toward symbolic representation in a series of six substages.

4. Substage 1 is essentially automatic pilot; substage 2 includes coordination of different modalities; in substage 3 the baby focuses more on the outside world; in substage 4 causal connections are understood and the object concept is grasped in a preliminary way; in substage 5 the baby begins to experiment more fully; and in substage 6 we see first signs of symbol usage.

5. Babies are able to learn by both classical and operant conditioning within the first few weeks of life, earlier than Piaget thought.

6. Newborns are also able to habituate to repeated stimuli, indicating that they have the ability to "recognize" that something has been experienced before.

7. In the first weeks of life, infants appear to be intent on locating objects; after about 2 months, they seem intent on identifying objects, so their method of scanning changes.

8. Newborns can also discriminate Mom from other people in the first weeks of life, first by sound and smell, somewhat later by sight alone. By 5 or 6 months they can discriminate among some emotional expressions.

9. From the earliest weeks, babies respond to the patterns of stimuli, or to relationships among stimuli, such as "big over small," or the sound of a particular story or melody. They also prefer to look at attractive rather than at less attractive faces.

10. Babies also show cross-modal transfer as early as 1 month, far earlier than Piaget supposed.

11. Piaget described a sequence of development in the child's understanding of the concept of object permanence—that objects continue to exist when they are out of sight or not being acted on by the child. In Piaget's experiments, babies began to show real comprehension of this only at about 8 months.

12. Newer research suggests that babies may have far more elaborate understanding of the properties of objects—including their permanence—at much earlier ages than Piaget supposed, although this is still under debate.

13. Babies are able to imitate some facial expressions in the first days of life. But they do not show deferred imitation until much later.

14. First words, at about 12 months of age, are preceded by a number of important steps.

15. Babies can discriminate among speech sounds in the first weeks. They can, in fact, make discriminations that adults cannot make.

16. Babies' earliest sounds are cries, followed at about 2 months by cooing, then by babbling at about 6 months. At 9 months babies typically use meaningful gestures and can understand a small vocabulary of spoken words.

17. After the first word, babies add words slowly for a few months and then rapidly. Most have a vocabulary of about 50 words by 18 months.

18. The earliest words are more often names for people or objects than they are words to describe actions.

19. Attempts to measure individual differences in sensorimotor development by constructing IQ-like tests have not been as successful as hoped; such tests are not strongly related to later measures of IQ.

20. Much more predictive are measures of more basic information processing skills in infancy, such as rate of habituation at 4 months, which is correlated with later IQ.

21. On the whole, Piaget seems to have underestimated the infant; there may be far more built-in at birth than Piaget supposed. But all would agree that there is progressive development, built on the base with which the baby begins. The early development culminates in the emergence of the ability to use symbols in play and in thought, at about 18 to 24 months of age.

Key Terms

babbling

Bayley Scales of Infant Development

cooing

cross-modal transfer

expressive language

expressive style

habituation

information processing

object permanence

receptive language

referential style

sensorimotor period

social referencing

Suggested Readings

Aslin, R. N. (1987). Visual and auditory development in infancy. In J. D. Osofsky (Ed.), *Handbook of infant development* (2nd ed.). New York: Wiley-Interscience. (Aslin has written a number of relatively recent summaries and reviews of the research on early perceptual development, of which this is perhaps the most easily understood by a nonexpert. Even so, this is quite technical and considerably more detailed than I have been in this chapter.)

Field, T. (1990). *Infancy.* Cambridge, MA: Harvard University Press. (One of an excellent series of books on topics in child development, written by experts but intended for lay readers. Field covers many of the topics I have discussed in this chapter, as well as in Chapter 6.)

Flavell, J. H. (1985). *Cognitive development* (2nd ed.). Englewood Cliffs, NJ: Prentice-Hall. (This is a first-rate basic text in the field, written by one of the major current figures in cognitive developmental theory. The introductory chapter and the chapter on infancy may be especially helpful if you find Piaget's theory somewhat hard to grasp.)

Haith, M. M. (1990). Progress in the understanding of sensory and perceptual processes in early infancy. *Merrill-Palmer Quarterly, 36,* 1–26. (In this relatively brief paper Haith looks back on the last 25 years of research on perceptual development. He comments not only on the knowledge gained but on the processes by which scientific progress has been made and the tasks still facing the field. Very interesting reading.)

SOCIAL AND PERSONALITY DEVELOPMENT IN INFANCY

6

At a social gathering several years ago I watched two young friends, Mark and Marcie, with their 4-month-old son Alexander. With very little effort, Alexander managed to attract everyone's attention. He looked around him, occasionally gave brief smiles, kicked his feet, shook a rattle, and cried once in a while. Those simple behaviors were enough to have all the adults in the room hovering over him, trying their best to entice a smile. I was not immune to his charms. I trotted out all my playing-with-baby tricks, raising my eyebrows, smiling broadly, calling his name, tickling him a bit on the cheek or on his feet, making clucking noises. My reward was one very small smile and a brief gaze.

Alex's parents, after four months of practice, were much more successful in this game. Either Mom or Dad could coax a smile from him within just a few seconds; either of them could easily soothe him if he cried.

My most immediate reaction to this scene was simple pleasure at seeing loving and attentive parents with their infant. But the psychologist in me was watching too. I could see all of Alex's social skills, his ability to entice. And I could see how much Alex and his parents had already learned about one another, how smoothly they performed a kind of "dance" of interaction. The baby brings his inborn and emerging physical and cognitive skills to this interaction; the parents bring their own skills and qualities as well as their instinctive responses to babies. To understand infants, we need to look at the development of these earliest relationships. We also need to look at the individual styles of behavior that each baby brings to the interaction with his caregivers.

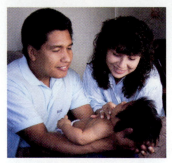

This mom and dad can probably easily coax a smile from their baby; even at this early stage they have learned each other's cues.

Think about your own relationships. In Bowlby's and Ainsworth's terms, which are attachments and which are affectional bonds?

Pick one of your attachment relationships and make a list of all the attachment behaviors you show toward that person. Are any of these the same as the kind of attachment behaviors we see in an infant?

Relationships between adult partners, like this couple, usually have all the hallmarks of a full attachment in Bowlby's terms.

Attachment Theory

The strongest theoretical influence in modern-day studies of infant-parent relationships is attachment theory, particularly the work of John Bowlby (1969, 1973, 1980, 1988a, 1988b), whose approach I mentioned briefly in Chapter 2. His ideas were rooted in psychoanalytic thought, particularly in the emphasis on the significance of the earliest relationship between mother and child. But he added important evolutionary and ethological concepts. In his view, babies are born with an innate tendency to create strong emotional bonds with their caregivers. Such relationships have *survival* value because they bring nurturance to the infant. They are built and maintained by an interlocking repertoire of instinctive behaviors that create and sustain proximity between parent and child or between other bonded pairs.

In Bowlby's writings and in the equally influential writings of Mary Ainsworth (1972, 1982; 1989; Ainsworth et al., 1978), there are several key concepts: affectional bond, attachment, and attachment behaviors.

Ainsworth defines an **affectional bond** as "a relatively long-enduring tie in which the partner is important as a unique individual and is interchangeable with none other. In an affectional bond, there is a desire to maintain closeness to the partner." (1989, p. 711.) An **attachment** is a subvariety of emotional bond in which a person's sense of security is bound up in the relationship. When you are attached, you feel (or hope to feel) a special sense of security and comfort in the presence of the other, and you can use the other as a "safe base" from which to explore the rest of the world.

In these terms, the child's relationship with the parent is an attachment, but the parent's relationship with the child is not. The parent presumably does not feel a greater sense of security in the presence of the infant or use the infant as a safe base. An adult's relationship with a very close friend or with an adult partner, however, typically is an attachment in the sense Ainsworth and Bowlby mean the term.

Because affectional bonds and attachments are internal states, we cannot see them directly. Instead, we deduce their existence by observing **attachment behaviors**, which are all those behaviors that allow a child or adult to achieve and retain proximity to someone else to whom he is attached. This could include smiling, making eye contact, calling out to the other person across a room, touching, clinging, crying. It is important to make clear that there is no one-to-one correspondence between the number of different attachment behaviors a child (or adult) shows on any one occasion and the strength of the underlying attachment. Attachment behaviors are elicited primarily when the individual has need of care or support or comfort. An infant is in such a needy state a good deal of the time. An older child, or an adult, will be likely to show attachment behaviors only when he is frightened or tired or otherwise under stress. It is the *pattern* of these behaviors, not the frequency, that tells us something about the strength or quality of the attachment or the affectional bond.

Attachment in Infancy

The attachment process is a two-way street. Both the baby and the parent develop bonds to each other, and we need to understand both processes. Let's begin with the parents.

The Parents' Bond to the Infant

If you read the popular press, I am sure you have come across articles proclaiming that mothers (or fathers) must have immediate contact with their newborn infant if they are to become properly bonded with the baby. This belief has been based primarily on the work of two pediatricians, Marshall Klaus and John Kennell (1976), who proposed the hypothesis that the first few hours after an infant's birth is a "critical period" for the mother's development of a bond to her infant. Mothers who are denied early contact, Klaus and Kennell thought, are likely to form weaker bonds and thus be at higher risk for a range of disorders of parenting.

Their proposal, as well as their supporting research, was one of many factors leading to significant changes in birth practices, including the now-normal presence of fathers at delivery. I would certainly not want to turn back the clock on such changes. But it now looks as if Klaus and Kennel's hypothesis is probably incorrect. Immediate contact does not appear to be either necessary or sufficient for the formation of a stable long-term affectional bond between parent and child (Myers, 1987).

A few studies show some short-term beneficial effects of very early contact. In the first few days after delivery, mothers with such contact may show more tender fondling or more gazing at the baby than is true of mothers who first held their babies some hours after birth (e.g., Campbell & Taylor, 1980; de Chateau, 1980). But there is little indication of a lasting effect. Two or three months after delivery, mothers who have had immediate contact with their newborns do not smile at them more or hold them differently than do mothers who had delayed contact.

Only in two subgroups of mothers is there a hint of a long-term effect. Among first-time mothers and among those who are at higher risk for problems with parenting—poverty-level mothers or very young mothers, for example—there are a few signs that early contact may make a difference.

For example, Susan O'Connor and her colleagues (O'Connor et al., 1980) randomly assigned some poverty-level mothers to a "rooming in" arrangement in which the mother cared for her infant in her own hospital room and thus had extended contact. Other mothers saw their infants only at feeding times. *Neither* group had immediate contact with the infant after birth, so the difference here is in the amount of contact in the first few days, not the timing of the first contact. These two groups were then tracked through the first 18 months of the children's lives. O'Connor was looking especially for any signs of "inadequacy of parenting," such as abuse of the child or the baby's failure to thrive. You can see the results in Table 6.1.

Obviously, very few mothers in either the rooming-in or normal-hospital groups showed inadequate parenting, but the rate was higher for the group that had had less contact with the infant in the early days. These findings raise the possibility that extended early contact may help *prevent* later parenting problems, but only among those mothers who are at high risk for such problems in the first place. For the majority of mothers, early contact does not seem to be an essential ingredient in the formation of a strong affectional bond between mother and infant.

A Second Step: Meshing Attachment Behaviors. Much more critical for the establishment of the parent's bond to the child is the opportunity for the parent and infant

If you were a hospital administrator and had to decide whether to have "rooming in" as a standard procedure for all mothers and babies, would you be persuaded by O'Connor's results? What other factors would you consider?

TABLE 6.1 Effect of Extended Early Contact on Adequacy of Parenting	Rooming-in Group (143 Cases)	Regular Hospital Care Group (158 Cases)
Number of children referred to Children's Protective Services for suspicion of abuse	1	5
Number of children hospitalized for illness or "failure to thrive"	1	8

Source: O'Connor et al., 1980, pp. 356–357.

Adults all over the world show this same "mock surprise" expression when they are talking to or playing with a baby. The mouth is open and turned up at the corners, the eyebrows are raised, the eyes are wide, and the forehead is wrinkled.

to develop a mutual, interlocking pattern of attachment behaviors—just what young Alex and his parents had already achieved. The baby signals his needs by crying or smiling; he responds to being held by being soothed or snuggling; he looks at the parents when they look at him. The parents, in their turn, enter into this two-person dance with their own (perhaps instinctive) repertoire of care-giving behaviors. They pick the baby up when he cries, respond to his signals of hunger or other need, smile at the baby when he smiles, gaze into his eyes when he looks at them. Some researchers and theorists have described this as the development of *synchrony* (e.g., Isabella, Belsky & von Eye, 1989).

One of the most intriguing things about this process is that we all seem to know how to do this particular dance and do it in very similar ways. In the presence of a young infant, most adults will automatically display a distinctive pattern of interactive behaviors, including smiling, raised eyebrows, and very wide-open eyes. And we all seem to use our voices in special ways with babies as well. In a study of mother-infant interactions among Chinese, German, and United States mothers, Hanus and Mechthild Papousek (1991) found that not only did all the mothers they listened to use a characteristically high-pitched and lilting voice, they also used the same intonation patterns. For example, they all tended to use a rising inflection when they wanted the baby to "take a turn" in the interaction, and a falling intonation when they wanted to soothe the baby.

But while we can perform all these attachment *behaviors* with many infants, we do not form a bond with every baby we coo at in the grocery store. For the adult, the critical ingredient for the formation of a bond seems to be the opportunity to develop real mutuality or synchrony—to practice the dance until the partners respond to each other smoothly and pleasurably. This takes time and many rehearsals, and some parents (and infants) become more skillful at it than others. In general, the smoother and more predictable the process becomes, the more satisfying it seems to be to the parents and the stronger their bond to the infant becomes. This second step appears to be *far* more important than the initial contact at birth in establishing a strong parental bond to the child. But this second process, too, can fail. I've explored some of the possible reasons for such a failure in the box on the opposite page.

Father-Child Bonds. Most of the research I have talked about has involved studies of mothers. Still, many of the same principles seem to hold for fathers as well. The father's bond, like the mother's, seems more dependent on the development of mutuality than on contact immediately after birth. Aiding the development of such mutuality is the fact that fathers seem to have the same repertoire of attachment behaviors as do mothers. In the early weeks of the baby's life, dads touch, talk to, and cuddle their babies in the same ways that mothers do (Parke & Tinsley, 1981).

Past these first weeks of life, however, we see signs of a kind of specialization of parents' behaviors with their infants and toddlers. Dads spend more time playing with the baby, with more physical roughhousing. Moms spend more time in routine care-giving and also talk and smile more at the baby (Parke & Tinsley, 1987). This does not mean that fathers have a weaker affectional bond with the infant; it does mean that the attachment behaviors they show toward the infant are typically somewhat different from those mothers show.

We do not yet know whether such sex differences in parenting behaviors are reflections of culturally based role definitions, or whether they might be instinctive, built-in differences. One crucial test would be to study families in which the father is the primary caregiver. So far we have only pale imitations of this crucial test—studies in which the father had been the primary caregiver or an equal caregiver for a few months of the child's early life. Unfortunately, the few studies of this type, done in Sweden, the United States, and Australia, have yielded totally contradictory results (Lamb et al., 1982; Field, 1978; Russell, 1982). For the moment, the question remains open.

THE REAL WORLD
Child Abuse and Other Consequences of Failure of Bonding

In the United States, in any given year about 3 percent of children suffer from neglect or from physical or sexual abuse (U.S. Bureau of the Census, 1990). Most such abuse is inflicted on older children; the average age of children in cases reported to Child Protective Services is 7. But in many cases the origins of later abuse or neglect may lie in a failure of the parent to form a strong affectional bond to the baby in the first months of life. How might such a failure occur?

The two-part system for fostering a strong bond between the parent and the infant is normally robust and effective. Most parents *do* form such bonds. But such a bond requires that both the infant and the parent have the necessary signals and skills. When either partner lacks the skills, the result can be a failure or weakening of the bond, with child abuse or neglect as one possible (though certainly not invariable) consequence.

On one side of the equation, the infant might lack the attachment behaviors needed to entice and hold the parent's attention and interaction. For example, Selma Fraiberg (1974, 1975) has studied a group of blind babies, who smile less than sighted infants and do not show mutual gaze. Most parents of blind infants, after several months of this, begin to think that their infant is rejecting them, or they conclude that the baby is depressed. These parents feel less strongly bonded to their blind infants than to their sighted infants. Similar problems can arise with parents of premature infants, who may be separated from their parents for the first weeks or months and then are likely to be quite unresponsive for the first weeks after they are home from the hospital.

Of course most blind or preterm infants, or others who are "different" in some way, do not end up being physically abused. Most parents manage to surmount these problems. But the rate of abuse is higher among preterm than term infants, and higher among babies who are sick a lot in the first few months (e.g., Sherrod et al., 1984).

A failure of bonding can just as well come from the parent's end of the system. A parent might lack "attachment skill" because she or he had been abused as a child and did not form a secure attachment with her or his own parents. The majority of parents who abuse their children were themselves abused as children—although it is important to emphasize that the reverse is not the case: the majority of adults who were abused children manage to break the cycle of violence and refrain from abusing their children (Zigler & Hall, 1989). Those who are unable to break this cycle are typically those who lack other social skills, who have no adequate social supports, or who are living under high levels of stress.

Another serious problem on the parents' side of the equation is depression, which not only disrupts the parent's nurturing behavior but affects the child's response as well. Babies interacting with depressed mothers or even with mothers who have been told to look depressed or "blank-faced," smile less and are more disorganized and distressed (e.g., Field et al., 1990; Cohn et al.,

1990; Gusella et al., 1988). The depressed mothers, for their part, are slower to respond to their infant's signals and are more negative—even hostile—to their infants (Rutter, 1990). Overall, these relationships appear to lack synchrony, that is, the mother and infant are not "dancing" well together. Furthermore, these deficiencies in the mother's behavior with the infant seem to persist even after the mother is no longer depressed—perhaps indicating that her bond with the infant is less firm. On the infant's side of the equation we also see generalization of the effect of the mother's depression. Tiffany Field and her colleagues (Field et al., 1988) have observed that 3-month-old babies with depressed mothers showed similar distressed or nonsynchronous behaviors when they interacted with a nondepressed adult.

Not all depressed mothers show this pattern of behavior. If they have a good marriage, good support from friends and other family, and if the baby has good interactive skills, depressed moms seem to be able to develop positive patterns of interaction with their babies (Teti, Gelfand & Pompa, 1990).

Probably you have noted a common theme in what I have said about the conditions that foster abuse, neglect, or poor parent-infant interactions. Any parent, regardless of depression or history of abuse, is more likely to abuse a child when her current life conditions are highly stressful. So abuse is more likely in families in which there is alcoholism in one parent (Famularo et al., 1986), large families, single-parent households, families living in poverty or in extremely crowded conditions (Garbarino & Sherman, 1980; Sack, Mason & Higgins, 1985; Pianta, Egeland & Erickson, 1989). Even these adverse conditions can be surmounted, though, if the parents have adequate emotional support, either from each other or from others outside the family.

Preventing child abuse that arises from such high stress levels or from parental depression has proven to be extremely difficult (Olds & Henderson, 1989). Intervention has been more successful in cases in which the problem seems to lie in the baby's lack of a full range of responses. For example, Fraiberg (1974) found that she could help the parents of blind babies to "read" the child's hand and body movements instead of waiting for smiles or eye contact. After such training, parents of blind babies found their attachment to the infant was strengthened.

The benefits of such training are not restricted to more secure attachments, either. Thomas Achenbach and his colleagues (Achenbach et al., 1990) have found that teaching parents to read the baby's signals was also helpful for the long-term development of low-birth-weight infants. Seven years after such instruction, the babies in the experimental group had mental test performance significantly higher than low-birth-weight babies whose families had had no intervention. In the long run, it may well be that the best strategies for preventing abuse will not be focused directly on the abuse but will instead focus on interventions that foster stronger and more secure attachments of parent to child, and child to parent.

Can you think of any other way a researcher might go about trying to figure out whether the differences between moms and dads in their typical way of interacting with babies are cultural or built-in?

The Development of the Infant's Attachment to the Parents

Like the parent's bond to the baby, the baby's attachment emerges gradually. Bowlby (1969) suggested three phases in the development of the infant's attachment, which I've sketched schematically at the top of Figure 6.1.

Phase 1: Nonfocused Orienting and Signaling.   Like Piaget, Bowlby thought the baby begins life with a set of innate behavior patterns that orient him toward others and signal his needs. Mary Ainsworth describes these as "proximity promoting" behaviors—they bring people closer. As you already know, the newborn can cry, make eye contact, cling, cuddle, and respond to care-giving efforts by being soothed. But at first, as Ainsworth says, "these attachment behaviors are simply emitted, rather than being directed toward any specific person" (1989, p. 710).

At this stage there is little evidence of an attachment. Nonetheless, the roots of attachment are to be found in this phase. The baby is building up expectancies, schemas, the ability to discriminate Mom and Dad from others. The smooth, predictable interactions that strengthen the parent's bond also form the base for the baby's emerging attachment.

Phase 2: Focus on One or More Figures.   By 3 months of age the baby begins to aim her attachment behaviors somewhat more narrowly. She may smile more to the people who regularly take care of her, and may not smile readily to a stranger. Yet despite the change, the infant does not yet have a full-blown attachment. There are still a number of people who are favored with the child's "proximity promoting" behaviors, and no one person, according to Bowlby, has become the "safe base." Children in this phase show no special anxiety at being separated from their parent and no fear of strangers (although take a look at the new study I've described in the "research report" on the opposite page for some counter evidence).

Phase 3: Secure-Base Behavior.   Bowlby thought that the baby forms a genuine attachment only at about 6 months of age. At the same time, the dominant mode of the baby's attachment behavior changes: She shifts from using mostly "come here" signals (proximity promoting) to what Ainsworth calls "proximity seeking," which we might think of as "go there" behaviors. Because the 6- to 7-month-old begins to be able to move about the world more freely by creeping and crawling, she can move *toward* the caregiver as well as enticing the caregiver to come to her. We also see a child of this age using the

Figure 6.1 This schematic may help you see how the various threads of the development of attachment are woven together.

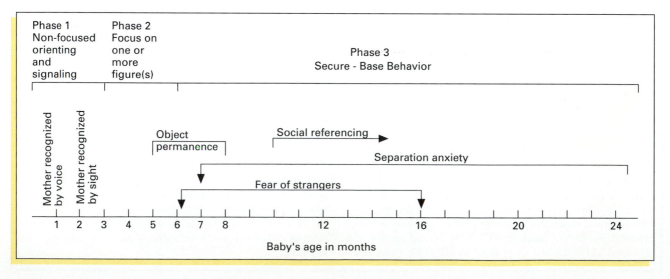

RESEARCH REPORT
New Findings on Early Attachment

Here is a good example of how new research can force the re-evaluation of theory. A Japanese researcher, Keiko Mizukami (Mizukami et al., 1990), proposes that babies develop clear attachments much earlier than Bowlby or Ainsworth suggested. The reason we don't readily see attachment in younger babies, Mizukami suggests, is that the 2- or 3-month-old cannot crawl or move about independently. Because the crucial test of an attachment is using the attachment figure as a safe base, the 2-month-old could never demonstrate that behavior even if an attachment were present.

Mizukami and his colleagues got around this problem by measuring babies' skin temperature, which tends to drop when the baby is under any kind of stress. Studying small groups of babies, they found that when the mother left the room, 8- to 16-week-old babies showed a drop in skin temperature. The drop was even larger if the mother was replaced by a stranger. However, if the mother remained with the baby when the stranger arrived, there was no equivalent sign of stress, all of which is consistent with the idea that babies as young as 2 to 4 months may already be using the mother as a ''safe base.'' If this finding is replicated, Bowlby, Ainsworth, and others may have to rethink the early stages of this developmental progression they propose.

"most important person" as a safe base from which to explore the world around her—one of the key signs that an attachment exists.

I should note that not all infants have a *single* attachment figure, even at this early point. Some may show strong attachment to both parents or to a parent and another caregiver, such as a baby-sitter or a grandparent. But even these babies, when under stress, usually show a preference for one of their favored persons over the others.

Once the child has developed a clear attachment, at about 6 to 8 months, several related behaviors also appear. One of these is social referencing, which I talked about in the last chapter. The 10-month-old uses his new abilities to discriminate among various facial expressions to guide his safe-base behavior. He begins to check out Mom's or Dad's expression before deciding whether to venture forth into some novel situation. At about the same age, babies also typically show both fear of strangers and separation protest.

Fear of Strangers and Separation Protest. Both these forms of distress are rare before 5 or 6 months, rise in frequency until about 12 to 16 months, and then decline. The research findings are not altogether consistent, but it looks as though fear of strangers normally appears first, while separation anxiety starts a bit later but continues to be visible for a longer period, a pattern I've marked in Figure 6.1.

Such an increase in fear and anxiety has been observed in children from a number of different cultures, and in both home-reared and day-care-reared children in the United States, all of which makes it look as if there are some basic cognitive or other age-related developmental timetables underlying this pattern (Kagan, Kearsley & Zelazo, 1978).

But while the general timing of these two phenomena may be common to virtually all children, the intensity of the fearful reaction is not. Children differ widely in how much fear they show toward strangers or toward novel situations. Some of this difference may reflect basic temperamental variations (Berberian & Snyder, 1982), a subject I'll take up in a moment. Heightened fearfulness may also be a response to recent upheaval or stress in the child's life, such as a recent move or a parent's job change (Thompson & Lamb, 1982). Whatever the origin of such variations in fearfulness, the pattern does eventually disappear in virtually all toddlers, typically by the middle of the second year.

Attachments to Mothers and Fathers

I pointed out earlier that both fathers and mothers appear to form strong bonds to their infants, although their behavior with infants varies somewhat. But what about the child's half of this relationship? Are infants and children equally attached to their fathers and mothers?

Dads like this one, who get involved with the day-to-day care of their babies, seem to reap the reward in a stronger attachment on the part of their babies.

In general, yes. From the age of 7 to 8 months, when strong attachments are first seen, infants prefer *either* the father or the mother to a stranger. And when both the father and the mother are available, an infant will smile at or approach either or both, *except* when he is frightened or under stress. When that happens, especially between 8 and 24 months, the child typically turns to the mother rather than the father (Lamb, 1981).

As you might expect, the strength of the child's attachment to the father at this early age seems to be related to the amount of time he has spent with the child. Gail Ross (Ross, Kagan, Zelazo & Kotelchuk, 1975) found she could predict a baby's attachment to the father by knowing how many diapers the dad changed in a typical week. The more diapers, the stronger the attachment! But greatly increased time with the father does not seem to be the only element. Michael Lamb and his Swedish colleagues have found that infants whose father was the major caregiver for at least a month in the first year of the child's life were nonetheless more strongly attached to their mothers than their fathers (Lamb, Frodi, Hwang & Frodi, 1983). For the father to be consistently *preferred* over the mother would probably require essentially full-time paternal care. As this option becomes more common in our society, it will be possible to study such father-child pairs to see if a preference for the father develops.

Internal Working Models of Attachment

Virtually all babies seem to go through the sequence I've described from preattachment to attachment. But the *quality* of the attachment they form to their parents differs. In Bowlby's terminology, infants create different **internal working models** of their relationship with parents and key others. This internal working model of attachment relationships includes such elements as the child's confidence (or lack of it) that the attachment figure will be available or reliable, the child's expectation of rebuff or affection, and the child's sense of assurance that the other is really a safe base for exploration.

The internal model begins to be formed late in the child's first year of life and continues to become more elaborated and firm through the first 4 or 5 years. By age 5, most children have clear internal models of the mother (or other caregiver), a self model, and a model of relationships. Once formed, such models shape and explain experiences and affect memory and attention. We notice and remember experiences that fit our model, and miss or forget experiences that don't match. In Piaget's terms, we more readily assimilate data that fit the model. More importantly, the model affects the child's behavior: The child essentially attempts to re-create, in each new relationship, the pattern with which he is familiar. Alan Sroufe gives a nice example that may make this point clearer:

> What is rejection to one child is benign to another. What is warmth to a second child is confusing or ambiguous to another. For example, a child approaches another and asks to play. Turned down, the child goes off and sulks in a corner. A second child receiving the same negative reaction skips on to another partner and successfully engages him in play. Their experiences of rejection are vastly different. Each receives confirmation of quite different inner working models. (1988, p. 23)

Secure and Insecure Attachments

All the theorists in this tradition share the assumption that the first attachment relationship is the most influential ingredient in the creation of the child's working model. Variations in that first attachment relationship are now almost universally described using Mary Ainsworth's category system (Ainsworth & Wittig, 1969; Ainsworth et al., 1978). She distinguishes between **secure attachment** and two types of **insecure attachment,** which she has assessed using a procedure called the **Strange Situation.**

The Strange Situation consists of a series of eight episodes in a laboratory setting. The child is first with the mother, then with the mother and a stranger, alone with the stranger, completely alone for a few minutes, reunited with the mother, left alone again, and then reunited first with the stranger and then the mother. Ainsworth suggested that children's reactions to this situation could be classified into three types: *securely attached*, *insecure/avoidant*, and *insecure/ambivalent* (also sometimes called *resistant*). Mary Main has suggested a fourth group, which she calls *insecure/disorganized/disoriented* (Main & Solo- man, 1985). I have listed some of the characteristics of the different types in Table 6.2.

These attachment types have been observed in studies in many different countries, and in every country secure attachment is the most common pattern (van IJzendoorn & Kroonenberg, 1988), occurring in 60 to 65 percent of all children studied. Where there is variability from one culture to the next, it is in the relative incidence of the two types of insecure attachment—differences I have explored in the "Across Cultures" discussion on pages 130–131.

In every culture, the probability that a child will be insecurely attached is much higher among children reared in poverty-level families, in families with a history of abuse, or in families in which the mother is diagnosed as seriously depressed (Spieker & Booth, 1988).

Because all the current work on the security of attachments has so many theoretical and practical ramifications, I need to take some time to explore some of the issues and implications.

Stability of Attachment Classification.   One of the key questions is whether security of attachment is stable over time. Does a child who is securely attached to his mother at 12 months still show the same secure attachment at 24 or 36 months? Is it still present at school age? This is a particularly important question for those researchers and therapists who are concerned about the possible permanence of effects of early abuse or neglect or other sources of insecure attachment. Can children recover from such early treatment? And is an initially securely attached child permanently buffered from the effects of later difficult life circumstances?

The answer—as usual!—is yes and no. When the child's family environment or life circumstances are reasonably consistent, the security or insecurity of attachment does remain stable. For example, Everett Waters (1978) found that only 2 out of the 50 infants he studied changed in their category of attachment security from 12 to 18 months. And in a stable, middle-class sample, Mary Main and her colleagues (Main, Kaplan & Cassidy,

---

TABLE 6.2   Behavior of Securely and Insecurely Attached Infants in the Strange Situation at 12 Months of Age

Securely attached.   Child shows low to moderate levels of proximity seeking to mother; does not avoid or resist contact if mother initiates it. When reunited with mother after absence, child greets her positively and can be soothed if upset. Clearly prefers mother to stranger.

Insecurely attached: detached/avoidant.   Child avoids contact with mother, especially at reunion after an absence. Does not resist mother's efforts to make contact, but does not seek much contact. Treats stranger and mother about the same throughout.

Insecurely attached: resistant/ambivalent.   Greatly upset when separated from mother, but mother cannot successfully comfort child when she comes back. Child both seeks and avoids contact at different times. May show anger toward mother at reunion and resists both comfort from and contact with stranger.

Insecurely attached: disorganized/disoriented.   Dazed behavior, confusion, or apprehension. Child may show strong avoidance following strong proximity seeking; may show simultaneously conflicting patterns, such as moving toward the mother but keeping gaze averted; may express emotion in a way that seems unrelated to the people present.

Sources: Ainsworth et al., 1978; Main & Solomon, 1985; Sroufe & Waters, 1977.

ACROSS CULTURES
Secure and Insecure Attachments in Different Cultures

If a secure or an insecure attachment is the product of particular patterns of parent-child interaction and if cultures differ in such patterns, then it would be reasonable to find varying proportions of secure, avoidant, and resistant attachments among children reared in different cultures.

In fact, researchers have found signs of just such cultural variation. The most thorough comparisons have come from a Dutch psychologist, Marinus van IJzendoorn, who has examined the results of 32 separate studies in eight different countries. He finds that the behavior of babies during the first few episodes in the Strange Situation, before the mother leaves the baby alone for the first time, is highly similar from one country to the next (Sagi, van IJzendoorn & Koren-Karie, 1991). In this situation, 12-month-old babies in Japan, Israel, Germany, the Netherlands,

Cross-Cultural Comparisons of Secure and Insecure Attachments

Country	Number of Studies	Percentage of Each Attachment Type		
		Secure	Avoidant	Ambivalent
West Germany	3	56.6	35.3	8.1
Great Britain	1	75.0	22.2	2.8
Netherlands	4	67.3	26.3	6.4
Sweden	1	74.5	21.6	3.9
Israel	2	64.4	6.8	28.8
Japan	2	67.7	5.2	27.1
China	1	50.0	25.0	25.0
United States	18	64.8	21.1	14.1
Overall Average	32	65.0	21.3	13.7

Source: *Based on Table 1 of van IJzendoorn & Kroonenberg, 1988, pp. 150–151.*

1985; Main & Cassidy, 1988) found strong correlations between ratings of security of attachment at 18 months and at 6 years. But when the child's circumstances change in some major way—such as when she starts going to day care or nursery school, or Grandma comes to live with the family, or the parents divorce or move—the security of the child's attachment may change as well, either from secure to insecure or the reverse (e.g., Thompson, Lamb & Estes, 1982, 1983). In poverty-level families, in which instability of circumstances is more common, changes in attachment security are also common (Vaughn et al., 1979).

The very fact that a child's security can change from one time to the next does not refute the notion of attachment as an internal working model. Bowlby suggested that for the first two or three years, the particular pattern of attachment a child shows is in some sense a property of each specific *relationship*. For example, recent studies of toddlers' attachments to mothers and fathers show that about 40 percent of the time the child is securely attached to one parent and insecurely attached to the other, with both possible combinations equally represented (Fox, Kimmerly & Schafer, 1991). It is the quality of each relationship that determines the child's security in that pair. If that relationship changes markedly, the security of the baby's attachment to that individual may change too. But by age 4 or 5, Bowlby argued that the internal working model becomes more general, more a property of the *child*, more generalized across relationships, and thus more resistant to change. At that point, the child tends to impose it upon new relationships, including relationships with teachers or peers.

Sweden, and the United States initially show interest in toys in the room and wander away from Mom. They show similar rates of proximity seeking and low rates of avoidance, all of which gives us confidence that the Strange Situation is tapping the same basic processes among children in many cultures.

Where differences exist it is in the babies' reactions to separation from and reunion with the mother—the crucial episodes for the classification of the security of the baby's attachment. You can see the percentage of babies classified in each group for each country in the table (left) (van IJzendoorn & Kroonenberg, 1988).

We need to be cautious about over-interpreting the information in this table, because in most cases there are only one or two studies from a given country, normally with quite small samples. The single study from China, for example, included only 36 babies. Still, the findings are thought-provoking.

The most striking thing about these data is actually the consistency rather than the difference. In each of the eight countries, a secure attachment is the most common pattern; in six of the eight, an avoidant pattern is the more common of the two forms of insecure attachment. Only in Israel and Japan is this pattern significantly reversed. Researchers and theorists have been struggling to explain these differences (Sagi, 1990; Main, 1990; Takahashi, 1986)

One possibility is that the Strange Situation is simply not an appropriate measure of attachment security in all cultures, van IJzendoorn's analysis notwithstanding. For example, because Japanese babies are rarely separated from their mothers in the first year of life, being left totally alone in the midst of the Strange Situation may be far more stressful for them, which might result in more intense, inconsolable crying and hence a classification of ambivalent attachment.

It is also possible that the *meaning* of a "secure" or "avoidant" pattern is different in different cultures, even if the percentages of each category are similar. Put another way, the secure baby in one culture may not have the same kind of internal working model as the secure baby in another culture. German researchers, for example, have suggested that an insecure avoidant classification in their culture may reflect not indifference by mothers but explicit training toward greater independence in the baby (Grossman et al, 1985).

On the other hand, research in Israel (e.g., Sagi, 1990) shows that the Strange Situation attachment classification predicts the baby's later social skills in much the same way as is found in U.S. samples, which suggests that the classification system is valid in both cultures.

At the moment the most plausible hypothesis is that the same factors in mother-infant interaction contribute to secure and insecure attachments in all cultures and that these patterns reflect similar internal models. But it will take more research like the Israeli work, in which the long-term outcomes of the various categories are studied, before we can be sure if this is correct.

Thus a child may "recover" from an initially insecure attachment or lose a secure one. But consistency over time is more typical, both because children's relationships tend to be reasonably stable for the first few years and because once the internal model is clearly formed, it tends to perpetuate itself.

Origins of Secure and Insecure Attachments. Where do these differences come from? For the development of a secure attachment, the common denominators seem to be both acceptance of the infant by the parents (e.g., Benn, 1986) and *contingent responsiveness* from the parents to the infant (Sroufe & Fleeson, 1986; Isabella, Belsky & von Eye, 1989; Pederson et al., 1990). Contingent responsiveness does not just mean that the parents love the baby or take care of the baby well, but rather that in their caregiving and other behavior toward the child they are sensitive to the child's own cues and respond appropriately. They smile when the baby smiles, talk to the baby when he vocalizes, pick him up when he cries, and so on. Parents of securely attached babies are also likely to be more emotionally expressive toward their babies—smiling more, using their voices in more expressive ways, touching the infant more (e.g., Egeland & Farber, 1984; Izard et al., 1991).

In contrast, mothers of babies rated as insecure/avoidant are likely to be "psychologically unavailable" to their infants (to use Alan Sroufe's phrase). Mothers may show such a withdrawn or neglecting pattern for a variety of reasons, but a common ingredient is depression in the mother—a phenomenon I talked about briefly in the "Real World" box on page 125.

If internal working models tend to persist and to affect later relationships, is this the same as saying that the first few years of life are a critical period for the creation of patterns of relationships? What counterevidence have you come across in this chapter?

THE REAL WORLD

Promoting Secure Attachments with Infant Carriers

In many parts of the world, particularly in the third world, mothers carry their babies with them most of the time, using some kind of sling or wrap that keeps the child against the mother's body—as the Masai mother is doing in the photo. In the United States, in recent years, variations on such a system have become a fairly common sight as well. Moms or dads are seen with a young infant snuggled against them, held by some kind of soft baby carrier. This not only allows moms or dads to have hands free to work or move while keeping the baby nearby, it also seems to foster a more secure attachment. Mary Ainsworth observed such a link in her studies in Uganda (Ainsworth, 1967). Now we have experimental data from the United States demonstrating the same effect.

Elizabeth Anisfeld and her colleagues (Anisfeld et al., 1990) gave each of a group of low-income mothers a gift right after the birth of their baby. Half were given a soft baby carrier, the other half received a plastic infant seat. Both groups were encouraged to use the item daily, and most did use the item at least some of the time. When the infants were tested in the Strange Situation at 13 months, Anisfeld found that 87 percent of those babies whose moms had carried them in the soft carrier were securely attached, compared to only 38 percent of the children of the moms

in the group that received the infant seat. Because the mothers had been assigned randomly to these two conditions, we can be more confident of the causal link between the expanded physical contact fostered by the baby carrier and the child's secure attachment.

The application to everyday life seems straightforward: More physical contact between baby and parents is beneficial, and a baby carrier is a particularly good way to achieve such contact. It is also a pleasure!

Infants rated as insecure/ambivalent are likely to have mothers who are inconsistent in their responses to the infant, rejecting the infant's bids for contact some of the time, responding positively at other times. Classifications in the fourth group, the insecure/disorganized/disoriented, are common among children who are maltreated as well as among those exposed to cocaine prenatally (Carlson et al., 1989; Lyons-Ruth et al., 1991; Rodning, Beckwith & Howard, 1991).

Long-Term Consequences of Secure and Insecure Attachment.   One of the reasons I have spent so much time talking about secure and insecure attachment is that this classification has proven to be extremely helpful in predicting a remarkably wide range of other behaviors in children, both as toddlers and in later childhood, as you can see in the summary list in Table 6.3. Those children rated as securely attached to their mothers have been found to be more sociable, more positive in their behavior toward others, and more emotionally mature in their approach to school and other nonhome settings.

Most of the information on which I have based Table 6.3 comes from studies of preschool or early elementary school children. But there is now at least one study in which children with known early attachment histories have been followed as far as preadolescence. Alan Sroufe and his colleagues, in a study I described briefly in Chapter 1, have now followed 32 of the several hundred children in his larger sample up to age 10 and 11 (Sroufe, 1989). These 32 were chosen specifically so that half had been securely attached as infants, and one-quarter had shown each of the two main types of insecure attachment.

Sroufe and his coworkers observed these children in a specially designed summer camp. The counselors rated each child on a range of characteristics, and observers noted how often children spent time together or with the counselors. Naturally, neither the counselors nor the observers knew what the children's initial attachment classification had been. The findings are clear: Those with histories of secure attachment were rated as

---

TABLE 6.3 Some Differences Between Securely and Insecurely Attached Children

Securely attached infants, at later ages, show a number of characteristics:

Sociability. They get along better with their peers, are more popular, have more friends. With strange adults they are more sociable, less fearful.

Self-esteem. They have higher self-esteem.

Relationships with siblings. They have better relationships with siblings, especially if both siblings are securely attached; if both are insecurely attached, the relationship is maximally antagonistic.

Dependency. They are less likely to seek attention from a teacher or other adult either by clinging or by being naughty.

Tantrums and aggressive behavior. They show less aggressive or disruptive behavior.

Compliance and good deportment. They are easier to manage in the classroom, requiring little overt control by the teacher but without high levels of docility.

Empathy. They show more empathy toward other children and toward adults. They do not show pleasure on seeing others' distress, which is fairly common among avoidant children.

Behavior problems. Results are mixed, but there are a number of studies that show that securely attached infants are less likely to show behavior problems at later ages.

Problem solving. They show longer attention span in free play, more confidence in attempting solutions to tasks with tools, use the mother or teacher more effectively as a source of assistance.

Sources: Cohn, 1990; Frankel & Bates, 1990; Greenberg & Speltz, 1988; Lütkenhaus, Grossman & Grossman, 1985; Matas, Arend & Sroufe, 1978; Plunkett, Klein & Meisels, 1988; Sroufe, 1988, 1989; Teti & Ablard, 1989.

more self-confident and as having more social competence. They complied more readily with counselor requests, expressed more positive emotions, and had a greater sense of their ability to accomplish things—a characteristic Sroufe and others call *agency*. Of the 8 children who had a history of attachment of the avoidant type, 5 showed patterns of either significant social isolation from peers or bizarre behavior; and all 8 of the children with histories of insecure attachment of the resistant or ambivalent type showed some pattern of deviant behavior. Four were markedly passive, 3 were notably hyperactive, and 1 was highly aggressive. Only 2 of the 16 securely attached children showed any of these deviant patterns.

I should emphasize again that these 32 children are the only ones yet studied over this length of time, and it is risky to build too tall a theoretical edifice on such a small empirical foundation. But Sroufe's data fit very well with the results from studies of younger children. Collectively the findings point to potentially long-term consequences of attachment patterns or internal working models of relationship constructed in the first year of life. But fluidity and change also occur, and we need to know much more about the factors that tend either to maintain or to alter the earliest models.

 ## The Development of the Sense of Self

During the same months that the baby is developing an attachment to Mom or Dad and creating an initial, primitive internal working model of attachment, she is also developing a parallel internal model of *self*. Just as she is figuring out that Mom or Dad continue to exist when they are out of sight, she is figuring out that *she* exists separately, and that she has qualities and properties.

Our thinking about infants' emerging sense of self has been strongly influenced by

ACROSS DEVELOPMENT
Links to Adult Attachments

Researchers who study attachment have begun to ask a new set of questions about the long-term consequences of early attachment patterns: Does the *parent's* internal model of attachment—which is presumably a product of his or her own early history—affect the security of the child's attachment?

Mary Main and her colleagues (Main, Kaplan & Cassidy, 1985) have devised an interview measure of the security of adult attachment in which adults are asked about their childhood experiences and their current relationship with their parents. In one question, adults are asked to choose five adjectives to describe their relationship with each parent and to say why they chose each adjective. They are also asked whether they ever felt rejected in childhood and how they feel about their parents currently. On the basis of the interview, the adult's internal working model of attachment is classified as being in one of three categories:

- *Secure-autonomous.* These individuals value attachment relations, see their early experiences as influential, but are objective in describing both good and bad qualities. Many remember positive early experiences, but it is also possible for someone who had experienced rejection to achieve this more tolerant and objective kind of model.
- *Dismissing.* These adults minimize the importance or the effects of their early experience. They may idealize their parents but have poor recall of their childhood, often denying negative experiences and emotions. Their emphasis is on their own personal strengths.
- *Preoccupied.* These individuals are still engrossed with their relationship with their parents, still actively struggling to please them or very angry at them. They are confused and ambivalent, but still engaged.

When these adult models are linked to the security of attachment displayed by the *children* of those adults, the expected pattern emerges: Adults with secure models of attachment to their own parents are much more likely to have infants or toddlers with secure attachments. Those with dismissing models are more likely to have infants with avoidant attachments, while adults with preoccupied attachments are more likely to have infants with ambivalent attachment (Main, Kaplan & Cassidy, 1985; Crowell & Feldman, 1988). Such a pattern has also been found in at least one prospective study in which the mother's attachment model was assessed *before* she gave birth to her first child (Fonagy, Steele & Steele, 1991).

In one recent study that illustrates how the mother's internal model can affect her behavior, Judith Crowell and Shirley Feldman observed moms with their preschoolers in a free-play setting. In the middle of the play period, the mother left the child alone for several minutes and then returned. Mothers who were themselves rated as secure in their attachment model were more likely to prepare the child ahead of time for the impending separation, had less difficulty themselves with the separation, and were most physically responsive to the child during reunion. Their children were least likely to avoid them during the reunion as well. Preoccupied moms were themselves more anxious about separating from the child, and prepared the child less. Dismissing mothers also prepared the child very little, but left without difficulty and remained physically distant from their children after returning to the playroom. Crowell and Feldman also noted that mothers with dismissing or preoccupied internal models interpreted the child's behavior very differently than did the secure moms.

> One mother observed her crying child through the observation window and said, ''See, she isn't upset about being left.'' At reunion, she said to the child, ''Why are you crying? I didn't leave.'' (1991, p. 604)

Thus the mother's own internal model not only affects her actual behavior, it affects the meaning she ascribes to the child's behavior, both of which will affect the child's developing model of attachment.

---

both Freud and Piaget, each of whom assumed that the baby began life with no sense of separateness. Freud emphasized what he called the *symbiotic* relationship between the mother and young infant in which the two are joined together as if they are one. He believed that the infant did not understand himself to be separate from the mother. Piaget emphasized that the infant's understanding of the basic concept of object permanence was a necessary precursor for the child's attaining *self*-permanence—a sense of himself as a stable, continuing entity. Both of these aspects of early self development reappear in current descriptions of the emergence of the sense of self. Michael Lewis, for example (1990, 1991; Lewis & Brooks-Gunn, 1979), divides the process into two main steps or tasks.

The First Step: The Subjective Self

Lewis argues that the child's first task is to figure out that he is separate from others and that this separate self endures over time and space. He calls this aspect of the self concept the *subjective self*, or sometimes the *existential self* because the key awareness seems to be that "I exist." Agreeing with Freud, Lewis places the beginnings of this understanding in the first 2 or 3 months of life. At that time, the baby grasps the basic distinction between self and everything else. In Lewis's view, the roots of this understanding lie in the myriad everyday interactions the baby has with the objects and people in his world that lead the baby to understand that he can have effects on things. When the child touches the mobile, it moves; when he cries, someone responds; when he smiles, his mother smiles back. By this process the baby separates self from everything else and a sense of *I* begins to emerge.

But it is not until the baby also grasps the concept of object permanence that we can really say that a subjective self has really emerged, and that does not occur until perhaps 9 to 12 months. Only then does the baby understand, at least in some preliminary way, that he has some permanence, that he exists in time and space.

The Second Step: The Objective Self

But this is not the end of the story. It is not enough merely to understand yourself as an agent in the world or a person who has experiences. For a full sense of self, the toddler must also understand herself to be an *object* in the world. Just as a ball has properties—roundness, the ability to roll, a certain feel in the hand—so the self also has qualities or properties, such as gender, size, a name, or qualities like shyness or boldness, coordination or clumsiness. It is this *self-awareness* that is the hallmark of the second phase of identity development. Lewis refers to this as the *objective self*, or sometimes the *categorical self*, because once the child achieves self-awareness the process of defining the self involves placing herself in a whole series of categories.

It has not been easy to determine just when a child has developed such self-awareness. The most commonly used procedure involves a mirror. First the baby is placed in front of a mirror to see how she behaves. Most infants of about 9 to 12 months will look at their own images, make faces, or try to interact with the baby-in-the-mirror in some way. After allowing this free exploration for a time, the experimenter, while pretending to wipe the baby's face with a cloth, puts a spot of rouge on the baby's nose, and then again lets the baby look in the mirror. The crucial test of self-recognition, and thus of awareness of the self, is whether the baby reaches for the spot on her *own* nose, rather than the nose on the face in the mirror.

The results from one of Lewis's studies using this procedure are in Figure 6.2. As you can see, none of the 9- to 12-month-old children in this study touched their noses, but

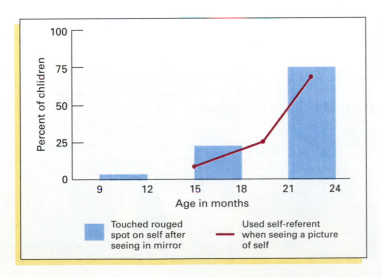

Figure 6.2 Mirror recognition and self-naming develop at almost exactly the same time. (*Source:* Lewis & Brooks, 1978, pp. 214–215.)

by 21 months, three-quarters of the children showed that level of self-recognition. The figure also shows the rate at which children refer to themselves by name when they are shown a picture of themselves, which is another commonly used measure of self-awareness. You can see that this development occurs at almost exactly the same time as self-recognition in a mirror. Both are present by about the middle of the second year of life, a finding confirmed by other investigators (e.g., Bullock & Lütkenhaus, 1990).

We can see signs of this new self-awareness in other behavior as well, such as the 2-year-old's determined rejection of help and insistence on doing things for herself, or in the newly proprietary attitude the child takes toward toys ("Mine!"). Looked at this way, much of the legendary "terrible twos" can be understood as an outgrowth of self-awareness.

Emergence of Emotional Expression.   These developmental shifts in the child's understanding of self are matched by parallel progressions in the baby's expression of emotions. Newborns already have a range of facial expressions that match happy or unhappy circumstances. By 3 or 4 months of age, adult observers are able to distinguish several other emotional expressions in the baby's repertoire: interest, anger, surprise, and sadness. A clear facial expression representing fear is distinguishable a few months later (Izard et al., 1980; P. Harris, 1989). But it is only early in the second year of life, at about the same time that a child shows self-recognition in the mirror, that we see the emergence of the so-called "self-conscious" or "social" emotions, like embarrassment or empathy (Lewis et al., 1989).

Early Self-Definitions.   Having achieved an understanding of herself as *object* with qualities or properties, the toddler now begins to *define* herself, to label herself in various ways. One of the earliest dimensions of such self-definition is gender. Two-year-olds can label themselves accurately as boys or girls, and their behavior begins to diverge in clear ways at about this age. For example, if you observe children while they play in a room stocked with a wide range of attractive toys, 2- and 3-year-old girls are more likely to play with dolls or at various housekeeping games, including sewing, stringing beads, or cooking. Boys the same age will more often choose to play with guns, toy trucks, fire engines, and with carpentry tools (Fagot, 1974; O'Brien & Huston, 1985). At the same ages we also see the beginnings of a preference for playmates of the same gender (Maccoby, 1988, 1990; Maccoby & Jacklin, 1987)—a pattern that gets progressively stronger through the preschool and early elementary school years.

Toddlers also categorize themselves on other simple dichotomous dimensions, such as big versus little, smart versus dumb, good or bad. At this early stage, they see themselves as one or the other, not both at different times.

In Bowlby's language, what seems to be happening here is that the child is creating an internal model of self, just as he creates an internal model of relationships. He first

When a toddler grabs a toy from a playmate, as this one is doing, it may be more a reflection of the youngster's new awareness of herself and her territory than any increased selfishness or "terrible two-ness."

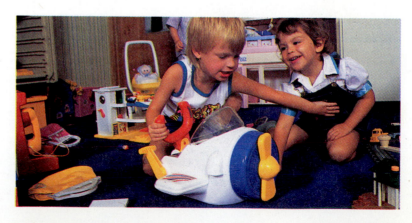

learns that he exists separately, that he has effects on the world. Then he begins to understand that he is also an object in the world, with properties, including size and gender. The internal model of self, or the self-scheme as it is often labeled, does not develop fully at this early age. But the toddler is already building up an image of himself, his qualities, his abilities. Like the internal model of attachment, this self-model or self-scheme affects the choices the toddler makes—such as choosing to play with other children of the same gender—as well as influencing the way the toddler will interpret experiences. In this way the internal model is not only strengthened but tends to carry forward.

Individual Differences Among Babies: Temperament

In developing both their self-scheme and their internal model of attachment, babies do not begin with a blank slate. Each baby starts life with certain built-in qualities, patterns of response, and styles of interacting. These built-in patterns affect the way others respond to each infant as well as shaping the way each baby is likely to understand or interpret her experiences.

Psychologists normally use the word **personality** to describe these differences in the way children and adults go about relating to the people and objects in the world around them. Like the concept of intelligence, the concept of personality is designed to describe *enduring individual differences* in behavior. Whether we are gregarious or shy, whether we plunge into new things or hold back, whether we are independent or dependent, whether we are confident or uncertain—all of these (and many more) are usually thought of as elements of personality.

Discussions of personality differences in infants are nearly always couched in terms of the concept of **temperament,** which refers to a *subset* or portion of personality traits, the individual's "emotional reactivity or behavioral style in interacting with the environment" (W. Carey, 1981). Babies range from placid to vigorous in their response to any kind of stimulation. They also differ in their rate of activity, their emotional dispositions (irritable or sunny), in their preference for social interactions or solitude, in the regularity of their daily rhythms, and in many other ways. The term *temperament* thus describes *how* the child reacts rather than what he can do or why.

Psychologists who study temperament in infants have not yet agreed on how best to describe the key dimensions of difference. Jerome Kagan has focused on only one dimension, inhibition, which he thinks is the foundation of what we later see as shyness; Buss and Plomin (1984, 1986), whose approach has been used in studies of adults as well as infants, argue for three crucial dimensions: emotionality, activity, and sociability. Rothbart (1989a) proposes two dimensions, reactivity and self-regulation, while Thomas and Chess (1977) describe nine dimensions—all of which you can see in Table 6.4.

It is not yet clear which of these views, if any, will eventually be most widely accepted, but the most influential thus far has been the Thomas and Chess formulation. So let me say more about their category system.

As you can see in Table 6.4, Thomas and Chess describe nine dimensions. They have found, however, that babies' behaviors on these nine dimensions tend to fall into three clusters. It is these clusters, in particular, that have been conceptually influential. The three temperamental types are:

Look carefully at the four category systems in Table 6.4. Is there any common ground?

- *The Easy Child.* Easy children approach new events positively. They try new foods without much fuss, for example. They are also regular in biological functioning, with good sleeping and eating cycles, are usually happy, and adjust easily to change.

- *The Difficult Child.* By contrast, the difficult child is less regular in body functioning and is slow to develop regular sleeping and eating cycles. These children react vigor-

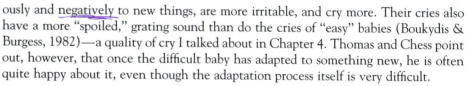

TABLE 6.4	**Some of the Dimensions of Temperament Suggested by Various Theorists**		
Thomas and Chess	**Buss and Plomin**	**Rothbart**	**Kagan**
Activity level *Rhythmicity* *Approach/withdrawal* *Adaptability to new experience* *Threshold of responsiveness* *Intensity of reaction* *Quality of mood* (+ or −) *Distractibility* *Persistence*	*Activity level:* variations in tempo, vigor, and endurance *Emotionality:* variations in the tendency to become distressed or upset easily or intensely (either with fear or anger) *Sociability:* variations in the tendency to seek and be gratified by rewards from social interaction; high level of responsivity toward others	*Reactivity:* variations in arousability of motor activity, affect, and such physiological responses as endocrine and autonomic nervous system *Self-regulation:* variations in processes that modulate reactivity, including attention, withdrawal, behavioral inhibition, self-soothing	*Inhibition:* degree of approach or withdrawal to new situations or objects or unfamiliar persons

Sources: Buss, 1989; Rothbart, 1989a; Kagan, Reznick & Snidman, 1990; Thomas & Chess, 1977.

ously and negatively to new things, are more irritable, and cry more. Their cries also have a more "spoiled," grating sound than do the cries of "easy" babies (Boukydis & Burgess, 1982)—a quality of cry I talked about in Chapter 4. Thomas and Chess point out, however, that once the difficult baby has adapted to something new, he is often quite happy about it, even though the adaptation process itself is very difficult.

- *The Slow-to-Warm-Up Child.* Children in this group are not as negative in responding to new things or new people as are difficult children. Rather, they show a kind of passive resistance. Instead of spitting out new food violently and crying, the slow-to-warm-up child may let the food dribble out and may resist mildly any attempt to feed her more of the same. These infants show few intense reactions, either positive or negative, although once they have adapted to something new, their reaction is usually fairly positive.

This category system is not the only one in use, but it has been remarkably influential, especially the description of the difficult child.

Chess and Thomas, as well as the other theorists who study temperament in babies, assume that these differences are built in at birth, as a result of either genetic patterning or prenatal experience. They are not saying that there is a "sociability" gene or an "intensity of reaction" gene. Instead, they see the behavioral differences as reflections of underlying variations in the ways a child's brain, nervous system, or hormone system operates (Rothbart, 1989b; Gunnar, 1990).

Kagan's work is the best example of this type of argument. He proposes that differences in behavioral inhibition are based on differing thresholds for arousal of those parts of the brain, the amygdala and the hypothalamus, that control responses to uncertainty. Arousal of these parts of the brain leads to increases in muscle tension and heart rate. Shy or inhibited children are thought to have a *low* threshold for such a reaction. That is, they more readily become tense and alert in the presence of uncertainty, perhaps even interpreting a wider range of situations as uncertain (Kagan, Reznick & Snidman, 1990; Kagan & Snidman, 1991). What we inherit, then, is not "shyness" or some equivalent, but a tendency for the brain to react in particular ways.

Finally, most of those who study temperament in infants assume that such dispositions persist through childhood and into adulthood. No theorist is proposing that the initial temperamental dispositions remain unchanged by experience. The individual's eventual

If this young fellow has as sunny a disposition at other times as he shows here, we'd say he had an "easy" temperament. Because they elicit different kinds of treatment from their caregivers, easy babies have quite different experiences in infancy and childhood and may therefore develop a quite different internal model of self.

pattern of behavior (phenotype) is a product of both the original genetic blueprint (genotype) and the subsequent experience. Temperament thus does not inevitably determine personality. Rather, temperamental variations are the building blocks of personality. They create a kind of "bias" in the system toward particular patterns. Given such a bias, there should be at least *some* stability of temperament over time. Such stability ought to show itself in the form of modest correlations between measures of a given temperamental dimension from one age to another.

Let me take a closer look at the evidence for some of these assumptions about temperament in infants.

The Inheritance of Temperament

The strongest evidence for the genetic basis of both infant temperament and later personality is that identical twins are quite a lot more alike in their temperament than are fraternal twins. This is true in studies of adults even when the identical twins have been reared apart—a set of findings I have explored in the "Research Report" on page 140—and it is true in studies of children and infants over age 1. One fairly typical set of results comes from a study by Buss and Plomin of 228 pairs of identical twins and 172 pairs of fraternal twins whose temperament was rated when they were 5 years old (Buss & Plomin, 1984). The correlations between the temperaments of fraternal twins on the dimensions of emotionality, activity, and sociability ranged from .53 to .63, while those of fraternal twins ranged from −.13 to +.12, a pattern of results that points to a strong genetic component.

Two other kinds of evidence, however, weaken this strong genetic argument: (1) studies of twins in the first year of life do *not* show this pattern; identical twin infants are no more alike than are fraternal twin infants (Gunnar, 1990), and (2) among adopted children, the correlations between the temperament of the child and that of the natural parent is not much higher than the correlation with adoptive parents' temperament (Scarr & Kidd, 1983). Most experts have concluded that there is good evidence for at least some genetic component in our usual measures of temperament; most also agree that this genetic influence gets *stronger* with age.

Consistency of Temperament over Time

In infancy, "difficultness," sociability, and activity level all seem to be at least moderately stable. Cranky 2-month-olds tend to be cranky at age 9 or 12 months; babies who smile more are friendlier later (e.g., Rothbart, 1986). In later childhood there is consistency across even larger time periods. For example, among the subjects in the sample originally selected by Thomas and Chess and now followed into adulthood, correlations between temperament scores obtained four years apart in elementary school averaged about .42 (Hegvik, McDevitt & Carey, 1981), while the correlation between a rating made in early adolescence and another in early adulthood was a robust .62 (Korn, 1984). But temperament scores on these same subjects as infants were not predictive of temperament in either elementary school or adulthood (Chess & Thomas, 1990).

This discontinuity between infancy and later temperament scores is extremely interesting—and poses some serious theoretical challenges. But there is no lack of potential explanations. Just as measures of infant intelligence may simply be measuring very different aspects of functioning than do later IQ tests, so the infant and childhood temperament measures may be simply assessing different things. Emotionality ratings in infancy, for example, are heavily influenced by how much a baby cries. In older children and adults, crying is not so much a part of the rating. Or, it could be that in early infancy, temperament measures are strongly affected by the infant's prenatal and birth experience and that this overrides genetic patterning, whereas childhood measures are purer reflections of genetic differences.

RESEARCH REPORT
The Inheritance of Personality Patterns: Evidence from Adults

In the past decade, a number of methodologically careful new studies of adult twins have repeatedly demonstrated that identical twins are more like one another than are fraternal twins on a whole host of measures of personality (Loehlin, 1992).

For example, Robert Plomin and his colleagues (Plomin et al., 1988) have taken advantage of the existence of an amazingly extensive and up-to-date twin registry in Sweden that includes 25,000 pairs of twins born between 1886 and 1958. From this set, they were able to identify 99 pairs of identical twins and 229 pairs of fraternal twins who had been reared apart, and then to compare them with matched pairs of twins reared together. On measures of emotionality and activity, identical twins were more similar than fraternal twins whether they had been reared together or not. The results were less clear for sociability.

A smaller but much more famous study in the United States is the Minnesota Twin Study (e.g., Tellegen et al., 1988; Bouchard, 1984)—a study that has been the subject of a great many articles in popular magazines like *Time* and *Fortune*. These researchers have been particularly interested in identical twins reared apart, frequently arranging for them to meet one another for the first time. On standard personality tests they find the now-familiar pattern: identical twins are simply much more like one another than are fraternal twins, even when the identical twins did not grow up together. This was true on measures such as positive and negative emotionality (which may be similar to Buss and Plomin's dimension of emotionality), but also on less obvious measures, such as a sense of "social potency" or a sense of well-being. Even a measure of traditionalism—an affinity for traditional values and a strong allegiance to established authority—shows slightly higher correlations among identical than among fraternal twins.

What has intrigued the popular press much more, though, are the less precise but striking descriptions of the similarities in clothing preferences, interests, posture and body language, speed and tempo of talking, favorite jokes, and hobbies in pairs of identical twins reared apart.

> One male pair who had never previously met arrived in England sporting identical beards, haircuts, wire-rimmed glasses and shirts. . . . One pair had practically the same items in their toilet cases, including the same brand of cologne and a Swedish brand of toothpaste. . . . [One pair] had the same fears and phobias. Both were afraid of water and had adopted the same coping strategy: backing into the ocean up to their knees. (Holden, 1987, p. 18)

It is difficult to imagine what sort of genetic process could account for similar preferences in hairstyles or toothpaste. But we can't merely dismiss these results because they are hard to explain. At the very least, these findings point to strong genetic components in many of the elements of personal style and emotional responsiveness that temperament researchers are trying to identify and track in infants.

It is also possible, of course, that whatever inborn temperamental differences we see in infancy are shaped and changed by the parents' responses to the child. For example, Fish, Stifter, and Belsky (1991) have recently studied changes and continuities in crying patterns in a small sample of infants. They found that those babies who had cried a great deal as newborns but cried at much lower levels at 5 months had mothers who were highly responsive and sensitive to the infant compared to mothers whose infants remained at high levels of crying across those months. Thus the responsive mother may have reshaped the baby's inborn temperamental behavior. However one explains this intriguing discontinuity, the fact remains that temperament in children age 2 and older *does* show at least some consistency over periods of years, even decades.

Temperament and Environment

Babies with different temperaments not only react differently to the world around them, they also trigger different reactions from the people taking care of them. But the process is complex. Buss and Plomin (1984) have proposed that in general, children in the middle range on temperament dimensions typically adapt *to* their environment, while those children whose temperament is extreme—like extremely difficult children—force their environment to adapt to them. So, for example, temperamentally difficult children are punished more (Rutter, 1978) than are more adaptable children. But even this statement is too simple. The parent's own child-rearing skills, the stress she experiences, and the amount of social or emotional support she has, all affect her ability to deal with an irritable or difficult child.

For example, Susan Crockenberg (1981, 1986) has found that babies with difficult temperaments are more likely to be insecurely attached *only* if their mothers see themselves as having inadequate social support. Equivalently difficult babies whose mothers have adequate support are no more likely than are easy babies to be insecurely attached. Similarly, Mavis Hetherington (1989) reports that in divorcing families, children with difficult temperaments show more problem behavior in response to the divorce, but this is especially true if the mother is also depressed and has inadequate social support. Those difficult children whose divorcing mothers were not depressed did not show heightened levels of problems. Thus the child's temperament clearly seems to have an impact, but the effect is not simple or straightforward.

These examples illustrate that what we see in the child's development is a complex outcome of the interaction of a great many elements in the system—the child's innate qualities, the skills and patterns the parents bring to the equation, and the setting in which the whole family is embedded. But of course we also need to look beyond the family as well. When I talk about older children, it will be even more important to look at settings outside the family, because schools, playgrounds, Boy Scout or Girl Scout troops, and other places where children gather all play a part in shaping the child's development. But even in infancy, forces outside the family have an impact. This is especially true today, as we see the majority of infants in the United States and in many other countries spending at least part of their time in nonhome care. So let us take a short journey into the subject of day care and its effects on infants and toddlers.

> The statement that difficult babies are more often punished is open to several possible interpretations. What are they?

▶ Beyond the Family: The Effects of Day Care on Infants and Toddlers

The increase in women's labor force participation over the past several decades represents a remarkably rapid and massive social change. In 1972, only 24 percent of women in the United States with children under age 1 were in the labor force; by 1988, that figure had more than doubled. The *majority* of such women now work outside the home at least part-time (U.S. Bureau of the Census, 1990). So it is now typical for infants as well as school-age children to spend some time in nonparental care.

Who Is Taking Care of the Children?

Day care is not a unitary phenomenon. Parents make a wide variety of care arrangements for their children, as you can see from Figure 6.3 (page 142), which shows the care arrangements of all children under age 5 in the United States in 1986 whose mothers were employed at least part-time outside the home. The most common pattern is obviously for a child to be cared for in another person's home, sometimes by a relative but more often by another mother who takes in a few children for care—a pattern usually called *family day care*. Care in the child's own home by someone other than a parent is next most common, with day-care *centers* actually the least common. But this pattern varies somewhat by age. For 3- and 4-year-olds, center care is the most frequent choice; for infants under 1 year of age, care by a relative and family day care are much more common (Hayes, Palmer & Zaslow, 1990).

These three types of care differ from one another in systematic ways. For example, center care typically provides the most cognitive enrichment, while family day care typically provides the least; both center care and family day care give the child an opportunity to play with same-age peers, while at-home care does not (Clarke-Stewart, 1987). Such variations make it very difficult to talk about global effects of day care, because the systems are quite different. Furthermore, the bulk of the research evidence is based on studies of

Figure 6.3 Child care arrangements for children 5 and under in the United States in 1986. The most common arrangement is what is usually called *family day care,* that is, care in someone else's home. (*Source:* U.S. Bureau of the Census, 1990, Table 616.)

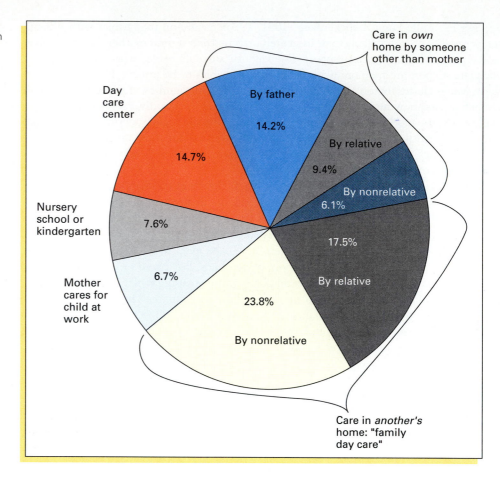

children in center care, and we cannot be sure that these findings will generalize to children in family day care or with at-home care by someone other than a parent.

Another difficulty in drawing clear conclusions arises from the fact that children enter day care at various ages and that the stability of their care varies enormously. Some children move often from one arrangement to another, others remain with the same caregiver for many years. Such differences are bound to change the outcomes for the child, and they make the research problem even more complex. Despite these problems, the enormous practical relevance of the questions involved here has forced psychologists to try to draw some conclusions—resulting at the moment in a very hot debate.

Effects of Day Care on Cognitive Development and Personality

Intensive, cognitively enriched day care, especially in the first year of life, appears to enhance children's intellectual development (Ramey & Haskins, 1981a, 1981b; Ramey, Yeates & Short, 1984; Ramey & Campbell, 1987; Ramey, Lee & Burchinal, 1989). Children in such programs, especially children from poverty-level families, typically show significantly higher IQs than are found among equivalent children reared at home. Some enhancement of cognitive functioning is also found in studies of more typical day care centers (e.g., Clarke-Stewart, 1984; Caldwell, 1986; Burchinal, Lee & Ramey, 1989). Studies in Sweden confirm such a positive effect as well: among 13-year-olds, those who had spent the most time in Sweden's very good quality day care centers had better school performance throughout elementary school compared to those totally home-reared or those with only minimal day care experience (Andersson, 1992).

If we look at the broader array of care arrangements experienced by the average child—day-care homes, baby-sitters, grandmother care, or a bit of each at different times—there are fewer signs of positive cognitive outcomes. One recent large study, in fact, shows *negative* effects on the child's 3-year vocabulary of being cared for by someone other than mother in the first nine months of life (Baydar & Brooks-Gunn, 1991). Such a negative outcome is clearly not an inevitable consequence of such early alternate care, because the intensive, enriched programs show the opposite effect. But in fact, most alternative care is not highly cognitively enriched. We obviously need to know a good deal more about the conditions of alternate care that do or do not foster good cognitive development.

Findings on the impact of day care on children's personality are even more varied. There are a few studies that show that children who have been in day care, compared to those reared by parents at home, are more aggressive with peers and less compliant with teachers and parents at later ages (e.g., Haskins, 1985; Belsky & Eggebeen, 1991). Other researchers have found no such effect (e.g., Lamb et al., 1988), while still others, such as Andersson in his studies in Sweden, have found that children in day care are actually more sociable and skillful with peers at later ages (e.g., Andersson, 1989, 1992). Tiffany Field, for example, has recently found that children who had been in *stable, good quality* day care as infants and preschoolers had more friends, were more popular, more assertive but less aggressive at grade school age than comparable children who had been reared entirely at home (Field, 1991).

Clearly there is no universal effect here. But the very fact that *some* day-care experiences seem to increase aggressiveness and noncompliance has raised a few red flags. How should we interpret such findings? Might it reflect the fact that teachers in many day-care centers, in an effort to encourage children to be independent, have also inadvertently reinforced aggressiveness and excessive assertiveness? Maybe. When one day-care center whose children had shown heightened aggressiveness altered their program to place greater emphasis on the development of positive social skills, the increase in aggressiveness disappeared (Finkelstein, 1982).

Alternatively, some have interpreted the aggressiveness not as signs of deviance or maladjustment, but rather as a sign that children in day care learn to think for themselves more and are less docile (e.g., Clarke-Stewart, 1990). Others argue that the key may be the quality of the day care, not day care itself, as indicated by the very positive outcomes

How would a learning theorist explain the fact that children in some day-care centers are later more aggressive, while in other centers no such effect is seen?

The majority of infants in the United States now experience at least some nonparental care, many of them in group settings like this one.

Field observed for children who had been in stable, good quality care. Still others, such as Jay Belsky—a psychologist who has generally taken the most pessimistic view of all the findings on day care—conclude that these hints of behavioral maladjustment among children in day care should be taken very seriously (Belsky, 1990) because they may reflect more basic difficulties in the child, such as problems with attachment.

Effects of Day Care on Children's Attachments to Parents

The hottest debate concerns just this question of attachment, a point I mentioned briefly in Chapter 2. Specifically, can an infant or toddler develop a secure attachment to her mother or father if she is repeatedly separated from them? We know that the majority of infants develop secure attachments to their fathers, even though the father typically goes away every day to work, so it is clear that such regular separations do not *preclude* secure attachment. Still, perhaps separation from both parents on a daily basis might adversely affect the security of the child's attachment.

We can narrow the window of uncertainty a good deal if we consider the child's age at the time she or he first enters day care. All parties to the current dispute agree that children who enter day care after about 18 months of age show *no* consistent loss of security of attachment to their parents. Where there is disagreement is about those infants who enter day care before 12 months of age.

Given that the child's central attachment is being formed in these early months, it seems entirely reasonable to wonder whether repeated separations would interfere with the process. Until about 5 years ago, most psychologists reading the relevant research had concluded that there was no demonstrable effect. But then Belsky, in a series of papers and in testimony before a Congressional committee, sounded an alarm (Belsky, 1985, 1987, 1990; Belsky & Rovine, 1988). Combining data from several studies, he concluded that there was a heightened risk of an insecure attachment among infants who enter day care before their first birthday. Controversy erupted. In the past few years, the hubbub has quieted some, and Belsky's central empirical conclusion has been widely accepted. Summing across the findings from 16 studies involving more than 1200 infants, Alison Clarke-Stewart (1990) finds that 36 percent of the infants in day care over 20 hours per week are classed as insecurely attached, compared to 29 percent of those infants reared entirely at home or in day care less than 20 hours per week. This is not a huge difference, but it is statistically significant. The present controversy swirls around how to interpret or explain this difference.

Belsky has his supporters. Alan Sroufe, one of the major figures in studies of early attachment, points out that we know that security of attachment is fostered both by the child's sense of the responsiveness of care and by the opportunity for parent and child to fine-tune their interactive dance. Both of these may be disrupted by placing the child in day care, although clearly in the majority of cases, parents find ways to counteract such disruptions, because the majority of children in day care are nonetheless securely attached (Sroufe, 1990).

On the other side of the argument are ranged a group of researchers who either don't believe that there is a serious problem to be dealt with or who argue that there are so many confounding variables that it is impossible to draw any clear conclusion. Here's a sampling of their arguments:

- The percentage of insecurely attached infants noted among those in day care is virtually identical to the worldwide average found by van IJzendoorn and Kroonenberg (1988) in their cross-cultural analysis of attachment studies. Some psychologists argue from this that the level of insecurity observed in United States day-care infants simply does not reflect a major problem (e.g., R. Thompson, 1990; Clarke-Stewart, 1990).

- The Strange Situation may not be an appropriate measure of attachment security for children in day care. To assess security, the child must be at least mildly stressed—otherwise we simply don't see enough attachment behaviors to judge the security of the child's attachment. A child in day care, who is used to repeated separations from Mom, may simply not experience the episodes of the Strange Situation as stressful, and thus may show behavior that looks like avoidance but is really an indication of relative comfort in the situation (e.g., Clarke-Stewart, 1990). Belsky's counterargument (Belsky & Braungart, 1991) is that if you look at the babies' actual behavior during the Strange Situation, especially the reunion episode, day-care babies show just as much fussing, whimpering, and crying as do home-reared babies, which means they were indeed experiencing stress.

- There is a serious problem of self-selection involved in any comparison of day-care and parent-reared infants. Mothers who work are different in other ways from mothers who do not. More are single mothers, more prefer to work or find child care onerous. A related problem is that children in the poorest quality day care, or who are moved

---

SOAP BOX
The Need for a New Family Policy in the United States

In her discussion of family policy, Louise Silverstein (1991) makes a number of compelling points:

> In 1990, fewer than 7% of American families reflected the two-parent model of husband as breadwinner and mother as homemaker (Braverman, 1989). Thus, the question of *whether* mothers should work is essentially irrelevant to modern family life. Mothers *do* work, and "child care is now as essential to family life as the automobile and the refrigerator." (Scarr et al., 1990, p. 26) (p. 1028)

> However, the United States remains the only one of 75 industrialized nations that does not have a government-sponsored family policy that provides some form of paid maternity benefits, parental leave, and subsidized child care. (p. 1025)

Silverstein's central argument is that psychologists have contributed to this lack of official support for the modern family by continuing to focus so much research attention on the question of the potential ill effects of mothers' employment or of day care. Instead, she argues, we must devote our research attention to the "negative consequences of the lack of affordable, government-subsidized, high-quality programs" (p. 1030).

A panel convened by the National Academy of Sciences to study child care in the United States echoes these concerns. Their basic conclusions include:

> 1. Existing child care services in the United States are inadequate to meet current and likely future needs of children, parents, and society as a whole. . . . The general accessibility of high-quality, affordable child care has immediate and long-term implications for the health and well-being of children, parents, and society as a whole. . . .

> 2. Of greatest concern is the large number of children who are presently cared for in settings that do not protect their health and safety and do not provide appropriate developmental stimulation (Hayes, Palmer & Zaslow, 1990, p. xii).

Whether or not psychologists must bear a share of the blame for our current situation, it is striking that we in the United States have apparently not faced up to the facts of modern family life or to the consequences of those facts for family needs. As I see it, one need is for a maternal leave policy that would allow more mothers (or fathers) to spend the early months of their child's life caring for the child full-time. Among other things, such a policy would permit more women to breast-feed for more months, which would have clear health benefits for children.

A second need is for good-quality, subsidized child care. The subsidy might come from private employers, some of whom have already recognized that on-site day-care programs benefit the company as well as families by reducing absenteeism and increasing worker productivity. In other cases, some kind of government subsidy seems essential. In France, for example, virtually all 3-, 4-, and 5-year-old children are in free preschools, paid for out of taxes earmarked for this purpose. French infants and toddlers can also be placed in a variety of day-care settings, partially funded by family allowances and direct government subsidies (Richardson & Marx, 1989). I am not arguing that we should copy the French system directly. I am arguing that we need an integrated, committed approach to the problem of providing quality care for young children.

often from one care arrangement to another, are also likely to come from families that are least stable (e.g., Howes & Stewart, 1987; Howes, 1990). For either reason, it is impossible to attribute the heightened levels of insecure attachment to the day-care experience rather than to home experiences.

For all these reasons, Alison Clarke-Stewart (1990) concludes that "at the present time . . . it is not appropriate to interpret the difference, as Belsky appears to, as suggesting that these children are emotionally insecure" (p. 69).

One can also argue that Belsky is focusing on the wrong issue or asking the wrong question. For the vast majority of families, the question is not Should I put my child in day care? but rather, Given that I have to work to help support my family, how do I find *good* quality, *affordable* care for my child? Clearly not all day care is bad; the great majority of children in such care show no ill effects; some show definite benefits. Given these realities, what psychologists should be asking is whether we know what makes good quality care. In fact, there has been some attempt to answer just this question. I've summarized what we know in Table 6.5, a list that might serve as a starting point in your evaluation of alternatives if and when you face this dilemma with your own children.

> What are some of the other differences you might expect between working and nonworking mothers of infants? How might those differences affect the likelihood that a child would be securely or insecurely attached?

TABLE 6.5 Some Characteristics of Day-Care Settings that Affect Outcomes for Children

Teacher/child ratio.   In general, the lower the better, and the younger the child, the smaller the ratio should be. For children younger than 2, the ratio should be no higher than 1:4; for 2- to 3-year-olds, ratios between 1:4 and 1:10 appear to be OK, although children at the younger end of this range will benefit from a lower ratio.

Group size.   Regardless of how many adults there are with each group of children, the smaller the number of children cared for together—whether in one room in a day-care center or in a home—the better for the child. Thus, a group of 30 children cared for by 5 adults is not as good as three smaller groups of 10 children cared for by 1 adult each. For infants, the best current information suggests a maximum of 6 to 8 per group; for 1- to 2-year-olds, between 6 and 12 per group. For older children, groups as large as 15 or 20 appear to be OK.

Amount of personal contact with adults.   In general, the more time the child spends in one-to-one interaction with an adult, the better, although when the child is cared for by a baby-sitter at home, it is possible to have too much adult contact. In a day-care home or center, however, amount of personal contact with an adult is an important feature.

Stability of relationship with caregiver.   A center with a stable staff would be preferable to one with high staff turnover, because children who have an opportunity to develop an enduring relationship with a single adult appear to do better.

Richness of verbal stimulation.   Regardless of the variety of toys available, the complexity and variety of the language used with the child will stimulate faster language and cognitive development.

Space, cleanliness, and colorfulness.   The overall physical organization of the space seems to make a difference. Children show more creative play and exploration in colorful, clean environments that are well adapted to child play. Lots of expensive toys are not critical, but there must be activities that children will find engaging, and space to move.

Caregiver's knowledge of child development.   Children's development is better in day-care centers or homes in which the caregivers have specific training in human development.

Marital status of caregivers.   Among family day-care providers, those caregivers who are single and thus responsible for all the care of the home as well as the children spend more time in housekeeping and thus less time with the children than is true of married caregivers.

Sources: C. Anderson et al., 1981; Clarke-Stewart, 1987; Hayes, Palmer & Zaslow, 1990; Hunt, 1986; Long, Peters & Garduque, 1985; Ruopp & Travers, 1982; Smith & Spence, 1981; Howes, Phillips & Whitebook, 1992.

Summary

1. In attachment theory, an important distinction is made between an affectional bond (an enduring tie to a uniquely viewed partner) and an attachment, which additionally involves the element of security and a safe base. An attachment is deduced from the existence of attachment behaviors.

2. The parents' bond to the infant may develop in two phases, but the second of these appears to be far more significant than the first: (1) an initial strong bond may be formed in the first hours of the child's life; (2) the bond may be strengthened by the repetition of mutually reinforcing and interlocking attachment behaviors.

3. A failure by parents to form a bond to the infant can occur either because the infant lacks the needed enticing skills, or the parent lacks skills. In either case the consequence may be neglect or abuse.

4. Fathers as well as mothers form strong bonds to their infants, but fathers show more playful behaviors with their children than do mothers.

5. Bowlby proposed that the child's attachment to the caregiver develops through a series of steps, beginning with rather indiscriminate aiming of attachment behaviors toward anyone within reach, through a focus on one or more figures, and finally "secure-base behavior," beginning at about 6 months of age, which signals the presence of a clear attachment.

6. In the second half of the first year, babies also typically show fear of strangers and protest at separation from their favored person.

7. Children typically develop strong attachments to both father and mother.

8. Children differ in the security of their first attachments, and thus in the internal working model they develop. The secure infant uses the parent as a safe base for exploration and can be readily consoled by the parent.

9. Studies in many countries suggest that a secure attachment is the most common pattern everywhere, but cultures differ in the frequency of different types of insecure attachment.

10. The security of the initial attachment is reasonably stable; a secure attachment is fostered by contingent responsiveness and acceptance by the parent.

11. Securely attached children appear to be more socially skillful, more curious and persistent in approaching new tasks, and more mature.

12. In the same months the infant is also developing the first step of a sense of self, the subjective self. The infant understands himself to exist separately and to be able to cause things to happen.

13. In the second year of life the baby develops a sense of self as a lasting object with properties, such as gender, size, and so on.

14. Babies differ in their basic temperaments, their style of responding to objects and people.

15. Theorists have not yet agreed on the best way to describe the dimensions of temperament, but Chess and Thomas's three-part category system of easy, difficult, and slow-to-warm-up babies has been most influential.

16. Temperamental differences appear to have at least a moderate genetic component and to be at least somewhat stable both during infancy and between preschool and adulthood.

17. Infants are also affected by experiences outside the family, in particular by day care, now a common experience for infants in the United States.

18. Some day-care settings enhance children's cognitive development. This is especially true for infants from poverty-level families.

19. Effects of nonfamily care on children's temperament or personality are less clear. The effects vary depending on the specific quality of the care setting.

20. Recent research shows that infants in day care have slightly higher incidence of insecure attachment to the mother than is true of infants reared at home. There is a significant dispute about how this difference should be interpreted.

Key Terms

affectional bond	insecure attachment	secure attachment
attachment	internal working model	Strange Situation
attachment behaviors	personality	temperament

Suggested Readings

Bowlby, J. (1988b). *A secure base.* New York: Basic Books. (This splendid small book, Bowlby's last before his recent death, includes a number of his most important papers as well as new chapters that bring his theory up to date. See particularly Chapters 7 and 9.)

Cicchetti, D., & Carlson, V. (Eds.) (1989). *Child maltreatment.* Cambridge, England: Cambridge University Press. (This is not light reading, but it is an excellent source of current information. It includes scholarly papers by many of the major researchers in the area of child abuse, including a number of papers that summarize our current knowledge about causes and consequences of abuse.)

Grusec, J. E., & Lytton, H. (1988). *Social development. History, theory, and research.* New York: Springer-Verlag. (This is the most recent of several good texts on social development. A very good source for further detail on almost any of the topics I've covered in this chapter.)

Schaffer, H. R. (1990). *Making decisions about children. Psychological questions and answers.* Oxford: Basil Blackwell. (This is an unusual and potentially very helpful book. Schaffer has taken up a series of practical questions about children's early development, many of which touch on issues I talked about in this chapter, such as whether early contact is essential for the parent's bond or whether the mother's employment has any detrimental effect on the child. For each question, he summarizes a few key studies and then provides his own conclusion.)

SUMMING UP INFANT DEVELOPMENT

Why Interludes?

Since this is the first of these "interludes," let me say a word about their purpose. Because this book is organized chronologically, with a set of chapters describing each age period, you might think that you will automatically gain a sense of the basic characteristics of each era. But because psychological research tends to focus on only one system at a time, such as attachment or perceptual skills

or language, my descriptions tend to follow the same pattern. In these interludes, I want to try to put the baby (or child or adult) back together, to look at all the threads at once.

A second purpose is to examine, albeit briefly, some of the external influences on the basic processes. In particular, I want to be sure that we keep coming back to the effects of the larger social system in which the child/adult is developing.

In each interlude, then, I will ask the same three questions: What are the *basic characteristics* of development in that period? What are the *central processes* that seem to be shaping those developmental patterns? What other forces affect or *influence* those processes?

Basic Characteristics of Infancy

The table below summarizes the various developmental patterns I've de-

A Summary of the Threads of Infant Development

Aspect of Development	Age in Months											
	0	2	4	6	8	10	12	14	16	18	20	22
Physical development		Increase in cortical involvement	Reaches for objects	Sits	Stands; crawls		Walks alone			Dendritic and synaptic "pruning"		
Perceptual development	Many perceptual skills present at birth	Visually discriminates Mom from stranger; scans to identify object	Discriminates patterns of sounds and sights; cross-modal transfer	Discriminates facial expressions								
Cognitive development	Possibly imitation of some facial gestures		Beginning of object permanence		Object permanence well established; coordinates actions to solve problems			Deferred imitation; finds *new* solutions to problems			Beginning internal manipulation of symbols	
Language development		Coos		Babbles	Meaningful gestures; understands a few words		First word			Vocabulary of 3–50 words		
Social/ personality development		Spontaneous social smiling	Early signs of attachment; self/other differentiation		Clear attachment	Stranger fear and anxiety			Plays with peers	Clear evidence of self-awareness		

scribed in the past three chapters. The rows in the table correspond to the various threads of development; what we need to do now is read up and down the table in addition to looking across the rows.

The overriding impression one gets of the newborn—despite her remarkable skills and capacities—is that she is very much on automatic pilot. There seem to be built-in rules or schemas that govern the way the infant looks, listens, explores the world, and relates to others.

One of the really remarkable things about these rules is how well designed they are to lead both the child and the caregivers into the "dance" of interaction and attachment. Think of an infant being breast-fed. The baby has the needed rooting, sucking, and swallowing reflexes to take in the milk; in this position, the mother's face is at just about the optimum distance from the baby's eyes for the infant to focus; the mother's facial features, particularly her eyes and mouth, are just the sort of visual stimuli that the baby is most likely to look at; the baby is particularly sensitive to the range of sounds of the human voice, particularly the upper register, so the higher-pitched, lilting voice most mothers use is easily heard by the infant.

Sometime around 6 to 8 weeks there seems to be a change, with these automatic, reflexive responses giving way to behavior that looks more volitional. The child now looks at objects differently, apparently trying to identify what an object is rather than merely where it is; at this age she also begins to reliably discriminate one face from another, smiles more, sleeps through the night, and generally becomes a more responsive creature.

These changes in the baby alter the parent-infant interaction patterns as well. As the child stays awake for longer periods, and smiles and makes eye contact more, exchanges between parent and child become more playful and smoother paced.

Somewhere in the middle of the first year, between roughly 6 and 8 months, there seems to be another shift, marked by the emergence of a remarkably wide range of new skills or behaviors: (1) The baby forms a strong central attachment, followed a few months later by separation anxiety and fear of strangers. (2) The infant begins to move around independently (albeit very slowly and haltingly at first). (3) The baby babbles, then begins to use meaningful gestures, to engage in imitative gestural games, and to comprehend individual words. (4) The baby understands, in at least a preliminary way, that objects and people can continue to exist even when they are out of sight. At the very least, these changes profoundly alter the parent-child interactive system, requiring the establishment of a new equilibrium.

The baby continues to build gradually on this set of new skills—learning a few spoken words, learning to walk, consolidating the basic attachment—until 18 or 20 months of age, at which point the child's language and cognitive development appear to take another major leap forward—a

set of changes I'll be talking about in chapters yet to come.

Central Processes

So what is causing all these changes? Any short list of such causes is inevitably going to be a gross oversimplification. Still, undaunted, let me suggest four key processes that seem to me to be shaping the patterns shown in the table.

Physical Maturation.   First and most obviously, the biological clock is ticking very loudly indeed during these early few months. Only at adolescence, and again in old age, do we see such an obvious maturational pattern at work. In infancy it is the prepatterned growth of neural dendrites and synapses that appears to be the key. The shift in behavior we see at 2 months, for example, seems to be governed by just such built-in changes, as synapses in the cortex develop sufficiently to control behavior more fully.

Important as this built-in program is, it nonetheless *depends on* the presence of a minimum "expectable" environment (Greenough, Black & Wallace, 1987). The brain may be wired to create certain synapses, but the process has to be triggered by exposure to particular kinds of experience. Because such a minimum environment exists for virtually all infants, the perceptual, motor, and cognitive developments we see are virtually identical from one baby to the next. But that does not mean that the environment is unimportant.

The Child's Explorations.   A second key process is the child's own exploration of the world around her. She is born *ready* to explore, to learn from her experience, but she still has to learn the specific connections between seeing and hearing, to tell the differences between Mom's face and someone else's, to pay attention to the sounds emphasized in the language she is hearing, to discover that her actions have consequences, and so on and on.

Clearly, physiological maturation and the child's own exploration are intimately linked in a kind of perpetual feedback loop. The rapid changes in the nervous system, bones, and muscles permit more and more exploration, which in turn affects the child's perceptual and cognitive skills, which in turn affect the architecture of the brain.

For example, there is now a good deal of evidence that the ability to crawl—a skill that rests on a whole host of maturationally based physical changes—profoundly affects the baby's understanding of the world. Before the baby can move independently, he seems to locate objects only in relation to his own body; after he can crawl, he begins to locate objects with reference to fixed landmarks (Campos & Bertenthal, 1989). This shift, in turn, probably contributes to the infant's growing understanding of himself as an object in space.

Attachment. A third key process seems obviously to be the relationship between the infant and the caregiver(s). I am convinced that Bowlby is right about the built-in *readiness* of all infants to create an attachment. But in this domain, the quality of the specific experience the child encounters seems to have a more formative effect than is true for other aspects of development. A wide range of environments are "good enough" to support physical, perceptual, and cognitive growth in these early months. But for the establishment of a secure central attachment, the acceptable range seems to be narrower.

Still, attachment does not develop along an independent track. Its emergence is linked both to maturational change and to the child's own exploration. For example, the child's un-

derstanding of object permanence may be a necessary precondition for the development of a basic attachment. As John Flavell puts it, "However could a child persistently yearn and search for a specific other person if the child were still cognitively incapable of mentally representing that person in the person's absence?" (1985, p. 135).

We might also turn this hypothesis on its head and argue that the process of establishing a clear attachment may cause, or at least affect, the child's cognitive development. For example, securely attached youngsters appear to persist longer in their play and develop the object concept more rapidly (e.g., Bates et al, 1982). Such a connection might exist because the securely attached child is simply more comfortable exploring the world around him from the safe base of his secure person. He thus has a richer and more varied set of experiences, which may stimulate more rapid cognitive (and neurological) development.

Internal Working Models. We could also think of attachment as being a subcategory of a broader process, namely the creation of internal working models. Seymour Epstein (1991) proposes that what the baby is doing is nothing less than beginning to create a "theory of reality." In Epstein's view, such a theory includes at least four elements:

A belief about the degree to which the world is a place of pleasure or pain

A belief about the extent to which the world is meaningful—predictable, controllable, and just versus capricious, chaotic, or uncontrollable

A belief about whether people are desirable or threatening to relate to

A belief about the worthiness or unworthiness of the self

The roots of this theory of reality, so Epstein and others argue (e.g., Bretherton, 1991), lie in the experiences of infancy, particularly the experiences with caregivers and other humans. Indeed, Epstein suggests that the beliefs created in infancy are likely to be the most basic and therefore the most durable and resistant to change at later ages. Not all psychologists would agree with Epstein about the broadness of the infant's "theory" of reality. But virtually all would now agree that the baby begins to create at least two significant internal models, one of the self and one of relationships with others (attachment). Of the two, the attachment model seems to be the most fully developed at 18 or 24 months; the model of the self undergoes many elaborations in the years that follow. It is only at about age 6 or 7 that the child seems to have a sense of his *global* worth—a characteristic we usually call self-esteem (Harter, 1985, 1988).

Influences on the Basic Processes

Perhaps the most important thing for you to remember about infant development is how robust and well-buffered it is (Masten, Best & Garmezy, 1990). Nonetheless, infants can be deflected from this common trajectory by several kinds of circumstances.

Organic Damage. The most obvious potential influence is some kind of damage to the physical organism, either from genetic anomalies, inherited disease, or teratogenic effects in utero. But even here, there is an interaction between nature and nurture. Recall from Chapter 3 that the long-term consequences of such damage may be more or less severe, depending on the richness and supportiveness of the environment the baby grows up in.

Family Environment. There are (at least) two ways to analyze the effect of the family environment. One way is to try to define an "ideal" environment—one that maximally supports, enriches, and furthers optimal development in the infant. Research in this tradition confirms that the ideal environment is one with a variety of objects for the baby to explore, at least some free opportunity to explore, and with loving, responsive, and sensitive adults who talk to the infant often and respond to the infant's cues (e.g., Bradley et al., 1989).

Alternatively, we can look at the effects of very poor environments. Many theorists such as Horowitz, whose model I showed in Figure 1.4, argue that most environments are sufficient to support normal development. Only environments which deviate widely from the norm will cause serious and lasting problems, especially if the infant brings some vulnerability to the process as well. Severe neglect or abuse would fall into this category, as might deep or lasting depression in a parent, or persisting upheaval or stress in family life. Paradoxically, both these ways of looking at the family seem accurate to me. For most aspects of development in infancy, most environments are "good enough" for normal growth. But that

does not mean that all babies whose family environment is above the cut-off point will develop optimally. Variations in enrichment, in responsiveness, in loving support affect not only the pattern of attachment but probably also the child's motivation, the content of his self-concept, his willingness to explore as well as his specific knowledge. We see the consequences of such differences further down the developmental road, when the child is facing the challenging tasks of school and the demands of relating to other children.

Influences on the Family. I've made the point before, but let me make it again: The baby is embedded in the family, but the family is part of a larger economic, cultural, and social system, all of which can have both direct and indirect effects on the infant. Let me give you just two examples.

The most obvious point is that the parents' overall economic circumstances may have a very wide-ranging impact on the baby's life experience. Poor families are less able to provide a safe and secure environment. Their infants are more likely to be exposed to environmental toxins such as lead, less likely to have regular health care, including immunizations, and more likely to have nutritionally inadequate diets. If they place their infant in day care, they may be unable to

afford good quality care, and they are more likely to have to shift their baby from one care arrangement to another. Collectively, these are large differences. We do not see the effects immediately; babies reared in poverty-level families do not look much different from babies reared in more affluent circumstances. But the differences begin to be obvious at age 2 or 3 or 4.

Another example, one that cuts across all social classes, is the effect of the parents' own social support on the infant's development. Mothers or fathers who feel that they have adequate support are more likely to have securely attached infants, are better able to handle the extra strain of a low-birth-weight infant or an infant with a difficult temperament, and so forth (e.g., Crockenberg, 1981). This effect can even be demonstrated experimentally.

Jacobson and Frye (1991) randomly assigned 46 poverty-level mothers either to a control group or to an experimental support group that met both prenatally and for the first year after delivery. When Jacobson and Frye evaluated the infants' attachment at 14 months, they found that the babies whose moms had been in the support group were more securely attached than those whose moms had had no such special help.

One Last Word. One of the strongest impressions one gets from so much of the current research on babies is that they are far more capable than we had thought. They appear to be born with many more skills, many more templates for handling their experiences. But they are not 6-year-olds, and we need to be careful not to get too carried away with our statements about how much the baby can do. As you will see in the next two chapters, the preschooler makes huge strides in every area.

PHYSICAL AND COGNITIVE DEVELOPMENT IN THE PRESCHOOL CHILD

7

Watch an 18-month-old playing near his Mom or Dad, and you'll notice that he doesn't go too far away. He may also glance at the parent regularly, as if checking to make sure the safe base is still there. Watch the same child a few years later and he is probably playing in a separate room, maybe with a chum. He may call out to Mom or Dad once in a while, asking them to come and see something he has created. Or he may wander past Mom or Dad periodically, but he is comfortable being further away. Changes like this may be less dramatic and obvious than the physical and cognitive changes in infancy, but they are nonetheless profound. In the years from 2 to 6 the child moves from still-dependent toddler, able to communicate only in very primitive ways, to a remarkably competent, communicative, social creature, ready to begin school.

▶ Physical Changes Between 2 and 6

In Chapter 4, I chronicled the many rapid changes in the infant's body. When we look at physical changes between 2 and 6 years, the story is much briefer. In the nervous system, new synapses are still formed as the child explores the world more fully, and some myelinization still continues. But the rate of change is vastly slower than what occurs in the early months of life.

Similarly, changes in height and weight are far slower in these preschool years than in infancy. Between about age 2 and adolescence, children add about 2 to 3 inches per year in length and about 6 pounds in weight.

Motor Development

These more gradual changes nonetheless combine to enable the child to make steady progress in motor development. The changes are not so dramatic as the beginning of walking. But they are significant because they enable toddlers and preschoolers to acquire skills that markedly increase their independence and exploratory ability.

Table 7.1, which parallels Table 4.3, shows the major locomotor, nonlocomotor, and manipulative skills that emerge in these preschool years. You can see that by age 5 or 6, the child is able to move confidently in all directions, to ride a tricycle, and to use her hands for quite small motions and actions, including picking up, holding, and using small objects such as pencils or scissors. Children of 5 and 6 also have the hand-eye coordination to kick and bat at balls—abilities that may be important for those parents who are eager to have their children acquire specific sports skills.

Health in the Preschool Years

Physicians distinguish between *acute* and *chronic* illnesses. The former are all those illnesses lasting less than three months, such as colds and flu. The latter are illnesses lasting longer than three months, often for years or even permanently, such as diabetes, muscular dystrophy, or asthma.

Acute illnesses are common among young children, just as they are among infants. In the United States, the average preschooler has four to six brief bouts of sickness each year, with colds and flu the most common types (Parmelee, 1986). In contrast, only one

---

TABLE 7.1   Milestones of Motor Development from 2 to 6

Age	Locomotor Skills	Nonlocomotor Skills	Manipulative Skills
18–24 mos	Runs (20 mos); walks well (24 mos); climbs stairs with both feet on each step	Pushes and pulls boxes or wheeled toys; unscrews lid on a jar	Shows clear hand preference; stacks 4 to 6 blocks; turns pages one at a time; picks things up without overbalancing
2–3 yrs	Runs easily; climbs up and down furniture unaided	Hauls and shoves big toys around obstacles	Picks up small objects (e.g., Cheerios); throws small ball forward while standing
3–4 yrs	Walks upstairs one foot per step; skips on both feet; walks on tiptoe	Pedals and steers a tricycle; walks in any direction pulling a big toy	Catches large ball between outstretched arms; cuts paper with scissors; holds pencil between thumb and first two fingers
4–5 yrs	Walks up *and* downstairs one foot per step; stands, runs and walks well on tiptoe		Strikes ball with bat; kicks and catches ball; threads beads but not needle; grasps pencil maturely
5–6 yrs	Skips on alternate feet; walks a thin line; slides, swings		Plays ball games quite well; threads needle and sews stitches

Sources: Connolly & Dalgliesh, 1989; The Diagram Group, 1977; Fagard & Jacquet, 1989; Mathew & Cook, 1990; Thomas, 1990.

THE REAL WORLD
Motor Development and Toys

If you have ever tried to buy a toy for a child, you know how bewildering it can be to walk into a store and see aisles and aisles of bright, attractive items. You want to find something that is right for your child's skills, but how do you know what makes a good toy, and what toys are good at what ages?

The first rule of thumb is to consider the safety of the toys. For infants and toddlers, this means avoiding toys with small pieces that might be swallowed or pieces that might come off (like sewn-on eyes for dolls, or small caps). Also avoid toys with sharp edges. Beyond the concern for safety, the choice of toys can be guided partly by basic information on perceptual and motor development.

Birth to Six Months. Little babies use their hands and their eyes to play, so a good choice is something that is bright, safe to hold on to, and hooked to the crib so it won't fall. Mobiles and "cradle gyms" fit the category, and so do soft toys tied to the sides of the crib.

6 to 12 Months. More mobile older babies are interested in toys that let them try out their new large muscle skills. Probably the best thing for a child this age is to "child-proof" your house, removing hazards like sharp objects and poisons so the child can explore freely. Playpens are probably not as good, although they may sometimes be necessary for safety reasons.

Infants of this age also enjoy stacking and nesting toys. Measuring cups and pots and pans are often better for this than are expensive baby toys.

Second Year. Give a toddler an expensive toy and chances are she will show at least as much interest in the box it came in than in the toy itself. Big boxes that can be crawled into I have found to be a particular hit. Toddlers also like toys with wheels, but *push* toys are better than *pull toys* because the child can see the object while it moves. Near the end of the year, toward the second birthday, the child can sometimes handle a big crayon or pencil and may enjoy "drawing." For obvious reasons, washable colors are preferred!

Third Year. When in doubt, get something with wheels. Kiddie cars, tricycles, and other riding toys are favorites among large toys, and cars and trucks (for both sexes) among small ones. Building toys also start to be interesting, especially those with many possibilities, like wooden blocks. Homemade blocks are just as satisfactory as expensive kits from a store. Remember, though, that for children this age the construction pieces have to be fairly large. Little bitty beads, or the smaller size Legos, or very small blocks are too small for the grasping skills of most children in this age range. They need objects that can be picked up in the whole hand.

Coloring and drawing are also usually great favorites, as are those messy classics, painting and Play-Doh. As with younger children, "washable" is an important label to look for.

Fourth to Seventh Year. Small muscle coordination develops rapidly during this period, and the child can manage toys like beads to be strung on a string, and scissors—although typical children's scissors are too dull for much accuracy; a sharp pair of scissors is a great gift for a child old enough to use them safely. Jacks, marbles, and checkers are also good choices for older children in this age group because they require the very kind of small motor skill the child now has, as well as stimulating interactions with other children and challenging the child's intellectual skills.

Large muscle skills are improving too in these years. Children in this age range can manage many kinds of sports equipment *if* you select appropriate sizes: lightweight hockey sticks or tennis rackets and larger-than normal balls. By the end of this period, the child can often manage a bicycle or at least start on one with training wheels. In all this, of course, it is important not to press too hard, too early, for highly skilled behavior.

Toys that stimulate fantasy are also greatly enjoyed by children in this age range, including dolls or other figures that represent some well-known fantasy, dress-up clothes or costumes, toy doctor kits, puppets.

As a general rule, at every age steer clear of expensive, complex toys that do only one or two things, such as robots that only whir and walk. Children are intrigued the first time but rapidly lose interest, and such toys are not adaptable to other forms of play.

in ten preschoolers has any kind of chronic illness (Starfield & Pless, 1980). The most common types are allergies, asthma, chronic bronchitis or sinusitis, eczema, visual and hearing impairments, and diabetes (U.S. Bureau of the Census, 1990; Starfield, 1991).

Another danger for children is accidents. In any given year, about a quarter of all children under 5 in the United States have at least one accident that requires some kind of medical attention (U.S. Bureau of the Census, 1990). Accidents are also the major cause of death between the ages of 1 and 5 (Starfield, 1991). At every age, such accidents are more common among boys than among girls. Among preschoolers, home-based accidents are most common—falls, cuts, accidental poisonings, and the like. Automobile accidents are the second leading source of injuries among children this age, although the rate of serious injury and death from such accidents has been dropping dramatically in recent years because of new laws mandating the use of restraint devices for infants and toddlers traveling in cars (Christophersen, 1989).

One of the most interesting findings on childhood illness is that a pattern of repeated illness in childhood—even just unusually frequent colds—is correlated with higher rates of illness in adolescence and poorer health in adulthood (e.g., Power & Peckham, 1990). The correlation is by no means perfect. Many "sickly" children are quite healthy as adults. And, of course, because we are dealing here with correlational evidence, we must be careful about making causal statements. But we can make a risk statement: a pattern of frequent or chronic early illness increases the probability of health problems later.

How many different explanations can you think of for such a link between childhood illness and adult health?

▶ Talking in Sentences: The Next Steps in Language Development

When we left the infant in Chapter 5, he was just beginning to use a few individual words. This is no small accomplishment, but what happens to language in the following year is even more remarkable. The toddler moves with amazing rapidity from single words to simple and then complex sentences. By age 3, most children have acquired all the basic tools needed to form sentences and make conversation (Bloom, 1991).

To understand this remarkable development, we need to know both how children come to string words into sentences and how they come to understand the meaning of the words they are using. In the terminology used by linguists, we need to understand both *syntax* (grammar) and *semantics* (word meaning). Let's start with grammar.

The Development of Grammar

In analyzing the way young children begin to form sentences, most linguists follow the lead of Roger Brown, who divided the process into several steps or phases (Brown, 1973).

Stage I Grammar.   The first step, which Brown called Stage I grammar, has several distinguishing features: the sentences are *short*—generally two or three words—and they are *simple*. Nouns, verbs and adjectives are usually included, but virtually all the purely grammatical markers (which linguists call **inflections**) are missing. At the beginning, for example, children learning English do not normally use the *s* for plurals or put the *ed* ending on verbs to make the past tense, nor do they use the *'s* of the possessive or auxiliary verbs like *am* or *do*.

Simple though they may be, even these earliest sentences seem to be based on rules. Not adult rules, to be sure, but rules nonetheless. Two-year-olds focus on certain types of words and put them together in particular orders. They also manage to convey a variety of different meanings with their Stage I sentences.

For example, young children frequently use a sentence made up of two nouns, such as *Mommy sock* or *sweater chair* (Bloom, 1973). We might conclude from this that a "two noun" form is a basic grammatical characteristic of early child language. But that misses the complexity. For instance, the child in Bloom's study who said "Mommy sock" said it on two different occasions. The first time was when she picked up her mother's sock and the second was when the mother put the child's own sock on the child's foot. In the first case, *Mommy sock* seems to mean "Mommy's sock" (a possessive relationship). But in the second instance the child seems to convey "Mommy is putting a sock on me," which is an *agent* (Mommy)–*object* (sock) relationship.

Stage II Grammar.   Stage II begins when the child begins to use any of the grammatical inflections, such as plurals, past tenses, auxiliary verbs, prepositions, and the like—a change that most often occurs between ages 2 and 3. You can get a better feeling for

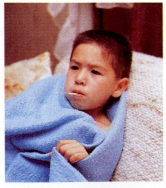

The average preschooler is sick with an "acute" illness about six times a year.

the sound of the change from Table 7.2, which lists some of the sentences of a little boy named Daniel, recorded by David Ingram (1981). The left-hand column lists some of Daniel's sentences at about 21 months of age, when he was still using the simplest forms; the right-hand column lists some of his sentences only 2½ months later (age 23–24 months), when he had just moved into Stage II.

You can get some sense from the table that Daniel did not add all the inflections at once. In this sample, he uses only a few, mostly the *s* for plural. It turns out that within each language community, children seem to add inflections and more complex word orders in fairly predictable sequences. Among children learning English, Roger Brown (1973) has found that the earliest inflection is most often the *ing* added onto a verb, such as in *I playing*, or *doggie running*. Then come (in order) prepositions like *on* and *in*, the plural *s* on nouns, irregular past tenses (such as *broke* or *ran*), possessives, articles (*a* and *the* in English), the *s* that we add to third person verbs such as *he wants*, regular past tenses like *played* and *wanted*, and the various forms of the auxiliary verb, as in *I am not going*.

There are also predictable sequences in the child's developing use of questions and negatives. In each case, the child seems to go through periods when he creates types of sentences that he has not heard adults use, but that are consistent with the particular set of rules he is using. For example, in the development of questions there is a point at which the child gets a *wh* word (*who, what, when, where, why*) at the front end of a sentence, but doesn't yet have the auxiliary verb put in the right place, such as: *Why it is resting now?* Similarly, in the development of negatives, there is a stage in which the *not* or *n't* or *no* is put in, but the auxiliary verb is omitted, as in *I not crying*, or *there no squirrels*.

Overregularization.   Another intriguing phenomenon of this second phase of sentence construction that underlines the rule-making and rule-following quality of even the earliest sentences is **overregularization** or overgeneralization. In English, this is especially

TABLE 7.2 Examples of Daniel's Stage I and Stage II Sentences

Stage I Sentences (Age: 21 Months)	Stage II Sentences (Age 23 Months)	
a bottle	a little boat	cat there
broke-it	doggies here	boat here
here bottle	give you the book	it's a boy
horse doggie	it's a robot	it's cat
broke it	little box there	no book
it a bottle	oh cars	oh doggie
kitty cat	sit down	this a bucket
oh a doggie	that flowers	there's a boat there
poor Daddy	those little boat	what those?
thank you	what's that?	what this?
that hat?	where going?	where the boat?
that monkey		
want a bottle		
want bottle		
want that?		

Source: Reprinted by permission of the publisher from "Early patterns of grammatical development" by D. Ingram, in R. E. Stark (Ed.), *Language behavior in infancy and early childhood*, Tables 6 and 7, pp. 344–345. Copyright 1981 by Elsevier Science Publishing Co., Inc.

clear in children's creation of past tenses like *wented* or *goed* or *ated*. Stan Kuczaj (1977, 1978) has found that young children initially learn a small number of irregular past tenses and use them correctly for a short time. But then rather suddenly the child seems to discover the rule of adding *ed* and overgeneralizes this rule to all verbs. This type of "error" is particularly common among children between ages 3 and 5.

What I've said so far describes what happens when a child learns a *single* language. But what about children who are exposed to two or more languages from the beginning? How confusing is this for a child? And how can parents ease the process? I've discussed the problems of bilingual children in the "real world" box below.

The Development of Word Meaning

To understand language development, it is not enough to know how children learn to string words together to form sentences. We also have to understand how the words in those sentences come to have meaning. Linguists are still searching for good ways to

---

THE REAL WORLD
Bilingual Children

There are at least two important practical questions surrounding the issue of bilingualism:

- Should parents who speak different native languages try to expose their children to both, or will that only confuse the child and make any kind of language learning harder? What's the best way to do this?
- If a child arrives at school age without speaking the dominant language of schooling, what is the best way for the child to acquire that second language?

Learning Two Languages at the Same Time. Parents should have no fears about exposing their child to two or more languages from the very beginning. Such simultaneous exposure does seem to result in slightly slower early steps in word learning and sentence construction, but bilingual children catch up rapidly.

The best way to help a child to learn two languages fluently is to speak both languages to the child from the beginning, *especially* if the two languages come at the child from different sources. For example, if Mom's native language is English and Dad's is Italian, Mom should speak only English to the infant/ toddler and Dad should speak only Italian. (The parents will of course speak to each other in whatever language they have in common). If both parents speak both languages to the child, or mix them up in their own speech, this is a much more difficult situation for the child, and language learning will be delayed (McLaughlin, 1984). Two languages can also be learned simultaneously if one language is always spoken at home and the other in a day care center or with playmates or in some other outside situation.

Bilingual Education. For many children, the need to be bilingual begins only when they enter school. In the United States today there are 2.5 million school-age children for whom English is not the primary language of the home (Hakuta & Garcia, 1989). Many of those children arrive at school with little or no facility in English. Educators have had to grapple with the task of teaching children a second language at the same time that they are trying to teach them subject matter such as reading and mathematics. The problem for the schools has been to figure out the best way to do this. Should the child be immediately immersed in the new language? Should the child learn basic academic skills in his native language and only later learn English as a second language? Or is there some combination of the two that will work?

The research findings are messy. Still, one thread does run through it all: neither full immersion nor English-as-a-second-language programs is as effective as truly bilingual programs in which the child is given at least some of her basic instruction in subject matter in her native language in the first year or two of school, but is also exposed to the second language in the same classroom (Padilla et al., 1991; Willig, 1985). After several years of such combined instruction, the child then makes a rapid transition to full use of the second language for all instruction. Interestingly, in her analysis of this research, Ann Willig has found that the ideal arrangement is very much like what works best at home with toddlers: If some subjects are always taught in one language, and other subjects in the other language, children learn both most easily. But if each sentence is translated, children do not learn the new language as quickly or as well.

Note, though, that even such ideal bilingual education programs will not be effective for children who come to school without good spoken language in their native tongue. Learning to read in any language requires that the child have a fairly extensive awareness of the structure of language —a point I'll be exploring more fully in Chapter 9. Any child who lacks such awareness— because she has been exposed to relatively little language, was not read to or talked to in infancy and preschool years—will have difficulty learning to read, whether the instruction is given in the native language or in English.

describe (or explain) children's emerging word meaning. So far, several sets of questions have dominated the research.

Which Comes First, the Meaning or the Word?   The most fundamental question is whether the child learns a word to describe a category or class he has *already* created through his manipulations of the world around him, or whether the existence of a word forces the child to create new cognitive categories. This may seem to be a highly abstract argument, but it touches on the fundamental issue of the relationship between language and thought. Does the child learn to represent objects to himself *because* he now has language, or does language simply come along at about this point and make the representations easier?

Not surprisingly, the answer seems to be both (Greenberg & Kuczaj, 1982; Clark, 1983; Cromer, 1991). On the cognitive side of the argument are several pieces of evidence I described in Chapter 5, such as the fact that young babies are able to remember and imitate objects and actions over periods of time—long before they have language to assist them.

Further evidence of cognitive primacy comes from the study of the child's use of various prepositions like *in*, *between*, or *in front of*, each of which seems to be used spontaneously in language only after the child has understood the concept (Johnston, 1985).

At the same time, children's language seems to affect their concepts too. As Russian psychologist Lev Vygotsky noted years ago (1962), there is a point somewhere in the child's second year when she "discovers" that objects have names. In part this discovery itself seems to rest on a new cognitive ability, the ability to categorize things. In one longitudinal study, for example, Alison Gopnik and Andrew Meltzoff (1987) found that the "naming explosion" typically occurs just after, or at the same time as, children first show spontaneous categorization of mixed sets of objects. Having discovered "categories," the child may now rapidly learn the names for already existing categories. At the same time, the naming explosion means that the child is likely to learn a whole lot of new words, too, which may help to create new categories, new mental schemes.

Extending the Class.   But what kind of categories does the child create? Suppose your 2-year-old, on catching sight of the family tabby, says, "See kitty." No doubt you will be pleased that the child has the right word applied to the animal. But what does the word *kitty* mean to the child? Does he think it is a name only for that particular fuzzy beast? Or does he think it applies to all furry creatures, or all things with four legs, or things with pointed ears, or what?

One way to figure out the kind of class or category the child has created is to see what other creatures or things he also calls *kitty*. That is, we can ask how the class is

To many students, discussions of the relationship between language and thought seem abstruse and uninteresting. See if you can put into your own words why this issue might be important or interesting. Can you think of a reason why it would matter, in real life, whether language or thought dominates?

Katherine, at 16 months, is just about the right age for what Vygotsky calls the "naming explosion." Here she is responding to a question from her mother: "Where are Daddy's teeth?"

extended in the child's language. If the child has a kitty category based on furriness, then many dogs and perhaps sheep would also be called kitty. If having a tail is a crucial feature, then sheep might be excluded, as would some breeds of cat. Or perhaps the child uses the word *kitty* only for the family cat. This would imply a very narrow category indeed. The general question for researchers has been whether children tend to use words narrowly or broadly, overextending or underextending them.

Our current information tells us that children *overextend* their early words more often than they *underextend* them, so we're more likely to hear the word *kitty* applied to dogs or guinea pigs than we are to hear it used for just one animal or for a very small set of animals or objects (Clark, 1983). All children seem to show overextensions, but the particular classes the child creates are unique to each child. There doesn't seem to be any tendency for all children to use the word *kitty* to apply to all four-footed animals or to all furry creatures or whatever. Some examples of overextensions, collected by Eve Clark (1975), are in Table 7.3.

These overextensions *may* tell us something about the way children think, such as that they have broad classes. But linguists like Clark remind us that part of the child's problem is that he simply doesn't know very many words. A child who wants to call attention to a horse may not know the word *horse*, so may say "dog" instead. Overextensions may thus arise from the child's desire to communicate and may not tell us that the child fails to make the discriminations involved (Clark, 1977, 1987).

Parents may also contribute to a child's overextensions. Carolyn and Cynthia Mervis (1982) found that mothers use the labels that they think the child will understand, rather than using the more precise labels. So they may call leopards and lions "kitty cats," or a toy fire engine a "car." Such a pattern may aid communication between mother and child, but it also may contribute to what we hear as overextensions in the child's early language.

Constraints on Word Learning. One of the most fundamental questions about word meanings, the subject of hot debate among linguists in recent years, is just how a child figures out which part of some scene a word may refer to. The classic example: A child sees a brown dog running across the grass with a bone in its mouth. An adult points and says *doggie*. From such an encounter the toddler is somehow supposed to figure out that

---

TABLE 7.3 Examples of Overextensions in the Language of Several Different Young Children

Word	Object or event for which the word was originally used	Other objects or events to which the word was later applied
mooi	moon	cakes, round marks on windows, writing on windows and in books, round shapes in books, tooling in leather book covers, round postmarks, letter O
buti	ball	toy, radish, stone spheres at park entrance
sch	sound of train	all moving machines
em	worm	flies, ants, all small insects, heads of timothy grass
fafer	sound of trains	steaming coffeepot, anything that hissed or made a noise
baw	ball	apples, grapes, eggs, squash, bell, clapper, anything round
va	white plush dog	muffler, cat, father's fur coat

Source: Reprinted with permission from Eve V. Clark, "Knowledge, context, and strategy in the acquisition of meaning." In *Georgetown University Round Table 1975; Developmental psycholinguistics: Theory and applications.* Edited by Daniel P. Dato. Copyright 1975 by Georgetown University, Washington, D.C., pp. 83–84.

If this mom or dad were to point toward the grass and say ''grass,'' how would this 2-year-old know whether the word meant ''green'' or ''dirt'' or ''there'' or ''grass''?

doggie refers to the animal, and not to running, or bone, or dog-plus-bone, or brownness, or ears, or grass, or any other combination of elements in the whole scene.

Many linguists have proposed that a child could only conceivably cope with this monumentally complex task if he operated with some built-in biases or *constraints* (e.g., Markman, 1989; Markman & Hutchinson, 1984; Waxman & Kosowski, 1990; Woodward & Markman, 1991). For example, the child may have a built-in initial assumption that words refer to objects *or* events but not both, or an assumption that words refer to whole objects and not to their parts or attributes.

Another possible built-in assumption or constraint is the *principle of contrast*, namely, that every word has a different meaning, so if a different word is used, it must refer to some different object or a different aspect of an object (Clark, 1983, 1987, 1990). For example, in a widely quoted study, Carey and Bartlett (1978) interrupted a play session with 2- and 3-year-old children by pointing to two trays and saying, "bring me the chromium tray, not the red one, the chromium one." These children already knew the word *red* but did not know the word *chromium*. Nonetheless, most of the children were able to follow the instruction by bringing the nonred tray. Furthermore, a week later about half of the children remembered that the word *chromium* referred to some color and that the color was "not red." Thus they learned the meaning by contrast.

Many linguists do not accept the idea of built-in constraints. Doubters such as Katherine Nelson (1988) point out that most of the research on language constraints has been done with children who were well past the one-word stage of language. It is possible that such biases, if they exist, are not built in but emerge as the child is learning language. Furthermore, Nelson suggests that the child rarely encounters a situation in which the adult points vaguely and gives some word. Most often, the child tries a sound or word and the adult guesses what the child may mean. Or the child points and the adult supplies the word. Thus the language the child hears is typically responsive to the child's own actions and emerging categories. The constraints on the process are the child's own conceptual system and the ability of the adult to interpret the child's meaning rather than some built-in tendencies within the child.

This debate reflects another facet of the broader nature/nurture argument. We've already seen in research on early perceptual development that quite a lot seems to be built in at birth. To what extent may this also be true of language? Is a baby born already programmed in some fashion to acquire language? Or does the child construct language based on specific experience?

On the basis of this very brief presentation, do you find yourself persuaded by Clark's constraint argument, or Nelson's counterargument? What more would you want to know?

Explaining Language Development

Explaining how a child learns language has proven to be one of the most compelling and one of the most difficult challenges within developmental psychology. This may surprise you. I suspect that most of you just take for granted that a child learns to talk by listening to the language she hears. What is magical or complicated about that? Well, the more you think about it, the more amazing and mysterious it becomes. For one thing, as Steven Pinker (1987) points out, there is a veritable chasm between what the child hears as language input and the language the child must eventually speak. The input consists of some set of sentences spoken to the child, with intonation, stress, and timing. They are spoken in the presence of objects and events, and the words are given in a particular order. All that may be helpful, even essential. But what the child must acquire from such input is nothing less than a set of rules for *creating* sentences. And the rules are not directly given in the sentences she hears. How does the child accomplish this feat? Theories abound. Let me start on the nurture end of the theoretical continuum.

Imitation and Reinforcement.   The earliest theories of language were based either on learning theory or on the common-sense idea that language was learned by imitation. Imitation obviously has to play some part, because the child learns the language she hears. Babbling drifts toward the sounds in the heard language; children imitate sentences they hear; they learn to speak with the accent of their parents. And those babies who show the most imitation of actions and gestures are also those who learn later language most quickly (Bates et al., 1982). So the tendency to imitate may be an important ingredient. Still, imitation alone can't explain all of language acquisition because it cannot account for the creative quality of the child's language. In particular, children consistently create types of sentences and forms of words that they have never heard—words like *goed* or *beated*.

Reinforcement theories such as Skinner's (1957) fare no better. Skinner argued that parents shape language through systematic reinforcements, gradually rewarding better and better approximations of adult speech. But in fact there is little evidence that parents do anything like this. Instead, parents are remarkably forgiving of all sorts of peculiar constructions and meaning (Brown & Hanlon, 1970; Hirsh-Pasek, Trieman & Schneiderman, 1984). In addition, children learn many forms of language, such as plurals, with relatively few errors, so some process other than shaping has to be involved.

Newer Environmental Theories: Talking to the Child.   Still, it seems obvious that what is said to the child has to play *some* role in the process. At the simplest level, we know that children whose parents talk to them often, read to them regularly, and respond to the child's own verbalizations, have children who begin to talk a little sooner. So at least the *rate* of development is affected by the amount of input.

The quality of the parents' language may also be important. In particular, we know that adults talk to children in a special kind of very simple language, often called **motherese**. This simple language is spoken in a higher-pitched voice and at a slower pace than is talk between adults. The sentences are short, with simple, concrete vocabulary, and they are grammatically simple. When speaking to children, parents also repeat a lot, with minor variations ("Where is the ball? Can you see the ball? Where is the ball? There is the ball!"). They may also repeat the child's sentence but in a slightly longer, more grammatically correct form—a pattern referred to as *expansion* or *recasting*.

Parents don't talk this way to children in order to teach them language. They do so with the hope that they will communicate better that way. Indeed, many of us unconsciously fall into this same pattern of speech when talking to the elderly or the handicapped or hospitalized patients—anyone in a dependent position. When used with adults, motherese is experienced as patronizing, but it may well be very useful, even necessary, for the child's language acquisition.

We can't hear what this mom is saying, but chances are she is talking to her daughter in some form of motherese, using short, simple sentences in a high-pitched, lilting voice. Children prefer this form of speech, and it may help them identify regularities in language.

We know, for example, that babies as young as a few days old can discriminate between motherese and adult-directed speech and *that they prefer to listen to motherese* (Cooper & Aslin, 1990). In particular, it seems to be the higher pitch of motherese that babies prefer (Fernald & Kuhl, 1987). Once the child's attention is drawn by this special tone, the very simplicity and repetitiveness of the adult's speech may help the child to pick out repeating grammatical forms (Hoff-Ginsberg, 1986).

Children's attention also seems to be drawn to recast sentences. In one recent study, for example, Farrar (1992) found that 2-year-old children were two to three times as likely to imitate a correct grammatical form after they had heard their mother recast their own sentences than they were when that same correct grammatical form appeared naturally in the mother's conversation. Experimental studies confirm this effect of recastings. Children who are deliberately exposed to higher rates of specific types of recast sentences seem to learn those grammatical forms more quickly (Keith Nelson, 1977).

Sounds good, doesn't it? But there are some holes in this theory. For one thing, while children who hear more expansions learn grammar sooner, children who rarely hear such forms nonetheless acquire a complex grammar, albeit more slowly. And while motherese does seem to occur in the vast majority of cultures and contexts, it does not occur in *all*. For example, Pye (1986) could find no sign of motherese in one Mayan culture, and studies in the United States show it is greatly reduced among depressed mothers (Bettes, 1988). Children of these mothers nonetheless learn language. Thus while motherese may be helpful, it cannot be *necessary* for language.

Innateness Theories.   On the other side of the theoretical spectrum we have the innateness theorists, who argue that much of what the child needs for learning language is built in to the organism. Early innateness theorists like Noam Chomsky (1965, 1975, 1986, 1988) were especially struck by two phenomena: the extreme complexity of the task the child must accomplish, and the apparent similarities in the steps and stages of children's early language. Recent studies of children learning many other languages now make it clear that there is more variability than first appeared—a set of findings I've described in the "across cultures" box on page 164. Nonetheless, innateness theories are alive and well and highly influential.

The most influential current innateness theorist is Dan Slobin (1985a, 1985b), who assumes a basic language making capacity in any child, made up of a set of fundamental *operating principles.* Just as the newborn infant seems to come programmed with "rules to look by," so Slobin is arguing that infants and children are programmed with "rules to listen by."

You've already encountered a good deal of evidence in Chapter 5 that is consistent with this proposal. We know that from earliest infancy, babies focus on individual sounds

If there were *no* similarity across children or across languages in early language learning, that would obviously argue strongly against an innateness theory. But just how much similarity does there have to be for a theory of built-in biases or constraints to still make sense? This is a complex question, but think about it.

ACROSS CULTURES
Universals and Variations in Early Language

In the early years of research on children's language development, linguists and psychologists were strongly impressed by the apparent similarities in the vocabularies and early sentences children constructed. You'll remember some of the cross-cultural comparisons of early vocabulary from Chapter 5, which show strong similarities. Studies in a wide variety of language communities, including Turkish, Serbo-Croatian, Hungarian, Hebrew, Japanese, a New Guinean language called Kaluli, German, and Italian, have revealed other important similarities:

- The prelinguistic phase seems to be identical in all language communities. All babies coo, then babble; all babies understand language before they can speak it; babies in all cultures begin to use their first words at about 12 months.
- In all language communities studied so far, a one-word phase precedes the two-word phase, with the latter beginning at about 18 months.
- Language learning is affected by the child's own actions. So, for example, in every language studied so far, when children first add verb inflections such as the past tense, they are more likely to add them to verbs that describe actions that bring visible results, such as *drop*, *fall*, *break*, or *spill*.
- In all languages studied so far, prepositions describing locations are added in essentially the same order. Words for *in*, *on*, *under*, and *beside* are learned first. Then the child learns the words *front* and *back* (Slobin, 1985a).
- Children seem to pay more attention to the ends of words than the beginnings, so they learn suffixes before they learn prefixes.

At the same time there are marked differences among languages and in children's early attempts to construct sentences in the language they are hearing. For example:

- The specific word order that a child uses in early sentences is not the same for all children in all languages. In some languages a noun/verb sequence is fairly common, in others a verb/noun sequence may be heard.
- Particular inflections are learned in highly varying orders from one language to another. Japanese children, for example, begin very early to use a special kind of marker, called a *pragmatic* marker, that tells something about the feeling or the context. For instance, in Japanese, the word *yo* is used at the end of a sentence when the speaker is experiencing some resistance from the listener; the word *ne* is used when the speaker expects approval or agreement. Japanese children begin to use these markers very early, much earlier than other inflections appear in most languages.
- Most strikingly, there are languages in which there seems to be no uninflected Stage 1 grammar at all. Children learning Turkish, for example, use essentially the full set of noun and verb inflections by age 2 and never go through a stage of using uninflected words. Their language is simple, but it is rarely ungrammatical from the adult's point of view (Aksu-Koc & Slobin, 1985).

Obviously any theory of language acquisition must account for both the common ground and the wide variations from one language to the next.

and on syllables in the stream of sounds they hear, that they pay attention to sound rhythm, and that they prefer speech of a particular pattern, namely motherese. Slobin also proposes that babies are preprogrammed to pay attention to the beginnings and endings of strings of sounds and to stressed sounds. Together, these operating principles would help to explain some of the features of children's early grammars.

The fact that this model is consistent with the growing information about apparently built-in perceptual skills and processing biases is certainly a strong argument in its favor. But it is still early days in the exploration of this approach, and there are other compelling alternatives. In particular, there are theorists who argue persuasively that what is important is not the built-in biases, but the child's *construction* of language as part of the broader process of cognitive development. In this view, the child is a "little linguist," applying her emerging cognitive understanding to the problem of language, searching for regularities and patterns.

Constructivist Theories of Language. Melissa Bowerman (1985) is the clearest proponent of this view. She puts the proposition this way: "When language starts to come in, it does not introduce new meanings to the child. Rather, it is used to express only those meanings the child has already formulated independently of language" (1985, p. 372).

If this is true, then we should observe clear links between achievements in language development and the child's broader cognitive development. For example, symbolic play, such as drinking from an empty cup, and imitation of sounds and gestures both appear at about the same time as the child's first words, suggesting some broad "symbolic" understanding that is reflected in a number of behaviors. In children whose language is significantly delayed, both symbolic play and imitation are normally delayed, too (Snyder, 1978; E. Bates, O'Connell & Shore, 1987; Ungerer & Sigman, 1984).

A second example occurs later: at about the point at which two-word sentences appear, we can also see children begin to combine several gestures into a sequence in their pretend play, such as pouring imaginary liquid, drinking, then wiping the mouth. Those children who are the first to show this sequencing in their play are also the first to show two- or three-word sentences in their speech (Bates et al., 1987; Shore, 1986; Brownell, 1988).

Obviously, we do not have to choose between Slobin's and Bowerman's approaches. Both may be true. The child may begin with built-in operating principles that aim the child's attention at crucial features of the language input. The child then processes that information according to her initial (perhaps built-in) strategies or schemes. But then she modifies those strategies or rules as she receives new information. The result is a series of rules for understanding and creating language. The strong similarities we see among children in their early language constructions come about both because all children share the same initial processing rules and because most children are exposed to very similar input from the people around them. But because the input is not identical, because languages differ, language development follows less and less common pathways as the child progresses.

As these brief descriptions of theory make clear, linguists and psychologists who have studied language have clearly made progress. We know a lot more now about how *not* to explain language. But we have not yet cracked the code. The fact that children learn complex and varied use of their native tongue within a few years remains both miraculous and largely mysterious.

The broader changes in the child's cognitive skills over the same years seem less mysterious, but we continue to learn more about the remarkable cognitive accomplishments of the preschool child as well as the limitations on her thinking.

▶ Changes in Thinking Between 2 and 6

Let me begin, as I did in Chapter 5, with a look at Piaget's view of the cognitive changes during these years, because his thinking has formed the framework of so much of our research on this age period.

Piaget's View of the Preoperational Period

According to Piaget, at about age 2 the child begins to use *symbols*—images or words or actions that *stand for* something else. What is more, she can now manipulate those symbols mentally. Both these changes mark the beginning of what Piaget calls the **preoperational period**.

We can see this shift clearly in children's pretend play, which I talk about in the "research report" on page 166. Among preschoolers, a broom may become a horsie, or a block may become a train. We can also see such symbol use in the emergence of language at about the same time. And we see the child's improving ability to manipulate these symbols internally in such things as her improving memory or in her ability to search more systematically for lost or hidden objects.

RESEARCH REPORT
Young Children's Play

If you watch young children during some unstructured time—when they are not eating or napping or being "organized" by the adults—you'll see them building towers out of blocks, moving dolls around in the doll house, making "tea" with the tea set, racing toy trucks across the floor, dressing up in grown-up clothes, putting puzzles together. They are, in a word, *playing*. This is not trivial or empty activity; it is the stuff on which much of cognitive development seems to be built.

The form of this play changes in very visible ways during the years from 1 to 6. Psychologists who have observed these changes describe several distinct types of play, emerging in a series of steps or stages (Rubin, Fein & Vandenberg, 1983). The stages flow together a good deal; children show several of these kinds of play at any one time. Still, the several types of play typically develop in the following order:

Sensorimotor Play.   The child of 12 months or so spends most of her play time exploring and manipulating objects using all the sensorimotor schemes in her repertoire. She puts things in her mouth, shakes them, stacks them, moves them along the floor. In this way she comes to understand what objects can do.

Constructive Play.   Such exploratory play with objects does continue past 12 months, especially with some totally new object, but by age 2 or so children begin to use objects to build or construct things—creating a block tower, putting together a puzzle, making something out of clay or with Tinkertoys. Such "constructive" play makes up nearly half of the play of children aged 3 to 6 (Rubin, Fein & Vandenberg, 1983).

First Pretend Play.   Pretend play also begins at about this same time. A child's first sign of such pretending is usually something like using a toy spoon to "feed" himself or a toy comb to comb his hair. The toys are still used for their actual or typical purposes

(the spoon for feeding), and the actions are still oriented to the *self*, but there is pretend involved. Between 15 and 21 months, there is a shift: The recipient of the pretend action now becomes another person or a toy. The child is still using objects for their usual purposes (such as drinking from a cup), but now she is using the toy cup with a doll instead of herself. Dolls are especially good toys for this kind of pretend, because it is not a very large leap from doing things to yourself to doing things with a doll. So children dress and undress dolls, feed them imaginary food, comb their hair.

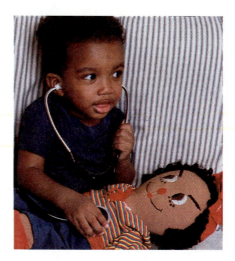

Substitute Pretend Play.   Between 2 and 3 years of age children begin to use objects to stand for something altogether different. They may comb the doll's hair with a baby bottle while saying that it is a comb, or use a broom to be a "horsie", or make "trucks" out of blocks. Constructive play, in which toys are used for their "real" purposes, does not disappear. But by age 4 or 5, children spend as much as 20 percent of their play time in this new, complicated kind of pretending (Field, De Stefano & Koewler, 1982).

Sociodramatic Play.   Somewhere in the preschool years children also begin to play parts or take roles. They play "daddy and mommy," "cowboys and indians," "doctor and patient," "train conductor and passengers" and many similar roles. You can see this among children as young as 2 or 3 when they are playing with their brothers or sisters; it appears a bit later in the play of nonsibling pairs or groups, perhaps at age 3 or 4. Children clearly get great delight out of these often-elaborate fantasies. Equally important, by playing roles, by pretending to be someone else, they also become more and more aware of how things may look or feel to someone else, and their egocentric approach to the world declines.

Beyond the accomplishment of symbol use, Piaget's description of the thinking of the preschool child was oddly negative in tone. He focused mostly on all the things the preschool age child still cannot do. More recent research has given us a much more positive view. I can contrast the two views most clearly by describing several key dimensions of the toddler's thinking, first through Piaget's eyes and then through the eyes of recent researchers.

Perspective Taking: Egocentrism.   Piaget's observations led him to conclude that children in this preoperational stage look at things entirely from their own perspective, from their own frame of reference, a quality Piaget called **egocentrism** (Piaget, 1954). The child is not being selfish; rather she simply thinks (assumes) that everyone sees the world her way.

Figure 7.1 shows a photo of a classic experiment illustrating this kind of egocentrism. The child is shown a three-dimensional scene with mountains of different sizes and colors. From a set of drawings, he picks out the one that shows the scene the way he sees it. Most preschoolers can do this without much difficulty. Then the examiner asks the child to pick out the drawing that shows how someone *else* sees the scene, such as the little doll figure, or the examiner. At this point preschool children have a problem. Most often they pick the drawing that shows their *own* view of the mountains (e.g., Gzesh & Surber, 1985; Flavell et al., 1981). For the child to be able to succeed at this task, according to Piaget, he must "decenter"—he must shift from using himself as the only frame of reference.

Understanding Identities.   In a similar way, Piaget thought that the preschool child needed to acquire another whole level or layer of understanding of the identity of objects. The sensorimotor infant eventually understands that objects continue to exist even when they are out of sight. But there are other aspects of objects that also remain constant despite apparent changes—that are *conserved*, in Piaget's language—and these new constancies baffle the preschool child.

I described some of Piaget's tests of the concept of conservation in the "research report" in Chapter 2. Table 7.4 lists all six of the different conservations Piaget studied. In every case, his measurement technique involved first showing the child two equal sets of objects, getting the child to agree they were equal in some key respect such as weight or quantity or length or number, and then shifting or deforming one of the objects and asking the child if they were still the same in some way. Children rarely show any of these forms of conservation before age 5, which Piaget took to be a sign that they were still captured by the *appearance* of change, and did not focus on the underlying, unchanging aspect.

Classification.   Piaget was also interested in the child's ability to classify objects—to put things in sets or types and to use abstract or formal properties, such as color or shape or even verbal labels, as a basis for such classification. Piaget studied this by giving young children sets of objects or picture cutouts of people, animals, or toys, and asking the child to put together the things that "go together" or "are similar" (Piaget & Inhelder, 1959). Two- and 3-year-old children, faced with such an array, will usually make designs or pictures. At perhaps 4, children begin showing more systematic sorting and grouping of objects, using first one dimension, such as shape, and later two or more dimensions at once, such as size *and* shape.

Despite this big advance, there is still some distance to go. In particular, the preoperational child still does not grasp the principle of **class inclusion**: She does not understand that some classes are fully contained within other classes. Dogs are part of the larger class of animals, roses are part of the class of flowers, and so forth.

For a child to show that she understands class inclusion it is not enough for her simply to use words like *animal* to refer to more than one kind of creature. She must also under-

Figure 7.1 This kind of experimental situation is similar to one Piaget used to study egocentrism in children. The child is first asked to pick out the picture that shows how the two mountains look to him, and then to pick out the picture that shows how the mountains look to the little clay man. Preschool children typically pick the same picture both times — the one that shows how it looks from their perspective.

Can you think of any examples of egocentrism in your own behavior? What about buying someone else the gift you were hoping to receive yourself? Other examples?

TABLE 7.4 Types of Conservation Studied by Piaget

Type	Method of Assessment
Number	Two rows with equal numbers of pennies or buttons, laid out parallel to one another with the items matching. Then one row is stretched out longer or squeezed together, or rearranged in some other way, and the child is asked, "Are there the same number?"
Length	Two pencils of identical length are laid one above the other so that they match perfectly; then one is displaced to the right or left so that one pencil's point sticks out further than the other. The child is asked if they are now the same length.
Quantity	Two identical beakers, with equal amounts of water; one is then poured into another glass, either tall and thin or short and squat. The child is asked if there is still the same amount to drink in each.
Substance or mass	Two equal balls of clay, one of which is then squashed or molded into another shape, such as a sausage or a pancake. The child is then asked if there is now the same amount of clay in each.
Weight	Two equal balls of clay, as for conservation of substance. They are weighed on a balance scale so that the child sees that they weigh the same. One is then deformed into another shape and the child asked if they still "have the same amount of weight."
Volume	Again two balls of clay are used, placed in two equal beakers of water so that the child sees that they displace the same amount of water. Then one ball is deformed, and the child asked if they will still "take up the same amount of space."

stand the logical relationships—a point I also talked about in the "research report" in Chapter 2. Piaget did not think that this understanding came until about age 7.

Newer Views of the Preoperational Child

In Chapter 5 I pointed out again and again that Piaget had underestimated babies' abilities to discriminate, compare, and imitate. The same point emerges very strongly from recent research on the thinking of children from ages 2 to 6. Children in this age range appear to be a good deal more cognitively skillful than Piaget's research had suggested.

Perspective Taking. Research on perspective taking, for example, shows that children as young as 2 and 3 have at least *some* ability to understand that other people see things or experience things differently than they do. For example, children this age will adapt their speech or their play to the demands of their companion. They play differently with older or younger playmates, and talk differently to a younger or a handicapped child (Brownell, 1990; Guralnick & Paul-Brown, 1984).

But such understanding is clearly not perfect at this young age. John Flavell has proposed that there are two levels of such perspective-taking ability. At Level 1, the child knows *that* some other person experiences something differently. At Level 2, the child develops a whole series of complex rules for figuring out precisely *what* the other person sees or experiences (Flavell, 1985; Flavell, Green & Flavell, 1990). Two- and 3-year-olds have Level 1 knowledge but not Level 2. We begin to see some Level 2 knowledge in 4- and 5-year-olds.

This clear shift in perspective-taking ability is but one aspect of what appears to be a broad change at about age 4. Let me give you some other examples.

John Flavell has shown that before about age 4, children confuse appearance and reality. If you show them a sponge that has been painted to look like a rock, they will either say that the object looks like a sponge and is a sponge, or that it looks like a rock and is a rock. But 4- and 5-year-olds can distinguish the two; they realize that it looks like a rock but *is* a sponge (Flavell, 1986). Thus the older child now understands that the same object can be represented differently, depending on one's point of view.

Using the same type of materials, investigators have also asked if a child can grasp the principle of a *false belief*. After the child has felt the sponge/rock and has answered questions about what it looks like and what it "really" is, you can ask something like this: "John [a playmate of the subject's] hasn't touched this, he hasn't squeezed it. If John just sees it over here like this, what will he think it is? Will he think it's a rock or will he think that it's a sponge?" (Gopnik & Astington, 1988, p. 35). By and large, 3-year-olds think that John will believe it is a sponge, while 4- and 5-year-olds realize that because John hasn't felt the sponge, he will have a false belief that it is a rock. Thus the child of 4 or 5 understands that someone else can believe something that isn't true. Further support for the fundamental nature of this shift comes from cross-cultural studies of children in Japan, China, and from a pygmy tribe in Cameroon, all of whom show precisely the same shift between age 3 and 5 (Avis & Harris, 1991; Flavell et al., 1983; Gardner et al, 1988).

Evidence like this has led a number of theorists (e.g. Astington & Gopnik, 1991; Harris, 1989; Perner, 1991) to propose that the 4-year-old has developed a new and more sophisticated **theory of mind**. The child this age has begun to understand that you cannot predict what other people will do solely from observing the situation itself; the other person's desires and beliefs also enter into the equation. So the child develops various theories about other people's ideas, beliefs, and desires and about how these will affect behavior.

Such a theory of mind does not spring forth full-blown at age 4. Three-year-olds understand some aspects of the links between people's thinking and their behavior. They know that a person who wants something will try to get it. They also know that that people will feel sad if they fail and happy if they succeed (Wellman, 1988). But they do not yet understand about others' beliefs or the effects such beliefs will have on the others' feelings. It is this new aspect of the theory of mind that we can see emerging at about 4 or 5.

The theories of mind of the 3- and 4-year-old differ in other ways as well. The 3-year-old seems to assume that there is a single "world" to be known, and that everyone knows it in the same way. The 4-year-old assumes that there are many worlds, and that other people not only know (or experience) different things, but that it is possible to "know" or believe something that is not true, and to change one's belief. The 4-year-old can remember that he used to think something different—that he used to think that the sponge was a rock but no longer believes that—a first hint of the development of the ability to be *aware* of what one knows and thinks.

The work on the child's theory of mind has not only opened up a fascinating new area of research, it has clearly demonstrated that the preschool child is vastly less egocentric than Piaget supposed. By age 4, and in more limited ways at earlier ages, the child has a remarkably sophisticated ability to understand other points of view and can predict other people's behavior based on deductions about their beliefs or feelings. I don't know about you, but I find this an amazing achievement.

Understanding Identities.   In contrast to the work on perspective taking, studies of conservation have generally confirmed Piaget's basic observations. Although younger children can demonstrate some understanding of conservation if the task is made very simple (e.g., Gelman, 1972; Wellman, 1982), most children cannot consistently solve conservation problems until age 5 or 6 or later.

Even more interesting is the discovery that conservation and perspective taking are part of the same basic process, namely the understanding of the relationship between appearance and reality. To understand conservation is to understand that something can

Consider your own theory of mind. What assumptions do you make about the way other people's behavior is affected by their beliefs or feelings or ideas? You operate on the basis of such a theory all the time, but can you articulate it?

These 3-year-olds already have some idea that other people's actions are affected by their feelings and ideas, but they probably do not yet understand false belief.

change in appearance but still stay the same "for real," just as the sponge looks like a rock but is really a sponge. Flavell has studied this in various ways beyond the sponge/rock problem or the classical conservation tasks. He has shown children objects under colored lights so that the apparent color changes; he has put masks on animals to make them look like another animal. In these studies, 2- and 3-year-olds consistently judge things by their appearance; by age 5, the child begins to be able to separate the appearance from the underlying reality and knows that some object isn't "really" red even though it looks red under a red-colored light, or that a cat with a dog mask is still "really" a cat (e.g., Flavell, Green & Flavell, 1989; Flavell et al., 1987; Taylor & Hort, 1990). Thus the child's ability to solve conservation problems at age 5 or 6 seems to rest on a more general awareness of the difference between appearance and reality.

Classification Skills. This ought to sound like a familiar refrain by now: Young children classify better than Piaget thought, particularly if you simplify the task or if you make it clear that you want them to use some kind of superordinate category for classifying. For example, Sandra Waxman and Rochel Gelman (1986) told 3- and 4-year-olds that a puppet really liked pictures of food (or animals, or furniture). The children were then given 12 pictures and asked to put the ones the puppet would like in one bin and the ones the puppet would not like in another bin. When they were given the category label in this way, these young children could quite easily classify the pictures into food and nonfood categories, or furniture and nonfurniture categories.

Even 2-year-olds may be capable of such classification. In one study, Sugerman (1979, cited in Gelman & Baillargeon, 1983) gave toddlers sets of toys that included two groups, such as four dolls and four rings. She found that they tended to move the toys in these two groups into different piles or sets during play, which suggests that they already treat them as categories or classes to some extent.

All in all, this research shows that the basic understanding that things-go-together-in-groups is present by at least age 2 (and perhaps earlier). But whether the child can display this understanding will depend on the way you set up the task. Piaget happened to pick a relatively difficult version of the task, so he ended up underestimating the child's understanding.

Class inclusion, however, is another matter. Post-Piagetian researchers have consistently found that real understanding of class inclusion does not appear until age 7 or 8, just as Piaget originally suggested (e.g., McCabe et al., 1982).

Overview of the Preoperational Child

If we add up the different bits of information I've just given you, two points seem clear. First, it is obvious that Piaget underestimated the preoperational child. Preschool children are capable of forms of logic that Piaget thought impossible at this stage. Not only can they classify objects by form or function, they are markedly less egocentric than Piaget believed. By age 4, most children have devised an unexpectedly sophisticated theory of others' minds.

However, while such performances can be *elicited*, 2-, 3-, and 4-year-old children do not necessarily show these more sophisticated understandings spontaneously. In order for the preschool child to demonstrate these relatively advanced forms of thinking, you have to make the task quite simple, eliminate distractions, or give special clues. The fact that children this age can solve these problems at all is striking, but it is still true that preschool children think differently from older children. The very fact that they can perform certain tasks *only* when the tasks are made very simple or undistracting is evidence for such a difference. In general, their attention is more likely to be captured by appearance, by externals. They do not seem to experience the world or think about it with as general a set of rules or principles as we see in older children and thus they do not easily generalize something they have learned in one context to a similar but not identical situation. It is precisely such a switch to general rules that Piaget thought characterized the transition to the next stage, that of concrete operations—a development I'll be talking about in Chapter 9.

▶ Individual Differences in Language and Cognitive Functioning

The sequences and patterns of language and cognition I've been describing give you a general picture, but it is nonetheless a somewhat misleading picture. There are also important variations from one child to the next, particularly in the rate of development the child shows, and in the child's relative ability to perform intellectual tasks. We see such differences not only in the speed of the child's language development, but in measures of cognitive power such as IQ tests.

Differences in Rate of Language Development

Some children begin using individual words at 8 months, others not until 18 months; some do not use two-word sentences until age 3 or even later. You can see the range of normal variation very clearly in the behavior of the three children Roger Brown has studied intensively, Eve, Adam, and Sarah. Figure 7.2 shows the average sentence length (referred to by linguists as the *mean length of utterance*, or MLU) of each of the children at each age. I have drawn a line at the MLU level which normally accompanies a switch

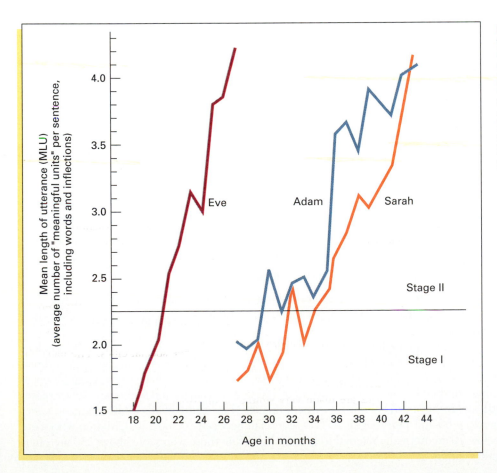

Figure 7.2 Children go through the various steps and stages of language development at markedly different rates. Eve reached Stage II grammar (noted by the horizontal line across the graph) at about 21 months, while Adam and Sarah were much slower. (*Source:* R. Brown, 1973, *A First Language*, Cambridge, MA: Harvard University Press, p. 55. Reprinted by permission.)

from Stage I to Stage II grammar. You can see that Eve made this transition at about 21 months, while Adam and Sarah passed over this point about a year later.

Variations within this range are *not* predictive of later IQ. Thus you should not worry if your child seems to be late in language development (nor be especially ecstatic if your baby begins to use words at 8 months). Such variations seem to have at least some genetic basis (e.g., Mather & Black, 1984; Plomin & DeFries, 1985a, 1985b), but they are also at least partly a response to differences in the richness of the language environment. Among adoptive families, for example, those who read to their children more and talk to them more have children who develop language more quickly.

Differences in Intelligence Among Preschoolers

In Chapter 5, I mentioned that so-called infant IQ tests were not strongly related to later measures of IQ. But I did not give you a full description of such later measures, nor define IQ. It is now time to do both.

Remember from Chapter 5 that the study of intelligence is part of the "cognitive power" tradition. Those who approached the study of thinking in this way were struck by the obvious variations among individuals in their ability to think, analyze, or learn new material. These researchers sought ways to measure and to understand those differences.

The First IQ Tests. The first modern intelligence test was created by Binet and Simon (1905). From the beginning, the test had a practical purpose, which was to identify children who might have difficulty in school. For this reason, the tests Binet and Simon devised were very much like some school tasks, including measures of vocabulary, comprehension of facts and relationships, and mathematical and verbal reasoning. Can the child describe the difference between wood and glass? Can the young child touch his nose, his ear, his head? Can he tell which of two weights is heavier?

Lewis Terman and his associates at Stanford University (Terman, 1916; Terman & Merrill, 1937) modified and extended many of Binet's original tests when they translated and revised the test for use in the United States. The several Terman revisions, called the **Stanford-Binet**, consist of a series of six individual tests for children of each age. A child taking the test is given the age tests beginning below his actual age, then those for his age, then those for each successively older age until the child reaches a level at which he fails all six tests. Terman initially described a child's performance in terms of a score called an **intelligence quotient,** later shortened to IQ. This score was computed by comparing the child's chronological age (in years and months) with his *mental age,* defined as the level of questions he could answer correctly. A child who could solve the problems for a 6-year-old but not those for a 7-year-old would have a mental age of 6. The formula used to calculate the IQ was

$$\frac{\text{Mental age}}{\text{Chronological age}} \times 100 = \text{IQ}$$

This formula results in an IQ above 100 for children whose mental age is higher than their chronological age and an IQ below 100 for children whose mental age is below their chronological age.

This old system for calculating the IQ is not used any longer, even in the modern revisions of the Stanford-Binet. Nowadays, IQs from all tests are calculated by a direct comparison of a child's performance with the average performance of a large group of other children his own age. But an IQ of 100 is still average, and higher and lower scores still mean above and below average performance. Two-thirds of all children achieve scores between 85 and 115; roughly 95% of scores fall between 70 and 130. Children who score below 70 are normally referred to as **retarded**, while those who score above 130 are often called **gifted**.

RESEARCH REPORT
The Wechsler Intelligence Scale for Children (WISC)

Unlike the Binet, which has separate tests for children of each age, on the WISC-R all children are given the same ten subtests or problems. Each subtest begins with very easy items and moves steadily toward more difficult items. A child begins with the easy ones and continues until she misses some specified number. The ten are divided into two groups, those that rely heavily on verbal abilities, and those that involve less language ability and test the child's perceptual skills and nonverbal logic, collectively called *performance* tests.

Verbal Tests

- *General Information:* "How many eyes have you?"
- *General Comprehension:* "What is the thing to do when you scrape your knee?"
- *Arithmetic:* "James had ten marbles and he bought four more. How many marbles did he have altogether?"
- *Similarities*: "In what way are a pear and an orange alike?"
- *Vocabulary:* "What is an emerald?"

Performance Tests

- *Picture Completion:* The child is shown pictures of familiar objects in which a part has been left out. He has to identify the missing part, such as a comb with a tooth missing.
- *Picture Arrangement:* Pictures like the frames of a comic strip are laid out in the wrong order in front of the child. The child has to figure out the right order to make a story.
- *Block Design:* Sets of blocks that are red and white on different sides, and half red/half white on the other sides are given to the child. Using these blocks, he has to copy designs. The first problems involve only four blocks; harder problems include nine blocks.
- *Object Assembly:* Large pictures of familiar objects, such as a horse or a face, have been cut up into pieces rather like a jigsaw puzzle with larger pieces. The child has to put them together in the correct configuration as rapidly as possible.
- *Coding:* A series of abstract symbols, such as balls and stars, are each shown with a paired symbol, such as a single line. The child then has several rows of the first set of symbols and must fill in the paired symbol next to each one.

Modern IQ Tests. The tests used most frequently by psychologists today are the Revised Stanford-Binet and the Wechsler Intelligence Scales for Children (Revised), usually called the **WISC-R,** which was developed by David Wechsler (1974). To give you some idea of the sort of items included in tests like these, I've described the WISC-R in some detail in the "research report" above.

Stability and Predictive Value of IQ Tests. Because these tests were originally designed to predict a child's ability to perform in school, it is obviously crucial to know whether they do this job well. The research findings on this point are quite consistent: the correlation between a child's test score and her current or later grades in school is about .50 to .60 (Carver, 1990; Brody, 1992). This is a strong but by no means perfect correlation. It tells us that on the whole, children with top IQ scores will also be among the high achievers in school, and those who score low will be among the low achievers. Still, some children with high IQ scores don't shine in school, while some lower IQ children do.

I am *not* saying here that IQ *causes* good or poor performance in school—although that is one possibility and one that has been widely believed. All we are sure of is that the two events—high or low IQ scores and high or low school performance—tend to go together, so that we can use one to predict the other.

At the same time, IQ scores are less stable than you probably think. If two tests are given a few months or a few years apart, the scores are likely to be very similar. The correlations between adjacent-year IQ scores in middle childhood, for example, are typically in the range of .80 (Honzik, 1986). Yet this high level of predictability masks an interesting fact: most children show quite wide fluctuations in their scores. Robert McCall and his colleagues (McCall, Appelbaum & Hogarty, 1973), for example, looked at the test scores of a group of 80 children who had been given IQ tests at regular intervals from the time they were 2½ until they were 17. The *average* difference between the highest

This second grader is working on the Block Design subtest of the WISC.

Given what I have said so far about IQ tests, do you think it would be worth-while to have every pre-school child tested? How would you use such scores? What would be the draw-backs of such universal testing?

and the lowest score achieved by each child in this group was 28 points, and one child in seven showed a shift of more than 40 points.

Such wide fluctuations are more common in young children. The general rule of thumb is that the older the child, the more stable the IQ score becomes, although even in older children, scores may still show fluctuations in response to major stresses such as parental divorce or changing schools or the birth of a sibling.

The fact that such wide variations can occur calls into question a common school practice of using a fixed cutoff score for determining eligibility for special programs, such as those for gifted or retarded children, particularly if only a single test score is used. For example, if the cutoff for eligibility for a gifted program is an IQ of 135, a child might obtain a score of 130 at one testing, be declared ineligible, and not be tested again later, even though the child might score above 135 on another occasion.

Limitations of IQ tests.   Before I move on to the question of the possible origins of differences in IQ, it is important to emphasize a few key limitations of such tests or the scores derived from them.

IQ tests do not measure underlying competence. An IQ score cannot tell you (or a teacher, or anyone else) that your child has some specific, fixed, underlying capacity. They can measure only performance on some given day.

The scores are not etched on a child's forehead at birth, never to change. IQ scores become quite stable in late childhood, but individual children can and do shift, particularly in response to any stress in their lives.

Perhaps most important, traditional IQ tests simply do not measure a whole host of skills that are likely to be highly significant for getting along in the world. IQ tests were originally designed to measure only the specific range of skills that are needed for success in school. This they do reasonably well. What they do not tell us is how good a particular person may be at other cognitive tasks requiring skills such as creativity, insight, street smarts, reading social cues, or understanding spatial relationships (Gardner, 1983; Sternberg, 1985, 1986, 1991).

Explaining Differences in IQ

You will not be surprised to discover that the arguments about the origins of differences in IQ nearly always boil down to a dispute about nature versus nurture. When Binet and Simon wrote the first IQ test, they did not assume that intelligence as measured on an IQ test was fixed or inborn. But many of the American psychologists who revised and promoted the use of the tests *did* believe that intellectual capacity is inherited and largely fixed at birth. Those who took this view, and those who believed that the environment was crucial in shaping a child's intellectual performance, have been arguing for at least 60 years. Let me walk you through some of the major points.

Evidence for the Importance of Heredity.   Both twin studies and studies of adopted children show strong hereditary influences on IQ. Bouchard and McGue (1981), in a comprehensive synthesis of the twin studies, estimate that the correlation between the IQ scores of identical twins who have grown up together is .85 (a *very high* correlation), while the correlation between scores of same-sex fraternal twins reared together is about .58 (lower, but still fairly substantial). The correlations for identical twins reared apart falls somewhere in between, ranging from .60 to .70 in different studies (Bouchard & McGue, 1981; Brody, 1992). This is precisely the pattern of correlations we would expect if there was a strong genetic element at work.

In adoption studies, the most common finding is that adopted children's IQs can be predicted better from knowing the IQs or the level of education of their birth parents than from knowing the IQs or education of their adoptive parents (Brody, 1992; Loehlin, Horn & Willerman, 1989; Phillips & Fulker, 1989; Scarr & Weinberg, 1983), a pattern of findings that also supports a genetic explanation.

Evidence for the Importance of Environment.   Adoption studies also provide support for an environmental influence on IQ scores, because the actual *level* of IQ scores of adopted children is clearly affected by the environment in which they have grown up. Early studies of adopted children involved mostly children born to poverty-level parents who were adopted into middle-class families. Such children typically have IQs that are 10 to 15 points higher than that of their birth mother (Scarr & Kidd, 1983), suggesting that the effect of the middle-class adoptive family was to raise the child's IQ. But this doesn't tell us whether a *less* stimulating adoptive family would *lower* the IQ of a child born to average or above-average IQ parents. That piece of information is now available from a French study by Christiane Capron and Michel Duyme (1989). They identified a group of 38 children, all adopted in infancy, who represent all possible combinations of high and low social class and education in the birth parents and the adoptive parents. Table 7.5 shows the children's IQ scores in adolescence. If you look across both rows, you can see that there is a difference of 11 or 12 points between the IQs of children reared in upper-class homes and those reared in lower-class families, no matter what the social class level or education of the birth parents. At the same time, the data also show a genetic effect, because the children *born to* upper-class parents have higher IQs than do those from lower-class families, no matter what kind of rearing environment they encountered.

Combining the Information.   Virtually all psychologists would now agree that heredity is a highly important influence on IQ scores. Studies around the world consistently yield estimates that roughly half of the variation in IQ within the population is due to heredity (Plomin, 1989; Plomin & Rende, 1991). The remaining half is clearly due to environment or to interactions between environment and heredity.

One useful way to conceptualize this interaction is with the concept of *reaction range*. The basic idea is that genes establish some range of possible reactions, upper and lower boundaries of functioning. Where a child will fall within those boundaries will be determined by environment. Richard Weinberg (1989) estimates that the reaction range for IQ is about 20 to 25 points. That is, given some specific genetic heritage, each child's actual IQ test performance may vary by as much as 20 or 25 points, depending on the richness or poverty of the environment in which he grows up. When we change the child's environment for the better, the child moves closer to the upper end of his reaction range. When we change the environment for the worse, the child's effective intellectual performance falls toward the lower end of his reaction range. Thus even though intelligence as measured on an IQ test is highly heritable, the absolute score within the reaction range is determined by environment. But just what is it about family environments that seems to make a difference?

Specific Family Characteristics and IQ.   When we watch the ways individual families interact with their infants or young children, and then follow the children over time to see which ones later have high or low IQs, we can begin to get some sense of the kinds of specific family interactions that foster higher scores. At least five dimensions of family interaction or stimulation seem to make a difference. Families with higher IQ children

1. provide an *interesting and complex physical environment* for the child, including play materials that are appropriate for the child's age and developmental level (e.g., Bradley et al., 1989).

2. are *emotionally responsive* to and *involved* with their child. They respond warmly and contingently to the child's behavior, smiling when the child smiles, answering the child's questions, and in myriad ways respond to the child's cues (e.g., Barnard et al., 1989; Bradley & Caldwell, 1976, 1984).

3. *talk to their child,* using language that is descriptively rich and accurate (e.g., Sigman et al., 1988).

TABLE 7.5 IQ Scores at Adolescence for Capron and Duyme's Adopted Children

		Social Class of Adoptive Parents	
		High	Low
Social Class of Biological Parents	High	119.60	107.50
	Low	103.60	92.40

Source: Capron & Duyme, 1989, Table 2, p. 553.

4. *avoid excessive restrictiveness*, punitiveness, or control, instead giving the child room to explore, even opportunities to make mistakes (e.g., Yeates et al., 1983; Bradley et al., 1989).

5. *expect* their child to do well and to develop rapidly. They emphasize and press for school achievement (e.g. Entwisle & Alexander, 1990).

You may have figured out that there is a methodological problem in research of this type. Because parents provide *both* the genes and the environment, we can't be sure that these environmental characteristics are really causally important. Perhaps this is the kind of environment that brighter parents provide, but the genes and not the environment cause the higher IQs in their children. The way around this problem is to look at the link between environmental features and IQ in adopted children. Fortunately, we have a few studies of this type, and they point to the same critical environmental features. That is, among adoptive families, those that behave in the ways listed above have adopted children who score higher on IQ tests (e.g. Plomin, Loehlin & DeFries, 1985).

School Experience and Special Interventions. Home environments and family interactions are not the only source of environmental influence. Many children also spend a very large amount of time in group care settings, including day care, special programs like Head Start, or regular preschools. How much effect do these environments have on the child's intellectual growth?

On a theoretical level, this question is of interest because it may tell us something about early experience in general and about the resilience of children. Are the effects of an initially impoverished environment permanent, or can they be offset by an enriched experience, such as a special preschool? At a practical level, programs like Head Start are based squarely on the assumption that it *is* possible to modify the trajectory of a child's intellectual development, especially if you intervene early.

Attempts to test this assumption have led to a messy body of research. In particular, children are rarely assigned randomly to Head Start or non–Head Start groups (V. Lee et al., 1990), making interpretation difficult. Still, there is some agreement on the effects. Children enrolled in Head Start or other enriched preschool programs, compared to similar children without such preschool, normally show a gain of about 10 IQ points during the year of the Head Start experience. This IQ gain typically fades and then disappears within the first few years of school (McKey et al., 1985), but there is nonetheless a clear residual effect. Children with Head Start or other enriched preschool experience are less likely to be placed in special education classes, somewhat less likely to repeat a grade, and somewhat more likely to graduate from high school (Darlington, 1991; Haskins, 1989). So although the children with preschool experience do not typically *test* much higher (and do *not* differ in IQ), they *function* better in school.

Children who attend enrichment programs like this Austin, Texas, Head Start program, typically do not show lasting gains in IQ, but they are more likely to succeed in school.

Even larger and more lasting effects are found when the special program is begun in infancy rather than at age 3 or 4 or 5. The best-designed and most meticulously reported of the infancy interventions has been carried out by Craig Ramey and his colleagues at the University of North Carolina (Ramey & Haskins, 1981a, 1981b; Ramey, Yeates & Short, 1984; Ramey & Campbell, 1987; Ramey, Lee & Burchinal, 1989). Infants from poverty-level families whose mothers had low IQs were randomly assigned either to a special day-care program, eight hours a day, five days a week, or to a control group, which received nutritional supplements and medical care but were reared largely at home. The special care program, which began when the infants were 6 to 12 weeks of age and lasted until they began kindergarten, involved very much the kinds of "optimum" stimulation I just described.

The IQ scores of the children at various ages are shown in Figure 7.3. You can see that the children who had been enrolled in the special program had significantly higher IQ scores than the control children, even a year and a half after the end of the enrichment

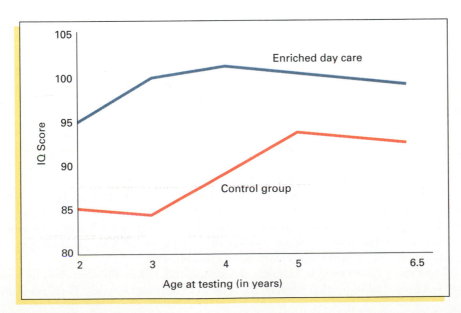

Figure 7.3 In Ramey's study, the experimental group children attended a special enriched day care program from about age 1 month to 5 years. The control group children were reared largely at home. All came from poverty-level families. The experimental group continued to have a significantly higher IQ even a year and a half after the program ended.

Suppose Ramey were to follow the children in his study until they were in high school, and discovered that the IQ differences between those who had been in the special enriched program and those in the control group had disappeared. What would be the implications of such a finding?

program. They also performed better on achievement tests in first grade and were less likely to be held back for a second year in kindergarten. Without intervention, many of the children from the "control" families were performing at a level that would be considered subnormal or retarded; over 30 percent repeated kindergarten. Thus, without negating the importance of heredity in IQ, it is clear that the child's home or school environment can effect the level of intellectual functioning the child achieves.

Group Differences in IQ: Race and Sex Differences

So far I have sidestepped two difficult issues, namely racial and sex differences in IQ or cognitive power. Because these issues can easily be blown out of proportion, I do not want to place too much emphasis on either topic. But you need to see what we know, what we don't know, and how we are trying to explain both kinds of differences.

Racial Differences in IQ. A number of racial differences in intellectual performance have been found, including consistently higher performance on achievement tests—particularly math tests—by Asian and Asian-American children (Stevenson et al., 1990; Sue & Okazaki, 1990). But the basic finding that has given researchers and theorists the most difficulty is that in the United States, black children score lower than white children on measures of IQ. The difference, which we begin to see when children are about 2 or 3 years old, is on the order of 12 IQ points (Brody, 1992).

Some scientists have argued for the hypothesis that some portion of this test score difference is due to basic genetic differences between the races (e.g., Jensen, 1980). Other scientists, granting that IQ is highly heritable, point out that the 12 point difference falls well within the presumed reaction range of IQ. They emphasize that there are sufficiently large differences in the environments in which black and white children are reared to account for the average difference in score (e.g., Brody, 1992).

Some of the most convincing research supporting the latter view comes from Sandra Scarr and her colleagues (Scarr & Kidd, 1983; Weinberg, Scarr & Waldman, 1992). For example, she has found that black children adopted at an early age into white middle-class families and thus reared in the majority environment scored only slightly less well on IQ tests than did white children adopted into the same families.

Findings like these persuade me that the IQ difference we see is primarily a reflection of the fact that the tests, and the school, are designed by the majority culture to promote a particular form of intellectual activity and that many black or other minority families rear their children in ways that do not maximize (or emphasize) this particular set of skills. In a similar vein, Harold Stevenson has argued that the differences between Asian and Caucasian children in performance on mathematics achievement tests results not from genetic differences in capacity but from differences in cultural emphasis on the importance of academic achievement, number of hours spent on homework, and differences in the quality of the math instruction in the schools (Stigler, Lee & Stevenson, 1987; Stevenson & Lee, 1990).

The fact that we may be able to account for such racial differences in IQ or achievement test performance by appealing to the concept of reaction range and to cultural or subcultural variations does not make the differences disappear, nor does it make them trivial. But perhaps it puts such findings into a less explosive framework.

Sex Differences in IQ. There are *no* consistent differences in total IQ scores between boys and girls. It is only when we break down the total score into several separate skills that some patterns of sex differences emerge. On average, boys are better at numerical reasoning and at spatial visualization tasks like those in Figure 7.4. Girls are slightly better on verbal tasks and at arithmetic computation (Jacklin, 1989).

Two crucial points need to be made about these differences. First, on *every* measure there is a great deal of overlap between the scores of males and females. There are many

Some psychologists have argued that the reason blacks achieve lower IQ scores than whites is that the tests are systematically biased against blacks or other minority group members. What kind of research results would demonstrate such a bias? What kind would argue against it?

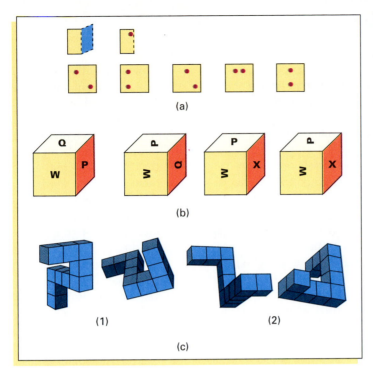

Figure 7.4 All three of these items test aspects of spatial visualization. Item *a* represents folded paper. A hole is punched through all the thicknesses. Which figure shows what the paper would look like when it is unfolded? In *b*, you must figure out which of the three cubes on the right could be a different view of the cube on the left. Item *c* is a measure of mental rotation. In each pair, would the two figures be the same if they were appropriately rotated? It is tests of this last subability that show the largest sex differences. (*Source:* Halpern, 1986, Figure 3.1, page 50, and Figure 3.2, p. 52.)

girls good at spatial visualization and many boys good at verbal reasoning. Second, the *absolute size of the differences is mostly very small* and has been decreasing over recent decades (Feingold, 1988; Brody, 1992). For example, even though it is true that girls typically do better on measures of verbal skill, sex accounts for only about *one percent* of the variation in scores. On measures of spatial visualization, gender accounts for perhaps five percent of the variation in scores (Halpern, 1986; Sanders, Soares & D'Aquila, 1982).

As with total IQ scores, there are probably both environmental and biological forces at work in creating these patterns. Biological influences have been most often argued in the case of sex differences in spatial abilities, where there may be both genetic differences and—more speculatively—differences in brain functioning resulting from prenatal variations in hormones (e.g., Newcombe & Baenninger, 1989).

In contrast, environmental influences are most often cited to explain the small sex differences in mathematical or verbal reasoning. Especially in the case of mathematics there is considerable evidence that girls' and boys' skills are systematically shaped by a series of environmental factors, including amount of exposure to math and the attitudes of parents and teachers toward girls' math achievement (Parsons, Adler & Kaczala, 1982; Holloway & Hess, 1985).

The Measurement of Intelligence: A Last Look

One of the questions that students often ask at this point is whether, given all the factors that can affect a test score, it is worth bothering with IQ tests at all. I think that these tests do assess some important aspects of children's intellectual performance and that they can be helpful in identifying children who may have difficulties in school. But it is worth emphasizing again that they do *not* measure a lot of other things we may be interested in. An IQ test is a specialized tool, and like many such tools, it has a fairly narrow range of appropriate use. I wouldn't want to throw out this tool, but we have to keep its limitations very firmly in mind when we use it.

Summary

1. Physical development is slower from age 2 to age 6 than in infancy, but it is still steady. Motor skills continue to improve gradually.

2. Preschool children average four to six acute illnesses each year. Chronic illnesses are less common.

3. Language development moves at a rapid pace between ages 2 and 3. Children begin forming two-word sentences and then move swiftly to more complex sentences, adding various grammatical inflections. A variety of meanings are conveyed even in the simplest sentences.

4. From the earliest sentences, children's language is creative, including forms and combinations the child has not heard but that follow apparent rules.

5. Studies of word meaning suggest that many words are learned only when the child already understands the underlying concept. Children's early word categories are more often overextended than underextended.

6. Some theorists argue that children have built-in constraints on their word learning, such as the principle of contrast.

7. Simple imitation or reinforcement theories of language development are not adequate to explain the phenomenon. More complex environmental theories, emphasizing the role of environmental richness or motherese, are more helpful, but also not sufficient.

8. Innateness theories, positing built-in operating principles, or "rules to listen by," are more persuasive, but they omit the role of the child as analyzer and synthesizer of linguistic information.

9. Piaget marked the beginning of the preoperational period at the point when the child, at about 18 to 24 months, begins to use mental symbols. Despite this advance, the preschool child still lacks many sophisticated cognitive characteristics. In Piaget's view, such children are still egocentric, lack understanding of conservation, and have only primitive classification abilities.

10. Recent research on the cognitive functioning of preschoolers makes it clear that Piaget underestimated these children. They are much less egocentric than he thought and in fact have remarkably sophisticated theories of mind by age 4 or 5. At about that age children also understand the difference between appearance and reality.

11. Language development proceeds at varying speeds in different children, with faster development associated with linguistically richer environments.

12. Children also differ in cognitive power, as measured by standard intelligence tests. Scores on such tests are predictive of school performance and are at least moderately consistent over time.

13. Differences in IQ have been attributed to both heredity and environment. Twin and adoption studies make it clear that at least half of the variation in IQ scores is due to genetic differences, the remainder to environment and the interaction of heredity and environment.

14. Qualities of the environment that appear to make a difference include the complexity of stimulation, the responsiveness and involvement of parents, the relative lack of restrictiveness, and high expectations for the child's performance.

15. Children's IQs can be raised by providing specially stimulating early environments, such as enriched day care or preschools.

16. Several kinds of racial differences in IQ or test performance have been found consistently. Such differences seem most appropriately attributed to environmental variation rather than genetics.

17. Boys and girls do not differ in total IQ but do differ in some component skills. Boys are generally better at tasks requiring spatial visualization and at mathematical reasoning, girls at many verbal tasks.

Key Terms

class inclusion	intelligence quotient (IQ)	retarded
egocentrism	motherese	Stanford-Binet
gifted	overregularization	theory of mind
inflections	preoperational period	WISC-R

Suggested Readings

Flavell, J. H. (1985). *Cognitive development* (2nd ed.). Englewood Cliffs, NJ: Prentice-Hall. (I recommended this book in Chapter 5 and recommend it again here. It is a first-rate basic text, written by one of the major current figures in cognitive developmental theory.)

Gallagher, J. J., & Ramey, C. T. (1987). *The malleability of children.* Baltimore: Paul H. Brookes Publishing Co. (If you are interested in the impact of special programs on IQ, this is a recent and readable source. A paper by Ramey is included.)

Hakuta, K. (1986). *Mirror of language: The debate on bilingualism.* New York: Basic Books. (An elegant and comprehensible discussion of many of the issues about bilingualism and bilingual education I have discussed in the "real world" box on page 158.)

Rice, M. L. (1989). Children's language acquisition. *American Psychologist, 44,* 149–156. (A brief review of the current status of our knowledge about language development.)

8 SOCIAL AND PERSONALITY DEVELOPMENT FROM 2 TO 6

If you asked a random sample of adults to tell you the most important characteristics of children between the ages of 2 and 6, my hunch is that the first thing on the list would not be the child's growing physical skill or her newly developing theory of mind. New language abilities might make the list, but I'd lay odds that most people would first mention the "terrible twos"—the nay-saying, newly oppositional toddler who wants to do things for herself. This public characterization of the toddler is exaggerated, but it is still true that some of the most obvious changes during the preschool years are in the realm of social behavior.

Theoretical Perspectives

It was just such changes in the child's relationships with others and in personality that Freud and Erikson attempted to describe in their theories. I talked about both these theories in Chapter 2, but let me review briefly.

Freud's Views

Freud described two stages during these preschool years, each highlighting a different aspect of sexual sensitivity.

The Anal Stage: 1–3 Years.   The first of these two stages is the anal stage. As the trunk matures and comes under more voluntary control, the baby becomes more and more sensitive in the anal region. At about the same time, her parents begin to place great emphasis on toilet training and show pleasure when she manages to perform in the right place at the right time. These two forces together help to shift the major center of sexual energy from the oral to the anal erogenous zone.

The key to the child's successful completion of this stage, according to Freud, is whether the parents allow the child sufficient anal exploration and pleasure. If toilet training becomes a major battleground, however, then the child's sexual energy may become *fixated* in this mode, with the possible adult consequences of excessive orderliness, stinginess, or the opposite, such as extreme messiness.

The Phallic Stage: 3–5 Years.   At about 3 or 4 years of age the genitals increase in sensitivity, ushering in a new stage. One sign of this new sensitivity is that children of both sexes quite naturally begin to masturbate at about this age. This is also the stage in which the Oedipus conflict is said to occur, with its accompanying identification with the same-sexed parent—a process I described in some detail in Chapter 2.

There are several implications of Freud's view of this age period. First, each of these stages holds the possibility of a new facet of conflict between child and parents. In the anal stage, there may be conflict over toilet training, as the child asserts his independence (and his anal pleasure) by resisting the parents' attempts to control him. In the phallic stage, there may be increased conflict between the child and the parent of the same sex, as the child struggles to handle his Oedipal feelings.

Freud's theory also suggests the hypothesis that the absence of either parent, such as by divorce, may be especially harmful for children in this age range, because they need both parents present to accomplish a proper identification with the parent of the same sex.

> Would social learning theorists arrive at the same hypothesis about the relationship between age and effects of divorce?

Erikson's Views

Erikson does not discount the important role of parent-child interaction and conflict in these years, but he also emphasizes the impact of the child's growing physical and cognitive skills on his sense of independence.

Autonomy Versus Shame and Doubt: 2–3 Years.   In the first of the two stages Erikson proposes in this age range, the child's greater mobility forms the basis for the sense of independence or autonomy. But if the child's efforts at independence are not carefully guided by the parents and she experiences repeated failures or ridicule, the results of all the new opportunities for exploration may be shame and doubt instead of a basic sense of self-control and self-worth.

Initiative Versus Guilt: 4–5 Years.   The second of Erikson's two stages in these years, roughly equivalent to Freud's phallic stage, is again ushered in by new skills or abilities in the child. The 4-year-old is able to plan a bit, to take initiative in reaching particular goals. The child practices his new cognitive skills and attempts to conquer the world around him. He may try to go out into the street on his own; he may take a toy apart, find he can't put it back together, and throw the whole mess at his mother. It is a time of vigor of action and of behaviors that parents may see as aggressive. The risk is that the child may go too far in his forcefulness, or that the parents may restrict and punish too much—either of which can produce guilt. Some guilt is needed, because without it there would be no conscience or self-control. The ideal interaction between parent and child is certainly not total indulgence. But too much guilt can inhibit the child's creativity and free interactions with others.

Both theorists seem to be saying that the key to this period is the balance between the child's emerging skills and needs for autonomy, and the parent's need to protect the child and control the child's behavior. Thus the parent's task changes rather dramatically after the baby leaves infancy. In the early months of life, the key task for the parents is to provide enough warmth, predictability, and responsiveness to foster a secure attachment and support the basic physiological programming. But once the child becomes physically, linguistically, and cognitively more independent, the need to control becomes a central aspect of the parents' task. Too much control, and the child will not have sufficient

This preschooler seems to be feeling either shame or doubt—both emotions that Erikson thought were common at this stage.

opportunity to explore; too little control and the child will become unmanageable and fail to learn the social skills he will need to get along with peers as well as adults.

Other Theoretical Perspectives

Neither Freud nor Erikson talked much about the role of the child's peers in development, but in recent years a number of theorists have emphasized the vital significance of such encounters. Willard Hartup (1989) suggests that each child needs experience in two different kinds of relationships: *vertical* and *horizontal* relationships. A vertical relationship involves an attachment to someone who has greater social power or knowledge, such as a parent or a teacher. Such relationships are complementary rather than reciprocal; that is, the parent nurtures and controls the child, while the child's half of the relationship is made up of bids for attention and compliance or acquiescence. Horizontal relationships, in contrast, are reciprocal and egalitarian. The individuals involved, such as same-age peers, have equal social power.

Hartup's point is that these two kinds of relationships serve different functions for the child, and both are needed for the child to develop effective social skills. Vertical relationships are necessary to provide the child with protection and security. In these relationships the child creates his basic internal working models and learns fundamental social skills. But it is in horizontal relationships—in friendships and in peer groups as well as in relationships with siblings—that the child tries out those basic skills. And it is in horizontal relationships that the child acquires those social skills that can only be learned in a relationship between equals: cooperation, competition, and intimacy.

These two kinds of relationships obviously affect one another, but the theory and data tend to be separate, so let me begin by talking about the vertical relationships, in particular the core relationship between child and parent.

▶ Relationships with Parents in the Preschool Years

Attachment

You'll remember from Chapter 6 that by 12 months of age, the baby normally has established a clear attachment to at least one caregiver. The baby displays this attachment in a wide variety of attachment behaviors, including smiling, crying, clinging, social referencing, and "safe-base behavior." By age 2 or 3, the attachment appears no less strong, but many of these attachment behaviors have become less continuously visible. Children this age are cognitively advanced enough to understand Mom if she explains why she is going away and that she will be back, so their anxiety at separation wanes. They can even use a photograph of their mother as a "safe base" for exploration in a strange situation (Passman & Longeway, 1982), which reflects the major cognitive advance of symbolic representation. Of course, attachment behaviors have not completely disappeared. Three- and 4-year-olds still want to sit on Mom's or Dad's lap; they are still likely to seek some closeness or proximity when Mom returns from an absence. But in nonfearful or non-stressful situations, the child is able to wander farther and farther from her safe base without apparent distress.

Beyond this reduced prominence of attachment behaviors, two other changes seem to take place in the child's attachment in these years. First the relationship with the key person, typically the mother, undergoes a further change, based on a cognitive advance. Just as the first attachment probably requires that the baby understand that his mother will continue to exist when she isn't there, so now the preschooler grasps that the *relationship* continues to exist even when the partners are apart. Children this age are much less distressed at separation, but they get upset if they don't know what's happening or haven't shared in the planning (Marvin & Greenberg, 1982).

Off she goes, into greater independ-ence. Children this age, especially those with secure attachments, are far more confident about being at a distance from their safe base.

An even broader change, which I mentioned in Chapter 6, is the generalization of the child's internal model of attachment. Bowlby argued that the child's model becomes less a property of each individual relationship and more a property of relationships in some more general sense. Four- and 5-year-olds are thus more likely to apply their internal model to new relationships, including relationships with peers.

In sum, the preschooler's attachment to the parent(s) remains strong and central to the child's experience, but it changes in form in a number of significant ways as the child's cognitive abilities advance.

Compliance and Defiance

At the same time, the 2-year-old's greater autonomy brings him into more and more situations in which the parent wants one thing and the child another. Contrary to the popular image of the "terrible twos," 2-year olds actually comply with parents' requests more often than not. If they resist, it is most likely to be passively, by simply not doing what is asked. The child says "no" or actively defies the parent only a small percentage of the time (Kuczynski et al., 1987). Overt refusals become more common by age 3 or 4, as does active negotiation with the parent.

Many psychologists think there is an important distinction between simple refusals, or nay-saying ("I don't want to," or "No"), and defiance, in which the child's refusal is accompanied by anger, temper tantrums, or whining (e.g., Crockenberg & Litman, 1990). The former seems to be an important and healthy aspect of self-assertion, and has been linked both to secure attachments and to greater maturity (Matas, Arend & Sroufe, 1978). Defiance, on the other hand, has been linked to insecure attachment or to a history of abuse.

Direct defiance declines over the preschool years; we are less likely to see temper tantrums or whining or equivalent outbursts in a 6-year-old than in a 2-year-old, in part because the child's cognitive and language skills have developed to the point where negotiation has become more possible. We can see the effects of these same cognitive changes in the child's relationships with peers as well.

What effect do you think the child's increasingly complex theory of mind has on the child's relationship with her parents?

▶ Relationships with Peers

There is certainly no denying the centrality of the child's family experience for the child's emerging personality and social relationships, particularly in these early years when children still spend a good portion of their time with their parents and siblings. But over the years from 2 to 6, relationships with peers become increasingly important; past the age of 6, relationships with peers are arguably more significant even than parent-child relationships.

Children first begin to show some positive interest in other infants as early as 6 months of age. If you place two babies that age on the floor facing each other, they will look at each other, touch, pull each other's hair, imitate each other's actions, and smile

---

RESEARCH REPORT
Siblings and Their Differences

The great majority of children grow up with brothers and sisters. In the preschool years, in fact, interactions with siblings may be a more important part of a child's social world than at any other age. Until recently, most psychological research on siblings focused on a single issue, the effect of birth order. Did it matter to the child's development if he was the oldest, the youngest, or in the middle? The typical finding was that first-borns were more likely to be strongly achievement oriented and more anxious; later-born children were likely to be more sociable, more influenced by others' opinions. Recent studies of sibling relationships have turned away from this somewhat simplistic question toward several more interesting issues, including the following: (1) What is the nature of sibling relationships during the preschool years? and (2) Why are siblings often so very different from one another?

Sibling Relationships. Folklore, such as the story of Cain and Abel, might lead us to believe that rivalry or jealousy is the key ingredient of sibling relationships. But observations of preschoolers with their siblings points toward other ingredients. Toddlers and preschoolers help their brothers and sisters, imitate them, and share their toys. Judy Dunn (Dunn & Kendrick, 1982), in a detailed longitudinal study of a group of 40 families in England, observed that the older child often imitated a baby brother or sister; by the time the younger child was a year old, he or she began imitating the older sib, and from then on most of the imitation flows in that direction, with the younger child copying the older one.

At the same time, brothers and sisters also hit one another, snatch toys, threaten and insult each other. The older child in a pair of preschoolers is likely to be the leader and is therefore more likely to show both aggressive and helpful behaviors (Abramovitch, Pepler & Corter, 1982). For both members of the pair, however, the dominant feature seems to be ambivalence: both supportive and negative behaviors are evident in about equal proportions. In Abramovitch's research, such ambivalence occurred whether the pair were close in age or further apart, and whether the older child was a boy or a girl. Naturally there are variations on this theme; some pairs show mostly antagonistic or rivalrous behaviors, while some show mostly helpful and supportive behaviors. As yet we know little about what might promote these alternative patterns. But *most* siblings show both types of behavior.

Why Do Siblings Turn Out Differently? Given that two children grow up in the "same" family, why is it that they so often turn out so differently? Most of us assume that parents treat their children in very similar ways, but Judy Dunn (1991, 1992) has shown that that is a fallacy. Parents may express warmth and pride toward one child and scorn toward another, may be lenient toward one and strict with another. Here's an example from one of Dunn's observations, of 30-month-old Andy and his 14-month-old sister Susie.

> Andy was a rather timid and sensitive child, cautious, unconfident, and compliant. . . . Susie was a striking contrast—assertive, determined, and a handful for her mother, who was nevertheless delighted by her boisterous daughter. In [one] observation of Andy and his sister, Susie persistently attempted to grab a forbidden object on a high kitchen counter, despite her mother's repeated prohibitions. Finally, she succeeded, and Andy overheard his mother make a warm, affectionate comment on Susie's action: "Susie, you *are* a determined little devil!" Andy, sadly, commented to his mother, "*I'm* not a determined little devil!" His mother replied, laughing, "No! What are you? A poor old boy!" (Dunn, 1992, p. 6)

Not only are such episodes common in family interactions, children are highly sensitive to such variations in treatment. Notice how Andy had monitored his mother's interaction with Susie, and then compared himself to his sister. Children this age are already aware of the emotional quality of exchanges between themselves and their parents as well as the exchanges between their siblings and parents. Dunn finds that those who receive less affection and warmth from their mothers are likely to be more depressed, worried, or anxious than are their siblings. And the more differently the parents treat siblings, the more rivalry and hostility there is likely to be between the brothers and sisters.

Of course parents treat children differently for many reasons, including the child's age. Susie and Andy's mother may be accepting of Susie's naughty behavior simply because she is so young. They also respond to temperamental differences in the children. But whatever the cause, it now seems clear that such differences in treatment are an important ingredient in the child's emerging internal model of self and contribute greatly to variations in behavior between children growing up in the same families.

at each other. By 10 months these behaviors are even more evident. Children this age apparently still prefer to play with objects, but will play with each other if no toys are available. By 14 to 18 months, we begin to see two or more children playing together with toys—sometimes cooperating together, sometimes simply playing side by side with different toys. By 3 or 4, children show more organized play with each other, clearly preferring to spend time with peers rather than alone.

Most of what children do with each other in these early years is play, particularly constructive and pretend play. They build things together, play in the sandbox together, or play with dolls, trucks, or dress-up clothes. In all these interactions, we can also see both positive and negative behaviors, both aggression and altruism.

Aggression

The most common definition of **aggression** is behavior with the apparent intent to injure another person or object (Feshbach, 1970). Every child shows at least some behavior of this type, most often after some kind of frustration. But the form and frequency of aggression changes over the preschool years, as you can see in the summary in Table 8.1.

When 2- or 3-year-old children are upset or frustrated, they are most likely to throw things or hit each other. As their verbal skills improve, however, there is a shift away from such overt physical aggression toward greater use of verbal aggression, such as taunting or name-calling, much as their defiance of their parents shifts from physical to verbal strategies.

A related but distinct aspect of "negative" encounters between children is competition or **dominance.** Whenever there are too few toys for the number of children, not enough time with the teacher to go around, or some other scarcity of desired objects, there will be competition. Sometimes competition results in outright aggression. More often, competition results in the development of a clear **dominance hierarchy,** more popularly known as a *pecking order*. Some children seem to be more successful than others at asserting their rights to desired objects, either by threats, by simply taking the object away, by glaring at the other child, or other strategies.

Clear dominance hierarchies are already visible at preschool age (e.g., Strayer, 1980). That is, among a group of children who play together regularly, some regularly win out over nearly all other children. Others, lower in the dominance hierarchy, lose to everyone. Interestingly, among 3- and 4-year-olds, a child's place in the group dominance system

Think about the groups you belong to. Do they have clear dominance hierarchies? Now imagine a group of adults coming together for the first time. Within a few weeks there is likely to be a pecking order. What determined that order? How does a dominant person establish such dominance?

TABLE 8.1 Changes in the Form and Frequency of Aggression Between Ages 2 and 8		
	2- to 4-year-olds	**4- to 8-year-olds**
Physical aggression	At its peak from 2 to 4	Declines over the period from 4 to 8
Verbal aggression	Relatively rare at 2; increases as the child's verbal skill improves	Dominant form of aggression from 4 to 8
Goal of aggression	Primarily "instrumental aggression," aimed at obtaining or damaging an object rather than directly hurting someone else	More "hostile aggression," aimed at hurting another person or another's feelings
Occasion for aggression	Most often after conflicts with parents	Most often after conflicts with peers

Sources: Goodenough, 1931; Hartup, 1974; Cummings et al., 1986.

Six-year-old Christopher and his 4-year-old sister Helen may be less likely to get into this kind of a physical fight than they were a few years ago, but clearly this kind of physical aggression does not totally disappear in the pre-school years.

is *not* related to popularity or to positive interactions to or from the child. But among 5- and 6-year-olds, the dominance and popularity/friendship systems may be linked. In this age group, the dominant children are also the most popular—so long as they are not bullies (Pettit et al., 1990; Strayer, 1980). The overall picture that emerges is that past the age of 4 or 5, *socially competent* children are those who are at the middle to higher end of the dominance hierarchy, who are positive, helpful, and supportive of others, and who refrain from overt acts of physical aggression.

Prosocial Behavior

Another important facet of peer relationships is a set of behaviors psychologists call **prosocial behavior**: "Intentional, voluntary behavior intended to benefit another" (Eisenberg, 1990, p. 240). In everyday language, this is essentially what we mean by **altruism**. This class of behaviors, too, shows a developmental course.

We first see such altruistic behaviors between ages 1 and 2. Children this age will offer to help another child who is hurt, share a toy or other treasure, or try to comfort another child or adult who appears sad or distressed (Zahn-Waxler & Radke-Yarrow, 1982; Zahn-Waxler et al., 1992; Marcus, 1986). Children this young have only a very primitive understanding of the fact that others feel differently from themselves, but they obviously understand enough about the emotions of others to respond in supportive and sympathetic ways when they see other children or adults hurt or sad.

We don't yet have a good enough base of data to be sure about the developmental patterns past these early years. Some kinds of prosocial behaviors seem to increase with age. For example, if you give children an opportunity to donate some treat to another child who is described as needy, older children donate more than younger children do. Helpfulness, too, seems to increase with age up through adolescence. But not all prosocial behaviors show this pattern. Comforting another child, for example, seems to be more common among preschool and early elementary school children than older children (Eisenberg, 1988, 1990).

We also know that children vary a lot in the amount of such altruistic behavior they show—variations that seem to be related to interaction patterns within the family. I've translated some of the research into concrete advice in the "real world" box on page 189.

Friendships

Beginning as early as age 2, children also show some signs of individual friendships, and these relationships may be an especially important arena for learning about reciprocity

THE REAL WORLD
Rearing Helpful and Altruistic Children

A growing body of research (summarized in Eisenberg, 1992) points to several specific child-rearing strategies that are linked to higher rates of altruistic or thoughtful behavior in children.

Creating a Loving and Warm Family Climate. It won't surprise you that parents who behave in loving, nurturing and supportive ways toward their children have children who are more helpful, more empathetic, and more thoughtful of others. This effect is much clearer, though, when such warmth is combined with clear explanations.

Explaining Why and Giving Rules. More altruistic children have parents who state their rules and standards clearly. This effect is well illustrated in research by Carolyn Zahn-Waxler and her colleagues. They asked a group of 16 mothers of young children to keep daily diaries of every incident in which someone around the child showed distress, fear, pain, sorrow, or fatigue. For example, John's mother described an incident in which her 2-year-old son was visited by a friend, Jerry:

> Today Jerry was kind of cranky; he just started completely bawling and he couldn't stop. John kept coming over and handing Jerry toys, trying to cheer him up, so to speak. He'd say things like "Here, Jerry," and I said to John: "Jerry's sad; he doesn't feel good; he had a shot today." John would look at me with his eyebrows kind of wrinkled together like he really understood that Jerry was crying because he was unhappy, not that he was just being a crybaby. He went over and rubbed Jerry's arm and said "Nice Jerry" and continued to give him toys. (Zahn-Waxler et al, 1979, p. 321–322)

Zahn-Waxler found that mothers who both explained the consequences of the child's actions (e.g., "If you hit Susan it will hurt her") *and* who stated the rules clearly, explicitly, and with emotion ("You mustn't hit people!") had children who were much more likely to react to others with helpfulness or sympathy. The same point emerges from research with older children: Stating the *reason* for generosity or helpfulness—particularly if the reason focuses on the feelings of other people—increases the likelihood that a child will behave in a kind or helpful manner.

Many of us, as parents, spend a lot of time telling children what *not* to do. The research on altruism in children points to the importance of telling children *why* they should not do things, especially in terms of the potential impact on other people. Equally important is stating *positive* rules or guidelines, e.g., "It's always good to be helpful to other people," or "we should share what we have with people who don't have so much."

Having Children Do Helpful Things. Helpfulness is also fostered by giving children a chance to do really helpful things. Children can help cook (a nurturing activity), take care of pets, make toys to give to hospitalized or poor children, assist in making a casserole to take to the recently widowed neighbor, teach younger siblings how to play games. At school age, tutoring other children also seems to have this effect.

Obviously, not all children do such things spontaneously. They have to be asked, sometimes coerced. If the coercion is too strong, the effect changes: The child may now attribute his "good" behavior to the coercion ("Mother made me do it"), rather than to some inner trait of his own ("I am a helpful/kind person"). When that happens, the coerced altruistic actions do not seem to foster future altruism. So it matters how the doing of helpful things is managed.

Prosocial Attributions. A fourth strategy is to attribute your child's helpful or altruistic action to the child's own internal character: "You're such a helpful child!" or "You certainly do a lot of nice things for other people." This strategy begins to be effective with children at about age 7 or 8, at about the same time that they are beginning to develop generalized notions of their own personality. By explaining your child's actions in terms of a global internal quality of kindness or generosity or thoughtfulness, you may affect the child's self-scheme. Thereafter, the child will try to match his actions to his own self-scheme.

Modeling Thoughtful and Generous Behavior. Perhaps the most significant strategy is to demonstrate to your children exactly the generous, thoughtful, and helpful behavior you would like them to show. If there is a conflict between what you say and what you do, children will imitate your actions. So stating the rules or guidelines clearly will do little good if your own behavior does not match what you say. If your goal is for your child to develop an internalized value for altruism, it is clear that you will need to look at your own behavior first.

and intimacy. Carollee Howes (1983, 1987) has observed that children as young as 14 to 24 months old in day-care settings showed consistent preferences for one or more playmates over a full-year period. Using a somewhat stricter definition of friendship—that the pair spend at least 30 percent of their time together— Robert Hinde and his coworkers (Hinde et al., 1985) have found that in a group of 3 1/2-year-olds, only about 20 percent showed signs of a stable friendship; by age 4, half of these same children met the friendship criterion.

These early friendships seem to be less enduring and more based on proximity and shared play interests than is true of friendships in older children (Berndt, 1981). But preschool friend pairs nonetheless show more mutual liking, more reciprocity, more extended interactions, more positive and less negative behavior, and more supportiveness in a novel situation than is true between nonfriend pairs.

Such friendships are much more likely to be seen between same-sex pairs, even among children as young as age 2 or 3. John Gottman (1986) reports that perhaps 65 percent of friendships in preschool children in the United States are with a same-sex peer. Nonfriend interactions are also more likely to be with children of the same sex, beginning as early as age 2 1/2 or 3 (Maccoby, 1988, 1990; Maccoby & Jacklin, 1987). By school age, peer relationships are almost exclusively same-sex. You can see the early development of this preference in Figure 8.1, which shows the results of a study of preschool play groups by La Freniere, Strayer and Gauthier (1984). By age 3, about 60 percent of play groups were same-sex groupings and the rate rose from there.

This trend toward greater and greater sex-segregation in play is part of the broader process of the development of the child's sense of self, including his awareness of his own and others' gender.

> **How many explanations can you think of for the fact that children begin to prefer to play with same-sex peers as early as age 3 or 4?**

▶ The Emergence of the Sense of Self

When we left the 18- to 24-month-old in Chapter 6, he was beginning to develop what Lewis calls the *objective self.* The toddler already understands himself to be an object in the world, with various properties. Between 2 and 6 the child certainly continues to define herself in this way. By the end of this period, a child can give you quite a full description of herself on a whole range of dimensions. Still, these early self-concepts remain highly concrete. For example, Susan Harter (1988, 1990; Harter & Pike, 1984) has found that children between 4 and 7 have clear notions of their own competence on a range of physical, intellectual, and social tasks, such as solving puzzles, being able to count, knowing a lot in school, climbing or skipping or jumping rope, or having lots of friends. But

Figure 8.1 La Freniere and his colleagues counted how often preschool children played with same-sex or opposite-sex playmates. You can see that in this sample, children as young as two-and-a-half already showed at least some preference for same-sex playmates. *(Source:* La Freniere, Strayer, & Gauthier, 1984. Figure 1, p. 1961. Copyright by The Society for Research in Child Development, Inc.)

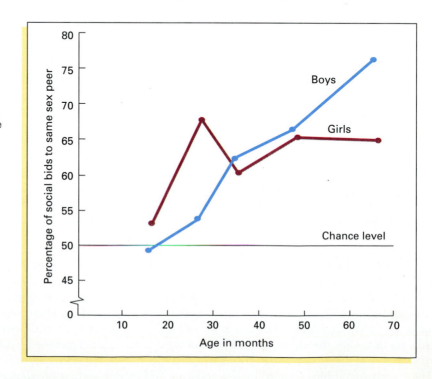

these separate aspects of the *self-scheme* or internal working model of the self have not yet coalesced into a global assessment of self-worth. For this reason, Harter argues that it is not appropriate to say of a preschooler that she has high or low self-esteem. She may have a high or low opinion of her ability to do some specific task, or her ability to relate to others in specific situations, but high or low self-esteem in a more global sense does not seem to emerge until about age 7.

The self-concept of a preschool child is concrete in another way as well; he tends to focus on his own visible characteristics—whether he's a boy or a girl, what he looks like, who he plays with, where he lives, what he is good at—rather than on more enduring, inner qualities. This pattern obviously parallels what we see in cognitive development at the same ages; it is in these same years that children's attention tends to be focused on the external appearance of objects rather than on their enduring properties.

The Social Self. Another facet of the child's emerging sense of self is an increasing awareness of himself as a player in the social game. By age 2, the toddler has already learned a variety of social "scripts"—routines of play or interaction with others in her world. Case (1991) points out that the toddler now begins to develop some implicit understanding of her own roles in these scripts. So she begins to think of herself as a "helper" in some situations, or as "the boss" when she is telling some other child what to do. You can see this clearly in children's sociodramatic play, as they begin to take explicit roles: "I'll be the daddy and you be the mommy," or "I'm the boss." As part of the same process, the preschool child also gradually understands her place in the network of family roles. She has sisters, brothers, father, mother, and so on.

The Gender Concept

One of the most fascinating aspects of the preschool child's emerging sense of self is the development of the child's sense of gender. The child has several related tasks. On the cognitive side, she must learn the nature of the gender category itself—that boyness or girlness is permanent, unchanged by such things as modifications in clothing or hair length. This understanding is usually called the **gender concept.** On the social side, she has to learn what behaviors go with being a boy or a girl. That is, she must learn the **sex role** appropriate for her gender.

The Development of the Gender Concept. There seem to be three steps in the child's understanding of the gender concept. First comes **gender identity,** which is simply a child's ability to label his own sex correctly and to identify other people as men or women, boys or girls. You already know from Chapter 6 that 2-year-olds can label themselves as boy or girl with reasonable accuracy (e.g., S. Thompson, 1975). By 2 1/2 or 3, most children can correctly label and identify the sex of others as well. Hair length and clothing seem to be the cues that children use for these early discriminations.

The second step is **gender stability,** which is the understanding that you stay the same gender throughout life. Researchers have measured this by asking children such questions as, "When you were a little baby, were you a little girl or a little boy?" or "When you grow up, will you be a mommy or a daddy?" Most children understand the stability aspect of gender by about age 4 (Slaby & Frey, 1975).

Finally, there is the development of true **gender constancy,** which is the recognition that someone stays the same gender even though he may appear to change by wearing different clothes or changing his hair length. For example, boys don't change into girls by letting their hair grow or wearing dresses. It may seem odd that a child who understands that he will stay the same gender throughout life (gender stability) can nonetheless be confused about the effect of changes in dress or appearance on gender. But numerous studies show this sequence, including studies of children growing up in other cultures, such as Kenya, Nepal, Belize, and Samoa (Munro, Shimmin & Munroe, 1984).

As their gender concept develops, children change their views about whether it is all right for little boys to play with dolls.

The underlying logic of this sequence may be a bit clearer if I draw a parallel between gender constancy and the concept of conservation. Conservation involves recognition that an object remains the same in some fundamental way even though it changes externally. Gender constancy is thus a kind of "conservation of gender" and is not typically understood until about 5 or 6, when the other conservations are first grasped (Marcus & Overton, 1978).

In sum, children as young as 2 or 2 1/2 know their own sex and that of people around them, but they do not have a fully developed concept of gender until they are 5 or 6.

The Development of the Sex Role.   The sex role has both a cognitive and a behavioral component. The child must understand what is "proper" or "normal" for people of each gender and must match her or his behavior to those norms.

By age 2 children already associate certain tasks and possessions with men and women, such as vacuum cleaner or stove and food with women and cars and tools with men (Weinraub et al., 1984). By age 3 or 4, children can assign occupations, toys, and activities to each gender, and by age 5, they begin to associate certain personality traits with males or females. They see women as weak, affectionate, gentle, appreciative, and softhearted, and men as aggressive, strong, cruel, and coarse. Cross-cultural studies in 28 different countries by John Williams and Deborah Best (1990) show that these same traits are part of both children's and adults' gender stereotypes in virtually all cultures, including non-Western countries such as Thailand, Pakistan, and Nigeria.

A very similar pattern is found in studies of children's ideas about what men and women (or boys and girls) *ought* to be like. A study by William Damon (1977) illustrates the point particularly clearly. He told a story to children aged 4 through 9 about a little boy named George who likes to play with dolls. George's parents tell him that only little girls play with dolls; little boys shouldn't. The children were then asked a batch of questions about this:

Why do people tell George not to play with dolls?

Are they right?

Is there a rule that boys shouldn't play with dolls?

What should George do?

Does George have a right to play with dolls? (p. 242).

Four-year-olds in this study thought it was OK for George to play with dolls. There was no rule against it and he should do it if he wanted to. Six-year-olds, in contrast, thought it was *wrong* for George to play with dolls. By about age 9, children had differentiated between what boys and girls usually do, and what is "wrong." One boy said, for example, that breaking windows was wrong and bad, but that playing with dolls was not bad in the same way: "Breaking windows you're not supposed to do. And if you play with dolls, well you can, but boys usually don't."

What seems to be happening is that the 5- or 6-year-old, having figured out that gender is permanent, is searching for a *rule* about how boys and girls behave (Martin & Halverson, 1981). She picks up information from watching adults, from TV, from listening to the labels that are attached to different activities (e.g., "Boys don't cry"). Initially children treat these as absolute, moral rules. Later they understand that these are social conventions, at which point sex-role concepts become more flexible and stereotyping declines somewhat.

Sex differences in behavior follow a similar pattern. They begin to be visible as early as age 2 or 3, when children begin to show both some preference for same-sex playmates and preference for sex-stereotyped toys. They become stronger over the preschool years and are fully and rigidly established by age 6 or 7.

In Western cultures, it is far more common for young girls to be "tomboys" than it is for boys to show "girlish" behavior. Does this mean girls have a less clear gender concept? What do you think might be causing such a difference?

Explaining Sex-Role Development.   Theorists from most of the major traditions have tried their hand at explaining this pattern of development. Freud relied on the concept of identification to explain the child's adoption of appropriate sex-role behavior, but his theory founders on the fact that children begin to show clearly sex-typed behavior long before age 4 or 5, when Freud thought identification occurred.

Social learning theorists, such as Mischel (1966, 1970), have emphasized the role of parents in shaping children's sex-role behavior and attitudes, a proposal quite well supported by research. Parents do seem to reinforce sex-typed activities in children as young as 18 months old, not only by buying different kinds of toys for boys and girls but by responding more positively when their sons play with blocks or trucks or when their daughters play with dolls (Fagot & Hagan, 1991; Lytton & Romney, 1991). Such differential reinforcement is particularly clear with boys. There is also new evidence suggesting that toddlers whose parents are more consistent in rewarding sex-typed toy choice or play behavior and whose mothers favor traditional family sex roles, learn accurate gender labels earlier than do toddlers whose parents are less focused on the gender-appropriateness of the child's play (Fagot & Leinbach, 1989; Fagot, Leinbach & O'Boyle, 1992)—findings clearly consistent with the predictions of social learning theory.

By age 2 or 3 we already see clear sex-role differences in children's toy choices. Left to their own devices, boys like this will select blocks or trucks to play with. Girls the same age are more likely to choose dolls or tea sets or dress-up clothes.

Still, helpful as it is, a social-learning explanation is probably not sufficient. In particular, there is less differential reinforcement of boy- versus girl-behavior than you'd expect, and probably not enough to account for the very early and robust discrimination children seem to make on the basis of gender. Even children whose parents seem to treat their young sons and daughters in highly similar ways nonetheless learn gender labels and show same-sex playmate choices.

A third alternative, based strongly on Piagetian theory, is Lawrence Kohlberg's suggestion that the crucial aspect of the process is the child's understanding of the gender concept (1966; Kohlberg & Ullian, 1974). Once the child realizes that he is a boy or she is a girl forever, then it becomes highly important for the child to learn how to behave in a way that fits the category he or she belongs to. Specifically, Kohlberg predicts that we should see systematic same-sex imitation only *after* the child has shown full gender constancy. Most studies designed to test this hypothesis have supported Kohlberg. Children do seem to become much more sensitive to same-sex models after they have understood gender constancy (e.g., Ruble, Balaban & Cooper, 1981). But Kohlberg's theory cannot handle the obvious fact that children show clear differential sex-role behavior, such as toy preferences, long before they have achieved full understanding of the gender concept.

The most fruitful current explanation is usually called **gender schema** theory (e.g., Bem, 1981, Martin & Halverson, 1981, 1983; Martin, 1991; Ruble, 1987). Just as the self-concept can be thought of as a "scheme" in Piaget's sense, or a "self-theory," so the child's understanding of gender can be seen in the same way. The gender schema begins to develop as soon as the child notices the differences between male and female, knows his own gender, and can label the two groups with some consistency—all of which happens by age 2 or 3. Perhaps because gender is clearly an either/or category, children seem to understand very early that this is a key distinction, so the category serves as a kind of magnet for new information (Maccoby, 1988). In Piaget's terms, once the child has established even a primitive gender scheme, a great many experiences are assimilated to it. Thus, as soon as this scheme begins to be formed, children may begin to show preference for same-sex playmates or for gender-stereotyped activities (Martin & Little, 1990).

Preschoolers first learn some broad distinctions about what kinds of activities or behavior go with each gender, both by observing other children and through the reinforcements they receive from parents. Then, between age 4 and 6 the child learns a more subtle and complex set of associations for his or her *own* gender—what children of his own gender like and don't like, how they play, how they talk, what kinds of people they associate with. Only at about age 8 to 10 does the child develop an equivalently complex view of the opposite gender (Martin, Wood & Little, 1990).

The key difference between this theory and Kohlberg's is that for a gender schema to be formed it is not necessary that the child understand that gender is permanent. When gender constancy is understood at about 5 or 6, the child develops a more elaborated rule or schema of "what people who are like me do" and treats this "rule" the same way she treats other rules—as absolutes. Later, the child's application of the "gender rule" becomes more flexible. She knows, for example, that most boys don't play with dolls, but that they *can* do so if they like.

Sex Differences in Social Interactions. Before I leave this subject, I want to say just a word about a new body of research that I find especially fascinating—studies that show that as early as age 3 or 4, boys and girls not only differ in the toys they play with and the playmates they choose, but in the ways they interact with those playmates.

Maccoby (1990) describes the girls' pattern as an *enabling style*. Enabling includes such behaviors as supporting the partner, expressing agreement, making suggestions. All these behaviors tend to foster a greater equality and intimacy in the relationship and keep the interaction going. In contrast, boys are more likely to show what Maccoby calls a *constricting* or *restrictive* style. "A restrictive style is one that tends to derail the interaction—to inhibit the partner or cause the partner to withdraw, thus shortening the interaction or bringing it to an end" (p. 517). Contradicting, interrupting, boasting, or other forms of self-display are all aspects of this style. You can get some sense of the difference from two examples drawn from Campbell Leaper's observations (1991) of pairs of previously unacquainted 7-year-olds, given in Table 8.2. Leaper's labels for these two exchanges are "cooperative" and "domineering," but they seem clearly to match Maccoby's distinction between enabling and restrictive styles.

These two patterns begin to be visible in the preschool years. For example, Maccoby (1990) points out that beginning as early as age 3 or 4, boys and girls use quite different strategies in their attempts to influence each other's behavior. Girls generally ask questions or make requests; boys are much more likely to make demands or phrase things using

TABLE 8.2 Examples of Enabling and Constricting Styles of Interaction

Girls' Interaction		Boys' Interaction	
Jennifer	Let's go play on the slide [sliding noises]	Andy	Mm, I don't like this
Sally	Okay [sliding noises] I'll do a choo-choo train with you	Patrick	[4 sec. silence; coughs, laughs]
		Andy	Do this
		Patrick	[4 sec. silence]
Jennifer	Okay	Andy	Do this
Sally	You can go first	Patrick	I wish I could go
Jennifer	Ch (gasp)	Andy	Do this. Kick your chair [kicking sounds]. Kick your chair!
Sally	Ch (gasp)		
		Patrick	I can't
		Andy	Mm huh (sigh)
		Patrick	[7 sec. silence]

Source: Leaper, 1991, from Tables 2 and 3, page 800.

imperatives ("Give me that!"). The really intriguing finding is that even at this early age, boys simply don't comply very much with the girls' style of influence attempt. So playing with boys yields little positive reinforcement for girls, and they begin to avoid such interactions and band together.

Similar differences in relationship style are evident in older children and adults. Girls and women have more intimate relationships with their friends. And in pairs or groups, girls and women seem to focus their attention on actions that will keep the interaction going. Adult men are more likely to be task-oriented, women to be relationship-oriented. I'll have much more to say about these differences in later chapters. For now I only want to point out that these subtle and profound differences seem to begin in very early childhood. What we do not yet understand is just how such differences might arise in children as young as 3 or 4.

Do your observations of adult relationships match the distinction Maccoby is making here? What do you think happens when a man and a woman interact in some nonromantic encounter? Is the resulting style some combination of enabling and constricting, or does one style dominate?

Individual Differences in Social Behavior and Personality

So far I've been talking primarily about shared developmental patterns. But I am sure it is obvious to you that in the preschool years, children's relationships, social behavior, and personalities become even more divergent than was true among infants. Some toddlers and preschoolers are highly aggressive, defiant, difficult to manage (Patterson, Capaldi & Bank, 1991; Campbell & Ewing, 1990). Some are shy and retiring, while others are sociable and outgoing. These differences obviously have a variety of sources. Inborn temperament seems to play some role, although by this age the child's temperamental tendencies have also been shaped by the parents' behavior. The security or insecurity of the child's first attachment is also part of the equation, as you have already seen in Table 6.4. Yet another causal element seems to be the parents' style of child rearing—the way they deal with the need to discipline and control the child, the extent to which they show affection and warmth, the contingency of their responses.

Temperament Differences

As I mentioned in Chapter 6, variations in the child's temperament, such as "easiness" or "difficultness," become reasonably stable by the preschool years. We also now begin to see a link between difficultness of temperament and both concurrent and future behavior problems: 3- or 4-year-olds with difficult temperament are more likely to show heightened aggressiveness, delinquency, or other forms of behavior problems in school, as teenagers, and as adults (Chess & Thomas, 1984). It is important to understand, though, that this is a *probability* statement. The majority of preschoolers who are classed as having difficult temperaments do *not* develop later behavior problems, although the likelihood of such an outcome is greater. Probably the easiest way to think of it is that a difficult temperament creates a *vulnerability* in the child. If this vulnerable child has supportive and loving parents who are able to deal effectively with the child's difficultness, the trajectory is altered and the child does not develop broader social problems. But if the parents do not like the child or lack suitable child-rearing skills, or if the family is facing other stresses, the vulnerable, difficult child is highly likely to emerge from the preschool years with serious problems relating to others (J. Bates, 1989).

The Impact of the Family: Styles of Parenting

The research on temperament gives us but one of many illustrations of the importance of understanding the family's role in the child's emerging personality or social behavior. Psychologists have struggled over the years to identify the best ways of describing the many dimensions along which families may vary. At the moment, the most fruitful conceptualization is one offered by Diana Baumrind (1967, 1971, 1973), who focuses on four

If this tantrum by young Frank is part of a regular pattern of difficult behavior, then the chances are higher that he will later have behavior problems in elementary school or adolescence. But such an outcome is not inevitable. Many difficult children change their behavior sufficiently to allow them to get along well with their peers at later ages.

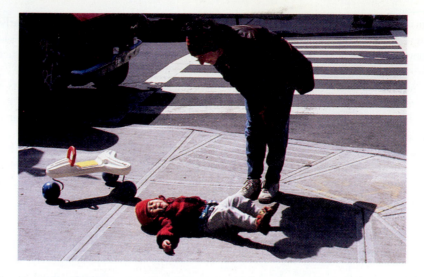

aspects of family functioning: nurturance or warmth, firmness and clarity of control, level of maturity demands, and degree of communication between parent and child.

Each of these four dimensions has been independently shown to be related to various child behavior. Children with nurturant and warm parents, as opposed to those with more rejecting parents, are more securely attached in the first two years of life, have higher self-esteem, are more empathetic, more altruistic, more responsive to others' hurts or distress, have higher measured IQs in preschool and elementary school, and are less likely to show delinquent behavior in adolescence or criminal behavior in adulthood (e.g., Maccoby, 1980; Schaefer, 1989; Simons, Robertson & Downs, 1989; Stattin & Klakenberg-Larsson, 1990). High levels of affection can even buffer the child against the negative effects of otherwise disadvantageous environments. Joan McCord, for example (1982), has found that among boys growing up in poverty-level, single-parent families, those whose mothers were rejecting were three times as likely to become delinquent or criminal as were those with affectionate and warm mothers.

The degree and clarity of the parents' control over the child has also been shown to be significant. Parents with clear rules, consistently applied, have children who are much less likely to be defiant or noncompliant—a pattern you'll remember from Gerald Patterson's research, which I talked about in Chapter 1 (Figure 1.3). Such children are also more competent and sure of themselves (Baumrind, 1973), and less aggressive (Patterson, 1980).

Equally important is the *form* of control the parent uses. The most optimal outcomes for the child occur when the parent is not overly restrictive, explains things to the child, and avoids the use of physical punishments such as spanking—a control strategy I've discussed in the "real world" box on the opposite page.

We also find more optimal outcomes for children whose parents have high expectations, high "maturity demands" in Baumrind's language. Such children have higher self-esteem, show more generosity and altruism toward others, and lower levels of aggression.

Finally, open and regular communication between parent and child has been linked to more positive outcomes. Listening to the child is as important as talking. Ideally, the parent needs to convey to the child that what the child has to say is *worth* listening to, that his ideas are important and should be considered in family decisions. Children from such families have been found to be more emotionally and socially mature (Bell & Bell, 1982; Baumrind, 1971, 1973).

While each of these characteristics of families may be significant individually, in fact they do not occur in isolation. They occur in combinations and patterns. Baumrind has identified three such patterns or styles:

- The **permissive style** is high in nurturance but low in maturity demands, control, and communication.
- The **authoritarian style** is high in control and maturity demands, but low in nurturance and communication.
- The **authoritative style** is high in all four.

Eleanor Maccoby and John Martin (1983) have proposed a variation of Baumrind's category system, shown in Figure 8.2, that I find even more helpful. They categorize families on two dimensions, the degree of demand or control and the amount of acceptance/rejection. The intersection of these two dimensions creates four types, three of

---

THE REAL WORLD
To Spank or Not to Spank

The short, emphatic answer to the question, ''Should I spank my child?'' is *no*. I know that this is easier to say than to do—and I admit to having applied a hand to my own children's rear ends on one or two occasions, even knowing that it would do little good and some potential damage. Yet the information we have about the effects of physical punishment, including spanking, seems to me to be so clear that a firm answer to the question is possible.

In the short term, spanking a child usually *does* get the child to stop the particular behavior you didn't like, and it seems to have a *temporary* effect of reducing the chance that the child will repeat the bad behavior. Because that's what you wanted, it may seem like a good strategy. But even in the short term there are some negative side effects. The child may have stopped misbehaving, but after a spanking he is undoubtedly crying, which is unpleasant. Crying is also a behavior that further spanking does not decrease: It is virtually impossible to get children to stop crying by spanking them! So you have exchanged one unpleasantness for another, and the second unpleasantness (crying) can't be dealt with by using the same form of punishment.

Another short-term side effect is that *you* are being reinforced for spanking whenever the child stops misbehaving after you spank her. Thus you are being ''trained'' to use spanking the next time, and a cycle is being built up.

In the longer term, the effects are clearly negative. First, when you spank, the child observes you using physical force or violence as a method of solving problems or getting people to do what you want. You thus serve as a model for a behavior you do *not* want your child to use with others.

Second, by repeatedly pairing your presence with the unpleasant or painful event of spanking, you are undermining your own positive value for your child. Over time, this means that you are less able to use *any* kind of reinforcement effectively. Eventually even your praise or affection will be less powerful in influencing your child's behavior. That is a very high price to pay.

Third, there is frequently a strong underlying emotional message that goes with spanking—anger, rejection, irritation, dislike of the child. Even very young children read this emotional message quite clearly (Rohner, Kean & Cournoyer, 1991). Spanking thus helps to create a family climate of rejection instead of warmth, with all the attendant negative consequences.

Finally, there is research evidence that children who are spanked more often show higher levels of aggression and less popularity with their peers, lower self-esteem, and more emotional instability (Rohner et al., 1991). They are less compliant with adults (Power & Chapieski, 1986). These are not outcomes parents intend for their children.

I am *not* saying that you should never punish a child. I *am* saying that *physical punishment,* such as spanking, is rarely (if ever) a good way to go about it. But what other forms of control will work? The most effective punishments—those that produce long-term changes in the child's behavior without unwanted or negative side effects—are those used *early* in some sequence of misbehavior, with the lowest level of emotion possible, and the mildest level of punishment possible (Patterson, 1975; Holden & West, 1989). Taking a desired toy away when the child *first* uses it to hit the furniture (or a sibling), or consistently removing small privileges when a child misbehaves will change the child's behavior, especially if the parent is also warm, clear about the rules, and consistent. It is far less effective to wait until the screams have reached a piercing level, or until the fourth time a teenager has gone off without telling you where she's going, and then weighing in with yelling, loud comments, and strong punishments.

If you have been brought up in a family in which spanking was the standard method, you may simply not know other ways. If you find yourself in this position, a parenting class—often offered by community colleges or other community organizations—might be of help.

Figure 8.2 Maccoby and Martin expanded on Baumrind's categories in this two-dimensional category system. The new parental style described here is the neglecting type. (*Source:* Adapted from E. E. Maccoby & J. A. Martin, 1983. Socialization in the context of the family: Parent-child interaction. In E. M. Hetherington [Ed.], *Handbook of child psychology*, Figure 2, p. 39. New York: Wiley.)

		Degree of acceptance or rejection	
		High acceptance: responsive	Low acceptance (rejection): unresponsive
Degree of demand and control	High	Authoritative-reciprocal	Authoritarian; power-assertive
	Low	Indulgent; permissive	Neglecting; ignoring; indifferent; uninvolved

which correspond quite closely to Baumrind's authoritarian, authoritative, and permissive types. Maccoby and Martin's conceptualization adds the fourth type, the **neglecting**, or uninvolved, style, which current research tells us may be the most detrimental of the four. Let me talk briefly about each style.

The Authoritarian Type.   Children growing up in authoritarian families—with high levels of demand and control but relatively low levels of warmth or responsiveness—typically are less skilled with peers than are children from other types of families and have lower self-esteem. Some of these children appear subdued; others may show high aggressiveness or other indications of being out of control. Which of these two outcomes occurs may depend in part on how skillfully the parents use the various disciplinary techniques. Patterson finds that the "out of control" child is most likely to come from a family in which the parents are authoritarian by inclination but lack the skills to enforce the limits or rules they set.

These effects are not restricted to preschool age children. In a study of nearly 8000 high school students, Sanford Dornbusch and his coworkers (Dornbusch et al., 1987; Lamborn et al., 1991) have found that teenagers from authoritarian families have poorer grades in school and more negative self-concepts than do teenagers from authoritative families.

The Permissive Type.   Children growing up with indulgent or permissive parents, too, show some negative outcomes. Dornbusch finds that they do slightly worse in school during adolescence, are likely to be more aggressive—particularly if the parents are specifically permissive toward aggressiveness—and to be somewhat immature in their behavior with peers and in school. They are less likely to take responsibility and are less independent.

It is somewhat surprising that children reared in permissive families are *less* independent and take *less* responsibility. You might think that such children have been specifically encouraged and reinforced for independence and decision making. Can you think of any reason why this pattern of results might occur?

The Authoritative Type.   The most consistently positive outcomes have been associated with the authoritative pattern, in which the parents are high in both control and warmth, setting clear limits but also responding to the child's individual needs. Children reared in such families typically show higher self-esteem, are more independent but at the same time more likely to comply with parental requests, and may show more altruistic behavior as well. They are self-confident and achievement oriented in school and get better grades (Dornbusch et al., 1987; Steinberg, Elmen & Mounts, 1989; Lamborn et al., 1991; Crockenberg & Litman, 1990).

The Neglecting Type.   In contrast, the most consistently negative outcomes are associated with the fourth pattern, the neglecting or uninvolved type. You may remember from the discussion of secure and insecure attachments in Chapter 6 that one of the family characteristics often found in children rated as insecure/avoidant is the "psychological unavailability" of the mother. The mother may be depressed, or she may be overwhelmed by other problems in her life and simply not have made any deep emotional connection with the child. Whatever the reason, such children continue to show disturbances in their relationships with peers and with adults for many years. At adolescence, for example, youngsters from neglecting families are more impulsive and antisocial, less competent with their peers, and much less achievement oriented in school (Block, 1971; Pulkkinen, 1982; Lamborn et al., 1991).

Several conclusions from this research are important. First, it seems clear that children are affected by the family "climate" or style. It seems highly likely that these effects persist well into adulthood, although we do not have the sort of longitudinal data we would need to be sure. Second, many of us are accustomed to thinking about family styles as if permissive and authoritative patterns were the only options. But research on the authoritarian pattern shows clearly that one can be *both* affectionate and firm, and that children respond to this combination in very positive ways.

Family Structure: Divorce and Other Variations

I cannot leave this discussion of family style and family functioning without at least some mention of the impact of divorce and other variations in family structure. For those

ACROSS CULTURES
Ethnic Differences in Styles of Parenting

It is important for us to know something about the incidence of these various styles of parenting among the major ethnic groups in our culture. If we were to find, for example, that the authoritative pattern is found only among white families, then we could not be sure whether the more positive outcomes associated with this style were simply the result of belonging to the majority culture or whether they were really a consequence of the way the parents behaved. The best evidence on this point comes from a study of adolescents rather than preschoolers, but it is nonetheless worth a look at this stage.

The findings come from the large study by Dornbusch and his colleagues that I have already mentioned (Steinberg et al., 1991). They have a sample of roughly 10,000 ninth- through twelfth-grade students, chosen so as to be representative of four different ethnic groups: white, black, Hispanic, and Asian. Each subject answered questions about the acceptance, control, and autonomy they received from their parents; those families described by the

students as above the average on all three dimensions were classed as authoritative. You can see the percentages of such families for the four ethnic groups in the table below, broken down further by the social class and intactness of the family.

You can see that an authoritative pattern is most common among white families and least common among Asians. But you can also see that in all groups, authoritative parenting is more common among the middle class than the working class, and (with one exception) more common in intact families than in single-parent or stepparent families. Furthermore, these researchers find that the relationship between authoritative parenting and positive outcomes occurred in all ethnic groups. In all four groups, for example, teenagers from authoritative families had better grades in school, more self-reliance, and less delinquency than did those from nonauthoritative families. Findings like these further underline the meaningfulness of this category system for every ethnic group.

	Percentage of Authoritative Families			
	Working Class		Middle Class	
Ethnic Group	Intact[a]	Not Intact	Intact	Not Intact
White	17.2	11.5	25.0	17.6
Black	13.4	12.2	14.0	16.0
Hispanic	10.7	9.8	15.8	12.9
Asian	7.5	6.1	15.6	10.8

[a]"Intact" means the child is still living with both biological parents; "not intact" may mean single parent, step-family, or any family configuration other than both natural parents.
Source: Steinberg et al., 1991, from Table 1, p. 25.

of us who live in cultures with high divorce rates, this is an issue of profound practical importance.

What may shock you is just how rare it is in the United States today for an individual to spend her entire childhood and adolescence living with both natural parents. Extrapolating from a longitudinal study of over 5000 families who have been followed since 1968, Sandra Hofferth (1985) estimates that only 30 percent of white children in the United States born in 1980 will still be living with their two natural parents at age 17. For black children, the figure is only 6 percent. Other estimates, based on cross-sectional comparisons, are somewhat more optimistic (e.g., Bumpass, 1984; Norton & Glick, 1986), but it would appear that at least 60 percent of today's children are likely to spend at least *some* time in a single-parent household, and perhaps 35 percent will spend at least a part of their childhood living with a stepparent.

Figure 8.3 shows the other types of family structures Hofferth predicts for the children born in 1980, so you can see the very large variety. Further complexities are added by the fact that most families change from one structure to another, sometimes repeatedly. Divorced mothers, for example, may have live-in relationships with one or more men before a remarriage, or may live for a while with their own parents. All in all, it is clear that the *majority* of children today experience at least two different family structures, often many more than that in the course of their growing up.

Research on the effects of such structures on family interaction patterns and on children has not kept pace with the rate of change in families. In particular, although the research base is growing, we still know relatively little about the many varieties of stepparent families. We know a good deal more about the effects of divorce.

Impact of Divorce.   Any change in the family structure is accompanied by dislocation and stress. In the case of divorce or separation, when an adult is subtracted from the family, the dislocation seems to be especially severe. In the several years immediately after a divorce, children become more defiant, more negative, more aggressive or depressed or angry. If they are of school age, their school performance typically drops for at least a while (Hetherington, 1989, 1991a, 1991b; Hetherington, Cox & Cox, 1978; Amato & Keith, 1991; Allison & Furstenberg, 1989). There is some disagreement about how long this negative effect may last for the child. Some investigators report lingering effects 5 and 10 years later (e.g., Wallerstein, 1984, 1989). Others do not find such lasting effects (e.g., Hetherington, 1989), but all agree that in the short run, children are disturbed.

These negative effects seem to be considerably larger for boys than for girls, although girls show more disruption at adolescence than do boys (Hetherington, 1991a, 1991b; Amato & Keith, 1991). Among younger children, boys are more likely to show increases in problem behavior, such as aggression or noncompliance, and they have more school problems than do girls from divorced families.

But contrary to the hypothesis derived from Freudian theory, there is no indication that the disruptive effect is more pronounced for children in the Oedipal period. Preschool-age children do typically show the clearest and most overt distress, such as prolonged crying or sleeping or eating disturbances. Teenagers are more likely to show anger or aggression. But neither the intensity of the problem nor the long-term consequences seem to be greater for children of any particular age.

Divorcing parents, too, are greatly disrupted. They may show wide mood swings, experience problems at work or poor health (Hetherington, 1989). Their parenting style also changes, becoming much less authoritative, almost neglectful.

Interestingly, it appears that many of these negative effects for both the adult and the children are mitigated when the mother has another adult in the home—her own mother, a friend, a live-in boyfriend (Dornbusch et al, 1985; Kellam, Ensminger & Turner,

If children in the Oedipal period do not show more negative reactions to their parents' divorce, what might this say about Freud's theory about this stage?

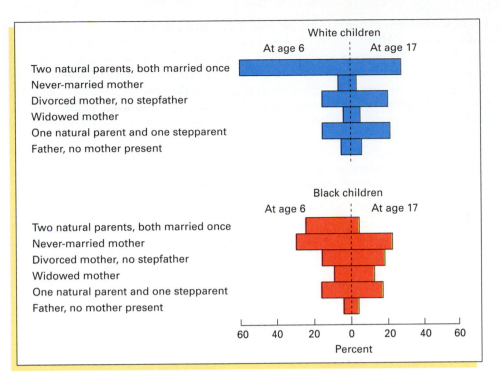

Figure 8.3 These figures show Sandra Hofferth's estimates of the percentage of children born in the United States in 1980 who will be in each of several family types or structures at age 6 and at age 17. Combining the data for blacks and whites, Hofferth estimates that only about a quarter of children will spend all of their childhood with both natural parents. (*Source:* Hofferth, 1985, Tables 1 and 2, pp. 99–100, 102–103.)

THE REAL WORLD
Softening the Effects of Divorce

Given the rate of divorce in our culture, a significant percentage of you reading these words will go through a divorce when you have children still living at home. There is no way to eliminate all the disruptive effects of such an event on your children, but I can give you some suggestions for minimizing or shortening those negative consequences. Here are some specific things you can do that are likely to soften the blow:

1. Try to keep the number of separate changes the child has to cope with to a minimum. If at all possible, keep the children in the same school, in the same home, the same day-care setting, etc. (Rutter, 1975).

2. Maintain your own network of support, and use that network liberally. Stay in touch with friends, seek out others in the same situation, join a support group. In whatever way you can, nurture yourself and your own needs (Hetherington & Camera, 1984).

3. Help your children stay in touch with the noncustodial parent. If you are the noncustodial parent, maintain as much contact as possible with your child(ren), calling regularly, seeing them regularly, attending school functions, and so on. Surprisingly, the evidence on this point is actually quite mixed; some studies show no positive benefit to the child of continued regular contact with the noncustodial parent (Emery, 1988). The difficulty in interpreting these results is that contact with the noncustodial parent is often confounded with the quality of the relationship between the now-divorced parents, which leads to the next point.

4. If you and your ex-spouse continue to have conflict, try very hard not to fight in front of the children. Conflict between the spouses itself seems not to be inevitably detrimental; it is the conflict that the child actually sees and hears that adds to the child's level of stress and disruption (Emery, 1988). If such conflict is low, then increased contact with the noncustodial parent seems most likely to be beneficial to the child.

5. Whatever else you do, do not use the child as a go-between or talk disparagingly about your ex-spouse to your child. Children who feel caught in the middle between the two parents are more likely to show various kinds of negative symptoms, such as depression or behavior problems (Buchanan, Maccoby & Dornbusch, 1991).

In the midst of your own emotional upheaval from a divorce, these are not easy prescriptions to follow. But if you are able to do so, your children will suffer less.

1977), which suggests that a two-adult system in a family may simply be more stable or easier to manage. However—and this is an important however—there are various hints that this buffering effect of a second adult in the home may *not* extend to stepparent family structures (mother/stepfather or father/stepmother). For example, Dornbusch finds that stepparent families show higher levels of authoritarian and lower levels of authoritative child-rearing styles (Dornbusch et al., 1987), and the children have lower school grades and higher rates of delinquency than do children in two-natural-parent families. Other studies of large samples of step-families do not always paint this same slightly negative picture (Schaffer, 1990). But findings like this illustrate once again just how complex the family system really is and how much we still have to learn about the ways in which families support or disrupt their children's development.

Summary

1. Freud and Erikson each described two stages of personality development during the preschool years, the anal and phallic stages in Freud's theory, and autonomy and initiative in Erikson's theory.

2. Both vertical relationships, such as with parents and teachers, and horizontal relationships with peers are highly important in these years. Only in play with peers can the child learn about reciprocal relationships, both co-operative and competitive.

3. The child's attachment to the parent(s) remains strong, but attachment behaviors become less visible as the child gets older, except in stressful situations.

4. Preschoolers also show more refusals and defiance of parental influence attempts than do infants. Outright defiance, however, declines from age 2 to 6.

5. Both these changes are clearly linked to the child's language and cognitive gains.

6. Play with peers is visible before age 2 and becomes increasingly central through the preschool years. Aggression with peers is also evident, more physical in the 2- and 3-year-old, more verbal in the 5- and 6-year-old.

7. Children as young as 2 also show altruistic behavior toward others, and this behavior seems to grow as the child's ability to take another's perspective increases.

8. Short-term friendships, mostly based on proximity, are evident in children in this age range. The majority of such pairs are same-sex.

9. The preschooler continues to define himself along a series of objective dimensions, but does not yet have a global sense of self-esteem.

10. Between ages 2 and 6, most children move through a series of steps in their understanding of gender constancy, first labeling their own and others' gender, then understanding the stability of gender, and finally understanding the constancy of gender at about age 5 or 6.

11. In these same years, children begin to learn what is "appropriate" behavior for their gender. By age 5 or 6, most children have developed fairly rigid rules about what boys or girls are supposed to do or be.

12. Neither Freud's nor Kohlberg's explanations of gender development has fared well. Social learning explanations are more persuasive, because parents do appear to do some differential reinforcement of sex-appropriate behavior. The most useful current theory is gender schema theory, which combines some elements of Piagetian and social learning models.

13. As early as age 3 or 4, boys and girls show different patterns or styles of interaction with peers, a difference that continues well into adulthood.

14. Children also differ widely in social behavior and personality. Temperament plays some role. Children with more difficult temperament are more likely to show later behavior problems or delinquency.

15. Parental styles are also significant. Authoritative parenting, combining high warmth, clear rules and communication, and high maturity demands, is associated with the most positive outcomes. Neglecting parenting is associated with the least positive. Two other patterns, each with specific effects, are the authoritarian and the permissive.

16. Family structure also affects children. Following a divorce, children typically show disrupted behavior for several years. Parental styles also change, becoming less authoritative.

Key Terms

aggression

altruism

authoritarian style

authoritative style

dominance

dominance hierarchy

gender concept

gender constancy

gender identity

gender schema

gender stability

neglecting style

permissive style

prosocial behavior

sex role

Suggested Readings

Eisenberg, N. (1992). *The caring child.* Cambridge, MA: Harvard University Press. (This is one of a series of excellent books aimed at the thoughtful lay reader rather than fellow professors.)

Grusec, J. E., & Lytton, H. (1988). *Social development. history, theory, and research.* New York: Springer-Verlag. (I recommended this in Chapter 6 and recommend it again here as an excellent, current text.)

Hartup, W. W. (1989). Social relationships and their developmental significance. *American Psychologist, 44,* 120–126. (Hartup has always been one of my favorite authors. His style is clear, his ideas interesting. Here he gives a brief review of some of the current work on social interactions.)

Lickona, T. (1983). *Raising good children.* Toronto: Bantam Books. (One of the very best "how to" books for parents I have ever seen, with excellent, concrete advice as well as theory. His emphasis is on many of the issues I raised in the "real world" box on rearing altruistic children.)

Maccoby, E. E. (1990). Gender and relationships. A developmental account. *American Psychologist, 45,* 513–520. (In this brief paper, Maccoby reviews the accumulating evidence suggesting that boys and girls show quite different styles of interaction, beginning in the preschool years.)

SUMMING UP PRESCHOOL DEVELOPMENT

Basic Characteristics of the Preschool Period

The table (page 205) summarizes the changes in children's abilities and behaviors between ages 2 and 6. The sense one gets of this period is that the child is making a slow but immensely important shift from dependent baby to independent child. The toddler or preschooler can now move around easily, can communicate more and more clearly, has a sense of himself as a separate person with specific qualities, and has the beginning cognitive and social skills that allow him to interact more fully and successfully with playmates. At the same time the child's thinking is *decentering*, becoming less egocentric and less tied to the outside appearances of things.

In the beginning, these newfound skills and new independence are not accompanied by impulse control. Two-year-olds are pretty good at doing; they are lousy at *not* doing. They see something, they go after it; when they want something, they want it *now!* If frustrated, they wail or scream or shout (isn't language wonderful?). A large part of the conflict parents experience with children at this age comes about because the parent *must* limit the child, not only for the child's own survival but also to help teach the child impulse control (Escalona, 1981).

The preschool years also stand out as the period in which the seeds are sown for the child's—and perhaps the adult's—social skills and personality. The attachment process in infancy continues to be formative because it helps to shape the internal working model of social relationships the child creates. But in the years from 2 to 6, this early model is revised, consolidated, and established more firmly.

The resultant interactive patterns tend to persist into elementary school and beyond. The 3-, 4-, or 5-year-old who develops the ability to share, to read others' cues well, to respond positively to others, and to control aggression and impulsiveness is likely to be a socially successful, popular 8-year-old. In contrast, the noncompliant, hostile preschooler is far more likely to become an unpopular, aggressive school child (Campbell et al., 1991; Patterson, Capaldi & Bank, 1991).

Central Processes

There are clearly many forces at play in creating these changes, beginning with two immense cognitive advances in this period: the 18- or 24-month-old child's new ability to use symbols, and the rapid development, between ages 3 and 5, of a more sophisticated theory of mind.

Symbol Use. The development of symbol use is reflected in many different aspects of the child's life. We see it in the rapid surge of language development, in the child's approach

to cognitive tasks, and in play, where the child is now able to pretend by having an object *stand for* something else. The ability to use language more skillfully in turn affects social behavior in highly significant ways, such as in the increasing use of verbal rather than physical aggression and the use of negotiation with parents in place of tantrums or defiant behavior.

Theory of Mind. The emergence of the child's more sophisticated theory of mind has equally broad effects, especially in the social arena, where the child's newfound abilities to read and understand others' behaviors form the foundation for new levels of interactions with peers and parents. It is probably not accidental that individual friendships between children are first visible at about the time that they also show the sharp drop in egocentrism that occurs with the emergence of the theory of mind.

We also see the seminal role of cognitive changes in the growing importance of several basic schemes. Not only does the 2- or 3-year-old have a more and more generalized internal model of attachment, she also develops a self-scheme and a gender-scheme, each of which forms part of the foundation of both social behavior and personality.

Play with Peers. Important as these cognitive changes are, they are clearly not the only causal forces. Equally central is the child's play with peers, which is itself made possible by the new physical and cognitive skills we see in the 2-year-old. When children play together, they expand one another's experience with objects and suggest new ways of pretending to one another, thus fostering still further cognitive growth. Conflict and disagreement are also key parts of chil-

A Summary of the Threads of Development During the Preschool Years

Aspect of Development	Age in Years				
	2	3	4	5	6
Physical development	Runs easily; climbs stairs one step at a time	Rides tricycle; uses scissors; draws	Climbs stairs one foot per step; kicks and throws large ball	Hops and skips; some ball games with more skill	Jumps rope; skips; may ride bike
Cognitive development	Symbol use; 2- and 3-step play sequences	Classification mostly by function	Beginning systematic classification by shape or size or color	Conservation of number and quantity	
		Ability to take others' physical perspective; beginning theory of mind	More advanced theory of mind; understands false belief		
Language development	2-word sentences	3- and 4-word sentences and grammatical markers	Continued improvement of inflections, past tense, plurals, passive sentences, and other language complexities		
Self/ personality development	Self-definition based on comparisons of size, age, gender			Self-definition based on physical properties or skills	
	Gender identity		Gender stability		Gender constancy
	Erikson's stage of autonomy vs. shame and doubt		Erikson's stage of initiative vs. guilt		
	Freud's anal stage		Freud's phallic stage		
Social development	Attachment behavior less and less overt, primarily shown under stress				
	Multistep turn-taking sequences in play with peers	Some altruism; beginning same-sex peer choice	Beginning signs of individual friendships	Negotiation, rather than defiance, more common with parents	
	Aggression primarily physical		Aggression more and more verbal		
				Sociodramatic play	Roles in play

dren's play, not only affecting the child's emerging social skills, but also stimulating the growth of theory of mind (Bearison, Magzamen & Filardo, 1986). When two children disagree about how to explain something, or insist on their own different views, it enhances each child's awareness that there *are* other perspectives, other ways of thinking or playing.

Of course, play with other children is also a part of the child's developing gender schema. Noticing whether other people are boys or girls, and what toys boys and girls play with, is itself the first step in the long chain of sex-role learning.

Family Interactions. It is also in social interactions, especially those with parents, that the child's initial social behaviors are modified or reinforced. The parents' style of discipline becomes critical here. Gerald Patterson's work shows clearly that parents who lack the skills to control the toddler's impulsivity and demands for independence are likely to end up strengthening noncompliant and disruptive behavior, even if the parents' intention is the reverse (Patterson,

Capaldi & Bank, 1991; Patterson & Bank, 1989).

Influences on the Basic Processes

The family's ability to support the child's development in these years is affected not only by the skills and knowledge the parents bring to the process, but also by the amount of stress they are experiencing from outside forces and the quality of support they have in their personal lives (e.g., Crockenberg & Litman, 1990; Morisset et al., 1990). In particular, mothers who are experiencing high levels of stress are more likely to be punitive and negative toward their children, with resulting increases in the children's defiant and noncompliant behavior (Webster-Stratton, 1988; Campbell et al., 1991). Susan Campbell's longitudinal study of a group of such noncompliant children (Campbell et al., 1991; Campbell et al., 1986;

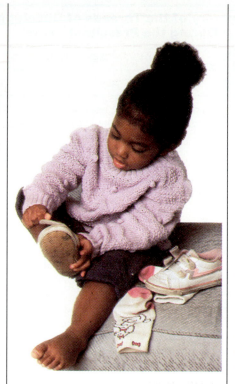

Campbell & Ewing, 1990) shows that just such maternal negativity is implicated in the persistence of noncompliant behavior into elementary school. Among the 3-year-olds who were labeled as "hard-to-manage," those who improved by age 6 had mothers who had been less negative.

The mother's stress is obviously not the only factor in her level of negativity toward the child. Depressed mothers are also more likely to show such behavior (Conrad & Hammen, 1989), as are mothers from working-class or poverty-level families, who doubtless experienced such negativity and harsh discipline in their own childhoods. But stress and lack of personal social support are part of the equation. Thus the preschooler, like children of every age, is affected by broader social forces outside the family as well as by the family interaction itself.

PHYSICAL AND COGNITIVE DEVELOPMENT FROM 6 TO 12

The years of middle childhood, marked on one side by the beginning of schooling and on the other by the onset of puberty, are often passed over rather briefly, as if they were somehow insignificant. Far less research has been done on children this age than on either preschoolers or adolescents. Even theorists often give less emphasis to this period. Freud, for example, referred to this as the "latency" period, as if development had gone underground. Yet it is clear that there are major cognitive advances in these years and that patterns and habits established during this time will affect not only adolescent experience, but also adulthood.

The beginning of formal schooling is itself a remarkable change. To be sure, an ever-growing proportion of children have been in day care or preschool. These children already have experience with being away from home for a good part of each day, which may make the transition to school less dramatic. But even for these children, school represents a major change in the level of expectation for performance that the child must try to meet. School signifies the beginning of the time when the child is expected to learn all those specific competencies and roles that are part of his culture, including the three Rs. Erikson focused on precisely this aspect of the period from 6 to 12, calling this stage *industry versus inferiority.*

We are also beginning to realize that learning appropriate social skills with one's peers is a highly significant part of the child's task in these years. This learning obviously begins in the preschool years, but the child's success or lack of success in establishing patterns of good social relationships in the elementary school years appears to have pervasive consequences, not just for the school child's sense of self-worth, but for adult lives as well—all of which I will talk about in some detail in the next chapter. In this chapter, let us look at what is happening physically and cognitively during these important early school years.

▶ Physical Changes at School Age

Perhaps one reason that middle childhood has been such a neglected area of study is that there is no remarkable physical change in children in this period. Change is steady but not striking. The growth patterns established in the late preschool years continue, with

What hypotheses can you generate to explain why middle childhood has been less studied than any other age period of childhood?

Children all over the world start school at about the same age. Here you can see a Czech classroom, and one in an aboriginal school in Australia.

This overweight child not only has different kinds of encounters with his peers, he is also more likely to be fat as an adult, with accompanying increased health risks.

Are obese children fat because they get less exercise, or do they exercise and move less because they are fat and it takes more effort? How could you design a study that would let you decide between these two alternatives?

2 to 3 inches and about 6 pounds added each year. Most of the significant motor skills have been developed in at least basic form by age 6 or 7, so what we see between 6 and 12 is increasing speed, better and better coordination, and greater skill at specific physical tasks.

Girls in this age range have slightly more body fat and slightly less muscle tissue than do boys, and girls are still ahead of boys in their overall rate of maturation. But in these years, girls and boys are remarkably similar in strength and speed.

What does begin during this period is the set of changes that eventually lead to puberty. Pubertal hormone changes may begin as early as age 8 in girls and at 9 or 10 for boys. But although the process begins in the school years, it is not until adolescence that we see it in full flower, so I will save the discussion of these pubertal changes until Chapter 11, where I will describe the whole process in one connected discussion.

Health

The rate of illnesses in these years is slightly lower than what we see in preschool children, but most elementary school youngsters have acute illnesses four to six times each year, mostly colds and flu. As at every age, children who are experiencing high levels of stress or family upheaval are more likely to become ill. For example, a large nationwide study in the United States shows that children living in mother-only families have more asthma, more headaches, and a generally higher vulnerability to illnesses of many types (Dawson, 1991).

Other Health Hazards: Obesity. Acute or chronic diseases are not the only health hazards for children. Beyond accidents, which continue to be the major cause of death among children in this age range, one of the most significant risks is obesity. In the United States, roughly 15 percent of elementary school children meet the usual definition of obesity, which is a body weight 20 percent or more above the normal weight for height.

Obesity is a significant long-term health problem. Among adults, the obese have shorter life expectancies and higher risk of heart disease and high blood pressure. We also know that there is a correlation between obesity in childhood and obesity in adulthood. Only about a fifth of obese babies are still obese as adults, but by school age the relationship has become much stronger (Roche, 1981; Grinker, 1981). An obese child has two and a half times the risk of being an obese adult. This does not mean, by the way, that all fat adults were fat children—about half of obese adults were *not* fat as children—but being obese in childhood greatly increases the risk (Shonkoff, 1984; Price et al., 1990).

Obesity in childhood or adulthood appears to have three basic causes: heredity, activity level, and diet. Children clearly seem to inherit a tendency toward fatness or leanness. Both twin and adoption studies show this effect. Adult identical twins, for example, have extremely similar adult weights even if they are reared apart, while fraternal twins differ much more in weight (Stunkard et al., 1990). Similarly, adopted children reared by obese parents are less likely to be obese than are the natural children of obese parents (Stunkard et al., 1986).

Whether a child with a genetic propensity to fatness will actually become obese, however, depends on both diet and exercise. Obese children (and adults) take in more calories than do their thinner peers, and they probably exercise less—although there is now some dispute about this conclusion. Early research by Mayer (1975), among others, suggested that obese children simply don't move as much, even when doing the same things thinner children are doing. More recent work suggests that this is true of obese adults, but not of fat children (e.g., Waxman & Stunkard, 1981). Thus, for children, it appears to be the combination of an efficient metabolism that uses every calorie taken in, and a higher intake of calories, that produces obesity.

Still, inactivity may play some role. One group of researchers, studying a national sample of over 6000 children, estimate that the prevalence of obesity increases roughly 2 percent for each additional hour of television a child or teenager watches per day, even when prior weight, family influences, and other background variables are taken into account (Dietz & Gortmaker, 1985). These investigators are not arguing that watching TV makes you fat; they are suggesting that the more TV a child watches, the less exercise he is getting and the greater the likelihood that the youngster will eat high-fat junk food.

Obesity obviously affects a child's social experiences during the school years, which may have effects detectable into adulthood. At the same time, I should point out that *fear* of fatness may also become a significant problem for some children, especially girls, particularly those from white middle-class families. Serious eating disorders such as bulimia and anorexia don't become common until adolescence, but many school-age children are already well aware of current cultural norms of thinness, particularly for women. Some normal-weight girls of 8 or 9 are already preoccupied with their weight, even dieting. When they hit puberty, with its large increase in body fat, a significant fraction of these girls develop eating disorders as a way of trying to control their weight and fat level. The balancing act required for the parents of an overweight child, then, is to try to help the child develop better eating and exercise habits without so emphasizing the importance of thinness that the child develops pathological patterns of dieting. In either case, it is clear that both health habits and body images established in these early years will tend to persist into adolescence and adulthood, with potentially pervasive health consequences.

◗ Cognitive Changes

In the cognitive arena there is more significant change going on during middle childhood, especially in the early years of this period, at the time the child starts school. Piaget saw this set of changes as being as striking, and as significant, as the acquisition of symbol usage at age 2.

Piaget's View of Concrete Operations

The new skills we see at age 5, 6, or 7 build on all the small changes we have already seen in the preschooler, but from Piaget's perspective there is a great leap forward that occurs when the child discovers or develops a set of general "rules" or "strategies" for examining and interacting with the world. Piaget calls this new set of skills **concrete operations**. By an "operation," Piaget means any of a set of powerful, abstract, internal schemes such as reversibility, addition, subtraction, multiplication, division, and serial ordering. Each of these is a kind of internal rule about objects and their relationships. The child now understands the *rule* that adding something makes it more and subtracting makes it less; she understands that objects can belong to more than one category at once and that categories have logical relationships.

Of all the operations, Piaget thought the most critical was *reversibility*—the understanding that both physical actions and mental operations can be reversed. The clay sausage in the conservation experiment can be made back into a ball, the water can be poured back into the shorter, fatter glass. This understanding of the basic reversibility of actions lies behind many of the gains made during this period. For example, if you possess the operation of reversibility, then knowing that A is larger than B also tells you that B is smaller than A. The ability to understand hierarchies of classes, such as *Fido, spaniel, dog,* and *animal,* also rests on this ability to go backward as well as forward in thinking about relationships.

Many of these operations seem to be acquired between ages 5 and 7. Signs of this shift in mental gears can be seen in the same lines of development I described in Chapter 7: identities, classification, and logic.

Identities in the Concrete Operations Period.   By age 6, virtually all children understand at least the conservation of quantity and number; conservation of weight is typically understood by age 7 or 8. Any one of a number of different operations may be used by a child in arriving at such understanding: reversibility ("If I changed it back it would be the same"), addition or subtraction ("You didn't add any so it has to be the same"), or compensation (paying attention to more than one thing at a time, such as "It's bigger around, but it's thinner, so it's the same").

Classification.   Similarly, children typically grasp the principle of class inclusion somewhere around age 7 or 8, a shift you can see especially clearly in the results of one of my favorite older studies. Mosher and Hornsby (1966) showed 6- to 11-year-old children a set of 42 pictures of animals, people, toys, and machines. The experimenter said he was thinking of one of the pictures, and the child was to figure out which one by asking questions that could be answered "yes" or "no."

There are several ways to figure out which questions to ask. You could point to one picture after another, asking, "Is it this one?" until you hit on the right one. Mosher and Hornsby called this *hypothesis scanning*. Or you could classify the pictures mentally into a hierarchy of groups, and then ask about one group at a time. You might start, for example, by asking, "Is it a toy?" If the answer is "yes," you might then ask about the subcategories: "Is it a red toy?" Mosher and Hornsby called this second strategy *constraint seeking*. You can see from Figure 9.1 that 6-year-olds relied essentially on guessing. By age 8, however, most children used the more cognitively advanced constraint strategy, reflecting the shift to what Piaget calls concrete operations.

Logic in the Concrete Operations Period.   Piaget argued that during these years the child develops the ability to use **inductive logic,** which involves moving from the particular to the general. The child of this age can now go from his own experience to a general principle. For example, he may have observed in his play that when you add another toy to a set and then count it, it always has one more. The 4- or 5-year-old would stop there. But the 7- or 8-year-old moves from such observations to the general principle that adding always makes more of something.

Elementary school children are pretty good observational scientists and will enjoy cataloging, counting species of trees or birds, or figuring out the nesting habits of guinea pigs. They are not yet good at **deductive logic,** which moves from the general to the specific, such as starting with a theory and then generating hypotheses from that theory. This is harder than inductive logic because it may require imagining things that you may never have experienced—something the concrete operations child typically does not do.

Figure 9.1   When 6-year-olds play "twenty-questions" with sets of pictures, their questions are nearly all in the form of a specific hypothesis or guess ("Is it this one?"). Eight-year-olds are more likely to use a constraint strategy, based on their ability to classify the pictures into hierarchically organized groups, asking questions like "Is it a toy?" (*Source:* Mosher & Hornsby, 1966, p. 91.)

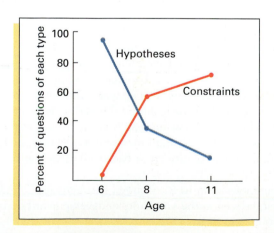

Thus, even though the child of this age is cognitively quite advanced, she is still tied to some degree to the concrete, to her own observations and experience.

An important practical application of this characteristic of thinking in the elementary school child is that children this age learn science (and other subjects) most easily if the material is presented "concretely," with plenty of opportunity for hands-on experience and inductive experimentation. They learn less well when scientific concepts or theories are presented in a deductive fashion (e.g., Saunders & Shepardson, 1987).

Post-Piagetian Work on the Concrete Operations Period

Unlike researchers who have studied the first two of Piaget's stages, those who have followed up on Piaget's descriptions of the concrete operational period have generally supported Piaget's observations on the timing of various developments. They have found, as had Piaget, that conservation of quantity and mass develop early in this period, followed by conservation of weight and then conservation of volume; they have found that children in this age range do indeed show inductive logic but typically fail on tasks that demand deductive logic (e.g., Markovitz, Schleifer & Fortier, 1989); they have found that over the years of concrete operations, children develop the ability to create hierarchical classification systems and use them to solve problems—as illustrated by the "twenty-questions" study.

You can see many of these changes in the findings from a longitudinal study of concrete operations tasks by Carol Tomlinson-Keasey and her colleagues (Tomlinson-Keasey et al., 1978). They followed a group of 38 children from kindergarten through third grade, testing them with five tasks each year: conservation of mass, weight, and volume, class inclusion, and hierarchical classification. The results, in Figure 9.2, show that the children got better at all five tasks over the three-year period, with two spurts, one between the end of kindergarten and the start of first grade (about the age that Piaget thought that concrete operations really began) and another during second grade.

You can also see in Figure 9.2 that these different tasks were not equally easy. Conservation of mass was easier than conservation of weight, with conservation of volume the hardest of the three. Class inclusion was also generally harder than conservation of mass. In fact, they found that conservation of mass seemed to be a necessary precursor for the development of class inclusion.

Findings like these raise some very fundamental questions about the validity of Piaget's concept of stages. Remember that Piaget thought that each stage was a cohesive whole, a structure that affected all aspects of thinking. If that is true, then we ought to find that a child of any given age applies very similar logic to a whole range of problems. In the case of concrete operations, we ought to find that a child applies operational logic to just about any task we give her. But researchers have generally *not* found such consistency from one task to another, just as Tomlinson-Keasey and her colleagues did not.

Instead, researchers have found that a child may perform at one stage on one task and at another stage on a second task, even though the two tasks appear to tap the same basic cognitive structure in Piaget's model (e.g., Uzgiris, 1973; Martorano, 1977; Keating & Clark, 1980; Flavell, 1982a, 1982b). The news is not all bad for Piaget's stage concept. You may remember from earlier chapters that there seems to be quite a lot of cross-task consistency in toddlers and at age 4. At about 18 to 24 months of age, children string two words together into sentences at about the same time that we first see strings of two pretend actions in the child's play and the first turn-taking and cooperation in their interactions with other children, all of which we might think of as *combinatorial* skill (Brownell, 1986; Brownell & Carriger, 1990). Even in retarded children these several skills seem to develop together, although at a later age (Siebert, Hogan & Mundy, 1986), all of which sounds remarkably stagelike.

In your everyday life, how do you use inductive logic? How do you use deductive logic?

Figure 9.2   In this longitudinal study, children were given the same set of concrete operations tasks five times, beginning in kindergarten and ending in third grade. (*Source:* Tomlinson-Keasey et al., 1979, adapted from Table 2, p. 1158.)

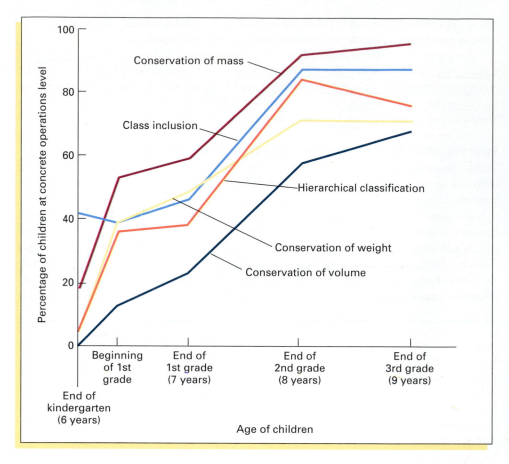

Similarly, between ages 4 and 5, children perform very consistently on a variety of tasks designed to assess their theory of mind, suggesting that there is some broad, stagelike development going on. But past the age of 5 or 6, there is much less evidence for such cross-task consistency. Adding to the doubts about Piaget's concept of stages is the evidence from a related body of research on *expertise.*

Studies of Expertise.   If children are applying broad forms of logic to all their experiences, the amount of specific knowledge a child has about a set of material shouldn't make a lot of difference to the form of logic she uses. A child who has never seen pictures of dinosaurs but who understands hierarchical classification ought to be able to create classifications of dinosaurs about as well as a child who had played with dozens of dinosaur models. A child who understands the principle of transitivity (that if A is greater than B, and B is greater than C, then A is greater than C) ought to be able to demonstrate this ability with sets of strange objects as well as with a set of toys familiar to her. But in fact that seems not to be the case.

There is now a great deal of research showing that specific knowledge makes a huge difference. Children and adults who know a lot about a subject or a set of materials—whether it is dinosaurs, baseball cards, mathematics, or whatever—think about that information very differently from novices. Experts categorize information in their special area in more complex and hierarchical ways, they apply more advanced forms of logic to material in that area, and they are better at remembering information on that topic. For example, a study in Germany of second- and fourth-grade children who were soccer fans, compared to those who rarely watched soccer games, showed that the experts remembered lists of soccer-related words better (Schneider & Bjorklund, 1992). Furthermore, such expertise seems to generalize very little to similar tasks. In the German study, for example, there were no differences between the soccer fans and the nonfans in their memory for lists of non-soccer-related words.

Some of the most interesting work on expertise has been done by Michelene Chi and her colleagues (e.g., Chi, Hutchinson & Robin, 1989; Chi & Ceci, 1987). In her most famous study (1978), she showed that expert chess players can remember the placement of chess pieces on a board much more quickly and accurately than novice chess players, *even when the expert chess players are children and the novices are adults.*

Because young children are novices at almost everything, while older children are more expert at many things, perhaps the difference in apparent cognitive strategies or functioning between younger and older children is just the effect of more specific knowledge, more experience, and *not* the result of stagelike changes in fundamental cognitive structures.

Some Neo-Piagetian Replies. Those who advocate the usefulness of stage concepts have not given up without a fight. Some have argued that we should not expect cross-task consistency at the beginning of a new stage, but only at the end, when the new structure is fully realized.

> Think about your own areas of expertise and the areas about which you have little knowledge. Can you see any differences in the *way* you think about these different areas, in the form of logic you use, or the way you go about remembering?

ACROSS CULTURES
The Effect of Schooling on Children's Thinking

Another specific experience that could affect the development of what Piaget calls concrete operations is schooling itself. It may well be that schooling starts at about age 6 or 7 in cultures all over the world precisely because adults have implicitly recognized that children this age are now ready to learn more abstract material. But it is also possible that it is schooling itself that helps to stimulate or trigger the transition to more abstract forms of thinking. If this is true, then we ought to find that children who do not attend school are delayed in acquiring concrete operational skills.

Researchers have attempted to test this hypothesis by studying children in societies or cultures in which schooling is not compulsory or is not universally available. By comparing similar groups of children, some of them in school and some of them not, it may be possible to discover the role that schooling plays in cognitive development.

A wide variety of such studies—in Mexico, Peru, Colombia, Liberia, Zambia, Nigeria, Uganda, Hong Kong, and many other countries—have led to the conclusion that schooling does indeed play a causal role in the development of at least some kinds of complex thinking. Schooled children, compared to unschooled children the same age, are better at memory tasks, especially those that require the construction of new mental categories or the use of other advanced mnemonic devices; they are better at classification tasks, especially those that involve some basis for classification other than color or function, and they are better able to shift from one basis of classification to another; they are more likely to understand the principle of conservation. Most broadly, schooled children appear to be better at generalizing a learned concept or principle to a new setting (Rogoff, 1981).

A good example of recent research on schooling is Harold Stevenson's study of the Quechua Indian children of Peru (Stevenson and Chen, 1989; Stevenson et al., 1991). He and his associates tested 6- to 8-year-old children in rural areas as well as in city barrios, and in each setting they tested some who had been in school for about six months and some who had not yet started school or who were living in an area where a school was not available. Stevenson found that in both rural and urban areas, schooled children performed better on virtually all tasks, including a measure of seriation and a measure of concept formation. These differences remained even if the parents' level of education, the nutritional status of the child, and the amount of educational enrichment offered at home were taken into account. Only on measures of memory, such as the ability to repeat back a set of numbers that had been read to the child, were there no differences.

This does not mean that schooling is the only way for children to acquire complex forms of thinking. Specific experience in a particular area can also promote expertise. For example, Geoffrey Saxe (1988) has found that 10-year-old unschooled street vendors in Brazil have devised their own strategies for solving arithmetic problems and do so with much better accuracy than do unschooled Brazilian children who have no street-vendor experience. At the same time, street vendors have difficulty solving school-type arithmetic problems.

Schooling thus exposes children to many specific skills and classes of knowledge, all of which increase their expertise in many areas. But schooling also appears to stimulate the development of more abstract, flexible, generalized strategies for remembering and solving problems.

Other replies to the critics have been in the form of slightly modified versions of stage theories. For example, Kurt Fischer (1980; Fischer & Pipp, 1984; Fischer & Canfield, 1986) proposes a series of "developmental levels," but sees them as representing the *optimal level*, the upper limit of performance of which the child is then capable under maximally supportive conditions—clear instructions, familiar content, high levels of motivation, and so on. In Fischer's theory, the optimal level rises discontinuously with age in a series of spurts, as a result of the emergence of new strategies or the integration of old strategies. At any given moment, however, a child's actual performance on different kinds of tasks will vary a great deal, depending on the child's expertise or the clarity or simplicity of the instructions, or other situational factors. Thus Fischer proposes stagelike changes at an underlying level of competence, but more variability at the visible level of performance.

Whether Fischer's proposals or some other model will ultimately provide the framework for a persuasive stage theory, I simply can't tell at this point. What is clear now is that Piaget's version of structurally distinct, cohesive stages of cognitive development is not an accurate description of the process. Instead of stages, cognitive development seems to be made up of a large number of apparently universal *vertical* sequences. In any given concept area, such as number concepts, concepts of gender, ideas about appearance and reality, or in hundreds of other areas, children seem to learn the basic rules or strategies in the same order. To quote John Flavell "Sequences are the very wire and glue of development. Later cognitive acquisitions build on or are otherwise linked to earlier ones, and in their turn similarly prepare the ground for still later ones." (1982b, p. 18.)

Thus, while Piaget appears to have been at least partially off-target in talking about stages, his emphasis on sequences has been right on the mark. Further, I am convinced that Piaget was right in arguing that the changes in cognitive skill from preschooler to school-age child are more than merely quantitative increases in specific task knowledge and experience—although Piaget himself acknowledged that such experience was a critical ingredient in the developmental process. There seem to be real differences in the way 2-year-olds and 8-year-olds approach problems that are not merely differences in experience. But if those differences are not in the basic structures, as Piaget thought, just what might those differences consist of? A different theoretical approach, known as *information processing*, may offer some answers.

Information Processing: Another View of Cognitive Development

Theorists like Piaget, who study cognitive structure, ask what overall structure of logic the child uses in solving problems and how those structures change with age. The information processing theorists ask what the child is *doing* intellectually when faced with a task, what intellectual *processes* she brings to bear, and how those processes might change with age.

The basic metaphor underlying the entire information processing approach has been that of the human mind as computer. Like a computer, we can think of the "hardware" of cognition, such as the physiology of the brain, the nerves and connective tissue, and the "software" of cognition, which would be the set of strategies or "programs" using the basic hardware. To understand cognition in general, we need to understand both the processing capacity of the hardware and the nature of the programs required to perform any given task. To understand cognitive *development*, we need to discover whether there are any changes with age in the basic processing capacity of the system and/or in the nature of the programs used. Does the hardware get more powerful with age? Do new types of programs emerge with age? Alternatively, perhaps all the wiring and all the programs are there from the beginning, but the child needs to learn to use the basic programs on each set of material.

Before you read the next section, think about how you might try to discover whether there are any changes with age in the basic hardware of cognition. What differences might we see in behavior if such hardware changes were part of development?

THE REAL WORLD
Learning to Read

The importance of knowledge and expertise, so clear in recent work on cognitive development, also appears when we look at that real-life cognitive skill, learning to read. Somewhat to my surprise, researchers have found that IQ is not a good predictor of how easily a child will learn to read in first grade. Piagetian-like tasks, such as measures of a child's ability to solve classification, seriation, and conservation problems, are somewhat better predictors of reading (Arlin, 1981; Tunmer, Herriman & Nesdale, 1988). But the really crucial ingredient is the child's specific experience or expertise with language and with letters.

Two kinds of knowledge seem to be especially significant: (1) the child's ability to recognize individual letters, and (2) the child's awareness that spoken and written words are made up of individual sounds (Adams, 1990).

I already mentioned in Chapter 5 that very young babies pay attention to individual sounds, called *phonemes*. But the understanding that words are made up of strings of such sounds—an understanding referred to as *phonemic awareness*—seems to be a more advanced understanding, one that is essential to reading. Researchers have studied this in a variety of ways, such as by asking the child to tap a pencil once for each separate sound in a word read to him, or by asking the child to say the first sound in some word, such as the *b* at the start of *bear*, or to say a word like *pink* without the first sound. Rhyming tasks may also measure phonemic awareness. All the research, splendidly summarized in a recent book by Marilyn Adams (1990), shows that 5- and 6-year-old children who have more phonemic awareness learn to read much faster than do children with less such awareness.

Letter recognition and phonemic awareness also interact with more basic cognitive skills. For instance, Tunmer and his colleagues (Tunmer, Herriman & Nesdale, 1988) have found that the best predictor of reading skill at the end of first grade is the child's letter recognition at the beginning of the year. But among those children who began first grade with poor phonemic awareness or letter recognition, those with good concrete operational knowledge caught up much more quickly in reading than did children who lagged behind in these basic cognitive skills. Thus good skills in either area—language awareness or logical abilities—can form the foundation for reading, but of the two, language awareness seems to be the more central.

Where does such early language awareness come from? How does it happen that some 5- and 6-year-olds have extensive understanding of the way words are put together, while others have little? The answer seems to be quite simple: exposure and exper-tise. For a child to learn about letters and sounds, he has to have had a great deal of exposure to language, both written and spoken. Such children are talked to a lot as infants, read to regularly, may have toy letters to play with, are told the sounds that go with each letter, or may be quite specifically taught the alphabet at an early age.

Nursery rhymes are also frequently a significant part of the early experience of good readers. One recent study (Maclean, Bryant & Bradley, 1987) found that among a sample of children in England, those who knew more nursery rhymes at age 3½ later had greater phonemic awareness and learned to read more readily than did those who knew fewer rhymes. Because nursery rhyme knowledge was *not* predictive of the child's later mathematical ability in this study, it looks very much as if we are dealing here with a quite specific body of expertise.

Of all the types of early experience that may contribute to such expertise, the most crucial seems to be the experience of being read to, regularly and in a fashion that invites the child's attention and response. Families that do not engage in such reading or do not encourage other prereading experiences have children who have far more difficulty learning to read once they begin school.

For those lacking such expertise at the start of school, the only solution is to try to build a parallel base of knowledge through many of the same kinds of experiences that more expert readers have had at home. This means that poor readers need a great deal of exposure to sound/letter combinations. But they also need to learn how to recognize patterns of letters in words. One need not—indeed must not—choose between those two hotly contested educational systems, phonics and ''whole word'' training. Both are needed, along with instruction in syntax, so that the child will understand better what words *could* appear in certain places in sentences.

Adams also makes a persuasive case that the poor reader must have maximum possible success in oral reading, preferably with texts that are full of the sort of rhyme and repetition that will help to foster phonemic awareness and learning of language regularities. Programs with this emphasis, such as the Reading Recovery Program devised by Marie Clay (1979), have been highly successful with poor readers, while more drill-like phonics programs have not. In other words, poor readers seem to learn to read most easily through programs that to some degree mimic the naturally occurring home experiences of good readers: a great deal of reading, ''play'' with words, active questioning, and experimentation.

Changes in Processing Capacity. Any computer has physical limits to the number of different operations it can perform at one time; computers also differ in speed. As the brain and nervous system develop in the early years of life, with synapses formed and then pruned to remove the redundant ones, perhaps the capacity, the speed, or the efficiency of the system increases.

One type of evidence supporting this possibility comes from studies of memory span, which I mentioned briefly in Chapter 1 (see Figure 1.5). In such research, the subject hears a list of items—letters, numbers, or words—and is then asked to repeat the list back in the order it was given. Typically the first list is quite short. Each new list is then one item longer until a length is reached at which the subject can no longer remember accurately. Figure 9.3 shows combined results from a number of studies of memory for letters in children and adults (Dempster, 1981). You can see that memory span increases fairly steadily over the years of childhood.

This pattern of findings *might* show an increase in processing capacity with age. But it might also result from differences in experience or expertise. Younger children clearly have less experience with numbers, letters, and words. Perhaps their poorer performance on tests that measure memory span is simply another example of the fact that experts can do things better than novices. In fact, when researchers have tried to match the degree of experience by asking older children to remember new letterlike figures, much of the age difference in memory span disappears. Because of findings like these, most experts have now concluded that there is probably no basic increase in underlying capacity, but that there may well be improvements in efficiency. Improved efficiency then frees up more "memory space" for storage (Schneider & Pressley, 1989).

One kind of improved efficiency is simply greater speed. Robert Kail (1991a, 1991b) has shown that children's thinking and their response time gets faster with age. Furthermore, the pattern of age increase is virtually identical across many different types of problems or tasks, including such perceptual-motor tasks as tapping, simple response time to a stimulus (such as pressing a button as quickly as possible every time a number is flashed on a screen), and cognitive tasks such as mental addition or subtests from the WISC. The most plausible explanation for this common pattern is that there is a fun-

Figure 9.3 Psychologists have tried to measure basic memory capacity by asking subjects to listen to a list of numbers, letters, or words, and then to repeat back the list in order. This figure shows the number of such items children of various ages are able to remember and report accurately, based on a number of different studies. (*Source:* Dempster, 1981, from Figures 1, 2, and 3, pp. 66, 67, 68.)

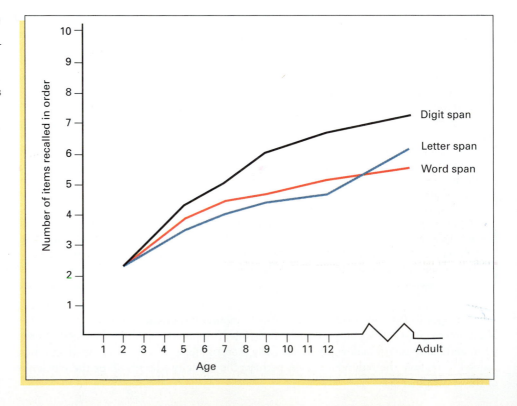

damental change in the physical system itself that allows greater and greater speed of both response and mental processing.

Another way in which processing could become more efficient with age is by increasing use of a variety of cognitive *strategies*—all those techniques we use to simplify or subdivide the cognitive tasks we face. A great deal of research within the information processing approach is aimed at understanding the emergence of just such strategies. A good example is the research on memory strategies.

Strategies for Remembering. If the normal maximum memory span is only 6 or 7 items, as the data in Figure 9.3 suggest, we would be in trouble if we had a longer list of items to recall, such as a grocery list, or a long list of errands to run. The solution is to use any one of a variety of memory strategies, some of which I've listed in Table 9.1. You can rehearse a longer list over and over to yourself; you can group the items in the list into clusters or chunks, such as "all the things I'll need for the macaroni and cheese recipe"; you can devise a story that ties all the items in your list together; or you can memorize the route you need to drive on your errands.

Just how early do children start using such strategies? Until fairly recently, most psychologists thought that spontaneous use of strategies did not appear until about age 6, at about the age when Piaget thought concrete operations began (e.g., Keeney, Cannizzo & Flavell, 1967). Current research has led to a slightly different set of conclusions. First, we can see some primitive signs of memory strategies under optimum conditions as early as age 2 or 3 (DeLoache, 1989; DeLoache et al., 1985), but with increasing age children use more and more powerful ways of helping themselves remember things. Second, for each strategy, children shift from a period in which they don't use it at all, to a period in which they will use it if reminded or taught, to one in which they use it spontaneously. Third, with increasing age, especially in the period from 6 to 12, children use these strategies more and more skillfully and generalize them to more and more situations. Thus, there are changes not only in the quantity of strategic use but in the quality.

TABLE 9.1 Some Common Information Processing Strategies Involved in Remembering

Rehearsal. Perhaps the most common strategy, involving either mental or vocal repetition, or repetition of movement (as in learning to dance). May occur in children as young as 2 years under some conditions.

Clustering. Grouping ideas or objects or words into clusters to help you remember them, such as "all animals," or "all the ingredients in the lasagna recipe," or "the chess pieces involved in the move called castling." This is one strategy that clearly benefits from experience with a particular subject or activity, because possible categories are learned, or are discovered in the process of exploring or manipulating a set of material. Primitive clustering occurs in 2-year-olds.

Elaboration. Finding shared meaning or a common referent for two or more things that need to be remembered. The helpful mnemonic for recalling the notes for the lines on the musical staff ("Every Good Boy Does Fine") is a kind of elaboration, as is associating the name of a person you have just met with some object or other word. This form of memory aid is not used spontaneously by all individuals and is not used skillfully until fairly late in development, if then.

Systematic searching. When you try to remember something, you can "scan" your memory for the whole domain in which it might be found. Three- and 4-year-old children can begin to do this to search for actual objects in the real world, but they are not good at doing this in memory. So search strategies may be first learned in the external world and then applied to inner searches.

Source: Flavell, 1985.

Experience with a teeter-totter, like this boy is getting, may be one source of knowledge about how balance scales work.

Rules for Problem Solving. Another area in which information processing researchers have found qualitative progressions is in problem solving. Some of the best-known work in this area has been Robert Siegler's studies of the development of *rules* (Siegler, 1976, 1978, 1981). Siegler's approach is a cross between Piagetian theory and information processing. He argues that cognitive development consists in acquiring a set of basic rules, which are then applied to a broader and broader range of problems on the basis of experience. There are no stages, only sequences.

In one test of this approach, Siegler uses a balance scale with a series of pegs on either side of the center, like the one in Figure 9.4. Disks can be placed on these pegs, and the child is asked to predict which way the balance will tip, depending on the location and number of disks. A complete solution requires the child to take into account both the number of disks on each side and the specific location of the disks. But children do not develop such a complete solution immediately. Instead, Siegler predicts that four rules will develop, in order.

Rule I, which is basically a "preoperational" rule, takes into account only one dimension, the number of weights. Children using this rule will predict that the side with more disks will go down, no matter which peg they are placed on. Rule II is a transitional rule. The child still judges on the basis of number, except when there are the same number of weights on both sides, and in that case takes distance from the fulcrum into account. Rule III is a kind of concrete operational rule. The child tries to take both distance and weight into account simultaneously, except that when the information is conflicting (such as when the side with weights closer to the fulcrum has more weights), the child simply guesses. Rule IV takes both weight and distance into account, using the correct formula (distance times weight for each side).

Siegler has found that virtually all children perform on this and similar tasks as if they were following one or another of these rules, and that the rules seem to develop in the given order. Very young children behave as if they don't have a rule (they guess or behave randomly so far as Siegler can determine); when a rule develops, it is always Rule I that comes first. But progression from one rule to the next is heavily dependent on experience. If children are given practice with the balance scale so that they can make predictions and then check which way the balance actually tips, many show rapid shifts upward in the sequence of rules.

Thus Siegler is attempting to describe a logical sequence children follow, not unlike the basic sequence of stages that Piaget describes, but Siegler shows that where a child's answers lie on this sequence depends not so much on age as on the amount of the child's experience with that particular material.

Metacognition and Executive Processes. A third area in which information processing researchers have been active is in studying how children come to know what they know. If I gave you a list of things to remember and then asked you later how you had gone about trying to remember it, you could tell me what you had done. You may even have consciously considered the various alternative strategies and then selected the best one. You could also tell me good ways to study or which kinds of tasks will be hardest and why. These are all examples of **metamemory** or **metacognition**—knowing about re-

Figure 9.4 This balance scale is similar to the one Siegler used. The scale was held in balance initially by a lever, while the experimenter placed weights on one or more of the pegs on either side. For each combination of weights, the child is asked to predict which way the scale will fall when the lever is released. (*Source:* From Siegler, 1981, p. 7.)

membering or knowing about knowing. Information processing theorists sometimes refer to these skills as **executive processes** because they involve planning and organizing in some central way, just as an executive may do.

It is clear that a child's performance on a whole range of tasks is likely to improve when such metacognitive skills are in operation, because she can now monitor her own performance or recognize when a particular strategy is called for and when it is not. The research shows that 4- and 5-year-old children do show some such monitoring (Schneider & Pressley, 1989), but it is rarely found earlier than that, and it clearly improves fairly rapidly after school age. Such executive skills may well form the foundation of many of the changes Piaget associated with the period of concrete operations.

A Summary of Developmental Changes in Information Processing. I can summarize all this evidence with a series of reasonable (albeit still tentative) generalizations.

1. There is probably *not* any increase in the basic processing capacity of the system, although there may be an increase in speed and other improvements in the efficiency with which the hardware is used.

2. The sheer amount of specific knowledge the child has about any given task increases as the child experiments, explores, studies things in school. This leads to more and more "expert" approaches to remembering and solving problems.

3. Genuinely new strategies are acquired, probably in some kind of order. In particular, in middle childhood the child seems to develop some "executive" or "metacognitive" abilities—she knows that she knows, and she can *plan* a strategy for the first time.

4. At school age, children also begin to apply existing strategies more flexibly to an expanding number of domains. An 8- or 9-year-old child who learns to rehearse on one kind of memory problem is much more likely to try it on a new memory problem than is a 5-year-old.

5. With increasing age, children can apply a wider range of different strategies to the same problem, so that if the first doesn't work, they can use a backup or alternative strategy. If you can't find your misplaced keys by retracing your steps, you try a backup, such as looking in your other purse or the pocket of your jacket, or searching each room of the house in turn. Young children do not do this; school age children and adolescents do.

Thus some of the changes that Piaget observed and chronicled with such detail and richness seem to be the result of increased experience with tasks and problems (a quantitative change, if you will). But there also seems to be a qualitative change in the complexity, generalizability, and flexibility of strategies used by the child, a change that accelerates during the school years.

▶ Individual Differences

In the midst of all this developmental regularity, there are—as always—wide individual variations. Because Piaget and his followers have not been very interested in such variations, most of what we know about individual differences in cognitive functioning in these school-age years comes from studies of IQ or school achievement. We also have fascinating new data on individual differences emerging from information processing research.

IQ Tests and Their Uses at School Age

By school age, IQ tests are very good predictors of later intellectual performance. One facet of this is that test scores become increasingly stable. Results from a longitudinal study by Wilson, for example, show correlations of .69 between IQ scores at age 6 and

Write down four good ways to study. In choosing one of these methods, does it matter what subject you are studying? How do you know all this? Do you think about it consciously when you are starting to study? The fact that you know these things and can think about them is evidence that you have metacognition, that you know what you know and how to think.

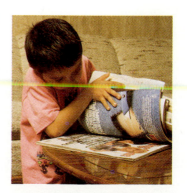

If this preschooler doesn't find what he's looking for on the first few tries, he will have trouble thinking of other possible places or ways to search. Elementary school children have more strategies and use them more flexibly.

age 15, and .80 between age 9 and age 15 (Brody, 1992). Results from the Berkeley/Oakland longitudinal studies are comparable. IQ scores from this age range also begin to be predictive of adult occupation and success, although those correlations become stronger at adolescence. This remarkable high degree of stability obviously reflects basic genetic differences as well as all the forms and varieties of environmental consistency I discussed in Chapter 1.

The most important use of IQ tests at elementary school, however, is not long-term prediction but rather identification of children who might need or benefit from special programs. Children whose speed of learning seems to be much faster or slower than normal may be given an IQ test to see if they might be retarded or gifted. Similarly, a child who is having difficulty learning to read but is otherwise doing OK may be given a test like the WISC-R or other special tests designed to diagnose specific learning disabilities or brain damage. In each case, the pattern of scores on the test as a whole or on individual subtests is then used along with other data to decide if the child should be in a special class.

Such uses of IQ tests are very close to what Binet envisioned nearly a hundred years ago. Nonetheless, such diagnostic functions for IQ tests have been the subject of a good deal of debate, much of it heated.

The Debate About IQ Tests in Schools. Everyone agrees that schools must often diagnose or sort children into groups. Clearly, some children do require additional assistance, and many benefit from special programs. The arguments center on whether IQ tests ought to be used as the central basis for such sorting. There are several strong reasons that they should not: First, IQ tests do not measure all the facets of a child's functioning that may be relevant. For example, clinicians have found that some children with IQs below 70, who would be considered retarded if the score alone were used for classification, nonetheless have sufficient social skills to enable them to function well in a regular classroom. If we use only the IQ score, some retarded children would be incorrectly placed in special classes. Second, there is the problem of the self-fulfilling prophecy of an IQ test score. Because many parents and teachers still believe that IQ scores are a permanent, unchanging feature of a child, once a child is labeled as "having" a particular IQ, that label tends to be difficult to remove later.

The most important negative argument is that tests may simply be biased in such a way that some subgroups of children are more likely to score high or low, even though their underlying ability is the same. For example, the tests may contain items that are not equally accessible to minorities and whites; taking such tests and doing well may also

There is little controversy over assigning children to special classes like this one for the hearing impaired. But there is a great deal of controversy about the best way to assign children to classes for the learning impaired or for the retarded.

require certain test-taking skills, motivations, or attitudes less common among some minority children, especially African-American children (R. Kaplan, 1985; Reynolds & Brown, 1984).

In response to these arguments, most major tests have been revised to eliminate all obvious types of bias. Yet a troubling fact remains: When IQ tests are used for diagnosis in schools, proportionately more minority than white children continue to be diagnosed as retarded or slow. This fact has led to a number of lawsuits, including *Larry P.* v. *Riles*, a case in which a group of parents of black children sued the California school system for bias. The parents argued that there was no underlying difference in basic ability between black and white children, so if differences in test scores led to larger numbers of black children being assigned to special classes, the tests must clearly be biased.

The school system argued that IQ tests don't measure underlying capacity, but only a child's existing repertoire of basic intellectual skills. In the terms I used in Chapter 7, this is like saying that an IQ test cannot tell you what the upper limit of some child's intellectual "reaction range" may be; all it can tell you is where the child is now functioning within that range. By school age, the child's level of functioning has already been affected by such environmental factors as prenatal care, diet, health, and family stability—all of which tend to be less than optimal among blacks in the United States. Thus, the test may accurately reflect a child's current abilities and be a proper basis for assigning the child to a special program, even though that child might have a greater underlying capacity or competence which could have been expressed under more ideal circumstances.

In this particular case, the judge ruled in favor of the parents and prohibited the use of standardized IQ test scores for placement in special classes in California. Other legal decisions have gone the other way (Elliott, 1988), so the legal question is not settled, although there are now many places in the United States in which the use of IQ tests for diagnosis and placement of African-American or other minority children is forbidden.

My own conclusion is that part of the difficulty arises from widespread confusion about what IQ and achievement tests are and are not. Because most adults believe that "intelligence is innate" and that IQ tests are meant to measure such innate ability, the score given to a child carries a heavy freight of excess meaning. At the same time, selection of children for special classes must still be done by *some* method. IQ tests seem to me to be more reliable and valid than the alternatives, such as less-well-standardized tests or teacher evaluations. I would not want a single IQ test used as the sole basis for a placement decision, especially early in elementary school when IQ test scores are still relatively variable. I would want to take into account the level of stress in the child's life at the time the test was given. But it seems foolish to me to throw out the tests altogether.

Do you agree with me? Why or why not?

Achievement Tests

Another type of test, widely used to measure intellectual skill at school age, is the **achievement test**, a type of measure with which nearly all of you doubtless have had personal experience. Achievement tests are designed to assess *specific* information learned in school, using items like those in Table 9.2. The child taking an achievement test doesn't end up with an IQ score, but his performance is still compared to that of other children in the same grade across the country.

How are these tests different from an IQ test? The original idea was that an IQ test was measuring the child's basic capacity, her underlying **competence,** while an achievement test was supposed to measure what the child had actually learned (her **performance).** This is an important distinction to which I have alluded before. Each of us presumably has some upper limit of ability—what we could do under ideal conditions, when we are maximally motivated, well, and rested. But because everyday conditions are rarely ideal, we typically perform below our hypothetical ability.

TABLE 9.2 Some Sample Items from a Fourth-Grade Achievement Test

---

Vocabulary

jolly old man

1. angry
2. fat
3. merry
4. sorry

Language Expression

Who wants _____ books?

1. that
2. these
3. them
4. this

Mathematics

What does the "3" in 13 stand for?

1. 3 ones
2. 13 ones
3. 3 tens
4. 13 tens

Reference Skills

Which of these words would be first in ABC order?

1. pair
2. point
3. paint
4. polish

Spelling

Jason took the *cleanest* glass.
right _____   wrong _____

Mathematics Computation

79	149	62
+14	− 87	× 3
____	____	____

Source: From Comprehensive Tests of Basic Skills, Form S. Reprinted by permission of the publisher, CTB/McGraw-Hill, Del Monte Research Park, Monterey, CA 93940. Copyright © 1973 by McGraw-Hill, Inc. All rights reserved. Printed in the USA.

In fact, it is *not possible* to measure competence. We can never be sure that we are assessing any ability under the best of all possible circumstances. We *always* measure performance. The authors of the famous IQ tests believed that by standardizing the procedures for administering and scoring the tests they could come close to measuring competence. Certainly it is good practice to design the best possible test and to administer it carefully. But it is important to understand that no test really measures "underlying" competence, only today's performance.

If you follow this logic to the end, you realize that all IQ tests are really achievement tests to some degree. The difference between tests called IQ tests and those called achievement tests is really a matter of degree. IQ tests include items that are designed to tap fairly fundamental intellectual processes like comparison or analysis; the achievement tests call for specific information the child has learned in school or elsewhere. College entrance tests, like the Scholastic Aptitude Tests (SATs, which many of you have taken recently) fall somewhere in between. They are designed to measure fairly basic "developed abilities," such as the ability to reason with words, rather than just specific knowledge. All three types of tests, though, measure aspects of performance and not competence.

The use of achievement tests in schools has been almost as controversial as the use of IQ tests. I've explored some of the arguments and counterarguments in the "real world" discussion on the opposite page.

Individual Differences in Information Processing

A quite different way of looking at individual differences has emerged from the information processing tradition. IQ tests are intended to measure differences in underlying ability by giving people fairly complex cognitive tasks, each of which may require a whole series of basic information processing strategies. Perhaps we could come closer to understanding individual differences in intelligence or intellectual performance if we shifted

THE REAL WORLD
Achievement Tests in Schools

The major arguments for using achievement tests in schools are that they provide parents and taxpayers with a way of assessing the quality of their schools, and they provide teachers with important information about the strengths and weaknesses of their class or individual students. The first of these is precisely the argument made recently by President Bush, who advocated the increased use of nationally administered achievement tests as a way to compare one state or one community with another and to measure the extent to which our schools are meeting our national educational goals.

But do such tests actually serve any of these purposes well? Maybe not. For one thing, when schools know that they are being evaluated based on test scores, there is a strong incentive to "teach to the test" (Corbett & Wilson, 1989). For another, teachers report that even when they do not spend time teaching specific material that is likely to be tested, they do spend more time on the general subject matter covered by the tests, and therefore have less time for skills that are not included in most achievement tests, such as discussing ideas, solving problems inductively, or engaging in creative activities (Darling-Hammond & Wise, 1985). The failure of most standardized tests to tap the child's ability to draw inferences, apply information, or ask good questions seems es-

pecially troublesome, because these are all problem-solving skills that appear to have long-range significance for adult success.

Overall, it seems clear that achievement tests will be useful as measures of the quality of schools only if there is a good match between what the tests measure and our basic educational goals. A community's, state's, or nation's children can be made to look bad or good, depending on the degree of such a match or on the level of difficulty of the test.

The usefulness of achievement tests is further undermined by the report from teachers that they rarely use test scores as a basis for diagnosing a specific child's strengths and weaknesses. Most feel that a child's day-to-day classroom performance yields better diagnostic information than a one-shot test under high stress conditions.

There is no easy solution to all this (Harvard Education Letter, September/October 1988). We need better tests that tap more basic problem-solving skills rather than merely rote learning; we need other ways of judging whether our schools are meeting our social mandate. At the very least, you need to be a very skeptical reader of those annual "school report cards" that purport to tell us how well a given school or school district is performing its job.

---

our attention to those more basic processes. The most common research strategy used by those taking this approach has been to look at the correlations between IQ scores and measures of specific information processing skills. This strategy has yielded a few preliminary connections.

Speed of Information Processing. One of the most basic sources of individual differences in IQ may be simply the speed with which an individual can perform basic information processing tasks, such as recognizing whether two letters or numbers are the same or different, or bringing some piece of information out of long-term memory. A number of different investigators have found just such a link: Subjects who are able to do basic recognition and memory tasks more quickly also have higher IQ scores on standard tests (e.g. Vernon, 1987). Most of this research has been done with adults, but the same link has also been found in a few studies with children (e.g., Keating, List & Merriman, 1985).

Furthermore, there are some clear suggestions that such speed-of-processing differences may be built in at birth. In particular, recall from Chapter 5 that measures of habituation and recognition memory taken when a baby is only 4 months old are correlated quite strongly with later IQ. It is difficult to imagine a set of experiences in the first few months of life that could have contributed to such differences in speed of habituation, so we are left with the obvious hypothesis that speed differences are present at birth.

Differences in Strategy Use. Comparisons of normal-IQ and retarded children have also pointed to important differences in information processing strategies. Retarded children show much less flexibility in their task approach than do normal-IQ children, and they generalize less well to new tasks. For example, Judy DeLoache (DeLoache & Brown, 1987) has compared the searching strategies of groups of 2-year-olds who were either developing normally or showed delayed development. When the search task was very

One of the synonyms of *intelligent* is *quick*. Do you think this reflects some basic assumption that speed of processing is a central ingredient of what we think of as intelligent behavior? Can one be very intelligent and slow?

simple, such as searching for a toy hidden in a distinctive location in a room, the two groups did not differ in search strategies or skill. But when the experimenter surreptitiously moved the toy before the child was allowed to search, normally developing children were able to search in alternative, plausible places, such as in nearby locations; delayed children simply persisted in looking in the place where they had seen the toy hidden. They either could not change strategies or did not have alternative, more complex strategies in their repertoires. Thus, it may well be that what distinguishes high-IQ from low-IQ children is not just speed but the ability to recognize what strategies are appropriate and to apply those strategies flexibly.

▶ The Impact of the Larger Culture

All the aspects of the larger culture that I have talked about in earlier chapters continue to affect the school-age child. The family's economic level, the parents' social network, the values of the particular subculture to which the child's family belongs are all still formative. But the most obvious nonfamily influence on the child between 6 and 12 is the school he attends. What do we know about the impact of school quality on the child's functioning?

School Quality

Real estate agents have always touted a "good school district" as a reason for settling in one town or neighborhood rather than another. Now we have research to show that the real estate agents were right: Specific characteristics of schools and of teachers do affect children's development.

Researchers interested in possible effects of good and poor schools have most often approached the problem by identifying unusually "effective" or "successful" schools (e.g., Rutter, 1983; Good & Weinstein, 1986). In this research, an effective school is defined as one in which pupils show one or more of the following characteristics at higher rates than you would predict, knowing the kind of families or neighborhoods the pupils come from: high scores on standardized tests, good school attendance, low rates of disruptive classroom behavior or delinquency, a high rate of later college attendance, or high self-esteem. Some schools seem to achieve such good outcomes consistently, year after year, so the effect is not just chance variation. When these successful schools are compared to others in similar neighborhoods that have less impressive track records, certain common themes emerge, which I've summarized in Table 9.3.

One of the marks of successful schools is that they assign regular homework. And one of the characteristics of academically successful children is that their parents supervise their homework, as this Native American father is doing.

> ## TABLE 9.3 Characteristics of Unusually Effective Schools
>
> *Qualities of pupils.* A *mixture* of backgrounds or abilities seems to be best, although the key appears to be to have a large enough concentration of pupils who come to school with good academic skills. Too great a concentration of children with poor skills makes it more difficult for the rest of the things on this list to occur.
>
> *Goals of the school.* Effective schools have a strong emphasis on academic excellence, with high standards and high expectations. These goals are clearly stated by the administration and shared by the staff.
>
> *Organization of classrooms.* Classes are focused on specific academic learning. Daily activities are structured, with a high percentage of time in actual group instruction. High expectations of performance are conveyed to pupils.
>
> *Homework.* Homework is assigned regularly, graded quickly.
>
> *Discipline.* Most discipline is handled within the classroom, with relatively little fallback to "sending the child to the principal." In really effective schools, not much class time is actually spent in discipline, because these teachers have very good control of the class. They intervene early in potentially difficult situations rather than imposing heavy discipline after the fact.
>
> *Praise.* Pupils receive high doses of praise for good performance or for meeting stated expectations.
>
> *Teacher experience.* Teacher *education* is not related to effectiveness of schools, but teacher *experience* is, presumably because it takes time to learn effective class management and instruction strategies.
>
> *Building surroundings.* Age or general appearance of the school building is not critical, but maintenance of good order, cleanliness, and attractiveness do have an effect.
>
> *School leadership.* Effective schools have strong leaders, and those leaders state their goals clearly and often.
>
> *Responsibilities for children.* In effective schools, children are more likely to be given real responsibilities—in individual classrooms and in the school as a whole.
>
> *Size.* As a general rule, smaller schools are more effective, in part because in such schools children feel more involved and are given more responsibility. This effect is particularly clear in studies of high schools.

Sources: Rutter, 1983; Linney & Seidman, 1989.

What strikes me when I read this list is the similarity between the qualities of effective schools and the qualities of effective parents I described in Chapter 8. Effective schools sound a lot like *authoritative schools*, rather than either permissive or authoritarian schools. There are clear goals and rules, good control, good communication, and high nurturance. Not surprisingly, a very similar pattern appears when researchers study effective classrooms: It is the "authoritative" teachers whose pupils do best academically. Such teachers have clear goals, clear rules, effective management strategies, and personal and warm relationships with their pupils (Linney & Seidman, 1989).

But as with any system, the quality of the whole is more than the sum of the quality of the individual parts. Each school also has an overall climate or ethos that makes a difference for the youngsters. The most positive school climate occurs when the principal provides clear and strong leadership, when there are widely shared goals, dedication to effective teaching, and concrete assistance provided for such teaching. In such schools, pupils and parents are respected, and there is usually a high rate of parent participation in school activities. If you are making a decision about a city or a neighborhood in which to rear your children, these are the qualities to look for.

ACROSS CULTURES
How Asian Teachers Teach Math and Science So Effectively

I mentioned briefly in Chapter 7 that children from many Asian countries consistently outperform U.S. children on tests of math and science. There are many possible reasons for this, including the greater emphasis Asian parents place on school achievement and the stronger belief by Asian parents that good results come from hard work. But part of the difference seems to arise from the way these subjects are taught. James Stigler and Harold Stevenson (1991), who have observed in 120 classrooms in Japan, Taiwan, and Minneapolis, are convinced that Asian teachers have devised a particularly effective mode of teaching.

Japanese and Chinese teachers approach mathematics and science by crafting a series of "master lessons," each organized around a single theme or idea, and each involving specific forms of student participation. These lessons are like good stories, with a beginning, a middle, and an end. They frequently begin with a problem posed for the students. Here is one example from a fifth-grade class in Japan:

> The teacher walks in carrying a large paper bag full of clinking glass. . . . She begins to pull items out of the bag, placing them, one-by-one, on her desk. She removes a pitcher and a vase. A beer bottle evokes laughter and surprise. She soon has six containers lined up on her desk. . . . The teacher, looking thoughtfully at the containers, poses a question: "I wonder which one would hold the most water?" Hands go up, and the teacher calls on different students to give their guesses: "the pitcher," "the beer bottle," "the teapot." The teacher stands aside and ponders: "Some of you said one thing, others said something different. . . . There must be some way we can find out who is correct. How can we know who is correct?" (Stigler & Stevenson, 1991, p. 14)

The lesson continues as the students agree on a plan for determining which will hold the most. At each step, the students are engaged in the process of figuring out how to test their guesses or hypotheses. Frequently in such lessons, students are divided into small groups, each with a task, which they then report back to the class as a whole, and results are tabulated on the board in a graph. At the end of the lesson, the teacher reviews the original problem and what students have learned. In this particular case, the children have learned something not only about measurement and about tabulation of results, but about the process of hypothesis testing.

In U.S. classrooms, in contrast, it is extremely uncommon for a teacher to spend 30 or 60 minutes on a single coherent math or science lesson involving the whole class of children and a single topic. It is much more common for children to be given seat work of some kind—problems to work on from a book or a work sheet, for example. Sometimes the teacher circulates through the room, providing individual assistance, but not always. There are also likely to be frequent interruptions in American classrooms, as some children go to band practice, or announcements are given over an intercom, or someone drops into the classroom to ask how many children will buy lunch that day. Furthermore, teachers in American classrooms shift more often from one topic to another during a single math or science "lesson." They might do a brief bit on addition, then talk about measurement, then about telling time, and back to addition. Asian teachers shift *activities* in order to provide variety, such as shifting from lecture format to small-group discussions; American teachers shift *topics* for the same apparent purpose.

One of the most striking contrasts in the Stigler and Stevenson study is the amount of time children in these different school cultures spend with the teacher leading the instruction. In the U.S. classrooms they observed, no one was leading any instruction 51 percent of the time: The children were working on their own or were moving from one activity to another. In contrast, only 9 percent of the time in Taiwan and 26 percent of the time in Japanese classrooms was spent without some group instruction being provided.

Stigler and Stevenson point out that there is nothing in the Asian type of teaching that is new to Western teachers. American educators frequently recommend precisely such techniques. "What the Japanese and Chinese examples demonstrate so compellingly is that when widely implemented, such practices can produce extraordinary outcomes." (p. 45.)

Summary

1. The period of middle childhood has been studied less than other age periods but is nonetheless highly significant for the child's development.

2. Physical development from 6 to 12 is steady and slow. The onset of puberty brings a whole host of hormonal changes.

3. Illnesses are less common during this period than at earlier ages but continue to be fairly regular. Other health problems include accidents and obesity.

4. Obesity appears to be caused by hereditary tendencies, by low levels of movement or exercise, and high-fat and high-calorie diets.

5. Piaget proposed a major change in the child's thinking at about age 6, when powerful "operations," such as reversibility, addition, or multiple classification were understood.

6. In the concrete operations period, the child also learns to use inductive logic but does not yet use deductive logic.

7. More recent research on this period confirms many of Piaget's descriptions of sequences of development but calls into question Piaget's basic concept of stages. There seems to be much less consistency of performance across cognitively similar tasks than Piaget's theory would require.

8. Studies of expertise also point to a more important role of specific task experience in the sophistication of the child's thinking than Piaget believed.

9. Research evidence does support the idea that cognitive development occurs in sequences, however, with the timing of each sequence affected by specific experience or expertise.

10. Information processing theorists have searched for the basic building blocks of cognition, both the "hardware" and the "software."

11. Most theorists conclude that there are no age-related changes in the capacity of the hardware, but that there are improvements in speed and efficiency.

12. One form of increased efficiency is the greater and greater use with age of various types of processing strategies, including strategies for remembering. Preschoolers use some strategies, but school-age children use them more frequently and more flexibly.

13. At school age, most children also develop some "executive skills," that is, the ability to monitor their own cognitive processes and thus to plan their mental activity.

14. Individual differences in cognitive functioning at school age have been measured primarily with IQ tests and with achievement tests. Both are controversial.

15. Both IQ tests and achievement tests must be understood as measures of performance, not competence.

16. Individual differences in information processing have also been studied. Speed of processing appears to be strongly correlated with IQ, as is flexibility and generality of strategy use.

17. Children's intellectual and social development is affected by the quality of the schools they attend. Successful or effective schools have many of the same qualities we see in authoritative families: clear rules, good control, good communication, and high warmth.

Key Terms

achievement tests	deductive logic	metacognition
competence	executive processes	metamemory
concrete operations	inductive logic	performance

Suggested Readings

Adams, M. J. (1990). *Beginning to read: Thinking and learning about print.* Cambridge, MA: The MIT Press. (This is a wonderful book about reading. If you are planning a career as a teacher, especially if you expect to teach early elementary school grades, you should go right out and buy a copy.)

Collins, W. A. (Ed.) (1984). *Development during middle childhood. The years from six to twelve.* Washington, D.C.: National Academy Press. (This book covers the exact age range I discuss in this chapter and the next. It includes chapters on most aspects of the child's functioning.)

10 SOCIAL AND PERSONALITY DEVELOPMENT FROM 6 TO 12

At age 8, Roger was prone to emotional outbursts, insisted on his own way when he played with other children, and bullied weaker children on the playground. At 13 he was arrested for shoplifting, and he dropped out of school at 17. As an adult, he had a hard time finding and keeping a job, and his marriage lasted only a few years. His wife claimed that she couldn't deal with his temper.

David, in contrast, was very shy at age 8. He rarely entered other groups of children when they were playing, although he would join in if asked or urged. He had a few friends in school, but he was mostly a loner. He went to college but had a very hard time settling on a career, and changed jobs frequently until his late twenties. His marriage has been stable, but he has been disappointed at his rate of progress in his job. His job supervisors say that David has a habit of withdrawing whenever they press him for something, or when the stress level at work gets high, so they are reluctant to promote him.

Both cases are fictitious, but the links between these types of childhood social behavior and adult outcomes are not. Certainly the cognitive changes I described in the last chapter play a central role in preparing the child for the demands of adolescence and adulthood. But it is probably in relationships, more than in cognition, that middle childhood has its greatest impact on the life course.

Let me build a bridge between cognition and social relationships by beginning with a look at how children in this age range *understand* themselves and their relationships. Such understandings form part of the basis of the relationships themselves.

▶ Children's Understanding of Self and Relationships

The Self-Concept at School Age

In Chapter 8 I pointed out that by age 5 or 6 most children define themselves along a whole range of dimensions. But these early self-descriptions are highly concrete, often quite situation specific. Over the elementary school years we see a shift toward a more abstract, more comparative, more generalized self-definition. A 6-year-old might describe herself as "smart" or "dumb"; a 10-year-old is more likely to give a comparative description, such as "smarter than most other kids," or "not as good at baseball as my friends"

(Ruble, 1987). At the same time, the child's self-concept also becomes less and less focused on external characteristics and more on stable, internal qualities (Harter, 1983, 1985).

A number of these themes are illustrated in the results of a study by Montemayor and Eisen (1977) of self-concepts in 9- to 18-year-olds. Each child was asked to give 20 answers to the question, Who am I? They found that the younger children in this study were still using mostly surface qualities to describe themselves, such as in this description by a 9-year-old:

> My name is Bruce C. I have brown eyes. I have brown hair. I have brown eyebrows. I am nine years old. I LOVE! Sports. I have seven people in my family. I have great! eye site. I have lots! of friends. I live on 1923 Pinecrest Dr. I am going on 10 in September. I'm a boy. I have a uncle that is almost 7 feet tall. My school is Pinecrest. My teacher is Mrs. V. I play Hockey! I'm almost the smartest boy in the class. I LOVE! food. I love fresh air. I LOVE school. (Montemayor & Eisen, 1977, pp. 317–318)

In contrast, look at the self-description of this 11-year-old girl in the sixth grade:

> My name is A. I'm a human being. I'm a girl. I'm a truthful person. I'm not very pretty. I do so-so in my studies. I'm a very good cellist. I'm a very good pianist. I'm a little bit tall for my age. I like several boys. I like several girls. I'm old-fashioned. I play tennis. I am a *very* good swimmer. I try to be helpful. I'm always ready to be friends with anybody. Mostly I'm good, but I lose my temper. I'm not well-liked by some girls and boys. I don't know if I'm liked by boys or not. (Montemayor & Eisen, 1977, p. 317–318)

This girl, like the other youngsters of this age in the Montemayor and Eisen study, not only describes her external qualities, she also emphasizes her beliefs, the quality of her relationships, and general personality traits. Thus, as the child moves through the years of middle childhood, her self-scheme becomes more complex, less tied to external features, more centered on feelings, on ideas.

It is also in these years that the child first combines individual judgments of her abilities in various arenas, such as in academics, sports, and relationships with peers, into a global judgment of self-worth or self-esteem (Harter, 1988).

Describing Other People

Children's descriptions of others move through highly similar changes, from the concrete to the abstract, from the ephemeral to the stable. If you ask 6- to 8-year-olds (or preschoolers) to describe others, they focus almost exclusively on external features—what the person looks like, where he lives, what he does. This description by a 7-year-old boy in England is typical:

> He is very tall. He has dark brown hair, he goes to our school. I don't think he has any brothers or sisters. He is in our class. Today he has a dark orange [sweater] and gray trousers and brown shoes. (Livesley & Bromley, 1973, p. 213)

When young children do use internal or evaluative terms to describe people, they are likely to use quite global terms, such as *nice* or *mean* or *good* or *bad*. Further, young children do not seem to see these qualities as lasting or general traits of the individual, applicable in all situations or over time (Rholes & Ruble, 1984). In other words, the 6- or 7-year-old has not yet developed a concept we might think of as "conservation of personality."

Beginning at about age 7 or 8, though, at just about the same time that children begin to describe themselves using more psychological terms and develop a global sense of self-worth, we see the emergence of similar ideas of global or enduring personality in others. The child focuses more on the inner traits or qualities of another person and

Before you go on and read any of the examples, take a moment and write down 20 answers to the ''Who am I?'' question yourself. Then after you have read the examples, go back and look at your own answers to the question again. What types of descriptions did you include?

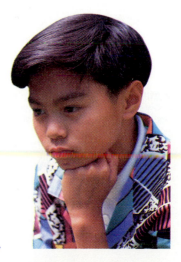

If you asked 4-year-olds and 8-year-olds to describe this boy, their descriptions would probably be quite different. The younger children would probably describe his physical characteristics; the older children might focus on his feelings or more enduring characteristics.

assumes that those traits will be visible in many situations (e.g., Gnepp & Chilamkurti, 1988). You can see the change in this description by a nearly-10-year-old:

> He smells very much and is very nasty. He has no sense of humour and is very dull. He is always fighting and he is cruel. He does silly things and is very stupid. He has brown hair and cruel eyes. He is sulky and 11 years old and has lots of sisters. I think he is the most horrible boy in the class. He has a croaky voice and always chews his pencil and picks his teeth and I think he is disgusting. (Livesley & Bromley, 1973, p. 217)

This description still includes many external, physical features, but it goes beyond such concrete, surface qualities to the level of personality traits, such as lack of humor and cruelty.

Less anecdotal evidence for some of these changes comes from a study by Carl Barenboim (1981). He asked 6-, 8-, and 10-year-olds to describe three people, and then a year later, asked them to do the same thing again. Thus, he has both longitudinal and cross-sectional information. Figure 10.1 shows age changes in two of the categories Barenboim used in his analysis. A *behavioral comparison* was any description that involved comparing a child's behaviors or physical features with another child or with a norm. Examples would be: "Billy runs a lot faster than Jason" or "She draws the best in our whole class." Statements that involved some internal personality construct were called *psychological constructs*, such as "Sarah is so kind" or "He's a real stubborn idiot!" You can see that behavioral comparisons peaked at around age 8 or 9, but that psychological statements rose steadily throughout middle childhood. Other research by Barenboim (1977) indicates that psychological constructs peak at 13 or 14, at which point they make up more than half of teenagers' descriptions of others.

Write down a description of your best friend. How does your description compare with the ones given by children? Can you define the difference in precise terms?

Concepts of Relationships

A very similar developmental progression emerges when we ask children to describe or define various kinds of relationships. Let me use descriptions of friendships as an illustration.

Among preschool children, friendships seem to be understood mostly in terms of physical characteristics. If you ask a young child how people make friends, the answer is

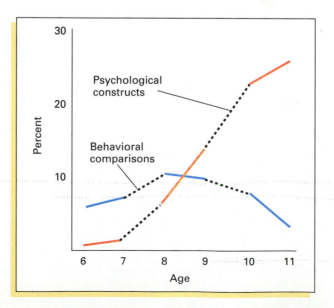

Figure 10.1   These data from Barenboim's study show the change in children's descriptions of their peers during the years of middle childhood. The colored lines represent longitudinal data, the dashed lines cross-sectional comparisons. *(Source:* Barenboim, 1981, Figure 1, p. 134.)

usually that they "play together," or spend time physically near each other (Selman, 1980; Damon, 1977, 1983). Friendship is understood to involve sharing toys or giving goods to one another.

Robert Selman's research (1980) and extensive studies by Thomas Berndt (1983, 1986) show that in elementary school this early view of friendship gives way to one in which the key concept seems to be *reciprocal trust*. Friends are now people who help and trust one another. Because this is also the age at which children's understanding of others becomes less external, more psychological, we shouldn't be surprised that friends are now seen as special people, with particular desired qualities other than mere proximity. In particular, the qualities of generosity and helpfulness become important parts of the definition of friendship for many children in this age range.

Linking Cognition and Social Behavior

The picture that emerges from putting all these jigsaw pieces together is of a child whose attention shifts from externals to internals. Just as the school child can understand conservation in part because he can set aside the *appearance* of change and focus on the underlying continuity, so the child of this same age looks beyond (or behind) physical appearance and searches for deeper consistencies that will help her to interpret both her own and other people's behavior.

Selman suggests another link between thinking and relationships in these years. The preschool child may have a theory of others' minds, but he does not yet understand that other people also read *his* mind. Put another way, the 4-year-old may understand the statement "I know that you know." But he does not yet understand the next step in this potentially infinite regress: "I know that you know that I know." This reciprocal aspect of perspective taking seems to be grasped some time in the early elementary school years. Selman's point is that only when the child understands reciprocity of perspective do we see really reciprocal relationships between friends. Only then do qualities like fairness and trust become central to children's ideas of friendship.

Just what is cause and what is effect is not so obvious. We should not necessarily assume that the cognitive horse is pulling the relationship cart, although that is one possibility. It is also plausible that the child learns important lessons about the distinction between appearance and reality, external and internal qualities, in play with peers and interactions with parents and teachers. Whichever way the causality runs, the central point is that children's relationships with others both reflect and shape their *understanding* of themselves and of relationships. With that in mind, let's look at the relationships themselves.

▶ Relationships in Middle Childhood

Relationships with Parents

Among elementary school children, as among preschoolers, visible attachment behaviors such as clinging or crying appear only in stressful situations, such as perhaps the first day of school, illness or upheaval in the family, or the death of a pet. Because fewer experiences are new and potentially stressful to the 7- or 8-year-old than to the preschooler, we see much less obvious safe-base behavior and less open affection from child to parent (Maccoby, 1984).

But it would be a great mistake to assume that the attachment has weakened. School children continue to use their parents as a safe base, continue to rely on their presence and support, continue to be strongly influenced by their parents' judgments.

What does change is the agenda of issues between parent and child. With preschoolers, parents are most concerned with teaching the child some level of physical indepen-

What factors other than the generally lower level of novelty or stress might account for the elementary-school child's rather sharp drop in overt affection displayed toward parents?

We are more likely to see parents and their school-age children doing something active together rather than showing overt affection, but that doesn't mean that the attachment of the child to the parent is any weaker than it was at earlier ages.

dence and controlling the child's behavior. They worry about toilet training, temper tantrums, defiance, and fights with siblings. Occasions requiring discipline are common. When the child reaches elementary school, disciplinary encounters decline. The agenda now includes such issues as the child's regular chores, the standards for the child's school performance, and the level of independence that will be allowed (Maccoby, 1984). Can Joe stop off at his friend's house after school without asking ahead of time? How far from home can Diana ride her bike? In many non-Western cultures, parents must also now begin to teach children quite specific tasks, such as agricultural work and care of younger children or animals, which may be necessary for the survival of the family.

When we look at the various ways parents try to accomplish all these tasks, we see the same parental styles as are evident among parents of preschoolers: authoritarian, authoritative, permissive, and neglecting. And in this age range, as at the earlier ages, it is clear that the authoritative style is by far the best for fostering and supporting the child's emerging competence.

Baumrind (1991) has provided illustrative data in a recent analysis of her small longitudinal sample. She classified each parent's style of interaction on the basis of extensive interviews and direct observation when the children were preschoolers. When the children were 9, she measured their level of social competence. Those rated "optimally competent" were seen as both assertive and responsible in their relationships, those rated

TABLE 10.1 Social Competence in 9-Year-Olds as a Function of Parental Style

Parental Style	Percentage of Children Rated as:		
	Competent	Partially Competent	Incompetent
Authoritative	85	15	0
Authoritarian	30	57	13
Permissive	8	67	25
Neglecting	0	47	53

Source: Baumrind, 1991, adapted from Table 5.1, p. 129.

"partially competent" typically lacked one of these skills, and those rated as "incompetent" showed neither. You can see in Table 10.1 that the children from authoritative families were nearly all rated as fully competent, while those from neglecting families were most often rated as incompetent.

Relationships with Peers

The biggest shift in relationships in the years of middle childhood is the increasing centrality of the peer group. The vertical relationships with parents or teachers obviously don't disappear, but playing with other kids is what 7-, 8-, 9-, or 10-year-old children prefer. Such activities—along with watching TV—take up virtually all children's time when they are not in school, eating, or sleeping (Timmer, Eccles & O'Brien, 1985).

What kids this age seem to like about their play groups is that they *do things* together. If you ask children this age what makes a group a group, they most often mention common activities—riding bikes together, jumping rope together, or whatever. They are much less likely to mention common attitudes or values as the basis for a group, or the role of group process. You can see this pattern in Figure 10.2, which shows the results of a study by Susan O'Brien & Karen Bierman (1988). They asked fifth, eighth, and eleventh grade subjects to tell them about the different groups of kids that hang around together at their school, and then to say how they could tell that a particular bunch of kids was a "group." For the fifth graders, the single best criteria of a "group" was that the kids did things together. For eighth-graders, shared attitudes and common appearance became much more important—yet another example of the broad shift from concrete to abstract views of relationships.

Sex Segregation.   The most striking thing about peer groups in this age range is probably not what kinds of activities they are engaged in, but how sex-segregated they are. Boys play with boys, girls play with girls, each in their own areas and at their own kinds of games. There are some ritualized "boundary violations" between these separate territories, such as chasing games (e.g., "You can't catch me, nyah nyah," followed by chasing accompanied by screaming by the girls) (Thorne, 1986). But on the whole, girls and boys actively avoid interacting with one another (Hartup, 1983). Given a forced choice between playing with a child of the opposite gender or a child of a different race,

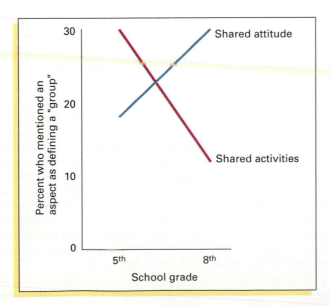

Figure 10.2 O'Brien and Bierman's results illustrate the change between elementary and high school in children's ideas about what defines a "group" of peers. (*Source:* O'Brien & Bierman, 1988, Table 1, p. 1363.)

In this age range, boys play with boys, girls with girls. It is also typical for boys this age to do something physical together, such as skateboarding.

researchers have found that elementary-school-age children will make the cross-race choice rather than the cross-gender choice (Maccoby & Jacklin, 1987).

<u>Friendships.</u>   This pattern is even more pronounced when we look at friendships. By age 7, sex segregation in friendships is almost total. In one study, parents reported that about a quarter of the friendships of their 5- or 6-year-olds but *none* of the friendships of their 7- or 8-year-olds were cross-sex (Gottman, 1986).

The quality of relationship between friends also varies by gender, although there are clearly some common themes that are true for both sexes. For one thing, both boys and girls have more friendships in middle childhood than they did as preschoolers. In one

ACROSS CULTURES
Gender Segregation in Other Cultures

Many of the statements I make about ''children's development'' are based exclusively on research done in the United States or other Western industrialized countries. It is always appropriate to ask whether the same developmental changes, the same behavioral patterns, would appear in children reared in very different environments. In the case of gender segregation, the answer seems quite clear: What we observe on U.S. school playgrounds is true all over the world.

A good example is an observational study of children in a Kipsigis settlement in rural Kenya (Harkness & Super, 1985). This particular settlement consists of 54 households engaged in traditional hoe agriculture and cattle raising. Women care for the children, cook, and carry firewood and water. Men are in charge of the cows, plow the fields when needed, maintain the dwellings, and participate in the political business of the community.

For this study, observers went to the settlement at different times of day to record the gender of each child's companions. They found little sex segregation among children younger than 6, but clear separation for children between 6 and 9. In this age group, two-thirds of boys' and three-fourths of girls' companions were of the same gender. The differences were even larger when

they looked at the sex of the child to which each youngster addressed his or her specific bids for attention: 72 percent of boys' and 84 percent of girls' bids were made to another child of the same gender.

These numbers reflect somewhat less sex segregation than we commonly observe in the United States. But what impresses me is that there is even this much in a culture in which children spend a good deal of their time in their own compound, with only siblings and half-siblings available as playmates.

This is not to say that context or culture have no effect. They clearly do. The Kipsigis encourage certain kinds of sex segregation by assigning somewhat different tasks to boys and girls. And in Western countries, children attending ''progressive'' schools in which equality of sex roles is a specific philosophy show less sex segregation in their play than is true in more traditional schools (Maccoby & Jacklin, 1987). But even in progressive schools, the majority of contacts are still with children of the same gender. All in all, it seems to be the case universally that when children this age are free to choose their playmates, they strongly prefer playmates of the same sex.

study, John Reisman and Susan Shorr (1978) found that second graders named about four friends each; by seventh grade this had increased to about seven friends each.

Many of these friendships are remarkably stable. Thomas Berndt, who has studied children's friendships extensively, finds that between half and three-quarters of close friendships in the elementary school years persist as long as a full school year; many last much longer (e.g., Berndt & Hoyle, 1985; Berndt, Hawkins & Hoyle, 1986), and such stability is as common among first graders as among eighth graders.

Children this age also treat their friends quite differently than they treat strangers. They are more *polite* to strangers or nonfriends. With pals they are more open, a quality expressed both in higher rates of supportive comments and higher levels of criticism.

But there are also intriguing differences in the quality of relationship in boys' and girls' friendships. Waldrop and Halverson (1975) refer to boys' relationships as *extensive* and to girls' relationships as *intensive*: Boys' friendship groups are larger and are more accepting of newcomers than are girls'. They play more outdoors and roam over a larger area in their play. Girlfriends are more likely to play in pairs or in smaller, more exclusive groups, and they spend more play time indoors or near home or school (Gottman, 1986).

At the level of actual interaction we also see differences, generally consistent with the distinction between restrictive and enabling styles I described in Chapter 8. Boys' groups and boys' friendships appear to be focused more on competition and dominance than are girls' friendships. In fact, among school-age boys, we see *higher* levels of competition between pairs of friends than between strangers, which is the opposite of what we see among girls. Friendships between girls also include more agreement, more compliance, and more self-disclosure than is true for boys.

Leaper's study, which I described in Chapter 8 (Table 8.2, page 194), illustrates the difference. He finds that "controlling" speech—a category that includes rejecting comments, ordering, manipulating, challenging, defying, refuting, or resisting the other's attempt to control—is twice as common in 7- and 8-year-old male friend pairs as among female pairs. Among the 4- and 5-year-olds in this study there were no sex differences in controlling speech.

None of this should obscure the fact that there are great similarities in the interactions

Do you still have any friends from your elementary school years? If not, why do you think those early friendships did not survive? If yes, what do you think differentiates an early friendship that survives from one that does not?

These two boys may well be good friends even though they are fighting. Among boys in middle childhood, aggression is *more* common between friends than between acquaintances or strangers.

of male and female friendship pairs. As one example, collaborative and cooperative exchanges are the most common forms of communication among both boys and girls. Neither should we necessarily conclude that boys' friendships are less important to them than are girls'. Nonetheless, it seems clear that there are differences in form and style that have enduring implications for the patterns of friendship over the full life span.

Aggression and Other Less Friendly Patterns.   I pointed out in Chapter 8 that physical aggression declines over the preschool years, while verbal aggression increases. These same trends continue in middle childhood. Both overt physical aggression and quarreling show further declines, while insults and derogation, aimed at damaging the other child's self-esteem rather than his body, increase (Hartup, 1984).

Researchers also find consistent sex differences in levels of aggression. At every age, boys show more aggression, more assertiveness, and more dominance. Boys are also overrepresented among children diagnosed with a *conduct disorder*, a designation that includes antisocial or aggressive behaviors such as argumentativeness, bullying, disobedience, high levels of irritability, and threatening and loud behavior.

Table 10.2 gives some highly representative data from a large, careful survey in Canada (Offord, Boyle & Racine, 1991) in which both parents and teachers completed checklists describing each child's behavior. In the table I've listed only the information provided by teachers, but parent ratings yielded parallel findings. It is clear that boys are described as far more aggressive on nearly any measure. In this same study, 6.5 percent of boys, but only 1.8 percent of girls, were diagnosed with a conduct disorder.

It seems inescapable that there is at least some biological basis for this sex difference. Eleanor Maccoby and Carol Jacklin (1974) summarize the arguments:

(1) Males are more aggressive than females in all human societies for which evidence is available. (2) The sex differences are found early in life, at a time when there is no evidence that differential socialization pressures have been brought to bear by adults to "shape" aggression differently for the two sexes. (3) Similar sex differences are found in man and subhuman primates. (4) Aggression is related to levels of sex hormones, and can be changed by experimental administration of these hormones. (pp. 242–243)

Taking all the evidence together, it seems probable that hormonal or other biological factors create higher rates of aggressiveness in boys to begin with. But nurture as well as nature is surely involved. In many cultures, including our own, important social influences may foster higher levels of aggression in boys (e.g., Brooks-Gunn & Matthews, 1979). You will remember from Chapter 8, for example, that fathers and mothers begin to re-

TABLE 10.2 Percentage of Boys and Girls Aged 4 to 11 Rated by Their Teachers as Displaying Each Type of Aggressive Behavior

Behavior	Boys	Girls
Mean to others	21.8	9.6
Physically attacks people	18.1	4.4
Gets in many fights	30.9	9.8
Destroys own things	10.7	2.1
Destroys others' things	10.6	4.4
Threatens to hurt people	13.1	4.0

Source: Offord, Boyle & Racine, 1991, from Table 2.3, p. 39.

inforce sex-stereotyped toy choice and behavior in their children at very early ages, and that this is particularly true of sons. Some evidence also suggests that young boys are punished or prohibited more often (Snow, Jacklin & Maccoby, 1983)—although of course this could be a response to rather than a cause of higher levels of aggression in boys.

At the same time, it is also true that the same family forces appear to foster high levels of aggression in both boys and girls. Highly aggressive children are most likely to come from families that display inconsistent discipline, rejection of the child, harsh punishment, and lack of parental supervision (Eron, Huesmann & Zelli, 1991). These are qualities that sound most like either neglecting or ineffectual authoritarian parenting styles. Thus, while the *rate* of aggression differs between the sexes, the family dynamic that contributes to it does not.

◗ Individual Differences

I've spent most of this chapter talking about common developmental patterns. But if we are to understand development, we must understand the individual pathways as well as the common ones. Sex differences represent one form of differential pathway. We also need to look at more individual variations, of which the two most important and pervasive in this age range appear to be variations in self-esteem and in popularity.

Self-Esteem

Preschool children certainly categorize themselves in various ways, but research by Susan Harter and others now shows that these categorizations do not coalesce into a *global* self-evaluation until about age 7 or 8 (Harter, 1988, 1990). Children at this age now readily answer questions about how well they like themselves as people, how happy they are, or how well they like the way are leading their lives. Such global evaluations are what is meant by **self-esteem**.

Harter argues that each child's level of self-esteem is a product of two internal assessments or judgments. First, each child experiences some degree of discrepancy between what he would like to be (or thinks he *ought* to be) and what he thinks he is. When that discrepancy is low, the child's self-esteem is generally high. When the discrepancy is high—when the child sees himself as failing to live up to his own goals or values—self-esteem will be much lower.

The standards are not the same for every child. Some value academic skills highly, others value sports skills or having good friends. The key to self-esteem, Harter proposes, is the amount of discrepancy between what is desired and what the child thinks he has

Hitting a home run will only raise this boy's self-esteem if he places a high value on being good at sports or at baseball specifically.

achieved. Thus, a child who values sports prowess but who isn't big enough or coordinated enough to be good at sports will have lower self-esteem than will an equally small or uncoordinated child who does not value sports skill so highly. Similarly, being good at something, like singing, playing chess, or being able to talk to your mother, won't raise a child's self-esteem unless the child values that particular skill.

The second major influence on a child's self-esteem, according to Harter, is the overall sense of support the child feels from the important people around her, particularly parents and peers. Children who feel that other people generally like them the way they are have higher self-esteem scores than do children who report less overall support.

Both these factors are clear in the results of Harter's own research, shown in Figure 10.3. She asked third-, fourth-, fifth-, and sixth-graders how important it was to them to do well in each of five domains, and how well they thought they actually did in each. The total discrepancy between these sets of judgments comprised the discrepancy score. Remember that a high discrepancy score indicates that the child didn't feel he was doing well in areas that mattered to him. The social support score was based on children's replies to a set of questions about whether they thought others (parents and peers) liked them as they were, treated them as a person, or felt that they were important. The data shown in the figure obviously support Harter's hypothesis. Among both the younger and older children in this study, global self-esteem was clearly and about equally related to both factors. Note that a low discrepancy score alone does not protect the child completely from low self-esteem if she lacks sufficient social support. And a loving and accepting family and peer group does not guarantee high self-esteem if the youngster does not feel she is living up to her own standards.

A particularly deadly combination occurs when the child perceives that the parents' support is *contingent* on good performance in some area—getting good grades, making the first-string football team, being popular with other kids. Then if the child does not measure up to the standard, he experiences both an increased discrepancy between ideal and achievement, and a loss of support from the parents.

Consistency of Self-Esteem over Time.   Cross-sectional studies like the one shown in Figure 10.3 can give us only a one-time snapshot of a child's self-esteem. It seems equally important to know whether low or high self-esteem tends to persist. Is a third grader with low self-esteem doomed to feel less than worthy for the rest of his life?

A number of short-term longitudinal studies of elementary-school-age children and teenagers show that global self-esteem is quite stable in the short term, but much less so over periods of several years. The correlation between two self-esteem scores obtained a few months apart is generally about .60. Over several years, this correlation drops to something more like .40 (Alsaker & Olweus, 1992). So it is true that a child with high self-esteem at age 8 or 9 is more likely to have a high self-esteem at age 10 or 11. But it is also true that there is a good deal of variation around that stability. Self-esteem seems to be particularly unstable in the years of early adolescence, around age 11 and 12. This makes sense in Harter's terms, since these are years when the standards children may set for themselves are likely to change as the youngsters move from elementary to junior high and from prepubescent to pubescent (Harter, 1990). In later adolescence, self-esteem appears to become more stable, although still not totally fixed.

Consequences of Variations in Self-Esteem.   The clearest research finding is that self-esteem is *strongly* negatively correlated with depression in both middle childhood and adolescence. The lower the self-esteem score, the more depressed the child describes himself to be. The correlations in several of Harter's studies range from −.67 to −.80— remarkably high for research of this type (Harter, 1988; Renouf & Harter, 1990). Bear in mind, though, that this is still correlational evidence. These findings don't prove that there is a causal connection between low self-esteem and depression. More persuasive is

Think about the following somewhat paradoxical proposition: If Harter's model of self-esteem is correct, then our self-esteem is most vulnerable in the area in which we may appear (and feel) the most competent. Does this fit with your experience?

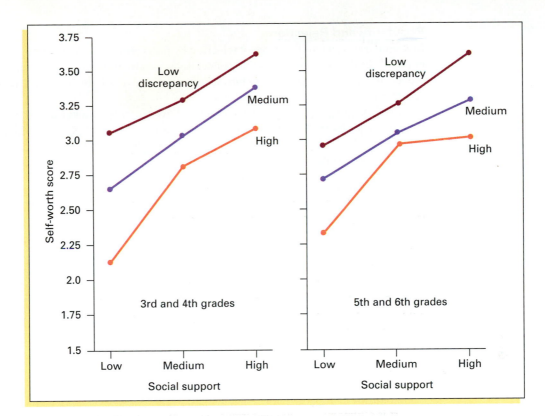

Figure 10.3 For both younger and older children in Harter's studies, self-esteem was about equally influenced by the amount of support the child saw herself as receiving from parents and peers, and by the degree of discrepancy between the value the child places on various domains and the skill she sees herself having in each of those domains. (*Source:* Harter, 1988, Figure 9.2, p. 227.)

Harter's finding from her longitudinal studies that when the self-esteem score rises or falls, the depression score drops or rises accordingly.

Origins of Differences in Self-Esteem.   Where do differences in self-esteem come from? Most obviously, parental and peer values help to shape the importance a child will place on some skill or quality. Peer (and general cultural) standards for appearance, for example, are powerful elements in self-esteem at every age. Similarly, the degree of emphasis parents place on the child performing well in school is an important element in the child's internal expectations in that area.

A child's perception of her own competence or acceptability is also shaped by her own direct experience of success or failure in various domains, such as schoolwork, creating relationships with peers, and sports or games. Labels and judgments from others are yet another element in the equation. Children who are repeatedly told that they are "pretty" or "smart" or "a good athlete" are likely to have higher self-esteem than are children who are told that they are "dumb" or "clumsy" or "a late bloomer." A child who brings home a report card with Cs and Bs on it and hears the parents say, "That's fine, honey. We don't expect you to get all As," draws conclusions both about the parents' expectations and about their judgments of his abilities.

Once again, then, we see the power of both the internal working model the child creates and the family and peer interactions that are the crucible in which the model is forged. Like the child's internal model of attachment, a child's self-scheme is not fixed in stone. It is responsive to changes in others' judgments as well as to changes in the child's own experience of success or failure. But once created, the model does tend to persist, both because the child will tend to choose experiences that will confirm and support his self-scheme and because the social environment —including the parents' evaluations of the child—tends to be at least moderately consistent.

Popularity and Rejection

In a similar way, a child's degree of rejection by peers tends to be consistent over the years of middle childhood and into adolescence. Rejected children tend to stay rejected; if they move out of this category, it is rare for them to move all the way to a high level of acceptance (Asher, 1990).

Psychologists who study rejected children have recently concluded that it is important to make a distinction between two groups of unpopular children. The most frequently studied are those children who are overtly rejected by peers. If you ask children to list peers they would *not* like to play with, or if you observe which children are avoided on the playground, you can get a measure of rejection of this type. The other type has come to be called *neglected*. Children in this category are reasonably well liked but lack individual friends and are rarely chosen as most preferred by their peers. Neglected children have been studied far less than have the rejected, but the preliminary evidence suggests that neglect is much less stable over time than is rejection (Asher, 1990). Still, neglected children appear to be more prone to depression and loneliness than are accepted children (Rubin et al., 1991).

Rejected children, in contrast, are much more likely to show conduct disorders, both in elementary school and at later ages, including adulthood. In fact, many researchers have now found that unpopularity with peers in elementary school is the best single predictor of long-term adult problems—a set of findings I have explored in the "across development" report on the opposite page. Because of such findings and because rejection is so clearly painful to the child, it is important for us to understand where such rejection comes from. Just why are some children rejected and others not?

Qualities of Rejected and Popular Children.   Some of the characteristics that differentiate popular and unpopular children are things outside a child's control. In particular, attractive children and physically larger children are more likely to be popular—perhaps merely a continuation of the preference for attractive faces that Langlois detected in young infants and that I described in Chapter 5. The most crucial ingredients, though, are not how the child looks but how the child behaves.

Popular children behave in positive, supporting, nonpunitive and nonaggressive ways toward most other children. They explain things and take their playmates' wishes into consideration (e.g., Ladd, Price & Hart, 1988; Black, 1992; Black & Hazen, 1990). Rejected children are aggressive, disruptive, and uncooperative (Coie, Dodge & Kupersmidt, 1990; Parkhurst & Asher, 1992). This conclusion emerges from research of a variety of kinds, including direct observation of groups of previously unacquainted children who spend several sessions playing with one another and then pick their favorite playmates from among the group (e.g., Coie & Kupersmidt, 1983; Dodge, 1983; Shantz, 1986). In these studies, children who are most consistently positive and supportive are those who end up being chosen as leaders or as friends. Those who consistently participate in conflicts are more often rejected.

Either as a cause or as a result of their rejection, rejected children also seem to have quite different internal working models of relationships and of aggression than do popular children. Kenneth Dodge (Dodge & Frame, 1982; Dodge et al., 1990; Dodge & Feldman, 1990) has shown that aggressive/rejected children are much more likely to see aggression as a useful way to solve problems. They are also much more likely to interpret someone else's behavior as hostile or attacking than is true for less aggressive or more popular children. Given an ambiguous event, such as being hit in the back with a kicked ball, aggressive or rejected children—especially boys—are much more likely to assume that the ball was thrown on purpose, and they retaliate. Of course such retaliation, in turn, is likely to elicit hostility from others, so their expectation that other people are hostile to them is further confirmed.

One reasonable hypothesis might be that neglected children would be more likely to have had insecure attachments as infants. Can you think of refinements of this hypothesis? And how could you test it?

This child would probably be classed as neglected rather than rejected. The long-term prognosis for such children is better than for rejected children, but they are more likely to be depressed in childhood and adolescence—as this boy seems to be.

ACROSS DEVELOPMENT
Long-Term Consequences of Childhood Aggression and Peer Rejection

Let me give you a sampling of the findings of a growing number of longitudinal studies that demonstrate a link between peer rejection or high aggressiveness (or both) in elementary school, and disturbances or behavior problems in adolescence and adulthood.

- Leonard Eron, in a 22-year longitudinal study, has found that a high level of aggressiveness toward peers at age 8 was related to various forms of aggressiveness at age 30, including "criminal behavior, number of moving traffic violations, convictions for driving while intoxicated, aggressiveness toward spouses, and how severely the subjects punished their own children" (Eron, 1987, p. 439).

- In the Concordia Project in French Canada, Lisa Serbin (Serbin et al., 1991) has studied several thousand children who were initially identified by their peers in grade 1, 4, or 7 as either highly aggressive, withdrawn, or both. A large comparison group of nonaggressive and nonwithdrawn children was also studied. Both aggressive girls and aggressive boys later showed poorer school achievement in high school. In adulthood, criminal offenses were much more likely among previously aggressive children than among the comparison group. For men, there was a 4 to 1 difference: 45.5 percent of the aggressive but only 10.8 percent of the nonaggressive had appeared in court. For women, the ratio was about 2 to 1 (3.8 percent versus 1.8 percent).

- Farrington (1991) has studied a group of 400 working-class boys in England, beginning when they were 8 and continuing into their thirties. Those who were rated by their teachers as most aggressive at age 8, 10, and 12, were more likely to describe themselves at 32 as getting into fights, carrying a weapon, or fighting police officers. They were also twice as likely as were less aggressive children to commit a violent offense (20.4 percent versus 9.8 percent), twice as likely to be unemployed, more likely to hit their wives, and half again as likely to have a drunk-driving conviction.

- Kupersmidt and Coie (1990), in a study of a small group of fifth graders who were followed to the end of high school, report that negative outcomes in high school—including poor school performance, regular truancy, dropping out of school, or

juvenile court appearance—were considerably more common among rejected children than among the popular. This effect was particularly evident for subjects who were highly aggressive as children and for those who were both aggressive and rejected.

- You may also remember a related study that I described in Chapter 1 (Figure 1.2, p. 10). Caspi and his colleagues (Caspi, Elder & Bem, 1987) found that boys in the Berkeley/Oakland longitudinal studies who were classed as "explosive" or ill-tempered in elementary school were more ill-tempered as adults, had lower levels of occupational success, and were more likely to divorce. Among women the relationships were less striking, but the spouses and children of women who had been ill-tempered girls perceived them as less adequate and more ill-tempered parents. They also tended to marry "down" in social class. Thus, both groups have adult lives we might reasonably describe as less successful.

There are obviously several ways we could explain such a link between early aggression or unpopularity and later behavior problems. The simplest explanation is that problems with peers arise out of high levels of aggression and that such aggression simply persists as the individual's primary mode of interaction. It is also possible that a failure to develop friendships itself causes problems that later become more general. Or, early aggression and later behavior problems could be linked through a seriously warped internal working model of relationships.

Whatever the explanation, the point to remember is that such deviant behavior does tend to persist and may have profound effects on an individual's entire life pattern. I will say yet again that this does not mean that it is impossible to deflect an individual from such a pathway, nor that individuals may not be resilient enough to recover from early patterns of deviance. None of these studies shows perfect continuity; all speak only of increased risks or increased probabilities. But it would be foolish to think that life begins all over again at age 20, with entirely new choices and a clean slate. Instead, we carry the traces of our childhood forward with us through our lives, in the form of established behavior patterns and powerful internal working models.

This body of research can also be linked to Gerald Patterson's work, whose model I described in Chapter 1 (Figure 1.3, page 12). Patterson is persuaded that a child's excess aggressiveness can be traced originally to ineffective parental control. Once the child's aggressiveness is well established, the child displays this same behavior with peers, is rejected by those peers, and is then driven more and more toward the only set of peers who will accept him, usually other aggressive or delinquent boys.

Happily, not all rejected children remain rejected or develop serious behavior problems or delinquency. And not all aggressive children are rejected. Recent research gives us a few hints about what may differentiate between these different subgroups. For example, among aggressive children, some also show fairly high levels of altruistic or pro-social behavior, and this mixture of qualities carries a much more positive prognosis than does aggression unleavened by helpfulness (Tremblay, 1991). Differences in the type of aggression a child shows may also prove to be predictive of later outcomes. Dodge (1991) suggests that children who show what he calls *proactive* aggression, who aggress in order to get their way or to obtain some desired end, may be more amenable to intervention or treatment than are children displaying *reactive* aggression, who aggress to retaliate against perceived wrong. The latter group seems intent on injuring the other person whereas the proactively aggressive child backs off as soon as his goal is achieved. Distinctions like these may help us not only to refine our predictions but to design better intervention programs for rejected/aggressive children.

The Role of the Larger Culture

As at earlier ages, the daily life of the school age child is shaped not just by the hours she spends in school or playing with pals. She is also affected by her family's economic circumstances, by the neighborhood she lives in, by the arrangements for her after-school care, and by the television programs she watches. Within the family, the pattern of interaction between parent and child is also affected by many of these same forces as well as by the quality of the parent's job, the amount of emotional support the parent(s) have from family or friends, and many other factors I've talked about in earlier chapters. Let me talk about two of these components of the larger culture that seem especially important in middle childhood: the effects of poverty and the effects of television.

The Effects of Poverty

Poverty has detrimental effects on children at every age, as I have said before. Poor mothers are much less likely to have adequate prenatal care, so their babies may get off to a poor start; poor children may have less adequate nutrition in their early years of life and may be exposed to more hazards, such as lead-based paint or other toxins. Those who live in poverty-ravaged urban areas are also likely to be exposed to street gangs and street violence, to drug pushers, to overcrowded homes and abuse. Whole communities have become like war zones.

In the United States, almost 13 million children live in urban poverty (Garbarino, Kostelny & Dubrow, 1991). More than one and a half million of these live in public housing developments, including some with the highest crime rates in the country. A recent survey in Chicago (Kotulak, 1990) revealed that nearly 40 percent of elementary and high school students in the inner city had witnessed a shooting, a third had seen a stabbing.

Black children are enormously overrepresented in the ranks of the poor. Overall, a black child in the United States has a 1 in 2 chance of being poor. If he is born to a single mother under the age of 25, his chances of poverty rise to 4 out of 5.

In the early years of childhood, when youngsters spend most of their time with a parent or other caregiver, or with siblings, they can be protected from some of the dangers inherent in many poverty environments. But in middle childhood, when children pass through the streets to travel to and from school and to play with their peers, they experience the impact of urban poverty and decay far more keenly. And of course, because they are likely to have missed out on many of the forms of intellectual stimulation that would allow them to succeed in school, they have high rates of problems and academic failures. One consequence of this is that less than half of urban poor children graduate from high school (Garbarino et al., 1991). The reasons for such school failures are complex, but there is little doubt that the chronic stress experienced by poor children is one highly significant component.

Yet among children exposed to such stresses, all are not equally vulnerable. Studies of resilient and vulnerable children (e.g., Masten, Best & Garmezy, 1990; Garmezy & Masten, 1991) suggest a series of characteristics or circumstances that seem to protect some children from the detrimental effects of repeated stresses and upheavals:

High IQ in the child

Competent adult parenting, such as an authoritative style

Effective schools

A secure initial attachment of the child to the parent

Most broadly, Garmezy and Masten argue that the key characteristic of the resilient child is what they call *competence*, which includes both cognitive and interpersonal skills. The child who has the sort of social skills needed to achieve at least moderate popularity with peers and to establish and maintain close friendships will be better able to weather the storms of family stress. The child with the cognitive skill to comprehend what is happening, who can figure out alternative strategies for dealing with problems, is also buffered from the worst effects of stress.

A good deal of the evidence supporting these generalizations comes from studies of children reared in poverty. For example, in a major longitudinal study in Kauai, Hawaii, Emmy Werner (Werner, Bierman & French, 1971; Werner & Smith, 1982) has found that a subset of those children born to and reared in poverty nonetheless became competent, able, autonomous adults. The families of these resilient children were clearly more authoritative, more cohesive, more loving than were the equivalently poor families whose children had less good outcomes. Thus, the stage for later resilience is set in infancy and early childhood.

RESEARCH REPORT
Latchkey Children

Many parents—including a great many living in poverty—find themselves unable to afford or arrange after-school care for their elementary school children. This leaves the child to care for herself in the hours between the end of school and a parent's return from work. Such children are referred to as *latchkey children*.

It has been very difficult to discover just how many latchkey children there are, in part because such a practice has had a lot of bad press, so parents are not always willing to acknowledge that their children care for themselves part of the time. Most current estimates are that between 5 and 10 percent of children between ages 6 and 13 in the United States spend at least some part of their days in "self-care" (Cain & Hofferth, 1989; U.S. Bureau of the Census, 1990). In families in which all the parental figures are working, the rate is about twice that (Cain & Hofferth, 1989).

Self-care is most likely for children 10 and over, and for only a short time each day, most often after school. Contrary to what you may assume, such care arrangements are *not* found primarily among families in poverty environments. On the contrary, they are more common among middle- and high-education white families in suburban or rural areas. In families of this type, there are less likely to be other adults living in the home or nearby who can supervise the child.

There is very little decent research to tell us what effect such self-care may have on children. The bulk of the evidence suggests that latchkey children do not differ from other kids in their school performance, self-concept, or susceptibility to peer pressure (Cole & Rodman, 1987) *if* the child has a clear routine, is in daily contact with the parent(s) by phone during the self-care hours, and has neighbors or others to turn to in case of need. When these conditions cannot be met—as may be the case for children living in public housing developments or in other environments without good support—self-care may simply exacerbate existing problems.

Among adolescents who lack supervision for parts of each day, those who stay in their own homes for the unsupervised hours seem to do better than those who spend the time "hanging out" or at a friend's house. The latter groups seem to be especially susceptible to peer pressure during the peer-sensitive years of early adolescence (Steinberg, 1986).

Overall, the relatively scant research literature suggests that self-care by children is not the unmitigated disaster that many popular press reports would have us believe. But there are enough red flags to suggest that we need to know a good deal more about the specific conditions needed to support children who must care for themselves for part of each day.

Similarly, studies of boys reared in high-crime inner-city neighborhoods show that high intelligence and at least a minimum level of family cohesion are key ingredients affecting a boy's chance of creating a successful adult life pattern (Long & Vaillant, 1984; McCord, 1982). Boys with low IQ or those reared in poverty-level families in which the parents were alcoholics or had strong antisocial tendencies were simply much less likely to develop the competence needed to bootstrap themselves out of their difficult circumstances.

Thus it is not the stress the family experiences *per se* that is causal, but rather the family's ability to cope with the stresses of their lives, to create a sufficiently supportive environment for the child to develop the needed intellectual and social competencies. But it is asking a very great deal of parents—very often single mothers under extreme financial and personal stress—to create such a supportive environment in the midst of urban poverty and violence. I am in full agreement with James Garbarino when he says:

> What is truly needed in America's urban war zones is restoration of a safe environment where children can have a childhood, and where parents can exert less energy on protecting children from random gunfire and more on helping children to grow. No one can eliminate all risk from the lives of families. But America does have the resources to make a real childhood a real possibility even for the children of the urban poor. But sometimes the war close to home is the most difficult to see. (Garbarino, Kostelny & Dubrow, 1991, p. 148)

Television and Its Effects

"By the time American children are 18 years old, they have spent more time watching television than in any other activity except sleep." (Huston et al., 1990.) United States' children spend more time watching TV than do children in most other countries, but TV ownership is above 50 percent of households in most of eastern and western Europe and in Latin America, so this is not an exclusively American phenomenon (Comstock, 1991).

In the United States, preschoolers watch TV two to four hours a day (Anderson et al., 1986). This rate typically rises still further in the elementary school years and then declines somewhat in adolescence (Comstock, 1991). High levels of viewing are more common among African-American children than among whites or Hispanics, and more common in families in which the parents are less well educated (Anderson, Mead & Sullivan, 1986).

Just what are children seeing during all those hours? Preschoolers see many programs designed specifically to be educational or informative, such as "Sesame Street" or "Mister Rogers' Neighborhood." As they get older, however, children increasingly watch cartoons, comedies, and adult-entertainment programs (Huston et al., 1990).

I can give you only a few tidbits from the vast amount of research designed to detect any effects such viewing may have on children and on adults. Still, a taste is better than no meal at all.

Positive Educational Effects of TV.   Programs specifically designed to be educational or to teach children positive values do indeed have demonstrable effects. This is particularly clear among preschoolers, for whom most such programming is designed. Children who watch "Sesame Street" more regularly, for example, develop larger vocabularies than do children who do not watch or watch less often (Rice et al., 1990), and those who watch programs that emphasize sharing, kindness and helpfulness, such as "Mister Rogers," "Sesame Street," or even "Lassie," show more kind and helpful behavior (Murray, 1980).

Negative Effects of TV on Cognitive Skills.   In elementary school and high school, however, there is evidence that higher levels of TV viewing are associated with *lower* scores on achievement tests, including measures of such basic skills as reading, arithmetic, and writing. This is particularly clear in the results of an enormous study in California that included over half a million sixth- and twelfth-graders (California Assessment Program, 1980). In this very large sample, the more hours the students watched TV, the lower their scores on standardized tests. This relationship was actually *stronger* among children from well-educated families, so it is not a result of the fact that working class or low-education families watch more TV. However, among children with limited English fluency, high levels of viewing were associated with somewhat higher school achievement. Thus, television can help to teach children things they did not already know, but among children with basic skills at the start of school, TV viewing time appears to have a negative effect on school performance.

Television and Aggression. By far the largest body of research has focused on the potential impact of TV on children's aggressiveness. There is no dispute about the high level of violence on TV, nor about the fact that this level has not declined in the past decades despite many public outcries. Nancy Signorielli (1986) estimates that in 1985, situation comedies averaged about two incidents of physical violence per hour, action/ adventure programs averaged eight. The rate is still higher in children's cartoons and would be far higher for all types of programs if verbal aggression were also counted.

Observers also agree that the "good guys" are just as likely to be violent as the "bad guys," and that violence on most TV programs is rewarded; people who are violent get what they want. In fact, violence is usually portrayed as a successful way of solving problems. Furthermore, the consequences of violence—pain, blood, and damage—are seldom shown, so the child is protected from seeing the painful and negative consequences of aggression and thus receives an unrealistic portrayal of those consequences.

Where there is still some dispute is over the possible *causal* effect such TV violence may have in children's levels of aggression. Demonstrating such a causal link is rather like demonstrating a causal link between smoking and lung cancer. Unequivocal findings would require an experimental design—a strategy ruled out for obvious ethical reasons. One cannot assign some people randomly to smoke for 30 years, nor assign some children to watch years of violent TV while others watch none.

How many different explanations can you think of for the relationship between amount of TV watching and school performance? What kind of data would you need to check the plausibility of each of your explanations?

In the United States, children between 6 and 12 spend more time watching TV than they do playing.

RESEARCH REPORT
Family Viewing Patterns

Statements about the average number of hours of children's viewing disguise very large variations among families not only in viewing patterns but also in attitudes about television. To a considerable extent, parents control their children's TV through explicit rules and through attitudes. About 40 percent of families regularly restrict the number of hours a child can watch; nearly half have consistent rules about what type or which specific programs a child may view (Comstock, 1991). In contrast, nearly 40 percent of parents of young children at least occasionally encourage TV watching in order to keep a child occupied.

Michelle St. Peters (St. Peters et al., 1991), in one recent study, found that she could classify families into one of four types, based on the degree of regulation of TV viewing parents imposed (high versus low) and the degree of encouragement they provided (high versus low):

Laissez-faire parents had few regulations but did not specifically encourage viewing.

Restrictive parents had high regulations and low encouragement.

Promotive parents had few regulations and high levels of encouragement for TV viewing.

Selective parents had high regulations but encouraged some specific types of viewing.

In a two-year longitudinal study of 5-year-olds and their parents,

St. Peters found that each of these four groups had quite different patterns of TV watching. As you would expect, children in restrictive families watched the least TV (11.9 hours per week). When they watched, it was most likely to be entertainment or educational programs aimed specifically at children (such as "Sesame Street," "Mister Rogers' Neighborhood," or "Walt Disney"). The heaviest viewers were children with parents classed as promotive (21.1 hours per week), and they watched not only children's programs but also adult comedy, drama, game shows, and action adventure. In laissez-faire families, children watched an intermediate number of hours (16.7), mostly devoted to child entertainment and comedy, a pattern similar to what appeared in the selective families, although the latter group watched more informative programs directed at children than did laissez-faire children.

The key point here is that families create the conditions for children's viewing and thus for what children learn from TV. Not only do parents establish a degree of regulation, they may also watch with the child and interpret what the child sees. A family that wishes to do so can take advantage of the beneficial things TV has to offer and minimize the aggressive, violent, or sexist content. The difficulty for many families, however, is that such a planned approach to TV may mean that the parents will have to give up their own favorite programs.

Some short-term experiments have been done in which one group of children is exposed to a few episodes of moderately aggressive TV while others watch neutral programs. These studies generally do show a short-term increase in aggression among those who watched the aggressive programs. But by and large, as is true of studies of smoking and lung cancer, we must rely on correlational evidence. And as always with correlational evidence, there is a problem of interpretation. For example, children who already behave aggressively may *choose* to watch more TV and more violent TV. And families in which TV is watched a great deal may also be more likely to use patterns of discipline that will foster aggressiveness in the child. One research example will make the point clear.

In his 22-year longitudinal study of aggressiveness from age 8 to 30, Leonard Eron (1987) has found that the best predictor of a young man's aggressiveness at age 19 was the violence of television programs he watched when he was 8. Twelve years later, when the men were 30, Eron found that the seriousness of criminal behavior was strongly related to the frequency of TV viewing at age 8, as you can see in Figure 10.4. The pattern is the same for women, by the way, but the level of criminal offenses is far lower, just as the level of aggression is lower among girls in childhood.

Eron also found that at age 8, boys who watched a lot of violent television were already more highly aggressive with their peers, indicating that aggressive boys choose to watch more violent TV. However, among the already aggressive 8-year-olds, those who watched the most TV were more delinquent or aggressive as teenagers and as adults (Huesmann, Lagerspetz & Eron, 1984; Eron, 1987).

Evidence like this suggests that the causality runs both ways: "aggressive children prefer violent television, and the violence on television causes them to be more aggressive" (Eron, 1987, p. 438). Eron goes on to say:

> It would, of course, be foolish to maintain that the specific programs these subjects watched at age 8 continued to influence their behavior 22 years later. . . . What was probably important about the programs these children watched were the attitudes and behavioral norms inculcated by continued watching of those and similar programs. . . . Thus, one who watches more aggressive sequences on television should have more aggressive strategies more strongly encoded and should respond more aggressively when presented with similar or relevant cues. (1987, p. 440)

Eron's conclusion is buttressed by results from several studies showing that children who watch a lot of violent TV are more likely to see aggression as a good way to solve problems. They are also more fearful and less trusting (Dominick & Greenberg, 1972; Comstock, 1991).

A minority of psychologists are not convinced that the data justify concluding that there is a causal link between violent TV and aggression in children or adults (e.g., Freedman, 1984). But the growing consensus is that such a causal link does indeed exist (e.g., Friedrich-Cofer & Huston, 1986; Comstock, 1991). Violent television is clearly not the only nor even the major cause of aggressiveness among children, but it is significant.

For parents, the clear message from all the research on TV is that television is an educational medium. Children learn from what they watch—vocabulary words, helpful behaviors, eating habits, and aggressive behaviors and attitudes. The overall content of television—violence and all—may indeed reflect general cultural values. But an individual family can pick and choose among the various cultural messages by controlling what the child watches on TV.

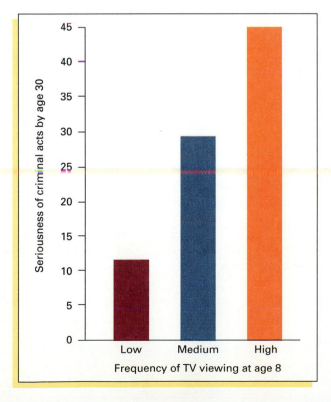

Figure 10.4 Eron finds a strong relationship between the amount of TV a group of boys watched when they were 8 and the average severity of criminal offenses they had committed by the age of 30. However, this finding alone does not prove there is a causal link between TV and later violence. (*Source:* Eron, 1987, Figure 3, p. 440.)

Summary

1. Patterns of relationships established in elementary school may have greater impact on adolescent and adult life patterns than do cognitive changes in these same years.

2. In middle childhood, the self-concept becomes more abstract, more comparative, more generalized.

3. Similar changes occur in children's descriptions of others and in their understanding of relationships such as friendships. Friendships are increasingly seen as reciprocal relationships in which generosity and trust are important elements.

4. These changes parallel the cognitive changes we see in the same years, particularly the child's reduced reliance on appearances.

5. Relationships with parents become less overtly affectionate, with fewer attachment behaviors, in middle childhood. The strength of the attachment, however, appears to remain strong.

6. Peer relationships become increasingly central. Gender segregation of peer group activities is at its peak in these years, and appears in every culture.

7. Individual friendships also become more common and more enduring; they are almost entirely sex-segregated. Boys' and girls' friendships appear to differ in quite specific ways. Boys' relationships are more extensive and more "restrictive," with higher levels of competition and aggression; Girls' relationships are more intensive and enabling, with more compliance and agreement.

8. Physical aggression declines, while verbal insults and taunts increase. Boys show markedly higher levels of aggression than do girls and higher rates of conduct disorders, a difference that doubtless has both biological and social origins.

9. Self-esteem appears to be shaped by two factors: the degree of discrepancy a child experiences between goals and achievements, and the degree of perceived social support from peers and parents.

10. Low self-esteem is strongly associated with depression in children this age.

11. Socially rejected children are most strongly characterized by high levels of aggression or bullying and low levels of agreement and helpfulness. Aggressive/rejected children are much more likely to show behavior problems in adolescence and a variety of disturbances in adulthood.

12. Rejected children are more likely to interpret others' behavior as threatening or hostile. Thus they have different internal models of relationship.

13. A large proportion of children, including the majority of black children, grow up in poverty and experience heightened danger and violence. The stress associated with this environment is one factor in poorer school performance.

14. Although it is difficult to establish causal relationships, most evidence points to a link between high levels of TV viewing and both current and later aggression.

15. TV may have some beneficial educational effects in teaching specific knowledge or attitudes, but heavy viewing is associated with lower levels of school achievement in nearly all groups.

Key Term

self-esteem

Suggested Readings

Asher, S. R., & Coie, J. D. (Eds.) (1990). *Peer rejection in childhood.* Cambridge: Cambridge University Press. (This edited volume contains papers by all the leading researchers on this important subject. The papers are aimed at an audience of fellow psychologists, so the technical level is fairly high. Still, it is a wonderful next source if you are interested in this subject.)

Comstock, G. (1991). *Television and the American child.* San Diego: Academic Press. (This is about as complete and current a book as you will find on this subject. The author, who is a respected professor of communications, not only analyzes an enormous array of research, he provides a great deal of actual data, so that you can see research results for yourself.)

SUMMING UP MIDDLE CHILDHOOD DEVELOPMENT

Basic Characteristics of Middle Childhood

The table below summarizes the changes and continuities of middle childhood. You can see from the table that there are many gradual changes: greater and greater physical skill, less and less reliance on appearance and more and more attention to underlying qualities and attributes, and greater and greater role of peers. The one period in which there seems to be a more rapid change is right at the beginning of middle childhood, at the point of transition from the preschooler to the school child. And of course at the other end of this age range, puberty causes another set of rapid changes.

The Transition Between 5 and 7. Some kind of transition into middle childhood has been noted in a great many cultures. There seems to be widespread recognition that a 6-year-old is somehow qualitatively different from a 5-year-old: more responsible, more able to understand complex ideas. Among the Kipsigis of Kenya, for example, the age of 6 is said to be the first point at which the child has *ng'omnotet*, translated as *intelligence* (Harkness & Super, 1985). The fact that schooling begins at this age seems to reflect an implicit or explicit recognition of this fundamental shift.

Psychologists who have studied development across this transition have pointed to a whole series of changes.

• Cognitively, there is a shift to what Piaget calls concrete operational thinking. The child now understands conservation problems, seriation, and class inclusion. More generally, the child seems to pay less attention to surface properties of objects and more to underlying continuities and patterns. We see this not only in children's understanding of physical objects but in their understanding of others, of relationships, and of themselves. In studies of information processing, we see a parallel rapid increase in the child's use of executive strategies.

• In self-concept, we first see a global judgment of self-worth at about age 7 or 8.

• In peer relationships, gender segregation becomes virtually complete by age 6 or 7, especially in individual friendships.

The apparent confluence of these changes is impressive and seems to

---

A Summary of the Threads of Development During Middle Childhood

Aspect of Development	Age in Years						
	6	7	8	9	10	11	12
Physical development	Jumps rope; skips; may ride bike	Rides two-wheeled bike	Rides bike well	Puberty begins for some girls		Puberty begins for some boys	
Cognitive development	Gender constancy; various concrete operations skills, including some conservation, class inclusion, various memory strategies, executive processes (metacognition)		Inductive logic; better and better use of concrete operations skills; conservation of weight			Conservation of volume	
Self/ personality development	Concept of self increasingly more abstract, less tied to appearance; descriptions of others increasingly focused on internal, enduring qualities						
		Global sense of self-worth					
		Friendship based on reciprocal trust					
	Gender segregation in play and friendships almost total						
	Enduring friendships appear, continue throughout these years						

provide some support for the existence of a Piaget-like stage. On the surface, at least, there seems to be some kind of change in the basic structure of the child's thinking that is reflected in all aspects of the child's functioning. But impressive as these changes are, it is not so clear that what is going on here is a rapid, pervasive, structural change to a whole new way of thinking and relating. Children don't make this shift all at once in every area of their thinking or relationships. For example, while the shift from a concrete to a more abstract self-concept may become noticeable at 6 or 7, it occurs quite gradually and is still going on at ages 11 and 12. Similarly, a child may grasp conservation of quantity at age 5 or 6, but typically does not understand conservation of weight until several years later.

Furthermore, expertise, or the lack of it, strongly affects the pattern of the child's cognitive progress. Thus, while I think most psychologists would agree that there is a set of important changes that normally emerges together at about this age, most would also agree that there is no rapid or abrupt reorganization of the child's whole mode of operating.

Central Processes

In trying to account for the developmental shifts we see during middle childhood, my bias has been to see the cognitive changes as most central, the necessary but not sufficient condition for the alterations in relationships and in the self-scheme during this period. A good illustration is the emergence of a global sense of self-worth, which seems to require not only a tendency to look beyond or behind surface characteristics, but also the use of inductive logic. The child appears to arrive at a global sense of self-worth by some summative, inductive process.

Similarly, the quality of the child's relationships with peers and parents seems to rest, in part, on basic cognitive understanding of reciprocity and perspective taking. The child now understands that others read him as much as he reads them. Children of 7 or 8 will now say of their friends that they "trust each other," something you would be very unlikely to hear from a 5-year-old.

Such a cognitive bias dominated theories and research on middle childhood for many decades, largely as a result of the powerful influence of Piaget's theory. This imbalance has begun to be redressed in recent years, as the central importance of the peer group and the child's social experience have been better understood. There are two aspects to this revision of thinking. First, we have reawakened to the (obvious) fact that a great deal of the experience on which the child's cognitive progress is based occurs in social interactions, particularly in play with other children. Second, we have realized that social relationships make a unique set of demands, both cognitive and interactive.

People, as objects of thought, are simply not the same as rocks, beakers of water, or balls of clay. Among many other things, people behave *intentionally*, and they can reveal or conceal information about themselves. Further, unlike relationships with objects, relationships with people are mutual and reciprocal. Other people talk back, respond to your distress, offer things, get angry.

Children also have to learn social scripts, those special rules that apply to social interactions, such as politeness rules, or rules about when you can and cannot speak, or rules about power or dominance hierarchies. Such scripts change with age, so at each new age the child must learn a new set of roles, a new set of rules about what she may and may not do. To be sure, these changes in the scripts are partly in *response* to the child's growing cognitive sophistication. But they also reflect changes in the child's role in the social system. One obvious example is the set of changes when children start school. The script associated with the role of "student" is simply quite different from the one connected with the role of "little kid." School classrooms are more tightly organized than are preschools or day care centers, expectations for obedience are higher, and there are more drills and routines to be learned. These changes are bound to affect the child's pattern of thinking.

Just what role physical change plays in this collection of developments I do not know. Clearly there *are* physical changes going on. Girls, in particular, begin the early steps of puberty during elementary school. But we simply don't know whether the rate of physical development in these years is connected in any way to the rate of the child's progress through the sequence of cognitive or social understandings. There has been virtually no research linking the first row in the table with any of the other rows. The one thing we know is that bigger, more coordinated, early developing children are likely to have slightly faster cognitive development and be somewhat more popular with peers. Obviously this is an area in which we need far more knowledge.

Influences on the Basic Processes: The Role of Culture

Most of what I have said about middle childhood—and about other ages as well—is almost entirely based on research on children growing up in Western cultures. I've tried to balance the scales a bit as I've gone along, but we must still ask, again and again, whether the patterns we see are specific to particular cultures, or whether they reflect underlying developmental processes common to all children everywhere.

In the case of middle childhood, there are some obvious differences in the experiences of children in Western cultures versus those growing up in villages in Africa, in Polyncsia, or in other parts of the world where families live by subsistence agriculture and schooling is not a dominant force

in children's lives (Weisner, 1984). In many such cultures, children of 6 or 7 are thought of as "intelligent" and responsible and are given almost adultlike roles. They are highly likely to be given the task of caring for younger siblings, and begin their apprenticeship in the skills they will need as adults, such as water carrying, agriculture or animal husbandry, learning alongside the adult. In some

west African and Polynesian cultures, it is also common for a child this age to be sent out to foster care, either with relatives or as an apprentice to a skilled tradesperson.

Such children obviously have a very different set of social tasks to learn in the middle childhood years. They do not need to learn how to relate to or make friends with strangers. Instead, from an early age they need to learn their place in an existing network of roles and relationships. For the Western child, the roles are less prescribed, the choices for adult life are far more varied.

Yet the differences in the lives of Western and non-Western children should not obscure the very real similarities. In all cultures, children this age develop individual friendships, segregate their play groups by gender, develop the cognitive underpinnings of reciprocity, learn the beginnings of what Piaget calls concrete operations, and acquire some of the basic skills that will be required for adult life. These are not trivial similarities. They speak to the power of the common process of development, even in the midst of obvious variation in experience.

11

PHYSICAL AND COGNITIVE DEVELOPMENT IN ADOLESCENCE

Most of us use the word *adolescence* as if the term applied to a fairly precise set of years, such as the teenage years or the time that starts with junior high school or the years from 12 to 20. But in fact, the relevant age range is fairly fuzzy on the edges. If we mean to include the physical process of puberty within the years of adolescence, then we need to think of adolescence as beginning before age 12, especially for girls, some of whom begin puberty at 8 or 9. And on the other end, it is not clear that it is still appropriate to refer to a young man of 18 with a job and a wife and child as an adolescent.

It makes more sense to think of adolescence as the period that lies psychologically and culturally between childhood and adulthood rather than as a specific age range. It is the period of transition in which the child changes physically, mentally, and emotionally into an adult. The timing of this transition differs from one society to another and from one individual to another within a culture. But every child must cross through such a transitional period to achieve adult status. In our culture, this transitional stage is often quite lengthy, lasting from perhaps 12 to 18—even later for those who go to college and thus postpone some aspects of full adult status.

Because the physical and emotional changes that are part of this transition are so striking, the period of adolescence has acquired a reputation as being full of *sturm und drang* ("storm and stress"). Such a description considerably exaggerates the degree of emotional upheaval most adolescents experience. But the *importance* of the process is difficult to exaggerate, beginning with the remarkable physical changes of puberty.

What do you think are some of the consequences of the lack of clear initiation rituals and of the relatively long period of adolescence in modern Western societies? How might our culture be different if we did have shared initiation rites?

▶ Physical Changes at Adolescence

The many body changes associated with puberty are largely controlled by hormones, which play a central role in the physical drama of adolescence.

ACROSS CULTURES
Adolescent Initiation Rituals

So important is the change in status from child to adult that many societies have both promoted and marked this passage with some kind of rite or ritual. There is an enormous amount of variability in the content of such rituals, but certain practices are especially common (Y. Cohen, 1964).

One such practice, more common for boys than for girls, is the separation of the child from the family, referred to by anthropologists as *extrusion*. The child may spend the day with his family but sleep elsewhere, or he may live in a separate dwelling with other boys or with relatives. Such a separation typically occurs quite early in adolescence, some time before the actual initiation ritual. In traditional Hopi and Navaho cultures, for example, boys typically sleep apart from the family beginning at age 8 or 10; in the Kurtatchi of Melanesia, boys go through an extrusion ceremony at about age 9 or 10, after which they sleep in a special hut used by boys and unmarried men (Cohen, 1964). This practice obviously symbolizes the separation of the child from the birth family, marking a coming of age. But it also emphasizes that the child ''belongs'' not just to the family but to the larger group of kin or societal/tribal members.

A related theme is the accentuation of differences between females and males. In many cultures, for example, nudity taboos begin only at adolescence. Before that age, it is quite OK for boys and girls to see one another naked; after that age it is not. In some cultures, adolescents are forbidden to speak to any opposite-sex siblings, a taboo that may extend until one of the siblings marries (Cohen, 1964). This practice seems to have at least two purposes. First and most obviously, it strengthens the incest taboo that is so important to avoid inbreeding. Second, it signifies the beginning of the time in life when males and females have quite different life patterns. Girls and boys have begun to learn gender-appropriate tasks long before adolescence, but at adolescence they take up those roles far more completely.

These two patterns may form the backdrop for the initiation ritual itself, which is usually briefer and more intense. During this time—usually in groups and separately for each sex—youth are indoctrinated by the elders into the customary practices of their tribe or society. They may learn special religious rituals or practices, such as the learning of Hebrew as preparation for the *bar mitzva* or *bas mitzva* in the Jewish tradition. They may learn the history and songs of their tribe or people. Often, there is drama and pageantry as part of the entire process.

Very frequently, physical mutilation or trials also play a part in the initiation. Boys may be circumcised, cut so as to create certain patterns of scars, or sent out into the wilderness to undergo spiritual purification or to prove their manhood by achieving some feat. This is less common in girls' initiation rituals, but physical trials or mutilation do occur, such as the removal of the clitoris, whipping, or scarification.

Among the Hopi, for example, both boys and girls go through specific rituals in which they are taught the religious ceremonies of the kachina cult and are whipped. After these ceremonies, they may participate fully in the adult religious practices. Among the Malekula of New Hebrides, boys are circumcised and secluded. Girls in this culture go through a kind of initiation just before they are married, rather than at puberty: they must have their two upper incisor teeth ceremonially knocked out, and they must be secluded for 10 days.

In modern United States culture, as in most other Western cultures, there are no universally shared initiation rites, but there are still many changes of status, and a few experiences that have some properties in common with traditional adolescent *rites de passage*. We do not deliberately separate adolescents from family or from adults, but we do send adolescents to a new level of school, thus effectively segregating them from all but their peers. Boot camp, for those who enter the military, is a more obvious parallel, because the recruits are sent to a separate location and undergo various physical trials before they are accepted.

Until relatively recent times, it was also common for adolescent boys and girls in our culture to attend separate schools. Even within coeducational schools, physical education classes were sex-segregated until very recently, as were such traditional gender-stereotyped classes as home economics and shop.

Various other changes in legal standing also mark the passage to adult status in modern Western cultures. Young people can have a driver's license at 16 and can see R-rated movies at 17. At 18 they can vote, marry, enter the military without parental consent, and be tried in adult rather than juvenile court for any legal offense—although legal access to alcohol is typically withheld until age 21.

These various remnants of ancient initiation patterns are considerably less condensed in modern society than is still true in many cultures around the world. One result of this is that the passage into adult status is much less clear for young people in most industrialized countries. Perhaps this is one reason why adolescents in our society often create their own separation and distinctness, such as by wearing unusual or even outlandish clothing or hairstyles.

In the initiation rite of the Kota tribe of the Congo, boys' faces are painted blue to make them appear ghostlike, to symbolize the phantom of their now-departed childhood.

TABLE 11.1 Major Hormones Involved in Physical Growth and Development

Gland	Hormone(s) Secreted	Function in Regulating Growth
Thyroid	Thyroxine	Affects normal brain development and overall rate of growth.
Adrenal	Adrenal androgen	Involved in some changes at puberty, particularly the development of secondary sex characteristics in girls.
Testes (in boys)	Testosterone	Crucial in the formation of male genitals prenatally; also triggers the sequence of primary and secondary sex characteristic changes at puberty in the male.
Ovaries (in girls)	Estradiol	Affects development of the menstrual cycle and breasts in girls but has less to do with other secondary sex characteristics than testosterone does for boys.
Pituitary	Growth hormone; activating hormones	Affects rate of physical maturation. Signals other glands to secrete.

Hormones

Hormones, which are secretions of the various **endocrine glands** in the body, govern pubertal growth and physical changes in several ways, summarized in Table 11.1. Of all the endocrine glands, the most critical is the **pituitary;** it provides the trigger for the release of hormones from other glands. For example, the thyroid gland only secretes thyroxine when it has received a signal to do so in the form of a specific thyroid-stimulating hormone secreted by the pituitary.

Of course, hormones play a central role in growth and development at earlier ages as well. Thyroid hormone (thyroxine) is present from about the fourth month of gestation and appears to be involved in stimulating normal brain development prenatally. Growth hormone is also produced by the pituitary beginning as early as 10 weeks after conception. Presumably it helps to stimulate the very rapid growth of cells and organs of the body. And as I mentioned in Chapter 3, testosterone is produced prenatally in the testes of the developing male and influences both the development of male genitals and some aspects of brain development.

After birth, the rate of growth is governed largely by thyroid hormone and pituitary growth hormone. Thyroid hormone is secreted in greater quantities for the first two years of life and then falls to a lower level and remains steady until adolescence (Tanner, 1978).

Secretions from the testes and ovaries, as well as adrenal androgen, remain at extremely low levels until about age 7 or 8, when adrenal androgen begins to be secreted—the first signal of the changes of puberty (Shonkoff, 1984). Following this first step there is a complex sequence of hormonal changes, laid out in a simplified schematic in Figure 11.1.

The timing of these changes varies a lot from one child to the next, but the sequence remains the same. The process begins with a signal from the hypothalamus, a small structure in the brain that plays a vital role in regulating a variety of behaviors, including eating, drinking, and sexual behavior. In the pubertal process, the thalamus signals to the pituitary gland, which then begins secreting increased levels of **gonadotropic hormones** (two in males, three in females). These in turn stimulate the development of the glands in the testes and ovaries that then begin to secrete more hormones, **testosterone** in boys and a form of **estrogen** called *estradiol* in girls. Over the course of puberty, the levels of

Figure 11.1 The action of the various hormones at puberty is exceedingly complex. This figure oversimplifies the process but gives you some sense of the sequence and the differences between the patterns for boys and girls. If you are interested in further details, a paper by Buchanan, Eccles, and Becker (1992) includes a brief, excellent review.

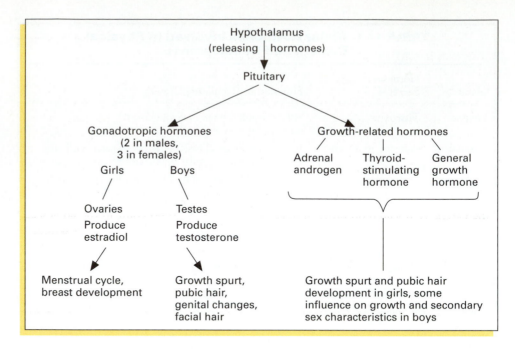

testosterone increase 18-fold in boys, while levels of estradiol increase 8-fold in girls (Nottelmann et al., 1987).

At the same time, the pituitary also secretes three other hormones that interact with the specific sex hormones and affect growth, although, as you can see in Figure 11.1, the interaction is a little different for boys and girls. In particular, the growth spurt and pubic hair development are more influenced by adrenal androgen in girls than in boys. Adrenal androgen is chemically very similar to testosterone, so it takes a "male" hormone to produce the growth spurt in girls. For boys, adrenal androgen is less significant, presumably because they already have male hormone in the form of testosterone floating about in their bloodstream.

It is somewhat misleading, by the way, to talk about "male" and "female" hormones. Both males and females have at least some of each (estrogen or estradiol, and testosterone or androgen); the difference is essentially in the relative proportion of the two. Within any one gender, these proportions differ as well, so some males have relatively more testosterone or less estrogen, while in others the two may be more balanced. Similarly, some girls may have a pattern of hormones that includes relatively more testosterone, while others may have relatively little.

Just how this hormonal process is turned off (or toned down) at the end of puberty is not as well understood (Dreyer, 1982). But in some fashion the level of both growth hormones and gonadotropic hormones produced in the pituitary drops to a lower level, and the rate of body change gradually tapers off at the adult levels.

All these hormonal changes are reflected in two sets of body changes: the well-known changes in sex organs and a much broader set of changes, in muscles, fat, bones, and body organs.

Height, Shape, Muscles, and Fat

Height.   One of the most dramatic changes is in height. You'll remember from earlier chapters that in infancy, the baby gains in height very rapidly, adding 10 to 12 inches in the first year. The toddler and school child grow much more slowly. The third phase begins with the dramatic adolescent spurt, triggered by the big increases in growth hormones. During this phase, the child may add 3 to 6 inches a year for several years. After the growth spurt, in the fourth phase, the teenager again adds height and weight slowly until his or her final adult size is reached. You can see the shape of the growth curve in Figure 11.2.

Shape.   At the same time, because the different parts of the child's body do not grow to full adult size at the same pace, the shape and proportions of the adolescent's body go through a series of changes. A teenager's hands and feet grow to full adult size earliest, followed by the arms and legs, with the trunk usually the slowest part to grow. So kids first outgrow their shoes, then their pants and long-sleeved shirts. But a bathing suit may continue to fit fine for quite some time, even when the rest of the body has changed. Because of this asymmetry in the body parts, we often think of an adolescent as "awkward" or uncoordinated. Interestingly, research does not bear that out. Robert Malina, who has done extensive research on physical development, has found no point in the adolescent growth process at which teenagers become consistently less coordinated or less skillful at physical tasks (Malina, 1990).

Children's heads and faces also change in childhood and adolescence. During the elementary school years, the size and shape of a child's jaw change when the permanent teeth come in. In adolescence both jaws grow forward and the forehead becomes more prominent. This set of changes often gives teenagers' faces (especially boys') an angular, bony appearance, quite unlike their earlier look—as you can see in the two pictures in Figure 11.3.

Muscles.   Muscle fibers, like bone tissues, go through a growth spurt at adolescence,

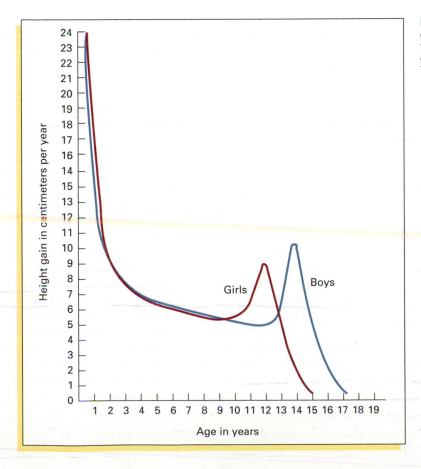

Figure 11.2 These curves show the gain in height for each year from birth through adolescence, with the adolescent growth spurt easily identifiable. (*Sources:* Tanner, 1978, p. 14; Malina, 1990).

Figure 11.3 These photos of the same boy before, during, and after puberty show the striking changes in the jaws and forehead that dramatically alter appearance in many teenage boys. The same changes occur in girls' faces but are not as dramatic. (*Source:* Tanner, 1962, Plate 1, p. 17.)

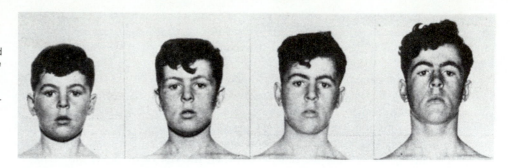

becoming thicker and denser. As a result, adolescents become quite a lot stronger in just a few years. Both boys and girls show this increase in muscle tissue and strength, but the increase is much greater in boys. Among adult men, about 40 percent of total body mass is muscle, compared to only about 24 percent in adult women.

Such a sex difference seems to be largely a result of hormone differences. But the contrast is increased—at least in our culture—by variations in levels of physical exercise among teenagers. Boys play more sports, move their bodies more, get more physical exercise. For example, when Tanner and his colleagues looked at changes in both arm muscle and calf muscle strength at adolescence, they found much larger sex differences in arm muscle gains than in leg muscles (Tanner, Hughes & Whitehouse, 1981). This pattern makes sense if we assume that arm muscle use varies more as a function of sports or other exercise than is true of leg muscles, which everyone uses for locomotion.

Fat. Another major component of the body is fat, most of which is stored immediately under the skin. This *subcutaneous fat* is first laid down beginning at about 34 weeks prenatally and has an early peak at about 9 months after birth. The thickness of this layer of fat then declines until about age 6 or 7, after which it rises until adolescence.

Once again there is a very large sex difference in these patterns. From birth, girls have slightly more fat tissue than boys, and this difference becomes gradually more marked during childhood, becoming particularly striking at adolescence. One current study of a large group of Canadian teenagers (Smoll & Schutz, 1990) shows that among girls in the 7th grade, 21.8 percent of body weight was made up of fat, while among 11th grade girls fat represented 24 percent. Among groups of boys the equivalent figures were 16.1 and 14.0. So during and after puberty, proportions of fat rise among girls and decline among boys, while the proportion of muscle tissue rises among boys and falls among girls.

As with muscle tissue, this sex difference in fat may be partially a life-style or activity-level effect; girls and women who are extremely athletic, such as long-distance runners or ballet dancers, typically have body fat levels that approximate those of the average boy. But if we compare equally fit boys and girls, boys still have lower fat levels.

Other Body Changes. Puberty also brings important changes in other body organs. In particular, the heart and lungs increase considerably in size, and the heart rate drops. Both of these changes are more marked for boys than for girls—another of the factors that increases the capacity for sustained effort by boys relative to girls. Before about age 12, boys and girls have similar physical strength, speed, and endurance, although even at these earlier ages, when there is a difference it favors the boys because of their lower levels of body fat. After puberty, boys have a clear advantage in all three (Smoll & Schutz, 1990).

Development of Sexual Maturity

The hormone changes of puberty also trigger the development of full sexual maturity, including changes in primary sex characteristics, such as the testes and penis in the male

What kind of research study could you design that would test further the hypothesis that the difference in muscle tissue between teenage boys and girls is primarily the result of differences in exercise or activity levels?

Assume that you are a member of a local school board, faced with a decision about whether to have teenage boys and girls play on the same competitive teams, such as volleyball, soccer, or baseball. Given all that I have said about sex differences in physical characteristics at puberty, how would you decide? Why?

and the ovaries, uterus, and vagina in the female, and in secondary sex characteristics, such as breast development in girls and body and facial hair and lowered voice pitch in boys.

Each of these physical developments occurs in a defined sequence. Each sequence is customarily divided into five stages, originally suggested by J. M. Tanner (1978). Stage 1 always describes the preadolescent stage, Stage 2 the first signs of pubertal change, Stages 3 and 4 the intermediate steps, and Stage 5 the final adult characteristic. Table 11.2 gives an example of these sequences for each sex.

Sexual Development in Girls.   Studies of preteens and teens in both Europe and North America (Malina, 1990) show that in girls, the various sequential changes are interlocked in a particular pattern. The first steps are typically the early changes in breasts and pubic hair development, followed by the peak of the growth spurt and by Stage 4 of both breast and pubic hair development. Only then does first menstruation occur, an event called **menarche** (pronounced men-ar-kee). Menarche typically occurs two years after the beginning of other visible changes and is succeeded only by the final stages of breast and pubic hair development. You can see the whole sequence in the upper part of Figure 11.4. Among girls in industrialized countries today, menarche occurs, on average, between ages 12½ and 13½; 95 percent of all girls experience this event between the ages of 11 and 15 (Malina, 1990).

Menarche does not signal full sexual maturity. It is possible to conceive shortly after menarche, but irregularity is the norm for some time. In as many as three-fourths of the cycles in the first year, and half the cycles in the second and third years after menarche, no ovum is produced (Vihko & Apter, 1980).

This initial irregularity of both ovulation and the timing of menstrual cycles has some significant practical consequences for sexually active teenagers. For one thing, such irregularity no doubt contributes to the widespread (but false) assumption among early-teenage girls that they cannot get pregnant because they are "too young." At the same time, menstrual irregularity makes any form of rhythm contraception unreliable, even among

TABLE 11.2 Examples of Tanner's Stages of Pubertal Development

Breast Development	Stage	Male Genital Development
No change except for some elevation of the nipple.	1	Testes, scrotum, and penis are all about the same size and shape as in early childhood.
Breast bud stage: Elevation of the breast and the nipple as a small mound. Areolar diameter is enlarged over Stage 1.	2	Scrotum and testes slightly enlarged. Skin of the scrotum is reddened and changed in texture but little or no enlargement of the penis.
Breast and areola both enlarged and elevated more than in Stage 2 but no separation of their contours.	3	Penis slightly enlarged, at first mainly in length. Testes and scrotum are further enlarged.
Areola and nipple form a secondary mound projecting above the contour of the breast.	4	Penis further enlarged, with growth in breadth and development of glans. Testes and scrotum further enlarged and scrotum skin still darker.
Mature stage. Only the nipple projects with the areola recessed to the general contour of the breast.	5	Genitalia are adult in size and shape.

Source: Petersen & Taylor, 1980, p. 127.

Figure 11.4 The typical sequence of pubertal development for girls (upper figure) and boys (lower figure), showing the *gains* in height at various ages as well as the average timing of various other body changes. Note how late in the sequence menarche occurs for girls and that girls are about 2 years ahead of boys. (*Sources:* Chumlea, 1982; Garn, 1980; Malina, 1990; Tanner, 1978.)

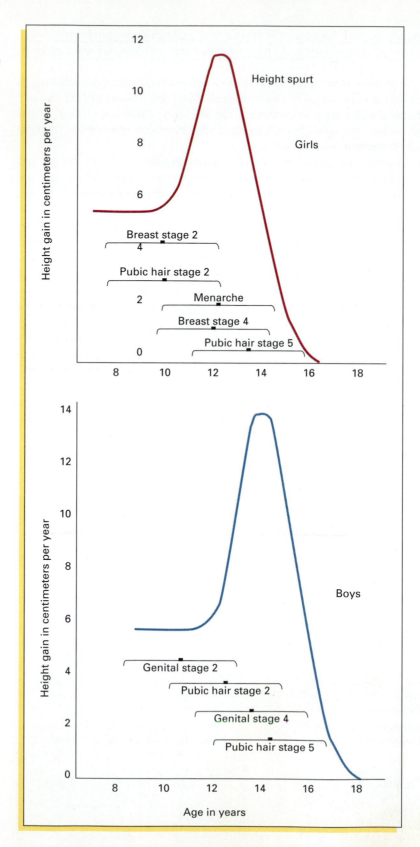

teenagers who have enough basic reproductive knowledge to realize that the time of ovulation is normally the time of greatest fertility—knowledge that is not widespread.

Sexual Development in Boys.   In boys, as in girls, the point of peak growth spurt typically comes fairly late in the sequence. Malina's data suggest that on average a boy completes Stages 2, 3, and 4 of genital development and Stages 2 and 3 of pubic hair development before the growth peak is reached (Malina, 1990). The development of a beard and the lowering of the voice come near the end of the sequence, as you can see in the lower part of Figure 11.4.

Precisely when in this sequence the boy begins to produce viable sperm is not entirely clear, although current evidence places this event sometime between ages 12 and 14, usually *before* the boy has reached the peak of the growth spurt (Brooks-Gunn & Reiter, 1990).

Two things are particularly interesting about these sequences. First, girls are clearly about two years ahead of boys in this developmental process. Most of you remember that period in late elementary school or junior high when the girls were suddenly taller than the boys and had the beginnings of secondary sex characteristics, while the boys were still definitely prepubertal. (A painful time for a lot of us.)

Also, while the order of development seems to be highly consistent *within* each sequence (such as breast development or pubic hair development), there is quite a lot of variability *across* sequences. I've given you the normative or average pattern, but individual teenagers often deviate from the norm. For instance, a boy may be in Stage 2 of genital development but already in Stage 5 of pubic hair development; a girl might move through several stages of pubic hair development before the first clear breast changes, or experience menarche much earlier in the sequence than normal. Physiologists have not figured out why this occurs, but it is an important point to keep in mind if you are trying to make a prediction about an individual teenager.

Health in Adolescence

Adolescents have fewer acute illnesses than do infants, toddlers, or school-age children, but death and accident rates rise at this age, largely because of the fact that teenagers are now driving. More than half of all teenage deaths are due to accidents, and most of these involve cars. Many of the fatal accidents are caused not by poor driving skills but by risk-taking behavior such as tailgating, speeding, or driving while intoxicated. In about half the cases in which a teenage driver is involved in a fatal auto accident, he or she has a blood alcohol level above .10—the legal limit for intoxication in most states (Millstein & Litt, 1990).

Another increasing risk among teenagers is suicide. Rates have tripled since 1960 and now represent about 12 percent of teen deaths. The rate is now about 15 deaths per 100,000 teenage males per year (Hawton, 1986)—not high in absolute numbers, but a disturbing trend. Also on the rise are two eating disorders, bulimia and anorexia nervosa, that have become remarkably common among teenage girls in many Western countries.

Bulimia and Anorexia.   **Bulimia** (sometimes called *bulimia nervosa*) is a pattern of "intense concern about weight, recurrent episodes of excessive overeating accompanied by a subjective sense of loss of control, and the use of vomiting, exercise, and/or purgative abuse to counteract the effects of binge eating" (Attie, Brooks-Gunn & Petersen, 1990, p. 410). Alternating periods of restrained and binge eating are common among individuals in all weight groups. Only when binge eating is combined with some kind of purging is the syndrome properly called *bulimia*.

The incidence of bulimia appears to have been increasing rather rapidly in recent decades, particularly among white teenage and young adult women. Current estimates vary quite a lot, but everyone agrees that at least 5 percent, and perhaps as many as 18

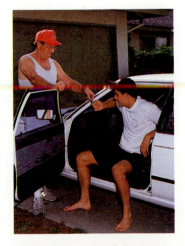

This dad is showing considerable trust to turn the keys to the family car over to his teenage son, given the accident rate of teen drivers.

THE REAL WORLD
How to Get Your Teenager to Stop Smoking, or Not to Start

Nearly half of eighth graders think there is no great risk to smoking a pack or two of cigarettes a day. By senior year, only about 30 percent still believe this, but by then many have a well-established smoking habit, difficult to break. It may seem from this that the right strategy with a young teen is to keep on talking about the long-term consequences of smoking. But teenagers (like many adults) feel invulnerable and immortal. They engage in many kinds of risky behaviors for the thrill of it and because they genuinely feel that nothing can happen to them. So it simply doesn't help very much to tell them about possible future problems. Several other strategies are much more successful.

Emphasize the Bad Breath. Tell them about all the negative *social* consequences of smoking. Their breath will smell bad, their teeth will turn yellow, their hair and clothes will smell like smoke all the time, and their ability to do well in athletics may be impaired. Tell them that teenagers themselves say that they find smokers less attractive. And tell teenage girls that smoking will not help them lose weight—a major reason for smoking for nearly all teenage girls—at least not enough to counterbalance the social costs.

Focus on the Manipulation. Remind your child that the cigarette companies are trying to manipulate them through their advertising. You may want to get them to look at specific ads and talk about the particular forms of manipulation involved. Because teenagers hate to be manipulated (by you or anyone else), this may be a successful argument.

Lobby the Schools. If the school your child attends has a designated smoking area, try to persuade them to abolish it and simply forbid smoking in any part of the school. In schools that allow smoking, 25 percent more of the students become smokers than is true in schools that forbid it on the grounds.

Pay Attention to Your Child's Friends. Teenagers whose friends smoke are more likely to take up the habit. You need to start paying attention to this *very* early—certainly by junior high school, when you may still have enough influence over the child's choice of friends to help steer the child toward a different crowd of kids.

Do Not Call Smoking an "Adult Choice." Many tobacco company programs ostensibly aimed at reducing teenage smoking tell teenagers that they are too young to smoke. But because teenagers want to do anything defined as "adult," this message may encourage smoking rather than the reverse. Instead, tell teenagers that they are old enough to know better; they are old enough to decide *not* to smoke.

percent of teenage girls are bulimic (Millstein & Litt, 1990). In contrast, less than 1 percent of college-age men show this syndrome (Attie et al., 1990; Howat & Saxton, 1988; Johnson et al., 1984; Pyle et al., 1983).

Anorexia nervosa is less common but potentially more deadly. It is characterized by "behavior directed toward weight loss, intense fear of gaining weight, body image disturbance, amenorrhea [cessation of menstruation], and an implacable refusal to maintain body weight" (Attie et al., 1990, p. 410). Ten to 15 percent of anorexic youth literally starve themselves to death. The incidence of anorexia has been hard to establish; the best current estimate is that it affects between 0.5 and 1 percent of girls or young women (Rolls, Federoff & Guthrie, 1991; Millstein & Litt, 1990), but is considerably more common among subgroups who are under pressure to maintain extreme thinness, such as ballet dancers.

The causes of both these disorders seem to lie, yet again, in the discrepancy between the young person's internal image of what kind or shape of body is desired, and her perception of her own body. Both syndromes seem to be increasing in frequency because of the currently intense emphasis in many Western countries on a very slender, almost prepubescent body shape as the ideal. From very early in life, girls, much more than boys, are taught both explicitly and implicitly that it matters if they are pretty or attractive, and that thinness is one of the critical variables in attractiveness. Current research, for example, shows that roughly three-fourths of teenage girls have dieted or are dieting, while boys rarely do so (Leon et al., 1989).

Those girls who most fully accept and internalize this model of beauty are most prone to develop bulimia or anorexia. For example, Ruth Striegel-Moore and her colleagues

(Striegel-Moore, Silberstein & Rodin, 1986) have found that bulimic girls and women are more likely than are nonbulimics to agree with statements like "Attractiveness increases the likelihood of professional success."

Both bulimia and anorexia seem to develop in adolescence, and not before that, precisely because one of the effects of puberty is to increase the amount of fat in the girl's body. This is particularly true of early developing girls, who characteristically acquire and retain higher fat levels than do later maturing girls. Thus an early developing girl who deeply believes that thinness is essential for beauty and that beauty is essential for happiness, especially if she sees her own body as failing to meet her internalized standard, seems at particularly high risk for developing bulimia or anorexia (Attie & Brooks-Gunn, 1989; Striegel-Moore et al., 1986; Rolls et al., 1991).

Research like this certainly points to the centrality of cognitive processes in every facet of the child's development—in health, in self-esteem, in social behavior. Those cognitive processes appear to go through yet another shift at adolescence, a change Piaget describes as the onset of **formal operations**.

How deeply entrenched are the societal patterns that contribute to these eating disorders, in your opinion? If you wanted to change our society in such a way that the incidence of bulimia and anorexia would go down, what changes would you make?

▌Cognitive Development at Adolescence

Piaget's View of Formal Operational Thought

Piaget's observations led him to conclude that this new level of thinking emerged fairly rapidly in early adolescence, between roughly 12 and 16. It has a number of key elements.

From the Actual to the Possible. One of the first steps in the process is for the child to extend her concrete operational reasoning abilities to objects and situations that she has not seen or experienced firsthand or that she cannot see or manipulate directly. Instead of thinking only about real things and actual occurrences, as the younger child can do, she must start to think about possible occurrences. This skill is obviously essential if the teenager is to think about the future systematically. The preschool child plays "dress up" by putting on real clothes. The teenager *thinks* about options and possibilities, imagining herself in different roles, going to college or not going to college, marrying or not marrying, having children or not. She can imagine future consequences of actions she might take now, so that some kind of long-term planning becomes possible (C. Lewis, 1981).

RESEARCH REPORT
An Australian Study Illustrating Sex Differences in Body Image Among Adolescents

Susan Paxton and her colleagues (Paxton et al., 1991) have recently reported on a study of Australian high school students that illustrates that the preoccupation with thinness among teenage girls is not restricted to the United States, and shows what that preoccupation can do to girls' body images.

A total of 562 teenagers, in grades 7 through 11, reported on their current weight and height and their judgment of that weight as underweight, good weight, or overweight. They also responded to questions about the effect it might have on their lives if they were thinner, and they described their weight control behaviors, including dieting and exercise.

Paxton reports a number of particularly interesting results. First of all, among teenagers who were actually normal weight for their height, 30.1 percent of the girls but only 6.8 percent of the boys described themselves as overweight. Thus the girls *perceive* themselves as too fat when they are actually normal. Furthermore, the majority of girls thought that being thinner would make them happier; a few even thought that being thinner would make them more intelligent. Boys, in contrast, thought that being thinner would actually have some negative effects.

Not surprisingly, these differences in the perception of thinness were reflected in dieting behavior in this sample. Twenty-three percent of the girls reported that they went on a crash diet at least occasionally; 4 percent said they did so once or twice a week. The comparable percentages for boys were 9 percent and 1 percent, respectively. More girls than boys also reported using diet pills, laxatives, and vomiting, although the rates were low for both sexes. Once again, we see internal models at work.

✱ **Systematic Problem Solving.** Another important feature of formal operations is the ability to search systematically and methodically for the answer to a problem. To study this, Piaget and his colleague Barbel Inhelder (Inhelder & Piaget, 1958) presented adolescents with complex tasks, mostly drawn from the physical sciences. In one of these tasks, subjects were given varying lengths of string and a set of objects of various weights that could be tied to the strings to make a swinging pendulum. They were shown how to start the pendulum by pushing the weight with differing amounts of force and by holding the weight at different heights. The subject's task was to figure out which one or which combination of length of string, weight of object, force of push, or height of push determines the "period" of the pendulum, which is amount of time for one swing. (In case you have forgotten your high school physics, the answer is that only the length of the string affects the period of the pendulum.)

If you give this task to a concrete operational child, she will usually try out many different combinations of length, weight, force, and height in an inefficient way. She might try a heavy weight on a long string, and then a light weight on a short string. Because both string length and weight have changed, there is no way to draw a clear conclusion about either factor.

In contrast, an adolescent using a formal operations approach is likely to be more organized, attempting to vary just one of the four factors at a time. She may try a heavy object with a short string, then with a medium string, then with a long one. After that, she might try a light object with the three lengths of string. Of course not all adolescents (or all adults, for that matter) are quite this methodical in their approach. But there is a very dramatic difference in the overall strategy used by 10-year-olds and 15-year-olds that marks the shift from concrete to formal operations.

✱ **Logic.** Another facet of this shift is the appearance of deductive logic in the child's repertoire of skills. I mentioned in Chapter 9 that the concrete operational child is able to use inductive reasoning, which involves arriving at a conclusion or a rule based on a lot of individual experiences. The more difficult kind of reasoning, deductive reasoning, involves if/then relationships: "If all people are equal, then you and I must be equal." Children as young as 4 or 5 can understand some such relationships if the premises given are factually true. But only at adolescence are young people able to understand and use the basic *logical* relationship (e.g., Ward & Overton, 1990).

A great deal of the logic of science is of this deductive type. We begin with a theory and propose, "If this theory is correct, then I should observe such and such." In doing this, we are going well beyond our observations. We are conceiving things that we have never seen that *ought* to be true or observable. We can think of this change as part of a general decentering process that began much earlier in cognitive development. The preoperational child gradually moves away from his egocentrism and comes to be able to take the physical or emotional perspective of others. During formal operations, the child takes another step by freeing himself even from his reliance upon specific experiences.

Post-Piagetian Work on Formal Operations

Most of the current work on formal operations has centered on two questions: (1) Is there really a change in the child's thinking at adolescence, and if so, when does it happen? (2) Why don't we see this change in every youngster?

✱ **Is There Really a Change?** All the recent research tells us that Piaget was correct about the existence of this new level of reasoning among adolescents. As Edith Neimark says (1982, p. 493), "An enormous amount of evidence from an assortment of tasks shows that adolescents and adults are capable of feats of reasoning not attained under normal circumstances by [younger] children, and that these abilities develop fairly rapidly during the ages of about 11 to 15."

Can you think of any real-life examples of tasks that demand this sort of systematic problem solving?

High school science classes, such as this one in Botswana, may be one of the first places where adolescents are required to use deductive logic—a skill Piaget did not think was present until the period of formal operations.

A cross-sectional study by Susan Martorano (1977), while not recent, is still a good illustration. She tested 20 girls at each of four grades (sixth, eighth, tenth, and twelfth) on 10 different tasks that require one or more of the formal operations skills. Some of her results are in Figure 11.5 (see page 266). You can see that older students generally did better, with the biggest improvement in scores occurring between eighth and tenth grades, between ages 13 and 15.

You can also see that the problems are not equally difficult, just as is true of the classic concrete operations tasks, which you may recall from Figure 9.2. Formal operations problems that required the child to consider two or more separate factors simultaneously were harder for Martorano's subjects than were problems that simply required the child to search for the logical possibilities. For example, the easiest problem, called *colored tokens*, asks the child how many different pairs of colors can be made using tokens of six different colors. This requires only thinking up and organizing possible solutions. The hardest problems require understanding multiple, simultaneous causation. The "balance" problem—which is very similar to the balance problem Siegler used to study the development of rules (recall Figure 9.4)—requires a youngster to predict whether or not two varying weights, hung at varying distances on either side of a scale, will balance. To solve this problem using formal operations, the teenager must consider both weight and distance simultaneously. Piaget's observations, and Martorano's results, suggest that this is a fairly late development.

Does Everybody Reach Formal Operations?   Apparently not. Piaget's own early evidence pointed to the possibility that many adolescents failed to develop formal operational reasoning. That possibility has been repeatedly confirmed in more recent research. Keating (1980) estimates that only about 50 to 60 percent of 18- to 20-year-olds in Western countries seem to use formal operations at all, let alone consistently. In Martorano's study, only 10 percent of the twelfth grade subjects showed formal operations on all the problems, and none of the younger students did. In non-Western countries the rates are even lower.

Why? There are several possibilities. One is that the usual methods of measuring formal operations are simply extremely difficult or unclear. When the instructions are made clearer, or the subjects are given hints or rules, they can demonstrate some aspects of formal operations (e.g., Danner & Day, 1977).

A second possibility is that expertise plays a central role. Most of us may have some

Figure 11.5 In this cross-sectional study, 20 girls of each age were tested on four different formal operations tasks. On three of the four tasks, you can see a rapid increase in skill between 13 and 15. The problems also obviously differ in difficulty. (*Source:* Martorano, 1977, p. 670. Copyright by the American Psychological Association.)

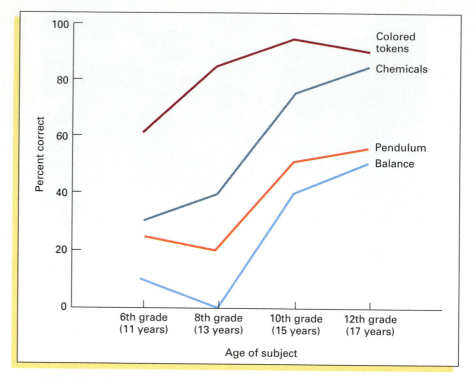

formal operational ability, but we only apply it to topics or tasks with which we are familiar. For example, I use formal operations reasoning about psychology because it is an area I know well. But I am a lot less skillful at applying the same kind of reasoning to fixing my car—about which I know next to nothing. Willis Overton and his colleagues (Overton et al., 1987) have found considerable support for this possibility in their research. They found that as many as 90 percent of adolescents could solve quite complex logic problems if they were stated using familiar content, while only half could solve an identical logical problem when it was stated in abstract language.

Still a third possibility is that most of our everyday experiences and tasks do not require formal operations. Concrete operations is quite sufficient most of the time. So we get into a cognitive rut, applying our usual mode of thinking to new problems as well. We can kick our thinking up a notch under some circumstances, especially if someone reminds us that it would be useful to do so, but we simply don't rehearse formal operations very much.

The fact that formal operations is found more often among young people or adults in industrialized cultures may be interpreted in the same way. Because of the high technology and the complexity of our lives, there is somewhat more demand for formal operational thought. By this argument, all nonretarded teenagers and adults are thought to have the *capacity* for formal logic, but only those whose lives demand its development will actually acquire it.

The Development of Moral Reasoning

Another aspect of cognitive development that interested Piaget and has continued to fascinate researchers is the child's reasoning about moral questions. How does a child decide what is good or bad, right or wrong, in his own and other people's behavior? When you serve on a jury, you must make such a judgment, as you do in everyday life: Should you give the store clerk back the excess change she handed you? Should you turn in a

Which of these explanations of the relative lack of formal operations among adolescents and adults do you find most persuasive? Think about your own experience. Do you use this type of thinking consistently, or only in certain situations? What sort of circumstances are most likely to trigger its use?

classmate you see cheating on an exam? What about someone who lies in a job interview? Does your judgment change if you know that the person desperately needs the job to support his handicapped child?

These questions do not become relevant only at adolescence or in adulthood. Children younger than adolescents clearly make such judgments as well. But because several key changes in moral reasoning appear to coincide with adolescence or with the emergence of formal operations reasoning, this is a good place to introduce you to this very intriguing body of theory and research.

Do you think that an expert car mechanic, like this one, uses formal operations in her work?

Lawrence Kohlberg's Theory.   Piaget was the first to offer a description of the development of moral reasoning (Piaget, 1932), but the theorist whose work has had the most powerful impact has been Lawrence Kohlberg (1964, 1976, 1980, 1981; Colby et al., 1983), who went beyond Piaget's original formulation. Kohlberg pioneered the practice of assessing moral reasoning by presenting a subject with a series of dilemmas in story form, each of which highlighted a specific moral issue, such as the value of human life. One of the most famous is the dilemma of Heinz:

> In Europe, a woman was near death from a special kind of cancer. There was one drug that the doctors thought might save her. It was a form of radium that a druggist in the same town had recently discovered. The drug was expensive to make, but the druggist was charging ten times what the drug cost him to make. He paid $200 for the radium and charged $2000 for a small dose of the drug. The sick woman's husband, Heinz, went to everyone he knew to borrow the money, but he could only get together about $1000 which is half of what it cost. He told the druggist that his wife was dying, and asked him to sell it cheaper or let him pay later. But the druggist said, "No, I discovered the drug and I'm going to make money from it." So Heinz got desperate and broke into the man's store to steal the drug for his wife. (Kohlberg & Elfenbein, 1975, p. 621)

After hearing this story, the child or young person is asked a series of questions, such as whether Heinz should have stolen the drug. What if Heinz didn't love his wife? Would that change anything? What if the person dying was a stranger? Should Heinz steal the drug anyway?

On the basis of answers to dilemmas like this one, Kohlberg concluded that there were three main levels of moral reasoning, with two substages within each level, as summarized in Table 11.3.

At Level I, **preconventional morality**, the child's (or teenager's or even adult's) judgments are based on sources of authority who are close by and physically superior to himself—usually the parents. Just as his descriptions of others at this same stage are largely external, so the standards the child uses to judge rightness or wrongness are external rather than internal. In particular, it is the outcome or consequence of his actions that determines the rightness or wrongness of those actions.

In Stage 1 of this level—the *punishment and obedience orientation*—the child relies on the physical consequences of some action to decide if it is right or wrong. If he is punished, the behavior was wrong; if he is not punished, it was right. He is obedient to adults because they are bigger and stronger.

In Stage 2—*individualism, instrumental purpose, and exchange*—the child begins to operate on the principle that you should do things that bring reward and avoid things that bring punishment. For this reason, the stage is sometimes called a position of *naive hedonism*. If it feels good or brings pleasant results, it is good. There is some beginning of concern for other people during this phase, but only if that concern can be expressed as something that benefits the child himself as well. So he can enter into agreements like "If you help me, I'll help you."

TABLE 11.3 Kohlberg's Stages of Moral Development

LEVEL 1: PRECONVENTIONAL MORALITY

Stage 1: Punishment and obedience orientation. The child decides what is wrong on the basis of what he is punished for. Obedience is valued for its own sake, but the child obeys because the adults have superior power.

Stage 2: Individualism, instrumental purpose, and exchange. The child follows rules when it is in his immediate interest. What is good is what brings pleasant results. Right is also what is fair, what is an equal exchange, a deal, an agreement.

LEVEL 2: CONVENTIONAL MORALITY

Stage 3: Mutual interpersonal expectations, relationships, and interpersonal conformity. The family or small group to which the child belongs becomes important. Moral actions are those that live up to others' expectations. "Being good" becomes important for its own sake, and the child generally values trust, loyalty, respect, gratitude, and keeping mutual relationships.

Stage 4: Social system and conscience (law and order). A shift in focus from the young person's family and close groups to the larger society. Good is fulfilling duties one has agreed to. Laws are to be upheld except in extreme cases. Contributing to society is also seen as good.

LEVEL 3: PRINCIPLED OR POSTCONVENTIONAL MORALITY

Stage 5: Social contract or utility and individual rights. Acting so as to achieve the "greatest good for the greatest number." The teenager or adult is aware that there are different views and values, that values are relative. Laws and rules should be upheld in order to preserve the social order, but they can be changed. Still, there are some basic nonrelative values, such as the importance of each person's life and liberty, that should be upheld no matter what.

Stage 6: Universal ethical principles. The adult develops and follows self-chosen ethical principles in determining what is right. Because laws usually conform to those principles, laws should be obeyed; but when there is a difference between law and conscience, conscience dominates. At this stage, the ethical principles followed are part of an articulated, integrated, carefully thought out and consistently followed system of values and principles.

Sources: After Kohlberg, 1976, and Lickona, 1978.

As illustration, here are some responses to variations of the Heinz dilemma, drawn from studies of children and teenagers in a number of different cultures, all of which would be rated as Stage 2:

> "He should steal the food for his wife because if she dies he'll have to pay for the funeral, and that costs a lot." (Taiwan)

> He should steal the drug because "he should protect the life of his wife so he doesn't have to stay alone in life." (Puerto Rico)

> [Suppose it wasn't his wife who was starving but his best friend. Should he steal the food for his friend?] "Yes, because one day when he is hungry his friend would help." (Turkey) (All quotes from Snarey, 1985, p. 221.)

At the next major level, **conventional morality**, there is a shift from judgments based on external consequences and personal gain to judgments based on rules or norms of a group to which the child belongs, whether that group is the family, the peer group, a church, or the nation. What the chosen reference group defines as right or good *is* right or good in the child's view, and the child internalizes these norms to a considerable extent.

Stage 3 (the first stage of Level 2) is the stage of *mutual interpersonal expectations, relationships, and interpersonal conformity* (sometimes also called the *good boy/nice girl* stage). Children at this stage believe that good behavior is what pleases other people. They value trust, loyalty, respect, gratitude, and maintenance of mutual relationships. Andy, a boy Kohlberg interviewed who was at Stage 3, said:

I try to do things for my parents, they've always done things for you. I try to do everything my mother says, I try to please her. Like she wants me to be a doctor and I want to, too, and she's helping me get up there. (Kohlberg, 1964, p. 401)

Another mark of this third stage is that the child begins to make judgments based on intentions as well as on outward behavior. If someone "means well" or "didn't mean to do it," their wrongdoing is seen as less serious than if they did it "on purpose."

Stage 4, the second stage of the conventional level, shows the child turning to larger social groups for her norms. Kohlberg labeled this the stage of *social system and conscience*. It is also sometimes called the *law and order orientation*. People reasoning at this stage focus on doing their duty, respecting authority, following rules and laws. The emphasis is less on what is pleasing to particular people (as in Stage 3) and more on adhering to a complex set of regulations. However, the regulations themselves are not questioned.

The transition to Level 3, **principled morality,** (also called *postconventional moral reasoning*) is marked by several changes, the most important of which is a shift in the source of authority. At Level 1 children see authority as totally outside themselves; at Level 2, the judgments or rules of external authority are internalized, but they are not questioned or analyzed; at Level 3, a new kind of personal authority emerges in which individual choices are made, with individual judgments based on self-chosen principles.

In Stage 5 at this level, called the *social contract* orientation by Kohlberg, we see the beginning of such self-chosen principles. Rules, laws, and regulations are not seen as irrelevant; they are important ways of ensuring fairness. But people operating at this level also see times when the rules, laws, and regulations need to be ignored or changed. Our American system of government is based on moral reasoning of this kind. We have provisions for changing laws and for allowing personal protests against a given law, such as during the civil rights protests of the 1960s, the Vietnam war protests of the 1960s and 1970s, or the protests against apartheid in the 1980s.

In his original writing about moral development, Kohlberg also included a sixth stage, the *universal ethical principles* orientation. People who reason in this way assume personal responsibility for their own actions, based upon fundamental and universal principles, such as justice and basic respect for persons. Kohlberg later waffled a good bit on whether such a stage was the logical and necessary end point of the sequence, and on whether people reasoning at such a level actually existed (e.g., Kohlberg, 1978; Kohlberg, Levine & Hewer, 1983; Kohlberg, 1984). If they exist at all, it seems likely that such universal ethical principles guide the moral reasoning of only a few very unusual individuals— perhaps those who devote their lives to humanitarian causes, such as Mother Teresa or Gandhi.

In all of this, it is important to understand that what determines the stage or level of a person's moral judgment is not the specific moral choice a young person or adult makes, but the kind of logic and the sources of authority the individual uses to justify that choice. For example, either choice (that Heinz should steal the drug or that he should not) could be justified with logic at any given stage. I've already given you some examples of a Stage 2 justification for Heinz's stealing the drug; here's a Stage 5 justification of the same choice, drawn from a study in India:

[What if Heinz was stealing to save the life of his pet animal instead of his wife?] "If Heinz saves an animal's life his action will be commendable. The right use of the drug is to administer it to the needy. There is some difference, of course— human life is more evolved and hence of greater importance in the scheme of nature—but an animal's life is not altogether bereft of importance. . ." (From Snarey, 1985, p. 223, drawn originally from Vasudev, 1983, p. 7.)

If you compare this answer to the ones I quoted before, you can clearly see the difference

Imagine a society in which everyone handled moral issues at Kohlberg's Stage 3. Now think about one in which everyone operated at Stage 5. How would those two societies be likely to differ?

Can you tell from this picture what stage or level of moral reasoning these antiapartheid protestors are using to support their actions?

in the *form* of reasoning used, even though the action being justified is precisely the same.

Kohlberg argued that this sequence of reasoning is both universal and hierarchically organized, just as Piaget thought his proposed stages of cognitive development were universal and hierarchical. That is, each stage follows and grows from the preceding one and has some internal consistency. Individuals should not move "down" the sequence, but only "upward" along the stages, if they move at all. Kohlberg did *not* suggest that all individuals eventually progress through all six stages, nor even that each stage is tied to specific ages. But he insisted that the order is invariant and universal. Let me take a critical look at these claims.

Age and Moral Reasoning.   Kohlberg's own findings, confirmed by many other researchers (Rest, 1983; Walker, de Vries & Trevethan, 1987; Colby et al., 1983), show that preconventional reasoning (Stages 1 and 2) is dominant in elementary school, and Stage 2 reasoning is still evident among many early adolescents. Conventional reasoning (Stages 3 and 4) emerges as important in middle adolescence and remains the most common form of moral reasoning in adulthood. Postconventional reasoning (Stages 5 and 6) is relatively rare, even in adulthood. For example, among men in their forties and fifties who have been part of the Berkeley longitudinal study, 13 percent were rated as using Stage 5 moral reasoning (Gibson, 1990). You can see the whole pattern of age changes in Figure 11.6, which shows the results from Kohlberg's own longitudinal study of 58 boys, first interviewed when they were 10, and now followed for more than 20 years (Colby et al., 1983).

Sequence of Stages.   The evidence also seems fairly strong that the stages follow one another in the sequence Kohlberg proposed. In the several long-term longitudinal studies of teenagers and young adults in the United States, Israel, and Turkey (Colby et al., 1983; Nisan & Kohlberg, 1982; Snarey, Reimer & Kohlberg, 1985), changes in the form of reasoning a subject used nearly always occurred in the hypothesized order. Subjects did not skip stages, and only about 5 to 7 percent of the time was there any indication of regression—a rate that is consistent with what we know about the reliability of the measures being used. Shorter-term longitudinal studies (Walker, 1989), show similar patterns of change. On the whole, I agree with James Rest (1983) that the evidence is "fairly compelling" that moral judgment changes over time in the sequence Kohlberg describes.

Universality.   But is this sequence of stages only a phenomenon of Western culture? Or has Kohlberg uncovered a genuinely universal process? Thus far, variations of Kohlberg's dilemmas have been used with children in 27 different cultural areas, including

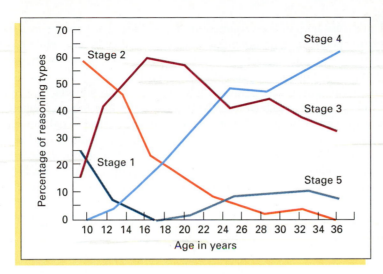

Figure 11.6 These findings are from Colby and Kohlberg's long-term longitudinal study of a group of boys who were asked about Kohlberg's moral dilemmas every few years from age 10 through early adulthood. As they got older, the stage or level of their answers changed, with conventional reasoning appearing fairly strongly at high school age. Postconventional or principled reasoning, though, was not very common at any age. (*Source:* Colby et al., 1983, Figure 1, p. 46. © The Society for Research in Child Development.)

both Western and non-Western, both industrialized and nonindustrialized (Snarey, 1985).

John Snarey, who has reviewed and analyzed these many studies, notes several things in support of Kohlberg's position: (1) In studies of children, an increase with age in the stage of reasoning used is found consistently. (2) The few longitudinal studies report "strikingly similar findings" (1985, p. 215), with subjects moving upward in the stage sequence with few reversals. (3) Cultures differ in the highest level of reasoning observed. In complex urban societies (both Western and non-Western), Stage 5 is typically the highest stage observed, while in those cultures Snarey calls "folk" societies, Stage 4 is typically the highest. Collectively, this evidence seems to provide quite strong support for the universality of Kohlberg's stage sequence.

Moral Development: A Critique. Kohlberg's theory about the development of moral reasoning has been one of the most provocative theories in all of developmental psychology. There have been over 1000 studies exploring or testing aspects of the theory, and several competing theories have been proposed. The remarkable thing is how well the theory has stood the test of this barrage of research and commentary. There does appear to be a clear set of stages in the development of moral reasoning, and these stages seem to be universal.

Still, the theory has not emerged unscathed. Some psychologists are less impressed than Snarey with the data on universality (e.g., Shweder, Mahapatra & Miller, 1987). Also troubling is the fact that so few teenagers or adults seem to reason at the postconventional level (Stages 5 or 6). The effective range of variation is from Stage 2 to Stage 4, which is not nearly so interesting or impressive as is the full range of stages (e.g., Shweder et al., 1987).

But by far the most vocal critics have been those who have pointed out that Kohlberg is really not talking about all aspects of "moral reasoning." Instead, as Kohlberg himself acknowledged in his later writings (Kohlberg, Levine & Hewer, 1983), he is talking about the development of reasoning about *justice and fairness*. We might also want to know about other ethical bases than justice, such as an ethic based on concern for others or for relationships. In this category, the best-known critic has been Carol Gilligan.

Gilligan's Ethic of Caring. Carol Gilligan (1982a, 1982b, 1987; Gilligan & Wiggins, 1987) is fundamentally dissatisfied with Kohlberg's focus on justice and fairness as the defining features of moral reasoning. Gilligan argues that there are, in fact, at least two distinct "moral orientations," justice and care. Each has its own central injunction: not to treat others unfairly (justice) and not to turn away from someone in need (caring).

Boys and girls learn both of these injunctions, but Gilligan has hypothesized that girls are more likely to operate from an orientation of caring or connection, while boys are more likely to operate from an orientation of justice or fairness. Because of these differences, they tend to perceive moral dilemmas quite differently.

Given the emerging evidence on sex differences in styles of interaction and in friendship patterns, which I talked about in both Chapters 8 and 10, Gilligan's hypothesis makes some sense. Perhaps girls, focused more on intimacy in their relationships, judge moral dilemmas by different criteria. But in fact, research on moral dilemmas has not shown that boys are more likely to use justice reasoning or that girls more often use care reasoning. Several studies of adults do show such a pattern (e.g., Lyons, 1983), but studies of children generally have not (Smetana, Killen & Turiel, 1991; Walker, de Vries & Trevethan, 1987).

For example, Walker (Walker et al., 1987) scored children's answers to moral dilemmas using both Kohlberg's fairness scheme and Gilligan's criteria for a care orientation. He found no sex difference for either hypothetical dilemmas like the Heinz dilemma or for the real-life dilemmas suggested by the children themselves. Only among adults did Walker find a difference, in the direction that Gilligan would expect.

Despite this lack of support for her central hypothesis regarding sex differences in the form of moral reasoning, I am not ready to discard all of Gilligan's views, primarily because the questions she is asking seem to me to fit so well with the newer research on sex differences in styles of relationship. The fact that we typically find no differences between boys and girls in their tendencies to use care versus justice orientations does not mean that there are not real differences in the assumptions males and females bring to relationships or to moral judgments.

Moral Judgment and Behavior.   Kohlberg's theory has also sometimes been criticized on the grounds that moral behavior does not always match the level of moral reasoning. Kohlberg never said that there should be a one-to-one correspondence between the two. Reasoning at Stage 4 (conventional reasoning) does not mean that you will never cheat or always be kind to your mother. Still, the form of reasoning a young person typically applies to moral problems should have at least *some* connection with real-life choices. Further, Kohlberg argued that the higher the level of reasoning a young person shows, the stronger the link to behavior ought to become. Thus young people reasoning at Stage 4 or Stage 5 should be more likely to follow their own rules or reasoning than should children reasoning at lower levels.

Do you think that a person's stage or level of moral reasoning has any impact on political behavior, such as voting or joining a political party? Can you generate a hypothesis about such a link and figure out how you might test that hypothesis?

For example, Kohlberg and Candee (1984) studied students involved in some of the precursors to the Vietnam war protests at Berkeley in the late 1960s. They interviewed and tested the moral judgment levels of a group that had participated at a sit-in in the university administration building, and a group randomly chosen from the campus population. Of those who thought it was morally right to hold a sit-in, nearly three-fourths of those reasoning at Stages 4 or 5 actually participated, compared to only about a quarter of those reasoning at Stage 3. Thus, the higher the stage of reasoning, the more consistent the behavior was with the reasoning.

In other studies, Kohlberg and others approached the question simply by asking whether there is a link between stage of moral reasoning and the probability of making some "moral choice," such as not cheating. For example, Kohlberg (1975) found that only 15 percent of students reasoning at the principled level (Stage 5) cheated when they were given an opportunity, while 55 percent of conventional level and 70 percent of preconventional students cheated.

Researchers have also compared the level of moral reasoning of groups that arguably differ in moral behavior, such as delinquents versus nondelinquents. In the great majority of cases, delinquents are found to reason at lower stages (Chandler & Moran, 1990;

Smetana, 1990), even when the two groups are carefully matched for education and social class.

Yet despite this abundance of evidence for a link between moral reasoning and behavior, no one has found the correspondence to be perfect. After all, in Kohlberg's studies, 15 percent of the principled moral reasoners did cheat, and a quarter of Stage 4 and Stage 5 reasoners who thought it morally right to participate in a sit-in did not do so. As Kohlberg said, "One can reason in terms of principles and not live up to those principles." (Kohlberg, 1975, p. 672.)

What else besides level of reasoning might matter? We don't have all the answers to that question yet, but some influences are clear. First, simple habits are involved. Every day, each of us faces small moral situations that we have learned to handle in a completely automatic way. Sometimes these automatic choices may be at a lower level of reasoning than we would use if we sat down and thought about it. I may make the same donation to a particular charity every year without stopping to consider whether I could now afford more, or whether that charity is really the place where my money could best be used.

Second, in any given situation, even though you might think it morally right to take some action, you may not see that action as morally *necessary* or obligatory. I might be able to make a good argument for the moral acceptability of a sit-in protest, but still not see it as my *own* duty or responsibility to participate.

A third element is the cost to the person of doing something helpful or of refraining from doing something morally "wrong," like cheating. If helping someone else has little cost in time, money, or effort, then most children and adults will help, regardless of their overall level of moral reasoning. But when there is some cost, we find a more consistent correlation between level of reasoning and behavior. This suggests the more general principle that moral reasoning becomes a factor in moral behavior only when there is something about the situation that heightens the sense of moral conflict, such as when there is a cost involved or when the individual feels personally responsible.

Finally, there are often competing motives or ethics at work as well, such as the pressure of a peer group or motives for self-protection or self-reward. In early adolescence, for example, when the impact of the peer group is particularly strong, we might expect a strong group effect on moral actions. So kids this age may be most susceptible to group decisions to go joyriding, to sneak beer into a party, or to soap the teachers' car windows on Halloween (Berndt, 1979), even when their own moral standards would argue against such behavior.

Thus moral *behavior* results from a complex of influences, of which the level of moral reasoning is only one element. Our knowledge about these links is improving, but we badly need to know more, both about group pressure and about all the other factors that lead each of us to behave in ways that are less thoughtful, considerate, or fair than we "know how" to do.

▶ Individual Differences

The developmental patterns I have been describing tell us—as usual—about the average or normal pattern. But they do not tell us about all the variation around that average. To add to my earlier discussions of individual differences, let me talk about one variation that seems especially significant among adolescents: early versus late puberty.

★ Early Versus Late Pubertal Development

Among adolescents, children of the same age may range from Stage 1 to Stage 5 in the steps of sexual maturation. These variations are not trivial, especially for a child who is unusually early or unusually late in development. What happens to a girl who begins to

Early developing girls, like the one on the right, report much less positive adolescent experiences and more depression than on-time or later developing girls, like the one on the left.

THE REAL WORLD
Application of Kohlberg's Theory to Education

A lot of what I have said about Kohlberg's theory may seem pretty abstract to you. In Kohlberg's own view, though, there were many potential practical implications for education. The question that interested him was whether children or young people can be taught higher stages of moral reasoning and, if so, whether such a change in moral reasoning would change their behavior in school.

We know from early research by Elliot Turiel (1966) that at least under some conditions, exposing young people to moral arguments one step above their own level of reasoning can lead to an increase in their level of moral judgment. Young people who attend college also continue to show increases in moral stage scores, while those who quit school after high school typically show no further increase (Rest & Thoma, 1985). Because arguments about moral and philosophical issues in class and over coffee (or a few beers) in the wee small hours of the night are one of the hallmarks of the college experience for many young people, perhaps it is the discussion—the exposure to other people's ideas, other people's logic, that makes a difference.

If that's true, what would happen if high school students were given systematic opportunities to explore moral dilemmas? Would that change them, too? Apparently it can.

One educational application has involved the creation of special discussion classes in which moral dilemmas similar to those Kohlberg devised are presented and argued. In the process, the teacher attempts to model higher levels of reasoning. Other programs are broader based, involving not just discussion, but also cross-age teaching (to encourage nurturance and caring), empathy training, cooperation games, volunteer service work, and the like. The dozens of studies on the effectiveness of programs of this kind show that on average, the programs succeed in shifting young people's moral reasoning upward about half a stage (Schaefli, Rest & Thoma, 1985). The largest effects are generally found in programs focusing exclusively on discussions of moral dilemmas, but broader-based programs work, too. Courses lasting longer than three or four weeks seem to work better than very short programs, and the effects are generally larger with older students—college students and even post-college age adults. Among high school students there is some impact, but it is not as large.

An even broader based educational application, designed to change students' moral behavior as much as their moral reasoning, has been the development of the so-called "just community." These experimental schools, typically set up as a "school

within a school," operate as a kind of laboratory for moral education (Higgins, 1991; Higgins, Power & Kohlberg, 1984; Kohlberg & Higgins, 1987; Power & Reimer, 1978).

Kohlberg insisted that the crucial feature of these just communities must be complete democracy: each teacher and student has one vote, and community issues and problems have to be discussed in open forum. Rules are typically created and discussed at weekly communitywide meetings. In this way, students become *responsible* for the rules and for one another.

In experimental schools following this model, Kohlberg and his coworkers found that students' level of Kohlbergian moral reasoning shifted upward, as did their reasoning about responsibility and caring. The link between moral reasoning and moral behavior was strengthened as well. For example, stealing and other petty crime virtually disappeared in one school after the students had repeatedly discussed the problem and arrived—painfully—at a solution that emphasized the fact that stealing damaged the whole community, and thus the whole community had to be responsible. For example, after one stealing episode the group agreed that if the stolen money was not returned (anonymously) by a specified date, each community member would be assessed 15 cents to make up the victim's loss (Higgins, 1991).

This effect of just communities makes sense when you think about the factors that seem to affect moral behavior. In these schools, two elements were added that would tend to support more moral behavior: a sense of personal responsibility and a group norm of higher moral reasoning and caring.

Among teenagers, the emotional impact of group pressure may be especially significant, in addition to whatever effect there may be from exposure to more mature arguments. If you are arguing your position about some moral dilemma but find yourself in the minority, the "social disequilibrium" you feel may help to make you more open to other arguments and thus to change your view. Certainly in experimental schools like those studied by Kohlberg, this added emotional impact is no doubt part of the process (Haan, 1985).

Classes in moral education have not proven to be the "quick fix" that many educators hoped for. The gains in moral reasoning are not huge and may not be reflected in increases in moral behavior in the school unless there is an effort to alter the overall moral atmosphere of the entire school. But these programs do show that there are provocative and helpful applications of at least some of the abstract developmental theories.

menstruate at 10 or a boy who does not go through a growth spurt until age 16? Do they turn out differently?

A recent burst of research on this question has led to an interesting and complex hypothesis that once again points to the importance of internal models. The general idea is that each young child or teenager has an internal model about the "normal" or "right" timing for puberty (Faust, 1983; Lerner, 1985, 1987; Petersen, 1987). Each girl has an internal model about the "right age" to develop breasts or begin menstruation; each boy has an internal model or image about when it is right to begin to grow a beard or for his voice to get lower. According to this hypothesis, it is the discrepancy between an adolescent's expectation and what actually happens that determines the psychological effect, just as it is the discrepancy between goals and achievements that determines self-esteem. Those whose development occurs outside the desired or expected range are likely to think less well of themselves, to be less happy with their bodies and with the process of puberty, perhaps have fewer friends, or experience other signs of distress.

In our culture today, most young people seem to share the expectation that pubertal changes will happen sometime between ages 12 and 14; anything earlier is seen as "too soon," anything later is thought of as late. If you compare these expectations to the actual average timing of pubertal changes, you'll see that such a norm includes girls who are average in development and boys who are *early*. So we should expect that these two groups—normal developing girls and early developing boys—should have the best psychological functioning. Early maturing boys may have an added advantage because they are more likely to be of the *mesomorphic* body type, with wide shoulders and a large amount of muscle. This body type is consistently preferred at all ages, and because boys with this body type tend to be good at sports, the early developing boy should be particularly advantaged.

Figure 11.7 shows the specific predictions graphically. Early boys should be best off, followed by average boys and girls. The least well off should be late developing boys and early developing girls. And in fact, that is generally what the newer research shows. Girls who are early developers (before 11 or 12 for major body changes) show consistently more negative body images, such as thinking themselves too fat (Tobin-Richards, Boxer & Petersen, 1983; Petersen, 1987; Simmons, Blyth & McKinney, 1983). Such girls are also more likely to get into trouble in school and at home (Magnusson, Stattin & Allen, 1986) and are more likely to be depressed (Rierdan & Koff, 1991). There are also hints that for girls, very late development is also somewhat negative, but the effect of lateness is not so striking for girls.

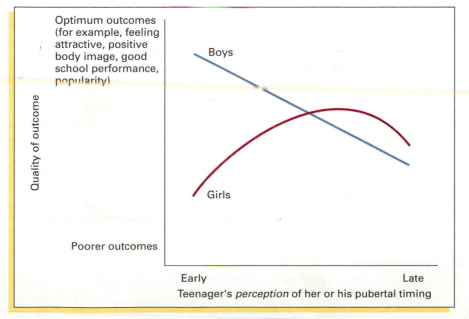

Figure 11.7 According to this model of the effects of early and late puberty, the best position for girls is to be "on time," while for boys the best position is to be "early." For both sexes, however, it is the *perception* of earliness or lateness, and not the actual timing, that is thought to be critical. (*Source:* adapted from Tobin-Richards et al., 1983, p. 137.)

Quality of outcome

Optimum outcomes (for example, feeling attractive, positive body image, good school performance, popularity)

Boys

Girls

Poorer outcomes

Early   Late
Teenager's *perception* of her or his pubertal timing

Among boys, as Figure 11.7 predicts, the relationship is essentially linear. The earlier the boy's development, the more positive his body image, the better he does in school, the less trouble he gets into, and the more friends he has (e.g., Duke et al., 1982).

In nearly all of these studies, earliness or lateness has been defined in terms of the actual physical changes. The results are even clearer when researchers have instead asked teenagers about their internal model of earliness or lateness. For example, Rierdan, Koff, and Stubbs (1989) have found that the negativeness of a girl's menarcheal experience was predicted by her *subjective* sense of earliness; those who perceived themselves as early reported a more negative experience. But such a negative experience was *unrelated* to the actual age of her menarche.

This link between the internal model and the outcome is especially vivid in a study of ballet dancers by Jeanne Brooks-Gunn (Brooks-Gunn & Warren, 1985; Brooks-Gunn, 1987). She studied 14- to 18-year-old girls, some of whom were serious ballet dancers studying at a national ballet company school. In this group, a very lean, almost prepubescent body is highly desirable. Given this, we would expect that among dancers, those who were very late in pubertal development would actually have a better image of themselves than those who were on time. And that is exactly what Brooks-Gunn found. Among nondancers the same age, normal-time menarche was associated with a better body image than late menarche, but exactly the reverse was true for the dancers.

Thus, it seems to be the discrepancy or mismatch between the desired or expected pattern and a youngster's actual pattern that is critical, not the absolute age of pubertal development. Because the majority of young people share similar expectations, we can see common effects of early or late development. But to predict the effect of early or late development in any individual teenager, we would need to know more about her or his internal model.

Do you remember your own puberty as very early, early, on time, or late? Do you think that perception had any effect on your overall experience of adolescence?

▶ The Larger Culture: Junior High and High School

Just as the school experience is formative in middle childhood, school is a central force in the lives of adolescents. But the effect is different in the two cases. In middle childhood, school experience is focused on learning a whole set of basic skills and specific knowledge—how to read, how to do mathematics, how to write. While there is certainly more specific knowledge conveyed to students in junior high and high school, and schooling may contribute to the development of formal operational thought, schooling serves a host of other functions in adolescence. Not only is it an arena in which teenagers can practice new heterosexual social skills, it is also the setting in which society attempts to shape young people's attitudes and behaviors to prepare them for adult life. High schools teach driver's education, "family life" education including sexuality, home economics, civics, current affairs. Guidance counselors may also help the teenager decide about college or about future job options, and organized sports programs offer opportunities for nonacademic success (or failure).

Despite this very broad range of educational roles played by the high school, it is academic success or school completion that most researchers have focused on and that society sees as one key measure of an adolescent's success or failure. So let me say a word or two about the two ends of the continuum, those who achieve academic success and those who drop out of school.

⚡Those Who Achieve

The best single predictor of a student's academic performance in high school is IQ. It is true that middle class kids are more likely to succeed in school and that children growing up in poverty environments are less likely to do well, but social class itself is only weakly related to school achievement. Within each racial group and each social class group, it is those with higher IQ who are most likely to get good grades, complete high school, and go on to college.

Furthermore, adolescent IQ and school grades both predict adult job success to at least some degree (Barrett & Depinet, 1991). Myriad studies of military jobs, for example, show correlations in the range of .45 to .55 between scores on IQ-like tests given when young men and women entered the military, and their later proficiency and success at a wide range of jobs (Hunter & Hunter, 1984).

Outside of the military, the same general relationship holds, although education plays a key intervening role. Students with higher IQ or better school performance in high school tend to go on to more years of additional education, and this is as true among children reared in poverty as it is among the middle class (Barrett & Depinet, 1991). Indeed, IQ scores are *better* predictors of a young person's eventual educational attainment than is the social class of the child's family (Brody, 1992). Those extra years of education, in turn, have a powerful effect on the career path a young person enters into in early adulthood (e.g., Rosenbaum, 1984; Featherman, 1980). Clearly, variations in the teenager's cognitive skill and academic progress have lasting reverberations.

That is not to say that family characteristics make no difference in fostering or failing to support a teenager's academic progress. They clearly do. You may remember a study by Dornbusch and his colleagues that I mentioned in Chapter 8, comparing the school performance of teenagers from authoritarian, authoritative, and permissive families (Dornbusch et al., 1987; Lamborn et al., 1991; Steinberg et al., 1991). These researchers found that adolescents from authoritative families did the best in school, and such a relationship held in each of the racial groups they studied—black, white, Asian and Hispanic. What this tells us is that regardless of the family's economic circumstances or racial group, teenagers do best in school if their parents set clear standards, expect the child to do well, are warm and supportive and have open lines of communication with the teenager. Interestingly, this connection was *least* clear in Asian-American families, whose children, as a group, do better in high school than any other racial group. Research by Stevenson and others (e.g., Stevenson et al., 1991), which I have mentioned before, suggests that Asian-American families (and perhaps Asian families in general) are more likely to emphasize the importance of effort and perseverance and to set high academic standards for their children—regardless of what other styles of parenting they may exhibit.

High school is not just an academic experience but also a somewhat sheltered place in which teenagers learn about many aspects of adult roles, try out new social relationships, and test themselves against one another intellectually and athletically.

Those Who Drop Out

Those who drop out before finishing high school in many ways represent the flip side of this picture. About 15 percent of students who enter high school in the United States fail to graduate. Boys are more likely to drop out than are girls, and among ethnic groups, Asian-Americans have the lowest dropout rates (less than 5 percent), with Native Americans the highest (23 percent). Whites (12 percent), African-Americans (17 percent), and Hispanics (19 percent) fall in between.

In the case of dropouts, social class is a far better predictor than is ethnicity. Kids growing up in poor families are considerably more likely to drop out of high school than are those from more economically advantaged families. But when you hold social class constant, there are essentially no differences in dropout rates among blacks, whites, and Hispanics. Indeed, among economically equal teenagers, blacks actually do somewhat better in school than do whites (Entwisle, 1990). This is an important piece of information, because many people assume that teenagers in some ethnic groups are somehow programmed by their culture to dislike school or to give up on schooling. In the United States, at the present time, that appears not to be the case.

Teenagers who drop out of school list many reasons for such a decision, including not liking school, poor grades, being suspended, or needing to find work to support a family. Girls who drop out most often do so because they plan to marry, are pregnant, or feel that school is simply not for them (Center for Educational Statistics, 1987). Lists of reasons like this, though, don't begin to capture the multifaceted nature of the decision to drop out. It is too simple, for example, to say that girls drop out because they are pregnant; some get pregnant because they are not interested in school and feel that they are ready for adult life. Low self-esteem also undoubtedly plays some role. In recent years, during economic hard times, many teenagers have also come to the conclusion that a high school diploma won't buy them anything in the job world—not a totally unreasonable view, given the poor job prospects for many high school graduates in many parts of the country (and the world) today (Rosenbaum, 1991).

Yet in the long term, teens who use such a rationale for dropping out of high school are wrong. Unemployment is higher among high school dropouts than in any other education group, and those who have work earn lower wages than do those with a high school diploma. The difference between these two groups is not as large as it once was; a man or woman with a high school diploma can no longer count on finding well-paid, skilled industrial jobs as was the case several decades ago. But a high school education still offers some advantage. Those who drop out enter a very different—and far less optimal—life trajectory.

Summary

1. Adolescence is defined not only as a time of pubertal change but as the transitional period between childhood and full adult role adoption.

2. Because of the importance of this transition, it is marked by rites and rituals in many cultures—although not in most modern Western countries.

3. The physical changes of adolescence are triggered by a complex set of hormonal changes, beginning at about age 8 or 9. Very large increases in gonado-

tropic hormones, including estrogen and testosterone, are central to the process.

4. Effects are seen in a rapid growth spurt in height and an increase in muscle mass and in fat. Boys add more muscle, and girls more fat.

5. In girls, mature sexuality is achieved in a set of changes beginning as early as age 8 or 9. Menarche occurs relatively late in the sequence.

6. Sexual maturity is later in boys, with

the growth spurt occurring a year or more after the start of genital changes.

7. Adolescents have fewer acute illnesses than younger children, but more deaths from accidents. They also have higher rates of suicide and two eating disorders, bulimia and anorexia.

8. Bulimia and anorexia both appear to be a response to the cultural emphasis on thinness and to a young person's judgment of the discrepancy between ideal and actual bodies.

9. Piaget proposed a fourth major level of cognitive development in adolescence, formal operational thought. It is characterized by the ability to apply basic operations to ideas and possibilities, in addition to actual objects.

10. Deductive logic and systematic problem solving are also part of formal operational thought.

11. Researchers have found clear evidence of such advanced forms of thinking in at least some adolescents. But formal operational thinking is not universal, nor is it consistently used even by those who possess the ability.

12. Another facet of adolescent thinking is the development of new levels of moral reasoning. Kohlberg proposes six stages of such reasoning, organized into three levels.

13. Preconventional moral reasoning includes reliance on external authority: what provokes punishment is bad; what feels good is good.

14. Conventional morality is based on rules and norms provided by outside groups, the family, church, or society. This is the dominant form of moral reasoning among teenagers and adults.

15. Principled or postconventional morality is based on self-chosen principles.

16. Only about 15 percent of adults reason at this level. Research evidence suggests that these levels and stages do develop in a specified order and that they are found in this same sequence in all cultures studied so far.

17. Kohlberg's model has been criticized on the grounds that it deals only with reasoning about justice and fairness. Gilligan suggests that people may also reason based on caring and connection, and that girls are more likely to use the latter model. Research does not support Gilligan on this point.

18. Moral reasoning is not perfectly correlated with moral behavior. Moral behavior is also affected by habits, by the degree of responsibility the individual feels, and by the cost associated with behaving morally.

19. Variations in rate of pubertal development have some psychological effects. In general, a large discrepancy between a teenager's concept of what is normal or desirable timing for puberty and his perception of his own timing, has negative effects. In United States culture today, girls who develop very early and boys who develop very late are most likely to report negative experiences.

20. Differences in IQ and school performance during adolescence are quite strongly predictive of both adult IQ and adult job success.

21. The school environment is one of the most formative in the adolescent's experience. Those who succeed academically in high school are those with higher IQs and those from authoritative families. Those who drop out are more likely to be poor or to be doing poorly in school.

Key Terms

anorexia nervosa	estrogen	pituitary gland
bulimia	formal operations	preconventional morality
conventional morality	gonadotropic hormones	principled morality
endocrine glands	menarche	testosterone

Suggested Readings

Feldman, S. S., & Elliott, G. R. (Eds.) (1990). *At the threshold. The developing adolescent.* Cambridge, MA: Harvard University Press. (An unusually good volume, with excellent papers by many of the leading adolescent researchers, reviewing aspects of adolescent experience. Among the many good papers is an absolutely splendid summary of the physical changes of puberty by Jeanne Brooks-Gunn and Edward Reiter.)

Hayes, C. D. (1987). *Risking the future. Vol. 1. Adolescent sexuality, pregnancy, and childbearing.* Washington, D.C.: National Academy Press. (This book summarizes the results of an extensive study done for the Committee on Child Development Research and Public Policy of the National Research Council. The chapter on trends in adolescent sexuality and fertility is especially thorough and informative.)

Kurtines, W. M., & Gewirtz, J. L. (Eds.) (1991). *Handbook of moral behavior and development.* Hillsdale, NJ: Lawrence Erlbaum Associates. (This is a massive three-volume work, prepared as a commemoration of the work of Lawrence Kohlberg. Volume 1 deals with theory, volume 2 with research, and volume 3 with application. If this area intrigues you, there is no more current, complete source.)

Malina, R. M. (1990). Physical growth and performance during the transitional years (9–16). In R. Montemayor, G. R. Adams, & T. P. Gullotta (Eds.), *From childhood to adolescence: A transitional period?* Newbury Park, CA: Sage. (To some extent Malina has picked up where Tanner has left off, providing us with updated information on normal physical growth. This particular paper focuses on puberty, but it contains references to much of Malina's work on other ages as well.)

Steinberg, L. & Levine, A. (1990). *You and your adolescent. A parent's guide for ages 10 to 20.* New York: Harper & Row. (This absolutely first-class book is clearly intended for parents, so it is not overly technical. But because it is written by one of the most innovative researchers studying adolescence, it is strongly based on research.)

Tanner, J. M. (1978). *Fetus into man. Physical growth from conception to maturity.* Cambridge, MA: Harvard University Press. (A detailed but very thorough and remarkably understandable small book that covers all but the most current information about physical growth.)

SOCIAL BEHAVIOR AND PERSONALITY AT ADOLESCENCE

12

I f your memories of your adolescence are anything like mine, then it is not just the physical changes of puberty that you remember. Certainly the fact that I grew 6 inches the year I was 12, towering over absolutely everyone, was a highly important event. I recall very vividly that I had little notion how long my arms and legs were from day to day, and I regularly hit people while making grand gestures; I recall my mother's despair at keeping me in clothes that fit; I know that this experience colored all my relationships and deeply affected my self-concept.

Significant as these physical changes were, my memories of those years are equally colored by another set of adolescent tasks: gaining some independence from my family and figuring out who I was, what I could or should do with my life. It is these tasks of independence and identity that are the central story of this chapter.

▶ Understanding the Self and Relationships at Adolescence

Let me begin, as I did in Chapter 10, by looking at the cognitive aspect of these tasks. How does the child's understanding of himself and his relationships change at adolescence?

The Self-Concept and Self-Esteem

One age-linked change occurs in self-esteem, which typically drops slightly at the beginning of adolescence, and then *rises* steadily and substantially (Harter, 1990; Wigfield et al., 1991). By the end of adolescence, the average 19- or 20-year-old has a considerably more positive sense of her global self-worth than she did at age 8 or 11.

By this age, most teenagers have a much more positive view of themselves than they did at age 10 or 12.

The brief drop in self-esteem at the onset of adolescence seems to be linked not so much to age as to changing schools at the same time as undergoing puberty (Harter, 1990). Researchers have noted it especially among students who shift to junior high school at seventh grade (Wigfield et al., 1991). When the transition process is more gradual, such as for children in a middle school that includes fifth through eighth grades, there is no parallel drop in self-esteem in early adolescence.

An equally significant change is in the nature of the teenager's self-definition, which becomes more and more abstract. You may remember the replies of a 9-year-old and an 11-year-old to the "Who am I?" question used in Montemayor and Eisen's study, which I quoted in Chapter 10 (page 229). Here's an answer by a 17-year-old to the same question:

> I am a human being. I am a girl, I am an individual. I don't know who I am. I am a Pisces. I am a moody person. I am an indecisive person. I am an ambitious person. I am a very curious person. I am not an individual. I am a loner. I am an American (God help me). I am a Democrat. I am a liberal person. I am a radical. I am a conservative. I am a pseudoliberal. I am an atheist. I am not a classifiable person (i.e. I don't want to be). (Montemayor & Eisen, 1972, p. 318)

Clearly, this girl's self-concept is even less tied to her physical characteristics or even her abilities than are those of the younger children. She is describing abstract traits or ideology.

You can see the change very graphically in Figure 12.1, based on the answers of all 262 subjects in the Montemayor and Eisen study. Each of the subjects' answers to the "Who am I?" question was placed in one or more specific categories, such as references to physical properties ("I am tall," "I have blue eyes"), or references to ideology ("I am a Democrat," "I believe in God," etc.). As you can see, appearance was a highly salient dimension in the preteen and early teen years, but became less dominant in late adolescence, at a time when ideology and belief became more salient. By late adolescence, most teenagers think of themselves in terms of enduring traits, beliefs, personal philosophy, and moral standards (Damon & Hart, 1988).

Recent research by Harter also shows that the self-concept becomes increasingly differentiated in adolescence, as the teenager comes to see herself somewhat differently in each of several roles: as a student, with friends, with parents, and in romantic relationships (Harter & Monsour, 1992). Self-concepts also become more flexible in the sense that categories are held less rigidly. One example of this is the greater flexibility adolescents show in their views about what is acceptable behavior for people of their gender.

Sex-Role Concepts in Adolescence. Seven- and 8-year-olds appear to treat gender categories as if they were fixed rules, but adolescents see that a wide range of behaviors occur among members of each gender group (Urberg & Labouvie-Vief, 1976; Huston-Stein & Higgens-Trenk, 1978). Indeed, a significant minority of teenagers and youths begin to define *themselves* with both masculine and feminine traits.

In the early days of research on masculinity and femininity, psychologists conceived of these two qualities as opposite ends of a single continuum. But work by Sandra Bem (1974) and Janet Spence and Robert Helmreich (1978) has shown that it is possible for an individual simultaneously to express both masculine and feminine sides of herself, to be both compassionate and independent, both gentle and assertive.

In this newer way of looking at sex roles, masculinity and femininity are conceived as two separate dimensions. Any person can be high or low on either one or both. The terms used to describe the four possible types created by this two-dimensional conception are shown in Figure 12.2. The two traditional sex roles are the masculine and the feminine combinations. But there are two new types that become evident when we think about

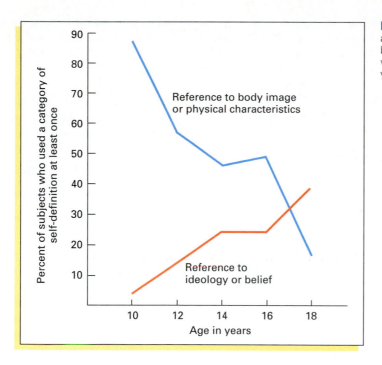

Figure 12.1 As they get older, children and adolescents define themselves less and less by what they look like and more and more by what they believe or feel. (*Source:* Montemayor & Eisen, 1977, from Table 1, p. 3l6.)

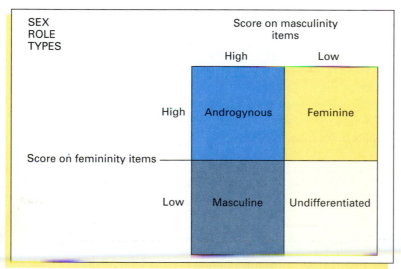

Figure 12.2 In this way of conceptualizing masculinity and femininity, each person expresses some level of each. When each dimension is dichotomized, four "types" are produced.

sex roles in this way: **androgynous** individuals describe themselves as having both masculine and feminine traits, and **undifferentiated** individuals describe themselves as lacking both.

Several studies show that roughly 25 to 35 percent of United States high school students define themselves as androgynous (Spence & Helmreich, 1978; Lamke, 1982a). More girls than boys seem to show this pattern, and more girls fall into the masculine category than boys in the feminine group.

More striking is the finding for *both* adolescent boys and girls, that either a masculine or an androgynous sex-role self-concept is associated with higher self-esteem (Lamke, 1982a, 1982b). This makes sense if we assume that both boys and girls value many of the qualities that are stereotypically masculine, such as independence and competence. Thus

Why should it make such a difference whether we think of masculinity and femininity as two ends of a single continuum, or as two separate dimensions?

a teenage boy can achieve high self-esteem and success with his peers by adopting a traditional masculine sex-role. For girls, though, adoption of a traditional feminine sex-role without some balancing "male" characteristics seems to carry a risk of lower self-esteem and even poorer relationships with peers (Massad, 1981).

Findings like these suggest the possibility that while the creation of rigid rules or schemas for sex roles is a normal—even essential—process in young children, a blurring of those rules may be an important process in adolescence, particularly for girls, for whom a more androgynous self-concept is associated with positive outcomes.

Identity in Adolescence

A somewhat different way to look at adolescent self-concept is through the lens of Erikson's theory. In this model, the central task or dilemma of adolescence is that of *identity versus role confusion*. Erikson argues that the child's early sense of identity comes partly unglued in early adolescence because of the combination of rapid body growth and the sexual changes of puberty. He refers to this period as one in which the adolescent mind is in a kind of *moratorium* between childhood and adulthood. The old identity will no longer suffice; a new identity must be forged, one that must serve to place the young person among the myriad roles of adult life—occupational roles, sexual roles, religious roles. Confusion about all these role choices is inevitable. Erikson puts it this way:

> In general it is primarily the inability to settle on an occupational identity which disturbs young people. To keep themselves together they temporarily overidentify, to the point of apparent complete loss of identity, with the heroes of cliques and crowds. . . . They become remarkably clannish, intolerant, and cruel in their exclusion of others who are "different," in skin color or cultural background . . . . and often in entirely petty aspects of dress and gesture arbitrarily selected as *the* signs of an in-grouper or out-grouper. It is important to understand . . . such intolerance as the necessary *defense against a sense of identity confusion*, which is unavoidable at [this] time of life. (1980, pp. 97–98)

The teenage clique or group thus forms a base of security from which the young person can move toward a unique solution of the identity process. Ultimately, each teenager must achieve an integrated view of himself, including his own pattern of beliefs, occupational goals, and relationships.

Nearly all the current work on the formation of adolescent identity has been based on James Marcia's descriptions of *identity statuses* (Marcia, 1966, 1980), which I described in Chapter 2. Recall that Marcia proposes that there are two key parts to any adolescent identity formation: a *crisis* and a *commitment*. Putting these two elements together creates four statuses: achieved identity, moratorium, foreclosure, and diffusion (recall Figure 2.2, page 30).

Whether every young person goes through some kind of identity crisis I cannot tell you, because there have been no longitudinal studies covering the relevant years. But there have been a number of cross-sectional studies, eight of which Alan Waterman (1985) has combined into a single analysis. Figure 12.3 on page 286 shows the pattern of results for *vocational identity*, one of the several facets of identity Erikson emphasized.

Several things are interesting about these results. First, notice that the identity achievement status occurs most typically not in high school but at college age. Also note that the moratorium status is relatively uncommon except in the early years of college. So if most young people are going through an identity crisis, that crisis is fairly late and not terribly long-lasting. Finally, it is interesting that about a third of young people at every age are in the foreclosure status, which may indicate that many young people simply do not go through a crisis at all, but follow well-defined grooves—a pattern we would

The implication in Marcia's formulation is that the foreclosure status is less developmentally mature—that one must go through a crisis in order to achieve a mature identity. Does this make sense to you?

ACROSS CULTURES
Ethnic Identity in Adolescence

For minority teenagers, especially nonwhite teens in a predominantly white culture, there is another aspect of creating an identity in adolescence: Such young people must also develop an ethnic or racial identity, which includes some or all of the following aspects (Phinney & Rosenthal, 1992):

Self-identification as a member of a group
Feelings of belonging and commitment to a group
Positive (or negative) attitudes toward the group
A sense of shared values and attitudes
Learning of specific ethnic traditions or practices, such as language, customs, and behaviors

Ethnic identity differs from most aspects of ego identity in the sense in which Erikson and Marcia speak of it because there is no choice about it. An occupational identity—even a sex role identity—may be chosen. But a minority youth does not have a choice about the specific identity chosen, only about the content of it.

Jean Phinney (1990; Phinney & Rosenthal, 1992) has proposed that in adolescence, the development of a complete ethnic identity moves through three rough stages. The first stage is an "unexamined ethnic identity," equivalent to what Marcia calls a foreclosed status. For some subgroups, such as African-Americans and Native Americans, this unexamined identity frequently includes the negative images and stereotypes common in the wider culture. Many youngsters in these and other minority groups initially prefer the dominant white culture or wish they had been born into the majority. An African-American journalist, Sylvester Monroe, who grew up in an urban housing project, clearly describes this initial negative feeling:

If you were black, you didn't quite measure up. . . . For a black kid there was a certain amount of self-doubt. It came at you indirectly. You didn't see any black people on television, you didn't see any black people doing certain things. . . . You don't think it out but you say, "well, it must mean that white people are better than we are. Smarter, brighter—whatever." (Quoted in Spencer & Dornbusch, 1990)

Not all minority teenagers arrive at such negative views of their own group. Individual youngsters may have very positive ethnic images if that is the content of the identity conveyed by parents or others around the child. The key is that this view of the young person's ethnic self is not arrived at independently but comes from outside sources, much as conventional moral judgments are based on outside authority.

The second stage is the "ethnic identity search," parallel to the crisis in Marcia's analysis of ego identity. This search is typically triggered by some experience that makes ethnicity salient—

perhaps an example of blatant prejudice or merely the widening experience of high school. At this point the young person begins to compare her own ethnic group with others, to arrive at her *own* judgments.

This exploration stage is eventually followed by a resolution of the conflicts and contradictions—analogous to Marcia's status of identity achievement. This is not necessarily an easy process. Some African-American adolescents, for example, who wish to try to compete in and succeed in the dominant culture, may experience ostracism from their black friends, who accuse them of "acting white" and betraying their blackness. Some Hispanics report similar experiences. Some resolve this by keeping their own ethnic group at arm's length; others deal with it by creating essentially two identities, as expressed by one young Chicano interviewed by Phinney:

Being invited to someone's house, I have to change my ways of how I act at home, because of culture differences. I would have to follow what they do. . . . I am used to it now, switching off between the two. It is not difficult. (Phinney & Rosenthal, 1992, p. 160)

Some resolve the dilemma by wholeheartedly choosing their own ethnic group's patterns and values, even though that may limit their access to the larger culture.

In both cross-sectional and longitudinal studies, Phinney has found that African-American teens and young adults do indeed move through these steps or stages toward a clear ethnic identity. Furthermore, there is evidence that among black, Asian-American, and Mexican-American teens and college students, those who have reached the second or third stage in this process—those who are searching or who have reached a clear identity—have higher self-esteem and better psychological adjustment (Phinney, 1990) than do those who are still in the "unexamined" stage. In contrast, among Caucasian students, ethnic identity has essentially no relationship to self-esteem or adjustment.

This stagelike model may be a decent beginning description of the process of ethnic identity formation. But let us not lose sight of the fact that the details and the content of the ethnic identity will differ markedly from one subgroup to another. Those groups that encounter more overt prejudice will have a different road to follow than will those who may be more easily assimilated; those whose own ethnic culture espouses values that are close to those of the dominant culture will have less difficulty resolving the contradictions than will those whose family culture is at greater variance with the majority. Whatever the specifics, it is clear that nonwhite and those from clearly defined ethnic groups have an important additional identity task in their adolescent years.

Figure 12.3 Waterman has combined data from eight different cross-sectional studies of identity statuses. Diffusion and foreclosure were the most common statuses among the younger teenagers, while an achieved identity was the most common status among the college juniors and seniors in these studies. (*Source:* Waterman, 1985. From Table 2, p. 18.)

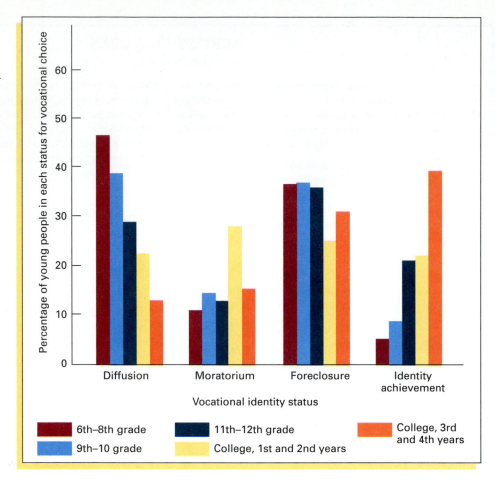

expect to be very common in nonindustrialized cultures in which children are expected to follow directly in their parents' occupational and sex-role footsteps.

Collectively, these findings suggest that the identity crisis occurs somewhat later than Erikson originally proposed. But this conclusion requires one qualification: It seems likely that young people who go to work immediately after high school will face the need for an occupational identity earlier than is true for those who go to college. Attending college is in some sense a postponement of full adult status. The years in college are a period in which students are actively encouraged to question, doubt, and try out alternatives. Those who go directly into the working world do not have that luxury. In one of the few studies of noncollege youth, Gordon Munro and Gerald Adams (1977) found that 45 percent of those who were already working were in the "identity achievement" status for occupational identity, which is higher than the levels shown in Figure 12.3 for college students.

Summary of Developmental Changes in Self-Concept

Let me combine the bits of information I have given in several chapters and sum up the developmental progression in self-concept. The young child develops first a primitive sense of her own separateness. This is followed quickly by an understanding of her own constancy and of herself as an actor or agent in the world. By 18 to 24 months, most children achieve self-awareness; they grasp the fact that they are also *objects* in the world. At that point, children begin to define themselves in terms of their physical properties (age, size, gender), and their activities and skills. Over the period of concrete and formal operations (from age 6 through adolescence), the content of the child's self-concept becomes gradually more abstract, less and less tied to outward physical qualities, more based on the assumption of enduring inner qualities. During late adolescence, the whole self-concept also appears to undergo a kind of reorganization, with a new, future-oriented, sexual, occupational, and ideological identity created.

Concepts of Relationships

In parallel fashion, the teenager's understanding of others and of relationships becomes more and more abstract, less and less tied to externals. For example, teenagers' descriptions of other people contain more comparisons of one trait with another or one person with another, more recognition of inconsistencies and exceptions, more shadings of gray than

---

RESEARCH REPORT
Gender, Identity, and Intimacy

One of the recurrent questions in studies of identity formation has been whether males and females achieve identity in the same way. The evidence is mixed. For occupational and religious identity, there appears to be no sex difference; male and female teenagers and college students are equally likely to have reached "identity achievement" status in these domains (Waterman, 1985). In two other domains, however, there are slight signs of difference. Girls and young women are more likely to have an achieved identity or to be in moratorium in the area of social roles, while males may be slightly more likely to have individuated political views.

Sex differences in the identity process might appear in another way as well. You'll remember from Chapter 2 that Erikson placed the identity dilemma in adolescence and the intimacy dilemma in early adulthood. In his view, one must complete the identity process before one can achieve intimacy. But some have argued that for women, identity is achieved *through* intimacy—an argument supported by the finding of greater identity achievement in the area of social roles for teenage girls and young adult women.

Another way this linkage has been explored has been to assess both identity status and a parallel "intimacy status" in groups of teenagers or young adults. Like the identity statuses, the most often used formulation of intimacy status is a two by two category system, with the degree of commitment (high versus low) along one axis, and the quality of the relationship (deep versus superficial) along the other, as in the table below.

If Erikson is correct that identity has to come first, we should be more likely to see intimate relationships among those with an achieved identity or in moratorium. But if identity and intimacy are related differently in males and females, we might find that intimacy and identity are unrelated among women.

I know of only two studies in which the connections between identity and intimacy status have been examined separately for males and females, and the results are contradictory. One (Kacerguis & Adams, 1980) found that achievement of occupational identity was a good predictor of intimacy status for *both* male and female college students, thus confirming Erikson. The other (Hodgson & Fischer, 1979) found different patterns for men and women undergraduates. In this study, 19 of 21 college women who were rated as identity achievers were also rated as showing intimacy in their relationships. However, 15 out of 29 women who had *not* reached identity achievement status were also rated as showing intimacy. Among the young men in this same study, only 3 showed intimacy without identity. So in this late 1970s sample, men who had not achieved identity in any area were quite unlikely to have achieved intimacy, but the same was not true for young women.

It may well be that such a finding was more typical a decade or two ago. We'd need current studies to check this. But the possibility is interesting, especially in view of the evidence I've already described suggesting that relationships differ in both form and function for males and females.

Intimacy Statuses

		Degree of Commitment	
		High	**Low**
Quality of Relationship	**Deep**	Intimate	Preintimate
	Superficial	Pseudointimate	Stereotyped

we hear in descriptions given by younger children (Shantz, 1983). As illustration, here's a description by a 15-year-old:

> Andy is very modest. He is even shyer than I am when near strangers and yet is very talkative with people he knows and likes. He always seems good tempered and I have never seen him in a bad temper. He tends to degrade other people's achievements, and yet never praises his own. He does not seem to voice his opinions to anyone. He easily gets nervous. (Livesley & Bromley, 1973, p. 221)

We see similar changes in children's descriptions of friendships, which become more qualified, more shaded. Damon's research suggests that in late adolescence, young people understand that even very close friendships cannot fill every need and that friendships are not static: they change, grow, or dissolve, as each member of the pair changes. A really good friendship, then, is one that *adapts* to these changes. At this age, young people say things about friendship like "trust is the ability to let go as well as to hang on" (Selman, 1980, p. 141).

In an intriguing series of interviews, Robert Selman (1980) has also studied friendships by asking children and adolescents how they settle disagreements or arguments with friends. Table 12.1 lists some of the answers given by children of various ages, illustrating the kind of progression I have been describing.

▶ Relationships at Adolescence

All these cognitive changes in the child's understanding of herself and her relationships form an important part of the foundation of the child's actual relationships, although the causality clearly runs both ways: relationships affect the child's thinking just as much as the changes in the child's understanding affect her relationships. In adolescence, the key relationships continue to be with parents and with peers.

Relationships with Parents

Adolescents have two apparently contradictory tasks in their relationships with their parents: to establish autonomy from the parents and to maintain their sense of relatedness with their parents. We can see both processes at work when we look at teen/parent

---

Can you recognize your own thinking in these comments? How would you describe your ways of settling arguments with your friends?

TABLE 12.1 Comments by Children of Various Ages About How to Solve Disagreements or Arguments Between Friends

"Go away from her and come back later when you're not fighting." (age 5)

"Punch her out." (age 5)

"Around our way the guy who started it just says he's sorry." (age 8)

"Well if you say something and don't really mean it, then you have to mean it when you take it back." (age 8½)

"Sometimes you got to get away for a while. Calm down a bit so you won't be so angry. Then get back and try to talk it out." (age 14)

"If you just settle up after a fight that is no good. You gotta really feel that you'd be happy the way things went if you were in your friend's shoes. You can just settle up with someone who is not a friend, but that's not what friendship is really about." (age 15½)

"Well, you could talk it out, but it usually fades itself out. It usually takes care of itself. You don't have to explain everything. You do certain things and each of you knows what it means. But if not, then talk it out." (age 16)

Source: Selman, 1980, pp. 107–113.

relationships. The push for autonomy shows itself in increases in conflict between parent and adolescent; the maintenance of connection is seen in the continued strong attachment of child to parent.

Increases in Conflict. The rise in conflict has been documented by a number of researchers (e.g., Steinberg, 1988; Montemayor, 1982; Paikoff & Brooks-Gunn, 1991). In the great majority of families, it seems to consist of an increase in mild bickering or conflicts over everyday issues, such as rules and regulations, dress codes, dating, grades, or housekeeping. Teenagers and their parents interrupt each other more often, and become more impatient with each other.

This increase in discord is widely found, but we need to be careful not to assume that it signifies a major disruption of the quality of the parent-child relationships. Steinberg estimates that only 5 to 10 percent of the families studied in the United States experience a substantial or pervasive deterioration in the quality of the parent-child relationship in these years of early adolescence.

But if the rise in conflict doesn't signal that the relationship is falling apart, what does it mean? A number of theorists have suggested that this rise in parent-child discord at adolescence, far from being a negative event, may instead be developmentally healthy and necessary—a part of the process of individuation and separation (Steinberg, 1988, 1990; Hill, 1988). Among primates, we see the same kind of increase in conflict, especially between adult males and the newly adolescent males. The young males begin to make competitive gestures and may be driven off into a brief period of independent life before returning to the troop. Among humans, we have some evidence that the increase in family conflict is linked not with age but with the hormonal changes of puberty, which would lend further support to the argument that this is a normal and even necessary process.

For example, in a short-term longitudinal study, Laurence Steinberg (1988) followed a group of teenagers over a one-year period, assessing their stage of puberty and the quality of their relationship with their parents at the beginning and end of the year. He found that as the pubertal stages began, family closeness declined, parent-child conflict rose, and autonomy in the child went up. Other researchers (e.g., Inoff-Germain et al., 1988) have taken this a step further by measuring actual hormone levels and showing links between the rise of the various hormones of puberty and the rise in aloofness toward or conflict with parents. Among girls, conflict seems to rise after menarche (Holmbeck & Hill, 1991).

The pattern of causes is obviously complex. Hormonal changes themselves may be causally linked to increases in assertiveness, perhaps especially among boys. But parents' reactions to pubertal changes may also be highly important parts of the mix. Visible pubertal changes, including menarche, change parents' expectations for the child and increase their concern about guiding and controlling the adolescent to help her avoid the shoals of too-great a level of independence.

In fact, there is good evidence that adolescence may actually be more stressful to *parents* than to the young people themselves (Gecas & Seff, 1990). Almost two-thirds of parents perceive adolescence as the most difficult stage of parenting, because of both loss of control over the adolescent and fear for the adolescent's safety caused by the youngster's increased independence.

In the midst of the increased conflict, and perhaps partially as a result of it, the overall level of the teenager's autonomy within the family increases steadily throughout the adolescent years. Parents give the youngster more and more room to make independent choices and to participate in family decision making. Steinberg argues that this "distancing" is a normal—even an essential—part of the adolescent development process.

Attachment to Parents. Paradoxically, neither the temporarily heightened family conflict nor the "distancing" from the parents seems to signify that the young person's underlying emotional attachment to the parent has disappeared or even greatly weakened.

Why might parents find their children's adolescence to be so stressful? How many hypotheses can you generate to explain such a finding? Do you think this is true in every culture, or is this likely to be true only of industrialized countries?

Teenagers may spend less time with their parents than they did when they were younger, but most continue to have strong attachments to Mom and Dad.

Results from a study by Fumiyo Hunter and James Youniss (1982) illustrate the point clearly.

Hunter and Youniss had groups of fourth-, seventh-, and tenth-graders, and college students answer eight different questions about their relationships with mother, father, and best same-sexed friend. Figure 12.4 shows the average score, on a 4-point scale, for those questions that dealt with the "intimacy" of the relationship (e.g., "we talk about problems," or "my mother knows how I feel") and for questions about the nurturance of the relationship (e.g., "My father gives me what I need," or "My best friend helps me to solve my problems"). The results show that intimacy with the mother and father went down during adolescence, while intimacy with the friend rose. But young people across this age range saw their parents as consistently high sources of nurturing.

This basic pattern is confirmed in other research (e.g., Furman & Buhrmester, 1992; Lempers & Clark-Lempers, 1990). For example, Greenberg reports that a teenager's sense of well-being or happiness is more strongly correlated with the quality of his attachment

Figure 12.4 Hunter and Youniss's results suggest that the attachment to the parents remains strong even while peer attachments strengthen and peer relationships become more intimate. (*Source:* F. T. Hunter & J. Youniss. Changes in functions of three relations during adolescence. *Developmental Psychology,* 1982, *18,* Figures 2 and 3, pp. 809, 810. Copyright 1982 by the American Psychological Association. Reprinted by permission of the publisher and author.)

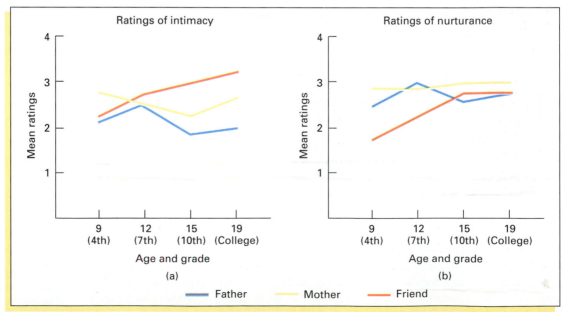

to the parent than to the quality of his attachments to his peers (Greenberg, Siegel & Leitch, 1983). Collectively, this evidence points to the fact that the central relationship with and attachment to the parent continues to be highly significant in adolescence, even while the teenager is becoming more autonomous.

Relationships with Peers

At the same time, there is no gainsaying the fact that peer relationships become far more significant at adolescence than they have been at any earlier stage, and perhaps more so than they will be at any later time in the life span. Teenagers spend more than half their waking hours with other teenagers, and less than 5 percent of their time with either parent. Of the roughly 40 percent of their hours that can be counted as leisure time, they spend two-fifths socializing with friends, most of that time talking (Csikszentmihalyi & Larson, 1984).

These friendships are quite stable. They also become more complex and psychologically richer. Adolescent friendships are increasingly intimate, in the sense that friends more and more share their inner feelings and secrets and are more knowledgeable about each other's feelings—a pattern found in studies in Russia as well as the United States (Kon & Losenkov, 1978). Loyalty and faithfulness also become more valued characteristics of friendship in adolescence (Berndt & Perry, 1990).

This set of changes is more than just a shift in how kids spend their time. More centrally, the *function* of the peer group and peer friendships changes. In elementary school, peer groups are mostly the setting for mutual play and for all the learning about relationships and the natural world that is part of such play. But the teenager uses his friends and his peer group in another way. He is struggling to make a slow transition from the protected life of the family to the independent life of adulthood, and the peer group becomes the *vehicle* for that transition. As Erikson pointed out, the clannishness and intense conformity to the group is a normal—even an essential—part of the process.

Age Changes in Conformity.   Peer-group conformity seems to intensify at about age 13 or 14 and then wanes slowly as the teenager begins to arrive at a sense of identity that is more independent of the peer group. For example, Thomas Berndt (1979) asked young people what they would do in a series of hypothetical situations in which their peers wanted to do something different from what they wanted or from what they knew was right. Some of the situations described helpful or prosocial actions, some neutral, and some mildly antisocial. An example of one of these antisocial situations follows.

What stage in Dunphy's sequence of peer group structures would you say these Venezuelan teenagers are illustrating?

Can you make any reasonable guesses about what qualities would characterize teenagers who are most and least susceptible to peer pressure? Personality characteristics? Intellectual skills? Family backgrounds?

You are with a couple of your best friends on Halloween. They're going to soap windows, but you're not sure you should or not. Your friends all say you should because there's no way you could get caught. What would you *really* do? (Berndt, 1979, p. 610)

You can see in Figure 12.5 that there were no age differences in peer influences for either neutral or prosocial situations, but there were for antisocial dilemmas. The peak of susceptibility to peers was in ninth grade, roughly age 14.

Lest you think that all 13- and 14-year-olds run amok with their peers, I should point out three things. First, in Berndt's study, the maximum score on the conformity scale was 10, so the level of conformity these teenagers reported is quite low. Second, teenagers report that peer pressure is more likely to be *against* misconduct than toward it (Brown, Clasen & Eicher, 1986). Third, susceptibility to negative peer pressure is lower among young people who are close to their parents (Steinberg & Silverberg, 1986). Thus, while peer influence is particularly strong in these adolescent years, there are important mitigating factors, too.

Changes in Peer-Group Structure. Over the same years the structure of the peer group also changes. The now-classic early study is Dunphy's observation of the formation, dissolution, and interaction of teenage groups in a high school in Sydney, Australia, between 1958 and 1960 (Dunphy, 1963). He identified two important subvarieties of groups, using labels that have become widespread in writing on adolescence. The first type, which Dunphy called **cliques,** were made up of four to six young people who appeared to be strongly attached to one another. Cliques had strong cohesiveness and high levels of intimate sharing. In the early years of adolescence, these cliques were almost entirely same-sex groups—left over from the preadolescent pattern. Gradually, however, the cliques combined into larger sets he called **crowds,** made up of several cliques, some male and some female. Finally, the crowd broke down again into heterosexual cliques, and finally into loose associations of couples. In Dunphy's study, the period of the fully developed crowd was roughly between ages 13 and 15—the very years when we see the greatest conformity to peer pressure.

Not all current observers of teenage peer groups agree with Dunphy that the crowd

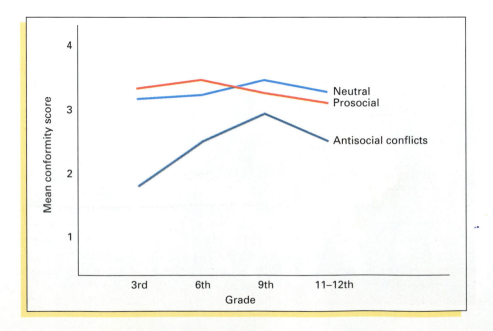

Figure 12.5 Berndt asked young people what they would do in hypothetical situations in which their peers wanted to do something different from what they wanted or from what they knew was right. Among these subjects, those in ninth grade were most susceptible to peer influence. (*Source:* Berndt, 1979, Figure 1, p. 611.)

is made up simply of a collection of cliques. Bradford Brown (1990), for example, uses the term *crowd* to refer to the "reputation-based" group with which a young person is identified, either by choice or by designation by peers. Groups with labels like *jocks*, *brains*, *nerds*, or *populars* are crowds in Brown's sense of the term. Cliques, in contrast, are always groups that the individual teenager chooses. But Brown would agree with Dunphy that in early adolescence, cliques are almost entirely same-sex; by late adolescence they have become mixed in gender.

Whatever labels are applied, there is agreement among theorists that the peer group performs the highly important function of helping the teenager make the shift from unisexual to heterosexual social relationships. The 13- or 14-year-old can begin to try out her new heterosexual skills in the somewhat protected environment of the crowd or clique; only after some confidence is developed do we see the beginnings of committed heterosexual pair relationships.

Heterosexual Relationships in Adolescence

Of all the changes in social relationships in adolescence, the most profound is the shift from the total dominance of same-sex friendships to heterosexual relationships. There is a very large cultural element in all this, of course. There are still many cultures in the world in which heterosexual contact during puberty or before marriage is tightly controlled and chaperoned; others in which there are no restrictions at all. Most Western cultures fall in between, with the current United States culture leaning strongly toward the no-restriction end of the continuum.

Dating and clear heterosexual (or homosexual) coupling comes fairly late in adolescence and represents the end point of the whole sequence of peer group structures.

The heterosexual relationships we see in early and middle adolescence are clearly part of the preparation for assuming a full adult sexual identity. Physical sexuality is part of that role, but so are the skills of personal intimacy with the opposite sex, including flirting, communicating, and reading the form of social cues used by the other gender.

In Western societies, these skills are learned first in larger groups and then in dating pairs. Studies of United States adolescents in the 1980s suggest that dating begins most typically at 15 or 16, as you can see from Table 12.2 (page 295), which shows results from a representative sample of Detroit teenagers (Thornton, 1990). This same study, with data collected in roughly 1980, shows that more than half of both boys and girls have become sexually active by the time they are 18.

Such a pattern of sexual activity is confirmed in other research. Collectively, the evidence suggests that in the United States today, about half of boys and a quarter to a third of girls aged 15 to 17 are no longer virgins. Among 18- and 19-year-olds, the rate of sexual activity is considerably higher, with approximately 75 percent of boys and 60 percent of girls having had at least one experience of intercourse (Sonenstein, Pleck & Ku, 1989; Hofferth, Kahn & Baldwin, 1987). At every age, the rates among black teenagers are considerably higher than among either whites or Hispanics. For example, among young men included in the 1988 National Survey of Adolescent Males, a nationally representative sample of nearly 2000 young men between the ages of 15 and 19, 80.6 percent of blacks were sexually active, compared to 56.8 percent of whites and 59.7 percent of Hispanics (Sonenstein, Pleck & Ku, 1989). Similar discrepancies are found among girls (Hofferth et al., 1987).

Early dating and early sexual activity are also more common among the poor of every ethnic group and among those who experience relatively early puberty. Among girls, for example, those with early menarche are more likely to initiate sexual activity early than are same-age peers who have not yet reached menarche. Religious teachings and individual attitudes about the appropriate age for sexual behavior also make a difference, as does family structure. Girls from divorced or remarried families, for example, report higher levels of sexual experience than do girls from intact families, and those with strong religious identity report less (Bingham, Miller & Adams, 1990; Miller & Moore, 1990).

THE REAL WORLD
Sexual Orientation Among Adolescents

Heterosexual experience is not the only kind teenagers may have. Homosexual contact is also fairly common, especially for boys and especially in childhood or early adolescence. Research on homosexuality in teenagers is not common, but indications are that perhaps 15 percent of boys and 10 percent of girls have at least one homosexual contact; Two to 3 percent report continuing homosexual relationships (Dreyer, 1982). Among adults, homosexuality appears to characterize 4 to 6 percent of the population in Western countries (for which we have the best data), although some estimates range as high as 17 percent (Gonsiorek & Weinrich, 1991).

Recent evidence has strengthened the hypothesis that a homosexual orientation may be built in, either genetically or through hormone patterning in utero. For example, Carl Roberts and his colleagues (Roberts et al., 1987) studied a group of boys who showed strong preference for female toys and playmates from their earliest years of life. When Roberts compared these boys to a group of boys with more typical masculine sex-role behaviors, he found little evidence that the more feminine boys had been specifically reinforced for these behaviors, nor that their fathers were providing models for such behavior. What Roberts found instead was that the feminine boys were more feminine in appearance from earliest babyhood and that three-fourths of them became homosexual or bisexual in orientation as adults.

Studies of girls who have experienced heightened levels of androgen prenatally also show behavioral effects of prenatal conditions. These ''androgenized'' girls, in comparison to their normal sisters, are later found to be more interested in rough-and-tumble play, more often prefer to play with boys, show less interest in dolls or babies, have fewer fantasies about being a mother (Meyer-Bahlburg, Ehrhardt & Feldman, 1986), although we have no data concerning their sexual preference as adolescents or adults.

Most convincing is a recent twin study by Bailey and Pillard

(1991) showing that sexual preference is much more similar among identical than among fraternal twins. In this sample, when one twin was homosexual, the probability that the second twin would also be homosexual was 52 percent among identical twins but only 22 percent among fraternal twins. By comparison, the equivalent ''concordance rate'' was only 11 percent among pairs of biologically unrelated boys adopted into the same families.

Such biological evidence does not mean that there are no environmental causes of a homosexual orientation. No behavior is entirely controlled by either nature or nurture, as I have said many times. At the very least, the twin study shows that identical twins do not invariably have the same sexual orientation. Something beyond biology must be at work, although we do not yet know what environmental factors may be contributory.

Whatever the cause, a homosexual orientation is clearly a minority preference, with high levels of prejudice and stereotyping associated with it and high risk for a variety of adolescent problems. In one study, for example, four-fifths of gay teens interviewed in Minneapolis had deteriorating school performance, and more than a quarter dropped out of high school (Remafedi, 1987a). They must also cope with the decision about whether to ''come out'' about their sexual orientation. Those who do come out are far more likely to tell peers than parents, although there is a risk attached to the decision to tell peers. In his Minneapolis study, Remafedi found that 41 percent of gay male youths had lost a friend over the issue of sexual orientation (Remafedi, 1987b). Some research suggests that as many as two-thirds of gay youth have not disclosed their orientation to their parents (Rotheram-Borus, Rosario & Koopman, 1991).

There is obviously much that we do not know about gay or lesbian youth. But it is a reasonable hypothesis that the years of adolescence may be particularly stressful for this subgroup. Like ethnic minority youth, homosexual teens have an additional task facing them in forming a clear identity.

Hormone levels also play some part, although the link seems to be more straightforward in boys than in girls. In boys, the likelihood of sexual activity is correlated with the amount of testosterone in the bloodstream. Among girls, sexual interests but not sexual behavior are associated with testosterone levels, which suggests that social influences are more involved in their sexual behavior than is true for boys (Brooks-Gunn & Furstenberg, 1989).

Sexual Knowledge and Contraceptive Use. Despite these heightened levels of sexual activity, it is remarkable how little teenagers know about physiology and reproduction. At best, only about half of white and a fifth of black teenagers can describe the time of greatest fertility in the menstrual cycle (Morrison, 1985). Many are convinced they cannot get pregnant because they are "too young." Perhaps in part because of such ignorance, less than half of teenage girls use contraceptives the first time they have intercourse (Hofferth, 1987a).

Increased knowledge about AIDS, however, seems to be changing this picture, albeit

TABLE 12.2 Dating and Sexual Behavior Among Adolescents in the United States

Age	First Date		Age	First Intercourse	
	Males (%)	Females (%)		Males (%)	Females (%)
13 or younger	21.2	8.6			
14	17.9	16.2			
15	21.2	33.6	15 or younger	21.7	8.5
16	29.5	29.3	16	15.4	10.7
17–18	7.2	10.0	17	17.0	18.6
			18	9.3	15.7
			Never	36.7	46.5

Source: Thornton, 1990, Table 1, pp. 246–247.

slowly. Data from the National Survey of Adolescent Males in 1988, for example, show that condom use among teenage urban males doubled between 1979 and 1988 (Sonenstein, Pleck & Ku, 1989; Pleck, Sonenstein & Ku, 1990), and was somewhat more likely among young men who judged the risk of AIDS to be high. Nonetheless, even in 1988, only 57 percent of young men reported using condoms during their last sexual encounter, and only 5 to 10 percent used condoms consistently (Pleck, Sonenstein & Ku, 1991)—numbers that will bring little comfort to epidemiologists concerned about the rise in HIV infection among adolescents.

Teen Pregnancy. Given the statistics on sexual activity and contraceptive use, we shouldn't be surprised that the rate of teenage pregnancy is high. Approximately one million teenage girls become pregnant every year (roughly one in ten girls) and about half of these pregnancies are carried to term. Perhaps ten thousand of these babies are born every year to girls under 15. The most striking version of these statistics is an estimate by Sandra Hofferth that 44 percent of all girls will be pregnant at least once before the age of 20 (Hofferth, 1987a). Those who choose to deliver their babies are likely to have a very different adult life trajectory than do teenagers who do not give birth—a set of findings I've examined in the "across development" discussion.

In the face of rising rates of HIV infection and AIDS among adolescents, and in light of the long-term life risks associated with teenage childbearing, we may need to rethink our attitudes about the timing, importance, and content of sex education in the schools. Abstinence may indeed be a valuable message, but it surely cannot be the only one. The sexual horse is out of the barn. Urging that the barn door be closed will not solve the problem.

▶ Individual Differences

Variations in Family Relationships

I have already talked at length in Chapter 8 about differences in family interactive style and their effects on children and teenagers (pages 195–202). Among adolescents, as among younger children, authoritative parenting is consistently associated with more positive outcomes for the child. I mentioned one aspect of this relationship in Chapter 11, making the point that teenagers whose parents use an authoritative style do better in school than do those whose parents use authoritarian or other styles. It turns out that the

If you were put in charge of designing a sex education program for public schools, what would you do? How early would you begin? What would you teach? What educational methods do you think would be most effective, and why?

ACROSS DEVELOPMENT
Long-Term Life Consequences for Adolescent Mothers

The popular press in recent years has bombarded us with articles about an ''epidemic'' of teenage pregnancies and what we ought to do about it. But it is not so clear that ''epidemic'' is an appropriate description (Vinovskis, 1988). Birth rates have actually dropped among the entire population, including teenagers. What has increased steadily since the 1960s is the rate of births to *unmarried* teens (Furstenberg, 1991). Thus, it is not that more and more teenagers are bearing children, but that more and more teenage girls choose to rear their children without marrying.

Whether this is a worrisome trend or not depends not only on one's religious or moral beliefs, but also on evidence about the long-term consequences of adolescent childbearing for the adult lives of women. The bulk of that evidence points to quite negative consequences (Hofferth, 1987b; Furstenberg, Brooks-Gunn & Morgan, 1987; Teti, Lamb & Elster, 1987). In the majority of studies, teenage childbearing is associated with:

More children, more closely spaced
Fewer years of total education throughout adult life
Lower levels of occupational success
Lower income in adulthood
Higher likelihood of divorce in adult life

Some longitudinal data from the Panel Study of Income Dynamics (Moore et al., 1981) in the figure below illustrate the point. You can see that those women who had their first child at 17 or younger had much lower probabilities of completing high school than did those who began childbearing later. And we know from many studies that those who fail to complete high school

have far fewer occupational and economic opportunities in adult life.

There is a catch in all this, of course—a major methodological problem that some of you will have seen. Girls who have their first child as teenagers are already different in a host of ways from those who delay childbearing. They are more likely to be poor, to come from families with low levels of education, and to have lower IQs. Many dropped out of school *before* they got pregnant. So perhaps all these poorer adult life outcomes are the result of these initial differences and not the teenage childbearing at all.

One can partially get around this problem with statistical controls or by comparing only early- and late-childbearing girls from the same social class. When researchers have done either of these things, they find that the differences in long-term outcomes are diminished but do not disappear (Furstenberg, 1991). Another alternative is to compare sisters, one of whom has had her first child as a teenager, the other after 20. The one such comparison, on a small sample (Geronimus, 1991), showed no differences in adult incomes or probability of being employed in early adult life, but the later-childbearing sisters were more likely to have completed schooling beyond high school—a difference that may have repercussions in later adult life.

At the moment the best conclusion seems to be that early childbearing does indeed have costs attached to it, but that the size of the cost varies a good deal from one girl to the next, depending on the amount of family support she can muster and her own skills and resources. At the very least, it clearly changes the set of choices the girl has in early adult life.

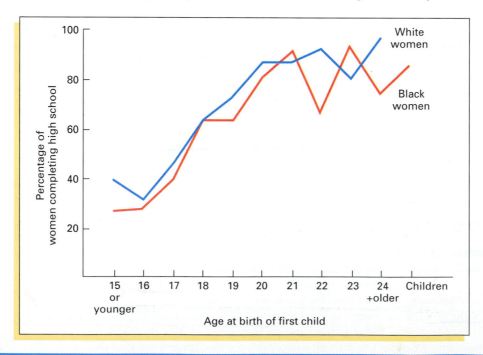

same benefit of authoritative parenting is also found when we look at other aspects of emotional and mental health.

Table 12.3 shows one set of results from the very large, multiethnic study by Dornbusch and his colleagues (Lamborn et al., 1991). Roughly 10,000 high school students, in Wisconsin and California, reported on their family patterns and on their own behavior and school performance. It is clear in the table that the outcomes were best for the students who described their families as authoritative, and least good for those from neglectful families, with teenagers from authoritarian and permissive families falling in between. More detailed studies of subgroups of these families show that those families who give their teenagers too much autonomy too soon have youngsters who have lower grades and lower levels of effort in school. Joint decision making between parents and teenagers—a hallmark of authoritative parenting—was linked to higher school performances and fewer personal problems, regardless of social class or ethnic group membership (Dornbusch et al., 1990).

Family Structure.   Family structure, too, continues to be an important factor in the teenager's life. But in adolescence we see an interesting exception to the typical pattern of effects. You'll remember from Chapter 8 that boys are usually more negatively affected than girls by parental divorce or remarriage. Among adolescents, it is girls who show more distress, both in families in which the girl lives with her still-single mother and in stepparent families (Vuchinich, Hetherington & Vuchinich, 1991; Hetherington, 1989, 1991b). Adolescent girls, but apparently not preschool- or elementary-school age girls, have more trouble interacting with the new stepfather than do their brothers and treat him more as an intruder. They are resistant, critical, sulky, and try to avoid contact with him, despite the obvious effort of many stepfathers to be thoughtful and nonauthoritarian. Girls in this situation are also likely to become depressed and more likely than are boys in stepfamilies to get involved with drugs.

Why this pattern occurs is not so obvious. The daughter may feel displaced from a special or more responsible position in the family system that she held after her parents' divorce and before the mother's remarriage; she may feel disturbed by the mother's romantic and clearly sexual involvement with the stepfather. In contrast, the teenage boy may have more to gain by the addition of the stepfather. The boy acquires a male role model and may be able to discard some of the adultlike responsibilities he held in the divorced family system. Whatever the explanation, findings like these remind us once again that family systems are astonishingly complex. Simple categories like "intact" and "stepparent" families will need to give way, ultimately, to more fine-grained analyses that

---

TABLE 12.3 Average Scores on Various Measures of Adolescent Behavior for Teenagers from Families with Different Styles of Discipline and Control

Outcome Measure	Style of Parenting			
	Authoritative	Authoritarian	Permissive	Neglectful
Self-reliance	3.09_a	2.96_b	3.03_a	2.98_b
Psychological symptoms	2.36_a	2.46_a	2.43_a	2.65_b
School misconduct	2.16_a	2.26_b	2.38_c	2.43_c
Drug use	1.41_a	1.38_a	1.69_b	1.68_b

Source: Lamborn et al., 1991, Table 9 and Table 10, p. 1060 & 1961.
Note: Numbers with different subscripts are significantly different from one another.

Chances are the daughter in this step-family is more likely to be upset and disturbed by her mother's remarriage and late baby than is her brother.

take into account not only the child's age and gender, but family style, the history and sequence of family structures, the presence of other relatives in the system, and so forth.

Deviant Behavior Patterns Among Adolescents

A similar level of complexity of analysis is needed to understand the origins of two of the most common types of deviant behavior among adolescents, depression and juvenile delinquency. Delinquency gets more press, but depression is an equally significant problem.

Depression.   For many years, psychiatrists thought that depression was an exclusively adult phenomenon. But there is now abundant evidence that depression is actually quite common in adolescence and occurs at least occasionally among younger children. Both Thomas Achenbach and Michael Rutter, in separate large studies—one in the United States and one in England—have found that approximately 10 percent of preadolescent children are described by parents or teachers as appearing miserable, unhappy, sad, or depressed (Achenbach & Edelbrock, 1981; Rutter, Tizard & Whitmore, 1970/1981). Among teenagers, the rate rises to perhaps 40 percent. When teenagers themselves are asked about their state of mind, perhaps a fifth of them describe moderate to severe levels of depressed mood (Siegel & Griffin, 1984; Gibbs, 1985).

When depressive episodes last six months or longer and are accompanied by other symptoms such as disturbances of sleeping and eating and difficulty concentrating, they are usually referred to as **clinical depression** or a *depressive disorder*. Recent epidemiological studies tell us that such severe forms of depression are relatively rare in preadolescents but are quite surprisingly common among adolescents. Estimates range fairly widely, but at least 2 percent and perhaps as many as 10 percent of teenagers can be diagnosed as clinically depressed (Cantwell, 1990).

Interestingly, among preadolescents, boys are somewhat more likely to be described as unhappy or depressed; among teenagers (as among adults) girls more often report high or chronic levels of depression (e.g., Baron & Perron, 1986; Nolen-Hoeksema, Girgus & Seligman, 1991)—one of the few types of psychopathology or deviant behavior that is more common among females.

Although teenagers and preadolescents who describe themselves as depressed do not invariably display all the symptoms of a full-blown clinical depression as seen in adulthood, depressed youngsters do show the same kind of hormonal and other endocrine changes during their depressed episodes as is true of adults, so we know that depression in children is a real and potentially serious clinical state, not just a "normal" or transitory unhappiness (Burke & Puig-Antich, 1990).

THE REAL WORLD
Adolescent Suicide and Its Prevention

One possible accompaniment of depression is suicide. Suicide is very uncommon in children before adolescence. Even among children between 10 and 14, fewer than 1 child in 100,000 in the United States commits suicide each year. But among those between 15 and 19, the rate is nine times higher, and this rate has been rising steadily in the United States in past decades (Hawton, 1986).

The likelihood of suicide is about four times as high among adolescent boys as among girls, and nearly twice as high among whites as among nonwhites *except* for Native American youth, who attempt and commit suicide at higher rates than any other group (Blum et al., 1992). Among white teenage boys aged 15 to 19, roughly 15 out of every 100,000 kill themselves each year. The rate among Native Americans is 26.3 per 100,000. In absolute terms, all of these teen suicides account for less than 1000 deaths per year, far less than the number of deaths by auto accidents in the same age range. But it does represent an ultimate form of deviant behavior.

In contrast, suicide *attempts* are estimated to be three to nine times more common in girls than in boys. Girls, more often than boys, use self-poisoning methods, and these types of suicide attempts are typically less successful than are the methods used by males.

It is obviously very difficult to uncover the contributing factors in successful or completed suicides, because the crucial individual is no longer available to be interviewed. Researchers and clinicians are forced to rely on secondhand reports by parents or others about the mental state of the suicide before the act—reports that are bound to be at least partially invalid, because in many cases the parents or friends had no suspicion that a suicide attempt was imminent. Nonetheless, it does seem clear that some kind of psychopathology is a common ingredient, including but not restricted to depression. Behavior problems such as aggression are also common in the histories of completed suicides, as is a family history of psychiatric disorder or suicide, or a pattern of drug or alcohol abuse (Hawton, 1986). But these factors alone are not enough to explain suicidal behavior. David Shaffer and his colleagues, in their recent analysis of the problem of suicide prevention (Shaffer et al., 1988) suggest at least three other elements that seem to be involved: (1) Some triggering stressful event: Studies of suicides suggest that among adolescents, this triggering event is often a disciplinary crisis with the parents or some rejection or humiliation, such as breaking up with a girlfriend or boyfriend, or failure in some valued activity. (2) Some altered mental state, which might be an attitude of hopelessness, or reduced inhibitions from alcohol consumption, or rage (Swedo et al., 1991). Among girls, in particular, the sense of hopelessness seems to be common: a feeling that the world is against them *and they can't do anything about it.* (3) There must be an opportunity—a loaded gun available in the house, a bottle of sleeping pills in the parents' medicine cabinet, or the like.

Attempts to prevent teen suicide have not been notably successful. Despite the fact that most suicides and suicide attempters have displayed significantly deviant behavior for some period of time before the event, most do not find their way to mental health clinics or other professionals, and increasing the availability of such clinics has not proven effective in reducing suicide rates.

Other prevention efforts have focused on education, such as providing information to all high school students about risk factors in the hope that students might recognize a problem in a friend. Special training in coping abilities has also been offered, so that teenagers might be able to find some nonlethal solution to their problems. The few studies that have evaluated such programs do not show that student attitudes had been much changed as a result (Shaffer et al., 1988).

These discouraging results are not likely to change until we know a great deal more about the developmental pathways that lead to this particular form of psychopathology. What makes one teenager particularly vulnerable and another able to resist the temptation? What combination of stressful circumstances is most likely to trigger a suicide attempt, and how do those stressful circumstances interact with the teenager's personal resources? Only when we can answer questions of this kind will we be on the road to understanding teenage suicide.

So why is there such an increase in depression at this age? And why do some children show this problem, while most do not? One possible pathway is suggested by the clear finding that children growing up with depressed parents are much more likely than are those growing up with nondepressed parents to develop depression themselves. Indeed, after reviewing this evidence, Downey and Coyne conclude that "depression is the *only* diagnosable disorder for which children of depressed parents show significantly heightened risk" (1990, p. 59, emphasis added). Of course, this could indicate a genetic factor at work here, a possibility supported by at least a few studies of twins and adopted children (Burke & Puig-Antich, 1990). Or, we could understand this link between parental and child depression in terms of the changes in the parent-child interaction that are caused by the parent's depression.

This teenager seems to be going through the common experience of the "blues," or depressed mood. As many as 10 percent of teenagers experience more protracted and serious episodes of depression.

I mentioned in Chapter 6 that depressed mothers are much more likely than are nondepressed mothers to have children who are insecurely attached. In particular, their behavior with their child is so nonresponsive that it seems to foster in the child a kind of helpless resignation. Such a sense of helplessness has been found to be strongly related to depression in both adults and adolescents (Dodge, 1990). We also now have even more direct evidence of the link between attachment and adolescent depression from a study by Rogers Kobak and his colleagues (Kobak, Sudler & Gamble, 1991), who used the adult attachment classification I described in the "across development" box in Chapter 6. In their small sample of 48 adolescents, those who were classed as having dismissive or preoccupied attachments also described more depressive symptoms than did those with secure current attachments to their parents.

Of course, not all children of depressed parents are themselves depressed. About 60 percent show no abnormality at all. Whether a child in such a family moves along a pathway toward depression or not seems to be a function of a whole series of protective or disruptive factors:

- If the parent's depression is short-lived or is medically treated so that the symptoms are less severe, the child has a much better chance of avoiding depression herself (e.g., Billings & Moos, 1983).

- The more other forms of stress the family experiences in addition to one parent's depression, such as an illness, family arguments, work stress, loss of income, job loss, or marital separation, the more likely the child is to show depressive symptoms.

- The more emotional and practical support the family receives from others, the less likely the child is to show depressive symptoms (Billings & Moos, 1983).

Thus, the family system can buffer the child from the effects of a parent's depression far more effectively if there are adequate social supports for the parents and not too many other stresses.

Having a depressed parent is not the only pathway that seems to lead to significant depression in an adolescent. Heightened stresses and life changes in the child's own life—such as parents' divorce, the death of a parent or another loved person, or the father's loss of job (Miller, Birnbaum & Durbin, 1990)—may also be contributing factors.

Such individual life stresses may also help to explain the sex differences in depression among adolescents. Anne Petersen (Petersen, Sarigiani & Kennedy, 1991) has recently proposed that girls typically experience more challenges or stresses during adolescence than do boys. In particular, she argues that girls are more likely to encounter simultaneous stressful experiences in adolescence, such as pubertal changes combined with a shift in schools. In her own longitudinal study, Peterson finds that when such synchronous stresses are taken into account, the sex difference in adolescent depression disappears. That is, in this study, depression was *not* more common among girls than among boys when both groups had encountered equal levels of life stress or simultaneous stressful experiences.

Yet another causal factor for adolescent depression is social isolation from peers in early elementary school (Hymel et al., 1990). Peer *rejection* is associated with what psychopathologists call *externalizing* problems—delinquency, conduct disorders, and the like—while isolation from peers is linked to *internalizing* problems such as depression.

You'll remember from Chapter 10 that low self-esteem is also part of the equation. Harter's studies tell us that a young person who feels she (or he) does not measure up to her own standards is much more likely to show symptoms of a clinical depression than is a child or adolescent whose self-esteem is higher.

We can also link the increase in depression at adolescence to the cognitive changes that occur at this age. For example, we know that adolescents are much more likely to

Can you think of any other possible explanations of the higher rates of depression among teenage girls than teenage boys? What sort of study would you have to do to test your hypotheses?

define themselves and others in *comparative* terms—to judge against some standard, or to see themselves as "less than" or "more than" some other person. We also know that at adolescence, appearance becomes highly salient, and that a great many teenagers are convinced that they do not live up to the culturally defined appearance standards. Self-esteem thus drops in early adolescence, and depression rises.

Harter's work is certainly helpful here, but it does not tell us why some teenagers are likely to see themselves as inadequate or to respond to such a sense of inadequacy with depression, while others do not. We have a number of pieces of this puzzle, but we have not yet been able to fit them together into a complete picture.

✦ Juvenile Delinquency.   Delinquency, classed as an externalizing disorder, belongs in the general category of *conduct disorders* I described in Chapter 10. Those children labeled as delinquent show not only the high levels of the bullying, argumentativeness, or disobedience that are common to all conduct disorders, but also some deliberate violation of the law.

Some antisocial or delinquent behaviors, such as fighting, threatening others, cheating, lying, or stealing, are just as common in 4- and 5-year-olds as they are in adolescents (Achenbach & Edelbrock, 1981). In adolescence, however, these behaviors often become more serious, more lethal, more consistent a pattern.

It is extremely difficult to estimate how many teenagers engage in such behavior. One way to gauge the magnitude of the problem is to look at the number of arrests—although arrest rates are arguably only the tip of the iceberg. Over one million juveniles are arrested each year, which is 3 to 4 percent of all youngsters between ages 10 and 17. The rate of arrests, in fact, is higher among those 16 to 18 than in any other age group across the entire life span. A good portion of these arrests are for relatively minor infractions: shoplifting, vandalism, or the like. But 28 percent of all those arrested for serious crimes—including murder, burglary, rape, and arson—are under 18 (U.S. Bureau of the Census, 1990).

Self-reports of delinquency by adolescents suggest even higher rates. Twenty-five to 40 percent of high school students say they have stolen something of relatively low value; 6 percent of boys say they have stolen a car; 12 percent of boys and 7 percent of girls say they have used a weapon to attack someone, and 10 to 15 percent of teenage boys say they have committed a burglary (Achenbach, 1982).

Just as conduct disorders are much more common among preschool- and elementary-school-age boys, delinquent acts and arrests are far more common among boys. Among those actually arrested, the ratio is more than 4 to 1; in self-reports the ratios vary, but the more physically violent the act, the larger the discrepancy.

All delinquents seem to share certain characteristics. In particular, like unpopular children at earlier ages, delinquent teenagers have deficits in *social* understanding. They are less skilled in reading others, in learning the social rules (Schonfeld et al., 1988). Delinquents are also likely to have parents (especially fathers) who are also antisocial or criminal. But within this basic set of similarities, psychologists have identified two distinct subgroups: (1) *socialized-subcultural delinquents*, who hang around with bad companions, stay out late, have a strong allegiance to their peer group or gang, and may commit various crimes as part of their peer activities; (2) *unsocialized-psychopathic delinquents*, who are more often loners and who seem to lack conscience or guilt. These are young people who appear to enjoy conflict and who appear to have little trust in anyone.

Socialized delinquents most often come from poor neighborhoods and grow up in families with erratic discipline and little affection—a style that would be classed as ignoring or rejecting in the category system I have been describing (Achenbach, 1982). As I mentioned in Chapter 6, families in the same kind of poor neighborhoods whose children do *not* become delinquent are distinguished most by a single ingredient: high levels of maternal love. Young people whose mothers are loving and affectionate toward them are simply far less likely to show delinquency regardless of poverty conditions (Glueck & Glueck, 1972; McCord, McCord & Zola, 1959).

Psychopathic delinquency, in contrast, may be found equally often among teenagers from every social class level, and as often in intact families as in broken homes (Achenbach, 1982). It is characterized by high rates of a variety of different types of criminal acts, often beginning quite early in childhood.

Patterson's theoretical model (recall Figure 1.3, page 12) and a great deal of confirming evidence point to a complex of factors causing either type of delinquency. A significant early experience is failure in early parental discipline and/or direct reinforcement for aggressive behavior within the family (Patterson, Capaldi & Bank, 1991). Other influences on the system are the child's temperament, protective factors such as maternal loving affection, and the sustaining conditions, such as lack of social skills or poor peer acceptance (J. Bates et al., 1991). These rejected/antisocial youngsters then tend to band together, further supporting one another's antisocial behavior. At each step along this pathway there are diversion possibilities, but the further along one goes, the more difficult it becomes to deflect and the more persistent the deviant behavior becomes.

Drug and Alcohol Use and Abuse. Another facet of problem behavior in adolescence is substance abuse. In fact, delinquency, early sexual activity, and drug usage all tend to go together, forming a kind of cluster of deviant behavior. For example, in one longitudinal study of a sample of high school students from Colorado, Donovan and Jessor (1985) found correlations among boys of .54 between delinquent behavior and marijuana usage, .41 between delinquent behavior and drunken episodes, and .36 between delinquent acts and frequency of sexual experience. The correlations were similar for girls, but somewhat lower.

National data suggest that many types of drug use have been declining among teenagers in recent years. For example, 23 percent of teenagers in 1974 reported that they had used marijuana, compared to only 17.4 percent in 1988. In the same years, the percentage of teenagers who had ever used cocaine also declined slightly, from 3.6 to 3.4 percent (U.S. Bureau of the Census, 1990). Of course, these numbers may underestimate actual usage, because many respondents will not be honest about using illegal or disapproved-of drugs. Still, there is no reason to suppose that the pattern of decline is suspect, because underreporting should affect the numbers equally in each survey.

Decline or no, we should not become sanguine about drug or alcohol usage among adolescents. Widespread use of alcohol and other drugs is still one of the major health problems among adolescents, and there are signs that alcohol use in particular is once again rising among teenagers. It is also increasingly a problem among younger children as well. One large recent study of first-, fourth-, and seventh-grade boys in Pittsburgh showed that 7.8 percent of *first-graders* had tried beer at least once. Among fourth-graders the comparable figure was 12 percent, rising to 56.5 percent among seventh-graders (Van Kammen, Loeber & Stouthamer-Loeber, 1991). And a study of Oklahoma students revealed that 4.5 percent of middle school students and 19.2 percent of high school students used alcohol weekly. Among the high school students in this study, all but 28 percent had tried alcohol at least once or twice (Novacek, Raskin & Hogan, 1991).

In the Oklahoma study, the most frequent reason teenagers gave for using drugs was because they were depressed (Novacek et al., 1991), followed by a desire to escape from their problems and to relax and have a good time. Those who used drugs regularly did *not* seem to do so to enhance their sense of group belonging; rather, they did so to help them cope with the stresses of their lives or to feel good.

If we put these bits and pieces together with what we know about the life course of rejected children or those who become delinquent, what emerges is the conclusion that

By the end of high school, nearly three-fourths of all students will have tried alcohol at least once.

drug and alcohol use are probably *not* primarily a response to group pressure from other teens to adopt risky behavior. Instead, such use appears to be more common in teens who already show other problems, including other risky or illegal behavior. Furthermore, substance-abusing teens are highly likely to have shown behavior problems at earlier ages, to have had poor school records, early rejection by peers, neglect at home, or a combination of these early problems (Robins & McEvoy, 1990). By default, such children or teens are drawn to peers who share their patterns and their internal models of the world.

This is not to say that a parent should be unconcerned if a teenager seems to have fallen in with "bad companions." Teenage peer groups can and do seduce youngsters into riskier, less approved behavior than they might otherwise engage in. But the crucial aspect of this sequence may be the fact that a young person is drawn to such a group of peers in the first place, rather than any subsequent behavioral contamination by the group. Delinquency, drug and alcohol use or abuse, risky sexual behavior—all these are symptoms of deeper forms of deviance, many of which have their roots in earlier developmental periods.

> How might we go about sorting out the causality here? What kind of study would we need to do in order to tell whether it is the peer group that lures young people into drug and alcohol use, or the young people inclined toward such use who are drawn to like-minded peers?

▶ The Impact of the Larger Culture

The larger culture in which the teenager is embedded naturally continues to have a significant effect on the adolescent's development. Adolescents in most Western countries continue to watch several hours of television a day, although viewing does drop somewhat in the teenage years (Comstock, 1991). Cultural values and specific habits and attitudes are all communicated through this medium. The broad economic climate also affects families, in turn affecting teenagers. Studies in farm communities, for example, show that high school students in families with significant economic hardship are more likely to be depressed, to use drugs, or to be delinquent (Lempers & Clark-Lempers, 1990) than are youngsters from less economically pressed families.

For many youngsters in the United States, however, a new point of contact with the larger culture is added during adolescence: a job.

Joining the Work World

In earlier historical eras and in many cultures around the world today, teenagers were or are already considered adults and fulfill normal adult work responsibilities. They work or worked in the mines, in the fields, herding animals, fishing. Child labor laws changed this picture drastically in the last century in most industrialized countries. In such countries today, adolescents are in school for many hours each day and are not available for adult work—although the typical school year, with a long summer vacation, was intended quite explicitly to allow young people to join in the labor of farming and harvest during the growing season.

Yet increasingly, adolescents have jobs. Beginning in about 1950 in the United States, teenage employment rates have risen quite steadily. Today, one-half to two-thirds of all high school juniors have some kind of formal part-time job during at least part of the school year. The great majority of students have had at least some work experience before they graduate (Greenberger & Steinberg, 1986; Steinberg & Dornbusch, 1991).

For some, such work is an economic necessity. Others work in order to support their favorite hobbies or habits, or to earn the money to buy some item, such as a stereo or even a car, or to go out for pizza with their friends. Parents are frequently very supportive of such work on the grounds that it "builds character" and teaches young people about "real life" (Greenberger & Steinberg, 1986). Here's one parental voice:

> Let's face it. . . . some time in life, someone is going to tell you what to do. . . . I think work is the only place to learn to deal with it. . . . Parents can give you a little discipline, but it isn't accepted. . . . You can't learn that in school, because

What was your own work experience as a teenager? What lessons do you think you learned from that work, if any? In light of your own experience and the data from this study, would you want your own children to work when they are teenagers?

there is another so-called tyrant, the teacher. But then they get . . . a boss, and you get out there and learn it. (Greenberger & Steinberg, 1986, p. 39)

But are parents right about such beneficial effects of work? Does it really teach responsibility and reliability? Results of several decades of research have now cast real doubt on these assumptions. The evidence suggests, in contrast, that the more hours adolescents work, the more *negative* the consequences we see.

The best current study is Steinberg and Dornbusch's analysis (1991) of results from the same very large sample of Wisconsin and California youngsters I have described several times (e.g., Table 12.4). In this case, they have employment information from 5300 ninth- to twelfth-graders, data collected in 1987 and 1988. These subjects were asked a great many other questions as well—about their families, their school work, their attitudes toward school, class cutting, how much homework they did each day, delinquent acts, drug usage, and current employment. So the researchers were able to look at the relationships between the amount of paid work the teenager reported and these other variables.

Because this large sample included sizable numbers of black, Asian, and Hispanic teens, as well as those from families of varying economic levels, it was also possible to check to see if the links between employment and outcomes varied as a function of ethnicity or social class. Steinberg and Dornbusch found that it did not. Essentially the same patterns held for all the ethnic groups and for all levels of family economic or social status.

The patterns are easy to describe: The more hours per week a teenager works, the lower his grade point average, the less time he spends on homework, the less effort he reports putting into school work, the more classes he cuts, the more drug usage and delinquent behavior he reports, and the higher the levels of depression or other psychological distress he reports. In no ethnic or social-class subgroup are there positive effects. Figure 12.6 displays two of the findings to illustrate the size of the effects.

These are not comforting findings. There is little sign here that work is building character. And for students who work long hours outside of school, the effects are quite noticeably negative. One might argue, as some researchers have (e.g., Barton, 1989), that work itself may not be the causal factor. Perhaps students who are already disinterested in school or doing poorly academically choose to work more. But Steinberg and Dornbusch's results contradict this interpretation. They included a separate measure of the

Figure 12.6 These two results from the Steinberg and Dornbusch study of adolescent employment illustrate the repeated pattern of findings: the more hours students worked, the more negative the outcomes. (It may look as if a few hours of work each week is associated with better grades, but this apparent rise is not statistically significant.) (*Source:* Steinberg & Dornbusch, 1991, Figure 1, p. 308, & Figure 2, p. 310.)

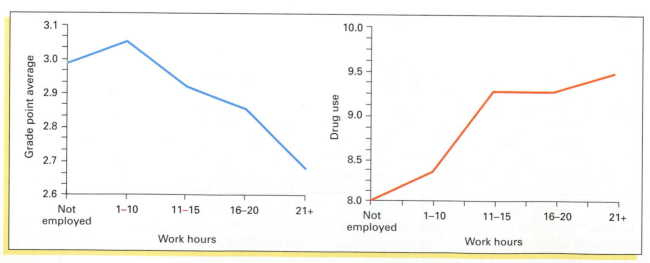

young person's attitude toward school and found the same relationship between hours worked and school performance for those who reported that they enjoyed and valued school as for those who said they did not.

It is difficult to escape the conclusion that teenage employment distracts young people from academic tasks, especially if the student works 10 or more hours each week. What is more, there appear to be few, if any, compensations: teens with jobs do not show higher self-reliance or self-esteem, as many theorists and policy planners had supposed. They also seem to learn some less-than-ideal lessons about the "real world," because they typically work in low-paying, repetitive, often meaningless jobs in which authority is arbitrary and unethical practices (such as stealing from your employer) common (Greenberger & Steinberg, 1986).

The one area in which we do see some positive benefit from adolescent employment is in prospects for future jobs and in later wages (Greenberger & Steinberg, 1986). For example, high school seniors who have had part-time jobs are more likely to report that they have full-time work lined up after their graduation. And those who see their jobs as providing skills that will be useful in the future seem to get some benefits and to be troubled by fewer negative side effects (Mortimer et al., 1992). But this minor benefit was seen primarily for those whose teenage employment was in skilled areas, such as skilled trades, factories, or health care. Students who have worked only in fast-food restaurants, retail sales, baby-sitting, or the like do not seem to have any leg up on future employment.

All of this does not mean that no teenager should ever work. There are obviously situations that will demand such employment, and certain types of skill training that may offer an important counterweight to the potential negative effects. But findings like these certainly should make parents pause before they (we) encourage teenagers to work on the grounds that it will build character.

Most teenage jobs are in low-level, low-responsibility, low-paying jobs like this one. Rather than teaching character and good work habits, as many parents suppose, such part-time work is linked to poorer school performance and higher delinquency and drug usage.

Summary

1. Self-esteem drops somewhat at the beginning of adolescence and then rises steadily through the teen years.

2. Self-definitions become still more abstract at adolescence, with more emphasis on enduring internal qualities and ideology.

3. Teenagers also increasingly define themselves in terms that include both masculine and feminine traits. When both are high, the individual is described as androgynous. High androgyny is associated with higher self-esteem in both male and female adolescents.

4. Erikson emphasized that adolescents must go through a crisis and a redefinition of the self. Many adolescents clearly do so, but we do not know whether all do.

5. Concepts of relationships also undergo change, becoming more flexible, more shaded. Friendships are increasingly seen as adaptive and changeable.

6. Adolescent-parent interactions typically become somewhat more conflicting in early adolescence, a phenomenon possibly linked to the physical changes of puberty. But the attachment to parents remains strong.

7. Peer relationships become increasingly important, both quantitatively and qualitatively. Theorists emphasize that peers serve an important function as a bridge between the dependence of childhood and the independence of adulthood.

8. Teenagers are most vulnerable to the pressure of their peers in fairly early adolescence. At this same time, peer groups shift from same-sex cliques to mixed sex crowds.

9. Dating normally begins slightly later, although there is wide variability.

10. Sexual activity among teenagers has become increasingly common in the United States and many other indus-

trialized countries. At every age, boys report more sexual activity than girls, and blacks report more than whites or Hispanics.

12. Knowledge of reproductive biology or contraception is comparatively low, and rates of teen pregnancy are high. Long term adult life outcomes for teenage girls who bear children appear to be quite different than for those who do not.

13. Authoritative family interactions continue to be the optimal pattern at adolescence. Teenagers in such families are more self-reliant, are less apt to use drugs, and have higher self-esteem than do those in neglecting or authoritarian families.

14. The parents' remarriage during the child's adolescence appears to have a more negative effect for girls than for boys.

15. Rates of depression increase sharply at adolescence and are higher among girls than boys. Depressed teens are more likely to come from families with at least one depressed parent, but there are other pathways, including poor peer acceptance in elementary school, low self-esteem, and high levels of life change or stress at adolescence.

16. Delinquent acts also increase at adolescence, especially among boys. Several types of delinquents have been identified, with different developmental pathways.

17. Correlated with delinquency is drug and alcohol use, but the majority of teens—including those not otherwise delinquent—report some alcohol use.

18. Part-time employment by teenagers has become very common. There is no indication that employment "builds character." Instead, it is associated with lower school performance and higher rates of delinquent behavior.

Key Terms

androgyny	cliques	undifferentiated
clinical depression	crowds	

Suggested Readings

Feldman, S. S., & Elliott, G. R. (Eds.) (1990). *At the threshold. The developing adolescent.* Cambridge, MA: Harvard University Press. (Once again I recommend this first-rate edited volume. It includes many excellent chapters addressing issues I have touched on in this chapter.)

Greenberger, E., & Steinberg, L. (1986). *When teenagers work. The psychological and social costs of adolescent employment.* New York: Basic Books. (A persuasive, clearly written, surprising book about the effects of teenage employment.)

Hayes, C. D. (Ed.) (1987). *Risking the future. Adolescent sexuality, pregnancy, and childbearing.* Vol. 1. Washington, D.C.: National Academy Press. (This book is the final report of a special panel on adolescent pregnancy and childbearing created by the National Research Council. It contains excellent reviews of the research on all aspects of adolescent sexuality and pregnancy, as well as a discussion of long-term outcomes for early sexuality and early pregnancy. A second volume in this set includes more detailed working papers.)

SUMMING UP ADOLESCENCE

Basic Characteristics of Adolescence

After reading the last two chapters, I think you will agree that it makes sense to divide the period of years from 12 to about 20 into two subperiods, one beginning at 11 or 12, the other perhaps at 16 or 17. Some label these as *adolescence* and *youth* (e.g., Kenis-ton, 1970), others as *early* and *late* adolescence (e.g., Brooks-Gunn, 1988). However we label them, there are distinct differences.

Early adolescence is, almost by definition, a time of transition, a time in which there is significant change in virtually every aspect of the child's functioning. Late adolescence is more a time of consolidation, when the young person establishes a cohesive new identity, with clearer goals and role commitments. Norma Haan (1981a) offers a helpful way of thinking about this difference, based on Piaget's concepts of assimilation and accommodation. Early adolescence, she says, is a time dominated by as-

---

A Summary of the Threads of Development During Early and Late Adolescence

Aspect of Development	Age in Years								
	12	13	14	15	16	17	18	19+
	Early Adolescence					Late Adolescence (Youth)		
Physical development	Major pubertal change begins for boys		Boys' height spurt				Puberty completed for boys	
		Girls' height spurt	Average age of menarche		Puberty completed for girls			
Cognitive development	Beginning formal operations: systematic analysis; some deductive logic				Consolidated formal operations (for some)			
	Kohlberg's Stage 3 ("good boy, nice girl" orientation) continues to dominate							
					Kohlberg's Stage 4 ("law and order") for a few			
			Descriptions of self and others begin to include exceptions, comparisons, special conditions; deeper personality traits					
Personality and social development	Self-esteem declines	Self-esteem begins to rise and continues to rise for remainder of adolescence						
	Rate of depression rises sharply and remains high						Clear identity achievement for perhaps half	
	Erikson's stage of identity vs. role diffusion							
	Cliques		Crowds	Pairs				
	Parent-child conflict peaks at beginning of puberty		Maximum impact of peer group pressure	Normal time for first dating				

similation, while late adolescence is primarily a time of accommodation.

The 12- or 13-year-old is assimilating an enormous amount of new physical, social, and intellectual experiences. While the experiences are being absorbed, but before they are digested, the young person is in a more or less perpetual state of disequilibrium. Old patterns and old schemes no longer work very well, but new ones have not been established. It is during this early period that the peer group is so centrally important. Ultimately, the 16- or 17- or 18-year-old begins to make the needed accommodations, pulls the threads together, and establishes a new identity, new patterns of social relationships, new goals and roles.

I've summarized the various aspects of development in these two periods in the table on page 307, but let me say a bit more about each.

Early Adolescence

In some ways the early years of adolescence have a lot in common with the early years of toddlerhood. Two-year-olds are famous for their negativism and for their constant push for more independence. At the same time, they are struggling to learn a vast array of new skills. Teenagers show many of these same qualities, albeit at much more abstract levels. We see a parallel rise in conflict or negativism with parents, much of which centers around issues of independence—they want to come and go when they please, listen to the music they prefer at maximum volume, and wear the clothing and hair styles that are currently "in."

Like the negativism of the 2-year-old, it is easy to overstate the depth or breadth of the conflict between young teenagers and their parents. It is important to keep in mind that we are not talking here about major turmoil, but only a temporary increase in disagreements or disputes. The depiction of adolescence as full of *sturm und drang* is as much an exaggeration as is the phrase "terrible twos." But both ages are characterized by a new push for independence, which is inevitably accompanied by more confrontations with parents over limits.

While this push for independence is going on, the young adolescent is also facing a whole new set of demands and skills to be learned—new social skills, new levels of cognitive complexity found in formal operations tasks. The sharp increases in the rate of depression and the drop in self-esteem we see at the beginning of adolescence seem to be linked to this surplus of new demands and changes. A number of investigators have found that those adolescents who have the greatest number of simultaneous changes at the beginning of puberty—changing to junior high school, moving to a new town or new house, perhaps a parental separation or divorce—also show the greatest loss in self-esteem, the largest rise in problem behavior, and the biggest drop in grade point average (e.g., Eccles & Midgley, 1990; Simmons, Burgeson & Reef, 1988). Young adolescents who can cope with these changes one at a time show fewer symptoms of stress.

Facing major stressful demands, the 2-year-old uses Mom (or some other central attachment figure) as a safe base for exploring the world, returning for reassurance when fearful. Young adolescents seem to do the same with the family, using it as a safe base from which to explore the rest of the world, including the world of peer relationships. Parents of young adolescents must try to find a difficult balance between providing the needed security, often in the form of clear rules and limits, and still allowing independence—just as the parent of a 2-year-old must walk the fine line between allowing exploration and keeping the child safe. Among teenagers, as among toddlers, the most confident and successful are those whose families manage this balancing act well.

Still a third way in which theorists have likened the young teenager to the 2-year-old is in egocentrism. David Elkind (1967) suggested some years ago that there is a rise in egocentrism in adolescence. This new egocentrism, according to Elkind, has two facets: (1) the belief that "others in our immediate vicinity are as concerned with our thoughts and behavior as we ourselves are" (Elkind & Bowen, 1979, p. 38), which Elkind describes as having an *imaginary audience*; (2) the possession of a *personal fable*, a tendency to consider their own ideas and feelings unique and singularly important. This is typically accompanied by a sense of invulnerability—a feeling that may lie behind the adolescent's apparent attraction to high-risk behavior, such as unprotected sex, drugs, drinking, high-speed driving, and the like.

Elkind's own research (e.g., Elkind & Bowen, 1979) shows that preoccupation with others' views of the self—what he calls imaginary audience behavior—peaks at about age 13 to 14. Teenagers this age are most likely to say that if they went to a party where they did not know most of the kids, they would wonder *a lot* about what the other kids were thinking of them. They also report that they worry a lot when someone is watching them work and feel desperately embarrassed if they discover a grease spot on their clothes or have newly erupted pimples. Of course, younger children and adults may also worry about these things, but they seem to be much less disturbed or immobilized by these worries than are 13- and 14-year-olds.

You'll recall that this is the same age at which teens seem to be most susceptible to peer pressure, and it is the peak age for the type of peer group Dunphy calls the crowd.

Drawing a parallel between the early adolescent and the toddler makes sense in that both age groups face the task of establishing a separate identity. The toddler must separate herself from the symbiotic relationship with Mom or central caregiver. She must figure out not only that she is separate but that she has abilities and qualities. Physical maturation also allows her new levels of independent exploration. The young adolescent must separate himself from his family and from his identity as a child, and begin to form a new identity as an adult. This, too, is accompanied by major maturational changes that make new levels and kinds of independence possible. In both cases, these changes are accompanied by a kind of self-preoccupation and by increases in confrontations with caregivers.

Late Adolescence

To carry the basic analogy further, late adolescence is more like the preschool years. Major changes have been weathered, and a new balance has been achieved. The physical upheavals of puberty are mostly complete, the family system has changed to allow more independence and freedom, and the beginnings of a new identity have been created. This period is not without its strains. For most young people, a clear identity is not achieved until college age, if then, so the identity process continues. And the task of forming emotionally intimate sexual or presexual partnerships is a key task of late adolescence. Nonetheless, I think Haan is correct in stating that this later period is more one of accommodation than assimilation.

At the very least, we know that it is accompanied by rising levels of self-esteem and declining levels of family confrontation or conflict.

Central Processes and Their Connections

In other interludes, I have suggested that changes in one or another of the facets of development may be central to the constellation of transformations we see at a given age. In infancy, underlying physiological changes along with the creation of a first central attachment appear to have such key causal roles; in the preschool years, cognitive changes seem especially dominant, while among school age children, both cognitive and social changes appear to be formative. In adolescence, there is significant change in *every* domain. At this point, we simply do not have the research data that clarify the basic causal connections among the transformations in these various areas. Still, we have *some* information about linkages.

The Role of Puberty

The most obvious place to begin is with puberty itself. Puberty not only defines the beginning of early adoles-

cence, it clearly affects all other facets of the young person's development, either directly or indirectly.

Direct effects might be seen in several ways. Most clearly, the surges of pubertal hormones stimulate sexual interest while they also trigger body changes that make adult sexuality and fertility possible. These changes seem inescapably causally linked to the gradual shift from same-sex peer groupings to heterosexual crowds and finally to heterosexual pair relationships.

Hormones and Family Relationships. Hormone changes may also be directly implicated in the increases in confrontation or conflict between parents and children, and the rise in various kinds of aggressive or delinquent behavior. Steinberg's research suggests such a direct link because he finds pubertal stage and not age to be the critical variable in predicting the level of adolescent-parent conflict. Other investigators have found that in girls, the rise in estradiol at the beginning of puberty is associated with increases in verbal aggression and a loss of impulse control, while in boys, increases in testosterone are correlated with increases in irritability and impatience (Paikoff & Brooks-Gunn, 1990). But there are also many studies in which no such connection is found (e.g., Coe, Hayashi & Levine, 1988), which has led most theorists to conclude that the connections between pubertal hormones and changes in adolescent social behavior are considerably more complicated than we had first imagined.

One of the complications is that the physical changes of puberty have highly significant indirect effects as well. When the child's body grows and becomes more like that of an adult, the parents begin to treat the child differently, and the child begins to see himself as a soon-to-be-adult. Both of these changes may be linked to the brief rise in parent-adolescent confrontation and may help to trigger some of the searching self-examinations that are part of this period of life.

The adolescent's pubertal changes also require other adaptations from the parents that change the family dynamics. It can be very confusing to deal with a young teenager who seems simultaneously to demand both more independence, authority, and power, and more nurturance and guidance. What is more, the presence of a sexually charged pubescent teen may re-awaken the parents' own unresolved adolescent issues, just when they are themselves facing a sense of physical decline in their forties or fifties. Teenagers may stay up late, severely restricting private time for parents. Perhaps, then, it is not surprising that many parents (particularly fathers) report that marital satisfaction is at its lowest ebb during their children's adolescence (Rollins & Galligan, 1978). Taking all this together, you can see why it is so difficult to sort out the direct and indirect effects of pubertal hormone changes on social behavior.

Puberty and Cognitive Change. Equally difficult to demonstrate is the possible link between the physical changes of puberty and cognitive changes, particularly the shift to formal operations. That there must be *some* connection between the two seems plausible. As J. M. Tanner says:

> There is clearly no reason to suppose that the link between maturation of [brain] structure and appearance of [cognitive] function suddenly ceases at age 6 or 10 or 13. On the contrary, there is every reason to believe that the higher intellectual abilities also appear only when maturation of certain structures is complete. (Tanner, 1970, p. 123)

But if there is a connection, it is clearly not an invariable one because we know that not all adolescents (or adults) ever develop formal operational thinking. So brain changes at puberty cannot be the sole cause of the development of these most abstract forms of thinking. Neurological or hormonal changes at adolescence may be *necessary* for further cognitive gains—although even that has not been clearly established—but they cannot be *sufficient* conditions for such developments.

The Role of Cognitive Changes at Adolescence

An equally attractive possibility to many theorists has been the proposition that it is the cognitive changes that are central. No one is arguing that the cognitive shift from concrete to formal operations is causing pubertal changes. But many have argued that cognitive development is central to many of the other changes we see at adolescence, including changes in the self-concept, the process of identity formation, increases in level of moral reasoning, and changes in peer relationship.

There is ample evidence, for example, that the more abstract nature

of the child's self-concept and of his descriptions of others is intimately connected to the broader changes in cognitive functioning (Harter, 1990). The emergence of concrete operations at 7 or 8 is reflected in the child's use of trait labels to describe himself and others; the emergence of formal operations is reflected in self-descriptions that focus more and more on interior states, and descriptions of others that are both flexible and based on subtle inferences from behavior.

A somewhat broader proposal about connections between cognitive and other changes at adolescence comes from Kohlberg (1973, 1976). He hypothesized that the child first moves to a new level of logical thought, then applies this new kind of logic to relationships as well as objects, and only then applies this thinking to moral problems. More specifically, Kohlberg argued that at least some formal operations and at least some mutual perspective taking in relationships are necessary (but not sufficient) for the emergence of conventional moral reasoning. Full formal operations and still more abstract social understanding may be required for postconventional reasoning.

The research examining such a sequential development is scant, but it supports Kohlberg's hypothesis. Lawrence Walker (1980) found that among a group of fourth- to seventh-graders he had tested on concrete and formal operations tasks, social understanding, and moral reasoning, one-half to two-thirds were reasoning at the same level across the different domains, which makes the whole thing look unexpectedly "stagelike." But when a child was ahead in one progression, the sequence was always that the child developed logical thinking first, then more advanced social understanding, and then the parallel moral judgments. Thus, a young person still using concrete operations is unlikely to use postconventional moral reasoning. But the coherence is not automatic. The basic cognitive understanding makes advances in social and moral reasoning *possible*, but does not guarantee them. Experience in relationships and with moral dilemmas is necessary too.

One moral of this (if you will excuse the pun) is that just because a young person or adult shows signs of formal operations does *not* necessarily mean that he or she will show sensitive, empathetic, and forgiving attitudes toward friends or family. It's a point worth keeping in mind.

Some ability to use formal operations may also be necessary but not sufficient for the formation of a clear identity. One of the characteristics of formal operations thinking is the ability to imagine possibilities that you have never experienced and to manipulate ideas in your head. These new skills may help to foster the broad questioning of old ways, old values, old patterns that are a central part of the identity formation process. Several studies show that among high school and college students, those in Marcia's identity achievement or moratorium statuses are much more likely also to be using formal operations reasoning than are those in the diffusion or foreclosure statuses (Leadbeater & Dionne, 1981; Rowe & Marcia, 1980). In Rowe and Marcia's study, the *only* individuals who showed full identity achievement were those who were also using full formal operations. But the converse was not true. That is, there were a number of subjects who used formal operations who had not yet established a clear identity. Thus, formal operations thinking may *enable* the young person to rethink many aspects of his life, but it does not guarantee

that he will do so.

Overall, we are left with the impression that both the physical changes of puberty and the potential cognitive changes of formal operations are central to the phenomenon of adolescence, but the connections between them and their impact on social behavior are still largely a mystery. I know it is frustrating to have me keep saying that we don't know, but that's an accurate statement of our current knowledge.

Influences on the Basic Processes

There is not space or time enough to detail all the many factors that will influence the teenager's experience of adolescence. Many I have already mentioned, including such cultural variations as the presence or absence of initiation rites, the timing of the child's pubertal development, and the degree of personal or familial stress. But one more general point is worth making: Adolescence, like every other developmental period, does not begin with a clean slate. The individual youngster's own temperamental qualities, behavioral habits, and internal models of interaction, established in earlier years of childhood, obviously have a profound effect on the experience of adolescence. Examples are easy to find.

• Sroufe's longitudinal study, which I described in Chapter 6 (Sroufe, 1989), shows that those who had been rated as having a secure attachment in infancy were more self-confident and more socially competent with peers at the beginning of adolescence.
• Delinquency and heightened aggressiveness in adolescence rarely appear afresh; they are nearly always presaged by earlier behavior problems and by inadequate family control as early as the years of toddlerhood (Di-

shion et al., 1991; Robins & McEvoy, 1990).
• Depression in adolescents is more likely among those who enter adolescence with lower self-esteem (Harter, 1988).

Avshalom Caspi and Terrie Moffitt (1991) make the more general point that *any* major life crisis or transition, including adolescence, has the effect of *accentuating* earlier personality or behavioral patterns rather than creating new ones. This is not unlike the observation that the child's attachment to the parent is only revealed when the child is under stress. Similarly, Caspi and Moffitt argue that in times of stress, old patterns—particularly old problems—are exacerbated. For example, they point out that girls with very early puberty, on average, have higher rates of psychological problems than do those with normal-time puberty. But closer analysis reveals that it is only the early puberty girls who already had social problems before puberty began whose pubertal experience and adolescence is more negative. Very early puberty does not increase psychological problems for girls who were psychologically healthier to begin with.

I think this is an important point for understanding all the various transitions of adult life. Not only do we carry ourselves with us as we move through the roles and demands of adult life, but those existing patterns may be most highly visible when we are under stress. This does not mean that we never change or learn new and more effective ways of responding. But we must never lose sight of the fact that by adolescence, and certainly by adulthood, our internal working models and our repertoire of coping behaviors are already established, creating a bias in the system. Another way of putting it is that while change is possible, continuity is the default option.

13

PHYSICAL AND COGNITIVE DEVELOPMENT IN EARLY ADULTHOOD

Because I completed my Ph.D. when I was just 24 and was thus "off time" in some respects, for most of my twenties and thirties I had a strong sense of being young. I was nearly always the youngest person—and of course nearly always the only woman—in groups of professional colleagues. In the early years I was often younger than many of the graduate students. Because I defined myself in this way, as a "young Turk," it was a particular shock, as my forties approached, to realize that I was approaching what I thought of as middle age.

No doubt each of us has our own definition of *young adult* or of *middle age* or *old age*. These definitions not only change over historical time, they may differ from one subgroup to another. Even among social scientists, there is no clear agreement on how we should divide up the years of adulthood. Physical and cognitive change in adulthood is more gradual and more variable from one individual to the next than is true in childhood. So it is not so obvious how we ought to divide up the years. By convention, most lifespan researchers make one division at 60 or 65, the age at which most adults in industrialized countries retire from paid work. The most common second age division is at about 40 or 45. This second demarcation point can be justified on any of several grounds.

- It allows one to divide the adult years into three roughly equal parts: early adulthood from 20 to 40, middle adulthood from 40 to about 65, and late adulthood from 65 until death.

- It reflects a set of role changes that often (but not always) occur in the early forties, when children begin to leave home and careers typically reach their peak.

- It reflects the fact that optimum physical and cognitive functioning, clearly present in one's twenties and thirties, begins to wane in some noticeable and measurable ways in the forties and fifties. The slope of change may be very gradual, but it is clearly moving downward after age 40. This results not only in an increase in disease and disability rates, but also in an increased *awareness* of physical decline in one's forties.

For all these reasons, I'm going to define *young adulthood* as the period from 20 to 40. But you should remember always that this is an arbitrary division and that there is quite

When you think about adult life, do you mentally divide it into segments of some kind? Where are the break points in your own mind? When does "middle age" start? When does "old age" begin? Do you think that your expectations or definitions are likely to have any effect on how you interpret the experiences in your life?

wide variability in the occurrence of some of these defining events and gradual change across the supposedly transitional years.

▶ Maturation and Aging

Another way in which the study of adults differs from the study of children has to do with the role of maturation and the other forms of shared change I talked about in Chapter 1. For one thing, when we study children's development, we are looking at increases, at improvements. When we study adults, especially when we study their physical and cognitive functioning, we begin to ask questions about loss of function or decline. Can we use the same theoretical models, the same ways of thinking and analyzing to study decline as we use to study increases?

Even at 30, adults may find that it takes a bit more work to get into or stay in shape than it did at 20.

Answers to such questions are influenced by just how one defines development. When we talk about the child's development, there is clearly direction and order to the change. The baby goes from sitting to crawling to walking; the adolescent moves through the steps of pubertal change; the child moves cognitively from concrete to abstract, from egocentric to relational. We can also agree that physical maturation forms the substrate of many of these developmental changes. When we study changes over the adult years, there is much less agreement about whether we are looking at *development* in the same sense.

Certainly there are widely (but not universally) shared role changes in adult life, many of which occur in early adulthood. But is there any direction, any pattern, to the changes we see in adults that we might reasonably think of as development? Do people get smarter, wiser, more stable, or slower as they age? And in all of this, what role does maturation play?

Superficially, it seems obvious that there are shared, inevitable physical changes in adulthood, normally referred to as *aging*, all of which seem self-evidently maturational in nature. I look at myself in the mirror and can readily see such changes, including white hair and more lines in my face. Many of us past the age of 40 believe we can detect similar changes in our thinking: it seems to take longer to remember names, and learning new things seems to take more time, more effort.

Physiologists and psychologists do not dispute these observations; there *is* a biological clock, and it clearly ticks more and more loudly as one moves through adult life. But recent research is beginning to tell us that some of what we have attributed to inevitable physical aging may have other causes, including disease and disuse. At the heart of the question is a methodological dilemma.

How Do We Study Physical Aging?   Suppose we want to know something about changes in heart or lung function over the years of adulthood. What happens to blood pressure or aerobic capacity or the ability of the heart to pump blood? Do these systems change in inevitable ways as we get older?

Data from cross-sectional studies seem to answer "yes" to this question. Such research shows that in older adults, the heart is less and less efficient and that our capacity for taking in and transmitting oxygen declines steadily. But there is a built-in difficulty with such comparisons. We also know that older adults are more likely to suffer from heart *disease.* So in random cross-sectional samples, each succeeding age group will have a larger and larger proportion of subjects who suffer from heart disease (e.g., Christensen et al., 1992). So how much of the "change" in heart function that we see in the cross-sectional comparison is really aging, and how much is simply the presence of more disease?

Longitudinal research will not help in this case. If we started with a random group of 20-year-olds and measured their heart and lung function every 10 years for 60 years, it would still be the case that at each succeeding testing point, a larger percentage of the subjects would be suffering from heart disease.

We know that heart disease itself is *not* a normal part of aging, because not everyone shows this disease process. The obvious solution is to look at age changes only in adults who are disease-free. In this way we may get some sense of the basic, underlying aging process, uncomplicated by disease. When we do that, we find *some* changes correlated with age, but they are much smaller. At the very least, it begins to look as if disease-free aging is slower and later than many of us had supposed. And some changes we thought were part of normal aging turn out not to exist at all when we look at disease-free adults.

I am not trying to create a picture of rosy optimism. The sand does indeed fall through the hourglass; death does come to us all. But it is important to try to sort out just what changes are really part of normal aging, and which are due to other, perhaps preventable, causes. These caveats are important even when we look at physical and cognitive functioning in early adulthood, when performance is at its peak by any measure. The newer research does not dispute such an advantage for the young, but it does point to the possibility that the difference between young and older adults is smaller than we had thought. With that background in mind, let's look at some of the evidence.

▶ Physical Functioning in Early Adulthood

At the end of adolescence, physical growth is complete and the body is clearly at its peak. Young adults perform better than do the middle-aged or old on virtually every physical measure. The adult in her twenties and thirties has more muscle tissue; maximum calcium in her bones; more brain mass; better eyesight, hearing, and smell; greater oxygen capacity; and a more efficient immune system. She is stronger, faster, and better able to recover from exercise or to adapt to changing body conditions, such as changes in temperature or light levels. I'll be talking about a number of these individual changes in more detail in Chapters 15 and 17, when I talk about the physical status of middle-aged and older adults. But to give you a sense of the overall shape and sweep of the differences, I've summarized them in Table 13.1.

Most of the summary statements in the table are based on both longitudinal and cross-sectional data, which gives considerably more strength to the conclusions. But many studies have not controlled for the health of the subjects, so it is possible that some of the differences are actually smaller, or occur later, than it now appears. Still, the pattern is certainly consistent: Adults achieve and maintain peak physical functioning until about age 40, at which time there begin to be measurable or noticeable changes in most aspects of performance. The underlying physiological change processes probably begin well before age 40; in some cases, such as the loss of mass of the thymus gland involved in immune system function, the change begins shortly after adolescence. But in most cases we do not detect a significant drop in physical *function* until middle age. Let me flesh out this brief summary with a few more detailed examples.

Heart and Lungs. The most common measure of overall aerobic ability is **maximum oxygen uptake (VO$_2$ max)**, which reflects the ability of the body to take in and transport oxygen to various body organs. When this is measured at rest, there are only minimal decrements associated with age. But when VO$_2$ max is measured during exercise, there is a systematic decline with age of about 1 percent a year. I've given some typical results from both cross-sectional and longitudinal studies of women in Figure 13.1 on page 316. Similar results are found with men (Lakatta, 1990; Kozma, Stones & Hannah, 1991).

Similarly, under resting conditions there are no age differences in the quantity of blood flow from the heart (cardiac output), but under exercise conditions, there is a significant decline, with 65-year-olds putting out 25 to 30 percent less than 25-year-olds (Lakatta, 1985; Rossman, 1980). Heart rate shows a similar pattern: no age differences in resting conditions, but a *smaller* rise in heart rate during exercise with increasing age.

This Yosemite Park ranger is probably in better shape now than he will be at any other time in his life.

TABLE 13.1 A Summary of Age Changes in Physical Functioning

Body Function	Age at Which Change Begins to be Clear or Measurable	Nature of Change
Vision	40–45	Lens of eye thickens and loses accommodative power, resulting in poorer near vision and more sensitivity to glare.
Hearing	About 50	Loss of ability to hear very high and very low tones.
Smell	About 40	Decline in ability to detect and discriminate among different smells.
Taste	None	No apparent loss in taste discrimination ability.
Muscles	About 50	Loss of muscle tissue, particularly in "fast twitch" fibers used for bursts of strength or speed, resulting in loss of strength.
Bones	After menopause in women; later in men	Loss of calcium in the bones, called *osteoporosis*. Also wear and tear on bone joints, called *osteoarthritis*, more marked after about 60.
Heart and lungs	35 or 40	No age difference on measures taken at rest; decline in most aspects of function when measured during or after exercise.
Nervous system	40–45	Loss of density of dendrites; loss of gray matter of brain; drop in brain weight; slower synaptic speed.
Immune system	Adolescence	Loss in size of thymus; reduction in number and maturity of T cells.
Reproductive system	Mid 30s for women	Increase reproductive risk and lowered fertility.
Cellular elasticity	Gradual	Gradual loss in most cells, including skin, muscle, tendon, and blood vessel cells. Faster deterioration in cells exposed to sunlight.
Height	40	Compression of disks in the spine, with resulting loss of height of 1 to 2 inches by age 80.
Weight	Nonlinear pattern	In United States studies, maximum weight in middle adulthood. Fat also redistributed at mid-life, when fat is lost in the face, legs, and lower arms, and added in upper arm, belly, and buttocks—the famous middle-aged spread.
Skin	40	Increase in wrinkliness, due to loss of elasticity; sweat- and oil-secreting glands become less efficient.
Hair	About 50	Becomes thinner and may gray.

Sources: Bartoshuk & Weiffenbach, 1990; Bornstein, 1988; Braveman, 1987; Doty et al., 1984; Duara, London & Rapoport, 1985; Finch, 1986; Fozard, 1990; Hallfrisch et al., 1990; Kallman, Plato & Tobin, 1990; Kozma, Stones & Hannah, 1991; Lakatta, 1985, 1990; Lim et al., 1992; McFalls, 1990; Miller, 1990; Rossman, 1980; Selmanowitz, Rizer & Orentreich, 1977; Shock, 1985; Wilkinson & Allison, 1989.

One exception to this pattern appears to be blood pressure. You know that when your blood pressure is tested, you are given two numbers. The higher number represents systolic pressure, which is the force of the blood when your heart is contracting. On this measure there are age differences even under resting conditions. Systolic pressure is lowest

Figure 13.1 The continuous line shows VO$_2$ max averages for cross-sectional comparisons; the arrows show changes on the same measure for groups of women studied longitudinally. The two sets of findings match remarkably. Note that the largest drop was between age 40 and 50. (*Source:* Plowman, Drinkwater & Horvath, 1979, Figure 1, p. 514.)

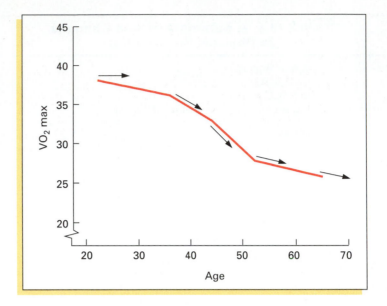

in adults in their twenties and thirties and then rises steadily with age, apparently as a result of loss of elasticity in the blood vessels, a reflection of a much more general loss of elasticity in tissues in all parts of the body (the cause of those wrinkles I see in my mirror).

Because we know that all these aspects of cardiovascular functioning can be improved with exercise, it is possible that the pattern of results I've been describing is still not a reflection of aging per se, but rather the effect of an increasingly sedentary life-style among older adults—a possibility I'll be coming back to in Chapters 15 and 17.

Strength and Speed. The collective effect of the changes in muscles and cardiovascular fitness is a general loss of strength and speed with age. Figure 13.2, on page 318, shows both cross-sectional and nine-year longitudinal changes in grip strength in a group of men who participated in the Baltimore Longitudinal Studies of Aging. Clearly, strength was at its peak in the twenties and early thirties, and then declined steadily. Once again I need to point out that such a difference might be the result of the fact that younger adults are more physically active or more likely to be engaged in activities or jobs that demand strength. Arguing against this conclusion, however, are studies of physically active older adults, who also show loss of muscle strength over time (e.g., Phillips et al., 1992). Even more persuasive are results of studies of top athletes, described in the "real world" box on the opposite page. Even among these highly conditioned individuals, the clear pattern is that there is loss of both strength and speed with age.

Reproductive Capacity. I pointed out in Chapter 3 that the risk of miscarriage and other complications of pregnancy is higher in a woman's thirties than in her twenties. Fertility—the ability to conceive—is also at its highest in the late teens and early twenties, and then drops steadily (McFalls, 1990). For example, in one large national study in the United States in 1982 in which *infertility* was defined as the "inability to conceive after one or more years of unprotected intercourse" (McFalls, 1990, p. 511), only 7 percent of women aged 20 to 24 were infertile, compared to 15 percent of those between 30 and 34, and 28 percent of those between 35 and 39 (Mosher, 1987; Mosher & Pratt, 1987).

Among men, fertility does not follow the same pattern. There is not much research, but it appears that there is essentially no change over the years of early adulthood in a man's capacity to impregnate. There is some decline after age 40, but (as I'll describe in detail in Chapter 15) there is no equivalent of menopause among men, who may be able to impregnate well into late life.

THE REAL WORLD
Age and Peak Sports Performance

One of the most obvious ways to test the principle that human bodies are at their physical peak in early adulthood is to look at sports performance. World-class performers in any sport are pushing their bodies to the limit of their abilities in some area. If early adulthood is really the peak, we should find that most world record holders or top performers are in their twenties or perhaps early thirties. Another strategy is to look at the average performance of top athletes in each of several age groups, including those over 35 or 40, nowadays referred to as "masters athletes." Both analyses lead inescapably to the same conclusion: athletic performance peaks early in life, although there is some variability from one kind of sport to another.

Swimmers, for example, reach their peak very early, at about age 17 for women and about 19 for men. Golfers peak the latest, at about age 31 (Schulz & Curnow, 1988). Runners lie in between, with top performances in the early or middle twenties. The longer the distance, the later the peak, as you can see in the figure, which represents the average age at which each of a series of top male athletes ran his fastest time.

Cross-sectional comparisons of the top performances of competitors of different ages lead to the same conclusion. For example, in Germany there are national swimming championships held each year, with awards to the top performers in each 5-year age range from 25 through 70. The best times become steadily slower with age (Letzelter, Jungermann & Freitag, 1986; Ericsson, 1990).

Of course, it is possible that such a decline is an illusion created by cohort differences of some kind. For one thing, not many adults continue national or world-class competition into their forties, fifties, or beyond, so the older competitors are drawn from much smaller groups. Fortunately, we can confirm the same general effects with a few small longitudinal studies of athletes who have continued to compete at maximum level over many years. These few studies show smaller declines with age than do the cross-sectional comparisons. In particular, top performers may maintain nearly peak performances well into their thirties. Paavo Nurmi, a famous Finnish long-distance runner, ran his fastest 10,000 meter time at 27 but was still running world-class times at 35. But there is nonetheless a decline (Ericsson, 1990), even for such top performers. Kareem-Abdul Jabbar may have continued to be a fine basketball player into his forties, but he was not as good at 40 as at 25, and he retired at 40 precisely because his performance level was dropping noticeably.

At the same time, it is also true that older athletes can perform far better than many of us may have supposed. World records for age groups over 40 ("Masters" categories) continue to drop; in many sports, current 50-year-olds are performing at higher levels than did Olympic athletes of a hundred years ago. The human body, at any age, is more responsive to training than researchers even a decade ago had presumed. But it is still true that for those who achieve and maintain a high level of fitness throughout adult life, peak performance will come in early adulthood.

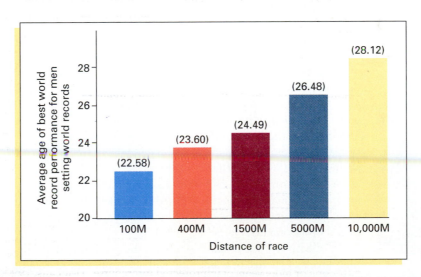

Immune System Functioning. The immune system, so critical in our ability to fight off disease, includes several types of cells created in the bone marrow (B cells) and in the thymus gland (T cells). Collectively, they protect the body by producing antibodies that react to foreign organisms, such as viruses or other infections, and by producing special cells that reject or consume harmful or mutant cells. It is T cells that are most deficient

Figure 13.2 These data, from the Baltimore Longitudinal Study of Aging, show both cross-sectional data (dots) and longitudinal data (lines) for grip strength among men. Once again, there is striking agreement between the two sets of information. (*Source:* Kallman, Plato & Tobin, 1990, Figure 2, p. M84.)

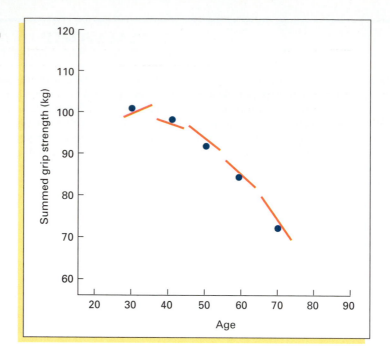

If an increase in the risk of disease is a normal part of aging, then why does it still make sense to study normal aging by studying only *healthy* adults?

The immune system functions less well when you are under stress, such as when you are studying for exams.

in AIDS, and it is T cells that decline most in number and efficiency with age (Miller, 1990). As the thymus gland shrinks, it apparently becomes less and less able to produce effective T cells. As a consequence, these cells become decreasingly efficient at "recognizing" a foreign cell, so that some disease cells, such as cancer cells, may not be fought effectively. In addition, the body produces fewer antibodies with increasing age. Together these changes mean that adults become more and more susceptible to disease as they age—a *highly* significant aspect of the aging process.

Yet, as with studies of studies of heart function, we need to be careful not to draw sweeping conclusions about normal aging of the immune system. There is a new and growing body of evidence showing striking connections between psychological stress or depression and the functioning of the immune system (Dorian & Garfinkel, 1987; Weisse, 1992). Medical students show lower levels of one subvariety of T cells ("natural killer" T cells) in the month before final exams than in the month after (Kiecolt-Glaser & Glaser, 1988). Widowhood and other major losses are associated with a sharp drop in immune system functioning in the weeks immediately after the loss, with a slow recovery (e.g., Willis et al., 1987; Schleifer et al., 1983).

Chronic stress, such as continuously high demands in one's job, also appears to have an effect on immune function. Faced with such stress, the initial response is a kind of mobilization, and immune system functioning actually improves for a short time, followed by a drop (Dorian & Garfinkel, 1987).

Collectively, this research points to the possibility that life experiences that demand high levels of change or adaptation will affect immune system functioning. Over a period of years and many stresses, the immune system becomes less and less efficient. It may well be that there are basic changes in the immune system with age *irrespective* of the level of stress. But it is also possible that what we think of as normal aging of the immune system is a response to cumulative stress. If so, then we might expect those adults who have encountered higher levels of stress to have higher rates of disease and shorter life expectancies. That is, they should "age" faster—an expectation born out by research on disease and death rates, to which we now turn.

Physical Health

When we look directly at age differences in physical health and death rates, the research follows the expected pattern. Most obviously, the older you are, the higher the likelihood that you will die in any given year. For those in the period of young adulthood, roughly 1 out of every 1000 will die each year; for those between ages 65 and 75, the rate is more like 30 out of every 1000 (U.S. Bureau of the Census, 1990; Kaplan, 1992). Furthermore, when young adults die, they are far more likely to die by accident, suicide, or homicide than from disease. Disease only becomes the most common cause of death starting in the late thirties and early forties, when heart disease and cancer become common.

Measures of chronic illness or disability show the same pattern, a fact that is especially clear in a set of survey data analyzed by James House and his colleagues (House, Kessler & Herzog, 1990; House et al., 1992). This nationally representative sample of 3617 adults in the United States was asked in 1986 about chronic health conditions and about their ability to perform daily tasks.

Figure 13.3 shows two sets of results from this study, with the relationship between disease or disability and age computed separately for four different social class groups. Panel A shows the number of chronic conditions out of a possible list of ten (e.g., arthritis/rheumatism, lung disease, high blood pressure, heart attack or heart trouble, diabetes, cancer, etc.). Panel B shows the degree of reported limitation of daily activities, on a scale in which 5 indicates that a person's daily activities are not at all limited by health-related problems, and a 1 indicates that they are limited a great deal.

Figure 13.3 Both chronic conditions (panel a) and degree of limitation in daily activities (panel b) change systematically with age over adulthood, but the change is obviously steeper and larger among poor and working class adults. (*Source:* House et al., 1990, Figure 1, p. 396 and Figure 3, p. 397.)

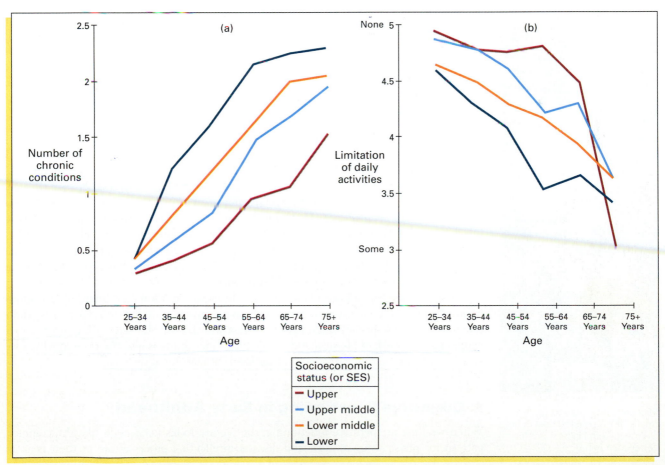

Two things are obvious in these figures. First, health clearly declines with age and disability increases—no big surprise. Second, these effects are larger and earlier among lower class adults than among the upper class. Among the highest social class group, defined as those with 16 or more years of education and an income of $20,000 or more (in 1986 dollars), there is especially gradual change.

What might be the cause of such social class differences? House and his colleagues looked at several possible sources, including health habits, such as drinking and smoking, and life stresses, such as financial troubles, losing a job, a divorce, moving, or the like. They found, as have others (e.g., James et al., 1992), that working class adults—black and white—had poorer health habits and higher levels of stress. When these differences are subtracted statistically, the social class differences apparent in Figure 13.3 become considerably smaller, although they do not disappear altogether (House et al., 1992). In particular, the upper class adults continue to have a clear health advantage, even when health habits and stress have been subtracted.

These data, then, not only substantiate what you already knew—that the risk of disease or disability rises with age. They also provide support for the hypothesis that cumulative stress may be one of the causal factors, because adults with lower levels of chronic stress "age" more slowly.

Overall, it is inescapably true that physical performance and health are at their peak during the years of young adulthood. But the reasons for this advantage to the young are more complicated than you might have guessed. What we think of broadly as "aging" is in fact a complex process, affected by a host of factors, including stress and activity.

Alcohol and Drug Abuse.   One exception to the generalization that young adults have the best health is the pattern of age differences in alcohol and drug abuse. Alcoholism and significant drug addiction is at its peak between 18 and about 40, after which it declines gradually. The rates are higher for men than for women, but the age pattern is very similar in both genders (Anthony & Aboraya, 1992). One large study in the United States finds the rate of alcohol abuse or dependence at about 6 percent among those in young adulthood, compared to 4 percent in middle adulthood, and 1.8 percent for those over 65 (Regier et al., 1988).

Mental Health

Another exception to the pattern of optimal health in young adulthood is found in studies of age differences in mental health problems. Studies in a number of developed countries show that the risk of emotional disturbance of almost any kind is *highest* between the ages of 25 and 44 and lowest in middle age (Regier et al., 1988; Kessler et al., 1992). This pattern holds for depression, anxiety disorders, substance abuse, and schizophrenia. There is still a good deal of disagreement about the pattern in late adulthood, but some investigators have found another rise in problems such as depression among those 75 and older (e.g., Kessler et al., 1992; Lewinsohn et al., 1991), although this has not been found in every study, and not for every type of disturbance.

Setting aside the dispute about the possible rise of emotional problems in late adulthood, the clearest conclusion from research on age and mental health is that early adulthood is a time of especially high personal stress and risk. So the time of life in which we experience our peak of physical and intellectual functioning is also the time in which we may be most prone to depression or other forms of emotional distress.

Michael Jordan, like all of us, is clearly at his physical best in his twenties—but his best is a lot better than mine!

What other explanations can you think of for the health advantage of the upper and middle classes? Can you think of a way to test your hypotheses?

Cognitive Functioning in Early Adulthood

When we look at cognitive functioning, the picture looks very much like the common pattern for physical functioning and disease: intellectual processes are at their peak in early adulthood, but the rate of decline is slower than most researchers had originally concluded. There is also much wider variability in the rate and pattern of decline than early researchers had presumed, differences that appear to be caused by a variety of environmental and life-style factors, as well as heredity. Once again, then, uncovering the basic pattern of cognitive aging has proven complex and difficult. Let's begin with some of the basic findings.

IQ

Early studies, relying on cross-sectional evidence, showed what looked like a steady decline in total IQ over the adult years, with the peak at about age 30 and a steady drop thereafter. Longitudinal data, on the other hand, give us a much more optimistic picture. The best single source of evidence is a remarkable cross-sequential study by Schaie, referred to as the Seattle Longitudinal Study (Schaie, 1983b, 1989, 1990; Schaie & Hertzog, 1983).

Schaie began in 1956 with a set of cross-sectional samples, 7 years apart, covering the ages from 25 to 67. Some of these subjects were then retested every 7 years, and at each new 7-year interval, a whole new set of cross-sectional samples was selected, some of whom were then also followed longitudinally. This enables Schaie to look at IQ changes over 7-, 14-, 21-, or 28-year intervals for several sets of subjects, each from a slightly different cohort. Figure 13.4 shows one set of cross-sectional comparisons in 1977, and 14-year longitudinal results smoothed over the whole age range. The test involved in this case is a measure of global intelligence on which the average score is set at 50 points (equivalent to an IQ of 100 on most other tests).

You can see that the cross-sectional comparisons show a steady drop in IQ. But the longitudinal evidence suggests that overall intelligence test scores actually rise in early adulthood and then remain quite constant until perhaps age 60, when it begins to decline.

A slightly different picture emerges if you break the total IQ measure down into components. One component is what Cattell and Horn have called **crystallized intelligence**, which includes verbal abilities and other skills that depend on specific knowledge and education (Cattell, 1963; Horn, 1982; Horn & Donaldson, 1980). Schaie's results, and the results of many other investigators, suggest that on measures of such abilities, intellectual performance is maintained through middle adulthood. So we continue to remember words we have learned, continue to be able to read newspaper articles and understand their meaning, continue to be able to solve problems in our area of work. But

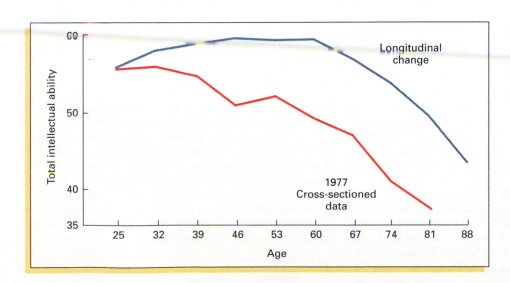

Figure 13.4 These results from the Seattle Longitudinal Study show both cross-sectional and longitudinal data for the measure of overall intellectual skill (mean score = 50). (*Source:* Schaie, 1983b, Tables 4.5 and 4.9, pp. 89 and 100.)

on tests that measure abilities less dependent on education or experience and more on speed of response or on abstract reasoning, called **fluid intelligence** by Horn and Cattell, the decline occurs earlier, in middle adulthood. If you give adults a measure of arithmetic skill, for example, in which the score is determined by the number of problems you can do correctly in a given space of time, there is a significant average decrement in performance beginning at about age 40. Similarly, measures of the ability to visualize objects rotated in space—a skill most of us do not practice regularly—shows early decrements.

But as with health or disability, there are wide individual variations in these patterns. In Schaie's studies, on every test, whether of a crystallized or fluid ability, there were at least some subjects who showed no decline at all during middle and late adulthood. Other subjects showed early and rapid drops, even on such crystallized skills as vocabulary (Schaie, 1989; 1990).

Memory.   The pattern of results from studies of memory ability over the adult years is very similar. On average, young adults perform better than older adults on virtually all measures of memory, but there are wide individual variations in the rate of decline. The average decline is sometimes—but not always—smaller when real-life memory tasks rather than artificial laboratory problems are used.

Measures of short-term memory—recalling something for only a short time, such as a phone number you've just looked up in the phone book and then call immediately— generally show a drop with age, as you've already seen in the results shown in Figure 1.5 (page 10). Age differences are still larger when we look at measures of long-term memory—items you have intended to store in your mind for longer periods or permanently, such as a friend's phone number or a poem you wanted to memorize or vocabulary words in a new language. Both the process of getting memories into this long-term storage (a process called *encoding* by memory theorists) and the process of retrieving them again seem to be impaired among older adults compared to young adults (Salthouse, 1991). With age we become both slower and less efficient in our memory processes—a set of findings I'll have much more to say about in Chapter 17.

Changes in Cognitive Structure

A more optimistic note has been sounded by a number of post-Piagetian theorists (reviewed by Richards & Commons, 1990) who argue that adulthood also brings another kind of developmental change, a reorganization of the structure of thought into some type of "postformal" thinking—an approach I mentioned briefly in Chapter 2. Gisela Labouvie-Vief (1980, 1990), for example, argues that formal operations is not the final stage of development. With its emphasis on the exploration of all logical possibilities, formal

---

RESEARCH REPORT
Continuities in IQ Scores in Adulthood

In the main part of the chapter I have talked about *changes* in IQ over the years of adulthood. But it is also interesting to ask about continuities. Does each person's IQ score tend to stay in roughly the same range? That is, is a high-IQ teenager still likely to be among those with the highest IQ scores in young adulthood or middle age?

The answer is clearly yes. The correlations between IQ scores at different ages in adulthood, even ages decades apart, are normally extremely high. For example, in the Berkeley/Oakland longitudinal studies, the correlation between IQ scores at age 17 and in middle age was .83 for males and .77 for females (Eichorn, Hunt & Honzik, 1981). Comparable correlations have been found in studies of other cohorts, so this strong consistency is not unique to this particular sample (e.g., Owens, 1966; Kangas & Bradway, 1971). This does not mean that there is no change in the absolute level of IQ after adolescence. In the Berkeley sample, for example, 11 percent of the subjects gained as many as 13 IQ points between age 17 and their mid-forties, while another 11 percent lost as many as 6 points. But it is still true that those with higher IQ scores in adolescence have a strong probability of having a higher IQ at age 30, 40, 50, and beyond.

thought may well be the optimal structure in very early adulthood, at a time when the individual is forming her identity, making choices, learning new ideas and skills. But past that early point, Labouvie-Vief thinks that the demands of adult life force two kinds of changes in the structure of adult thought.

First, there is a shift to a more *pragmatic* form of thinking. Each adult learns to solve the problems and meet the challenges associated with the roles she is filling and the jobs she is called on to perform. In Labouvie-Vief's view, this does not represent a *loss* of cognitive function but a necessary structural change, because it is essentially impossible to approach every problem, every day, with full formal operational thinking. As she puts it, the "endless generating of 'ifs' and 'whens,' no longer may be adaptive" (Labouvie-Vief, 1980, p. 153).

In her more recent writing, Labouvie-Vief also argues that past earliest adulthood, we begin to shift our way of understanding from an analytic mode, which is focused on facts and aimed at arriving at clear answers, to a mode that is more reliant on imagination and metaphor and open to paradox and uncertainty. We not only become less certain about many choices, we understand that certainty is not possible in many situations and for many problems faced in everyday adulthood. You may be able to use some aspects of formal operations in choosing among several different day care options for your child, but the decision about whether to place your child in day care in the first place is not so obviously amenable to formal logic. Your feelings may be ambivalent, the choices not clearcut.

Patricia Arlin (1975, 1989, 1990) describes postformal adult thinking in a somewhat different way. In her terminology, Piaget's stage of formal operations is a stage of *problem solving*. The new stage that may emerge in early adulthood is characterized by *problem finding*. This new mode is optimal for dealing with problems in which there is no clear solution or for which there are multiple solutions. It includes much of what we normally call creativity. A person operating at this stage is able to generate many possible solutions to ill-defined problems or to see old problems in new ways. Arlin argues that problem finding is a clear stage, following formal operations, but that it is achieved by only a small number of adults, such as those involved in advanced science or arts.

Still a third view of postformal thinking comes from William Perry (1970), whose theory offers a nice synthesis of Kohlberg's theory of moral reasoning, Piaget's views, and Loevinger's stages of ego development. Perry suggests that in early adulthood, many young people move through a series of steps or stages in their ways of thinking about the world.

- First, young people see everything in polar terms. Authority is external, and questions have right answers. This is very similar to Kohlberg's level of conventional morality or Loevinger's conformist stage. Virtually all teenagers, and many adults, continue to think about the world in this way.

- Some young people, perhaps especially those in college who are exposed to many other points of view, shift from this polar view to a position in which they accept several alternative views as coexistent. But in this intermediate stage they still feel that there *is* a right answer, only that they do not know it yet.

- The next step is relativism. The college student or adult shifts to an assumption that all knowledge is relative; there is no absolute truth. This is similar to Stage 5 in Kohlberg's sequence of moral development and to Loevinger's self-aware level.

- Finally, Perry thinks that some young people arrive at their own specific views and values, to which they commit themselves.

The driving force for this sequence of shifts is both exposure to other people's views and experience with the sort of real-life dilemmas for which there is no clear right an-

List four personal problems you have had to solve in the past six months. What kind of logic or thought process did you use to solve each one? Did your mode of thinking vary as a function of the nature of the problem?

What kind of thinking might this young couple be using as they struggle to balance their finances? Analytic? Pragmatic? Concrete or formal operations?

swer—the very sort of experience that Labouvie-Vief thinks pushes adults toward pragmatic rather than formal reasoning.

Many of these new theories of postformal thought are intriguing, but they remain highly speculative, with little empirical evidence to back them up. More generally, there is little agreement on whether these new types of thinking represent "higher" forms of thought, built on the stages Piaget describes, or whether it is more appropriate simply to describe them as a "different" form of thinking that may or may not emerge in adulthood. What I think is important about this work is the emphasis on the fact that the normal problems of adult life, with their inconsistencies and complexities, cannot always be addressed fruitfully using formal operations logic. It seems entirely plausible that adults will be pushed toward more pragmatic, relativistic forms of thinking, using formal operational thinking only occasionally, if at all. Labouvie-Vief's point, which I think is correct, is that we should not think of this change as a *loss* or a deterioration, but rather as a reasonable adaptation to a different set of cognitive tasks.

▶ A Model of Physical and Cognitive Aging

Many of the various bits and pieces of information I've given you about both physical and cognitive changes in adulthood can be fruitfully combined in a single model, proposed by Nancy Denney (1982, 1984) and shown in Figure 13.5. She argues that there is a common curve of rising and then falling skill on nearly any physical or cognitive measure, reflected in the basic shape of the curves shown. But she also proposes that there is a large variation in absolute *level* of performance, as a function of the amount an individual "exercises" some ability or skill. The word *exercise* is used here very broadly. It refers not only to physical exercise but also mental exercise and to the degree to which some specific task may have been performed before. Many laboratory tests of memory, for example, such as memorizing lists of names, would tap unexercised abilities. Everyday memory tasks, such as recalling details from a newspaper column a person had just read, would tap much more exercised abilities.

The gap between the curve for unexercised abilities and the curve for maximally exercised abilities represents the degree of *improvement* that would be possible for any given skill. Any skill that is not fully exercised can be improved, even in old age, if the individual begins to exercise that ability. There is clear evidence, for example, that aerobic capacity (VO_2 max) can be increased at any age if subjects begin a program of physical exercise (e.g., Blumenthal et al., 1991). Nonetheless, in Denney's model, the maximum

Figure 13.5 Denney's model suggests both a basic decay curve and a fairly large gap between actual level of performance on exercised and unexercised abilities. (*Source:* Denney, 1982, 1984.)

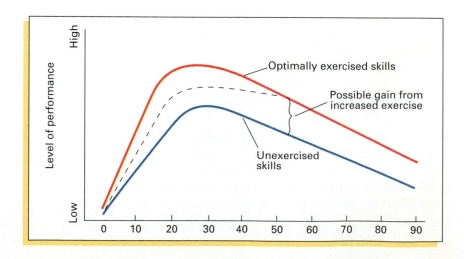

level you will be able to achieve, even with optimum exercise, will decline with age, just as performance of top athletes declines, even with optimum training regimens. One implication of this is that when you are young, you can get away with physical sloth or poor study habits and still perform well; as you get older, this becomes less and less true, because you are fighting against the basic decay curve of aging.

The dotted line on the figure represents a hypothetical curve for a skill that is less than optimally exercised, but still used fairly regularly. Many verbal skills would fall into this category, as would problem-solving skills or everyday tasks. Because skills like these are demanded in a great many jobs, they are heavily exercised in our twenties and thirties, and are well maintained, creating a flat-topped curve similar to what Schaie finds for vocabulary and other exercised or crystallized abilities. But if Denney is correct, then at some point even optimum exercise will no longer maintain these abilities at that same level, and some decline is found—just as Schaie reports.

This model obviously does not handle all the facts I've given you. In particular, Denney's model does not easily handle the wide degree of variation from one individual to the next in the pattern of maintenance or decline over age. To handle findings like these, one might assume some variation among individuals in the shape of the basic underlying decay curve or a larger gap between exercised and unexercised abilities. Or perhaps the basic curve is simply much flatter than Denney proposes, with a later point of decay.

What the model does do is emphasize—correctly I think—that there *is* some kind of underlying decay curve. Early adulthood is the period of maximum potential in nearly every physical and intellectual arena, a time of greatest ease of performance. But those in middle adulthood may perform as well or better than the average young adult in arenas in which they maintain a high level of exercise. With increasing age, this high level of function requires more and more effort, however, until eventually a point is reached at which even maximum effort will no longer maintain peak function. Indeed Schaie's data tell us that those adults who have the *highest* level of performance in middle adulthood are likely to show the *largest* declines in old age, because they are already functioning at top speed and can only go down. This is equivalent to the finding that world-class athletes notice the effects of aging at earlier ages than do weekend warriors, because they are already at peak function.

▶ Individual Differences

One possible source of the individual variations in both physical and cognitive aging is the set of health habits followed in early and middle adulthood. It may seem, when you are 25 or 30, that you can get away with any kind of neglect or abuse of your body. But it ain't so.

Health Habits and Their Long-Term Effects

The best evidence for the long-term effects of various health practices comes from a major longitudinal epidemiological study in a single county of California, the Alameda County Study (Berkman & Breslow, 1983; Kaplan, 1992). The study began in 1965, when a random sample of all residents of the county, a total of 6928 subjects, completed an extensive questionnaire about many aspects of their lives. These subjects were contacted again in 1974 and 1983, at which points they described their health and disability. The researchers also monitored death records and were able to specify the time of death of each of the subjects who died between 1965 and 1983. They could then link health practices reported in 1965 to later death, disease, or disability.

Suppose a blue-collar worker who had never been past high school decides, at age 40, to go to college. She goes to school for four years, gets a degree in English literature, and becomes a high school teacher. What line on Denney's curve might you predict for this person's score on a vocabulary test?

The researchers identified seven health practices that they thought might be critical: physical exercise, smoking, drinking, over- or under-eating, snacking, eating breakfast, and regular sleep. Table 13.2 lists the optimum behavior for each of these habits, as defined in this study.

Data from the first 9 years of the Alameda study show that five of these seven practices were independently related to the risk of death. Only snacking and breakfast eating were unrelated to mortality. When the five strong predictors were combined in the 1974 data, the pattern shown in Figure 13.6 appeared. At every age, for both men and women, those with poorer health habits had a higher risk of mortality. Not surprisingly, these health habits were also related to disease and disability rates over the 18 years of the study. Those who described poorer health habits in 1965 were more likely to report disability or disease symptoms in 1974 and in 1983 (Guralnik & Kaplan, 1989).

Because young people are much less likely to die or to get sick, the impact of health habits may seem quite trivial in the years of early adulthood. Besides, when you're young, you feel invulnerable. But for those of you who are still young adults, and whose health habits are less than optimal, remember that there is no free lunch. Not only is it difficult to break well-established habits, but the effect of poor habits seems to be cumulative. In particular, poor health habits in early adulthood may set into motion or contribute to hastening the development of specific diseases, such as heart disease or cancer. There may be no symptoms during the years from 20 to 40, but the process has begun.

For example, the effect of a high cholesterol diet—a health habit that the Alameda researchers did not include in their study because its importance was not so well known in 1965—appears to add up over time. Research on heart disease also suggests cumulative effects of smoking. Fortunately, it is also true that if you quit smoking, the risk eventually drops down to the same level as that of a person who never smoked. And a radical lowering of fat levels in your diet may reverse the process of cholesterol buildup in the blood vessels (Ornish, 1990). So there is a payoff for changing your health habits, even in your twenties and thirties.

Other Personal Factors That Affect Health and Cognition

I've already mentioned one other factor that may affect health at any age. Stress significantly reduces the efficiency of the immune system in the short term, which increases the risk of disease. Fortunately, there are also protective factors—elements that may reduce the risk of disease and increase a person's sense of happiness or well-being. High on this list are social support and a sense of personal control.

So how many Twinkies are you eating? How many hours of sleep are you getting? Are you exercising? Smoking? There's no time like the present. . . .

TABLE 13.2 Optimum Health Practices as Defined in the Alameda County Study	
Health Practice	Optimum Level
Physical Activity	Participate often in at least two or three of the following: swimming, walking, sports, gardening, fishing, or hunting.
Smoking	Never smoked.
Weight	Weight no more than 30% above, nor 10% below the amounts listed in standard life insurance weight tables.
Alcohol	No more than 16 drinks per month.
Eating Breakfast	Daily or almost daily.
Snacking	Eat between meals seldom, rarely, or never.
Sleep pattern	Usually sleep 7 or 8 hours a night.

Source: Berkman & Breslow, 1983.

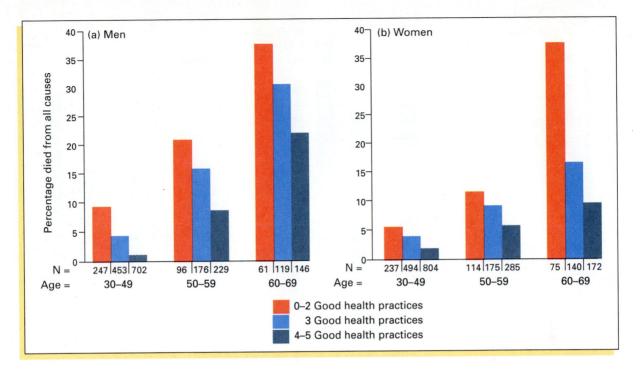

Social Support. There is now abundant research showing that adults with adequate social support have lower risk of disease, death, and depression than do adults with weaker social networks or less supportive relationships (e.g., Cohen, 1991; Berkman & Breslow, 1983; Berkman, 1985). This effect is particularly clear when an individual is under high stress. That is, the negative effect of stress on health and happiness is smaller for those individuals with adequate social support than for those whose social support is weak. This pattern of results is usually described as the *buffering* effect of social support.

Social support has been defined and measured in myriad ways. In early studies, including the Alameda study, it was typically defined in terms of such objective criteria as marital status and frequency of reported contact with friends and relatives. Recent studies suggest that subjective measures may be more powerful; a person's *perception* of the adequacy of his social contacts and emotional support is more strongly related to physical and emotional health than are most objective measures (Sarason, Sarason & Pierce, 1990). This greater potency of the subjective sense of support is entirely consistent with what I have been saying about the significance of internal models in shaping behavior and attitudes. It is not the objective amount of contact with others that is important, but how that contact is understood or interpreted. In fact, Barbara Sarason and her colleagues (Sarason, Pierce & Sarason, 1990) propose a specific link between attachment and the sense of support, suggesting that the tendency to perceive support as being "out there" and "sufficient" is related to the security of a person's basic attachment. The more secure the attachment, the greater our sense of social support is likely to be.

The importance of social support for health can again be illustrated with some of the findings from the Alameda study, shown in Figure 13.7. In this case, the social network index reflects an objective measurement: number of contacts with friends and relatives, marital status, church and group membership. But even using this less-than-perfect measure of support, the relationship is vividly demonstrated.

Of course it is possible that social support is not the crucial variable here. Perhaps people with low social support are different in other ways that are significant for health,

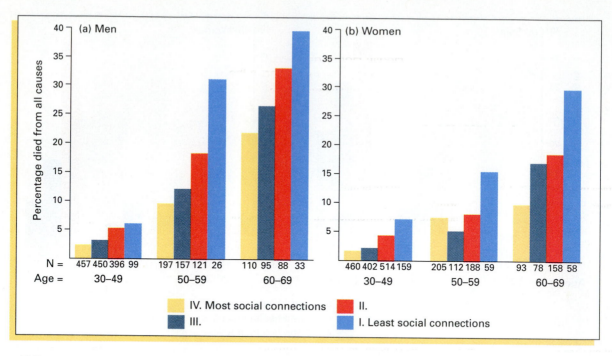

N =	457	450	396	99	197	157	121	26	110	95	88	33
Age =	30–49				50–59				60–69		

Legend:
- IV. Most social connections
- III.
- II.
- I. Least social connections

Figure 13.7 The extensiveness of a person's social network is predictive of the risk of death over the next decade, an example of the potency of the impact of social support on health. (*Source:* Berkman & Breslow, 1983, Figure 4–3, p. 130.)

such as health habits or social class. Berkman (1985) checked out these possibilities in the Alameda data and found that the link between support and risk of death persisted even when initial physical health status, social class, smoking, alcohol consumption, level of physical activity, weight, race, and life satisfaction were taken into account.

Studies using more subjective measures of support yield similar results: those adults, both young and old, who feel sufficiently supported by their family and friends are less likely to become sick under stressful conditions (e.g., Cohen, 1991; Cohen & Wills, 1985).

Whether there are any age differences in the strength of these relationships is not so clear. Examples of the buffering effect of social support can be found in studies of adults of every age group. But there is at least some theoretical reason to suppose that social support may be especially critical in young adulthood. According to Erikson and others, the early years of adult life are focused on the task of creating satisfying intimate relationships both with a marital or cohabiting partner and with friends. We also have evidence that the *lack* of such intimacy is especially disturbing in these early years. More young adults describe themselves as lonely, for example, than is true of any other age group (Parlee, 1979), which may be a major contributing factor to the high rate of depression among young adults. Given the centrality of this issue in early adulthood, one might hypothesize that a social support measure would be more strongly related to health in this age group than at other ages. So far as I know, there is no study that tests this possibility, but it is a hypothesis worth exploring.

A Sense of Control. Another personal characteristic that affects physical and mental health is an individual's sense of control. Different facets of the sense of control have been emphasized by various theorists. Bandura (1977b, 1982c, 1986) talks about it in terms of **self-efficacy**, the belief in one's ability to perform some action or to control one's behavior or environment, to reach some goal or make something happen. Such a belief is one aspect of what I have called the internal model of the self, and it is affected by one's whole history of experience with mastering tasks and overcoming obstacles.

RESEARCH REPORT

Health Habits and Overall Health in Blacks and Whites in the United States

National survey data from 1985 (U.S. Bureau of the Census, 1990) indicate that poor health habits are found at the same rates among blacks and whites. The figure below shows differences on five different health habits reported by 42,000 individuals in face-to-face interviews. The Census Bureau divides the data into three groups: white, black, and "other," with the latter group including primarily Hispanics and Asians. There are ethnic differences on every health habit measured, but no one ethnic group has consistently worse health habits. Blacks are more likely to smoke, to be overweight, and to get too little sleep, but they are less likely to drink to excess and to be sedentary.

Results from a smaller study of 2030 adults living in a single county in North Carolina (James et al., 1992) confirm and extend the national data: blacks were more likely to smoke and be overweight. But these patterns varied depending on age, sex, and education. For example, among men, those most likely to smoke were low education blacks; among women, the most likely to smoke were young (18- to 34-year-old) white women with low education. High levels of exercise were least common among low-education blacks, both male and female, but among men, well-educated blacks were *most* likely to exercise regularly.

So while blacks may report more poor health practices in some studies, education rather than race may actually be a more significant factor in predicting health habits. Certainly that is true for overall health status, among blacks as well as among whites. You've already seen the social class differences in disease and disability. The North Carolina study tells us that the same pattern holds for both blacks and whites. In both groups, adults with high school education or less reported poorer health than did those with more than high school, although in every case, the worst health was reported by low education blacks. Thus minority status adds to health risk, but social class or education is a significant variable across the board.

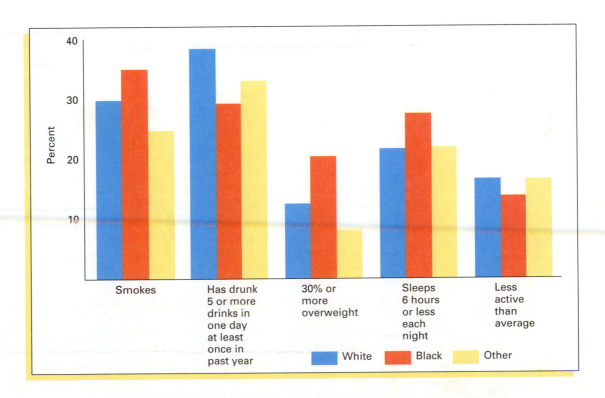

Rotter (1966) expresses another aspect of the same broad idea in his concept of **locus of control**. He differentiates between internal and external locus of control orientations. An individual with an internal orientation believes that things happen to him because of what he himself has done; those with an external locus believe that they have no control over what happens to them, that control lies in others or in the system. There is some indication from studies in Finland that adults become somewhat more external in their orientation with age, since they feel less able to control health and their children as they get older (Nurmi, Pulliainen & Salmela-Aro, 1992). But at any age there are wide individual variations in the tendency toward an internal or external sense of control.

Martin Seligman (1991) expresses a similar idea in his concepts of optimism and helplessness. The pessimist, who feels helpless, believes that misfortune is his own fault and that there is nothing he can do about it. The optimist believes there is always some solution and that he can work it out with his own effort.

All of these concepts appear to tap aspects of what Rodin (1990) refers to as *perceived control*. Do I believe that I can accomplish some task or solve some problem by dint of effort, or do I feel manipulated by the system and unable to cope? All these researchers propose that the basic sense of control/efficacy/optimism arises in childhood and adolescence as a result of our early experiences of effectiveness and success or failure and frustration.

Research on the links between a sense of control and health shows that those with a more helpless attitude or with a low sense of self-efficacy are more likely to become depressed and more likely to become ill (Seligman, 1991; Syme, 1990). The most striking demonstration of this connection is from the 35-year Grant study of a group of Harvard men who were first interviewed in their freshman year, in 1938–1940. Researchers were able to use interview material from a contact with these men when they were 25 to assess their degree of pessimism. Their later physical health from age 30 to 60 was then rated by physicians who examined the subjects every five years. Pessimism was not related to health at 30, 35, or 40, but at every assessment from 45 to 60, those who had had a more pessimistic approach at age 25 had significantly poorer health, and this was true even if physical and mental health at age 25 was controlled statistically (Peterson, Seligman & Vaillant, 1988). Pessimism or a lack of control thus may reflect a basic personality characteristic that affects the choices adults make and their interpretation of experience.

A person's sense of control is also clearly influenced by specific circumstances. Epidemiologist Leonard Syme (1990) points to research in both Sweden and the United States showing that the rate of heart disease is unusually high among workers whose job has high demand but low discretion and latitude. That is, when the stress is high but the ability to make choices and control the situation is low, disease rates go up. Because the jobs held by many working class and lower class adults are likely to be of this type, while jobs held by the highest social class group are likely to allow more personal control, perhaps the concept of control can help to explain the large social class differences in disease rates you saw in Figure 13.3.

Finally, it is also possible to show that experimentally increasing someone's sense of control improves his health—a rare case in which we have both cross-sectional, longitudinal, and experimental evidence on the same point (Rodin, 1986). In the earliest and best-known study of this kind, Judith Rodin and Ellen Langer (1977) found that mortality rates of nursing home residents were lower among those who had been given control over even quite simple aspects of their daily lives, such as whether to have scrambled eggs or omelettes for breakfast, or whether to sign up to attend a movie.

It seems quite likely that children growing up in poverty-level families or in circumstances in which they rarely have much control over their lives may be more likely to develop a low sense of self-efficacy or little optimism. The point is that these psychological processes and enduring personality characteristics affect not only our roles and relationships, they affect our physical health as well, beginning in early adulthood.

Summary

1. Although it is an arbitrary division, we can segment the adult years into three periods, with young adulthood comprising the years from 20 to about 40.

2. Sorting out the effects of basic maturational change (which we call *aging*) from other causes of change in adult life has proven difficult. Both disease and reduced activity may also contribute to observed patterns.

3. Nonetheless, it is clear that between 20 and 40, adults are at their peak both physically and cognitively. In these years a person has more muscle tissue, more calcium in the bones, more brain mass, better sensory acuity, greater aerobic capacity, and a more efficient immune system.

4. These differences are smaller when we study only healthy individuals longitudinally, but there is still some decline.

5. Studies of heart and lung function show no age change under resting conditions, but performance declines with age when tests are given during or after exercise.

6. A number of these changes contribute to a loss of speed with age—both speed in moving and response time to some stimulus. This decline is observed even (or especially) in top athletes.

7. Changes in the immune system may be especially critical in accounting for what we think of as the aging process,

because they mean the older adult is more susceptible to disease.

8. Increases in disease and disability with age are earlier and larger for lower-class than upper-class adults, even when health habits and stress levels are taken into account.

9. In contrast, mental health is *worse* in early adulthood; young adults are more likely to be depressed, anxious, or lonely than are the middle aged.

10. Measures of cognitive skill, like physical skill, show declines with age, but the decline is quite late for well exercised abilities like vocabulary, everyday memory problems, and normal problem solving.

11. There *may* also be a change in cognitive structure in adult life, with several varieties of post-formal-operational stages suggested by theorists.

12. Exercise of either physical or cognitive abilities can improve performance at any age, although the upper limit may decline over time.

13. There are wide individual variations in the rate of physical and cognitive loss. Some of this difference seems to be explained by varying health habits. Adults with good health habits have lower risk of death and disease at any age.

14. Social support and a sense of personal control also affect the rate of disease and death, especially in the face of stress.

Key Terms

crystallized intelligence

fluid intelligence

locus of control

maximum oxygen uptake

self-efficacy

Suggested Readings

Seligman, M. E. P. (1991). *Learned optimism.* New York: Alfred A. Knopf. (A very readable description of Seligman's influential theory of optimism and learned helplessness, written for the lay reader. A wide-ranging and thought-provoking book.)

Salthouse, T. A. (1991). *Theoretical perspectives on cognitive aging.* Hillsdale, NJ: Lawrence Erlbaum Associates. (An extremely thorough, detailed analysis of all the evidence on cognitive changes from early to late adulthood. This book is not for the casual reader, but it is an excellent source of further references on virtually any aspect of this complex subject.)

Schneider, E. L., & Rowe, J. W. (Eds.) (1990). *Handbook of the biology of aging,* 3rd ed. San Diego, CA: Academic Press. (A compendium of technical papers describing current knowledge about various facets of biological aging, including changes in the brain, the circulatory system, and the immune systems.)

SOCIAL AND PERSONALITY DEVELOPMENT IN EARLY ADULTHOOD

14

If the biological clock is all but inaudible during the years of early adulthood, the social clock is all but deafening. In early adulthood, each of us takes our place in our society. For nearly all of us, this means acquiring, learning, and performing the three roles central to adult life: worker, spouse, and parent.

The details of timing and content of these roles obviously differ from one culture to another and from one cohort to another. In rural subsistence cultures, work and marriage come much earlier than in most industrialized cultures. And in our own culture, there has been quite a lot of variability from one cohort to the next in the modal age for marriage or bearing children. In the United States, for example, the modal age for first marriage has risen dramatically in recent years. In 1975, 40 percent of women's first marriages occurred before age 20; in 1986, the rate was only half that (U.S. Bureau of the Census, 1990). But regardless of such changes in the cultural norms, it is still true that in early adulthood we must each turn outward from our preoccupation with self-definition and take on a series of roles that involve intricate relationships with other people.

▶ Leaving Home ✴

One accompaniment, or precursor, of this role-acquisition process is leaving home. Of course, some young people (more often young women) leave home at the time of marriage, so there is no intervening period of independent or semi-independent living. Increasingly, however, young men and women in developed countries move through a transitional phase, living apart from their family but not yet married or cohabiting (Goldscheider & DaVanzo, 1989). College provides precisely this kind of transitional phase for large numbers of young people; others leave home to set up independent households, a pattern especially common among young adults who are working full-time.

Attachment to Parents

Leaving home is more than just setting up a separate residence. It also involves a highly significant psychological emancipation process in which the young person distances himself emotionally from his parents to at least some degree. In essence, the young adult must transfer his most central attachment from the parent(s) to one or more peers (Hazan et al., 1991). As Robert Weiss puts it:

> If children are eventually to form their own households, their bonds of attachment to the parents must become attenuated and eventually end. Otherwise, independent living would be emotionally troubling. The relinquishing of attachment to parents appears to be of central importance among the individuation-achieving processes of late adolescence and early adulthood. (1986, p. 100)

Do you buy Weiss's argument? How might you go about trying to determine whether adults are still attached to their parents, as *attachment* has been defined by Ainsworth (discussed in Chapter 6)?

Many theorists dispute Weiss's contention that the attachment to the parent is fully given up in adult life (e.g., Cicirelli, 1991). Certainly adults continue to maintain regular contact with their parents throughout their lives and experience deep grief at the parent's death. When we are under great stress, we may also long to have our parents there to comfort us—all signs that some form of attachment continues to exist. But there is clearly a pulling back from this bond in early adulthood, necessary if the relationship to an intimate partner is going to become the central attachment of one's emotional life—and necessary if the young adult is going to be able to see the parent more objectively, as a person and not just as a parent. As Corinne Nydegger puts it, "The task [of the young adult] . . . is to attain emotional emancipation from the parents, while remaining engaged as a son or daughter." (Nydegger, 1991, p. 102.)

Such an emancipation occurs for most adults in their early twenties. If you ask children and adults questions like, Who is the person you don't like to be away from? or, Who is the person you know will always be there for you? children and teenagers most often list their parents, while adults most often name their spouse and almost never mention their parents (Hazan et al., 1991).

This transition does not occur abruptly. Of the various elements of an attachment, the first to shift seems to be proximity seeking. In adolescence we already see a preference

The moment of leaving home is not necessarily easy, but every young person must come to it eventually, whether it is to go off to college, to set up an independent household, or to marry.

by young people for spending time with (being near) their peers. But adolescents still think of their parents as their safe base. In early adulthood, most of us shift this safe-base aspect of the central attachment to a spouse or other peer (Hazan et al., 1991; Hazan & Shaver, 1990).

Let me say again that I am not at all trying to propose here that parents become unimportant to adult life. A large fraction of adults, in fact, describe their relationships with their parents as "very close and intimate" (Rossi, 1989); in middle and later adult life, grown children also take on the task of caring for their aging parents—sometimes out of a sense of obligation but more frequently out of a sense of deep affection and caring. But for most adults, the parent-child relationship ceases to be the *central* attachment.

Interestingly, it begins to look as if securely attached young people have an easier time making this transition than do those with anxious, ambivalent attachments. Among college students, for example, one study shows that those who were still "absorbed" by their relationship with their parents and with their need to become independent experienced greater stress and more physical and psychological symptoms than did those with a more secure relationship to their parents (Zirkel & Cantor, 1990). So, just as an infant with a secure attachment feels more comfortable physically moving away from the parent and exploring new territory, the young adult with a secure attachment finds it easier to move away from the parent psychologically.

▶ Finding a Partner

You'll remember that Erikson lists *intimacy versus isolation* as the key task of early adulthood, where intimacy is defined as "the ability to fuse your identity with someone else's without fear that you're going to lose something yourself" (Erikson, in Evans, 1969). Each of us, to fulfill this task, needs to find a partner, a single individual with whom we can find or create an intimate, secure attachment. That core relationship then forms the secure base from which each adult can move out into the adult world of work; it also obviously creates the nuclear family in which the next generation of children will be reared. An individual who fails to create such an intimate relationship, such a focal adult attachment, will lack that secure base and will experience a sense of isolation or loneliness. Indeed, you may remember from the last chapter that loneliness is at its peak in the earliest years of adulthood, years when so many young people are betwixt and between, having turned partly away from family but not yet having found an intimate partnership.

You may have noticed that I have consistently used the word *partner* rather than spouse. I have done so quite deliberately, because I want to include homosexual and cohabiting heterosexual partnerships as well as marital partners in this discussion. We know far less about the latter two groups than about married couples, but the available research suggests that many of the same processes are involved in all three types of relationship.

The Process of Choosing

What attracts us to one person and not another? Why do some pairs break up, while others continue to the point of commitment? We have a lot more heat than light on these questions. There has been an enormous amount of research but not many clear answers. The most popular theories describe mate selection as proceeding through a series of filters or steps (Perlman & Fehr, 1987). Bernard Murstein (1970, 1976, 1986), for example, suggests that when you meet someone new, you apply three filters, in the order listed:

1. *External characteristics*: Does this person match you in quality of appearance, apparent social class, or manners?

2. *Attitudes and beliefs*: Is there a match with your ideas in basic areas, such as sex, religion, or politics?

3. *Role fit*: Does this person's ideas about relationships match your own? Do you have similar ideas about appropriate sex roles? Are you compatible sexually? For example, if one partner is eager for a high level of personal self-disclosure and the other is reticent about revealing his feelings, a poor match would exist on this last filter.

The research suggests that all these elements are important, but the sequence is probably not nearly as rigid as Murstein suggested. All three facets may be part of your reaction from the very beginning. What is clear from sociological research is that the strongest single element in attraction and mate selection is similarity. We are drawn to those we see as like ourselves—in age, education, social class, ethnic group membership, religion, attitudes, interests, or temperament. Sociologists describe this as a process of *assortive mating*, or *homogamy*, and there is ample evidence that likes (rather than opposites) attract, and that partnerships based on homogamy are much more likely to endure than are those in which the partners differ markedly (Murstein, 1986).

In addition, there is some evidence that there is a kind of exchange process involved in choosing a partner. Each of us has certain assets to offer to a potential mate. Exchange theorists (Edwards, 1969) argue that we each try for the best bargain, the best exchange, we can manage. According to this model, women frequently exchange their sexual and domestic services for the economic support offered by a man (Schoen & Wooldredge, 1989). In choosing a partner, this means that women are likely to be more concerned with the job prospects or economic status of a potential mate, while men are more focused on attractiveness. Recent survey data from the United States provide some support for this view (South, 1991). A national sample of over 2000 unmarried adults were asked to indicate how willing they would be to marry someone with various characteristics, such as someone who was not good looking, someone younger than themselves, someone with less or more education than themselves, and someone who earns more or less than themselves.

In this survey, white, black, and Hispanic men were all less willing than were women to marry someone who was not good-looking, but more willing to marry someone with less education or lower income. Women in this sample were more likely to want to marry someone older than themselves, while men preferred someone younger, both patterns that are consistent with exchange theories of mate selection. Overall, women seem to aim to

Does Murstein's model make sense to you? When you meet someone new, do you have a sort of mental checklist? What's on that list?

Social scientists have not done very well at devising theories to explain lovely moments of romance like this one.

"marry up" economically or socially and are very concerned about the future economic prospects of a potential mate, while men are less concerned about such questions and more willing to marry "down" on any trait except attractiveness.

Creating a Relationship

All of that sounds as if choosing a partner is a pretty cold-blooded, rational process. But let us not forget the powerful role of sexual attraction and the equally profound role of personality and attachment patterns in shaping both our choices of mates and the pattern of relationship we create with those partners. In particular, the role of internal working models of attachment in partner selection and relationship formation has been the focus of a whole burst of research in the past few years (e.g., Collins & Read, 1990; Feeney & Noller, 1990; Hazan & Shaver, 1987, 1990; Kobak & Sceery, 1988; Mikulincer & Nachshon, 1991; Simpson, 1990; Simpson, Rholes & Nelligan, 1992). I find this new work fascinating because it helps to connect the often separate research on child and adult development. It also underlines yet again the importance of internal working models in shaping our behavior in a wide variety of situations.

The basic argument is that each of us tends to re-create in our partnership relationships the pattern we carry in our internal model of attachment. That does not mean that the security of the very first attachment in infancy is carried forward, unaltered. In the "across development" box in Chapter 6 (page 134), I pointed out that change in these internal models clearly can occur. In particular, some adults with insecure attachment histories are able to analyze and accept their childhood relationships and create a new internal model. But whether a young adult's internal model is the product of redefinition or unchanged early assumptions, it will still affect his expectations for a partner, the sort of partner he chooses, the way he will behave with his partner, and the stability of the relationship.

The new research tells us that adults with secure attachment models are inclined to trust others, to see their partner as their friend as well as lover, to show little jealousy and little anxiety about whether their affection will be or is reciprocated. They give more support to their partners in tense or anxious situations, and they seek comfort from their partner more easily. Adults with an anxious attachment model are unsure of themselves in relationships, are anxious about whether their feelings are reciprocated, are jealous and preoccupied with their relationship. Those with avoidant internal models are less happy in their relationships, less trusting, avoid closeness, disclose little about themselves, and are less accepting of the other person. In a tense or anxious situation, they seek less support and provide less reassurance. Perhaps, expecting rejection, they hold back from commitment.

These differences have been found in a number of studies of college students as well as a few studies of older adults. Cindy Hazan and Phillip Shaver (1987, 1990) measured types of internal models straightforwardly by asking each of their subjects to choose one of the three descriptions of relationships given in Table 14.1. In a sample of over six hundred adults of varying ages, they found 56 percent described themselves as secure (option 1), 25 percent chose option 2 (avoidant) and 19 percent chose option 3 (anxious or ambivalent), remarkably similar to the incidence of these three types in children. They also found that adults of the three types differed, as expected, in the way they described their most important partnership relationship and in their expectations about relationships. In several studies, Hazan and Shaver have also found that avoidant types are most likely to describe themselves as lonely (Hazan & Shaver, 1987, 1990). Research in Australia, using an Eriksonian theoretical framework, suggests that loneliness is more common among those young adults who have not yet achieved emotional intimacy (Boldero & Moore, 1990), a finding that is consistent with the Hazan and Shaver results.

> ### TABLE 14.1 Attachment Descriptions Used by Hazan and Shaver in Their Research
>
> Which of the following best describes your feelings?
>
> 1. I find it relatively easy to get close to others and am comfortable depending on them and having them depend on me. I don't often worry about being abandoned or about someone getting too close to me.
>
> 2. I am somewhat uncomfortable being close to others; I find it difficult to trust them completely, difficult to allow myself to depend on them. I am nervous when anyone gets too close, and often, love partners want me to be more intimate than I feel comfortable being.
>
> 3. I find that others are reluctant to get as close as I would like. I often worry that my partner doesn't really love me or won't want to stay with me. I want to merge completely with another person, and this desire sometimes scares people away.

Source: Hazan & Shaver, 1987, Table 2, p. 515.

In addition, like tends to pick like. When both members of dating couples are asked about their internal models, researchers find that securely attached adults tend to pick secure partners, although anxiously attached individuals are not more likely to pick one another (Collins & Read, 1990).

The least happy relationships among young dating couples seem to be of two varieties. One of these is any combination with an anxiously attached woman, perhaps because such women may show greater clinging and jealousy, characteristics many men find off-putting. Thus the anxiously attached woman tends to create an unstable, unhappy relationship, just as she expects. The other unhappy combination is any pairing with an avoidant man (Collins & Read, 1990; Simpson, 1990), once again fulfilling the avoidant man's expectation that relationships have little to offer.

Attachment history is not the only ingredient in this particular soup, just as homogamy is not the only basis for initial attraction. Sexual attraction and love are immensely complex processes, of which we understand only a fraction. Correlations between attachment models and relationship qualities or actual partnership behaviors are modest, at best. But the recent research has pointed us in a new and fruitful direction. What we now need is longitudinal research within this framework so that we can see what role attachment models may play in the process of commitment to a partner and in the quality and stability of long-term partner relationships.

Partnerships over Time

Once a marriage or a cohabiting partnership has been formed, what happens to the relationship over the ensuing years? Are there any predictable changes, any developmental patterns?

We have surprisingly little information. Part of the problem is that cross-sectional studies, which might otherwise be a way to get some sense of marital changes over time, suffer in this case from a major methodological problem: if we compare 5-year marriages with 15-year marriages, the older group necessarily includes only enduring marriages. Couples who divorce between the 5th and 15th year are omitted from the studies. We may end up knowing something about the characteristics of *lasting* marriages/partnerships, but not about relationships in more general terms. Furthermore, duration of marriage is normally confounded with age. A 20-year marriage is typically a marriage between adults in their forties, and we could not be sure that characteristics of the relationship were the result of changes in relationships in general or of being 40. To avoid this particular difficulty, we would need to study marriages that began at various ages, following each pair over time. No one has done such a study, or even anything close to it. The best infor-

Think about some of the other possible combinations of attachment types. What might be the strengths or pitfalls of each of these types of relationship?

We can't tell from this photo what this young woman's internal model of attachment may be, but we know that her model will affect her expectations, and her behavior, with her boyfriend.

mation we have comes from a small set of longitudinal studies that cover only the first few years of marriage. Still, these few studies reveal some interesting changes in the actual interactions between partners in the early months.

The best single piece of research I know of is by Ted Huston and his colleagues (Huston, McHale & Crouter, 1986), who studied 168 couples in their first marriages. Each partner was interviewed at length within the first three months of the marriage, and then again after one year. The researchers also phoned each partner repeatedly in the weeks surrounding these time points, each time asking what the subject had done with his or her spouse over the past 24 hours. Figure 14.1, which gives comparisons on 3 of the 15 measures, shows that the rate of various kinds of positive interactions or pleasing behaviors declined over time. There were parallel declines in incidents of shared physical affection other than sex, but *no* change in the rate of negative or displeasing behaviors during these early months—although other longitudinal studies show an increase in reported distress over periods as long as three years (e.g., Kurdek, 1991). In Huston's study, the same pattern appeared whether the couple had children during the first year of marriage or not, which makes it look as if these are changes associated with the relationship itself and not a function of the strain associated with adding children to the family.

In this first year, satisfaction drops because pleasing behaviors decline. Because the sharing of feelings also declined, perhaps what we are seeing here is a basic drop in the psychological intimacy of the relationship. Wouldn't it be interesting to know whether this same pattern would occur in couples in which both partners had secure internal working models of attachment?

Good and Bad Marriages

Most of the rest of what we know about partnerships in the years of early adulthood comes from studies of the causes of divorce. Because, by current estimates, between half and two-thirds of all first marriages in the United States will end in divorce (e.g., Martin & Bumpass, 1989), this is clearly a vitally important subject. I've summarized some of the main conclusions from this very large body of research in Table 14.2, and you'll want to read the list carefully.

Two points stand out for me when I read this list. First, many of the most powerful influences on marital success exist before a marriage even begins. Each partner brings to the relationship certain skills, resources, and traits that affect the emerging partnership system. Couples with better resources—more education, better ability to solve problems,

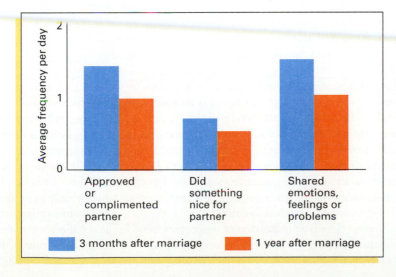

Figure 14.1 Most couples become less satisfied with their marriages in their first year together. The reason for such a decline is clear when you look at actual interactions, which become much less positive and supportive. (*Source:* Huston, McHale & Crouter, 1986, from Table 7.4, p. 124.)

TABLE 14.2 Characteristics of Successful Marriages

Personal Characteristics of Partners in More Stable Marriages
They married after age 20, but before age 30.

They have relatively high levels of education and/or come from middle-class families.

They are more religious or of the same religious background.

They have high levels of self-esteem.

They are low in the personality characteristic labeled "neuroticism," which includes a tendency toward hostility, impulsiveness, and anxiety.

They have not cohabited before marriage or have lived together only a short time.

Their parents were less likely to have divorced.

Qualities of the Interactions of Couples in Successful Marriages
They like each other and consider themselves friends.

They agree on roles and like the way the spouse is filling his/her role.

They are good at reading each other's signals. In dissatisfied marriages, husbands seem to read the wife less well than she reads him.

They have low levels of negative and high levels of positive or supportive interactions.

They are good at conflict resolution; they are less likely to avoid problems and less likely to criticize the partner.

Sources: Booth & Edwards, 1985; Bowen & Orthner, 1983; Filsinger & Thoma, 1988; Gottman & Levenson, 1984; Gottman & Porterfield, 1981; Halford, Hahlweg & Dunne, 1990; Heaton & Pratt, 1990; Kelly & Conley, 1987; Kurdek, 1991; Lauer & Lauer, 1985; Martin & Bumpass, 1989; Noller & Fitzpatrick, 1990; Schafer & Keith, 1984; White, 1990; Wilson & Filsinger, 1986.

better health (including low rates of alcoholism) and greater self-esteem—are more able to weather the storms and stresses of marriage. The personality characteristics of the partners seem to be especially important. For example, Kelly and Conley (1987), in a remarkable longitudinal study of 300 couples who were engaged in 1930 and studied until 1980, found that the single best predictor of divorce was a high level of a personality pattern called *neuroticism* in either partner—a pattern very similar to what Thomas and Chess describe as a "difficult" temperament. Among those who stayed together, the level of neuroticism of the partners was negatively correlated with marital satisfaction.

But a marriage is more than the sum of the qualities or assets of the two individuals. Equally important for the success of marriage is the quality of the actual interactions that develop between the couple. Adults who have good communication skills, or low neuroticism, are likely to create better interaction patterns. But it is the positiveness or negativeness of the actual interaction that seems to be critical, however that is achieved. Research by John Gottman shows especially clearly that the single biggest difference between happy and unhappy couples is the relative niceness or nastiness of daily conversations. For a stable positive interactive system, Gottman suggests that the ratio of nice to nasty needs to be at least 4 to 1 or better (Gottman, 1991). When the ratio falls below that, the system becomes "chaotic" and will tend to amplify problems rather than dampen them down. Just as a baby with a difficult temperament is hard to soothe, a couple with a chaotic or distressed system finds it difficult to soothe themselves and arguments escalate out of control. In this state, they are more susceptible to stress of almost any kind.

What is the direction of causality in all this? Do couples become unhappy because they are more negative, or more negative because they are already unhappy? Both may happen, but it looks as if the more common route is that couples become unhappy because they are negative. The best indication of this comes from studies of therapeutic interventions with unhappy couples: couples who are trained to increase their rate of positive interactions typically show increases in their marital satisfaction (O'Leary & Smith, 1991).

Think about your most recent unsuccessful relationship—a dating relationship that did not last, a marriage that ended in divorce. Was there a point in the relationship when it became "chaotic" in Gottman's sense—when the ratio of negative to positive encounters became so poor that it spiraled out of control? Was the change gradual?

THE REAL WORLD

Cohabitation and Its Effect on Subsequent Marriage

In the 1970s and 1980s, the average age at first marriage in the United States began to go up rapidly, and the number of young people listed as ''never married'' rose in tandem. For example, in 1970, only about 20 percent of men and 10 percent of women aged 25 to 29 had never married; in 1988 the corresponding percentages were 43 percent and 30 percent (U.S. Bureau of the Census, 1990). These figures might mean that young adults are simply more reluctant to marry today, perhaps because they want to establish careers before they marry. The alternative possibility, supported by the research, is that young people are forming committed partnerships just as early and as often, but many more are choosing to cohabit instead of marry (Bumpass, Sweet & Cherlin, 1991; Bumpass & Sweet, 1989).

In the United States and in most Western industrialized countries, rates of cohabitation have quadrupled since 1970. In a large United States survey in 1988, Bumpass and Sweet (1989) found that nearly half of all adults in their early thirties had cohabited at least once. Sixty percent of these cohabitations resulted in marriage.

In effect, cohabitation is becoming a common step in the process of courtship and marriage, although this is more true in some subgroups than in others. You may think that cohabitation is largely a behavior of college students, but the data say otherwise. While more than a quarter of college students have cohabited before marriage, the rate is much higher among those with *less* education. Put more technically, there is a strong negative correlation between education and the likelihood of cohabiting. Bumpass and his colleagues argue that this results because lower-education adults are less likely to have the economic resources to marry. Racial differences in cohabitation also run partially counter to stereotypic expectations: if you control for education, blacks are *less* likely to cohabit than are non-Hispanic whites. Hispanics have the lowest rates of the three groups (Bumpass & Sweet, 1989).

When cohabiting couples are asked to give justifications for cohabitation, the most frequently endorsed reason is that it allows them to be sure they are compatible before marriage (Bumpass et al., 1991). In Murstein's sense, many couples now argue that cohabiting is a final ''filter'' before marriage, a last chance to see if it will work before making the final commitment. The clear assumption on the part of the majority of cohabiters is that living together will improve the chances of a successful marriage, because the wrinkles will have been worked out ahead of time, and less compatible pairs will decide not to marry.

Interestingly, the research shows exactly the opposite. Couples who cohabited before marriage are *more* likely to divorce later and are *less* satisfied with their marriages than are those who married without living together ahead of time (Booth & Johnson, 1988; Trussell & Rao, 1989; White, 1987; DeMaris & Rao, 1992). Of course it is also true that about 40 percent of couples who cohabit do not marry. In earlier eras, many would have married and later divorced. So cohabitation may indeed be preventing some divorces. But among cohabiters who do marry, divorce rates are higher than among noncohabiters. Why might this be so?

The most likely explanation is that it is not cohabiting itself that ''spoils'' people for marriage, but that people who choose to cohabit are different to begin with. Cohabitors, as a group, seem more willing to flout tradition in any of a variety of ways. They espouse less traditional sex roles, are less likely to attend church, and less likely to agree that one ought to stick with a marriage no matter how bad it is (DeMaris & Leslie, 1984). The group of adults who do not cohabit before marriage, on the other hand, contains a large percentage of individuals who are more traditional in their attitudes, including their attitudes about divorce.

This research, then, does not tell us that cohabiting makes later marriages worse. But neither does it tell us that cohabiting makes later marriages better, as most cohabiters believe.

As a final point, although none of this research on marital satisfaction has used an attachment theory framework, I am nonetheless struck by the parallel between the qualities of a successful marriage and the qualities of a secure attachment. In good marriages, there is a high level of the same kind of responsiveness to the other's signals that we see between securely attached infants and their parents. Satisfied partners take turns, read each other's cues, and respond positively. Whatever internal model of attachment an individual may bring to a marriage, the ability of the partners to create such a mutually interlocking and supportive interactive system seems to be critical in the survival of the marriage.

Social Networks: Friendships and Kin Relationships

Creating a partnership may be the most central task of the stage of intimacy, but it is certainly not the only reflection of that basic process. In early adult life, each of us creates

RESEARCH REPORT
Homosexual Partnerships

Contrary to current cultural myths, the majority of homosexual partnerships are enduring rather than short-term relationships. Between 40 and 60 percent of gay men are in long-lasting partnerships; among lesbians, the figure is closer to 75 percent (Peplau, 1991).

Letitia Peplau, who has been one of the most active researchers in this area, also reports that homosexuals are as likely as are heterosexuals to be satisfied with their partnership relationship. What does differentiate the two types of partnership is the nature of the power relationships between the two. Homosexual couples are more egalitarian than are heterosexual couples. There is no tendency within a same-sex pair for one to adopt the male sex role and the other the female; rather, they share power more equally. This is particularly true of lesbian couples. Gay male partnerships are more likely to have power differentials, with the man who earns the most money having the greatest power and

control in the relationship (Blumstein & Schwartz, 1983)—a pattern that also exists in heterosexual couples.

Some of the same factors that affect the success of marriages seem to be important in the endurance of gay partnerships. Like marriages, gay couples experience a drop in their relationship satisfaction in the early months of their partnership (Kurdek & Schmitt, 1986). And like marriages, gay relationships are more likely to last if the two partners share similar backgrounds and are equally committed to the relationship (Peplau, 1991). Although there is no research to support this, I assume that the interactional patterns that characterize lasting marriages would also typify lasting homosexual pairings.

All this means that gay partnerships are far more like heterosexual relationships than they are different. The urge to form a single, central, committed attachment in early adult life is present in all of us, gay or straight.

what Toni Antonucci (1990, 1991) calls a **convoy** of relationships, a "protective layer . . . of family and friends, who surround the individual and help in the successful negotiation of life's challenges" (Antonucci & Akiyama, 1987a, p. 519). It includes family members, a partner if you have one, and friends. For most of us, this convoy remains quite stable over our adult years. It may not be the same people in it at all times, but both the size of our convoy and our satisfaction with the support we receive from it seem to remain fairly constant (e.g., Antonucci, 1990).

Relationships with Family Members

Even though the attachment to parents may be attenuated, most adults still see or talk to their parents regularly. Figure 14.2 shows some typical data, organized by family life cycle stage. In the sample of about 200 young adults reflected in the figure, virtually all were in touch with their parents at least once a month; nearly half were in touch weekly. Contact with siblings was less frequent.

Figure 14.2 Despite the process of physical and emotional emancipation that occurs in young adulthood, virtually all adults are in contact with their parents at least monthly. (*Source:* Leigh, 1982, from Table 2, p. 202.)

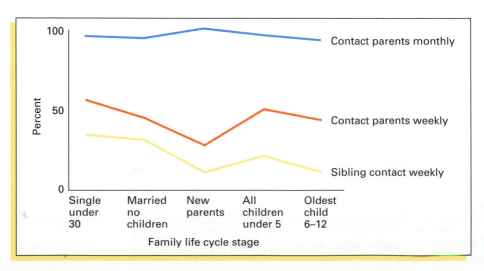

The amount and kind of contact an adult has with kin are strongly influenced by proximity. Adults who live within two hours of their parents and siblings see them far more often than is true of those who live at longer distance. But long distance does not prevent a parent or sibling from being part of an individual adult's convoy. These relationships can provide support in times of need, even if physical contact is infrequent.

Friendships in Early Adulthood

Friends, too, can be important members of a convoy. We choose our friends as we choose our partner, from among those we see as like ourselves in education, social class, interests, family background, or family life-cycle stage. Cross-sex friendships are more common among adults than they are among 10-year-olds, but they are still outnumbered by same-sex friendships. Young adults' friends are also overwhelmingly drawn from their own age group. Beyond this basic filter of similarity, close friendship seems to rest on mutual openness and personal disclosure.

There are some hints that the number of friends in the convoy may be at a peak in the earliest years of adult life, and then drop somewhat in one's thirties (e.g., Farrell &

ACROSS CULTURES
Kin Relationships in Black and Hispanic Families

You may well wonder whether the description of young adult kin relationships I've given you is equally valid for all subgroups or subcultures. In fact it is not. In the United States, both black and Hispanic family relationships differ from those in the Anglo culture.

Hispanic Kin Relationships.   Among Hispanics, particularly Mexican-Americans, the convoy is strongly dominated by family ties, a pattern strengthened by the fact that Hispanic families typically choose to live nearer to one another than is true of Anglos. Given a choice, many non-Hispanics move *away* from kin networks in early adulthood while Hispanics move *toward* them (Vega, 1990). In the Hispanic culture, extensive kin networks are the rule rather than the exception, with frequent visiting and exchange not only with parents, children, and siblings, but with grandparents, cousins, aunts, and uncles (Keefe, 1984). These frequent contacts are not only perceived as enjoyable, they are seen as vital signs of the closeness of kin relationships. It is not enough to write or talk on the phone; to maintain close ties you need to see and touch your relatives and friends. Among Hispanics, an individual's self-esteem may also be more strongly related to the valuation given by the kin group. William Madsen describes the difference this way:

> When an Anglo fails, he thinks first of how this failure will affect him and his status in society. When a Chicano fails, his first evaluation of the failure is in terms of what it will do to his family and how it will affect his relationship to other family members. (1969, p. 224)

There is some indication that this pattern is stronger in first-generation immigrants, who rely almost exclusively on family members for emotional support and problem solving. Second-generation immigrants seem to have more extensive nonkin networks. But in both generations, the extended family clearly plays a more central role in the daily life of Hispanics than it does in the Anglo culture.

Black Kin Relationships.   The same is true of African-Americans, although the reasons are somewhat different. There is a whole set of demographic differences between black and white families in the United States that create markedly different kin contacts. Young adult blacks are much less likely to marry than are whites. Many live in cohabiting relationships, but many others live in multigeneration households with their parents, grandparents, or other relatives. The National Survey of Black Americans, a nationally representative sample studied in 1980, showed that 21.8 percent of all black families were of this extended type. Among black families headed by a young adult the rate was 50 percent, most of these consisting of two generations of adult women and one or more children (Hatchett, Cochran & Jackson, 1991). Over the period of young adulthood, six out of ten black women live in such a household at least for a period of time, compared to only about 30 percent of white women (Beck and Beck, 1989). As a result, parent-adult child relationships seem to be particularly central to young adult convoys in African-American culture, especially the relationship between mothers and their adult daughters.

Frequent and supportive contact with kin and other network members is also a significant part of the daily life of most black adults who do not live in extended family households. In one large national survey of black Americans (Taylor, 1986), 37 percent reported that they had contact with family members nearly every day. African-Americans also are more likely to form what have been called pseudokin networks or ''fictive'' kin relationships—close familylike relationships with neighbors or peers, in which a wide variety of aid is exchanged (Taylor et al., 1990).

Rosenberg, 1981). Perhaps it is easier to make friends in those early years before all the many roles have been fully adopted—before one has married and had children, before the pressures of a job make time scarce. So friendships formed in your early twenties may last through your twenties and thirties, but you may make few new close friends in your thirties, and you may lose a few to moves or lack of contact. This is largely speculative, however, because we have essentially no appropriate longitudinal data covering these years.

Sex Differences in Early Adult Friendships. Much less speculative is the information about sex differences in friendship patterns. As in childhood, there are very striking sex differences in both the number and quality of friendships in the convoy. Women have more close friends, and their friendships are more intimate, with more self-disclosure and more exchange of emotional support. Young men's friendships, like those of boys and older men, are more competitive. Male friends are less likely to agree with each other or ask for or provide emotional support to one another (Maccoby, 1990; Antonucci, 1990). Adult women friends talk to one another; adult men friends do things together.

My favorite illustrative quote comes from a 38-year-old male executive interviewed by Robert Bell (1981).

> I have three close friends I have known since we were boys and they live here in the city. There are some things I wouldn't tell them. For example, I wouldn't tell them much about my work because we have always been highly competitive. I certainly wouldn't tell them about my feelings of any uncertainties with life or various things I do. And I wouldn't talk about any problems I have with my wife or in fact anything about my marriage and sex life. But other than that I would tell them anything. [After a brief pause he laughed and said:] That doesn't leave a hell of a lot, does it? (pp. 81–82)

I am not saying that men's friendships are lacking in either number or quality. Men *do* have close friends, and they are satisfied with those friendships. Yet clearly they are different. In particular, men's friendships may be less likely to meet *intimacy* needs than is true for women's pairs. Indeed, both men and women appear to satisfy their intimacy needs in relationships with women (Reis, 1986). For most men, this need is met in marriage; many more men than women have no close or intimate confidant other than their spouse.

Not surprisingly, women also typically fill the role of "kin-keeper" (Rosenthal, 1985). They write the letters, make the phone calls, arrange the gatherings. It is my daughter-in-law and not my son who writes to say thank-you for gifts and who calls to tell me how my grandson is doing. In later stages of adult life, it is also the women who are likely to take on the role of caring for aging parents—a pattern I'll have much more to say about in Chapter 16.

Taken together, these facts mean that women have a much larger "relationship role" than do men. In virtually all cultures it is part of the female role to be responsible for maintaining the emotional aspects of relationships, with a spouse, with friends, with family, and—of course—with children.

Make a list of all your own friends, and rate each one on intimacy on a 5-point scale, where 5 is the most intimate and 1 is not at all intimate. Do you have any cross-gender friendships? If so, are your friendships with women more intimate than your friendships with men? What do you do with your friends? Does your experience match the research findings?

▶ Parenthood ✈

The second major new role acquired in early adulthood is that of parent. Nine out of every ten adults will become a parent, most in their twenties or thirties. For most, the role of parent brings profound satisfaction, a greater sense of purpose and self-worth, and a feeling of being grown-up. It may also bring a sense of shared joy between husband and wife (Hoffman & Manis, 1978; Umberson & Gove, 1989). In one large study, 80 percent

One of the basic differences between men's friendships and women's friendships is that men are more likely to do things together, while women are more likely to talk.

of the parents sampled said their lives had been changed for the better by the arrival of children (Hoffman & Manis, 1978). But it is also true that the birth of the first child signals a whole series of changes in adult lives, particularly in sex roles and in marital relationships, and not all these changes are without strain.

Changes in Sex Roles. One change is an intensification of traditional sex roles that seems to be triggered by the birth of the first child. Anthropologist David Gutmann refers to this as the **parental imperative** (1975). Because human children are remarkably vulnerable and slow growing, they require a long period of both physical and emotional support. Gutmann argues that as a species, we are "wired" to divide up those two responsibilities, with mothers taking on the task of emotional support and fathers taking on the role of physical support and protection. According to Gutmann, even couples with an egalitarian philosophy will move toward a more traditional division of roles after the birth of the first child. Women, he argues, will be more and more oriented toward "hearth," while the man faces outward toward the world, figurative spear in hand. One man interviewed by Daniels and Weingarten (1988) illustrates the point:

> The baby's coming was a good thing, because it drove home to me that I had to have a better job. And I knew I'd need an education to get one. I transferred to the evening shift so I could go to college during the day. The hours were hard, I was under a lot of pressure, and I missed my family, but it was something I had to do. (p. 38)

Gutmann's own anthropological research among the Navaho, the Mayan, and the Druze generally supports his claim. There is also some support from research in the United States.

For example, Cowan and Cowan (1988) report that after the birth of a woman's first child, her tendency to define herself as "worker" or "student" decreases significantly. For men, the roles of worker or student remain highly salient even after the birth of a child. These researchers also find that women assume more responsibility for household tasks and care of the child than either partner had predicted before the child was born (Cowan et al., 1991). Not every study supports Gutmann's hypothesis (e.g., Feldman & Aschenbrenner, 1983; Cunningham & Antill, 1984), but it raises some intriguing issues, especially in light of the assumptions by many women that complete equality of roles within marriage is possible.

More firmly established is the effect of the arrival of the first child on marital (or partnership) satisfaction: It goes down, at least initially (Glenn, 1990). Figure 14.3 gives one typical set of findings, which show that satisfaction is highest before children appear and then drops and remains relatively low as long as there are children in the home, rising again during the "postparental" and retirement stages. The best documented portion of this pattern is the drop in marital satisfaction after the birth of the first child, for which we have both longitudinal and cross-sectional evidence.

You've already seen in Figure 14.1 that, on average, *all* marriages decline in positive exchanges over the first year, whether children are born during that interval or not. Other research tells us that the advent of a child adds further role conflicts and role strains. Recall that role conflict exists when a person is attempting to fill two or more roles that are physically or psychologically incompatible with each other. New parents discover that the roles of parent and spouse are at least partially incompatible. There are not enough hours in a day, and the hours that the child demands are usually subtracted from the hours spent with the partner (Cowan et al., 1991). New parents report that they now have much less time for each other—for conversation, for sex, for simple affection or even routine chores done together (Belsky, Spanier & Rovine, 1983; Belsky, Lang & Rovine, 1985).

Many new parents also experience considerable role strain—that sense that you do not know how to fill the role you find yourself in. And this sense of strain is exacerbated

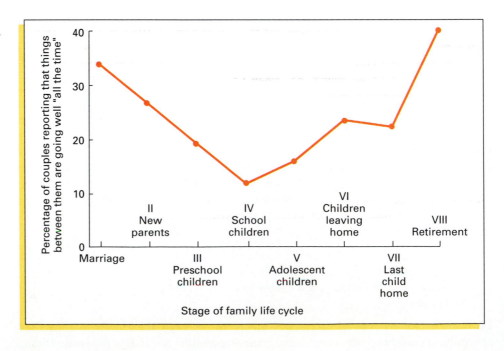

Figure 14.3 This pattern of change in marital satisfaction over the stages of the family life cycle is one of the most well documented in family sociology research. (*Source:* Rollins & Feldman, 1970, Tables 2 & 3, p. 24. Copyright 1970 by the National Council on Family Relations, 1910 West Country Road B, Suite 147, St. Paul, MN 55113.)

These parents are doubtless delighted with the arrival of young Selma, who was 5 weeks old when this photo was taken, but they may also feel a bit overwhelmed by this new role.

by anything that increases family stress, such as economic hardship, pressure from work, or a baby with a difficult temperament (Sirignano & Lachman, 1985).

▶ The Role of Worker ✈

Adding to the strain is the fact that a large percentage of young adults are simultaneously filling a third time-consuming and relatively new role, that of worker. Young people take on this role in part to support themselves economically. But that is not the only reason for the centrality of this role. Satisfying work also seems to be an important ingredient in happiness or life satisfaction for both men and women (Tait, Padgett & Baldwin, 1989; Tamir, 1982). Indeed, among women, those who work are generally more satisfied with their lives and physically healthier than those who do not work at all outside the home (e.g., Betz & Fitzgerald, 1987).

Virtually all men take on the role of worker, as do the majority of women in today's younger cohorts, although women still are likely to work for fewer years of their adult life. Current estimates are that women born in 1980 will spend nearly 30 years working outside the home, compared to only 12 years for the cohort born in 1940. But the average for men is more like 40 years (Spenner, 1988), so there is still a sex difference in work role experience. We also know far more about the work experiences of men than of women. So if it seems as if I keep saying "he" when I talk about workers, it is not because only men work, but because men have been the focus of most of the research.

Before we look at what we know about career steps and sequences in early adulthood, let me back up a step. How do young people choose an occupation?

Choosing an Occupation

As you might imagine, a plethora of factors influences a young person's choice of job or career: gender, ethnic group, intelligence, school performance, personality and self-concept, family background and values, and education. Let me talk briefly about four of these: family, education/intelligence, gender, and personality.

Family Influences. The general rule—with many exceptions—is that young people tend to choose occupations at the same general social class level as their parents. In part this effect operates through the medium of education: Middle-class families are more likely to encourage their children to go on for further education past high school. Such added education, in turn, makes it more likely that the young person will qualify for middle-class jobs, for which a college education is frequently a required credential (Featherman, 1980).

What explanations can you think of for the observation that working women are healthier and happier than nonworking women? How could you test your hypotheses?

Families also influence job choices through their value systems. In particular, parents who value academic and professional achievement are far more likely to have children who attend college and choose professional-level jobs. This effect is not just social-class difference in disguise. Among working-class families, it is those who place the strongest emphasis on their children's achievements whose children are most likely to move up into middle-class jobs (Gustafson & Magnusson, 1991).

2 Education and Intelligence. Education and intelligence also interact very strongly to influence not just the specific job a young person will choose, but also career success over the long haul. I mentioned some of these links in Chapter 11, but let me reiterate. It works like this: The higher your intelligence, the more years of education you are likely to complete; the more education you have, the higher the rung of the career ladder on which you enter the job market; the higher the rung of entry, the further you are likely to go up the career ladder over your lifetime (Kamo et al., 1991; Farmer et al., 1990; Featherman, 1980).

Intelligence has direct effects on job choice and job success as well. Brighter students are more likely to choose technical or professional careers, and highly intelligent workers are more likely to advance, even if they enter the system on a lower rung of the career ladder (e.g., Dreher & Bretz, 1991).

3 Gender. Specific job choice is also strongly affected by gender. Despite the women's movement and despite the vast increase in the proportion of women working, it is still true that sex role definitions designate some jobs as "women's jobs" and some as "men's jobs." Male jobs are more varied, more technical, and higher in both status and income (e.g., doctor, business executive, carpenter). Women's jobs are concentrated in service occupations, typically lower status and lower paid (e.g., teacher, nurse, secretary) (Betz & Fitzgerald, 1987). One-third of all working women occupy clerical jobs; another quarter are in health care, teaching, or domestic service. These differences have not disappeared even in fields in which the proportion of men and women is becoming more balanced. For example, more men are becoming nurses, but they tend to be concentrated in specific subspecialties or in supervisory ranks.

Children learn these cultural definitions of "appropriate" jobs for men and women in their early years, just as they learn all the other aspects of sex roles. So it is not surprising that most young women and men choose jobs that fit these sex-role designations (e.g., Schulenberg, Goldstein & Vondracek, 1991). Cross-sex job choices are much more common among young people who see themselves as androgynous or whose parents hold unconventional occupations. For instance, young women who choose traditionally masculine careers are more likely to have a mother who has had a long-term work commitment and are more likely to define themselves either as androgynous or masculine (Betz & Fitzgerald, 1987; Fitzpatrack & Silverman, 1989).

4 Personality. A fourth important influence on job choice is the young person's personality. John Holland, whose work has been the most influential in this area (1973, 1985), proposes six basic personality types and six parallel work environments, which I've summarized in Table 14.3. Holland's basic hypothesis is that each of us tends to choose, and be most successful at, an occupation that matches our personality.

Research in non-Western as well as Western cultures, and with blacks, Hispanics, and Native Americans as well as whites in the United States, has generally supported Holland's proposal (e.g., Kahn et al., 1990; Eberhardt & Muchinsky, 1984; Meier, 1991). Ministers, for example, generally score highest on the social scale, engineers highest on the investigative scale, and car salespersons on the enterprising scale (Benninger & Walsh, 1980; Walsh, Horton & Gaffey, 1977).

People whose personality matches their job are also more likely to be satisfied with their work, although, interestingly, job *success* is only very weakly related to personality/

TABLE 14.3 Holland's Personality and Work Environment Types

Type	Personality	Appropriate Work Environment
Artistic	Prefers unstructured, individual activity; asocial.	Free, unsystematized, ambiguous activities to produce art or performance.
Enterprising	Likes organizing and directing others; usually highly verbal and dominating, persuasive and high in leadership.	Manipulation of others, such as in sales.
Conventional	Likes clear guidelines, structured activities, and subordinate role; accurate and precise.	Ordered, precise, systematic manipulation of data; e.g., record keeping, filing, bookkeeping, organizing.
Social	Likes to work with people and dislikes intellectual or highly ordered activity; needs attention.	Caring for, training, serving, enlightening others.
Investigative	Likes ambiguous, challenging tasks involving abstract thinking, planning, organizing; usually low in social skills.	Creative investigation or observation of physical, biological, or cultural phenomena.
Realistic	Likes mechanical activities and tool use; aggressive, masculine, physically strong; usually low in verbal or interpersonal skills.	Systematic or ordered manipulation of tools, machines, or animals.

Source: Holland, 1973.

job match (Assouline & Meir, 1987). It is obviously quite possible to succeed at a job that is a poor match for your personality, but you're likely to be less happy with such a job in the long run.

Jobs over Time

Once the job or career has been chosen, what kinds of experiences do young adults have in their work life? Do they become more or less satisfied with their work over time? Are there clear career steps that we might think of as stages or shared steps on the ladder?

Job Satisfaction. Many studies show that job satisfaction is at its *lowest* in early adulthood and rises steadily until retirement, a pattern that has been found in repeated surveys among both male and female respondents (Glenn & Weaver, 1985).

We know this is not just a cohort effect because similar findings have been reported over many years of research, and we know that it is not entirely culture specific since it has been found in many industrialized countries. But what might cause it? Some research (e.g., Bedeian, Ferris & Kacmar, 1992) points to the conclusion that what we have here is not an age effect but the effect of job tenure. Older workers are likely to have had their jobs longer, which may contribute to several sources of satisfaction, including better pay, more job security, and more authority. But there may also be some genuine age effects at work, too. The jobs young people hold are likely to be dirtier, physically harder, or less complex and less interesting (Spenner, 1988). Part of this difference is the result of in-experience, but it may also reflect the greater strength and physical hardiness of the young.

One other possible explanation for the pattern of increasing job satisfaction with age is self-selection. By middle age, many workers have tried and discarded several jobs and have arrived at an occupation that suits them (White & Spector, 1987).

Before you read further, see if you can think of several different reasons why job satisfaction might increase with age.

Job satisfaction rises steadily through the years of young adulthood, for both men and women.

Career Ladders. Within any given career path, workers also tend to move from step to step up some sort of job sequence or career ladder. In academic jobs, the sequence is from instructor to assistant professor to associate and then full professor. In an automobile plant the ladder may go from assembly line worker to foreman to general foreman to superintendent and on up. In the corporate world, there may be many rungs in a clear management ladder.

What kind of progress up such a ladder do young adults typically make? To answer such a question properly, of course, we need longitudinal studies. There are not many of these, but fortunately there are a few, including a 20-year study of AT&T managers (Bray & Howard, 1983), and a 15-year study of workers in a large company, called ABCO by the investigator, James Rosenbaum (1984).

This research suggests several generalizations about the developmental progression of work careers in early adulthood. First, college education makes a very large difference, as I already pointed out. Even with intellectual ability controlled, those with a college education advance further and faster.

Second, *early* promotion is associated with greater advancement over the long haul. In the particular company Rosenbaum studied, 83 percent of those who were promoted within the first year eventually got as far as lower management, while only 33 percent of those who were first promoted after three years of employment got that far.

Third, and perhaps most important, most work advancement occurs early in a career path, after which a plateau is reached. Rosenbaum's results make the point clearly. Company policy in the ABCO company was that all workers—whether they had a college degree or not—should enter at the submanagement level. The first upward step was to the job of foreman, with lower management the second possible step. Figure 14.4 shows the percentages of workers who made these career moves at each age. Both steps obviously occurred early; by age 40, virtually all the promotions that were going to occur had already happened. The same pattern occurs in other career paths as well, such as accounting and the academic world (Spenner, 1988), so this is not unique to business career ladders.

Such a pattern *may* be unique, however, to adults who enter a profession in their twenties and stay in it through most of their adult lives. There are at least a few hints in research with women—whose work histories are frequently much less stable than this— that it may be time-in-career rather than age that is the critical variable for the timing of promotions. There may be a window of 10 or 15 years between the time you enter a profession and the time you reach a plateau. If you begin in your twenties, you are likely

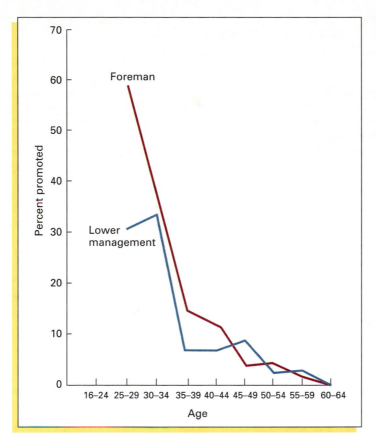

Figure 14.4 Rosenbaum's longitudinal study of promotions in a large corporation illustrates the general pattern that promotions occur early in adult life; by one's mid-thirties or early forties, most workers have reached a plateau in their work progress. (*Source:* Rosenbaum, 1984, Figure 3.1, p. 80.)

to have peaked by your mid-thirties. But if you begin when you are 40, you still might have 15 years in which to advance.

Another View of Work Sequences. Another way to describe the work experience of young adults is in terms of a series of stages. First comes the **trial** or **establishment stage**, typically between ages 20 and 30—equivalent to the earliest phase of the early adult life structure proposed by Levinson, which you may remember from Chapter 2 (Figure 2.3, page 38). In this period, the young person is deciding on his job or career and may try out several different options, perhaps returning to school for further training. Once in a given occupation, the young person in this earliest stage must learn the ropes, perhaps moving through the early steps in some career ladder as he masters the needed skills.

Next comes the **stabilization stage**, roughly from age 30 to 45. Having chosen an occupation and learned the ropes, the worker now focuses on fulfilling whatever aspirations or goals he may have set for himself. The young scientist pushes himself to win a Nobel Prize; the young attorney bucks for partner; the young business executive tries to move as far up the ladder as he can; the young blue-collar worker may strive for job stability or for promotion to foreman. It is in these years that most promotions do in fact occur, although it is also in these years that the job plateau is reached.

Women's Work Patterns

Some of what I have said about work patterns so far is as true for women as it is for men. Women's work satisfaction goes up with age (and with job tenure), just as men's does, for example. But women's work experience in early adulthood differs from men's in one

THE REAL WORLD
Mentors and Their Role in Early Adult Work Experience

Daniel Levinson, whose theory I introduced in Chapter 2, proposes that one of the key experiences of the era of early adulthood is the relationship with a **mentor**. In Levinson's terms, a mentor is normally an individual 8 to 15 years older than the young adult, who takes the younger worker under his (or her) wing, teaching him the ropes, advising and promoting his career. Practically speaking, a mentor may obviously be important for the young person's progress up some career ladder. Psychologically, Levinson thought the mentor served the function of assisting the young person to move from the dependency of youth to the full independence of one's thirties or forties. Just as the peer group provides transitional support in adolescence, helping the teenager to move toward social independence, so the mentor serves a similar function in the work world.

This concept has entered our everyday parlance; it has even become a verb: *to mentor*. But there is surprisingly little research on the mentoring process. We do not know whether the majority of young adults have mentors in their workplace, nor whether mentoring is important either for professional advancement or for psychological maturity. (Nor, for that matter, do we know much about how important the role of mentor may be for the mentor.)

In Levinson's own study of men, relatively few described mentors, a finding confirmed in several studies of women designed to test Levinson's theory (Roberts & Newton, 1987). Studies of business executives, in contrast, suggest that mentoring may be common. In one study, 83 percent of a group of 140 male and female middle- and upper-level executives said they had had a mentor, although less than half said their mentor had been highly significant in their career advancement (Shapiro & Farrow, 1988). The difference may lie in the way mentoring is defined. I am not sure that Levinson would count as a mentor someone who had not played a significant role in one's career advancement.

Given the paucity of evidence and the somewhat contradictory findings, what can I tell you about the potential importance of a mentor to your own career? Certainly, having a mentor cannot hurt, and it may well help in career advancement. If for no other reason, it would be worth your while to try to cultivate such a relationship. What I simply do not know is whether such a relationship is either necessary or sufficient for psychological maturity. Probably it is not, but it may nonetheless bring real satisfactions.

strikingly important respect: it is far less likely to be continuous. This difference, in turn, has a wide range of repercussions for women's work roles.

In 1988 in the United States, two-thirds of all women between the ages of 25 and 64 were in the labor force at least part-time. The rate is lower among Hispanic women and about equal for blacks and whites. But in every ethnic group, the more education a woman has, the more likely she is to work. Among women with at least four years of college, 80.8 percent are in the labor force (U.S. Bureau of the Census, 1990).

Nonetheless, most women do not work continuously over the years of early adulthood. Studies of several different cohorts of women in the United States suggest that only a fifth to a quarter of women are continuously employed throughout early adult life (Sörensen, 1983; U.S. Bureau of the Census, 1984; Moen, 1985). Most of the rest move in and out of the work force at least once, often many times.

Women's work patterns are obviously changing rapidly; it is possible that a larger percent of current cohorts of 20- and 30-year-old women will work continuously. But because it is women who bear, nurse, and (primarily) rear children, it is most often women who stay home with children for at least a brief period during their early adult years, and that fact seems unlikely to change totally.

One way we might think of women's work patterns is to think of them as having an extra stage we could call *in-and-out*. For some women this stage comes first, almost as part of the trial stage. For others it comes after the trial stage but before the stabilization stage. To compare the promotion history of women and men, we would have to subtract this in-and-out period from women's history, and compare only the years spent in continuous work. Unfortunately, no one has done that kind of research, so we cannot be sure whether women's work pathways would follow the same patterns as do men's. But we do have some indication that the discontinuous aspect of women's work patterns does affect their job success and work achievement.

For example, women who work continuously have higher salaries and achieve higher levels in their jobs than do those who have moved in and out of employment (Van Velsor & O'Rand, 1984). We also have some indication that among women who have not worked continuously, those who have had several short bursts of work during their in-and-out stage do better economically than those who were unemployed for a single long stretch, even when the total months or years of employment are the same in the two groups (Gwartney-Gibbs, 1988). Very likely these short bursts of work allow the woman to keep up her work skills, especially if the woman works at the same type of job each

ACROSS CULTURES
Job Patterns for U.S. Women of Different Ethnic Groups

A fascinating new book by Teresa Amott and Julie Matthaei (1991) about the history and work patterns of women in nine different U.S. ethnic groups gives us a glimpse into women's varying work experiences. The figure below shows one summary of the differences. For this analysis, jobs were classified into four categories by status. For comparison purposes, the pattern of jobs for European-American men is also given.

The four job categories are as follows:

Level 1: managers, professional persons, supervisors, owners of businesses or farms
Level 2: technologists, precision production workers, artisans, repair persons, transportation workers
Level 3: health technicians, salespersons, clerical personnel, machine operators, assemblers, inspectors
Level 4: service employees, cleaners, helpers, unskilled laborers

The figure makes clear that Asian-American women have caught up to and now exceed European women in their access to higher-level occupations. This seems to have occurred primarily through education. Asian families had always placed a high value on *male* education; in the past decades this value has been extended to female education, with the result that Asian woman have access to more upper-level jobs that have high educational entrance requirements.

The group which has lagged most in both occupational involvement and success are Chicanas, not only because of the immigration pattern over many decades, which placed many Chicanos and Chicanas in low-paying agricultural jobs, but also because their culture has had a strong emphasis on the importance of family life and the woman's central place in that life.

If you are interested in this area, I can strongly recommend Amott and Matthaei's book. Their most central point is that the work and family experiences of women in the United States is powerfully affected by the specific history and cultural values of their ethnic group.

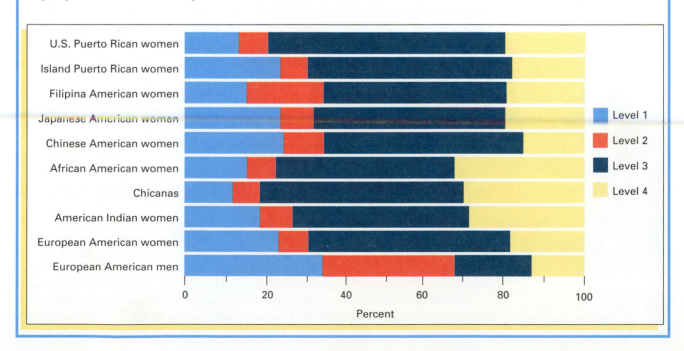

time she reenters the labor market. Part-time work also seems to serve some of the same function. Clearly there are strategies that can help a woman maximize her work success while still spending some period with her family, but it takes a good deal of thought and planning.

Combining Work and Family Roles

This point raises the more general question of how individuals, and couples, manage to combine the roles of worker and parent, or worker and spouse. It is interesting, and testimony to our cultural patterns, that we think it quite uncomplicated for a man to be worker, parent, and spouse, but we think it is problematic for a woman to be all three. Women do in fact *feel* more role conflict between these three roles than men do, for several clear reasons.

The most obvious reason is that if you add up the hours spent in family work (child care, cleaning, cooking, shopping, and so on) and in paid employment, employed women are working more hours a week than are their husbands or partners. Women do considerably more of the family tasks than men do, even when both partners work full-time (e.g., Geerken & Gove, 1983; Shelton, 1990; Rexroat & Shehan, 1987). You can see the net effect of this in Figure 14.5, which is based on data from the Panel Study of Income Dynamics, a study of over 5000 families in 1976. Among childless couples, there is an almost even distribution of labor; but when children are young, women are simply putting in more hours. Among other things, this pattern provides further evidence for Gutmann's notion of the *parental imperative*. Sex roles become more traditional after the birth of a child.

More recent studies do show that there has been some move toward greater equality in some subgroups. For instance, men who are more philosophically committed to sex-role equality do take on more household work and child care (e.g., Perry-Jenkins & Crouter, 1990). But across the board, it is still the case that full-time working women do considerably more hours of household work than do their working partners. Data from the National Survey of Families and Households in 1987 and 1988, for example (Coltrane & Ishii-Kuntz, 1992), indicate that only about one-fifth of household work is done by husbands in these current families. Even when today's women do less of the work themselves, they are still *in charge of* seeing that it gets done (Maret & Finlay, 1984).

Women also feel more conflict between family and work roles because of the way sex roles are defined in most cultures. The woman's role is to be relationship-oriented, to care for, to nurture. To the extent that a woman has internalized that role expectation—and most of us have—she will define herself, and judge herself, more by how well she performs such caring roles than by how well she performs on the job. Joseph Pleck argues that this means that the boundaries between work and family roles are therefore "asymmetrically permeable" for the two sexes (Pleck, 1977). That is, for a woman, family roles spill over into her work life. She not only takes time off from her job when children are born, she stays home with the sick child, takes time off to go to a teacher's conference or a PTA meeting, and thinks about her family tasks during her work day. These simultaneous, competing demands are the very definition of role conflict.

For men, it is almost as if work and family roles are sequential rather than simultaneous. Men are workers during the day, husbands and fathers when they come home. Women are mothers and wives all day, even when they work. If the two roles conflict for men, it is more likely to be the work role that spills over into family life than the other way around (Duxbury & Higgins, 1991).

Not all the intersections of family and work roles are so problematic for women. For example, working women have more power in their partnerships than do nonworking women (e.g., Blumstein & Schwartz, 1983; Spitze, 1988). The more equal the earnings

For young women only: What plans do you now have to combine work and family? Might your planning or your thinking change as a result of what you have just read?

Women are working in larger and larger numbers, but fewer than a third work continuously during the early adult years.

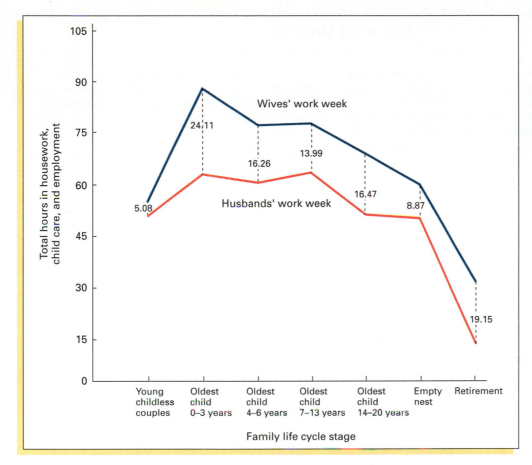

Figure 14.5 When both partners work full-time, women still do more housework and child care, so that their total work week is many hours longer—contributing significantly to women's greater sense of role conflict between work and family roles. Note that the gap is greatest right after the birth of the first child—perhaps a time when the man is most likely to be intensely committed to his career. (*Source:* Rexroat & Shehan, 1987, Fig. 1, p. 746.)

of the partners, the more equality there is in decision making and in household work (Brayfield, 1992). But it remains true that the most striking single fact about work and family roles in this age of high women's employment is that women, more than men, struggle to resolve the conflict between the two. It is also clear that this conflict is vastly greater during early adulthood, when children are young and needing constant care, than it is in middle or later adult life. In many respects it is this maximally complex intersection of spousal, parental, and work roles that is the defining feature of early adult life.

Personality Continuity and Change ✈

Perhaps because of the mutual impact of these several major roles, we also see some very interesting, shared changes in personality qualities over the years of early adulthood. That is not to say that we all become alike. On the contrary, basic temperament or personality traits show strong continuity over this 20-year period. But overlaid on top of that continuity is a set of shared changes. Let me start by looking at the continuities.

Personality Continuity

In earlier chapters I have talked about various facets of personality studied in children, including such temperamental dimensions as difficultness, activity level, or sociability. Echoes of these same qualities are found in studies of adult personality, especially in the work of Robert McCrae and Paul Costa (1990; Costa & McCrae, 1980a, 1980b, 1988; Costa et al., 1986).

THE REAL WORLD
Strategies for Coping with Family/Work Conflict

Are you overwhelmed by the many competing demands of work and family? Are there some days when you despair? I cannot offer you a magic formula for eliminating such conflict or despair, but there are some strategies that help. I'm going to phrase this as advice to women, because it is women who experience the greatest role conflict. But there is no reason why men could not profit from the same points.

• *Redefine or restructure family roles.* Douglas Hall (1972, 1975) has found that women who find ways to redistribute basic household tasks to other family members (husband and children), or who simply give up doing some tasks, experience less stress and conflict. You might want to make a list of all the household chores that you do and that your partner does and go over the list jointly, eliminating whatever items you can cross out and reassigning the others. Men *can* clean toilets; clutter can be dealt with less frequently (or, heaven forbid, not at all), meals can perhaps be simpler. Depending on economic resources, help can also be hired.

• *Redefine your concept of what you* ought *to be.* An even more basic strategy is to try to change your ideas about sex roles themselves. Where is it written that only women can stay home with a sick child? It is probably written in your internal model of your self, or your gender schema. Many women find it difficult to give up such tasks even when they cause severe role conflict, because such nurturing is part of their image of themselves. As one woman, whose husband was very involved in the care of their infant, said:

I love seeing the closeness between him and the baby, especially since I didn't have that with my father, but if he does well at his work *and* his relationship with the baby, what's my special contribution? (Cowan & Cowan, 1987, p. 168)

It may be worth your while to try to discover whether the current division of labor in your own household exists because of resistance to participation by husband or children, or because of your own inner resistance to changing your view of yourself and your basic contribution to the family unit.

• *Take a class in time management.* I am sure you have already been given lots of advice about how it could all be managed if you just handled things better. Easier said than done! But there actually are techniques that help, many of which are taught in workshops and classes in most cities. Even though attending such a workshop will temporarily add to your role conflict, it is worth the time.

What does *not* work is simply to try harder to do it all yourself. Women who continue to try to perform all three roles at a high level report maximum strain and stress. Something has to give, whether it is your standards for housework or your sense of your female role. And even then, combining all these roles is inherently full of opportunities for conflict. At best, the balance is delicate. At worst, it is overwhelming.

These researchers have identified five dimensions or traits, each of which shows considerable stability both from one situation to another and over time: **neuroticism, extraversion** (whose opposite is introversion), **openness to experience, agreeableness,** and **conscientiousness**. There is now agreement among personality researchers that these "big five" traits, described in Table 14.4, capture the bulk of variation in personality among individuals.

If you think about parallels between these five and some of the temperament dimensions described by infancy researchers, the overlap is clear: "difficultness" of temperament sounds like an aspect of neuroticism; "easiness" of temperament reflects agreeableness; activity level reflects one aspect of extraversion, as does sociability. If there is order in the universe, we ought to find at least *some* correlation between such temperamental qualities measured in early childhood and the five personality dimensions in adulthood. As yet we have no longitudinal data that would allow us to check this expectation, but I am sure that eventually such evidence will be available. Meanwhile, we *do* have a good deal of evidence about the stability of these five traits in adulthood, one set of which I've given on the right hand side of Table 14.4.

These results come from a six-year longitudinal study of a group of 983 men and women, aged 21 to 76 at the time of the first testing (Costa & McCrae, 1988). The numbers I've given you are the correlations between test scores on the first and second tests, given six years apart. Clearly people continue to perceive themselves, or describe

TABLE 14.4 The "Big Five" Personality Traits Identified by McCrae and Costa, and Their Stability Over Time

Trait	Quality of Individual High in That Trait	Stability Over 6 Years
Neuroticism	Worrying, temperamental, self-pitying, self-conscious, emotional, and vulnerable.	.83
Extraversion	Affectionate, talkative, active, fun-loving, passionate, and a joiner.	.82
Openness to experience	Imaginative, creative, original, curious, liberal; willing to explore inner feelings.	.83
Agreeableness	Soft-hearted, trusting, generous, acquiescent, lenient, good-natured.	.63
Conscientiousness	Conscientious, hard-working, well-organized, punctual, ambitious, persevering.	.79

Source: McCrae & Costa, 1990, adapted from Table 1, p. 3, and from Costa & McCrae, 1988, Table 4.

themselves, in very much the same ways over periods of this length. The correlations were essentially the same for women as for men, and for younger adults (age 25 to 56) as for older adults (57 to 84). Other evidence suggests that the correlations are likely to be a bit smaller if we measure over longer periods of time, such as several decades, but the consistency is still remarkably robust (Helson & Moane, 1987; Haan, Millsap & Hartka, 1986)

All of this means that we take ourselves along on our journey through adult life. We approach the new roles of early adulthood in ways that reflect our basic personality traits. In particular, individuals high in neuroticism seem to have a particularly difficult time with many of life's tasks. They are consistently higher on measures of maladjustment or unhappiness, less satisfied with their lives (McCrae & Costa, 1990), and more likely to divorce, as you have already seen in the results from Kelly and Conley's longitudinal study (1987).

Adults high in neuroticism also deal less well with stress. Faced with a significant life change, they are more likely to describe it (and experience it) as a crisis and to show enduring consequences. For example, in one of his studies of the effect of the Great Depression, Elder (Liker & Elder, 1983) found that irritable men (presumably high in neuroticism) became more and more irritable under severe economic stress. Less neurotic men showed initial negative reactions and then bounced back. You may also remember from Chapter 1 (Figure 1.2, p. 7) the description of Elder's study of explosive and ill-tempered boys. These youngsters carried this trait with them into adult life and, as a consequence, were less successful in both work and family roles. In contrast, adults high in extraversion are consistently more satisfied with their lives.

Can you think of other possible effects of these personality traits on a young adult's experience with the roles I've been talking about here? Which personality traits would you expect to be associated with greater marital stability? Which might predict good physical health?

Changes in Personality

Even while these consistent traits exist, it also appears to be the case that there is an interesting set of shared changes in personality in early adulthood. You've already seen an example of such simultaneous consistency and change in the last chapter: average IQ goes up in early adulthood (recall Figure 13.4) even while the correlation between IQ scores at two different adult ages is extremely high. Simultaneous consistency and change can occur because of the way we compute correlations like the ones in Table 14.4. When we give a group of people the same test on two different occasions, the correlation between them is high if the *rank order* remains the same, that is, if those who are high at the first testing are still high at the second testing. But the whole group could rise or fall at the same time without altering the rank order.

McCrae and Costa do not think that there is any change. They find none on measures of their five personality traits. But several important longitudinal studies, using more in-depth methods of measuring personality and covering a larger number of years of adult life, do suggest a set of changes that make theoretical and intuitive sense to me. In young adulthood, we see increases in a cluster of characteristics including confidence, self-esteem, independence, and achievement orientation.

The best single set of data comes from the Berkeley/Oakland longitudinal sample, a study I have talked about several times. You'll recall that several hundred subjects were studied from childhood into their fifties and sixties (Haan, 1981b; Haan, Millsap & Hartka, 1986). Personality characteristics were measured with an unusual technique, called a *Q-sort*. A Q-sort consists of a set of words or phrases that might describe an individual, such as "satisfied with self" or "bullies others," or "socially poised." A skilled rater, using all the information available about each subject at a given age (interview material, data from direct observations or comments by other psychologists who have observed the subject, test results), sorts this set of words or phrases into nine separate piles. Pile 1 contains the statements *least* characteristic of the individual and pile 9 contains those that are the most. As an added feature, the rater is required to create a normal distribution across the nine piles; only a very few items are allowed in the most extreme piles (piles 1 and 9) and the bulk must be placed in the middle piles. This method is not unique to the Berkeley studies; among other things, a Q-sort strategy is now widely used as an alternative to the Strange Situation as a method of assessing the security of a child's attachment. What is important for you to remember about this technique is that it reflects the *relative weight* or *relative visibility* of a characteristic at a given time in the life span rather than the absolute level of some quality.

Figure 14.6 shows the pattern of change with age in a cluster of Q-sort items relating to aspects of assertiveness versus submissiveness. Figure 1.1 in Chapter 1 (page 4) showed the changes in another cluster, self-confidence versus the sense of being victimized. You ought to go back and look at that figure again. You'll see that both assertiveness and self-

Figure 14.6 Scores for the assertiveness cluster of Q-sort items in the Berkeley/Oakland longitudinal studies. (*Source:* Haan, Millsap & Hartka, 1986, Figure 2, p. 228.)

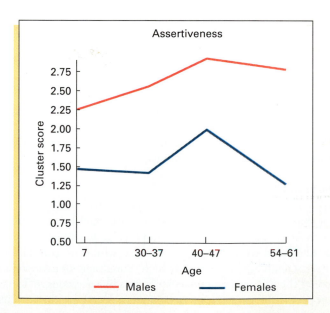

confidence rose in early adulthood among these subjects, especially between ages 30 and 40. In the same years there was also an increase in a cluster Haan calls "cognitively committed," which includes aspects of ambition, valuing independence, and valuing intellect.

Other researchers report similar changes. In a study of women graduates of Mills College, Helson and Moane (1987; Helson, Mitchell & Moane, 1984) found few personality changes between 21 and 27, but between 27 and 43 the women increased in dominance (including aspects of confidence) and independence. The AT&T managers studied by Bray and Howard (1983) also showed a decline in dependency and an increase in the need for autonomy over the 20 years of the study, covering the ages from roughly 20 to 40.

Findings like these suggest the possibility that in early adulthood there is a basic shift toward greater autonomy, greater achievement striving, greater self-confidence and personal assertiveness. The young adult not only becomes physically independent of his family, he becomes increasingly psychologically independent as well. And as he masters the various roles of early adult life, he becomes more confident, more able to assert his individuality.

Other theorists have talked about the underlying change in early adulthood in terms of a shift from an external to an internal definition of oneself (e.g., Loevinger, 1976, 1984). In our twenties, we each struggle to learn all the culturally defined and demanded roles. In that sense, we allow ourselves to be defined by external criteria. But these roles are not always a good fit, so eventually we begin to push at the edges, to find our own individuality.

Daniel Levinson (1978) uses the term *detribalization* to describe this change. By the end of early adulthood, he says, the adult

> becomes more critical of the tribe—the particular groups, institutions and traditions that have the greatest significance for him, the social matrix to which he is most attached. He is less dependent upon tribal rewards, more questioning of tribal values. (p. 242)

It seems to me that this set of changes is not in conflict with the consistency in basic personality traits described by McCrae and Costa. An extraverted 20-year-old will still be an extraverted 40-year-old, even though at 40 she is *also* more independent and self-confident than she was. As I see it, a basic set of *developmental* changes is overlaid on consistent personality traits. The way in which each of us handles the tasks of early adult life will be affected by our personality or temperament; an individual high in neuroticism will respond differently than will someone with a less prickly approach to life. But all of us are affected by the shared tasks of early adulthood—by the need to become independent of family and to learn a large set of new role skills.

▶ Individual Differences

If the acquisition of the "big three" roles in early adulthood is central to the rhythm and shape of this period of life, then what happens to people who do not adopt all three roles, such as adults who do not marry (or cohabit) or those who do not have children? And does the timing of these events matter?

Those Who Do Not Marry

Marriage, or (presumably) long-term cohabitation, brings certain advantages. Married young adults are happier, healthier, live longer, and have lower rates of a variety of psychiatric problems (Lee, Seccombe & Shehan, 1991; Coombs, 1991; Glenn & Weaver,

We don't know why this man has remained unmarried. We do know that because he is single he is at higher risk for a variety of physical and emotional problems. Of course, if he has other sources of significant emotional support, he may be buffered from such negative consequences.

1988) than do adults without committed partners. The least well off on virtually all measures are unmarried men, while the best off are married men. The two groups of women fall in between, with married women at a slight advantage over the unmarried. But unmarried women are considerably healthier and happier than are unmarried men.

One possible explanation of this pattern is that some sort of self-selection is occurring. People who are healthy and happy are simply more likely to marry. Logical as it may sound, researchers have found little support for this explanation (Coombs, 1991). Instead, there is support for an explanation based on the notion of social support. The argument is that married adults are less vulnerable to both disease and emotional distress because they are buffered by the support from their central attachment to their partner. Married men derive particular benefits precisely because men are less likely to have close confidants outside of marriage and because wives, more than husbands, provide emotional warmth and support to their spouse.

I hasten to add that this does not mean that all single adults are lonely and unhappy. The differences I've described are averages, and there are many exceptions. Many adults are single by preference; many have found alternative sources of support. Never-married women, for example, are more likely to maintain very close contact with their parents, perhaps retaining that central attachment in a less attenuated form (e.g., Allen & Pickett, 1987). They are also more likely than are their married peers to have full-time, continuous careers and to be more successful and better paid as a result (Sörensen, 1983). Still, there is no doubt that being unmarried changes the shape of early adulthood in significant ways and carries certain psychological risks.

Those Who Do Not Have Children

Having no children also changes the shape of adult life, both in marriages and in work patterns. Without the presence of children, there is a much smaller dip in the curve of marital satisfaction. As is true of all marriages, those without children are likely to experience some drop in the first months and years of marriage (as you've seen in Figure 14.1), but over the whole range of years of adult life the curve is much flatter than the one shown in Figure 14.3 (Houseknecht, 1987; Ishii-Kuntz, & Seccombe, 1989). In their twenties and thirties, childless couples consistently report higher cohesion in their marriages than do couples with children. When there is no parenthood role to fulfill, there is more time and energy for the partnership role.

Interestingly, once the children have left home, this difference may reverse. There is at least one study that shows that among postparental adult couples (mostly in their fifties and sixties), marital satisfaction is *higher* among those with children than among the childless (Houseknecht & Macke, 1981). Another difference is in the role of worker, especially for women. Like never-married women, childless married women are much more likely to have full-time continuous careers and to be more committed to the goal of career success (Houseknecht, 1987; Hoffman & Manis, 1978).

Overall, then, childlessness has the expected effects on the way young adults distribute their energy among the main roles. At a deeper level, however, childlessness may demand a different kind of adaptation. One very interesting analysis comes from a 40-year longitudinal study of a group of inner-city but nondelinquent boys who had originally served as a comparison group for a study of delinquent youth (Snarey et al., 1987). Of the 343 married men still part of this sample in their late forties, 29 had fathered no child. Snarey and his colleagues found that the way a man responded to this childlessness was predictive of his psychological health at age 47. At that age, each man was rated on his degree of what Erikson calls *generativity*. A man was considered to be generative if he had taken responsibility for the growth and well-being of other adults through some kind of mentoring or other teaching or supervising. Among those with no children, those who

Do these results mean that every adult has to have some nurturing experience with children to achieve maturity or optimum mental health at later ages? What other explanations can you think of?

were rated as most generative were likely to have responded to their childlessness by finding some kind of substitute child to nurture. They adopted a child, became Big Brothers, or got involved with the rearing of someone else's child, such as a niece or nephew. Those childless men rated as nongenerative were more likely to have chosen a pet as a child substitute.

This is only a single study—and I do not want to build too large a speculative edifice on top of it—but it raises the possibility that some aspects of psychological growth in early adulthood may depend either on the task of bearing and rearing children or on some reasonable substitute that calls forth one's nurturing and caring qualities.

The Effect of Timing

Finally, let me say just a bit about the effect that variations in timing may have on a person's experience of early adulthood. The most general point is that being "off time" or out of sequence in the adoption of any of the major roles of early adult life seems to exact some price. I've already talked about the long-term life histories of those who have their first child very early (Chapter 12, page 296). Very early marriage (under age 20) is also linked to higher risks of later divorce.

Even the sequence in which you add key roles seems to make a difference. Dennis Hogan (1981), in an analysis of 1973 Census Bureau data on over 35,000 men, found the lowest divorce rates among those who had followed the normative sequence: finishing school, then finding a job, and then getting married. The highest divorce rates were for those who married first, even when that marriage was fairly late and even among men with high levels of education.

Norms obviously differ from one culture to another and from one cohort to another. The "on time" age for marriage is now much older in the United States than it was even a decade ago, and there is no surety that the "ideal" sequence Hogan identified would still be the optimal sequence today. The point is not that the major roles of early adulthood are best acquired in a fixed order but that they are easier to learn and succeed at if they are acquired in the *accustomed* order and at the accustomed time.

Childless men (or women) can satisfy their need to nurture and care for others through any of a variety of alternative means, including programs like Big Brothers.

Summary

1. The central tasks of young adult life are the acquisition and learning of three major new roles: partner/spouse, parent, and worker.

2. The process begins with leaving home, which involves both physical and emotional separation from parents. Some theorists think young people must severely attenuate their basic attachment to the parent.

3. The new central attachment becomes the one to one's partner, who may then serve as a safe base for ventures out into the world of work.

4. Choices of partner are most heavily influenced by similarity, including—perhaps—similarity in security or insecurity of attachment. At the least, attachment models appear to influence the form of relationship we create and the assumptions we make about others.

5. Committed partnerships—marriage or long-term cohabitation—tend to decline in quality in the first year, as the rate of positive interactions drops.

6. Enduring relationships, compared to those that end in divorce or separation, are found among those who enter the relationship with good resources (education, problem-solving ability, etc.), and among those who create positive communication strategies. Good marriages look like secure attachments; poor or failing marriages look like insecure attachments.

7. Each adult also creates a convoy of relationships, including family and friends as well as partner. Relationships

with family members tend to be steady and supportive, even if less central than they were at earlier ages.

8. Friendships may be larger in number in early adulthood than at other ages. There are also clear sex differences in the form and frequency: women have more friends and more intimate relationships.

9. Parenthood brings both joy and the stress of a new role to learn. On average, marital satisfaction declines after the birth of the first child and remains low for most of early adulthood. At the same time there is typically an accentuation of traditional sex roles within the partnership, called by Gutmann the "parental imperative."

10. The specific job or career an adult chooses is affected by his or her education, intelligence, family background and resources, family values, personality, and gender. The majority of adults choose jobs that fit the cultural norms for their social class and gender. More intelligent young people, or those with more education, are more upwardly mobile.

11. Adults also tend to choose, and be happier in, jobs that fit their particular personality.

12. Job satisfaction rises steadily throughout early adulthood, in part because young-adult jobs are less well paid, more repetitive, less creative, and less powerful.

13. Within any given occupation or career, job advancement tends to occur fairly early in adult life; most promotions have been received by age 35 or 40.

14. We can think of the work role career as having two stages in early adulthood: a trial (or establishment) stage in which alternative pathways are explored, and a stabilization stage in which the career path is established.

15. For women, there is frequently an additional "in-and-out" stage in which family responsibilities alternate with out-of-home work periods. The more continuous a woman's work history, the more successful she is likely to be at her job.

16. When both partners work, the family responsibilities are not equally divided: women continue to perform more of this work and feel more role conflict.

17. Certain aspects of personality are highly consistent during adulthood, particularly the five traits identified by McCrae & Costa: neuroticism, extraversion, openness to experience, agreeableness, and conscientiousness.

18. There also appear to be shared changes in personality. Between 30 and 40, young adults become more independent, more confident, more assertive, more oriented toward achievement, more individualistic, and less governed by social rules.

19. These patterns differ somewhat in adults who do not adopt one or more of the key roles, such as those who do not marry or those without children. Unmarried adults are, on average, less happy and more prone to illness. Childless adults do not experience the same degree of decline in marital quality as do those with children.

20. The timing and sequencing of the several major young adult roles are also important. Any significant deviation from the normative timing and sequence exacts a price.

Key Terms

agreeableness	extraversion	parental imperative
conscientiousness	mentor	stabilization stage
convoy	neuroticism	trial stage
establishment stage	openness to experience	

Suggested Readings

Betz, N. E., & Fitzgerald, L. F. (1987). *The career psychology of women.* Orlando, FL: Academic Press. (A very thorough and detailed presentation of current knowledge of women's work patterns in the United States: career choices, career progress, and work/family conflict.)

Gilmour, R., & Duck, S. (Eds.) (1986). *The emerging field of personal relationships.* Hillsdale, NJ: Lawrence Erlbaum Associates. (A particularly useful collection of papers on relationships in early (and later) adulthood. Included is Ted Huston's longitudinal study of early marriage, a good paper by Reis on sex differences in personal relationships, and others.)

McCrae, R. R., & Costa, P. T., Jr. (1990). *Personality in adulthood.* New York: The Guilford Press. (This relatively brief book not only lays out McCrae and Costa's ideas about personality traits, it reports on their very extensive body of longitudinal research.)

SUMMING UP EARLY ADULT DEVELOPMENT

Basic Characteristics of Early Adulthood

In our youth-oriented and youth-admiring culture, many of us think of young adulthood as the easiest or best years of life. Physically, that is certainly true. The body is at its peak in the years from 20 to 40. Any aspect of mental functioning that is based on physiological speed or efficiency is also at its peak, as is clear in the summary in the table below. But socially and emotionally these years are probably more stressful and more difficult than any other part of adulthood.

These are the years in which more separate roles must be learned than at any other age, and in which there are likely to be more separate life changes than in any other era. Demographer Ronald Rindfuss (1991) refers to the years from 20 to 30 as "demographically dense" because there is more action in these years—more marriages, divorces, geographical moves, births, school leavings, and periods of unemployment than at any other time of life.

Adults themselves place many of the tasks of this age high on their list of important events of their lives. If you ask older adults to think back over their entire adult life and identify the most important events, they list more events in early adulthood as significant (Martin & Smyer, 1990). We can also see signs of the stress involved in this constellation of tasks in the high rates of emotional distress and loneliness described by young adults compared to those in middle age or early old age.

Because the prescriptions about the several key adult roles come from outside ourselves, this is also the time in our adult lives when we are most defined by external criteria. Not only do we measure ourselves against such criteria ("Am I a good mother?" "Am I going to get the promotion?"), we identify ourselves in terms of the roles we occupy.

In the language of Jane Loevinger's theory, this is a *conformist* stance,

---

A Summary of the Threads of Development in Early Adulthood

Aspect of Development	Age in Years				
	20	25	30	35	40
Physical Development	Peak function on virtually all measures; maximum health; best time for childbearing; athletic performance at its peak in most sports.			Athletic prowess clearly begins to decline for top performers; some decline for ordinary folks (not operating at top levels) but the decline is less noticeable.	
Cognitive Development	Maximum performance on any mental task requiring speed; maximum memory ability on most measures.		*Increasing* IQ and improving performance on any "crystallized" intelligence test, such as vocabulary or problem solving.		
Social and Personality Development	Erikson's stage of Intimacy versus Isolation; dominant in 20s, still central in 30s.				
	Typical timing for the acquisition of three major new roles: spouse, parent, and worker.				
	Maximum sense of role conflict among these roles.				
Work	Trial or establishment stage: searching for right work.		Stabilization stage: time of most promotions; plateau usually reached by 40.		
Partnership	Searching for partner.	Finding partner and marriage.	Decline in marital satisfaction after birth of first child and throughout rest of young adulthood.		
Personality	Peak time for definition of self in terms of the roles occupied.		Increasing self-confidence, assertiveness, independence; detribalization; greater individualization.		
	Continuity throughout this period on 5 major personality characteristics: neuroticism, extraversion, openness to experience, conscientiousness, and agreeableness.				
Emotional Health	Highest levels of depression and loneliness in one's 20s.				

characterized not only by external sources of authority but also by a tendency to think in "us/them," stereotyped ways about others and about one's own emotional life. Evidence from the longitudinal studies I described in Chapter 14 suggests that this way of understanding ourselves, so characteristic of the first part of early adulthood, gives way in our late thirties or early forties to what Loevinger calls the *self-aware level*, and eventually to the *conscientious stage*—both perhaps aspects of what Levinson calls "detribalization." Having learned the key roles, we begin to free ourselves from their constraints; we figure out how to fulfill our various duties and still express our own individuality.

Of course I cannot say that young adults in every culture will necessarily become more self-confident, assertive, and independent by the time they are 40. We simply don't have the research to back up such an assertion. But it looks as if it may be a common thread, perhaps a basic part of the normal progress of adult life. But why?

Several possibilities occur to me. One is that over the years of young adulthood, many of us discover that following the rules, doing what you are "supposed to do," does not necessarily bring reward. You don't always get the promotion you worked so hard for; you may not find a mate, even though you have done all the "right" things. Having children may not bring consistent satisfaction or joy, as you may have expected. Inevitable disillusionments like these may lead many individuals to question the rules, to doubt the eternal correctness of role prescriptions.

Another push toward questioning comes from the expertise that many adults develop in their work roles. We may pursue job or career because it is part of what is expected of us, but in the process we may discover our own talents and capacities. Such a discovery increases our self-confidence and may turn us more toward an inward and away from an outward definition of self. In the process, we may also become aware of those parts of ourselves that our collective roles do not allow us to express, and we may search for ways to express those parts.

This individualization process may begin in early adulthood and be in full bloom by age 40. But it is still true that the years of early adulthood are more dominated by the social clock, by the demands and strictures of the central social roles, than will be true at any other time in adult life.

Central Processes

When asked about the keys to successful adult life, Freud is reported to have said *love and work*. Freud was clearly correct. We know that those adults who are satisfied with their work and with their relationships are also satisfied with their lives in general. But it begins to look as if love is the more important of the two. For instance, the single most significant predictor of a person's overall life satisfaction (at any adult age) is each person's reported happiness in marriage and family relationships (Campbell, 1981; Glenn & Weaver, 1981; Sears, 1977). Work satisfaction, although significant, is apparently not as central

as satisfaction in love.

The centrality of love relationships is also underlined in the new work on internal models of attachment. Hazan and Shaver (1990), in an extremely interesting extension of attachment theory, have proposed that we can think of the relationship of love and work in adulthood in the same way that Bowlby and Ainsworth think of attachment and exploration in a young child. Bowlby believes that both the tendency to become attached and the tendency to explore are innate. Of the two, however, attachment is the more central. The exploration system can only operate optimally if the attachment system is not aroused. When the child has a secure attachment, the attachment figure can be used as a safe base for exploration. But if the child is anxious about the attachment, that anxiety dominates and the child explores less freely.

Among adults, so Hazan and Shaver argue, work is the equivalent of exploration. It is the major source of a sense of competence, just as is true of a child's exploration. And like the child's exploration, adult work is best accomplished when the adult has a safe emotional base from which to move outward into the world.

In their preliminary research, Hazan and Shaver (1990) have found support for this thesis. They asked their adult subjects both about the quality of their basic sense of attachment (using the descriptions I listed in Table 14.1), and about many facets of their work experience. In a sample of several hundred adults ranging in age from 18 to 79, they found clear differences between the three attachment types.

Securely attached adults are less worried about work failure and less likely to feel unappreciated. They do not let work demands interfere with their relationships or health, and they enjoy their vacations.

Anxiously attached adults, lacking the safe base of a secure relationship, continue to be preoccupied with attachment issues and thus have little energy left to focus on work tasks. They describe themselves as worried about their job performance, "prefer to work with others but feel underappreciated and fear rejection for poor performance. They are also easily distracted, have trouble completing projects, and tend to slack off after receiving praise" (p. 277).

Avoidant subjects like to work alone and are inclined to become "workaholics," seldom taking vacations and not enjoying them when they take them. They use work to avoid social life or intimate relationships.

These parallels between the attachment system and work behaviors and feelings are striking. They suggest that one's approach to work is deeply affected by the strengths or deficiencies of one's internal model of attachment or relationships. This single study, of course, does not prove the basic hypothesis that love is more central than work. Ultimately we will need longitudinal studies in which young people's attachment security and work attitudes are assessed at regular intervals throughout adult life. Only in this way can we figure out whether early adulthood attachment status predicts later job attitudes or success. But my hunch is that Hazan and Shaver are entirely correct about the relative roles of love and work in adult life. Certainly their view is consistent with Erikson's theory, with his emphasis on *intimacy* as the central task of young adulthood.

Influences on the Basic Processes

Each of us brings to the tasks of adult life certain advantages and disadvantages. High on the list would be each individual's history of secure or insecure attachment carried forward from childhood. Research tells us, for example, that adults who lost a parent in childhood—to death or divorce—are at greater risk for a variety of problems, including depression, separation or divorce themselves, and poorer physical health (Harris, Brown & Bifulco, 1990; Amato & Keith, 1991). More directly, we now have at least fragments of evidence that adults who describe their early childhood relationships with parents as rejecting or ambivalent (who are thus more often insecurely attached) have more trouble establishing secure adult relationships. If Hazan and Shaver are correct, they may also have more troubled work experiences as well.

Family Social Class. Attachment history is clearly not the only element in this equation. Other aspects of family background have powerful effects. Most clearly, children growing up in poverty or working-class families are likely to complete fewer years of schooling, a difference with long-term repercussions for adult occupational experiences.

Bear in mind, though, that this is a *probability* statement. Lower education, and thus less successful work histories, are more *likely* for this subgroup, but they are not inevitable. It is also possible for young people to escape from the constrictions and deprivations of a disorderly or poverty-stricken childhood, a fact clearly shown in the results from one of the long-term longitudinal studies I described in Chapter 14. As part of an investigation of delinquency and its roots and consequences, several hundred nondelinquent boys from inner-city, multiproblem families were studied as a comparison group (Snarey, et al., 1987; Glueck & Glueck, 1968). When these nondelinquent teens were followed into middle age, most of them turned out to be stable, with decent incomes (Long and Vaillant, 1984). Yet it was also true that the more disadvantaged the man's family had been—the more disorganized, dependent on social agencies, neglecting or abusing—the more likely it was that the man would remain in the lower class as an adult. Those who worked their way out of the lowest social class levels were those whose families were poor but more stable and well organized. These researchers did not use Baumrind's system of categorizing families, but one might guess that an authoritative early family history would be most likely to support a move out of poverty. Thus the underclass does not invariably perpetuate itself in each new generation; there are avenues or pathways for change. But a disorderly or deprived family background is like starting adulthood with at least one strike against you.

Personality. Another significant predictor of the ability to master the various tasks of early adult life is the individual's personality. A high level of neuroticism seems to be especially detrimental. Indeed, it is possible that some of the differences Hazan and Shaver (and others) have ascribed to internal models of attachment are really basic personality variance in disguise. The anxiously attached person, for example, may also be a person who scores high on measures of neuroticism. Similar arguments made about the link between temperament and attachment security in infancy have not been well supported; many temperamentally "difficult" infants establish secure attachments, although there is some sign that an insecure attachment is somewhat more likely for such difficult babies. What we need now, in studies of adults, is separate measurement of attachment security and personality traits. Are there adults who are high in neuroticism but secure in attachment? Do such adults have a different pattern of adult experiences than other highly neurotic adults? My own sense is that these two ways of looking at individual differences in adults overlap somewhat but not fully. Each is independently significant. But that's an empirical question yet to be answered.

Personal Choices.   The pathway through early adulthood is also affected by a set of personal choices each of us makes, including such things as health practices and choices about the timing of adopting the various key roles. The effects of health practices may be largely invisible in early adulthood, as I pointed out in Chapter 13. But the health chickens come home to roost later in adult life, in the form of higher rates of disease and disability for those with poor health habits.

The effects of variation in timing, in contrast, may already be visible in early adulthood. The sequence and timing of marriage, parenthood, and work experiences create what various authors have called *pathways, trajectories,* or *anchor points* of adult life (O'Rand, 1990; Hagestad, 1990; Elder, 1991). One example is the woman who works before marriage or childbearing, who will have higher lifetime earnings than will a woman who marries and has her children before she moves into the labor force. Similarly, delaying childbearing into one's thirties has a ripple effect on all subsequent family life stages. For one thing, it increases the likelihood of being "squeezed" in middle adulthood, with one's children still needing support at the same time as one acquires responsibility for aging parents.

Being off-time in the sense of bucking the norm also has its price, as I have pointed out before. Why might

this be true? One possibility is that "off-timeness" operates through yet another internal model, what Mildred Seltzer and Lillian Troll call the *expected life history.* When asked, most young adults have no difficulty writing their own projected life story. Each of us carries around a model for the "normal" or "expectable" sequence of events in our lives, or the goals we expect to reach at particular ages. It is a road map for our future. "I will finish school, then marry, then have three children, then go to work. By the time I'm 50, my kids will have left home and I'll be able to really focus on my career"; or, "I don't want to marry until I'm about 30 because I'm determined to be the youngest partner in my law firm before then."

These expectations have their origins both in specific family patterns and in the social role expectations of a given cohort in a particular culture. When they work out, expectations can help each of us anticipate stressful events and reduce their negative impact because we have prepared ahead of time. A perfect example is retirement, which looks like a major upheaval but which rarely has any negative effects, presumably because it is something anticipated and planned.

When our adult life does *not* follow our expectations, however, Seltzer and Troll argue that there is a psy-

chological price to be paid. In my generation, college women expected to marry soon after they finished college. It was certainly what I expected, and when it didn't happen that way it required a major readjustment of my thinking—and some pain, I might add. Not to marry at 21 or 22 was to be off-time, to break an expected mold. It carried the message of failed femininity.

The negative effect of being off-time may also be observable for a much simpler reason: in a given culture, some sequences may simply be objectively more difficult. For example, women who are widowed when they are still in their thirties have a considerably harder time adjusting to the loss than do women widowed in their sixties or seventies (Ball, 1976–77). This *could* result because early widowhood is a deviation from the expected life history. But the greater adaptational difficulty of young widows may occur because the younger woman is more likely to have young children to support and may not have adequate economic resources.

Whether we think of the process in terms of yet another impact of internal models or as a function of more objective stresses associated with certain timing or sequences, the significant point is that the choices we make and the chance events we are dealt in our early adult life may shape our experiences for many decades.

Whether a person thinks of young adulthood as a time of struggle or a time of opportunity may be more a reflection of basic optimism or pessimism. What is objectively true is that in these years we are physically more energetic, quicker, and stronger than at any other time in our lives—capacities that are needed if we are to master the complex tasks we are asked to learn and perform in these years.

PHYSICAL AND COGNITIVE CHANGES IN MIDDLE ADULTHOOD

The middle years of adulthood are an interesting time from the point of view of physical and cognitive functioning. In our culture at least, most of us *believe* that the great downhill physical and mental slide begins in these middle years. We think we will start having trouble remembering things in our forties and fifties (Ryan, 1992); we think that our physical bodies will begin to decay in those same years. Some of that does indisputably occur. Memory does get less efficient in some situations in mid-life; vision and hearing get worse; we slow down slightly and become somewhat weaker. But what is surprising in all of this is that the amount of loss is far less than folklore would have us believe, at least *among adults who are otherwise healthy*. For healthy adults, maintenance or very gradual loss is what we see in the middle years.

> Why do you think there is such a widespread belief in our culture that significant physical decline begins in middle adulthood? What would it take to change this belief?

Physical Functioning in Middle Adulthood

Those adults who have survived to the age of 40 can expect to live a good many more years. The technical term is **life expectancy**, which refers to the average number of years remaining for a person of a given age. Figure 15.1 shows the life expectancy at age 40 for men and women, black and white, in the United States as of 1986. You can see that women can expect to live longer than men and that whites can expect to live longer than blacks. The Census Bureau has not regularly reported this same information separately for Hispanics, but current estimates are that the life expectancy for this sub-group is only slightly below that of whites and well above the numbers for blacks (Markides & Mindel, 1987).

Life expectancy, by the way, is not the same as **life span**. The latter phrase refers to the upper boundary, the maximum number of years any member of a given species could expect to live. The life span of humans—the upper boundary—seems to be about 110 years. At this point in human history, life expectancy is a good deal less than the life span. But there has been a very rapid and striking increase in life expectancy in developed countries over the past few decades, most of which is a result of increases at the upper end of the age span rather than reductions in infant mortality. In 1940 in the United

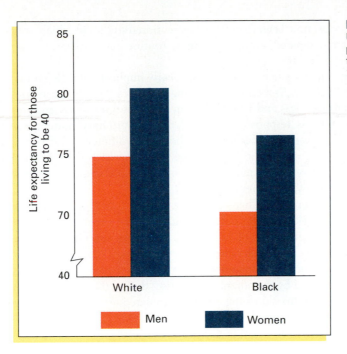

Figure 15.1 Life expectancy at age 40 in the United States in 1986. Women obviously can expect to live longer than men, and whites longer than blacks. (*Source:* U.S. Bureau of the Census, 1990, Table 104, p. 73.)

States, life expectancy for a woman of 65 was 78.6 years; by 1986 that figure had risen to 83.6 (Brock, Guralnik & Brody, 1990). The gain for men has been smaller, 2.5 years rather than 5, but for both sexes the gains have been impressive. Indeed some physicians and physiologists have argued that improvements in health care and health habits will ultimately mean that the great majority of adults will be able to live to the full potential life span.

All of this is encouraging news for those entering middle adulthood, because the majority of 40-year-olds (in industrialized countries, at least) are only at the midpoint of their lives. What kind of changes in their bodies can these 40-year-olds expect over the succeeding 25 years?

Changes in the Physical Body

For a quick overview of the common physical changes of middle age, go back and take another look at Table 13.1 (page 315), which summarizes most of the evidence. For many physical functions, measurable change/decline may begin in the forties or fifties, but it moves at a very gradual rate through middle adulthood, increasing in rate only after age 65 or even 75. For others, change or decline is already substantial in the middle adult years—a set of changes I need to talk about in more detail.

Reproductive System.   If you were asked to name a single significant physical change occurring in the years of middle adulthood, chances are you'd list menopause—especially if you're a woman. The more general term is **climacteric**, which refers to the loss of reproductive capacity over the years of middle or late adulthood in both men and women.

In men, the climacteric is extremely gradual, with a slow loss of reproductive capacity, although this varies widely from one man to the next, and there are documented cases of men in their nineties fathering children. On average, there seems to be a decline in the quantity of viable sperm produced, beginning perhaps at about age 40. There is also a very gradual shrinkage of the testes, and the volume of seminal fluid declines after about age 60.

The causal factor appears to be an equally gradual decline in testosterone levels, beginning in early adulthood and continuing well into old age (Gray et al., 1991). Because such a decline has now been found in cross-sectional studies in which only healthy adults of each age are compared, as well as in more routine comparisons, we can be reasonably confident of the finding.

Declines in key sex hormones are also clearly implicated in the set of changes we call **menopause** in women. As menopause—literally the cessation of the menses—approaches, the ovaries produce less and less of two key hormones, estrogen and progesterone, and become less and less responsive to stimulation by pituitary hormones, which help to regulate levels of estrogen. Figure 15.2 shows the difference between pre- and post-menopausal women in estradiol and estrone, both of which are subvarieties of estrogen. Progesterone decreases even more, from roughly 10,000 picograms per milliliter before menopause to roughly 200 after.

You'll remember from Chapter 11 that several forms of estrogen, secreted by the ovaries, increase rapidly during puberty, triggering the onset of menstruation as well as stimulating the development of breast and secondary sex characteristics. In the adult woman, estrogen levels are high during the first 14 days of the menstrual cycle, stimulating the release of ova and the preparation of the uterus for possible implantation. Progesterone, which is secreted by the adrenal gland, rises during the second half of the menstrual cycle, and stimulates the sloughing off of accumulated material in the uterus each month if no conception has occurred.

When estrogen levels begin to decline in the years just before menopause, there may first be some irregularity in menstruation, because the estrogen signal to the ovary to release an ovum may be insufficient. For a period of years, estrogen levels may fluctuate from one monthly cycle to the next, so that menstruation remains unpredictable. Eventually estrogen levels drop to a consistently low level, insufficient to trigger release of an ovum, and menstruation ceases: menopause. The average age of menopause for both blacks and whites in the United States, and for women in other parts of the world in which studies have been done—including Europe, South Africa, India, and New Guinea—is typically 49 or 50, although malnourished women appear to enter menopause earlier. And even among well-nourished women, as many as 8 percent experience premature menopause before the age of 40 (Weg, 1987a).

The reduction in estrogen also has effects on genital and other tissue. The breasts become less firm, there is some loss of tissue in the genitals, the uterus shrinks somewhat in size, and the vagina becomes both shorter and smaller in diameter. The walls of the

---

What kind of effect might these changes have on sexual behavior or attitudes toward sex in middle-aged women and men?

Figure 15.2 One of the central changes of the climacteric for women is the decline in both forms of estrogen. This decline not only helps to produce menopause, it also increases the rate of bone loss and the risk of heart disease. (*Source:* Harman & Talbert, 1985, from Table 3, p. 466.)

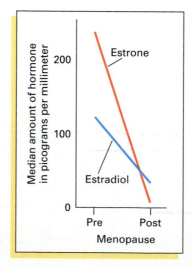

vagina also become somewhat thinner and less elastic, and produce less lubrication during intercourse (Weg, 1987b).

Not all of these changes are immediately noticeable to the woman progressing through menopause. The most noticeable symptom is yet another consequence of the rapid change in hormones, the *hot flash* or *hot flush*—a rapidly spreading, hot sensation, accompanied by a flush on the chest and face, typically followed by profuse sweating. Insomnia or difficulty sleeping is a frequent accompaniment, because flashes are more common at night than during the day.

The causes of this very common phenomenon are not yet fully understood. The most likely possibility is that they are triggered by pulses of one of the two pituitary hormones— luteinizing hormone, or LH—whose job it is to signal to the ovaries to produce more estrogen. When the ovaries fail to respond, there is no estrogen to balance the pituitary hormone and the hot flash results. Eventually the pituitary stops secreting LH at such high levels and the hot flashes disappear (Kletzky & Borenstein, 1987).

Between half and three-quarters of women in the pre- or postmenopausal (referred to as *perimenopausal*) period report at least some hot flashes. Of those who have them, 85 percent will have them for more than a year; a third or more will have them for five years or more (Kletsky & Borenstein, 1987). They are certainly not fatal, but they can be socially

---

RESEARCH REPORT
Why Do Women Live Longer Than Men?

Women do not have an advantage over men in every culture or in every era. Whenever or wherever rates of death in pregnancy and childbirth are very high, women's life expectancies are typically the same or lower than men's. But where maternal mortality has been reduced, women begin to show quite large advantages in longevity (Verbrugge & Wingard, 1987). Both biological and social explanations have been offered.

The most convincing biological argument is that women may be physically less vulnerable to some or all diseases. I pointed out in Chapters 3 and 4 that boys are more vulnerable to a host of problems prenatally and in the first year of life. Differences in longevity among middle-aged and older adults may simply reflect the same variation in basic vulnerability. Men are more likely to inherit sex-linked recessive diseases, they may be more vulnerable to fragile-X syndrome, and their relative lack of estrogen may make them more vulnerable to heart disease. The difference in heart disease risk is especially striking. Between ages 45 and 54, 237 men out of every 100,000 die of heart disease, compared to only 74 women (Verbrugge, 1989). Past menopause, when women's estrogen levels decline, this difference in rates of heart disease diminishes, although it does not totally disappear even in late old age. The specific effect of estrogen may be to improve the density of ''good'' cholesterol, the high-density lipoproteins, and reduce the rate of ''bad'' cholesterol, low-density lipoproteins (Hazzard, 1985), although this conclusion is still speculative.

The social factors are more numerous (Verbrugge, 1984, 1985, 1989) and perhaps equally important. First, women's work exposes them to fewer environmental hazards. This may become less true over the next few cohorts, as we see greater equality in occupational opportunity. But among current middle-aged and elderly cohorts it is clearly the case that there are more men who have been exposed to such hazards as asbestos, smoke, and chemicals of various kinds. Physically dangerous jobs, such as police officer, fire fighter, or logger, are also more frequently done by men.

Women also seek health care more regularly. They are more likely to get regular checkups, even when they are feeling well, and seek help earlier in an illness than do men, which improves their chances of amelioration or cure (Verbrugge & Wingard, 1987). And they generally have better health habits, beginning early in adulthood. They take vitamins more often, and they are less likely to smoke or to drink heavily. In the Alameda County study, which I referred to often in Chapter 13, Berkman and Breslow (1983) found that women were more likely to be overweight but less likely to drink or smoke heavily. Sex differences in smoking are much smaller now than they were when today's elderly were young. So we might expect that sex differences in death from such smoking-related diseases as lung cancer and heart disease will eventually decline.

When longevity of men and women is compared after all these social factors have been controlled, the size of the sex difference is reduced, but it is not eliminated. In particular, sex differences in the risk of death from heart disease remain large even when health habits and occupation have been removed from the equation (Verbrugge & Wingard, 1987). This means either that the social explanations are not sufficient or that we do not yet know all the social factors that may be important. Women's more intimate social networks, for example, may buffer them more fully from the effects of stress. We don't yet know all the answers, but the question is fascinating.

THE REAL WORLD
The Pros and Cons of Hormone Replacement Therapy

Most of the physical symptoms of the menopause, including hot flashes, thinning of the vaginal wall, and loss of vaginal lubrication, can be dramatically reduced by taking estrogen and progesterone orally. Because women readers may eventually have to decide whether to follow such a regimen, let me tell you a little about what we know and don't know.

Hormone replacement therapy has had a somewhat checkered history over the past few decades. In the 1950s and 1960s, estrogen therapy became extremely common. In some surveys, as many as half of all postmenopausal women in the United States reported using replacement estrogen, many of them over periods of ten years or more (Stadel & Weiss, 1975). In the 1970s, however, new evidence showed that the risk of endometrial cancer (cancer of the lining of the uterus) increased 3 to 10 times in women taking replacement estrogen (Nathanson & Lorenz, 1982). Not surprisingly, when this information became available, the incidence of such therapy dropped dramatically.

The third act in this drama was the discovery that a combination of estrogen and progesterone, at quite low dosages, had the same benefits as estrogen alone and eliminated the increased risk of endometrial cancer. Two other benefits of estrogen therapy have also been identified. First, it clearly retards the bone loss of osteoporosis. Second, it looks as if estrogen also reduces the risk of heart disease, in large part by increasing the levels of high-density lipoproteins and lowering the levels of low-density lipoproteins (Ross et al., 1987).

The possibility of a link between estrogen and heart disease was first suggested by the fact that rates of heart attacks are very low in premenopausal women but rise substantially postmenopausally. The hypothesis has been strengthened by a number of epidemiological studies that show that women taking replacement estrogen have about *half* the risk of dying of heart disease as do postmenopausal women not receiving estrogen (Ross et al., 1987; Barrett-Connor & Bush, 1991). *However*, nearly all of this research has involved women taking only estrogen; the combination of estrogen and progesterone appears to have a weaker beneficial effect, although we have only limited research on this question. This sounds almost too good to be true, doesn't it? Why

shouldn't every postmenopausal woman be on a program of hormone replacements? There are two counter arguments. First, many women consider the process of aging, including the changes of menopause, to be natural physical processes with which they do not want to tinker. Second, there are still questions to be answered about side effects of extended hormone therapy, especially the possibility of a link between hormones and breast cancer. Assessments of the current data point to the conclusion that

> long-term use of estrogen replacement therapy in moderately high doses does carry with it a sizeable increase in breast cancer risk, that small doses for a short time convey no measurable increase in risk, and that the effect of smaller doses for long periods of time is not adequately studied but is unlikely to be substantial. (Henderson, Ross & Pike, 1987, p. 270)

Note that both dosage and length of use appear to be important. Because most current hormone replacement therapy regimens involve very low dosage, it is possible that there is no increased risk involved. But we need more data to be sure, particularly studies in which the effects of estrogen/progesterone combinations are investigated. Meanwhile, many physicians counsel against hormone replacement for women who have had breast cancer or for those who are at especially high risk for this form of cancer, such as those with a mother or sister who has had breast cancer.

In the face of these various pros and cons, my own decision was first to reject hormone replacement. I argued that menopause was a natural process, that millions of other women had survived hot flashes and so could I. But after four years of 10 to 30 flashes a day, and after the newer evidence on heart disease protection appeared, I changed my mind. At the same time, I also made a commitment to become more regular about physical exams, particularly mammograms. For me this has been a good compromise. You will have to make your own choice, in light of the evidence available at the time you face the decision.

disconcerting and may be seriously disruptive of one's sleep. If that sounds autobiographical, it is, because I'm one of the minority with long-term, frequent hot flashes. My first experience with them was on a trip to China when I was 46. Our Chinese hosts kept commenting on how red my face was. True enough!

One other issue about the climacteric in women deserves some mention. It has been part of our folklore for a very long time that menopause involves major emotional upheaval as well as clear physical changes. Women were presumed to be emotionally volatile, angry, depressed, even shrewish during these mid-life years. Five years ago I felt comfortable saying that these presumptions were myth. Now there are fragments of information suggesting that there may be an increase in certain kinds of psychological symptoms in some women in the years immediately *before* actual menopause, although the research is scant and the results not entirely consistent.

One bit of evidence comes from a large epidemiological study of emotional disorders in the United States—a study I have mentioned before (Regier et al., 1988). When the subjects in this study are grouped not by decades but by single years, the results suggest that for women, but not for men, there is a rather abrupt rise in depression beginning at about age 35 and peaking at about 43 or 44 (Anthony & Aboraya, 1992). At the peak, the rate of significant depression is about 4.5 percent. Several other smaller studies similarly point to increases in irritability in the late thirties or early forties (Dennerstein, 1987). The difficulty with many of these studies, including Regier's epidemiological study, is that age rather than menopausal status is normally the independent variable. So what we have here is some sign of an increase in problems for women right around age 40. But we do not know whether such an increase is linked to the hormonal changes prior to menopause or to some other set of social conditions common at that age. Furthermore, we have other studies that show no increases in symptoms in these same years (Eisdorfer & Raskind, 1975; Weg, 1983). For example, Bernice Neugarten (1976) studied 100 normal women, aged 43 to 53, assessing them on a whole range of psychological symptoms and traits, including anxiety, depression, level of life satisfaction and self-esteem. Menopausal status was *unrelated* to any of these variables. More research of this type, with much larger samples of women, is needed to settle the question. For now, the jury is still out.

Vision and Hearing. A second physical change that clearly occurs in the middle years is a loss of visual acuity. Most of us will need reading glasses or bifocals by the time we are 45 or 50. Two changes in the eyes, collectively called **presbyopia**, are involved. First, the lens of the eye thickens. In a process that begins in childhood but produces noticeable effects only in middle adulthood, layer after layer of slightly pigmented material is added to the lens. Because light coming into the eye must pass through this thickened, slightly yellowed material, the total light reaching the retina drops, which reduces a person's overall sensitivity, particularly to short-wavelength colors such as blue, bluegreen, and violet (Bornstein, 1988).

Because of this thickening, it is also harder and harder for the muscles surrounding the eye to change the shape of the lens to adjust the focus. In a young eye, the shape of the lens is adjusted for each distance, so no matter how near or far away some object may be, the light rays passing through the eye converge on the retina in the back of the eye, giving a sharp image. But as the thickening increases, elasticity of the lens declines and it is no longer possible to make these fine adjustments. Many images becomes blurry (Briggs, 1990). In particular, the ability to focus clearly on near objects deteriorates rapidly in one's forties and early fifties. As a result, middle-aged adults often hold books and other items farther and farther away, because only that way can they get a clear image. Finally, of course, it is no longer possible to read the print at the distance at which you can focus, and you are driven to wearing reading glasses or bifocals—a change that requires both physical and psychological adjustment.

These changes appear to be universal and unavoidable—a genuinely natural part of aging. They also seem to occur at about the same rate whether you begin with glasses immediately or put off wearing glasses as long as possible. These same changes also affect the ability to adapt quickly to variations in levels of light or glare, such as passing headlights when driving at night or in the rain. So driving and equivalent activities may become more stressful.

The equivalent process in hearing, called **presbycusis**, has measurable effects on hearing acuity somewhat later in life. The loss is primarily in the ability to hear high and very low frequency sounds, and it appears to result from basic wear and tear. The auditory nerves and the structures of the inner ear gradually degenerate. Little loss is apparent, on

By age 45 or 50, nearly everyone will need to use glasses, especially for reading.

Any weight-bearing exercise will help prevent osteoporosis, but walking seems to be especially beneficial.

If you were in charge of public health programs and wanted to convince young adults that they should not listen to loud music over earphones because of risks of early and extensive hearing loss, how would you go about persuading them? What arguments do you think would work?

average, until about age 50, and only a small percentage of middle-aged adults require hearing aids—in contrast to glasses, which are required by the majority (Fozard, 1990). However, the amount of hearing loss is considerably greater in adults who work or live in very noisy environments (Baltes, Reese & Nesselroade, 1977)—or who listen regularly to very loud music. Rock musicians, I understand, suffer from very early presbycusis.

Bones.   Another change that begins to be quite large in middle adulthood is a change in the bones. Between age 40 and 70, women lose about 20 percent and men about 10 percent of bone mass. This change, called **osteoporosis**, results from a loss of calcium in the bone, leaving the bones more brittle and porous. Among women, there is very little bone loss before menopause. After menopause, there is rapid loss. Studies in Italian women, for example, show that the loss of calcium in the spine is roughly 4 percent per year in the first three years after menopause, slowing to about 2 percent a year thereafter. Loss in other bones is slower (Ortolani et al., 1991). The collective effect of these losses is a significantly heightened risk of fractures (Lindsay, 1985). Among older women—and men—such fractures can be a major cause of disability and reduced activity, so this is not a trivial change.

In women, it is clear that bone loss is linked quite directly to estrogen levels. We know that estrogen drops dramatically after menopause, and it is the timing of menopause rather than age that signals the increase in rate of bone loss. We also know that replacing the lost estrogen with artificial estrogen reduces the rate of bone loss to premenopausal levels (Duursma et al., 1991), all of which makes the link quite clear.

While the overall pattern of bone loss seems to be a normal part of aging, the amount of such loss nonetheless varies quite a lot from one individual to another. I've listed the known risk factors in Table 15.1.

Other than artificial hormones, the most constructive action you can take to prevent osteoporosis is regular exercise, particularly weight-bearing exercise such as walking. In one recent study, for example, postmenopausal women who began a program of walking, jogging, or stair climbing, for an hour, three times a week, showed an *increase* in bone mineral content of 5.2 percent within nine months, compared to a loss of 1.4 percent in the nonexercising comparison group (Dalsky et al., 1988). But this benefit fades if the exercise is not maintained.

Changes in Health: Disease and Death

Another way to look at changes in the physical body over these middle years is to look at health. What kinds of diseases and disabilities do we see in middle-aged adults? And if they die, what do they die of?

Illness and Disability.   The number of truly healthy adults declines in mid-life. Perhaps half of adults between 40 and 65 have either some diagnosed disease or disability, or a significant but undiagnosed problem, such as the early stages of heart disease. Young adults have more *acute* illnesses, including colds, flu, infections, and digestive disorders. But middle-aged adults have more chronic diseases and disabilities. You can see the difference quite clearly in Table 15.2, which shows rates by age for selected acute and chronic problems.

The same story emerges when we look at the behavioral effects of disease or disability. If you ask adults about their ability to perform various normal daily activities, you find that about 23 percent of adults between 45 and 64 say they have at least some minor limitation in their daily activity, such as trouble lifting heavy objects. But very few have so much disability that they are unable to care for themselves physically (Verbrugge, 1984). After age 65, significant activity limitation becomes much more common.

Deaths.   Given these numbers, it is not surprising that disease, rather than violence (accident or homicide), for the first time becomes the largest cause of death in middle adulthood. Table 15.3 lists the three main causes of death for men and women for two

TABLE 15.1 Risk Factors for Osteoporosis

Race. Blacks are at higher risk than are whites, for reasons not known.

Gender. Women have considerably higher risk than males.

Weight. Those who are light for their height are at higher risk. This is thought to result from the beneficial effect of additional weight-bearing exercise that comes simply from carrying around a few more pounds.

Timing of Climacteric. Women with early menopause, and those who have had their ovaries removed, are at higher risk, presumably because their estrogen levels decline at earlier ages.

Family History. Those with a family history of osteoporosis are at higher risk.

Diet. Those with diets low in calcium and high in either caffeine or alcohol are at higher risk, although it is *not* clear that a substantial increase in calcium intake among postmenopausal women will reduce the risk.

Exercise. Those with a sedentary life-style are at higher risk. Prolonged immobility, such as bed rest, also increases rate of bone loss. Increasing exercise reduces the rate of bone loss.

Sources: Goldberg & Hagberg, 1990; Gordon & Vaughan, 1986; Lindsay, 1985; Smith, 1982.

TABLE 15.2 Age Differences in Incidence of Common Acute and Chronic Illnesses in the United States in 1987

Average Rate per 100 Population	Age group		
	25–44	45–64	65 +
Acute illnesses:			
Respiratory problems	28.2	21.4	14.3
Infections	18.2	7.8	5.5
Chronic illnesses:			
Heart conditions	4.1	12.6	28.5
High blood pressure	6.2	25.2	39.2
Arthritis	5.3	27.3	46.4

Source: U.S. Bureau of the Census, 1990, Tables 189 and 190, p. 118.

TABLE 15.3 Leading Causes of Death for Middle-Aged Men and Women in the United States in 1988

Rank	Men	Women
	Age 45 to 54	
1	Heart Disease (221)[a]	Cancer (161)
2	Cancer (171)	Heart Disease (72)
3	Accidents (47)	Cardiovascular diseases (19)
	Age 55 to 64	
1	Heart Disease (627)	Cancer (374)
2	Cancer (524)	Heart Disease (244)
3	Cerebrovascular diseases (59)	Cerebrovascular diseases (47)

[a]The number in parentheses is the number of deaths from that cause in 1988, per 100,000 population in that age range.

Source: U.S. Bureau of the Census, 1990, Table 117, p. 81.

periods in middle adulthood. Several points are plain in this simple set of data. First, the total death rate from all causes nearly triples in these years, from 486 per 100,000 from age 45 to 54, to 1246 between ages 54 and 64.

Second, women have much lower death rates than men—yet another reflection of the basic sex difference in life expectancy I have already talked about. But what is not evident in either Table 15.2 or Table 15.3 is a fascinating paradox: women live longer, but they have *more* diseases and disabilities. Women are more likely to describe their health as poor, they have more chronic conditions such as arthritis, and have more limitations in their daily activities.

This difference is already present in early adulthood, and it grows larger over age. By old age, women are substantially more likely to be chronically ill (Verbrugge & Wingard, 1987). In early adulthood, this gender difference in disease rate can be largely attributed to health problems associated with childbearing. At later ages, the difference cannot be explained in this same way.

How can this be? How is it possible that men die younger but are healthier while they are alive? Lois Verbrugge, who has been the leading researcher exploring such questions, (Verbrugge, 1984, 1989; Verbrugge & Wingard, 1987) suggests that the apparent paradox can be resolved if we consider the specific diseases from which men and women suffer, and the diseases they die from. It's obvious from Table 15.3 that the primary killer diseases are cancer and heart disease, and men contract these diseases *earlier* in their lives. Because both these diseases often act quickly, men are less likely to have prolonged periods of disability before their deaths.

Women die of these same diseases, but they contract them later, and live longer once they contract them, possibly because they seek treatment sooner. At the same time, women are also much more likely to suffer from *nonfatal* chronic diseases, particularly arthritis, a disease that may be linked to the greater bone loss women experience following menopause. The net effect of these two changes is that women are likely to spend many more years of adulthood with some kind of disability (Kaplan, Anderson & Wingard, 1991).

Before I leave this rather depressing subject of death and disease, let me say a bit more about each of the two leading causes of death in this age range: heart disease and cancer.

Coronary Heart Disease.   The rate of **coronary heart disease** (usually abbreviated CHD) has been dropping rapidly in the United States in recent years, but it is still the leading cause of death both in the United States and in the developed world (White et al., 1986). CHD covers a variety of physical problems, but the key change is in the arteries. In individuals suffering from CHD, the arteries become clogged with fibrous and calcified tissue, a process called *atherosclerosis.* Eventually, key arteries may become completely blocked, producing what lay people call a *heart attack* if the blockage is in the coronary arteries, or a *stroke* if the blockage is in the brain. Atherosclerosis is *not* a normal part of aging. It is a disease, increasingly common with age, but not inevitable.

Some types of people are more at risk than others for CHD. Our best information comes from a number of very long-term epidemiological studies, such as the Framingham study, in which the health and habits of large numbers of individuals have been tracked over time. In the Framingham study, 5209 adults were first studied in 1948, when they were aged 30 to 59. Their health (and mortality) since then has been assessed repeatedly (e.g., Dawber, Kannel & Lyell, 1963; Kannel & Gordon, 1980; Anderson, Castelli & Levy, 1987). In this way it has been possible to identify those characteristics that predicted later CHD. The left-hand side of Table 15.4 lists the well-established risk factors emerging from the Framingham and equivalent studies, along with a few others that are more speculative.

What evidence could I muster to support a claim that women are tougher than men? What counterarguments could you offer?

> ### TABLE 15.4 Risk Factors for Heart Disease and Cancer
>
> | Risk | Heart Disease | Cancer |
> |---|---|---|
> | Smoking | Major risk; the more you smoke, the greater the risk. Quitting smoking reduces the risk. | Substantially increases risk for lung cancer; also implicated in pancreatic cancer. |
> | Blood pressure | Systolic pressure above 140 linked to higher risk; the higher the BP, the higher the risk. | No known risk. |
> | Weight (Obesity) | Increased risk with any weight more than 30% above normal weight-for-height. | Increased risk of breast cancer with greater weight. |
> | Cholesterol | Clear risk for total cholesterol of 200 or more; an elevated level of low-density lipoproteins seems to be the culprit. | No known risk. |
> | Low levels of exercise | Inactive adults have roughly twice the risk. | Inactivity is associated with higher risk of colon cancer.[a] |
> | Diet | High-fat diet linked to increased risk.[a] | High-fat diet increases risk; high-fiber diet decreases risk.[a] |
> | Heredity | 7 to 10 times the risk for those with first-degree relatives with CHD. | Some involvement, but mechanisms not entirely clear.[a] |

[a]These items are less well established.

Sources: Benfante & Reed, 1990; Berlin & Colditz, 1990; Chamberlain & Galton, 1990; Fozard, Metter & Brant, 1990; Kannel & Gordon, 1980; Kritchevsky, 1990; McGandy, 1988; Shipley, Pocock & Marmot, 1991.

Because lists like these have appeared in numerous popular magazines and newspapers, there's not likely to be much that is news here. What is important to understand, though, is that these risks are cumulative in the same way that the health habits investigated in the Alameda County study seem to be cumulative: the more high-risk behaviors or characteristics you have, the higher your risk of heart disease. Furthermore, the effect is not just additive. For example, high cholesterol is three times more serious in a heavy smoker than in a nonsmoker (Tunstall-Pedoe & Smith, 1990).

Cancer. When we look at the second major killer disease of middle (and old) age, there are both parallels and differences with CHD. Figure 15.3 compares death rates for cancer and CHD over the full adult age range, combining the numbers for men and women. In middle adulthood, there are obviously few differences in the likelihood of dying of these two diseases. But in later years, cancer deaths rise fairly slowly, while CHD deaths rise dramatically.

The two diseases are similar, though, in that neither strikes in a totally random fashion. Indeed, as you can see in Table 15.4, some of the same risk factors are involved in both. Of the cancer risk factors I've listed on the right-hand side of the table, the most controversial concerns diet, especially the role of dietary fat. While some experts estimate that as many as 35 percent of all cancer death is attributed to diet (Bal & Foerster, 1991), others think the case is not yet completely proven (e.g., Carroll, 1991).

At the risk of sounding like a broken record, let me say once more that most of the risk factors listed in Table 15.4 are at least partially under your own control. It helps to have established good health habits in early adulthood, but it is also clear from the research that improving your health habits in middle age can reduce your risks of either cancer or heart disease.

RESEARCH REPORT
Type A Behavior and Coronary Heart Disease

If you read the popular literature on heart disease, you'll know that I have left out of Table 15.4 one of the most-discussed potential risk factors, usually called **Type A behavior** or the **Type A personality**. I've left it out quite deliberately, because there is a good deal of dispute about just how risky this behavior pattern really is.

The Type A personality pattern was first described by two cardiologists, Meyer Friedman and Ray Rosenman (1974; Rosenman & Friedman, 1983). They were struck by the apparent consistency with which patients who suffered from heart disease shared several other characteristics, including competitive achievement striving, a sense of time urgency, and hostility or aggressiveness. These people, whom they named Type A, were perpetually comparing themselves to others, always wanting to win. They scheduled their lives tightly, timed themselves in routine activities, and often tried to do such tasks faster each day. And they had frequent conflicts with their coworkers and family. Type B people, in contrast, were thought to be less hurried, more laid back, less competitive, less hostile.

Early research by Friedman and Rosenman suggested that Type A behavior was linked to heightened levels of cholesterol and hence to heightened risk of CHD, even among people who did not suffer from observable heart disease. Contradictory results from more extensive studies since then, however, have forced some modifications in the original hypothesis (e.g., Booth-Kewley & H. Friedman, 1987; Matthews, 1988; Miller et al., 1991).

For one thing, all facets of the Type A personality, as originally described, do not seem to be equally significant for CHD. The most consistent link has been found between CHD and hostility, with hard-driving competitiveness showing weaker links. Time pressure is not consistently related to CHD at all.

What is more, among individuals who are *already* at high risk of CHD—because of smoking, high blood pressure, or the like—knowing about levels of hostility does not add to the accuracy of your prediction about heart disease. If two adults both have high blood pressure and high cholesterol, for example, they are both equally at risk of heart disease, even if one of them displays high levels of hostility and the other does not. It is only among people who do *not* show other risk factors that Type A personality traits add helpful information to the prediction. The effect is fairly small, but in large samples of low-risk adults, those who are hostile and competitive are slightly more likely to develop CHD than are those who are more easygoing.

I think that most people who have analyzed this research would now agree that there is *some* kind of connection between personality and CHD. What is less clear is just which aspect(s) of personality are most strongly predictive. Recent work suggests that measures of neuroticism or depression may be even better risk predictors than hostility (Booth-Kewley & Friedman, 1987; Cramer, 1991). So stay tuned: this story is not over yet.

Figure 15.3 In the middle adult years, deaths from cancer and heart disease are about equally prevalent, but in old age, death from heart disease rises precipitously. (*Source:* U.S. Bureau of the Census, 1990, from Table 117, p. 81.)

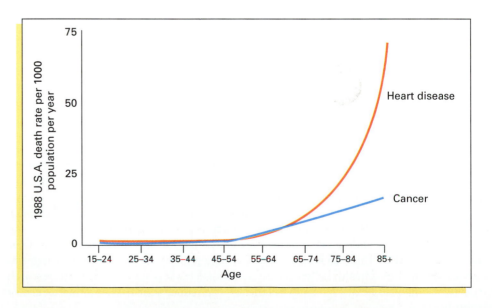

ACROSS CULTURES
Typical Diets and Cancer Rates Around the World

Aside from animal studies, which demonstrate a clear causal link between high-fat diets and cancer rates, (Weisburger & Wynder, 1991), some of the strongest evidence for a link between diet and cancer comes from cross-national comparisons. For example, the typical Japanese diet contains only about 15 percent fat, while the typical U.S. diet is closer to 40 to 45 percent fat. Cancer (and CHD) is much less frequent in Japan. The possibility of a causal link between the two is further strengthened by the observation that in those areas in Japan in which Western dietary habits have been most adopted, cancer rates have risen to nearer Western levels (Weisburger & Wynder, 1991).

Comparisons of diet and cancer rates in many nations show similar patterns. This is especially clear in results from a study of United Nations data by Hugo Kesteloot and his colleagues (Kesteloot, Lesaffre & Joossens, 1991). They have obtained two kinds of information for each of 36 countries: (1) the death rates from each of several types of cancer, and (2) the estimated per-person intake of fat from dairy products or lard. Only dairy and lard fat are included because these are the major sources of saturated fats, thought to be more strongly implicated in disease. Note that the unit of analysis for this study is a *country* and not an individual. The figure below shows the relationship between deaths from rectal cancer and fat consumption, one of the clearest connections. In this case the correlation between the two is .64. The equivalent correlations for other types of cancer were: .60 for breast cancer in women; .70 for prostate cancer in men; .43 for colon cancer in men and .47 in women. For all cancers combined, the correlations were .58 in men and .65 in women. The correlations between national fat intake and deaths from *heart disease* were also significant: .55 for men and .35 for women.

The relationship between dietary fat, other risk factors, and cancer is obviously complex, and there is much yet to be learned. But cross-national comparisons of this type have generated highly useful hypotheses.

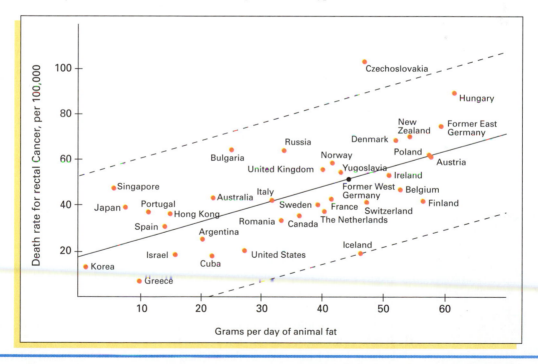

Mental Health in Middle Age

I mentioned in Chapter 13 that most types of emotional disturbance are considerably more common in early adulthood than in the middle years of adult life. Let me give you only one concrete example, drawn from Regier's major recent epidemiological study (Regier et al., 1988). Regier and his colleagues interviewed 18,571 adults living in five different parts of the United States about their psychological symptoms over the previous month. The researchers then identified those subjects whose replies were consistent with standard diagnostic criteria for various forms of disorders, such as substance abuse, depression, anxiety, or the like. In this survey, 3 percent of those aged 25 to 44 were classed as suffering from a major depressive episode, compared to 2 percent among those between 45 and 64. The rate dropped further, to .7 percent, in those over 65. The pattern is essentially the same for both women and men, although the rates are higher for women at every age.

These findings raise questions about the existence of that widely discussed event, the mid-life crisis.

Proffessinial White Males

Mid-Life Crisis: Fact or Fallacy?   The concept of a mid-life crisis was not invented by popular writers out of whole cloth. It has been part of several major theories of adult development, including Jung's and Levinson's. Levinson argues that each person must confront a constellation of tasks at mid-life that virtually guarantee a crisis of some kind: the awareness of one's own mortality, recognition of new physical limitations and health risks, and major changes in most roles. Confronting all these tasks, according to Levinson, is highly likely to exceed an adult's ability to cope, thus creating a crisis.

When researchers look at the actual evidence, they often come to diametrically opposite conclusions. David Chiriboga concludes that "there is mounting evidence from research studies that serious mid-life problems are actually experienced by only 2 percent to 5 percent of middle agers" (1989, p. 117). Lois Tamir, reading the same evidence, concludes that mid-life is a time of important psychological transition marked with "deep-seated self-doubts or confusion" (1989, p. 161).

My own conclusion is far more like Chiriboga's than like Tamir's. I already mentioned, in discussing the emotional consequences of menopause, that there is a peak of depression in women at about middle age. But note that even at the peak, at about age 44, the rate is only about 4.5 percent—hardly evidence for a universal crisis. I'm also impressed by results of several studies by personality researchers, Paul Costa and Robert McCrae (1980a; McCrae & Costa, 1984). They devised a mid-life crisis scale, including items about inner turmoil, marital or job dissatisfaction, and a sense of failing power. They then compared the responses of over 500 men in a cross-sectional study of subjects ranging in age from 35 to 70. They could find no age at which scores were significantly high. Others who have devised mid-life crisis scales have arrived at the same conclusion (e.g., Farrell & Rosenberg, 1981), as have those who have studied responses to stress (e.g., Pearlin, 1975).

Of course, it is possible that some kind of crisis is common in mid-life but that it occurs at a different age for each person. That would mean that there would be no *single* age with a peak of problems, and it could explain Costa and McCrae's results. But studies like Regier's are hard to explain away so easily, because they are combining 10- or 20-year periods in their age groups. If a crisis were more common in mid-life than in early adulthood, we ought to see some sign of it in increased rates of depression or anxiety when all mid-life adults are compared to all young adults. But we simply do not find that (Hunter & Sundel, 1989).

Longitudinal studies do not lend much comfort to mid-life crisis advocates either. Norma Haan, for example, could find no indication that any kind of crisis was common at mid-life among the subjects included in the Berkeley/Oakland longitudinal study (Haan, 1981b).

Only for one subgroup is there any confirming evidence: white men from the middle class, especially those with professional occupations. Lois Tamir (1982), in a national sample of about 1000 men who ranged in age from 25 to 69, found that college-educated men in the 45 to 49 age range reported more drinking problems, more prescription drug use (such as sleeping pills or tranquilizers), less reported "zest" and more "psychological immobilization."

If you wanted to design the absolutely best study on mid-life crisis, what would you need to do? What kind of sample, research design, and measures would you need to include?

The only subgroup of adults who show any signs of a mid-life crisis are white, middle-class, well-educated men. Even among men in this group, though, a "crisis" is by no means universal at mid-life. It may well reflect the experiences of quite specific cohorts studied so far by researchers.

Whether this pattern is characteristic only of a particular cohort we cannot tell from this one study. But even if this result were common in a number of cohorts, it would not begin to persuade me that a crisis is a necessary, or even a very common, experience of the middle years of adulthood. Certainly there are stresses and tasks that are unique to this period, but there is little sign that these stresses and tasks are more likely to overwhelm an adult's coping resources at this age than at any other.

Cognitive Functioning in Middle Adulthood

LOSS OF SPEED

In Chapter 13 I described the basic shape of cognitive changes in the middle years, contrasting it with what happens in early adulthood. If you'll go back and look at Figure 13.4 (page 321), and at Denney's model (Figure 13.5, page 324), you'll remember that in middle adulthood, most of us maintain or even gain in skill on any task that is highly practiced or based on specific learning. So our vocabularies get better, and our problem-solving ability is generally maintained. On tasks that demand speed or require underused or unpracticed skills, such as a timed arithmetic test or a test dealing with three-dimensional spatial representations, declines are measurable and significant during the middle adult years. Still, even in these domains the absolute size of the loss is quite small for most adults in this age range. Werner Schaie, whose Seattle Longitudinal Study has given us the most complete evidence on this point, says,

> It is my general conclusion that reliably replicable age changes in psychometric abilities of more than trivial magnitude cannot be demonstrated prior to age 60, but that reliable decrement can be shown to have occurred for all abilities by age 74. (1983b, p. 127)

Memory

A similar statement could be made about changes in memory during middle adulthood. There are some losses, but when an adult is dealing with familiar material, the decline is fairly gradual during these years, although more noticeable after perhaps 55 or 60. The decline is earlier and larger when the material is less familiar, when a memory must be retained over an interval, or when there is some distraction. A good illustration of a number of these points comes from a recent study by Robin West and Thomas Crook (1990).

The memory task West and Crook used is a variant of a familiar, everyday task: remembering telephone numbers. Subjects sat in front of a computer screen, on which a series of 7-digit or 10-digit telephone numbers appeared, one at a time. The subject said each number as it appeared, the number then disappeared from the screen, and the subject had to dial the number she had just seen on a push-button phone attached to the computer. On some trials, the subjects got a busy signal when they first dialed and then had to dial the number over again. Figure 15.4 shows the relationship between age and the correct recall of the phone numbers under these four conditions.

Notice that there is essentially no decline with age in immediate recall of a normal 7-digit telephone number. This is the equivalent of what you do when you look a number up in the phone book, say it to yourself as you read it, and then dial it immediately. When the length of the number increases to the 10-digit length we use for long-distance numbers, however, you can see a decline with age, beginning at about age 60. And when there is even a brief delay, the decline occurs earlier. West and Crook think that the busy signal acts as a distractor as well as a delay, and that the distraction may be more of a problem for the older adult.

The telephone number task is an example of a measure of *primary*, or *short-term, memory*—where some item is to be held in memory for perhaps 30 seconds. *Secondary*, or

Figure 15.4 In these results from West and Crook's study of memory for telephone numbers, notice that there is no loss of memory in middle adulthood for the most common condition: a seven digit number dialed immediately. But if the number of digits increases or if you have to remember the number a bit longer, some decline in memory begins around age 50 or 60. (*Source:* West & Crook, 1990, from Table 3, page 524.)

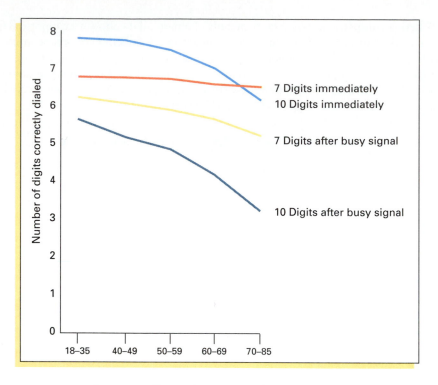

long-term, memory refers to recall over longer periods, from minutes to years. Do we find the same kinds of changes with age in long-term memory? On the whole, yes. Both the process of getting information into longer-term storage (a process called *encoding*), and the process of getting it out when you need it (*retrieval*) become gradually less efficient and speedy with age, but most of the drop occurs after age 60 rather than at mid-life, much as Schaie finds with measures of overall cognitive skill. We see this pattern when subjects are asked to put names to familiar faces (a retrieval task) or to learn lists of words and remember them several days later (an encoding task) (Salthouse, 1991).

The literature on memory change with age also offers a few tidbits in support of Labouvie-Vief's view that what happens to cognition in adulthood is not only a decline in capacity but also a change in emphasis or structure. Labouvie-Vief (1985), as you may recall from Chapter 13, suggests that in adulthood we tend to shift away from the logical or formal-operational approach that dominates in adolescence and at college age, to a more pragmatic approach aimed at solving everyday problems. In memory, this might be reflected in a decline in memory for surface detail but a compensatory memory for themes or meaning. A study by Cynthia Adams (1991) yields some confirmation.

Adams asked adults of various ages to read a story and then to recall it, in writing, immediately afterward. Younger adults were more likely to report specific events or actions in the story, while the middle-aged adults recalled more of the psychological motivations of the characters and offered more interpretations of the story in their recall. What this may mean is that the encoding process changes as we get older. We may simply not attempt to encode detail, but we may store broader or more summary information.

Yet even if we assume that the type of information encoded changes from early to middle adulthood, it is still not clear how we should explain such a change. It could mean "loss in the service of growth," as Labouvie-Vief suggests. Or it could indicate "decline with compensation." That is, we might go for essence rather than detail because that has proven the most informative, or because gradual loss in the efficiency and speed of memory processes has pushed us that way.

Remembering what you read in a newspaper is no more difficult in middle age than in early adulthood, but middle-aged adults may focus less on details and more on basic themes.

If all of what I have just said about changes in memory during middle adulthood seems overly decorated with words like "perhaps," "somewhat" and "may be," it is not accidental. There is an *enormous* literature on memory changes with age, but it suffers from two flaws that make it difficult to draw conclusions about the middle adult years. First, a very large proportion of the research compares only young and old adults and does not test the middle-aged at all. Second, the vast majority of the studies are cross-sectional rather than longitudinal. So we simply do not know much about what happens to individual memory over these years or how much individual variability there may be in the process. If we can extrapolate from Schaie's studies of IQ and specific cognitive skills, it seems reasonable to expect wide variation from one adult to the next. Some of us will experience significant memory loss in mid-life; many others will have none.

Using Intellectual Skills: Creative Productivity at Mid-Life

A somewhat different question about cognitive functioning in the middle years of adulthood—one that may have more direct relevance for our work life—has to do with creativity or productivity. Are middle-aged business executives as good (or better) at problem solving in their work? Are middle-aged scientists as creative as young ones?

Early research by Lehman (1953), which has been widely quoted, pointed to the conclusion that peak creativity, like peak physical functioning, occurred in early adulthood. Lehman arrived at this conclusion by identifying a series of major scientific discoveries over the past several hundred years, and then determining how old each scientist was at the time of that discovery. Most were quite young, especially in science and mathematics. The classic example is Einstein, who was 26 when he developed the special theory of relativity.

These are interesting patterns, but Lehman's method seems to me to be a backwards way to go at the question. The alternative is to study scientists or other problem solvers over their whole working lives and see whether the ordinary (non-Einsteinian) person is more productive and creative in early or middle adult life. Dean Simonton (1991) has moved a step in this direction by looking at the lifetime creativity and productivity of thousands of notable scientists from the nineteenth and earlier centuries. He was able to identify the age at which these individuals (nearly all men) published their first significant work, their best work, and their last work. In every scientific discipline represented in this unusual sample, the average age for the person's best work was right around age 40. But the curve is quite flat at the top. Most of these people were still publishing significant, even outstanding, research through their forties and into their fifties. In fact, Simonton proposes that the reason the best work is done at about 40 is not that the mind works better at that age, but that productivity is at its highest at that time. Chance alone would suggest that the best work will come during the time when the most work is being done.

Lifetime creative output of modern-day scientists follows a similar pattern. Mathematicians, psychologists, physicists, and other scientists born in this century have consistently shown their peak productivity—the most papers published in a single year—when they were about age 40. But when you look at research quality, such as by counting the number of times each research paper is cited by peers, you find that quality remains high through age 50 or even 60 (Horner, Rushton & Vernon, 1986; Simonton, 1988).

Among musicians or other artists, peak creativity may occur later or be maintained far longer. Simonton (1989) asked judges to rate the aesthetic qualities of musical compositions by the 172 composers whose works are most often performed. Late-in-life works ("swan songs") were most likely to be evaluated as masterpieces by the judges.

It is also possible to approach the question of age and creativity or professional effectiveness experimentally. Siegfried Streufert and his colleagues (Streufert et al., 1990) have done this in a particularly interesting study. They created sets of four-person

Dr. Rosalyn Yalow, who won the Nobel Prize for Medicine in 1977, continued to be highly productive and to do high-quality work throughout her middle adult years—a pattern common among scientists.

decision-making teams made up of mid-level managers from state and federal governments and private industry. On 15 of the teams, the participants were all between ages 28 and 35. Members of another 15 teams were middle-aged (aged 45 to 55), and another 15 teams included only older adults (aged 65 to 75). Each team was given a wonderfully complex simulated task: they were asked to manage an imaginary developing country called Shamba. They were given packets of information about Shamba ahead of time, and they could request additional information during their group work via a computer—which was of course programmed so as to make the experience of the different groups as much alike as possible, although the participants did not know that. Every group faced a crisis in Shamba at about the same time in their work; the computer later specified a particular resolution of that crisis, no matter what solutions the group had proposed.

Streufert recorded all the questions, suggestions, and plans generated by each group, from which he created a series of measures of activity rate, speed, depth, diversity, and strategic excellence of each group's performance. The young groups and the middle-aged groups differed significantly on only 3 out of the 16 measures. The younger groups did more things (made more decisions and took more actions); they asked for more additional information (often excessively, to the point of overload); they suggested a greater diversity of actions. But on measures of the use of strategy, planning, handling emergencies, and using the information they obtained, there were no differences between the young and middle-aged. In contrast, the oldest groups performed less well by virtually every measure. Their interactions tended to be task-oriented but diffuse. Middle-aged teams, in contrast, asked for just about the right amount of information—not too much to overload the system but enough to make good decisions—and used the information effectively.

Although this is only a single study, cross-sectional rather than longitudinal in design, it points in the same direction as does the literature on age and scientific productivity. Middle-aged adults appear to retain their ability to do high-level productive work or problem solving.

If creativity, productivity, and ability to deal with complex problems all decline past the years of midlife, does this mean that our political leaders should all be younger than 65? Why or why not?

▶ **Individual Differences** ✈

You've already encountered a good deal of information about individual differences in this chapter, especially in the discussion of risk factors and health habits associated with heart disease and cancer. Other information suggests that many of the same characteristics that are linked to increased or decreased risk of these two diseases are also linked to the rate of change or maintenance of overall health and intellectual skill in the middle years.

One example comes from Schaie's analysis of data from the Seattle Longitudinal Study (Schaie, 1983b). He has found that those subjects who have some kind of cardiovascular disease—either CHD or high blood pressure—show earlier and larger declines on intellectual tests than do those who are disease free. Other researchers have found similar linkages. Even adults whose blood pressure is controlled by medication seem to show earlier declines (Schultz et al., 1986; Sands & Meredith, 1992). Schaie cautions us about taking these findings too far. The size of the effect is quite small, and it may operate indirectly rather than directly. Adults with cardiovascular disease may become physically less active as a response to their disease. The lower level of activity, in turn, may affect the rate of intellectual decline.

Exercise and Health. This raises the possibility that exercise may be one of the critical factors in determining an individual adult's overall physical health and cognitive performance during these years. Denney's model, which you met in Chapter 13, points to just such a connection. Let me give you two examples to expand on the point.

Michael Pollock (Pollock et al., 1987) has assessed the physical functioning of an unusual group of 22 men who were all successful competitive runners or walkers when they were first tested. At that time, they were middle-aged or older, and all ran 20 or 30 miles a week as part of their training. Ten years later, all these men were still running regularly, but some of them continued to compete in races and others did not. The competitive group also ran more miles per week, 35.9 compared to 22.3 for the less competitive subgroup. Figure 15.5 shows what happened to the VO_2 max (maximum oxygen uptake) scores of these two groups over the ten years.

You can see that the most intense levels of continuing exercise were associated either with maintenance or smaller loss of VO_2 max over the ten-year interval. In particular, continuing high-level runners who had been in their forties and fifties at the beginning of the ten years maintained their VO_2 max, while their age-mates who had dropped down a notch in training showed a decline. For those in their sixties at the start of the study, intensity of exercise obviously made much less difference; both groups declined. Across all ages, the competitive group also had slower pulse and lower systolic blood pressure.

This is a *very* small and selective sample. We obviously need more research of this type to be sure of these conclusions, but the findings are consistent with Denney's overall model and with the hypothesis that vigorous physical activity can help to maintain excellent health over the years of middle adulthood.

Physical exercise also seems to help maintain cognitive abilities in these same years, very likely because it helps to maintain cardiovascular fitness (e.g., Clarkson-Smith & Hartley, 1989, 1990a). Among physically healthy middle-aged and older adults, those who are more physically active, doing gardening, heavy housework, or aerobic exercise such as walking, running, or swimming, have higher scores on tests of reasoning, reaction time, and short-term memory.

Caution lights should have gone off in your head at this point: Studies like these have a potentially major flaw in that they compare people who *choose* to be active with those who choose not to be. It seems likely that those who exercise are different in other ways from those who do not, although in most of these studies the researchers have been careful to match the two groups as well as possible on variables they thought might make

Before you read any further, figure out the flaw in this research strategy.

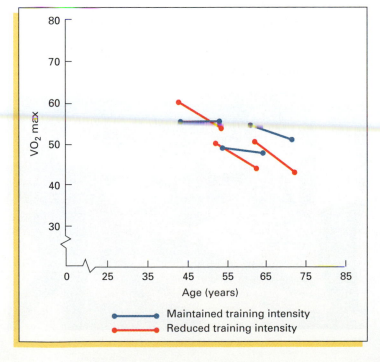

Figure 15.5 Each line in this figure represents the aerobic fitness of a small number of men studied over a 10-year period. All were competitive runners at the start of the study. Half of them remained competitive; the other half continued to run but not compete. Those who maintained the highest level of exercise maintained their aerobic fitness best. (*Source:* Pollock et al., 1987, adapted from Figure 2, p. 729.)

Maintained training intensity
Reduced training intensity

a difference, including physical health and education level. A better test would be to assign some people randomly to exercise groups and some not, and then see if there are any changes in their cognitive functioning.

In fact there are a few such studies, from which the results have been quite mixed. Everyone finds that exercise increases measures of physical functioning, such as VO$_2$ max, even in very aged adults. Some also show that exercise improves thinking (e.g., Elsayed, Ismail & Young, 1980), while others do not (e.g., Madden et al., 1989; Emery & Gatz, 1990). In most cases, the experimental exercise program lasts only a few months, and that may not be sufficient to make any difference in mental functioning. Were I making a bet at this point, based in the fragmentary evidence we now have, I'd bet that there is some effect of long-term exercise on cognitive performance, but that it isn't a very large effect. Still, because we already know that exercise provides some protection against both heart disease and some kinds of cancer, prudence alone would argue for building it into your life. So walk already!

In my enthusiasm for preventive actions such as exercise, I should not forget to reemphasize the larger importance for mid-life health and mental ability of those ubiquitous demographic variables, social class and race. If you go back and look at Figure 13.3 (page 319), you'll see that social class is a more significant predictor of variations in health in middle age than at any other time of adult life. Virtually all young adults are healthy, while most older adults have some chronic problems or restrictions in daily activities. It is in the middle of adulthood that occupational level and education affect the pattern. Figure 13.3 does not break this pattern down by race, but separate research suggests that the same link between social class and health is found among Hispanic-Americans and African-Americans (Markides & Lee, 1991; James et al., 1992; Chatters, 1991).

Ethnicity and Health.   Ethnic status itself is also linked both to overall health and to the incidence of specific diseases. Blacks and Hispanics not only have shorter life expectancies, they have poorer overall health than do whites in the United States. Among the middle-aged, nearly 40 percent of blacks describe their health as fair or poor. The comparable figures are 28 to 30 percent for Hispanics and roughly 20 percent for whites (Markides & Mindel, 1987). A number of factors contribute to such a difference, including the lower overall social class of minorities, with all that entails, less access to health care, greater stress, and perhaps poorer health habits.

There are also differences in incidence of specific diseases, not all of them to the disadvantage of minorities. Hispanic men, for example, have lower rates of both heart

If we are to believe the research, these middle-aged square dancers will probably have better retention of their cognitive abilities over the next decades than will their sedentary peers. But is this because the people who *choose* to be active are different in other ways that cause better mental performance, or is the exercise itself the cause?

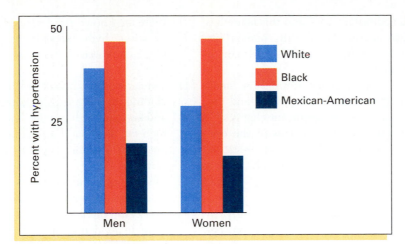

Figure 15.6 Combined data from two large national studies illustrate the standard finding of higher rates of hypertension among blacks and lower rates among Hispanics. (*Source:* Sorel, Ragland & Syme, 1991, from Table 3, p. 375.)

disease and cancer than do white men. Hispanic women, regrettably, do not have this same advantage (Markides & Mindel, 1987). Black men show the reverse pattern: they are *more* likely to die of heart disease than are white men. In addition, blacks have higher rates of two other significant diseases: cancer and high blood pressure. Blacks have higher incidence of most types of cancer, including breast, uterine, prostate, and stomach cancers, and have poorer survival rates once cancer is diagnosed, perhaps because they receive medical care later in the illness (Chatters, 1991). In the United States, 51 percent of white cancer patients survive at least five years; in blacks the comparable figure is 38 percent (U.S. Bureau of the Census, 1990).

Blacks are also more likely than whites to suffer from high blood pressure, more properly called **hypertension**, most often defined as a systolic pressure above 140, or a *diastolic* pressure (the lower number you are given) above 90. Figure 15.6 shows the combined findings from two large national surveys in the United States of adults between age 25 and 65 (Sorel, Ragland & Syme, 1991). You can see that blacks have higher rates than whites and that this difference is considerably larger among women than among men. You can also see that among Mexican-Americans, rates of hypertension are markedly *lower* than in either of the other two groups. This is an especially important piece of information. It suggests that poverty alone cannot be the explanation of higher rates of hypertension among blacks, because Mexican-Americans also have high rates of poverty.

There is no good agreement as yet on the cause of blacks' higher levels of hypertension. Blacks in Africa do not have the same unusually high rates, which argues against a genetic explanation. One possibility is that it may be linked to weight differences. Williams (1992) reports that in one set of national survey data, the race difference in hypertension among women could be entirely explained as a function of higher rates of obesity in blacks. But in the national survey data shown in in Figure 15.6, the racial differences remain even when body mass is taken into account. Clearly we need to know a good deal more about the unique health problems of blacks, Hispanics, and other minority groups, and their causes, if we are to be able to design effective heath-care programs for adults of all ages.

Other than differences in timeliness of medical care, what other explanations can you think of for higher rates of cancer in African-Americans? How could you test your hypotheses?

Physicians and epidemiologists have not yet uncovered the reason for the higher rates of hypertension among blacks in the United States.

Summary

1. Most adults believe that significant physical and mental decline begins in the years of middle adulthood, al-

though in fact the changes are fairly small and gradual.

2. At age 40, life expectancy is for 35 to

40 additional years, and this figure has been increasing steadily; human life span, in contrast, is likely to remain at about 110.

3. Many physical functions show small changes in the forties, fifties, and sixties; a few show significant changes.

4. Added layers to the lens of the eye, with accompanying loss of elasticity, reduce visual acuity noticeably in one's forties or fifties. Hearing loss is more gradual.

5. Bone mass declines significantly in middle age, especially in women, beginning just before menopause. Faster bone loss occurs in women with early menopause, who are underweight, exercise little, and have low-calcium diets.

6. The loss of reproductive capacity, called the *climacteric* in both men and women, occurs very gradually in men but rapidly in women. Men gradually produce fewer viable sperm and a smaller quantity of seminal fluid.

7. Menopause typically occurs between 45 and 55, as a result of a series of hormone changes, including rapid declines in both estrogen and progesterone. One major symptom is the hot flash.

8. The rate of illness and death rises noticeably in middle adulthood. Young adults have more acute illnesses; middle-aged adults have more chronic illnesses. Women have significantly more illnesses than men, even though they die at later ages.

9. The two major causes of death in middle adulthood are cancer and heart disease. Death rates for both these diseases are higher among men.

10. Coronary heart disease is not a normal part of aging; it is a disease for which there are known risk factors, including smoking, high blood pressure, high blood cholesterol, obesity, and high-fat diet.

11. Cancer, too, has known risk factors, including smoking, high-fat diet, obesity, and an inactive life-style. The role of a high-fat diet has been controversial, but most evidence supports its causal contribution.

12. Middle-aged adults have lower rates of emotional disturbances of virtually every kind than do young adults. There is little evidence of any widespread "mid-life crisis."

13. Cognitive skills are generally retained well in the middle adult years, except for unexercised abilities or those that require speed. IQ generally goes up, as does vocabulary.

14. Some memory loss occurs, but the loss is quite small until fairly late in the middle years, at least on most measures.

15. Creative productivity also appears to remain high during middle adulthood, at least for adults in challenging jobs, on whom most of this research has been done.

16. The importance of exercise is a continuing theme in research on both physical and cognitive functioning in middle adulthood. Adults who maintain high levels of exercise appear to retain their skills better than do those who are more sedentary.

17. On all measures of both physical and mental functioning, working-class or poverty-level adults show poorer maintenance or more decline.

18. Minority group members also tend to have poorer health; e.g., blacks have higher cancer rates and higher rates of hypertension.

Key Terms

climacteric	life span	presbyopia
coronary heart disease (CHD)	menopause	Type A behavior
	osteoporosis	Type A personality
hypertension	presbycusis	
life expectancy		

Suggested Readings

Charness, N. (Ed.) (1985). *Aging and human performance*. Chichester, England: Wiley. (This is an excellent source, not only because it contains summary chapters on many of the topics I've covered here, but because it has an extensive bibliography.)

Jackson, J. S. (Ed.) (1991). *Life in black America*. Newbury Park, CA: Sage Publications. (The papers in this book summarize the results from studies of several national samples of black Americans in the late 1970s and 1980s. Many of the chapters cover material that I have dealt with elsewhere in this book, but there are several papers relevant to physical and cognitive functioning over the whole adult age range.)

Mishell, D. R., Jr. (Ed.) (1987). *Menopause: Physiology and pharmacology*. Chicago: Year Book Medical Publishers. (If you want to know more about this important mid-life physical change, this is a wonderful source. The papers are detailed, but written in language that is not too technical for a nonphysician.)

16

SOCIAL AND PERSONALITY DEVELOPMENT IN MIDDLE ADULTHOOD

When I look at social and personality development in these middle years of adult life, what is most striking is how much less tightly the garment of social roles now fits. In the metaphor I have been using all along, the social clock is ticking much less loudly. Many of the same roles that dominate early adult life continue, of course. Most middle-aged adults are spouses, parents, and workers. But by age 40 or 50, these roles have changed in important ways. Children begin to leave home, which dramatically alters and reduces the intensity of the role of parent; job promotions have usually topped out, so there is less need to learn new work skills. And because both parenting and working are less demanding, there is more time for a marriage or partnership relationship.

Collectively, these changes mean that many people find their middle adult years to be less stressful and happier than the first 20 years of adult life. I am aware as I write those words that I have a vested interest in their truth; I am 52, in the precise middle of the years I have defined as middle adulthood. But vested interest or no, both the data and my own experience support the proposition that these are, in many ways, the optimum time of adult life.

At the same time, a third truth about these years is that there is far more variability in individuals' experiences than was the case earlier. You've already seen in Chapter 15 that large differences in health begin to be apparent in this age range. We can also see wider variations in what we might think of as psychological growth. Some adults, by mid-life, have begun to go through the process Levinson calls detribalization; others have not. Some have achieved what Erikson calls generativity, others have not. These variations then affect the adult's ability to deal with the new stresses and strains of these middle years.

To illustrate all these points, let me look at some of the same roles and relationships I described in Chapter 14.

Partnerships at Mid-Life

Several lines of evidence suggest that, on average, marital satisfaction rises in mid-life, reaching higher levels than at any time since very early marriage. You've already seen one example in the data in Figure 14.3 (page 346), and this curve is quite typical. The most likely explanation of this pattern is simply that role overload declines as the children begin to leave home, leaving husbands and wives with more time to spend together. For some couples, menopause also removes the possibility of further pregnancies, a change that may increase sexual freedom and satisfaction.

The same kind of pattern emerges if you ask not about satisfaction but about problems. Joseph Veroff and his colleagues (Veroff, Douvan & Kulka, 1981) have evidence on this point from two sets of cross-sectional national samples, one set studied in 1957 and one in 1976, together creating a cross-sequential study. You can see in the left-hand side of Figure 16.1 that in both surveys, older adults were less likely to describe problems with their marriage—although it is interesting that every age group reported fewer problems in 1976 than had been true in 1957.

Of course, results like this could mean that over time, the more troubled marriages end in divorce. As these poor relationships are weeded out of the pool of marriages, it is not surprising that older couples report fewer problems. Alternatively, it could be that marital satisfaction rises with age because problems have genuinely declined in intact marriages.

The other side of the same coin, however, is that there are signs that middle-aged marriages may also involve fewer positive interactions: fewer episodes of physical affection, fewer episodes of self-disclosure or encouragement. You can see one such sign in another set of results from Veroff's study. In 1976 they added a question about the frequency of physical affection between partners. Data on the right half of Figure 16.1 shows that the percentage of individuals who reported high rates of such affection with their spouse went down with age.

A remarkably similar pattern emerged from another cross-sectional study, by Clifford Swensen and his colleagues (Swensen, Eskew & Kohlhepp, 1981), one of my favorite pieces of research in this area. Swensen interviewed 776 adults spanning the family life

Can you think of any kind of research design that would get around the problem of the confounding of age and length of marriage in studies on changes in marital quality with age? How could we discover whether the increase in marital satisfaction at mid-life is really related to "mid-lifeness" rather than to long marriages?

Figure 16.1 Both problems and affection appear to decline in marriages over time, judging from these cross-sectional comparisons. Some have interpreted this pattern as indicating that marriages become more "devitalized" or empty with time; others see it as a sign of more companionable marriages in mid-life. What we do know is that couples report that they are more satisfied with their marriages in middle adulthood. (*Source:* Veroff, Douvan & Kulka, 1981, Table 4.20, p. 193, and Table 4.21, p. 185.)

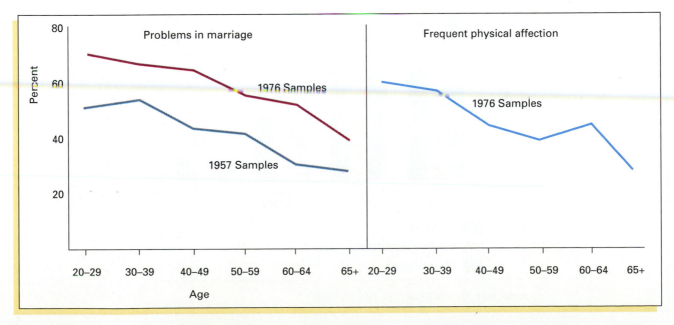

RESEARCH REPORT
Another Look at Love Relationships Across Adulthood

Another way to try to uncover basic developmental patterns in love relationships is to compare descriptions of partnerships by young, middle-aged, and older couples, all of whom have satisfying, loving relationships. That is, you hold constant the level of satisfaction and ask whether there are changes in the *components* of satisfaction.

Reedy, Birren, and Schaie (1981) used this strategy in a study of 102 happily married couples, divided equally among young couples (average age: 28.2), middle-aged couples (average age: 45.4), and older couples (average age: 64.7). Each partner in each couple was asked to complete a Q-sort with a set of 108 statements that might describe their relationship with their spouse. You'll remember that in a Q-sort, the statements have to be distributed following a normal distribution, so each subject had to identify those few statements that were most true, those few that were least true, and place the rest in relative spots in between.

Six different facets of a relationship were reflected in the 108 statements:

Communication: e.g., "He (she) finds it easy to confide in me."
Sexual Intimacy: e.g., "We try to please each other physically."
Respect: e.g., "We share common goals for our lives."
Help and play behaviors: e.g., "We spend a great deal of time together."

Emotional security: e.g., "I really feel I can trust him (her)."
Loyalty: e.g., "The future is sure to be perfect as long as we are together."

Reedy and her colleagues found that emotional security and respect were the two most important components of love at every age, but there were nonetheless subtle differences in the relative importance of the various facets, as you can see in the figure. Older couples placed somewhat more emphasis on emotional security and loyalty, somewhat less on communication and sexual intimacy.

The patterns of differences displayed in the figure may seem quite small, but each is a statistically significant age difference. In part, the size of the difference is dictated by the Q-sort technique itself, because each person must use the same distribution of scores. Thus the sum of the scores on all six facets must add to the same number for each age group. So what we are looking for, and what Reedy found, are those slight variations in the relative importance of these different aspects of a loving partnership.

Because these are cross-sectional comparisons, we cannot be sure that they do not merely reflect cohort differences in values or attitudes about marriage. But the findings are also consistent with the view that passion and sexual intimacy become less important in partnerships with increasing age, while tender, affectionate feelings and loyalty become more important.

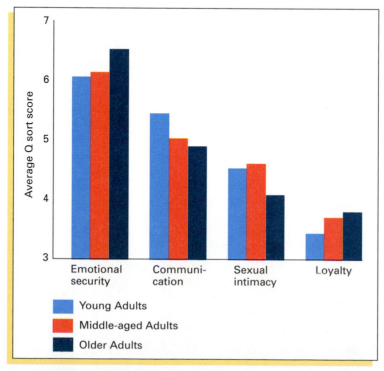

(*Source:* Reedy, Birren & Schaie, 1981, Table 1, p. 58.)

cycle stages from newlyweds to postretirement couples. Two scales were used to describe each person's marriage. A "love scale" measured expressions of affection, self-disclosure, moral support and encouragement, material support, and toleration of the less pleasant aspects of the other person. A "marital problems" scale assessed the degree of problems in six separate areas: child rearing and home labor, personal care and appearance (e.g., "Does your partner leave more mess than you like?"), money management, problem solving and decision making, relationships with relatives and in-laws, and expressions of affection. Figure 16.2 shows their results.

In these marriages, scores on the love scale declined steadily with age, while marital problems were highest among those with young children at home. If overall marital satisfaction is some kind of net difference between love and problems, then you can see that the life stage in which the couple has young children at home would involve the least satisfaction. Couples in this group report high problems and low expressions of love. Mid-life couples, in contrast, appear to have a balance tilted toward satisfaction. But they may do so not because expressions of love are particularly high, but because problems decline.

Some observers have described these middle-aged marriages as *devitalized* or *empty,* although one might argue equally that they could be called *companionable.* They are less likely to be actively unhappy, but they seem not to be very intimate. Because partners of this age clearly turn to one another in times of stress, and grieve when the spouse dies,

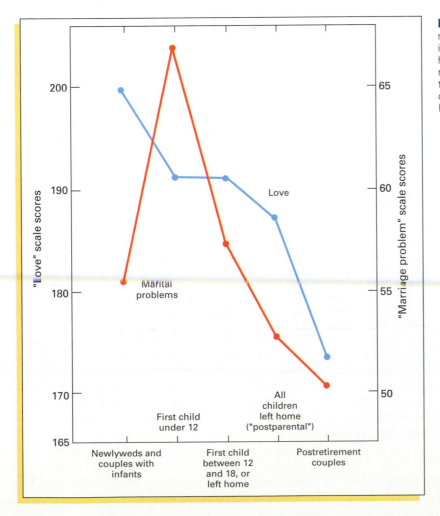

Figure 16.2   This suggests even more clearly that the greater marital satisfaction couples report in middle adulthood comes about mostly because the rate of problems has dropped, rather than that the rate of affection has increased. (*Source:* Swensen, Eskew & Kohlhepp, 1981, Figure 1, p. 848.)

there is little sign that the basic attachment has weakened or disappeared. But it may be accurate to say that overt attachment behaviors in the absence of stress become less frequent, just as we see in young children, whose attachment remains powerful but becomes less visible over a period of years.

Let me caution yet again that all of this is highly speculative, based as it is on cross-sectional data. The few longitudinal studies we have involve very small numbers of subjects and suffer from the usual confounding of age and length of marriage. One such study of a group of 17 couples followed for 40 years does point to the existence of a period of "empty love" somewhere in early middle age, with a shift toward a deeper or more intimate relationship in late middle age. But this curvilinear pattern described only 7 of the 17 couples. Five more had marriages that had been consistently high in love and affection over 40 years, 3 were neutral at every time point, and 2 were mostly negative. We have no way of knowing how typical these 17 couples may be of enduring marriages, but the results do point to the conclusion that there are many pathways through the marriage relationship. On average, marital satisfaction may rise and fall in a particular pattern. But that does not describe every marriage. There is no developmental necessity to a rise in satisfaction in the middle years nor to any devitalization in the same period. Nonetheless, it is true that as a group, middle-aged adults describe themselves as being more satisfied with their marriages than do young adults.

▶ Parents and Children ✦

When I talked about the relationship between young adults and their families, I was talking almost entirely about connections up the chain of family generations. When we look at family relationships in middle age, we have to look in both directions: down the generational chain to relationships with grown or nearly grown children, and up the chain to relationships with now-aging parents.

One of the striking effects of increased life expectancy in developed countries is that we are likely to spend many more years with both upward and downward family relationships. For example, Watkins, Menken, and Bongaarts (1987) estimate that in 1800, a woman could expect both her parents to be dead by the time she was 37. In 1980, the average woman could expect to have one parent still living until she was 57. Today, roughly half of all 60-year-old women still have living mothers, and this pattern will only become stronger as life expectancy increases still further.

Each of the positions in a family's generational chain has certain role prescriptions (Hagestad, 1986, 1990), and we expect to move in an orderly way through those roles. In middle adulthood, in current cohorts at least, the family role involves not only maximum amounts of assistance given in both directions in the generational chain, but also the maximum responsibility for maintaining affectional bonds, producing what is sometimes called the mid-life "squeeze," or the "sandwich generation."

Such a squeeze is illustrated particularly well in a set of findings from early research by Reuben Hill (Hill, 1965). He interviewed three generations in each of 100 families, each including a set of grandparents over the age of 60, middle-aged parents between age 40 and 60, and one married child between age 20 and 40. He asked the family members how much help they gave to the other generations and how much they received. Figure 16.3 shows that in every area except assistance with illness, the middle generation gave more help than they received.

You can also deduce from the figure that the middle-aged adults in this sample gave different kinds of help up and down the generational chain. To their children they gave mostly financial help and child-care assistance. To their parents they gave help with household management, illness care, and emotional support.

To bring this fact home to you even more clearly, you might want to make some inquiries in your own family. Find out how old your parents each were when their last living parent died (if, indeed, that has yet occurred). And how old were your *grandparents* when they became the oldest in the lineage? Can you go back one more step in the lineage?

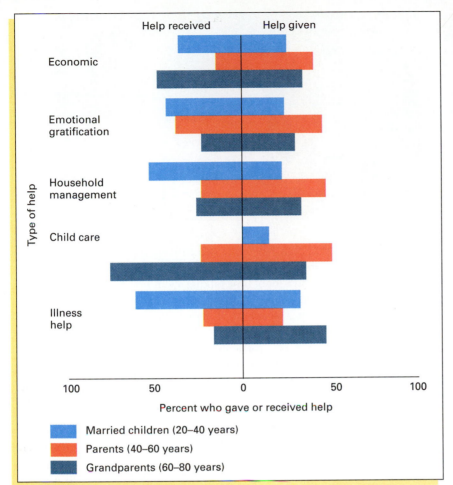

Figure 16.3 The phenomenon of the mid-life "squeeze" or the "sandwich generation" is illustrated by these data from Hill's three-generation family study. Middle-aged adults give more help in four of the five categories, and they receive less help than do their elder parents. (*Source:* Hill, 1965, from Table 3, p. 125.)

We see the same sorts of variations in the types of interactions with parents and children in a newer three-generation family study by sociologist Gunhild Hagestad (1984). She was interested not so much in patterns of aid but in attempts to influence those of other generations in the family. Middle-aged adults in this sample of 148 families typically spent more effort trying to influence their children than their parents, but both occurred fairly regularly. Their most successful influences on their aging parents came in the form of practical advice about where to live, and how to manage the household and money. Attempts to change their parents' views about social issues, or to comment on family dynamics, largely fell on deaf ears.

Influence attempts toward their young-adult children were aimed mostly at shaping the child's transition into all the key adult roles. So they talked about educational choices, work, money, and personal life-style.

Influence attempts do not radiate exclusively from the middle generation, either. Both the young adult children and the aging grandparents in this study tried to influence the middle-aged parent generation, with varying success. I was amused to read in Hagestad's account that parents, whatever their age, keep trying to influence their children, and that children, whatever their age, continue to resist such influence and advice. But advice from child to parent is much more likely to be successful. Only about a third of the influence attempts from parents to children were effective, while about 70 percent of the influence attempts in the other direction were positively received.

Three generations of adults in the same family, like this grandfather, son, and grown grandson, are now the rule rather than the exception. Probably these three men have certain subjects they talk about regularly, a shared agenda of their relationship.

Hagestad also found that each family seemed to have a particular agenda or set of themes that cropped up again and again in their descriptions of interactions across the generations. Some families spend a lot of time talking about money; others never mention this subject. Some focus on family dynamics or on health issues. Themes like this are particularly clear if you look at all-male or all-female lineages. In more than half the families Hagestad studied, the three generations of women regularly talked about some aspect of interpersonal relationships—particularly family dynamics—while such a theme never appeared in the male lineages. Grandfathers, fathers, and grown sons were more likely to talk about work, education, or money with one another. Other studies of multigeneration families, both in the United States and in Germany, confirm these same patterns. When women family members have conflicts, it is most likely to be over how members of the family ought to relate to one another. When fathers, sons, and grandsons have conflicts, they are likely to be about nonfamily issues, such as politics or social issues (Lehr, 1982; Hagestad, 1985).

I am particularly fond of Hagestad's research because it gives us a small window into the complex workings of family relationships across several generations. We can gain still further understanding of family relationships for middle-aged adults by looking separately at specific relationships either down or up the generational chain. Research on the "empty nest," on grandparenthood, and on care of aging parents begins to give us a picture of this sandwich generation.

What is the conversational glue that holds your own family together? Do the male lineage chains talk about different things than do the females?

The Departure of the Children: The "Empty Nest"

The timing of this stage in the family life cycle is obviously dependent on a person's (or couple's) age when the last child was born. Among women born between 1940 and 1949 in the United States—those now in their forties and early fifties—the last child was born on average at about age 26. If we assume that this last child will have left home by the time he or she is 24 or 25, then women in this cohort will be roughly 50 when the last child leaves. Because men are typically somewhat older at marriage, they will be 53 to 55 when the last child leaves. Obviously, those who delay childbearing will push this empty nest stage to a later age.

Hagestad's work reinforces the obvious fact that the role of parent does not cease when the child leaves home. Support and advice continue to be expected and offered. But the content of the parental role in this postparental phase is clearly quite different from what it was when the children were still at home. On a day-to-day basis, the child is not there to be fed or cleaned up after. As a result, there is much more time for the spousal roles, a change which undoubtedly contributes to the higher reported marital satisfaction in this stage of family life. Interestingly (and quite sensibly), there also seems to be some sign of a weakening of the so-called parental imperative. Go back and look again at Figure 14.5. You can see that in this postparental phase, husbands and wives are much more equal in their total work/family contributions than was true at earlier phases.

But wait a minute. Isn't the empty-nest stage supposed to be a *more* stressful time, rather than less, especially for women? Folklore would have it that most women will be depressed or upset at this time of their lives because of the loss of the centrality of the role of mother. Of course, it is possible that such a pattern exists in some cultures, but it seems not to be true of U.S. culture, at least not for the great majority of middle-aged women.

Suicide rates do go up for women in mid-life, but the rise begins between 31 and 40, when children are still at home, and then drops for those women over 50, which is when the empty nest typically occurs. Similarly, the blip on the curve of depression among mid-life women appears in the late thirties and early forties, before the children have left home. Alcohol abuse also declines in women in their forties and fifties (U.S. Bureau of the Census, 1984). More to the point, when women are specifically asked about positive and negative transitions in their lives, those who list the departure of the last child as significant are more likely to describe this event as positive than negative (Harris, Ellicott & Holmes, 1986).

Those few women who do experience some distress in this role transition appear to be those whose sense of self-identity has been heavily invested in the role of mother. Women in this age range who are in the labor force are much more likely to experience the empty nest as positive. The general rule is that the more roles you have to fill, the more likely you are to experience role conflict or role overload. In early adulthood, when the role of parent is added, we see a large increase in such strains; when the role of parent is dramatically reduced in complexity in this postparental period, strain declines.

Grandparenthood

At the same time, the majority of us add a family role in middle adulthood, that of grandparent. In the United States, about three-fourths of all adults become grandparents before they are 65, and most now live long enough to see those grandchildren grow up (Hagestad, 1988; Cherlin & Furstenberg, 1986). Coming from a long-lived family, I knew all four of my grandparents. The earliest of their four deaths was when I was 16, the last when I was in my late forties, by which time there were grown great-grandchildren in the lineage. My own first grandchild is now a year old, so we have four generations in the

Once the kids are grown and gone, many couples find more time for each other and more pleasure—including laughter—in their relationship.

family once again. (My father, on learning of the birth of my sister's first grandson, his first great-grandchild, said, "I love having great-grandchildren. What I find hard is realizing that I'm the father of a grandmother!") Four- and five-generation families are now becoming common, even in this era of later childbirth in the younger generations.

The median age for women to become grandmothers in the United States is between 42 and 45 (Sprey & Matthews, 1982), although this age range may change in future cohorts as the average age of childbearing rises. Still, this is clearly a normative experience of middle adulthood.

Most grandparents see or talk to their grandchildren regularly. They may write, call, or visit as often as every couple of weeks. Current generations of grandparents generally describe warm, loving relationships with their grandchildren, in contrast to the much more formal or authoritarian relationships they recall with their own grandparents.

Still, all grandparents are not the same. A number of researchers have described distinct styles of grandparenting. Andrew Cherlin and Frank Furstenberg (1986) suggest three:

1. Remote: These grandparents typically see their grandchildren relatively infrequently and have little direct influence over their grandchildren's lives. The most common reason for this remoteness is physical distance, but there are many grandparents who live nearby but are still emotionally detached. One grandmother interviewed by Cherlin and Furstenberg, when asked what it has meant to her to be a grandmother, said—in a formal, distant voice —

> Well, I'm grateful that I've lived long enough to see the children. And I'm grateful that my children are carrying out the principles, the goals, the ideals that I wanted to put into them. And I hope that my grandchildren put it into their children. You know, to lead the good life, be educated, and to continue your education long after you get out of school. (p. 54)

2. The companionate relationship: In sharp contrast is this statement by another woman in the same study:

> When you have grandchildren, you have more love to spare. Because the discipline goes to the parents and whoever's in charge. But you just have extra love and you will tend to spoil them a little bit. And you know, you give. (p. 55)

Grandparents with this attitude create very warm, pleasurable relationships with their grandchildren, labeled as *companionate* by Cherlin and Furstenberg. Yet these grandparents also say that they are glad they no longer have the day-to-day responsibility. They can love the grandchildren and then send them home.

3. The involved relationship: The third type includes grandparents who are much more actively involved in the rearing of their grandchildren. Some of them live in three-generation households with one or more of their children and grandchildren; some have nearly full-time involvement in the care of the grandchildren. But there are also involved relationships in which the grandparent has no responsibility for the grandchild's care but sees the grandchild(ren) very frequently and creates an unusually close link.

Among younger grandparents, there appears to be a fourth type identified by some researchers as a "fun seeker" (Neugarten & Weinstein, 1964; McCready, 1985). These grandparents focus on playful, leisure-time activities with their grandchildren—taking them on outings or playing games with them.

In Cherlin and Furstenberg's study of a national sample of over 500 grandparents, 55 percent were classed as companionate, 29 percent as remote, and 16 percent as involved.

Young Rosa seems delighted with her grandfather, with whom she seems to have what Cherlin & Furstenberg would call a "companionate" relationship.

They also found that the pattern differed by age and by gender. Grandmothers were more likely to establish emotionally warm, companionate relationships, as were younger grandparents of both sexes (Cherlin & Furstenberg, 1986; Bengtson, 1985). Grandparents over 65 were more likely to be remote, sometimes because their health was no longer good enough to be able to tolerate the presence of very young children on a regular basis.

Other investigators have found robust ethnic differences in styles of grandparenting. In particular, Hispanic-American grandparents are far more likely to establish companionate relationships. They see their grandchildren more often, provide more help, and are more satisfied with their relationships with their grandchildren than are Anglos (Bengtson, 1985). At least one study of southern rural black and white grandfathers shows similar differences, with black grandfathers describing closer and more frequent contact with their grandchildren than did whites of similar social class (Kivett, 1991).

The marital status of the grandparent's own child also affects the grandparent-grandchild relationship. Grandparents with divorced or unmarried daughters are particularly likely to be strongly involved in their grandchildren's lives (Aldous, 1985). In African-American families, in particular, middle-aged grandmothers are quite likely to be involved as surrogate parents, providing major caregiving to their grandchildren (Cherlin & Furstenberg, 1986). In 1984, for example, more than a fifth of all black women in the United States lived in households with at least one grandchild, compared to only about 5 percent of white women (Beck & Beck, 1989). In a great many cases, these arrangements develop when the daughter is very young when she gives birth to the grandchild. The grandmother takes over a major childrearing role as an aid to her daughter, to allow the daughter to finish school, or to hold down a job. That it is indeed an aid is suggested by the fact that teenage mothers who have this kind of assistance from their own mothers (or other relatives) complete more years of education and have more successful work careers later in their adult lives (Taylor et al., 1990).

The role of grandparent obviously brings many middle-aged and older adults a good deal of pleasure and satisfaction. What is more interesting to me, though, is the repeated finding that an adult's overall life satisfaction seems affected very little by the quality of relationships with grandchildren. Grandparents who see their grandchildren more often do not describe themselves as happier than those who see them less often (Palmore, 1981). This does not mean that grandparents are displeased with the role. It means instead that for most adults in middle age, grandparenthood is not central to their lives, to their sense of self, or to their overall morale. In this, it is quite unlike the roles of spouse or parent, new roles in early adulthood that have highly significant effects on overall happiness or life satisfaction.

Caring for an Aging Parent

Another role that *may* be added at mid-life, and that does have a powerful effect on overall life satisfaction is that of major caregiver to one's aging parents. It turns out to be remarkably hard to discover just what percentage of middle-aged adults provide such care. Virtually all the evidence we have is based on studies of elderly adults, who are asked about the kind and amount of care they receive from their children. But this does not tell us what we need to know about the typical experience of the middle-aged adult. What we need to ask instead is what percentage of the middle-aged are providing care. For example, we know that among the elderly who have an adult child, 18 percent actually live with one of those children (Hoyert, 1991; Crimmins & Ingegneri, 1990). But because most elders have more than one child, it is not true that 18 percent of middle-aged children have a parent living with them. Nor is it true that all of those home-sharing elders are disabled or in need of regular care. So this strategy will not tell us how many of the middle-aged are providing regular or extensive care to an elder parent.

Think of a design for a study to check the hypothesis that health differences can explain most of the age differences in styles of grandparenting.

Better information comes from a small number of studies in which representative samples of middle-aged and older adults have been asked how much and what kind of assistance they give and receive (e.g., Rosenthal, Matthews & Marshall, 1989; Spitze & Logan, 1990). In one such study, Spitze and Logan interviewed 1200 middle-aged adults in upstate New York. Figure 16.4 shows that in this sample, less than 20 percent of adults between 40 and 65 were providing as much as three hours per week of assistance to an older parent. In about a quarter of these cases—roughly 5 percent—the parent lived with the middle-aged child.

Such numbers may be misleadingly low for two reasons. In the first place, they do not tell us what percentage of middle-aged adults will *ever* have the role of primary or significant caregiver for their parent. In addition, of course, it is quite possible that the percentage of adults who will need to take on this role will rise in the next decades, as life expectancy continues to increase and as more older adults live for more years with disabilities. But even with these caveats, it looks as if only a minority of adults ever fill such a role.

Not all middle-aged adults are equally likely to be in this minority. Those who are most likely to care for an aging parent are only children, the unmarried, those not employed full time, and daughters—a pattern I've discussed in more detail in the "real world" box on the opposite page.

The Effects of Caregiving.   In the past decade, there have been dozens of studies exploring the impact on the caregiver of tending to the daily needs of a parent (or spouse) who is disabled, frail, or demented. In the large majority of studies, the recipient of care has been diagnosed with Alzheimer's disease or some other dementia. Such individuals gradually lose their ability to perform ordinary daily tasks. They may ultimately be unable to dress or feed themselves and may not recognize their caregivers.

The demands on the caregiver may be extreme. The patient may need to be carried or lifted; household chores will need to be taken care of. In some cases the patient requires constant surveillance. Providing such care, especially if the caregiver is also trying to meet the needs of her (or his) own job and family, may drain both energy and finances.

Not surprisingly, such a demanding role takes its toll. A recent review of all the available studies (Schulz, Visintainer & Williamson, 1990) shows that both spouses and children serving as caregivers are more depressed than are matched comparison groups of adults of the same age and social class. There are weaker indications that caregivers are more likely to become ill than are noncaregiving comparison groups. A few studies even

If you compared a group of middle-aged men who provide regular caregiving to their aging parents to a group of men who do not provide such care, what differences might you expect to find between the two groups? Age? Occupation? Personality?

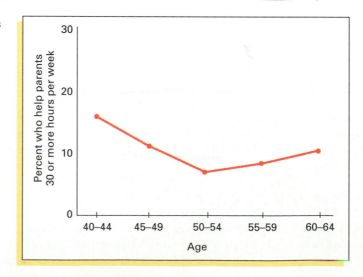

Figure 16.4 Relatively few middle-aged adults are involved in extensive caregiving for one or both parents at any one time. But these cross-sectional data do not tell us what percentage of adults will fill such a role at *some time* in their lives. (*Source:* Spitze & Logan, 1990, from Table 2, p. 189.)

THE REAL WORLD
Who Helps When an Elder Becomes Frail or Disabled?

Faced with an aging parent who needs some kind of regular assistance, who takes on the task, and why? The simple answer is that women do—daughters and daughters-in-law. Daughters are two to four times as likely as sons to provide assistance with daily living (Dwyer & Coward, 1991). The more complex answer is that families negotiate the caregiving task along a number of dimensions, including competing demands and availability of resources. Within a group of siblings, the one most likely to take on the task of caregiving is the one who has no children still at home, who is not working or not married, and who lives closest to the aging parent (Stoller, Forster & Duniho, 1992). The child with the strongest attachment to the parent is also most likely to provide help, although this effect is usually overridden by proximity and time availability (Whitbeck, Simons & Conger, 1991).

Most of these factors, in today's society, combine to make a daughter or daughter-in-law the most likely candidate for the role of caregiver. In today's middle-aged cohorts, women are more likely to be unemployed and less likely to be married because both widowed and divorced women are less likely to remarry than are widowed or divorced men. Furthermore, within the family system, the strongest attachment is likely to be the one between mother and daughter. And since it is most likely to be an elder mother who requires assistance, this once again points to daughters as the most likely caregiver.

Furthermore, proximity to the elder, which may seem like an independent element in the equation, is not a random process. Daughters, perhaps because of their greater emotional closeness or their socialization toward the role of kin-keeping, are more likely to live near their parents. And parents, when they approach their later years, are more likely to move to be close to a daughter than a son.

Yet sons are quite often involved in the care of an elder. There is some evidence that older men living alone are more likely to turn to a son than to a daughter (Stoller, 1990). And if a son is unmarried, he is more likely to take on the caregiving role than is his married sister (Stoller et al., 1992).

Despite such notable exceptions, it is still inescapable that women are far more likely than are men to take on the role of caregiver to an aging parent, just as women are more likely to take on the role of caregiver within a marriage, and with children. Whether this will change in the next few decades, as many more middle-aged women enter or remain in the labor force, we will have to wait and see. But my hunch is that, just as the balance of housework has not changed much in response to radical changes in women's work patterns, caregiving patterns are not likely to change rapidly either.

show that immune system function declines in efficiency among regular caregivers (Kiecolt-Glaser et al., 1987; Dura & Kiecolt-Glaser, 1991).

It is important, though, to keep these statements in perspective. For one thing, many of the studies have recruited subjects from among those participating in Alzheimer's family support groups. Such groups may attract precisely those individuals who find the task of caregiving to be highly stressful. For another, most caregivers report periods when they are very low in mood and despairing because of the burden they are bearing, but few show

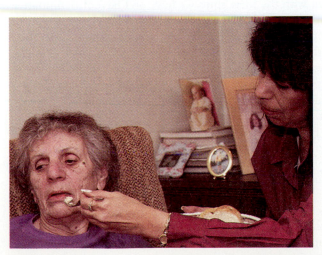

Daughters, far more than sons, are likely to take on the role of significant caregiver for a disabled or demented parent, as this daughter has done for her mother, who suffers from Alzheimer's disease.

all the signs of a full clinical depression. Third, these studies tell us almost nothing about the amount of burden that may be felt by a son or daughter (or spouse) caring for a nondemented but somewhat disabled older person. Finally, and not surprisingly, the sense of burden can be significantly mitigated by having enough outside sources of support, including friends to talk to, siblings who share the caregiving task, and a supportive spouse (Schulz & Williamson, 1991; Brody et al., 1992).

I am not trying to minimize the enormity of the task that may be involved for an individual middle-aged son or daughter (or elderly spouse) caring full-time for a demented or extremely frail elder. There are clearly costs, sometimes very great costs. But such a burden is *not* a normal part of the experience of current cohorts of middle-aged adults, at least in developed countries.

For the majority of middle-life adults, the pattern is far less extreme and far more positive. We give more assistance to our parents than we did at earlier ages, but we also continue to see them regularly for ceremonial and celebratory occasions and continue to feel affection as well as filial responsibility. Our parents are also important *symbolically*, because so long as they are alive, they occupy the niche of "elder" in the family lineage. When they are gone, each generation moves up a notch in the sequence of family generations, and those in the middle generation must come to terms with the fact that they are now "next in line" for death.

▶ Friends in Mid-Life

There is scant information about friendships in middle adulthood, but what little we have seems to suggest that friendships may be less central to the life of the middle-aged adult than they are in early or in late adulthood. The total number of friends people describe is high in one's twenties and then seems to drop and remain low through middle adulthood. In the later years, past 65 or so, the number of friends people list as part of their personal network or "convoy" rises again (Dickens & Perlman, 1981; Antonucci & Akiyama, 1987a; Farrell & Rosenberg, 1981). The frequency with which adults see their friends follows the same pattern. In one cross-sectional study in Detroit (Stueve & Gerson, 1977), 73 percent of young single adults reported that they saw their friends at least weekly; among those in the postparental stage, only 39 percent said they saw their friends that often.

In part, this pattern seems to reflect the fact that adults in their thirties, forties, and fifties are still engrossed in other roles. But it also may reflect the fact that in middle age, we are more likely to be content with the friendships we have and have little initiative to create new ones. In general, it appears to be the case that friends who are known longer are seen *less* often, and middle-aged adults have typically known their friends longer than is true for younger adults. Yet these same long-term friendships are also more intimate. So perhaps the best way to describe the pattern of friendships in the middle years of adulthood is that we tend not to have many but that they are close and do not require frequent contact to maintain that closeness. They readily survive benign neglect, but they are not therefore less important.

Individual Differences in Friendship Patterns. The sex differences in friendship patterns I have already described several times continue to be evident among middle-aged adults. Women have more intimate friends; men have larger, looser collections of friends with whom they engage in mutually enjoyable activities but with whom they share fewer of their feelings or problems.

Beyond that, there are indications that the ability to create and maintain friendships is itself a stable aspect of personality (Costa, Zonderman & McCrae, 1985). Costa and McCrae measured this friendship dimension with a set of questions about number, close-

Of course the other alternative is that friendships are simply less important in middle adulthood. Which possibility do you think makes the most sense, and why? What kind of data would we need to settle this question?

ness, and intimacy of friendships, and absence of loneliness. In longitudinal studies of adult men, they found that such descriptions were fairly stable over periods as long as 12 years. Even more impressive is the fact that consistency was essentially the same whether a man had moved during the interval or not.

We have no equivalent longitudinal data about friendships in adult women, but I would be surprised if the pattern differed substantially. I think that Costa and McCrae are correct in their assertion that each of us has some basic ability or tendency to form good friendships, and that we take this ability with us wherever we go as we move through the years of adult life. It would also be very interesting to know whether this ability or personality trait is related to the security of an adult's internal working model of attachment.

▶ Work in Mid-Life

In work life, as in family roles, middle adulthood is a time in which roles are generally well-learned. At the same time, most adults experience few work promotions in these years. They have reached a plateau. You might expect that this last fact would lead to lower work satisfaction, but it does not. Instead, job satisfaction and income are typically at their peak, as is a sense of power or clout in the job. Lois Tamir, who has studied men's work attitudes cross-sectionally, suggests two explanations for this apparent paradox. On the one hand, many men have achieved genuine success and status by mid-life and are quite reasonably satisfied. Alternatively, middle-aged men may become resigned to the idea that they are unlikely to be promoted further, and so they convince themselves that they have achieved sufficient status, or they change their expectations, their work values.

Tamir's cross-sectional study of a nationally representative sample of men offers further evidence for the second of these explanations, as you can see in Table 16.1. Among young adult men in this study (aged 25 to 39), job satisfaction was linked to various measures of personal satisfaction, while among the middle-aged it was not. Middle-aged men, in other words, have begun to disengage from their work as a primary source of personal fulfillment or satisfaction, even while they are likely to be more pleased with the work itself than they have been at any earlier age.

Whether the same is true of women workers at mid-life is not so clear. For those women who begin to work steadily only in their thirties or forties, the middle adult years may be the time of most rapid work advancement rather than a time of maintenance of previous gains. For such women, we might expect that work satisfaction would play the same role in overall life satisfaction as it does for young adult men.

TABLE 16.1 Job Satisfaction and Life Satisfaction in Different Age Groups of Men		
	Age Group	
Correlation Between Job Satisfaction and:	Young (25–39)	Middle-Aged (40–49)
Overall life satisfaction	.31[a]	.04
Zest	.43[a]	.09
Self-esteem	.26[a]	−.02

[a]This correlation is significant at the .001 level, which means that if there were really no link between the two variables, such a correlation would occur by chance only once in every 1000 samples of this size.

Source: Tamir, 1982, Tables 4.14, 4.15, and 4.16, pp. 91 & 92.

Interestingly, though, a shift to full-time employment when the nest is finally empty is not a very common pattern for women, at least in current cohorts. In Phyllis Moen's study (1991), based on 10-year longitudinal data from the Michigan Panel Study of Income Dynamics, most middle-aged women had begun working while their children were still at home. Few began work for the first time at the point at which the last child left home. The life transition that was far more likely to send a woman into the work force full-time in her middle adult years was divorce or widowhood.

All of this suggests that the work lives of middle adult women continue to be far more variable than is true of men of the same age. We are almost entirely lacking in any knowledge of the psychological effect of work on women in this age group. We know they are more satisfied with their work than are younger women, but do they have a greater sense of authority or clout in their jobs at this age? We know that middle-aged women who work have somewhat higher life satisfaction than women who don't (e.g., Betz & Fitzgerald, 1987). But we do not know whether the same pattern of relationship between work satisfaction and life satisfaction that Tamir observed in men would hold for women as well. My own guess is that among women who had worked continuously, the pattern might be the same. But I doubt that that is true for women whose work history is more variable, or those who only hit their occupational stride in their forties and fifties.

Preparation for Retirement

Many middle-aged adults also begin to prepare for retirement in various ways, often as early as 15 years before their anticipated retirement date. One aspect of such preparation is a gradual reduction in work load. For example, Figure 16.5 shows the percentages of men and women in a random national sample of 1339 adults who worked 45 or more hours per week, or who had retired for nonhealth reasons (Herzog, House & Morgan, 1991). You can see that by age 55, more adults begin to retire, and those who were employed are working fewer hours.

As they get nearer to the normative time for retirement, middle-aged adults also increase both formal and informal preparations for that transition (Evans, Ekerdt & Bossé, 1985; Newman, Sherman & Higgins, 1982). They talk to their spouses or with friends or

I have interpreted Figure 16.5 as meaning that in middle adulthood, there is a kind of winding down of involvement with work. Are there other possible interpretations or explanations of these data?

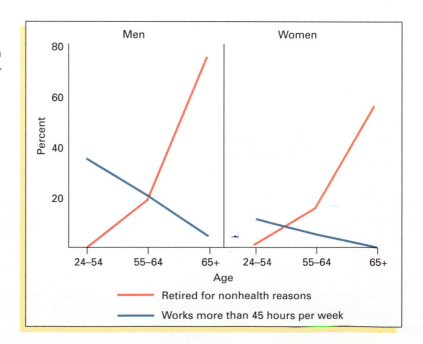

Figure 16.5 Most of us think of 65 as "retirement age," but in fact, many adults begin a gradual process of withdrawal from work well before that age. (*Source:* Herzog, House & Morgan, 1991, Table 1, p. 205.)

coworkers about retirement options and read more articles in the popular press. A minority also take part in such formal preparations as attending financial planning seminars, asking the Social Security Administration how much income they can expect at retirement age, investigating their pension plan at work in more detail, or seeking professional retirement planning guidance.

Such preparations are more likely among workers who are looking forward to retirement, who are dissatisfied with their work, or have a retired friend (Evans, Ekerdt & Bossé, 1985). There are also a few studies that indicate that men are more likely to prepare for retirement than are working women (Kroeger, 1982), although I do not know if that would still be true with more current samples. Those who dread retirement do the least planning, but even in this group, the incidence of informal planning increases as the time of retirement approaches.

If we combine all these pieces of information about work patterns in middle adulthood, the picture we get shows a gradual reduction in the centrality of the work role in an adult's life. This seems to be true both literally and psychologically. The number of hours worked tends to go down (although I wish someone would tell that to my 60+ hours-per-week professor husband, who works more hours at age 54 than he did ten years ago), and thoughts about retirement rise. Perhaps more centrally, satisfaction with one's work becomes less critical for feelings of happiness or well-being than is true in the earlier decades of adult life. Like family roles, then, the work role becomes much less intense in middle age.

▶ Personality in Mid-Life ✳

There are also suggestions of such a lowering of intensity in research on personality in the middle adult years. Most observers agree that over the years from 40 to 65 there is a shift away from the achievement striving, the independence, assertiveness and individualism that we see peaking at about mid-life. But personality theorists have not agreed on just how to characterize the direction of change. Let me describe five different views of the process.

Interiority.   Bernice Neugarten (1977) proposed that the shift is toward what she called *interiority*. She believed that in old age, adults turn away from their preoccupation with the outer world and become much more focused on interior processes—on reminiscence, on understanding their own life. Carol Ryff (Ryff & Baltes, 1976; Ryff, 1982) has described a similar process using somewhat different terminology. She argues that over the years of middle adulthood there is a shift from *instrumental values* to *terminal values*. Instrumental values have to do with desirable types of conduct—*being* something, such as ambitious or capable or courageous. Terminal values have to do with desirable end states—*having* something, such as happiness or a sense of accomplishment.

Ryff's own research offers some support for this view. In several studies, she has found that women in their forties and fifties are more likely to choose instrumental values, while those in their sixties and seventies select terminal values. But she found no such difference for men.

Ego Integrity.   Erikson's theory offers another model. You'll remember from Chapter 2 that he proposes two stages that affect these middle adult years: *generativity versus stagnation* and *ego integrity versus despair.* Generativity, which is the dominant stage from perhaps age 30 through roughly age 50, reflects the centrality of the task of nurturing the next generation, of passing on the flame in some fashion. It is expressed not only in bearing or rearing one's own children, but in more symbolic ways through teaching, serving as mentor, or taking on leadership roles in various civic, religious, or charitable organizations. It includes both nurturance and an awareness of one's own authority and power to influence others.

Erikson thought that bearing and rearing children was one way to develop the quality of generativity, but it is not the only way, nor the only expression of that quality. Generativity also includes the quality of feeling one's power and worth, and can be expressed through serving as mentor or civic leader, or through creative endeavor.

The task of achieving ego integrity, which may begin in one's fifties or sixties, is not unlike Neugarten's notion of interiority. To succeed at this task, the individual must come to terms with what she has done with her life, to find meaning in her choices, and to accept the "inalterability of the past" (Erikson et al., 1986, p. 56). If Erikson's view is correct, we might see signs of a shift away from individual achievement striving and toward a more reflective attitude in late middle age.

There are hints of changes of this kind, but the findings are much less clear than is the case for the set of changes I described in early adult life. One hint comes from the Berkeley/Oakland longitudinal studies. If you go back and look at Figure 14.6 and at the parallel figure from Chapter 1 (Figure 1.1), you'll see that while self-confidence continues to rise through the fifties, assertiveness peaks in the forties and then drops. In that same study, a measure of outgoingness also peaked in the forties among women and then dropped, as did the measure the Berkeley researchers call *cognitively committed*, which includes aspects of ambition, valuing independence, and valuing intellect. In this sample then, there is some sign of a sea change around age 50, after which there are indications of a decline in assertiveness, ambition, and outgoingness. Whether these changes continue into later decades we cannot tell from this study, because the sample has not yet been studied at ages beyond the mid-fifties.

Flexibility and Tenacity.   Another intriguing set of findings that cast the personality changes of this era in somewhat different terms comes from research in Germany by Jochen Brandstädter and Bernard Baltes-Götz (1990). They have studied a group of 1228 married couples ranging in age from 34 to 63. Among the measures they included is one they call *tenacious goal pursuit*, and another they call *flexible goal adjustment*. An individual high in tenacious goal pursuit is one who would agree with statements like these (p. 216):

> The harder a goal is to achieve, the more desirable it often appears to me.

> Even if everything seems hopeless, I still look for a way to master the situation.

Someone high in flexible goal adjustment would agree with the following (pp. 215–216):

> In general, I'm not upset very long about an opportunity passed up.

> I can adapt quite easily to changes in a situation.

> I usually recognize quite easily my own limitations.

Figure 16.6 shows cross-sectional differences on both these measures in this German sample. Tenacious goal pursuit went down in middle adulthood, while flexible goal adjustment rose. In a similar vein, cross-sectional studies in the United States generally show slight increases in introversion over the years of adulthood (e.g., Costa et al., 1986; Leon et al., 1979).

Maturity of Defense Mechanisms.   Still another way to look at personality change in these middle years is to focus on defense mechanisms. In Chapter 2 I mentioned George Vaillant's general theoretical proposal that what happens with development is a gradual shift away from the most reality-distorting defense mechanisms. To test this notion, Vaillant divided the defenses into three types: (1) immature, such as projection, distortion, and denial, (2) neurotic, such as repression, intellectualization, and displacement; and (3) mature, such as suppression, humor, and altruism. He then analyzed the types of defenses used by 100 of the Harvard men in the Grant study at various ages. The results generally confirmed his expectations: these men used more and more mature defenses as they aged. By middle adulthood, mature defenses comprised about 40 percent of the total. Similar results have emerged both from Haan's studies of the Berkeley/Oakland subjects and Helson and Moane's longitudinal study of Mills College women graduates (Haan, 1976; Helson & Moane, 1987).

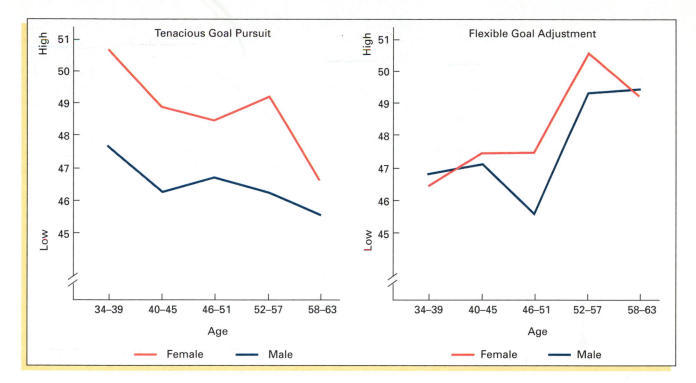

Figure 16.6 These cross-sectional data from a large study in Germany suggest one aspect of the "mellowing" of personality that may occur in middle adulthood. (*Source:* Brandstädter & Baltes-Götz, 1990, Figure 7.6, p.216, and Figure 7.7, p. 217.)

All of these studies show gradual changes in the maturity of defenses, beginning in early adulthood. So this is not a process unique to middle age. But by middle adulthood, many adults have become considerably better able to handle anxieties and stresses without resorting to the most reality-distorting forms of defense.

Sex-Role Crossover.   A rather different view of personality change in middle adulthood comes from anthropologist David Gutmann, whose ideas you have already met in the concept of the parental imperative. His studies of many cultures led him to conclude that sex roles change again in late middle age. At that time, Gutmann argues, men's and women's roles "cross over," with men beginning to express more feminine qualities and women expressing more masculine qualities. Women become more assertive, men more passive. He says:

> Paradoxically, these gender reversals are most evident in those culture areas that also sponsor the fierce machismo of younger men, for example, rural Mexico and the American Southwest. Thus, as Indian women age, they can enter the ritual dances that are closed to younger women. By the same token, without feeling shame or censure, older Indian men can join the ranks of the women. (1987, p. 95)

There are many other examples. Older Iroquois women become "manly-hearted" and can hold religious and political office for the first time in their lives. Japanese women over 60, Gutmann reports, acquire a whole range of freedoms, including implicit permission to make bawdy jokes in mixed company; older women in Lebanese villages become similarly bawdy, aggressive, and controlling toward males.

These various views of personality change in the middle years of adulthood do not paint a single coherent picture, even though they all point to *some* kind of change in personality past mid-life. The adult in her sixties seems less intense, less preoccupied with achieving specific goals, perhaps slightly more introverted, perhaps more willing or able to adapt to circumstances, more able (or willing) to express all facets of herself.

But by no means all the evidence fits with even this very general description. For example, Schaie and Willis (1991) find that adults in their sixties become *less* flexible in their attitudes and their thinking. And Carol Ryff could find no sign of greater interiority among older adults when she attempted to measure Neugarten's concept directly. And of course we should not forget all the evidence showing that many personality traits are highly consistent over middle adulthood, including the five traits McCrae and Costa have identified.

There are several possible reasons why the findings should be so difficult to add up. First, there is really very little research on personality change in the years of middle adulthood. Longitudinal studies, for example, tend to begin either in early adulthood or at age 60 or so, and they rarely cover the middle adult years.

In addition, individual variability seems to be higher in middle adulthood (and higher still in old age) than is true in early adulthood (Nelson & Dannefer, 1992). Perhaps because of the power of the central roles, young adults are much more likely to march to the same drummer; by middle adulthood, there are many different beats. Trajectories have diverged. Most adults this age are healthy, but some are not; some have achieved their work goals, while others have not. Some achieve generativity and move toward grappling with the task of integrity. Some have given up immature defense mechanisms while others have not. In Loevinger's terms, some shift from the conformist stance of early adulthood to a more individualistic stance. Some later move on to a stage she calls *autonomous*, in which the individual moves from a preoccupation with self toward greater humanitarian concern. All these variations mean that there is much less likely to be a *shared* pattern of personality change. There may be an underlying pathway described by a shift toward lessened achievement strivings, less intensity, more introversion, and more mature defenses. But even if the path itself is shared—a point on which not all observers or theorists would agree—not all adults will move the same distance along it, which makes it far more difficult to detect the direction of change. What we need now is a more subtle look at personality continuity and change in these middle years, one that takes into account the wider degree of variability, the different levels of growth or development.

▶ Individual Differences

A look at individual differences in adult life experiences may give us one kind of window on the variability of middle adult patterns. The pathway an adult follows, or the degree of movement along any one pathway, is affected by a whole range of factors, including individual family history and personality—which I've explored in the "across development" box—as well as the stresses and crises each person has had to cope with.

All of us deal with some stresses, including the daily hassles of working with annoying coworkers, a long commute, racial or ethnic or gender prejudice that may be directed our way, an in-law we simply can't bear, or whatever. By mid-life, many of us have also encountered specific crises, such as a divorce, poor health, early widowhood, losing a job, or moving. What are the effects of such crises on adult life patterns?

One effect you have already read about: high levels of stress, whether from chronic hassles or specific crises, are associated with poorer immune function and poorer health. But many significant crises have an impact on other areas of the adult's life as well. Let me say just a bit more about two particularly common such crises, divorce and unemployment.

Divorce

Between 40 and 50 percent of current cohorts of young adults in the United States will eventually divorce (Glick & Lin, 1986). In Chapter 8 I talked about the substantial effects divorce has on children. Certainly it is no less disruptive for adults, and it may have significant consequences for the patterning or sequencing of adult roles.

ACROSS DEVELOPMENT
Predictions of Psychological Adjustment at Mid-Life from Earlier Measures of Personality and Family Background

Can we tell what kind of middle adulthood a person is likely to have, based on what we know about his childhood, adolescence, or early adult life? To answer this question we obviously need long-term longitudinal data, of which we have very little. But there are some extremely interesting fragments of information, from both the Berkeley/Oakland study and the Grant study of Harvard men.

In both studies, middle-aged psychological health was judged by comparing each subject to an ideal of some kind. In the Berkeley study, a Q-sort pattern was established which defined an ideally healthy middle-aged adult as warm, compassionate, dependable, responsible, insightful, productive, candid, and calm. Each subject's own descriptive Q-sort was then compared to this ideal.

In the case of the Grant study, George Vaillant (1975; Vaillant & Vaillant, 1990) identified specific behaviors or accomplishments he considered signs of psychological adjustment, including enjoyment of one's job, stable marriage, steady advance in career, low level of illness, regular vacations, and low use of alcohol or other drugs. Each man in this study was then compared to these standards.

In the Berkeley study, those who were closer to the ideal of psychological health at 40 and 50 had grown up with more open-minded, intellectually competent parents, who had stable marriages and used more reasonable and consistent types of control with their child. (In Baumrind's terms, these families might well be described as authoritative.) Their mothers were warm, pleasant, poised, and nondefensive. As teenagers, these better adjusted adults were more adept in their relationships with both peers and adults (Livson & Peskin, 1981; Peskin & Livson, 1981; Hightower, 1990).

Similarly, men in the Grant study who were better adjusted at mid-life had come from warmer families and had better relationships with both their fathers and mothers in childhood than had less well adjusted middle-aged men. Collectively, these findings suggest the not-so-surprising conclusion that those who start out well are likely to continue along that path. And "starting well" seems to include the components of warmth from parents and good social skills. But none of these links between childhood and adulthood is incredibly strong. There are many adults who start well who do not look so put together at 45 or 50, and many who came from unstable or difficult childhoods who nonetheless look healthy at middle age.

One possible explanation for such discontinuities comes from yet another analysis of the Berkeley data, this time by Florine Livson (1976, 1981). She began by identifying a group of adults who had all been rated as high in overall psychological health when they were 50. Because all these subjects had also been rated on the same scale when they were 40, Livson was able to identify two subsets: those who were rated as psychologically healthy or mature at *both* 40 and 50, (called "stable") and those who had been rated as less integrated or optimal in functioning at 40 but who had got it together by the time they were 50 (called "improvers"). She then asked whether these two groups had different histories.

What she found was that those men and women who had shown stable patterns of psychological health in middle age were those whose temperament or personality as teenagers and young adults happened to be a good match for the prevailing sex roles and societal norms of their era. The stable women had been extroverted as teenagers, settled happily for being wives and mothers, had little personal ambition—a pattern that fit well with the expectations for their cohort. The stable men were achievement oriented and fairly conformist. They moved into adulthood, taking on the various roles, feeling comfortable with the expectations that they achieve and support their families.

In contrast, those who looked less healthy at 40 but good at 50 had been teenagers and young adults who did not fit easily into the roles assigned them. The men had been unconventional teenagers, often with artistic interests, often emotionally more expressive than the norm. They had tried to fit themselves into the norms for their culture, but by 40 they were unhappy. At that stage they kicked over the traces to at least some extent, and allowed some of their humor and creativity to flower. Similarly, the improver women had been more intellectual as teenagers (not so acceptable for girls of that generation), but had married at the usual time. By 40, they were irritable, thin-skinned, unhappy. When their children left home, they went back to school or found jobs they liked, and by 50 they had found avenues to express themselves more fully.

This analysis suggests that the *match* between the demands or expectations of a particular era and an individual's own temperament or interests may play a major role in shaping adult personality or psychological health. Those who fit easily into the niche assigned to them will move more comfortably through the early decades of adult life. Those who do not match well—either because they lack certain skills or because of basic temperament—will struggle far more. Some will not succeed in that struggle, perhaps turning to drugs or alcohol, becoming depressed, or moving through a series of unsuccessful relationships. Others, though, like the "improvers" Livson identified, will respond to the struggle with personal growth and will eventually find ways to express their own qualities. This may be particularly possible in middle age, when "detribalization" becomes acceptable, when the roles fit more loosely. For some, then, middle age offers an opportunity for individual expression that may not be so apparent in early adult life.

Psychological Effects. At a psychological level, divorce is clearly a major stressor. It is associated with increases in both physical and emotional illness. Recently separated or divorced adults have more automobile accidents, are more likely to commit suicide, lose more days at work because of illness, and are more likely to become depressed (Bloom, White & Asher, 1979; Menaghan & Lieberman, 1986; Stack, 1989). They also report strong feelings of failure and a loss of self-esteem, as well as loneliness (Chase-Lansdale & Hetherington, 1990). These negative effects are strongest in the first months after the separation or divorce, much as we see the most substantial effects for children during the first 12 to 24 months.

Longer-term effects vary far more. Some adults seem to grow from the experience and show better psychological functioning five or ten years later than they had shown before the divorce. Others seem to be worse off psychologically, even ten years later (Wallerstein, 1986). There is some indication that those who remarry are likely to be happier than those who remain single—yet another bit of evidence supporting the general conclusion that marriage (or a stable partnership) is linked to better mental and physical health. Yet for those whose second marriage ends in divorce, the negative consequences can be substantial (Spanier & Furstenberg, 1987). At the moment, the most we can say is that there is a great deal of heterogeneity in adults' responses to divorce. And we know very little about the factors that might predict good or poor long-term reactions, except that we know that those adults with adequate social support are less disrupted in the short term (Chase-Lansdale & Hetherington, 1990).

Economic Effects. The psychological effects of divorce are often significantly exacerbated by serious economic effects, particularly for women. Because most men have had continuous work histories, they commonly leave a marriage with far greater earning power than do women. Women not only typically lack high earning capacity, they also usually retain custody of any children, with attendant costs. Several longitudinal studies in both the United States and European countries such as Germany show that divorced men generally improve in their economic position, while divorced women are strongly adversely affected. Estimates of the degree of women's loss range from 71 percent to about 20 percent of income after divorce, but all studies show at least some negative short-term effect, with the average being a drop of about 40 to 50 percent in total family income or per capita income (Holden & Smock, 1991; Morgan, 1991: Burkhauser et al., 1991). This negative economic effect does not disappear quickly, if at all. The most reliable means of economic recovery is remarriage, which brings most women back to near or above pre-divorce levels. For those women who do not remarry, however, the economic effects are more lasting. The data in Figure 16.7 are quite typical. They come from a panel study of over 5000 women, aged 30 to 44 at the start of the study, who were reinterviewed regularly for 15 years (Morgan, 1991). You can see that widowed and separated women, as well as those divorced, show a rapid drop in income, and that the lower level of income remains even seven to eight years after the marital transition occurred.

Such a long-term economic loss from divorce seems to be especially likely for working-class women, or those with relatively low levels of education. Women who were earning above-average incomes before their divorce are more likely to recover, even if they do not remarry (Holden & Smock, 1991).

I do not want to minimize the stressful effects of this kind of economic hardship on divorcing women, but I find it very interesting that, despite their relative lack of economic stress, divorced men nonetheless seem to show more psychological symptoms than do divorced women. The difference may be linked to women's more intimate and extensive social support networks, which they use to very good effect in the aftermath of a divorce.

Age Differences in the Effects of Divorce. Because half of all divorces occur within the first seven years of marriage, the majority of divorces actually occur during early

Another possible explanation of all these findings is that people who are already more depressed or unhealthy are more likely to divorce. What kind of evidence would you have to have to rule out this explanation?

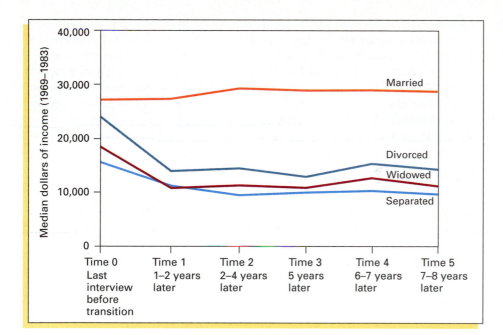

Figure 16.7 Women who move out of marriage because of divorce, widowhood, or separation show a large average drop in income. Unless they remarry, they are unlikely to recover to the same financial level they enjoyed during their marriage. (*Source:* Morgan, 1991, Figure 4.1, p. 75.)

adulthood rather than middle adulthood (Uhlenberg, Cooney & Boyd, 1990). Only about a quarter occur when the couple is over the age of 40. But divorce among middle-aged and older adults appears to be more emotionally disruptive than it is for younger adults (Bloom, White & Asher, 1979). This is precisely the opposite of what we see for widowhood, which is psychologically much more difficult if it occurs early in life. Both these patterns, of course, are consistent with the notion that being "off-time" for any kind of life change or transition is more stressful. Divorce is not easy at any time, but among young adults in today's cohorts it is at least fairly common and is thus "on-time."

It might also be that the economic impact of divorce—at least for women—is more severe during the middle years, although we have no data that I know of to test this hypothesis. Certainly there are many middle-aged women in current cohorts who have little or no work experience. After a divorce, such women—often called "displaced home-makers"—have very poor job prospects. They also have lower chances of remarriage than do younger divorced women (Chase-Lansdale & Hetherington, 1990).

Life Pathways. For many adults, divorce also affects the sequence and timing of family roles. Even though some divorced women have further children in a subsequent marriage, the average number of years of childbearing for divorced women is only slightly longer than what we see in women who remain married (Norton, 1983). In some cases, however, the total number of years of child *rearing* may be significantly larger for the divorced, especially for divorced men who remarry younger women with young children. One effect of this is to reduce the number of years a man (or woman) may have between the departure of the last child and the time when elder parents may need economic or physical assistance.

Divorce also brings a whole new set of roles. For a custodial parent, divorce means taking on some parental roles previously filled by the now-departed spouse. A divorced woman is also likely to take on a greatly expanded job role. And both men and women, custodial parent or not, must now deal with all the chores the spouse used to attend to, whatever they may have been in their relationship—fixing the leak in the roof, doing the grocery shopping, or taking clothes to the cleaners.

Remarriage, which occurs for about 80 percent of divorced adults, frequently brings the remarkably complex role of stepparent. If there are several sets of children involved, there may be stages added to the standard family role cycle. A women with children in elementary school may now find herself suddenly also the parent of teenagers, which demands different skills. Each of these changes seems to be accompanied by a new period of adaptation, often with considerable upheaval. If we think about this in Levinson's theoretical language, this means divorced/remarried adults have fewer opportunities to create stable life structures and have more periods of transition or crisis. It changes the *rhythm* of adult life, for good or ill.

Unemployment

Involuntary unemployment has effects that are remarkably similar to those of divorce. Adults who have been laid off from work or who are on extended strikes show heightened levels of anxiety and depression and higher risk of physical illness in the months after the job loss (Kessler, Turner & House, 1988; Liem & Liem, 1988; Price, 1992). Such effects are not unique to workers in the United States. Equivalent results have been found in studies in England, Denmark, and in other Western developed countries (e.g., Warr, Jackson & Banks, 1988; Iversen & Sabroe, 1988). You can see an example of this effect in Figure 16.8, which shows results from a study comparing 146 unemployed and 184 employed men and women in Michigan during the middle 1980s (Kessler, Turner & House, 1988).

Interestingly, just as remarriage alleviates many of the stresses associated with divorce, reemployment seems to restore health, emotional stability, and the sense of well-being quite rapidly.

The causal chain linking unemployment and emotional or physical distress is both direct and indirect. The financial strain of job loss is itself a major contributor to the heightened levels of anxiety and depression. When job loss occurs without significant financial strain—such as when the spouse continues to work at a well-paying job, or the family has other resources—the effect of job loss is only about half as great (Kessler, Turner & House, 1988). But there are also indirect effects through changes in family relationships and from loss of self-esteem. Most strikingly, marital relationships deteriorate rapidly after

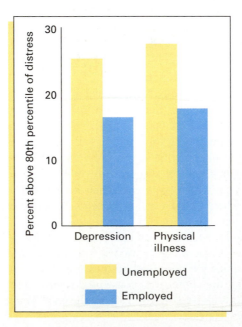

Figure 16.8 Adults who are involuntarily unemployed report more psychological distress on nearly every measure, including both depression and physical illness, as in this study in Michigan. (*Source:* Kessler, Turner & House, 1988, from Table 2, p. 74.)

one or the other spouse has been laid off. The number of hostile or negative interactions increases, and the number of warm and supportive interactions declines, so that the crucial ratio of positive to negative becomes worse and worse. Separation or divorce become much more common as a result (Conger et al., 1990; Elder & Caspi, 1988).

You may wonder whether there isn't some self-selection here. You may remember from Caspi and Elder's research, which I mentioned in Chapter 1 (Caspi, Elder & Bem, 1987, 1988; Caspi & Elder, 1988), that ill-tempered children are more likely to change jobs often as adults. They may also be laid off more often and thus be overrepresented in the ranks of the unemployed. But we know that this cannot be the whole story, because we see the same pattern of distress and discord in situations in which everyone employed in a single factory has been laid off, with no selection for the personality of the worker (e.g., Iversen & Sabroe, 1988). Longitudinal studies also show that even among those who were psychologically very stable and healthy before becoming unemployed, being laid off increases problems (Warr et al., 1988).

Age Differences. These negative effects of unemployment are seen in both young and middle-aged adults, but those between 30 and 60 seem to show the largest effects— the greatest increases in physical illness and the biggest drops in mental health (Warr et al., 1988). Those in the middle-aged group also show the longest period of deterioration in their status, compared to the younger groups who show a drop and then stabilize quickly. This pattern makes some sense in terms of the stages of men's work lives I talked about in Chapter 14. During the trial stage, young adults between 18 and 29 may interpret periods of unemployment as a normal part of the trial and error process of finding the right job. But in the stabilization stage, workers may interpret job loss quite differently— either as a sign of personal failure or as an unrecoverable loss of security. Younger workers are also more likely to be unmarried, with fewer economic responsibilities, and they may be able to return to live with their parents during their unemployed period. So for them, the stress is less pronounced.

Racial Differences. The dynamics of job loss appear to be much the same for workers of every racial group. Black unemployed, like other unemployed groups, show higher rates of distress and illness and lower levels of life satisfaction (Bowman, 1991). But unem-

In December of 1991, General Motors announced that over 74,000 employees would be laid off over the next few years. These men, who have just heard that they may lose their jobs, are likely to exhibit many symptoms of stress over the months to come.

ployment is clearly more common among blacks than whites in the United States and in most European countries (Bowman, 1991). Vonnie McLoyd, who has studied the effects of black unemployment, says,

> Even in the best of times, the official unemployment rate of black workers typically is twice that of white workers. Blacks' increased vulnerability to unemployment is attributable to several factors, including lesser education, lesser skill training, less job seniority, fewer transportable job skills, and institutional barriers. (1990, p. 316)

What is more, recent structural changes in the U.S. economy have made the problem worse, because there has been heavy job loss in manufacturing and other blue-collar job sectors in which black men are most likely to be employed. Black women, more often employed in the service sector, have been less severely affected by these recent changes. The effect of this pattern of change has been to increase still further the number of black families headed by women.

The magnitude of the effect of unemployment may also be larger for blacks than whites because it is so often accompanied by a lack of any sense of personal control over the situation. When jobs become increasingly scarce, even hard work and diligence will not necessarily pay off in reemployment. A sense of victimization is a common result, as is increased ill health and depression. Because many blacks, confronted with chronic racism or chronic urban poverty, are already functioning at very high levels of stress, unemployment increases the risks proportionately more. Go back and look again at Figure 13.3 (page 319), because it illustrates the impact of these cumulative stresses on the physical health of blacks versus whites over the adult years.

The Role of Social Support. As with all types of stress, the effects of unemployment can be partially buffered by having adequate social support. For instance, in a short-term longitudinal study of men who had been laid off because their companies had gone out of business, Kasl and Cobb (1982) found that those men who had adequate support from wives and friends showed fewer emotional and physical symptoms than did those with lower levels of perceived support. The irony, of course, is that one of the effects of unemployment is to weaken the marital relationship, which may be the central source of social support for many men.

The Effects of Timing

The pattern of effects of both divorce and unemployment fit the general principle that being "off-time" or atypical in your life trajectory has specific psychological costs. Divorce is more stressful in older cohorts, in which it is less common; losing your job is less stressful in your twenties, when it is fairly common, than in middle life, when it is off-time.

There are other mid-life examples of this same principle. If your children do not leave the nest by the time they are 25 or so, you are likely to feel extra strain, even a sense of failure (Hagestad, 1986). Those who become grandparents unusually early or unusually late seem to be less comfortable with the role (Troll, 1985; Burton & Bengtson, 1985). Those whose parents die early find themselves unexpectedly thrust into the role of family "elders" before they are ready for that designation. As one 40-year-old man whose parents had both just died said, "I'm too young to be next in line!" (Hagestad, 1986).

All of these are examples in which the person's life does not follow the pattern of the "expected life history." We may not be consciously aware of this set of expectations, this internal model of the "normal" or "expected" adult life, but we seem to be significantly and negatively affected by any violations of the anticipated pattern. Most generally, any time you experience a major life event at a time that is not typical for your generation, you are likely to experience heightened depression (Hurwicz et al., 1992).

ACROSS CULTURES
Very Early Grandparenthood in Black Families

The impact of being "off-time" is vividly illustrated in a study by Linda Burton and Vern Bengtson (1985) of a group of 41 black families in Los Angeles, each of which included a new mother, a grandmother, and a great-grandmother. Each generation was divided into those who were "early" and those who were "on-time" for being in that particular role. For the grandmothers, being on-time was defined as becoming a grandmother between 42 and 57; early grandmothers had all acquired the role before they were 38, several of them in their twenties. The large majority of these grandmothers had at least a high school education; few were on welfare. So these are mostly working-class or middle-class families.

What is striking is how different the experience of grandmotherhood was for those who were early as opposed to those who were on time. Early grandmothers reported far more strain and distress. In part this occurs because these young grandmothers are still in early adulthood themselves, with all that that signifies about role conflict and role overload. Many of these early grandmothers still had their own young children at home to rear. They were distressed to have the role of grandparent added to the list, especially if they expected to have to take on some of the task of rearing this grandchild.

But the off-timeness itself also seems to be disturbing. These women associate grandparenthood with being "old," and they do not want to feel old.

> I could break my daughter's neck for having this baby. I just got a new boyfriend. Now he will think I'm too old. It was bad enough being a mother so young—now a grandmother too! (Burton & Bengtson, 1985, p. 61)

So speaks a 28-year-old grandmother. Another who became a grandmother at 27 said, "I'm too young to be a grandmother. You made this baby, you take care of it" (p. 61). Many of these very early grandmothers did end up helping to rear their new grandchildren, but clearly they were less than thrilled by this task. In contrast, women in this study who became grandmothers at the normative time were much more willing to participate in the new child's care and much more pleased about becoming grandmothers.

There are clearly many confounding factors involved here. Very early grandmothers must, of necessity, have been early mothers themselves, so they are a different group to begin with. But these results are consistent with what else we know about the impact of being on-time or off-time in major life transitions.

Are All Crises Negative?

In Chinese, the characters that form the word *crisis* mean both "danger" and "opportunity" (Levinson, 1990). Mindful of this point, perhaps we ought to look to see whether crisis also has a less negative side. Indeed, many theories of adult development have as one of their cornerstone concepts the notion that stress or crisis can be transformative rather than (or in addition to) being disruptive. Erikson's theory has some of this element, as does Carl Jung's. Morton Lieberman and Harvey Peskin (1992) suggest several examples:

> The envy of youth in middle age may mobilize untapped resources of caring . . . ; the keener awareness of death in middle age may permit a more equanimous attitude toward one's mortality, a lessening of strivings for perfection, and a new realization of creative potential . . . ; the death of a loved parent may help free the survivor to become more his or her own person. (p. 132)

Whether some kind of stress or crisis is *required* for growth is another matter, although some such link makes a certain amount of sense. Just as it is pain that usually tells us that something is wrong with our physical body, so unhappiness or anguish may be necessary to get our attention, to tell us that we need to change in some way. Marriages may become deeper and more intimate if the couple has been through difficult times and learned how to communicate better; early widowhood may force a young woman to develop her own skills in a way she would not have done otherwise.

Yet it is also clear that psychological pain or suffering does not invariably (or even often) lead to personal growth. Stress is most often related to increased distress. David Chiriboga has some evidence for both kinds of effects of stress in several longitudinal studies of a sample that initially included a group of high school seniors, a group of newlyweds, a group of adults about age 50, and a group nearing retirement. All these

Can you think of any instances in your own life in which you have learned something constructive, or grown in some fashion, because of a crisis? Can you also think of an opposite example—an instance in which you have experienced a crisis or a major life change which led to distress or suffering but which did not seem to bring any redeeming growth?

groups were then reinterviewed 3, 5, 7, and 11 years later (Chiriboga, 1984; Chiriboga & Cutler, 1980; Chiriboga & Dean, 1978).

In all four age groups, Chiriboga found the usual negative effects of stress: those who experienced more life changes, particularly changes that involved losses in close personal relationships, showed higher rates of depression, poorer health, and lower life satisfaction. But he also found a few signs that some stresses were linked to lower levels of problems later. Among younger men, for example, those who had worried a lot about problems at work later had *lower* levels of depression; among older men, those who experienced a collection of small changes Chiriboga calls "disharmony," including changes in political or religious beliefs, or anticipation of impending stress, described *fewer* emotional problems at later ages. In the same vein, Norma Haan, in her analysis of the results of the Berkeley/Oakland study (1982), has found that adults who were physically ill more often over their adult years were rated as more empathetic and more tolerant of ambiguity in late middle age.

I am not at all trying to downplay the stressful effects of major life changes or crises. But I do want to raise the possibility that pain or crisis or stress may be necessary—although not sufficient—for some kinds of psychological growth, just as the oyster creates a pearl only if there is a grain of sand inside the shell. At the very least, I find this a comforting hypothesis because it suggests that there is always something to be gained from every painful experience. I would find life a good deal more discouraging if I did not believe that such growth is possible.

Summary

1. There are a number of signs that the years of middle adulthood are less stressful and happier than early adulthood.

2. Marital satisfaction is typically higher at mid-life than earlier. This appears to be due primarily to a drop in problems or negative encounters.

3. Middle-aged adults have significant family interactions both up and down the generational chain, creating a "generational squeeze" or "sandwich generation." Middle adults provide more assistance in both directions, and they attempt to influence both preceding and succeeding generations.

4. Individual families appear to have particular sets of topics or activities that serve as conversational glue between the generations.

5. There is little sign that middle-aged parents experience negative reactions at the time of the "empty nest," when the last child leaves home. On the contrary, the reduction in role demands may contribute to the rise in life satisfaction at this age.

6. The majority of adults become grandparents in middle age. Most have warm, affectionate relationships with their grandchildren, although there are also many remote relationships. A minority of grandparents are involved in day-to-day care of grandchildren.

7. Only a minority of middle-aged adults seem to take on the role of significant caregiver for an aging parent. Those who do, particularly if the parent suffers from some form of dementia, report considerable burden and suffer increased depression.

8. Women are twice as likely as men to fill the role of caregiver to a frail elder.

9. Friendships appear to be somewhat less numerous in middle adulthood, although there is no sign that friendships are less intimate or less important. The ability to create and maintain friendships appears to be a somewhat stable trait over the years of adulthood.

10. The majority of middle-aged adults work at least part-time, but the centrality of the work role appears to wane somewhat, and work satisfaction is less

clearly linked to overall life satisfaction than at earlier ages.

11. The number of hours worked, on average, also declines as retirement age approaches.

12. Personality changes during middle adulthood are less clearly shared than are changes seen in early adulthood. There are some signs of "mellowing," a lowering of intensity and striving, but there is more variability in personality traits in middle adulthood than at earlier ages.

13. Variations in experiences of life changes and crises may account for some of the variation in personality patterns. Divorce, for example, increases emotional distress and physical illness and may permanently alter the role path and the financial status of an adult, particularly for divorced women.

14. Job loss also brings increased risk of emotional distress and physical illness,

both directly via loss of economic security and indirectly via deterioration of marital relationships and loss of self-esteem.

15. The negative impact of both divorce and job loss appears to be larger among middle-aged adults than among young adults. For both types of crisis, negative consequences are mitigated for those adults with adequate social support.

16. Any role change or crisis that is off-time, that deviates from normative expectations for that cohort or for the culture, is associated with higher levels of stress, including very early grandparenthood, early death of one's parents, or late departure of grown children from the home.

17. Some theorists argue that crises may lead to growth as well as to distress. Indeed, crisis or significant life change may be necessary for psychological growth to occur. This remains an open question.

Suggested Readings

Block, M. R., Davidson, J. L. & Grambs, J. D. (1981). *Women over forty. Visions and realities*. New York: Springer. (Not a new book, but a good review of information about middle-aged and older women.)

Cherlin, A. J. & Furstenberg, F. F. Jr. (1986). *The new American grandparent*. New York: Basic Books. (A nicely written book, aimed at the lay reader rather than fellow psychologists, that describes the authors' own and others' research on grandparents.)

Farrell, M. P. & Rosenberg, S. D. (1981). *Men at midlife*. Boston: Auburn House. (Also not new, but very interesting. This is a report of a study of about five hundred young- and middle-adult men in the northeastern United States. It includes case study descriptions of individual men as well as discussions of marriages, friendships, and other roles among mid-life men.)

Hagestad, G. O. (1984). The continuous bond: A dynamic, multigenerational perspective on parent-child relations between adults. In M. Perlmutter (Ed.), *Minnesota symposia on child psychology*, Vol. 17 (pp. 129–158). Hillsdale, NJ: Lawrence Erlbaum Associates. (All of Hagestad's papers are excellent; if you are interested in family interactions and cross-generational relations you might profitably read any of her papers listed in the bibliography at the end of the book. This one is particularly good.)

Vaillant, G. E. (1977). *Adaptation to life: How the best and brightest came of age*. Boston: Little, Brown. (This is a fascinating report of the lives of 100 of the men included in the Grant study of Harvard men. At the time this book was written, the men had been followed into early middle age. There are many intriguing case studies, which will give you a feel for the wide variations in adult pathways.)

SUMMING UP MIDDLE ADULTHOOD

Basic Characteristics of the Middle Adult Period

I've summarized the changes seen in these middle adult years in the table below, but the summary doesn't capture the most interesting aspects of this age period. What strikes me most about this period is how full of paradoxes it seems.

The most obvious paradox lies in the juxtaposition of high levels of marital and work satisfaction with a growing awareness of physical decline. A second lies in the fact that the tight grip of family and work roles loosens considerably in these years, but that this is also a time in which we acquire several new roles over which we have little personal control. We enter the postparental stage when the last child leaves home; we become grandparents when our children have children; we take on the task of caring for aging parents only if they become too ill or disabled to care for themselves. While we may have some influence over the process of our children leaving home, we have little or no influence over the timing of grandchildren or over our parents' health or disability.

The easing of the demands of such central roles as parent and worker is also part of another paradox because this change creates an increased sense of choice. There are more options about how to fill individual roles and fewer clear rules about how we must behave. At the same time, middle adults also seem to feel some decline in their sense of personal control. Brandstädter and Baltes-Götz (1990) have both longitudinal and cross-sectional data from their study in Germany showing that between age 40 and age 60, adults increasingly feel that their ability to achieve their goals is affected by conditions beyond their control. But in this same group of adults, there was also an increase between 40 and 60 in the sense that their ability to reach personal goals is dependent on their own actions. Thus there is *both* an increased sense of choice, *and* an increased awareness that there are uncontrollable forces at work, such as potential decline in one's own health or in the health of one's parents.

It may seem impossible that both these things could be simultaneously true, but if you think about specific examples it makes perfectly good sense. As I move through my forties and fifties, I may feel more and more that maintaining good friendships requires effort on my part, but I also re-

A Summary of the Threads of Development During Middle Adulthood				
Aspect of Development	**Age in Years**			
	40 **45**	**50**	**55**	**65**
Physical Development	Many types of physical changes become visible between 40 and 50, including vision changes, decline in aerobic capacity, skin changes; slowing of nervous system, and hence reaction time.	Menopause in women. Increased bone loss. Increased loss of muscle tissue.		Increased rate of hearing loss.
Cognitive Development	IQ increases to about age 50 or 55, then shows very gradual decline. Earlier loss on less practiced skills, e.g., spatial visualization. Little change in memory until fairly late in this period, although there is some loss of speed of recall.			
Personality Development	Erikson's stage of generativity.	Erikson's stage of ego integrity versus despair.		
	Some signs of "mellowing" after the peak of individuality, assertiveness, and confidence at 40–45.			
Social Relationships	Empty nest: last child leaves home.			
	Grandparent role acquired by most adults.			
	May take on role as caregiver of aging parent.			
	Work roles become less prominent; gradual decline in hours worked; preparation for retirement.			
	Heightened marital satisfaction.			

alize that I have no control over the timing of the death of my friends; I may become increasingly aware that my day-to-day health is affected by whether I exercise and watch my diet, and still have a growing awareness of the extent to which I have no control over basic disease processes.

Central Processes

What obviously lies behind these apparent paradoxes is a set of changes in the centrality of the biological and social clocks in this middle adult period. In early adulthood, the social clock is positively deafening, while the biological clock is all but inaudible. In middle adulthood, the two are far more balanced in their effects: the social clock becomes less and the biological clock more significant. The weakening of the social clock gives rise to that increased sense of choice and personal control, while the rise of the biological clock contributes to the sense of loss of control.

The Biological Clock

It is certainly during these years that the first signs of aging become visible to most of us. We may need to wear glasses for the first time; hair begins to turn white; skin becomes more noticeably wrinkled; it becomes harder to climb several flights of stairs or to regain fitness after losing it. I pointed out repeatedly in Chapter 15 that most of these changes are quite gradual and that there is wide individual variability in their timing. But it is impossible to move through the middle adult years without awareness of *some* physical decline or deterioration.

David Karp (1988) has documented the growing awareness of this change in a wonderfully evocative series of interviews with men and women in their fifties. This is by no means a random sample. All of the 72 subjects were white, all worked in pro-

fessional occupations. We simply don't know whether working-class or minority adults would describe their experiences in the same terms. Still, this study gives us a rare in-depth view of the experiences of middle-aged adults, for whom, as Karp says, "the fact of aging seems to be one of life's great surprises" (p. 729).

The surprise is sprung from both the body and the culture. The body messages include all the many manifestations of slowing down. One of the men Karp interviewed said:

I'm getting more creakiness. I'm snoring at night. I can still appreciate beauty in a woman certainly, but you know, the testosterone is not quite there. I've also been noticing it with my kid over the last few years. My kid was playing baseball and I wasn't getting down for the ground balls as much. We'd go down to the field and I'd say, "John, instead of those ground

balls, why don't you hit me some fly balls." And I wouldn't go out so far because it was harder for me to throw the balls in. I noticed those changes. (p. 730)

The cultural messages may be more subtle, but they are potent. Younger adults begin to treat you as an "older person," which may mean that you get either more respect or less, depending on the circumstances. Or you may find yourself eligible for various programs for "senior citizens." As just one example, I was quite shocked to be invited to join the American Association of Retired Persons when I turned 50. "Wait just a minute! I'm not retired yet."

There are also the generational reminders that come from the increasing infirmity or death of one's own parents. One of Karp's subjects said, "as I see my father becoming physically impaired I know it's going to happen to me eventually" (p. 731).

There are also generational reminders from now-adult children and from young people encountered at work. Most of us in this age range have become aware that young people seem much younger than they used to! Yet the paradox remains, because virtually all of Karp's subjects said that they still *felt* young on the inside. The inner picture of ourselves we have at 40 or 50 or 60 does not yet include the gray hair, the wrinkles, the slower body. So there are repeated moments of shock, when the body reminders and the cultural and generational reminders jog our awareness yet again that we are, indeed, aging.

The Social Clock

At the same time, adults in middle age frequently feel a sense of being at the height of their powers, of having learned the ropes and now being able to make things happen. One of Karp's subjects put it this way: "I'm more seeing myself as not just a beginner . . . but as having arrived" (p. 729). Others talk of an increased sense of the value of accumulated experience, even wisdom. Many talk of seeing their life in a more holistic way, from a larger perspective—perhaps a beginning of the process Erikson calls ego integrity.

This increased sense of knowledge, wisdom, and perspective seems to be one of the fruits of having learned the roles of early adulthood and then of having found one's own individuality through the process Levinson calls *detribalization*. But a greater sense of control and choice also emerges because at least some of the dominant roles of early adulthood have become considerably less demanding. In particular, the role of parent, which consumes an enormous amount of time and energy for perhaps 20 years, now becomes far more occasional and part-time. Inevitably this means that middle-aged adults have more time and energy for other roles, including the role of spouse or partner. The gradual reduction in the dominance of the

work role over these same years also means that there is more time and energy for other roles, perhaps including involvement in community activities or with friends. Many middle-aged adults reap the benefits of these changes in the form of increased marital and work satisfaction.

Influences on the Basic Processes

The extent to which any given adult will experience middle adulthood in these ways is obviously affected by a whole host of things, three of which seem particularly significant: health, the timing of family and work events, and the existence of crises and unanticipated life changes.

Health.   Probably the biggest single factor influencing the individual experience of middle adulthood is health. Most adults are still quite healthy in these years. But for the minority who experience significant ill health in their fifties and sixties, the recognition of physical aging is far more profound, and the sense of choice and control is far less apparent.

Among the Harvard men in the Grant study, for example, the two events that were most likely to shift a man in mid-life from good to poor psychological adjustment were either a significant deterioration of health or alcoholism (Vaillant, 1990).

Similarly, those who retire in their fifties and sixties are most likely to do so because of ill health. Such adults may find themselves in straightened financial circumstances, perhaps with inadequate pensions. And certainly their sense of control and choice is much lower than what we see in an individual who can select the timing of her or his retirement. Not surprisingly, adults who retire early because of ill health also enjoy their retirement far less and are more likely to be depressed (Palmore et al., 1985).

The Timing of Family and Work Roles.   Another highly significant influence on the experience of middle adulthood is the precise timing of various family or work events, most potently the timing of childbearing. There are both cohort and individual differences in such timing. For ex-

ample, women born in 1920 in the United States gave birth to their last child at the average age of about 31. For such women, the postparental period began at roughly age 55. Because these same women had a life expectancy of about 73 years, they could expect to live only about 18 years after their last child left home. In contrast, the average woman born in 1950, now entering middle adulthood, had her last child at the age of 25 and could expect to live to the age of about 80, which gives a net increase of 13 postparental years, half of which are in middle adulthood.

The same logic obviously applies to individuals. Those who bear their children late are reducing their postparental years and thus delaying the point in their lives at which the social clock becomes less dominant. These are not trivial differences, and they contribute greatly to the wide degree of variability in adults' experience of middle adulthood.

The same logic no doubt applies to the timing of various work experiences, such as promotions, although we have less direct evidence here. Someone who is still moving up an occupational ladder in her (or his) forties and fifties may continue to place the work role in a central position in her life far more than is true of someone whose career topped out at 35. Bray and Howard's study of AT&T managers (1983), for example, shows that those men who had moved furthest up the corporate hierarchy were more satisfied with their jobs in their forties and fifties. Interestingly, however, they were not more satisfied with their lives overall and were not better adjusted.

Findings like these underline yet again the wide variability among middle-aged adults in their experience of these years. There are obviously many pathways that can lead to life satisfaction in middle age. For some, satisfaction continues to be found through work. Many more adults seem to find it in their partnership or in other family and personal relationships.

Crises. Middle adulthood, like early adulthood, is also shaped by the various unanticipated life changes and crises each adult must confront. The years from 40 to 65 are very different for a divorced woman with few job skills than for a woman of the same age in an intact marriage who has a successful career. They are different for a man who is laid off from his steady job at age 50 and who cannot readily find other work than they are for a man who experiences no interruption in employment. Economic differences are not the only effects of such variations, although they may be substantial. Those who have experienced many crises, many losses, are more likely to experience episodes of ill health and are less likely to feel that they have control over their own choices and opportunities. And of course, both ill health and a sense of helplessness have widespread repercussions in many other areas of life.

Yet it may well be how an adult copes with such crises, rather than the crises themselves, that is most significant in shaping the experience of middle adulthood. In Vaillant's study of the Harvard men who participated in the Grant Study, for example, one of the best predictors of good health and emotional adjustment at age 65 was the *lack* of use of mood-altering drugs (such as tranquilizers) or alcohol at age 45 (Vaillant & Vaillant, 1990). Another good predictor was the maturity of the defense mechanisms the men had used at 45. Those who looked worst at 65 were those who had been most likely to deal with middle-aged crises by denial or repression, while those who were well-adjusted and healthy at 65 had used less reality-distorting defenses. The 45-year-olds who had turned to drugs or alcohol and who used less mature forms of defense had not actually faced any more crises than had the more mature men. But they had dealt with those crises, those strains, quite differently.

So what determines how an individual deals with crisis or life strains? One obvious answer is personality. McCrae and Costa have some evidence that adults who are high in neuroticism are more likely to react to crises in self-defeating ways. And you've already seen Caspi's data, from the Berkeley/Oakland studies, showing that childhood or adolescent personality patterns such as shyness or ill-temper predict a number of aspects of the adult life course. I also mentioned in the "across development" box in Chapter 16 that both Vaillant and the Berkeley researchers have found that those adults who look healthiest and most psychologically mature at age 40 or 50 are those who came from warmer families and who had higher self-esteem in adolescence or early adulthood.

But personality is not destiny. All the relevant correlations are comparatively small, so there are clearly many adults who begin with several strikes against them who nonetheless respond well to the normal crises of adult life and move into and through middle adulthood with grace and growth. And there are many who appear to have everything going for them who falter in the face of normal (or extraordinary) crises and begin a downward spiral, often including alcohol or drugs or depression. As yet we know painfully little about what may cause such variations. But I think this is one of the crucial questions if we are to understand either middle adulthood or the whole of adult life.

17

PHYSICAL AND MENTAL CHANGES IN OLD AGE

We turn now, finally, to the seventh of the "seven ages of man," the time of old age. Shakespeare, who is credited with the notion of seven ages, had a dim view of this final stage of the life span. He described it in *As You Like It* as "second childishness, and mere oblivion, sans [without] teeth, sans eyes, sans taste, sans everything." This is certainly no longer an accurate description of the years of old age in many parts of the world. But most life span theorists do at least agree with Shakespeare that old age is the seventh stage.

One of the most striking demographic changes in the past few decades—ranking right up there with the massive increase in women's labor force participation—has been the rapid graying of the population of the world. Because life expectancy has increased significantly, and because birth rates have declined in many countries, the percentage of the total population over age 65 has increased and will continue to increase dramatically. Figure 17.1 shows the pattern of increase for several individual countries, projected up to the year 2025. This change has been more pronounced in developed countries, but some increase has occurred in every part of the world (Myers, 1990). One major contributor to this pattern has been the existence of the Baby Boom cohorts, born after World War II and now entering middle adulthood, who will greatly swell the ranks of the elderly after the year 2010. By 2040, when most of the baby boomers will have died, the rate of expansion of the elderly population will drop sharply.

This demographic change will have a variety of effects, both obvious and subtle, on the culture of every country affected by it. Pension plans, including Social Security in the United States, will be severely strained; health care costs will rise dramatically; hospitals, nursing homes, and other health care delivery systems will come under increasing pressure. We will also undoubtedly see changes in the style or form of advertising on television and elsewhere, as ads are increasingly aimed at the elderly, as well as a shift in political

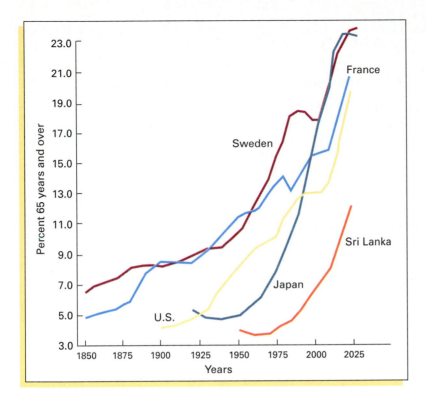

Figure 17.1 The rapid recent rise in the percentage of older adults in the population is not restricted to the United States. (*Source:* Myers, 1990, Figure 2–2, p. 27.)

power. Within families, smaller families and longer-lived elders may mean that a larger and larger percentage of middle-aged adults will need to take on the role of caregiver for a frail elder. Every segment of society will have to adjust in some fashion to this remarkable change in the age distribution of the population.

▶ Subgroups of the Elderly

It would be a mistake, though, to think of the elderly as a single group. Bernice Neugarten (1974, 1975) suggested one category system that has been widely adopted by gerontologists. She distinguished between the **young old** and the **old old**. In Neugarten's terms, the young old are those between 55 and 75, while the old old are those over 75. In most current usage, adults in their fifties and early sixties are still thought of as being in middle adulthood, and the term *young old* is used only to describe those between 65 and 75. But the point is still significant. Furthermore, the old old are the fastest growing segment of the population in the United States at present, so we need to know far more about this group (Longino, 1988).

One of the things that differentiates these two subgroups is the risk of significant disability or ill health. In addition, there are a number of measures of physical and mental functioning that show a more rapid decline beginning at about age 75, including total IQ, hearing loss, and aerobic capacity.

I do not want to overemphasize this distinction. If psychologists and gerontologists have learned anything in the past few decades of research, it is that the process of aging is highly individual. Some adults at 65 are already disabled; others are still full of vim and vigor at 85 or older. Perhaps it would be better, in fact, to distinguish between healthy and unhealthy elderly. Still, frailty is far more likely in an individual over the age of 75 than in one between 65 and 75. The distinction between young old and old old may thus

Can you think of other effects that this increase in the proportion of elders will have on society?

The graying of the population is a fact of life in most countries in the world.

help us to keep in mind that aging is not something that happens rapidly at age 65, and that the social and physical needs and abilities of elders may vary enormously.

Physical Changes in Late Adulthood

Life Expectancy

Let's begin with the most basic information: how much longer can a person of 65 expect to live? You've already seen some basic figures on life expectancy at age 40 in Figure 15.1. Table 17.1 adds to that information by telling you the number of additional years a person in the United States could expect to live if she had survived to age 65, 75, 85, or 95. The table also shows the average number of years of *active life expectancy*, that is, the number of additional years without a disability that would interfere with a person's ability to take care of her own daily needs.

Several things are clear from these data. First, as usual, they show that women live longer than men. This difference gets slightly smaller with increasing age, but it does not disappear. Second, these numbers illustrate yet again a point I made in Chapter 15, that women may live longer but they are more often disabled. A woman of 65 can expect to spend roughly twice as many years with some kind of disability as is true for a man. Still, three-quarters of her remaining time is likely to be free of such disability, so the picture is not as gloomy as it may look at first.

Physical Changes in Specific Body Systems

I have already sketched the overall pattern of change and decline in various body systems during adulthood in Chapters 13 and 15, so I do not need to belabor the point here. For virtually all systems, some loss of function begins at about age 40 and continues gradually through the remainder of life—a pattern very like the general shape of the curve Denney proposes in her overall model of cognitive and physical change in adulthood (Figure 13.5, page 324). There may be an acceleration of the decline after 75 or 80, but that does not appear to be true for every system.

Some of these gradual changes result in significant change or loss of function during middle adulthood, such as the changes in vision and in bone mass in women. Others do not typically lead to noticeable or significant functional change until past 65. Let me talk about a few of the latter group in more detail.

Changes in the Brain.   If you look back at Table 13.1, you'll see that there are four main changes in the brain during the adult years: a reduction in brain weight, a loss of gray matter, a loss of density in the dendrites, and slower synaptic speed.

TABLE 17.1 Life Expectancy and Active Life Expectancy for Adults over 65 in the United States

| At Age | Women | | Men | |
	Total Life Expectancy	Active Life Expectancy	Total Life Expectancy	Active Life Expectancy
65	18.57	13.61	14.44	11.87
75	11.70	6.97	8.97	6.44
85	6.44	2.25	5.15	2.55
95	3.65	0.35	3.22	0.64

Source: From Manton & Stallard, 1991, Table 4, p. S179.

THE REAL WORLD
Institutionalization Among Older Adults

Table 17.1 tells us that the average older adult will spend at least a few years with some kind of disability. How often does disability mean nursing home care? There are both optimistic and pessimistic answers to that question, depending on what statistics you look at.

One of the more optimistic statistics is that only 4.6 percent of all adults over 65 in the United States are in any kind of institutional care (Brock, Guralnik & Brody, 1990). More women are in nursing homes than men in both age groups, and many more of the old old receive such care, but this figure may be lower than you would have guessed.

A somewhat rosy view is also conveyed by the estimate, based on a study of a very large representative sample of all adults eligible for Medicare in the United States (Manton & Stallard, 1991), that the average 65-year-old American man can expect to spend about half a year in an institution before he dies. The average woman can expect to spend about one and a third years. But neither of these statistical approaches answers what is perhaps the most important question: What is the probability that any given 65-year-old will spend any time in a nursing home or other institution? In the United States, that probability is about .40 (Kane & Kane, 1990), a figure that suggests a more pessimistic view. If we put these three pieces of data together, it looks as if some kind of institutional care is common but by no means

universal in the years of late adulthood, and that such care is most often fairly brief. Only a quarter of those over 65 can expect to spend as long as a year in a nursing home.

When we look at the actual experiences of those in nursing homes, again there are both rosy and gloomy pictures. It is true that placement in a nursing home is often followed by death within a relatively short space of time. But it is *not* true that nursing home care necessarily *shortens* a person's life over what it might have been in home care or some other setting. Only when an older adult has been *involuntarily* moved to an institution (or to any other living situation) is there evidence that the move itself is a causal factor in rapid decline and death.

Involuntarily institutionalized elders show much higher death rates in the ensuing months and years than do equivalent elders who remain at home (Lawton, 1985, 1990), although even this effect is not inevitable. When the institution itself is one with high levels of warmth, individuation, and opportunity for choice and control, even an involuntary move need not accelerate the process of physical or mental decline.

The moral of the story is that it would be wise for each of us to plan ahead for our own older years, so that, should some kind of institutional care become necessary—as it well might—we will have maximum say in the matter.

Whether an older adult's experience in an institution is positive or negative will depend a great deal on whether the move was voluntary and anticipated.

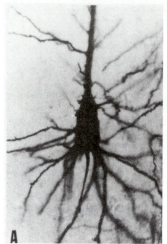

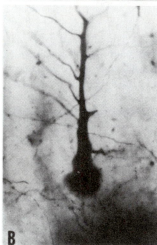

Figure 17.2 Changes in the density of dendrites with age are clear in these photos of a neuron from a normal mature adult (A) and in an 80-year-old (B). (*Source:* Scheibel, 1992, Figure 5, p. 160.)

The most central of these changes is the loss of dendritic density. You'll remember from Chapter 4 that there is a pruning of dendrites late in the first year of life, as redundant or unused pathways are eliminated. The loss of dendrites in middle and late adulthood does not seem to be pruning of this same type. Rather, there appears to be a real loss of useful dendritic connections. Figure 17.2 illustrates the change.

This dendritic loss is apparently not equally distributed over the brain. In some brain regions there may actually be continued increases in dendritic density in old age, as if to compensate for the loss in neighboring neurons (Scheibel, 1992). But there is little doubt that overall, the synaptic structure of the brain becomes less dense and less efficient. The reduction of total brain weight and the specific loss of gray matter both appear to be consequences of this reduced density of dendrites, rather than independent phenomena (Lim et al., 1992).

Dendritic loss also results in a gradual slowing of synaptic speed, with consequent slowing of reaction time in many everyday tasks. There is enough redundancy in neural pathways that it is nearly always possible to find some route from neuron A to neuron B, or from neuron A to some muscle cell. But with the increasing loss of dendrites, the shortest route may be lost, so reaction time increases. David Morgan (1992) refers to this process as a loss of "synaptic plasticity."

One final change in the nervous system, about which there is a good deal of dispute among physiologists, is the loss of neurons themselves. For many years the standard statement in texts was that 100,000 neurons were lost every day in adult life. This statement, largely based on early work by Brody (1955), has recently been called into question, because a number of new studies show no loss at all. But even if there really is a daily loss of 100,000 neurons, there is such a vast number of neurons in the brain that the proportion lost over a lifetime would be very small. Current estimates are that there are perhaps one *trillion* neurons in the brain (Morgan, 1992). A loss of 100,000 per day, even if it began at birth and lasted for a life span of 100 years, would be only about 4 billion neurons, leaving 96 percent still intact.

Precisely because there is such a vast number of neurons and dendrites, there are enormous redundancies built into the system. When dendritic loss begins, the initial effects on behavior are quite small. It is really only in very late old age that they accumulate to the point where some everyday activities become markedly difficult. Albert Scheibel puts it well:

The remarkable plasticity that neural tissue appears to maintain, even into advanced age, and the redundancy of neuronal circuits provide, in most cases, a good deal of functional margin, even in the presence of age-related structural change. In the long run, it is the loss of interconnectivity among neurons, individually and collectively, that eventually compromises computational power and produces symptoms. (1992, p. 168)

Changes in the Senses: Hearing. You've already read about the changes in vision in the forties and fifties (presbyopia) that mean that virtually all adults need at least reading glasses while still in middle adulthood. Normal hearing loss (presbycusis) begins at a similar age but doesn't add up to functionally significant loss for most adults until somewhat later. National statistics in the United States suggest that about 13 to 14 percent of middle aged adults have some hearing impairment, while for those over 65 this rate doubles (U.S. Bureau of the Census, 1990). Table 17.2 breaks this down further for the young old and the old old, showing the steady rise in hearing problems. The table also shows that, unlike many other disabilities of old age, men are more likely to experience auditory problems than are women. This sex difference is normally attributed to differential exposure to noise, because more men—at least in current cohorts of older adults

TABLE 17.2 Percentage of Older Adults with Hearing Impairment					
	Those with Hearing Impairment			Those Who Use Hearing Aids		
Age Group	Total	Male	Female	Total	Male	Female
65–74	23.2	30.3	17.7	5.7	7.0	4.7
75–84	34.3	43.2	29.5	10.7	13.6	8.9
85+	51.4	a	a	19.0	a	a

[a]No separate gender data are provided for this age group.

Source: U.S. Bureau of the Census, 1990, Table 192, p. 119.

in developed countries—have worked in environments with high levels of noise.

Hearing impairments common in older adults include several difficulties:

- *High-frequency sounds (presbycusis).* Presbycusis itself involves a loss of ability to hear high-frequency sounds at normal loudness. For the range of sounds in normal human speech (between 500 and 2000 hertz), the loss after age 60 is such that a given sound has to be about 1 to 2 decibels louder each year for the individual to report that he hears it. Evidence for this comes from both cross-sectional and longitudinal data (Fozard, 1990).

- *Word discrimination.* Even when the sound is loud enough, older adults have more difficulty identifying individual words they have just heard. This loss seems to be independent of presbycusis (Schieber, 1992).

- *Hearing under noise conditions.* When there is noise, the loss of ability to discriminate individual words is even greater. One effect of this is that older adults have a more difficult time at parties or in large mixed groups where there is a background of noise or other conversations.

- *Tinnitus,* a persistent ringing in the ears, also increases in incidence with age, although it appears to be independent of the other changes just described. Roughly 10 percent of adults over 65 experience this problem (U.S. Bureau of the Census, 1990). This *may* be caused by exposure to noise, but that is not well established.

Even mild hearing loss can pose communication problems in some situations. Those with such problems may also be perceived by others as disoriented or suffering from poor memory, especially if the person with the hearing loss is unwilling to admit the problem and ask for a repeat of some comment or instruction. Nonetheless, it is not the case that the older adult with a hearing impairment is necessarily socially isolated or unhappy. Mild and moderate hearing loss, even if uncorrected with a hearing aid, is simply not correlated with measures of general social, emotional, or psychological health of elderly adults. It is only when the loss is severe that we see an increase in social or psychological problems, including heightened rates of depression (Corso, 1987; Schieber, 1992).

Presbycusis and the other changes in hearing seem to result from gradual degeneration of virtually every part of the auditory system. Older adults secrete more ear wax, which may block the ear canal; the bones of the middle ear become calcified and less elastic; the cochlear membranes of the inner ear become less flexible and less responsive; and there are degenerations of the nerve pathways to the brain (Schieber, 1992). Basic wear and tear seems to be the culprit.

Changes in the Senses: Smell and Taste.   As with the question of loss of neurons, there is now a good deal of dispute about whether we lose taste buds in old age. Older

How do you think a hearing impairment is likely to affect the life of an older adult? Other than wearing a hearing aid, how could a person with a moderate impairment adapt his life so as to reduce the impact of the disability?

A third or more of older adults have some significant hearing loss. Whether this loss interferes with daily living depends on how severe it is and how well the individual can compensate. This man appears to be handling the problem well with the use of a hearing aid.

research showed considerable loss; newer research does not (Schieber, 1992). But there is agreement that the threshold for taste—the amount of some flavor that has to be present before you can tell that it is there—rises with age for both salty and bitter flavors, although not for sweet or sour tastes. These changes are not large and vary quite a lot from one individual to another (Schieber, 1992).

Changes in smell, however, are much larger and clearer. The best information comes from a cross-sectional study by Richard Doty and his colleagues (Doty et al., 1984), who tested nearly 2000 children and adults on their ability to identify 40 different smells—everything from pizza to gasoline. You can see in Figure 17.3 that young and middle-aged adults had equally good scores on this smell identification test, but that after age 60 there was a rapid decline.

These losses of taste and smell can reduce many pleasures in life. But they can also have practical health consequences. Smell enhances the pleasure of food, so as smell (and taste) becomes less acute, elders are less motivated to prepare tasty food. A loss of ability to detect salt may be particularly problematic because a person who experiences such a loss may add more salt to her food in order to taste it. High salt intake, in turn, may contribute to high blood pressure in some individuals.

Sleep Changes.   Sleep patterns also seem to shift in old age, with significant consequences for daily routines. Adults older than 65 typically wake up more frequently in the night and show decreases in rapid eye movement (REM) sleep—the lighter sleep state in which dreaming occurs. Older adults are also more likely to wake early in the morning and go to bed early at night. They become "morning people" instead of "night people" (Richardson, 1990; Hoch et al., 1992; Monk et al., 1991). And because their night sleep is more often interrupted, older adults also nap more during the day in order to accumulate the needed amount of sleep.

These changes are seen in almost every older person, even those who are clearly healthy. So this is not just a result of unhealthy older adults having trouble sleeping. It is a widely shared set of physical changes.

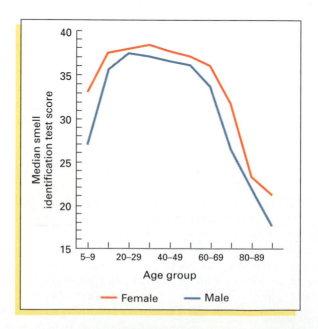

Figure 17.3 Doty's data show a very rapid drop, starting at about age 65, in the ability to identify smells. (*Source:* Doty et al., 1984.)

▶ Health and Disability ▶

All the physical changes I have described, here and in Chapters 13 and 15, and all the bad health habits that come home to roost, contribute to a major increase in health problems and disabilities in the years after age 65. One illustration of the size of the change comes from Vaillant's very long-term longitudinal study of the Harvard men in the Grant study. Eighty percent of them were rated as being in "excellent health" at age 40, but only 22 percent were given the same rating at 63 (Vaillant, 1990). When large numbers of adults are asked to give their own rating of their health, the results are similar. For example, in a recent study of a national sample of adults, 52.3 percent of those aged 45 to 64 rated their health as "excellent" or "very good" compared to only 35.2 percent of those over 65 (Verbrugge, 1989).

Ill health can manifest itself in several ways. For some (more often men) it means the rapid onset and rapid progress of some fatal disease, such as cancer or a fatal heart attack. Death from pneumonia, which becomes increasingly common in old age, also generally follows this rapid pattern. Many such individuals have few symptoms and little or no period of disability before the onset of disease. Others (more often women) have a number of symptoms of disease for a longer period of time, which may result in various minor or major physical disabilities. Because I have already talked about both cancer and heart disease in Chapter 15, let me focus my attention here on the second pattern, particularly on physical disabilities such as arthritis, and on the various dementias, including Alzheimer's disease, which frequently involve long periods of mental disability.

Physical Disabilities ▶

One widely used measure of ill health or disability involves asking individuals whether they are able to perform certain "activities of daily living." Figure 17.4 shows the percentage of those over 65 in the United States—not including those in nursing homes or other institutions—who report that they have trouble with two categories of such activities: personal care and "instrumental" activities like cooking and doing housework.

The incidence of such disabilities obviously rises with age. But it would be a mistake to assume that functional disability is universal even among the old old. It certainly is

What are some of the implications for *society* of the fact that older women live more years with disability than do men?

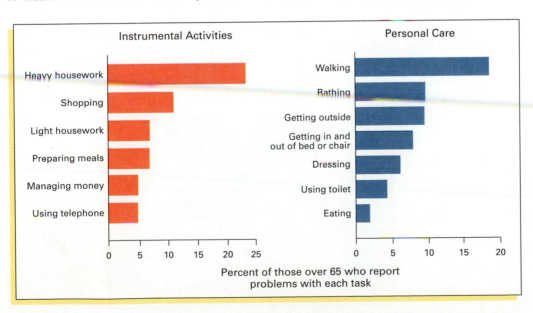

Figure 17.4 Many, but by no means all, older adults have difficulty with these everyday self-care and instrumental activities. (*Source:* Brock, Guralnik & Brody, 1990, Figures 5 and 6, pages 18 & 19.)

The cane tells us that this Greek woman has some physical disability, but it certainly looks as if she is still able to take care of her daily tasks.

not. For example, in a recent national sample of 1791 community-dwelling adults aged 80 or older, 67 percent had no difficulty lifting 10 pounds, 57 percent had no difficulty climbing 10 steps, 49 percent had no difficulty walking a quarter of a mile, and 47 percent had no problem stooping, crouching, or kneeling. A third of these 80-year-olds had no difficulty with any of these tasks (Harris et al., 1989). Nor should you assume that once an older person develops a disability, he is stuck with it forever. It is true that if you follow a group of elders over several years, those with some form of functional disability initially have higher death rates and higher rates of disability over the next few years (Harris et al., 1989). But there are at least some, even among those over 80, who improve in their physical functioning from one observation to the next.

The physical problems or diseases that are most likely to contribute to such functional disability are arthritis and cardiovascular problems, including both chronic heart disease and hypertension. Table 17.3 gives the current incidence of these problems in the United States.

Not everyone with these problems is disabled, but the risk of some kind of functional disability is two to three times higher among those who suffer from these diseases than among those elders who do not (Verbrugge, Lepkowski & Konkol, 1991). Because women are considerably more likely to have some level of arthritis, and somewhat more likely to have hypertension, they are also more often disabled in the various movements and tasks

TABLE 17.3 Incidence of Major Chronic Illnesses in Older Americans in 1987		
	Age	
Condition	**65–74**	**75 +**
Arthritis	46.4%	51.2%
Hypertension	39.2	33.7
Heart disease	28.5	32.2

Source: Brock, Guralnik & Brody, 1990, Table VII, p. 15.

of daily living that are necessary for independent life (Verbrugge, 1984, 1985, 1989; Brock, Guralnik & Brody, 1990). When we put these bits together with the fact that women are more likely to be widowed and thus would lack a partner who could assist with these daily living tasks, it should not be surprising that there are more women than men living with their children or in nursing homes.

Mental Disabilities: Alzheimer's Disease and Other Dementias

Another major disease symptom that is found predominantly among those over 65 is **dementia**, a term used for any global deterioration of intellectual functions, including loss of memory, judgment, social functioning, and control of emotions. Strictly speaking, dementia is a symptom and not a disease. It can be caused by a wide variety of conditions, including Alzheimer's disease, Parkinson's disease, depression, multiple small strokes (called *multi-infarct dementia*), multiple blows to the head (such as among boxers), a single head trauma, some kinds of tumor, advanced alcoholism, vitamin B_{12} deficiency, advanced stages of AIDS, and some kinds of infections (Horvath & Davis, 1990; Anthony & Aboraya, 1992). Of all these, the two most common forms are **Alzheimer's disease,** (sometimes also called *senile dementia of the Alzheimer's type*, or SDAT) which accounts for half or more of all cases, and multi-infarct dementia.

I have given you this list of possible causes of dementia so you will understand that not all older adults who show progressive problems with memory and problem solving are necessarily suffering from Alzheimer's disease.

Unfortunately, there is at present no way of conclusively diagnosing Alzheimer's; only at autopsy can a pathologist be certain that that was the problem. But many of the other causes of dementia *can* be diagnosed before death, and many can be ameliorated or even cured, which makes differential diagnosis very important. For example, both depression and problems with repeated small strokes may be treated with medication. Differential diagnosis may also be highly important for family members. Because a propensity to Alzheimer's disease seems to be at least partly heritable, while most other causes of dementia are not, sons and daughters may want to be sure of the source of any dementia in their aging parent. I have one friend, for example, whose mother is in a nursing home suffering from severe dementia. My friend intends to have the specific diagnosis confirmed by autopsy after her mother's death, if only so that she can make more intelligent plans now for the possibility that she might suffer from a similar symptom in her own old age.

Incidence of Dementias Among the Elderly.   Researchers have not yet come to complete agreement on just how common dementia is among older adults. The most common figure, based on more than 50 epidemiological studies in many different developed countries (including the United States, Sweden, France, Great Britain, Italy, and Japan) is that roughly 5 percent of those over 65 exhibit significant symptoms of dementia (Anthony & Aboraya, 1992). These same studies also show a clear rise in risk with advancing age. Dementia occurs at a low rate—1 to 3 percent—among the young old. The rate then rises steeply, affecting perhaps 5 to 8 percent of those between ages 75 and 84, and perhaps as many as 15 percent of those older than 85.

Results from at least one recent study, however, suggest that these rate estimates may be too low. Denis Evans and his colleagues (Evans et al., 1989), in a carefully selected and carefully tested sample in Boston, found that 3 percent of those between ages 56 and 74, 18.7 percent of those between 75 and 84, and fully 47.2 percent of those over 85 were classified as "probable Alzheimer's." At this stage we simply do not know whether these numbers reflect an aberration of the particular sample Evans studied, or whether other, equally detailed surveys would reveal similarly high rates. Settling this question has obvious practical importance for all of us.

Think for a minute about the practical implications of this. What differences would it make to society if the real rate of dementia among those over 75 were 8 percent or 20 percent?

ACROSS CULTURES
Ethnic Group Differences in Health and Disability in Late Adulthood in the United States

All the figures I have given you on health and disability in the aged are average numbers for the entire United States population. But it is important to ask whether these figures are equally valid for all minority groups. You will not be surprised to know that they are not. But it is not the case that all minority groups are disadvantaged. Each minority group has a different pattern of death and disability. Before I give you some of the details, I need to emphasize that in most cases we cannot sort out the differential roles of ethnicity and social class. Those minority groups that show the highest rates of disability and the shortest life expectancy are generally also those with higher percentages of older adults living in poverty, and both factors undoubtedly affect the pattern we see.

The least healthy group of elders appear to be Native Americans. Indeed, some authors contend that the ''elder American Indian may be the most significantly deprived individual in the country'' (Stanford & Du Bois, 1992), although there is little national data to support this assertion. One fact we do have is that Native Americans have the shortest life expectancy of any minority group in the United States. Native American elders are also more likely than are other groups to suffer from several potentially disabling diseases, most notably diabetes and alcoholism. In many tribes, 20 percent of the middle-aged and elderly have been diagnosed with diabetes, linked to high rates of obesity as well as genetic propensity (Markides & Mindel, 1987). Markides and Mindel conclude that

despite the lack of adequate data on such indicators as self-rated health, restriction of activity, and bed-disability days, there is little doubt that Native Americans are disadvantaged on all such variables. These disadvantages are no doubt related to physically demanding labor, poor nutrition, unsanitary living conditions, as well as poor access to adequate medical care. (p. 90)

African-American elders are also disadvantaged in health, as you already know from earlier chapters. Blacks have shorter life expectancies, higher rates of disability, and higher rates of certain diseases, such as hypertension. A relative disadvantage continues in elderly blacks, but the size of the disadvantage diminishes somewhat. One sign of this is that among those who reach the age of 75, life expectancy is *longer* among blacks than whites, a crossover effect that is particularly clear for elderly black women (Johnson, Gibson & Luckey, 1990). Similarly, while more older blacks describe their health as fair or poor than is true for older whites, the difference is smaller than was true in middle adulthood. But these facts do not mean that blacks are getting healthier as they age. Instead, this pattern of findings seems to be another illustration of one of the classic pitfalls of cross-sectional comparisons. Only those blacks who are relatively healthier survive to late adulthood.

In contrast to the story for both Native Americans and African

---

The Characteristics of Alzheimer's Disease. Dementia of the Alzheimer's type is caused by a specific set of changes in brain structure, including most prominently a kind of tangling of dendritic fibers within nerve cell bodies, illustrated in Figure 17.5. All aging adults appear to have some of these neurofibrillary tangles, but the number of them is vastly higher among those exhibiting symptoms of dementia. The effect is to short-circuit many of the neural pathways, making memory and other everyday activities increasingly difficult.

The early stages of Alzheimer's disease usually move very slowly, beginning with subtle memory difficulties, repetitions during conversations, and disorientation in unfamiliar settings. Then memory for recent events begins to go. Memory for distant events or for well-rehearsed daily routines is often retained until late in the illness, presumably because these memories can be accessed through many alternate neural pathways. Eventually, however, an individual with Alzheimer's disease may fail to recognize family members, may be unable to remember the names of common objects, or may forget how to perform such routine activities as toothbrushing or dressing. Some patients also show angry outbursts, others an increased level of dependency and "clinginess" to family or friends (Raskind & Peskind, 1992).

Researchers do not yet understand the etiology (the origins or causes) of this disorder. Just as we do not know why cancer cells, which are present in low numbers in all of us,

Americans, the health of elderly Hispanic-Americans and Asian-Americans appears to be equal to or better than that of majority whites. For example, Hispanic 65-year-olds have slightly longer life expectancies than do non-Hispanic whites. Part of this difference appears to be due to a lower rate of heart disease and hypertension among Hispanics, particularly Hispanic men. They also have fewer limitations of activity due to chronic conditions. The other side of the coin is that elderly Hispanics are more likely to die from infectious diseases, flu, pneumonia, or diabetes than are other groups. The difference in diabetes rates is particularly large: two to five times more Mexican-Americans suffer from this disease than the general U.S. population, a difference not entirely explainable by obesity patterns (Markides, Coreil & Rogers, 1989). As yet, we know very little about the role social class or education may play in these patterns, although there are a few hints that the close kin networks in Hispanic families may serve as a protective, buffering factor for both mental and physical health among all members of this minority, whether elderly or not (Stanford & Du Bois, 1992).

Elderly Asian-Americans, particularly those of Chinese and Japanese ancestry, appear to have the best health and mortality pattern of any group, although this conclusion is based on relatively little data. We do know that Asian-Americans as a group have longer life expectancies, but this pattern is largely carried by Japanese-Americans and Chinese-Americans, both well-acculturated groups with high levels of education and social class. More recent Asian immigrant groups do not enjoy the same advantage. We know far less about the day-to-day health status of elderly Asians, although there are at least a few studies of inner-city Asians, such as those in Chinatowns in San Francisco or Los Angeles, that suggest that elders in these settings may have considerably poorer health and higher rates of disability than is typical for Asians in other areas (Markides & Mindel, 1987).

What general conclusions can we draw from these various profiles of health in different ethnic groups? First, it seems clear that the elderly in all ethnic groups have not shared equally in the recent improvements in health and health care in the United States. But it is not yet clear how much of this variation is due to social class differences, and how much to overt or subtle forms of discrimination.

Second, there are signs that there may be ethnic differences in genetic propensities for particular diseases, such as diabetes, coronary heart disease, or hypertension. We cannot be sure that these differences are genetic. The different groups may also vary in diet, in other health habits, and in access to health care. But the possibility is worth a good deal of further research. Finally, we know far too little about the impact of specific cultural patterns on health among the elderly. What role does family structure or social support play? Is it the case that the supportive family systems typically created by Hispanics and the extended family patterns created by blacks provide a buffering effect of some kind? And what role does acculturation play? Among Hispanics, there are hints that those who are *most* acculturated have the highest rates of depression and other emotional disturbance (Stanford & Du Bois, 1992). Is this widely true, and is it true in other groups? We have more questions than answers.

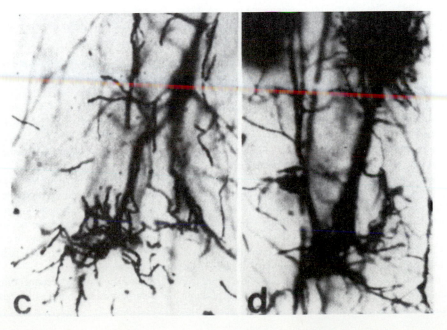

Figure 17.5 Compare these neurons, from a patient who died of Alzheimer's disease, with the normal aging neuron shown in Figure 17.2. (*Source:* Scheibel, 1992, figure 6, p. 162.)

suddenly multiply rapidly, we do not know why the normal, very slow increase of neurofibrillary tangles and other changes in the brain accelerate in Alzheimer's patients. But we do have some information about the *risk factors* for developing Alzheimer's, which I've explored in the research report below.

Mental Health

I have been careful to talk about Alzheimer's disease and other dementias as a separate category apart from the discussion of mental health in old age. The great majority of cases of dementia are caused by physical *diseases* and do not properly belong in the category of psychological disorders or emotional disturbances. Depression, which is a psychological disorder, can cause some symptoms of dementia, but most depressed individuals do not exhibit significant dementia.

RESEARCH REPORT
Risk Factors for Alzheimer's Disease

Studies of risk factors for any disease are often a first step in understanding the causes of that disease. Knowing that high levels of cholesterol are a risk factor for heart disease points researchers toward studies of cholesterol biochemistry; knowing that a high fat diet is a risk factor for cancer suggests new lines of research. Similarly, early studies of Alzheimer's risk factors have helped to set the research agenda of those trying to understand the origins of this disease.

As yet we have no large-scale longitudinal epidemiological studies of Alzheimer's disease. So we must base our understanding of risk factors on the alternative strategy of *case-control* studies. In such a design, individuals who suffer from some disorder (cases) are compared to a matched set of individuals who do not (controls). In the case of Alzheimer's disease, European researchers have recently increased the power of the case-control method by pooling data from eleven different studies of this type (Van Duijn, Stijnen & Hofman, 1991; Kokmen, 1991). The significant risks identified in these 11 studies were:

• *Family history of dementia, Down syndrome, or Parkinson's disease*. The strongest single risk factor is having at least one first-degree relative (grandparent, parent, sibling) with symptoms of dementia. Alzheimer's patients had 3½ times as many such relatives as did control subjects. Parkinson's disease, which also produces dementia, was also more than twice as common among the first-degree relatives of Alzheimer's patients (Van Duijn et al., 1991). The really intriguing finding in this set is the link with Down syndrome. Researchers have found that neurofibrillary tangles and other neurological changes associated with Alzheimer's also appear in Down syndrome adults, although at much earlier ages, by age 30 or 40. This link suggests that whatever genetic component there may be in Alzheimer's may lie on chromosome 21, because that is the chromosome with multiple copies in Down syndrome. This possibility has now been confirmed by early genetic studies (Raskind & Peskind, 1992). Please note, though, that results like this do *not* mean that all Alzheimer's patients have inherited the disease. Familial history is more common in patients who develop Alzheimer's early in life. But in the majority of Alzheimer's cases, particularly those with late-onset Alzheimer's, there is *no* family history, just as in the majority of breast cancer cases there is no family history, despite the fact that family history increases the risk.

• *Head trauma*. The Alzheimer's patients in the combined case-control studies were 1.8 times as likely as the comparison subjects to have had at least one episode of a head injury resulting in unconsciousness (Mortimer et al., 1991).

• *Maternal age*. Alzheimer's patients had 1.7 times the likelihood of having a mother who was 40 or older at the time of their birth, compared to control subjects (Rocca et al., 1991). This finding further strengthens the link with Down syndrome, which is also more common among children born to older mothers. In addition, the European researchers found a slightly increased risk for those whose mothers were very young—between 15 and 19, although this was not found in every study they included.

These three risks are the clearest. Other possible links are with a history of hypothyroidism or epilepsy, and a negative relationship with the presence of migraine headache: Alzheimer's patients were slightly *less* likely to have had a history of severe headache or migraine. There were also some signs that Alzheimer's patients were more likely to have had a history of depression, although this was true only for those whose Alzheimer's had begun fairly late in life.

No relationship was found between Alzheimer's disease and smoking, alcohol consumption, or exposure to environmental hazards such as solvents and lead. There have been various speculations about the possible role of aluminum exposure because higher-than-normal concentrations of aluminum are found in cells in Alzheimer's patients, but there are no good case-control studies to confirm or disconfirm such a hypothesis.

Ultimately, better techniques for diagnosis and treatment may emerge from the research that is stimulated by findings like these.

Just how common the various forms of psychological disorders may be in late adulthood is a matter of some dispute. For some disorders, such as schizophrenia or alcohol or drug abuse, the data are clear: older adults have lower rates of problems than any other age group. Where there is still uncertainty is in the case of depression.

The earliest studies of age differences in depression suggested that older adults were at higher risk for such disorders than any other age group, contributing to a widespread cultural stereotype of the inevitably depressed elder. This view slowly gave way in the face of newer epidemiological studies that suggested the exact opposite—that late adulthood was a time of particularly *low* incidence of depression and other emotional disturbances (e.g., Regier et al., 1988). Now this rosier conclusion, too, is being called into question in the face of growing evidence that the incidence of depression remains low until perhaps age 70 or 75, after which it rises significantly (e.g., Kessler et al., 1992; Lewinsohn et al., 1991). At the same time, the incidence of *major* depressive episodes seems to decline steadily over the years of late adulthood (Anthony & Aboraya, 1992). Thus, adults over 70 are less likely to have an extended period of deep depression, but are somewhat more likely to experience "the blues."

Part of the difficulty in arriving at a clear conclusion in this area arises from the fact that the typical measures of depression include questions about physical symptoms such as sleep disturbances, loss of appetite, and low energy levels as well as questions about mood. Since elderly adults are more likely to experience such physical symptoms, independent of any depressed mood, they end up with higher scores on self-report measures of depression. In addition, the early stages of dementia may also have symptoms of depression. When you remove these confounding elements from the data, the rise in depression past age 70 or 75 is much smaller, but does not disappear (Blazer et al., 1991).

The causes of depression in the elderly are not difficult to predict: inadequate social support, inadequate income, emotional loss such as bereavement, and nagging health problems. In Dan Blazer's study of 4000 adults aged 65 and older, 13.4 percent of those with incomes below $5000 had high scores on a depression scale, compared to only 5.5 percent of those with incomes over $15,000 (Blazer et al., 1991). Blazer and his colleagues argue that age itself is not the causal variable at work here. The risk factors for depression are essentially the same at every age, including poor health and lack of social support. To the extent that these risk factors are more likely to be present among the old old, depression rates will rise. When these risk factors are addressed or held constant, the rate of depression is actually lower among the elderly than among other age groups.

I know that this mix of contradictory research findings is confusing, so let me underline the one point I want you to carry away with you from the research on mental health in old age: increased depression is not at all an inevitable aspect of old age. Depression is no more a necessary part of "normal aging" than is heart disease. Even in the face of poor health, bereavement, or economic difficulties, the majority of older adults do not become depressed or anxious.

▶ The Effects of Physical Changes and Disease on Behavior in Late Adulthood

All the changes in the physical body that become more visible in the years of late adulthood may be interesting to physicians and physiologists, but for most of us they become important only when they affect our daily lives. I've described a number of such effects as I've gone along, such as the increased difficulty with activities of daily living that may accompany disabilities, or problems with understanding conversations in crowded or noisy conditions. But let me just say another word or two about the kinds of behavioral changes that may be troubling to those in late adulthood.

General Slowing

The biggest single effect is a general sense of slowing down. One of the changes that lies behind this experience is clearly the dendritic loss at the neural level, but arthritic changes in the joints, loss of elasticity in the muscles, and many other changes contribute. Writing things down takes longer (Schaie and Willis, 1991), tying your shoes takes longer, adapting to changes in temperature or changes in light conditions takes longer. Even tasks that involve words, which otherwise tend to show little loss with age, nonetheless are done more slowly (Lima, Hale & Myerson, 1991; Madden, 1992).

One of the arenas in which such changes add up to really significant differences in functioning is in a complex motor activity like driving. Young adults have more auto accidents than any other age group, primarily because they drive too fast. But older adults have more accidents *per mile driven* (Evans, 1988; Owsley et al., 1991). When adults of various ages are asked about their driving experiences, older adults are more likely to report that they have trouble reading street signs, responding to quick movements by other vehicles, or reacting appropriately when a vehicle appears unexpectedly on the periphery. They also say that they have more trouble judging their own speed and that the instrument panel is too dim (Kline et al., 1992). Some of these are obviously effects of the changes in the eye that occur with aging. But many seem to be related to the general slowing of reaction time. It becomes harder and harder for older drivers to respond appropriately to rapidly changing conditions.

Sexual Activity

Another behavior that is affected by the cumulative physical changes of aging is sexual behavior. Like all the changes I've been describing, the age of 65 does not mark an abrupt change in sexual activity. Figure 17.6 will give you some sense of the gradual change, with results taken from both cross-sectional and longitudinal studies. The cross-sectional data come from a nationally representative sample of 807 adults interviewed in the late 1980s (Marsiglio & Donnelly, 1991). The longitudinal data are from the Duke longitudinal studies (Palmore, 1981), in which several hundred adults were interviewed on two occasions, six years apart. The figure includes only those subjects in both studies who were married and thus had an available sexual partner. Notice how similar the findings are from these two sources, despite the fact that the data were collected 20 years apart, and that one is a random sample and the other is not.

Do you think that there should be an upper age limit for driver's licenses? Why or why not?

This woman may well be a skillful driver, but many of the physical changes associated with aging are likely to make it harder for her to adapt rapidly to changing driving conditions.

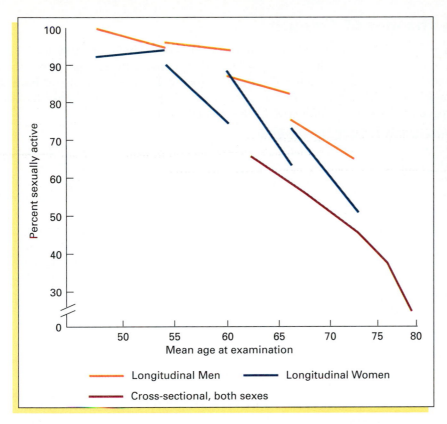

Figure 17.6 The red and blue lines in this figure all reflect longitudinal data. Each of these lines describes a group of adults interviewed twice, six years apart. The cross-sectional data, shown in the purple line, reflect interview responses of 800 adults of different ages interviewed only once. Both sets of information show that the number of adults, of those with an available sexual partner, who report that they had had sexual intercourse in the past month declines steadily in late adulthood. But it does not drop to zero, even among the old old. (*Sources:* Palmore, 1981, Figure 6–3, p. 87; Marsiglio & Donnelly, 1991, data from Table 2, p. S341.)

The data tell us that by age 70, only about half of *married* adults are still sexually active. Among those who are, frequency of intercourse (or masturbation) also declines, although not as rapidly. Those 75 and older who are still sexually active report having had intercourse nearly three times a month, which is about half the rate reported by those in their fifties.

This decline in sexual activity doubtless has many causes, most of them not yet well understood. With increasing age, both men and women report more and more problems with sexual arousal, although we have very sketchy and widely varying estimates of the frequency of this problem. Among men aged 60 to 65, estimates of impotence vary from 18 percent to 40 percent; among those over 80, the rate of arousal problems among both men and women is as high as 60 percent or more (Rossman, 1980; Keil et al., 1992). The changes of menopause may also contribute to declining sexual activity because the reduction in vaginal lubrication and the thinning of the walls of the vagina may make intercourse painful for some women—although, paradoxically, regular sexual activity seems to reduce both these effects.

Overall health is another major factor. Blood pressure medication sometimes produces impotence as a side effect; chronic pain may affect sexual desire. There may also be disinterest in or boredom with one's sexual partner, and there may be some effect of social stereotypes that portray old age as an essentially asexual period of life.

What is striking to me, though, is not so much that there is a decline in sexual activity as that many older adults, despite the physical changes, nonetheless continue to find pleasure in sexual activity. The more general point is that while many everyday activities may become more difficult in late adulthood, most adults nonetheless find ways to adapt, with inventiveness and some grace.

▶ Theories of Aging

By now you have read what must seem like endless descriptions of physical change and decline, all roughly described as "aging." But what is driving the change? *Why* does aging occur? There is still no universally accepted theory. For the moment, we have to be content with alternative explanations, which come in two basic subvarieties: biologically programmed aging and destructive environmental conditions.

Biologically Programmed Aging

Many biologists argue that aging occurs at the cellular level, resulting from a series of deteriorations in the efficiency of cellular functioning. For example, breaks in DNA strands are a common event within cells. In the vast majority of cases, the breakage is repaired, so the cell continues to function effectively. But over time, the small fraction of unrepaired DNA mounts up. As cells with such damaged material accumulate in individual organs, "aging" occurs (Tice & Setlow, 1985). It is also possible that the *ability* to repair damaged DNA declines with age (e.g., Hartnell, Morley & Mooradian, 1989).

Other cell-level changes include a loss of elasticity, a reduced ability to produce fully mature T cells in the immune system, and changes in cell proteins that result in lowered efficiency. The research that leads to these general statements has taken us a long way toward understanding physical aging, but it does not solve the deeper theoretical puzzle. We are still left with the question of why these changes should occur with age at all.

Genetic Limits. One theory that does touch on this deeper question begins with the observation that each species appears to have a characteristic maximum life span. For humans this seems to be about 110 or 120 years; for turtles it is far longer, and for chickens, far less. This persuaded biologists like Hayflick (1977, 1987) that there may be some genetic process that limits life span. Hayflick bolstered this argument with his observation—since replicated in many laboratories throughout the world—that embryo cells placed in nutrient solution would divide only a fixed number of times, after which the cell colony would degenerate. Human embryo cells will double about 50 times; those from the Galapagos tortoise double roughly 100 times, while a chicken cell will double only about 25 times. Furthermore, cells taken from human adults will double only about 20 times, as if they had already "used up" some of their genetic capacity. The theoretical proposal that emerges from such observations is that each species has some "Hayflick limit," after which cells simply no longer have any capacity to replicate themselves accurately (Norwood, Smith & Stein, 1990). There may also be species-specific limits on other cell functions, such as the ability to repair DNA, all of which contribute to the process we call aging.

Destructive Environmental Conditions

Cells might also be less efficient in their functioning because they have been damaged by external forces. Biologists who hold this view argue that the organism is not programmed to self-destruct. Rather, it is exposed constantly to random events that can damage individual cells. In particular, all of us live with background levels of radiation that might contribute to cellular damage, especially damage to the DNA. Such "hit theories" of aging were once very popular. But recent experimental research, in which animals have been deliberately exposed to varying levels of radiation, does not offer much support (Cristofalo, 1988; Tice & Setlow, 1985). Those animals that lived under higher levels of radiation did not exhibit signs of faster cellular aging, although they were more prone to diseases of various kinds.

What both these broad theoretical approaches have in common is the assumption that aging occurs at the cellular level and results from the gradual accumulation of small errors in cellular functioning. Such errors could result from external forces, from the operation of some kind of internal genetic clock, or from wear and tear from day-to-day usage of body parts—like the changes in the cells of the inner ear that are responsive to variations in noise exposure. What we see as aging is the product of all these factors. Vincent Cristofalo summarizes it in a compatible but slightly different way:

> One way to envision the organism's aging scenario is that each cell and tissue type has its own aging trajectory. Death occurs when homeostasis in one of the more rapidly aging components of the organism falls beyond the point necessary to maintain the organism. (1988, p. 126)

Does it matter, in any practical sense, which of these two theories is correct?

▶ Cognitive Changes in Late Adulthood ✎

If middle adulthood is the period in which adults maintain most of their cognitive abilities, late adulthood is the period in which those abilities decline more noticeably. Among the young old (65 to 75), these changes are still fairly small and there are still a few tasks, such as vocabulary knowledge, which show little or no average decline. But among the old old, there are average declines on virtually all measures of intellectual skill, with the largest declines on any measure that involves speed or unexercised abilities (Cunningham & Haman, 1992). Recall Schaie's comment that I quoted in Chapter 15, that "reliable decrement can be shown to have occurred for all abilities by age 74" (Schaie, 1983b, p. 127).

Memory

Changes in memory are also more clearly apparent in old age, although this effect varies depending on the familiarity of the material and the length of time it must be remembered. If your own long-term memory is working, you'll recall the West and Crook study I described in Chapter 15, in which adults were asked to remember a telephone number displayed briefly on a computer screen and then to dial the number from memory. This kind of simple short-term (or *primary*) memory task shows little decline even in very late adulthood. Where we see a loss with age is on *secondary* memory tasks, both in encoding and retrieval. The encoding side of this—the input process—would include such things as trying to memorize a phone number, learn a song or poem by heart, or learn a list of items to buy at the grocery store. The retrieval or output side would include problems like remembering someone's name, remembering the grocery list when you get to the store, recalling whether you were supposed to meet your friend Mary for lunch on Tuesday or Wednesday, remembering the name of the street on which the doctor's office is located, or the like.

Encoding Processes. Interestingly enough, the older adult has very much the same kind of difficulty in encoding as we see in preschool children—a failure to use efficient strategies for remembering new information. Given a list of items to memorize, older adults are less likely to use such efficient strategies as placing the items into logical groupings (a process memory specialists call "chunking"), or even basic rehearsal, although older adults—again like young children—can and do use such strategies when they are reminded to do so (Sugar & McDowd, 1992). This suggests that at least part of the difference may not be inability but disuse. Older adults, in fact, are much more likely to use such external aids as list-making to help them remember things, so they may be simply out of practice in the use of many kinds of internal memory strategies. Still, this can't be all the explanation because even with such reminders, younger adults normally outperform older adults on memory tasks.

Retrieval. When it comes to getting things out of memory, older adults are also at a disadvantage, although not on every task. When the task is one of *recognition*, older adults do about as well as younger adults. If all you have to do is say whether you have seen something before, or whether a particular name goes with a given picture, older

This French baker has little trouble remembering the recipe for bread he's been baking all his life, but he might find it takes longer to memorize a new recipe than it did when he was 25.

adults are OK. It is when they must spontaneously *recall* some item of information that they have difficulty. With increasing age, older adults experience more and more "tip of the tongue" phenomena, when they know they know something, such as a person's name, but cannot remember it (Maylor, 1990, 1991). So long-term memories become less accessible as we get older.

Familiar and Unfamiliar Material. Most of what we know about memory differences between young and older adults has been based on rather artificial laboratory tasks, such as memorizing lists of words. Perhaps older adults are really just as capable of feats of memory if the items to be remembered are more familiar or more meaningful.

I said in Chapter 15 that on such meaningful tasks there is little change in middle age. Among older adults the pattern is more mixed. In general, older adults perform more poorly on meaningful memory tasks, just as they do on laboratory tasks, but there are a few exceptions to this statement.

A number of studies show that under at least some conditions, older adults can do as well as younger adults at remembering some passage they have read. This equality of performance is particularly likely if the passage describes information with which both age groups are equally familiar (Hultsch & Dixon, 1990), although there is some indication that a delay in recall interferes more with older than younger adults. Other research suggests that older adults are just as good at *prospective* memory tasks, where you need to remember to do something in the future, such as making a phone call or paying a bill on a particular date (e.g., Poon & Schaffer, 1982). They are also just as good at remembering highly salient pieces of information, such as whether they voted in an election fours years ago, or the opening time of the cafeteria where they have dinner once a week (Sinnott, 1986; Herzog & Rogers, 1989).

But older adults are not as good at many other meaningful or familiar memory tasks, such as recalling whether they have performed some activity or not, such as turning off the burner on the stove before they left the house, or where specific buildings are located in a familiar town (Kausler & Lichty, 1988; Evans et al., 1984).

Further Caveats. This is an old tune by now, but let me sing it again anyway: Virtually all of this research is cross-sectional, and we know from studies in other areas of cognitive functioning that cross-sectional comparisons routinely suggest larger declines with age than do longitudinal data. In the case of memory studies, this difference is aggravated by the typical strategy of comparing college students to older adults who have less than a college education. In the few cases in which comparisons have been made between noncollege young and old adults, the differences in performance seem to be much smaller. For example, in studies of the use of memory strategies, researchers find that both noncollege young adults and older adults use fewer good memory strategies than do college students (Sugar & McDowd, 1992).

Despite these caveats, I nonetheless think it is inescapable that there is a real decline in memory performance in the late years of adulthood, although this decline is not uniform across all types of memory tasks (West, Crook & Barron, 1992). It is harder to get new things into memory and harder to get them out. Some of this may reflect the basic loss of processing speed that is part of aging (Salthouse & Babcock, 1991). There may be a loss in actual processing capacity as well (Babcock & Salthouse, 1990). Whatever the ultimate explanation, there seems clearly to be some average loss.

Problem Solving

Very nearly the same summary could be written about changes in problem-solving skill in old age. Laboratory tasks used to study this ability are varied, but one typical one involves asking a subject to figure out what combination of button pushings will turn on a light. On such tasks, younger adults do quite a lot better than older adults, using more optimal strategies and arriving at solutions sooner. This age difference appears even if the subjects are encouraged to take notes and keep track of the combinations they have already tried. Older adults under such conditions take fewer and apparently less effective notes (Kluwe, 1986)—a particularly interesting result because it suggests that the compensatory processes used by older adults, like note-taking, are not fully effective.

You might well argue, as some researchers have as well, that these are pretty artificial tasks. How do elderly adults do on more familiar or more practically relevant problems? Nancy Denney approached this issue by asking a group of older adults to help her identify a set of real-life problems that older adults might typically face. Here's one problem on a topic suggested by the elders:

> Let's say that a 67-year-old man's doctor has told him to take it easy because of a heart condition. It's summertime and the man's yard needs to be mowed but the man cannot afford to pay someone to mow the lawn. What should he do? (Denney & Pearce, 1989, p. 439)

How many solutions to this problem can you think of?

Denney then posed ten such problems to groups of adults of various ages from 20 to 79 and counted the number of safe and effective solutions proposed by each subject. On this task—intentionally biased to favor the older subjects—adults between 30 and 50 had the best scores, while those over 50 did least well (Denney & Pearce, 1989; Denney, Tozier & Schlotthauer, 1992). Longitudinal studies of problem solving, as is true of longitudinal studies of IQ changes, suggest that the decline occurs later than 50, but that there is still a decline. For example, among the subjects in the Baltimore Longitudinal Study of Aging, tested on a battery of problem-solving tests on two occasions six years apart, there were declines only after age 70 (Arenberg, 1974; Arenberg & Robertson-Tchabo, 1977).

Rainer Kluwe, after reviewing all the research on age changes in problem-solving ability, concludes that in older adults "the solution search, given well-defined problems, is not very well organized, it is inefficient, redundant, and finally not very successful" (1986, p. 519). Some of this may reflect cohort differences, but clearly not all of it. A real decline does occur, just as is true for memory.

Two More Encouraging Views

Such a pessimistic, albeit realistic, appraisal of the evidence can be balanced with two other sets of information, one suggesting that training can have a significant effect, and the other emphasizing the compensating effect of wisdom.

These senior citizens in Texas, lobbying their legislators, are demonstrating one form of problem solving. But research tells us that older adults on average are likely to think of fewer and less varied solutions to everyday problems.

Training Effects.   There is now an extensive body of research that shows that with appropriate training, older adults can significantly improve their performance on a variety of cognitive tasks, including memory tests (Kliegl, Smith & Baltes, 1989; Verhaeghen, Marcoen & Goossens, 1992), and IQ-like tests (Gratzinger et al., 1990; Kliegl, Smith & Baltes, 1989; Dittmann-Kohli et al., 1991). There is even one longitudinal study, involving some of the older subjects in the Seattle Longitudinal Study, showing that among adults in their seventies, the effects of such training persist over periods as long as six years (Willis & Nesselroade, 1990).

But—and this is a big *but*—these training gains do not bring the older adult's performance up to that of a young adult. When both older and younger adults are given the same kind of training, the most common result is to enlarge rather than to shrink the age difference. A study by Reinhold Kliegl and his colleagues in Germany is typical (Kliegl, Smith & Baltes, 1990; Baltes & Kliegl, 1992).

Kliegl tested 18 young college students and 19 older adults, with the two groups roughly equivalent in tested intelligence. The older adults, all physically healthy, ranged in age from 65 to 80, with an average age of 71.7 years. The task used was a traditional laboratory memory task in which the subject is presented with a list of 30 words to remember, each presented for some fixed length of time, with the time ranging from 20 seconds per word down to 1 second per word. When the whole list has been presented, the subject must try to write down as many of the words as possible.

After a pretest, each subject in Kliegl's study was given extensive training on a mnemonic strategy called the Method of Loci. In this method, you first memorize some sequence of images, such as buildings along your route to work, or a set of streets that occur in sequence. You create vivid images for each item in this series, and then you hook each item in the word list to one of the sequence of images. In Kliegl's study, the subjects were first given a set of pictures of 30 familiar buildings in Berlin and asked to memorize this set, in sequence, with a vivid mental image for each one. Only when every subject could repeat back this sequence in 90 seconds did they begin to use this sequence as an aid in remembering lists of words. In training sessions, each subject attempted to use the method, with the length of presentation of each word in the word lists gradually shortened as the subject got better at the task. Between lists, the experimenter asked the subject what images he or she had used, and suggested possible improvements. These training sessions were interspersed with test sessions to check on the subject's progress. Figure 17.7 shows the results from these test sessions.

The results are full of suggestive information. Note that the older adults showed clear improvement over time with both long and medium presentation times, but showed no improvement under the most difficult condition, the very short presentation times. This suggests that there are simply processing limits for the older adults that cannot be exceeded, even with training. More significantly, note that in every case the younger adults benefitted more from training than did the elders.

If we relate these findings to Denney's overall model, shown in Figure 13.5 (page 324), we might conclude that Denney has underestimated the degree to which the unpracticed and the practiced ability lines converge in later adulthood. The difference between these two lines, which a number of authors refer to as "reserve capacity" (e.g., Baltes & Baltes, 1990a), appears to be smaller in older adulthood than in the young. But there is *some* reserve capacity at every age that can be mobilized. This is true for measures of physical functioning, such as VO_2 max (maximum oxygen uptake), which improves with exercise even among the very old, and for measures of cognitive performance, which improve with practice at every age.

Interestingly, there is evidence from a recent study by this same research group that older adults in the very earliest stages of dementia have little or no reserve capacity. In

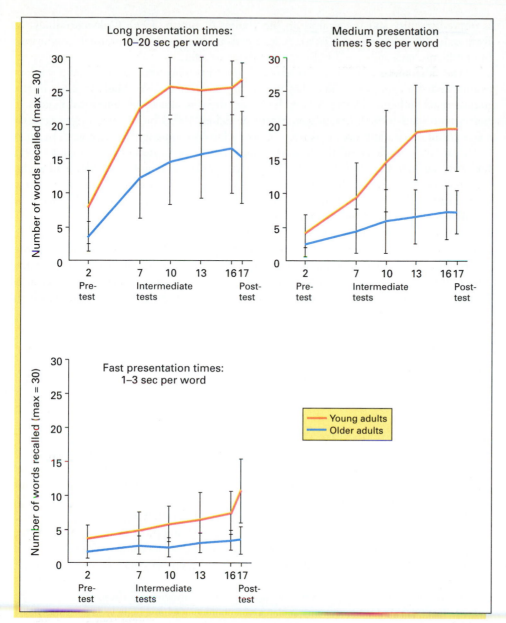

Figure 17.7 These fascinating results from Kliegl's study show that older adults can indeed improve their memory performance after training, but they don't gain as much as do younger adults, suggesting that the reserve capacity is smaller in old age than in young adulthood. (*Source:* Kliegl et al., 1990, Figure 2, p. 899.)

this one study, such individuals did not show significant gains in performance after extended training (M. Baltes, Kühl & Sowarka, 1992). Perhaps, then, in the early stages of some dementing disease, adults first push themselves to use all the reserve capacity they can muster, and only then begin to show the memory and other cognitive losses that characterize early dementia.

Wisdom.   Theorists who study cognition in older adults have also recently begun to examine more systematically the concept of wisdom. Are there some ways in which elders have advantages over the young because of their accumulation of knowledge and skills? As yet there is no agreed-upon definition of wisdom, but most authors emphasize that it goes beyond mere accumulations of facts. It reflects understanding of "universal truths" or basic laws or patterns; it is knowledge that is blended with values and meaning systems; it is knowledge based on the understanding that clarity is not always possible, that there is unpredictability and uncertainty in life (Baltes & Smith, 1990; Csikszentmihalyi & Rathunde, 1990; Sternberg, 1990a). A wise person, then, will have unusual insight into life problems, unusually good judgment or advice to offer.

Are older adults more wise? Virtually all theorists who have written about wisdom assume that they are, or assume that if wisdom exists, it is more likely to exist in the middle aged and the elderly. As yet, however, there is almost no empirical evidence. Baltes and Smith (1990; Staudinger, Smith & Baltes, 1992) have a few fragments that suggest that older adults are *as good* as younger adults on some measures of wisdom, such as the ability to understand the lessons or meaning to be gained from a single person's life. And Lucinda Orwoll (Orwoll & Perlmutter, 1990) has found that older adults who are singled out as wise by others are indeed different from their peers. They are more likely to be rated as high in what Erikson calls ego integrity, and they are more likely to show a global perspective—a concern for humanity as a whole.

But these very small pieces of evidence do not tell us whether some kind of wisdom is a benefit of aging for most adults, or even if there are more wise individuals among the elderly than are to be found among younger groups. But this line of theory and research does point to renewed interest on the part of psychologists in aspects of cognitive functioning that cannot be readily measured by standard IQ or memory tests, and on which older adults *might* have some advantage.

▶ Individual Differences

The single word to describe individual variations in patterns of physical and mental change in old age is *huge*. Some adults are already displaying significant disability and significant cognitive losses by their fifties and sixties; others seem to keep all their mental marbles, and most of their physical vigor, well into their seventies and eighties—even nineties. As an illustration, take a look at the data in Figure 17.8, which shows the scores on a measure of vocabulary knowledge (a crystallized skill) for four individual subjects in Schaie's Seattle Longitudinal Study, each tested five times over 28 years. The degree of variability is striking, and it makes one wonder how meaningful it is to talk about patterns of shared, "normal" aging of cognitive functioning.

Or consider the finding from a seven-year longitudinal study by Sherry Willis of 102 older adults, first tested when they were between ages 62 and 86. Over the ensuing seven years, when most of the subjects shifted from being young old to being old old, 62 percent of the group showed either stability or actual improvement in competence on everyday intellectual tasks (Willis et al., 1992).

There have been two approaches to attempting to understand these variations. The first of these, labeled with the rather depressing name of the **terminal drop** hypothesis, centers on the suggestion that all adults retain excellent function until a period a few years before death, at which time they drop rather precipitously in physical and mental functioning. The second approach involves a search for individual characteristics, such as family heredity and life-style, that may predict differences in rate or pattern of aging.

Terminal Drop

Kleemeier (1962) first proposed the idea of terminal drop to describe patterns of change in cognitive functioning in old age. He suggested that intellectual skill is maintained virtually unchanged until five to seven years before death, at which time there is a rapid drop. When we compare groups of individuals cross-sectionally or when we follow individuals longitudinally, each successive age group contains more and more individuals who are in this period of terminal drop, and thus the average score will tend to go down. But if Kleemeier is right, then the average pattern doesn't tell us anything about the individual pattern. The only way to test Kleemeier's hypothesis is to track backward from death for

Make a list of the people you think of as wise. How old are they? Is old age necessary for wisdom? If not, how do you think wisdom is acquired?

Is this Katmandu grandmother more wise than she was as a young woman? How might such wisdom be apparent in her behavior?

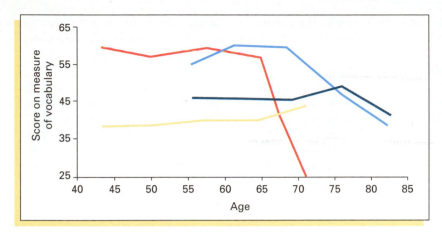

Figure 17.8 Each of the lines in this figure represents the scores on a vocabulary test for a single individual over a period of 28 years. Clearly there is great variability. Also interesting is the fact that no one of these subject's performance matches the average pattern of change on this measure. (*Source:* Schaie, 1989b, Figures 5.13 and 5.14, pp. 82–83.)

individuals for whom we have regular data at previous ages. This has now been done with data from several longitudinal studies.

Analyzing data from the Duke longitudinal studies, Palmore and Cleveland (1976) looked at the pattern of earlier test scores for 178 deceased men. They found no indication of terminal drop for their many measures of physical functioning, all of which showed gradual decline. But they did find a pattern of terminal drop for total IQ, which tended to remain stable until a few years before each man's death. Equivalent studies of other longitudinal samples (e.g., Johansson & Berg, 1989; Siegler, McCarty & Logue, 1982; White & Cunningham, 1988) suggest that the terminal drop pattern is more common on measures of well exercised (crystallized) abilities. Declines on unexercised (fluid) abilities are typically more gradual, following the pattern of physical change.

But terminal drop is clearly not the whole story. For most physical changes, and at least some cognitive changes, the decline is gradual for each person. Yet it is still true that this decline begins much earlier in some individuals than in others. Available explanations of such differences focus on both heredity and on life-style variations.

Heredity

Some general tendency to "live long and prosper" (to quote Mr. Spock from "Star Trek") is clearly inherited. Identical twins are more similar in length of life than are fraternal twins, and adults whose parents and grandparents are long-lived are also more likely to have long lives (Plomin & McClearn, 1990). The amount of illness prior to death also seems to be linked to genetic patterns. In the Swedish twin studies, for example, identical twins have more similar rates of illness than do fraternal twins (Pedersen & Harris, 1990). Similarly, Vaillant, studying the Harvard men in the Grant study sample, has found a small but significant correlation between the longevity of each man's parents and grandparents and his own health at age 65. Only about a quarter of those whose oldest grandparent had lived past 90 had any kind of chronic illness at age 65, compared to nearly 70 percent of those whose oldest grandparent had died at 78 or younger (Vaillant, 1991).

Just what it is that might be inherited is not entirely clear. One possibility is that different individuals may have slightly different "Hayflick limits," or there may be variations in the basic rate of physical maturation. The latter possibility is supported by the finding that among women, those with naturally occurring menopause earlier than age 50 have shorter life expectancies than do those with post-50 menopause. Women from the same kinds of backgrounds who have early menopause because of surgical removal of the ovaries do *not* show shortened life expectancies (Snowdon et al., 1989).

Whatever the explanation, I want to emphasize that the effect of heredity on longevity, or on health in late life, does not appear to be enormous. If your grandparents all

One of the favored few who maintain high levels of functioning throughout late adulthood, Bess Whitehead Scott of Austin, Texas, seems fit as a fiddle on her one hundredth birthday.

died when they were in their sixties or seventies, this need not mean that you will die early or necessarily be troubled with chronic problems. But there is some connection.

Life-Style and Health

What is likely to be far more important for your experience of late adulthood is your health, along with all the life-style factors I have talked about in earlier chapters, including health habits, mental and physical exercise, and adequacy of social support.

Health.   The single largest factor determining the trajectory of an adult's physical or mental status over the years past 65 is health. Those who are already suffering from one or more chronic diseases at 65 show far more rapid declines than do those who begin late adulthood with no disease symptoms. In part, of course, this is an expression of disease processes themselves. Cardiovascular disease results, among other things, in restricted blood flow to many organs, including the brain, with predictable effects on an adult's ability to learn or remember (Schaie, 1983b). And of course, those suffering from the early stages of Alzheimer's disease or another disease that causes dementia will experience far more rapid declines in mental abilities than will those free of such disease.

Ill health also has an indirect effect through its influence on health habits, particularly exercise. Those who have disabilities that prevent them from exercising regularly are likely to show earlier or more rapid decline in many physical and mental functions because of that secondary lack of exercise.

Health Habits.   Health habits also have direct effects, even among those who are not disabled. The same health habits that were important predictors of longevity and health in early adulthood continue to be significant predictors among the elderly. For example, a 17-year follow-up of those subjects in the Alameda County epidemiological study who had been 60 or over at the start of the study shows that smoking, low levels of physical activity, and too low or too high weight are linked to increased risk of death over the succeeding 17 years (Kaplan, 1992). Many other large epidemiological studies confirm such connections (e.g., Paffenbarger et al., 1987).

Even among older adults living in poverty, whose general risk of poor health is high, individual health habits are related to illness. James Lubben (Lubben, Weiler & Chi, 1989) has studied the incidence of hospitalization among a group of California elders, all Medicaid recipients, all with incomes of $550 a month or less in 1982. Hospital use in the following year was significantly higher among those who smoked and those who engaged in physical activity less than once a week. In this case, neither diet nor current weight was related to hospitalization.

Of course, it is not always possible to sort out the causality in studies like these. Those elders who are already feeling ill or disabled are less likely to exercise, and these are the same individuals who are more likely to be hospitalized. But because these are prospective longitudinal data, it is possible to control for the individual's health status at the start of the study, and when you do so, the relationships remain.

There are many ways to maintain physical fitness in old age. In China you often see the elderly practicing Tai Chi in the early morning. In the United States we have aerobics classes.

Physical Exercise.   Perhaps the most crucial variable is physical exercise, which has been clearly linked not only to greater longevity but also to better maintenance of various physical functions. For instance, Roberta Rikli and Sharman Busch (1986) studied a group of 65-year-old women who had been physically active for at least the past ten years, and compared them to a group of more sedentary women the same age. The active women had better reaction times, better flexibility, and better balance than did the inactive women. Indeed, the active women in this study had scores on these measures that were comparable to performances of inactive young women. Because similar results are obtained in studies in which older adults have been assigned randomly to exercise and nonexercise groups (e.g., Blumenthal et al., 1991), we know that differences like this are not merely the result of self-selection.

Physical exercise also seems to help maintain higher levels of cognitive performance among the elderly, although not every researcher finds this, as I pointed out in Chapter 15. One particularly clear study comes from Robert Rogers and his colleagues (Rogers, Meyer & Mortel, 1990), who followed a group of 85 men from age 65 through age 69. All were well educated and in good health at the start of the study, with no symptoms of heart disease or dementia. In the succeeding four years, a third of the men chose to continue working, mostly at fairly high-level jobs. Another third retired but remained physically active, while the remaining group retired and became physically (and mentally) inactive. The inactive subjects showed progressive declines on a measure of blood flow to the brain and performed significantly lower than either the active retired or the still-working men on a battery of cognitive tests—a set of results shown in Figure 17.9.

If anything, physical exercise seems to be even more important in the later years than at earlier ages. When you are young, you can get away with being sedentary. Your body will still run efficiently even if you neglect it (e.g., Poehlman, Melby & Badylak, 1991). But with increasing age, optimum function rests to a surprising degree on maintaining at least a moderate level of physical activity. Some authors have suggested that as much as half of the decline in various aspects of physical (and perhaps cognitive) functioning in old age could be prevented through improved life-style, particularly exercise. Yet only about 5 to 10 percent of adults over 65 in the United States are physically active (O'Brien & Vertinsky, 1991). Reasons given for not exercising are many, including poor health, arthritic pain, time demands from an ailing spouse, culturally based assumptions about what is appropriate behavior for older persons, embarrassment about exposing an aging body to others in an exercise program, lack of available facilities, lack of transportation to suitable fitness sites, fears of various kinds, and plain lethargy.

Mental Exercise. The effects of mental exercise on cognitive functioning among the elderly have been harder to pin down, but there are at least a few bits of evidence suggesting that mental fitness may be as important as physical fitness. For example, those older subjects in the Duke longitudinal studies who reported participating in many intellectual activities at the start of the study (such as reading, playing games, or doing hobbies) *increased* in verbal skills over the following six-year period, while those who were less active showed a decline (Busse & Wang, 1971). In another study, researchers found that older adults who play bridge regularly had higher scores on tests of both memory and reasoning compared to non–bridge players. The two groups did not differ in education,

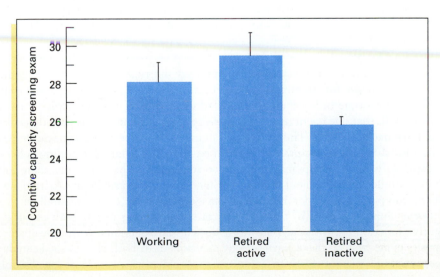

Figure 17.9 In this longitudinal study of healthy men, those who became inactive after they retired performed significantly worse on tests of mental ability four years later. (*Source:* Rogers, Meyer & Mortel, 1990, Figure 2, p. 126.)

THE REAL WORLD
Practical Advice for Maintaining Mental and Physical Fitness in Old Age

After reading everything I have said in the chapters on adulthood, you could probably write this list as well as I can. But let me restate the obvious, and tell you how I have tried to implement my own advice.

1. *Establish good health habits early.* Don't wait until you are old to change your health habits. Make changes now, whatever your age. Stop smoking (or don't start); eat a lower fat diet, particularly one low in cholesterol; keep your weight within 30 percent of the guidelines for your height and build (and remember that this is a pretty wide range; I'm not arguing for perfect svelte bodies here; I'm only arguing against obesity); get enough sleep. Not all of these have been easy for me to implement. I quit smoking when I was 30, and my weight has always been within 30 percent of norms (although it *does* fluctuate more than I would like and I am tired of worrying about it!). Because I am a vegetarian, my diet is fairly naturally low in cholesterol, but I have recently increased my efforts to cut down on fat intake. Sleep is the hardest item on this list, because there do not seem to be enough hours in the day.

2. *Exercise your body regularly.* This could be listed under health habits, but it is so important that it is worth listing separately. Begin now, whatever age you are. You don't have to become a long-distance runner or a champion swimmer. You only need to do some aerobic exercise for at least a half hour three times a week. Walking regularly is the easiest way to accomplish this goal, especially if you get into the habit of walking instead of driving to local appointments or to nearby stores. My own regimen includes a brisk 2½-mile walk every morning before breakfast, and then I walk for most errands that are within a range of about 20 minutes. It adds up to about 20 miles of walking a week.

3. *Exercise your mind regularly.* Don't stop with your formal education. Keep learning new things. Learn a new language; memorize poetry; learn to play a mentally challenging game like chess or bridge and play it regularly; read the newspaper every day; do crossword puzzles. Challenge your mind, and do so in as wide a variety of ways as you can. Many of these things have been regular parts of my adult life, but there is always room for more. My current challenge is to become fluent in German by spending a sabbatical year in Germany. My husband, whose native tongue is German, has promised not to speak English to me at all. The first few months are likely to be difficult!

4. *Stay in touch with friends and family.* If you do not maintain your social "convoy," it won't be there when you need it, whether the need occurs in old age or at some earlier point. Maintenance of the convoy requires not only that you take time to gather with friends and relatives, it also means taking time to respond to *others'* times of need. Taking my own advice, I recently splurged both time and money and spent a long weekend in a distant state with a group of three of my dearest women friends. We walked, talked, ate, talked some more, ate some more (all low-fat, of course!), ran on the beach. We plan to make it a yearly tradition, and I wonder why I didn't take steps to create such a tradition long ago.

5. *Find ways to reduce or control chronic stress.* There are all kinds of books about stress management on bookstore shelves. If you are chronically stressed, you may want to look at one or more of those. My own specific advice is to take time each day, even if it is only five minutes, for "centering" yourself. This might be through prayer or meditation or simply sitting quietly and breathing deeply. My own routine includes several such moments during the day—and when I do not leave time for them, I notice the difference in my level of tension.

6. *Take vacations.* Longer breaks also seem to be important. Vaillant has consistently included an item about vacations in his measure of optimum psychosocial functioning, a measure he finds to be linked to a variety of aspects of health. I try for two 10-day interludes a year, but I confess that I do not always manage that much.

---

health, exercise levels, or life satisfaction, and they did not differ on other measures of physical or cognitive functioning that have a less obvious relationship to bridge playing, such as reaction time or vocabulary size (Clarkson-Smith & Hartley, 1990b). Only on cognitive skills that one might reasonably expect to be sharpened by regular bridge playing was a difference observable. Thus, the effects of intellectual exercise may be quite specific. Memorizing things helps maintain your memory; tasks that demand reasoning help maintain those skills; reading helps maintain your vocabulary, and the like. Sadly, there appears to be no intellectual equivalent of basic aerobic activity—no single intellectual activity that you can participate in for 30 minutes three times a week to stay mentally fit.

Social Support.   Finally, the adequacy of social support affects both physical and cognitive functioning in old age, just as it does at earlier points in the life span. Two examples come from studies I have already mentioned: In both the Alameda study and in Lubben's study of poor elderly in California, those elders who were more socially isolated at the start of the study had a higher risk of illness or death in the subsequent years than did those with more adequate social networks, independent of their health status or health habits.

I cannot emphasize enough just how large the differences are in the quality of both physical and intellectual functioning among those over 65. Even among those over 75—the old old—there are enormous differences. Every longitudinal study of the elderly has found at least a few subjects who show no decline at all in their mental abilities. What all of this suggests is the intriguing possibility that decline may be the typical, but not the *invariable*, accompaniment of aging. If that is true, then it holds out the hope that by understanding the causes of good or poor maintenance of skills in the last years of life, we may be able to increase greatly the number of adults who are able to keep all their mental (and physical) marbles until very near death. That is a hope well worth vigorous research pursuit.

Summary

1. The percentage of the population above 65 has been increasing rapidly in the past decades, and it will continue to increase into the next century.

2. Those over 65 can be helpfully divided into the young old (65–75) and the old old (75+).

3. In the United States, a woman of 65 can expect to live an average of another 18.5 years, while a man can expect nearly 12 more years. More of those years will include disability for women than for men.

4. Changes in the brain associated with aging include most centrally a loss of dendritic density in neurons, which has the effect of slowing reaction time for almost all tasks.

5. Loss of hearing is more common and more noticeable after 65; it includes loss of hearing for high sounds, some loss of ability to discriminate words, and greater difficulty hearing under noise conditions.

6. There is less loss of taste discrimination than smell. The latter declines significantly in late adulthood.

7. Older adults also show different sleep patterns: less REM sleep, earlier waking, and more frequent waking in the night.

8. The rate of physical disability also increases, but at every age there are at least some adults who have no restriction in activity. Arthritis, hyperten-sion, and heart disease are most likely to cause disability.

9. Dementia is rare before late adulthood, becoming steadily more common with advancing age, affecting 15 percent or more of those over 85. The most common cause is Alzheimer's disease.

10. Risk factors for Alzheimer's disease include any family history of dementia, Down syndrome, or Parkinson's disease; a mother over 40; a blow to the head.

11. Most forms of emotional disturbance are less frequent in late adulthood. The exception is depression, which rises in frequency past age 70 or 75, although this is not true among those in good health, who have adequate support.

12. The most noticeable effect of all the physical changes of aging on day-to-day behavior is a general slowing of all responses.

13. Many older adults continue to be sexually active, although this becomes less common with increasing age.

14. There is as yet no widely accepted theory of the aging process. Current alternatives emphasize the possible existence of genetic limiting conditions, and/or the cumulative effects of damage to or malfunction within cells.

15. On virtually all measures of cognitive functioning, reliable decrements are found after about age 70. Loss is earlier on speeded or unexercised tasks.

16. This is reflected on most tests of memory, although older adults are as good as younger adults on short-term memory tasks and on some kinds of familiar memory problems.

17. Problem solving shows a similar pattern, although even on familiar material older adults appear to be less skillful at finding varied solutions.

18. Even in late adulthood, however, adults have reserve capacity—the ability to improve performance on any cognitive task with training, although younger adults have *more* reserve capacity.

19. Some authors suggest that older adults are wiser, but research on this question is in its infancy.

20. There are vast individual differences in the timing and pace of all the physical and mental changes described.

21. For some types of ability, skills may be retained at peak level until a few years before death (the terminal drop hypothesis). For others, the decline is more gradual.

22. The timing and rate of decline is affected by heredity, by overall health, by current and prior health habits, particularly physical and mental exercise, and by availability of adequate social support. Skills that are not used regularly show more rapid decline. Thus, "use it or lose it."

Key Terms

Alzheimer's disease	old old	young old
dementia	terminal drop	

Suggested Readings

Birren, J. E., Sloane, R. B. & Cohen, G. D. (Eds.) (1992). *Handbook of mental health and aging* (2nd ed.). San Diego, CA: Academic Press. (This is a wonderful compendium, both up to date and complete. Some of the papers assume a fairly technical vocabulary, but if nothing else this book will provide the most current bibliography on virtually every topic related to mental health in old age.)

Bond, J. & Coleman, P. (Eds.) (1990). *Aging in society. An introduction to social gerontology.* London: Sage Publications. (A very good general source on many aspects of aging, written primarily by British researchers, which means that it provides a welcome look at the process of aging in elders outside the United States.)

Markides, K. S. & Mindel, C. H. (1987). *Aging and ethnicity.* Newbury Park, CA: Sage Publications. (A good comprehensive discussion of differences in aging experiences for blacks, Hispanics, Native Americans, and Asians in the United States.)

Sternberg, R. J. (Ed.) (1990b). *Wisdom. Its nature, origins, and development.* Cambridge, England: Cambridge University Press. (The best single current source on this interesting subject, although there is far more theorizing than data offered.)

SOCIAL AND PERSONALITY DEVELOPMENT IN LATE ADULTHOOD

18

It may seem that the physical and mental changes in late adulthood are so striking and so pervasive that they necessarily dominate any discussion of these final years of life. Certainly the biological clock *is* far louder in these years. But the changes in roles and relationships are perhaps just as striking. If early adulthood is the period when we add complex, time-consuming roles, and middle adulthood is the period when those roles are redefined and renegotiated, then late adulthood is the time when many of them are shed.

▶ Overall Changes in Roles in Late Adulthood

The role of worker is given up at retirement; the role of daughter or son is given up when the last parent dies; widowhood means giving up the role of spouse. Many smaller roles a person may have filled in religious or community organizations may also be given up in these later years in favor of younger people. An older adult may step down from the position as chair of the local United Way fund drive or as head of the program committee for the garden club or as member of a local school board.

Moreover, as sociologist Irving Rosow has pointed out (1985), the roles that do remain in late adulthood have far less content, far fewer duties or expectations. Most older adults continue to occupy the role of parent, but in these late years, the role is typically far less complicated, less demanding. Unless you had your children very late, or they have encountered unusual difficulties in getting established in their own lives, by the time you are 65 your last child is long since launched and fully independent. Similarly, in other arenas, elders may occupy roles that have titles, but fewer duties. A retired university professor, for instance, may have the title of *emeritus professor*, a position which carries a

Can you think of other examples of "empty" roles occupied by older adults? Can you think of counter-examples—roles filled by older adults that are not empty, that have clear rules and expectations attached to them?

few benefits and essentially no obligations. In other organizations, an older individual may be given the title of honorary chairman.

In a practical sense, this loss of role content means that for many older adults, the routines of life are no longer structured by specific roles. But is this good or bad? Some, including Rosow, see this loss of role definition as carrying with it a distinct risk of isolation or alienation. Other social scientists see distinct advantages to this "roleless" time in late life.

One such advantage is a greater "[licence] for eccentricity" (Bond & Coleman, 1990, p. 78). Because they do not have to fit into the sometimes tight confines of role expectations, older adults feel far freer to express their own individuality—in dress, language, or personal preferences. I think this change begins before age 65; the gradual assertion of just such individuality seems to be characteristic of middle adulthood as well. But certainly in late adulthood there is a kind of institutionalized acceptance of eccentricity.

To see which of these two visions of late adulthood may be more valid, we need to look more closely at the changes in roles and relationships among older adults. One good place to begin is with a look at demographic changes in household composition and patterns of assistance. In middle adulthood, the majority of adults still live with a spouse or partners. In late adulthood that becomes less and less common.

▶ Demographic Changes: Living Arrangements in Late Adulthood

Figure 18.1 shows marital statuses for the young old and the old old. For comparison purposes, I've also given marital statuses for those in late middle age.

Several things ought to jump out at you immediately from this figure. First, there is clearly a drop in the percentage of married adults as we move into late adulthood. But

Figure 18.1 Among all elders, but most dramatically among older women, there is a decline in the likelihood of living with a spouse. (*Source:* U.S. Bureau of the Census, 1990, from Table 49, p. 42.)

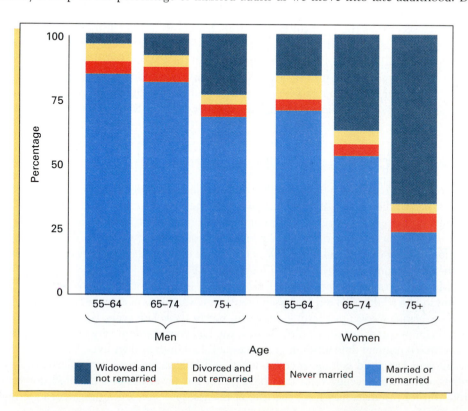

even more clearly, this change is vastly larger and more rapid for women than for men. Because men typically marry younger women, and because women live longer than men, the normal expectation for a man is that he will have a spouse or intimate partner until he dies. The normal expectation for a woman is that she will eventually be without such a partner, often for many years. It is hard to exaggerate the importance of that difference for the experience of late adulthood for men and women.

This same difference is also clearly reflected in the second set of data, in Figure 18.2, which shows the living arrangements of older adults. The majority of men over 65 live with their spouse. For those elders who are not married, living alone is the most common choice, although this is slightly more likely among older women than older men (Brock, Guralnik & Brody, 1990; Crimmins & Ingegneri, 1990).

Most of the unmarried elders who live alone do so out of preference (Pampel, 1983). There are a number of indications that in the United States, and in other countries with adequate basic financial support for older citizens, single older adults choose living alone over living with relatives, even when their health has declined. A particularly intriguing set of data comes from a study by Jacqueline Worobey and Ronald Angel (1990), who interviewed 2498 unmarried men and women over 70. Each of these subjects had been contacted twice, once in 1984 and once in 1986, so it was possible for Worobey and Angel to look at changes in living arrangements for those whose health stayed the same, improved, or declined. Of those who lived alone at the start of the study and whose health declined over the next two years, 81 percent of the men and 76 percent of the women still lived alone two years later.

That does not mean that health has no impact on living arrangements. It clearly does. In the United States, older adults with significant health problems are more likely to live with their children or with other relatives than are those who are healthier (e.g., Stinner, Byun & Paita, 1990; Choi, 1991). But it is simply not true that most elders with

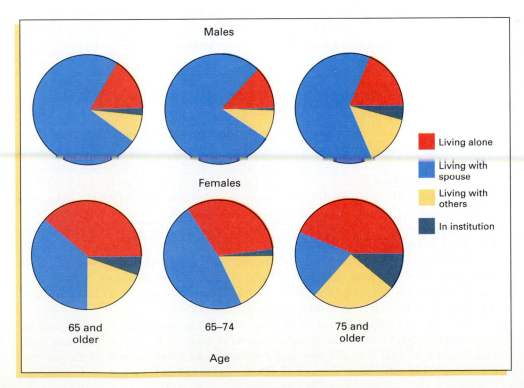

Figure 18.2 For those elders who are not living with a spouse, living alone is the most common alternative in every group except single men over 75. (*Source:* Brock, Guralnik & Brody, 1990, Figure 2, p. 8.)

Affection and mutual pleasure between married couples clearly does not disappear in old age. Frank and Palmina Canovi, married over 70 years, were both over 100 when this photo was taken.

mild or moderate disability or health problems live with relatives. Most appear to prefer to live alone and do so as long as possible—at least in our culture in current cohorts. In other cultures, the pattern is often quite different. In Japan, for example, only 7 percent of adults over 60 live alone, and only 29 percent live with a spouse only. Over half live with a child (Tsuya & Martin, 1992).

Other than health, the factors that affect the probability that a single older adult in the United States will live with a child or with other relatives include:

- *Income*. Those with lower incomes are more likely to live with family, although this difference is not large (Choi, 1991). Many elders with marginal or below-poverty-level incomes live alone.

- *Ethnicity*. White elders are considerably more likely to live alone than are African-American or Hispanic elderly—yet another manifestation of the broader ethnic differences in family living patterns I have already described. In one recent study, Choi (1991) found that 73 percent of white widows over 65, but only 56 percent of nonwhite widows, lived alone. Equivalent differences exist for single older men (e.g., Stinner et al., 1990).

- *Number of daughters and sons*. The more children an elder has, the more likely he or she is to live with a child, but this is more true of daughters than of sons. That is, elders with more daughters are more likely to live with a child than are those with few daughters, but having more sons does not increase the likelihood (Soldo, Wolf & Agree, 1990).

What do all these statistics suggest about the roles and relationships of older adults? First and foremost, of course, they point to a sharp divergence of experience between men and women in these later years. They also tell us that we will need to look beyond the spousal or partnership relationship if we are to understand the pattern of social interactions that are central to the aging individual. With so many unmarried elders, relationships with children and other family members may become more central. With so many elders living alone, relationships with friends may also become more significant. So let's look at these three sets of relationships: partnerships, kin, and friends.

Relationships in Late Adulthood

Partner Relationships

We have little information about marriage relationships in late adulthood that would change what I have already said about such relationships in mid-life. Cross-sectional comparisons tell us that marital satisfaction is higher in these late years than when children are still at home or being launched. But this satisfaction may have a somewhat different basis in late adulthood than is true of the high marital satisfaction of the early years of marriage. Late-adulthood marriages are based less on passion and mutual disclosure and more on loyalty, familiarity, and mutual investment in the relationship (Bengtson, Rosenthal & Burton, 1990).

Despite such possible differences, there are still common themes when we look at particularly successful partnerships at any age. Such relationships appear to be ones in which the partners view each other as best friends, agree on life goals, and maintain humor and playfulness in their relationships (Lauer & Lauer, 1986).

I do not want to run the risk of leaving you with the impression that most late-life marriages are somehow desiccated husks, drained of their life and juice, with only habit and loyalty left. That may well be true for some, but we have evidence to the contrary for many. You'll recall from Chapter 17 (Figure 17.6) that at least half, and probably a

THE REAL WORLD
Deciding on Nursing-Home Care

In Chapter 17 I talked a bit about the numbers of older adults living in nursing homes and other institutions. Who are those institutionalized elders? And how do they and their families make the decision that this is the best alternative care?

Older adults express little liking for nursing-home care as an option. In one study of elders in Virginia, for example, several thousand subjects were asked which care arrangements they would prefer should they become sick or disabled. The two preferred options, both approved by 68 percent, were care by a relative in one's own home or paid in-home care. The least preferred choice was moving to the home of a child or other relative (20 percent) with nursing-home care seen as acceptable by only a slightly larger number, 25 percent (McAuley & Blieszner, 1985). Nursing-home care is widely perceived as impersonal and lacking in dignity and personal control (e.g., Biedenharn & Normoyle, 1991). In some subcultures, especially among Hispanics, nursing-home care also carries the connotation that the family did not care enough to provide assistance. As a result, elderly Hispanics are even less likely than are whites to spend any time in an institution and far more likely to live in multigeneration households (Burr & Mutchler, 1992).

The economics of nursing-home care also make it unattractive for many older adults. Such care now costs $2000 to $3000 a month, costs not covered by Medicare or most health insurance plans. A stay of as long as a year will exhaust the disposable assets of the majority of older adults. To be eligible for Medicaid coverage for such care, all disposable assets must first be used up, which may leave a surviving spouse in very difficult financial straits. Many states now have laws that permit certain assets, such as a home, to be transferred to a surviving spouse so that this asset need not be used up before the partner in the nursing home is eligible for Medicaid—a procedure that leaves the surviving spouse in somewhat better financial condition. But there may still be significant impoverishment.

In the face of such personal preferences and economic realities, family members make the decision for nursing home placement with great reluctance, only after all other options have been ruled out or exhausted. It is an immensely difficult decision, fraught with guilt and distress.

Not surprisingly, the likelihood of nursing home placement varies considerably from one subgroup to another. The most likely candidate for institutional care is an old old, white, unmarried woman with no or few children, significant disability or dementia, and few economic resources—whose care is thus paid for by Medicaid (Hanley et al., 1990; Cohen, Tell & Wallack,

1986; McFall & Miller, 1992). Nursing-home care is especially likely if the elder is no longer able to toilet or feed herself, although even among those who are disabled to this extent, home care rather than institutional care is still the most common arrangement. Similarly, a fifth of residents in nursing homes or other institutions suffer from moderate to severe dementia (Siegler & Lewis, 1984), but this does not mean that all elders with dementia are in institutions. Most are not.

The problem for individual families is to try to balance the needs of everyone in the system: the need of the older adult for independence and control; the financial support available; the needs of younger family members who have lives of their own to lead. Susan Kushner Resnick's description of the family decision with and for her 90-year-old grandmother conveys the complexity and the distress:

> Nobody wanted to send her to the home, as it's called. After she broke her hip, she went there to recover, but she never got well enough to leave. The alternatives were worse than institutionalization. She could stay in her apartment only with 24-hour nursing care. The expense was the first deterrent; the second, her fear of the possibility that one night the nurse would call in sick and she would have to stay alone. We discussed sending her to her daughter's (my mother's) house, but since both of my parents work, she wouldn't have gotten constant care. Besides, the sandwich generation wasn't equipped for the strain of catering night and day to an elderly person. So it was decided. ''I know I need to stay here,'' Nana told me . . . ''but I *hate* to break up my house.'' (Resnick, 1992, p. 22)

What often tips the balance, one way or the other, is whether any family member is able or willing to provide assistance, and whether other community services can help fill the service gap. In the case of Resnick's grandmother, sufficient support was not feasible. But for other families, Meals on Wheels, visiting nurses, adult day-care services or the equivalent may make it possible for family members to continue to care for a frail or demented elder.

Certainly if average nursing home care were of much higher quality than it now is, with built-in opportunities for personal control and challenging activities and first-rate medical care, and if such care were covered by Medicare or other national health insurance, choosing such a care option might be less difficult. But until we reach that optimistic point, the choice of nursing home care—for oneself or for an aging parent—is likely to continue to be wrenching and painful.

majority, of late-life couples are still sexually active. Older couples also spend more time with each other than with family or friends, and although much of this time is indeed spent in passive activities or basic maintenance—watching TV, doing housework, running errands—it is also true that those married elders who spend more time with their spouse report that they are happier (e.g., Larson, Mannell & Zuzanek, 1986).

Further evidence of the deep bonds that continue to exist in late-life marriages is the remarkable degree of care and assistance older spouses give each other when one or the other is disabled or demented. Among married elders with some kind of disability, by far the largest source of assistance is the spouse, not children or friends. Many husbands and wives continue to care for severely ill or demented spouses over very long periods of time. And many elderly couples in which both spouses suffer from significant disabilities nonetheless continue to care for one another "til death do them part."

Late adult marriages may thus be less romantic, less emotionally intense than is true of the early years of marriage, but they are typically satisfying and highly committed.

It is the *loss* of the partnership/marriage relationship through the death of the spouse or partner that alters this pattern for so many older adults, as you have already seen in Figure 18.1. The gender difference in marital status among elders is further increased by a higher rate of remarriage for older men than for women, a pattern found both among the widowed and the divorced at every age. A fifth of single men over 65 remarry, compared to only 2 percent of women. Older unmarried men are also more likely to date and more likely to cohabit (Bulcroft & Bulcroft, 1991).

I will be talking about the grief and loss of widowhood in the chapter on death and dying. Here I want only to reemphasize what I have said before about the impact of marriage (or other central partnership) on other aspects of physical and psychological functioning. Married older adults, like married adults of any age, have certain distinct advantages: they have higher life satisfaction, better health, and lower rates of institutionalization. Such differential advantages are generally greater for married older men than for married older women, again as is true among younger adults. This difference might be interpreted as indicating that marriage affords more benefits to men than to women. Or we might conclude that men rely more on their marriage relationship for social support and are thus more affected by its loss. Whatever the explanation, it seems clear that among older women, marital status is less strongly connected to health or life satisfaction, *except* that marital status is strongly connected to financial security among older women. As I'll describe in detail shortly, widows and other unmarried older women are significantly more likely to live in poverty than are other elders, and poverty has obvious effects on both the sense of well-being and health.

How many different explanations can you think of for the fact that older single men are more likely to remarry than are women?

More older men are married not only because they are outlived by their wives, but also because they are more likely to remarry if they are widowed, as this man is doing. And—typically—he is marrying a woman younger than himself, increasing the likelihood that she will be widowed in her turn.

At the risk of repeating myself, I want to emphasize yet again how profound is the difference between the normal experience of older men and women. Women *expect* to be widowed; men do not. Women expect to spend some time living alone; men do not. In fact, it is quite possible that this difference in expectation plays some role in the differential impact of marital status on older men and women. We know that unexpected or unplanned life changes are generally more difficult to handle than are expected or planned changes. Women may thus prepare psychologically for singleness, while men do not. But this difference aside, the terrain of relationships in late adulthood is radically different for men and for women.

Relationships with Children and Other Kin

Folklore and popular press descriptions of late adulthood suggest that family, particularly children and grandchildren, form the core of the social life of older adults, perhaps especially those older adults who are widowed. There is some support for such a view, but there are also some curious disconfirmations.

It is true that the great majority of older adults who have at least one living child see their child(ren) and grandchild(ren) regularly. For example, in one very large national sample of over 11,000 adults aged 65 and over, 63 percent reported that they saw at least one of their children once a week or more often; another 16 percent saw a child one to three times a month, and only a fifth saw their children as rarely as once a month or less (Crimmins and Ingegneri, 1990). Such regular contact is made easier by the fact that even in the United States, where distances are large and mobility has been high, three-fourths of elders have at least one child living within an hour's travel. Very similar figures are reported by researchers in other developed countries, such as England (Jerrome, 1990), so this pattern is not unique to the United States.

Patterns of Aid. Part of that regular contact is, of course, in the form of aid to and from the elder person—a pattern I already described in Chapter 16. The great majority of the aid needed by older adults, and that cannot be provided by a spouse, is provided by other family members, particularly children (e.g., Antonucci & Akiyama, 1987b; Antonucci, 1990). One representative set of numbers comes from the National Survey of Families and Households, a quite recent large national sample that includes over 1500 adults over 65 who have at least one living child. In this group, 52 percent were receiving some household help, and 21 percent were receiving some financial help from at least one child (Hoyert, 1991).

Not surprisingly, the same factors that contribute to the likelihood of an elder living with a child also predict the amount of non-live-in help an older adult will receive from her children: blacks and Hispanics are more likely to receive help than are whites, and those with lower incomes receive more help, as do those with more children. Unmarried older women receive the most help from their children.

Emotional Connections. But relationships between older parents and their children cannot be reduced simply to the exchange of aid. A great deal of the interaction is social as well as functional, and the great majority of older adults describe their relationships with their adult children in positive terms. Most see their children not only out of obligation or duty but because such contacts are pleasurable, and a very large percentage describe at least one child as a confidant (Connidis & Davies, 1992). There are obviously exceptions—parent-child relationships that are distant, cold, or fraught with strain and difficulty. But in the main, elders describe their relationships with their children as being close and compatible (Cicirelli, 1983).

Children and Life Satisfaction. The puzzle comes when we look at the correlation between an older adult's contacts with her children and her overall level of satisfaction with her life. Given the obvious centrality of relationships with children in the daily life of most elders, it seems entirely reasonable to assume that those who have more frequent contact with their offspring will report higher levels of happiness or life satisfaction. But this is *not* what researchers have found, at least in studies in the United States. Those who see their children more often, or report more positive interactions, do not describe themselves as happier or healthier overall than do those who have less frequent or less positive relationships with their children (e.g., Lee & Ellithorpe, 1982; Seccombe, 1987; Markides & Krause, 1985). Contact with children is also unrelated to self-esteem or to loneliness among elders (Lee & Shehan, 1989; Lee & Ishii-Kuntz, 1987).

One possible explanation of this apparent paradox might be that combining results for married and unmarried elders in these correlations is confusing the issue. Married elders have each other and thus do not need their children's emotional support in order to feel satisfied. If that's true, we might expect to find that contact with children is critical for overall happiness or sense of well-being only for unmarried elders. But once again that's not what the research shows. The lack of connection between contact with children and well-being holds for older widows as well as for those with spouses still living.

Another possible explanation is that the relationship with one's children is still full of role prescriptions, even in old age. It may be friendly, but it is not chosen in the same way that a relationship with a friend is. With your friend, you may feel free to "be yourself," you may feel accepted as who you are. With your children, you may feel the need to live up to their demands and expectations.

Several small research studies support this possibility. For instance, Maria Talbott (1990) interviewed 55 older widows at some length about their relationships with their children. These women said many positive things about those relationships, but they described certain negatives as well. Some felt neglected by their children, some felt unappreciated, some were afraid of bothering or burdening their children.

In a rather different type of study, Reed Larson and his colleagues (Larson, Mannell & Zuzanek, 1986) had a group of 92 older adults, both men and women, wear pagers for a week. During the day, each subject was paged about once every two hours. When paged, the subject wrote down who he was with, what he was doing, and how happy, cheerful, friendly, sociable, alert, energetic, active, or excited he felt at that moment. Larson found that when subjects were paged while interacting with their children, they described fewer positive emotions than they did when they were beeped while interacting with friends. These older adults also described quite different activities with the two groups. When with children, they were most likely to report doing housework; with friends they most often reported socializing or eating.

Think about the oldest generation in your family. How would you describe the family role that those aging parents (or grandparents) fill? What are the family's expectations? Can you detect potential sources of strain in this role?

This 95-year-old clearly gains much pleasure from this family gathering on her birthday. Research tells us, though, that such family contact does not seem to be an essential ingredient of an older adult's overall morale.

ACROSS CULTURES
Older Mexican-Americans' Relationships with Their Children

Given the greater centrality and significance of family interactions in Hispanic families, you might expect to find that in this ethnic group, life satisfaction among older adults is positively linked to family contact. But at least one recent study of Mexican-Americans in San Antonio, Texas, suggests otherwise.

Renee Lawrence, Joan Bennett, and Kyriakos Markides (1992) studied a group of 321 older Hispanic adults, all of whom had an adult child and at least one grown grandchild living in the same community. They found that those who had the most frequent contact with their adult children reported the *most* psychological distress, including depression and such physical symptoms of distress as trouble sleeping and poor appetite. This need not mean that contact with family makes elders more distressed. Such a correlation could also occur since those elders who are most physically frail are likely to have the most frequent contact with their children. Indeed, when the researchers took that into account they found that the negative effect disappeared. But no positive effect emerged, either. Among those who were not physically dependent on their children, frequency of contact was not linked to satisfaction or to lower levels of depression.

It was only when they looked at the emotional content of the relationship that Lawrence et al. found signs of positive effects of association with children. The more affection an elder felt for his adult children, the *less* distress he reported. But affection, like frequency of contact, was not related to the older adult's overall satisfaction with life or happiness.

These results are highly consistent with findings from studies of Anglos in the United States, despite the differences between the two cultures in the basic patterns of family interaction. Contact with children appears to be neither necessary nor sufficient for happiness or life satisfaction among older adults, although having an affectionate, confidant relationship with one or more children may help to prevent some kinds of emotional distress. Whether this is true elsewhere in the world I do not know because equivalent research is not available. But at least we know that this pattern of findings is not unique to Caucasian-Americans.

Yet another possibility is that one of the potential negatives about relationships with children in late adulthood is that these relationships are not *reciprocal*, not balanced. For instance, several studies by Linda Thompson and Alexis Walker (Thompson & Walker, 1984; Walker & Thompson, 1983) show that there is greater attachment and affection between mothers and daughters when the relationship is perceived as equal in giving and receiving. To the extent that parent-child relationships in late adulthood become *less* reciprocal—as they typically do—the aging parent may experience those relationships as less satisfying and thus less contributory to high morale.

Finally, it is quite possible that in most of this research we have focused on the wrong aspect of family relationships in trying to understand their role in older adult lives. Just as other research on social support tells us that it is *satisfaction* with one's level of support rather than the objective amount of support that is linked to health, so it may well be that satisfaction with family contacts would be linked to overall satisfaction. The only study I know of to have approached the question in this way does indeed show precisely this. Crohan and Antonucci (1989), in a study of 718 American adults aged 50 to 95, found that satisfaction with family relationships was correlated with overall life satisfaction, while *quantity* of contact with family was not.

Social scientists are still trying to unravel this particular skein of results. For now, the best I can tell you is that family relationships, while essential for many aspects of care and assistance for older adults, are full of ripples and eddies, demands and inequities, as well as pleasures.

Siblings.   I have not said much about sibling relationships between adults, primarily because brothers and sisters do not ordinarily loom large in adults' social networks. Most adults have at least one living sibling, and most report that they have at least moderately close relationships with their brothers and sisters. But few would place a brother or sister in the center circle of their social network (Cicirelli, 1982; Goetting, 1986). Most write or call occasionally and see one another on family occasions, but they are not exceptionally close. Faced with an important decision, few adults say that they would turn to a sibling for advice, and few provide each other with financial or other assistance at any

RESEARCH REPORT
Late Life Relationships Among the Never-Married or Childless

Research on the experiences of never-married or married-but-childless elders adds further to the somewhat contradictory information about the potential importance or unimportance of relationships with children in late adulthood. Snippets of information point in quite opposite directions.

On the negative side, in the United States and other industrialized countries, widowed men without children are more prone to suicide, alcoholism, and accidental death, while widowed childless women are more likely to be institutionalized (Aldous & Klein, 1991). Childless widowed elders—both men and women—are also more likely to live alone and more likely to have low levels of contact with others. In one national survey in 1974 (Bachrach, 1980), a quarter of those over 65 who were childless and living alone reported having had no contact with any other person in the previous two days, compared to only 10 percent of those living alone who had at least one child. These statistics paint a rather bleak picture of the late years of childless adults.

On the other hand, there are several studies showing that childless elderly are no less satisfied with their lives than are those with children (e.g., Glenn & McLanahan, 1981). Those who are still married find satisfaction within that relationship. There is even one study showing that marital satisfaction is higher among those elders without children than among those who have at least one child (Lee, 1988). And those who never married, perhaps

especially never-married women, have often created rich networks of other relationships, with kin, with friends, with the children of kin or friends. One older never-married woman interviewed by Robert Rubinstein (Rubinstein et al., 1991) described such a network of friends:

> Family has had practically no meaning to me. Very little. My friends have been my family. And there are people out there in Michigan who really feel that I am a part of their family. We call each other up on the phone. They're concerned. (p. S275)

Some of the women in this study did express some concern about their ability to care for themselves in late old age without the support of children or grandchildren. But these women had found creative ways to fill their needs for companionship and social support, beyond or in place of traditional family ties.

These apparently contradictory findings are a good illustration of why it is so difficult to draw broad generalizations about the elderly. There are obviously many pathways, each with potentially positive adaptations. Childless single men may be the most vulnerable subgroup precisely because they appear to find it more difficult to create alternative or compensatory relationships (Brubaker, 1990). But the lack of marriage or children is not at all an inevitable recipe for discontent in old age.

age. There are a few small studies suggesting that sibling relationships are closer among some ethnic groups, such as Italian-Americans and African-Americans (Gold, 1990; Johnson, 1982). But even in these groups the number of emotionally intimate sibling relationships appears to be fairly small.

Interestingly, though, there are a few signs that relationships with siblings may become more important in late adulthood than they were earlier, although this effect may be restricted to relationships with sisters. Victor Cicirelli, in a small study of 83 older adults (1989), asked his subjects to rate their degree of closeness with each of their living siblings on a 5-point scale. He also measured each subject's level of depression as a negative indicator of overall well-being. Table 18.1 shows what emerged when Cicirelli correlated

TABLE 18.1 Correlations of Closeness with Sibling and Depression in Cicirelli's Study

	Correlation
Men with sisters	$-.51^{a}$
Women with sisters	$-.30^{a}$
Men with brothers	$-.21$
Women with brothers	$.09$

[a]These correlations are statistically significant at the .05 level, which means that a correlation this large would have been found by chance only five times out of a hundred in samples this size if there really were no relationship between the two variables.
Source: Cicirelli, 1989, Table 2, p. 214.

these two measures separately for the four combinations of sibling gender. You can see that those older adults who described close relationships with their sisters were less depressed. Relationships with brothers were uncorrelated with depression.

Similarly, Shirley O'Bryant (1988) has found that among recently widowed older women, the availability of a sister nearby was second only to health as a predictor of a widow's overall adjustment to the loss of her spouse. Contact with brothers had no beneficial effect, and neither did contact with children.

These findings point once again to the differential role of women as kin-keepers, as providers of emotional support. In late adulthood, sisters may sometimes take the place of a spouse as a close confidant.

Friends and Other Members of the Convoy

Relationships with friends in later life are less ambivalent than are relationships with family, although they may be equally complex in other ways. Although we do not have good evidence (and *no* decent longitudinal data), it is reasonable to assume that the number of friendships may diminish gradually from age 65 onward. Most close friends at this age are friends of long standing (Litwak, 1989; Blieszner, 1989); as they die, the network becomes smaller. Widowed adults may also lose contact with still-married friends.

At the same time, there is mounting evidence that contact with friends—unlike contact with family members—is a significant ingredient in overall life satisfaction, in self-esteem, and in amount of loneliness reported by older adults (Adams & Blieszner, 1989; Antonucci, 1990; Jerrome, 1990; Lee & Ishii-Kuntz, 1987; Lee & Shehan, 1989). This is particularly true of unmarried elders, but it is at least somewhat true for those still married as well.

Friends meet different kinds of needs than do family members for older adults. For one thing, they create relationships that are likely to be more reciprocal or equitable, and we know that such equitable relationships are more valued and least stressful (e.g., Roberto & Scott, 1986). Friends provide companionship, opportunities for laughter, sharing of activities. In one recent Canadian study, for example, friends were second only to spouses as sources of companionship among those over 65 (Connidis & Davies, 1992). And because friends generally come from the same cohort, they also share history and culture, the same favorite old songs, the same jokes, the same social experiences. Friends may also provide significant assistance with daily tasks, such as shopping or housework (e.g., Adams, 1986), although they typically provide less help of this kind than do family members.

Gender Differences in Friendships and in Network Structure. As at earlier ages, women and men appear to form different kinds of social networks. Older men's friendships involve less disclosure and less intimacy, although they may list as many or even more friends than do women (Wright, 1989). A particularly helpful set of data to illustrate these differences comes from Toni Antonucci's national survey of network systems in adults aged 50 and over (Antonucci & Akiyama, 1987b). In order to make the two gender groups comparable, she included only men and women who were married and had at least one living child. Antonucci found no differences in the number of friends men and women identified, but she did find several other differences, which she summarizes:

> The differences between men and women in some ways are quite simple: men rely on their spouse; women rely on children and friends in addition to their spouse. (Antonucci & Akiyama, 1987b, p. 748)

It would be very helpful to have an equivalent set of data for unmarried older men and women with living children. Lacking a spouse, does a man turn more to his children, or perhaps to a sister? Or does he then extend his friendship network? Research on the impact of widowhood on men suggests indirectly that many men may do none of these. Widowed

Why might it be the case that most friends in late adulthood are friends of long standing? Are there social barriers to creating new friendships in old age? Are there psychological barriers?

In late adulthood, friends seem to play a special role, perhaps because they share the same background and memories—like favorite old tunes.

men appear to be at greater risk for a variety of health problems and emotional distress than are widowed women—indications that their social support systems are not sufficient to buffer them from this major stress. But it would be good to have more direct information about the role of friends among unmarried older adults.

Ethnic Group Differences: Social Networks among African-American Elderly. Not only do older blacks appear to have somewhat warmer relationships with their siblings and higher rates of coresidence with their children, they also show two other creative patterns of social network use. They create strong relationships with fictive kin, a pattern I described in the box in Chapter 14. In African-American groups, friends often acquire a status like that of a close sibling, aunt, uncle, or grandparent. Among elders of all ethnic groups, such fictive kin may be important sources of both emotional and instrumental support (Mac Rae, 1992), but the pattern is particularly prevalent among African-Americans (e.g., Johnson & Barer, 1990).

A second network pattern seen more among African-American elders than among white elders is the use of their church as a significant source of social support. For example, among black older women in one large national sample, those who regularly participated in social events at a church were more likely to give and receive high levels of help from friends rather than from children (Hatch, 1991). Other research suggests that among black elders more than among whites, participation in church social activities is linked to higher levels of well-being (Walls & Zarit, 1991; Bryant & Rakowski, 1992). Given the fact that many more African-American elders than whites are unmarried, heads of households, or poor, both the use of fictive kin and the reliance on church support seem effective strategies for increasing overall social support.

An Overview of Relationships in Late Adulthood

Two things stand out for me in looking at relationship patterns in late adulthood. First of all, there is a great deal of continuity in relationships from earlier periods of life. Women continue to create larger and more intimate networks and continue their role as kin keepers; men continue to rely more on their spouse as confidant. Blacks and other minorities continue to create more extended families, and they rely more on families for a variety of assistance. This continuity exists at an individual level as well: those who have many friends and extensive networks in early and middle adulthood are likely to continue

Participation in church activities is more likely to be a central aspect of the support system of older African-Americans than is true for other older groups in the United States.

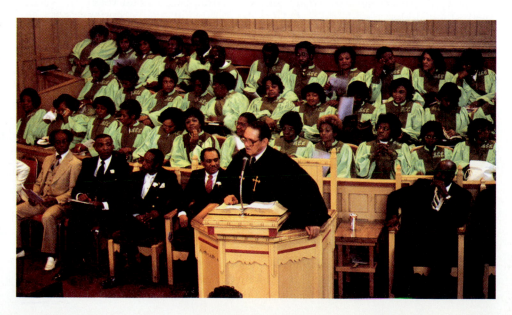

to create such networks in old age (McCrae and Costa, 1990), while those who are more solitary or introverted are likely to persist in that pattern.

The second thing that strikes me is that this continuity occurs despite significant attrition in the older adult's personal convoy. The majority of older women are widowed; both older men and women lose friends and siblings to death. Yet most older adults adapt to these changes remarkably well and continue to maintain active social contacts throughout the remainder of their lives. They see friends and family, and they continue to attend church or other organizations. The limiting condition for social activity in late adulthood is far more likely to be physical disability than death of partner or friends. This persistence of social contacts in old age speaks not only to the continuing importance of such interactions for adults' sense of connection and well-being, but also to the robust capacity for adaptation that remains in late life.

▶ Work in Late Adulthood: The Process of Retirement

A similarly robust capacity for adaptation marks the transition from work to retirement. While this transition certainly does involve the loss of a major role, virtually all the folklore about the negative effects of this particular role loss turns out to be wrong, at least for current cohorts in developed countries. Our knowledge about the whole process has been greatly enhanced by the availability of a series of excellent longitudinal studies, each following a group of men or women from before retirement into the years past retirement. In a particularly helpful analysis, Erdman Palmore and his colleagues (Palmore et al., 1985) have combined the results of seven such studies, yielding a sample of over 7000 adults, each interviewed at least twice, and often many more times than that. I will draw heavily on their findings, because this is by far the largest set of longitudinal information available.

The Timing of Retirement

One inaccurate piece of folklore is that 65 is the normal age of retirement. As recently as 1970 in the United States, 65 was indeed the most common age of retirement for men. But in recent decades, both in the United States and in most industrialized countries, the average age of retirement has been getting younger and younger. In one recent cross-national comparison, Alex Inkeles and Chikako Usui (1989) note that in 13 of the 34 capitalist and communist nations they surveyed, 60 is the official pensionable age; in another 17 countries, 65 is the official age at which an older worker becomes entitled to a pension, but in nearly all cases there is some support for those who retire earlier. For example, in the United States, 65 is the age at which an individual becomes eligible for full Social Security benefits, but reduced benefits can be received starting at age 62. Other retirement programs allow still earlier benefits. In part because of these opportunities, the average age of retirement has dropped quite rapidly. Figure 18.3 shows what the picture looks like now, expressed in terms of work-force participation rates in the United States population. Fewer than half of men are still in the work force at 65, with the rapid decline beginning at about 60. The pattern for women is clearly similar (Clark, 1988; Hayward, Grady & McLaughlin, 1988).

Reasons for Retirement

Results from Palmore's combined analysis along with other evidence point to a series of factors that contribute to the decision to retire.

Health.   Health status is one of the strongest predictors of *early* retirement. Among workers aged 60 to 67, poor health raises the probability of retirement by 14 to 18 percent and lowers the average age of retirement from one to three years (Sammartino, 1987). This effect is seen among Hispanics and African-Americans as well as among whites

Before you read the section on retirement, think about your own attitudes toward this life change. Do you expect it to be positive and enjoyable, or do you anticipate it with dread or some anxiety? What do you think has shaped your attitudes?

Figure 18.3 This set of information comes from the Bureau of Labor Statistics for 1986. You can see that the majority of men and women have stopped work before age 65, a pattern that has been prompted in part by the availability of many types of pensions at 60 or 62. (*Source:* Bee, 1992, Figure 9–9, p. 317; original source: Clark, 1988, data from Table 3, p. 174.)

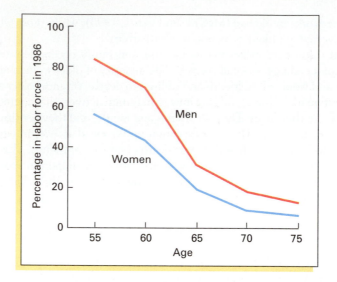

Some people never retire. Dr. Julius Manes, 87 when this photo was taken, worked as a physician until his death at 88. Anna Bobbitt Gardner is, at age 80, Director of the Academy of Musical Arts in Boston.

(Stanford et al., 1991), and in other countries than the United States (e.g., McDonald & Wanner, 1990). Among those who retire at more normative times, such as at 65, however, health is a less powerful factor, presumably because most of those who retire later are in good health. Their retirement decision is affected by a variety of other factors.

Age. Age itself is an important ingredient in the equation because in many occupations there are either mandatory retirement rules or clear expectations from employers or family members. Internal models also play an important part. If 62 or 65 is the "right" time for retirement in a person's "expected life history," then there is a strong tendency to retire at that age, regardless of health.

Family Composition. Whatever an adult's age, those who are still supporting minor children retire later than do those in the postparental stage. Thus, men and women who bear their children very late, or those who acquire a second, younger family in a second marriage, or those rearing grandchildren, are likely to continue to work until these children are launched.

Pension Programs. Equally important, both for early and for on-time retirement, is the availability of adequate financial support after retirement. Those who anticipate pension support in addition to Social Security retire earlier than do those who have no such financial backup.

Anticipated pension and health frequently work in opposite directions, because many working-class men and women who have worked in unskilled jobs can expect little supplementary retirement income *and* are in poor health. In general, working-class adults retire *earlier* than do middle- and upper-class workers, responding to ill health and normative pressures, but there is a significant subgroup of poor or working-class adults, including many minority adults, who continue working well past the normal retirement ages in order to supplement their incomes.

On the other end of the social class scale, health and pension adequacy work against one another in the opposite way. Adults in this group generally have better health and better pensions. They also tend to have more interesting jobs. The three factors combine to produce somewhat later retirement for this more socially favored group.

Work Characteristics. This leads to the more general point that those who like their work and are highly work-committed, including many self-employed adults, retire later—often quite a lot later—than do those who are less gratified with their work. Those in challenging and interesting jobs are likely to postpone retirement until they are pushed by ill-health or attracted by some special financial inducement. For them, availability of normal pension programs is less of an influence (Hayward & Hardy, 1985).

Women Versus Men. None of these factors, except age, is as good a predictor of retirement among women as it is among men (Palmore et al., 1985). Women do indeed retire at about the same ages as do men, but neither financial benefits nor health nor job characteristics tell you very much about who will retire early and who will postpone this life change. No one has a very good explanation of this difference in predictability. It might reflect the fact that women's retirement timing is more affected by their partners' retirement than is the reverse; it might reflect the fact that women in current cohorts of 50- and 60-year-olds are relatively newer to the work force than are men and less bored with their jobs or with working. We'll have to wait and see whether later cohorts of women with more extended work histories behave differently.

The Effects of Retirement

A particularly striking example of negative myths about retirement came to my attention several years ago. A one-page reprint of an article about retirement was handed around among faculty at a large university. Among other things, it said, "There is no way to describe adequately the letdown many people feel when they retire from a responsible executive post." It went on to predict that faculty who retired would experience a desperate search for other sources of meaning in their lives, followed by depression and illness.

There may well be some self-fulfilling prophecy at work here. It is indeed true that some adults adjust badly to retirement and that such poor adjustment is more likely (but not inevitable) among highly work-committed adults. But as a general rule, gloomy expectations about negative effects of retirement are unfounded.

Effects on Income. Retired adults in the United States have five potential sources of income, four of which are government pensions, such as Social Security; other pensions, such as those offered through an employer, including military pensions and those for government workers; earnings from continued work; and income from savings or other assets. For those living below the poverty line, the fifth source is public assistance beyond Social Security, including food stamps and Supplemental Security Income. You can see how these various sources contribute to household income for older adults in the United States in Table 18.2. These data are from 1984, but there is little reason to believe that the distribution of income sources has changed much. Social Security is clearly the largest

TABLE 18.2 Percentage of Household Income from Various Sources for Adults over Age 65 in the United States in 1984

Source	All Households (%)	Total Household Income			
		<$5000 (%)	$5000–$9,999 (%)	$10,000–$19,999 (%)	20,000+ (%)
Social Security	38	77	71	48	20
Other pensions	13	2	7	16	15
Earnings	16	0	4	10	23
Assets	28	4	10	21	39
Public assistance	1	14	3	0	0
Other	4	3	5	5	3

Source: Ycas & Grad, 1987, Table 4, p. 8.

RESEARCH REPORT
Choosing Not to Retire

A minority of adults choose not to retire at all or to do so only very gradually. You can see signs of this group if you go back and look again at Figure 16.5 (page 404). You can see that in this large sample, 4.3 percent of men over 65 were still working more than 45 hours per week. In the same sample, nearly another tenth were working 29 to 45 hours per week. These continuing workers include several subsets. One subgroup is made up of those who simply continue at the kind of work they have always done, like college professors or politicians. A second subgroup includes those who officially retire from their previous job or line of work, but who take up what is sometimes called a *bridge job*—a new type of employment, often part-time, and very frequently in some totally different line of work, that makes a bridge between full-time work and full retirement. One recent analysis of longitudinal data from the Retirement History Study (Quinn & Burkhauser, 1990) suggests that as many as a fifth of workers continue working for at least several years past the typical retirement age in one or the other of these patterns.

Who are these nonretirees? We know almost nothing about women who choose not to retire or who retire only very gradually, but we know a little about men who follow such patterns. Some are men with low levels of education and poor retirement benefits who simply cannot afford to quit work. They continue at part-time work, as they can find it, to supplement Social Security.

A larger fraction of nonretirees, however, especially among those who continue in the same line of work past retirement age,

appear to come from the other end of the social-class spectrum: they are highly educated, healthy professionals in challenging, high-level occupations. Many are self-employed. They continue work because they find their work interesting, or because their sense of identity is still strongly tied to their occupation. One piece of empirical support for this generalization comes from the National Longitudinal Surveys. Before retirement age, the researchers had asked all the subjects: ''If, by some chance, you were to get enough money to live comfortably without working, do you think that you would work anyway?'' Nearly three-fourths of those who later shunned retirement had answered yes (Parnes et al., 1985).

Of course not all men (or women) who were highly work-committed in their forties, fifties, and early sixties shun retirement. Many do stop work at the typical ages. One of the things that differentiates those who choose to stop paid work from those who do not is their expectations about retirement itself. Highly work-committed men who expect retirement to be unpleasant are far more likely to keep on working. They may have few interests or hobbies outside their work. Equally work-committed men who anticipate retirement with more pleasure are more likely to stop work. Overall then, those who shun retirement do so either because of economic necessity, or to ease themselves gradually into a nonworking state, or because they continue to find their work more satisfying than they expect retirement to be.

---

single source of retirement income overall; for nearly half of older Americans (46 percent) it is the *only* source of income (Ycas & Grad, 1987).

These numbers, though, do not tell us anything about the average level of income for older adults in comparison to their own incomes before retirement. It will not surprise you to know that on average, incomes decline at retirement. Data from Palmore's combined analysis suggest that the drop is on the order of about 25 percent. But this figure misrepresents the actual financial status of retired persons to a considerable degree. In the United States, as in many developed countries, many retired adults own their own homes and thus have no mortgage payments; their children are launched; they are eligible for Medicare, as well as for many special senior-citizen benefits. When you adjust for all these factors, you find that, *on average*, retired adults in the United States, Australia, and most European countries have incomes that are 85 to 100 percent of preretirement levels (Smeeding, 1990). (The most striking exception to this statement, by the way, is Britain, where as many as 60 percent of elders have incomes at or near poverty levels. [Walker, 1990]). For some, particularly some of the working poor, income may actually increase after retirement. A combination of Social Security and Supplemental Security Income (SSI) may be more than these individuals were able to earn in their working years (Palmore, et al., 1985).

Twenty years ago I could not have written such an upbeat summary. But significant improvements in Social Security benefits in the United States (and equivalent improvements in many other countries), including regular cost-of-living increases, have meant

Compare your current budget to what you might anticipate when you are 65 or older. Where would your expenses be less? In what areas might your expenses rise in late adulthood?

that in the past few decades the relative financial position of the elderly has improved more than any other age group in the population. For example, in 1970, 24.6 percent of all adults over 65 in the United States were living below the poverty line; in 1988, only 12 percent were at that low economic level. In contrast, 20.4 percent of children lived in poverty in 1988 (U.S. Bureau of the Census, 1990).

But such low rates of poverty among the elderly are misleading, as are the figures on adequate average incomes—in this case, both figures are deceptively positive. A large percentage of older adults fall into a category Smeeding (1990) calls "'tweeners," those with incomes just above the poverty line. In 1988, a fifth of all older couples, and two fifths of single elders, were in this category. For singles, this group was defined by an income between $5700 and $11,400 per year; for couples, the equivalent range was $7200 to $14,400. These adults are "not well off enough to be financially secure, while not poor enough to qualify for the means-tested elderly safety net" (Smeeding, 1990, p. 372).

The fact that twice as many single as married elders fall into this group is one sign of a more pervasive difference. Table 18.3, which shows poverty rates for different sub-groups of elders, makes the point even more clearly. If I broke it down still further, by ethnic group, you would see that at every age and for every marital category, black and Hispanic elders have higher rates of poverty than do whites. Among the aged, the sub-group at highest risk for poverty is black unmarried women, of whom as many as 70 percent live in poverty (U.S. Bureau of the Census, 1989a). And because women live longer than men do, nearly three-fourths of the elderly poor are women.

Many of these financially impoverished older women are not really "retired"; they were never employed. Most rely exclusively on Social Security income or on other forms of public assistance. If the woman did not work, but her deceased husband earned Social Security credits, her income is a fraction of that to which her husband was entitled. While he was still alive, their combined pensions would have been enough to raise them above the poverty level; when she is widowed, his pension disappears and she is left with only her own reduced share. In 1987, the average Social Security benefit for a widow(er) was $455 a month, or $5460 a year, which is just at the poverty line.

Some of this sex difference in poverty levels among the elderly is likely to shrink in later cohorts, because many more women will have been in the labor force and thus will have accumulated retirement benefits of their own. But for now, this feminization of poverty is very striking among the elderly.

In the face of these statistics, it is easy to become discouraged about the financial status of the elderly. But let us also not forget the more positive points with which I began this section: (1) overall adequacy of income does *not* decline, on average, after retirement;

TABLE 18.3 Incidence of Poverty for Various Subgroups of Older Adults in the United States in 1986

	All 65 +	65–74	75–84	85 +
Total poverty rates	12.6	10.6	15.5	18.8
Men	8.5	7.5	9.2	16.6
Married men	5.9	5.5	6.1	9.7
Women	15.6	13.0	19.2	19.7
Married women	6.1	5.5	7.6	10.7
Widowed women	21.3	19.8	20.3	23.4

Source: Smeeding, 1990, Table 19–3, p. 369; original source is House Ways and Means Committee, 1988.

and (2) elderly adults in the United States are better off financially today than they have ever been.

Effects on Health. The longitudinal studies tell us quite clearly that health simply does not change—for better or worse—because of retirement. When ill health accompanies retirement, the causal sequence is nearly always that the individual retired *because* he or she was in poor health. There is simply no indication that among those in good health at retirement age, retirement itself has any effect on health status over the succeeding years (Palmore et al., 1985). This clear set of research results is interesting because it suggests that for the vast majority of adults, retirement is not a highly stressful life change. That conclusion is buttressed further by studies of the impact of retirement on attitudes and mental health.

Effects on Attitudes and Mental Health. The bulk of the evidence suggests that retirement has essentially no impact on overall life satisfaction or subjective well-being. Longitudinal studies that have included such measures show little difference in scores before and after retirement, and there is little sign of any increase in depression among

---

THE REAL WORLD
Moving South: Residential Mobility After Retirement

One of the effects of retirement for most adults is an increase in choices about where to live. When your job or your spouse's job no longer ties you to a specific place, you can choose to move to sunnier climes or to live nearer to one of your children. Many of you may have the notion, as did I, that such a move is common among older adults. Somewhat to my surprise, I find that it is not.

There *is* a small burst of residential moves right around retirement age, so it is clear that some older adults do indeed choose to take advantage of their greater freedom in this way. But this burst only brings the rate of moves to about 1 percent a year (Longino, 1990). There is another burst of moves roughly ten years later, beginning at about age 75.

Charles Longino (1990; Longino et al., 1991; Jackson et al., 1991; Litwak & Longino, 1987), who has been the most diligent investigator of residential moves among the elderly, suggests that there are three types of moves. The first, which he calls an *amenity* move, is the one most of us think of when we think of older adults changing residences. If an older adult makes such a move, it is almost always right around the time of retirement. Most typically, amenity moves are in a direction *away* from the older person's children, frequently to a warmer climate—Florida, California, and Arizona being the most popular destinations in the United States. In Canada, amenity moves are most often westward, particularly to British Columbia; in Britain, the equivalent move is to the seaside.

Those who make such amenity moves are likely to be still married, relatively healthy, with adequate or good retirement income. Often the relocating pair have vacationed in the new location, many have planned the move carefully over a number of years (e.g., Cuba & Longino, 1991). Most—but not all—report higher levels of life satisfaction or morale after such a move, although there are some who move back to their home base because they find themselves too isolated from kin. These days, a growing number of older adults try to split the difference with a pattern of *seasonal migration*, spending winter months in sunnier areas and summer months at home, nearer to family. One survey of older residents of upstate New York found that 14 percent had spent at least part of the winter in another state, usually in the Sun Belt (Krout, 1983).

The second type of move, which Longino calls *compensatory migration* or a *kinship migration*, occurs when the older adult—most often a widow living alone—has developed a sufficient level of chronic disability that she is having serious difficulty managing an independent household. When a move of this type occurs, it is nearly always a shift to be closer to a daughter or son or some other relative who can provide regular assistance. In some cases this means moving in with that daughter or son, but often the move is to an apartment or house nearby, or into a special retirement community in which the individual lives independently but has supportive services available. My maternal grandparents spent the last several decades of their lives living in such a retirement community.

The final type of migration in late adulthood is what Longino calls *institutional migration*, a move to nursing home care. Three of my four grandparents made such a move for the final few weeks of their lives, when their health had deteriorated to the point where they needed regular nursing care that no one in the family could provide for them.

Of course, very few older adults actually move three times. Longino's point is that these are three very different kinds of moves, made by quite different subsets of the population of elderly and at different time points in the years of late adulthood. Amenity moves are usually early, kinship or compensatory moves are likely to be mid- to late-old age, while institutional moves are clearly late in life. Only the first of these reflects the increase in choices and options that may open up during the retirement years.

those recently retired (Palmore et al., 1985). For most, retirement is not perceived as a stress at all.

One recent study has provided some particularly clear evidence on this point. Raymond Bossé and his colleagues (Bossé et al., 1991) have been studying a group of over 1500 men over a period of years. In the most recent contact, the subjects were asked to indicate which of 31 possibly stressful life events had occurred to them in the past year and to rate the overall stressfulness of each of these events. Retirement was ranked thirtieth out of 31 in overall stressfulness, below even such items as "move to a less desirable residence," or "decrease in responsibilities or hours at work or where you volunteer." Of those who had retired in the previous year, seven out of ten said that they found retirement either not at all or only a little stressful. Those men in the sample who were still working were almost twice as likely to list work problems as retired men were to list retirement problems.

Among the 30 percent of retired men in this study who did list some problems with retirement, poor health, and poor family finances were the most likely causes. Those with marital problems were also likely to describe more daily hassles in their retirement life.

Other evidence suggests that those who respond least well to retirement are those who had the least control over the process. Those who are forced to retire—either by poor health, by mandatory retirement policies, because their jobs were eliminated, or for any other reason—when they would prefer to be working, and those who are still working when they would prefer to be retired, are both likely to report lower satisfaction and higher levels of stress (Herzog, House & Morgan, 1991). Retirement is also likely to be more stressful for those whose economic situation is poor or for those who must cope simultaneously with retirement and with other major life changes, such as widowhood (Stull & Hatch, 1984). But for those for whom retirement is anticipated and on-time, this role loss is not stressful.

One of the other bits of folklore about retirement is that it is hard on wives, who must adjust to the full-time presence of a husband who previously was out of the house most of the day. How could you design a study that would tell you whether this is true or not?

▶ Personality Changes in Late Adulthood

If the personality changes of young adulthood can be described as "individuation," and those of middle adulthood (more tentatively) as "mellowing," how might we describe the changes of late adulthood? Does mellowing simply continue? Are there other changes?

If this retiring man is at all typical, he is under 65, has planned at least a little bit for his retirement, and will experience few stresses associated with the transition.

Several theorists have hypothesized specific forms of change, but there is little agreement and very little data. Still, you should at least be familiar with the alternative views.

Erikson's View of Integrity

Erikson thought that the task of achieving ego integrity began in middle adulthood but that it was most central in late adulthood. To achieve it, the older adult must come to terms with who she is and has been, with how her life has been lived, the choices that were made, the opportunities gained and lost. It also involves coming to terms with death and accepting its imminence.

We have essentially no longitudinal or even cross-sectional data to tell us whether older adults are more likely than younger or middle-aged adults to achieve such self-acceptance. What we have instead are a few bits of information suggesting that those who have achieved it are less fearful of death and most likely to reminisce happily about their lives.

In one such study, Maxine Walaskay (Walaskay, Whitbourne & Nehrke, 1983–84) used a method very like Marcia's Ego Identity Interview to classify older adults into one of four statuses:

Integrity achieved. The individual is aware of her own aging, able to accept her own unique life as it was lived, and able to adjust to changes.

Despair. The person has come to a negative evaluation of her own life, does not accept it, sees life as "too short" to make up for mistakes.

Foreclosed. The individual is content with her current life but resists any self-exploration, any assessment of the whole lifetime.

Dissonant. The person is just beginning to try to resolve the integrity dilemma and is full of ambivalence.

When Walaskay classified a group of 40 older adults based on her interviews, and then also assessed their fear of death and their overall life satisfaction, she found that those in the achieved and foreclosed statuses were most satisfied with their lives, and least anxious about death.

Such a study is suggestive, but barely more than that. Because the integrity and foreclosed statuses were little different in satisfaction or fear, it is not at all clear that acceptance of one's own life is a necessary ingredient for contentment with current life or even adaptation to old age. It would be useful to have more research of this kind, but I am not convinced that Erikson is correct that integrity versus despair is the most helpful conceptualization of the central personal task of old age.

Reminiscence and Life Review

One offshoot of Erikson's theory has been the notion that reminiscence is a necessary, healthy part of old age. If a positive view of one's whole life is to be achieved, perhaps it is essential to look back on one's past years. Robert Butler used the phrase **life review** (Butler, 1963) to describe such a process.

Unfortunately, despite two decades of research on Butler's ideas (Haight, 1988), we are still full of ignorance about this process. Just as Walaskay found that both integrated and foreclosed adults were likely to be satisfied with their lives, research on reminiscence suggests that either high or low levels of reminiscence can be found among well-adjusted and contented older adults (e.g., Coleman, 1986). There is simply no indication that high levels of reminiscence are necessary to achieve such contentment, nor do we know whether reminiscence actually increases in old age, and if so, at what point in late adulthood it rises in importance.

Disengagement Theory

Another theory that has had a good deal of influence on gerontologists is **disengagement theory**, first proposed by Cumming and Henry (1961) to describe what they saw as a central psychological process of old age. As reformulated by Cumming (1975), disengagement theory has three aspects:

Shrinkage of life space. As we age, we interact with fewer and fewer others, fill fewer and fewer roles.

Increased individuality. In the roles and relationships that remain, the older individual is less and less governed by strict rules or expectations.

Acceptance—even embrace—of these changes. The healthy older adult actively disengages from roles and relationships, turning more and more inward and away from interactions with others.

The first two of these points seem largely beyond dispute. What has been controversial about disengagement theory is the third point. Cumming and Henry argued that the normal and *healthy* response to the shrinkage of roles and relationships is for the older adult to step back still further, to stop seeking new roles, to spend more time alone, to turn inward.

The research evidence on this last point has been decidedly mixed. On the one hand, Cumming and Henry appear to be quite wrong in concluding that isolation or withdrawal is the healthier choice. On the contrary, all the evidence suggests that those who disengage the *least* are the happiest, have the highest morale, and live the longest (e.g., Bryant & Rakowski, 1992; Palmore, 1981; Holahan, 1988). The effect is not large, but it has been found consistently.

On the other hand, there is some support for disengagement theory in the observation that older adults seem to be more content with solitude than is true at earlier ages. Recall the point I made in Chapter 14 that older adults are *least* likely to describe themselves as lonely, while young adults are most likely. It is also true that every in-depth study of life styles of older adults identifies at least a few who lead contented, socially isolated lives, sometimes engaged in an all-consuming hobby (e.g., Maas & Kuypers, 1974; Rubinstein, 1986).

Some older adults are quite content with solitary lives.

Clearly, then, it is possible to choose a highly disengaged life-style in late adulthood and to find satisfaction in it. But it is *not* the case that such disengagement is necessary for overall mental health in old age. For most adults, the opposite is true. For most, some level of social involvement is both a sign, and probably a cause, of higher morale and lower levels of depression or other psychiatric symptoms. Roles and relationships may rule our lives less in late adulthood than at earlier ages, but they still seem to be an essential ingredient for emotional balance, at least for most of us.

Each of these three approaches has been influential; none has been ultimately satisfactory as a description of late adult personality. As is the case with health and physical status in these same years, the clearest truth is probably that there is immense diversity in adults' ways of approaching and responding to old age. There may be, at some deeper level, some kind of search for integrity, some kind of disengagement. But if so, we have not yet found the best way of capturing such a process in our theoretical or empirical sights.

◗ Individual Differences

In recent years one of the guiding themes in the gerontology literature has been the concept of *successful aging* (e.g., Baltes & Baltes, 1990b), defined in terms of long life, good physical and mental health, good retention of mental abilities, social competence, a sense of personal control, and overall satisfaction with one's life. Researchers and theorists have begun to ask what characteristics of an individual might predict such good outcomes. I have already talked about the predictors of longevity and of physical and cognitive health in Chapter 17. Many of the same factors appear when we look at an outcome such as life satisfaction, as you can see from the list in Table 18.4.

If we look for patterns within this list, it doesn't take long to identify social support as a critical ingredient in several of the patterns described in the table. For example, one of the reasons that lower-income or lower-social-class adults have lower overall satisfaction is that they have weaker social support networks. If you compare subgroups of middle- and lower-class adults who have equivalent social support, there are no differences in satisfaction (Murrell & Norris, 1991).

We can see the tracks of social support also in the link between extraversion and life satisfaction: extraverted adults tend to create larger and more intimate social networks (e.g., Krause, Liang & Keith, 1990). Social support plays a similar role in the correlation between life changes and satisfaction. Those who have an adequate network are at least partially buffered from the worst effects of stressful life events.

A second thread running through the items in Table 18.4 is that old friend, a sense of control (Rodin, 1986), a personal characteristic I talked about in Chapter 13. For example, financial strain among the elderly appears to be linked to overall life satisfaction or depression primarily through the loss of any sense of control over one's life—a link found in studies in both Japan and the United States (Krause, Jay & Liang, 1991). Even life events that seem objectively highly stressful may have little negative effect if the individual feels he has some choice. So *involuntary* retirement or *involuntary* institutionalization have negative effects, while planned and chosen retirement or move to a nursing home do not.

As a final point, let me emphasize yet again that what is critical in almost all cases is an individual's *perception* of her situation: perceived adequacy of social support, perceived adequacy of income, and self-ratings of health are all better predictors of life satisfaction or morale than are any objective measures. This may mean that one adaptive response to the many losses and declines of late adulthood is to lower one's standards, to expect less and thus to be satisfied with less. When an older adult describes himself as

TABLE 18.4 Predictors of Life Satisfaction in Older Adults

DEMOGRAPHIC FACTORS

Income/Social class	Those with higher income are more likely to be satisfied with their lives, even when you hold constant other factors, such as health.
Education	More highly educated adults are slightly more satisfied, but the difference is small.
Gender	There is essentially no difference, despite the higher level of aches and pains and the larger number of widows among older women.
Marital status	Married adults consistently report higher life satisfaction.
Race/Ethnicity	There appears to be no general tendency for blacks, Hispanics, or other minority groups to have lower (or higher) life satisfaction beyond the effect of social class and income. For this outcome, at least, there appears to be no "double jeopardy" among aging minorities. Those who are poor and black, for example, are not more dissatisfied than any other group.

PERSONAL QUALITIES

Personality	Extraverted adults, and those low in neuroticism, are consistently more satisfied with their lives.
Sense of control	The greater the sense of control, the greater the life satisfaction. This may be especially significant in late adulthood, when the objective amount of control may decline.
Social interaction	Those with more contact with others, especially more intimate and supportive contact, are more satisfied.
Health	Those with better self-perceived health are more satisfied. Note, though, that self-perceived health is not at all perfectly correlated with health as a physician might rate it.
Religion	Those who describe themselves as more religious also describe themselves as more satisfied.
Negative life change	The more negative life changes an elder has recently had to deal with, the lower his life satisfaction is likely to be.

Sources: Antonucci, 1991; Diener, 1984; George, 1990; Gibson, 1986; Koenig, Kvale & Ferrell, 1988; Markides & Mindel, 1987; Murrell & Norris, 1991; Willits & Crider, 1988.

being in "good health" he is unlikely to mean precisely the same thing that he meant when he was 25. But what seems to be critical for overall emotional balance, for a sense of satisfaction with one's life, is the degree of discrepancy between what one expects and what one has. Because such expectations are another example of internal models, we see yet again the importance of understanding such internal models if we are to understand any individual's course of development from birth to death.

Summary

1. Late adulthood is a time when many large and small roles are shed. Remaining roles have less content. This may offer greater license for individuality and for choice.

2. Many older adults lose the role of spouse because of the high rate of widowhood. This is far more common among older women, however, among whom the majority are widowed.

3. Among those elders who are not married, living alone is the most common living arrangement among elders in the United States, typically from preference. The minority who live with a child are most likely to be drawn from

any of several subgroups: those with low income, minority elderly, especially African-Americans, and those who have many daughters.

4. Spousal relationships in late adulthood are, on average, high in marital satisfaction, with strong loyalty and mutual affection. If one spouse is disabled, the healthier spouse is likely to provide care.

5. Married elders, as a group, are somewhat healthier and more satisfied with their lives than are single elders; this difference is larger among men than women.

6. The majority of elders have at least one living child, and most see their child(ren) regularly and with some pleasure. But the amount of contact with children is *not* correlated with older adults' overall level of life satisfaction or morale.

7. There is some indication that relationships with siblings, particularly sisters, may become more significant in late adulthood than at earlier ages.

8. Degree of contact with friends *is* correlated with overall life satisfaction among older adults. Women in this age group continue to have larger social networks. Men rely more on their spouse for social support, while women rely on both friends and children.

9. Among African-Americans, social networks often include fictive kin in central helping roles. Older blacks in the United States also rely on church groups for support and assistance more than is true of other groups.

10. The average age of retirement is now closer to 62 than 65 in the United States and in many developed countries. Early retirement is most often caused by ill health. On-time retirement is affected by family responsibilities, adequacy of anticipated pension income, and satisfaction with one's job.

11. Income typically declines with retirement, but income *adequacy* does not decline so much. Improvements in Social Security mean that elder adults are now better off financially than ever before, but 12 percent live in poverty and another quarter have near-poverty incomes. Among elders, women and minorities are most likely to live in poverty.

12. Retirement appears not to be a stressful life change for the great majority. It is not causally connected to any deterioration in physical or mental health. The minority who find it stressful are likely to be those who feel they have least control over the process.

13. No theory of personality change in late adulthood has been well supported by existing evidence. Erikson's concept of integrity and Butler's concept of life review have been influential, but research does not indicate they are prevalent or necessary.

14. The concept of disengagement has similarly been found wanting; high life satisfaction and good mental health are found most often among elders who disengage the *least*.

15. One aspect of successful aging is high life satisfaction, found most often among elders who are married, have adequate income, are somewhat extroverted in personality, who feel they have good control over their lives, perceive their own health to be good, and are satisfied with the amount and quality of social interaction they have.

16. Adequacy of perceived social support and a sense of control appear to be especially crucial.

Key Terms

disengagement theory   life review

Suggested Readings

Binstock, R. H. & George, L. K. (Eds.) (1990). *Handbook of aging and the social sciences*, 3rd ed. San Diego: Academic Press. (This is the latest edition of a handbook series that provides first-rate up-to-date summaries of research and theory on a whole range of subjects relevant to this chapter. The material is often dense, but this is a splendid source of current references.)

Bond, J. & Coleman, P. (Eds.) (1990). *Aging in society*. London: Sage Publications. (I recommended this book in Chapter 17 and do so again here. It not only provides a very good review of research on retirement, living arrangements, intimate relationship, and many other topics, it also offers a non–United States perspective, because the authors are all British and rely on British research as well as studies in the United States and other countries.)

Markides, K. S. & Mindel, C. H. (1987). *Aging and ethnicity*. Newbury Park, CA: Sage Publications. (This is the best book I have found on this subject.)

Schulz, J. H. (1988). *The economics of aging* (4th ed.). Dover, MA: Auburn House. (Everything you ever wanted to know about the economic status of the elderly.)

SUMMING UP LATE ADULTHOOD

Key Characteristics of Late Adulthood

As usual, I've briefly summarized this age period in a table, which shows that there are some distinct differences between the young old and the old old. Functionally significant decrements in many types of cognitive skills, for example, are not found until past age 75, and many physical measures show an accelerated rate of change at about the same time.

Yet despite the apparent clarity of the information in the table, this is an extremely difficult age period to talk about or to summarize. Depending on which facts you choose to emphasize, you can arrive at a fairly rosy description or a quite depressing one. Of late, social scientists have been tilting toward more optimistic statements, partly because newer research shows fewer inevitable declines. A case can be made that the central fact about late adulthood is that *both* the optimistic and the pessimistic views are correct—for some people. Joseph Quinn makes the point very clearly:

Never begin a sentence with "The elderly are . . ." or "The elderly do . . . ." No matter what you are discussing, some are, and some are not; some do, and some do not. The most important characteristics of the aged is their diversity. The average can be very deceptive, because it ignores the tremendous dispersion around it. Beware of the mean. (Quinn, 1987, p. 64)

Quinn is absolutely correct. There is enormous variability among older adults in physical and mental status, in vigor, wisdom, satisfaction, zest, loneliness, and economic security. For those elders at the more positive ends of these various continua, late adulthood can be a time of choice and opportunity. Edwin Shneidman (1989), writing about the decade of one's seventies, seems to be describing this subgroup when he says:

Consider that when one is a septuagenarian, one's parents are

A Summary of the Threads of Development in Late Adulthood

Aspect of Development	"Young Old" 65	75	"Old Old" 85	95
Physical Development	Significant decline in hearing, speed of response; continued gradual decline on most physical measures. Incidence of disease and disability increased.	Accelerated decline on most physical measures, although there is wide individual variability even at this age.		
Cognitive Development	On crystallized abilities generally little loss; gradual decline on many fluid abilities.	Reliably measurable decline on all cognitive measures, on average, but wide individual variability. Some indication of "terminal drop" for crystallized abilities.		
Personality Development	No clear understanding of the process of personality change in late adulthood; Erikson suggests ego integrity as key task; Neugarten suggests interiority. Cumming and Henry suggest disengagement. None of these has strong empirical support.			
		Rise in incidence of depression in very late adulthood, although this appears not to be caused by age itself.		
Social Relationships and Roles	Continued high rate of social involvement; degree of social involvement in general related to life satisfaction. Retirement for most working adults.	Some decline in social involvement for those whose physical disabilities make mobility more problematic.		

gone, children are grown, mandatory work is done; health is not too bad, and responsibilities are relatively light, with time, at long last, for focus on the self. These can be sunset years, golden years, an Indian Summer, a period of relatively mild weather for both soma and psyche in the late autumn or early winter of life, a decade of greater independence and increased opportunities for further self-development. (1989, p. 684)

At the other end of the continuum are older adults who live below or close to poverty level, with significant physical ailments, for whom these last years are anything but an Indian summer.

No single summary statement can encompass this degree of diversity. Yet Quinn is also wrong, because there *are* some common patterns, nonetheless. Yes, a small percentage of older adults retain excellent physical and mental functioning into late old age, but age *normally* brings a significant slowing of responses, wear and tear on the joints, higher rates of disease, and all the other physical changes I have described in detail. And no matter how unusually fit an older adult may be, he or she *cannot* run as fast as a 25-year-old.

All the emphasis on those adults who retain good fitness thus risks leaving the impression that for some people the sands do not fall through the hourglass. The fact that the biological clock does not tick equally loudly for all older adults cannot mask or disguise the fact that biological change/loss becomes more and more of an issue for everyone in these later years. Those who retain good function do so with greater effort and more care as they age. They more often operate near the limits of their reserve capacity than is true of younger adults.

Paul and Margaret Baltes (1990a)

have suggested a framework for thinking about successful aging that I think clarifies this point particularly well. They define successful aging as a process of "*selective optimization with compensation*" (p. 21). In this view, an older adult maintains maximum levels of functioning through three strategies:

• *Selection*: restricting the range of domains or arenas of operation, concentrating energy and time on those demands and needs that are most central. So an older adult might give up mountain climbing but walk regularly, or serve on only one committee instead of three, or rest up before a demanding activity.

• *Optimization*: enriching and augmenting their reserves by learning new strategies and keeping old skills well practiced, such as by taking classes, reading the paper regularly, maintaining levels of physical fitness with good diet and exercise.

• *Compensation*: compensating for losses in various simple as well as creative ways, such as wearing glasses or a hearing aid, driving less often at night or when roads are crowded, or writing more lists rather than relying on internal memory systems.

The very fact that compensation is required to adjust well to old age is a crucial point. Yet it is also the case that a great many adults *do* compensate and adjust to their changing physical and social circumstances, often with inventiveness and humor. A personal example has made this very clear to me. My father, now 78, carries with him a fat notebook in which he keeps lists of things to do, items to buy, times of appointments, address, phone numbers. He refers to this notebook as his "brains," which always makes me laugh. If he momentarily loses track of this notebook, he asks, "Where are my brains?" Yet because of this highly successful compensatory device, he does not forget appointments, has frequently used phone numbers handy when he needs them, and is able to move efficiently through his days. He is still frustrated by tip-of-the-tongue problems with his memory; he walks slowly. But he *has* compensated successfully for many of his various limitations and disabilities so that he can still be active and do many of the things that matter to him.

Central Processes

The most central process in all of this is clearly the set of physical changes that makes up normal aging. These changes begin their slow march in young adulthood or even adolescence. But for most of us, it is only in late adulthood that the changes accumulate enough that we need to compensate, or increase in rate to the point that we experience a rapid decline in some function. Recent research does tell us that at least some of the changes we had attributed to inevitable aging may be preventable or avoidable altogether—such as increases in cholesterol. But let us not swing too far in the other direction and conclude that there is no such thing as physical aging. Neurons lose dendrites; fewer mature T cells are produced by the immune system; damage to DNA in individual cells accumulates. Eventually, one or more body systems cannot continue to function, and we experience disease and ultimately death.

What makes this biological decline easier to deal with is the simultaneous change in the demands of many social roles. Older adults can adapt to physical or mental losses in part because they are less constrained by role expectations, including the role of parent and that of worker.

Of course it is not accidental that the weakening of the grip of social roles occurs at the time when the body is becoming less reliable. Young adults take on the burden of key social roles because they are physically fit to do so, because this is the optimum time for childbearing and child rearing, the

time of greatest physical strength. This very same timing means that 30 or 40 years later, when late adulthood is reached, children will be grown and the younger generation(s) can take up the physical and mental burdens of work and intense family life.

Given the intertwining of these two sequences of change, it is easy to see how Cumming and Henry arrived at disengagement theory. They perceived a kind of harmony in the entire system: in old age, social obligations are gradually withdrawn and no new roles are offered. It makes some sense to assume that the older adult would naturally respond to this social loss by withdrawing still further. But while such symmetry may make conceptual sense, it turns out not to make psychological sense. Older adults may be freed of most role prescriptions, but they do not lose their desire for intimacy or for emotional support from

others; they may be less likely to be lonely than are younger adults, but it is still true that those elders who lack supportive and intimate human relationships are at greater risk for illness and depression.

This observation leads us to the more general point that despite the physical changes of aging and the near inaudibility of the social clock, many of the same basic psychological processes that we see in teenagers, young adults, and middle-aged adults are still operative in old age. For example, life satisfaction is predicted by essentially the same factors at every age: adequate social support, a sense of control, low incidence of off-time or unplanned life changes, and adequate financial conditions. Among young adults, work satisfaction is a more significant ingredient in the equation, and among older adults, health rises to near the top of the list. But the common ingredients are notable.

Wallace Stegner makes the point particularly well in his book *The Spectator Bird*—one of the best novels about aging I have ever read. One of the characters, a doctor in his early eighties, when asked if he feels like an old man, replies that he does not. He feels like a young man who has something wrong with him.

That inner sense that you are "the same" but that somehow your body has changed is a common sensation in middle and late adulthood. It becomes disconcerting to look in a mirror, not only because the physical changes themselves may be not-so-charming to see, but because of the sense of shock that the "older" person in the mirror is really you. Such a sense of dislocation between the physical changes and a less-changing inner self arises not only because we each take ourselves with us through adult life—our personality traits, our internal working models, our physical characteristics—but also because the same fundamental psychological processes are operative at every age. There are different shadings, to be sure. But we respond to stress in similar ways, regardless of age; we create attachments and use our central attachment figures in much the same ways, regardless of age.

Influences on the Basic Processes

I've made these points before, but let me state them yet again, if only for emphasis. The largest influences on the experiences of late adulthood are factors that begin far earlier in life.

In your sixties you may be able to choose when to retire; you can choose where you will live and how you will spend your time. But all those decisions will be heavily influenced by your health, and that in turn is strongly related to all the earlier health decisions you made (or did not make). To be sure, not everyone has a great deal of choice about early health decisions. A man or woman may spend many years working in an unhealthy environment—mining, working with chemicals or asbestos, or the like—because that is the only work that is available to support the family. Many children and younger adults also do not have access to good health care or to a decent diet, deficits that will have repercussions at later ages. But whether we are talking about personal health choices like smoking or unavoidable health risks taken earlier in life, it is clear that all the health chickens come home to roost in late life. And no single thing will affect the shape of late adulthood more than the individual's health. Those in robust health retain better intellectual abilities, they are able to maintain physical function better because they are more able to get adequate exercise, and they have more options for "optimization with compensation."

The timing of earlier roles also affects the shape of later adult life, especially for those Neugarten calls the *young old*. Those who had their children late are likely to have a quite different experience between 65 and 75 than will those whose childbearing was completed by age 25 or 30. The former group may find themselves working past normal retirement age because of financial needs of not-yet-launched children. And because such late-in-life children are more recently launched when the older adults reach a point at which they may need financial or other assistance, there is likely to be more conflict of roles.

A third early-established pattern that can affect the experience of late adulthood is the quality of intimate relationships—not only with a spouse or partner, but with friends. Those older adults who have a confidant weather the various stresses of aging more easily and buoyantly than do those who lack such a confidant. But confidants are not to be found hanging on trees, ready for plucking when you need them. They are created and nurtured over many years. Women seem to deal with the many changes of old age more easily than do men in no small part because they are more likely to have created a network of such intimate relationships throughout their lives.

There is at least one major exception to the argument that the major influences on late adulthood are patterns established much earlier in life. Within the period of late adulthood, successful aging also depends very much on that wise old principle, "Use it or lose it." In almost every arena of life, retention of capacity in late adulthood depends on repeated use, on practice. This is far less true at earlier ages, when the body and the mind may operate well despite neglect and disuse. But in late adulthood, optimization depends on regular use. The mind remains sharp to the extent that we use it; the body retains function to the extent that we exercise it; social relationships remain supportive to the extent that we nurture them with regular contact. The habit of such use can certainly be established at earlier ages. All to the good. But even those who have neglected their bodies, their minds, and their relationships can change these patterns in late adulthood, and by so doing they can achieve a more "successful" aging.

In the end, successful aging does not mean cheating death or necessarily living for more years. It does mean using the available years to the fullest extent. That this is possible is attested to by the minority of older adults who retain fitness and zest. I fully intend to become such a zestful, eccentric old lady.

19 DYING, DEATH AND BEREAVEMENT

The "last dance," the "end of the journey." These are among the many ways of describing death. We began our own journey in this book by studying the beginning of human life at conception; we must end it by talking about dying and death.

Death can come at any age, but for most of us in industrialized societies, death comes in late adulthood. Three-fourths of children born today can expect to die after age 65 (Marshall & Levy, 1990). So a good deal of what I will say about dying and death will concern older adults. But the story must begin earlier, with our understanding of and attitudes toward dying and death.

▶ The Meaning of Death over the Life Span

As an adult, you understand that death is irreversible, that it comes to everyone, and that it means a cessation of all function. But how early do children understand these aspects of death?

Children's Understanding of Death

Results from a variety of studies suggest that pre-school-age children typically understand none of these aspects of death. They believe that death can be reversed, such as through prayer, magic, or wishful thinking; they believe that dead persons can still feel or breathe; and they believe that death can be avoided by at least some people, such as those who are clever or lucky, or members of their own family (Speece & Brent, 1984; Lansdown & Benjamin, 1985). At about school age, just at about the time that Piaget described as the beginning of concrete operations, most children seem to understand both the permanence and universality of death.

To illustrate the shift, here are three responses given by children to an interview about death after they had heard a story about two children who used to go into a candy store kept by an old lady who died.

> A 5-year-old: Someone came into the shop to kill her. She'll see them again and she'll die again. She can try to get up.

> A 7-year-old: They never come alive again. You can't move because your heart has stopped. People wish you can come alive but you can't. Children can't die because they start at one and go to 100.

These boys, comforting each other in front of their mother's grave, are likely to have far more developmentally mature concepts of death than would others their age who have not encountered death first-hand.

A 9-year-old: Their heart can't take it any longer and they die. Babies can die of cancer, kidney problems. Heaven is much nicer than down here. (All quotes from Lansdown & Benjamin, 1985, p.20)

The first of these children has not yet understood the permanence of death; the second has not understood the universality of it; the third seems to have grasped all three, although the excerpt given is not extensive enough to be sure. Researchers have tried hard to connect the child's understanding of these aspects of the concept of death with the emergence of various facets of concrete operations. Some investigators have found that those children who understand conservation are also more likely to understand the permanence or universality of death. But not everyone has found such a link (Speece & Brent, 1984). Instead, as is true of so many other concepts at this age, the child's specific experience seems to make a good deal of difference. Four- and 5-year-olds who have had direct experience with death of a family member are more likely to have understood the permanence and loss of function associated with death than are those who have had no such personal experience (Stambrook & Parker, 1987).

The Meanings of Death in Adulthood

In adulthood, the concept of death goes well beyond the simple understanding of inevitability and universality. Most broadly, death has important social meaning. The death of any one person changes the roles and relationships of everyone else in that family. When an elder dies, everyone else in that particular lineage moves up one step in the generational system. If a middle-aged person dies, it may dislocate that same generational system because there is now no one in the "sandwich generation" to take on tasks of elder care. If it is a young adult or a child who dies, then the parents lose part of their role as parent. Beyond the family, death of individuals also affects other roles, by making room for younger adults to take on significant tasks. Retirement serves some of the same function because the older adult "steps aside" for the younger. But death brings many permanent changes in social systems.

Kalish (1985) lists four other meanings that death may have for adults.

Death as an Organizer of Time.   At an individual level, the prospect of death may shape one's view of time. Bernice Neugarten has suggested that in middle age, most

Death not only brings grief, it changes roles within families. This young man may well have to take on family responsibilities at an unusually early age.

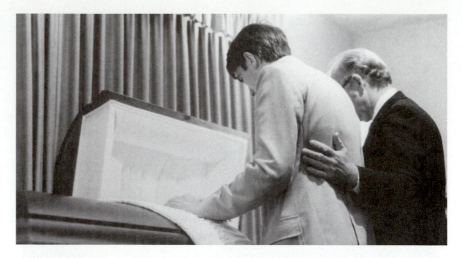

individuals switch in the way they think of time, from "time since birth" to "time till death" (1968, 1970), a shift clearly reflected by this middle-aged subject:

> Before I was 35, the future just stretched forth. There would be time to do and see and carry out all the plans I had. . . . Now I keep thinking, will I have time enough to finish off some of the things I want to do? (Neugarten, 1970, p.78)

When you think of your own age, do you think of time since birth, time till death, or both? If you think in terms of time till death, can you remember when you switched to this view, and why?

Such an "awareness of finitude"—to use Victor Marshall's phrase (1975)—is not a part of every middle-aged or older adult's view of death. Pat Keith (1981–82), in a study of a group of adults aged 72 and older, found that only about half thought in terms of "time remaining." Interestingly, those that did think of death in these terms had less fear of death. Other research confirms this: those middle-aged and older adults who continue to be preoccupied with the past and avoid thinking about their own eventual death are more likely to be fearful and anxious about death (Pollack, 1979–80).

Death as Punishment.   Children are quite likely to think of death as punishment for being bad—a kind of ultimate Stage 1 moral reasoning. But this view and its reverse (that long life is the reward for being good) are still common in adults. For example, Kalish and Reynolds (1976) found that 36 percent of adults in their study agreed with the statement that "most people who live to be 90 years old or older must have been morally good people." Such a view is strengthened by religious teachings that emphasize a link between sin and death.

Death as Transition.   Many adults see death as a transition from one form of life to another, from physical life to some kind of immortality. In the United States, roughly 70 percent believe in some kind of life after death (Klenow & Bolin, 1989–90). Such a belief is more common among women than men and more common among Catholics and Protestants than among Jews, but there is no age difference. Twenty-year-olds are just as likely to report such a belief as are those over 60.

Death as Loss.   The most pervasive meaning of death, for most adults, is that of loss. I do not mean here merely the understanding that the body functions stop at death. Beyond that is the awareness that death means loss of relationships, loss of taste or smell, loss of pleasure. Death means I'll never taste another brownie, or hear another beautiful piece of music, or hold hands with my lover, or laugh, or cry.

The type of loss that most concerns a person does seem to vary by age. Young adults are more concerned about loss of opportunity to experience things and about the loss of family relationships; older adults worry more about the loss of time to complete *inner* work. We can see such differences in the results of a study by Richard Kalish (Kalish &

Reynolds, 1976), who interviewed roughly 400 adults, equally divided into four ethnic groups: African-American, Japanese-American, Mexican-American, and Anglo-American. Among many other questions, he asked, "If you were told that you had a terminal disease and six months to live, how would you want to spend your time until you died?" Table 19.1 shows both the ethnic differences and the age differences in response to this question.

The largest ethnic difference Kalish and Reynolds found was that the Mexican-Americans in this sample were far more likely to say that they would increase the time they would spend with family or other loved ones. The age differences were more substantial. Younger adults were more likely to say they would seek out new experiences; older adults were considerably more likely to say they would turn inward—an interesting form of support for disengagement theory.

Fear of Death

If death is understood as punishment or loss, then it may be something to be feared. Fear of death has been one of the most studied aspects of attitudes toward death, and the research has consistently shown that middle-aged adults are most afraid, while older adults are the least afraid. Young adults typically fall in between (Riley & Foner, 1968; Gesser, Wong & Reker, 1987–88). The difference between the middle-aged and the aged is especially clear from a study by Vern Bengtson and his colleagues (Bengtson, Cuellar & Ragan, 1977), who have interviewed a sample of adults aged 45 to 74, chosen to represent the population of the city of Los Angeles. Figure 19.1 shows the percentage of each age group who said they were very afraid or somewhat afraid of death. The fact that the shape of the curve is so remarkably similar for all three ethnic groups who participated in this study makes the results even more impressive. And although these are cross-sectional results, similar patterns emerged from cross-sectional comparisons done in the 1960s and the 1980s, which makes the conclusion that much more credible.

This peak of fear of death in the middle adult years is entirely consistent with the proposals of a number of theorists, including Levinson, that confronting the inevitability of one's own death is one of the major psychological tasks of middle age. Awareness of that inevitability is presumably triggered by all those signs of body aging that begin to be apparent in these middle years, as well as by the death of elderly parents. These events combine to break down our defenses against awareness of death, and we become more consciously afraid.

TABLE 19.1 What Would You Do If You Knew You Were to Die in Six Months? Age and Ethnic Group Differences in Reply

	Ethnic Groups				Age Groups		
	Afr.-Amer.	Jap.-Amer.	Mex.-Amer.	Angl.-Amer.	20–39	40–59	60+
Make a marked change in life-style (e.g., travel, sex, experiences)	16	24	11	17	24	15	9
Center on inner life (e.g., read, contemplate, pray)	26	20	24	12	14	14	37
Focus concern on others; be with loved ones	14	15	38	23	29	25	12
Attempt to complete projects, tie up loose ends	6	8	13	6	11	10	3
No change in life-style	31	25	12	36	17	29	31

Source: Kalish & Reynolds, 1976, p. 205, item 037.

Figure 19.1 The remarkable similarity in the pattern of results for these three ethnic groups in southern California lends support to the generalization that older adults are less afraid of death than are the middle-aged. (*Source:* Bengtson, Cuellar & Ragan, 1977, Figure 1, p. 80.)

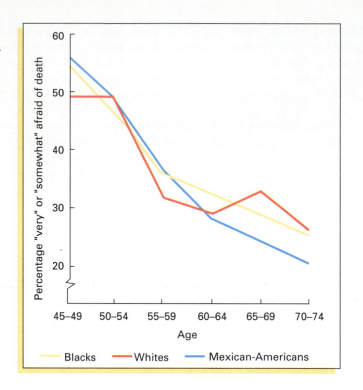

Is it possible that older adults are just as afraid of death as are the middle-aged, but that they simply deal with it differently? Can you think of any way you could study such a possibility?

Older adults do not become less concerned with death. On the contrary, the elderly think and talk more about death than do those at any other age. Death to the older person is highly salient. But it is apparently not as frightening as it was at middle life, perhaps because most individuals, having faced the inevitability, have come to terms with it. Older adults are more likely to fear the period of uncertainty *before* death than they are to fear death itself. They are anxious about where they may live, who will care for them, whether they will be able to cope with the loss of control and independence that may be part of the last months or years of life (Marshall & Levy, 1990).

Other Predictors of Fear of Death.   Two characteristics, other than age, correlated with fear of death, are religiosity and neuroticism. The most typical finding is that adults who are deeply religious or attend church regularly report less fear of death than do those who are less religious, although there are a few studies showing that those who are deeply irreligious are also low in fear of death (Kalish, 1985). The most fearful, then, may be those who are uncertain about, or uncommitted to, any religious or philosophical tradition. Those who feel they have some purpose or meaning are less afraid (Durlak, 1972).

Adults who score high on scales of neuroticism are also more fearful of death (Frazier & Foss-Goodman, 1988–89), as are those who feel that they have not accomplished what they had hoped in their lives or are disappointed in themselves (Neimeyer & Chapman, 1980–81; Pollack, 1979–80). In Erikson's terms, research results like these suggest that those who have achieved intimacy, generativity, and integrity will be less fearful of death than those who have not successfully resolved the various psychological tasks of adult life. If we think of it that way, then all of life is in some sense a preparation for death.

▶ Preparation for Death

Preparation for death occurs on a number of other levels as well. At a practical level, a person can obtain life insurance or make out a will. Such preparations become more common as you move toward late adulthood and thus closer to the inevitability of death. For example, 61 percent of men between ages 18 and 24 have life insurance, compared to 86 percent of men between 55 and 64 (U.S. Bureau of the Census, 1989b). Far fewer people prepare for death by making out a will; only about 30 percent of adults in the United States have done so. But it is still true that older adults are more likely than younger ones to have taken this step. In Kalish and Reynolds' study (1976), only 10 percent of those aged 20 to 39 had made out a will, compared to 39 percent of those 60 and older. Similarly, older adults are more likely to have made arrangements for their own funeral or burial.

At a somewhat deeper level, adults may prepare for death through some process of reminiscence, such as the life review Butler suggested. I mentioned in the last chapter that we have little evidence that older adults typically or necessarily go through such a review process. But for some, such a review may be an important aspect of "writing the final chapter," or legitimizing one's life in some fashion (Marshall & Levy, 1990). Two of my four grandparents, for instance, in their eighties wrote autobiographies for circulation within the family. I find the documents fascinating not only because they tell me more than I knew before about my grandparents' lives and about family history, but also because of the self-justification and self-explanations they contain. I know of no research that would tell me how common such explicit review may be, but such acts may form an important part of the preparation for death for at least some elders.

Deeper still, there may be unconscious changes that occur in the years just before death that we might think of as a type of preparation. I mentioned the physical and mental changes associated with the concept of "terminal drop" in Chapter 17. Research by Morton Lieberman has pointed to the possibility that there may be terminal psychological changes as well (Lieberman, 1965; Lieberman & Coplan, 1970).

Lieberman studied a group of older adults longitudinally, interviewing and testing each subject regularly over a period of three years. At the end of the study, Lieberman kept track of the subjects and noted the time of their death. In this fashion he was able to identify one group of 40 subjects who had all died rather soon (within one year) after the end of the interviewing, and to compare them with another group of 40 who had survived at least three years after the end of the testing. The two groups were matched by age, sex, and marital status at the start of the study. By comparing the psychological

Adults prepare for death in various ways, such as buying life insurance or writing a will, as this middle-aged woman is doing.

test scores of these two groups during the course of the three years of testing, he could detect changes that might take place near to death.

He found that those nearer to death not only showed terminal drop on tests of memory and learning, they also became less emotional, less introspective, less aggressive or assertive, more conventional, docile, and dependent, and more warm. All these characteristics increased over time, a pattern that did not occur among those the same age who were further from death. Thus, it was not that initially conventional, docile, dependent, unintrospective adults died sooner, but that these qualities became accentuated in those who were close to death.

This is only a single study. As always in such cases, we need to be careful about drawing sweeping conclusions from limited evidence. But the results are intriguing and suggestive. They paint a picture of a kind of psychological preparation for death—conscious or unconscious—in which the individual gives up tilting at windmills, becomes less active physically and psychologically. These near-death individuals do not necessarily become less involved with other people, but there is nonetheless a kind of "disengagement" that seems to occur.

Given these findings, is it possible that Cumming and Henry were correct about disengagement being a natural process toward the end of life, but placed it too early and too sweepingly in the years of late adulthood?

▶ The Process of Dying

Elizabeth Kübler-Ross (1969) drew very similar conclusions based on her work with terminally ill adults and children. In her early writings, she proposed that those who know they are dying move through a series of steps or stages, arriving finally at the stage she calls *acceptance*. This model of stages of dying has had many critics; even Kübler-Ross herself, in her later writings, no longer argues that dying moves through clear or sequential stages (Kübler-Ross, 1974). Instead, she now talks of emotional tasks rather than stages. But because her original ideas have been immensely influential and her terminology is still widely used, you need to have at least some familiarity with these concepts.

Kübler-Ross's Stages of Dying

Based on her observations of hundreds of dying patients, Kübler-Ross suggested five stages: denial, anger, bargaining, depression, and acceptance.

Denial.   Many people, confronted with a terminal diagnosis, react with some variant of "Not me!" "It must be a mistake," "I'll get another opinion," or "I don't feel sick." All these are forms of denial, a psychological defense that may be highly useful in the early hours and days after such a diagnosis, since it helps to deal with the shock of knowing one is near death. Kübler-Ross thought that these extreme forms of denial faded within a few days, to be replaced by anger.

Anger.   Anger often expresses itself in thoughts like "It's not fair!" but it may also be expressed toward God, toward the doctor who should have done something sooner, toward nurses or family members. The anger seems to be a response not only toward the terminal diagnosis itself, but also to the sense of loss of control and helplessness that many patients feel in impersonal medical settings.

Bargaining.   Stage 3 is an interesting new form of defense in which the patient tries to make "deals" with doctors, nurses, family, or God. "If I do everything you tell me, then I'll live till spring." Kübler-Ross has described a particularly compelling example of this: A patient with terminal cancer wanted to live long enough to attend the wedding of her eldest son. The hospital staff, to help her try to reach this goal, taught her self-hypnosis to deal with her pain, and she was able to attend the wedding. Kübler-Ross goes on to describe the aftermath: "I will never forget the moment when she returned to the hospital. She looked tired and somewhat exhausted and—before I could say hello—said, 'Now don't forget I have another son!' " (1969, p. 83).

Depression.   Bargaining may be a successful defense for a while, but eventually—so Kübler-Ross thought—it breaks down in the face of all the signs of declining physical status. At this point, stage 4 becomes evident as the patient becomes depressed. Many dying persons sink into despair, often lasting for long periods. In Kübler-Ross's view, this depression or despair is a necessary preparation for the final step of acceptance. In order to reach acceptance, the dying person must grieve for all that will be lost with death.

Acceptance.   When such grieving is finally done, the individual is ready to die. A particularly eloquent expression of acceptance comes from Stewart Alsop (1973), a writer who, after being diagnosed with leukemia, kept a diary of the last years of his life. In one of the very late entries in this journal he says, "A dying man needs to die as a sleepy man needs to sleep, and there comes a time when it is wrong, as well as useless, to resist" (Alsop, 1973, p. 299).

Criticisms and Alternative Views

There is no doubt about the enormous influence this description of the dying process has had on physicians, nurses, social workers, and others who work with dying individuals and their families. Not only did Kübler-Ross provide a common language, she made central to the debate the need for compassion from health-care workers and for dignity for the dying person. The emergence of alternative programs for the dying, such as the hospice movement—about which I'll say more in a moment—can be clearly traced to Kübler-Ross's writings.

But Kübler-Ross's original suggestion that the dying process necessarily involved these five emotions, occurring in a fixed sequence, has been widely criticized and largely discarded. The criticisms are of several types.

Method Problems.   Methodological criticisms have focused on the fact that Kübler-Ross's descriptions of dying stages were based on observations of perhaps 200 patients. She provided no systematic information about how often she saw them, over what length of time. She did not even give their ages, although it is clear that many were middle-aged or young adults, for whom a terminal diagnosis was clearly "off-time." Virtually all were cancer patients. It is not at all clear that the same reactions would necessarily occur among much older adults or among those experiencing other types of disease, such as heart disease or pneumonia. Thus, even if there are stages of dying in the responses of some adults, that may be true of only a particular subset.

Culture Specificity.   A second criticism has centered around the question of whether such reactions to dying are specific to this culture or are a universal human response. Most social scientists would now agree that reactions to dying are strongly culturally conditioned. In some Native American cultures, tradition calls for death to be faced and accepted with one's whole being and with composure. Because it is part of nature's cycle, it is not to be feared or fought. In some Plains Indian tribes, for example, a death song is composed to describe the individual's life and to complete the cycle (DeSpelder & Strickland, 1983).

In Mexican culture, death is seen as a mirror of the person's life. Thus, your death, your way of dying, tells much about what kind of person you have been. And unlike the dominant U.S. culture, in which death is feared and thoughts of it are repressed, in Mexican culture death is discussed frequently, even celebrated in a national feast day, the Day of the Dead (DeSpelder & Strickland, 1983). It seems inescapable that such cultural variations will affect an individual's reaction to his own impending death.

Are There Stages?   The most potent criticism of Kübler-Ross's stages of dying, though, is that there may be no stages at all, even in this culture and among the type of patient she originally described. Clinicians and researchers who have observed dying patients more systematically than did Kübler-Ross have not always found all five of the

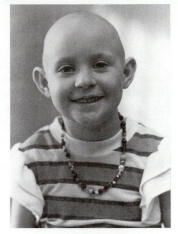

Children use some of the same defenses to deal with their own potential deaths as do adults. Young cancer patients, like this cheerful-looking young girl, may deny or bargain: "If I take my medicine I'll be able to go back to school in the fall."

If you wanted to discover whether there really are widely shared stages in people's reactions to dying, what kind of study would you have to do? How might you study stages of dying in those who die from something other than a disease with a clear terminal diagnosis?

ACROSS CULTURES
The Good Death in Kaliai

It is important to be aware that our own cultural ways of dealing with death are not universal. So let me give you an example of a radically different set of death rituals, found among the Kaliai, a small Melanesian group in Papua New Guinea (Counts, 1976–77). The Kaliai see death not as an end to life but as a transition between different life states. Those who have passed through this transition become powerful, superhuman beings—ordinarily invisible to the living person, but with their own form and duties.

In Kaliai beliefs, all deaths are caused by some malevolent agent or cause—someone or something that the dying person has offended in some fashion, be it another living person who may kill directly or through sorcery, a ghost, or a superhuman being. No matter how careful a life one may lead, it is impossible to avoid giving offense to someone or something, so eventually death will come.

A ''good death'' is one in which the transition from human to superhuman has been done properly, which means that all social relationships have been brought into balance. In this cultural system, all social relationships involve exchanges of material goods through lending and gift giving. To die with these exchanges in balance, the individual must make preparations as death approaches, making sure that he owes nothing nor is owed anything. If a person dies unexpectedly, the family must complete this process, or the transition to the superhuman status—called *antu*—cannot be completed.

Any person who feels that he is near death moves from his house into a temporary shelter. At that point he does two things. He attempts to thwart death by all possible means, including appeasing whoever he thinks he may have offended and using whatever medicines or cures may be offered. And he begins to bring to closure all his social relationships, so that when death comes he is fully prepared. Family members gather during this dying process, all of them speculating at length about who the killer might be, what transgressions the victim might be guilty of. If the victim recovers, he or she simply resumes normal life; everyone assumes that somehow the killer's feelings were somehow assuaged. If the victim dies, then the family members prepare the body for funeral rites, crying a grieving chant.

My purpose in describing this unusual cultural approach to death is not just to intrigue you with the range of human diversity, but to point out that in any culture, death customs flow naturally from beliefs about the causes and meaning of death. This is as true of our own culture or subcultures as it is of the Kaliai. Those who believe in the possibility of miracle cures will be more likely to go to Lourdes; those who believe that death can be thwarted with proper medical care will react differently to a diagnosis of a serious illness than will someone who sees illness as God's choice or who believes in the law of karma. Each of us, and each culture or subculture collectively, has beliefs about death, dying, and afterlife that will affect the way we approach our own death, as well as the way we react to the death of those close to us.

---

emotions she described, and not in the order specified. Of the five, only depression appears to be a common thread among dying persons in Western culture. There is little sign that the majority of dying persons move toward the kind of acceptance or disengagement that Alsop describes (Baugher et al., 1989–90). Instead, some remain active and involved right up to the end. Edwin Shneidman (1980, 1983) puts it well:

> I reject the notion that human beings, as they die, are somehow marched in lock step through a series of stages of the dying process. On the contrary, in working with dying persons, I see a wide panoply of human feelings and emotions, of various human needs, and a broad selection of psychological defenses and maneuvers—a few of these in some people, dozens in others—experienced in an impressive variety of ways. (1980, p. 110)

But if not stages, how should we conceptualize the dying process? Shneidman suggests that we think of "themes" that may appear many times over the course of dying, including terror, passive uncertainty, fantasies of being rescued, incredulity, feelings of unfairness, fight against pain, and many others. Charles Corr (1991–92) has recently suggested a "task-based" approach. In his view, coping with dying is like coping with any other problem or dilemma: there are certain tasks you need to take care of. He suggests four such tasks for the dying person.

1. satisfying bodily needs and minimizing physical stress
2. maximizing psychological security, autonomy, and richness in living

3. sustaining and enhancing those interpersonal attachments significant to the dying person

4. identifying, developing, or reaffirming sources of spiritual energy, and thereby fostering hope

Corr is not denying the importance of the various emotional themes described by Shneidman. Rather, he is arguing that for health professionals who deal with dying individuals, it is more helpful to think in terms of the patient's tasks, because the dying person may need help in performing some or all of them.

Whichever model one uses, what *is* clear is that there are no lockstep stages, no common patterns that typify most or all reactions to impending death. There are common themes, but they are blended together in quite different patterns by each of us as we face this last task.

Individual Adaptations to Potential Death

Such individual variations in response to impending death have themselves been the subject of a good deal of research interest in the past few decades. Those who work with cancer patients, in particular, have not only been struck by the wide range of patients' reactions to a cancer diagnosis, but also by potential links between the type of reaction and how long an individual survives after a terminal diagnosis.

The most influential single study in this area has been the work of Steven Greer and his colleagues (Greer, Morris & Pettingale, 1979; Pettingale, et al., 1985). They have followed a group of 57 women diagnosed with early stages of breast cancer. Three months after the original diagnosis, each woman was interviewed at some length, and her reaction to the diagnosis and to her treatment was classed in one of four groups:

1. *Denial:* Rejection of evidence about diagnosis; insistence that surgery was just precautionary.

2. *Fighting spirit:* An optimistic attitude, accompanied by a search for more information about the disease. They plan to fight the disease with every method available.

3. *Stoic acceptance:* Acknowledging the diagnosis but without seeking any further information; ignoring the diagnosis and carrying on their normal life as much as possible.

4. *Helpless/hopeless:* Overwhelmed by diagnosis; see themselves as dying or gravely ill; devoid of hope.

Greer then checked on the survival rates of these four groups 5 and 10 years after the diagnosis. Table 19.2 shows the 10-year results, which are quite striking. Fifty-five percent of those whose initial reaction had been either denial or fighting spirit were still alive 10 years later, while only 22 percent of those whose initial reaction had been either stoic acceptance or helplessness/hopelessness were still alive. Because the four groups had not differed initially in the stage of their disease or in treatment, it is difficult to escape the possibility that differences in psychological response may be causal factors in disease progress.

Similar results have emerged from studies of patients with melanoma (a particularly deadly form of skin cancer), as well as other cancers (Temoshok, 1987). In general, those who report more fatigue, less hostility, and more helplessness, and who fail to express negative feelings die *sooner* (O'Leary, 1990). Those who struggle the most, who fight the hardest, who express their anger and hostility openly, and who also find some sources of joy in their lives, live longer. In some ways, the data suggest that "good patients"—those who are obedient and not too questioning, who don't yell at their doctors or make life difficult for those around them—are in fact likely to die sooner. Difficult patients, who question and challenge those around them, last longer.

TABLE 19.2 Differences in 10-year Outcomes Among Women Cancer Patients with Differing Psychological Responses to Initial Diagnosis

Psychological Response 3 Months After Operation	Outcome 10 Years Later			
	Number Alive with No Recurrence	Number Alive with Metastases	Number Dead	Total
Denial	5	0	5	10
Fighting spirit	6	1	3	10
Stoic acceptance	7	1	24	32
Helplessness/ hopelessness	1	0	4	5

Source: Pettingale et al., 1985, Table page 750.

Furthermore, there are now a few studies linking these psychological differences to immune system functioning. A particular subset of immune cells thought to be an important defense against cancer cells, called NK cells, have been found to occur at lower rates among those patients who report *less* distress and who seem better adjusted to their illness (O'Leary, 1990).

Despite the consistency of these results, two important cautions are nonetheless in order before we leap to the conclusion that a fighting spirit is the optimum response to any disease. First, there are some careful studies in which no link has been found between depression/stoic acceptance/helplessness and more rapid death from cancer (e.g., Cassileth, Walsh & Lusk, 1988; Richardson et al., 1990).

Second, it is not clear that the same psychological response is necessarily optimum for every form of disease. Early studies of AIDS patients, for example, are quite contradictory. Some show that those who respond with the least tension and anxiety have the best immune system function; others indicate that survival time is positively related to a patient's emotional openness and reactivity—results closer to the findings from studies of cancer patients (O'Leary, 1990). Even more questions remain concerning the role of psychological responses to heart disease. There is a certain irony in the fact that many of the qualities that appear to be optimal among cancer patients could be considered as reflections of a Type A (or perhaps A−) personality. Because the Type A personality is a *risk* factor for heart disease, it is not so obvious that a "fighting spirit" response to a diagnosis of advanced heart disease would necessarily be the most desirable. This research does tell us, though, that there are indeed connections between psychological defenses or ways of coping and physical functioning, even in the very last stages of life.

The Role of Social Support. Another important ingredient in an individual's response to imminent death is the amount of social support he or she may have available. Not only do those with positive and supportive relationships describe lower levels of pain and less depression during their final months of illness (Carey, 1974; Hinton, 1975), they also live longer. For example, heart attack patients who live alone are more likely to have a second attack than are those who live with someone else (Case et al, 1992), and those with significant levels of atherosclerosis live longer if they have a confidant than if they do not (Williams et al., 1992).

What is particularly impressive is that this link between social support and length of survival has also been found in *experimental* studies in which patients with equivalent diagnoses and equivalent medical care have been randomly assigned either to an experimental group in which subjects participate in regular support group sessions or to a control group in which subjects have no such specially created support system. In one such study of a group of 86 women with metastatic breast cancer (that is, cancer that had spread beyond the original site), David Spiegel (Spiegel, et al., 1989) found that the average length of survival was 36.6 months for those in the support group, compared to 18.9 months in the control group. Thus, just as social support helps to buffer children and adults from some of the negative effects of many kinds of nonlethal stress, so it seems to perform a similar function for those facing death.

Where Death Occurs: Hospitals and Hospices

In the United States and other industrialized countries, the great majority of adults die in hospitals rather than at home or even in nursing homes. Naturally, the exact pattern varies a good deal from one person to the next. Some with known progressive diseases, such as cancer, are in and out of the hospital for months or years before death; at the other end of the continuum are those who are hospitalized with an acute problem, such as a heart attack or pneumonia, and die within a short space of time, having had no prior hospitalization. In between fall those who may have experienced several different types of care in the last weeks or months, including hospitalization, home health care, and nursing home care. Despite such diversity, it is still true that the majority of deaths, particularly among the elderly, are preceded by some weeks of hospitalization (Shapiro, 1983).

In recent years, however, an alternative form of terminal care has become prominent—**hospice care**. The hospice movement was given a good deal of boost by Kübler-Ross's writings because she emphasized the importance of a "good death" or a "death with dignity," in which the patient and the patient's family have more control over the entire process. Many health care professionals, particularly in England and the United States,

It is one thing to find that support groups extend life among those with terminal illnesses. It is another to explain why, or by what mechanism. What hypotheses can you generate about why social support works in this way?

THE REAL WORLD
Saying Good-bye

The Kaliai of New Guinea have ritualized systems for completing social relationships when death approaches. In most industrialized countries, we have no such widely accepted rituals, but because the human need for closure and ritual is so strong, many adults nonetheless create some method of saying farewell.

A recent study in Australia by Allan Kellehear and Terry Lewin (1988–89), gives us a glimpse of the variety of good-byes devised by the dying. They interviewed 90 terminally ill cancer patients, all of whom expected to die within one year or less. Most had known of their cancer diagnosis for at least a year prior to the interview, but had only recently been given a short-term prognosis. As part of the interview, each of these 90 people was asked if she (or he) had already said farewell to anyone, and to describe any plans she had for future farewells. To whom did she want to say good-bye, and how would those good-byes be handled?

About a fifth of these people planned no farewells. Another three-fifths thought it was important to say good-bye, but wanted to put it off until very near the end so as to distress family and friends as little as possible. They hoped that there would then be time for a few final words with spouse, children, and close friends.

The remaining fifth began their farewells much earlier, and used many different avenues. Some planned special visits with family members or friends, to have "one last talk." Some wrote to friends or family, expressing in writing their feelings and their farewells. Some made special gifts. One woman sent photos and personal treasures to all her sisters; another made dolls to give to friends, family, and medical staff. In a particularly touching farewell gesture, another woman, who had two grown daughters but no grandchildren, knitted a set of baby clothes for each daughter, for the grandchildren she would never see.

Kellehear and Lewin make the important point that all these farewells are a kind of gift. They signal to the other person that they are worthy of a last good-bye. They may be a balancing of the relationship slate just as much as the balancing of physical gifts and obligations is among the Kaliai.

Farewells also may allow the dying person to disengage more readily when death comes closer and to warn others that death is indeed approaching. It may thus help the living to begin a kind of anticipatory grieving and in this way to prepare better for the loss.

began to suggest that such a good death could be better achieved if the dying person were at home or in a homelike setting, in which contact with family and other friends would be part of the daily experience.

From such suggestions came hospice care, first implemented in England (Saunders, 1977), later spreading to many other countries. There are now more than 1200 hospice programs in the United States, all of which share a basic guiding philosophy (Bass, 1985): (1) Death should be viewed as normal, not to be avoided but to be faced and accepted. (2) The patient and family should be encouraged to prepare for the death by examining their feelings, planning for their later life, talking openly about the death. (3) The family should be involved in the patient's care as much as this is physically possible, not only because this gives the patient the emotional support of those who love her, but because it allows each family member to come to some resolution of her or his relationship with the dying person. (4) The *control* over the patient's care should be in the hands of the patient and the family. They decide what types of medical treatment they will ask for or accept; they decide whether the patient will remain at home or be hospitalized. (5) Medical care should be primarily palliative rather than curative. The emphasis is on controlling pain and maximizing comfort, not on invasive or life-prolonging measures.

Three somewhat different types of programs following these general guidelines have been developed. The most common types of hospice programs are home-based programs, in which there is one central family caregiver—most frequently the spouse—who provides hour-to-hour care for the dying person with the support and assistance of specially trained nurses or other staff who visit regularly, provide medication, and help the family deal psychologically with the impending death. A second type is a special hospice center in which a small number of patients in the last stages of a terminal disease are cared for in as homelike a setting as possible. Finally, there are hospital-based hospice programs that provide palliative care following the basic hospice philosophy, with daily involvement of family members in the patient's care, but within a hospital setting. It is interesting that these three options parallel so closely the basic birth options now available as well: home delivery, birthing centers, and hospital-based birthing rooms. The fourth choice, both at birth and at death, is traditional hospital care.

Research on Hospice Care.   The choice of traditional hospital care versus hospice care is most often made on philosophical rather than medical grounds. But it is still worth

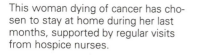

This woman dying of cancer has chosen to stay at home during her last months, supported by regular visits from hospice nurses.

asking whether there are any differences between the two types of care in patients' or families' experiences. Two large recent studies suggest that the differences are small, although they tilt slightly toward hospice care.

The National Hospice Study (Greer et al., 1986; Morris et al., 1986) analyzed the experiences of 1754 terminally ill cancer patients treated in 40 different hospices and 14 conventional hospitals. Half the hospice programs were home-based, half hospital-based. The researchers looked at the patient's reported pain and satisfaction with care and at the central caregiver's quality of life and satisfaction. Given the fact that these patients were not assigned randomly to hospice or conventional hospital care but chose their own form of care, what is remarkable is how few differences there were between the two. There were no differences in patients' reported pain, length of survival, or satisfaction with care. The major difference was that family members were most satisfied with hospital-based hospice care, while those with home-based hospice care reported the highest sense of burden.

In a second, smaller study, Robert Kane and his colleagues (Kane et al., 1984; Kane et al., 1985) assigned subjects randomly either to hospice or normal hospital care. The hospice care in this case was a combination of home-based and hospital-based. Most patients remained at home but spent brief periods in the hospital-hospice ward, either when the family needed a break or when the patient's care became too complex to handle at home. As in the National Hospice Study, Kane found no differences between these two groups in reports of pain or length of survival. But he did find that patients in the hospice group were more consistently satisfied with the quality of care they received and with their degree of control over their own care. Similarly, the family members in the hospice group in Kane's study were more satisfied with their own involvement with the patient's care and had lower levels of anxiety than did family members of the hospital-treatment group.

Taken together, these two studies suggest that if you use purely physical yardsticks, there are essentially no differences in these two types of terminal care. Control of pain and survival duration do not differ. Where differences exist, it is on measures of attitudes or feelings. On some—but not all—such measures, those in hospice care, and their families are slightly more satisfied. At the same time, there are clear signs that home-based hospice care is a considerable burden, especially on the central caregiver, who may spend as much as 19 hours a day in physical care.

To my way of thinking, the most positive aspect of hospice care is that it offers a choice for the dying individual, just as the rise in birth centers has increased the choices for prospective parents. Because a sense of control appears to be an important ingredient in a person's satisfaction with life, having some control over the conditions of one's death is also likely to be an important ingredient in coping with this last of life's transitions.

Given what you have just read and your own philosophical assumptions, do you think you would choose hospice care for your own death or urge it on a spouse or parent in the last stages of a terminal illness? Why or why not?

▶ After Death: Rituals and Grieving

No matter where or how an individual dies, he is likely to leave behind family members and friends as well as a larger culture, which must deal with that death in some fashion. In virtually every culture, the immediate response is some kind of funeral ritual.

Funerals and Other Ceremonies

When I was a good deal younger and was dragged along to various funerals by my parents, I thought that these occasions were entirely empty gestures—a set of rituals that were dictated by the culture but that had no function at all. What was the point, I thought, in coming together in this way just to put a dead body into the ground? As I have gotten older and have been through funerals for closer family members, I have come to understand that such rituals exist in every culture precisely because they serve many vital functions. As Marshall and Levy put it:

> Rituals provide a . . . means through which societies simultaneously seek to control the disruptiveness of death and to make it meaningful. . . . The funeral exists as a formal means to accomplish the work of completing a biography, managing grief, and building new social relationships after the death. (1990, p. 246; 253)

Funerals help family members to manage their grief by giving them a specific set of roles to play. Each culture defines these roles differently. In some, family members wear black, in others they wear white; in some they are expected to bear the loss stoically, in others they are expected to wail and cry openly. But whatever the specifics, there are rules to guide the first few days or weeks after the death. Those rules tell you what to wear, whom you must talk to, what plans you must (or must not) make, who should be fed. You may hold a wake, or sit shiva, or plan the funeral or a memorial service.

For friends and acquaintances, too, there are guiding rules, at least for those first few days. Food may be brought, letters of condolence may be written, help offered, wakes and funerals attended.

Funerals and other rituals also bring family members together as no other occasion—with the possible exception of weddings—is likely to do. I was particularly struck by this at the funeral of my father's mother, who died about six years ago. Among those who came to the memorial service were several cousins I had not seen for at least 30 years. Not only was I quite unprepared for the strong sense of family connection I felt for and with these strangers, I found myself greatly drawn to one of the cousins I barely knew. We have since created a warm friendship that I expect to last for the rest of our lives.

In this way, death rituals can strengthen family ties, clarify the new lines of influence or authority within a family, pass on the flame in some way to the next generation. At the same time, death rituals are also designed to help the survivors understand the meaning of death itself, in part by emphasizing the meaning of the life of the person who has died. It is not accidental that most death rituals include testimonials, biographies, witnessing. By telling the story of the person's life, by describing that life's value and meaning, the death can be more readily accepted. In a sense, a funeral is often like a "life review," and serves for the living some of the same purpose that Butler thought it served for the elderly person approaching death.

Each culture has its own funeral rituals. In Yugoslavia, where this photo was taken recently, it is clearly the custom for mourners to wear black.

Finally, death rituals may give some transcendent meaning to death itself, by placing it in some philosophical or religious context. In this way, they provide comfort to the bereaved by offering answers to that inevitable question, Why?

Beyond the Immediate Rituals: Grieving

The ritual of a funeral, in whatever form it occurs, can provide a structure and comfort in the days immediately following a death. But what happens when that structure is gone? How do we each handle the sense of loss? Answering that question requires a look at the epidemiology of grief as well as at individual variations in reaction to loss by death.

Epidemiology of Grieving: The Example of Widowhood. As a general rule, the most difficult death to recover from is the death of a spouse. Being widowed is regularly listed as the most stressful single event on lists of negative life changes. Epidemiological studies support this generalization. In the year following bereavement, the incidence of depression rises substantially, while rates of death and disease rise slightly in the widowed (Stroebe & Stroebe, 1986; Reich, Zautra & Guarnaccia, 1989). This pattern is found in both large epidemiological studies and in smaller, detailed studies of small samples. Fortunately, we even have a few longitudinal studies in which it is possible to examine *pre*widowhood levels of depression or disease. For example, Fran Norris and Stanley Murrell (1990) have interviewed a sample of 3000 adults, all 55 and older, five times over 2½ years. Forty-eight of those adults experienced the death of a spouse during the interval, which allowed Norris and Murrell to look at depression and health status before and immediately after bereavement and to compare this pattern to what occurred in those who were not bereaved in the same interval.

Norris and Murrell found no differences between the widowed and nonwidowed on their measure of physical health, but they found large differences on a measure of depression, as you can see in Figure 19.2. The widowed had been more depressed before the death of their spouse, presumably because at least some already knew the spouse was ill. But depression rose sharply within the six months after the spouse's death, and then dropped again.

Other research confirms that the first six months are the most difficult. Two years after widowhood, most studies show no differences between the widowed and nonwidowed on global measures of physical or mental health (e.g., McCrae & Costa, 1988).

Think about the various funerals or equivalent death rituals you have attended. Do they seem to have served the purposes I've described? Do some forms of funeral seem to do a better job of meeting these needs than others?

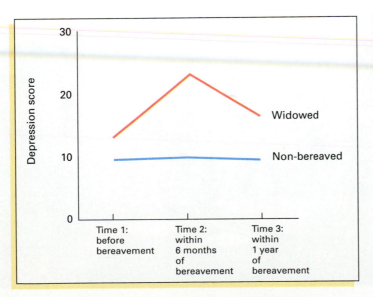

Figure 19.2 The peak of depression occurred here in the months just after widowhood, but depression also remained significantly higher one year after the spouse's death. (Source: Norris & Murrell, 1990, from Table 1, p. 432.)

These effects do vary somewhat by both age and gender. I pointed out in the interlude summarizing young adulthood that younger widows and those whose spouse died either suddenly or after a very short illness show higher levels of problems than do those who are widowed "on-time" or after a time of preparation (Ball, 1976–77). I've also mentioned several times that widowhood is a more negative experience for men than for women. The risk of death from either natural causes or suicide in the months immediately after widowhood is significantly greater among men than among women (Stroebe & Stroebe, 1986), even when higher male death rates at most ages are taken into account. This difference is most often interpreted as yet another sign of the importance of social support. Because a man is more likely to have only his spouse as close confidant, at her death he will more likely lack the buffering effect of social support from other sources.

Stages of Grief.   Data like these tell us that widowhood or the loss of a parent or child is highly stressful for most people. But they do not tell us anything about the experience of grief on an individual level. Given the fondness of psychologists for stage theories of almost any process, you won't be surprised that a number of authors have proposed that grief proceeds in a number of stages, highly similar to the stages of dying Kübler-Ross originally described. As with the stages of dying, there are many criticisms of these stage theories of grief. It is nonetheless worth your while to have at least a passing knowledge of them, if only because—like the stages of dying—they have affected the thinking of therapists, social workers, and others who work with the bereaved.

John Bowlby, whose work on attachment you already know, has proposed four stages of grieving (1980). Catherine Sanders, in a more recent formulation (1989), has proposed five, but there is a great deal of overlap. I've combined the two into a single summary in Table 19.3.

Some quotes from actual grieving individuals may give you a more complete taste of the experience. In the first period of shock or numbness, people say things like:

> I feel so vague. I can't keep my mind on anything for very long.

> I'm afraid I'm losing my mind. I can't seem to think clearly.

> It was so strange. I was putting on my makeup, combing my hair, and all the time it was as if I were standing by the door watching myself go through these motions. (Sanders, 1989, p. 47, 48, 56)

Studies of widows by Helena Lopata (1981, 1986) suggest that some "sanctification" of the deceased is almost universal, perhaps because by remembering their husband as saintly the widow is telling herself that she was worthy of the love of such a person.

TABLE 19.3 Stages of Grief Proposed by Bowlby and Sanders

Stage	Bowlby's Label	Sanders' Label	General Description
1	Numbness	Shock	Characteristic of the first few days, occasionally longer; disbelief, confusion, restlessness, feelings of unreality, a sense of helplessness.
2	Yearning	Awareness of loss	The bereaved person tries to recover the lost person; may actively search or wander as if searching; may report that they see the dead person. Also full of anxiety and guilt, fear, frustration. May sleep poorly and weep often.
3	Disorganization and despair	Conservation/ withdrawal	Basically this is the period of depression and despair; searching ceases and the loss is accepted, but acceptance of loss brings depression or a sense of helplessness. Often accompanied by great fatigue and a desire to sleep all the time.
4	Reorganization	Healing and renewal	Sanders sees two periods here; Bowlby only one. Both see this as the step in which the individual takes control again. There is some forgetting, some sense of hope, increased energy, better health, better sleep patterns, reduction of depression.

Sources: Bowlby, 1980; Sanders, 1989.

In the stage of awareness of loss or yearning, when anger is a common ingredient, people say things like, "His boss should have known better than to ask him to work so hard." Bowlby also suggests that this period is equivalent to what we see in young children who have been temporarily separated from their closest attachment figure. They will literally search for this favored person, going from room to room. In adults who are widowed, some of the same searching goes on—sometimes physically, sometimes mentally.

In the stage of disorganization and despair, the restlessness of the previous period disappears and there is instead a great lethargy. One 45-year-old whose child had just died described her feelings:

> I can't understand the way I feel. Up to now, I had been feeling restless. I couldn't sleep. I paced and ranted. Now, I have an opposite reaction. I sleep a lot. I feel fatigued and worn out. I don't even want to see the friends who have kept me going. I sit and stare, too exhausted to move. . . . Just when I thought I should be feeling better, I am feeling worse. (Sanders, 1989, p. 73)

Bowlby and Sanders argue that these reactions are likely to occur at the loss of any person to whom we are attached, whether partner, parent, or child (e.g., Douglas, 1990–91). The death of a friend, a grandchild, or someone who might be part of our convoy but not an intimate confidant is less likely to trigger this array of emotions.

These descriptions of the grieving process are highly evocative. But as with the concept of stages of dying, we need to ask two important questions about these proposed stages of grieving: (1) Do they really occur in fixed stages? and (2) Does everyone feel all these feelings, in whatever sequence? The answer to both questions seems to be no.

Alternative Views of the Grief Process. There is now a growing set of "revisionist" views of grieving that give a rather different picture than either Bowlby or Sanders offers. First, naturally enough, there are many researchers and theorists who find that grieving simply does not occur in fixed stages, with everyone following the same pattern (Wortman & Silver, 1990). There may be common themes, such as anger, guilt, depression, or restlessness, but they may not appear in a fixed order.

One compromise suggestion I particularly like is a proposal from Selby Jacobs and his colleagues (Jacobs et al., 1987–88) that each of the key themes in the grieving process may have a likely trajectory, such as the pattern shown in Figure 19.3. The basic idea, obviously, is that many themes are present at the same time, but that one or another may dominate in an approximate sequence. Thus we might well find that disbelief is highest immediately after the death, and that depression peaks some months later, which will make the process look stagelike, but in fact, both elements are present throughout.

Jacobs does not argue that every bereaved person necessarily follows a pathway that looks like this. Some might move more quickly, others more slowly through these various themes. In contrast, other revisionist theorists and researchers contend that for some adults, grieving itself simply does not include these elements. Camille Wortman and Roxane Silver (Wortman & Silver, 1987, 1989, 1990; Silver & Wortman, 1980) have amassed an impressive amount of evidence to support such a view.

Wortman and Silver dispute two points about the traditional view of grieving: that distress is an inevitable response to loss and that *failure* to experience distress is a sign that the individual has not grieved "properly." The psychoanalytic view, represented in Bowlby's approach and dominant for many decades, holds that lack of overt distress must indicate significant repression or denial of painful feelings. Ultimately, according to this view, such denial or repression will have negative consequences. Bowlby argues that those who express their pain, who "allow themselves to grieve," are behaving in an ultimately healthy way.

If this formulation is correct, we should find that those widows or other grieving individuals who show the *most* distress immediately after the death should have the best long-term adjustment, while those who show the least immediate distress should evidence some kind of residual problem later on. But the data do not support this expectation. On the contrary, those who show the highest levels of distress immediately following a loss are typically the ones who are still depressed several years later, while those who show little distress immediately show no signs of delayed problems.

After reviewing this body of research, Wortman and Silver (1990) conclude that

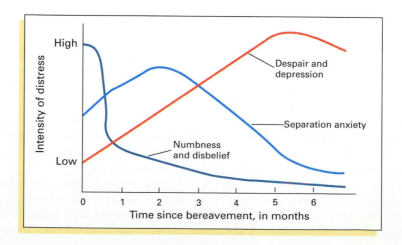

Figure 19.3 Jacobs offers this model as an alternative to strict stage theories of grieving. At any given moment, many different emotions or themes may be apparent, but each may have a particular, common trajectory. (*Source:* Jacobs et al., 1987–88, Figure 1, p. 43.)

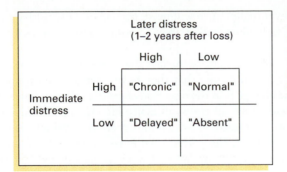

Figure 19.4 If we divide widows according to the amount of immediate distress and the amount of long-term distress they exhibit or report, then four types emerge, as described by Wortman and Silver. The "normal" type, with high immediate distress followed by recovery is depicted by psychoanalytic theory as the only healthy response. But research does not support that. (*Source:* Wortman & Silver, 1990.)

there are at least four distinct patterns of grieving, as laid out in Figure 19.4. Furthermore, they discovered that the pattern they call "absent" grief is remarkably common. In their own study, 26 percent of bereaved subjects showed essentially no distress either immediately after the death or several years later. In other studies the percentage of individuals who show such a nongrief pattern is as high as 77 percent. In Wortman and Silver's study and in all the other research of this type, the least common pattern is delayed grief. Only 1 to 5 percent of adults show such a response to loss. Thus, there is little support for either aspect of the traditional view: high levels of distress are neither an inevitable nor a necessary aspect of the grieving process. Many adults seem to handle the death of a spouse, a child, or a parent without significant dislocation, although *on average* it remains true that widowed or other bereaved persons are higher in depression, lower in life satisfaction, and at greater risk for illness than are the nonbereaved.

As yet we know little about what may differentiate among those who show these different types of grief response. There is some indication that abrupt losses—unexpected and off-time—are most likely to trigger chronic distress. Equally interesting are the few studies that suggest that those with an ambivalent attachment to the deceased are more likely to have longer-term difficulties (Parkes & Weiss, 1983; Wortman & Silver, 1990). Those with secure attachments certainly feel the loss but are able to recover more quickly.

Other factors that may exacerbate the problem of dealing with a loss through death are other concurrent life changes or stresses and a lack of available social support—both recurrent themes in research on the impact of all types of stress. Some bereaved persons also appear to find considerable strength from their religious or philosophical beliefs, such as a belief that all things are part of God's plan. But those who believe that hard work and virtue will be rewarded may have an especially difficult time coping with loss. Thus, religious beliefs may be highly significant but may either reduce or exacerbate the severity of a grief reaction.

Wortman and Silver's research is important for a variety of reasons. Not only does it cause us to question accepted wisdom and look again at the empirical evidence—always a valuable process—it also directs our attention to the wide variety of grieving responses and the *normality* of a nondistressed response. It simply does not appear to be the case that everyone needs to "work through" a whole host of negative emotions. Nor is it true that everyone recovers from a loss eventually. Some continue to show significant distress years after the death. Obviously, we need to understand more about where these differences come from. But in the meantime, I hope that mere knowledge of such variations will make you more sensitive in your response to friends or family members who are dealing with the loss of some loved person. Those who express little distress may not be repressing but may be coping in other ways. They are not likely to take kindly to suggestions from you that they should "get it all out" or "take time to grieve." Equally, those who are significantly depressed may not be pleased to be told something like, "It's hard now but

If you were designing a study to examine the differences between adults who show little or no grief after the death of a loved one, compared to those who show chronic grief, what characteristics would you want to be sure to study? Personality traits? Attachment pattern? Work status? History of depression? What else?

you'll get over it eventually." You will need, instead, to be sensitive to the signals you are getting from the individual, rather than imposing your own view of the normal grief process.

Finally, let us not lose sight of the fact that loss can also lead to growth. Indeed, the majority of widows say not only that they have changed as a result of their husband's death, but that the change is in the direction of greater independence, greater skill (Wortman & Silver, 1990). Like all crises, all major life changes, bereavement can be an opportunity as well as, or instead of, a disabling experience. Which way we respond is likely to depend very heavily on the patterns we have established from early childhood: our temperament or personality, our internal working models of attachment and self, our intellectual skills, and the social network we have created. Ultimately, we respond to death—our own or someone else's—as we have responded to life.

Summary

1. Until about age 6 or 7, children do not understand that death is permanent, inevitable, and involves loss of function.

2. Among adults, death has many meanings: a signal for changes in familial roles; a punishment for failing to live a good life; a transition to another state, such as a life after death; as loss of opportunity and relationships. Awareness of death may also serve as an organizer of time.

3. Fear of death appears to peak in midlife, after which it drops rather sharply. Older adults talk more about death but are less afraid.

4. Highly religious adults are typically less afraid of death, while those with high scores on a neuroticism scale are more fearful.

5. Many adults prepare for death in practical ways, such as by buying life insurance or writing a will. Reminiscence may also serve as some preparation. There are also some signs of deeper personality changes immediately before death, including more dependence and docility, less emotionality and assertiveness.

6. Kübler-Ross suggested five stages of dying: denial, anger, bargaining, depression, and acceptance. Research fails to support the assertion that all adults show all five or that the stages necessarily occur in this order. The most common ingredient is depression.

7. Research with cancer patients suggests that those who are most docile and accepting or most hopeless in response to diagnosis and treatment have shorter life expectancies. Those who fight hardest, even in angry ways, live longer.

8. Dying adults with better social support, either from family and friends or through specially created support groups, also live longer than those who lack such support.

9. The great majority of adults in industrialized countries die in hospitals. Hospice care for the dying, however, is becoming more common.

10. Hospice care emphasizes patient and family control of the process and palliative rather than curative treatment. Some studies suggest that patients and families are slightly more satisfied with hospice than hospital care, but home-based hospice care is highly burdensome for the caregiver.

11. Funerals and other rituals after death serve important functions, including defining roles for the bereaved, bringing family together, and giving meaning to the deceased's life and death.

12. On average, bereaved individuals show heightened levels of sickness, death, and depression in the months immediately after the death of an attachment figure.

13. Theories of stages of grieving, such as Bowlby's, have not been widely sup-

ported by recent research. A significant number of bereaved adults show no heightened depression or problems, either immediately or later. Others show persistent problems even after many years.

Key Term

hospice care

Suggested Readings

Feifel, H. (Ed.) (1977). *New meanings of death*. New York: McGraw Hill. (This book is not new, but it is a remarkably good collection of papers. Included is one of the very early descriptions of hospice care by Cicely Saunders, as well as papers by other key theorists and researchers in this area, such as Robert Kastenbaum, Edwin Shneidman, and Richard Kalish.)

Kalish, R. A. (1985). The social context of death and dying. In R. H. Binstock & E. Shanas (Eds.), *Handbook of aging and the social sciences* (2nd ed.). New York: Van Nostrand Reinhold. (This is a more recent summary of a great deal that is known about death and dying.)

ANOTHER LOOK AT THE BASIC ISSUES

In each of the interludes I have tried to suggest some of the key qualities or themes that characterize each age period in the years from birth to death. But even that summing and analyzing process may have left you without a sense of the full sweep of development over all those years. So I want to close the circle of this book by returning, at least briefly, to some of the issues I raised in Chapters 1 and 2: continuity and change, individual differences and variability, and theories of development.

Continuity and Change

Continuity and change are the very warp and woof—the essential ingredients—of development. Certainly your experience of yourself and of your own development is made up of both. You feel yourself as the same person from moment to moment, from year to year, and at the same time you feel that you have changed. You are not the same at 25 or 45 as you were at 12. If you ask most middle-aged or older adults if they would like to be 20 again, most laugh and say something like, "Heavens, no!" They will then go on to tell you how much they have learned that they didn't know then and wouldn't want to do without. So both continuity and change exist simultaneously—one of the central truths about development.

Continuity

Among the many sources of continuity is inborn temperament. Certainly there is much about individual personality that is not genetically determined or even biologically influenced. But babies are born with certain response biases, certain patterns of reaction to events. Depending on how people respond to the baby, on what is reinforced and what is not,

these initial biases may be strengthened or modified. By middle childhood, certainly by adolescence or adulthood, stable patterns have been established. These enduring personality patterns, in turn, affect the way each of us responds to the many events we encountered over our lifetime.

Those of us who have a more difficult temperament or who are high in neuroticism are likely to have a very different life course than others. Such people respond more negatively to almost any kind of stress, have more problems creating enduring relationships, and are less likely to be satisfied with their lives. In contrast, those high in extraversion or cheerfulness seem far more likely to create stable and satisfying relationships, recover more quickly from stressful experiences, and generally have higher morale.

In a similar way, internal models of the self, of gender, and of attachment tend to create continuity. Of course, internal models are not independent of personality. A temperamentally "difficult" child is somewhat more likely to develop an insecure attachment to mother or father, creating a kind of double disadvantage for some children. But internal models are not merely another description of personality. I am talking here about an individual's *understanding*, the meaning he or she attaches to experiences, the expectations he or she may have about others, about relationships, and about the self. These are *cognitions* as well as feelings. And they appear to be immensely powerful.

Such constructed meaning systems are not fixed at some point in childhood, never to change. We have only to look at Mary Main's work on in-

ternal models of attachment in adults to see evidence for the possibility of change. If you go back and look at the box in Chapter 6 (page 134) you'll see that the *secure-autonomous* category of adult attachment is sometimes found in adults who describe quite unloving or even abusive childhoods. They recognize that their childhood experiences were formative but are able to be objective about them. We know far too little about how such a reassessment or transformation may have taken place. But it is important to recognize that such change *can* occur. Continuity may be the default option, but it is not invariable.

At the risk of overstating the case, I think the new emphasis on internal models is the single most significant theoretical advance in the field of developmental psychology in the past several decades. We have come to understand that environments do not "happen" to people, do not shape behavior in some automatic way, at any age. The intervening process is the individual's understanding of each experience. We obviously need to know a great deal more about how the basic internal models are formed and change and how they affect choices and behavior. But I believe we are now on the right track.

Change

At the same time, development is also about change, both shared and individual. Shared change, which has been the focus of most theories of development and a great deal of the research, is shaped throughout life by the twin processes I have referred to as the *biological clock* and the *social clock*. But these two influences are rarely balanced in their effect. In childhood, biological maturation plays an enormously powerful role. Indeed, the whole rhythm of childhood is very much governed by such maturation: from physically helpless infant to more mature toddler; from nonverbal toddler to verbally fluent 4-year-old; from sexually immature to post-pubescent adolescent. Of course, experience makes a difference, and the child's own activity is critical in shaping the process of development. But beneath all the other formative processes, the biological clock is ticking away, loudly and in common form for virtually every child.

The social clock is not totally absent in these early years of life. There are some shared changes in social roles, such as the shift from preschool to school-age child, that have profound effects on the child's development. But the shared patterns of change we observe in children are far more a product of biological maturation and of the fact that virtually all children experience similar early environments than they are of clearly defined changes in social roles.

In early adulthood, the relative potency of these two influences reverses almost completely. Once fully past puberty, there begins a period of 20 or more years when the physical mechanism operates at peak form. In these years the social clock defines the developmental hours, shaping the sequence of life changes that the great majority of us share: a change from single to married, from child to parent, from dependent to independent.

In middle adulthood, perhaps for the only time in the life span, these two major influences are in approximate balance. The internal biological changes we label as aging begin to be more apparent, while social definitions become less stringent or constricting. In very late adulthood, the biological processes again dominate. Notice that there is no single age

period in which *both* biological and social clocks are extremely strong influences. Rather, there is a kind of alternation, a predictable ebb and flow, creating one kind of shared rhythm of change over the life span.

Theories of Development

I am sure it is obvious to you by now that no one theory of development has adequately described this entire process over the whole life span. Stage theories have been highly attractive to many observers and researchers because they appear to create orderliness out of what might otherwise seem like confusing changes. But they have become less and less attractive because research fails to show strongly age-linked stages in a great many instances. Even in childhood, when stagelike changes seem especially likely, there are measurable variations in the timing of certain cognitive shifts as a function of specific experience or expertise. In adulthood, stage theories are even less well substantiated.

There are nonetheless two stage-like theoretical concepts that I think have merit. First, if not stages, then surely there are *sequences*. Throughout development, we find strong evidence of shared sequences of development or experience. There is a sequence in children's understanding of the gender concept or of the concept of conservation; there is a sequence in the emergence of moral reasoning; there is a family life cycle sequence that begins as soon as an adult becomes a parent for the first time; there is the sequence of generations within a family, as each of us moves from the young adult generation, to the "sandwich generation" and finally to the status of elder within a given family; there are sequences in job experiences, perhaps even in changes within partnership relationships.

It is probably true that only those sequences that are at least partially rooted in maturational change are *universally* experienced. But within any given culture or cohort, lifespan development proceeds along many common pathways.

A related concept that I think is enormously useful in understanding development, perhaps particularly adult development, is Levinson's notion of alternating periods of stable life structures and transition. I do not agree that the *content* of these alternating periods is anywhere near as fixed or universal as Levinson suggested. Not everyone has a mid-life crisis or a transition at age 30. But the idea that there is an alternation of stability and transition seems to me to capture one aspect of the developmental process very well. Just as there is a basic rhythm created by the ebb and flow of the social and biological clocks, so there is a second basic rhythm created by the alternation of stability and change.

We can see this in children as well as adults. The transition of toddlerhood, for example, with its multiple adaptations (language, independent locomotion, establishment of a clear attachment) is followed by a period of several years in which both the child's behavior and the child's relationships with his parents are more predictable; the transition from age 5 to 7, when the child begins school, is followed by several years in which the child and the family create a more stable life structure. Even among infants, change does not seem to occur at a continuous rate. There are times of rapid change and times of greater stability, such as the period from about 2 months to perhaps 6 months and the period from about 8 months to perhaps 12 months.

In adulthood, the timing of the transitions and stable life structures may vary more from one individual to the next, depending on culture, on cohort, on the timing of marriage and childbearing, or on unique experiences. But a basic alternation between stability and transition seems to be a common thread in virtually all lives.

Many things may trigger a transition. In childhood and adolescence, physiological changes are at the root of some, such as the obvious example of puberty. In adulthood, changes in health or in the *awareness* of biological aging may also be important. But role changes are more likely to provoke shifts out of a stable life structure in adulthood, as may unexpected or off-time life changes, such as the loss of a job.

In each of these transitions, I think there is an opportunity for growth, precisely because the transition may call the internal models into question or force you to face new issues. Puberty triggers a whole new set of questions about independence and autonomy; marriage forces each of us to deal with the habits and internal models we bring to relationships. Middle age may cause you to question that most unexamined assumption, the feeling of invincibility or immortality. People living through crisis or transition sometimes say "I am beside myself." It is a revealing phrase, reflecting, perhaps, that sense of being momentarily outside of one's normal frame. There may well be pain involved, a sense of dislocation and loss, but there may also be an opportunity to *change* the frame, to reshape the internal models. In Piaget's terms, there is, in each such transition, an opportunity to *decenter*, to experience the world less and less egocentrically. Not everyone takes that opportunity. Many of us come to and through these points of transition without reexamining our assumptions or taking up the new tasks. But growth at some deeper level seems especially

possible at these transitional points.

Jane Loevinger, whose theory I mentioned in Chapter 2 and elsewhere, argues for just such a *potential* sequence of changes, such as the shift that may occur from the typical conformist stance of young adulthood to what she calls the conscientious stage. Loevinger's basic proposition is that there is a pathway laid out, a growth sequence, but that not everyone moves the same distance along it. This is analogous to what we see in the development of moral reasoning, where there appears to be a sequence of understandings that everyone follows but at somewhat different rates, stopping at different points along the way.

If we combine the concept of sequences with Levinson's concept of alternations between stability and transition, we end up with something vaguely like a stage theory but without the assumption that everyone will necessarily experience the transitions at the same time and without the idea that each transition will necessarily result in growth. For some, a transition results in depression, alcoholism, or perhaps even regression to earlier forms of coping. For others, the disequilibrium is followed by a return to the previous status quo. But there is an *opportunity* for change and growth at each turn of the spiral.

Individual Differences

These common patterns or rhythms should not and cannot disguise the other central fact about lifespan development, namely that there are enormous individual differences in timing and pathways. Such differences become especially visible during any period of the life span in which the biological clock is relatively unintrusive. Early in life and in the very last years of life, the common ground

is more apparent. But at every age there are wide variations, even in something so basic as the rate of maturation itself. As Uhlenberg and Chew (1986) explain:

> The life course experiences of individuals are almost as unique as their fingerprints—no two being identical. (p. 23)

Here's one more example of the magnitude of the variation, to add to the many I have already given: Rindfuss (Rindfuss, Swicegood & Rosenfeld, 1987) has studied a large sample of adults who graduated from high school in 1972. For the first eight years after graduation, the researchers noted whether each of the nearly 14,000 subjects had passed into or out of specific role statuses, such as work, education, marriage, or military service. There were 1100 different combinations of sequence and timing among the men in this study, and 1800 different combinations among the women. Virtually all these adults did indeed acquire one or more of these roles, but not in the same order or at the same age. When you compound such variations in timing and sequence with already-existing variations in personality, in internal models, in education, and in health, it is clear why sociologists and psychologists begin to talk of "fingerprints" or "trajectories" rather than "common paths."

If that is the case, then in what sense can we talk about "normal development" at all? I hope you will agree with me that it makes a good deal of sense to talk about common paths or normal development in *childhood*. In the first 12 to 15 years of life we see not only common maturational changes, we also see highly similar cultural responses to those maturational patterns. Babies are held and talked to; toddlers the world over are given more freedom; children in virtually all cultures begin schooling somewhere around age 6 or 7; rites of passage to adulthood are common themes of adolescent experience. The details vary, but there are clearly shared sequences and experiences.

But what about adulthood? Does it make sense to talk about "adult development" at all? As you will have gathered from what I have said already, I believe it does, but not with precisely the same meaning as when we say "child development." In adulthood, there is the much fainter but still present maturational timetable we call *aging* that provides a very rough common shape to adult experience. Key family and work roles also create a pattern that is widely shared, both within given cultures or cohorts and across cultures. At a deeper level, there are also the shared rhythms of the balance between social and biological clocks and the ebb and flow of transition and stability. Finally, there may be a common potential pathway of growth of the kind Loevinger has described. These different rhythms are, at heart, what is meant by adult development. But upon that base, there is an almost infinite variety of life patterns.

A musical metaphor may make the point clearer. The basic shared rhythms are like the beat of a song or the percussion part in a symphony. Every melody, every orchestration, must be built upon that beat, so every song, every symphony, will sound somewhat alike. But your song and mine will have different melodies. Whether the song is harmonious or disharmonious, whether new themes are introduced without dissonance or only with discord, will depend on all the factors I have described throughout this book. But each of us will create a song, a life. May you enjoy writing your song as much as I have enjoyed creating mine.

GLOSSARY

accommodation That part of the adaptation process by which a person modifies existing schemes to fit new experiences, or creates new schemes when old ones no longer handle the data.

achievement test A test usually given in schools, designed to assess a child's learning of specific material taught in school, such as spelling or arithmetic computation.

affectional bond A "relatively long-enduring tie in which the partner is important as a unique individual and is interchangeable with none other" (Ainsworth, 1989, p. 711).

age strata Groupings by age within any given society, such as "toddlers," "teenagers," or "the elderly," each with its own norms and expectations.

aggression Usually defined as intentional physical or verbal behaviors directed toward a person or an object with the intent to inflict damage on that person or object.

agreeableness One of the five major personality traits described by McCrae and Costa, characterized by good-naturedness, trust, generosity, and acquiescence.

alpha-fetoprotein test (AFP) A prenatal diagnostic test frequently used to screen for the risk of neural tube defects.

altruism Behavior of a person who gives or shares objects, time, or goods with others, with no obvious self-gain.

Alzheimer's disease The most common form of dementia, caused by specific changes in the brain, particularly a large increase in neurofibrillary tangles, resulting in gradual and permanent loss of memory and other cognitive functions.

amniocentesis A medical test for genetic abnormalities in the embryo/fetus that may be done at about 15 weeks of gestation.

amnion The sac or bag, filled with liquid, in which the embryo and fetus floats during prenatal life.

androgyny A self-concept including, and behavior expressing, high levels of both masculine and feminine qualities.

anorexia nervosa Disease characterized by "behavior directed toward weight loss, intense fear of gaining weight, body image disturbance. . . . and an implacable refusal to maintain body weight" (Attie et al., 1990, p. 410).

Apgar score A rating system for newborns with a maximum of 10 points, based on assessment of heart and respiratory rates, muscle tone, response to stimulation, and color.

assimilation That part of the adaptation process that involves the "taking in" of new experiences or information into existing schemes. Experience is not taken in "as is," however, but is modified (or interpreted) somewhat so as to fit the preexisting schemes.

attachment The positive affective bond between one person and another, such as the child for the parent or the parent for the child.

attachment behavior The collection of (probably) instinctive behaviors of one person toward another that bring about or maintain proximity and caregiving, such as the smile of the young infant; behaviors that reflect an attachment.

authoritarian parental style One of the three styles described by Baumrind, characterized by high levels of control and maturity demands and low levels of nurturance and communication.

authoritative parental style One of the three styles described by Baumrind, characterized by high levels of control, nurturance, maturity demands, and communication.

axon The long appendagelike part of a neuron; the terminal fibers of the axon serve as transmitters in the synaptic connection with the dendrites of other neurons.

babbling The vocalizing, often repetitively, of consonant-vowel combinations by an infant, typically beginning at about 6 months of age.

Bayley Scales of Infant Development The best-known and most widely used test of infant "intelligence."

being motives Class of motives suggested by Maslow. Includes the desire to discover and understand one's own potential and that of others and to give love.

biological clock A phrase used to describe the fundamental sequence of biological changes that occur with age, beginning with conception and moving through old age.

bulimia Disease or disorder characterized by "intense concern about weight, recurrent episodes of excessive overeating accompanied by a subjective sense of loss of control, and the use of vomiting, exercise, and/or purgative abuse to counteract the effects of binge eating" (Attie et al., 1990, p. 410).

cephalocaudal From the head downward. Describes one recurrent pattern of physical development in infancy.

cesarean section Delivery of the child through an incision in the mother's abdomen rather than vaginally.

chorionic villus sampling A technique for prenatal genetic diagnosis involving taking a sample of cells from the placenta. Can be performed earlier in the pregnancy than amniocentesis.

chromosome A string of DNA containing signals and instructions for a wide variety of normal developmental processes and unique individual characteristics. Each human cell contains 46 chromosomes arranged in 23 pairs.

classical conditioning One of three major types of learning. An automatic unconditioned response such as an emotion or a reflex comes to be triggered by a new cue, called the conditioned stimulus (CS), after the CS has been paired several times with the original unconditioned stimulus.

class inclusion   The relationship between classes of objects, such that a subordinate class is included in a superordinate class, as bananas are part of the class "fruit."

climacteric   The general term used to describe the period (in both men and women) in which reproductive capacity is lost during adulthood. Menopause is another word to describe the climacteric in women.

clinical depression   *See* **depression.**

clique   Term used to describe a group of 6–8 teenage friends with strong attachment bonds and high levels of group solidarity and loyalty.

cohort   A group of persons of approximately the same age who have shared similar major life experiences, such as cultural training, economic conditions, or type of education.

competence   The behavior of a person as it would be under ideal or perfect circumstances. It is not possible to measure competence directly.

concrete operations   The stage of development proposed by Piaget between ages 6 and 12, in which mental operations such as subtraction, reversibility, and multiple classification are acquired.

conditioned stimulus   In classical conditioning, the stimulus that, after being paired a number of times with an unconditioned stimulus, can trigger the unconditioned response.

conscientiousness   One of the five major personality traits described by McCrae and Costa, characterized by punctuality, ambition, conscientiousness, and perseverance.

control group   The group of subjects in an experiment that receives either no special treatment or some neutral treatment.

conventional morality   The second level of moral judgment proposed by Kohlberg, in which the person's judgments are dominated by considerations of group values and laws.

convoy   Term used by Antonucci to describe the set of individuals who make up a person's intimate social network and who travel with the individual through the various stages of adulthood.

cooing   An early stage during the prelinguistic period, from about 1–4 months of age, when vowel sounds are repeated, particularly the *uuu* sound.

coronary heart disease (CHD)   General term used by physicians to describe a set of disease processes in the heart and circulatory system, including most noticeably a narrowing of the arteries with plaque (atherosclerosis).

correlation   A statistic used to describe the degree or strength of a relationship between two variables. It can range from +1.00 to −1.00. The closer it is to 1.00 the stronger the relationship being described.

cortex   The convoluted gray portion of the brain that governs most complex thought, language and memory, among other functions.

critical period   A period of time during development when the organism is especially responsive to and learns from a specific type of stimulation. The same stimulation at other points in development has little or no effect.

cross-modal transfer   The ability to coordinate information from two senses, or to transfer information gained through one sense to another sense at a later time, such as identifying visually something you had previously explored only tactually.

cross-sectional design   A research design in which separate groups of individuals of different ages are compared on the same measures at the same time point.

crowd   A larger and looser group of friends than a clique, with perhaps 20 members; normally made up of several cliques joined together.

crystallized intelligence   That aspect of intelligence that is primarily dependent on education and experience: knowledge and judgment acquired through experience.

deductive logic   Reasoning from the general to the particular, from a rule to an expected instance, or from a theory to a hypothesis. Characteristic of formal operational thought.

defense mechanisms   Normal methods of dealing with anxiety proposed by Freud that are largely unconscious and at least somewhat distorting of reality. Includes such mechanisms as repression, intellectualization, projection, and suppression.

deficiency motives   Class of motives proposed by Maslow, including basic instincts or drives that involve correction of some imbalance or creation of homeostasis. Includes biological needs, need for safety, need for love and affection, and need for self-esteem.

dementia   Any global deterioration of intellectual functions, including memory, judgment, social functioning, and control of emotions. A symptom and not a disease, caused by a wide variety of conditions, including most commonly Alzheimer's disease and multiple small strokes.

dendrites   The branchlike part of a neuron that forms one half of a synaptic connection to other nerves. Dendrites develop rapidly in the final three prenatal months and the first year after birth.

deoxyribonucleic acid   Called DNA for short, this is the chemical of which genes are composed.

dependent variable   The variable in an experiment that is expected to show the impact of manipulations of the independent variable.

depression   A combination of sad mood, sleep and eating disturbances, and difficulty concentrating. When all these symptoms are present, it is usually called *clinical depression*.

dilation   The first stage of childbirth, when the cervix opens sufficiently to allow the infant's head to pass into the birth canal.

disengagement theory   Theory proposed by Cumming and Henry, suggesting that the normal and psychologically healthy response to the loss of roles and role content in late adulthood is a gradual withdrawal or disengagement from social interactions.

dominance   The degree to which an individual can regularly "win-out" in social encounters. Pecking order.

dominance hierarchy   A set of dominance relationships in a group describing the rank order of "winners" and "losers" in social encounters.

Down syndrome   A genetic anomaly in which every cell contains three copies of chromosome 21 rather than two. Children born with this genetic pattern are usually mentally retarded and have characteristic physical features.

effacement   The flattening of the cervix that, along with dilation, allows the delivery of the infant.

ego   In Freudian theory, that portion of the personality that organizes, plans, and keeps the person in touch with reality. Language and thought are both ego functions.

egocentrism   A cognitive state in which the individual (typically a child) sees the world only from his own perspective, without awareness that there are other perspectives.

endocrine glands   These glands, including the adrenals, the thyroid, the pituitary, the testes, and the ovaries, secrete hormones governing overall physical growth and sexual maturing.

equilibration   The third part of the adaptation process, as proposed by Piaget, involving a periodic restructuring of schemes into new structures.

establishment stage   *See* **trial stage.**

estrogen   The female sex hormone secreted by the ovaries.

executive processes   Proposed subset of information processes involving organizing and planning strategies. Similar in meaning to *metacognition.*

experiment   A research design in which the experimenter systematically manipulates some variable of interest, assigning subjects randomly to one or more experimental and control groups.

experimental group   The group (or groups) of subjects in an experiment that is given some special treatment that is expected to produce some hypothesized consequence.

expressive language   The term used to describe the child's skill in speaking and communicating orally.

expressive style   One of two styles of early language proposed by Nelson, characterized by low rates of nounlike terms and high use of personal-social words and phrases.

extinction   A decrease in the strength of some response after nonreinforcement.

extraversion   One of the five major personality traits identified by McCrae and Costa, characterized by tendency toward affection, talkativeness, activity, passion, being a joiner and fun-loving.

fallopian tube   The tube down which the ovum travels to the uterus and in which conception usually occurs.

fetal alcohol syndrome (FAS)   A pattern of physical and mental abnormalities, including mental retardation and minor physical anomalies, found often in children born to alcoholic mothers.

fluid intelligence   That aspect of intelligence reflecting fundamental biological processes and depending less on specific experience.

fontanels   The "soft spots" in the skull present at birth. These disappear when the several bones of the skull grow together.

foreclosure   One of four identity statuses proposed by Marcia, involving an ideological or occupational commitment without having gone through a reevaluation.

formal operations   Piaget's name for the fourth and final major stage of cognitive development, occurring during adolescence, when the child becomes able to manipulate and organize ideas as well as objects.

gametes   Sperm and ova. These cells, unlike all other cells of the body, contain only 23 chromosomes rather than 23 pairs.

gender concept   The understanding of one's own gender, including the permanence and constancy of gender.

gender constancy   The final step in developing a gender concept, in which the child understands that gender doesn't change even though there are external changes like clothing or hair length.

gender identity   The first step in gender concept development, in which the child labels herself correctly and categorize others correctly as male or female.

gender schema   A fundamental schema created by children beginning at age 18 months or younger by which the child categorizes people, objects, activities, and qualities by gender.

gender stability   The second step in gender concept development, in which the child understands that a person's gender continues to be stable throughout the lifetime.

gene   A uniquely coded segment of DNA in a chromosome that affects one or more specific body processes or developments.

genotype   The pattern of characteristics and developmental sequences mapped in the genes of any specific individual.

gifted   Normally defined in terms of very high IQ (above 140 or 150), but may also be defined in terms of remarkable skill in one or more specific areas, such as mathematics or memory.

glial cells   One of two major classes of cells making up the nervous system, glial cells provide the firmness and structure, the "glue" to hold the system together.

gonadotropic hormones   Hormones produced in the pituitary gland that stimulate the sex organs to develop.

habituation   An automatic decrease in the intensity of a response to a repeated stimulus, which enables the child or adult to ignore the familiar and focus attention on the novel.

hospice care   A relatively new pattern of care for terminally ill patients in which the majority of care is provided by family members, with control of care and care-setting in the hands of the patient and family. May be at home or in special wards or separate institutions.

hypertension   Technical term for the disease of high blood pressure. Most often defined as a systolic pressure above 140, or a diastolic pressure (the lower number you are given) above 90.

id   In Freudian theory, the first, primitive portion of the personality; the storehouse of basic energy, continually pushing for immediate gratification.

identification   The process of taking into oneself ("incorporating") the qualities and ideas of another person, which Freud thought was the result of the Oedipal crisis at age 3–5. The child attempts to make himself like his parent of the same sex.

identity   Term used in Erikson's theory to describe the gradually emerging sense of self, changing through a series of eight stages.

identity achievement   One of four identity statuses proposed by Marcia, involving the successful resolution of an identity "crisis," resulting in a new commitment.

identity diffusion   One of four identity statuses proposed by Marcia, involving neither a current reevaluation nor a firm personal commitment.

identity statuses   Four statuses described by James Marcia that are defined by a person's position on two dimensions: the presence or absence of an identity crisis, and the presence or absence of a commitment to some value or role.

independent variable   A condition or event that an experimenter manipulates in some systematic way in order to observe the impact of that variation on subjects' behavior.

inductive logic   Reasoning from the particular to the general, from experience to broad rules. Characteristic of concrete operational thinking.

inflections   The grammatical "markers" such as plurals, possessives, past tenses, and equivalent.

information processing   Phrase used to refer to a new, third, approach to the study of intellectual development that focuses on changes with age and on individual differences in fundamental intellectual processes.

insecure attachment   Includes both ambivalent and avoidant patterns of attachment in children; the child does not use the parent as a safe base and is not readily consoled by the parent if upset.

intelligence quotient (IQ)   Originally defined in terms of a child's mental age and chronological age, IQs are now computed by comparing a child's performance with that of other children of the same chronological age.

internal models   Phrase now used by a number of theorists to describe an internalized meaning system created by a child or adult, such as an internal model of attachment or of the self. An alternate version is *internal working model*.

intrinsic reinforcements   Those inner sources of pleasure, pride, or satisfaction that serve to increase the likelihood that an individual will repeat the behavior that led to the feeling.

libido   The term used by Freud to describe the pool of sexual energy in each individual.

life expectancy   The average number of years a person of some designated age (e.g., at birth or age 65) can expect still to live.

life review   Process proposed by Butler as an essential ingredient in successful aging; reminiscence to examine and assess one's life.

life span   The theoretical maximum number of years of life for a given species. It is assumed that even major new improvements in health care will not allow us to exceed this limit.

life structure   A key concept in Levinson's theory: The "underlying pattern or design of a person's life at a given time," including roles, relationships, and behavior patterns.

locus of control   Theoretical concept proposed by Rutter describing beliefs about whether control and cause of experiences is internal to oneself or external.

longitudinal design   A research design in which the same subjects are observed or assessed repeatedly over a period of months or years.

low birth weight (LBW)   Any baby born below 2500 grams is given this label, including both those born too early (preterm) and those who are "small for date."

maturation   The sequential unfolding of physical characteristics, governed by instructions contained in the genetic code and shared by all members of the species. Similar in meaning to the less-precise phrase *biological clock*.

maximum oxygen uptake (VO2 max)   The amount of oxygen that can be taken into the bloodstream and hence carried to all parts of the body. A major measure of aerobic fitness, VO_2 max decreases with age but can be increased again with exercise.

medulla   A portion of the brain that lies immediately above the spinal cord; largely developed at birth.

menarche   Onset of menstruation in girls.

menopause   Term used to refer to the point in the female climacteric when menstruation completely ceases. More generally, the term is frequently used as a synonym for the entire climacteric period in women.

mentor   An older adult who may take on the role of guide or supporter for a younger person. Levinson proposes that such a relationship creates a bridge from the dependency of youth to the independence of middle age.

metacognition   General and rather loosely used term describing an individual's knowledge of his own thinking processes. Knowing what you know, and how you go about learning or remembering.

metamemory   A subcategory of metacognition; knowledge about your own memory processes.

midbrain   A section of the brain lying above the medulla and below the cortex that regulates attention, sleeping, waking, and other "automatic" functions. Largely developed at birth.

modeling   A term used by Bandura and others to describe observational learning.

moratorium   One of four identity statuses proposed by Marcia, involving a present crisis but no commitment as yet.

motherese   The word linguists often use to describe the particular pattern of speech by adults to young children. The sentences are shorter, simpler, repetitive, and higher pitched.

myelin   Material making up a sheath that develops around most axons. This sheath is not completely developed at birth.

myelinization   The process by which myelin is added.

negative reinforcement   The strengthening of a behavior that occurs because of the removal or cessation of an unpleasant stimulus.

neglecting parental style   A fourth style of parenting characterized by low levels of nurturance, control, communication, and maturity demands.

neuron   The second major class of cells in the nervous system, neurons are responsible for transmission and reception of nerve impulses.

neuroticism   One of the five major personality traits identified by McCrae and Costa, characterized by the tendency toward worry, temperament, self-pity, self-consciousness, emotionality, and vulnerability.

object permanence   The understanding that an object continues to exist even when it is temporarily out of sight. More generally, the basic understanding that objects exist separate from one's own action on them.

observational learning   Learning of motor skills, attitudes, or other behaviors through observing someone else perform them.

old old   Term now used fairly commonly by gerontologists to describe those over age 75.

openness to experience   One of the five major personality traits identified by McCrae and Costa, characterized by tendency toward imagination, creativity, originality, curiosity, liberality, and a preference for variety.

operant conditioning   One of the three major types of learning in which the probability of a person performing some behavior is affected by positive or negative reinforcements.

operations   Piaget's term for the new and powerful class of mental schemes he saw as developing between roughly ages 5 and 7, including reversibility, addition, and subtraction.

ossification   The process of hardening by which soft tissue becomes bone.

osteoporosis   Loss of bone mass with age, characterized by increased brittleness and porousness.

overregularization   The tendency on the part of children to make the language regular, such as using past tenses like "beated" or "goed."

ovum   The gamete produced by a woman, which, if fertilized by a sperm from the male, forms the basis for the developing organism.

parental imperative   Phrase used by David Gutmann to describe a possibly "wired in" pattern of intensification of sex-role differentiation after the birth of the first child.

partial reinforcement   Reinforcement of behavior on some schedule less frequent than every occasion.

performance   The behavior shown by a person under actual circumstances. Even when we are interested in competence, all we can ever measure is performance.

permissive parental style   One of the three styles described by Baumrind, characterized by high levels of nurturance and low levels of control, maturity demands, and communication.

personality   The collection of individual, relatively enduring, patterns of reacting to and interacting with others that distinguishes each child or adult.

phenotype   The expression of a particular set of genetic information in a specific environment; the observable result of the joint operation of genetic and environmental influences.

pituitary gland   One of the endocrine glands that plays a central role in controlling the rate of physical maturation and sexual maturing.

placenta   An organ that develops during gestation between the fetus and the wall of the uterus. The placenta filters nutrients from the mother's blood, acting as liver, lungs, and kidneys for the fetus.

positive reinforcement   Strengthening of a behavior by the presentation of some pleasurable or positive stimulus.

preconventional morality   The first level of morality proposed by Kohlberg, in which moral judgments are dominated by consideration of what will be punished and what feels good.

preoperational period   Piaget's term for the second major stage of cognitive development, from age 2 to 6, marked at the beginning by the ability to use symbols.

presbycusis   Normal loss of hearing with aging, especially of high-frequency tones, resulting from basic wear and tear on the auditory system.

presbyopia   Normal loss of visual acuity with aging, especially of ability to focus the eyes on near objects, resulting from buildup of layers on the lens and loss of elasticity.

principled morality   The third level of morality proposed by Kohlberg, in which considerations of justice, individual rights, and contracts dominate moral judgment.

prosocial behavior   *See* **altruism.**

proximodistal   From the center outward. With *cephalocaudal*, describes the pattern of physical changes in infancy.

psychosexual stages   The stages of personality development suggested by Freud, including the oral, anal, phallic, latency, and genital stages.

psychosocial stages   The stages of personality development suggested by Erikson, including trust, autonomy, initiative, industry, identity, intimacy, generativity, and ego integrity.

punishment   Unpleasant consequences, administered after some un-desired behavior by a child or adult, with the intent of extinguishing the behavior.

rapid eye movement (REM) sleep   One of the characteristics of sleep during dreaming, which occurs during the sleep of newborns, too.

receptive language   Term used to describe the child's ability to understand (receive) language, as contrasted to his ability to express language.

referential style   Second style of early language proposed by Nelson, characterized by emphasis on objects and their naming and description.

reflexes   Automatic body reactions to specific stimulation, such as the knee jerk or the Moro reflex. Many reflexes remain among adults, but the newborn also has some "primitive" reflexes that disappear as the cortex is fully developed.

resilience   A characteristic of an individual child or adult, product of both in-born and acquired characteristics, that enables that person to adapt successfully to the environment despite stress, threat, or challenging circumstances.

retarded   Label for an individual with very low IQ, typically below 70.

role   A concept from sociology; The "job description" for some social position or status, such as teacher, employer, baseball manager, wife, man, or whatever. All individuals occupy multiple roles.

role conflict   The experience of occupying two or more roles that are somewhat incompatible, either logistically or psychologically.

role strain   The experience of occupying a role for which you are not properly equipped in skills or personal qualities.

scheme   Piaget's word for the basic actions of knowing, including both physical actions (sensorimotor schemes, such as looking or reaching) and mental actions, such as classifying, comparing, or reversing. An experience is assimilated to a scheme, and the scheme is modified or created through accommodation.

secure attachment   Demonstrated by the child's ability to use the parent as a safe base and to be consoled after separation, when fearful, or when otherwise stressed.

self-efficacy   Theoretical concept proposed by Bandura; the belief in one's capacity to cause some intended event to occur or to perform some task.

self-esteem   A global judgement of self-worth; how well you like who you perceive yourself to be.

sensitive period   Similar to a critical period except broader and less specific. A time in development when a particular type of stimulation is especially important or effective.

sensorimotor period   Piaget's term for the first major stage of cognitive development, from birth to about 18 months, when the child moves from reflexive to voluntary action.

sequential designs   A family of research designs that involve multiple cross-sectional or multiple longitudinal studies or both.

sex role   The "job description" for a particular gender. Knowledge of the role is displayed not only in differential behavior, but in the concept of what is appropriate behavior for each gender.

social clock   The sequence of roles and expected social experiences that unfold in common patterns over the life span, such as moving from one school grade to the next, from school to independent life, from work to retirement.

social referencing   Using another person's reaction to some situation as a basis for deciding one's own reaction. A baby does this when she checks her parent's facial expression or body language before responding positively or negatively to something new.

stabilization stage   One way of thinking about the stages of work life in early adulthood. The trial or establishment stage in one's twenties is followed by the stabilization stage in one's thirties, during which a plateau of achievement is usually reached.

Stanford-Binet   The best-known American intelligence test. It was written by Louis Terman and his associates based upon the first tests by Binet and Simon.

states of consciousness   Five main sleep/awake states have been identified in infants, from deep sleep to active awake states.

Strange Situation   A series of episodes used by Mary Ainsworth and others in studies of attachment. The child is observed with the mother, with a stranger, left alone, and when reunited with stranger and mother.

sudden infant death syndrome (SIDS)   Unexpected death of an infant who otherwise appears healthy. Also called *crib death*. Cause is unknown.

superego   In Freudian theory, the "conscience" part of personality, which develops as a result of the identification process. The superego contains the parental and societal values and attitudes incorporated by the child.

synapse   The point of communication between the axon of one neuron and the dendrites of another, where nerve impulses are passed from one neuron to another, or from a neuron to some other type of cell, such as a muscle cell.

temperament   An individual's typical style of response to experiences. Temperament differences may be genetic in origin and are somewhat stable over time.

teratogen   Any outside agent (such as a disease or a chemical) that significantly increases the risk of deviations or abnormalities in prenatal development.

terminal drop   Phrase used to describe a theory that mental and physical functioning remains at a steady level during late adulthood until a point roughly five years from death, after which there is a rapid decline.

testosterone   The primary male hormone, secreted by the testes in males.

theory of mind   Phrase used to describe one aspect of the thinking of 4- and 5-year olds when they show signs of understanding not only that other people think differently, but something about the way others' minds work.

trial stage   One way of thinking about stages in the work life in early adulthood. The trial stage (also called the establishment stage) is the period in one's twenties when various careers or jobs may be tried, and/or needed skills acquired in some occupation.

Type A behavior   Behavior of an individual with a Type A personality.

Type A personality   A combination of competitiveness, a sense of time urgency, and hostility or aggressiveness, which may be associated with higher risk of coronary heart disease.

ultrasound   A form of prenatal diagnosis in which high-frequency sound waves are used to provide a picture of the moving fetus. Can be used to detect many physical deformities, such as neural tube defects, multiple pregnancies, and gestational age.

unconditioned response   In classical conditioning this is the basic unlearned response that is triggered by the unconditioned stimulus.

unconditioned stimulus   In classical conditioning this is the cue or signal that automatically triggers (without learning) the unconditioned response.

undifferentiated   One of four types proposed by Bem and others to describe variations in gender self-concept. An undifferentiated individual describes herself or himself as low in both masculine and feminine traits.

uterus   The female organ in which the blastocyst implants itself and within which the embryo/fetus develops. Popularly referred to as the *womb*.

vulnerability   A characteristic of an individual child or adult, product of both in-born and acquired characteristics, that increases the likelihood that he or she will respond to stress in nonadaptive or pathological ways.

WISC-R   The Wechsler Intelligence Scale for Children, Revised. Another well-known American IQ test that includes both verbal and performance (nonverbal) subtests.

young old   Phrase now used by many gerontologists to describe those between roughly 60 and 75.

REFERENCES

Note: The numbers in boldface at the end of each entry refer to the chapter(s) or interlude(s) in which that source is cited.

Abrahams, B., Feldman, S. S., & Nash, S. C. (1978). Sex role self-concept and sex role attitudes: Enduring personality characteristics or adaptations to changing life situations? *Developmental Psychology, 14,* 393–400. **1**

Abramovitch, R., Pepler, D., & Corter, C. (1982). Patterns of sibling interaction among preschool-age children. In M. E. Lamb & B. Sutton-Smith (Eds.), *Sibling relationships: Their nature and significance across the lifespan* (pp. 61–86). Hillsdale, NJ: Erlbaum. **8**

Abrams, B., Newman, V., Key, T., & Parker, J. (1989). Maternal weight gain and preterm delivery. *Obstetrics and Gynecology, 74,* 577–1989. **3**

Achenbach, T. M. (1982). *Developmental psychopathology* (2nd ed.). New York: Wiley. **12**

Achenbach, T. M., & Edelbrock, C. (1981). Behavioral problems and competencies reported by parents of normal and disturbed children aged four to sixteen. *Monographs of the Society for Research in Child Development, 46* (Serial No. 188). **12**

Achenbach, T. M., Phares, V., Howell, C. T., Rauh, V. A., & Nurcombe, B. (1990). Seven-year outcome of the Vermont intervention program for low-birthweight infants. *Child Development, 61,* 1672–1681. **6**

Adams, C. (1991). Qualitative age differences in memory for text: A life-span developmental perspective. *Psychology and Aging, 6,* 323–336. **15**

Adams, M. J. (1990). *Beginning to read: Thinking and learning about print.* Cambridge, MA: The MIT Press. **9**

Adams, R. G. (1986). Emotional closeness and physical distance between friends: Implications for elderly women living in age-segregated and age-integrated settings. *International Journal of Aging and Human Development, 22,* 55–76. **18**

Adams, R. G., & Blieszner, R. (Eds.) (1989). *Older adult friendship.* Newbury Park, CA: Sage Publications. **18**

Adler, A. (1948). *Studies in analytical psychology.* New York: Norton. **2**

Ainsworth, M. D. S. (1967). *Infancy in Uganda: Infant care and the growth of love.* Baltimore: Johns Hopkins University Press. **6**

Ainsworth, M. D. S. (1972). Attachment and dependency: A comparison. In J. L. Gewirtz (Ed.), *Attachment and dependency* (pp. 97–138). Washington, D. C.: V. H. Winston. **6**

Ainsworth, M. D. S. (1982). Attachment: Retrospect and prospect. In C. M. Parkes & J. Stevenson-Hinde (Eds.). *The place of attachment in human behavior* (pp. 3–30). New York: Basic Books. **6**

Ainsworth, M. D. S. (1989). Attachments beyond infancy. *American Psychologist, 44,* 709–716. **6**

Ainsworth, M. D. S., Blehar, M., Waters, E., & Wall, S. (1978). *Patterns of attachment.* Hillsdale, NJ: Erlbaum. **6**

Ainsworth, M. D. S., & Wittig, B. A. (1969). Attachment and exploratory behavior of one-year-olds in a strange situation. In B. M. Foss (Ed.), *Determinants of infant behavior* (Vol. 4). London: Methuen. **6**

Aksu-Koc, A. A. & Slobin, D. I. (1985). The acquisition of Turkish. In D. I. Slobin (Ed.), *The crosslinguistic study of language acquisition. Vol. 1: The data* (pp. 839–878). Hillsdale, NJ: Erlbaum. **7**

Aldous, J. (1985). Parent-adult child relations as affected by the grandparent status. In V. L. Bengtson & J. F. Robertson (Eds.), *Grandparenthood* (pp. 117–132). Beverly Hills, CA: Sage Publications. **16**

Aldous, J., & Klein, D. M. (1991). Sentiment and services: Models of intergenerational relationships in mid-life. *Journal of Marriage and the Family, 53,* 595–608. **18**

Allen, K. R., & Pickett, R. S. (1987). Forgotten streams in the family life course: Utilization of qualitative retrospective interviews in the analysis of lifelong single women's family careers. *Journal of Marriage and the Family, 49,* 517–526. **14**

Allison, P. D., & Furstenberg, F. F. Jr. (1989). How marital dissolution affects children: Variations by age and sex. *Developmental Psychology, 25,* 540–549. **8**

Alsop, S. (1973). *Stay of execution.* New York: Lippincott. **19**

Alsaker, F. D., & Olweus, D. (1992). Stability of global self-evaluations in early adolescence: A cohort longitudinal study. *Journal of Research on Adolescence, 2,* 123–145. **10**

Amato, P. R., & Keith, B. (1991). Parental divorce and the well-being of children: A meta-analysis. *Psychological Bulletin, 110,* 26–46. **8, Int5**

Amott, T., & Matthaei, J. (1991). *Race, gender, and work. A multicultural economic history of women in the United States.* Boston, MA: South End Press. **14**

Anderson, B., Mead, N., & Sullivan, S. (1986). *Television: What do national assessment results tell us?* Princeton, NJ: Educational Testing Service. **10**

Anderson, C. W., Nagle, R. J., Roberts, W. A., & Smith, J. W. (1981). Attachment to substitute caregivers as a function of center quality and caregiver involvement. *Child Development, 52,* 53–61. **6**

Anderson, D. R., Lorch, E. P., Field, D. E., Collins, P. A., & Nathan, J. G. (1986). Television viewing at home: Age trends in visual attention and time with TV. *Child Development, 57,* 1024–1033. **10**

Anderson, K. M., Castelli, W. P., & Levy, D. (1987). Cholesterol and mortality. 30 years of follow-up from the Framingham study. *Journal of the American Medical Association, 257,* 2176–2180. **15**

Andersson, B. (1989). Effects of public day-care: A longitudinal study. *Child Development, 60,* 857–886. **6**

Andersson, B. (1992). Effects of day-care on cognitive and socioemotional competence of thirteen-year-old Swedish school children. *Child Development, 63,* 20–36. **6**

Anisfeld, E., Casper, V., Nozyce, M., & Cunningham, N. (1990). Does infant carrying promote attachment? An experimental study of the effects of increased physical contact on the development of attachment. *Child Development, 61,* 1617–1627. **6**

Anisfeld, M. (1991). Neonatal imitation. *Developmental Review, 11*, 60–97. **5**

Anthony, J. C., & Aboraya, A. (1992). The epidemiology of selected mental disorders in later life. In J. E. Birren, R. B. Sloane & G. D. Cohen (Eds.) *Handbook of mental health and aging* (2nd ed.) (pp. 28–73). San Diego, CA: Academic Press. **13, 15, 17**

Antonucci, T. C. (1990). Social supports and social relationships. In R. H. Binstock & L. K. George (Eds.), *Handbook of aging and the social sciences* (3rd ed.) (pp. 205–226). San Diego: Academic Press. **14, 18**

Antonucci, T. C. (1991). Attachment, social support, and coping with negative life events in mature adulthood. In E. M. Cummings, A. L. Greene & K. H. Karraker (Eds.), *Life-span developmental psychology. Perspectives on stress and coping* (pp. 261–276). Hillsdale, NJ: Erlbaum. **14, 18**

Antonucci, T. C., & Akiyama, H. (1987a). Social networks in adult life and a preliminary examination of the convoy model. *Journal of Gerontology, 42*, 519–527. **14, 16**

Antonucci, T. C., & Akiyama, H. (1987b). An examination of sex differences in social support among older men and women. *Sex Roles, 17*, 737–749. **18**

Apgar, V. A. (1953). A proposal for a new method of evaluation of the newborn infant. *Anesthesiology Annals, 32*, 260–267. **4**

Arenberg, D. (1974). A longitudinal study of problem solving in adults. *Journal of Gerontology, 29*, 650–658. **17**

Arenberg, D., & Robertson-Tchabo, E. A. (1977). Learning and aging. In J. E. Birren & K. W. Schaie (Eds.), *Handbook of the psychology of aging*. New York: Van Nostrand Reinhold. **17**

Arlin, P. (1981). Piagetian tasks as predictors of reading and math readiness in Grades K-1. *Journal of Educational Psychology, 73*, 712–721. **9**

Arlin, P. K. (1975). Cognitive development in adulthood: A fifth stage? *Developmental Psychology, 11*, 602–606. **13**

Arlin, P. K. (1989). Problem solving and problem finding in young artists and young scientists. In M. L. Commons, J. D. Sinnott, F. A. Richards & C. Armon (Eds.), *Adult Development, Vol. 1. Comparisons and applications of developmental models* (pp. 197–216). New York: Praeger. **13**

Arlin, P. K. (1990). Wisdom: The art of problem finding. In R. J. Sternberg (Ed.), *Wisdom. Its nature, origins, and development* (pp. 230–243). New York: Cambridge University Press. **13**

Asher, S. R. (1990). Recent advances in the study of peer rejection. In S. R. Asher & J. D. Coie (Eds.), *Peer rejection in childhood* (pp. 3–16). Cambridge: Cambridge University Press. **10**

Asher, S. R., & Coie, J. D. (Eds.) (1990). *Peer rejection in childhood*. Cambridge: Cambridge University Press. **10**

Aslin, R. N. (1987). Visual and auditory development in infancy. In J. D. Osofsky (Ed.), *Handbook of infant development*, (2nd ed.). (pp. 5–97). New York: Wiley-Interscience. **5**

Assouline, M., & Meir, E. I. (1987). Meta-analysis of the relationship between congruence and well-being measures. *Journal of Vocational Behavior, 31*, 319–332. **14**

Astbury, J., Orgill, A. A., Bajuk, B., & Yu, V. Y. H. (1990). Neurodevelopmental outcome, growth and health of extremely low-birthweight survivors: How soon can we tell? *Developmental Medicine and Child Neurology, 32*, 582–589. **3**

Astington, J. W., & Gopnik, A. (1991). Theoretical explanations of children's understanding of the mind. In G. E. Butterworth, P. L. Harris, A. M. Leslie & H. M. Wellman (Eds.), *Perspectives on the child's theory of mind* (pp. 7–31). New York: Oxford University Press. **7**

Attie, I., & Brooks-Gunn, J. (1989). Development of eating problems in adolescent girls: A longitudinal study. *Developmental Psychology, 25*, 70–79. **11**

Attie, I., Brooks-Gunn, J., & Petersen, A. (1990). A developmental perspective on eating disorders and eating problems. In M. Lewis & S. M. Miller (Eds.), *Handbook of developmental psychopathology* (pp. 409–420). New York: Plenum. **11**

Avis, J., & Harris, P. L. (1991). Belief-desire reasoning among Baka children: Evidence for a universal conception of mind. *Child Development, 62*, 460–467. **7**

Babcock, R. L., & Salthouse, T. A. (1990). Effects of increased processing demands on age differences in working memory. *Psychology and Aging, 5*, 421–428. **17**

Bachrach, C. A. (1980). Childlessness and social isolation among the elderly. *Journal of Marriage and the Family, 42*, 627–638. **18**

Baer, D. M. (1970). An age-irrelevant concept of development. *Merrill-Palmer Quarterly, 16*, 238–245. **2**

Bailey, J. M., & Pillard, R. C. (1991). A genetic study of male sexual orientation. *Archives of General Psychiatry, 48*, 1089–1096. **12**

Baillargeon, R. (1987). Object permanence in very young infants. *Developmental Psychology, 23*, 655–664. **5**

Baillargeon, R., & DeVos, J. (1991). Object permanence in young infants: Further evidence. *Child Development, 62*, 1227–1246. **5**

Baillargeon, R., Spelke, E. S., & Wasserman, S. (1985). Object permanence in five-month-old infants. *Cognition, 20*, 191–208. **5**

Baird, P. A., Sadovnick, A. D., & Yee, I. M. L. (1991). Maternal age and birth defects: A population study. *The Lancet, 337*, 527–530. **3**

Bal, D., & Foerster, S. B. (1991). Changing the American diet. *Cancer, 67*, 2671–2680. **15**

Ball, J. F. (1976–77). Widow's grief: The impact of age and mode of death. *Omega, 7*, 307–333. **Int5, 19**

Baltes, M. M., Kühl, K., & Sowarka, D. (1992). Testing for limits of cognitive reserve capacity: A promising strategy for early diagnosis of dementia? *Journal of Gerontology: PSYCHOLOGICAL SCIENCES, 47*, P165–167. **17**

Baltes, P. B., & Baltes, M. M. (1990a). Psychological perspectives on successful aging: The model of selective optimization with compensation. In P. B. Baltes & M. M. Baltes (Eds.), *Successful aging* (pp. 1–34). Cambridge, England: Cambridge University Press. **17, Int7**

Baltes, P. B., & Baltes, M. M. (Eds.) (1990b). *Successful aging*. Cambridge, England: Cambridge University Press. **18**

Baltes, P. B., & Kliegl, R. (1992). Further testing of limits of cognitive plasticity: Negative age differences in a mnemonic skill are robust. *Developmental Psychology, 28*, 121–125. **17**

Baltes, P. B., & Smith, J. (1990). Toward a psychology of wisdom and its ontogenesis. In R. J. Sternberg (Ed.), *Wisdom. Its nature, origins, and development* (pp. 87–120). Cambridge, England: Cambridge University Press. **17**

Baltes, P. B., Reese, H. W., & Lipsitt, L. P. (1980). In M. R. Rosenzweig & L. W. Porter (Eds.), *Annual review of psychology*. Palo Alto, CA: Annual Reviews, Inc. **1**

Baltes, P. B., Reese, H. W., & Nesselroade, J. R. (1977). *Life-span developmental psychology: Introduction to research methods*. Monterey, Ca: Books/Cole. **15**

Bamford, F. N., Bannister, R. P., Benjamin, C. M., Hillier, V. F., Ward, B. S., & Moore, W. M. O. (1990). Sleep in the first year of life. *Developmental Medicine and Child Neurology, 32*, 718–724. **4**

Bandura, A. (1977a). *Social learning theory*. Englewood Cliffs, NJ: Prentice-Hall. **2**

Bandura, A. (1977b). Self-efficacy: Toward a unifying theory of behavioral change. *Psychological Review, 84*, 91–125. **13**

Bandura, A. (1982a). The psychology of chance encounters and life paths. *American Psychologist, 37*, 747–755. **1**

Bandura, A. (1982b). The self and mechanisms of agency. In J. Suls (Ed.), *Psychological perspectives on the self*, Vol. 1. (pp. 3–40). Hillsdale, NJ: Erlbaum. **2**

Bandura, A. (1982c). Self-efficacy mechanism in human agency. *American Psychologist, 37*, 122–147. **13**

Bandura, A. (1986). *Social foundations of thought and action: A social cognitive theory*. Englewood Cliffs, NJ: Prentice-Hall. **2, 13**

Bandura, A. (1989). Social cognitive theory. *Annals of child development*, 6, 1–60. **1, 2**

Barenboim, C. (1977). Developmental changes in the interpersonal cognitive system from middle childhood to adolescence. *Child Development, 48*, 1467–1474. **10**

Barenboim, C. (1981). The development of person perception in childhood and adolescence: From behavioral comparisons to psychological constructs to psychological comparisons. *Child Development, 52*, 129–144. **10**

Barnard, K. E., Bee, H. L., & Hammond, M. A. (1984). Developmental changes in maternal interactions with term and preterm infants. *Infant Behavior and Development, 7* 101–113. **3**

Barnard, K. E., & Eyres, S. J. (1979). *Child health assessment. Part 2: The first year of life*. (DHEW Publication No. HRA 79–25). Washington, D. C.: U.S. Government Printing Office. **4**

Barnard, K. E., Hammond, M. A., Booth, C. L., Bee, H. L., Mitchell, S. K., & Spieker, S. J. (1989). Measurement and meaning of parent-child interaction. In J. J. Morrison, C. Lord & D. P. Keating (Eds.), *Applied developmental psychology* (Vol. 3.) (pp. 40–81). San Diego: Academic Press. **7**

Baron, P., & Perron, L. M. (1986). Sex differences in the Beck depression inventory scores of adolescents. *Journal of Youth and Adolescence, 15*, 165–171. **12**

Barrett, D. E., Radke-Yarrow, M., & Klein, R. E. (1982). Chronic malnutrition and child behavior: Effects of early caloric supplementation on social and emotional functioning at school age. *Developmental Psychology, 18*, 541–556. **4**

Barrett, G. V., & Depinet, R. L. (1991). A reconsideration of testing for competence rather than for intelligence. *American Psychologist, 46*, 1012–1024. **11**

Barrett-Connor, E., & Bush, T. L. (1991). Estrogen and coronary heart disease in women. *Journal of the American Medical Association, 265*, 1861–1867. **15**

Barton, P. (1989). *Earning and learning: The academic achievement of high school juniors with jobs*. Princeton, NJ: Educational Testing Service. **12**

Bartoshuk, L. M., & Weiffenbach, J. M. (1990). Chemical senses and aging. In E. L. Schneider & J. W. Rowe (Eds.) *Handbook of the biology of aging* (3rd ed.) (pp. 429–444). San Diego, CA: Academic Press. **13**

Bass, D. M. (1985). The hospice ideology and success of hospice care. *Research on Aging, 7*, 307–328. **19**

Bates, E., Bretherton, I., Beeghly-Smith, M., & McNew, S. (1982). Social bases of language development: A reassessment. In H. W. Reese & L. P. Lipsitt (Eds.), *Advances in child development and behavior* (Vol. 16) (pp. 8–68). New York: Academic Press. **Int1, 7**

Bates, E., Bretherton, I., & Snyder, L. (1988). *From first words to grammar. Individual differences and dissociable mechanisms*. Cambridge, England: Cambridge University Press. **5**

Bates, E., Camaioni, L., & Volterra, V. (1975). The acquisition of performatives prior to speech. *Merrill-Palmer Quarterly, 21*, 205–226. **5**

Bates, E., O'Connell, B., & Shore, C. (1987). Language and communication in infancy. In J. D. Osofsky (Ed.), *Handbook of infant development* (2nd ed.) (pp. 149–203). New York: Wiley. **5, 7**

Bates, J. E. (1989). Applications of temperament concepts. In G. A. Kohnstamm, J. E. Bates & M. K. Rothbart (Eds.), *Temperament in childhood* (pp. 321–356). Chichester, England: Wiley. **8**

Bates, J. E., Bales, K., Bennett, D. S., Ridge, B., & Brown, M. M. (1991). Origins of externalizing behavior problems at eight years of age. In D. J. Pepler & K. H. Rubin (Eds.), *The development and treatment of childhood aggression* (pp. 93–120). Hillsdale, NJ: Erlbaum. **12**

Baugher, R. J., Burger, C., Smith, R., & Wallston, K. (1989–90). A comparison of terminally ill persons at various time periods to death. *Omega, 20*, 103–115. **19**

Baumrind, D. (1967). Child care practices anteceding three patterns of preschool behavior. *Genetic Psychology Monographs, 75*, 43–88. **8**

Baumrind, D. (1971). Current patterns of parental authority. *Developmental Psychology Monograph, 4* (1, Part 2). **8**

Baumrind, D. (1973). The development of instrumental competence through socialization. In A. D. Pick (Ed.), *Minnesota Symposium on child psychology* (Vol. 7) (pp. 3–46). Minneapolis: University of Minnesota Press. **8**

Baumrind, D. (1991). Effective parenting during the early adolescent transition. In P. A. Cowan & M. Hetherington (Eds.), *Family transitions* (pp. 111–163). Hillsdale, NJ: Erlbaum. **10**

Baydar, N., & Brooks-Gunn, J. (1991). Effects of maternal employment and child-care arrangements on preschoolers' cognitive and behavioral outcomes: Evidence from the children of the National Longitudinal Survey of Youth. *Developmental Psychology, a27*. 932–945. **6**

Bayley, N. (1969). *Bayley scales of infant development*. New York: Psychological Corporation. **5**

Bearison, D. J., Magzamen, S., & Filardo, E. K. (1986). Socio-cognitive conflict and cognitive growth in young children. *Merrill-Palmer Quarterly, 32*, 51–72. **Int2**

Beck, R. W., & Beck, S. H. (1989). The incidence of extended households among middle-aged black and white women: Estimates from a 15-year panel study. *Journal of Family Issues, 10*, 147–168. **14, 16**

Beckwith, L., & Rodning, C. (1991). Intellectual functioning in children born preterm: Recent research. In L. Okagaki & R. J. Sternberg (Eds.), *Directors of development* (pp. 25–58). Hillsdale, NJ: Erlbaum. **3**

Bedeian, A. G., Ferris, G. R., & Kacmar, K. M. (1992). Age, tenure, and job satisfaction: A tale of two perspectives. *Journal of Vocational Behavior, 40*, 33–48. **14**

Bee, H. L. (1992). *The journey of adulthood*. New York: Macmillan. **18**

Bee, H. L., Barnard, K. E., Eyres, S. J., Gray, C. A., Hammond, M. A., Spietz, A. L., Snyder, C., & Clark, B. (1982). Prediction of IQ and language skill from perinatal status, child performance, family characteristics, and mother-infant interaction. *Child Development, 53*, 1135–1156. **5**

Bell, L. G., & Bell, D. C. (1982). Family climate and the role of the female adolescent: Determinants of adolescent functioning. *Family Relations, 31*, 519–527. **8**

Bell, R. R. (1981). *Worlds of friendship*. Beverly Hills, CA: Sage. **14**

Belsky, J. (1985). Prepared statement on the effects of day care. In Select Committee on Children, Youth, and Families, House of Representatives, 98th Congress, Second Session, *Improving child care services: What can be done?* Washington, D. C.: U.S. Government Printing Office. **6**

Belsky, J. (1987). *Science, social policy and day care: A personal odyssey*. Paper presented at the biennial meetings of the Society for Research in Child Development, Baltimore, April. **6**

Belsky, J. (1990). The "effects" of infant day care reconsidered. In N. Fox & G. G. Fein (Eds.), *Infant day care: The current debate* (pp. 3–40). Norwood, NJ: Ablex. **6**

Belsky, J., & Braungart, J. M. (1991). Are insecure-avoidant infants with extensive day-care experience less stressed by and more independent in the strange situation? *Child Development, 62,* 567–571. **6**

Belsky, J., & Eggebeen, D. (1991). Early and extensive maternal employment and young children's socioemotional development: Children of the National Longitudinal Survey of Youth. *Journal of Marriage and the Family, 53,* 1083–1110. **6**

Belsky, J., Lang, M. E., & Rovine, M. (1985). Stability and change in marriage across the transition to parenthood: A second study. *Journal of Marriage and the Family, 47,* 855–865. **14**

Belsky, J., & Rovine, M. (1988). Nonmaternal care in the first year of life and the security of infant-parent attachment. *Child Development, 59,* 157–167. **6**

Belsky, J., Spanier, G. B., & Rovine, M. (1983). Stability and change in marriage across the transition to parenthood. *Journal of Marriage and the Family, 45,* 567–577. **14**

Bem, S. L. (1974). The measurement of psychological androgyny. *Journal of Consulting and Clinical Psychology, 42,* 155–162. **12**

Bem, S. L. (1981). Gender schema theory: A cognitive account of sex-typing. *Psychological Review, 88,* 354–364. **8**

Benfante, R., & Reed, D. (1990). Is elevated serum cholesterol level a risk factor for coronary heart disease in the elderly? *Journal of the American Medical Association, 263,* 393–396. **15**

Bengtson, V. L. (1985). Diversity and symbolism in grandparent roles. In V. L. Bengtson & J. F. Robertson (Eds.), *Grandparenthood.* Beverly Hills, CA: Sage. **16**

Bengtson, V. L., Cuellar, J. B., & Ragan, P. K. (1977). Stratum contrasts and similarities in attitudes toward death. *Journal of Gerontology, 32,* 76–88. **19**

Bengtson, V., Rosenthal, C., & Burton, L. (1990). Families and aging: Diversity and heterogeneity. In R. H. Binstock & L. K. George (Eds.), *Handbook of aging and the social sciences* (3rd ed.) (pp. 263–287). San Diego: Academic Press. **18**

Benn, R. K. (1986). Factors promoting secure attachment relationships between employed mothers and their sons. *Child Development, 57,* 1224–1231. **6**

Benninger, W. B., & Walsh, W. B. (1980). Holland's theory and non-college-degreed working men and women. *Journal of Vocational Behavior, 17,* 81–88. **14**

Berberian, K. E., & Snyder, S. S. (1982). The relationship of temperament and stranger reaction for younger and older infants. *Merrill-Palmer Quarterly, 28,* 79–94. **6**

Berch, D. B., & Bender, B. G. (1987, December). Margins of sexuality. *Psychology Today, 21,* 54–57. **3**

Berg, J. M. (1974). Aetiological aspects of mental subnormality. In A. M. Clarke & A. D. B. Clarke (Eds.), *Mental deficiency: The changing outlook* (3rd ed.) (pp. 82–117). New York: Free Press. **3**

Berg, W. K., & Berg, K. M. (1987). Psychophysiological development in infancy: State, startle, and attention. In J. D. Osofsky (Ed.), *Handbook of infant development* (2nd ed.) (pp. 238–317). New York: Wiley-Interscience. **4**

Berkman, L. F. (1985). The relationship of social networks and social support to morbidity and mortality. In S. Coen & S. L. Syme (Eds.), *Social support and health* (pp. 241–262). Orlando, FL: Academic Press. **13**

Berkman, L. F., & Breslow, L. (1983). *Health and ways of living. The Alameda County Study.* New York: Oxford University Press. **13, 15**

Berkowitz, G. S., Fiarman, G. S., Mojica, M. A., Bauman, J., & de Regt, R. H. (1989). Effect of physician characteristics on the cesarean birth rate. *American Journal of Obstetrics and Gynecology, 161,* 146–149. **3**

Berkowitz, G. S., Skovron, M. L., Lapinski, R. H., & Berkowitz, R. L. (1990). Delayed childbearing and the outcome of pregnancy. *New England Journal of Medicine, 322,* 659–664. **3**

Berlin, J. A., & Colditz, G. A. (1990). A meta-analysis of physical activity in the prevention of coronary heart disease. *American Journal of Epidemiology, 132,* 612–628. **15**

Berndt, T. J. (1979). Developmental changes in conformity to peers and parents. *Developmental Psychology, 15,* 608–616. **11, 12**

Berndt, T. J. (1981). Age changes and changes over time in prosocial intentions and behavior between friends. *Developmental Psychology, 17,* 408–416. **8**

Berndt, T. J. (1983). Social cognition, social behavior, and children's friendships. In E. T. Higgins, D. N. Ruble & W. W. Hartup (Eds.), *Social cognition and social development. A sociocultural perspective* (pp. 158–192). Cambridge, England: Cambridge University Press. **10**

Berndt, T. J. (1986). Children's comments about their friendships. In M. Perlmutter (Ed.), Cognitive perspectives on children's social and behavioral development. *Minnesota Symposia on Child Psychology,* Vol. 18 (pp. 189–212). Hillsdale, NJ: Erlbaum. **10**

Berndt, T. J., Hawkins, J. A., & Hoyle, S. G. (1986). Changes in friendship during a school year: Effects on children's and adolescents' impressions of friendship and sharing with friends. *Child Development, 57,* 1284–1297. **10**

Berndt, T. J., & Hoyle, S. G. (1985). Stability and change in childhood and adolescent friendships. *Developmental Psychology, 21,* 1007–1015. **10**

Berndt, T. J., & Perry, T. B. (1990). Distinctive features and effects of early adolescent friendships. In R. Montemayor, G. R. Adams & T. P. Gullotta (Eds.), *From childhood to adolescence. A transitional period?* (pp. 269–287). **12**

Bertenthal, B. I., & Campos, J. J. (1987). New directions in the study of early experience. *Child Development, 58,* 560–567. **4**

Bettes, B. A. (1988). Maternal depression and motherese: Temporal and intonational features. *Child Development, 59,* 1089–1096. **7**

Betz, N. E., & Fitzgerald, L. F. (1987). *The career psychology of women.* Orlando, FL: Academic Press. **14, 16**

Biedenharn, P. J., & Normoyle, J. B. (1991). Elderly community residents' reactions to the nursing home: An analysis of nursing home-related beliefs. *The Gerontologist, 31,* 107–115. **18**

Billings, A. G., & Moos, R. H. (1983). Comparisons of children of depressed and nondepressed parents: A social-environmental perspective. *Journal of Abnormal Child Psychology, 11,* 463–486. **12**

Binet, A., & Simon, T. (1905). Methodes nouvelles pour le diagnostic du niveau intellectual des anormaux. *L'Anee Psychologique, 11,* 191–244. **7**

Bingham, C. R., Miller, B. C., & Adams, G. R. (1990). Correlates of age at first sexual intercourse in a national sample of young women. *Journal of Adolescent Research, 5,* 18–33. **12**

Binstock, R. H., & George, L. K. (Eds.) (1990). *Handbook of aging and the social sciences* (3rd ed.) San Diego, CA: Academic Press. **18**

Birren, J. E., Sloane, R. B., & Cohen, G. D. (Eds.), (1992). *Handbook of mental health and aging,* 2nd ed. San Diego, CA: Academic Press. **17**

Black, B. (1992). Negotiating social pretend play: communication differences related to social status and sex. *Merrill-Palmer Quarterly, 38,* 212–232. **10**

Black, B., & Hazen, N. L. (1990). Social status and patterns of communication in acquainted and unacquainted preschool children. *Developmental Psychology, 26,* 379–387. **10**

Blackman, J. A. (1990). Update on AIDS, CMV, and herpes in young children: Health, developmental, and educational issues. In M. Wolraich & D. K. Routh (Eds.), *Advances in developmental and behavioral pediatrics*, (Vol. 9) (pp. 33–58). London: Jessica Kingsley Publishers. **3**

Blazer, D., Burchett, B., Service, C., & George, L. K. (1991). The association of age and depression among the elderly: An epidemiologic exploration. *Journal of Gerontology: MEDICAL SCIENCES, 46*, M210–215. **17**

Blieszner, R. (1989). Developmental processes of friendship. In R. G. Adams & R. Blieszner (Eds.), *Older adult friendship* (pp. 108–128). Newbury Park, CA: Sage Publications. **18**

Block, J. (1971). *Lives through time*. Berkeley, CA: Bancroft. **8**

Block, J. (1987). *Longitudinal antecedents of ego-control and ego-resiliency in late adolescence*. Paper presented at the biennial meetings of the Society for Research in Child Development, Baltimore, April. **2**

Block, M. R., Davidson, J. L., & Grambs, J. D. (1981). *Women over forty. Visions and realities*. New York: Springer. **16**

Bloom, B. L., White, S. W., & Asher, S. J. (1979). Marital disruption as a stressful life event. In C. Levinger & O. C. Moles (Eds.), *Divorce and separation. Context, causes, and consequences*. New York: Basic Books. **16**

Bloom, L. (1973). *One word at a time*. The Hague: Mouton.

Bloom, L. (1991). *Language development from two to three*. Cambridge, England: Cambridge, University Press. **7**

Blum, R. W., Harmon, B., Harris, L., Bergeisen, L., & Resnick, M. D. (1992). American Indian-Alaska Native youth health. *Journal of the American Medical Association, 267*, 1637–1644. **12**

Blumenthal, J. A., Emery, C. F., Madden, D. J., Schniebolk, S., Walsh-Riddle, M., George, L. K., McKee, D. C., Higginbotham, M. B., Cobb, RR., & Coleman, R. E. (1991). Long-term effects of exercise on physiological functioning in older men and women. *Journal of Gerontology: PSYCHOLOGICAL SCIENCES, 46*, P352–361. **13, 17**

Blumstein, P., & Schwartz, P. (1983). *American couples*. New York: William Morrow. **14**

Boldero, J., & Moore, S. (1990). An evaluation of de Jong-Giervald's loneliness model with Australian adolescents. *Journal of Youth and Adolescence, 10*, 133–147. **14**

Bond, J., & Coleman, P. (Eds.) (1990). *Aging in society*. London: Sage Publications. **17, 18**

Booth, A., & Edwards, J. N. (1985). Age at marriage and marital instability. *Journal of Marriage and the Family, 47*, 67–75. **14**

Booth, A., & Johnson, D. (1988). Premarital cohabitation and marital success. *Journal of Family Issues, 9*, 255–272. **14**

Booth-Kewley, S. & Friedman, H. S. (1987). Psychological predictors of heart disease: A quantitative review. *Psychological Bulletin, 101*, 343–362. **15**

Bornstein, M. H. (Ed.) (1987). *Sensitive periods in development. Interdisciplinary perspectives*. Hillsdale, NJ: Erlbaum. **1**

Bornstein, M. H. (1988). Perceptual development across the life cycle. In M. H. Bornstein & M. E. Lamb (Eds.), *Developmental psychology: An advanced textbook* (2nd ed.). Hillsdale, NJ: Erlbaum. **13, 15**

Bornstein, M. H. (1989). Stability in early mental development: From attention and information processing in infancy to language and cognition in childhood. In M. H. Bornstein & N. A. Krasnegor (Eds.), *Stability and continuity in mental development* (pp. 147–170). Hillsdale, NJ: Erlbaum. **5**

Borthen, I., Lossius, P., Skjaerven, R., & Pergsjo, P. (1989). Changes in frequencey and indications for cesarean section in Norway, 1967–1984. *Acta Obstet Gynecol Scand, 68*, 589–593. **3**

Bossé, R., Aldwin, C. M., Levenson, M. R., & Workman-Daniels, K. (1991). How stressful is retirement? Findings from the normative aging study. *Journal of Gerontology: PSYCHOLOGICAL SCIENCES, 46*, P9–14. **18**

The Boston Women's Health Collective (1984). *The New Our Bodies, Ourselves: A book by and for women* (2nd ed.). New York: Simon & Schuster. **3**

Botwinick, J., & Storandt, M. (1974). *Memory, related functions and age*. Springfield, IL: Charles C. Thomas. **1**

Bouchard, T. J., Jr. (1984). Twins reared apart and together: What they tell us about human diversity. In S. Fox (Ed.), *The chemical and biological bases of individuality*. New York: Plenum Press. **6**

Bouchard, T. J. Jr. , & McGue, M. (1981). Familial studies of intelligence: A review. *Science, 212*, 1055–1059. **1, 7**

Boukydis, C. F. Z., & Burgess, R. L. (1982). Adult physiological response to infant cries: Effects of temperament, parental status, and gender. *Child Development, 53*, 1291–1298. **6**

Bowen, G. L., & Orthner, D. K. (1983). Sex-role congruency and marital quality. *Journal of Marriage and the Family, 45*, 223–230. **14**

Bowerman, M. (1985). Beyond communicative adequacy: From piecemeal knowledge to an integrated system in the child's acquisition of language. In K. E. Nelson (Ed.). *Children's language* (Vol. 5) (pp. 369–398). Hillsdale, NJ: Erlbaum. **7**

Bowlby, J. (1969). *Attachment and loss* (Vol. 1), *Attachment*. New York: Basic Books. **1, 6**

Bowlby, J. (1973). *Attachment and loss* (Vol. 2), *Separation, anxiety, and anger*. New York: Basic Books. **6**

Bowlby, J. (1980). *Attachment and loss* (Vol. 3), *Loss, sadness, and depression*. New York: Basic Books. **1, 6, 19**

Bowlby, J. (1988a). Developmental psychiatry comes of age. *The American Journal of Psychiatry, 145*, 1–10. **6**

Bowlby, J. (1988b). *A secure base*. New York: Basic Books. **6**

Bowman, P. J. (1991). Joblessness. In J. J. Jackson (Ed.) *Life in black America* (pp. 156–178). Newbury Park, CA: Sage Publications. **16**

Brackbill, Y., McManus, K., & Woodward, L. (1985). *Medication in maternity*. Ann Arbor: University of Michigan Press. **3**

Bradley, R. H., & Caldwell, B. M. (1976). The relation of infants' home environment to mental test performance at fifty-four months: A follow-up study. *Child Development, 47*, 1172–1174. **7**

Bradley, R. H., & Caldwell, B. M. (1984). 174 children: A study of the relationship between home environment and cognitive development during the first 5 years. In A. W. Gottfried (Ed.), *Home environment and early cognitive development: Longitudinal research* (pp. 5–56). New York: Academic Press. **7**

Bradley, R. H., Caldwell, B. M., Rock, S. L., Barnard, K. E., Gray, C., Hammond, M. A., Mitchell, S., Siegel, L., Ramey, C. D., Gottfried, A. W., & Johnson, D. L. (1989). Home environment and cognitive development in the first 3 years of life: A collaborative study involving six sites and three ethnic groups in North America. *Developmental Psychology, 25*, 217–235. **Int1, 7**

Brandstädter, J., & Baltes-Götz, B. (1990). Personal control over development and quality of life perspectives in adulthood. In P. Baltes & M. M. Baltes (Eds.), *Successful aging* (pp. 197–224). Cambridge, England: Cambridge University Press. **16, Int6**

Braveman, N. S. (1987). Immunity and aging immunologic and behavioral perspectives. In M. W. Riley, J. D. Matarazzo, & A. Baum (Eds.), *Perspectives in behavioral medicine. The aging dimension*. Hillsdale, NJ: Erlbaum. **13**

Braverman, L. B. (1989). Beyond the myth of motherhood. In M. McGoldrick, C. M. Anderson, & F. Walsh (Eds.), *Women and families* (pp. 227–243). New York: Free Press. **6**

Bray, D. W., & Howard, A. (1983). The AT&T longitudinal studies of managers. In K. W. Schaie (Ed.), *Longitudinal studies of adult psychological development*. New York: Guilford Press. **14, Int6**

Brayfield, A. A. (1992). Employment resources and housework in Canada. *Journal of Marriage and the Family, 54*, 19–30. **14**

Breitmayer, B. J., & Ramey, C. T. (1986). Biological nonoptimality and quality of postnatal environment as codeterminants of intellectual development. *Child Development, 57*, 1151–1165. **3**

Bretherton, I. (1991). Pouring new wine into old bottles: The social self as internal working model. In M. R. Gunnar & L. A. Sroufe (Eds.). *Self processes and development. The Minnesota symposia on child development* (Vol. 23) (pp. 1–42). Hillsdale, NJ: Erlbaum. **1, Int1**

Briggs, R. (1990). Biological aging. In J. Bond & P. Coleman (Eds.), *Aging in society* (pp. 48–61). London: Sage Publications. **15**

Brock, D. B., Guralnik, J. M., & Brody, J. A. (1990). Demography and the epidemiology of aging in the United States. In E. L. Schneider & J. W. Rowe (Eds.), *Handbook of the biology of aging*, (3rd ed.) (pp. 3–23). San Diego, CA: Academic Press. **15, 17, 18**

Brody, E. M., Litvin, S. J., Hoffman, C., & Kleban, M. H. (1992). Differential effects of daughters' marital status on their parent care experiences. *The Gerontologist, 32*, 58–67. **16**

Brody, H. (1955). Organization of the cerebral cortex. III. A study of aging in the human cerebral cortex. *Journal of Comparative Neurology, 102*, 511–556. **17**

Brody, N. (1992). *Intelligence* (2nd ed.). San Diego, CA: Academic Press. **7, 9, 11**

Bronfenbrenner, U. (1979). *The ecology of human development*. Cambridge, MA: Harvard University Press. **1**

Bronfenbrenner, U. (1986). Ecology of the family as a context for human development: Research perspectives. *Developmental Psychology, 22*, 723–742. **1**

Bronfenbrenner, U. (1989). Ecological systems theory. *Annals of child development, 6*, 187–249. **1**

Brooks-Gunn, J. (1987). Pubertal processes and girls' psychological adaptation. In R. M. Lerner & T. T. Foch (Eds.), *Biological-psychosocial interactions in early adolescence* (pp. 123–154). Hillsdale, NJ: Erlbaum. **11**

Brooks-Gunn, J. (1988). Commentary: Developmental issues in the transition to early adolescence. In M. R. Gunnar & W. A. Collins (Eds.), *Development during the transition to adolescence. Minnesota symposia on child psychology* (Vol. 21) (pp. 189–208). Hillsdale, NJ: Erlbaum. **Int4**

Brooks-Gunn, J., & Furstenberg, F. F., Jr. (1989). Adolescent sexual behavior. *American Psychologist, 44*, 249–257. **12**

Brooks-Gunn, J., & Matthews, W. S. (1979). *He and she: How children develop their sex-role identity*. Englewood Cliffs, NJ: Prentice-Hall. **3, 10**

Brooks-Gunn, J., & Reiter, E. O. (1990). The role of pubertal processes. In S. S. Feldman & G. R. Elliott (Eds.), *At the threshold. The developing adolescent* (pp. 16–53). Cambridge, MA: Harvard University Press. **11**

Brooks-Gunn, J., & Warren, M. P. (1985). The effects of delayed menarche in different contexts: Dance and nondance students. *Journal of Youth and Adolescence, 13*, 285–300. **11**

Brown, B. B. (1990). Peer groups and peer cultures. In S. S. Feldman & G. R. Elliott (Eds.), *At the threshold. The developing adolescent* (pp. 171–196). Cambridge, MA: Harvard University Press. **12**

Brown, B. B., Clasen, D. R., & Eicher, S. A. (1986). Perceptions of peer pressure, peer conformity dispositions, and self-reported behavior among adolescents. *Developmental Psychology, 22*, 521–530. **12**

Brown, J. L. (1987). Hunger in the U.S. *Scientific American, 256*(2), 37–41. **3**

Brown, R. (1973). *A first language: The early stages*. Cambridge, MA: Harvard University Press. **7**

Brown, R., & Hanlon, C. (1970). Derivational complexity and order of acquisition. In J. R. Hayes (Ed.), *Cognition and the development of language* (pp. 155–207). New York: Wiley. **7**

Brownell, C. A. (1986). Convergent developments: Cognitive-developmental correlates of growth in infant/toddler peer skills. *Child Development, 57*, 275–286. **9**

Brownell, C. A. (1988). Combinatorial skills: Converging developments over the second year. *Child Development, 59*, 675–685. **7**

Brownell, C. A. (1990). Peer social skills in toddlers: Competencies and constraints illustrated by same-age and mixed-age interaction. *Child Development, 61*, 836–848. **7**

Brownell, C. A., & Carriger, M. S. (1990). Changes in cooperation and self-other differentiation during the second year. *Child Development, 61*, 1164–1174. **9**

Brubaker, T. H. (1990). Families in later life: A burgeoning research area. *Journal of Marriage and the Family, 52*, 959–981. **18**

Bryant, S., & Rakowski, W. (1992). Predictors of mortality among elderly African-Americans. *Research on Aging, 14*, 50–67. **18**

Buchanan, C. M., Eccles, J. S., & Becker, J. B. (1992). Are adolescents the victims of raging hormones: Evidence for activational effects of hormones on moods and behavior at adolescence. *Psychological Bulletin, 111*, 62–107. **11**

Buchanan, C. M., Maccoby, E. E., & Dornbusch, S. M. (1991). Caught between parents: Adolescents' experience in divorced homes. *Child Development, 62*, 1008–1029. **8**

Buehler, J. W., Kaunitz, A. M., Hogue, C. J. R., Hughes, J. M., Smith, J. C., & Rochat, R. W. (1986). Maternal mortality in women aged 35 years or older: United States. *Journal of the American Medical Association, 255*, 53–57. **3**

Bulcroft, R. A., & Bulcroft, K. A. (1991). The nature and functions of dating in later life. *Research on Aging, 13*, 244–260. **18**

Bullock, M., & Lütkenhaus, P. (1990). Who am I? Self-understanding in toddlers. *Merrill-Palmer Quarterly, 36*, 217–238. **6**

Bumpass, L. (1984). Children and marital disruption: A replication and update. *Demography, 41*, 71–82. **8**

Bumpass, L. L., & Sweet, J. A. (1989). National estimates of cohabitation. *Demography, 26*, 615–625. **14**

Bumpass, L. L., Sweet, J. A., & Cherlin, A. (1991). The role of cohabitation in declining rates of marriage. *Journal of Marriage and the Family, 53*, 913–927. **14**

Burchinal, M., Lee, M., & Ramey, C. (1989). Type of day-care and preschool intellectual development in disadvantaged children. *Child Development, 60*, 128–137. **6**

Burke, P., & Puig-Antich, J. (1990). Psychobiology of childhood depression. In M. Lewis & S. M. Miller (Eds.), *Handbook of developmental psychopathology* (pp. 327–340). New York: Plenum. **12**

Burkhauser, R. V., Duncan, G. J., Hauser, R., & Berntsen, R. (1991). Wife or Frau, women do worse: A comparison of men and women in the United States and Germany after marital dissolution. *Demography, 28*, 353–360. **16**

Burr, J. A., & Mutchler, J. E. (1992). The living arrangements of unmarried elderly Hispanic females. *Demography, 29*, 93–112. **18**

Burton, L. M., & Bengtson, V. L. (1985). Black grandmothers: Issues of timing and continuity of roles. In V. L. Bengtson & J. F. Robertson (Eds.), *Grandparenthood* (pp. 61–78). Beverly Hills, CA: Sage Publications. **16**

Bushnell, I. W. R. (1982). Discrimination of faces by young infants. *Journal of Experimental Child Psychology, 33*, 298–308. **5**

Buss, A. (1989). Temperaments as personality traits. In G. A. Kohnstamm, J. E. Bates & M. K. Rothbart (eds.), *Temperament in childhood* (pp. 49–58). Chichester, England: Wiley. **6**

Buss, A. H., & Plomin, R. (1984). *Temperament: Early developing personality traits*. Hillsdale, NJ: Erlbaum. **6**

Buss, A. H., & Plomin, R. (1986). The EAS approach to temperament. In R. Plomin & J. Dunn (Eds.), *The study of temperament: Changes, continuities and challenges* (pp. 67–80). Hillsdale, NJ: Erlbaum. **6**

Busse, E. W., & Wang, H. S. (1971). The multiple factors contributing to dementia in old age. In *Proceedings of the Fifth World Congress of Psychiatry*, Mexico City. [Reprinted in E. Palmore (Ed.), *Normal aging II*. Durham, NC: Duke University Press, 1974.] **17**

Butler, R.N. (1963). The life review: An interpretation of reminiscence in the aged. *Psychiatry, Journal for the Study of Interpersonal Processes, 26*. Reprinted in B. L. Neugarten (Ed.), *Middle age and aging*. Chicago: University of Chicago Press, 1968. **18**

Butterfield, E. C., Siladi, D., & Belmont, J. M. (1980). Validating theories of intelligence. In H. W. Reese & L. P. Lipsitt (Eds.), *Advances in child development and behavior* (Vol. 15) (pp. 96–152). New York: Academic Press. **5**

Cain, V. S., & Hofferth, S. L. (1989). Parental choice of self-care for school-age children. *Journal of Marriage and the Family, 51*, 65–77. **10**

Caldwell, B. M. (1986). Day care and early environmental adequacy. In W. Fowler (Ed.), *Early experience and the development of competence, New Directions for Child Development, 32*, 11–30. **6**

California Assessment Program (1980). *Student achievement in California schools. 1979–1980 annual report: Television and student achievement*. Sacramento: California State Department of Education. **10**

Campbell, A. (1981). *The sense of well-being in America*. New York: McGraw-Hill. **Int5**

Campbell, S. B. & Ewing, L. J. (1990). Follow-up of hard-to-manage preschoolers: Adjustment at age 9 and predictors of continuing symptoms. *Journal of Child Psychology and Psychiatry, 31*, 871–889. **8, Int2**

Campbell, S. B., Ewing, L. J., Breaux, A. M., & Szumowski, E. K. (1986). Parent-referred problem three-year-olds: Follow-up at school entry. *Journal of Child Psychology and Psychiatry, 27*, 473–488. **Int2**

Campbell, S. B., & Taylor, P. M. (1980). Bonding and attachment: Theoretical issues. In P. M. Taylor (Ed.). *Parent-infant relationships* (pp. 3–24). New York: Grune & Stratton. **6**

Campbell, S. B., Pierce, E. W., March, C. L., & Ewing, L. J. (1991). Noncompliant behavior, overactivity, and family stress as predictors of negative maternal control with preschool children. *Development and Psychopathology, 3*, 175–190. **Int2**

Campos, J. J., & Bertenthal, B. I. (1989). Locomotion and psychological development in infancy. In F. J. Morrison, C. Lord & D. P. Keating (Eds.), *Applied developmental psychology* (Vol. 3) (pp. 229–258). San Diego: Academic Press. **Int1**

Cantwell, D. P. (1990). Depression across the early life span. In M. Lewis & S. M. Miller (Eds.), *Handbook of developmental psychopathology* (pp. 293–310). New York: Plenum. **12**

Capron, C., & Duyme, M. (1989). Assessment of effects of socio-economic status on IQ in a full cross-fostering study. *Nature, 340*, 552–554. **7**

Capute, A. J., Palmer, F. B., Shapiro, B. K., Wachtel, R. C., Ross, A., & Accardo, P. J. (1984). Primitive reflex profile: A quantification of primitive reflexes in infancy. *Developmental Medicine and Child Neurology, 26*, 375–383. **4**

Capute, A. J., Palmer, F. B., Shapiro, B. K., Wachtel, R. C., Schmidt, S., & Ross, A. (1986). Clinical linguistic and auditory milestone scale: Prediction of cognition in infancy. *Developmental Medicine & Child Neurology, 28*, 762–771. **4, 5**

Carey, R. G. (1974). Living until death: A program of service and research for the terminally ill. *Hospital Progress*, reprinted in E. Kübler-Ross (Ed.), *Death. The final stage of growth*. Englewood Cliffs, NJ: Prentice Hall, 1975. **19**

Carey, S., & Bartlett, E. (1978). Acquiring a single new word. *Papers and Reports on Child Language Development, 15*, 17–29. **7**

Carey, W. B. (1981). The importance of temperament-environment interaction for child health and development. In M. Lewis & L. A. Rosenblum (Eds.), *The uncommon child* (pp. 31–56). New York: Plenum. **6**

Carlson, V., Cicchetti, D., Barnett, D., & Braunwald, K. (1989). Disorganized/disoriented attachment relationships in maltreated infants. *Developmental Psychology, 25*, 525–531. **6**

Caron, A. J., & Caron, R. F. (1981). Processing of relational information as an index of infant risk. In S. Friedman & M. Sigman (Eds.). *Preterm birth and psychological development* (pp. 219–240). New York: Academic Press. **5**

Carroll, K. K. (1991). Dietary fats and cancer. *American Journal of Clinical Nutrition, 53*, 1064S-1067S. **15**

Carter, C. S. (1988). Patterns of infant feeding, the mother-infant interaction and stress management. In T. M. Field, P. M. McCabe, & N. Schneiderman (Eds.), *Stress and coping across development* (pp. 27–46). Hillsdale, NJ: Erlbaum. **4**

Carver, R. P. (1990). Intelligence and reading ability in grades 2–12. *Intelligence, 14*, 449–455. **7**

Case, R. (1991). Stages in the development of the young child's first sense of self. *Developmental Review, 11*, 210–230. **8**

Case, R. B., Moss, A. J., Case, N., McDermott, M., & Eberly, S. (1992). Living alone after myocardial infarction. Impact on prognosis. *Journal of the American Medical Association, 267*, 515–519. **19**

Caspi, A., Bem, D. J., & Elder, G. H. Jr., (1989). Continuities and consequences of interactional styles across the life course. *Journal of Personality, 57*, 375–406. **1**

Caspi, A., & Elder, G. H. Jr. (1988). Childhood precursors of the life course: Early personality and life disorganization. In E. M. Hetherington, R. M. Lerner & M. Perlmutter (Eds.), *Child development in life-span perspective*. Hillsdale, NJ: Erlbaum. **1, 16**

Caspi, A., Elder, G. H. Jr., & Bem, D. J. (1987). Moving against the world: Life-course patterns of explosive children. *Developmental Psychology, 23*, 308–313. **1, 10, 16**

Caspi, A., Elder, G. H., Jr., & Bem, D. J. (1988). Moving away from the world: Life-course patterns of shy children. *Developmental Psychology, 24*, 824–831. **1, 16**

Caspi, A., & Moffitt, T. E. (1991). Individual differences are accentuated during periods of social change: The sample case of girls at puberty. *Journal of Personality and Social Psychology, 61*, 157–168. **Int4**

Cassileth, B. R., Walsh, W. P., & Lusk, E. J. (1988). Psychosocial correlates of cancer survival: A subsequent report 3 to 8 years after cancer diagnosis. *Journal of Clinical Oncology, 6, 1753–1759*. **19**

Cattell, R. B. (1963). Theory of fluid and crystallized intelligence: A critical experiment. *Journal of Educational Psychology, 54*, 1–22. **13**

Center for Educational Statistics (1987). *Who drops out of high school? From high school and beyond*. Washington, DC: Office of Educational Research and Improvement, U.S. Department of Education. **11**

Cernoch, J. M., & Porter, R. H. (1985). Recognition of maternal axillary odors by infants. *Child Development, 56*, 1593–1598. **5**

Chamberlain, J. C., & Galton, D. J. (1990). Genetic susceptibility to atherosclerosis. *British Medical Bulletin, 46*, 917–940. **15**

Chandler, M., & Moran, T. (1990). Psychopathology and moral development: A comparative study of delinquent and nondelinquent youth. *Development and Psychopathology, 2*, 227–246. **11**

Charness, N. (Ed.) (1985). *Aging and human performance*. Chichester, England: Wiley. **15**

Chase-Lansdale, P. L., & Hetherington, E. M. (1990). The impact of divorce on life-span development: Short and long term effects. In P. B. Baltes, D. L., Featherman & R. M. Lerner (Eds.), *Life-span development and behavior* (Vol. 10) (pp. 107–151). Hillsdale, NJ: Erlbaum. **16**

Chatters, L. M. (1991). Physical health. In J. S. Jackson (Ed.), *Life in black America* (pp. 199–220). Newbury Park, CA: Sage Publications. **15**

Cherlin, A., & Furstenberg, F. F. (1986). *The new American grandparent*. New York: Basic Books. **16**

Chess, S., & Thomas, A. (1984). *Origins and evolution of behavior disorders: Infancy to early adult life*. New York: Brunner/Mazel. **8**

Chess, S., & Thomas, A. (1990). Continuities and discontinuities in temperament. In L. N. Robins & M. Rutter (Eds.), *Straight and devious pathways from childhood to adulthood* (pp. 205–220). Cambridge, England: Cambridge University Press. **6**

Chi, M. T. (1978). Knowledge structure and memory development. In R. S. Siegler (Ed.). *Children's thinking: What develops?* (pp. 73–96). Hillsdale, NJ: Erlbaum. **8**

Chi, M. T. H., & Ceci, S. J. (1987). Content knowledge: Its role, representation, and restructuring in memory development. In H. W. Reese (Ed.), *Advances in child development and behavior* (Vol. 20) (pp. 91–142). Orlando, FL: Academic Press. **9**

Chi, M. T. H., Hutchinson, J. E., & Robin, A. F. (1989) How inferences about novel domain-related concepts can be constrained by structured knowledge. *Merrill-Palmer Quarterly, 35*, 27–62. **9**

Chiriboga, D. A. (1984). Social stressors as antecedents of change. *Journal of Gerontology, 39*, 468–477. **16**

Chiriboga, D. A. (1989). Mental health at the midpoint: Crisis, challenge, or relief? In S. Hunter & M. Sundel (Eds.), *Midlife myths. Issues, findings, and practice implications*. Newbury Park, CA: Sage. **15**

Chiriboga, D. A., & Cutler, L. (1980). Stress and adaptation: Life span perspectives. In L. W. Poon (Ed.), *Aging in the 1980s. Psychological issues*. Washington, D.C.: American Psychological Association. **16**

Chiriboga, D. A., & Dean, H. (1978). Dimensions of stress: Perspectives from a longitudinal study. *Journal of Psychosomatic Research, 22*, 47–55. **16**

Choi, N. G. (1991). Racial differences in the determinants of living arrangements of widowed and divorced elderly women. *The Gerontologist, 31*, 496–504. **18**

Chomsky, N. (1965). *Aspects of a theory of syntax*. Cambridge, MA: MIT Press. **7**

Chomsky, N. (1975). *Reflections on language*. New York: Pantheon Books. **7**

Chomsky, N. (1986). *Knowledge of language: Its nature, origin, and use*. New York: Praeger. **7**

Chomsky, N. (1988). *Language and problems of knowledge*. Cambridge, MA: MIT Press. **7**

Christensen, K. J., Moye, J., Armson, R. R., & Kern, T. M. (1992). Health screening and random recruitment for cognitive aging research. *Psychology and Aging, 7*, 204–208. **13**

Christophersen, E. R. (1989). Injury control. *American Psychologist, 44*, 237–241. **7**

Chumlea, W. C. (1982). Physical growth in adolescence. In B. B. Wolman (Ed.), *Handbook of developmental psychology* (pp. 471–485). Englewood Cliffs, NJ: Prentice-Hall. **11**

Cicchetti, D., & Carlson, V. (1989). *Child maltreatment*. Cambridge, England: Cambridge University Press. **6**

Cicirelli, V. G. (1982). Sibling influence throughout the lifespan. In M. E. Lamb & B. Sutton-Smith (Eds.), *Sibling relationships*. Hillsdale, NJ: Erlbaum. **18**

Cicirelli, V. G. (1983). Adult children and their elderly parents. In Brubaker, T. H. (Ed.), *Family relationships in later life*. Beverly Hills, CA: Sage. **18**

Cicirelli, V. G. (1989). Feelings of attachment to siblings and well-being in later life. *Psychology and Aging, 4*, 211–216. **18**

Cicirelli, V. G. (1991). Attachment theory in old age: Protection of the attached figure. In K. Pillemer & K. McCargner (Eds.), *Parent-child relationships throughout life* (pp. 25–42). Hillsdale, NJ: Lawrence Erlbaum Press. **14**

Clark, E. V. (1975). Knowledge, context, and strategy in the acquisition of meaning. In D. P. Date (Ed.), *Georgetown University round table on language and linguistics*. Washington, DC: Georgetown University Press. **7**

Clark, E. V. (1977). Strategies and the mapping problem in first language acquisition. In J. Macnamara (Ed.). *Language learning and thought* (pp. 147–168). New York: Academic Press, 1977. **7**

Clark, E. V. (1983). Meanings and concepts. In J. H. Flavell & E. M. Markman (Eds.), *Handbook of child psychology: Cognitive development* (Vol. 3) (pp. 787–840). New York: Wiley. (P. H. Mussen, General Editor) **7**

Clark, E. V. (1987). The principle of contrast: A constraint on language acquisition. In B. MacWhinney (Ed.), *Mechanisms of language acquisition* (pp. 1–34). Hillsdale, NJ: Erlbaum. **7**

Clark, E. V. (1990). On the pragmatics of contrast. *Journal of Child Language, 41*, 417–431. **7**

Clark, R. L. (1988). The future of work and retirement. *Research on aging, 10*, 169–193. **18**

Clarke-Stewart, A. (1984). Day care: A new context for research and development. In M. Perlmutter (Ed.), *Minnesota symposia on child psychology* (Vol. 17) (pp. 61–100). Hillsdale, NJ: Erlbaum. **6**

Clarke-Stewart, A. (1987). The social ecology of early childhood. In N. Eisenberg (Ed.), *Contemporary topics in developmental psychology* (pp. 292–318). New York: Wiley-Interscience. **6**

Clarke-Stewart, A. (1990). "The 'effects' of infant day care reconsidered" reconsidered: Risks for parents, children, and researchers. In N. Fox & G. G. Fein (Eds.), *Infant day care: The current debate* (pp. 61–86). Norwood, NJ: Ablex. **2, 6**

Clarkson-Smith, L., & Hartley, A. A. (1989). Relationships between physical exercise and cognitive abilities in older adults. *Psychology and Aging, 4*, 183–189. **15**

Clarkson-Smith, L., & Hartley, A. A. (1990a). Structural equation models of relationships between exercise and cognitive abilities. *Psychology and Aging, 5*, 437–446. **15**

Clarkson-Smith, L., & Hartley, A. A. (1990b). The game of bridge as an exercise in working memory and reasoning. *Journal of Gerontology: PSYCHOLOGICAL SCIENCES, 45*, P233–238. **17**

Clay, M. M. (1979). *The early detection of reading difficulties* (3rd ed.). Portsmouth, NH: Heinemann. **9**

Coe, C., Hayashi, K. T., & Levine, S. (1988). Hormones and behavior at puberty: Activation or concatenation? In M. R. Gunnar & W. A. Collins (Eds.), *Development during the transition to adolescence. Minnesota symposia on child psychology*, (Vol. 21) (pp. 17–42). Hillsdale, NJ: Erlbaum. **Int4**

Cohen, M. A., Tell, E. J., & Wallack, S. S. (1986). Client-related risk factors of nursing home entry among elderly adults. *Journal of Gerontology, 41*, 785–792. **18**

Cohen, S. (1991). Social supports and physical health: Symptoms, health behaviors, and infectious disease. In E. M. Cummings, A. L. Greene, & K. H. Karraker (Eds.), *Life-span developmental psychology. Per-*

spectives on stress and coping (pp. 213–234). Hillsdale, NJ: Erlbaum. **13**

Cohen, S., & Wills, T. A. (1985). Stress, social support, and the buffering hypothesis. *Psychological Bulletin, 98,* 310–357. **1, 13**

Cohen, Y. A. (1964). *The transition from childhood to adolescence.* Chicago: Aldine. **11**

Cohn, D. A. (1990). Child-mother attachment of six-year-olds and social competence at school. *Child Development, 61,* 151–162. **6**

Cohn, D. A., Silver, D. H., Cowan, P. A., Cowan, C. P., & Pearson, J. L. (1991). Working models of childhood attachment and marital relationships. Paper presented at the biennial meetings of the Society for Research in Child Development, Seattle, WA. **1**

Cohn, J. F., Campbell, S. B., Matias, R., & Hopkins, J. (1990). Face-to-face interactions of postpartum depressed and nondepressed mother-infant pairs at 2 months. *Developmental Psychology, 26,* 15–23. **6**

Coie, J. D., Dodge, K. A., & Kupersmidt, J. B. (1990). Peer group behavior and social status. In S. R. Asher & J. D. Coie (Eds.) *Peer rejection in childhood* (pp. 17–59). Cambridge: Cambridge University Press. **10**

Coie, J. D. & Kupersmidt, J. B. (1983). A behavioral analysis of emerging social status in boys groups. *Child Development, 54,* 1400–1416. **10**

Colby, A., Kohlberg, L., Gibbs, J., & Lieberman, M. (1983). A longitudinal study of moral judgment. *Monographs of the Society for Research in Child Development, 48* (1–2, Serial No. 200). **11**

Cole, D. A. (1991). Change in self-perceived competence as a function of peer and teacher evaluation. *Developmental Psychology, 27,* 682–688. **10**

Cole, D. A., & Rodman, H. (1987). When school-age children care for themselves: Issues for family life educators and parents. *Family Relations, 36,* 92–96. **10**

Coleman, P. (1986). *Ageing and reminiscence processes: Social and clinical implications.* Chichester, England: Wiley. **18**

Coleman, P. (1990). Psychological aging. In J. Bond & P. Coleman (Eds.), *Aging in society* (pp. 89–122). London: Sage Publications.

Collin, M. F., Halsey, C. L. & Anderson, C. L. (1991). Emerging developmental sequelae in the "normal" extremely low birth weight infant. *Pediatrics, 88,* 115–120. **3**

Collins, N. L., & Read, S. J. (1990). Adult attachment, working models, and relationship quality in dating couples. *Journal of Personality and Social Psychology, 58,* 644–663. **14**

Collins, W. A. (Ed.) (1984). *Development during middle childhood. The years from six to twelve.* Washington, D.C.: National Academy Press. **9**

Colombo, J., & Mitchell, D. W. (1990). Individual differences in early visual attention: Fixation time and information processing. In J. Colombo & J. Fagen (Eds.), *Individual differences in infancy: Reliability, stability, prediction* (pp. 193–228). Hillsdale, NJ: Erlbaum. **5**

Coltrane, S., & Ishii-Kuntz, M. (1992). Men's housework: A life course perspective. *Journal of Marriage and the Family, 54,* 43–57. **14**

Comstock, G. (1991). *Television and the American child.* San Diego, CA: Academic Press. **10, 12**

Conger, R. D., Elder, G. H., Jr., Lorenz, F. O., Conger, K. J., Simons, R. L., Whitbeck, L. B., Huck, S., & Melby, J. N. (1990). Linking economic hardship to marital quality and instability. *Journal of Marriage and the Family, 52,* 643–656. **16**

Connidis, I. A., & Davies, L. (1992). Confidants and companions: choices in later life. *Journal of Gerontology: SOCIAL SCIENCES, 47* S115–122. **18**

Connolly, K., & Dalgleish, M. (1989). The emergence of a tool-using skill in infancy. *Developmental Psychology, 25,* 894–912. **4, 7**

Conrad, M., & Hammen, C. (1989). Role of maternal depression in perceptions of child maladjustment. *Journal of Consulting and Clinical Psychology, 57,* 663–667. **Int2**

Coolsen, P., Seligson, M., & Garbarino, J. (1985). *When school's out and nobody's home.* Chicago: National Committee for Prevention of Child Abuse. **10**

Coombs, R. H. (1991). Marital status and personal well-being: A literature review. *Family Relations, 40,* 97–102. **14**

Cooper, R. P., & Aslin, R. N. (1990). Preference for infant-directed speech in the first month after birth. *Child Development, 61,* 1584–1595. **7**

Corbett, H. D., & Wilson, B. (1989). Two state minimum competency testing programs and their effects on curriculum and instruction. In R. Stake (Ed.), *Effects of changes in assessment policy, Vol. 1, Advances in program evaluation.* Greenwich, CT: JAI Press. **9**

Corr, C. A. (1991–92). A task-based approach to coping with dying. *Omega, 24,* 81–94. **19**

Corso, J. F. (1987). Sensory-perceptual processes and aging. In K. W. Schaie (Ed.), *Annual Review of Gerontology and Geriatrics,* Vol. 7 (pp. 29–56). New York: Springer. **17**

Cossette, L., Malcuit, G., & Pomerleau, A. (1991). Sex differences in motor activity during early infancy. *Infant Behavior and Development, 14,* 175–186. **4**

Costa, P. T., Jr., & McCrae, R. R. (1980a). Still stable after all these years: Personality as a key to some issues in adulthood and old age. In P. B. Baltes & O. G. Brim, Jr. (Eds.), *Life-span development and behavior.* New York: Academic Press. **14, 15**

Costa, P. T., & McCrae, R. R. (1980b). Influence of extraversion and neuroticism on subjective well-being: Happy and unhappy people. *Journal of Personality and Social Psychology, 38,* 668–678. **14**

Costa, P. T. Jr., & McCrae, R. R. (1988). Personality in adulthood: A six-year longitudinal study of self-reports and spouse ratings on the NEO personality inventory. *Journal of Personality and Social Psychology, 54,* 853–863. **14**

Costa, P. T., Jr., McCrae, R. R., Zonderman, A. B., Barbano, H. E., Lebowitz, B., & Larson, D. M. (1986). Cross-sectional studies of personality in a national sample: 2. Stability in neuroticism, extraversion, and openness. *Psychology and Aging, 1,* 144–149. **14, 16**

Costa, P. T., Jr., Zonderman, A. B., & McCrae, R. R. (1985). Longitudinal course of social support among men in the Baltimore Longitudinal Study of Aging. In I. G. Sarason & B. R. Sarason (Eds.), *Social support: Theory, research and applications* (pp. 137–154). Dordrecht, Netherlands: Martinus Nijhoff Publishers. **16**

Counts, D. R. (1976–77). The good death in Kaliai: Preparation for death in western New Britain. *Omega, 7,* 367–372. **19**

Cowan, C. P., & Cowan, P. A. (1987). Men's involvement in parenthood: Identifying the antecedents and understanding the barriers. In P. W. Berman & F. A. Pedersen (Eds.), *Men's transitions to parenthood. Longitudinal studies of early family experience.* Hillsdale, NJ: Erlbaum. **14**

Cowan, C. P., & Cowan, P. A. (1988). Who does what when partners become parents: Implications for men, women, and marriage. *Marriage & Family Review, 13,* 1 & 2. **14**

Cowan, C. P., Cowan, P. A., Heming, G., & Miller, N. B. (1991). Becoming a family: Marriage, parenting, and child development. In P. A. Cowan & M. Hetherington (Eds.), *Family transitions* (pp. 79–109). Hillsdale, NJ: Erlbaum. **14**

Cramer, D. (1991). Type A behavior pattern, extraversion, neuroticism and psychological distress. *British Journal of Medical Psychology, 64,* 73–83. **15**

Crimmins, E. M., & Ingegneri, D. G. (1990). Interaction and living arrangements of older parents and their children. *Research on Aging, 12*, 3–35. **16, 18**

Cristofalo, V. J. (1988). An overview of the theories of biological aging. In J. E. Birren & V. L. Bengtson (Eds.), *Emergent theories of aging.* New York: Springer. **17**

Crockenberg, S. B. (1981). Infant irritability, mother responsiveness, and social support influences on the security of infant-mother attachment. *Child Development, 52*, 857–865. **6, Int1**

Crockenberg, S. B. (1986). Are temperamental differences in babies associated with predictable differences in care-giving? *New Directions for Child Development, 31*, 53–74. **6**

Crockenberg, S. B., & Litman, C. (1990). Autonomy as competence in 2-year-olds: Maternal correlates of child defiance, compliance, and self-assertion. *Developmental Psychology, 26*, 961–971. **8, Int2**

Crohan, S. E., & Antonucci, T. C. (1989). Friends as a source of social support in old age. In R. G. Adams & R. Blieszner (Eds.), *Older adult friendship* (pp. 129–146). Newbury Park, CA: Sage Publications. **18**

Cromer, R. F. (1991). *Language and thought in normal and handicapped children.* Oxford, England: Basil Blackwell. **7**

Crowell, J. A., & Feldman, S. S. (1988). Mothers' internal models of relationships and children's behavioral and developmental status: A study of mother-child interaction. *Child Development, 50*, 1273–1285. **6**

Crowell, J. A., & Feldman, S. S. (1991). Mothers' working models of attachment relationships and mother and child behavior during separation and reunion. *Developmental Psychology, 27*, 597–605. **6**

Csikszentmihalyi, M., & Larson, R. (1984). *Being adolescent: Conflict and growth in the teenage years.* New York: Basic Books. **12**

Csikszentmihalyi, M., & Rathunde, K. (1990). The psychology of wisdom: An evolutionary interpretation. In R. Sternberg (Ed.), *Wisdom. Its nature, origins, and development* (pp. 25–51). Cambridge, England: Cambridge University Press. **17**

Cuba, L., & Longino, C. F. Jr. (1991). Regional retirement migration: The case of Cape Cod. *Journal of Gerontology: SOCIAL SCIENCES, 46*, S33–42. **18**

Cumming, E. (1975). Engagement with an old theory. *International Journal of Aging and Human Development, 6* 187–191. **18**

Cumming, E., & Henry, W. E. (1961). *Growing old.* New York: Basic Books. **18**

Cummings, E. M., Hollenbeck, B., Iannotti, R., Radke-Yarrow, M., & Zahn-Waxler, C. (1986). Early organization of altruism and aggression: Developmental patterns and individual differences. In C. Zahn-Waxler, E. M. Cummings, & R. Iannotti (Eds.), *Altruism and aggression* (pp. 165–188). Cambridge, England: Cambridge University Press. **8**

Cunningham, A. S., Jelliffe, D. B., & Jelliffe, E. F. P. (1991). Breast-feeding and health in the 1980s: A global epidemiologic review. *The Journal of Pediatrics, 118*, 659–666. **4**

Cunningham, J. D., & Antill, J. K. (1984). Changes in masculinity and femininity across the family life cycle: A reexamination. *Developmental Psychology, 20*, 1135–1141. **14**

Cunningham, W. R., & Haman, K. L. (1992). Intellectual functioning in relation to mental health. In J. E. Birren, R. B. Sloane, & G. D. Cohen (Eds.), *Handbook of mental health and aging,* (2nd ed.) (pp. 340–355). San Diego, CA: Academic Press. **17**

Dalsky, G. P., Stocke, K. S., Ehsani, A. A., Slatopolsky, E., Waldon, C. L., & Birge, S. J. (1988). Weight-bearing exercise training and lumbar bone mineral content in postmenopausal women. *Annals of Internal Medicine, 108*, 824–828. **15**

Damon, W. (1977). *The social world of the child.* San Francisco: Jossey-Bass. **8, 10**

Damon, W. (1983). The nature of social-cognitive change in the developing child. In W. F. Overton (Ed.)., *The relationship between social and cognitive development* (pp. 103–142). Hillsdale, NJ: Erlbaum. **10**

Damon, W., & Hart, D. (1988). *Self understanding in childhood and adolescence.* New York: Cambridge University Press. **12**

Daniels, P., & Weingarten, K. (1988). The fatherhood clock. The timing of parenthood in men's lives. In P. Bronstein & C. P. Cowan (Eds.), *Fatherhood today. Men's changing role in the family* (pp. 36–52). New York: Wiley-Interscience. **14**

Dannefer, D. (1984a). Adult development and social theory: A paradigmatic reappraisal. *American Sociological Review, 49*, 100–116. **2**

Dannefer, D. (1984b). The role of the social in life-span developmental psychology, past and future: Rejoinder to Baltes and Nesselroade. *American Sociological Review, 49*, 847–850. **2**

Dannefer, D. (1988). What's in a name? An account of the neglect of variability in the study of aging. In J. E. Birren & V. L. Bengtson (Eds.), *Emergent theories of aging.* New York: Springer. **2**

Danner, F. W., & Day, M. C. (1977). Eliciting formal operations. *Child Development, 48*, 1600–1606. **11**

Darling-Hammond, L., & Wise, A. E. (Jan, 1985). Beyond standardization: State standards and school improvement. *Elementary School Journal*, 315–336. **9**

Darlington, R. B. (1991). The long-term effects of model preschool programs. In L. Okagaki & R. J. Sternberg (Eds.), *Directors of development* (pp. 203–215). Hillsdale, NJ: Erlbaum. **7**

Dasen, P., & Heron, A. (1981). Cross-cultural tests of Piaget's theory. In H. C. Triandis & A. Heron (Eds.), *Handbook of cross-cultural psychology* (Vol. 4) *Developmental psychology* (pp. 295–342). Boston: Allyn and Bacon. **5**

Dasen, P. R., Inhelder, B., Lavallee, M., & Retschitzki, J. (1978). *Naissance de l'intelligence chez l'enfant Baoulé de Côte d'Ivoire.* Berne: Hans Huber. **5**

Dawber, T. R., Kannel, W. B., & Lyell, L. P. (1963). An approach to longitudinal studies in a community: The Framingham study. *Annals of the New York Academy of Science, 107*, 539–556. **15**

Dawson, D. A. (1991). Family structure and children's health and well-being: Data from the 1988 National Health Interview Survey on child health. *Journal of Marriage and the Family, 53*, 573–584. **9**

DeCasper, A. J., & Fifer, W. P. (1980). Of human bonding: Newborns prefer their mothers' voices. *Science, 208*, 1174–1176. **5**

DeCasper, A. J., & Sigafoos, A. D. (1983). The intrauterine heartbeat: A potent reinforcer for newborns. *Infant Behavior and Development, 6*, 19–25. **5**

DeCasper, A. J., & Spence, M. J. (1986). Prenatal maternal speech influences newborns' perception of speech sounds. *Infant Behavior and Development, 9*, 133–150. **5**

de Chateau, P. (1980). Effects of hospital practices on synchrony in the development of the infant-parent relationship. In P. M. Taylor (Ed.), *Parent-infant relationships* (pp. 137–168). New York: Grune & Stratton. **6**

DeLoache, J. S. (1989). The development of representation in young children. In H. W. Reese (Ed.), *Advances in child development and behavior* (Vol. 22) (pp. 2–37). San Diego, CA: Academic Press. **9**

DeLoache, J. S., & Brown, A. L. (1987). Differences in the memory-based searching of delayed and normally developing young children. *Intelligence, 11*, 277–289. **9**

DeLoache, J. S., Cassidy, D. J., & Brown, A. L. (1985). Precursors of mnemonic strategies in very young children's memory. *Child Development, 56*, 125–137. **9**

DeMaris, A., & Leslie, G. R. (1984). Cohabitation with the future spouse: Its influence upon marital satisfaction and communication. *Journal of Marriage and the Family, 46,* 77–84. **14**

DeMaris, A., & Rao, K. V. (1992). Premarital cohabitation and subsequent marital stability in the United States: A reassessment. *Journal of Marriage and the Family, 54,* 178–190. **14**

Dempster, F. N. (1981). Memory span: Sources of individual and developmental differences. *Psychological Bulletin, 89,* 63–100. **9**

Dennerstain, L. (1987). Psychological changes. In D. R. Mischell, Jr. (Ed.), *Menopause: Physiology and pharmacology* (pp. 115–126). Chicago: Year Book Medical Publishers, Inc. **15**

Denney, N. W. (1982). Aging and cognitive changes. In B. B. Wolman (Ed.), *Handbook of developmental psychology.* Englewood Cliffs, NJ: Prentice-Hall. **13**

Denney, N. W. (1984). Model of cognitive development across the life span. *Developmental Review, 4,* 171–191. **13**

Denney, N. W., & Pearce, K. A. (1989). A developmental study of practical problem solving in adults. *Psychology and Aging, 4,* 438–442. **17**

Denney, N. M., Tozier, T. L., & Schlotthauer, C. A. (1992). The effect of instructions on age differences in practical problem solving. *Journal of Gerontology: PSYCHOLOGICAL SCIENCES, 47,* P142–145. **17**

Dennis, W. (1960). Causes of retardation among institutional children: Iran. *Journal of Genetic Psychology, 96,* 47–59. **4**

Den Ouden, L., Rijken, M., Brand, R., Verloove-Vanhorick, S. P., & Ruys, J. H. (1991). Is it correct to correct? Developmental milestones in 555 "normal" preterm infants compared with term infants. *Journal of Pediatrics, 118,* 399–404. **4**

de Regt, R. H., Minkoff, H. L., Feldman, J., & Schwarz, R. H. (1986). Relation of private or clinic care to the cesarean birth rate. *New England Journal of Medicine, 315,* 619–624. **3**

DeSpelder, L. A., & Strickland, A. L. (1983). *The last dance. Encountering death and dying.* Palo Alto, CA: Mayfield. **19**

The Diagram Group. (1977). *Child's body.* New York: Paddington. **4, 7**

Diamond, A. (1991). Neuropsychological insight into the meaning of object concept development. In S. Carey & R. Gelman (Eds.). *The Epigenesis of mind. Essays on biology and cognition* (pp. 67–110). Hillsdale, NJ: Erlbaum. **5**

Dickens, W. J., & Perlman, D. (1981). Friendship over the life-cycle. In S. Duck & R. Gilmour (Eds.), *Personal relationships 2. Developing personal relationships.* New York: Academic Press. **16**

Dickerson, J. W. T. (1981). Nutrition, brain growth and development. In K. J. Connolly & H. F. R. Prechtl (Eds.). *Maturation and development: Biological and psychological perspectives.* Clinics in Developmental Medicine No. 77/78, (pp. 110–130). London: Heinemann. **4**

Diener, E. (1984). Subjective well-being. *Psychological Bulletin, 95,* 542–575. **18**

Dietz, W. H., & Gortmaker, S. L. (1985). Do we fatten our children at the television set? Obesity and television viewing in children and adolescents. *Pediatrics, 75,* 807–812. **9**

Dishion, T. J., Patterson, G. R., Stoolmiller, M., & Skinner, M. L. (1991). Family, school, and behavioral antecedents to early adolescent involvement with antisocial peers. *Developmental Psychology, 27,* 172–180. **1, Int4**

Dittman-Kohli, F., Lachman, M. E., Kliegl, R., & Baltes, P. B. (1991). Effects of cognitive training and testing on intellectual efficacy beliefs in elderly adults. *Journal of Gerontology: PSYCHOLOGICAL SCIENCES, 46,* P162–164. **17**

DiVitto, B., & Goldberg, S. (1979). The effects of newborn medical status on early parent-infant interaction. In T. Field, A. Sostek, S. Goldberg & H. H. Shuman (Eds.), *Infants born at risk.* New York: Spectrum. **3**

Dodge, K. A. (1983). Behavioral antecedents of peer social status. *Child Development, 54,* 1386–1399. **10**

Dodge, K. A. (1990). Developmental psychopathology in children of depressed mothers. *Developmental Psychology, 26,* 3–6. **12**

Dodge, K. A. (1991). The structure and function of reactive and proactive aggression. In D. J. Pepler & K. H. Rubin (Eds.), *The development and treatment of childhood aggression* (pp. 201–218). Hillsdale, NJ: Erlbaum. **10**

Dodge, K. A., Coie, J. D., Pettit, G. S., & Price, J. M. (1990). Peer status and aggression in boys groups: Developmental and contextual analysis. *Child Development, 61,* 1289–1309. **10**

Dodge, K. A., & Feldman, E. (1990). Issues in social cognition and sociometric status. In S. R. Asher & J. D. Coie (Eds.) *Peer rejection in childhood* (pp. 119–155). Cambridge: Cambridge University Press. **10**

Dodge, K. A., & Frame, C. L. (1982). Social cognitive biases and deficits in aggressive boys. *Child Development, 53,* 620–635. **10**

Dominick, J. R., & Greenberg, B. S. (1972). Attitudes toward violence: The interaction of television exposure, family attitudes, and social class. In G. A. Comstock & E. A. Rubenstein (Eds.), *Television and social behavior* (Vol. 3) (pp. 314–335). Washington, DC: U.S. Government Printing Office. **10**

Donovan & Jessor, R. (1985). Structure of problem behavior in adolescence and young adulthood. *Journal of Consulting and Clinical Psychology, 53,* 890–904. **12**

Dorian, B., & Garfinkel, P. E. (1987). Stress, immunity and illness—a review. *Psychological Medicine, 17,* 393–407. **13**

Dornbusch, S. M., Carlsmith, J. M., Bushwall, S. J., Ritter, P. L., Leiderman, H., Hastdorf, A. H., & Goss, R. T. (1985). Single parents, extended households, and the control of adolescents. *Child Development, 56,* 326–341. **8**

Dornbusch, S. M., Ritter, P. L., Liederman, P. H., Roberts, D. F., & Fraleigh, M. J. (1987). The relation of parenting style to adolescent school performance. *Child Development, 58,* 1244–1257. **8, 11**

Dornbusch, S. M., Ritter, P. L., Mont-Reynaud, R., & Chen, Z. (1990). Family decision making and academic performance in a diverse high school population. *Journal of Adolescent Research, 5,* 143–160. **12**

Doty, R. L., Shaman, P., Appelbaum, S. L., Bigerson, R., Sikorski, L., & Rosenberg, L. (1984). Smell identification ability: Changes with age. *Science, 226,* 1441–1443. **13, 17**

Douglas, J. D. (1990–91). Patterns of change following parent death in midlife adults. *Omega, 22,* 123–137. **19**

Downey, G., & Coyne, J. C. (1990). Children of depressed parents: An integrative review. *Psychological Bulletin, 108,* 50–76. **12**

Dreher, G. F., & Bretz, R. D., Jr. (1991). Cognitive ability and career attainment: Moderating effects of early career success. *Journal of Applied Psychology, 76,* 392–397. **14**

Dreyer, P. H. (1982). Sexuality during adolescence. In B. B. Wolman (Ed.). *Handbook of developmental psychology* (pp. 559–601). Englewood Cliffs, NJ: Prentice-Hall. **11, 12**

Duara, R., London, E. D., & Rapoport, S. I. (1985). Changes in structure and energy metabolism of the aging brain. In C. E. Finch & E. L. Schneider (Eds.), *Handbook of the biology of aging* (2nd ed.) New York: Van Nostrand Reinhold. **13**

Duke, P. M., Carlsmith, J. M., Jennings, D., Martin, J. A., Dornbusch, S. M., Gross, R. T., & Siegel-Gorelick, B. (1982). Educational correlates of early and late sexual maturation in adolescence. *Journal of Pediatrics, 100,* 633–637. **11**

Duncan, G. J., & Morgan, J. N. (1985). The panel study of income dynamics. In G. H. Elder Jr. (Ed.), *Life course dynamics. Trajectories and transitions, 1968–1980.* Ithaca: Cornell University Press. **1**

Dunn, J. (1991). The developmental importance of differences in siblings' experiences within the family. In K. Pillemer & K. McCartney (Eds.), *Parent-child relations throughout life* (pp. 113–124). Hillsdale, NJ: Erlbaum. **8**

Dunn, J. (1992). Siblings and development. *Current Directions in Psychological Science, 1*, 6–9. **8**

Dunn, J., & Kendrick, C. (1982). Siblings and their mothers: Developing relationships within the family. In M. E. Lamb & B. Sutton-Smith (Eds.), *Sibling relationships: Their nature and significance across the lifespan* (pp. 39–60). Hillsdale, NJ: Erlbaum. **8**

Dunphy, D. C. (1963). The social structure of urban adolescent peer groups. *Sociometry, 26*, 230–246. **12**

Dura, J. R., & Kiecolt-Glaser, J. K. (1991). Family transitions, stress, and health. In P. A. Cowan & M. Hetherington (Eds.), *Family transitions* (pp. 59–76). Hillsdale, NJ: Erlbaum. **16**

Durlak, J. A. (1972). Relationship between attitudes toward life and death among elderly women. *Developmental Psychology, 8*, 146. **19**

Duursma, S. A., Raymakers, J. A., Boereboom, F. T. J., & Scheven, B. A. A. (1991). Estrogen and bone metabolism. *Obstetrical and Gynecological Survey, 47*, 38–44. **15**

Duvall, E. M. (1962). *Family development* (2nd ed.). New York: Lippincott. **2**

Duxbury, L. E., & Higgins, C. A. (1991). Gender differences in work-family conflict. *Journal of Applied Psychology, 76*, 60–74. **14**

Dwyer, J. W., & Coward, R. T. (1991). A multivariate comparison of the involvement of adult sons versus daughters in the care of impaired parents. *Journal of Gerontology: SOCIAL SCIENCES, 56*, S259–269. **16**

Eaton, W. O., & Enns, L. R. (1986). Sex differences in human motor activity level. *Psychological Bulletin, 100*, 19–28. **4**

Eberhardt, B. J., & Muchinsky, P. M. (1984). Structural validation of Holland's hexagonal model: Vocational classification through the use of biodata. *Journal of Applied Psychology, 69*, 174–181. **14**

Eccles, J. S., & Midgley, C. (1990). Changes in academic motivation and self-perception during early adolescence. In R. Montemayor, G. R. Adams, T. P. Gullotta (Eds.), *From childhood to adolescence: A transitional period?* (pp. 134–155). Newbury Park, CA: Sage. **Int4**

Edwards, J. N. (1969). Familial behavior as social exchange. *Journal of Marriage and the Family, 31*, 518–526. **14**

Egeland, B., & Farber, E. A. (1984). Infant-mother attachment: Factors related to its development and changes over time. *Child Development, 55*, 753–771. **6**

Eichorn, D. H., Hunt, J. V., & Honzik, M. P. (1981). Experience, personality, and IQ: Adolescence to middle age. In D. H. Eichorn, J. A. Clausen, N. Haan, M. P. Honzik & P. H. Mussen (Eds.), *Present and past in middle life* (pp. 89–116). New York: Academic Press. **13**

Eichorn, D. H., Clausen, J. A., Haan, N., Honzik, M. P., & Mussen, P. H. (Eds.) (1981). *Present and past in middle life.* New York: Academic Press. **1**

Eisdorfer, C., & Raskind, M. (1975). Aging, hormones and human behavior. In B. Eleftheriou & R. Sprott (Eds.), *Hormonal correlates of behavior, Vol. 1, A lifespan view.* New York: Plenum Press. **15**

Eisenberg, N. (1988). The development of prosocial and aggressive behavior. In M. H. Bornstein & M. E. Lamb (Eds.), *Developmental psychology: An advanced textbook* (2nd ed.) (pp. 461–496). Hillsdale, NJ: Erlbaum. **8**

Eisenberg, N. (1990). Prosocial development in early and mid-adolescence. In R. Montemayor, G. R. Adams, & T. P. Gullotta (Eds.), *From childhood to adolescence: A transitional period?* (pp. 240–268). Newbury Park, CA: Sage. **8**

Eisenberg, N. (1992). *The caring child.* Cambridge, MA: Harvard University Press. **8**

Elder, G. H., Jr. (1974). *Children of the great depression.* Chicago: University of Chicago Press. **1**

Elder, G. H., Jr. (1978). Family history and the life course. In T. Hareven (Ed.), *Transitions: The family and the life course in historical perspective* (pp. 17–64). New York: Academic Press. **1**

Elder, G. H., Jr. (1991). Family transitions, cycles, and social change. In P. Cowan & M. Hetherington (Eds.), *Family transitions* (pp. 31–58). Hillsdale, NJ: Erlbaum. **Int5**

Elder, G. H., Jr., & Caspi, A. (1988). Economic stress in lives: Developmental perspectives. *Journal of Social Issues, 44*, 25–45. **16**

Elder, G. H., Jr., Liker, J. K., & Cross, C. E. (1984). Parent-child behavior in the Great Depression: Life course and intergenerational influences. In P. B. Baltes & O. G. Brim, Jr. (Eds.) *Life-span development and behavior* (Vol. 6) (pp. 111–159). New York: Academic Press. **1**

Elkind, D. (1967). Egocentrism in adolescence. *Child Development, 38*, 1025–1034. **Int4**

Elkind, D., & Bowen, R. (1979). Imaginary audience behavior in children and adolescents. *Developmental Psychology, 15*, 38–44. **Int4**

Elliott, R. (1988). Tests, abilities, race, and conflict. *Intelligence, 12*, 333–350. **9**

Elsayed, M., Ismail, A. H., & Young, R. S. (1980). Intellectual differences of adult men related to age and physical fitness before and after an exercise program. *Journal of Gerontology, 35*, 383–387. **15**

Emery, C. F., & Gatz, M. (1990). Psychological and cognitive effects of an exercise program for community-residing older adults. *The Gerontologist, 30*, 184–192. **15**

Emery, R. E. (1988). *Marriage, divorce, and children's adjustment.* Newbury Park, CA: Sage. **8**

Entwisle, D. R. (1990). Schools and the adolescent. In S. S. Feldman & G. R. Elliott (Eds.), *At the threshold. The developing adolescent* (pp. 197–224). Cambridge, MA: Harvard University Press. **11**

Entwisle, D. R., & Alexander, K. L. (1990). Beginning school math competence: Minority and majority comparisons. *Child Development, 61*, 454–471. **7**

Entwisle, D. R., & Doering, S. G. (1981). *The first birth.* Baltimore: Johns Hopkins University Press. **3**

Epstein, S. (1991). Cognitive-experiential self theory: Implications for developmental psychology. In M. R. Gunnar & L. A. Sroufe (Eds.) *Self process and development. The Minnesota symposia on child development* (Vol. 23) (pp. 79–123). Hillsdale, NJ: Erlbaum. **1, Int1**

Ericsson, K. A. (1990). Peak performance and age: An examination of peak performance in sports. In P. Baltes & M. M. Baltes (Eds.), *Successful aging* (pp. 164–196). Cambridge: Cambridge University Press. **13**

Erikson, E. H. (1959). *Identity and the life cycle.* New York: Norton. (Republished, 1980). **2**

Erikson, E. H. (1964). *Insight and responsibility.* New York: Norton. **2**

Erikson, E. H. (1974). *Dimensions of a new identity: The 1973 Jefferson lectures in the humanities.* New York: Norton. **2**

Erikson, E. H. (1980). *Identity and the life cycle.* New York: Norton. (Original work published 1959) **12**

Erikson, E. H., Erikson, J. M., & Kivnick, H. Q. (1986). *Vital involvement in old age.* New York: W. W. Norton. **16**

Eron, L. D. (1987). The development of aggressive behavior from the perspective of a developing behaviorism. *American Psychologist, 42*, 435–442. **10**

Eron, L. D., Huesmann, L. R., & Zelli, A. (1991). The role of parental variables in the learning of aggression. In D. J. Pepler & K. H. Rubin

(Eds.), *The development and treatment of childhood aggression* (pp. 169–188). Hillsdale, NJ: Erlbaum. **10**

Escalona, K. S. (1981). The reciprocal role of social and emotional developmental advances and cognitive development during the second and third years of life. In E. K. Shapiro & E. Weber (Eds.), *Cognitive and affective growth: Developmental interaction* (pp. 87–108). Hillsdale, NJ: Erlbaum. **Int2**

European Collaborative Study (1991). Children born to women with HIV-1 infection: Natural history and risk of transmission. *The Lancet, 337,* 253–260. **3**

Evans, D. A., Funkenstein, H. H., Albert, M. S., Scherr, P. A., Cook, N. R., Chown, M. J., Hebert, L. E., Hennekens, C. H., & Taylor, J. O. (1989). Prevalence of Alzheimer's disease in a community population of older persons. *Journal of the American Medical Association, 262,* 2551–2556. **17**

Evans, G. W., Brennan, P. L., Skorpanich, M. A., & Held, D. (1984). Cognitive mapping and elderly adults: Verbal and location memory for urban landmarks. *Journal of Gerontology, 39,* 452–457. **17**

Evans, L. (1988). Older driver involvement in fatal and severe traffic crashes. *Journal of Gerontology: SOCIAL SCIENCES, 43,* S186–193. **17**

Evans, L., Ekerdt, D. J., & Bossé, R. (1985). Proximity to retirement and anticipatory involvement: Findings from the Normative Aging Study. *Journal of Gerontology, 40,* 368–374. **16**

Evans, R. I. (1969). *Dialogue with Erik Erikson.* New York: Dutton. **2**

Fagan, J. F. III (1984). The intelligent infant: Theoretical implications. *Intelligence, 8,* 1–9. **5**

Fagan, J. F. III, & McGrath, S. K. (1981). Infant recognition memory and later intelligence. *Intelligence, 5,* 121–130. **5**

Fagan, J. F. III, & Shepherd, P. A. (1986). *The Fagan Test of Infant Intelligence: Training manual.* Cleveland, OH: Infantest Corporation. **5**

Fagard, J., & Jacquet, A. (1989). Onset of bimanual coordination and symmetry versus asymmetry of movement. *Infant Behavior and Development, 12,* 229–235. **4, 7**

Fagot, B. I. (1974). Sex differences in toddlers' behavior and parental reaction. *Developmental Psychology, 10,* 544–558. **6**

Fagot, B. I., & Hagan, R. (1991). Observations of parent reactions to sex-stereotyped behaviors: Age and sex effects. *Child Development, 62,* 617–628. **8**

Fagot, B. I., & Leinbach, M. D. (1989). The young child's gender schema: Environmental input, internal organization. *Child Development, 60,* 663–672. **8**

Fagot, B. I., Leinbach, M. D., & O'Boyle, C. (1992). Gender labeling, gender stereotyping, and parenting behaviors. *Developmental Psychology, 28,* 225–230. **8**

Famularo, R., Stone, K., Barnum, R., & Whatron, R. (1986). Alcoholism and severe child maltreatment. *American Journal of Orthopsychiatry, 56,* 481–485. **6**

Farmer, Y. M., Reis, L. M., Nickinovich, D. G., Kamo, Y., & Borgatta, E. F. (1990). The status attainment model and income. *Research on Aging, 12,* 113–132. **14**

Farrar, M. J. (1992). Negative evidence and grammatical morpheme acquisition. *Developmental Psychology, 28,* 90–98. **7**

Farrell, M. P., & Rosenberg, S. D. (1981). *Men at midlife.* Boston: Auburn House. **14, 15, 16**

Farrington, D. P. (1991). Childhood aggression and adult violence: Early precursors and later life outcomes. In D. J. Pepler & K. H. Rubin (Eds.), *The development and treatment of childhood aggression* (pp. 5–30). Hillsdale, NJ: Erlbaum. **10**

Faust, M. S. (1983). Alternative constructions of adolescent growth. In J. Brooks-Gunn & A. C. Petersen (Eds.), *Girls at puberty. Biological and psychosocial perspectives* (pp. 105–126). New York: Plenum Press. **11**

Featherman, D. L. (1980). Schooling and occupational careers: Constancy and change in worldly success. In O. G. Brim, Jr. & J. Kagan (Eds.), *Constancy and change in human development.* Cambridge, MA: Harvard University Press. **11, 14**

Feeney, J. A., & Noller, P. (1990). Attachment style as a predictor of adult romantic relationships. *Journal of Personality and Social Psychology, 58,* 281–291. **14**

Feifel, H. (Ed.) (1977). *New meanings of death.* New York: McGraw-Hill. **19**

Feingold, A. (1988). Cognitive gender differences are disappearing. *American Psychologist, 43,* 95–103. **7**

Feldman, S. S., & Aschenbrenner, B. (1983). Impact of parenthood on various aspects of masculinity and femininity: A short-term longitudinal study. *Developmental Psychology, 19,* 278–289. **14**

Feldman, S. S., & Elliott, G. R. (Eds.) (1990). *At the threshold. The developing adolescent.* Cambridge, MA: Harvard University Press. **11, 12**

Fernald, A., & Kuhl, P. (1987). Acoustic determinants of infant preference for motherese speech. *Infant Behavior and Development, 10,* 279–293. **7**

Feshbach, S. (1970). Aggression. In P. H. Mussen (Ed.), *Carmichael's manual of child psychology* (Vol. 2, 3rd ed.) (pp. 159–260). New York: Wiley. **8**

Field, T. (1990). *Infancy.* Cambridge, MA: Harvard University Press. **5**

Field, T. M. (1977). Effects of early separation, interactive deficits, and experimental manipulations on infant-mother face-to-face interaction. *Child Development, 48,* 763–771. **4**

Field, T. M. (1978). Interaction behaviors of primary versus secondary caretaker fathers. *Developmental Psychology, 14,* 183–185. **6**

Field, T. M. (1982). Social perception and responsivity in early infancy. In T. M. Field, A. Huston, H. C. Quay, L. Troll, & G. E. Finley (Eds.), *Review of human development* (pp. 20–31). New York: Wiley. **5**

Field, T. M. (1991). Quality infant day-care and grade school behavior and performance. *Child Development, 62,* 863–870. **6**

Field, T. M., De Stefano, L., & Koewler, J. H. III (1982). Fantasy play of toddlers and preschoolers. *Developmental Psychology, 18,* 503–508. **7**

Field, T. M., Healy, B., Goldstein, S., & Guthertz, M. (1990). Behavior-state matching and synchrony in mother-infant interactions of nondepressed versus depressed dyads. *Developmental Psychology, 26,* 7–14. **6**

Field, T. M., Healy, B., Goldstein, S., Perry, S., Bendell, D., Schanberg, S., Zimmerman, E. A., & Duhn, C. (1988). Infants of depressed mothers show "depressed" behavior even with nondepressed adults. *Child Development, 59,* 1569–1579. **6**

Field, T. M., Woodson, R., Greenberg, R., & Cohen, D. (1982). Discrimination and imitation of facial expressions by neonates. *Science, 218,* 179–181. **5**

Filsinger, E. E., & Thoma, S. J. (1988). Behavioral antecedents of relationship stability and adjustment: A five-year longitudinal study. *Journal of Marriage and the Family, 50,* 785–795. **14**

Finch, C. E. (1986). Issues in the analysis of interrelationships between the individual and the environment during aging. In A. B. Sorensen, F. E. Weinert, & L. R. Sherrod (Eds.), *Human development and the life course: Multidisciplinary perspectives.* Hillsdale, NJ: Erlbaum. **13**

Finkelstein, N. W. (1982). Aggression: Is it stimulated by day care? *Young Children, 37,* 3–9. **6**

Fischer, K. W. (1980). A theory of cognitive development: The control and construction of hierarchies of skills. *Psychological Review, 87,* 477–531. **9**

Fischer, K. W., & Bidell, T. (1991). Constraining nativist inferences about cognitive capacities. In S. Carey & R. Gelman (Eds.) *The epigenesis of mind: Essays on biology and cognition* (pp. 199–236). Hillsdale, NJ: Erlbaum. **5**

Fischer, K. W., & Canfield, R. L. (1986). The ambiguity of stage and structure in behavior: Person and environment in the development of psychological structures. In I. Levin (Ed.), *Stage and structure: Reopening the debate* (pp. 246–267). Norwood, NJ: Ablex. **9**

Fischer, K. W., & Pipp, S. L. (1984). Processes of cognitive development: Optimal level and skill acquisition. In R. J. Sternberg (Ed.). *Mechanisms of cognitive development* (pp. 45–80). New York: W. H. Freeman. **9**

Fish, M., Stifter, C. A., & Belsky, J. (1991). Conditions of continuity and discontinuity in infant negative emotionality: Newborn to five months. *Child Development, 62,* 1525–1537. **6**

Fiske, M. (1980). Changing hierarchies of commitment in adulthood. In N. J. Smelser & E. H. Erikson (Eds.), *Themes of work and love in adulthood.* Cambridge, MA: Harvard University Press. **2**

Fitzpatrick, J. L., & Silverman, T. (1989). Women's selection of careers in engineering: Do traditional-nontraditional differences still exist? *Journal of Vocational Behavior, 34,* 266–278. **14**

Flavell, J. H. (1982a). On cognitive development. *Child Development, 53,* 1–10. **9**

Flavell, J. H. (1982b). Structures, stages, and sequences in cognitive development. In W. A. Collins (Ed.). *The concept of development: The Minnesota symposia on child psychology* (Vol. 15) (pp. 1–28). Hillsdale, NJ: Erlbaum. **9**

Flavell, J. H. (1985). *Cognitive development* (2nd ed.). Englewood Cliffs, NJ: Prentice-Hall. **2, 5, Int1, 7, 9**

Flavell, J. H. (1986). The development of children's knowledge about the appearance-reality distinction. *American Psychologist, 41,* 481–425. **7**

Flavell, J. H., Everett, B. A., Croft, K., & Flavell, E. R. (1981). Young children's knowledge about visual perception: Further evidence for the Level 1–Level 2 distinction. *Developmental Psychology, 17,* 99–103. **7**

Flavell, J. H., Green, F. L., & Flavell, E. R. (1989). Young children's ability to differentiate appearance-reality and Level 2 perspectives in the tactile modality. *Child Development, 60,* 201–213. **7**

Flavell, J. H., Green, F. L., & Flavell, E. R. (1990). Developmental changes in young children's knowledge about the mind. *Cognitive Development, 5,* 1–27. **7**

Flavell, J. H., Green, F. L., Wahl, K. E., & Flavell, E. R. (1987). The effects of question clarification and memory aids on young children's performance on appearance-reality tasks. *Cognitive Development, 2,* 127–144. **7**

Flavell, J. H., Zhang, X-D, Zou, H., Dong, Q., & Qi, S. (1983). A comparison of the appearance-reality distinction in the People's Republic of China and the United States. *Cognitive Psychology, 15,* 459–466. **7**

Folven, R. J., & Bonvillian, J. D. (1991). The transition from nonreferential to referential language in children acquiring American Sign Language. *Developmental Psychology, 27,* 806–816. **5**

Fonagy, P., Steele, H., & Steele, M. (1991). Maternal representations of attachment during pregnancy predict the organization of infant-mother attachment at one year of age. *Child Development, 62,* 891–905. **6**

Fox, N. A., Kimmerly, N. L., & Schafer, W. D. (1991). Attachment to mother/attachment to father: A meta-analysis. *Child Development, 62,* 210–225. **6**

Fozard, J. L. (1990). Vision and hearing in aging. In J. E. Birren & K. W. Schaie (Eds.), *Handbook of the psychology of aging* (3rd ed.) (pp. 150–171). San Diego, CA: Academic Press. **13, 15, 17**

Fozard, J. L., Metter, E. J., & Brant, L. J. (1990). Next steps in describing aging and disease in longitudinal studies. *Journal of Gerontology: PSYCHOLOGICAL SCIENCES, 45,* P116–127. **15**

Fraiberg, S. (1974). Blind infants and their mothers: An examination of the sign system. In M. Lewis & L. A. Rosenblum (Eds.), *The effect of the infant on its caregiver* (pp. 215–232). New York: Wiley. **6**

Fraiberg, S. (1975). The development of human attachments in infants blind from birth. *Merrill-Palmer Quarterly, 21,* 315–334. **6**

Frankel, K. A., & Bates, J. E. (1990). Mother-toddler problem solving: Antecedents in attachment, home behavior, and temperament. *Child Development, 61,* 810–819. **6**

Frankenberg, W. K., Dodds, J. B., Fandal, A. W., Kazuk, E., & Cohrs, M. (1975). *Denver developmental screening test: Reference manual.* Denver: University of Colorado Medical Center. **5**

Frazier, P. H., & Foss-Goodman, D. (1988–89). Death anxiety and personality: Are they truly related? *Omega, 19,* 265–274. **19**

Freedman, D. G. (1979). Ethnic differences in babies. *Human Nature, 2,* 36–43. **4**

Freedman, J. L. (1984). Effect of television violence on aggressiveness. *Psychological Bulletin, 96,* 227–246. **10**

Freud, S. (1905). Three contributions to the theory of sex. *The basic writings of Sigmund Freud* (A. A. Brill, trans.). New York: Random House (Modern Library). **2**

Freud, S. (1920/1965). *A general introduction of psychoanalysis* (J. Riviere, trans.). New York: Washington Square Press. **2**

Friedman, M., & Rosenman, R. H. (1974). *Type A behavior and your heart.* New York: Knopf. **15**

Friedrich-Cofer, L., & Huston, A. C. (1986). Television violence and aggression: The debate continues. *Psychological Bulletin, 100,* 364–371. **10**

Fu, Y.-H, Pizzuti, A., Fenwick, R. G. Jr., King, J., Rajnarayan, S., Dune, P. W., Dubel, J., Nasser, G. A., Ashizawa, T., de Jong, P., Wieringa, B., Korneluk, R., Perryman, M. B., Epstein, H. F., & Caskey, C. T. (1992). An unstable triplet repeat in a gene related to Myotonic muscular dystrophy. *Science, 225,* 1256–1258. **3**

Furman, W., & Buhrmester, D. (1992). Age and sex differences in perceptions of networks of personal relationships. *Child Development, 63,* 103–115. **12**

Furstenberg, F. F., Jr. (1991). As the pendulum swings: Teenage childbearing and social concern. *Family Relations, 40,* 127–138. **12**

Furstenberg, F. F. Jr., Brooks-Gunn, J., & Morgan, S. P. (1987). *Adolescent mothers in later life.* Cambridge, England: Cambridge University Press. **12**

Gallagher, J. J., & Ramey, C. T. (1987). *The malleability of children.* Baltimore: Paul H. Brookes Publishing. **7**

Garbarino, J., & Sherman, D. (1980). High-risk neighborhoods and high-risk families: The human ecology of child maltreatment. *Child Development, 51,* 188–198. **6**

Garbarino, J., Kostelny, K., & Dubrow, N. (1991). *No place to be a child. Growing up in a war zone.* Lexington, MA: Lexington Books. **10**

Gardner, D., Harris, P. L., Ohmoto, M., & Hamasaki, T. (1988). Japanese children's understanding of the distinction between real and apparent emotion. *International Journal of Behavioral Development, 11,* 203–218. **7**

Gardner, H. (1983). *Frames of mind: The theory of multiple intelligence.* New York: Basic Books. **7**

Garmezy, N., & Masten, A. S. (1991). The protective role of competence indicators in children at risk. In E. M. Cummings, A. L. Green & K. H. Karraker (Eds.), *Life-span developmental psychology. Perspectives on stress and coping* (pp. 151–174). Hillsdale, NJ: Erlbaum. **1, 10**

Garmezy, N., & Rutter, M. (Eds.) (1983). *Stress, coping, and development in children.* New York: McGraw-Hill. **1**

Garn, S. M. (1980). Continuities and change in maturational timing. In O. G. Brim, Jr., & J. Kagan (Eds.), *Constancy and change in human development* (pp. 113–162). Cambridge, MA: Harvard University Press. **4, 11**

Gecas, V., Seff, M. A. (1990). Families and adolescents: A review of the 1980s. *Journal of Marriage and the Family, 52,* 941–958. **12**

Geerken, M., & Gove, W. R. (1983). *At home and at work. The family's allocation of labor.* Beverly Hills, CA: Sage. **14**

Gelman, R. (1972). Logical capacity of very young children: Number invariance rules. *Child Development, 43,* 75–90. **7**

Gelman, R., & Baillargeon, R. (1983). A review of some Piagetian concepts. In J. H. Flavell & E. M. Markman (Eds.), *Handbook of child psychology: Cognitive development* (Vol. 3) (pp. 167–230). New York: Wiley. (Paul H. Mussen, General Editor). **7**

Gentner, D. (1982). Why nouns are learned before verbs: Linguistic relativity versus natural partitioning. In S. A. Kuczaj II (Ed.), *Language development, Vol. 2. Language, thought, and culture* (pp. 301–334). Hillsdale, NJ: Erlbaum. **5**

George, L. K. (1990). Social structure, social processes, and social-psychological states. In R. H. Binstock & L. K. George (Eds.), *Handbook of aging and the social sciences,* 3rd ed. (pp. 186–204). San Diego, CA: Academic Press. **18**

Geronimus, A. T. (1991). Teenage childbearing and social and reproductive disadvantage: The evolution of complex questions and the demise of simple answers. *Family Relations, 40,* 463–471. **12**

Gesell, A. (1925). *The mental growth of the preschool child.* New York: Macmillan. **1**

Gesser, G., Wong, P. T. P., & Reker, G. T. (1987–88). Death attitudes across the life-span: The development and validation of the death attitude profile (DAP). *Omega, 18,* 113–128. **19**

Gibbs, J. T. (1985). Psychosocial factors associated with depression in urban adolescent females: Implications for assessment. *Journal of Youth and Adolescence, 14,* 47–60. **12**

Gibson, D. M. (1986). Interaction and well-being in old age: Is it quantity or quality that counts? *International Journal of Aging and Human Development, 24,* 29–40. **18**

Gibson, D. R. (1990). Relation of socioeconomic status to logical and sociomoral judgment of middle-aged men. *Psychology and Aging, 5,* 510–513. **11**

Gilligan, C. (1982a). New maps of development: New visions of maturity. *American Journal of Orthopsychiatry, 52,* 199–212. **11**

Gilligan, C. (1982b). *In a different voice: Psychological theory and women's development.* Cambridge, MA: Harvard University Press. **11**

Gilligan, C. (1987). Adolescent development reconsidered. *New Directions for Child Development, 37,* 63–92. **11**

Gilligan, C., & Wiggins, G. (1987). The origins of morality in early childhood relationships. In J. Kagan & S. Lamb (Eds.), *The emergence of morality in young children* (pp. 277–307). Chicago: The University of Chicago Press. **11**

Gilmour, R., & Duck, S. (Eds.) (1986). *The emerging field of personal relationships.* Hillsdale, NJ: Erlbaum. **14**

Gleitman, L. R., & Gleitman, H. (1992). A picture is worth a thousand words, but that's the problem: The role of syntax in vocabulary acquisition. *Current Directions in Psychological Science, 1,* 31–35. **5**

Glenn, N. D. (1990). Quantitative research on marital quality in the 1980s: A critical review. *Journal of Marriage and the Family, 52,* 818–831. **14**

Glenn, N. D., & McLanahan, S. (1981). The effects of offspring on the psychological well-being of older adults. *Journal of Marriage and the Family, 43,* 409–421. **18**

Glenn, N. D., & Weaver, C. N. (1981). The contribution of marital happiness to global happiness. *Journal of Marriage and the Family, 43,* 161–168. **Int5**

Glenn, N. D., & Weaver, C. N. (1985). Age, cohort, and reported job satisfaction in the United States. In A. S. Blau (Ed.), *Current perspectives on aging and the life cycle. A research annual.* Vol 1. *Work, retirement and social policy.* Greenwich, CT: JAI Press. **14**

Glenn, N. D., & Weaver, C. N. (1988). The changing relationship of marital status to reported happiness. *Journal of Marriage and the Family, 50,* 317–324. **14**

Glick, P. C., & Lin, S. (1986). Recent changes in divorce and remarriage. *Journal of Marriage and the Family, 48,* 737–747. **16**

Glueck, S., & Glueck, E. (1968). *Delinquents and nondelinquents in perspective.* Cambridge, MA: Harvard University Press. **Int5**

Glueck, S., & Glueck, E. (1972). *Identification of pre-delinquents: Validation studies and some suggested uses of Glueck Table.* New York: Intercontinental Medical Book Corp. **12**

Gnepp, J., & Chilamkurti, C. (1988). Children's use of personality attributions to predict other people's emotional and behavioral reactions. *Child Development, 50,* 743–754. **10**

Goetting, A. (1986). The developmental tasks of siblingship over the life cycle. *Journal of Marriage and the Family, 48,* 703–714. **18**

Gold, D. T. (1990). Late-life sibling relationships: Does race affect typological distribution? *The Gerontologist, 30,* 741–748. **18**

Goldberg, A. P., & Hagberg, J. M. (1990). Psychical exercise in the elderly. In E. R. Schneider & J. W. Rowe (Eds.), *Handbook of the biology of aging* (3rd ed.) (pp. 407–428). San Diego: Academic Press. **15**

Goldberg, S. (1972). Infant care and growth in urban Zambia. *Human Development, 15,* 77–89. **5**

Goldfield, B. A., & Reznick, J. S. (1990). Early lexical acquisition: Rate, content, and the vocabulary spurt. *Journal of Child Language, 17,* 171–183. **5**

Goldscheider, F. K., & DaVanzo, J. (1989). Pathways to independent living in early adulthood: Marriage, semiautonomy, and premarital residential independence. *Demography, 26,* 597–614. **14**

Gonsiorek, J. C., & Weinrich, J. D. (1991). The definition and scope of sexual orientation. In J. C. Gonsiorek & J. D. Weinrich (Eds.), *Homosexuality. Research implications for public policy.* Newbury Park, CA: Sage Publications. **12**

Good, T. L., & Weinstein, R. S. (1986). Schools make a difference. Evidence, criticisms, and new directions. *American Psychologist, 41,* 1090–1097. **9**

Goodenough, F. L. (1931). *Anger in young children.* Minneapolis: University of Minnesota Press. **8**

Goodsitt, J. V., Morse, P. A., Ver Hoeve, J. N., & Cowan, N. (1984). Infant speech recognition in multisyllabic contexts. *Child Development, 55,* 903–910. **5**

Gopnik, A., & Astington, J. W. (1988). Children's understanding of representational change and its relation to the understanding of false belief and the appearance-reality distinction. *Child Development, 59,* 26–37. **7**

Gopnik, A., & Meltzoff, A. (1987). The development of categorization in the second year and its relation to other cognitive and linguistic developments. *Child Development, 58,* 1523–1531. **7**

Gordon, G. S., & Vaughan, C. (1986). Calcium and osteoporosis. *Journal of Nutrition, 116,* 319–322. **15**

Gottman, J. M. (1986). The world of coordinated play: Same- and cross-sex friendship in young children. In J. M. Gottman & J. G. Parker (Eds.), *Conversations of friends. Speculations on affective development* (pp. 139–191). Cambridge, England: Cambridge University Press. **8, 10**

Gottman, J. M. (1991). Chaos and regulated change in families: A metaphor for the study of transitions. In P. A. Cowan & M. Hetherington (Ed.s), *Family transitions* (pp. 247–272). Hillsdale, NJ: Erlbaum. **14**

Gottman, J. M., & Levenson, R. W. (1984). Why marriages fail: Affective and physiological patterns in marital interaction. In J. C. Masters & K. Yarkin-Levin (Eds.), *Boundary areas in social and developmental psychology.* New York: Academic Press. **14**

Gottman, J. M., & Porterfield, A. L. (1981). Communicative competence in the nonverbal behavior of married couples. *Journal of Marriage and the Family, 43,* 817–824. **14**

Gratzinger, P., Sheikh, J. I., Friedman, L., & Yesavage, J. A. (1990). Cognitive interventions to improve face-name recall: The role of personality trait differences. *Developmental Psychology, 26,* 889–893. **17**

Gray, A., Berlin, J. A., McKinlay, J. B., & Longcope, C. (1991). An examination of research design effects on the association of testosterone and male aging: Results of a meta-analysis. *Journal of Clinical Epidemiology, 44,* 671–684. **15**

Greenberg, J., & Kuczaj, S. A. II. (1982). Towards a theory of substantive word-meaning acquisition. In S. A. Kuczaj II (Ed.), *Language development. Vol. l. Syntax and semantics* (pp. 275–312). Hillsdale, NJ: Erlbaum. **7**

Greenberg, M. T., & Speltz, M. L. (1988). Attachment and the ontogeny of conduct problems. In J. Belsky & T. Nezworski (Eds.), *Clinical implications of attachment* (pp. 177–218). Hillsdale, NJ: Erlbaum. **6**

Greenberg, M. T., Siegel, J. M. & Leitch, C. J. (1983). The nature and importance of attachment relationships to parents and peers during adolescence. *Journal of Youth and Adolescence, 12,* 373–386.

Greenberger, E. & Steinberg, L. (1986). *When teenagers work. The psychological and social costs of adolescent employment.* New York: Basic Books. **12**

Greenough, W. T., Black, J. E., & Wallace, C. S. (1987). Experience and brain development. *Child Development, 58,* 539–559. **3, 4, Int1**

Greer, D. S., Mor, V., Morris, J. N., Sherwood, S., Kidder, D., & Birnbaum, H. (1986). An alternative in terminal care: Results of the National Hospice Study. *Journal of Chronic Diseases, 39,* 9–26. **19**

Greer, S., Morris, T., & Pettingale, K. W. (1979). Psychological response to breast cancer: Effect on outcome. *Lancet, 2,* 785–787. **19**

Grinker, J. A. (1981). Behavioral and metabolic factors in childhood obesity. In M. Lewis & L. A. Rosenblum (Eds.), *The uncommon child* (pp. 115–150). New York: Plenum. **9**

Grossmann, K., Grossmann, K. E., Spangler, G., Suess, G., & Unzner, L. (1985). Maternal sensitivity and newborns' orientation responses as related to quality of attachment in northern Germany. In I. Bretherton & E. Waters (Eds.), *Growing points of attachment theory and research* (pp. 233–256). *Monographs of the Society of Research in Child Development, 50* (1–2, Serial No. 209). **6**

Grusec, J. E., & Lytton, H. (1988). *Social development. History, theory, and research.* New York: Springer-Verlag. **6, 8**

Gunnar, M. R. (1990). The psychobiology of infant temperament. In J. Colombo & J. Fagen (Eds.), *Individual differences in infancy: Reliability, stability, prediction* (pp. 387–410). Hillsdale, NJ: Erlbaum. **6**

Guralnick, M. J., & Paul-Brown, D. (1984). Communicative adjustments during behavior-request episodes among children at different developmental levels. *Child Development, 55,* 911–919. **7**

Guralnik, J. M. & Kaplan, G. A. (1989). Predictors of healthy aging: Prospective evicence from the Alameda County Study. *American Journal of Public Health, 79,* 703–708. **13**

Gusella, J. L., Muir, D., & Tronick, E. Z. (1988). The effect of manipulating maternal behavior during an interaction on three- and six-month-olds' affect and attention. *Child Development, 59,* 1111–1124. **6**

Gustafson, S. B., & Magnusson, D. (1991). *Female life careers: A pattern approach.* Hillsdale, NJ: Erlbaum. **14**

Gutmann, D. (1975). Parenthood: A key to the comparative study of the life cycle. In N. Datan & L. H. Ginsberg (Eds.), *Life-span developmental psychology. Normative life crises.* New York: Academic Press. **14**

Gutmann, D. (1987). *Reclaimed powers. Toward a new psychology of men and women in later life.* New York: Basic Books. **16**

Gwartney-Gibbs, P. A. (1988). Women's work experience and the "rusty skills" hypothesis: A reconceptualization and reevaluation of the evidence. In B. A. Gutek, A. H. Stromberg, & L. Larwood (Eds.), *Women and work. An annual review* (Vol. 3). Newbury Park, CA: Sage. **14**

Gzesh, S. M., & Surber, C. F. (1985). Visual perspective-taking skills in children. *Child Development, 56,* 1204–1213. **7**

Haan, N. (1976). ". . . change and sameness . . . " reconsidered. *International Journal of Aging and Human Development, 7,* 59–65. **16**

Haan, N. (1981a). Adolescents and young adults as producers of their own development. In R. M. Lerner & N. A. Busch-Rossnagel (Eds.), *Individuals as producers of their own development.* New York: Academic Press. **Int4**

Haan, N. (1981b). Common dimensions of personality development: Early adolescence to middle life. In D. H. Eichorn, J. A. Clausen, N. Haan, M. P. Honzik & P. H. Mussen (Eds), *Present and past in middle life.* New York: Academic Press. **14, 15**

Haan, N. (1982). The assessment of coping, defense, and stress. In L. Goldberger & S. Breznitz (Eds.), *Handbook of stress. Theoretical and clinical aspects.* New York: The Free Press. **16**

Haan, N. (1985). Processes of moral development: Cognitive or social disequilibrium? *Developmental Psychology, 21,* 996–1006. **11**

Haan, N., Millsap, R., & Hartka, E. (1986). As time goes by: Change and stability in personality over fifty years. *Psychology and Aging, 1,* 220–232. **1, 14**

Hack, M., Breslau, N., Weissman, B., Aram, D., Klein, N., & Borawski, E. (1991). Effect of very low birth weight and subnormal head size on cognitive abilities at school age. *New England Journal of Medicine, 325,* 231–237. **3**

Hagestad, G. O. (1984). The continuous bond: A dynamic, multigenerational perspective on parent-child relations between adults. In M. Perlmutter (Ed.), *Minnesota symposia on child psychology* (Vol. 17). Hillsdale, NJ: Erlbaum. **16**

Hagestad, G. O. (1985). Continuity and connectedness. In V. L. Bengtson (Ed.), *Grandparenthood.* Beverly Hills, CA: Sage. **16**

Hagestad, G. O. (1986). Dimensions of time and the family. *American Behavioral Scientist, 29,* 679–694. **16**

Hagestad, G. O. (1988). Demographic change and the life course: Some emerging trends in the family realm. *Family Relations, 37,* 405–410. **16**

Hagestad, G. O. (1990). Social perspectives on the life course. In R. H. Binstock & L. K. George (Eds.), *Handbook of aging and the social sciences* (3rd ed.) (pp. 151–168). San Diego, CA: Academic Press. **Int5, 16**

Haight, B. K. (1988). The therapeutic role of a structured life review process in homebound elderly subjects. *Journal of gerontology: PSYCHOLOGICAL SCIENCES, 43*, P40–44. **18**

Haith, M. M. (1980). *Rules that babies look by.* Hillsdale, NJ: Erlbaum. **1, 5**

Haith, M. M. (1990). Progress in the understanding of sensory and perceptual processes in early infancy. *Merrill-Palmer Quarterly, 36*, 1–26. **5**

Hakuta, K. (1986). *Mirror on language: The debate on bilingualism.* New York: Basic Books. **7**

Hakuta, K., & Garcia, E. E. (1989). Bilingualism and education. *American Psychologist, 44*, 374–379. **7**

Halford, W. K., Hahlweg, K., & Dunne, M. (1990). The cross-cultural consistency of marital communication associated with marital distress. *Journal of Marriage and the Family, 52*, 487–500. **14**

Hall, D. T. (1972). A model of coping with role conflict: The role behavior of college educated women. *Administrative Science Quarterly, 17*, 471–486. **14**

Hall, D. T. (1975). Pressures from work, self, and home in the life stages of married women. *Journal of Vocational Behavior, 6*, 121–132. **14**

Hallfrisch, J., Muller, D., Drinkwater, D., Tobin, J., & Adres, R. (1990). Continuing diet trends in men: The Baltimore Longitudinal Study of Aging (1961–1987). *Journal of Gerontology: MEDICAL SCIENCES, 45*, M186–191. **13**

Halpern, D. F. (1986). *Sex differences in cognitive abilities.* Hillsdale, NJ: Erlbaum. **7**

Hanley, R. J., Alecxih, L. M. B., Wiener, J. M., & Kennell, D. L. (1990). Predicting elderly nursing home admissions: Results from the 1982–1984 national long-term care survey. *Research on Aging, 12*, 199–228. **18**

Harkness, S., & Super, C. M. (1985). The cultural context of gender segregation in children's peer groups. *Child Development, 56*, 219–224. **10, Int3**

Harman, S. M., & Talbert, G. B. (1985). Reproductive aging. In C. E. Finch & E. L. Schneider (Eds.), *Handbook of the biology of aging* (2nd ed). New York: Van Nostrand Reinhold. **15**

Harris, P. L. (1989). *Children and emotion. The development of psychological understanding.* Oxford: Basil Blackwell. **6, 7**

Harris, R. L., Ellicott, A. M., & Holmes, D. S. (1986). The timing of psychosocial transitions and changes in women's lives: An examination of women aged 45 to 60. *Journal of Personality and Social Psychology, 51*, 409–416. **2, 16**

Harris, T., Brown, G. W., & Bifulco, A. (1990). Loss of parent in childhood and adult psychiatric disorder: A tentative overall model. *Development and Psychopathology, 2*, 311–328. **Int5**

Harris, T., Kovar, M. G., Suzman, R., Kleinman, J. C., & Feldman, J. J. (1989). Longitudinal study of physical ability in the oldest-old. *American Journal of Public Health, 79*, 698–702. **17**

Harter, S. (1983). Developmental perspectives on the self-system. In E. M. Hetherington (Ed.), *Handbook of child psychology: Socialization, personality, and social development* (Vol. 4) (pp. 275–386). New York: Wiley. (P. H. Mussen, General Editor). **10**

Harter, S. (1985). Competence as a dimension of self-evaluation: Toward a comprehensive model of self-worth. In R. L. Leahy (Ed.), *The development of the self* (pp. 55–122). Orlando, FL: Academic Press. **Int1, 10**

Harter, S. (1988). The determinations and mediational role of global self-worth in children. In N. Eisenberg (Ed.), *Contemporary topics in developmental psychology* (pp. 219–242). New York: Wiley-Interscience. **Int1, 8, 10, Int4**

Harter, S. (1990). Processes underlying adolescent self-concept formation. In R. Montemayor, G. R. Adams, & T. P. Gullotta (Eds.), *From childhood to adolescence: A transitional period?* (pp. 205–239). Newbury Park, CA: Sage. **8, 10, 12, Int4**

Harter, S., & Monsour, A. (1992). Developmental analysis of conflict caused by opposing attributes in the adolescent self-portrait. *Developmental Psychology, 28*, 251–260. **12**

Harter, S., & Pike, R. (1984). The Pictorial Perceived Competence Scale for Young Children. *Child Development, 55*, 1969–1982. **8**

Hartnell, J. M., Morley, J. E., & Mooradian, A. D. (1989). Reduction of alkali-induced white blood cell DNA unwinding rate: A potential biomarker of aging. *Journal of Gerontology: BIOLOGICAL SCIENCES, 44*, B125-B130. **17**

Hartup, W. W. (1974). Aggression in childhood: Developmental perspectives. *American Psychologist, 29*, 336–341. **8**

Hartup, W. W. (1983). Peer relations. In E. M. Hetherington (Ed.), *Handbook of child psychology. Vol. 3: Socialization, personality, and development* (pp. 103–196). New York: Wiley. (P. H. Mussen Series Editor). **10**

Hartup, W. W. (1984). The peer context in middle childhood. In W. A. Collins (Ed.), *Development during middle childhood. The years from six to twelve* (pp. 240–282). Washington, DC: National Academy Press. **10**

Hartup, W. W. (1989). Social relationships and their developmental significance. *American Psychologist, 44*, 120–126. **8**

Harvard Education Letter (September/October, 1988). Testing: Is there a right answer? IV (5), 1–kins, R. (1985). Public school aggression among children with varying day-care experience. *Child Development, 56*, 689–703. **6**

Haskins, R. (1985). Public school aggression among children with varying day-care experience. *Child Development, 56*, 689–703. **6**

Haskins, R. (1989). Beyond metaphor: The efficacy of early childhood education. *American Psychologist, 44*, 274–282. **7**

Hatch, L. R. (1991). Informal support patterns of older African-American and white women. *Research on Aging, 13*, 144–170. **18**

Hatchett, S. J., Cochran, D. L., & Jackson, J. S. (1991). Family life. In J. S. Jackson (Ed.), *Life in black America.* Newbury Park, CA: Sage Publications. **14**

Hawton, K. (1986). *Suicide and attempted suicide among children and adolescents.* Beverly Hills, CA: Sage. **11, 12**

Hayes, C. D. (1987). *Risking the future, Vol. 1: Adolescent sexuality, pregnancy, and childbearing.* Washington, DC: National Academy Press. **11, 12**

Hayes, C. D., Palmer, J. L., & Zaslow, M. J. (1990). *Who cares for America's children?* Washington, DC: National Academy Press. **6**

Hayflick, L. (1977). The cellular basis for biological aging. In C. E. Finch & L. Hayflick (Eds.), *Handbook of the biology of aging.* New York: Van Nostrand Reinhold. **17**

Hayflick, L. (1987). Origins of longevity. In H. R. Warner, R. N. Butler, R. L. Sprott & E. L. Schneider (Eds.), *Aging, Vol 31, Modern biological theories of aging.* New York: Raven Press. **17**

Hayward, M. D., Grady, W. R., & McLaughlin, S. D. (1988). The retirement process among older women in the United States. Changes in the 1970s. *Research on Aging, 10*, 358–382. **18**

Hayward, M. D., & Hardy, M. A. (1985). Early retirement processes among older men: Occupational differences. *Research on Aging, 7*, 491–518. **18**

Hazan, C., & Shaver, P. (1987). Romantic love conceptualized as an attachment process. *Journal of Personality and Social Psychology, 52*, 511–524. **14**

Hazan, C., & Shaver, P. (1990). Love and work: An attachment-theoretical perspective. *Journal of Personality and Social Psychology, 59*, 270–280. **14, Int5**

Hazan, C., Hutt, M., Sturgeon, J., & Bricker, T. (1991). The process of relinquishing parents as attachment figures. Paper presented at the biennial meetings of the Society for Research in Child Development, Seattle. 14

Hazzard, W. R., (1985). The sex differential in longevity. In R. Andres, E. L. Bierman & A. W. R. Hazzard (Eds.), *Principles of geriatric medicine* (pp. 72–81). New York: McGraw Hill. 15

Heagarty, M. C. (1991). America's lost children: Whose responsibility? *The Journal of Pediatrics, 118,* 8–10. 3

Heaton, T. B., & Pratt, E. L. (1990). The effects of religious homogamy on marital satisfaction and stability. *Journal of Family Issues, 11,* 191–207. 14

Hegvik, R. L., McDevitt, S. C., & Carey, W. B. (1981). *Longitudinal stability of temperament characteristics in the elementary school period.* Paper presented at the meeting of the International Society for the Study of Behavioral Development, Toronto, August. 6

Helson, R., Mitchell, V., & Moane, G. (1984). Personality and patterns of adherence and nonadherence to the social clock. *Journal of Personality and Social Psychology, 46,* 1079–1096. **1, 14**

Helson, R., & Moane, G. (1987). Personality change in women from college to midlife. *Journal of Personality and Social Psychology, 53.* **14, 16**

Henderson, B. E., Ross, R. K., & Pike, M. C. (1987). Menopause, estrogen treatment, and carbohydrate metabolism. In D. R. Mishell, Jr. (Ed.), *Menopause: Physiology and Pharmacology* (pp. 253–260). Chicago: Year Book Medical Publishers. 15

Henneborn, W. J., & Cogan, R. (1975). The effect of husband participation on reported pain and the probability of medication during labour and birth. *Journal of Psychosomatic Research, 19,* 215–222. 3

Herzog, A. R., & Rogers, W. L. (1989). Age differences in memory performance and memory ratings as measured in a sample survey. *Psychology and Aging, 4,* 173–182. 17

Herzog, A. R., House, J. S., & Morgan, J. N. (1991). Relation of work and retirement to health and well-being in older age. *Psychology and Aging, 6,* 202–211. **16, 17, 18**

Hess, E. H. (1972). "Imprinting" in a natural laboratory. *Scientific American, 227,* 24–31. 1

Hetherington, E. M. (1989). Coping with family transitions: Winners, losers, and survivors. *Child Development, 60,* 1–14. **6, 8, 12**

Hetherington, E. M. (1991a). The role of individual differences and family relationships in children's coping with divorce and remarriage. In P. A. Cowen & M. Hetherington (Eds.), *Family transitions* (pp. 165–194). Hillsdale: Erlbaum. 8

Hetherington, E. M. (1991b). Presidential address: Families, lies, and videotapes. *Journal of Research on Adolescence, 1,* 323–348. **8, 12**

Hetherington, E. M., & Camera, K. A. (1984). Families in transition: The process of dissolution and reconstitution. In R. D. Parke, R. N. Emde, H. P. McAdoo, & G. P. Sackett (Eds.), *Review of child development research: Vol. 7. The family* (pp. 398–440). Chicago: University of Chicago Press. 8

Hetherington, E. M., Cox, M., & Cox, R. (1978). The aftermath of divorce. In M. H. Stevens, Jr., & M. Mathews (Eds.), *Mother/child, father/child relationships* (pp. 149–176). Washington, DC: National Association for the Education of Young Children. 8

Higgins, A. (1991). The just community approach to moral education: Evolution of the idea and recent findings. In W. M. Kurtines & J. L. Gewirtz (Eds.), *Handbook of moral behavior and development, Vol. 3, Application* (pp. 111–141). Hillsdale, NJ: Erlbaum. 11

Higgins, A., Power, C., & Kohlberg, L. (1984). The relationship of moral atmosphere to judgments of responsibility. In W. M. Kurtines & J. L. Gewirtz (Eds.), *Morality, moral behavior, and moral development*

(pp. 74–108). New York: Wiley-Interscience. 11

Hightower, E. (1990). Adolescent interpersonal and familial precursors of positive mental health at midlife. *Journal of Youth and Adolescence, 19,* 257–275. 16

Hill, J. P. (1988). Adapting to menarche: Familial control and conflict. In M. R. Gunnar & W. A. Collins (Eds.), *Development during the transition to adolescence. Minnesota Symposia on Child Psychology* (Vol. 21) (pp. 43–78). Hillsdale, NJ: Erlbaum. 12

Hill, R. (1965). Decision making and the family life cycle. In E. Shanas & G. F. Streib (Eds.), *Social structure and the family: Generational relations.* Englewood Cliffs, NJ: Prentice-Hall. 16

Hinde, R. A., Titmus, G., Easton, D., & Tamplin, A. (1985). Incidence of "friendship" and behavior toward strong associates versus nonassociates in preschoolers. *Child Development, 56,* 234–245. 8

Hinton, J. (1975). The influence of previous personality on reactions to having terminal cancer. *Omega, 6,* 95–111. 19

Hirsch, H. V. B., & Tieman, S. B. (1987). Perceptual development and experience-dependent changes in cat visual cortex. In M. H. Bornstein (Ed.), *Sensitive periods in development: Interdisciplinary perspectives* (pp. 39–80). Hillsdale, NJ: Erlbaum. 1

Hirshberg, L. M., & Svejda, M. (1990). When infants look to their parents: I. Infants' social referencing of mothers compared to fathers. *Child Development, 61,* 1175–1186. 5

Hirsh-Pasek, K., Trieman, R., & Schneiderman, M. (1984). Brown and Hanlon revisited: Mothers' sensitivity to ungrammatical forms. *Journal of Child Language, 11,* 81–88. 7

Hoch, C. C., Buysse, D. J., Monk, T. H., & Reynolds, C. F. III. (1992). Sleep disorders and aging. In J. E. Birren, R. B. Sloane & G. D. Cohen (Eds.), *Handbook of mental health and aging,* (2nd ed.) (pp. 557–582). San Diego, CA: Academic Press. 17

Hodgson, J. W., & Fischer, J. L. (1979). Sex differences in identity and intimacy development in college youth. *Journal of Youth and Adolescence, 8,* 37–50. 12

Hofferth, S. L. (1985). Updating children's life course. *Journal of Marriage and the Family, 47,* 93–115. 8

Hofferth, S. L. (1987a). Teenage pregnancy and its resolution. In S. L. Hofferth & C. D. Hayes (Eds.), *Risking the future. Adolescent sexuality, pregnancy, and childbearing. Working papers* (pp. 78–92). Washington, DC: National Academy Press. 12

Hofferth, S. L. (1987b). Social and economic consequences of teenage childbearing. In S. L. Hofferth & C. D. Hayes (Eds.), *Risking the future. Adolescent sexuality, pregnancy, and childbearing. Working papers* (pp. 123–144). Washington, DC: National Academy Press. 12

Hofferth, S. L., Kahn, J. R., & Baldwin, W. (1987). Premarital sexual activity among U.S. teenage women over the past three decades. *Family Planning Perspectives, 19,* 46–53. 12

Hoff-Ginsberg, E. (1986). Function and structure in maternal speech: Their relation to the child's development of syntax. *Developmental Psychology, 22,* 155–163. 7

Hoffman, L. W., & Manis, J. D. (1978). Influences of children on marital interaction and parental satisfactions and dissatisfactions. In R. M. Lerner & G. B. Spanier (Eds.), *Child influences on marital and family interaction.* New York: Academic Press. 14

Hogan, D. P. (1981). *Transitions and social change. The early lives of American men.* New York: Academic Press. 14

Holahan, C. K. (1988). Relation of life goals at age 70 to activity participation and health and psychological well-being among Terman's gifted men and women. *Psychology and Aging, 3,* 286–291. 18

Holden, C. (September, 1987). Genes and behavior: A twin legacy. *Psychology Today,* 18. 6

Holden, G. W., & West, M. J. (1989). Proximate regulation by mothers: A demonstration of how differing styles affect young children's behavior. *Child Development, 60,* 64–69. 8

Holden, K. C., & Smock, P. J. (1991). The economic costs of marital dissolution: Why do women bear a disproportionate cost? *Annual Review of Sociology, 17,* 51–78. 16

Holland, J. L. (1973). *Making vocational choices: A theory of careers.* Englewood Cliffs, NJ: Prentice-Hall. 14

Holland, J. L. (1985). *Making vocational choices* (2nd ed.). Englewood Cliffs, NJ: Prentice-Hall. 14

Holloway, S. D., & Hess, R. D. (1985). Mothers' and teachers' attributions about children's mathematics performance. In I. E. Sigel (Ed.), *Parental belief systems. The psychological consequences for children* (pp. 177–200). Hillsdale, NJ: Erlbaum. 7

Holmbeck, G. N., & Hill, J. P. (1991). Conflictive engagement, positive affect, and menarche in families with seventh-grade girl. *Child Development, 62,* 1030–1048. 12

Honigfeld, L. S., & Kaplan, D. W. (1987). Native-American post-neonatal mortality. *Pediatrics, 80,* 575–578. 4

Honzik, M. P. (1986). The role of the famiy in the development of mental abilities: A 50-year study. In N. Datan, A. L. Greene, & H. W. Reese (Eds.), *Life-span developmental psychology. Intergenerational relations* (pp. 185–210). Hillsdale, NJ: Erlbaum. 7

Hook, E. (1982). The epidemiology of Down syndrome. In S. Pueschel & J. Rynders (Eds.), *Down syndrome: Advances in biomedicine and the behavioral sciences* (pp. 11–88). Cambridge, MA: Ware Press. 3

Horn, J. L. (1982). The aging of human abilities. In B. B. Wolman (Ed.), *Handbook of developmental psychology.* Englewood Cliffs, NJ: Prentice-Hall. 13

Horn, J. L., & Donaldson, G. (1980). Cognitive development in adulthood. In O. G. Brim, Jr., & J. Kagan (Eds.), *Constancy and change in human development.* Cambridge, MA: Harvard University Press. 13

Horner, K. W., Rushton, J. P., & Vernon, P. A. (1986). Relation between aging and research productivity of academic psychologists. *Psychology and Aging, 1,* 319–324. 15

Horowitz, F. D. (1987). *Exploring developmental theories: Toward a structural/behavioral model of development.* Hillsdale, NJ: Erlbaum. 1

Horowitz, F. D. (1990). Developmental models of individual differences. In J. Colombo & J. Fagen (Eds.), *Individual differences in infancy: Reliability, stability, prediction* (P. 3–18). Hillsdale, NJ: Erlbaum. 1

Horvath, T. B., & Davis, K. L. (1990). Central nervous system disorders in aging. In E. R. Schneider & J. W. Rowe (Eds.), *Handbook of the biology of aging* (3rd ed.) (pp. 306–329). San Diego, CA: Academic Press. 17

House, J. A., Kessler, R. C., & Herzog, A. R. (1990). Age, socioeconomic status, and health. *The Milbank Quarterly, 68,* 383–411. 13

House, J. S., Kessler, R. C., Herzog, A. R., Mero, R. P., Kinney, A. M., & Breslow, M. J. (1992). Social stratification, age, and health. In K. W. Schaie, D. Blazer & J. M. House (Eds.), *Aging, health behaviors, and health outcomes* (pp. 1–32). Hillsdale, NJ: Erlbaum. 13

Houseknecht, S. K. (1987). Voluntary childlessness. In M. B. Sussman & S. K. Steinmetz (Eds.), *Handbook of marriage and the family.* New York: Plenum. 14

Houseknecht, S. K., & Macke, A. S. (1981). Combining marriage and career: The marital adjustment of professional women. *Journal of Marriage and the Family, 43,* 651–661. 14

Howat, P. M., & Saxton, A. M. (1988). The incidence of bulimic behavior in a secondary and university school population. *Journal of Youth and Adolescence, 17,* 221–321. 11

Howes, C. (1983). Patterns of friendship. *Child Development, 54,* 1041–1053. 8

Howes, C. (1987). Social competence with peers in young children: Developmental sequences. *Developmental Review, 7,* 252–272. 8

Howes, C. (1990). Can the age of entry into child care and the quality of child care predict adjustment in kindergarten? *Developmental Psychology, 26,* 292–303. 6

Howes, C., Phillips, D. A., & Whitebook, M. (1992). Thresholds of quality: Implications for the social development of children in center-based child care. *Child Development, 63,* 449–460. 6

Howes, C., & Stewart, P. (1987). Child's play with adults, toys, and peers: An examination of family and child-care influences. *Developmental Psychology, 23,* 423–430. 6

Hoyert, D. L. (1991). Financial and household exchanges between generations. *Research on Aging, 13,* 205–225. 16, 18

Huesmann, L. R., Lagerspetz, K., & Eron, L. D. (1984). Intervening variables in the television violence-aggression relation: Evidence from two countries. *Developmental Psychology, 20,* 746–775. 10

Hultsch, D. F., & Dixon, R. A. (1990). Learning and memory in aging. In J. E. Birren & K. W. Schaie (Eds.), *Handbook of the psychology of aging* (3rd ed.) (pp. 259–274). San Diego, CA: Academic Press. 17

Hunt, C. E., & Brouillette, R. T. (1987). Sudden infant death syndrome: 1987 perspective. *Journal of Pediatrics, 110,* 669–678. 4

Hunt, J. McV. (1986). The effect of variations in quality and type of early child care on development. *New Directions for Child Development, 32,* 31–48. 6

Hunter, F. T., & Youniss, J. (1982). Changes in functions of three relations during adolescence. *Developmental Psychology, 18,* 806–811. 12

Hunter, J. E., & Hunter, R. F. (1984). Validity and utility of alternative predictors of job performance. *Psychological Bulletin, 86,* 721–735. 11

Hunter, S., & Sundel, M. (1989). *Midlife myths. Issues, findings, and practice implications.* Newbury Park, CA: Sage. 15

Huntington, L., Hans, S. L., & Zeskind, P. S. (1990). The relations among cry characteristics, demographic variables, and developmental test scores in infants prenatally exposed to methadone. *Infant Behavior and Development, 13,* 533–538. 4

Hurwicz, M, Duryam, C. C., Boyd-Davis, S. L., Gatz, M., & Bengtson, V. L. (1992). Salient life events in three-generation families. *Journal of Gerontology: PSYCHOLOGICAL SCIENCES, 47,* P11–13. 16

Hurwitz, E., Gunn, W. J., Pinsky, P. F., & Schonberger, L. B. (1991). Risk of respiratory illness associated with day-care attendance: A nationwide study. *Pediatrics, 87,* 62–69. 4

Huston, A. C., Wright, J. C., Rice, M. L., Kerkman, D., & St. Peters, M. (1990). Development of television viewing patterns in early childhood: A longitudinal investigation. *Developmental Psychology, 26,* 409–420. 10

Huston, T. L., McHale, S. M., & Crouter, A. C. (1986). When the honeymoon's over: Changes in the marriage relationship over the first year. In R. Gilmour & S. Duck (Eds.), *The emerging field of personal relationships.* Hillsdale, NJ: Erlbaum. 14

Huston-Stein, A., & Higgens-Trenk, A. (1978). Development of females from childhood through adulthood: Career and feminine role orientations. In P. B. Baltes (Ed.), *Life-span development and behavior,* (Vol. 1) (pp. 258–297). New York: Academic Press. 12

Hutt, S. J., Lenard, H. G., & Prechtl, H. F. R. (1969). Psychophysiological studies in newborn infants. In L. P. Lipsitt & H. W. Reese (Eds.), *Advances in child development and behavior, Vol. 4* (pp. 128–173). New York: Academic Press. 4

Hutto, C., Parks, W. P., Lai, S., Mastrucci, M. T., Micthcll, C., Munoz, J., Trapido, E., Master, I. M., & Scott, G. B. (1991). A hospital-based prospective study of perinatal infection with human immunodeficiency virus type 1. *Journal of Pediatrics, 118,* 347–353. 3

Hymel, S., Rubin, K. H., Rowden, L., & LeMare, L. (1990). Children's peer relationships: Longitudinal prediction of internalizing and externalizing problems from middle to late childhood. *Child Development, 61,* 2004–2021. 12

Ingram, D. (1981). Early patterns of grammatical development. In R. E. Stark (Ed.), *Language behavior in infancy and early childhood* (pp. 327–358). New York: Elsevier/North-Holland. **7**

Inhelder, B., & Piaget, J. (1958). *The growth of logical thinking from childhood to adolescence*. New York: Basic Books. **11**

Inkeles, A., & Usui, C. (1989). Retirement patterns in cross-national perspective. In D. I. Kertzer & K. W. Schaie (Eds.), *Age structuring in comparative perspective* (pp. 227–262). Hillsdale, NJ: Erlbaum. **18**

Inoff-Germain, G., Arnold, G. S., Nottelmann, E. D., Susman, E. J., Cutler, G. B. Jr., & Chrousos, G. P. (1988). Relations between hormone levels and observational measures of aggressive behavior of young adolescents in family interactions. *Developmental Psychology, 24*, 129–139. **12**

Isabella, R. A., Belsky, J., & von Eye, A. (1989). Origins of infant-mother attachment: An examination of interactional synchrony during the infant's first year. *Developmental Psychology, 25*, 12–21. **6**

Ishii-Kuntz, M. & Seccombe, K. (1989). The impact of children upon social support networks throughout the life course. *Journal of Marriage and the Family, 51*, 777–790. **14**

Istvan, J. (1986). Stress, anxiety, and birth outcomes. A critical review of the evidence. *Psychological Bulletin, 100*, 331–348. **3**

Iversen, L., & Sabroe, S. (1988). Psychological well-being among unemployed and employed people after a company closedown: A longitudinal study. *Journal of Social Issues, 44*, 141–152. **16**

Izard, C. E., Haynes, O. M., Chisholm, G., & Baak, K. (1991). Emotional determinants of infant-mother attachment. *Child Development, 62*, 906–917. **6**

Izard, C. E., Huebner, R. R., Risser, D., McGinnes, G. C., & Dougherty, L. M. (1980). The young infant's ability to produce discrete emotional expressions. *Developmental Psychology, 16*, 132–140. **6**

Jacklin, C. N. (1989). Female and male: Issues of gender. *American Psychologist, 44*, 127–133. **7**

Jackson, D. J., Longino, C. F., Jr., Zimmerman, R. S., & Bradsher, J. E. (1991). Environmental adjustments to declining functional ability. Residential mobility and living arrangements. *Research on Aging, 13*, 289–309. **18**

Jackson, E., Campos, J. J., & Fischer, K. W. (1978). The question of decalage between object permanence and person permanence. *Developmental Psychology, 14*, 1–10. **5**

Jackson, J. S. (Ed.) (1991). *Life in black America*. Newbury Park: Sage Publications. **15**

Jacobs, S. C., Kosten, T. R., Kasl, S. V., Ostfeld, A. M., Berkman, L., & Charpentier, P. (1987–88). Attachment theory and multiple dimensions of grief. *Omega, 18*, 41–52. **19**

Jacobson, S. W., & Frye, K. F. (1991). Effect of maternal social support on attachment: Experimental evidence. *Child Development, 62*, 572–582. **Int1**

James, S. A., Keenan, N. L., & Browning, S. (1992). Socioeconomic status, health behaviors, and health status among blacks. In K. W. Schaie, D. Blazer & J. M. House (Eds.), *Aging, health behaviors, and health outcomes* (pp. 39–57). Hillsdale, NJ: Erlbaum. **13, 15**

Jensen, A. R. (1980). *Bias in mental testing*. New York: The Free Press. **7**

Jerrome, D. (1990). Intimate relationships. In J. Bond & P. Coleman (Eds.), *Aging in society* (pp. 181–208). London: Sage Publications. **18**

Johansson, B., & Berg, S. (1989). The robustness of the terminal decline phenomenon: Longitudinal data from the digit-span memory test. *Journal of Gerontology: PSYCHOLOGICAL SCIENCES, 44*, P184–186. **17**

Johnson, C., Lewis, C., Love, S., Lewis, L., & Stuckey, M. (1984). Incidence and correlates of bulimic behavior in a female high school population. *Journal of Youth and Adolescence, 13*, 15–26. **11**

Johnson, C. L. (1982). Sibling solidarity: Its origin and functioning in Italian-American families. *Journal of Marriage and the Family, 44*, 155–167. **18**

Johnson, C. L., & Barer, B. M. (1990). Families and networks among older inner-city blacks. *The Gerontologist, 30*, 726–733. **18**

Johnson, H. R., Gibson, R. C., & Luckey, I. (1990). Health and social characteristics. Implications for services. In Z. Harel, E. A. McKinney & M. Williams (Eds.), *Black aged* (pp. 131–145). Newbury Park, CA: Sage Publications. **17**

Johnston, J. R. (1985). Cognitive prerequisites: The evidence from children learning English. In D. I. Slobin (Ed.), *The crosslinguistic study of language acquisition: Vol. 2. Theoretical issues* (pp. 961–1004). Hillsdale, NJ: Erlbaum. **7**

Jonas, O., Chan, A., & MacHarper, T. (1989). Caesarean section in south Australia, 1986. *Australia and New Zealand Journal of Obstetrics and Gynaecology, 29*, 99–106. **3**

Jones, K. L., Smith, D. W., Ulleland, C. N., & Streissguth, A. P. (1973). Pattern of malformation in offspring of chronic alcoholic mothers. *Lancet, 1*, 1267–1271. **3**

Jung, C. G. (1916). *Analytical psychology*. New York: Moffat, Yard. **2**

Jung, C. G. (1939). *The integration of personality*. New York: Holt, Rinehart & Winston. **2**

Kacerguis, M. A., & Adams, G. R. (1980). Erikson stage resolution: The relationship between identity and intimacy. *Journal of Youth and Adolescence, 9*, 117–126. **12**

Kagan, J., & Snidman, N. (1991). Temperamental factors in human development. *American Psychologist, 46*, 857–862. **6**

Kagan, J., Kearsley, R., & Zelazo, P. (1978). *Infancy: Its place in human development*. Cambridge, MA: Harvard University Press. **6**

Kagan, J., Reznick, J. S., & Snidman, N. (1990). The temperamental qualities of inhibition and lack of inhibition. In M. Lewis & S. M. Miller (Eds.), *Handbook of developmental psychopathology* (pp. 219–226). New York: Plenum Press. **6**

Kahn, S. B., Alvi, S., Shaukat, N., Hussain, M. A., & Baig, T. (1990). A study of the validity of Holland's theory in a non-western culture. *Journal of Vocational Behavior, 36*, 132–146. **14**

Kail, R. (1991a). Developmental change in speed of processing during childhood and adolescence. *Psychological Bulletin, 109*, 490–501. **9**

Kail, R. (1991b). Processing time declines exponentially during childhood and adolescence. *Developmental Psychology, 27*, 259–266. **9**

Kalish, R. A. (1985). The social context of death and dying. In R. H. Binstock & E. Shanas (Eds.), *Handbook of aging and the social sciences*. (2nd ed.) New York: Van Nostrand Reinhold. **19**

Kalish, R. A., & Reynolds, D. K. (1976). *Death and ethnicity: A psychocultural study*. Los Angeles: University of Southern California Press. Reprinted 1981, Farmingdale, NJ: Baywood Publishing Co. **19**

Kallman, D. A., Plato, C. C., & Tobin, J. D. (1990). The role of muscle loss in the age-related decline of grip strength: Cross-sectional and longitudinal perspectives. *Journal of Gerontology: MEDICAL SCIENCES, 45*, M82–88. **13**

Kamo, Y., Ries, L. M. Farmer, Y., M., Nickinovich, D. G., & Borgatta, E. F. (1991). Status attainment revisited. The National Survey of Families and Households. *Research on Aging, 13*, 124–143. **14**

Kandall, S. R., & Gaines, J. (1991). Maternal substance use and subsequent Sudden Infant Death Syndrome (SIDS) in offspring. *Neurotoxicology and Teratology, 13*, 235–240. **4**

Kandel, E. R. (1985). Nerve cells and behavior. In E. R. Kandel & J. H. Schwartz (Eds.), *Principles of neural science* (2nd ed.) (pp. 13–24). New York: Elsevier. **3**

Kane, R. L., & Kane, R. A. (1990). Health care for older people: Organizational and policy issues. In R. H. Binstock & L. K. George (Eds.),

Handbook of aging and the social sciences, (3rd ed.) (pp. 415–437). San Diego, CA: Academic Press. **17**

Kane, R. L., Klein, S. J., Bernstein, L., Rothenberg, R., & Wales, J. (1985). Hospice role in alleviating the emotional stress of terminal patients and their families. *Medical Care, 23,* 189–197. **19**

Kane, R. L., Wales, J., Bernstein, L., Leibowitz, A., & Kaplan, S. (1984). A randomized controlled trial of hospice care. *Lancet,* 890–894. **19**

Kangas, J., & Bradway, K. (1971). Intelligence at middle age: A thirty-eight-year follow-up. *Developmental Psychology, 5,* 333–337. **13**

Kannel, W. B., & Gordon, T. (1980). Cardiovascular risk factors in the aged: The Framingham study. In S. G. Haynes & M. Feinleib (Eds.), *Second conference on the epidemiology of aging.* U.S. Department of Health and Human Services, NIH Publication No. 80–969. Washington, DC: U.S. Government Printing Office. **15**

Kaplan, G. A. (1992). Health and aging in the Alameda County study. In K. W. Schaie, D. Blazer & J. M. House (Eds.), *Aging, health behaviors, and health outcomes* (pp. 69–88). Hillsdale, NJ: Erlbaum. **13, 17**

Kaplan, R. M. (1985). The controversy related to the use of psychological tests. In B. B. Wolman (Ed.), *Handbook of intelligence. Theories, measurements, and applications* (pp. 465–504). New York: Wiley. **9**

Kaplan, R. M., Anderson, J. P., & Wingard, D. L. (1991). Gender differences in health-related quality of life. *Health Psychology, 10,* 86–93. **15**

Karmiloff-Smith, A. (1991). Beyond modularity: Innate constraints and developmental change. In S. Carey & R. Gelman (Eds.), *The epigenesis of mind. Essays on biology and cognition* (pp. 171–197). Hillsdale, NJ: Erlbaum. **5**

Karp, D. A. (1988). A decade of reminders: Changing age consciousness between fifty and sixty years old. *The Gerontologist, 28,* 727–738. **Int6**

Kasl, S. V., & Cobb, S. (1982). Variability of stress effects among men experiencing job loss. In L. Goldberger & S. Breznitz (Eds.), *Handbook of stress. Theoretical and clinical aspects.* New York: The Free Press. **16**

Kataria, S., Frutiger, A. D., Lanford, B., & Swanson, M. S. (1988). Anterior fontanel closure in healthy term infants. *Infant Behavior and Development, 11,* 229–233. **4**

Kausler, D. H., & Lichty, W. (1988). Memory for activities: Rehearsal-independence and aging. In M. L. Howe & C. J. Brainerd (Eds.), *Cognitive development in adulthood: Progress in cognitive development research* (pp. 93–131). New York: Springer-Verlag. **17**

Kaye, Katherine, Elkind, L., Goldberg, D., & Tytun, A. (1989). Birth outcomes for infants of drug abusing mothers. *New York State Journal of Medicine, 89,* 256–261. **3**

Keating, D. P. (1980). Thinking processes in adolescence. In J. Adelson (Ed.), *Handbook of adolescent psychology* (pp. 211–246). New York: Wiley. **11**

Keating, D. P., & Clark, L. V. (1980). Development of physical and social reasoning in adolescence. *Developmental Psychology, 16,* 23–30. **9**

Keating, D. P., List, J. A., & Merriman, W. E. (1985). Cognitive processing and cognitive ability: Multivariate validity investigation. *Intelligence, 9,* 149–170. **9**

Keefe, S. E. (1984). Real and ideal extended familism among Mexican Americans and Anglo Americans: On the meaning of "close" family ties. *Human Organization, 43,* 65–70. **14**

Keeney, T. J., Cannizzo, S. R., & Flavell, J. H. (1967). Spontaneous and induced verbal rehearsal in a recall task. *Child Development, 38,* 935–966. **9**

Keil, J. E., Sutherland, S. E., Knapp, R. G., Waid, L. R., & Gazes, P. C. (1992). Self-reported sexual functioning in elderly blacks and whites. *Journal of Aging and Health, 4,* 112–125. **17**

Keith, P. M. (1981–82). Perceptions of time remaining and distance from death. *Omega, 12,* 307–318. **19**

Kellam, S. G., Ensminger, M. E., & Turner, R. J. (1977). Family structure and the mental health of children: Concurrent and longitudinal community-wide studies. *Archives of General Psychiatry, 34,* 1012–1022. **8**

Kellehear, A., & Lewin, T. (1988–89). Farewells by the dying: A sociological study. *Omega, 19,* 275–292. **19**

Kelly, E. L., & Conley, J. J. (1987). Personality and compatibility: A prospective analysis of marital stability and marital satisfaction. *Journal of Personality and Social Psychology, 52,* 27–40. **14**

Keniston, K. (Autumn, 1970). Youth: A "new" stage in life. *American Scholar, 8,* 631–654. **Int4**

Kessler, R. C., Foster, C., Webster, P. S., & House, J. S. (1992). The relationship between age and depressive symptoms in two national surveys. *Psychology and Aging, 7,* 119–126. **13, 17**

Kessler, R. C., Turner, J. B., & House, J. S. (1988). Effects of unemployment on health in a community survey: Main, modifying, and mediating effects. *Journal of Social Issues, 44,* 69–85. **16**

Kessner, D. M. (1973). *Infant death: an analysis by maternal risk and health care.* Washington, DC: National Academy of Sciences. **3**

Kesteloot, H., Lesaffre, E., & Joossens, J. V. (1991). Dairy fat, saturated animal fat, and cancer risk. *Preventive Medicine, 20,* 226–236. **15**

Kiecolt-Glaser, J. K., & Glaser, R. (1988). Behavioral influences on immune function: Evidence for the interplay between stress and health. In T. M. Field, P. M. McCabe, & N. Schneiderman (Eds.), *Stress and coping across development.* Hillsdale, NJ: Erlbaum. **13**

Kiecolt-Glaser, J. K., Glaser, R., Suttleworth, E. E., Dyer, C. S., Ogrocki, P., & Speicher, C. E. (1987). Chronic stress and immunity in family caregivers of Alzheimer's disease patients. *Psychosomatic Medicine, 49,* 523–535. **16**

Kilpatrick, S. J., & Laros, R. K. (1989). Characteristics of normal labor. *Obstetrics and Gynecology, 74,* 85–87. **3**

Kitchen, W. H., Doyle, L. W., Ford, G. W., Murton, L. J., Keith, C. G., Rickards, A. L., Kelly, E., & Callanan, C. (1991). Changing two-year outcome of infants weighing 500 to 999 grams at birth: A hospital study. *Journal of Pediatrics, 118,* 938–943. **3**

Kivett, V. R. (1991). Centrality of the grandfather role among older rural black and white men. *Journal of Gerontology: SOCIAL SCIENCES, 46,* S250–258. **16**

Klaus, H. M., & Kennell, J. H. (1976). *Maternal-infant bonding.* St. Louis, MO: Mosby. **6**

Kleemeier, R. W. (1962). Intellectual changes in the senium. *Proceedings of the Social Statistics Section of the American Statistics Association, 1,* 290–295. **17**

Klenow, D. J., & Bolin, R. C. (1989–90). Belief in an afterlife: A national survey. *Omega, 20,* 63–74. **19**

Kletzky, O. A., & Borenstein, R. (1987). Vasomotor instability of the menopause. In D. R. Mishell, Jr. (Ed.), *Menopause: Physiology and pharmacology.* (pp. 53–66). Chicago: Year Book Medical Publishers. **15**

Kliegl, R., Smith, J., & Baltes, P. B. (1989). Testing-the-limits and the study of adult age differences in cognitive plasticity of a mnemonic skill. *Developmental Psychology, 25,* 247–256. **17**

Kliegl, R., Smith, J., & Baltes, P. B. (1990). On the locus and process of magnification of age differences during mnemonic training. *Developmental Psychology, 26,* 894–904. **17**

Kline, D. W., Kline, T. J. B., Fozard, J. L., Kosnik, W., Schieber, F., & Sekuler, R. (1992). Vision, aging, and driving: The problem of older drivers. *Journal of Gerontology: PSYCHOLOGICAL SCIENCES, 47,* P27–34. **17**

Kluwe, R. H. (1986). Psychological research on problem-solving and aging. In A. B. Sörensen, F. E. Weinert & L. R. Sherrod (Eds.), *Human development and the life course: Multidisciplinary perspectives* (pp. 509–534). Hillsdale, NJ: Erlbaum. **17**

Kobak, R. R., & Sceery, A. (1988). Attachment in late adolescence: Working models, affect regulation, and representations of self and others. *Child Development, 59,* 135–146. **14**

Kobak, R. R., Sudler, N., & Gamble, W. (1991). Attachment and depressive symptoms during adolescence: A developmental pathways analysis. *Development and Psychopathology, 3,* 461–474. **12**

Koenig, H. G., Kvale, J. N., & Ferrell, C. (1988). Religion and well-being in later life. *The Gerontologist, 28,* 18–28. **18**

Kohlberg, L. (1964). Development of moral character and moral ideology. In M. L. Hoffman & L. W. Hoffman (Eds.), *Review of child development research* (Vol. 1) (pp. 283–332). New York: Russell Sage Foundation. **2, 11**

Kohlberg, L. (1966). A cognitive-developmental analysis of children's sex-role concepts and attitudes. In E. E. Maccoby (Ed), *The development of sex differences* (pp. 82–172). Stanford, CA: Stanford University Press. **8**

Kohlberg, L. (1973). Continuities in childhood and adult moral development revisited. In P. B. Baltes & K. W. Schaie (Eds.) *Life-span developmental psychology: Personality and socialization* (pp. 180–204). New York: Academic Press. **Int4**

Kohlberg, L. (1975). The cognitive-developmental approach to moral education. *Phi Delta Kappan,* June, 670–677. **11**

Kohlberg, L. (1976). Moral stages and moralization: The cognitive-developmental approach. In T. Lickona (Ed.), *Moral development and behavior: Theory, research, and social issues* (pp. 31–53). New York: Holt. **2, 11, Int4**

Kohlberg, L. (1978). Revisions in the theory and practice of moral development. *New Directions for Child Development, 2,* 83–88. **11**

Kohlberg, L. (1980). *The meaning and measurement of moral development.* Worcester, MA: Clark University Press. **11**

Kohlberg, L. (1981). *Essays on moral development. Vol. 1. The philosophy of moral development.* New York: Harper & Row. **2, 11**

Kohlberg, L. (1984). *Essays on moral development. Vol. II: The psychology of moral development.* San Francisco: Harper & Row. **2, 11**

Kohlberg, L., & Candee, D. (1984). The relationship of moral judgment to moral action. In W. M. Kurtines & J. L. Gewirtz (Eds.), *Morality, moral behavior, and moral development* (pp. 52–73). New York: Wiley. **11**

Kohlberg, L., & Elfenbein, D. (1975). The development of moral judgments concerning capital punishment. *American Journal of Orthopsychiatry, 54,* 614–640. **11**

Kohlberg, L., & Higgins, A. (1987). School democracy and social interaction. In W. M. Kurtines & J. L. Gewirtz (Eds.), *Moral development through social interaction* (pp. 102–130). New York: Wiley-Interscience. **11**

Kohlberg, L., Levine, C., & Hewer, A. (1983). Moral stages: A current formulation and a response to critics. *Contributions to human development 10.* Basel: S. Karger. **11**

Kohlberg, L., & Ullian, D. Z. (1974). Stages in the development of psychosexual concepts and attitudes. In R. C. Friedman, R. M. Richart & R. L. Vande Wiele (Eds.), *Sex differences in behavior* (pp. 209–222). New York: Wiley. **8**

Kokmen, E. (1991). The EURODEM collaborative re-analysis of case-control studies of Alzheimer's disease: Implications for clinical research and practice. *International Journal of Epidemiology, 20* (Suppl. 2), S65-S67. **17**

Kon, I. S., & Losenkov, V. A. (1978). Friendship in adolescence: Values and behavior. *Journal of Marriage and the Family, 40,* 143–155. **12**

Kopp, C. B. (1983). Risk factors in development. In M. M. Haith & J. J. Campos (Eds.), *Handbook of child psychology: Infancy and developmental psychobiology* (Vol. 2) (pp. 1081–1188). New York: Wiley. (P. H. Mussen, General Editor). **3**

Kopp, C. B. (1990). Risks in infancy: appraising the research. *Merrill Palmer Quarterly, 36,* 117–140. **3**

Korn, S. J. (1984). Continuities and discontinuities in difficult/easy temperament: Infancy to young adulthood. *Merrill-Palmer Quarterly, 30,* 189–199. **6**

Korner, A. F., Hutchinson, C. A., Koperski, J. A., Kraemer, H. C., & Schneider, P. A. (1981). Stability of individual differences of neonatal motor and crying patterns. *Child Development, 52,* 83–90. **4**

Kotulak, R. (1990, September 28). Study finds inner-city kids live with violence. *Chicago Tribune, 1,* 16. **10**

Kozma, A., Stones, M. J., & Hannah, T. E. (1991). Age, activity, and physical performance: An evaluation of performance models. *Psychology and Aging, 6,* 43–49. **13**

Krause, N., Jay, G., & Liang, J. (1991). Financial strain and psychological well-being among the American and Japanese elderly. *Psychology and Aging, 6,* 170–181. **18**

Krause, N. Liang, J., & Keith, V. (1990). Personality, social support, and psychological distress in later life. *Psychology and Aging, 5,* 315–326. **18**

Kritchevsky, D. (1990). Nutrition and breast cancer. *Cancer, 66,* 1321–1325. **15**

Kroeger, N. (1982). Preretirement preparation: Sex differences in access, sources, and use. In M. Szinovacz (Ed.), *Women's retirement* (pp. 95–112). Beverly Hills, CA: Sage Publications. **16**

Krout, J. A. (1983). Seasonal migration of the elderly. *The Gerontologist, 23,* 295–299. **18**

Kübler-Ross, E. (1969). *On death and dying.* New York: Macmillan. **19**

Kübler-Ross, E. (1974). *Questions and answers on death and dying.* New York: Macmillan. **19**

Kuczaj, S. A. II. (1977). The acquisition of regular and irregular past tense forms. *Journal of Verbal Learning and Verbal Behavior, 49,* 319–326. **7**

Kuczaj, S. A. II. (1978). Children's judgments of grammatical and ungrammatical irregular past tense verbs. *Child Development, 49,* 319–326. **7**

Kuczynski, L., Kochanska, G., Radke-Yarrow, M., & Girnius-Brown, O. (1987). A developmental interpretation of young children's noncompliance. *Developmental Psychology, 23,* 799–806. **8**

Kuhl, P. K. (1983). Perception of auditory equivalence classes for speech in early infancy. *Infant Behavior and Development, 6,* 263–285. **5**

Kupersmidt, J. B., & Coie, J. D. (1990). Preadolescent peer status, aggression, and school adjustment as predictors of externalizing problems in adolescence. *Child Development, 61,* 1350–1362. **10**

Kurdek, L. A. (1991). Predictors of increases in marital distress in newlywed couples: A 3-year prospective longitudinal study. *Developmental Psychology, 27,* 627–636. **14**

Kurdek, L. A., & Schmitt, J. P. (1986). Early development of relationship quality in heterosexual married, heterosexual cohabiting, gay, and lesbian couples. *Developmental Psychology, 22,* 305–309. **14**

Kurtines, W. M., & Gewirtz, J. L. (Eds.) (1991). *Handbook of moral behavior and development.* Vol. 1 Theory, Vol. 2. Research, Vol 3. Application. Hillsdale, NJ: Erlbaum. **11**

Labouvie-Vief, G. (1980). Beyond formal operations: Uses and limits of pure logic in life-span development. *Human Development, 23,* 141–161. **2, 13**

Labouvie-Vief, G. (1985). Cognition and aging. In J. E. Birren & K. W. Schaie (Eds.), *The handbook of the psychology of aging* (pp. 500–530). New York: Van Nostrand Reinhold. **15**

Labouvie-Vief, G. (1990). Modes of knowledge and the organization of development. In M. L. Commons, C. Armon, L. Kohlberg, F. A. Richards, T. A. Grotzer & J. D. Sinnott (Eds.), *Adult development*, Vol. 2, *Models and methods in the study of adolescent and adult thought*. New York: Praeger. **2, 13**

Ladd, G. W., Price, J. M., & Hart, C. H. (1988). Predicting preschoolers' peer status from their playground behaviors. *Child Development, 59,* 986–992. **10**

La Freniere, P., Strayer, F. F., & Gauthier, R. (1984). The emergence of same-sex affiliative preferences among preschool peers: A developmental/ethological perspective. *Child Development, 55,* 1958–1965. **8**

Lakatta, E. G. (1985). Heart and circulation. In C. E. Finch & E. L. Schneider (Eds.), *Handbook of the biology of aging* (2nd ed.) New York: Van Nostrand Reinhold. **13**

Lakatta, E. G. (1990). Heart and circulation. In E. L. Schneider & J. W. Rowe (Eds.), *Handbook of the biology of aging* (3rd ed.) (pp. 181–217). San Diego, CA: Academic Press. **13**

Lamb, M. E. (1981). The development of father-infant relationships. In M. E. Lamb (Ed.), *The role of the father in child development* (2nd ed.) (pp. 459–488). New York: Wiley. **6**

Lamb, M. E., Frodi, M., Hwang, C., & Frodi, A. M. (1983). Effects of paternal involvement on infant preferences for mothers and fathers. *Child Development, 54,* 450–458. **6**

Lamb, M. E., Frodi, A. M., Hwang, C., Frodi, M., & Steinberg, J. (1982). Mother- and father-infant interaction involving play and holding in traditional and nontraditional Swedish families. *Developmental Psychology, 18,* 215–221. **6**

Lamb, M. E., Hwang, C., Bookstein, F. L., Broberg, A., Hult, G., & Frodi, M. (1988). Determinants of social competence in Swedish preschoolers. *Developmental Psychology, 24,* 58–70. **6**

Lamborn, S. D., Mounts, N. S., Steinberg, L., & Dornbusch, S. M. (1991). Patterns of competence and adjustment among adolescents from authoritative, authoritarian, indulgent, and neglectful families. *Child Development, 62,* 1049–1065. **8, 11, 12**

Lamke, L. K. (1982a). Adjustment and sex-role orientation. *Journal of Youth and Adolescence, 11,* 247–259. **12**

Lamke, L. K. (1982b). The impact of sex-role orientation on self-esteem in early adolescence. *Child Development, 53,* 1530–1535. **12**

Langlois, J. H., Ritter, J. M., Roggman, L. A., & Vaughn, L. S. (1991). Facial diversity and infant preferences for attractive faces. *Developmental Psychology, 27,* 79–84. **5**

Langlois, J. H., Roggman, L. A., Casey, R. J., Ritter, J. M., Rieser-Danner, L. A., & Jenkins, V. Y. (1987). Infant preferences for attractive faces: Rudiments of a stereotype? *Developmental Psychology, 23,* 263–369. **5**

Langlois, J. H., Roggman, L. A., & Rieser-Danner, L. A. (1990). Infants' differential social responses to attractive and unattractive faces. *Developmental Psychology, 26,* 153–159. **5**

Lansdown, R., & Benjamin, G. (1985). The development of the concept of death in children aged 5 - 9 years. *Child care, health and development, 11,* 13–30. **19**

Larson, R., Mannell, R., & Zuzanek, J. (1986). Daily well-being of older adults with friends and family. *Psychology and Aging, 1,* 117–126. **18**

Lauer, J. C., & Lauer, R. H. (June, 1985). Marriages made to last. *Psychology Today, 19,* (6), 22–26. **14**

Lauer, R. H., & Lauer, J. C. (1986). Factors in long-term marriages. *Journal of Family Issues, 7,* 382–390. **18**

Lawrence, R. H., Bennett, J. M., & Markides, K. S. (1992). Perceived intergenerational solidarity and psychological distress among older Mexican Americans. *Journal of Gerontology: SOCIAL SCIENCES, 47,* S55–65. **18**

Lawton, M. P. (1985). Housing and living environments of older people. In R. H. Binstock & E. Shanas (Eds.), *Aging and the social sciences* (2nd ed.). New York: Van Nostrand Reinhold. **17**

Lawton, M. P. (1990). Residential environment and self-directedness among older people. *American Psychologist, 45,* 638–640. **17**

Leadbeater, B. J., & Dionne, J. (1981). The adolescent's use of formal operational thinking in solving problems related to identity resolution. *Adolescence, 16,* 111–121. **Int4**

Leaper, C. (1991). Influence and involvement in children's discourse: Age, gender, and partner effects. *Child Development, 62,* 797–811. **8**

Lee, G. R. (1988). Marital satisfaction in later life: The effects of non-marital roles. *Journal of Marriage and the Family, 50,* 775–783. **18**

Lee, G. R., & Ellithorpe, E. (1982). Intergenerational exchange and subjective well-being among the elderly. *Journal of Marriage and the Family, 44,* 217–224. **18**

Lee, G. R., & Ishii-Kuntz, M. (1987). Social interaction, loneliness, and emotional well-being among the elderly. *Research on Aging, 9,* 459–482. **18**

Lee, G. R., Seccombe, K., & Shehan, C. L. (1991). Marital status and personal happiness: An analysis of trend data. *Journal of Marriage and the Family, 53,* 839–844. **14**

Lee, G. R., & Shehan, C. L. (1989). Social relations and the self-esteem of older persons. *Research on Aging, 11,* 427–442. **18**

Lee, V. E., Brooks-Gunn, J., Schnur, E., & Liaw, F. (1990). Are Head Start effects sustained? A longitudinal follow-up comparison of disadvantaged children attending Head Start, no preschool, and other preschool programs. *Child Development, 61,* 495–507. **7**

Lehman, H. C. (1953). *Age and achievement*. Princeton, NJ: Princeton University Press. **15**

Lehr, U. (1982). Hat die Grosfamilie heute noch eine Chance? *Der Deutsche Artz, 18,* Sonderdruck. **16**

Leigh, G. K. (1982). Kinship interaction over the family life span. *Journal of Marriage and the Family, 44,* 197–208. **14**

Lempers, J. D., & Clark-Lempers, D. (1990). Family economic stress, maternal and paternal support and adolescent distress. *Journal of Adolescence, 13,* 217–229. **12**

Leon, G. R., Gillum, B., Gillum, R., & Gouze, M. (1979). Personality stability and change over a 30-year period—middle age to old age. *Journal of Consulting and Clinical Psychology, 47,* 517–524. **16**

Leon, G. R., Perry, C. L., Mangelsdorf, C., & Tell, G. (1989). Adolescent nutritional and psychological patterns and risk for the development of an eating disorder. *Journal of Youth and Adolescence, 18,* 273–282. **11**

Lerner, R. M. (1985). Adolescent maturational changes and psychosocial development: A dynamic interactional perspective. *Journal of Youth and Adolescence, 14,* 355–372. **11**

Lerner, R. M. (1986). *Concepts and theories of human development* (2nd ed.). New York: Random House. **2**

Lerner, R. M. (1987). A life-span perspective for early adolescence. In R. M. Lerner & T. T. Foch (Eds.), *Biological-psychosocial interactions in early adolescence* (pp. 9–34). Hillsdale, NJ: Erlbaum. **11**

Lester, B. M. (1987). Prediction of developmental outcome from acoustic cry analysis in term and preterm infants. *Pediatrics, 80,* 529–534. **4**

Lester, B. M., Corwin, M. J., Sepkoski, C. Siefer, R., Peucker, M., McLaughlin, S., & Golub, H. L. (1991). Neurobehavioral syndromes in cocaine-exposed newborn infants. *Child Development, 62,* 674–705. **3**

Lester, B. M., & Dreher, M. (1989). Effects of marijuana use during pregnancy on newborn cry. *Child Development, 60,* 765–771. **4**

Letzelter, M., Jungermann, C., & Freitag, W. (1986). Schwimmleistungen im Alter [Swimming performance in old age]. *Zeitschrift fur Gerontologie, 19,* 389–395. **13**

Levinson, D. J. (1978). *The seasons of a man's life.* New York: Knopf. **2, 14**

Levinson, D. J. (1980). Toward a conception of the adult life course. In N. J. Smelser & E. H. Erikson (Eds.), *Themes of work and love in adulthood.* Cambridge, MA: Harvard University Press. **2**

Levinson, D. J. (1986). A conception of adult development. *American Psychologist, 41,* 3–13. **2**

Levinson, D. J. (1990). A theory of life structure development in adulthood. In C. N. Alexander & E. J. Langer (Eds.), *Higher stages of human development* (pp. 35–54). New York: Oxford University Press. **2, 16**

Lewinsohn, P. M., Rohde, P., Seeley, J. R., & Fischer, S. A. (1991). Age and depression: Unique and shared effects. *Psychology and Aging, 6,* 247–260. **13, 17**

Lewis, C. C. (1981). How adolescents approach decisions: Changes over grades seven to twelve and policy implications. *Child Development, 52,* 538–544. **11**

Lewis, M. (1990). Social knowledge and social development. *Merrill-Palmer Quarterly, 36,* 93–116. **6**

Lewis, M. (1991). Ways of knowing: Objective self-awareness of consciousness. *Developmental Review, 11,* 231–243. **6**

Lewis, M., & Brooks, J. (1978). Self-knowledge and emotional development. In M. Lewis & L. A. Rosenblum (Eds.), *The development of affect* (pp. 205–226). New York: Plenum. **6**

Lewis, M., & Brooks-Gunn, J. (1979). *Social cognition and the acquisition of self.* New York: Plenum. **6**

Lewis, M., & Brooks-Gunn, J. (1981). Visual attention at three months as a predictor of cognitive functioning at two years of age. *Intelligence, 5,* 131–140. **5**

Lewis, M., & Sullivan, M. W. (1985). Infant intelligence and its assessment. In B. B. Wolman (Ed.) *Handbook of intelligence* (pp. 505–599). New York: Wiley-Interscience. **5**

Lewis, M., Sullivan, M. W., Stanger, C., & Weiss, M. (1989). Self development and self-conscious emotions. *Child Development, 60,* 146–156. **6**

Lickona, T. (1978). Moral development and moral education. In J. M. Gallagher & J. A. Easley, Jr. (Eds.), *Knowledge and development* (Vol. 2) (pp. 21–74). New York: Plenum. **11**

Lickona, T. (1983). *Raising good children.* Toronto: Bantam Books. **8**

Lieberman, M. A. (1965). Psychological correlates of impending death: Some preliminary observations. *Journal of Gerontology, 20,* 182–190. **19**

Lieberman, M. A., & Coplan, A. S. (1970). Distance from death as a variable in the study of aging. *Developmental Psychology, 2,* 71–84. **19**

Lieberman, M. A., & Peskin, H. (1992). Adult life crises. In J. E. Birren, R. B. Sloane & G. D. Cohen (Eds.), *Handbook of mental health and aging* (2nd ed.) (pp. 119–143). **16**

Liem, R., & Liem, J. H. (1988). Psychological effects of unemployment on workers and their families. *Journal of Social Issues, 44,* 87–105. **16**

Liker, J. K., & Elder, G. H. (1983). Economic hardship and marital relations in the 1930s. *American Sociological Review, 48,* 343–359. **14**

Lim, K. O., Zipursky, R. B., Watts, M. C., & Pfefferbaum, A. (1992). Decreased gray matter in normal aging: An in vivo magnetic resonance study. *Journal of Gerontology: BIOLOGICAL SCIENCES, 47,* B26–30. **13, 17**

Lima, S. D., Hale, S., & Myerson, J. (1991). How general is general

slowing? Evidence from the lexical domain. *Psychology and Aging, 6,* 416–425. **17**

Lindsay, R. (1985). The aging skeleton. In M. R. Haug, A. B. Ford & M. Sheafor (Eds.), *The physical and mental health of aged women.* New York: Springer. **15**

Linney, J. A., & Seidman, E. (1989). The future of schooling. *American Psychologist, 44,* 336–340. **9**

Lipshultz, S., Frassica, J. J., & Orav, E. J. (1991). Cardiovascular abnormalities in infants prenatally exposed to cocaine. *Journal of Pediatrics, 118,* 44–51. **3**

Lipsitt, L. P. (1982). Infant learning. In T. M. Field, A. Houston, H. C. Quay, L. Troll & G. E. Finley (Eds.), *Review of human development* (pp. 62–78). New York: Wiley. **5**

Litwak, E. (1989). Forms of friendships among older people in an industrial society. In R. G. Adams & R. Blieszner (Eds.), *Older adult friendship* (pp. 65–88). Newbury Park, CA: Sage Publications. **18**

Litwak, E., & Longino, C. F. Jr. (1987). Migration patterns among the elderly: A developmental perspective. *The Gerontologist, 27,* 266–272. **18**

Livesley, W. J., & Bromley, D. B. (1973). *Person perception in childhood and adolescence.* London: Wiley. **10, 12**

Livson, F. B. (1976). Patterns of personality development in middle-aged women: A longitudinal study. *International Journal of Aging and Human Development, 7,* 107–115. **16**

Livson, F. B. (1981). Paths to psychological health in the middle years: Sex differences. In D. H. Eichorn, J. A. Clausen, N. Haan, M. P. Honzik & P. H. Mussen (Eds.), *Present and past in middle life.* New York: Academic Press. **16**

Livson, N., & Peskin, H. (1981). Psychological health at 40: Prediction from adolescent personality. In D. H. Eichorn, J. A. Clausen, N. Haan, M. P. Honzik & P. H. Mussen (Eds.), *Present and past in middle life.* New York: Academic Press. **16**

Lo, Y. D., Patel, P., Wainscoat, J. S., Sampietro, M., Gillmer, M. D. G., & Fleming, K. A. (December 9, 1989). Prenatal sex determination by DNA amplification from maternal peripheral blood. *The Lancet,* 1363–1365. **3**

Loehlin, J. C. (1989). Partitioning environmental and genetic contributions to behavioral development. *American Psychologist, 44,* 1285–1292. **1**

Loehlin, J. C. (1992). *Genes and environment in personality development.* Newbury Park, CA: Sage. **6**

Loehlin, J. C., Horn, J. M., & Willerman, L. (1989). Modeling IQ change: Evidence from the Texas Adoption Project. *Child Development, 60,* 993–1004. **7**

Loevinger, J. (1976). *Ego development.* San Francisco: Jossey-Bass. **2, 14**

Loevinger, J. (1984). On the self and predicting behavior. In R. A. Zucker, J. Aronoff & A. I. Rabin (Eds.), *Personality and the prediction of behavior.* New York: Academic Press. **14**

Long, F., Peters, D. L., & Garduque, L. (1985). Continuity between home and day care: A model for defining relevant dimensions of child care. In I. E. Sigel (Ed.), *Advances in applied developmental psychology* (Vol. 1) (pp. 131–170). Norwood, NJ: Ablex. **6**

Long, J. V. F., & Vaillant, G. E. (1984). Natural history of male psychological health. XI: Escape from the underclass: *The American Journal of Psychiatry, 141,* 341–346. **10, Int5**

Longino, C. F. Jr. (1988). Who are the oldest Americans? *The Gerontologist, 28,* 515–523. **17**

Longino, C. F. Jr. (1990). Geographical distribution and migration. In R. H. Binstock & L. K. George (Eds.), *Handbook of aging and the social sciences* (3rd ed.) (pp. 45–63). San Diego, CA: Academic Press. **18**

Longino, C. F., Jr., Jackson, D. J., Zimmerman, R. S., & Bradsher, J. E.

(1991). The second move: Health and geographic mobility. *Journal of Gerontology: SOCIAL SCIENCES, 46, S218–224.* **18**

Lopata, H. Z. (1981). Widowhood and husband sanctification. *Journal of Marriage and the Family, 43,* 439–450. **19**

Lopata, H. Z. (1986). Time in anticipated future and events in memory. *American Behavioral Scientist, 29,* 695–709. **19**

Lozoff, B. (1989). Nutrition and behavior. *American Psychologist, 44,* 231–236. **4**

Lubben, J. E., Weiler, P. G., & Chi, I. (1989). Health practices of the elderly poor. *American Journal of Public Health, 79,* 731–734. **17**

Lütkenhaus, P., Grossmann, K. E., & Grossmann, K. (1985). Infant-mother attachment at twelve months and style of interaction with a stranger at the age of three years. *Child Development, 56,* 1538–1542. **6**

Lyons, N. P. (1983). Two perspectives: On self, relationships, and morality. *Harvard Educational Review, 53,* 125–145. **11**

Lyons-Ruth, K., Repacholi, B., McLeod, S., & Silva, E. (1991). Disorganized attachment behavior in infancy: Short-term stability, maternal and infant correlates, and risk-related subtypes. *Development and Psychopathology, 3,* 388–396. **6**

Lytton, H., & Romney, D. M. (1991). Parents' differential socialization of boys and girls: A meta-analysis. *Psychological Bulletin, 109,* 267–296. **8**

Maas, H. S., & Kuypers, J. A. (1974). *From thirty to seventy.* San Francisco: Jossey-Bass. **18**

Maccoby, E. E. (1980). *Social development. Psychological growth and the parent-child relationships.* New York: Harcourt Brace Jovanovich. **8**

Maccoby, E. E. (1984). Middle childhood in the context of the family. In W. A. Collins (Ed.), *Development during middle childhood. The years from six to twelve* (pp. 184–239). Washington, DC: National Academy Press. **10**

Maccoby, E. E. (1988). Gender as a social category. *Developmental Psychology, 24,* 755–765. **6, 8**

Maccoby, E. E. (1990). Gender and relationships. A developmental account. *American Psychologist, 45,* 513–520. **6, 8, 14**

Maccoby, E. E., & Jacklin, C. N. (1974). *The psychology of sex differences.* Stanford, CA: Stanford University Press. **10**

Maccoby, E. E., & Jacklin, C. N. (1987). Gender segregation in childhood. In H. W. Reese (Ed.), *Advances in child development and behavior* (Vol. 20) (pp. 239–288). Orlando, FL: Academic Press. **6, 8, 10**

Maccoby, E. E., & Martin, J. A. (1983). Socialization in the context of the family: Parent-child interaction. In E. M. Hetherington (Ed.), *Handbook of child psychology: Socialization, personality, and social development* (Vol. 4) (pp. 1–102). New York: Wiley. (P. H. Mussen, General Editor) **8**

MacGowan, R. J., MacGowan, C. A., Serdula, M. K., Lane, J. M., Joesoef, R. M., & Cook, F. H. (1991). Breast-feeding among women attending Women, Infants, and Children clinics in Georgia, 1987. *Pediatrics, 87,* 361–366. **4**

Maclean, M., Bryant, P., & Bradley, L. (1987). Rhymes, nursery rhymes, and reading in early childhood. *Merrill-Palmer Quarterly, 33,* 255–281. **9**

Mac Rae, H. (1992). Fictive kin as a component of the social networks of older people. *Research on Aging, 14,* 226–247. **18**

Madden, D. J. (1992). Four to ten milliseconds per year: Age-related slowing of visual word identification. *Journal of Gerontology: PSYCHOLOGICAL SCIENCES, 47,* P49–68. **17**

Madden, D. J., Blumenthal, J. A., Allen, P. A., & Emery, C. F. (1989). Improving aerobic capacity in healthy older adults does not necessarily lead to improved cognitive performance. *Psychology and Aging, 4,* 307–320. **15, 17**

Madsen, W. (1969). Mexican Americans and Anglo Americans: A comparative study of mental health in Texas. In S. C. Plog & R. B. Edgerton (Eds.), *Changing perspectives in mental illness* (pp. 217–247). New York: Holt, Rinehart & Winston. **14**

Magnusson, D., Stattin, H., & Allen, V. L. (1986). Differential maturation among girls and its relation to social adjustment: A longitudinal perspective. In P. B. Baltes, D. L. Featherman & R. M. Lerner (Eds.), *Life-span development and behavior* (Vol. 7) (pp. 136–173). Hillsdale, NJ: Erlbaum. **11**

Main, M. (1990). Cross-cultural studies of attachment organization: Recent studies, changing methodologies, and the concept of conditional strategies. *Human Development, 33,* 48–61. **6**

Main, M., & Cassidy, J. (1988). Categories of response to reunion with the parent at age 6: Predictable from infant attachment classifications and stable over a 1-month period. *Developmental Psychology, 24,* 415–426. **6**

Main, M., Kaplan, N., & Cassidy, J. (1985). Security in infancy, childhood, and adulthood: A move to the level of representation. In I. Bretherton & E. Waters (Eds.), Growing points of attachment theory and research. *Monographs of the Society for Research in Child Development, 50* (Serial No. 209, pp. 66–104.) **6**

Main, M., & Solomon, J. (1985). Discovery of an insecure disorganized/disoriented attachment pattern: Procedures, findings and implications for the classification of behavior. In M. Yogman & T. B. Brazelton (Eds.), *Affective development in infancy* (pp. 95–124). Norwood, NJ: Ablex. **6**

Malina, R. M. (1979). Secular changes in size and maturity: Causes and effects. In A. F. Roche (Ed.), *Secular trends in human growth, maturation, and development. Monographs of the Society for Research in Child Development, 44* (#179), 59–102.

Malina, R. M. (1982). Motor development in the early years. In S. G. Moore & C. R. Cooper (Eds.), *The young child. Reviews of research* (Vol. 3) (pp. 211–232). Washington, DC: National Association for the Education of Young Children. **4**

Malina, R. M. (1990). Physical growth and performance during the transition years (9–16). In R. Montemayor, G. R. Adams & T. P. Gullotta (Eds.), *From childhood to adolescence: A transitional period?* (pp. 41–62). Newbury Park, CA: Sage. **11**

Manton, K. G., & Stallard, E. (1991). Cross-sectional estimates of active life expectancy for the U.S. elderly and oldest-old populations. *Journal of Gerontology: SOCIAL SCIENCES, 46,* S170–182. **17**

Marcia, J. E. (1966). Development and validation of ego identity status. *Journal of Personality and Social Psychology 3,* 551–558. **2, 12**

Marcia, J. E. Identity in adolescence. (1980). In J. Adelson (Ed.), *Handbook of adolescent psychology* (pp. 159–187). New York: Wiley. **2, 12**

Marcus, D. E., & Overton, W. F. (1978). The development of cognitive gender constancy and sex role preferences. *Child Development, 49,* 434–444. **8**

Marcus, R. F. (1986). Naturalistic observation of cooperation, helping, and sharing and their association with empathy and affect. In C. Zahn-Waxler, E. M. Cummings, & R. Iannotti (Eds.), *Altruism and aggression. Biological and social origins* (pp. 256–279). Cambridge, England: Cambridge University Press. **8**

Maret, E., & Finlay, B. (1984). The distribution of household labor among women in dual-earner families. *Journal of Marriage and the Family, 46,* 357–364. **14**

Markides, K. S., Coreil, J., & Rogers, L. P. (1989). Aging and health among southwestern Hispanics. In K. S. Markides (Ed.), *Aging and health* (pp. 177–210). Newbury Park, CA: Sage Publications. **17**

Markides, K. S., & Krause, N. (1985). Intergenerational solidarity and psychological well-being among older Mexican Americans: A three-generations study. *Journal of Gerontology, 40,* 390–392. **18**

Markides, K. S., & Lee, D. J. (1991). Predictors of health status in middle-aged and older Mexican Americans. *Journal of Gerontology: SOCIAL SCIENCES, 46,* S243–249. **15**

Markides, K. S., & Mindel, C. H. (1987). *Aging and ethnicity.* Newbury Park, CA: Sage Publications. **15, 17, 18**

Markman, E. M. (1989). *Categorization and naming in children; Problems of induction.* Cambridge, MA: MIT Press, Bradford Books. **7**

Markman, E. M. & Hutchinson, J. (1984). Children's sensitivity to constraints on word meaning: Taxonomic vs. thematic relations. *Cognitive Psychology, 16,* 1–27. **7**

Markovitz, H., Schleifer, M., & Fortier, L. (1989). Development of elementary deductive reasoning in young children. *Developmental Psychology, 25,* 787–793. **9**

Marshall, V. W. (1975). Age and awareness of finitude in developmental gerontology. *Omega, 6,* 113–129. **19**

Marshall, V. W., & Levy, J. A. (1990). Aging and dying. In R. H. Binstock & L. K. George (Eds.), *Handbook of aging and the social sciences* (pp. 245–260). San Diego, CA: Academic Press. **19**

Marsiglio, W., & Donnelly, D. (1991). Sexual relations in later life: A national study of married persons. *Journal of Gerontology: SOCIAL SCIENCES, 46,* S338–344. **17**

Martin, C. L. (1991). The role of cognition in understanding gender effects. In H. W. Reese (Ed.), *Advances in child development and behavior* (Vol. 23) (pp. 113–150). San Diego, CA: Academic Press. **8**

Martin, C. L., & Halverson, C. F. Jr. (1981). A schematic processing model of sex typing and stereotyping in children. *Child Development, 52,* 1119–1134. **8**

Martin, C. L., & Halverson, C. F. Jr. (1983). The effects of sex-typing schemas on young children's memory. *Child Development, 54,* 563–574. **8**

Martin, C. L., & Little, J. K. (1990). The relation of gender understanding to children's sex-typed preferences and gender stereotypes. *Child Development, 61,* 1427–1439. **8**

Martin, C. L., Wood, C. H., & Little, J. K. (1990). The development of gender stereotype components. *Child Development, 61,* 1891–1904. **8**

Martin, P., & Smyer, M. A. (1990). The experience of micro- and macroevents. A life span analysis. *Research on Aging, 12,* 294–310. **Int5**

Martin, T. C., & Bumpass, L. L. (1989). Recent trends in marital disruption. *Demography, 26,* 37–51. **14**

Martorano, S. C. (1977). A developmental analysis of performance on Piaget's formal operations tasks. *Developmental Psychology, 13,* 666–672. **9, 11**

Marvin, R. S., & Greenberg, M. T. (1982). Preschoolers' changing conceptions of their mothers: A social-cognitive study of mother-child attachment. *New Directions for Child Development, 18,* 47–60. **8**

Maslow, A. H. (1968). *Toward a psychology of being* (2nd ed.). New York: Van Nostrand Reinhold. **2**

Maslow, A. H. (1970a). *Religions, values, and peak-experiences.* New York: Viking. (Original work published 1964). **2**

Maslow, A. H. (1970b). *Motivation and personality* (2nd ed.). New York: Harper & Row. **2**

Maslow, A. H. (1971). *The farther reaches of human nature.* New York: Viking. **2**

Massad, C. M. (1981). Sex role identity and adjustment during adolescence. *Child Development, 52,* 1290–1298. **12**

Masten, A. S., Best, K. M., & Garmezy, N. (1990). Resilience and development: Contributions from the study of children who overcome adversity. *Development and Psychopathology, 2,* 425–444. **1, Int1, 10**

Matas, L., Arend, R. A., & Sroufe, L. A. (1978). Continuity of adaptation in the second year: The relationship between quality of attachment and latter competence. *Child Development, 49,* 547–556. **6, 8**

Mather, P. L., & Black, K. N. (1984). Heredity and environmental influences on preschool twins' language skills. *Developmental Psychology, 20,* 303–308. **7**

Mathew, A., & Cook, M. (1990). The control of reaching movements by young infants. *Child Development, 61,* 1238–1257. **4, 7**

Matthews, K. A. (1988). Coronary heart disease and Type A behaviors: Update on and alternative to the Booth-Kewley and Friedman (1987) quantitative review. *Psychological Bulletin, 104,* 373–380. **15**

Maurer, D., & Maurer, C. (1988). *The world of the newborn.* New York: Basic Books. **3, 4**

Mayer, J. (1975). Obesity during childhood. In M. Winick (Ed.), *Childhood obesity* (pp. 73–80). New York: Wiley. **9**

Maylor, E. A. (1990). Recognizing and naming faces: Aging, memory retrieval and the tip of the tongue state. *Journal of Gerontology: PSYCHOLOGICAL SCIENCES, 45,* P215–226. **17**

Maylor, E. A. (1991). Recognizing and naming tunes: Memory impairment in the elderly. *Journal of Gerontology: PSYCHOLOGICAL SCIENCES, 46,* P207–217. **17**

McAuley, W. J., & Blieszner, R. (1985). Selection of long-term care arrangements by older community residents. *The Gerontologist, 25,* 188–193. **18**

McBride, G. (1991, Fall). Nontraditional inheritance—II. The clinical implications. *Mosaic, 22,* 12–25. **3**

McCabe, A. E., Siegel, L. S., Spence, I., & Wilkinson, A. (1982). Class-inclusion reasoning: Patterns of performance from three to eight years. *Child Development, 53,* 779–785. **7**

McCall, R. B. (1981). Early predictors of later IQ: The search continues. *Intelligence, 5,* 141–147. **5**

McCall, R. B., Appelbaum, M. I., & Hogarty, P. S. (1973). Developmental changes in mental performance. *Monographs of the Society for Research in Child Development, 38* (Serial No. 150). **7**

McCord, J. (1982). A longitudinal view of the relationship between parental absence and crime. In J. Gunn & D. P. Farrington (Eds.), *Abnormal offenders, delinquency, and the criminal justice system* (pp. 113–128). London: Wiley. **8, 10**

McCord, W., McCord, J., & Zola, I. K. (1959). *Origins of crime.* New York: Columbia University Press. **12**

McCrae, R. R., & Costa, P. T., Jr. (1984). *Emerging lives, enduring dispositions: Personality in adulthood.* Boston: Little, Brown. **15**

McCrae, R. R., & Costa, P. T., Jr. (1988). Psychological resilience among widowed men and women: A 10-year follow-up of a national sample. *Journal of Social Issues, 44,* No. 3, 129–142. **19**

McCrae, R. R., & Costa, P. T., Jr. (1990). *Personality in adulthood.* New York: The Guilford Press. **14, 18**

McCready, W. C. (1985). Styles of grandparenting among white ethnics. In V. L. Bengtson & J. F. Robertson (Eds.), *Grandparenthood.* Beverly Hills, CA: Sage. **16**

McDonald, P. L., & Wanner, R. A. (1990). *Retirement in Canada.* Toronto: Butterworths. **18**

McFall, S., & Miller, B. H. (1992). Caregiver burden and nursing home admission of frail elderly persons. *Journal of Gerontology: SOCIAL SCIENCES, 47* S73–79. **18**

McFalls, J. A. Jr. (1990). The risks of reproductive impairment in the later years of childbearing. *Annual Review of Sociology, 16,* 491–519. **3, 13**

McGandy, R. B. (1988). Atherogenesis and aging. In R. Chernoff & D. A. Lipschitz (Eds.), *Aging.* Vol. 35. *Health promotion and disease prevention in the elderly.* New York: Raven Press. **15**

McKey, R. H., Condelli, L., Granson, H., Barrett, B., McConkey, C., & Plantz, M. (1985, June). *The impact of Head Start on children, families and communities* (final report of the Head Start Evaluation, Synthesis and Utilization Project). Washington, DC: CSR. **7**

McLaughlin, B. (1984). *Second-language acquisition in childhood: Vol. 1. Preschool children* (2nd ed.). Hillsdale, NJ: Erlbaum. **7**

McLoyd, V. C. (1990). The impact of economic hardship on black families and children: Psychological distress, parenting, and socioemotional development. *Child Development, 61,* 311–346. **4**

Meier, S. T. (1991). Vocational behavior, 1988–1990: Vocational choice, decision-making, career development interventions, and assessment. *Journal of Vocational Behavior, 39,* 131–181. **14**

Meltzoff, A. N. (1988). Infant imitation and memory: Nine-month-olds in immediate and deferred tasks. *Child Development, 59,* 217–225. **5**

Meltzoff, A. N., & Borton, R. W. (1979). Intermodal matching by human neonates. *Nature, 282,* 403–404. **5**

Meltzoff, A. N., & Moore, M. K. (1983). Newborn infants imitate adult facial gestures. *Child Development, 54,* 702–709. **5**

Menaghan, E. G., & Lieberman, M. A. (1986). Changes in depression following divorce: A panel study. *Journal of Marriage and the Family, 48,* 319–328. **16**

Mervis, C. B., & Mervis, C. A. (1982). Leopards are kitty-cats: Object labeling by mothers for their thirteen-month-olds. *Child Development, 53,* 267–273. **7**

Meyer-Bahlburg, H. F. L., Ehrhardt, A. A., & Feldman, J. F. (1986). Long-term implications of the prenatal endocrine milieu for sex-dimorphic behavior. In L. Erlenmeyer-Kimling & N. E. Miller (Eds.), *Life-span research on the prediction of psychopathology* (pp. 17–30). Hillsdale, NJ: Erlbaum. **12**

Mikulincer, M., & Nachshon, O. (1991). Attachment styles and patterns of self-disclosure. *Journal of Personality and Social Psychology, 51,* 321–331. **14**

Miller, B. C., & Moore, K. A. (1990). Adolescent sexual behavior, pregnancy, and parenting: Research through the 1980s. *Journal of Marriage and the Family, 52,* 1025–1044. **12**

Miller, R. A. (1990). Aging and the immune response. In E. L. Schneider & J. W. Rowe (Eds.), *Handbook of the biology of aging* (3rd ed.) (pp. 157–180). San Diego, CA: Academic Press. **4**

Miller, S. M., Birnbaum, A., & Durbin, D. (1990). Etiologic perspectives on depression in childhood. In M. Lewis & S. M. Miller (Eds.), *Handbook of developmental psychopathology* (pp. 311–340). New York: Plenum. **12**

Miller, T. Q., Turner, C. W., Tindale, R. S., Posavac, E. J., & Dugoni, B. L. (1991) Reasons for the trend toward null findings in research on Type A behavior. *Psychological Bulletin, 110,* 469–495. **15**

Millstein, S. G., & Litt, I. R. (1990). Adolescent health. In S. S. Feldman & G. R. Elliott (Eds.), *At the threshold. The developing adolescent* (pp. 431–456). Cambridge, MA: Harvard University Press. **11**

Miranda, S. B., Fantz, R. L. (1974). Recognition memory in Down's syndrome and normal infants. *Child Development, 45,* 651–660. **5**

Mischel, W. (1966). A social learning view of sex differences in behavior. In E. E. Maccoby (Ed.), *The development of sex differences* (pp. 56–81). Stanford, CA: Stanford University Press. **8**

Mischel, W. (1970). Sex typing and socialization. In P. H. Mussen (Ed.), *Carmichael's manual of child psychology* (Vol. 2) (pp. 3–72). New York: Wiley. **8**

Mishell, D. R., Jr. (Ed.) (1987). *Menopause: Physiology and pharmacology.* Chicago: Year Book Medical Publishers. **15**

Mitchell, P. R., & Kent, R. D. (1990). Phonetic variation in multisyllable babbling. *Journal of Child Language, 17,* 247–265. **5**

Mitchell, E. A., Scragg, R., Stewart, A. W., Becroft, D. M. O., Taylor, B. J., Ford, R. P. K., Hassall, I. B., Barry, D. M. J., Allen, E. M., & Roberts, A. P. (1991). Results from the first year of the New Zealand cot death study. *New Zealand Medical Journal, Feb. 104,* 71–76. **4**

Mizukami, K., Kobayashi, N., Ishii, T., & Iwata, H. (1990). First selective attachment begins in early infancy: A study using telethermography. *Infant Behavior and Development, 13,* 257–271. **6**

Moen, P. (1985). Continuities and discontinuities in women's labor force activity. In G. H. Elder, Jr., (Ed.), *Life course dynamics.* (pp. 113–155) Ithaca, NY: Cornell University Press. **14**

Moen, P. (1991). Transitions in mid-life: Women's work and family roles in the 1970s. *Journal of Marriage and the Family, 53,* 135–150. **16**

Monk, T. H., Reynolds, C. F. III, Buysse, D. J., Hoch, C. C., Jarrett, D. B., Jennings, J. R., & Kupfer, D. J. (1991). Circadian characteristics of healthy 80-year-olds and their relationship to objectively recorded sleep. *Journal of Gerontology: MEDICAL SCIENCES, 46,* M171–175. **17**

Montemayor, R. (1982). The relationship between parent-adolescent conflict and the amount of time adolescents spend alone and with parents and peers. *Child Development, 53,* 1512–1519. **12**

Montemayor, R., & Eisen, M. (1977). The development of self-conceptions from childhood to adolescence. *Developmental Psychology, 13,* 314–319. **10, 12**

Moon, C., & Fifer, W. P. (1990). Syllables as signals for 2-day-old infants. *Infant Behavior and Development, 13,* 377–390. **5**

Moore, K. A., Hofferth, S. L., Wertheimer, R. F., Waite, L. J., & Caldwell, S. B. (1981). Teenage childbearing: Consequences for women, families, and government welfare expenditures. In K. G. Scott, T. Field & E. G. Robertson (Eds.), *Teenage parents and their offspring.* New York: Grune & Stratton. **12**

Moore, K. L. (1988). *The developing human. Clinically oriented embryology* (4th ed.). Philadelphia: W. B. Saunders. **3**

Morgan, D. G. (1992). Neurochemical changes with aging: Predisposition towards age-related mental disorders. In J. E. Birren, R. B. Sloane & G. D. Cohen (Eds.), *Handbook of mental health and aging* (2nd ed.) (pp. 175–200). San Diego, CA: Academic Press. **17**

Morgan, L. A. (1991). *After marriage ends. Economic consequences for midlife women.* Newbury Park, CA: Sage Publications. **16**

Morisset, C. E., Barnard, K. E., Greenberg, M. T., Booth, C. L., & Spieker, S. J. (1990). Environmental influences on early language development: The context of social risk. *Development and Psychopathology, 2,* 127–149. **Int2**

Morris, J. N., Mor, V., Goldberg, R. J., Sherwood, S., Greer, D. S., & Hiris, J. (1986). The effect of treatment setting and patient characteristics on pain in terminal cancer patients: A report from the National Hospice Study. *Journal of Chronic Diseases, 39,* 27–35. **19**

Morrison, D. M. (1985). Adolescent contraceptive behavior: A review *Psychological Bulletin, 98,* 538–568. **12**

Morrongiello, B. A. (1988). The development of auditory pattern perception skills. In C. Rovee-Collier & L. P. Lipsitt (Eds.), *Advances in infancy research* (Vol. 5) (pp. 137–173). Norwood, NJ: Ablex. **5**

Morse, P. A., & Cowan, N. (1982). Infant auditory and speech perception. In T. M. Field, A. Houston, H. C. Quay, L. Troll, & G. E. Finley (Eds.), *Review of human development* (pp. 32–61). New York: Wiley. **5**

Mortimer, J. A., Van Duijn, C. M., Chandra, V., Fratiglioni, L., Graves, A. B., Heyman, A., Jorm, A. F., Kokmen, E., Kondo, K., Rocca, W. A., Shalat, S. L., Soininen, H., & Hofman, A. (1991). Head trauma as a risk factor for Alzheimer's disease: A collaborative reanalysis of case-control studies. *International Journal of Epidemiology, 20* (Suppl 2), S28–35. **17**

Mortimer, J. T., Finch, M., Shanahan, M., & Ryu, S. (1992). Work experience, mental health, and behavioral adjustment in adolescence. *Journal of Research on Adolescence, 2,* 25–57. **12**

Mosher, F. A., & Hornsby, J. R. (1966). On asking questions. In J. S. Bruner, R. R. Olver & P. M. Greenfield (Eds.), *Studies in cognitive growth* (pp. 68–85). New York: Wiley. **9**

Mosher, W. D. (1987). Infertility: Why business is booming. *American Demography, July,* 42–43. **13**

Mosher, W. D., & Pratt, W. F. (1987). Fecundity, infertility, and reproductive health in the United States, 1982. *Vital Health Statistics,* Series 23, No. 14. National Center for Health Statistics, US Public Health Service. Washington: USGPO. **13**

Munro, G., & Adams, G. R. (1977). Ego-identity formation in college students and working youth. *Developmental Psychology, 13,* 523–524. **12**

Munroe, R. H., Shimmin, H. S., & Munroe, R. L. (1984). Gender understanding and sex role preference in four cultures. *Developmental Psychology, 20,* 673–682. **8**

Murray, J. L., & Bernfield, M. (1988). The differential effect of prenatal care on the incidence of low birth weight among blacks and whites in a prepaid health care plan. *New England Journal of Medicine, 319,* 1385–1391. **3**

Murray, J. P. (1980). *Television & youth. 25 years of research and controversy.* Stanford, CA: The Boys Town Center for the Study of Youth Development. **10**

Murrell, S. A., & Norris, F. H. (1991). Differential social support and life change as contributors to the social class-distress relationship in old age. *Psychology and Aging, 6,* 223–231. **18**

Murstein, B. I. (1970). Stimulus-Value-Role: A theory of marital choice. *Journal of Marriage and the Family, 32,* 465–481. **14**

Murstein, B. I. (1976). *Who will marry whom? Theories and research in marital choice.* New York: Springer. **14**

Murstein, B. I. (1986). *Paths to marriage.* Beverly Hills, CA: Sage. **14**

Myers, B. J. (1987). Mother-infant bonding as a critical period. In M. H. Bornstein (Ed.), *Sensitive periods in development: Interdisciplinary perspectives* (pp. 223–246). Hillsdale, NJ: Erlbaum. **6**

Myers, G. C. (1990). Demography of aging. In R. H. Binstock & L. K. George (Eds.), *Handbook of aging and the social sciences* (3rd ed.) (pp. 19–44). San Diego, CA: Academic Press. **17**

Naeye, R. L., & Peters, E. C. (1984). Mental development of children whose mothers smoked during pregnancy. *Obstetrics & Gynecology, 64,* 601–607. **3**

Nathanson, C. A., & Lorenz, G. (1982). Women and health: The social dimensions of biomedical data. In J. Z. Giele (Ed.), *Women in the middle years.* New York: Wiley. **15**

National Center for Health Statistics (1984). Advance report on final natality statistics, 1982. *Monthly Vital Statistics Report, 33* (No. 6), Supplement, Sept. 28, 1984. **4**

Neerhof, M. G., MacGregor, S. N., Retzky, S. S., & Sullivan, T. P. (1989). Cocaine abuse during pregnancy: Peripartum prevalence and perinatal outcome. *American Journal of Obstetrics and Gynecology, 161,* 633–638. **3**

Neimark, E. D. (1982). Adolescent thought: Transition to formal operations. In B. B. Wolman (Ed.), *Handbook of developmental psychology* (pp. 486–502). Englewood Cliffs, NJ: Prentice-Hall. **11**

Neimeyer, R. A., & Chapman, K. M. (1980–81). Self/ideal discrepancy and fear of death: The test of an existential hypothesis. *Omega, 11,* 233–239. **19**

Nelson, C. A. (1987). The recognition of facial expression in the first two years of life: Mechanisms of development. *Child Development, 58,* 889–909. **5**

Nelson, C. A. (1989). Past, current, and future trends in infant face perception research. *Canadian Journal of Psychology, 43,* 183–198. **5**

Nelson, E. A., & Dannefer, D. (1992). Aged heterogeneity: Fact or fiction? The fate of diversity in gerontological research. *The Gerontologist, 32,* 17–23. **16**

Nelson, Katherine. (1973). Structure and strategy in learning to talk. *Monographs of the Society for Research in Child Development, 38* (Serial No. 149). **5**

Nelson, Keith. (1977). Facilitating children's syntax acquisition. *Developmental Psychology, 13,* 101–107. **7**

Neugarten, B. L. (1968). The awareness of middle age. In B. L. Neugarten (Ed.), *Middle age and aging.* Chicago, IL: University of Chicago Press. **19**

Neugarten, B. L. (1970). Dynamics of transition of middle age to old age. *Journal of Geriatric Psychiatry, 4,* 71–87. **19**

Neugarten, B. L. (1974). Age groups in American society and the rise of the young-old. In F. R. Eisele (Ed.), *Political consequences of aging.* Philadelphia: American Academy of Political and Social Sciences. **17**

Neugarten, B. L. (1975). The future of the young-old. *The Gerontologist, 15,* 4–9. **17**

Neugarten, B. L. (1976). Adaptation and the life cycle. *The Counseling Psychologist, 6,* 16–20. **15**

Neugarten, B. L. (1977). Personality and aging. In J. E. Birren & K. W. Schaie (Eds.), *Handbook of the psychology of aging.* New York: Van Nostrand Reinhold. **16**

Neugarten, B. L. (1979). Time, age, and the life cycle. *American Journal of Psychiatry, 136,* 887–894. **1**

Neugarten, B. L., & Weinstein, K. (1964). The changing American grandparent. *Journal of Marriage and the Family, 26,* 199–204. **16**

Newcombe, N. S., & Baenninger, M. (1989). Biological change and cognitive ability in adolescence. In G. R. Adams, R. Montemayor & T. P. Gullotta (Eds.), *Biology of adolescent behavior and development* (pp. 168–194). Newbury Park, CA: Sage. **7**

Newman, E. S., Sherman, S. R., & Higgins, C. E. (1982). Retirement expectations and plans: A comparison of professional men and women. In M. Szinovacz (Ed.), *Women's retirement* (pp. 113–122). Beverly Hills: Sage Publications. **16**

Nightingale, E. O., & Goodman, M. (1990). *Before birth. Prenatal testing for genetic disease.* Cambridge, MA: Harvard University Press. **3**

Nilsson, L. (1990). *A child is born.* New York: Delacorte Press. **3**

Nisan, M., & Kohlberg, L. (1982). Universality and variation in moral judgment: A longitudinal and cross-sectional study in Turkey. *Child Development, 53,* 865–876. **11**

Nolen-Hoeksema, S., Girgus, J. S., & Seligman, M. E. P. (1991). Sex differences in depression and explanatory style in children. *Journal of Youth and Adolescence, 20,* 233–246. **12**

Noller, P., & Fitzpatrick, M. A. (1990). Marital communication in the eighties. *Journal of Marriage and the Family, 52,* 832–843. **14**

Norris, F. H., & Murrell, S. A. (1990). Social support, life events, and stress as modifiers of adjustment to bereavement by older adults. *Psychology and Aging, 5,* 429–436. **19**

Norton, A. J. (1983). Family life cycle: 1980. *Journal of Marriage and the Family, 45,* 267–275. **16**

Norton, A. J., & Glick, P. C. (1986). One parent families: A social and economic profile. *Family Relations, 35,* 9–18. **8**

Norwood, T. H., Smith, J. R., & Stein, G. H. (1990). Aging at the cellular level: The human fibroblastlike cell model. In E. R. Schneider & J. W. Rowe (Eds.), *Handbook of the biology of aging* (3rd ed.) (pp. 131–154). San Diego, CA: Academic Press. **17**

Nottelmann, E. D., Susman, E. J., Blue, J. H., Inoff-Germain, G., Dorn, L. D., Loriaux, D. L., Cutler, G. B., Jr., & Chrousos, G. P. (1987). Gonadal and adrenal hormone correlates of adjustment in early adolescence. In R. M. Lerner & T. T. Foch (Eds.), *Biological-psycho-*

social interactions in early adolescence (pp. 303–324). Hillsdale, NJ: Erlbaum. **11**

Novacek, J., Raskin, R., & Hogan, R. (1991). Why do adolescents use drugs? Age, sex, and user differences. *Journal of Youth and Adolescence, 20,* 475–492. **12**

Nowakowski, R. S. (1987). Basic concepts of CNS development. *Child Development, 58,* 568–595. **4**

Nurmi, J., Pulliainen, H., & Salmela-Aro, K. (1992). Age differences in adults' control beliefs related to life goals and concerns. *Psychology and Aging, 7,* 194–196. **13**

Nydegger, C. N. (1991). The development of paternal and filial maturity. In K. Pillemer & K. McCartney (Eds.), *Parent-child relations throughout life* (pp. 93–112). Hillsdale, NJ: Erlbaum. **14**

O'Brien, M., & Huston, A. C. (1985). Development of sex-typed play behavior in toddlers. *Developmental Psychology, 21,* 866–871. **6**

O'Brien, S. F., & Bierman, K. L. (1988). Conceptions and perceived influence of peer groups: interviews with preadolescents and adolescents. *Child Development, 59,* 1360–1365. **10**

O'Brien, S. J., & Vertinsky, P. A. (1991). Unfit survivors: Exercise as a resource for aging women. *The Gerontologist, 31,* 347–357. **17**

O'Bryant, S. L. (1988). Sibling support and older widows' well-being. *Journal of Marriage and the Family, 50,* 173–183. **18**

O'Connor, S., Vietze, P. M., Sandler, H. M., Sherrod, K. B., & Altemeier, W. A. (1980). Quality of parenting and the mother-infant relationships following rooming-in. In P. M. Taylor (Ed.), *Parent-infant relationships* (pp. 349–368). New York: Grune & Stratton. **6**

Offord, D. R., Boyle, M. C., & Racine, Y. A. (1991). The epidemiology of antisocial behavior in childhood and adolescence. In D. J. Pepler & K. H. Rubin (Eds.) *The development and treatment of childhood aggression* (pp. 31–54). Hillsdale, NJ: Erlbaum. **10**

Olds, D. L., & Henderson, C. R. Jr. (1989). The prevention of maltreatment. In D. Cicchetti & V. Carlson (Eds.), *Child maltreatment* (pp. 722–763). Cambridge, England: Cambridge University Press. **6**

O'Leary, A. (1990). Stress, emotion, and human immune function. *Psychological Bulletin, 108,* 363–382. **19**

O'Leary, K. D., & Smith, D. A. (1991). Marital interactions. *Annual Review of Psychology, 42,* 191–212. **14**

Oller, D. K. (1981). Infant vocalizations: Exploration and reflectivity. In R. E. Stark (Ed.), *Language behavior in infancy and early childhood* (pp. 85–104). New York: Elsevier/North-Holland. **5**

Olshan, A. F., Baird, P. A., & Teschke, K. (1989). Paternal occupational exposures and the risk of Down syndrome. *American Journal of Human Genetics, 44,* 646–651. **3**

O'Rand, A. M. (1990). Stratification and the life course. In R. H. Binstock & L. K. George (Eds.), *Handbook of aging and the social sciences* (3rd ed.) (pp. 130–148). San Diego, CA: Academic Press. **Int5**

Ornish, D. (1990). *Dr. Dean Ornish's program for reversing heart disease.* New York: Random House. **13**

Ortolani, S., Trevisan, C., Bianchi, M. L., Caraceni, M. P., Ulivieri, F. M., Gandolini, G., Montesano, A., & Polli, E. E. (1991). Spinal and forearm bone mass in relation to ageing and menopause in healthy Italian women. *European Journal of Clinical Investigation, 21,* 33–39. **15**

Orwoll, L., & Perlmutter, M. (1990). The study of wise persons: Integrating a personality perspective. In R. J. Sternberg (Ed.), *Wisdom. Its nature, origins, and development* (pp. 160–180). Cambridge, England: Cambridge University Press. **17**

Overton, W. F., Ward, S. L., Noveck, I. A., Black, J., & O'Brien, D. P. (1987). Form and content in the development of deductive reasoning. *Developmental Psychology, 23,* 22–30. **11**

Owens, W. A. (1966). Age and mental abilities: A second adult follow-up. *Journal of Educational Psychology, 57,* 311–325. **13**

Owsley, C., Ball, K., Sloane, M. E., Roenker, D. L., & Bruni, J. R. (1991). Visual/cognitive correlates of vehicle accidents in older drivers. *Psychology and Aging, 6,* 403–415. **17**

Padilla, A. M., Lindholm, K. J., Chen, A., Duran, R., Hakuta, K., Lambert, W., & Tucker, G. R. (1991). The English-only movement: Myths, reality, and implications for psychology. *American Psychologist, 46,* 120–130. **7**

Paffenbarger, R. S., Hyde, R. T., Wing, A. L., & Hsieh, C. (1987). Physical activity, all-cause mortality, and longevity of college alumni. *New England Journal of Medicine, 314,* 605–613. **17**

Page, D. C., Mosher, R., Simpson, E. M., Fisher, E. M. C., Mardon, G., Pollack, J., McGillivray, B., de la Chapelle, A., & Brown, L. G. (1987). The sex-determining region of the human Y chromosome encodes a finger protein. *Cell, 51,* 1091–1104. **3**

Paikoff, R. L., & Brooks-Gunn, J. (1990). Physiological processes: What role do they play during the transition to adolescence? In R. Montemayor, G. R. Adams & T. P. Gullotta (Eds.), *From childhood to adolescence. A transitional period?* (pp. 63–81). Newbury Park, CA: Sage. **Int4**

Paikoff, R. L., & Brooks-Gunn, J. (1991). Do parent-child relationships change during puberty? *Psychological Bulletin, 110,* 47–66. **12**

Palkovitz, R. (1985). Fathers' birth attendance, early contact, and extended contact with their newborns: A critical review. *Child Development, 56,* 392–406. **3**

Palmore, E. (1981). *Social patterns in normal aging: Findings from the Duke Longitudinal Study.* Durham, NC: Duke University Press. **1, 16, 17, 18**

Palmore, E. B., Burchett, B. M., Fillenbaum, G. G., George, L. K., & Wallman, L. M. (1985). *Retirement. Causes and consequences.* New York: Springer. **Int6, 18**

Palmore, E. B., & Cleveland, W., (1976). Aging, terminal decline, and terminal drop. *Journal of Gerontology, 31,* 76–81. **17**

Pampel, F. C. (1983). Changes in the propensity to live alone: Evidence from consecutive cross-sectional surveys, 1960–1976. *Demography, 20,* 433–447. **18**

Papousek, H., & Papousek, M. (1991). Innate and cultural guidance of infants' integrative competencies: China, the United States, and Germany. In M. H. Bornstein (Ed.), *Cultural approaches to parenting* (pp. 23–44). Hillsdale, NJ: Erlbaum. **5**

Parke, R. D., & Tinsley, B. R. (1981). The father's role in infancy: Determinants of involvement in caregiving and play. In M. E. Lamb (Ed.), *The role of the father in child development* (2nd ed.) (pp. 429–458). New York: Wiley. **6**

Parke, R. D., & Tinsley, B. R. (1984). Fatherhood: Historical and contemporary perspectives. In K. A. McCluskey & H. W. Reese (Eds.), *Life-span developmental psychology. Historical and generational effects* (pp. 203–248). Orlando, FL: Academic Press. **3**

Parke, R. D., & Tinsley, B. J. (1987). Family interaction in infancy. In J. D. Osofsky (Ed.), *Handbook of infant development* (2nd ed.) (pp. 579–641). New York: Wiley. **6**

Parkes, C. M., & Weiss, R. S. (1983). *Recovery from bereavement.* New York: Basic Books. **19**

Parkhurst, J. T., & Asher, S. R. (1992). Peer rejection in middle school: Subgroup differences in behavior, longliness, and interpersonal concerns. *Developmental Psychology, 28,* 231–241. **10**

Parlee, M. B. (1979, October). The friendship bond. *Psychology Today, 14,* 43–54, 113. **13**

Parmelee, A. H. Jr. (1986). Children's illnesses: Their beneficial effects on behavioral development. *Child Development, 57,* 1- 10. **7**

Parmelee, A. H., Jr., & Sigman, M. D. (1983). Perinatal brain development and behavior. In M. M. Haith & J. J. Campos (Eds.), *Handbook of child psychology: Infancy and developmental psychobiology* (Vol. 2) (pp. 95–156). New York: Wiley. (P. H. Mussen, General Editor) 3

Parmelee, A. H., Jr., Wenner, W. H., & Schulz, H. R. (1964). Infant sleep patterns from birth to 16 weeks of age. *Journal of Pediatrics, 65,* 576–582. 4

Parnes, H. S., Crowley, J. E., Haurin, R. J., Less, L. J., Morgan, W. R., Mott, F. L., & Nestel, G. (1985). *Retirement among American men.* Lexington, MA: Lexington Books. 18

Parsons, J. E., Adler, T. F., & Kaczala, C. M. (1982). Socialization of achievement attitudes and beliefs: Parental influences. *Child Development, 53,* 310–321. 7

Passman, R. H., & Longeway, K. P. (1982). The role of vision in maternal attachment: Giving 2-year-olds a photograph of their mother during separation. *Developmental Psychology, 18,* 530–533. 8

Patterson, G. R. (1975). *Families: Applications of social learning to family life.* Champaign, IL: Research Press. 2, 8

Patterson, G. R. (1980). Mothers: The unacknowledged victims: *Monographs of the Society for Research in Child Development, 45* (Serial No. 186.) 8

Patterson, G. R., & Bank, L. (1989). Some amplifying mechanisms for pathological processes in families. In M. R. Gunnar & E. Thelen (Eds.), *Minnesota symposia on child psychology* (Vol. 22) (pp. 167–209). Hillsdale, NJ: Erlbaum. Int2

Patterson, G. R., Capaldi, D., & Bank, L. (1991). An early starter model for predicting delinquency. In D. J. Pepler & K. H. Rubin (Eds.) *The development and treatment of childhood aggression* (pp. 139–168). Hillsdale, NJ: Erlbaum. 1, 8, Int2, 12

Patterson, G. R., DeBarsyshe, B. D., & Ramsey, E. (1989). A developmental perspective on antisocial behavior. *American Psychologist, 44,* 329–335. 1

Paxton, S. J., Wertheim, E. H., Gibbons, K., Szmjkler, G. I., Hillier, L., & Petrovich, J. L. (1991). Body image satisfaction, dieting beliefs, and weight loss behaviors in adolescent girls and boys. *Journal of Youth and Adolescence, 20,* 361–379. 11

Pearlin, L. (1975). Sex roles and depression. In N. Datan & L. H. Ginsberg (Eds.), *Life-span developmental psychology: Normative life crises.* New York: Academic Press. 15

Pearlin, L. I. (1980). Life strains and psychological distress among adults. In N. J. Smelser & E. H. Erikson (Eds), *Themes of work and love in adulthood.* Cambridge, MA: Harvard University Press. 2

Pearlin, L. I. (1982). Discontinuities in the study of aging. In T. K. Hareven & K. J. Adams (Eds.), *Aging and life course transitions: An interdisciplinary perspective.* New York: Guilford Press. 2

Pederson, D. R., Moran, G., Sitko, C., Campbell, K., Ghesquire, K., & Acton, H. (1990). Maternal sensitivity and the security of infant-mother attachment: A Q-sort study. *Child Development, 61,* 1974–1983. 6

Pedersen, N. L., & Harris, J. R. (1990). Developmental behavioral genetics and successful aging. In P. B. Baltes & M. M. Baltes (Eds.), *Successful aging* (pp. 359–380). Cambridge, England: Cambridge University Press. 17

Pence, A. R. (Ed.) (1988). *Ecological research with children and families. From concepts to methodology.* New York: Teachers College Press. 1

Peplau, L. A. (1991). Lesbian and gay relationships. In J. C. Gonsiorek & J. D. Weinrich (Eds.), *Homosexuality. Research implications for public policy* (pp. 177–196). Newbury Park, CA: Sage. 14

Perlman, D., & Fehr, B. (1987). The development of intimate relationships. In D. Perlman & S. Duck (Eds.), *Intimate relationships. Development, dynamics, and deterioration.* Newbury Park, CA: Sage. 14

Perner, J. (1991). On representing that: The asymmetry between belief and desire in children's theory of mind. In D. Frye & C. Moore (Eds.), *Children's theories of mind: Mental states and social understanding* (pp. 139–156). Hillsdale, NJ: Erlbaum. 7

Perry, W. B. (1970). *Forms of intellectual and ethical development in the college years.* New York: Holt, Rinehart & Winston. 13

Perry-Jenkins, M., & Crouter, A. C. (1990). Men's provider-role attitudes. Implications for household work and marital satisfaction. *Journal of Family Issues, 11,* 136–156. 14

Peskin, H., & Livson, N. (1981). Uses of the past in adult psychological health. In D. H. Eichorn, J. A. Clausen, N. Haan, M. P. Honzik, & P. H. Mussen (Eds.), *Present and past in middle life.* New York: Academic Press. 16

Petersen, A. C. (1987). The nature of biological-psychosocial interactions: The sample case of early adolescence. In R. M. Lerner & T. T. Foch (Eds.), *Biological-phychosocial interactions in early adolescence.* (pp. 35–62). Hillsdale, NJ: Erlbaum. 11

Petersen, A. C., Sarigiani, P. A., & Kennedy, R. E. (1991). Adolescent depression: Why more girls? *Journal of Youth and Adolescence, 20,* 247–272. 12

Petersen, A. C., & Taylor, B. The biological approach to adolescence. (1980). In J. Adelson (Ed.), *Handbook of adolescent psychology* (pp. 117–158). New York: Wiley. 11

Peterson, C., Seligman, M. E. P., & Vaillant, G. E. (1988). Pessimistic explanatory style is a risk factor for physical illness: A thirty-five-year longitudinal study. *Journal of Personality and Social Psychology, 55,* 23–27. 13

Petitto, L. A. (1988). "Language" in the prelinguistic child. In F. S. Kessell (Ed.) *The development of language and language researchers: Essays in honor of Roger Brown* (pp. 187–222). 5

Pettingale, K. W., Morris, T., Greer, S., & Haybittle, J. L. (March 30, 1985). Mental attitudes to cancer: An additional prognostic factor. *Lancet, P.* 85. 19

Pettit, G. S., Bakshi, A., Dodge, K. A., & Coie, J. D. (1990). The emergence of social dominance in young boys' play groups: Developmental differences and behavioral correlates. *Developmental Psychology, 26,* 1017–1025. 8

Phillips, K., & Fulker, D. W. (1989). Quantitative genetic analysis of longitudinal trends in adoption designs with application to IQ in the Colorado Adoption Project. *Behavior Genetics, 19,* 621–658. 7

Phillips, S. K., Bruce, S. A., Newton, D., & Woledge, R. C. (1992). The weakness of old age is not due to failure of muscle activation. *Journal of Gerontology: MEDICAL SCIENCES, 47,* M45–49. 13

Phinney, J. S. (1990). Ethnic identity in adolescents and adults: Review of research. *Psychological Bulletin, 108,* 499–514. 12

Phinney, J. S., & Rosenthal, D. A. (1992). Ethnic identity in adolescence: Process, context, and outcome. In G. R. Adams, T. P. Gullotta & R. Montemayor (Eds.), *Adolescent identity formation* (pp. 145–172). Newbury Park, CA: Sage. 12

Piaget, J. (1932). *The moral judgment of the child.* New York: Macmillan. 11

Piaget, J. (1952). *The origins of intelligence in children.* New York: Basic Books. (Original work published 1936). 2, 5

Piaget, J. (1954). *The construction of reality in the child.* New York: Basic Books. (Original work published 1937). 5, 7

Piaget, J. (1970). Piaget's theory. In P. H. Mussen (Ed), *Carmichael's manual of child psychology* (Vol. 1) (3rd ed.) (pp. 703–732). New York: Wiley. 2

Piaget, J. (1977). *The development of thought. Equilibration of cognitive structures.* New York: The Viking Press. 2

Piaget, J., & Inhelder, B. (1959). *La genèse des structures logiques élémentaires: Classifications et sériations.* Neuchâtel: Delachaux et Niestlé. 2, 7

Piaget, J., & Inhelder, B. (1969). *The psychology of the child*. New York: Basic Books. 2

Pianta, R., Egeland, B., & Erickson, M. F. (1989). The antecedents of maltreatment: Results of the Mother-Child Interaction Research Project. In D. Cicchetti & V. Carlson (Eds.), *Child maltreatment* (pp. 203–253). Cambridge, England: Cambridge University Press. 6

Pinker, S. (1987). The bootstrapping problem in language acquisition. In B. MacWhinney (Ed.), *Mechanisms of language acquisition* (pp. 399–442). Hillsdale, NJ: Erlbaum. 7

Pitkin, R. M. (1977). Nutrition during pregnancy: The clinical approach. In M. Winick (Ed.), *Nutritional disorders of American women*. New York: Wiley. 3

Pleck, J. (1977). The work-family role system. *Social Problems, 24*, 417–427. 14

Pleck, J. H., Sonenstein, F. L., & Ku, L. C. (1990). Contraceptive attitudes and intention to use condoms in sexually experienced and inexperienced adolescent males. *Journal of Family Issues, 11*, 294–312. 12

Pleck, J. H., Sonenstein, F. L., & Ku, L. C. (1991). Adolescent males' condom use: Relationships between perceived cost-benefits and consistency. *Journal of Marriage and the Family, 53*, 733–745.

Plomin, R. (1989). Environment and genes: Determinants of behavior. *American Psychologist, 44*, 105–111. 7

Plomin, R., & DeFries, J. C. (1985a). A parent-offspring adoption study of cognitive abilities in early childhood. *Intelligence,9*, 341–356. 7

Plomin, R., & DeFries, J. C. (1985b). *Origins of individual differences in infancy. The Colorado Adoption Project*. Orlando, FL: Academic Press. 7

Plomin, R., Loehlin, J. C., & DeFries, J. C. (1985). Genetic and environmental components of "environmental" influences. *Developmental Psychology, 21*, 391–402. 7

Plomin, R., & McClearn, G. E. (1990). Human behavioral genetics of aging. In J. E. Birren & K. W. Schaie (Eds.), *Handbook of the psychology of aging* (3rd ed.) (pp. 67–79). San Diego, CA: Academic Press. 17

Plomin, R., Pedersen, N. L., McClearn, G. E., Nesselroade, J. R., & Bergeman, C. S. (1988). EAS temperaments during the last half of the life span: Twins reared apart and twins reared together. *Psychology and Aging, 3*, 43–50. 1, 6

Plomin, R., & Rende, R. (1991). Human behavioral genetics. *Annual Review of Psychology, 42*, 161–190. 1, 7

Plomin, R., Rende, R., & Rutter, M. (1991). Quantitative genetics and developmental psychopathology. In D. Cicchetti & S. L. Toth (Eds.), *Internalizing and externalizing expressions of dysfunction: Rochester symposium on developmental psychopathology* (pp. 155–202). Hillsdale, NJ: Erlbaum. 1

Plowman, S. A., Drinkwater, B. L., & Horvath, S. M. (1979). Age and aerobic power in women: A longitudinal study. *Journal of Gerontology, 34*, 512–520. 13

Plunkett, J. W., Klein, T., & Meisels, S. J. (1988). The relationship of preterm infant-mother attachment to stranger sociability at 3 years. *Infant Behavior and Development, 11*, 83–96. 6

Poehlman, E. T., Melby, C. O., & Badylak, S. F. (1991). Relation of age and physical exercise status on metabolic rate in younger and older healthy men. *Journal of Gerontology: BIOLOGICAL SCIENCES, 46*, B54–58. 17

Pollack, J. M. (1979–80). Correlates of death anxiety: A review of empirical studies. *Omega, 10*, 97–121. 19

Pollock, M. L., Foster, C., Knapp, D., Rod, J. L., & Schmidt, D. H. (1987). Effect of age and training on aerobic capacity and body composition of master athletes. *Journal of Applied Physiology, 62*, 725–731. 15

Poon, L. W., & Schaffer, G. (1982). Prospective memory in young and elderly adults. Paper presented at the Annual Meetings of the American Psychological Association, Washington, D. C. 17

Poulson, C. L., Nunes, L. R. D., & Warren, S. F. (1989). Imitation in infancy: A critical review. In H. W. Reese (Ed.), *Advances in child development and behavior* (Vol. 22) (pp. 272–298). San Diego, CA: Academic Press. 5

Power, C., & Peckham, C. (1990). Childhood morbidity and adulthood ill health. *Journal of Epidemiology and Community Health, 44*, 69–74. 7

Power, C., & Reimer, J. (1978). Moral atmosphere: An educational bridge between moral judgment and action. *New Directions for Child Development, 2*, 105–116. 11

Power, T. G., & Chapieski, M. L. (1986). Child rearing and impulse control in toddlers: A naturalistic investigation. *Developmental Psychology, 22*, 271–275. 8

Prechtl, H. F. R., & Beintema, D. J. (1964). The neurological examination of the full-term newborn infant. *Clinics in Developmental Medicine, 12*. London: Hinemann. 4

Price, R. A., Stunkard, A. J., Ness, R., Wadden, T., Heshka, S., Kanders, B., & Cormillot, A. (1990). Childhood onset (age <10) obesity has high familial risk. *International Journal of Obesity, 14*, 185–195. 9

Price, R. H. (1992). Psychosocial impact of job loss on individuals and families. *Current Directions in Psychological Science, 1*, 9–11. 16

Pulkkinen, L. (1982). Self-control and continuity in childhood delayed adolescence. In P. Baltes & O. Brim (Eds.), *Life span development and behavior* (Vol. 4) (pp. 64–107). New York: Academic Press. 8

Pye, C. (1986). Quiche Mayan speech to children. *Journal of Child Language, 13*, 85–100. 7

Pyle, R., Mitchell, J., Eckert, E., Halverson, P., Neuman, P., & Goff, G. (1983). The incidence of bulimia in freshman college students. *International Journal of Eating Disorders, 2*, 75–85. 11

Quinn, J. F. (1987). The economic status of the elderly: Beware of the mean. *The Review of Income and Wealth, 1*, 63–82. **Int7**

Quinn, J. F., & Burkhauser, R. V. (1990). Work and retirement. In R. H. Binstock & L. K. George (Eds.), *Handbook of aging and the social sciences* (3rd ed.) (pp. 307–327). San Diego: Academic Press. 18

Ramey, C. T., & Campbell, F. A. (1987). The Carolina Abecedarian Project. An educational experiment concerning human malleability. In J. J. Gallagher & C. T. Ramey (Eds.), *The malleability of children* (pp. 127–140). Baltimore: Paul H. Brookes. 6, 7

Ramey, C. T., & Haskins, R. (1981a). The modification of intelligence through early experience. *Intelligence, 5*, 5–19. 6, 7

Ramey, C. T., & Haskins, R. (1981b). Early education, intellectual development, and school performance: A reply to Arthur Jensen and J. McVicker Hunt. *Intelligence, 5*, 41–48. 6, 7

Ramey, C. T., Lee, M. W., & Burchinal, M. R. (1989). Developmental plasticity and predictability: Consequences of ecological change. In M. H. Bornstein & N. A. Krasnegor (Eds.), *Stability and continuity in mental development* (pp. 217–234). Hillsdale, NJ: Erlbaum. 6, 7

Ramey, C. T., Yeates, K. W., & Short, E. J. (1984). The plasticity of intellectual development: Insights from inventive intervention. *Child Development, 55*, 1913–1925. 6, 7

Raskind, M. A., & Peskind, E. R. (1992). Alzheimer's disease and other dementing disorders. In J. E. Birren, R. B. Sloane & G. D. Cohen, (Eds.), *Handbook of mental health and aging* (2nd ed.) (pp. 478–515). San Diego, CA: Academic Press. 17

Razel, M. (1985). A reanalysis of the evidence for the genetic nature of early motor development. In I. E. Sigel (Ed.), *Advances in applied developmental psychology* (Vol. 1) (pp. 171–212). Norwood, NJ: Ablex. 4

Rea, M. F. (1990). The Brazilian national breastfeeding program: A success story. *International Journal of Gynecology and Obstetrics, 31* (Suppl. 1), 79–82. **4**

Reedy, M. N., Birren, J. E., & Schaie, K. W. (1981). Age and sex differences in satisfying love relationships across the adult life span. *Human Development, 24,* 52–66. **16**

Regier, D. A., Boyd, J. H., Burke, J. D., Rae, D. S., Myers, J. K., Kramer, M., Robins, L. N., George, L. K., Karno, M., & Locke, B. Z. (1988). One-month prevalence of mental disorders in the United States. *Archives of General Psychiatry, 45,* 977–986. **13, 15, 17**

Reich, J. W., Zautra, A. J., & Guarnaccia, C. A. (1989). Effects of disability and bereavement on the mental health and recovery of older adults. *Psychology and Aging, 4,* 57–65. **19**

Reinke, B. J., Holmes, D. S., & Harris, R. L. (1985). The timing of psychosocial changes in women's lives: The years 25–45. *Journal of Personality and Social Psychology, 48,* 1353–1364. **2**

Reis, H. T. (1986). Gender effects in social participation: Intimacy, loneliness, and the conduct of social interaction. In R. Gilmour & S. Duck (Eds.), *The emerging field of personal relationships.* Hillsdale, NJ: Erlbaum. **14**

Reisman, J. M., & Shorr, S. I. (1978). Friendship claims and expectations among children and adults. *Child Development, 49,* 913–916. **10**

Remafedi, G. (1987a). Adolescent homosexuality: Psychosocial and medical implications. *Pediatrics, 79,* 331–337. **12**

Remafedi, G. (1987b). Male homosexuality: The adolescent's perspective. *Pediatrics, 79,* 326–330. **12**

Renouf, A. G., & Harter, S. (1990). Low self-worth and anger as components of the depressive experience in young adolescents. *Development and psychopathology, 2,* 293–310. **10**

Resnick, S. K. (March 8, 1992). Moving on. *New York Times Magazine,* pp. 22–24. **18**

Rest, J. R., (1983). Morality. In J. H. Flavell & E. M. Markman (Eds.), *Handbook of child psychology: Cognitive development* (Vol. 3) (pp. 556–629). New York: Wiley. (P. H. Mussen, General Editor). **11**

Rest, J. R., & Thoma, S. J. (1985). Relation of moral judgment development to formal education. *Developmental Psychology, 21,* 709–714. **11**

Rexroat, C., & Shehan, C. (1987). The family life cycle and spouses' time in housework. *Journal of Marriage and the Family, 49,* 737–750. **14**

Reynolds, C. R., & Brown, R. T. (Eds.) (1984). *Perspectives on bias in mental testing.* New York: Plenum. **9**

Rholes, W. S., & Ruble, D. N. (1984). Children's understanding of dispositional characteristics of others. *Child Development, 55,* 550–560. **10**

Ricciuti, H. N. (1981). Developmental consequences of malnutrition in early childhood. In M. A. Lewis & L. A. Rosenblum (Eds.), *The uncommon child* (pp. 151–172). New York: Plenum. **4**

Rice, M. L. (1989). Children's language acquisition. *American Psychologist, 44,* 149–156. **7**

Rice, M. L., Huston, A. C., Truglio, R., & Wright, J. (1990). Words from "Sesame Street": Learning vocabulary while viewing. *Developmental Psychology, 26,* 421–428. **10**

Richards, F. A., & Commons, M. L. (1990). Postformal cognitive-developmental theory and research: A review of its current status. In C. N. Alexander & E. J. Langer (Eds.), *Higher stages of human development. Perspectives on adult growth* (pp. 139–161). New York: Oxford University Press. **13**

Richardson, G., & Marx, E. (1989). *A welcome for every child. How France achieves quality in child care.* Report of the Child Care Study Panel of the French-American Foundation, New York. **6**

Richardson, G. S. (1990). Circadian rhythms and aging. In E. R. Scheider & J. W. Rowe (Eds.), *Handbook of the biology of aging,* 3rd ed. (pp. 275–305). San Diego, CA: Acdemic Press. **17**

Richardson, J. L., Zarnegar, Z., Bisno, B., & Levine, A. (1990). Psychosocial status at initiation of cancer treatment and survival. *Journal of Psychosomatic Research, 34,* 189–201. **19**

Ridenour, M. V. (1982). Infant walkers: Developmental tool or inherent danger. *Perceptual and Motor Skills, 55,* 1201–1202. **4**

Rierdan, J., & Koff, E. (1991). Depressive symptomatology among very early maturing girls. *Journal of Youth and Adolescence, 20,* 415–425. **11**

Rierdan, J., Koff, E., & Stubbs, M. L. (1989). Timing of menarche, preparation, and initial menstrual experience: Replication and further analysis in a prospective study. *Journal of Youth and Adolescence, 18,* 413–426. **11**

Rikli, R., & Busch, S. (1986). Motor performance of women as a function of age and physical activity level. *Journal of Gerontology, 41,* 645–649. **17**

Riley, M. W., Foner, A. (1968). *Aging and society.* Vol. 1. *An inventory of research findings.* New York: Russell Sage Foundation. **19**

Riley, M. W. (1976). Age strata in social systems. In R. H. Binstock & E. Shanas (Eds.), *Handbook of aging and the social sciences.* New York: Van Nostrand Reinhold. **1**

Riley, M. W. (1986). Overview and highlights of a sociological perspective. In A. B. Sorensen, F. E. Weinert & L. R. Sherrod (Eds.), *Human development and the life course: Multidisciplinary perspectives* (pp. 153–176). Hillsdale, NJ: Lawrence Erlbaum. **1**

Rindfuss, R. R. (1991). The young adult years: Diversity, structural change, and fertility. *Demography, 28,* 493–512. **Int5**

Rindfuss, R. R., Swicegood, C. G., & Rosenfeld, R. A. (1987). Disorder in the life course: How common and does it matter? *American Sociological Review, 52,* 785–801. **Post**

Roberto, K. A., & Scott, J. P. (1986). Equity considerations in the friendships of older adults. *Journal of Gerontology, 41,* 241–247. **18**

Roberts, C. W., Green, R., Williams, K., & Goodman, M. (1987). Boyhood gender identity development: A statistical contrast of two family groups. *Developmental Psychology, 23,* 544–557. **12**

Roberts, P., & Newton, P. M. (1987). Levinsonian studies of women's adult development. *Psychology and Aging, 2,* 154–163. **14**

Robins, L. N., & McEvoy, L. (1990). Conduct problems as predictors of substance abuse. In L. N. Robins & M. Rutter (Eds.), *Straight and devious pathways from childhood to adulthood* (pp. 182–204). Cambridge, England: Cambridge University Press. **12, Int4**

Robinson, N. M. (1978). Perinatal life for mother and baby. Common problems of the perinatal period. In D. W. Smith, E. L. Bierman, & N. M. Robinson (Eds.), *The biologic ages of man* (2nd ed.) (pp. 97–106). Philadelphia: Saunders. **4**

Rocca, W. A., Van Duijn, C. M., Clayton, D., Chandra, V. Fratiglioni, L., Graves, A. B., Heyman, A., Jorm, A. F., Kokmen, E., Kondo, K., Mortimer, J. A., Shalat, S. L., & Soininen, H. (1991). Maternal age and Alzheimer's disease: A collaborative re-analysis of case-control studies. *International Journal of Epidemiology, 20* (Suppl. 2), S21–27. **17**

Roche, A. F. (1981). The adipocyte-number hypothesis. *Child Development, 52,* 31–43. **9**

Rodin, J. (1986). Aging and health: Effects of the sense of control. *Science, 233,* 1271–1275. **13, 18**

Rodin, J. (1990). Control by any other name: Definitions, concepts, and processes. In J. Rodin, C. Schooler & K. W. Schaie (Eds.), *Self-directedness: Cause and effects throughout the life course* (pp. 1–17). Hillsdale, NJ: Erlbaum. **13**

Rodin, J., & Langer, E. J. (1977). Long-term effects of a control-relevant intervention with the institutionalized aged. *Journal of Personality and*

Social Psychology, 35, 897–902. **13**

Rodning, C., Beckwith, L., & Howard, J. (1991). Quality of attachment and home environments in children prenatally exposed to PCP and cocaine. *Development and Psychopathology, 3,* 351–366. **6**

Rogers, J. (1991, Fall). Nontraditional inheritance - I. Mechanisms Mendel never knew. *Mosaic, 22,* 3–11. **3**

Rogers, R. L., Meyer, J. S., & Mortel, K. F. (1990). After reaching retirement age physical activity sustains cerebral perfusion and cognition. *Journal of the American Geriatric Society, 38,* 123–128. **17**

Rogoff, B. (1981). Schooling and the development of cognitive skills. In H. C. Triandis & A. Heron (Eds.), *Handbook of cross-cultural psychology, Vol. 4, Developmental psychology* (pp. 233–294). Boston: Allyn and Bacon. **9**

Rohner, R. P., Kean, K. J., & Cournoyer, D. E. (1991). Effects of corporal punishment, perceived caretaker warmth, and cultural beliefs on the psychological adjustment of children in St. Kitts, West Indies. *Journal of Marriage and the Family, 53,* 681–693. **8**

Rollins, B. C., & Feldman, H. (1970). Marital satisfaction over the family life cycle. *Journal of Marriage and the Family, 32,* 20–27. **14**

Rollins, B. C., & Galligan, R. (1978). The developing child and marital satisfaction of parents. In R. M. Lerner & G. M. Spanier (Eds.), *Child influences on marital and family interaction. A life-span perspective* (pp. 71–106). New York: Academic Press. **Int4**

Rolls, B. J., Fedoroff, I. C., & Guthrie, J. F. (1991). Gender differences in eating behavior and body weight regulation. *Health Psychology, 20,* 133–142. **11**

Rooks, J. P., Weatherby, N. L., Ernst, E. K. M., Stapleton, S., Rosen, D., & Rosenfield, A. (1989). Outcomes of care in birth centers. The national birth center study. *The New England Journal of Medicine, 321,* 1804–1811. **3**

Roosa, M. W. (1984). Maternal age, social class, and the obstetric performance of teenagers. *Journal of Youth and Adolescence, 13,* 365–374. **3**

Rose, S. A., & Ruff, H. A. (1987). Cross-modal abilities in human infants. In J. D. Osofsky (Ed.), *Handbook of infant development* (2nd ed.) (pp. 318–362). New York: Wiley-Interscience. **5**

Rosenbaum, J. E. (1984). *Career mobility in a corporate hierarchy.* New York: Academic Press. **11, 14**

Rosenbaum, J. E. (1991). Are adolescent problems caused by school or society? *Journal of Research on Adolescence, 1,* 301–322. **11**

Rosenblith, J. F., & Sims-Knight, J. E. (1989). *In the beginning. Development in the first two years of life.* Newbury Park, CA: Sage. **3, 4**

Rosenman, R. H., & Friedman, M. (1983). Relationship of Type A behavior pattern to coronary heart disease. In H. Selye (Ed.), *Selye's guide to stress research* (Vol 2). New York: Scientific and Academic Editions. **15**

Rosenthal, C. J., (1985). Kinkeeping in the familial division of labor. *Journal of Marriage and the Family, 49,* 965–974. **14**

Rosenthal, C. J., Matthews, S. H., & Marshall, V. W. (1989). Is parent care normative? The experiences of a sample of middle-aged women. *Research on Aging, 11,* 244–260. **16**

Rosow, I. (1985). Status and role change through the life cycle. In R. H. Binstock & E. Shanas (Eds.), *Handbook of aging and the social sciences* (2nd ed.). New York: Van Nostrand Reinhold. **18**

Ross, G., Kagan, J., Zelazo, P., & Kotelchuck, M. (1975). Separation protest in infants in home and laboratory. *Developmental Psychology, 11,* 256–257. **6**

Ross, R. K., Paganini-Hill, A., Mack, T. M., & Henderson, B. E. (1987). Estrogen use and cardiovascular disease. In D. R. Mishell, Jr. (Ed.), *Menopause: Physiology and pharmacology* (pp. 209–224). Chicago: Year Book Medical Publishers. **15**

Rossi, A. S. (1989). A life-course approach to gender, aging, and inter-generational relations. In K. W. Schaie & C. Schooler (Eds.), *Social structure and aging: Psychological processes.* Hillsdale, NJ: Erlbaum. (pp. 207–236). **14**

Rossman, I. (1980). Bodily changes with aging. In E. W. Busse & D. G. Blazer (Eds.), *Handbook of geriatric psychiatry.* New York: Van Nostrand Reinhold. **13, 17**

Rothbart, M. K. (1986). Longitudinal observation of infant temperament. *Developmental Psychology, 22,* 356–365. **6**

Rothbart, M. K. (1989a). Temperament in childhood: A framework. In G. A. Kohnstamm, J. E. Bates & M. K. Rothbart (Eds.), *Temperament in childhood* (pp. 59–75). Chichester, England: Wiley. **6**

Rothbart, M. K. (1989b). Biological processes in temperament. In G. A. Kohnstamm, J. E. Bates & M. K. Rothbart (Eds.), *Temperament in childhood* (pp. 77–110). Chichester, England: Wiley. **6**

Rotheram-Borus, M. J., Rosario, M., & Koopman, C. (1991). Minority youths at high risk: Gay males and runaways. In M. E. Colten & S. Gore (Eds.), *Adolescent stress. Causes and consequences* (pp. 181–200). New York: Aldine de Gruyter. **12**

Rotter, J. B. (1966). Generalized expectancies for internal versus external control of reinforcement. *Psychological Monographs, 80* (1, Whole No. 609). **13**

Rovee-Collier, C. (1986). The rise and fall of infant classical conditioning research: Its promise for the study of early development. In L. P. Lipsitt & C. Rovee-Collier (Eds.), *Advances in infancy research* (Vol. 4) (pp. 139–162). Norwood, NJ: Ablex. **5**

Rovet, J., & Netley, C. (1983). The triple X chromosome syndrome in childhood: Recent empirical findings. *Child Development, 54,* 831–845. **3**

Rowe, I., & Marcia, J. E. (1980). Ego identity status, formal operations, and moral development. *Journal of Youth and Adolescence, 9,* 87–99. **Int4**

Rowe, J. W., Wang, S. Y., & Elahi, D. (1990). Design, conduct, and analysis of human aging research. In E. R. Schneider & J. W. Rowe (Eds.), *Handbook of the biology of aging* (3rd ed.) (pp. 63–71). San Diego, CA: Academic Press. **1**

Rubin, K. H., Fein, G. G., & Vandenberg, B. (1983). Play. In E. M. Hetherington (Ed.), *Handbook of child psychology: Socialization, personality, and social development* (Vol. 4) (pp. 693–774). New York: Wiley. (Paul H. Mussen, General Editor) **7**

Rubin, K. H., Mymel, S., Mills, R. S. L., & Rose-Rasnor, L. (1991). Conceptualizing different developmental pathways to and from social isolation in childhood. In D. Cicchetti & S. L. Toth (Eds.) *Internalizing and externalizing expressions of dysfunction: Rochester symposium on developmental psychopathology* (Vol. 2) (pp. 91–122). Hillsdale, NJ: Erlbaum. **10**

Rubinstein, R. L. (1986). *Singular paths: Old men living alone.* New York: Columbia University Press. **18**

Rubinstein, R. L., Alexander, B. B., Goodman, M., & Luborsky, M. (1991). Key relationships of never married childless older women: A cultural analysis. *Journal of Gerontology: SOCIAL SCIENCES, 46,* S270–277. **18**

Ruble, D. N. (1987). The acquisition of self-knowledge: A self-socialization perspective. In N. Eisenberg (Ed.), *Contemporary topics in developmental psychology* (pp. 243–270). New York: Wiley-Interscience. **8, 10**

Ruble, D. N., Balaban, T., & Cooper, J. (1981). Gender constancy and the effects of sex-typed televised toy commercials. *Child Development, 52,* 667–673. **8**

Ruopp, R., & Travers, J. (1982). Janus faces day care: Perspectives on quality and cost. In E. F. Zigler & E. W. Gordon (Eds.), *Day care: Scientific and social policy issues* (pp. 72–101). Boston: Auburn House. **6**

Russell, G. (1982). Shared-caregiving families: An Australian study. In M. E. Lamb (Ed.), *Nontraditional families* (pp. 139–172). Hillsdale, NJ: Erlbaum. **6**

Rutter, M. (1975). *Helping troubled children.* New York: Plenum. **8**

Rutter, M. (1978). Early sources of security and competence. In J. S. Bruner & A. Garton (Eds.), *Human growth and development.* London: Oxford University Press. **6**

Rutter, M. (1983). School effects on pupil progress: Research findings and policy implications. *Child Development, 54,* 1–29. **9**

Rutter, M. (1987). Continuities and discontinuities from infancy. In J. D. Osofsky (Ed.), *Handbook of infant development* (2nd ed.) (pp. 1256–1296). New York: Wiley-Interscience. **1**

Rutter, M. (1990). Commentary: Some focus and process considerations regarding effects of parental depression on children. *Developmental Psychology, 26,* 60–67. **6**

Rutter, M., Tizard, J., & Whitmore, K. (1970/1981). *Education, health and behaviour.* Huntington, NY: Krieger. (Originally published 1970). **12**

Ryan, A. S., Rush, D., Krieger, F. W., & Lewandowski, G. E. (1991). Recent declines in breast-feeding in the United States, 1984 through 1989. *Pediatrics, 88,* 719–727. **4**

Ryan, E. G. (1992). Beliefs about memory changes across the adult life span. *Journal of Gerontology: PSYCHOLOGICAL SCIENCES, 47,* P41–46. **15**

Ryff, C. (1982). Self-perceived personality change in adulthood and aging. *Journal of Personality and Social Psychology, 42,* 108–115. **16**

Ryff, C., & Baltes, P. B. (1976). Value transition and adult development in women: The instrumentality-terminality sequence hypothesis. *Developmental Psychology, 12,* 567–568. **16**

Sack, W. H., Mason, R., & Higgins, J. E. (1985). The single parent family and abusive child punishment. *American Journal of Orthopsychiatry, 55,* 252–259. **6**

Sagi, A. (1990). Attachment theory and research from a cross-cultural perspective. *Human Development, 33,* 10–22. **6**

Sagi, A., van IJzendoorn, M. H., & Koren-Karie, N. (1991). Primary appraisal of the strange situation: A cross-cultural analysis of preseparation episodes. *Developmental Psychology, 27,* 587–596. **6**

Saigal, S., Szatmari, P., Rosenbaum, P., Campbell, D., & King, S. (1991). Cognitive abilities and school performance of extremely low birth weight children and matched term control children at age 8 years: A regional study. *Journal of Pediatrics, 118,* 751–760. **3**

Salthouse, T. A. (1991). *Theoretical perspectives on cognitive aging.* Hillsdale, NJ: Erlbaum. **13, 15**

Salthouse, T. A., & Babcock, R. L. (1991). Decomposing adult age differences in working memory. *Developmental Psychology, 27,* 763–776. **17**

Sameroff, A. J., & Cavanaugh, P. J. (1979). Learning in infancy: A developmental perspective. In J. D. Osofsky (Ed.), *Handbook of infant development* (pp. 344–392). New York: Wiley. **5**

Sammartino, F. J. (1987). The effect of health on retirement. *Social Security Bulletin, 50(2),* 31–47. **18**

Sanders, B., Soares, M. P., & D'Aquila, J. M. (1982). The sex difference on one test of spatial visualization: A nontrivial difference. *Child Development, 53,* 1106–1110. **7**

Sanders, C. M. (1989). *Grief. The mourning after.* New York: Wiley-Interscience. **19**

Sands, L. P., & Meredith, W. (1992). Blood pressure and intellectual functioning in late midlife. *Journal of Gerontology: PSYCHOLOGICAL SCIENCES, 47,* P81–84. **15**

Sarason, B. R., Pierce, G. R., & Sarason, I. G. (1990). Social support: The sense of acceptance and the role of relationships. In B. R. Sarason, I. G. Sarason & G. R. Pierce, *Social support: An interactional view* (pp. 97–128). New York: Wiley. **13**

Sarason, B. R., Sarason, I. G., & Pierce, G. R. (1990). Traditional views of social support and their impact on assessment. In B. R. Sarason, I. G. Sarason & G. R. Pierce, *Social support: An interactional view.* (pp. 9–25). New York: Wiley. **13**

Saunders, C. (1977). Dying they live: St. Christopher's Hospice. In H. Feifel (Ed.), *New meanings of death.* New York: McGraw-Hill. **19**

Saunders, W. L., & Shepardson, D. (1987). A comparison of concrete and formal science instruction upon science achievement and reasoning ability of sixth grade students. *Journal of Research in Science Teaching, 24,* 39–51. **9**

Saxe, G. B. (1988). The mathematics of child street vendors. *Child Development, 59,* 1415–1425. **9**

Scarr, S. (1992). Developmental theories for the 1990s: Development and individual differences. *Child Development, 63,* 1–19. **1**

Scarr, S., & Kidd, K. K. (1983). Developmental behavior genetics. In M. M. Haith & J. J. Campos (Eds.), *Handbook of child psychology: Infancy and developmental psychobiology* (Vol. 2) (pp. 345–434). New York: Wiley. (P. H. Mussen, General Editor) **3, 6, 7**

Scarr, S., Phillips, D., & McCartney, K. (1990). Facts, fantasies and the future of child care in the United States. *Psychological Science, 1,* 26–35. **6**

Scarr, S., & Weinberg, R. A. (1983). The Minnesota adoption studies: Genetic differences and malleability. *Child Development, 54,* 260–267. **1, 7**

Schaefer, E. S. (1989). Dimensions of mother-infant interaction: Measurement, stability, and predictive validity. *Infant Behavior and Development, 12,* 379–393. **8**

Schaefli, A., Rest, J. R., & Thoma, S. J. (1985). Does moral education improve moral judgment? A meta-analysis of intervention studies using the Defining Issues Test. *Review of Educational Research, 55,* 319–352. **11**

Schafer, R. B., & Keith, P. M. (1984). A causal analysis of the relationship between the self-concept and marital quality. *Journal of Marriage and the Family, 46,* 909–914. **14**

Schaffer, H. R. (1990). *Making decisions about children. Psychological questions and answers.* Oxford, England: Basil Blackwell. **6, 8**

Schaie, K. W. (1983a). What can we learn from the longitudinal study of adult psychological development? In K. W. Schaie (Ed.), *Longitudinal studies of adult psychological development.* New York: Guilford Press. **1**

Schaie, K. W. (1983b). The Seattle longitudinal study: A 21-year exploration of psychometric intelligence in adulthood. In K. W. Schaie (Ed.), *Longitudinal studies of adult psychological development.* New York: Guilford Press. **13, 15, 17**

Schaie, K. W. (1989). Individual differences in rate of cognitive change in adulthood. In V. L. Bengtson & K. W. Schaie (Eds.), *The course of later life. Research and reflections.* New York: Springer (pp. 65–86). **13, 17**

Schaie, K. W. (1990). Intellectual development in adulthood. In J. E. Birren & K. W. Schaie (Eds.), *Handbook of the psychology of aging* (3rd ed.) San Diego, CA: Academic Press. **13**

Schaie, K. W., & Hertzog, C. (1983). Fourteen-year cohort-sequential analyses of adult intellectual development. *Developmental Psychology, 19,* 531–543. **13**

Schaie, K. W., & Willis, S. L. (1991). Adult personality and psychomotor performance: Cross-sectional and longitudinal analyses. *Journal of Gerontology: PSYCHOLOGICAL SCIENCES, 46,* P275–284. **16, 17**

Scheibel, A. B. (1992). Structural changes in the aging brain. In J. E. Birren, R. B. Sloane, & G. D. Cohen, (Eds.), *Handbook of mental health and aging* (2nd ed.) (pp. 147–174). San Diego, CA: Academic Press. **17**

Schieber, F. (1992). Aging and the senses. In J. E. Birren, R. B. Sloane, & G. D. Cohen, (Eds.), *Handbook of mental health and aging* (2nd ed.) (pp. 252–306). San Diego, CA: Academic Press. **17**

Schleifer, S. J., Keller, S. E., Camerino, M., Thornton, J. C., & Stein, M. (1983). Suppression of lymphocyte stimulation following bereavement. *Journal of the American Medical Association, 250*, 374–377. **13**

Schneider, E. L., & Rowe, J. W. (Eds.) (1990). *Handbook of the biology of aging* (3rd ed.) San Diego, CA: Academic Press. **13**

Schneider, W., & Bjorklund, D. F. (1992). Expertise, aptitude, and strategic remembering. *Child Development, 63*, 461–473. **9**

Schneider, W., & Pressley, M. (1989). *Memory development between 2 and 20.* New York: Springer-Verlag. **9**

Schoen, R., & Wooldredge, J. (1989). Marriage choices in North Carolina and Virginia, 1969–71 and 1979–81. *Journal of Marriage and the Family, 51*, 465–481. **14**

Schonfeld, I. S., Shaffer, D., O'Connor, P., & Portny, S. (1988). Conduct disorder and cognitive functioning: Testing three causal hypotheses. *Child Development, 59*, 993–1007. **12**

Schramm, W. F., Barnes, D. E., & Bakewell, J. M. (1987). Neonatal mortality in Missouri home births, 1978–84. *American Journal of Public Health, 77*, 930–935. **3**

Schulenberg, J., Goldstein, A. E., & Vondracek, F. W. (1991). Gender differences in adolescents' career interests: Beyond main effects. *Journal of Research in Adolescence, 1*, 37–61. **14**

Schultz, N. R. Jr., Elias, M. F., Robbins, M. A., Streeten, D. H. P., & Blakeman, N. (1986). A longitudinal comparison of hypertensives and normotensives on the Wechsler Adult Intelligence Scale: Initial findings. *Journal of Gerontology, 41*, 169–175. **15**

Schulz, J. H. (1988). *The economics of aging* (4th ed.). Dover, MA: Auburn House Publishing Co. **18**

Schulz, R., & Curnow, C. (1988). Peak performance and age among superathletes: Track and field, swimming, baseball, tennis, and golf. *Journal of Gerontology: PSYCHOLOGICAL SCIENCES, 43*, 113–120. **13**

Schulz, R., Visintainer, P., & Williamson, G. M. (1990). Psychiatric and physical morbidity effects of caregiving. *Journal of Gerontology: PSYCHOLOGICAL SCIENCES, 45*, 181–191. **16**

Schulz, R., & Williamson, G. M. (1991). A 2-year longitudinal study of depression among Alzheimer's caregivers. *Psychology and Aging, 6*, 569–578. **16**

Scollon, R. (1976). *Conversations with a one-year-old.* Honolulu: University of Hawaii Press. **5**

Sears, R. R. (1977). Sources of life satisfactions of the Terman gifted men. *American Psychologist, 32* 119–128. **Int5**

Seccombe, K. (1987). Children. Their impact on the elderly in declining health. *Research on Aging, 9*, 312–326. **18**

Seidman, D. S., Ever-Hadani, P., & Gale, R. (1989). The effect of maternal weight gain in pregnancy on birth weight. *Obstetrics and Gynecology, 74*, 240–246. **3**

Seitz, V. (1988). Methodology. In M. H. Bornstein & M. E. Lamb (Eds.), *Developmental psychology: An advanced textbook* (2nd ed.) (pp. 51–84). Hillsdale, NJ: Erlbaum. **1**

Seligman, M. E. P. (1991). *Learned optimism.* New York: Alfred Knopf. **13**

Selman, R. L. (1980). *The growth of interpersonal understanding.* New York: Academic Press. **10, 12**

Selmanowitz, V. J., Rizer, R. L., & Orentreich, N. (1977). Aging of the skin and its appendages. In C. E. Finch & L. Hayflick (Eds.), *Handbook of the biology of aging.* New York: Van Nostrand Reinhold. **13**

Sepkoski, C. (1987). *A longitudinal study of the effects of obstetric medication.* Paper presented at the biennial meetings of the Society for Research in Child Development, Baltimore. **3**

Serbin, L., Moskowitz, D. S., Schwartzman, A. E., & Ledingham, J. E. (1991). Aggressive, withdrawn, and aggressive/withdrawn children in adolescence: Into the next generation. In D. J. Pepler & K. H. Rubin (Eds.), *The development and treatment of childhood aggression* (pp. 55–70). Hillsdale, NJ: Erlbaum. **10**

Shaffer, D., Garland, A., Gould, M., Fisher, P., & Trautman, P. (1988). Preventing teenage suicide: A critical review. *Journal of the American Academy of Child and Adolescent Psychiatry, 27*, 675–687. **12**

Shantz, C. U. (1983). Social cognition. In J. H. Flavell & E. M. Markman (Eds.), *Handbook of child psychology*, Vol. III, *Cognitive development* (pp. 495–555). New York: Wiley. (P. H. Mussen, Series Editor) **12**

Shantz, D. W. (1986). Conflict, aggression, and peer status: An observational study. *Child Development, 57*, 1322–1332. **10**

Shapiro, E. (1983). Impending death and the use of hospitals by the elderly. *Journal of the American Geriatric Society, 31*, 348–351. **19**

Shapiro, G. L., & Farrow, D. L. (1988). Mentors and others in career development. In S. Rose & L. Larwood (Eds.), *Women's careers. Pathways and pitfalls.* New York: Praeger. **14**

Shelton, B. A. (1990). The distribution of household tasks. Does wife's employment status make a difference? *Journal of Family Issues, 11*, 115–135. **14**

Sherrod, K. B., O'Connor, S., Vietze, P. M., & Altemeier, W. A. III. (1984). Child health and maltreatment. *Child Development, 55*, 1174–1183. **6**

Shiono, P. H., Klebanoff, M. A., & Rhoads, G. G. (1986). Smoking and drinking during pregnancy. Their effects on preterm birth. *Journal of the American Medical Association, 225*, 82–84. **3**

Shipley, M. J., Pocock, S. J., & Marmot, M. G. (1991). Does plasma cholesterol concentration predict mortality from coronary heart disease in elderly people? 18 year follow up in Whitehall study. *British Medical Journal, 303*, 89–92. **15**

Shneidman, E. S. (1980). *Voices of death.* New York: Harper & Row. **19**

Shneidman, E. S. (1983). *Deaths of man.* New York: Jason Aronson. **19**

Shneidman, E. S. (1989). The Indian summer of life. A preliminary study of septuagenarians. *American Psychologist, 44*, 684–694. **Int7**

Shock, N. W. (1985). Longitudinal studies of aging in humans. In C. E. Finch & E. L. Schneider (Eds.), *Handbook of the biology of aging* (2nd ed.). New York: Van Nostrand Reinhold. **13**

Shonkoff, J. P. (1984). The biological substrate and physical health in middle childhood. In W. A. Collins (Ed.), *Development during middle childhood. The years from six to twelve* (pp. 24–69). Washington, DC: National Academy Press. **9, 11**

Shore, C. (1986). Combinatorial play, conceptual development, and early multiword speech. *Developmental Psychology, 22*, 184–190. **7**

Shweder, R. A., Mahapatra, M., & Miller, J. G. (1987). Culture and moral development. In J. Kagan & S. Lamb (Eds.), *The emergence of morality in young children* (pp. 1–82). Chicago: The University of Chicago Press. **11**

Siebert, J. M., Hogan, A. E., & Mundy, P. C. (1986). On the specifically cognitive nature of early object and social skill domain associations. *Merrill-Palmer Quarterly, 32*, 21–36. **9**

Siegel, L. J., & Griffin, N. J. (1984). Correlates of depressive symptoms in adolescents. *Journal of Youth and Adolescence, 13*, 475–487. **12**

Siegler, I. C. (1983). Psychological aspects of the Duke Longitudinal Studies. In K. W. Schaie (Ed.), *Longitudinal studies of adult psychological development* (pp. 136–190). New York: Guilford Press. **1**

Siegler, I. C., & Lewis, M. A. (1984). Long-term care of the elderly. In D. Blazer & I. C. Siegler (Eds.), *A family approach to health care of the elderly.* Menlo Park, CA: Addison-Wesley. **18**

Siegler, I. C., McCarty, S. M., & Logue, P. E. (1982). Wechsler memory scale scores, selective attrition, and distance from death. *Journal of Gerontology, 37,* 176–181. **17**

Siegler, R. S. (1976). Three aspects of cognitive development. *Cognitive Psychology, 8,* 431–520. **9**

Siegler, R. S. (1978). The origins of scientific reasoning. In R. S. Siegler (Ed.). *Children's thinking: What develops?* (pp. 109–150). Hillsdale, NJ: Erlbaum. **9**

Siegler, R. S. (1981). Developmental sequences within and between concepts. *Monographs of the Society for Research in Child Development, 46,* (2, Serial No. 189). **2, 9**

Siegler, R. S. (1984). Mechanisms of cognitive growth: Variation and selection. In R. J. Sternberg (Ed.), *Mechanisms of cognitive development* (pp. 141–162). New York: W. H. Freeman. **2**

Siegler, R. S. (1986). Unities across domains in children's strategy choices. In M. Perlmutter (Ed.), *Perspectives on intellectual development. The Minnesota symposia on child psychology,* Vol. 19 (pp. 1–48). Hillsdale, NJ: Erlbaum. **5**

Siegler, R. S. (1988). Individual differences in strategy choices: Good students, not-so-good students, and perfectionists. *Child Development, 59,* 833–851. **2**

Siegler, R. S., & Jenkins, E. (1989). *How children discover new strategies.* Hillsdale, NJ: Erlbaum. **2**

Siegler, R. S., & Richards, D. D. (1982). The development of intelligence. In R. J. Sternberg (Ed.), *Handbook of human intelligence* (pp. 897–974). Cambridge: Cambridge University Press. **5**

Sigman, M., Cohen, S. E., Beckwith, L., Asarnow, R., & Parmelee, A. H. (1991). Continuity in cognitive abilities from infancy to 12 years of age. *Cognitive Development, 6,* 47–57. **5**

Sigman, M., Neumann, C., Carter, E., Cattle, D. J., D'Souza, S., & Bwibo, N. (1988). Home interactions and the development of Embu toddlers in Kenya. *Child Development, 59,* 1251–1261. **7**

Signorielli, N. (1986). Selective television viewing: A limited possibility. *Journal of Communication, 36* (No. 3), 64–81. **10**

Silver, R. L., & Wortman, C. B. (1980). Coping with undesirable life events. In J. Garber & M. E. P. Seligman (Eds.), *Human helplessness: Theory and applications.* New York: Academic Press. **19**

Silverstein, L. B. (1991). Transforming the debate about child care and maternal employment. *American Psychologist, 46,* 1025–1032. **6**

Simmons, R. G., Blyth, D. A., & McKinney, K. L. (1983). The social and psychological effects of puberty on white females. In J. Brooks-Gunn & A. C. Petersen (Eds.), *Girls at puberty. Biological and psychosocial perspectives* (pp. 229–272). New York: Plenum. **11**

Simmons, R. G., Burgeson, R., & Reef, M. J. (1988). Cumulative change at entry to adolescence. In M. R. Gunnar & W. A. Collins (Eds.), *Development during the transition to adolescence. Minnesota Symposia on Child Psychology,* Vol. 21 (pp. 123–150). Hillsdale, NJ: Erlbaum. **Int4**

Simons, R. L., Robertson, J. F., & Downs, W. R. (1989). The nature of the association between parental rejection and delinquent behavior. *Journal of Youth and Adolescence, 18,* 297–309. **8**

Simonton, D. K. (1988). Age and outstanding achievement: What do we know after a century of research? *Psychological Bulletin, 104,* 251–267. **15**

Simonton, D. K. (1989). The swan-song phenomenon: Last-works effects for 172 classical composers. *Psychology and Aging, 4,* 42–47. **15**

Simonton, D. K. (1991). Career landmarks in science: Individual differences and interdisciplinary contrasts. *Developmental Psychology, 27,* 119–130. **15**

Simpson, J. A. (1990). Influence of attachment styles on romantic relationships. *Journal of Personality and Social Psychology, 59,* 971–980. **14**

Simpson, J. A., Rholes, W. S., & Nelligan, J. S. (1992). Support seeking and support giving within couples in an anxiety-provoking situation: The role of attachment styles. *Journal of Personality and Social Psychology, 62,* 434–446. **14**

Sinnott, J. D. (1986). Prospective/intentional and incidental every day memory: Effects of age and passage of time. *Psychology and Aging, 1,* 110–116. **17**

Sirignano, S. W., & Lachman, M. E. (1985). Personality change during the transition to parenthood: The role of perceived infant temperament. *Developmental Psychology, 21,* 558–567. **14**

Skinner, B. F. (1957). *Verbal behavior.* New York: Prentice-Hall. **7**

Slaby, R. G., & Frey, K. S. (1975). Development of gender constancy and selective attention to same-sex models. *Child Development, 46,* 849–856. **8**

Slater, A. M., & Bremner, J. G. (Eds.), (1989). *Infant development.* Hillsdale, NJ: Erlbaum. **4**

Slobin, D. I. (1985a). Introduction: Why study acquisition crosslinguistically? In D. I. Slobin (Ed.), *The crosslinguistic study of language acquisition. Vol. 1: The data* (pp. 3–24). Hillsdale, NJ: Erlbaum. **1, 7**

Slobin, D. I. (1985b). Crosslinguistic evidence for the language-making capacity. In D. I. Slobin (Ed.), *The crosslinguistic study of language acquisition. Vol. 2: Theoretical issues* (pp. 1157–1256). Hillsdale, NJ: Erlbaum. **7**

Smeeding, T. M. (1990). Economic status of the elderly. In R. H. Binstock & L. K. George (Eds.), *Handbook of aging and the social sciences* (3rd ed.) (pp. 362–381). San Diego, CA: Academic Press. **18**

Smelser, N. J., & Erikson, E. H. (1980). *Themes of work and love in adulthood.* Cambridge, MA: Harvard University Press. **2**

Smetana, J. G. (1990). Morality and conduct disorders. In M. Lewis & S. M. Miller (Eds.), *Handbook of developmental psychopathology.* (pp. 157–180). New York: Plenum. **11**

Smetana, J. G., Killen, M., & Turiel, E. (1991). Children's reasoning about interpersonal and moral conflicts. *Child Development, 62,* 629–644. **11**

Smith, A. N., & Spence, C. M. (1981). National day care study: Optimizing the day care environment. *American Journal of Orthopsychiatry, 50,* 718–721. **6**

Smith, D. W., & Stenchever, M. A. (1978). Prenatal life and the pregnant woman. In D. W. Smith, E. L. Bierman & N. M. Robinson (Eds.), *The biologic ages of man* (2nd ed.) (pp. 42–77). Philadelphia: W. B. Saunders. **4**

Smith, E. L. (1982). Exercise for prevention of osteoporosis: A review. *Physician and Sportsmedicine, 10,* 72–83. **15**

Smoll, F. L., & Schutz, R. W. (1990). Quantifying gender differences in physical performance: A developmental perspective. *Developmental Psychology, 26,* 360–369. **11**

Snarey, J., Son, L., Kuehne, V. S., Hauser, S., & Vaillant, G. (1987). The role of parenting in men's psychosocial development: A longitudinal study of early adulthood infertility and midlife generativity. *Developmental Psychology, 23,* 593–603. **14, Int5**

Snarey, J. R. (1985). Cross-cultural universality of social-moral development: A critical review of Kohlbergian research. *Psychological Bulletin, 97,* 202–232. **11**

Snarey, J. R., Reimer, J., & Kohlberg, L. (1985). Development of social-moral reasoning among kibbutz adolescents: A longitudinal cross-sectional study. *Developmental Psychology, 21,* 3–17. **11**

Snow, M. E., Jacklin, C. N., & Maccoby, E. E. (1983). Sex-of-child differences in father-child interaction at one year of age. *Child Development, 54,* 227–232. **10**

Snowdon, D. A., Kane, R. L., Beeson, L., Burke, G. L., Sprafka, J. M., Potter, J., Iso, H., Jacobs, D. R. Jr., & Phillips, R. L. (1989). Is early natural menopause a biologic marker of health and aging? *American Journal of Public Health, 79*, 709–714. **17**

Snyder, L. (1978). Communicative and cognitive abilities and disabilities in the sensorimotor period. *Merrill-Palmer Quarterly, 24*, 161–180. **7**

Soldo, B. J., Wolf, D. A., & Agree, E. M. (1990). Family, households, and care arrangements of frail older women: A structural analysis. *Journal of Gerontology: SOCIAL SCIENCES, 45*, S238–249. **18**

Sonenstein, F. L., Pleck, J. H., & Ku, L. C. (1989). Sexual activity, condom use and AIDS awareness among adolescent males. *Family Planning Perspectives, 21*, 152–158. **12**

Sorel, J. E., Ragland, D. R., & Syme, S. L. (1991). Blood pressure in Mexican Americans, whites, and blacks. *American Journal of Epidemiology, 134*, 370–378. **15**

Sörensen, A. (1983). Women's employment patterns after marriage. *Journal of Marriage and the Family, 45*, 311–321. **14**

Sosa, R., Kennell, J. H., Klaus, M. H., Robertson, S., & Urrutia, J. (1980). The effect of a supportive companion on perinatal problems, length of labor and mother-infant interaction. *New England Journal of Medicine, 303*, 597–600. **3, 14**

South, S. J. (1991). Sociodemographic differentials in mate selection preferences. *Journal of Marriage and the Family, 53*, 928–940. **14**

Spanier, G. B., & Furstenberg, F. F., Fr. (1987). Remarriage and reconstituted families. In M. B. Sussman & S. K. Steinmetc (Eds.), *Handbook of marriage and the family* (pp. 419–434). New York: Plenum Press. **16**

Speece, M. W., & Brent, S. B. (1984). Children's understanding of death: A review of three components of a death concept. *Child Development, 55*, 1671–1686. **19**

Spelke, E. S. (1979). Exploring audible and visible events in infancy. In A. D. Pick (Ed.), *Perception and its development: A tribute to Eleanor J. Gibson* (pp. 221–236). Hillsdale, NJ: Erlbaum. **5**

Spelke, E. S. (1991). Physical knowledge in infancy: Reflections on Piaget's theory. In S. Carey & R. Gelman (Eds.) *The epigenesis of mind. Essays on biology and cognition* (pp. 133–169). Hillsdale, NJ: Erlbaum. **5**

Spelke, E. S., & Owsley, C. J. (1979). Intermodal exploration and knowledge in infancy. *Infant Behavior and Development, 2*, 13–27. **5**

Spence, J. T., & Helmreich, R. L. (1978). *Masculinity and femininity.* Austin, TX: University of Texas Press. **12**

Spencer, M. B., & Dornbusch, S. M. (1990). Challenges in studying minority youth. In S. S. Feldman & G. R. Elliott (Eds.), *At the threshold. The developing adolescent* (pp. 123–146). Cambridge, MA: Harvard University Press. **12**

Spenner, K. I. (1988). Occupations, work settings and the course of adult development: Tracing the implications of select historical changes. In P. B. Baltes, D. L. Featherman, & R. M. Lerner (Eds.), *Life-span development and behavior*, Vol. 9 (pp. 244–288). Hillsdale, NJ: Erlbaum. **14**

Spiegel, D., Bloom, J. R., Kraemer, H. C., & Gottheil, E. (October 14, 1989). Effect of psychosocial treatment on survival of patients with metastatic breast cancer. *The Lancet*, 888–891. **19**

Spieker, S. J., & Booth, C. L. (1988). Maternal antecedents of attachment quality. In J. Belsky &. T. Nezworski (Eds.), *Clinical implications of attachment* (pp. 95–135). Hillsdale, NJ: Erlbaum. **6**

Spitze, G. (1988). Women's employment and family relations: A review. *Journal of Marriage and the Family, 50*, 595–618. **14**

Spitze, G., & Logan, J. (1990). More evidence on women (and men) in the middle. *Research on Aging, 12*, 182–198. **16**

Sprey, J., & Matthews, S. H. (1982). Contemporary grandparenthood. A systematic transition. *Annals of the American Academy of Political Science, 464*, 91–103. **16**

Sroufe, L. A. (1988). The role of infant-caregiver attachment in development. In J. Belsky & T. Nezworski (Ed.), *Clinical implications of attachment* (18–40). Hillsdale, NJ: Erlbaum. **6**

Sroufe, L. A. (1989). Pathways to adaptation and maladaption: Psychopathology as developmental deviation. In D. Cicchetti, D. (Ed.), *The emergence of a discipline: Rochester symposium on developmental psychopathology* (Vol. 1) (pp. 13–40). Hillsdale, NJ: Erlbaum. **1, 6, Int4**

Sroufe, L. A. (1990). A developmental perspective on day care. In N. Fox & G. G. Fein (Eds.), *Infant day care: The current debate* (pp. 51–60). Norwood, NJ: Ablex. **6**

Sroufe, L. A., Egeland, B., & Kreutzer, T. (1990). The fate of early experience following developmental change: Longitudinal approaches to individual adaptation in childhood. *Child Development, 61*, 1363–1373. **1**

Sroufe, L. A., & Fleeson, J. (1986). Attachment and the construction of relationships. In W. W. Hartup & Z. Rubin (Eds.), *Relationships and development* (pp. 51–72). Hillsdale, NJ: Erlbaum. **6**

Sroufe, L. A., & Waters, E. (1977). Attachment as an organizational construct. *Child Development, 48*, 1184–1199. **6**

Stack, S. (1989). The impact of divorce on suicide in Norway, 1951–1980. *Journal of Marriage and the Family, 51*, 229–238. **16**

Stadel, B. V., & Weiss, N. S. (1975). Characteristics of menopausal women: A survey of King and Pierce Counties in Washington, 1973–74. *American Journal of Epidemiology, 102* (Sept), 209–216. **15**

Stambrook, M., & Parker, K. C. H. (1987). The development of the concept of death in childhood: A review of the literature. *Merrill-Palmer Quarterly, 33*, 133–158. **19**

Stanford, E. P., Happersett, C. J., Morton, D. J., Molgaard, C. A., & Peddecord, K. M. (1991). Early retirement and functional impairment from a multiethnic perspective. *Research on Aging, 13*, 5–38. **18**

Stanford, P., & Du Bois, B. C. (1992). Gender and ethnicity patterns. In J. E. Birren, R. B. Sloane & G. D. Cohen, (Eds.), *Handbook of mental health and aging* (2nd ed.) (pp. 99–119). San Diego, CA: Academic Press. **17**

Starfield, B. (1991). Childhood morbidity: Comparisons, clusters, and trends. *Pediatrics, 88*, 519–526. **4, 7**

Starfield, B., & Pless, I. B. (1980). Physical health. In O. G. Brim, Jr. & J. Kagan. *Constancy and change in human development* (pp. 272–324). Cambridge, MA: Harvard University Press. **7**

Stattin, H., & Klackenberg-Larsson, I. (1990). The relationship between maternal attributes in the early life of the child and the child's future criminal behavior. *Development and Psychopathology, 2*, 99–111. **8**

Staudinger, U. M., Smith, J., & Baltes, P. B. (1992). Wisdom-related knowledge in a life review task: Age differences and the role of professional specialization. *Psychology and Aging, 7*, 271–281. **17**

Stegner, W. (1976). *The spectator bird.* New York: Penguin Books. **Int7**

Stein, Z., Susser, M., Saenger, G., & Morolla, F. (1975). *Famine and human development: The Dutch hunger winter of 1944–1945.* New York: Oxford University Press. **3**

Steinberg, L. (1986). Latchkey children and susceptibility to peer pressure: An ecological analysis. *Developmental Psychology, 22*, 433–439. **10**

Steinberg, L. (1988). Reciprocal relation between parent-child distance and pubertal maturation. *Developmental Psychology, 24*, 122–128. **12**

Steinberg, L. (1990). Interdependence in the family: Autonomy, conflict and harmony in the parent-adolescent relationship. In S. S. Feldman & G. R. Elliott (Eds.), *At the threshold: The developing adolescent.* Cambridge, MA: Harvard University Press. **12**

Steinberg, L., & Dornbusch, S. M. (1991). Negative correlates of part-time employment during adolescence: Replication and elaboration. *Developmental Psychology, 27*, 304–313. **12**

Steinberg, L., Elmen, J. D., & Mounts, N. S. (1989). Authoritative parenting, psychosocial maturity, and academic success among adolescents. *Child Development, 60*, 1424–1436. **8**

Steinberg, L., & Levine, A. (1990). *You and your adolescent. A parent's guide for ages 10 to 20.* New York: Harper & Row. **11**

Steinberg, L., Mounts, N. S., Lamborn, S. D., & Dornbusch, S. D. (1991). Authoritative parenting and adolescent adjustment across varied ecological niches. *Journal of Research on Adolescence, 1*, 19–36. **8, 11**

Steinberg, L. D., & Silverberg, S. (1986). The vicissitudes of autonomy in early adolescence. *Child Development, 57*, 841–851. **12**

Stenchever, M. A. (1978). Labor and delivery. In D. W. Smith, E. L. Bierman, & N. M. Robinson (Eds.), *The biologic ages of man* (2nd ed.) (pp. 78–86). Philadelphia: W. B. Saunders. **3**

Sternberg, R. J. (1979). The nature of mental abilities. *American Psychologist, 34*, 214–230. **5**

Sternberg, R. J. (1985). *Beyond IQ: A triarchic theory of human intelligence.* New York: Cambridge University Press. **5, 7**

Sternberg, R. J. (1986). *Intelligence applied.* New York: Harcourt Brace Jovanovich. **7**

Sternberg, R. J. (1990a). Wisdom and its relations to intelligence and creativity. In R. J. Sternberg (Ed.), *Wisdom. Its nature, origins, and development* (pp. 142–159). Cambridge, England: Cambridge University Press. **17**

Sternberg, R. J. (Ed.) (1990b). *Wisdom. Its nature, origins, and development.* Cambridge, England: Cambridge University Press. **17**

Sternberg, R. J. (1991). Death, taxes, and bad intelligence tests. *Intelligence, 15*, 257–269. **7**

Stevenson, H. W., & Chen, C. (1989). Schooling and achievement: A study of Peruvian children. *International Journal of Educational Research, 13*, 883–894. **9**

Stevenson, H. W., Chen, C., Lee, S., & Fuligni, A. J. (1991). Schooling, culture, and cognitive development. In L. Okagaki & R. J. Sternberg (Eds.), *Directors of development* (pp. 243–268). Hillsdale, NJ: Erlbaum. **1, 9, 11**

Stevenson, H. W., & Lee, S. (1990). Contexts of achievement: A study of American, Chinese, and Japanese children. *Monographs of the Society for Research in Child Development, 55*, (1–2, Serial No. 221). **7**

Stevenson, H. W., Lee, S., Chen, C., Lummis, M., Stigler, J., Fan, L., & Ge, F. (1990). Mathematics achievement of children in China and the United States. *Child Development, 61*, 1053–1066. **7**

Stewart, J. F., Popkin, B. M., Guilkey, D. K., Akin, J. S., Adair, L., & Flieger, W. (1991). Influences on the extent of breast-feeding: A prospective study in the Philippines. *Demography, 28*, 181–199. **4**

Stigler, J. W., Lee, S., & Stevenson, H. W. (1987). Mathematics classrooms in Japan, Taiwan, and the United States. *Child Development, 58*, 1272–1285. **7**

Stigler, J. W., & Stevenson, H. W. (Spring, 1991). How Asian teachers polish each lesson to perfection. *American Educator*, pp. 12–20, 43–47. **9**

Stinner, W. F., Byun, Y., & Paita, L. (1990). Disability and living arrangements among elderly American men. *Research on Aging, 12*, 339–363. **18**

Stoller, E. P. (1990). Males as helpers: The role of sons, relatives, and friends. *The Gerontologist, 30*, 228–235. **16**

Stoller, E. P., Forster, L. E., & Duniho, T. S. (1992). Systems of parent care within sibling networks. *Research on Aging, 14*, 28–49. **16**

St. Peters, M., Fitch, M., Huston, A. C., Wright, J. C., & Eakins, D. J. (1991). Television and families: What do young children watch with their parents? *Child Development, 62*, 1409–1423. **10**

Strayer, F. F. (1980). Social ecology of the preschool peer group. In

A. Collins (Ed.), *Minnesota symposia on child psychology* (Vol. 13) (pp. 165–196). Hillsdale, NJ: Erlbaum. **8**

Streissguth, A. P., Aase, J. M., Clarren, S. K., Randels, S. P., LaDue, R. A., & Smith, D. F. (1991b). Fetal alcohol syndrome in adolescents and adults. *Journal of the American Medical Association, 265*, 1961–1967. **3**

Streissguth, A. P., Barr, H. M., Martin, D. C., & Herman, C. S. (1980a). Effects of maternal alcohol, nicotine, and caffeine use during pregnancy on infant mental and motor development at eight months. *Alcoholism: Clinical and Experimental Research, 4*, 152–164. **3**

Streissguth, A. P., Barr, H. M., & Sampson, P. D. (1990). Moderate prenatal alcohol exposure: Effects on child IQ and learning problems at age 7½ years. *Alcoholism: Clinical and Experimental Research, 14*, 662–669. **3**

Streissguth, A. P., Barr, H. M., Sampson, P. D., Darby, B. L., & Martin, D. C. (1989). IQ at age 4 in relation to maternal alcohol use and smoking during pregnancy. *Developmental Psychology, 25*, 3–11. **3**

Streissguth, A. P., Carmichael-Olson, H., Sampson, P. D., & Barr, H. M. (1991a). Alcohol vs. tobacco as prenatal correlates of child behavior: Follow-up to 11 years. Paper presented at the biennial meetings of the Society for Research in Child Development, Seattle, 1991. **3**

Streissguth, A. P., Landesman-Dwyer, S., Martin, J. C., & Smith, D. W. (1980b). Teratogenic effects of alcohol in humans and laboratory animals. *Science, 209*, 353–361. **3**

Streissguth, A. P., Martin, D. C., Barr, H. M., Sandman, B. M., Kirchner, G. L., & Darby, B. L. (1984). Intrauterine alcohol and nicotine exposure: Attention and reaction time in 4-year-old children. *Developmental Psychology, 20*, 533–541. **3, 4**

Streissguth, A. P., Martin, D. C., Martin, J. C., & Barr, H. M. (1981). The Seattle longitudinal prospective study on alcohol and pregnancy. *Neurobehavioral Toxicology and Teratology, 3*, 223–233. **3**

Streufert, S., Pogash, R., Piasecki, M., & Post, G. M. (1990). Age and management team performance. *Psychology and Aging, 5*, 551–559. **15**

Striegel-Moore, R. H., Silberstein, L. R., & Rodin, J. (1986). Toward an understanding of risk factors for bulimia. *American Psychologist, 41*, 246–263. **11**

Strobino, D. M. (1987). The health and medical consequences of adolescent sexuality and pregnancy: A review of the literature. In S. L. Hofferth & C. D. Hayes (Eds.), *Risking the future. Adolescent sexuality, pregnancy, and childbearing. Working papers* (pp. 93–122). Washington, DC: National Academy Press. **3**

Stroebe, W., & Stroebe, M. S. (1986). Beyond marriage: The impact of partner loss on health. In R. Gilmour & S. Duck (Eds.), *The emerging field of personal relations.* Hillsdale, NJ: Erlbaum. **2, 19**

Stueve, C. A., & Gerson, K. (1977). Personal relations across the lifecycle. In C. S. Fischer (Ed.), *Networks and places: Social relations in the urban setting* (pp. 78–98). New York: Free Press. **16**

Stull, D. E., & Hatch, L. R. (1984). Unravelling the effects of multiple life changes. *Research on Aging, 6*, 560–571. **18**

Stunkard, A. J., Sorensen, T. I. A., Hanis, C., Teasdale, T. W., Chakraborty, R, Schull, W. J., & Schulsinger, F. (1986). An adoption study of human obesity. *New England Journal of Medicine, 314*, 193–198. **9**

Stunkard, A. J., Harris, J. R., Pedersen, N. L., & McClearn, G. E. (1990). The body-mass index of twins who have been reared apart. *New England Journal of Medicine, 322*, 1483–1487. **9**

Sue, S., & Okazaki, S. (1990). Asian-American educational achievement: A phenomenon in search of an explanation. *American Psychologist, 45*, 913–920. **7**

Sugar, J. A., & McDowd, J. M. (1992). Memory, learning, and attention. In J. E. Birren, R. B. Sloane & G. D. Cohen, (Eds.), *Handbook of mental health and aging* (2nd ed.) (pp. 307–339). San Diego, CA: Academic Press. **17**

Swedo, S. E., Rettew, D. C., Kuppenheimer, M., Lum, D., Dolan, S., & Goldberger, E. (1991). Can adolescent suicide attempters be distinguished from at-risk adolescents? *Pediatrics, 88*, 620–629. **12**

Swensen, C. H., Eskew, R. W., & Kohlhepp, K. A. (1981). Stage of family life cycle, ego development, and the marriage relationship. *Journal of Marriage and the Family, 43*, 841–853. **16**

Syme, S. L. (1990). Control and health: An epidemiological perspective. In J. Rodin, C. Schooler & K. W. Schaie (Eds.) *Self-directedness. Cause and effects throughout the life course.* (pp. 213–229). Hillsdale, NJ: Erlbaum. **13**

Taffel, S. M., Placek, P. J., & Liss, T. (1987). Trends in the United States cesarean section rate and reasons for the 1980–85 rise. *American Journal of Public Health, 77*, 955–959. **3**

Tait, M., Padgett, M. Y., & Baldwin, T. T. (1989). Job and life satisfaction: A reevaluation of the strength of the relationship and gender effects as a function of the date of the study. *Journal of Applied Psychology, 74*, 502–507. **14**

Takahashi, K. (1986). Examining the strange-situation procedure with Japanese mothers and 12-month-old infants. *Developmental Psychology, 22*, 265–270. **6**

Talbott, M. M. (1990). The negative side of the relationship between older widows and their adult children: The mother's perspective. *The Gerontologist, 30*, 595–603. **18**

Tamir, L. M. (1982). *Men in their forties. The transition to middle age.* New York: Springer. **14, 15, 16**

Tamir, L. M. (1989). Modern myths about men at midlife: An assessment. In S. Hunter & M. Sundel (Eds.), *Midlife myths. Issues, findings, and practice implications.* Newbury Park, CA: Sage. **15**

Tanner, J. M. (1962). *Growth at adolescence* (2nd ed.). Oxford: Blackwell Scientific Publications. **11**

Tanner, J. M. (1970). Physical growth. In P. H. Mussen (Ed.), *Carmichael's manual of child psychology* (Vol. 1, 3rd ed.) (pp. 77–156). New York: Wiley. **Int4**

Tanner, J. M. (1978). *Fetus into man. Physical growth from conception to maturity.* Cambridge, MA: Harvard University Press. **3, 4, 11**

Tanner, J. M., Hughes, P. C. R., & Whitehouse, R. H. (1981). Radiographically determined widths of bone, muscle and fat in the upper arm and calf from 3–18 years. *Annals of Human Biology, 8*, 495–517. **11**

Taylor, M., & Hort, B. (1990). Can children be trained in making the distinction between appearance and reality? *Cognitive Development, 5*, 89–99. **7**

Taylor, R. J. (1986). Receipt of support from family among black Americans: Demographic and familial differences. *Journal of Marriage and the Family, 48*, 67–77. **14**

Taylor, R. J., & Chatters, L. M. (1991). Extended family networks of older black adults. *Journal of Gerontology: SOCIAL SCIENCES, 46*, S210–217. **1**

Taylor, R. J., Chatters, L. M., Tucker, M. B., & Lewis, E. (1990). Developments in research on black families: A decade review. *Journal of Marriage and the Family, 52*, 993–1014. **14, 16**

Tellegen, A., Lykken, D. T., Bouchard, T. J., Wilcox, K. J., Segal, N. L., & Rich, S. (1988). Personality similarity in twins reared apart and together. *Journal of Personality and Social Psychology, 54*, 1031–1039. **6**

Temoshok, L. (1987). Personality, coping style, emotion and cancer: Towards an integrative model. *Cancer Surveys, 6*, 545–567. **19**

Terman, L. (1916). *The measurement of intelligence.* Boston: Houghton Mifflin. **7**

Terman, L., & Merrill, M. A. (1937). *Measuring intelligence: A guide to the administration of the new revised Stanford-Binet tests.* Boston: Houghton Mifflin. **7**

Teti, D. M., & Ablard, K. E. (1989). Security of attachment and infant-sibling relationships: A laboratory study. *Child Development, 60*, 1519–1528. **6**

Teti, D. M., Gelfand, D. M., & Pompa, J. (1990). Depressed mothers' behavioral competence with their infants: Demographic and psychosocial correlates. *Development and Psychopathology, 2*, 259–270. **6**

Teti, D. M., Lamb, M. E., & Elster, A. B. (1987). Long-range socioeconomic and marital consequences of adolescent marriage in three cohorts of adult males. *Journal of Marriage and the Family, 49*, 499–506. **12**

Tew, M. (1985). Place of birth and perinatal mortality. *Journal of the Royal College of General Practitioners, 35*, 390–394. **3**

Thelen, E. (1981). Rhythmical behavior in infancy: An ethological perspective. *Developmental Psychology, 17*, 237–257. **4**

Thelen, E. (1989). The (re)discovery of motor development: Learning new things from an old field. *Developmental Psychology, 25*, 946–949. **4**

Thelen, E., & Ulrich, B. D. (1991). Hidden skills: A dynamic systems analysis of treadmill stepping during the first year. *Monographs of the Society for Research in Child Development, 56* (1, Serial No. 223). **4**

Thomas, A., & Chess, S. (1977). *Temperament and development.* New York: Brunner/Mazel. **6**

Thomas, R. M. (Ed.) (1990). *The encyclopedia of human development and education. Theory, research, and studies.* Oxford: Pergamon Press. **2, 4, 7**

Thompson, L., & Walker, A. J. (1984). Mothers and daughters: aid patterns and attachment. *Journal of Marriage and the Family, 46*, 313–322. **18**

Thompson, R. A. (1990). The effects of infant day care through the prism of attachment theory: A critical appraisal. In N. Fox & G. G. Fein (Eds.) *Infant day care: The current debate* (pp. 41–50). Norwood, NJ: Ablex. **6**

Thompson, R. A., & Lamb, M. E. (1982). Stranger sociality and its relationship to temperament and social experience during the second year. *Infant Behavior and Development, 5*, 277–287. **6**

Thompson, R. A., Lamb, M. E., & Estes, D. (1982). Stability of infant-mother attachment and its relationship to changing life circumstances in an unselected middle-class sample. *Child Development, 53*, 144–148. **6**

Thompson, R. A., Lamb, M. E., & Estes, D. (1983). Harmonizing discordant notes: A reply to Waters. *Child Development, 54*, 521–524. **6**

Thompson, S. K. (1975). Gender labels and early sex role development. *Child Development, 46*, 339–347. **8**

Thorne, B. (1986). Girls and boys together . . . but mostly apart: Gender arrangements in elementary schools. In W. W. Hartup & Z. Rubin (Eds.), *Relationships and development* (pp. 167–184). Hillsdale, NJ: Erlbaum. **10**

Thornton, A. (1990). The courtship process and adolescent sexuality. *Journal of Family Issues, 11*, 239–273. **12**

Tice, R. R., & Setlow, R. B. (1985). DNA repair and replication in aging organisms and cells. In C. E. Finch & E. L. Schneider (Eds.), *Handbook of the biology of aging* (2nd ed.). New York: Van Nostrand Reinhold. **17**

Timmer, S. G., Eccles, J., & O'Brien, K. (1985). How children use time. In F. T. Juster & F. P. Stafford (Eds.), *Time, goods, and well being* (pp. 353–369). Ann Arbor: Institute for Social Research, The University of Michigan. **10**

Tobin-Richards, M. H., Boxer, A. M., & Petersen, A. C. (1983). The psychological significance of pubertal change: Sex differences in perceptions of self during early adolescence. In J. Brooks-Gunn and A. C. Petersen (Eds.), *Girls at puberty. Biological and psychosocial perspectives* (pp. 127–154). New York: Plenum. **11**

Tomlinson-Keasey, C., Eisert, D. C., Kahle, L. R., Hardy-Brown, K., & Keasey, B. (1978). The structure of concrete operational thought. *Child Development, 50,* 1153–1163. **9**

Trehub, S. E., Bull, D., & Thorpe, L. A. (1984). Infants' perception of melodies: The role of melodic contour. *Child Development, 55,* 821–830. **5**

Trehub, S. E., & Rabinovitch, M. S. (1972). Auditory-linguistic sensitivity in early infancy. *Developmental Psychology, 6,* 74–77. **5**

Trehub, S. E., Thorpe, L. A., & Morrongiello, B. A. (1985). Infants' perception of melodies: Changes in a single tone. *Infant Behavior and Development, 8,* 213–223. **5**

Tremblay, R. E. (1991). Commentary. Aggression, prosocial behavior, and gender: Three magic words, but no magic wand. In D. J. Pepler & K. H. Rubin (Eds.), *The development and treatment of aggression* (pp. 71–78). Hillsdale, NJ: Erlbaum. **10**

Troll, L. E. (1985). The contingencies of grandparenting. In V. L. Bengtson & J. F. Robertson (Eds.) *Grandparenthood* (pp. 135–150). Beverly Hills, CA: Sage. **16**

Trussell, J., & Rao, K. V. (1989). Premarital cohabitation and marital stability: A reassessment of the Canadian evidence. *Journal of Marriage and the Family, 51,* 535–539. **14**

Tsuya, N. O., & Martin, L. G. (1992). Living arrangements of elderly Japanese and attitudes toward inheritance. *Journal of Gerontology: SOCIAL SCIENCES, 47,* S45–54. **18**

Tunmer, W. E., Herriman, M. L., & Nesdale, A. R. (1988). Metalinguistic abilities and beginning reading. *Reading Research Quarterly, 23,* 134–158. **9**

Tunstall-Pedoe, H., & Smith, W. C. S. (1990). Cholesterol as a risk factor for coronary heart disease. *British Medical Bulletin, 46,* 1075–1087. **15**

Turiel, E. (1966). An experimental test of the sequentiality of developmental stages in the child's moral judgment. *Journal of Personality and Social Psychology, 3,* 611–618. **11**

Uhlenberg, P., & Chew, K. S. (1986). The changing place of remarriage in the life course. In D. L. Kertzer (Ed.), *Current perspectives on aging and the life cycle* (Vol. 2, pp. 23–52). Greenwich, CT: JAI Press. **Post**

Uhlenberg, P., Cooney, T., & Boyd, R. (1990). Divorce for women after midlife. *Journal of Gerontology: SOCIAL SCIENCES, 45,* S3–11. **16**

Umberson, D., & Gove, W. R. (1989). Parenthood and psychological well-being. Theory, measurement, and stage in the family life course. *Journal of Family Issues, 10,* 440–462. **14**

Ungerer, J. A., & Sigman, M. (1984). The relation of play and sensorimotor behavior to language in the second year. *Child Development, 55,* 1448–1455. **7**

U.S. Bureau of the Census (1984). *Statistical Abstract of the United States: 1985.* (105th ed.) Washington, DC: U.S. Government Printing Office. **14, 16**

U.S. Bureau of the Census (1989a). Current Population Reports, Series P-23, No. 162, *Studies in Marriage and the Family.* Washington, DC: U.S. Government Printing Office. **18**

U.S. Bureau of the Census (1989b). *Statistical Abstract of the United States: 1989* (109th edition). Washington, DC: U.S. Government Printing Office. **19**

U.S. Bureau of the Census (1990). *Statistical abstract of the United States 1990* (110th ed.). Washington, DC: U.S. Government Printing Office. **3, 6, 7, 10, 12, 13, 14, 15, 17, 18**

U.S. Bureau of the Census (1991). *Statistical abstract of the United States 1991* (111th ed.). Washington, DC: U.S. Government Printing Office. **3**

Urberg, K. A., & Labouvie-Vief, G. (1976). Conceptualizations of sex roles: A life-span developmental study. *Developmental Psychology, 12,* 15–23. **12**

Uzgiris, I. C. (1973). Patterns of cognitive development in infancy. *Merrill-Palmer Quarterly, 19,* 21–40. **9**

Vaillant, G. E. (1975). Natural history of male psychological health. III. Empirical dimensions of mental health. *Archives of General Psychiatry, 32,* 420–426. **16**

Vaillant, G. E. (1977). *Adaptation to life: How the best and brightest came of age.* Boston: Little, Brown. **1, 2, 16**

Vaillant, G. E. (1990). Avoiding negative life outcomes: Evidence from a forty-five year study. In P. B. Baltes & M. M. Baltes (Eds.), *Successful aging* (pp. 332–358). Cambridge, England: Cambridge University Press. **Int6, 17**

Vaillant, G. E. (1991). The association of ancestral longevity with successful aging. *Journal of Gerontology: PSYCHOLOGICAL SCIENCES, 46,* P292–298. **17**

Vaillant, G. E., & Vaillant, C. O. (1990). Natural history of male psychological health, XII: A 45-year study of predictors of successful aging at age 65. *American Journal of Psychiatry, 147,* 31–37. **16, Int6**

Van de Perre, Simonon, A., Msellati, P., Hitimani, D., Vaira, D., Bazebagira, A., Van Goethem, C., Stevens, A., Karita, E., Sondag-Thull, D., Dabis, F., & Lepage, P. (1991). Postnatal transmission of human immunodeficiency virus type 1 from mother to infant. *New England Journal of Medicine, 325,* 593–598. **3**

Van Duijn, C. M., Stijnen, T., & Hofman, A. (1991). Risk factors for Alzheimer's disease: Overview of the EURODEM collaborative re-analysis of case-control studies. *International Journal of Epidemiology, 2* (Suppl. 2), S4–12. **17**

van IJzendoorn, M. H., & Kroonenberg, P. M. (1988). Cross-cultural patterns of attachment: A meta-analysis of the Strange Situation. *Child Development, 59,* 147–156. **6**

Van Kammen, W. B., Loeber, R., & Stouthamer-Loeber, M. (1991). Substance use and its relationship to conduct problems and delinquency in young boys. *Journal of Youth and Adolescence, 20,* 399–413. **12**

Van Velsor, E., & O'Rand, A. M. (1984). Family life cycle, work career patterns, and women's wages at midlife. *Journal of Marriage and the Family, 46,* 365–373. **14**

Vasudev, J. (1983). *A study of moral reasoning at different life stages in India.* Unpublished manuscript, University of Pittsburgh, PA. **11**

Vaughn, B. E., Egeland, B., Sroufe, L. A., & Waters, E. (1979). Individual differences in infant-mother attachment at twelve and eighteen months: Stability and change in families under stress. *Child Development, 50,* 971–975. **6**

Vega, W. A. (1990). Hispanic families in the 1980s: A decade of research. *Journal of Marriage and the Family, 52,* 1015–1024. **14**

Verbrugge, L. M. (1984). A health profile of older women with comparisons to older men. *Research on Aging, 6,* 291–322. **15, 17**

Verbrugge, L. M. (1985). An epidemiological profile of older women. In M. R. Haug, A. B. Ford & M. Sheafor, (Eds.), *The physical and mental health of aged women.* New York: Springer. **15, 17**

Verbrugge, L. M. (1989). Gender, aging, and health. In K. S. Markides (Ed.), *Aging and health.* Newbury Park, CA: Sage. **15, 17**

Verbrugge, L. M., Lepkowski, J. M., & Konkol, L. L. (1991). Levels of disability among U.S. adults with arthritis. *Journal of Gerontology: SOCIAL SCIENCES, 46,* S71–83. **17**

Verbrugge, L. M., & Wingard, D. L. (1987). Sex differentials in health and mortality. *Women and Health, 12*, 103–145. **15**

Verhaeghen, P., Marcoen, A., & Goossens, L. (1992). Improving memory performance in the aged through mnemonic training: A meta-analytic study. *Psychology and Aging, 7*, 242–251. **17**

Vernon, P. A. (Ed.), (1987). *Speed of information-processing and intelligence*. Norwood, NJ: Ablex. **9**

Veroff, J., Douvan, E., & Kulka, R. A. (1981). *The inner American. A self-portrait from 1957 to 1976*. New York: Basic Books. **16**

Victorian Infant Collaborative Study Group (1991). Eight-year outcome in infants with birth weight of 500–999 grams: Continuing regional study of 1979 and 1980 births. *Journal of Pediatrics, 118*, 761–767. **3**

Vihko, R., & Apter, D. (1980). The role of androgens in adolescent cycles. *Journal of Steroid Biochemistry, 12*, 369–373. **11**

Vinovskis, M. (1988). *An "epidemic" of adolescent pregnancy? Some historical and policy considerations*. New York: Oxford University Press. **12**

Vorhees, C. F., & Mollnow, E. (1987). Behavioral teratogenesis: Long-term influences on behavior from early exposure to environmental agents. In J. D. Osofsky (Ed.), *Handbook of infant development* (2nd ed.) (pp. 913–971). New York: Wiley-Interscience. **3**

Vuchinich, S., Hetherington, E. M., Vuchinich, R. A., & Clingempeel, W. G. (1991). Parent-child interaction and gender differences in early adolescents' adaptation to step families. *Developmental Psychology, 27*, 618–626. **12**

Vygotsky, L. S. (1962). *Thought and language*. New York: Wiley. **2, 7**

Wahlström, J. (1990). Gene map of mental retardation. *Journal of Mental Deficiency Research, 34*, 11–27. **3**

Walaskay, M., Whitbourne, S. K., & Nehrke, M. F. (1983–84). Construction and validation of an ego integrity status interview. *International Journal of Aging and Human Development, 18*, 61–72. **18**

Wald, E. R., Guerra, N., & Byers, C. (1991). Frequency and severity of infections in day care: Three-year follow-up. *Journal of Pediatrics, 118*, 509–514. **4**

Wald, N. J., Cuckle, H. S., Densem, J. W., Nanchahal, K., Royston, P, Chard, T., Haddow, J. E., Knight, G. J., Palomaki, G. E., & Canick, J. A. (1988). *British Medical Journal, 297*, 883–887. **3**

Walden, T. A. (1991). Infant social referencing. In J. Garber & K. A. Dodge (Eds.), *The development of emotion regulation and dysregulation* (pp. 69–88). Cambridge, England: Cambridge University Press. **5**

Waldrop, M. F., & Halverson, C. F. (1975). Intensive and extensive peer behavior: Longitudinal and cross-sectional analysis. *Child Development, 46*, 19–26. **10**

Walker, A. (1990). Poverty and inequality in old age. In J. Bond & P. Coleman (eds.), *Aging in Society* (pp. 229–249). London: Sage Publications. **18**

Walker, A. J., & Thompson, L. (1983). Intimacy and intergenerational aid and contact among mothers and daughters. *Journal of Marriage and the Family, 45*, 841–849. **18**

Walker, L. J. (1980). Cognitive and perspective-taking prerequisites for moral development. *Child Development, 51*, 131–139. **Int4**

Walker, L. J. (1989). A longitudinal study of moral reasoning. *Child Development, 60*, 157–160. **11**

Walker, L. J., de Vries, B., & Trevethan, S. D. (1987). Moral stages and moral orientations in real-life and hypothetical dilemmas. *Child Development, 58*, 842–858. **11**

Walker-Andrews, A. S., & Lennon, E. (1991). Infants' discrimination of vocal expressions: Contributions of auditory and visual information. *Infant Behavior and Development, 14*, 131–142. **5**

Wallerstein, J. (Jan 22, 1989). Children after divorce. Wounds that don't heal. *The New York Times Magazine*, 19–21, 41–44. **8**

Wallerstein, J. S. (1984). Children of divorce: Preliminary report of a ten-year follow-up of young children. *American Journal of Orthopsychiatry, 54*, 444–458. **8**

Wallerstein, J. S. (1986). Women after divorce: Preliminary report from a ten-year-follow-up. *American Journal of Orthopsychiatry, 56*, 65–77. **16**

Walls, C. T., & Zarit, S. H. (1991). Informal support from black churches and the well-being of elderly blacks. *The Gerontologist, 31*, 490–495. **18**

Walsh, W. B., Horton, J. A., & Gaffey, R. L. (1977). Holland's theory and college degreed working men and women. *Journal of Vocational Behavior, 10*, 180–186. **14**

Ward, S. L., & Overton, W. F. (1990). Semantic familiarity, relevance, and the development of deductive reasoning. *Developmental Psychology, 26*, 488–493. **11**

Warr, P., Jackson, P., & Banks, M. (1988). Unemployment and mental health: Some British studies. *Journal of Social Issues, 44*, 47–68. **16**

Waterman, A. S. (1985). Identity in the context of adolescent psychology. *New Directions for Child Development, 30*, 5–24. **12**

Waters, E. (1978). The reliability and stability of individual differences in infant-mother attachment. *Child Development, 59*, 483–494. **6**

Watkins, S. C., Menken, J. A., & Bongaarts, J. (1987). Demographic foundations of family change. *American Sociological Review, 52*, 346–358. **16**

Watson, J. D., & Crick, F. H. C. (1953). Molecular structure of nucleic acid. A structure for deoxyribose nucleic acid. *Nature, 171*, 737–738. **3**

Waxman, M. A., & Stunkard, A. J. (1981). Caloric intake and expenditure in obese boys. *Journal of Pediatrics, 96*, 187–193. **9**

Waxman, S., & Gelman, R. (1986). Preschoolers' use of superordinate relations in classification and language. *Cognitive Development, 1*, 139–156. **7**

Waxman, S. R., & Kosowski, T. D. (1990). Nouns mark category relations: Toddlers' and preschoolers' word-learning biases. *Child Development, 61*, 1461–1473. **7**

Webster-Stratton, C. (1988). Mothers' and fathers' perceptions of child deviance: Roles of parent and child adjustment and child deviance. *Journal of Consulting and Clinical Psychology, 56*, 909–915. **Int2**

Wechsler, D. (1974). *Manual for the Wechsler Intelligence Scale for Children, Revised*. New York: Psychological Corp. **7**

Weg, R. B. (1983). The physiological perspective. In R. B. Weg (Ed.), *Sexuality in the later years. Roles and behavior*. New York: Academic Press. **15**

Weg, R. B. (1987a). Demography. In D. R. Mischel Jr. (Ed.), *Menopause: Physiology and pharmacology* (pp. 23–40). Chicago: Year Book Medical Publishers. **15**

Weg, R. B. (1987b). Sexuality in the menopause. In D. R. Mischel Jr. (Ed.), *Menopause: Physiology and pharmacology* (pp. 127–138). Chicago: Year Book Medical Publishers. **15**

Wegman, M. E. (1991). Annual summary of vital statistics—1990. *Pediatrics, 88*, 1081–1092. **3, 4**

Weinberg, R. A. (1989). Intelligence and IQ: Landmark issues and great debates. *American Psychologist, 44*, 98–104. **7**

Weinberg, R. A., Scarr, S., & Waldman, I. D. (1992). The Minnesota transracial adoption study: A follow-up of IQ test performance. *Intelligence, 16*, 117–135. **7**

Weinraub, M., Clemens, L. P., Sockloff, A., Ethridge, T., Gracely, E., & Myers, B. (1984). The development of sex role stereotypes in the third year: Relationships to gender labeling, gender identity, sex-typed toy preference, and family characteristics. *Child Development, 55*, 1493–1503. **8**

Weisburger, J. H., & Wynder, E. L. (1991). Dietary fat intake and cancer. *Hematology/Oncology Clinics of North America, 5,* 7–23. **15**

Weisner, T. S. (1984). Ecocultural niches of middle childhood: A cross-cultural perspective. In W. A. Collins (Ed.) *Development during middle childhood. The years from six to twelve* (pp. 335–369). Washington, DC: National Academy Press. **10**

Weiss, R. S. (1986). Continuities and transformations in social relationships from childhood to adulthood. In W. W. Hartup & Z. Rubin (Eds.), *On relationships and development.* (pp. 95–110). Hillsdale, NJ: Erlbaum. **14**

Weisse, C. S. (1992). Depression and immunocompetence: A review of the literature. *Psychological Bulletin, 111,* 475–489. **13**

Wellman, H. M. (1982). The foundations of knowledge: Concept development in the young child. In S. G. Moore & C. C. Cooper (Eds.), *The young child. Reviews of research* (Vol. 3) (pp. 115–134). Washington, DC: National Association for the Education of Young Children. **7**

Wellman, H. M. (1988). First steps in the child's theorizing about the mind. In J. W. Astington, P. L. Harris, & D. R. Olson (Eds.), *Developing theories of mind* (pp. 64–92). New York: Cambridge University Press. **7**

Wen, S. W., Goldenberg, R. L., Cutter, G. R., Hoffman, H. J., Cliver, S. P., Davis, R. O., & DuBard, M. D. (1990). Smoking, maternal age, fetal growth, and gestational age at delivery. *American Journal of Obstetrics and Gynecology, 162,* 53–58. **3**

Werker, J. F., & Tees, R. C. (1984). Cross-language speech perception: Evidence for perceptual reorganization during the first year of life. *Infant Behavior and Development, 7,* 49–63. **5**

Werner, E. E. (1986). A longitudinal study of perinatal risk. In D. C. Farran & J. D. McKinney (Eds.), *Risk in intellectual and psychosocial development* (pp. 3–28). Orlando, FL: Academic Press. **1, 3**

Werner, E. E., & Smith, R. S. (1982). *Vulnerable but invincible: A study of resilient children.* New York: McGraw-Hill. **10**

Werner, E. E., Bierman, J. M., & French, F. E. (1971). *The children of Kauai.* Honolulu: University of Hawaii Press. **10**

Werner, H. (1948). *Comparative psychology of mental development.* Chicago: Follett. **2**

West, R. L., & Crook, T. H. (1990). Age differences in everyday memory: Laboratory analogues of telephone number recall. *Psychology and Aging, 5,* 529–529. **15**

West, R. L., Crook, T. H., & Barron, K. L. (1992). Everyday memory performance across the life span: Effects of age and noncognitive individual differences. *Psychology and Aging, 7,* 72–82. **17**

Whitbeck, L. B., Simons, R. L., & Conger, R. D. (1991). The effects of early family relationships on contemporary relationships and assistance patterns between adult children and their parents. *Journal of Gerontology: SOCIAL SCIENCES, 46,* S330–337. **16**

White, A. T., & Spector, P. E. (1987). An investigation of age-related factors in the age-job-satisfaction relationship. *Psychology and Aging, 2,* 261–265. **14**

White, J. (1987). Premarital cohabitation and marital stability in Canada. *Journal of Marriage and the Family, 49,* 641–647. **14**

White, L. K. (1990). Determinants of divorce: A review of research in the eighties. *Journal of Marriage and the Family, 52,* 904–912. **14**

White, L. R., Cartwright, W. S., Cornoni-Huntley, J., & Brock, D. B. (1986). Geriatric epidemiology. In C. Eisdorfer (Ed.), *Annual review of gerontology and geriatrics* (Vol. 6). New York: Springer. **15**

White, N., & Cunningham, W. R. (1988). Is terminal drop pervasive or specific? *Journals of Gerontology: PSYCHOLOGICAL SCIENCES, 43,* P141–144. **17**

Wiesenfeld, A. R., Malatesta, C. Z, & DeLoach, L. L. (1981). Differential parental response to familiar and unfamiliar infant distress signals. *Infant Behavior and Development, 4,* 281–296. **4**

Wigfield, A., Eccles, J. S., MacIver, D., Reuman, D. A., & Midgley, C. (1991). Transitions during early adolescence: Changes in children's domain-specific self-perceptions and general self-esteem across the transition to junior high school. *Developmental Psychology, 27,* 552–565. **12**

Wilcox, A. J., Weinberg, C. R., O'Connor, J. F., Baird, D. D., Schlaatterer, J. P., Canfield, R. E., Armstrong, E. G., & Nisula, B. C. (1988). Incidence of early loss of pregnancy. *New England Journal of Medicine, 319,* 189–194. **3**

Wilkinson, R. T., & Allison, S. (1989). Age and simple reaction time: decade differences for 5,325 subjects. *Journal of Gerontology: PSYCHOLOGICAL SCIENCES, 44,* P29–35. **13**

Williams, D. R. (1992). Social structure and the health behaviors of blacks. In K. W. Schaie, D. Blazer & J. S. House (Eds.), *Aging, health behaviors, and health outcomes* (pp. 59–64). Hillsdale, NJ: Erlbaum. **15**

Williams, J. E., & Best, D. L. (1990). *Measuring sex stereotypes. A multination study* (rev. ed.). Newbury Park, CA: Sage. **8**

Williams, R. B., Barefoot, J. C., Califf, R. M., Haney, T. L., Saunders, W. B., Pryor, D. B., Hlatky, M. A., Siegler, I. C., & Mark, D. B. (1992). Prognostic importance of social and economic resources among medically treated patients with angiographically documented coronary artery disease. *Journal of the American Medical Association, 267,* 520–524. **19**

Williamson, N. E. (1990). Breastfeeding trends and the breastfeeding promotion program in the Philippines. *International Journal of Gynecology & Obstetrics, 31* (Suppl. 1), 45–41. **4**

Willig, A. (1985). Meta-analysis of studies on bilingual education. *Review of Educational Research, 55,* 269–317. **7**

Willis, L., Thomas, P., Garry, P. J., & Goodwin, J. S. (1987). A prospective study of response to stressful life events in initially healthy elders. *Journal of Gerontology, 42,* 627–630. **13**

Willis, S. L., Jay, G. M., Diehl, M., & Marsiske, M. (1992). Longitudinal change and prediction of everyday task competence in the elderly. *Research on Aging, 14,* 68–91. **17**

Willis, S. L., & Nesselroade, C. S. (1990). Long-term effects of fluid ability training in old-old age. *Developmental Psychology, 26,* 905–910. **17**

Willits, F. K., & Crider, D. M. (1988). Health rating and life satisfaction in the later middle years. *Journal of Gerontology: SOCIAL SCIENCES, 43,* S172–176. **18**

Wilson, M. R., & Filsinger, E. E. (1986). Religiosity and marital adjustment: Multidimensional interrelationships. *Journal of Marriage and the Family, 48,* 147–151. **14**

Winick, M. (1980). *Nutrition in health and disease.* New York: Wiley. **3**

Woodward, A. L., & Markman, E. M. (1991). Review. Constraints on learning as default assumptions: Comments on Merriman and Bowman's "The mutual exclusivity bias in children's word learning." *Developmental Review, 11,* 137–163. **7**

World Health Organization (1981). *Contemporary patterns of breastfeeding. Report on the WHO collaborative study on breast-feeding.* Geneva: World Health Organization. **4**

Worobey, J. L., & Angel, R. J. (1990). Functional capacity and living arrangements of unmarried elderly persons. *Journal of Gerontology: SOCIAL SCIENCES, 45,* S95–101. **18**

Wortman, C. B., & Silver, R. C. (1987). Coping with irrevocable loss. In G. R. VandenBos & B. K. Bryant (Eds.), *Cataclysms, crises, and catastrophes: Psychology in action.* Washington, DC: American Psychological Association. **19**

Wortman, C. B., & Silver, R. C. (1989). The myths of coping with loss. *Journal of Consulting and Clinical Psychology, 57*, 349–357. **19**

Wortman, C. B., & Silver, R. C. (1990). Successful mastery of bereavement and widowhood: A life-course perspective. In P. B. Baltes & M. M. Baltes (Eds.), *Successful aging* (pp. 225–264). Cambridge, England: Cambridge University Press. **19**

Wright, P. H. (1989). Gender differences in adults' same- and cross-gender friendships. In R. G. Adams & R. Blieszner (Eds.), *Older adult friendship* (pp. 197–221). Newbury Park, CA: Sage Publications. **18**

Ycas, M. A., & Grad, S. (1987). Income of retirement-aged persons in the United States. *Social Security Bulletin, 50(7)*, 5–14. **18**

Yeates, K. O., MacPhee, D., Campbell, F. A., & Ramey, C. T. (1983). Maternal IQ and home environment as determinants of early childhood intellectual competence: A developmental analysis. *Developmental Psychology, 19*, 731–739. **7**

Zahn-Waxler, C., & Radke-Yarrow, M. (1982). The development of altruism: Alternative research strategies. In N. Eisenberg (Ed.), *The development of prosocial behavior* (pp. 109–138). New York: Academic Press. **8**

Zahn-Waxler, C., Radke-Yarrow, M., & King, R. A. (1979). Child-rearing and children's prosocial initiations toward victims of distress. *Child Development, 50*, 319–330. **8**

Zahn-Waxler, C., Radke-Yarrow, M., Wagner, E., & Chapman, M. (1992). Development of concern for others. *Developmental Psychology, 28*, 126–136. **8**

Zaslow, M. J., & Hayes, C. D. (1986). Sex differences in children's responses to psychosocial stress: Toward a cross-context analysis. In M. E. Lamb, A. L. Brown, & B. Rogoff (Eds.), *Advances in developmental psychology* (Vol. 4) (pp. 285–238). Hillsdale, NJ: Erlbaum. **3**

Zeskind, P. S., & Lester, B. M. (1978). Acoustic features and auditory perceptions of the cries of newborns with prenatal and perinatal complications. *Child Development, 49*, 580–589. **4**

Zigler, E., & Hall, N. W. (1989). Physical child abuse in America: Past, present, and future. In D. Cicchetti & V. Carlson (Eds.), *Child maltreatment* (pp. 38–75). Cambridge, England: Cambridge University Press. **6**

Zigler, E., & Hodapp, R. M. (1991). Behavioral functioning in individuals with mental retardation. *Annual Review of Psychology, 42*, 29–50. **3**

Zirkel, S., & Cantor, N. (1990). Personal construal of life tasks: Those who struggle for independence. *Journal of Personality and Social Psychology, 58*, 172–185. **14**

CREDITS

345(B) Paula Lerner/The Picture Cube. 347 Laura Dwight. 350 Bill Aron/Photo Edit. 354 David Young-Wolff/Photo Edit. 360 David Young-Wolff/Photo Edit. 361 Tony Freeman/Photo Edit. 365 Addison Geary/Stock Boston. 367 Madelaine Oton-Tarpey.

Chapter 15: 368 Tony Stone Images. 373 Tony Freeman/Photo Edit. 374 Bob Daemmrich. 380 Robert Brenner/Photo Edit. 382 Elizabeth Crews. 383 Jan Collsioo/Photoreporters. 386 Tony Freeman/Photo Edit. 387 Bob Daemmrich.

Chapter 16: 390 Richard Hutchings/InfoEdit. 396 Tony Freeman/Photo Edit. 397 Myrleen Ferguson/Photo Edit. 398 Laura Dwight. 401 Robert Brenner/Photo Edit. 405 Myrleen Ferguson/Photo Edit. 413 SIPA-Press. 419 Tony Stone Images. 420 Richard Hutchings/InfoEdit. 422 Merritt Vincent/Photo Edit.

Chapter 17: 423 Elizabeth Zuckerman/Photo Edit. 425 Don & Pat Valenti/Tony Stone Images. 426 From J. E. Birren, R. B. Sloane, & G. D. Cohen (Eds.), *Handbook of Mental Health and Aging*, 2nd ed. Academic Press, San Diego, CA, pp. 147–174. Used with permission. 427 M. Richards/Photo Edit. 430 Alan Oddie/Photo Edit. 433 From J. E. Birren, R. B. Sloane, & G. D. Cohen (Eds.), *Handbook of Mental Health and Aging*, 2nd ed. Academic Press, San Diego, CA, pp. 147–174. Used with permission. 436 Michael Newman/Photo Edit. 439 Mary Kate Denny/Photo Edit. 441 Bob Daemmrich. 444 Cary Wolinsky/Stock Boston. 445 Bob Daemmrich. 446(T) Suzanne Murphy/Tony Stone Images. 446(B) Bob Daemmrich.

Chapter 18: 451 Don & Pat Valenti/Tony Stone Images. 454 Paul Boyer. 456 Rhoda Sidney/Photo Edit. 458 Rhoda Sidney/Photo Edit. 461 Andras Dancs/Tony Stone Images. 462 Brent Jones. 464 Jamie Cope. 469 Alan Oddie/Photo Edit. 471 Judy Canty/Stock Boston. 477 Merritt Vincent/Photo Edit. 478 Don & Pat Valenti/Tony Stone Images.

Chapter 19: 480 Alan Oddie/Photo Edit. 481 Mark C. Walker/The Picture Cube. 482 H. Armstrong Roberts. 485 Michael Newman/Photo Edit. 487 The Picture Cube. 492 William Thompson/The Picture Cube. 494 Alexandra Boulet/SIPA-Press. 496 Robert Brenner/Photo Edit. 504 Alan Oddie/ Photo Edit.

◗ Literary, Figures, and Tables

Chapter 1: 4 Figure 1.1 "As time goes by: Change and stability in personality over fifty years" by N. Haan, R. Millsap, and E. Hartka from *Psychology and Aging*, 1, 220–232. Copyright © 1986 by the American Psychological Association. Reprinted by permission. 12 Figure 1.3 "A developmental perspective on antisocial behavior" by G. R. Patterson, B. D. DeBarshyshe, and E. Ramsey from *American Psychologist*, 44. Copyright © 1989 by the American Psychological Association. Reprinted by permission. 13 Figure 1.4 "The first two years of life: Factors related to thriving" by F. D. Horowitz from *The Young Child: Reviews of Research*, Vol. 3, edited by S. G. Moore and C. R. Cooper. Reprinted by permission of the publisher, The National Association from the Education of Young Children, Washington, DC.

Chapter 2: 38 Figure 2.3 From *The Seasons of a Man's Life* by Daniel J. Levinson et al. Copyright © 1978 by Daniel J. Levinson. Reprinted by permission of Alfred A. Knopf, Inc.

Chapter 3: 70 Figure 3.10 "Perinatal life for mother and baby: Labor and delivery" by M. A. Stenchever from *The Biologic Ages of Man*, 2nd ed., edited by D. W. Smith, E. L. Bierman, and N. M. Robinson. Copyright © 1978 by W. B. Saunders Company. Reprinted by permission.

Chapter 5: 104 Table "Infant preferences for attractive faces: Rudiments of a stereotype?" by J. H. Langlois, L. A. Roggman, R. J. Casey, J. M. Riter, L. A. Rieser-Danner, and V. Y. Jenkins from *Developmental Psychology*, 23, 363–369. Copyright © 1987 by the American Psychological Association. Reprinted by permission. 109 Figure 5.3 "Physical knowledge in infancy: Reflections on Piaget's theory" by E. S. Spelke from *The Epigenesis of Mind: Essays on Biology and Cognition* by S. Carey and R. Gelman, editors. Reprinted by permission of Lawrence Erlbaum Associates, Inc., and Susan Carey. 115 Figure 5.6 "Early lexical acquisition: Rate, content, and the vocabulary spurt" by B. A. Goldfield and J. S. Reznick from *Journal of Child Language*, 17, 171–183, 1990, figure 3 from page 177.

Chapter 7: 157 Table 7.2 "Early patterns of grammatical development" by David Ingram from *Language Behavior in Infancy and Early Childhood* edited by R. E. Stark. Reprinted by permission of David Ingram. 160 Table 7.3 "Knowledge, context and strategy in the acquisition of meaning" by E. V. Clark from *Georgetown University Round Table 1975: Developmental Psycholinguistics: Theory and Applications* edited by D. P. Dato. Reprinted by permission of Georgetown University Press. 171 Figure 7.2 Reprinted by permission of the publishers from *A First Language* by Roger Brown. Cambridge, MA: Harvard University Press. Copyright © 1973 by the President and Fellows of Harvard College. 176 Table 7.5 Data from "Assessment of effects of socioeconomic status on IQ in a full cross-fostering study" by C. Capron and M. Duyme. Reprinted with permission from *Nature*, 340, 552–554 and the author. Copyright © 1989 Macmillan Magazines Ltd. 177 Figure 7.3 "The Carolina Abecedarian Project: An Educational Experiment" by C. T. Ramey and F. A. Campbell in *The Malleability of Children* edited by J. J. Gallagher and C. T. Ramey. Reprinted by permission of Paul H. Brookes Publishing Company and Craig T. Ramey, Ph.D. 179 Figure 7.4 From *Sex Differences in Cognitive Abilities*, 2nd ed., by Diane F. Halpern. Copyright © 1992 by Diane F. Halpern. Reprinted by permission of Diane F. Halpern and Lawrence Erlbaum Associates, Inc.

Chapter 8: 190 Figure 8.1 "The emergence of same-sex affiliative preferences among preschool peers: A developmental/ethological perspective" by P. LaFrenière, F. F. Strayer, and R. Gauthier in *Child Development* 55. Copyright © by The Society for Research in Child Development, Inc. Reprinted by permission. 194 Table 8.2 "Influence and involvement in children's discourse: Age, gender and partner effects" by C. Leaper from *Child Development*, 62. Copyright © by The Society for Research in Child Development,

Inc. Reprinted by permission. **198** Figure 8.2 "Socialization in the context of the family: Parent-child interaction" by E. E. Maccoby and J. A. Martin in *Handbook of Child Psychology*, Volume IV edited by E. M. Hetherington. Copyright © 1983 by John Wiley & Sons, Inc. Reprinted by permission of John Wiley & Sons, Inc. **199** Table from "Research Report" on ethnic differences in family style by L. Steinberg, N. S. Mounts, S. D. Lamborn, and S. M. Dornbusch in *Journal of Research on Adolescence*, 1, 19–36. Reprinted by permission of Lawrence Erlbaum Associates, Inc., and Laurence Steinberg.

Chapter 9: 210 Figure 9.1 "On asking questions" from *Studies in Cognitive Growth* by J. S. Bruner, R. R. Olver, and P. M. Garfield. Reprinted by permission. **216** Figure 9.3 "Memory span: Sources of individual and development differences" by F. N. Dempster from *Psychological Bulletin*, 89, 63–100. Copyright © 1981 by American Psychological Association. Reprinted by permission of American Psychological Association and F. N. Dempster. **222** Table 9.2 Items from the Comprehensive Tests of Basic Skills, Form S, published by CTB Macmillan/McGraw-Hill, 2500 Garden Road, Monterey, CA 93940. Copyright © 1973 by McGraw-Hill Inc. The specific items used are Reading Vocabulary, Item 7; Spelling, Item 12; Language Expression, Item 27; Mathematics Computation, Items 5, 18, and 32; Mathematics Concepts, Item 1; Reference Skills, Item 1. Reproduced by permission of the publisher.

Chapter 10: 230 Figure 10.1 Adapted from "The development of person perception in childhood and adolescence: From behavioral comparisons to psychological constructs to psychological comparisons" by C. Barenboim from *Child Development*, 52. Copyright © by The Society for Research in Child Development. **239** Figure 10.3 "The determinants and mediation role of global self-worth in children" by S. Harter in *Contemporary Topics in Developmental Psychology* edited by N. Eisenberg. Copyright © 1988 by John Wiley & Sons, Inc. Reprinted by permission of John Wiley & Sons, Inc. **247** Figure 10.4 "The development of aggressive behavior from the perspective of a developing behaviorism" by L. D. Eron from *American Psychologist*, 42, 435–442. Copyright © 1987 by the American Psychological Association. Reprinted by permission of the American Psychological Association and L. D. Eron.

Chapter 11: 257 Figure 11.2 Reprinted by permission of the publishers from *Fetus into Man* by J. M. Tanner. Cambridge, MA: Harvard University Press. Copyright © 1978, 1989 by J. M. Tanner. **259** Table 11.2 "The biological approach to adolescence" by A. C. Petersen and B. Taylor in *Handbook of Adolescent Psychology* edited by J. Adelson. Copyright © 1980 by John Wiley & Sons, Inc. Reprinted by permission of John Wiley & Sons, Inc. **271** Figure 11.6 "Longitudinal Study of Moral Judgement" by A. Colby, L. Kohlberg, J. Gibbs, and M. A. Lieberman in *Monographs of the Society for Research in Child Development*, 48. Copyright © by The Society for Research in Child Development. Reprinted by permission.

Chapter 12: 290 Figure 12.4 "Changes in functions of three relations during adolescence" by Fumiyo Tao and J. Youniss from *Developmental Psychology*, 18. Copyright © 1982 by the American Psychological Association. Reprinted by permission. **292** Figure 12.5 "Developmental changes in conformity to peers and parents" by Thomas J. Berndt from *Developmental Psychology*. Copyright © 1979 by the American Psychological Association. Reprinted by permission. **297** Table 12.3 Adaptation of "Patterns of competence and adjustment among adolescents from authoritative, authoritarian, indulgent, and neglectful families" by S. D. Lamborn, N. S. Mounts, L. Steinberg, and S. M. Dornbusch from *Child Development*, 62. Copyright © by The Society for Research in Child Development, Inc. Reprinted by permission. **304** Figure 12.6 "Negative correlates of part-time employment during adolescence: Replication and elaboration" by L. Steinberg and S. M. Dornbusch from *Developmental Psychology*, 27, 304–313. Copyright © 1991 by the American Psychological Association. Reprinted by permission of the American Psychological Association and Laurence Steinberg.

Chapter 13: 316 Figure 13.1 "Age and aerobic power in women: A longitudinal study" by S. A. Plowman, B. L. Drinkwater, and S. M. Horvath from *Journal of Gerontology*, 34, 512–520, 1979. Copyright © 1979 by The Gerontological Society of America. Reprinted by permission. **319** Figure 13.3 "Age, socioeconomic status, and health" by J. S. House, R. C. Kessler, and A. R. Herzog from *The Milbank Quarterly*, 68. Reprinted by permission of *The Milbank Quarterly*. **327** Figure 13.6 From *Health and Ways of Living: The Alameda County Study* by Lisa F. Berkman and Lester Breslow. Copyright © 1983 by Oxford University Press, Inc. Reprinted by permission.

Chapter 14: 338 Table 14.1 "Romantic love conceptualized as an attachmnent process" by C. Hazan and P. Shaver from *Journal of Personality and Social Psychology*, 52, 511–524. Copyright © 1987 by the American Psychological Association. Reprinted by permission of the American Psychological Association and the author. **346** Figure 14.3 "Marital satisfaction over the family life cycle" by Boyd C. Rollins and Harold Feldman from *Journal of Marriage and the Family*, 1970, p. 32. Reprinted by permission of the National Council on Family Relations and Boyd C. Rollins. **351** Figure 14.4 from *Career Mobility in a Corporate Hierarchy* by James E. Rosenbaum. Reprinted by permission of Academic Press and James E. Rosenbaum. **353** Box "Race, gender, and work: A multicultural economic history of women in the United States" by T. Amott and J. Matthaie. Reprinted with permission of the publisher, South End Press, 116 Saint Botolph Street, Boston, MA 02115. **355** Figure 14.5 "The family life cycle and spouses' time in housework" by Cynthia Rexroat and Constance Shehan from *Journal of Marriage and the Family*, 49:4, 737–750. Copyright © 1987 by the National Council on Family Relations, 3989 Central Avenue NE, Suite 550, Minneapolis, MN 55421. Reprinted by permission. **357** Table 14.4 "Personality in adulthood" by R. R. McCrae and P. T. Costa, Jr. Reprinted by permission of The Guilford Press. **358** Figure 14.6 "As time goes by: Change and stability in personality over fifty years" by N. Haan, R. Millsap, and E. Hartka from *Psychology and Aging*, 1, 220–232. Copyright © 1986 by the American Psychological Association. Reprinted by permission.

Chapter 15: 379 Box, Figure 1, "Dairy fat, saturated animal fat, and cancer risk" by H. Kesteloot, E. Lesaffre, and J. V. Joossens from *Preventive Medicine*, 20, 226–236. Reprinted by permission of Academic Press and Hugo Kesteloot. **385** Figure 15.5 "Effect of age and training on aerobic capacity and body composition of master athletes" by M. L. Pollock, D. Foster, D. Knapp, J. L. Rod, and D. H. Schmidt from *Journal of Applied Physiology*, 62. Reprinted by permission of American Physiological Society.

Chapter 16: 393 Figure 16.2 "Stages of family life cycle, ego development, and the marriage relationship" by C. H. Swensen, R. W. Eskew, and K. A. Kohlhepp from *Journal of Marriage and the Family*, 43:4, 841–853. Copyright © 1981 by the National Council on Family Relations, 3989 Central Avenue NE, Suite 550, Minneapolis, MN 55421. Reprinted by permission. **407** Figure 16.6 Figures from *Successful Aging* by J. Brandstadter and B. Baltes-Gotz. Reprinted by permission of Cambridge University Press.

Chapter 17: 423 Figure 17.1 "Demography of aging" by George C. Myers from *Handbook of Aging and the Social Sciences*, 3rd ed., edited by R. H. Binstock and L. K. George. Data from the Center for Demographic Studies, Duke University. Reprinted by permission of Academic Press, Inc. **428** Figure 17.3 "Smell identification ability: Changes with age" by R. L. Doty et al. from *Science*, 226, 1441–1443, figure 1. Copyright © 1984 by the American Association for the Advancement of Science. Reprinted by permission of the AAAS and R. L. Doty. **429** Figure 17.4 "Demography and the epidemiology of aging in the United States" by D. B. Brock, J. M. Guralnik, and J. A. Brody from *Handbook of the Biology of Aging*, 3rd ed., edited by E. L. Schneider and J. W. Rowe, pp. 18–19. Reprinted by permission of Academic Press. **437** Figure 17.6 E. Palmore, *Social Patterns in Normal Aging: Findings from a Duke Longitudinal Study*, figure 6-3, p. 87. Copyright Duke University Press, 1981. Reprinted with

permission of the publisher. **443** Figure 17.7 "On the locus and process of magnification of age differences during mnemonic training" by R. Kliegl, J. Smith, and P. B. Baltes from *Developmental Psychology*, 26, 894–904. Copyright © 1990 by the American Psychological Association. Reprinted by permission of the American Psychological Association and Reinhold Kliegl. **445** Figure 17.8 "Individual differences in rate of cognitive change in adulthood" by K. W. Schaie from *The Course of Later Life, Research and Reflections* edited by V. L. Bengtson and K. W. Schaie. Copyright © 1989 by Springer Publishing Company. Reprinted by permission of Springer Publishing Company, Inc., New York, NY 10012.

Chapter 18: 453 Figure 18.2 "Demography and the epidemiology of aging in the United States" by D. B. Brock, J. M. Guralnik, and J. A. Brody from *Handbook of the Biology of Aging*, 3rd ed., edited by E. L. Schneider and J. W. Rowe, p. 8. Reprinted by permission of Academic Press. **455** Box, from "Moving On" by Susan Kishner Resnick in *The New York Times*, March 8, 1992. Copyright © 1992 by The New York Times Company. Reprinted by permission. **467** Table 18.3 "Economic status of the elderly" by T. M. Smeeding from *Handbook of Aging and the Social Sciences*, 3rd ed., edited by R. H. Binstock and L. K. George. Reprinted by permission of T. M. Smeeding.

Chapter 19: 484 Figure 19.1 "Stratum contrasts and similarities in attitudes toward death" by V. L. Bengtson, J. B. Cuellar, and P. K. Ragan from *Journal of Gerontology*, 32, 76–88, Figure 1, page 80. Copyright © 1977 by The Gerontological Society of America. Reprinted by permission. **490** Table 19.2 "Mental attitudes to cancer: An additional prognostic factor" by K. W. Pettingale, T. Morris, S. Greer, and J. L. Haybittle from *The Lancet*. Reprinted by permission of Keith W. Pettingale. **498** Figure 19.3 "Attachment theory and multiple dimensions of grief" by S. C. Jacobs et al. from *Omega, Journal of Death and Dying*, 18:1, 41–52, figure 1, page 43. Copyright © 1988 by Baywood Publishing Company, Inc. Reprinted by permission of Baywood Publishing Company, Inc., and Selby C. Jacobs, M.D.

Author and Subject Indexes

Author Index

SUBJECT INDEX